Encyclopedia
of the
American Constitution

Original 1986 Editorial Board

Encyclopedia
of the
American Constitution

SECOND EDITION

Edited by
LEONARD W. LEVY
and
KENNETH L. KARST

ADAM WINKLER, Associate Editor for the Second Edition

DENNIS J. MAHONEY, Assistant Editor for the First Edition
JOHN G. WEST, JR., Assistant Editor for Supplement I

MACMILLAN REFERENCE USA
An imprint of the Gale Group
New York

Copyright © 2000 by Macmillan Reference USA

Macmillan Library Reference USA
1633 Broadway
New York, NY 10019

Printed in the United States of America

Printing Number
10 9 8 7 6 5 4 3 2 1

Library of Congress Cataloging-in-Publication Data
Encyclopedia of the American Constitution / edited by Leonard W. Levy and Kenneth L.
Karst.—2nd ed. / Adam Winkler, associate editor for the second edition.
        p. cm.
    Includes bibliographical references and indexes.
    ISBN 0-02-864880-3 (hard cover : alk. paper)
        1. Constitutional law—United States—Encyclopedias.   I. Levy, Leonard Williams,
1923–   II. Karst, Kenneth L.   III. Winkler, Adam.
    KF4548 .E53   2000
    342.73—dc21   00-029203

This paper meets the requirements of ANSI-NISO Z39.48-1992 (Permanence of Paper).

Contents

Preface

(1986)

In the summer of 1787 delegates from the various states met in Philadelphia; because they succeeded in their task, we now call their assembly the Constitutional Convention. By September 17 the delegates had completed the framing of the Constitution of the United States. The year 1987 marks the bicentennial of the Constitutional Convention. This Encyclopedia is intended as a scholarly and patriotic enterprise to commemorate the bicentennial. No encyclopedia on the Constitution has heretofore existed. This work seeks to fill the need for a single comprehensive reference work treating the subject in a multidisciplinary way.

The Constitution is a legal document, but it is also an institution: a charter for government, a framework for building a nation, an aspect of the American civic culture. Even in its most limited sense as a body of law, the Constitution includes, in today's understanding, nearly two centuries' worth of court decisions interpreting the charter. Charles Evans Hughes, then governor of New York, made this point pungently in a 1907 speech: "We are under a Constitution, but the Constitution is what the judges say it is." Hughes's remark was, if anything, understated. If the Constitution sometimes seems to be chiefly the product of judicial decisions, it is also what Presidents say it is—and legislators, and police officers, and ordinary citizens, too. In the final analysis today's Constitution is the product of the whole political system and the whole history of the many peoples who have become a nation. "Constitutional law is history," wrote Professor Felix Frankfurter in 1937, "But equally true is it that American history is constitutional law."

Thus an Encyclopedia of the American Constitution would be incomplete if it did not seek to bridge the disciplines of history, law, and political science. Both in identifying subjects and in selecting authors we have sought to build those bridges. The subjects fall into five general categories: doctrinal concepts of constitutional law (about fifty-five percent of the total words); people (about fifteen percent); judicial decisions, mostly of the Supreme Court of the United States (about fifteen percent); public acts, such as statutes, treaties, and executive orders (about five percent); and historical periods (about ten percent). (These percentages are exclusive of the appendices—printed at the end of the final volume—and bibliographies.) The articles vary in length, from brief definitions of terms to treatments of major subjects of constitutional doctrine, which may be as long as 6,000 words, and articles on periods of constitutional history, which may be even longer. A fundamental concept like "due process of law" is the subject of three 6,000-word articles: Procedural Due Process of Law (Civil), Procedural Due Process of Law (Criminal), and Substantive Due Process of Law. In addition, there is a 1,500-word article on the historical background of due process of law. The standard length of an article on a major topic, such as the First Amendment, is 6,000 words; but each principal component of the amendment—Freedom of Speech, Freedom of the Press, Religious Liberty, Separation of Church and State—is also the subject of a 6,000-word article. There are also other, shorter articles on other aspects of the amendment.

The reader will find an article on almost any topic reasonably conceivable. At the beginning of the first volume there is a list of all entries, to spare the reader from paging through the volumes to determine whether particular entries exist. This list, like many another efficiency device, may be a mixed blessing; we commend to our readers the joys of encyclopedia-browsing.

The Encyclopedia's articles are arranged alphabetically and are liberally cross-referenced by the use of small capital letters indicating the titles of related articles. A reader may thus begin with an article focused on one feature of his or her field of inquiry, and move easily to other articles on other aspects of the subject. For example, one who wished to read about the civil rights movement of the 1950s and 1960s might begin with the large-scale subject of Civil Rights itself; or with a particular doctrinal topic (Desegregation, or Miscegenation), or an article focused on a narrower factual setting (Public Accommodations, or Sit-Ins). Alternatively, the reader might start with an important public act (Civil Rights Act of 1964), or with a biographical entry on a particular person (Martin Luther King, Jr., or Earl Warren). Other places to start would be articles on the events in particular eras (Warren Court or Constitutional History, 1945–1961 and 1961–1977). The reader can use any of these articles to find all the others, simply by following the network of cross-references. A Subject Index and a Name Index, at the end of the last volume, list all the pages on which the reader can find, for example, references to the freedom of the press or to Abraham Lincoln. Full citations to all the judicial decisions mentioned in the Encyclopedia are set out in the Case Index, also at the end of the final volume.

The Encyclopedia's approximately 2,100 articles have been written by 262 authors. Most of the authors fall into three groups: 41 historians, 164 lawyers (including academics, practitioners, and judges), and 53 political scientists. The others are identified with the fields of economics and journalism. Our lawyer-authors, who represent about three-fifths of all our writers, have produced about half the words in the Encyclopedia. Historian-authors, although constituting only about sixteen percent of all authors, produced about one-third of the words; political scientists, although responsible for only one-sixth of the words, wrote more than a quarter of the articles. Whether this information is an occasion for surprise may depend on the reader's occupation.

In addition to the interdisciplinary balance, the reader will find geographical balance. Although a large number of contributors is drawn from the

School of Law of the University of California, Los Angeles, the Claremont Colleges, and other institutions in California, most come from the Northeast, including twelve from Harvard University, thirteen from Yale University, and nine from Columbia University. Every region of the United States is represented, however, and there are many contributors from the South (Duke University, University of Virginia, University of North Carolina, University of Texas, etc.), from the Midwest (University of Chicago, University of Notre Dame, University of Wisconsin, University of Michigan, etc.), and from the Northwest (University of Oregon, Portland State University, University of Washington, etc.). There are several contributors from foreign countries, including Austria, Canada, and Great Britain.

Every type of academic environment is represented among the eighty-six colleges and universities at which the authors work. The contributors include scholars based at large public universities smaller state colleges, Ivy League universities, private liberal arts colleges, and religiously affiliated institutions. Not all of the authors are drawn from academia; one is a member of Congress and nine are federal judges. In addition, other government offices, research institutions, libraries, newspaper staffs, and law firms are represented.

Each article is signed by its author; we have encouraged the authors to write commentaries, in essay form, not merely describing and analyzing their subjects but expressing their own views. On the subject of the Constitution, specialists and citizens alike will hold divergent viewpoints. In inviting authors to contribute to the Encyclopedia, we have sought to include a range of views. The reader should be alert to the possibility that a cross-referenced article may discuss similar issues from a different perspective—especially if those issues have been the subject of recent controversy. We hope this awareness will encourage readers to read more widely and to expand the range of their interests concerning the Constitution.

Planning of the Encyclopedia began in 1978, and production began in 1979; nearly all articles were written by 1985. Articles on decisions of the Supreme Court include cases decided during the Court's October 1984 term, which ended in July 1985. Given the ways in which American constitutional law develops, some of the subjects treated here are moving targets. In a project like this one, some risk of obsolescence is necessarily present; at this writing we can predict with confidence that some of our authors will wish they had one last chance to modify their articles to take account of decisions in the 1985 term. To minimize these concerns we have asked the authors of articles on doctrinal subjects to concentrate on questions that are fundamental and of enduring significance.

We have insisted that the authors keep to the constitutional aspects of their various topics. There is much to be said about abortion or antitrust law, or about foreign affairs or mental illness, that is not comprehended within the fields of constitutional law and history. In effect, the title of every article might be extended by the phrase ". . . and the Constitution." This statement is emphatically true of the biographical entries; every author was admonished to avoid writing a conventional biography and, instead, to write an appreciation of the subject's significance in American constitutional law and history.

We have also asked authors to remember that the Encyclopedia will be used by readers whose interests and training vary widely, from the specialist in constitutional law or history to the high school student who is writing a paper. Not every article will be within the grasp of that student, but the vast majority of articles are accessible to the general reader who is neither historian nor lawyer nor political scientist. Although a constitutional specialist on a particular subject will probably find the articles on that specialty too general, the same specialist may profit from reading articles in other fields. A commerce clause expert may not be an expert on the First Amendment; and First Amendment scholars may know little about criminal justice. The deluge of cases, problems, and information flowing from courts, other agencies of government, law reviews, and scholarly monographs has forced constitutional scholarship to become specialized, like all branches of the liberal arts. Few, if any, can keep in command of it all and remain up to date. The Encyclopedia organizes in readable form an epitome of all that is known and understood on the subject of the Constitution by the nation's specialist scholars.

Because space is limited, no encyclopedia article can pretend to exhaust its subject. Moreover, an encyclopedia is not the same kind of contribution to knowledge as a monograph based on original research in the primary sources is. An encyclopedia is a compendium of knowledge, a reference work addressed to a wide variety of interested audiences: students in secondary school, college, graduate school, and law school; scholars and teachers of constitutional law and history; lawyers; legislators; jurists; government officials; journalists; and educated citizens who care about their Constitution and its history. Typically, an article in this Encyclopedia contains not only cross-references to other articles but also a bibliography that will aid the reader in pursuing his or her own study of the subject.

In addition to the articles, the Encyclopedia comprises several appendices. There is a copy of the complete text of the Constitution as well as of George Washington's Letter of Transmittal. A glossary defines legal terms that may be unfamiliar to readers who are not lawyers. Two chronologies will help put topics in historical perspective; one is a detailed chronology of the framing and ratification of the Constitution and the Bill of Rights, and the other is a more general chronology of American constitutional history. Finally, there are three indexes: the first is an index of court cases, with the complete citation to every case mentioned in the Encyclopedia (to which is attached a brief guide to the use of legal citations); the second is an index of names; and the third is a general topical index.

For some readers an encyclopedia article will be a stopping-point, but the articles in this Encyclopedia are intended to be doorways leading to ideas and to additional reading, and perhaps to the reader's development of independent judgment about the Constitution. After all, when the American Constitution's tricentennial is celebrated in 2087, what the Constitution has become will depend less on the views of specialists than on the beliefs and behavior of the nation's citizens.

LEONARD W. LEVY
KENNETH L. KARST
DENNIS J. MAHONEY

Acknowledgments

(1986)

The editors are grateful to our authors, to our editorial board, and to our advisory committee (all listed in the early pages of the Encycloiedia) for their labors and advice during these seven years.

The editors acknowledge with utmost appreciation the financial support given to this project by four institutions. The National Endowment for the Humanities made a major grant which the Weingart Foundation of Los Angeles matched. The Macmillan Publishing Company and The Claremont Graduate School also handsomely underwrote this encyclopedia. The earliest private funds came from a small group of southern California attorneys and foundations: The Times Mirror Foundation; James Greene, Judge Dyson William Cox and Janice T. Cox, Robert P. Hastings, James E. Ludlam, and J. Patrick Waley; Musick, Peeler & Garrett; and The Ralph B. Lloyd Foundation.

The Claremont Graduate School and University Center also provided facilities and logistical support for the Encyclopedia. Former President Joseph B. Platt gave the project his encouragement. Executive Vice-President Paul A. Albrecht significantly assisted our grant applications from the outset and remained helpful throughout the project. Associate Dean Christopher N. Oberg has seen to the efficient management of administrative aspects of the project. Sandra Glass, now of the Keck Foundation, provided invaluable aid while she was associated with The Claremont Graduate School. We are also grateful for the unflagging support of the School of Law of the University of California, Los Angeles, and its deans, William D. Warren and Susan Westerberg Prager.

A succession of graduate students at The Claremont Graduate School worked on the project as editorial assistants, research assistants, typists, and proofreaders. First was Dr. David Gordon, who also acted as assistant editor for one year, and who wrote over one hundred of the articles before going on to law school. Dr. Michael E. DeGolyer and Susan Marie Meyer served ably as editorial assistants. Others who worked on the project were Michael Walker, Kenneth V. Benesh, Susan Orr, Suzanne Kovacs, Dr. Steven Varvis, Dr. Patrick Delana, and Paul R. Huard.

The secretaries in the History Department of The Claremont Graduate School have typed thousands of letters and hundreds of articles, in addition to performing numerous other small tasks to keep the project going; particular thanks are due to Lelah Mullican. The Claremont Graduate School Academic Computing Center and its director, Gunther Freehill, showed us how to automate our record keeping and provided facilities for that purpose.

Most important, we gratefully acknowledge the support of Charles E. Smith, Vice-President and Publisher, Professional Books Division, Macmillan Publishing Company, and of Elly Dickason, our editor at Macmillan. Mr. Smith actively and continuously supported the project from its early days and by his prodding kept us on a Stakhanovite schedule. Ms. Dickason performed arduous labors with supreme professional skill and unfailing good humor.

Finally, we thank Elyse Levy and Smiley Karst for their own indispensable contributions to this project. A personal dedication page seems inappropriate for a reference work, otherwise this Encyclopedia would have been dedicated to them. Natalie Glucklich, Renee Karst, Aaron Harris, and Adam Harris, the grandchildren of the senior editors, entered the world without realizing that the Encyclopedia project was underway. They assisted not a whit, but we acknowledge our pleasure in seeing their names in print.

Preface

(1992)

The continuing deluge of problems and developments concerning the Constitution makes an updating of the *Encyclopedia of the American Constitution* desirable. The Supreme Court decides at least 250 cases annually, about 150 of them with full opinions. Before the bicentennial of the ratification of the Bill of Rights concludes, the Court will have decided about 1,500 cases since we finished the manuscript for the four-volume edition in mid-1985. New opinions of the Court are having a substantial impact on most of American constitutional law and the public policies that it reflects.

The Court itself is undergoing major changes in personnel. Chief Justice Warren Burger and Justices Lewis H. Powell, William J. Brennan, and Thurgood Marshall have retired. William H. Rehnquist now sits in the center seat; Antonin Scalia succeeded to Rehnquist's former position; Anthony Kennedy became Powell's successor; David H. Souter holds Brennan's old chair; and Clarence Thomas succeeds Marshall. Changes in personnel herald additional and significant changes in constitutional law. For example, the Senate Judiciary Committee hearings on the nomination of Robert H. Bork, in itself a landmark event, reflected a national concern on all sides for the integrity and impartiality of the Court and its interpretation of the Constitution.

As we finished editorial work on the Encyclopedia in 1985, the Department of Justice intensified a broad attack on the "judicial activism" of the Supreme Court, the finality of its decisions, and its incorporation doctrine, which makes the Bill of Rights applicable to the states. Soon after, the protracted Iran-Contra inquiries raised some of the most important constitutional issues since Watergate. New, important, and even sensational developments of concern to the Constitution have become almost common.

This Supplement to the Encyclopedia has enabled us to present many topics that we had originally neglected and to cover all major developments and decisions since 1985; it includes articles on the full range of developments in constitutional law. Because we wanted the Supplement to be a free-standing volume, as well as an additional volume to the original work, we instructed contributors to introduce each article with a short background to its topic and to write as if the Encyclopedia did not exist. In addition to articles on concepts such as abortion, affirmative action, establishment of religion, equal protection, and free speech, we have included analyses of major cases. We have treated new developments conceptually, topically, biographically, historically, and by judicial decision.

We continued our policy of getting a wide range of scholarly opinions. For the sake of variety, generally we did not ask the authors of the original articles to "update" their contributions; we sought different authors, sometimes of differing constitutional persuasions. The Supplement is an independent reference work.

The Supplement enables us to include articles on topics that we had omitted from the four-volume set, either as a result of editorial neglect or because some authors failed to produce the articles and too little time remained to replace them. As comprehensive as the Encyclopedia is, it has gaps that we have sought to close with this Supplement (e.g., Court-packing plans, the Judicial Conference of the United States, original intent, constitutional remedies, special prosecutors, entitlements, constitutional fictions, the civil rights movement, gender rights, legal culture, law and economic theory, ratifier intent, textualism, unenumerated rights, the Senate Judiciary Committee, and so on). The Supplement also gave us the opportunity to treat at greater length a variety of topics to which we originally allocated insufficient space. Although 1,500,000 words for the four-volume set was a huge amount, we found the publisher's limitations on length to be too constraining. An additional volume of over 400,000 words, which Macmillan approved for the Supplement, gave us space to redo overbrief articles, to repair omissions, and to update the entire work.

For the most part, the Supplement covers wholly fresh topics, not only those omitted from the original set but those that have come to attention since then. When we planned the Encyclopedia in the late 1970s, for example, the subject of original intent was far less discussed than it was a decade later. Other comparatively new topics include the relation of capital punishment to race, the anti-abortion movement, children and the First Amendment, critical legal studies, the right to die, vouchers, independent counsel, the balanced budget amendment, the controversy over creationism, Iran-Contra, ethics in government, criminal justice and technology, political trials, the Gramm-Rudman Act, patenting the creation of life, government as proprietor, the Attorney General's Commission on Pornography, the Boland Amendment, feminist theories, drug testing, joint-resolutions, constitutional realism, the Bail Reform Act of 1984, recent appointees to the Court, low-value speech, unenumerated rights, private discrimination, visas and free speech, and the Rehnquist Court. The updating of old topics, covering the period since 1985, also, of course, presents new material. We estimate that about seventy-five percent of the entries in the Supplement consist of new topics. Of the total 320 articles in this volume, 247 present entries not in the original Encyclopedia. Nevertheless, any encyclopedia is merely an epitome of knowledge, and we again labored under practical constraints on word lengths. Space is always limited. We do not mislead ourselves or readers by suggesting that we have managed to cover everything.

The articles in this Supplement, as in the original edition, are intended primarily to be doorways leading to ideas and to additional reading. Thus, all articles in this Supplement are elaborately cross-referenced to other related articles within the same covers and to articles in the original four-volume edition. Cross-references are indicated by words set in small capitals. . . .

As in the original edition, we believe readers will find any article on almost any topic reasonably conceivable or a cross-reference to related topics. The Supplement contains articles by 178 contributors. Most of the contributors are academic lawyers who teach constitutional law, but other professors of law have made contributions, as well as a few lawyers in private practice and five federal judges. In addition many historians and political scientists are among the contributors, as are ten deans and three associate deans. We sought as much interdisciplinary balance as the entries themselves permitted and, with respect to the location of the contributors, we sought geographical balance by recruiting authors from the whole of the nation, as well as from different sorts of institutions. The University of California, Los Angeles, continues to be the institution with the largest number of contributors, followed by Harvard University, University of Michigan, Yale University, University of Minnesota, University of Southern California, Georgetown University, University of Chicago, New York University, and Stanford University, in that order. All together, eighty-five institutions have been represented.

Every article is signed by its author. We have encouraged the authors to write commentaries in essay form, not merely describing and analyzing their subjects but expressing their own views. Specialists and ordinary citizens alike hold divergent viewpoints on the Constitution. Readers should be alert to the likelihood that a cross-referenced article may discuss similar issues from a different perspective, especially if the issues have been the subject of recent controversy.

LEONARD W. LEVY
KENNETH L. KARST
JOHN G. WEST, JR.

Acknowledgments

(1992)

We are grateful to our authors as well as to the members of the Editorial Board. We acknowledge with utmost appreciation the support given to this project by the Earhart Foundation, by The Claremont Graduate School and University Center and its officers, President John D. Maguire, former Vice-President Jerome Spanier, and especially former Vice-President Christopher Oberg. Three graduate students of The Claremont Graduate School served, indispensably, as editorial assistants: Mary Bellamy, Dana Whaley, and Jeffrey Schultz. The Macmillan Reference Division, headed by Philip Friedman, his editor in chief, Elly Dickason, and Senior Project Editor Martha Goldstein have done extraordinarily well and generously by us, earning our appreciation.

As before, the grandchildren of the senior editors assisted not a whit, but we acknowledge our pleasure in remembering them and especially in seeing in print the names of those who came into this world since Aaron, Renee, Natalie, and Adam. The new ones are Elon Glucklich, Jacob Harris, and Elijah Dylan Karst. We are pleased, too, to thank our wives, Elyse Levy and Smiley Karst, to whom this work might have been dedicated if a personal dedication page were appropriate for a reference work. Along with their names would be that of John West's sister Janet, a plucky woman who graduated from law school and passed her bar exam during the life of this project despite medical adversities.

Preface

(2000)

This second edition of the *Encyclopedia of the American Constitution* represents the compilation of twenty years' work. It gathers together in one source all of the articles written for the original four-volume set published in 1986; articles in the supplementary volume published in 1992; and new articles on developments in the 1990s. Our initial intention was to publish a second supplementary volume, but as publication drew near it became clear that the combination of the original work with two supplements, each with articles of relevance to researchers and students of particular topics, would be unwieldy. For example, one looking for an overview of Freedom of Speech would have had to look up articles in three separate volumes to form a complete picture. With this second edition, all articles on a single topic are placed together and dated, for easy retrieval in one search.

This edition contains 361 new articles by 237 authors. Some of these authors contributed to the original Encyclopedia or Supplement I or both, but we have sought to expand the list to include a new generation of scholars. As before, most of the contributors are academic lawyers, yet some articles are written by judges, practicing lawyers, historians, or political scientists. Every article is signed by its author. We have continued to encourage writers to use the essay form, expressing their own views as they wish. We recruited authors with the purpose of presenting a wide range of views. For new articles on some controversial subjects we have sought to provide contrasting views under the same title (e.g., Same-Sex Marriage, I and II; Workplace Harassment and Freedom of Speech, I and II).

The substantial new material of this edition focuses mainly on the constitutional issues arising since the publication of Supplement I in 1992. During this time, two new Justices have joined the U.S. Supreme Court: Justice Ruth Bader Ginsburg replaced Justice Byron R. White, and Justice Stephen G. Breyer replaced Justice Harry A. Blackmun. We have been saddened during these years by the deaths of Chief Justice Warren E. Burger, and Justices

William J. Brennan, Jr., Thurgood Marshall, Lewis F. Powell, Jr., and Harry A. Blackmun.

We have not only updated topics covered in earlier volumes, but also included a great many articles on topics not previously covered. Some of these articles represent relatively new subject matter (e.g., DNA testing and genetic privacy, the Internet and freedom of expression, the Twenty-Seventh Amendment). Others offer new perspectives on doctrinal or historical subjects of longer standing (e.g., deliberative democracy, economics of affirmative action, jury service as a political right, the Seneca Falls Convention).

During the past decade, the constitutional philosophy of the Rehnquist Court has become more identifiable, clarified by many decisions of significant constitutional import. Although easily labeled as "conservative," the Court has in fact been as activist as its recent predecessors in setting forth new doctrine. Nowhere is this more evident than in the Rehnquist Court's rulings scaling back the ability of criminal defendants to use the writ of habeas corpus to obtain federal judicial review, and its rulings in the area of federalism, where expansive notions of states' rights have cabined federal power for the first time since the days of the New Deal. In a notable decision, the Court refused to create a new constitutional right to die with the aid of a physician; in another, it clearly held for the first time that people using the public streets have a constitutional right to loiter without police interference. In other areas of vibrant national interest, such as free speech, abortion, voting rights, and affirmative action, the Court has continued generally along the paths of its predecessors, although often reshaping the precise contours of controlling doctrine.

Although the courts remain the primary subject of constitutional analysis, we have broadly defined the subject of this Encyclopedia to include legislative developments on issues of constitutional import (e.g., welfare rights); historically significant incidents that evaded judicial review (e.g., the impeachment of President William J. Clinton); and developments in the realm of theory (e.g., critical race theory). Such an approach corresponds to a recently expanded body of scholarly work challenging the view that the judiciary is the sole interpreter of the Constitution. The original volumes of the Encyclopedia shared this broad definition of constitutional law.

To encourage browsing we have continued the original practice of incorporating extensive cross-referencing into the articles. A cross-reference is indicated by small capitals, enabling the reader to know where he or she can turn to discover more on related topics. Often the reader who follows these signs will find the issues discussed from a different perspective. With only a handful of exceptions, this second edition's coverage of topics ended in mid-1999, when we "closed the book" at the end of the Supreme Court's October 1998 term.

We are grateful to Elly Dickason and Brian Kinsey of Macmillan Reference for their unfailing help throughout the planning and the editorial process that produced this second edition. We are indebted as well to the numerous authors who contributed to this project; both their patience and insight were requisite for the project's fulfillment. Finally, we owe everything to our loving wives, Elyse Levy, Smiley Karst, and Melissa Bomes, for their support and encouragement throughout the long years of editing this Encyclopedia.

LEONARD W. LEVY
KENNETH L. KARST
ADAM WINKLER

List of Articles

List of Contributors

(1986)

Benjamin Aaron
Professor of Law, Emeritus
University of California, Los Angeles

LABOR AND THE ANTITRUST LAWS

Henry J. Abraham
James Hart Professor of Government and Foreign Affairs
University of Virginia

AFFIRMATIVE ACTION
APPOINTMENT OF SUPREME COURT JUSTICES
BIDDLE, FRANCIS
FUNDAMENTAL RIGHTS
HARLAN, JOHN MARSHALL (1833–1911)
ORDERED LIBERTY

Norman Abrams
Professor of Law
University of California, Los Angeles

BALLEW V. GEORGIA
BURCH V. LOUISIANA
JURY SIZE
JURY UNANIMITY
LAW ENFORCEMENT AND FEDERAL–STATE RELATIONS

David Adamany
Professor of Law and Political Science, and President
Wayne State University

CAMPAIGN FINANCE
ELECTIONS, REGULATION OF
POLITICAL PARTIES IN CONSTITUTIONAL LAW
PRIMARY ELECTION

Lee A. Albert
Professor of Law
State University of New York, Buffalo

FEDERAL GRANTS-IN-AID

Francis A. Allen
Edson R. Sunderland Professor of Law
University of Michigan

RIGHT TO COUNSEL

Reginald Alleyne
Professor of Law
University of California, Los Angeles

EMPLOYMENT DISCRIMINATION

George Anastaplo
Professor of Law
Loyola University of Chicago Law School
Lecturer in the Liberal Arts
University of Chicago

POLITICAL PHILOSOPHY OF THE CONSTITUTION

Alison Grey Anderson
Professor of Law
University of California, Los Angeles

SECURITIES LAW AND THE CONSTITUTION

David A. Anderson
Rosenberg Centennial Professor of Law
University of Texas, Austin

GAG ORDER
NEW YORK TIMES CO. V. SULLIVAN
SEDITIOUS LIBEL

Michael Asimow
Professor of Law
University of California, Los Angeles

NATIONAL POLICE POWER
SIXTEENTH AMENDMENT

James R. Asperger
United States Attorney
Los Angeles

ARREST WARRANT
OVERRULING
SEARCH WARRANT
VAGRANCY LAWS

Carl A. Auerbach
Professor of Law
University of Minnesota, Twin Cities

SUBVERSIVE ADVOCACY

Barbara Allen Babcock
Ernest W. McFarland Professor of Law
Stanford Law School

ARGERSINGER V. HAMLIN
ASH, UNITED STATES V.
BETTS V. BRADY
ESCOBEDO V. ILLINOIS
FARETTA V. CALIFORNIA
FRUIT OF THE POISONOUS TREE
JOHNSON V. ZERBST
KIRBY V. ILLINOIS

LINEUP
MASSIAH V. UNITED STATES
POWELL V. ALABAMA
PRETRIAL DISCLOSURE
WADE, UNITED STATES V.

Stewart Abercrombie Baker
Attorney
Steptoe & Johnson, Washington, D.C.

STEVENS, JOHN PAUL

Lance Banning
Professor of History
University of Kentucky

MADISON, JAMES

Sotirios A. Barber
Professor of Government
University of Notre Dame

CHECKS AND BALANCES
DELEGATION OF POWER
ENUMERATED POWERS
GENERAL WELFARE CLAUSE
INHERENT POWERS
INTERGOVERNMENTAL IMMUNITY
INTERPOSITION
LIMITED GOVERNMENT
NECESSARY AND PROPER CLAUSE
TENTH AMENDMENT
UNWRITTEN CONSTITUTION

Edward L. Barrett, Jr.
Professor of Law
University of California, Davis

DIRECT AND INDIRECT TAXES
EXCISE TAX
FOREIGN COMMERCE
IMPORT-EXPORT CLAUSE
IMPOST
JURISDICTION TO TAX
ORIGINAL PACKAGE DOCTRINE
STATE REGULATION OF COMMERCE
STATE TAXATION OF COMMERCE
TAXING AND SPENDING POWERS

Paul M. Bator
John P. Wilson Professor of Law
University of Chicago

JUDICIAL SYSTEM, FEDERAL
JUDICIARY ACT OF 1789

Maurice G. Baxter
Professor of History
Indiana University

WEBSTER, DANIEL

Derrick A. Bell
Professor of Law
Harvard Law School

DESEGREGATION

Herman Belz
Professor of History
University of Maryland

CONSTITUTIONAL HISTORY, 1861–1865
CONSTITUTIONALISM AND THE AMERICAN FOUNDING
THEORIES OF THE UNION
WAITE, MORRISON R.

Paul Bender
Dean and Professor of Law
Arizona State University

RETROACTIVITY OF JUDICIAL DECISIONS

Michael Les Benedict
Professor of History
Ohio State University

CONSTITUTIONAL HISTORY, 1865–1877

Raoul Berger
Professor of Law, Emeritus
Harvard Law School

IMPEACHMENT

Walter Berns
*John M. Olin Distinguished Scholar in Constitutional
  and Legal Studies*
American Enterprise Institute
Professorial Lecturer
Georgetown University

CAPITAL PUNISHMENT CASES OF 1972
CAPITAL PUNISHMENT CASES OF 1976
NATURAL RIGHTS AND THE CONSTITUTION

Richard B. Bernstein
Research Curator, U.S. Constitution Exhibition
The New York Public Library

BALDWIN, ROGER N.
BOUDIN, LOUIS B.
BRANT, IRVING

CARR, ROBERT K.
COHEN, MORRIS R.
CRIMINAL SYNDICALISM LAWS
CROSSKEY, WILLIAM W.
CUSHMAN, ROBERT E.
HAMILTON, WALTON HALE
HOWE, MARK DEWOLFE
JENSEN, MERRILL
KELLY, ALFRED H.
MINTON, SHERMAN
ROSSITER, CLINTON
STORY, JOSEPH (with Henry Steele Commager)
SWISHER, CARL BRENT
TEN BROEK, JACOBUS
TUGWELL, REXFORD G.
WIGMORE, JOHN HENRY

Scott H. Bice
Professor of Law and Dean of the Law Center
University of Southern California

LEGISLATIVE INTENT

Joseph W. Bishop, Jr.
Richard Ely Professor of Law
Yale Law School

DECLARATION OF WAR
MILITARY JUSTICE
POLICE ACTION
STATE OF WAR

Charles L. Black, Jr.
Sterling Professor of Law, Emeritus
Yale Law School
Professor of Law
Columbia University

ADMIRALTY AND MARITIME JURISDICTION
EQUITY
STATE ACTION

Vincent Blasi
Corliss Lamont Professor of Civil Liberties
Columbia University

DEMONSTRATION
PUBLIC FORUM

Albert P. Blaustein
Professor of Law
Rutgers-Camden School of Law

INFLUENCE OF THE AMERICAN CONSTITUTION
  ABROAD

Maxwell Bloomfield
Professor of History and Law
Catholic University of America

COMMENTATORS ON THE CONSTITUTION

Grace Ganz Blumberg
Professor of Law
University of California, Los Angeles

HELVERING V. DAVIS
SOCIAL SECURITY ACT
STEWARD MACHINE COMPANY V. DAVIS

Lee C. Bollinger
Professor of Law
University of Michigan

BURGER, WARREN E.

Robert H. Bork
Judge
United States Court of Appeals for the District of
    Columbia Circuit

JUDICIAL REVIEW AND DEMOCRACY

Paul Brest
Kenneth and Harle Montgomery Professor of Clinical
    Legal Education
Stanford Law School

CONSTITUTIONAL INTERPRETATION
LEGISLATION

Ralph S. Brown
Simeon E. Baldwin Professor of Law, Emeritus
Yale Law School

LOYALTY OATH
LOYALTY-SECURITY PROGRAMS

Barbara Brudno
Attorney
Former Professor of Law
University of California, Los Angeles

WEALTH DISCRIMINATION

Harold H. Bruff
John S. Redditt Professor of Law
University of Texas, Austin

OFFICE OF MANAGEMENT AND BUDGET

Robert A. Burt
Southmayd Professor of Law
Yale University

FAMILY AND THE CONSTITUTION
MENTAL ILLNESS AND THE CONSTITUTION
MENTAL RETARDATION AND THE CONSTITUTION

Paul D. Carrington
Professor of Law and Dean of the Law School
Duke University

TRIAL BY JURY

Robert L. Carter
Judge
United States District Court, Southern District of
    New York

UNITED STATES DISTRICT COURTS

Gerhard Casper
William B. Graham Professor of Law and Dean of the
    Law School
University of Chicago

CONSTITUTIONALISM

Donald S. Chisum
Professor of Law
University of Washington, Seattle

PATENT

Jesse H. Choper
Dean and Professor of Law
University of California, Berkeley

SEPARATION OF CHURCH AND STATE

William Cohen
C. Wendell and Edith M. Carlsmith Professor of Law
Stanford Law School

CLERKS
DOUGLAS, WILLIAM O.
PREEMPTION

Henry Steele Commager
Professor of History, Emeritus
Amherst College

STORY, JOSEPH (with Richard B. Bernstein)

Richard C. Cortner
Professor of Political Science
University of Arizona

CONSTITUTIONAL HISTORY, 1961–1977

Robert M. Cover
Chancellor Kent Professor of Law
Yale Law School

TAFT COURT

Archibald Cox
Carl M. Loeb University Professor, Emeritus
Harvard University

FIRST AMENDMENT
HUGHES COURT
STONE COURT

William J. Cuddihy
Claremont, California

ASSISTANCE, WRIT OF
BONHAM'S CASE
CALVIN'S CASE
FOURTH AMENDMENT, HISTORICAL ORIGINS OF
GENERAL WARRANT
OTIS, JAMES, JR.
PAXTON'S CASE
WILKES CASES

David P. Currie
Harry N. Wyatt Professor of Law
University of Chicago

JUDICIAL POWER

Thomas Curry
Vicar for Priests
Archdiocese of Los Angeles

BACKUS, ISAAC
HOOKER, THOMAS
LELAND, JOHN
WILLIAMS, ROGER

Richard Danzig
Attorney
Latham, Watkins & Hills, Washington, D.C.

CONSCRIPTION (with Ira Nerken)

Robert Dawidoff
Associate Professor of History
Claremont Graduate School

ADAMS, HENRY
RANDOLPH, JOHN

Howard E. Dean
Professor of Political Science
Portland State University

JUDICIAL POLICYMAKING
MECHANICAL JURISPRUDENCE
THAYER, JAMES BRADLEY

Walter Dellinger
Professor of Law
Duke University

AMENDING PROCESS

John Patrick Diggins
Professor of History
University of California, Irvine

PROGRESSIVE CONSTITUTIONAL THOUGHT

Norman Dorsen
Stokes Professor of Law
New York University
President
American Civil Liberties Union

AMERICAN CIVIL LIBERTIES UNION
CIVIL LIBERTIES
DRAFT CARD BURNING
FLAG DESECRATION

Robert F. Drinan, S.J.
Professor of Law
Georgetown University
Former Member of Congress (1971–1981)

CIVIL DISOBEDIENCE

Murray Dry
Professor of Political Science
Middlebury College

ANTI-FEDERALIST CONSTITUTIONAL THOUGHT
STORING, HERBERT J.

Patrick Dutton
Attorney
Vinnedge, Lance & Glenn, Ontario, California

NEW JERSEY V. T. L. O.

Frank H. Easterbrook
Judge
United States Court of Appeals for the Seventh
    Circuit
Former Lee and Brena Freeman Professor of Law
University of Chicago

REHNQUIST, WILLIAM H.

Theodore Eisenberg
Professor of Law
Cornell University

AGE DISCRIMINATION
AGE DISCRIMINATION ACT
ANTIDISCRIMINATION LEGISLATION
ARLINGTON HEIGHTS V. METROPOLITAN HOUSING
    DEVELOPMENT CORP.
BANKRUPTCY ACT
BANKRUPTCY POWER
BANKRUPTCY REFORM ACT
BIVENS V. SIX UNKNOWN NAMED AGENTS OF THE
    FEDERAL BUREAU OF NARCOTICS
BUTZ V. ECONOMOU
CIVIL RIGHTS ACT OF 1866 (JUDICIAL
    INTERPRETATION)
CIVIL RIGHTS ACT OF 1957
CIVIL RIGHTS ACT OF 1960
CIVIL RIGHTS ACT OF 1964
CIVIL RIGHTS ACT OF 1968
CIVIL RIGHTS COMMISSION
CIVIL RIGHTS DIVISION
CIVIL RIGHTS REMOVAL
CIVIL RIGHTS REPEAL ACT
CLASSIC, UNITED STATES V.
COLOR OF LAW
DAMAGES
DAVIS V. PASSMAN
DEVELOPMENTALLY DISABLED ASSISTANCE AND BILL
    OF RIGHTS ACT
DOMBROWSKI V. PFISTER
EDELMAN V. JORDAN
EDUCATION AMENDMENTS OF 1972 (TITLE IX)
EDUCATION OF HANDICAPPED CHILDREN ACTS
EXECUTIVE IMMUNITY
EXECUTIVE ORDER
EXECUTIVE ORDER 11246
EXECUTIVE ORDERS 9980 AND 9981
EXHAUSTION OF REMEDIES
FEDERAL PROTECTION OF CIVIL RIGHTS
FEDERAL TORT CLAIMS ACT
FITZPATRICK V. BITZER
GRAVEL V. UNITED STATES

GRIFFIN V. BRECKINRIDGE
GRIGGS V. DUKE POWER CO.
GUEST, UNITED STATES V.
HAGUE V. CONGRESS OF INDUSTRIAL ORGANIZATIONS
HODGES V. UNITED STATES
HUTCHINSON V. PROXMIRE
IMBLER V. PACHTMAN
IMPLIED CONSTITUTIONAL RIGHTS OF ACTION
INSTITUTIONAL LITIGATION (with Stephen C. Yeazell)
JONES V. ALFRED H. MAYER CO.
JUDICIAL IMMUNITY
KATZENBACH V. MORGAN
LAKE COUNTRY ESTATES, INC. V. TAHOE REGIONAL
    PLANNING AGENCY
LARSON V. DOMESTIC AND FOREIGN COMMERCE
    CORPORATION
LAU V. NICHOLS
LEGISLATIVE IMMUNITY
MITCHUM V. FOSTER
MONELL V. DEPARTMENT OF SOCIAL SERVICES
MONROE V. PAPE
MUNICIPAL IMMUNITY
OPEN HOUSING LAWS
OREGON V. MITCHELL
OWEN V. CITY OF INDEPENDENCE
PALMER V. THOMPSON
PIERSON V. RAY
QUERN V. JORDAN
REHABILITATION ACT
REVISED STATUTES OF THE UNITED STATES
SCHEUER V. RHODES
SCREWS V. UNITED STATES
SECTION 1983, TITLE 42, UNITED STATES CODE
    (JUDICIAL INTERPRETATION)
SOUTH CAROLINA V. KATZENBACH
SPEECH OR DEBATE CLAUSE
STRICT CONSTRUCTION
STUMP V. SPARKMAN
TENNEY V. BRANDHOVE
UNITED STEELWORKERS OF AMERICA V. WEBER
VOTING RIGHTS ACT OF 1965 AND ITS AMENDMENTS
WAIVER OF CONSTITUTIONAL RIGHTS
WASHINGTON V. DAVIS
WOOD V. STRICKLAND

Daniel J. Elazar
President
Center for the Study of Federalism
Professor of Political Science
Temple University

FEDERALISM, THEORY OF

Ward E. Y. Elliott
Professor of Government
Claremont McKenna College

AVERY V. MIDLAND COUNTY
BAKER V. CARR
COLEGROVE V. GREEN
COLEMAN V. MILLER
DIRECT ELECTIONS
ELECTORAL COLLEGE
FIFTEENTH AMENDMENT (JUDICIAL
  INTERPRETATION)
GERRYMANDER
MULTIMEMBER DISTRICT
O'BRIEN V. BROWN
ONE PERSON, ONE VOTE
REPRESENTATION

Richard E. Ellis
Professor of History
State University of New York, Buffalo

CHASE, SAMUEL
CUSHING, WILLIAM
DUVALL, GABRIEL
ELLSWORTH, OLIVER
IREDELL, JAMES
JAY, JOHN
PATERSON, WILLIAM
TODD, THOMAS
WASHINGTON, BUSHROD

Thomas I. Emerson
Augustus E. Lines Professor of Law, Emeritus
Yale Law School

FREEDOM OF SPEECH
FREEDOM OF THE PRESS

David F. Epstein
Analyst
United States Department of Defense,
  Washington, D.C.

FEDERALIST, THE

Edward J. Erler
Professor of Political Science
California State University, San Bernardino

CONCURRENT POWERS
DISCRETE AND INSULAR MINORITIES
EX POST FACTO
FIREFIGHTERS LOCAL UNION NO. 1784 V. STOTTS

JUDICIAL LEGISLATION
O'CONNOR, SANDRA DAY
ROGERS V. LODGE

Robert K. Faulkner
Professor of Political Science
Boston College

BICKEL, ALEXANDER M.
LOCKE, JOHN
MARSHALL, JOHN

John D. Feerick
Professor of Law and Dean of the Law School
Fordham University

PRESIDENTIAL SUCCESSION

Don E. Fehrenbacher
Professor of History
Stanford University

CONSTITUTIONAL HISTORY, 1848–1861
DRED SCOTT V. SANDFORD

David Fellman
Vilas Professor of Political Science, Emeritus
University of Wisconsin, Madison

CRIMINAL PROCEDURE
FREEDOM OF ASSEMBLY AND ASSOCIATION

Martha A. Field
Professor of Law
Harvard Law School

ABSTENTION DOCTRINE
FORTAS, ABE

Paul Finkelman
Professor of History
State University of New York, Binghamton

ARTHUR, CHESTER A.
BATES, EDWARD
BENTON, THOMAS HART
BINGHAM, JOHN A.
BINNEY, HORACE
BIRNEY, JAMES G.
BLACK, JEREMIAH S.
BRECKINRIDGE, JOHN
BUCHANAN, JAMES
BUTLER, BENJAMIN F.
CARPENTER, MATTHEW H.
COMMONWEALTH V. JENNISON

CONKLING, ROSCOE
CRITTENDEN, JOHN J.
CURTIS, GEORGE T.
DAVIS, JEFFERSON
DOUGLAS, STEPHEN A.
FEDERAL TEST ACTS
FESSENDEN, WILLIAM PITT
FILLMORE, MILLARD
GARFIELD, JAMES A.
GARRISON, WILLIAM LLOYD
GRANT, ULYSSES SIMPSON
HAYES, RUTHERFORD B.
HAYNE, ROBERT YOUNG
JACKSON'S PROCLAMATION TO THE PEOPLE OF SOUTH
    CAROLINA
JACKSON'S VETO OF THE BANK OF THE UNITED
    STATES BILL
JOHNSON, REVERDY
JULIAN, GEORGE
PIERCE, FRANKLIN
PINKNEY, WILLIAM
PRIGG V. PENNSYLVANIA
SEWARD, WILLIAM H.
STANBERY, HENRY S.
STANTON, EDWIN M.
STEPHENS, ALEXANDER H.
STEVENS, THADDEUS
SUMNER, CHARLES
TARIFF ACT
TAYLOR, ZACHARY
TOOMBS, ROBERT A.
TRUMBULL, LYMAN
TYLER, JOHN
WHEATON, HENRY
WILMOT PROVISO
WIRT, WILLIAM
WOODBURY, LEVI

Louis Fisher
Specialist in American National Government
Congressional Research Service, The Library of
    Congress

CARTER, JIMMY
EMERGENCY POWERS
EXECUTIVE ORDER 10340
LEGISLATIVE VETO
PRESIDENTIAL ORDINANCE-MAKING POWER
PRESIDENTIAL SPENDING POWER
TRUMAN, HARRY S.
VETO POWER
YOUNGSTOWN SHEET & TUBE CO. V. SAWYER

Owen M. Fiss
Alexander M. Bickel Professor of Public Law
Yale Law School

FULLER COURT
RACIAL DISCRIMINATION

David H. Flaherty
Professor of History
University of Western Ontario

FUNDAMENTAL LAW (HISTORY)

Caleb Foote
Elizabeth Josselyn Boalt Professor of Law
University of California, Berkeley

BAIL

George Forsyth
Claremont, California

ADAMS, JOHN QUINCY

Marvin E. Frankel
Attorney
Kramer, Levin, Nessen, Kamen & Frankel
Former Judge
United States District Court, Eastern District of New
    York

GRAND JURY

John Hope Franklin
James B. Duke Professor of History, Emeritus
Duke University

SLAVERY AND THE CONSTITUTION

Paul A. Freund
Carl M. Loeb University Professor, Emeritus
Harvard Law School

SUPREME COURT (HISTORY)

Gerald E. Frug
Professor of Law
Harvard Law School

CITIES AND THE CONSTITUTION

Jaime B. Fuster
Member of Congress
Puerto Rico
Professor of Law
University of Puerto Rico

PUERTO RICO, CONSTITUTIONAL STATUS OF

David J. Garrow
Associate Professor of Political Science
City College of New York and City University
Graduate School

KING, MARTIN LUTHER, JR.

William Gillette
Professor of History
Rutgers University

FIFTEENTH AMENDMENT (FRAMING AND
RATIFICATION)

Ruth Bader Ginsburg
Judge
United States Court of Appeals for the District of
Columbia Circuit

REPRODUCTIVE AUTONOMY
SEX DISCRIMINATION

Robert Jerome Glennon
Professor of Law
University of Arizona

BROWN, HENRY BILLINGS
FRANK, JEROME N.

Carole E. Goldberg-Ambrose
Professor of Law
University of California, Los Angeles

AMERICAN INDIANS AND THE CONSTITUTION
CONCURRENT JURISDICTION
DECLARATORY JUDGMENT
DIVERSITY JURISDICTION
FEDERAL QUESTION JURISDICTION
FEDERAL RULES OF CIVIL PROCEDURE
REMOVAL OF CASES

Abraham S. Goldstein
Sterling Professor of Law
Yale Law School

RIGHT TO BE INFORMED OF ACCUSATION

Joel K. Goldstein
Attorney
Goldstein & Price, St. Louis

VICE-PRESIDENCY

David Gordon
Attorney
D'Ancona & Pflaum, Chicago

ACT OF STATE DOCTRINE
ADAMS V. TANNER
ADAMSON EIGHT-HOUR ACT
AGRICULTURAL ADJUSTMENT ACT OF 1933
AGRICULTURAL ADJUSTMENT ACT OF 1938
AGRICULTURAL MARKETING AGREEMENT ACT
ALLEN-BRADLEY COMPANY V. LOCAL UNION #3
ALLGEYER V. LOUISIANA
AMES, FISHER
APEX HOSIERY COMPANY V. LEADER
APPALACHIAN ELECTRIC POWER COMPANY V. UNITED
STATES
ARNOLD, THURMAN
BARTKUS V. ILLINOIS
BATES V. STATE BAR OF ARIZONA
BENTON V. MARYLAND
BIBB V. NAVAJO FREIGHT LINES, INC.
BITUMINOUS COAL ACT
BOB-LO EXCURSION COMPANY V. MICHIGAN
BREWSTER V. UNITED STATES
BURBANK V. LOCKHEED AIR TERMINAL
BURNS BAKING COMPANY V. BRYAN
BUSHELL'S CASE
CARTER, JAMES COOLIDGE
CHAE CHAN PING V. UNITED STATES
CHAMPION V. AMES
CHICAGO, BURLINGTON & QUINCY RAILROAD CO. V.
CHICAGO
CHICAGO, MILWAUKEE & ST. PAUL RAILWAY CO. V.
MINNESOTA
CHILD LABOR TAX ACT
CHINESE EXCLUSION ACT
CHOATE, JOSEPH H.
CIRCUIT COURTS OF APPEALS ACT
CLARK DISTILLING CO. V. WESTERN MARYLAND
RAILWAY CO.
CLAYTON ACT
CLEVELAND, GROVER
CODISPOTI V. PENNSYLVANIA
COPPAGE V. KANSAS
CORRIGAN V. BUCKLEY
COYLE V. SMITH
CUMMINGS, HOMER S.
DAVIS, JOHN W.
DAYTON-GOOSE CREEK RAILWAY COMPANY V.
UNITED STATES
DEAN MILK COMPANY V. CITY OF MADISON
DE MINIMIS NON CURAT LEX
DILLON, JOHN F.

POLLAK, WALTER H.
POLLOCK V. WILLIAMS
PRUDENTIAL INSURANCE COMPANY V. BENJAMIN
PURE FOOD AND DRUG ACT
RAILROAD CONTROL ACT
RAILROAD RETIREMENT ACT
RAYMOND MOTOR TRANSPORTATION COMPANY V.
   RICE
RIBNIK V. MCBRIDE
ROBINSON-PATMAN ACT
SELDEN, JOHN
SHERMAN ANTITRUST ACT
SHREVEPORT DOCTRINE
SIMON V. EASTERN KENTUCKY WELFARE RIGHTS
   ORGANIZATION
SMYTH V. AMES
SOUTH-EASTERN UNDERWRITERS ASSOCIATION V.
   UNITED STATES
STAFFORD V. WALLACE
STANDARD OIL COMPANY V. UNITED STATES
STETTLER V. O'HARA
STREAM OF COMMERCE DOCTRINE
SWIFT & COMPANY V. UNITED STATES
TENNESSEE VALLEY AUTHORITY ACT
TRANS-MISSOURI FREIGHT ASSOCIATION V.UNITED
   STATES
TYSON & BROTHER V. BANTON
ULTRA VIRES
UNITED MINE WORKERS V. CORONADO COAL
   COMPANY
UNITED MINE WORKERS V. UNITED STATES
VICINAGE
WABASH, ST. LOUIS & PACIFIC RAILWAY V. ILLINOIS
WAGNER ACT
WALZ V. TAX COMMISSION
WATER POWER ACT
WEBB-KENYON ACT
WICKERSHAM, GEORGE
WILSON V. NEW
WINSHIP, IN RE
WOLFF PACKING COMPANY V. COURT OF INDUSTRIAL
   RELATIONS
WOODS V. CLOYD W. MILLER COMPANY
WYTHE, GEORGE
YAKUS V. UNITED STATES
YAMASHITA, IN RE

William B. Gould
Charles A. Beardsley Professor of Law
Stanford Law School

LOCHNER V. NEW YORK
WORKERS' COMPENSATION LEGISLATION

Henry F. Graff
Professor of History
Columbia University

NIXON, RICHARD M.

Kent Greenawalt
Cardozo Professor of Jurisprudence
Columbia University

CONSCIENTIOUS OBJECTION
INCITEMENT TO UNLAWFUL CONDUCT

Jack Greenberg
Professor of Law
Columbia University
Former General Counsel
NAACP Legal Defense & Educational Fund

CIVIL RIGHTS
NAACP LEGAL DEFENSE & EDUCATIONAL FUND

Linda Greenhouse
Staff Writer
The New York Times

GOLDBERG, ARTHUR J.

Eugene Gressman
William Rand Kenan, Jr., Professor of Law
University of North Carolina, Chapel Hill

JUDICIAL CODE
MURPHY, FRANK
STAY OF EXECUTION
SUPREME COURT PRACTICE

Thomas C. Grey
Professor of Law
Stanford Law School

HIGHER LAW

Erwin N. Griswold
Partner
Jones, Day, Reavis & Pogue, Washington, D.C.
Former Dean
Harvard Law School
Former Solicitor General of the United States

SOLICITOR GENERAL

Gerald Gunther
William Nelson Cromwell Professor of Law
Stanford Law School

DOWLING, NOEL T.
HAND, LEARNED
JUDICIAL REVIEW

Nathan Hakman
Professor of Political Science
State University of New York, Binghamton

INTEREST GROUP LITIGATION

Kermit L. Hall
Professor of History and Law
University of Florida

BOND, HUGH LENNOX
BREWER, DAVID J.
CAMPBELL, JOHN A.
CIRCUIT COURTS
CRANCH, WILLIAM
GRIER, ROBERT C.
GROSSCUP, PETER S.
HASTIE, WILLIAM HENRY
MORROW, WILLIAM W.
NELSON, SAMUEL
PARDEE, DON ALBERT
PETERS, RICHARD
POLK, JAMES KNOX
SAWYER, LORENZO

Catherine Hancock
Associate Professor of Law
Tulane University

CRIMINAL CONSPIRACY
FAY V. NOIA
NO-KNOCK ENTRY
PORNOGRAPHY
TOWNSEND V. SAIN

Louis Henkin
University Professor
Columbia University

FOREIGN AFFAIRS

Harold W. Horowitz
Vice Chancellor for Faculty Relations and Professor of Law
University of California, Los Angeles

CHOICE OF LAW

A. E. Dick Howard
White Burkett Miller Professor of Law and Public Affairs
University of Virginia

BURGER COURT
MAGNA CARTA

Samuel P. Huntington
Director, Center for International Affairs
Eaton Professor of the Science of Government
Harvard University

CIVIL–MILITARY RELATIONS

James Willard Hurst
Vilas Professor of Law, Emeritus
University of Wisconsin, Madison

FREEDOM OF CONTRACT
TREASON

Harold M. Hyman
William P. Hobby Professor of History
Rice University

CHASE, SALMON P.
CIVIL RIGHTS ACT OF 1866 (FRAMING)
EMANCIPATION PROCLAMATION
HABEAS CORPUS ACT OF 1863
JOHNSON, ANDREW
MILLIGAN, EX PARTE
SLAUGHTERHOUSE CASES
TEXAS V. WHITE
THIRTEENTH AMENDMENT (FRAMING)
VALLANDIGHAM, EX PARTE
WADE-DAVIS BILL

Clyde E. Jacobs
Professor of Political Science, Emeritus
University of California, Davis

ELEVENTH AMENDMENT
SOVEREIGN IMMUNITY

Henry V. Jaffa
Henry Salvatori Research Professor of Political Philosophy
Claremont McKenna College and Claremont Graduate School

LINCOLN, ABRAHAM

Alan R. Jones
Professor of History
Grinnell College

COOLEY, THOMAS M.

Sanford H. Kadish
Morrison Professor of Law
University of California, Berkeley

PROCEDURAL DUE PROCESS OF LAW, CRIMINAL

Yale Kamisar
Henry K. Ransom Professor of Law
University of Michigan

POLICE INTERROGATION AND CONFESSIONS

John Kaplan
Jackson Eli Reynolds Professor of Law
Stanford Law School

CLARK, TOM C.
DRUG REGULATION
EVIDENCE
HARMLESS ERROR

Kenneth L. Karst
Professor of Law
University of California, Los Angeles

ABSOLUTISM (FREEDOM OF SPEECH AND PRESS)
ACCESS TO THE COURTS
ADEQUATE STATE GROUNDS
AKE V. OKLAHOMA
ALEXANDER V. HOLMES COUNTY BOARD OF
    EDUCATION
ALIEN
ALL DELIBERATE SPEED
ALLEN V. WRIGHT
ALLIED STRUCTURAL STEEL COMPANY V. SPANNAUS
AMBACH V. NORWICK
ANCILLARY JURISDICTION
APPEAL
APPELLATE JURISDICTION
ARNETT V. KENNEDY
ASHWANDER V. TENNESSEE VALLEY AUTHORITY
ATASCADERO STATE HOSPITAL V. SCANLON
BADGES OF SERVITUDE
BALDWIN V. FISH & GAME COMMISSION
BARROWS V. JACKSON
BELL V. MARYLAND
BEREA COLLEGE V. KENTUCKY
BIRTH CONTROL
BISHOP V. WOOD
BLUM V. YARETSKY
BOARD OF CURATORS V. HOROWITZ
BOARD OF EDUCATION V. PICO
BOARD OF REGENTS V. ROTH
BODDIE V. CONNECTICUT
BOLLING V. SHARPE
BOUNDS V. SMITH
BRANDEIS BRIEF
BREEDLOVE V. SUTTLES
BRIEF
BROADRICK V. OKLAHOMA

BROCKETT V. SPOKANE ARCADES, INC.
BROWN V. BOARD OF EDUCATION
BROWN V. SOCIALIST WORKERS '74 CAMPAIGN
    COMMITTEE
BROWN V. UNITED STATES
BUCHANAN V. WARLEY
BUCK V. BELL
BURTON V. WILMINGTON PARKING AUTHORITY
CALIFANO V. GOLDFARB
CALIFANO V. WESTCOTT
CAREY V. POPULATION SERVICES INTERNATIONAL
CARROLL V. PRESIDENT AND COMMISSIONERS OF
    PRINCESS ANNE
CENTRAL HUDSON GAS & ELECTRIC CORP. V. PUBLIC
    SERVICE COMMISSION
CERTIFICATION
CERTIORARI, WRIT OF
CHILLING EFFECT
CITY COUNCIL OF LOS ANGELES V. TAXPAYERS FOR
    VINCENT
CLAIMS COURT
CLEVELAND BOARD OF EDUCATION V. LAFLEUR
COLUMBIA BROADCASTING SYSTEM, INC. V. FEDERAL
    COMMUNICATIONS COMMISSION
COLUMBUS BOARD OF EDUCATION V. PENICK
COMITY, JUDICIAL
COMMERCE COURT
COMPANION CASE
COMPELLING STATE INTEREST
CONFERENCE
CONSENT DECREE
CONSTITUTIONAL COURT
COOPER V. AARON
CORNELIUS V. NAACP LEGAL DEFENSE AND
    EDUCATIONAL FUND, INC.
COURT OF CUSTOMS AND PATENT APPEALS
COURT OF INTERNATIONAL TRADE
COURT OF MILITARY APPEALS
CRAIG V. BOREN
CRAWFORD V. BOARD OF EDUCATION
DANDRIDGE V. WILLIAMS
DE FACTO/DE JURE
DEFUNIS V. ODEGAARD
DEPARTMENT OF AGRICULTURE V. MURRY
DIVORCE AND THE CONSTITUTION
DOCTRINE
DOUGLAS V. CALIFORNIA
DUN & BRADSTREET, INC. V. GREENMOSS BUILDERS,
    INC.
DUNN V. BLUMSTEIN
EDWARDS V. CALIFORNIA
EFFECTS ON COMMERCE
EISENSTADT V. BAIRD

UNCONSTITUTIONALITY
UNITED JEWISH ORGANIZATIONS V. CAREY
UNITED STATES COURT OF APPEALS FOR THE
    FEDERAL CIRCUIT
UNITED STATES TRUST CO. V. NEW JERSEY
VACCINATION
VALLEY FORGE CHRISTIAN COLLEGE V. AMERICANS
    UNITED FOR SEPARATION OF CHURCH AND STATE
VENUE
VLANDIS V. KLINE
WAINWRIGHT V. SYKES
WALKER V. BIRMINGHAM
WARD V. ILLINOIS
WATKINS V. UNITED STATES
WAYTE V. UNITED STATES
WENGLER V. DRUGGISTS MUTUAL INSURANCE
    COMPANY
WESBERRY V. SANDERS
WHALEN V. ROE
WIDMAR V. VINCENT
WILLIAMS V. VERMONT
YOUNGER V. HARRIS
ZABLOCKI V. REDHAIL

Don B. Kates, Jr.
Attorney
Benenson & Kates, San Francisco

SECOND AMENDMENT

Andrew L. Kaufman
Charles Stebbins Fairchild Professor of Law
Harvard Law School

CARDOZO, BENJAMIN N.

David Kaye
Professor of Law
Arizona State University

SOCIAL SCIENCE IN CONSTITUTIONAL LITIGATION
    (with Hans Zeisel)

Morton Keller
Spector Professor of History
Brandeis University

CONSTITUTIONAL HISTORY, 1877–1901
CONSTITUTIONAL HISTORY, 1901–1921

James H. Kettner
Professor of History
University of California, Berkeley

CITIZENSHIP (HISTORICAL DEVELOPMENT)

Edward Keynes
Professor of Political Science
Pennsylvania State University

VIETNAM WAR

Louis W. Koenig
Professor of Political Science
New York University

CABINET

Donald P. Kommers
Professor of Government and International Studies
University of Notre Dame

REGULATORY AGENCIES
SUBJECTS OF COMMERCE
SUPREMACY CLAUSE

Sheldon Krantz
Professor of Law and Dean of the School of Law
University of San Diego

CRUEL AND UNUSUAL PUNISHMENT

James E. Krier
Professor of Law
University of Michigan

ENVIRONMENTAL REGULATION AND THE
    CONSTITUTION

Samuel Krislov
Professor of Political Science
University of Minnesota, Twin Cities

AMICUS CURIAE
"ULYSSES," ONE BOOK ENTITLED, UNITED STATES V.

Philip B. Kurland
William R. Kenan Distinguished Service Professor
University of Chicago

APPOINTING AND REMOVAL POWER, PRESIDENTIAL
EXECUTIVE PRIVILEGE
IMPOUNDMENT OF FUNDS
PARDONING POWER
PRESIDENTIAL POWERS

Stanley I. Kutler
Fox Professor of American Institutions
University of Wisconsin, Madison

BAILEY V. DREXEL FURNITURE CO.
BRADLEY, JOSEPH P.
BUNTING V. OREGON

BUTLER, PIERCE (1866–1939)
CATRON, JOHN
CHARLES RIVER BRIDGE V. WARREN BRIDGE
  COMPANY
CHILD LABOR AMENDMENT
CLIFFORD, NATHAN
CURTIS, BENJAMIN R.
DAVIS, DAVID
DAY, WILLIAM R.
EAKIN V. RAUB
EXECUTIVE ORDERS 9835 AND 10450
GIBSON, JOHN BANNISTER
HAMMER V. DAGENHART
HUNT, WARD
KEATING-OWEN CHILD LABOR ACT
KENT V. DULLES
LEGAL TENDER CASES
MATTHEWS, STANLEY
MCREYNOLDS, JAMES C.
MISSISSIPPI V. JOHNSON
MULLER V. OREGON
PITNEY, MAHLON
SANFORD, EDWARD T.
STRONG, WILLIAM
SWAYNE, NOAH H.
TRUAX V. CORRIGAN
VAN DEVANTER, WILLIS
WEST COAST HOTEL COMPANY V. PARRISH

Wayne R. LaFave
David C. Baum Professor of Law
Professor in the Center for Advanced Study
University of Illinois, Urbana-Champaign

SEARCH AND SEIZURE

Jacob W. Landynski
Professor of Political Science
New School for Social Research

ADMINISTRATIVE SEARCH
AGNELLO V. UNITED STATES
AGUILAR V. TEXAS
ALMEIDA-SANCHEZ V. UNITED STATES
AUTOMOBILE SEARCH
BORDER SEARCH
BRINEGAR V. UNITED STATES
CALANDRA, UNITED STATES V.
CAMARA V. MUNICIPAL COURT
CARROLL V. UNITED STATES
CHIMEL V. CALIFORNIA
CONSENT SEARCH
DRAPER V. UNITED STATES
ELKINS V. UNITED STATES

EXIGENT CIRCUMSTANCES SEARCH
INFORMANT'S TIP
KER V. CALIFORNIA
MAPP V. OHIO
MARSHALL V. BARLOW'S, INC.
PLAIN VIEW DOCTRINE
ROBINSON, UNITED STATES V.
SCHNECKLOTH V. BUSTAMONTE
SEARCH INCIDENT TO ARREST
SILVER PLATTER DOCTRINE
SILVERTHORNE LUMBER CO. V. UNITED STATES
SPINELLI V. UNITED STATES
STONE V. POWELL
TERRY V. OHIO
UNREASONABLE SEARCH
WEEKS V. UNITED STATES
WOLF V. COLORADO
WONG SUN V. UNITED STATES
WYMAN V. JAMES

William Letwin
Professor of Economics
London School of Economics and Political Science

ECONOMIC REGULATION
EVIDENTIARY PRIVILEGE

Betsy Levin
Professor of Law and Dean of the Law School
University of Colorado

EDUCATION AND THE CONSTITUTION

Leonard W. Levy
Andrew W. Mellon All-Claremont Professor of the
  Humanities
Chairman, Graduate Faculty of History
Claremont Graduate School

ADAIR V. UNITED STATES
ADAMSON V. CALIFORNIA
ADKINS V. CHILDREN'S HOSPITAL
AGUILAR V. FELTON
ALBERTSON V. SUBVERSIVE ACTIVITIES CONTROL
  BOARD
AMERICAN INSURANCE COMPANY V. CANTER
ARTICLES OF CONFEDERATION
ASHTON V. CAMERON COUNTY WATER IMPROVEMENT
  DISTRICT
BALDWIN V. NEW YORK
BANCROFT, GEORGE
BANK OF AUGUSTA V. EARLE
BARRON V. CITY OF BALTIMORE
BAYARD V. SINGLETON

HOLMES V. WALTON
HOME BUILDING & LOAN ASSOCIATION V. BLAISDELL
HOUSTON, CHARLES H.
HOWARD, JACOB M.
HUMPHREY, HUBERT H.
HUMPHREY'S EXECUTOR V. UNITED STATES
HURTADO V. CALIFORNIA
HYLTON V. UNITED STATES
ILLINOIS V. GATES
IMMUNITY GRANT (SELF-INCRIMINATION)
INALIENABLE POLICE POWER
INCORPORATION DOCTRINE
JACOBS, IN RE
JENKINS V. ANDERSON
JOHNS, UNITED STATES V.
JOHNSON V. LOUISIANA
JONES V. SECURITIES & EXCHANGE COMMISSION
JUDGE PETERS, UNITED STATES V.
JUDICIARY ACT OF 1801
JUDICIARY ACTS OF 1802
KASTIGAR V. UNITED STATES
KEMMLER, IN RE
KIDD V. PEARSON
KILBOURN V. THOMPSON
KIRSCHBAUM V. WALLING
KOLENDER V. LAWSON
LA FOLLETTE, ROBERT M.
LAMONT V. POSTMASTER GENERAL OF THE UNITED
    STATES
LARKIN V. GRENDEL'S DEN, INCORPORATED
LEISY V. HARDIN
LICENSE CASES
LILBURNE, JOHN
LOAN ASSOCIATION V. TOPEKA
LOEWE V. LAWLOR
LOUISVILLE JOINT STOCK LAND BANK V. RADFORD
LYNCH V. DONNELLY
MACDONALD, UNITED STATES V.
MADDEN V. KENTUCKY
MADISON'S "MEMORIAL AND REMONSTRANCE"
MADISON'S NOTES OF THE DEBATES
MALLOY V. HOGAN
MANDAMUS, WRIT OF
MARBURY V. MADISON
MARCHETTI V. UNITED STATES
MARSH V. CHAMBERS
MARSHALL COURT
MARTIN V. HUNTER'S LESSEE
MARTIN V. MOTT
MARYLAND TOLERATION ACT
MASSACHUSETTS BAY, COLONIAL CHARTERS OF
MASSACHUSETTS CIRCULAR LETTER
MASSACHUSETTS CONSTITUTION

MAXWELL V. DOW
MAYOR OF NEW YORK V. MILN
MCCULLOCH V. MARYLAND
MCKEIVER V. PENNSYLVANIA
MCLAUGHLIN, ANDREW C.
MEIKLEJOHN, ALEXANDER
MICHIGAN V. SUMMERS
MILLETT V. PEOPLE OF ILLINOIS
MINNESOTA V. BARBER
MINOR V. HAPPERSETT
MIRANDA V. ARIZONA
MISSOURI PACIFIC RAILROAD V. HUMES
MOREHEAD V. NEW YORK EX REL. TIPALDO
MUELLER V. ALLEN
MURRAY'S LESSEE V. HOBOKEN LAND &
    IMPROVEMENT COMPANY
NEAL V. DELAWARE
NEW JERSEY V. WILSON
NEW JERSEY COLONIAL CHARTERS
NEW JERSEY PLAN
NEW YORK V. QUARLES
NEW YORK CHARTER OF LIBERTIES AND PRIVILEGES
NIX V. WILLIAMS
NORRIS V. ALABAMA
NORTHWESTERN FERTILIZER CO. V. HYDE PARK
NORTHWEST ORDINANCE
OGDEN V. SAUNDERS
OLIVER, IN RE
OLIVER V. UNITED STATES
OREGON V. ELSTAD
OROZCO V. TEXAS
OSBORN V. BANK OF THE UNITED STATES (with
    Kenneth L. Karst)
OVERT ACTS TEST
PACE V. ALABAMA
PALKO V. CONNECTICUT
PANAMA REFINING CO. V. RYAN
PARLIAMENTARY PRIVILEGE
PASSENGER CASES
PAYTON V. NEW YORK
PENNSYLVANIA COLONIAL CHARTERS
PENNSYLVANIA CONSTITUTION OF 1776
PENSACOLA TELEGRAPH CO. V. WESTERN UNION
    TELEGRAPH CO.
PEOPLE V. CROSWELL
PETITION OF RIGHT
PHILADELPHIA & READING RAILROAD CO. V.
    PENNSYLVANIA
PIQUA BRANCH OF THE STATE BANK OF OHIO V.
    KNOOP
PLESSY V. FERGUSON
POINTER V. TEXAS
POLLOCK V. FARMERS' LOAN & TRUST CO.

PREFERRED FREEDOMS
PRICE, UNITED STATES V.
PRODUCTION
PROPELLER GENESEE CHIEF V. FITZHUGH
PROVIDENCE BANK V. BILLINGS
PUBLIC FIGURE
RAILROAD RETIREMENT BOARD V. ALTON RAILWAY
   COMPANY
RAWLE, WILLIAM
REAGAN V. FARMERS' LOAN & TRUST CO.
REESE V. UNITED STATES
RESERVED POLICE POWER
REYNOLDS V. UNITED STATES
RHODE ISLAND V. INNES
RHODE ISLAND AND PROVIDENCE PLANTATIONS,
   CHARTER OF
RIGHT AGAINST SELF-INCRIMINATION
ROANE, SPENCER
ROBERTS V. CITY OF BOSTON
ROCHIN V. CALIFORNIA
ROGERS V. RICHMOND
ROSS, UNITED STATES V.
RULE OF REASON
RUMMEL V. ESTELLE
RUTGERS V. WADDINGTON
SCHALL V. MARTIN
SCHECHTER POULTRY CORP. V. UNITED STATES
SCHMERBER V. CALIFORNIA
SCHROEDER, THEODORE
SELECTIVE EXCLUSIVENESS
SHAW, LEMUEL
SIMS' CASE
SINKING FUND CASES
SOCIAL COMPACT THEORY
SOLEM V. HELM
SONZINSKY V. UNITED STATES
SOUTH DAKOTA V. NEVILLE
SPRINGER V. UNITED STATES
STAMP ACT CONGRESS, RESOLUTIONS OF
STEAGALD V. UNITED STATES
STONE V. FARMERS' LOAN & TRUST CO.
STONE V. MISSISSIPPI
STRAUDER V. WEST VIRGINIA
STUART V. LAIRD
STURGES V. CROWNINSHIELD
SULLIVAN, UNITED STATES V.
SUPREME COURT, 1789–1801
TAXATION WITHOUT REPRESENTATION
TENNESSEE V. GARNER
TEN POUND ACT CASES
TERRETT V. TAYLOR
TESTIMONIAL AND NONTESTIMONIAL COMPULSION
TEST OATH CASES

TEXAS V. BROWN
THORNTON V. CALDOR, INC.
TIEDEMAN, CHRISTOPHER G.
TOLERATION ACT
TREVETT V. WEEDEN
TUCKER, ST. GEORGE
TWINING V. NEW JERSEY
TWO SOVEREIGNTIES RULE
ULLMAN V. UNITED STATES
UNITED RAILWAYS & ELECTRIC CO. OF BALTIMORE V.
   WEST
VAN HORNE'S LESSEE V. DORRANCE
VEAZIE BANK V. FENNO
VERMONT CONSTITUTION OF 1777
VIRGINIA CHARTER OF 1606
VIRGINIA DECLARATION OF RIGHTS AND
   CONSTITUTION OF 1776
VIRGINIA PLAN
VIRGINIA STATUTE OF RELIGIOUS FREEDOM
VON HOLST, HERMANN EDUARD
WALKER, TIMOTHY
WALKER V. SAUVINET
WALLACE V. JAFFREE
WARE V. HYLTON
WARREN, CHARLES
WELSH V. WISCONSIN
WESTON V. CITY COUNCIL OF CHARLESTON
WHEELER, BURTON K.
WICKARD V. FILBURN
WILLIAMS V. FLORIDA
WILLIAMS V. MISSISSIPPI
WILLSON V. BLACK BIRD CREEK MARSH CO.
WONG KIM ARK, UNITED STATES V.
WOODRUFF V. PARHAM
WORTMAN, TUNIS
WRIGHT V. VINTON BRANCH OF MOUNTAIN TRUST
   BANK OF ROANOKE
WRIGHTWOOD DAIRY CO., UNITED STATES V.
WYNEHAMER V. PEOPLE OF NEW YORK
YARBROUGH, EX PARTE
YBARRA V. ILLINOIS
YELLOW DOG CONTRACT
YICK WO V. HOPKINS
ZENGER'S CASE

Wendy E. Levy
Deputy District Attorney
Los Angeles County

BARKER V. WINGO
KLOPFER V. NORTH CAROLINA
MCNABB-MALLORY RULE

Anthony Lewis
Columnist
The New York Times
Lecturer on Law
Harvard Law School

GIDEON V. WAINWRIGHT
PUBLIC TRIAL
WARREN, EARL

Hans A. Linde
Justice
Supreme Court of Oregon

STATE CONSTITUTIONAL LAW

Charles Lister
Attorney
Covington & Burling, Washington, D.C.

HARLAN, JOHN MARSHALL (1899–1971)

Charles A. Lofgren
Crocker Professor of American Politics and History
Claremont McKenna College

CURTISS-WRIGHT EXPORT CORPORATION, UNITED
    STATES V.
KOREAN WAR
MISSOURI V. HOLLAND
NATIONAL LEAGUE OF CITIES V. USERY
WAR POWERS

Gerald P. López
Professor of Law
Stanford Law School

CITIZENSHIP (THEORY)
IMMIGRATION AND ALIENAGE (with Kenneth L. Karst)
TREATY OF GUADALUPE HIDALGO (with Kenneth L.
    Karst)
TREATY ON THE EXECUTION OF PENAL SENTENCES

Richard Loss
Evanston, Illinois

CORWIN, EDWARD S.

Daniel H. Lowenstein
Professor of Law
University of California, Los Angeles

HATCH ACT

Theodore J. Lowi
John L. Senior Professor of American Institutions
Cornell University

POLITICAL PARTIES

Dennis J. Mahoney
Assistant Professor of Political Science
California State University, San Bernardino

ADAMS, SAMUEL
ADVICE AND CONSENT
AMNESTY
APTHEKER V. SECRETARY OF STATE
ARTICLES OF IMPEACHMENT OF ANDREW JOHNSON
ARTICLES OF IMPEACHMENT OF RICHARD M. NIXON
ASSOCIATION, THE
ATTAINDER OF TREASON
BAILEY V. ALABAMA
BALDWIN, ABRAHAM
BAREFOOT V. ESTELLE
BASSETT, RICHARD
BEACON THEATRES, INC. V. WESTOVER
BEARD, CHARLES A.
BECKER AMENDMENT
BEDFORD, GUNNING, JR.
BENIGN RACIAL CLASSIFICATION
BEVERIDGE, ALBERT J.
BICAMERALISM
BILL OF ATTAINDER
BILL OF CREDIT
BLAINE AMENDMENT
BLAIR, JOHN
BLOUNT, WILLIAM
BLUE RIBBON JURY
BOB JONES UNIVERSITY V. UNITED STATES
BORROWING POWER
BREARLY, DAVID
BRICKER AMENDMENT
BROAD CONSTRUCTION
BROOM, JACOB
BROWN V. ALLEN
BRYCE, JAMES
BUDGET
BUDGET AND ACCOUNTING ACT
BURGESS, JOHN W.
BURR, AARON
BUTLER, PIERCE (1744–1822)
CAPITATION TAXES
CARROLL, DANIEL
CARY, JOHN W.
CEASE AND DESIST ORDER
CHIPMAN, NATHANIEL
CLOSED SHOP

MONTESQUIEU
MORRIS, GOUVERNEUR
MORRIS, ROBERT
MURPHY V. FLORIDA
MURPHY V. FORD
MURRAY, WILLIAM
NATIONAL SECURITY ACT
NIXON V. ADMINISTRATOR OF GENERAL SERVICES
NORRIS, GEORGE W.
NOXIOUS PRODUCTS DOCTRINE
OBLIGATION OF CONTRACTS
OPINION OF THE COURT
ORDINANCE OF 1784
PAINE, THOMAS
PALMER RAIDS
PANAMA CANAL TREATIES
PENDLETON, EDMUND
PENDLETON ACT
PENN, WILLIAM
PEREZ V. UNITED STATES
PETIT JURY
PHILADELPHIA V. NEW JERSEY
PICKERING, JOHN
PIERCE, WILLIAM
PINCKNEY, CHARLES
PINCKNEY, CHARLES COTESWORTH
PINCKNEY PLAN
PITT, WILLIAM
PLURALITY OPINION
POCKET VETO
POCKET VETO CASE
POLICE POWER
POSSE COMITATUS ACT
POWELL, THOMAS REED
POWELL V. MCCORMACK
PRATT, CHARLES
PREAMBLE
PRIVACY ACT
PRIVILEGE FROM ARREST
PRIVY COUNCIL
PROHIBITION
QUIRIN, EX PARTE
RANDOLPH, EDMUND
RATIFICATION OF CONSTITUTIONAL AMENDMENTS
RATIO DECIDENDI
READ, GEORGE
RECALL
REFERENDUM
REID V. COVERT
RETROACTIVITY OF LEGISLATION
REVENUE SHARING
RIGHT-PRIVILEGE DISTINCTION (with Kenneth L. Karst)

RODNEY, CAESAR A.
ROOSEVELT, THEODORE
RUTLEDGE, JOHN
SCHICK V. REED
SCHNELL V. DAVIS
SCHOULER, JAMES
SEDITION
SELECTIVE DRAFT LAW CASES
SELECTIVE SERVICE ACTS
SERIATIM
SEVENTEENTH AMENDMENT
SEVENTH AMENDMENT
SHAYS' REBELLION
SHERMAN, ROGER
SMITH, J. ALLEN
SOUNDTRUCKS AND AMPLIFIERS
SOVEREIGNTY
SPAIGHT, RICHARD DOBBS
SPOT RESOLUTIONS
STARE DECISIS
STATE
STATES' RIGHTS
STATES' RIGHTS AMENDMENTS
SUBVERSIVE ACTIVITY
SWAIN V. ALABAMA
TAFT, ROBERT A.
TAYLOR, JOHN
TERRITORY
THIRD AMENDMENT
THORPE, FRANCIS N.
TITLES OF NOBILITY
TOCQUEVILLE, ALEXIS DE
TOWNSHEND ACTS
TROP V. DULLES
TUCKER, HENRY ST. GEORGE
TUCKER, JOHN RANDOLPH
TUCKER, N. BEVERLEY
TWELFTH AMENDMENT
TWENTIETH AMENDMENT
TWENTY-FIFTH AMENDMENT
TWENTY-FIRST AMENDMENT
TWENTY-FOURTH AMENDMENT
TWENTY-SECOND AMENDMENT
TWENTY-SIXTH AMENDMENT
TWENTY-THIRD AMENDMENT
VATTEL, EMERICH DE
VOLSTEAD ACT
WAR POWERS ACTS
WASHINGTON, GEORGE
WASHINGTON'S FAREWELL ADDRESS
WEEMS V. UNITED STATES
WELFARE BENEFITS
WILLIAMSON, HUGH

WILLIAMSON V. LEE OPTICAL CO.
WILLOUGHBY, WESTEL W.
WILSON, WOODROW
YATES, ROBERT
YOUNG, EX PARTE
ZEMEL V. RUSK

Daniel R. Mandelker
Stamper Professor of Law
Washington University, St. Louis

ZONING (with Barbara Ross)

Everett E. Mann, Jr.
Associate Professor of Public Policy and
    Administration
California State College, Bakersfield

FREEDOM OF INFORMATION ACT

Burke Marshall
Nicholas deB. Katzenbach Professor of Law
Yale Law School
Former Solicitor General of the United States

ATTORNEY GENERAL AND DEPARTMENT OF JUSTICE

Alpheus Thomas Mason
McCormick Professor of Jurisprudence, Emeritus
Princeton University

ROBERTS, OWEN J.
STONE, HARLAN F.
TAFT, WILLIAM HOWARD

Charles W. McCurdy
Associate Professor of History and Law
University of Virginia

BLATCHFORD, SAMUEL
FIELD, STEPHEN J.
FULLER, MELVILLE W.
GRAY, HORACE
JACKSON, HOWELL E.
LAMAR, L. Q. C.
MILLER, SAMUEL F.
MONETARY POWER
PECKHAM, RUFUS W.
SHIRAS, GEORGE, JR.
WAITE COURT
WOODS, WILLIAM B.

Gary L. McDowell
Associate Professor of Political Science
Newcomb College of Tulane University

CONGRESS AND THE SUPREME COURT

Carl McGowan
Senior judge
United States Court of Appeals for the District of
    Columbia Circuit

UNITED STATES COURTS OF APPEALS

Robert B. McKay
Professor of Law
New York University

REAPPORTIONMENT

Daniel J. Meador
James Monroe Professor of Law
University of Virginia

COKE, EDWARD

Bernard D. Meltzer
Distinguished Service Professor of Law, Emeritus
University of Chicago

RIGHT-TO-WORK LAWS

Wallace Mendelson
Professor of Government
University of Texas, Austin

CONTRACT CLAUSE

Frank I. Michelman
Professor of Law
Harvard Law School

PROCEDURAL DUE PROCESS OF LAW, CIVIL

Abner J. Mikva
Judge
U.S. Court of Appeals for the District of Columbia
    Circuit

PREVENTIVE DETENTION

Arthur S. Miller
Professor of Law, Emeritus
George Washington University

CONSTITUTIONAL REASON OF STATE
CORPORATIONS AND THE CONSTITUTION

Paul J. Mishkin
Emanuel S. Heller Professor of Law
University of California, Berkeley

HABEAS CORPUS

Robert H. Mnookin
Professor of Law
Stanford Law School

CHILDREN'S RIGHTS
GAULT, IN RE
GINSBERG V. NEW YORK
JUVENILE PROCEEDINGS

Henry P. Monaghan
Thomas Macioce Professor of Law
Columbia University

CONSTITUTIONAL COMMON LAW

Donald G. Morgan
Professor of Politics
Mount Holyoke College

JOHNSON, WILLIAM

Edmund S. Morgan
Sterling Professor of History
Yale University

CONSTITUTIONAL HISTORY BEFORE 1776

Richard E. Morgan
*William Nelson Cromwell Professor of Constitutional
Law and Government*
Bowdoin College

ABINGTON TOWNSHIP SCHOOL DISTRICT V. SCHEMPP
BOARD OF EDUCATION V. ALLEN
CANTWELL V. CONNECTICUT
CHURCH OF JESUS CHRIST OF LATTER DAY SAINTS V.
    UNITED STATES
COCHRAN V. LOUISIANA
COMMITTEE FOR PUBLIC EDUCATION AND RELIGIOUS
    LIBERTY V. REGAN
DAVIS V. BEASON
DOREMUS V. BOARD OF EDUCATION
ENGEL V. VITALE
EPPERSON V. ARKANSAS
EVERSON V. BOARD OF EDUCATION
FLAG SALUTE CASES
GIROUARD V. UNITED STATES
HAMILTON V. BOARD OF REGENTS OF THE
    UNIVERSITY OF CALIFORNIA

JACOBSON V. MASSACHUSETTS
LEMON V. KURTZMAN
LOVELL V. CITY OF GRIFFIN
McCOLLUM V. BOARD OF EDUCATION
MURDOCK V. PENNSYLVANIA
PRINCE V. MASSACHUSETTS
SCHWIMMER, UNITED STATES V.
SEEGER, UNITED STATES V.
SHERBERT V. VERNER
TORCASO V. WATKINS
WISCONSIN V. YODER
WOLMAN V. WALTER
ZORACH V. CLAUSEN

Paul L. Murphy
Professor of History and American Studies
University of Minnesota

ALIEN REGISTRATION ACT
ATOMIC ENERGY ACT
ATTORNEY GENERAL'S LIST
CHAFEE, ZECHARIAH, JR.
COMMUNIST CONTROL ACT
CONGRESSIONAL BUDGET AND IMPOUNDMENT
    CONTROL ACT
CONSTITUTIONAL HISTORY, 1921–1933
CONSTITUTIONAL HISTORY, 1945–1961
DISTRICT OF COLUMBIA REPRESENTATION
    AMENDMENT
DISTRICT OF COLUMBIA SELF-GOVERNING AND
    GOVERNMENT REORGANIZATION ACT
ECONOMIC STABILIZATION ACT
ELEMENTARY AND SECONDARY EDUCATION ACT
EMERGENCY PRICE CONTROL ACT
ESPIONAGE ACT
FEDERAL IMMUNITY ACT
FULL EMPLOYMENT ACT
HEALTH INSURANCE FOR THE AGED ACT (MEDICARE)
HOUSE COMMITTEE ON UN-AMERICAN ACTIVITIES
INTERNAL SECURITY ACT
JENCKS ACT
LANDRUM-GRIFFIN ACT
MUNDT-NIXON BILL
OMNIBUS CRIME CONTROL AND SAFE STREETS ACT
ORGANIZED CRIME CONTROL ACT
PENNSYLVANIA V. NELSON
REPORT OF THE CONFERENCE OF CHIEF JUSTICES ON
    FEDERAL–STATE RELATIONSHIPS
SEDITION ACT
SELECTIVE SERVICE ACT
SHEPPARD-TOWNER MATERNITY ACT
SOUTHERN MANIFESTO

STEEL SEIZURE CONTROVERSY
SUBVERSIVE ACTIVITIES CONTROL BOARD
TAFT-HARTLEY LABOR RELATIONS ACT
WATERGATE AND THE CONSTITUTION
YATES V. UNITED STATES

Walter F. Murphy
McCormick Professor of Jurisprudence
Princeton University

JUDICIAL STRATEGY
JUDICIAL SUPREMACY

William P. Murphy
Paul B. Eaton Professor of Law
University of North Carolina, Chapel Hill

FAIR LABOR STANDARDS ACT
MAXIMUM HOURS AND MINIMUM WAGES
    LEGISLATION

John M. Murrin
Professor of History
Princeton University

BRITISH CONSTITUTION

William E. Nelson
Professor of Law
New York University

FOURTEENTH AMENDMENT (FRAMING)

Ira Nerken
Attorney
Latham, Watkins & Hills, Washington, D.C.

CONSCRIPTION (with Richard Danzig)

Burt Neuborne
Professor of Law, New York University
Director of Litigation, American Civil Liberties Union

BLACKMUN, HARRY A.
LITIGATION STRATEGY

Roger K. Newman
Attorney
New York

BLACK, HUGO L.
CAHN, EDMOND

R. Kent Newmyer
Professor of History
University of Connecticut

BALDWIN, HENRY
BARBOUR, PHILIP P.
MCKINLEY, JOHN
MCLEAN, JOHN
TANEY COURT
TRIMBLE, ROBERT

Melville B. Nimmer
Professor of Law
University of California, Los Angeles

COPYRIGHT
PRIVACY AND THE FIRST AMENDMENT
SYMBOLIC SPEECH

W. John Niven
Professor of History
Claremont Graduate School

VAN BUREN, MARTIN

John T. Noonan, Jr.
Judge
United States Court of Appeals for the Ninth Circuit
Former Professor of Law
University of California, Berkeley

REAGAN, RONALD

John E. Nowak
Professor of Law
University of Illinois

BREACH OF THE PEACE
FELONY
SUBPOENA
TRESPASS

David M. Oshinsky
Professor of History
Rutgers University

MCCARTHYISM

Lewis J. Paper
Attorney
Washington, D.C.

BRANDEIS, LOUIS D.

Michael E. Parrish
Professor of History
University of California, San Diego

AFROYIM V. RUSK
BRIDGES V. CALIFORNIA
BURTON, HAROLD
BYRNES, JAMES F.
CLARKE, JOHN H.
COMMONWEALTH V. SACCO AND VANZETTI
CONSTITUTIONAL HISTORY, 1933–1945
DEBS V. UNITED STATES
ELFBRANDT V. RUSSELL
FRANKFURTER, FELIX
FROHWERK V. UNITED STATES
GERENDE V. BOARD OF SUPERVISORS OF ELECTIONS
GIBONEY V. EMPIRE STORAGE & ICE CO.
HUGHES, CHARLES EVANS
IRVIN V. DOWD
JACKSON, ROBERT H.
JOINT ANTI-FASCIST REFUGEE COMMITTEE V.
  MCGRATH
KENNEDY, JOHN F.
LINMARK ASSOCIATES V. WILLINGBORO
LOVETT, UNITED STATES V.
MCKENNA, JOSEPH
NIEMOTKO V. MARYLAND
PARKER V. LEVY
PROCUNIER V. MARTINEZ
ROBEL V. UNITED STATES
ROSENBERG V. UNITED STATES
RUTLEDGE, WILEY B.
SHAUGHNESSY V. UNITED STATES EX REL. MEZEI
STROMBERG V. CALIFORNIA
TENNESSEE V. SCOPES
WHITE, EDWARD D.
WHITTAKER, CHARLES
WIEMAN V. UPDEGRAFF

J. Francis Paschal
Professor of Law
Duke University

SUTHERLAND, GEORGE

Michael J. Perry
Professor of Law
Northwestern University

ABORTION AND THE CONSTITUTION

Merrill D. Peterson
*Thomas Jefferson Professor of History and Former
  Dean of Faculty*
University of Virginia

ADAMS, JOHN
ALIEN AND SEDITION ACTS
AMERICAN SYSTEM
BANK OF THE UNITED STATES ACTS
CALHOUN, JOHN C.
CLAY, HENRY
CONSTITUTIONAL HISTORY, 1789–1801
CONSTITUTIONAL HISTORY, 1801–1829
INTERNAL IMPROVEMENTS
JACKSON, ANDREW
JEFFERSON, THOMAS
LOUISIANA PURCHASE TREATY
PROCLAMATION OF NEUTRALITY
VIRGINIA AND KENTUCKY RESOLUTIONS
WHISKEY REBELLION

Leo Pfeffer
Professor of Constitutional Law
Long Island University
Former General Counsel American Jewish Congress

AMERICAN JEWISH CONGRESS
CHILD BENEFIT THEORY
CULTS AND THE CONSTITUTION
GOVERNMENT AID TO RELIGIOUS INSTITUTIONS
RELEASED TIME
RELIGION AND FRAUD
RELIGION IN PUBLIC SCHOOLS
RELIGIOUS LIBERTY
RELIGIOUS TEST FOR PUBLIC OFFICE
RELIGIOUS USE OF STATE PROPERTY
SUNDAY CLOSING LAWS

Louis H. Pollak
Judge
United States District Court, Eastern District of
  Pennsylvania

VOTING RIGHTS

Robert C. Post
Professor of Law
University of California, Berkeley

BRENNAN, WILLIAM J., JR.

Monroe E. Price
Professor of Law and Dean
Cardozo School of Law, Yeshiva University of New York

BROADCASTING
FAIRNESS DOCTRINE
PRISONERS' RIGHTS
STEWART, POTTER J.

C. Herman Pritchett
Professor of Political Science, Emeritus
University of California, Santa Barbara

CONGRESSIONAL MEMBERSHIP
VINSON COURT

A. Kenneth Pye
Samuel Fox Mordecai Professor of Law
Duke University

SPEEDY TRIAL

David M. Rabban
Professor of Law
University of Texas, Austin

ACADEMIC FREEDOM

Jeremy Rabkin
Professor of Political Science
Cornell University

LEGISLATIVE POWER

Norman Redlich
Dean and Judge Edward Weinfeld Professor of Law
New York University

NINTH AMENDMENT

Willis L. M. Reese
Charles Evans Hughes Professor of Law, Emeritus
Columbia University

FULL FAITH AND CREDIT

Donald H. Regan
Professor of Law and Professor of Philosophy
University of Michigan

PHILOSOPHY AND THE CONSTITUTION

John Phillip Reid
Professor of Law
New York University

COLONIAL CHARTERS
DOE, CHARLES

Deborah L. Rhode
Professor of Law
Stanford Law School

EQUAL RIGHTS AMENDMENT
NINETEENTH AMENDMENT

Charles E. Rice
Professor of Law
University of Notre Dame

FREEDOM OF PETITION

Kenneth F. Ripple
Judge
United States Court of Appeals for the Seventh Circuit
Professor of Law
University of Notre Dame

CHIEF JUSTICE, ROLE OF THE

John P. Roche
Professor of Civilization and Foreign Affairs and Former Dean of the Fletcher School of Law and Diplomacy
Tufts University

CONSTITUTIONAL CONVENTION OF 1787

Donald M. Roper
Professor of History
State University of New York, New Paltz

KENT, JAMES
LIVINGSTON, HENRY BROCKHOLST
THOMPSON, SMITH

Arthur Rosett
Professor of Law
University of California, Los Angeles

ANTITRUST LAW
PLEA BARGAINING
REED, STANLEY F.
UNCONSTITUTIONAL CONDITIONS

Barbara Ross
Attorney
Ross & Hardies, Chicago

ZONING (with Daniel R. Mandelker)

Ralph A. Rossum
Alice Tweed Tuohy Professor of Government
Claremont McKenna College

DENATURALIZATION
DEPORTATION
EXPATRIATION
NATURALIZATION
WILSON, JAMES

Eugene V. Rostow
Sterling Professor of Law, Emeritus
Yale Law School
*Distinguished Visiting Research Professor of Law and
    Diplomacy*
National Defense University

COMMANDER-IN-CHIEF
WAR, FOREIGN AFFAIRS, AND THE CONSTITUTION

W. W. Rostow
Professor of Economics and History
University of Texas, Austin

JOHNSON, LYNDON B.

Wilfrid E. Rumble
Professor of Political Science
Vassar College

LEGAL REALISM
POUND, ROSCOE
SOCIOLOGICAL JURISPRUDENCE

Robert A. Rutland
Editor-in-Chief, Papers of James Madison
University of Virginia

RATIFICATION OF THE CONSTITUTION

Stephen A. Saltzburg
Professor of Law
University of Virginia

REASONABLE DOUBT

Joseph L. Sax
*Philip A. Hart Distinguished University Professor of
    Law*
University of Michigan

TAKING OF PROPERTY

Frederick Schauer
Professor of Law
University of Michigan

NEW YORK TIMES CO. V. UNITED STATES

Harry N. Scheiber
Professor of Law
University of California, Berkeley

AFFECTED WITH A PUBLIC INTEREST
COMPETITIVE FEDERALISM
COOPERATIVE FEDERALISM
DUAL FEDERALISM
EMINENT DOMAIN
FEDERALISM, HISTORY OF
GRANGER CASES
NEBBIA V. NEW YORK
PUBLIC PURPOSE DOCTRINE
STATE POLICE POWER
VESTED RIGHTS
WEST RIVER BRIDGE COMPANY V. DIX

Arthur M. Schlesinger, Jr.
Schweitzer Professor in the Humanities
City University of New York

ROOSEVELT, FRANKLIN D.

Benno C. Schmidt, Jr.
President
Yale University

COMMERCIAL SPEECH
FREE PRESS/FAIR TRIAL
LIBEL AND THE FIRST AMENDMENT
PRIOR RESTRAINT AND CENSORSHIP
REPORTER'S PRIVILEGE
SHIELD LAWS
WHITE COURT

Gary T. Schwartz
Professor of Law
University of California, Los Angeles

ECONOMIC ANALYSIS AND THE CONSTITUTION

Herman Schwartz
Professor of Law
Washington College of Law, American University

ALDERMAN V. UNITED STATES
BERGER V. NEW YORK
ELECTRONIC EAVESDROPPING
GELBARD V. UNITED STATES
IRVINE V. CALIFORNIA

KATZ V. UNITED STATES
LOPEZ V. UNITED STATES
NARDONE V. UNITED STATES
NATIONAL SECURITY AND THE FOURTH AMENDMENT
OLMSTEAD V. UNITED STATES
ON LEE V. UNITED STATES
SILVERMAN V. UNITED STATES
UNITED STATES DISTRICT COURT FOR THE EASTERN
    DISTRICT OF MICHIGAN, UNITED STATES V.
WHITE, UNITED STATES V.
WIRETAPPING

Murray L. Schwartz
Professor of Law
University of California, Los Angeles

VINSON, FRED M.

David L. Shapiro
William Nelson Cromwell Professor of Law
Harvard Law School

ERIE RAILROAD CO. V. TOMPKINS
FEDERAL COMMON LAW, CIVIL
SWIFT V. TYSON

Martin Shapiro
Professor of Law
University of California, Berkeley

ABOOD V. DETROIT BOARD OF EDUCATION
ABRAMS V. UNITED STATES
ADDERLEY V. FLORIDA
ADLER V. BOARD OF EDUCATION OF CITY OF NEW
    YORK
AMERICAN COMMUNICATIONS ASSOCIATION V. DOUDS
BAD TENDENCY TEST
BALANCING TEST
BARENBLATT V. UNITED STATES
BEAUHARNAIS V. ILLINOIS
BRANDENBURG V. OHIO
BUCKLEY V. VALEO
CAPTIVE AUDIENCE
CHAPLINSKY V. NEW HAMPSHIRE
CLEAR AND PRESENT DANGER
COHEN V. CALIFORNIA
COMMUNIST PARTY OF THE UNITED STATES V.
    SUBVERSIVE ACTIVITIES CONTROL BOARD
COX V. LOUISIANA
COX V. NEW HAMPSHIRE
DE JONGE V. OREGON
DENNIS V. UNITED STATES
FEINER V. NEW YORK
FIGHTING WORDS

FIRST NATIONAL BANK OF BOSTON V. BELLOTTI
GIBSON V. FLORIDA LEGISLATIVE INVESTIGATION
    COMMISSION
GITLOW V. NEW YORK
HERNDON V. LOWRY
HUDGENS V. NATIONAL LABOR RELATIONS BOARD
KEYISHIAN V. BOARD OF REGENTS
KONIGSBERG V. STATE BAR
KOVACS V. COOPER
LAIRD V. TATUM
MARSH V. ALABAMA
MASSES PUBLISHING COMPANY V. PATTEN
MCCLOSKEY, ROBERT G.
MCGRAIN V. DAUGHERTY
MIAMI HERALD PUBLISHING COMPANY V. TORNILLO
NAACP V. BUTTON
NEAR V. MINNESOTA
RED LION BROADCASTING CO. V. FEDERAL
    COMMUNICATIONS COMMISSION
SCALES V. UNITED STATES
SCHENCK V. UNITED STATES
SCHWABE V. NEW MEXICO BOARD OF BAR
    EXAMINERS
SPEISER V. RANDALL
TERMINIELLO V. CHICAGO
THORNHILL V. ALABAMA
UPHAUS V. WYMAN
VIRGINIA STATE BOARD OF PHARMACY V. VIRGINIA
    CITIZENS CONSUMER COUNCIL
WHITNEY V. CALIFORNIA

Steven Shiffrin
Professor of Law
University of California, Los Angeles

BRANZBURG V. HAYES
COLUMBIA BROADCASTING SYSTEM, INC. V.
    DEMOCRATIC NATIONAL COMMITTEE
COOLIDGE V. NEW HAMPSHIRE
COX BROADCASTING CORP. V. COHN
FEDERAL COMMUNICATIONS COMMISSION V.
    PACIFICA FOUNDATION
GOVERNMENT SPEECH
GROUP LIBEL
KINGSLEY INTERNATIONAL PICTURES CORP. V.
    REGENTS
LISTENERS' RIGHTS
MARKETPLACE OF IDEAS
OBSCENITY
RIGHT TO KNOW
TWO-LEVEL THEORY
WARDEN V. HAYDEN

YOUNG V. AMERICAN MINI THEATERS, INC.
ZURCHER V. STANFORD DAILY

Bernard H. Siegan
Distinguished Professor of Law
University of San Diego

ECONOMIC LIBERTIES AND THE CONSTITUTION

Stanley Siegel
Professor of Law
University of California, Los Angeles

POSTAL POWER

Jay A. Sigler
Distinguished Professor of Political Science
Rutgers University

DOUBLE JEOPARDY

Thomas B. Silver
President
Public Research Syndicated

COOLIDGE, CALVIN
HARDING, WARREN G.

Aviam Soifer
Professor of Law
Boston University

BRANTI V. FINKEL
CAROLENE PRODUCTS COMPANY, UNITED STATES V.
GUILT BY ASSOCIATION
RICHMOND NEWSPAPERS, INC. V. VIRGINIA

Theodore J. St. Antoine
James E. and Sarah A. Degan Professor of Law
University of Michigan

BOYCOTT
PICKETING

Robert L. Stern
Attorney
Mayer, Brown & Platt, Chicago

COMMERCE CLAUSE
DARBY LUMBER COMPANY, UNITED STATES V.
WAGNER ACT CASES

Gerald Stourzh
Professor of History
University of Vienna

HAMILTON, ALEXANDER

Frank R. Strong
*Cary C. Boshamer University Distinguished Professor
of Law, Emeritus*
University of North Carolina

FUNDAMENTAL LAW AND THE SUPREME COURT
LAW OF THE LAND

Philippa Strum
Professor of Political Science
City University of New York (Brooklyn College and
the Graduate Center)

POLITICAL QUESTION DOCTRINE

William F. Swindler
John Marshall Professor of Law
Marshall-Wythe School of Law, College of William
and Mary

BLACKSTONE, WILLIAM

Nathan Tarcov
Associate Professor of Political Science
University of Chicago

POPULAR SOVEREIGNTY IN DEMOCRATIC POLITICAL
THEORY

Telford Taylor
Nash Professor of Law, Emeritus
Columbia University
*Dr. Herman George and Kate Kaiser Professor of
Constitutional Law*
Cardozo College of Law, Yeshiva University of New
York

LEGISLATIVE INVESTIGATION

Glen E. Thurow
Associate Professor of Politics
University of Dallas

DORMANT POWERS
EXCLUSIVE POWERS

Laurence H. Tribe
Tyler Professor of Constitutional Law
Harvard Law School

SUBSTANTIVE DUE PROCESS

Phillip R. Trimble
Professor of Law
University of California, Los Angeles

DAMES & MOORE V. REGAN
EXTRATERRITORIALITY

Mark Tushnet
Professor of Law
Georgetown University

MARSHALL, THURGOOD

Arvo Van Alstyne
Professor of Law
University of Utah

INVERSE CONDEMNATION
JUST COMPENSATION
PUBLIC USE

William W. Van Alstyne
Perkins Professor of Law
Duke University

IMPLIED POWERS
JUDICIAL ACTIVISM AND JUDICIAL RESTRAINT
SUPREME COURT (ROLE IN AMERICAN GOVERNMENT)

Jonathan D. Varat
Professor of Law
University of California, Los Angeles

ADVISORY OPINION
CASES AND CONTROVERSIES
COLLUSIVE SUIT
FLAST V. COHEN
INVALID ON ITS FACE
JUSTICIABILITY
MOOTNESS
OVERBREADTH
PUBLIC EMPLOYEES
RIPENESS
SIERRA CLUB V. MORTON
STANDING
STOCKHOLDER'S SUIT
STUDENTS CHALLENGING REGULATORY AGENCY
    PROCEDURES (SCRAP), UNITED STATES V.
TAXPAYERS' AND CITIZENS' SUITS
VAGUENESS
WHITE, BYRON R.

M. J. C. Vile
Professor History
University of Kent, Canterbury

SEPARATION OF POWERS

Clement E. Vose
John E. Andrus Professor of Government
Wesleyan University

TEST CASE

Kim McLane Wardlaw
Attorney
O'Melveny & Myers, Los Angeles

BANTAM BOOKS, INC. V. SULLIVAN
ERZNOZNIK V. CITY OF JACKSONVILLE
GANNETT CO., INC. V. DEPASQUALE
HERBERT V. LANDO
JACOBELLIS V. OHIO
KINGSLEY BOOKS, INC. V. BROWN
MEMOIRS V. MASSACHUSETTS
MILLER V. CALIFORNIA
NEBRASKA PRESS ASSOCIATION V. STUART
ROTH V. UNITED STATES
SNEPP V. UNITED STATES
STANLEY V. GEORGIA

Stephen L. Wasby
Professor of Political Science
State University of New York, Albany

SUPREME COURT DECISIONS, IMPACT OF

Lloyd L. Weinreb
Professor of Law
Harvard Law School

FAIR TRIAL
WARRANTLESS SEARCH

Robert Weisberg
Professor of Law
Stanford Law School

CAPITAL PUNISHMENT

Harry H. Wellington
Sterling Professor of Law
Yale Law School

LABOR AND THE CONSTITUTION

Peter Westen
Professor of Law
University of Michigan

COMPULSORY PROCESS, RIGHT TO
CONFRONTATION, RIGHT OF
HEARSAY RULE

Burns H. Weston
Bessie Dutton Murray Professor of Law
University of Iowa

BELMONT, UNITED STATES V.
EXECUTIVE AGREEMENTS

INTERNATIONAL EMERGENCY ECONOMIC POWERS
   ACT
MARSHALL PLAN
NORTH ATLANTIC TREATY
PINK, UNITED STATES V.
STATUS OF FORCES AGREEMENT
TREATY POWER
UNITED NATIONS CHARTER

G. Edward White
   Professor of Law
   University of Virginia

   HOLMES, OLIVER WENDELL, JR.
   WARREN COURT

James Boyd White
   *L. Hart Wright Professor of Law and Professor of
      English Language and Literature*
   University of Michigan

   ARREST
   BURDEN OF PROOF
   FEDERAL RULES OF CRIMINAL PROCEDURE
   JURY DISCRIMINATION

Charles H. Whitebread
   George T. Pfleger Professor of Law
   University of Southern California

   DISCOVERY
   INDICTMENT
   INFORMATION
   MERE EVIDENCE RULE
   MIRANDA RULES
   MISDEMEANOR
   PRESENTMENT
   PROBABLE CAUSE
   STOP AND FRISK
   VOIR DIRE

William M. Wiecek
   Congdon Professor of Public Law and Legislation
   Syracuse University

   ABLEMAN V. BOOTH
   ABOLITIONIST CONSTITUTIONAL THEORY
   ANNEXATION OF TEXAS
   BLACK CODES
   CHASE COURT
   CIVIL LIBERTIES AND THE ANTISLAVERY
      CONTROVERSY
   COMPROMISE OF 1850
   CONFISCATION ACTS
   CONQUERED PROVINCES THEORY

CONSTITUTIONAL HISTORY, 1829–1848
DANIEL, PETER V.
FORCE ACT
FORCE ACTS
FREEDMEN'S BUREAU
FUGITIVE SLAVERY
GROVES V. SLAUGHTER
GUARANTEE CLAUSE
JOINT COMMITTEE ON RECONSTRUCTION
KANSAS-NEBRASKA ACT
LECOMPTON CONSTITUTION
LINCOLN-DOUGLAS DEBATES
LINCOLN'S PLAN OF RECONSTRUCTION
LUTHER V. BORDEN
MAYSVILLE ROAD BILL
MCCARDLE, EX PARTE
MILITARY RECONSTRUCTION ACTS
MISSOURI COMPROMISE
MORRILL ACT
NASHVILLE CONVENTION RESOLUTIONS
NULLIFICATION
OMNIBUS ACT
PEONAGE
PERSONAL LIBERTY LAWS
POPULAR SOVEREIGNTY
PRIZE CASES
PROHIBITION OF SLAVE TRADE ACT
REPUBLICAN FORM OF GOVERNMENT
SECESSION
SLAVERY IN THE TERRITORIES
SOMERSET'S CASE
SOUTH CAROLINA ORDINANCE OF NULLIFICATION
SOUTH CAROLINA ORDINANCE OF SECESSION
STATE SUICIDE THEORY
STRADER V. GRAHAM
TANEY, ROGER BROOKE
TENURE OF OFFICE ACT
THREE-FIFTHS CLAUSE
WAYNE, JAMES M.

J. Harvie Wilkinson III
   Judge
   United States Court of Appeals for the Fourth Circuit

   POWELL, LEWIS F., JR.

Peter Woll
   Professor of Politics
   Brandeis University

   BUREAUCRACY

C. Vann Woodward
Sterling Professor of History, Emeritus
Yale University

COMPROMISE OF 1877

L. Kinvin Wroth
Professor of Law and Dean of the School of Law
University of Maine

COMMON LAW (ANGLO-AMERICAN)
RULE OF LAW

Stephen C. Yeazell
Professor of Law
University of California, Los Angeles

ADMINISTRATIVE LAW
CLASS ACTION
COLLATERAL ATTACK

CONTEMPT POWER, JUDICIAL
FAIR HEARING
INJUNCTION
INSTITUTIONAL LITIGATION (with Theodore
     Eisenberg)
JURISDICTION
NOTICE

Hans Zeisel
Professor of Law, Emeritus
University of Chicago

SOCIAL SCIENCE IN CONSTITUTIONAL LITIGATION
     (with David Kaye)

John Zvesper
Professor of Politics
University of East Anglia, Norwich

RIGHT OF REVOLUTION

List of Contributors

(1992)

Henry J. Abraham
James Hart Professor of Government and Foreign Affairs
University of Virginia

APPOINTMENTS CLAUSE

Norman Abrams
Professor of Law
University of California, Los Angeles

FEDERAL CRIMINAL LAW

T. Alexander Aleinikoff
Professor of Law
University of Michigan

IMMIGRATION AND ALIENAGE (UPDATE 1)

Ronald J. Allen
Professor of Law
Northwestern University

PROCEDURAL DUE PROCESS OF LAW, CRIMINAL (UPDATE)

Albert W. Alschuler
Professor of Law
University of Chicago

BAIL (UPDATE)
THIRD-PARTY CONSENT

Akhil Reed Amar
Professor of Law
Yale Law School

AMENDMENT PROCESS (OUTSIDE ARTICLE V)

Alison Grey Anderson
Professor of Law
University of California, Los Angeles

SOBELOFF, SIMON E.

Peter Arenella
Professor of Law
University of California, Los Angeles

FOURTH AMENDMENT

Lance Banning
Professor of History
University of Kentucky

FEDERALISTS

Edward L. Barrett
Professor of Law
University of California, Davis

INTERGOVERNMENTAL TAX IMMUNITIES

Norma Basch
Professor of History
Rutgers University

WOMAN SUFFRAGE
WOMEN IN CONSTITUTIONAL HISTORY

Sara Sun Beale
Professor of Law
Duke University

GRAND JURY (UPDATE)

Michael R. Belknap
Professor of Law
California Western School of Law

POLITICAL TRIALS

Herman Belz
Professor of History
University of Maryland

CONSTITUTIONAL HISTORY, 1980–1989

Robert W. Bennett
Dean and Professor of Law
Northwestern University of Law

INTERPRETIVISM
POVERTY LAW

Walter Berns
John M. Olin University Professor
Georgetown University

CONSERVATISM

Scott H. Bice
Professor and Dean of the Law Center
University of Southern California

DELEGATION OF POWER (UPDATE)

Lee C. Bollinger
Dean and Professor of Law
University of Michigan

COMMERCIAL SPEECH (UPDATE 1)
EXTREMIST SPEECH

Richard J. Bonnie
John S. Battle Professor of Law
University of Virginia

DRUG REGULATION (UPDATE 1)

Craig M. Bradley
Professor of Law and Harry T. Ice Faculty Fellow
Indiana University

REHNQUIST, WILLIAM H. (UPDATE 1)

Harold H. Bruff
John S. Redditt Professor of Law
University of Texas, Austin

JUDICIAL REVIEW OF ADMINISTRATIVE ACTS

David P. Bryden
Professor of Law
University of Minnesota

JUDICIAL ROLE

Robert A. Burt
Southmayd Professor of Law
Yale University

MENTAL ILLNESS AND THE CONSTITUTION (UPDATE)
PATIENTS' RIGHTS

John O. Calmore
Program Officer, Rights and Social Justice
Ford Foundation

RESIDENTIAL SEGREGATION

Lincoln Caplan
Staff Writer
New Yorker Magazine, Inc.

SOLICITOR GENERAL (UPDATE)

Clayborne Carson
Director and Senior Editor, The Martin Luther King, Jr., Papers Project
Stanford University

CIVIL RIGHTS MOVEMENT

Stephen L. Carter
Professor of Law
Yale University

RACIAL DISCRIMINATION (UPDATE 1)
SCIENCE, TECHNOLOGY, AND THE CONSTITUTION

Erwin Chemerinsky
Professor of Law
University of Southern California

HABEAS CORPUS (UPDATE 1)

Jesse H. Choper
Dean and Professor of Law
University of California, Berkeley

GOVERNMENT AID TO RELIGIOUS INSTITUTIONS
(UPDATE 1)

William Cohen
C. Wendell and Edith M. Carlsmith Professor of Law
Stanford University

ECONOMIC DUE PROCESS
ECONOMIC EQUAL PROTECTION
FOURTEENTH AMENDMENT, SECTION 5 (JUDICIAL
CONSTRUCTION)

Ruth Colker
C. J. Morrow Professor of Law
Tulane University

ABORTION AND THE CONSTITUTION (UPDATE 1A)

Daniel O. Conkle
Professor of Law
Indiana University School of Law

ESTABLISHMENT CLAUSE

Kimberlé Crenshaw
Professor of Law
University of California, Los Angeles

ANTIDISCRIMINATION LEGISLATION (UPDATE 1)
CIVIL RIGHTS (UPDATE 1)

Michael Kent Curtis
Associate Professor of Law
Wake Forest University

FOURTEENTH AMENDMENT, SECTION 5 (FRAMING)
INCORPORATION DOCTRINE AND ORIGINAL INTENT

George Dargo
Assistant Professor of Law
Duke University

JEFFERSONIANISM

Walter Dellinger
Professor of Law
Duke University

ADVICE AND CONSENT TO SUPREME COURT
NOMINATIONS (with Madeline Morris)
ARTICLE V CONVENTIONS CLAUSE
SCHOOL PRAYERS

George W. Dent
Professor of Law
Case Western University

RELIGION IN PUBLIC SCHOOLS (UPDATE 1)
VOUCHERS

David Dolinko
Professor of Law
University of California, Los Angeles

RIGHT AGAINST SELF-INCRIMINATION (UPDATE)

Rochelle C. Dreyfuss
Professor of Law
New York University School of Law

COMPUTERS (with David W. Leebron)

Robert F. Drinan, S.J.
Professor of Law
Georgetown University

HOUSE OF REPRESENTATIVES

Donald A. Dripps
Associate Professor of Law
University of Illinois

MIRANDA RULES (UPDATE)

Ronald Dworkin
Professor of Law
New York University and University College, Oxford

JURISPRUDENCE AND CONSTITUTIONAL LAW

Peter B. Edelman
Associate Dean and Professor of Law
Georgetown University

WELFARE RIGHTS

Theodore Eisenberg
Professor of Law
Cornell University

CONSTITUTIONAL REMEDIES

Richard E. Ellis
Professor of History
State University of New York, Buffalo

JACKSONIANISM

Edward J. Erler
Chair and Professor of Political Science
California State University, San Bernardino

CAPITAL PUNISHMENT AND RACE
RACE-CONSCIOUSNESS

Samuel Estreicher
Professor of Law
New York University

SUBSTANTIVE DUE PROCESS (UPDATE 1)
SUPREME COURT'S WORK LOAD

Julian N. Eule
Professor of Law
University of California, Los Angeles

DIRECT DEMOCRACY
DORMANT COMMERCE CLAUSE
TEMPORAL LIMITS ON LAWMAKING POWERS

Richard Fallon
Professor of Law
Harvard University

POWELL, LEWIS F., JR. (UPDATE)

Daniel A. Farber
Henry J. Fletcher Professor of Law
University of Minnesota

ENVIRONMENTAL REGULATION AND THE
   CONSTITUTION (UPDATE 1)
TAKING OF PROPERTY (UPDATE 1)

Paul Finkelman
Professor of Law
Brooklyn Law School

REPUBLICAN PARTY
WHIG PARTY

Edwin B. Firmage
Professor of Law
University of Utah

CONGRESSIONAL WAR POWERS

Peter Graham Fish
Professor of Political Science and Law
Duke University

JUDICIAL CONFERENCE OF THE UNITED STATES

Louis Fisher
Senior Specialist, Congressional Research Service
The Library of Congress

FEDERALISM AND SHARED POWERS
LINE-ITEM VETO
NONJUDICIAL INTERPRETATION OF THE
   CONSTITUTION
SENATE JUDICIARY COMMITTEE

William A. Fletcher
Professor of Law
University of California, Berkeley

ELEVENTH AMENDMENT (UPDATE 1)

William E. Forbath
Professor of Law
University of California, Los Angeles

LABOR MOVEMENT

Richard S. Frase
Professor of Law
University of Minnesota

CRIMINAL JUSTICE SYSTEM

Paul A. Freund
Karl M. Loeb University Professor, Emeritus
Harvard University

WYZANSKI, CHARLES E., JR.

Barry Friedman
Professor of Law
Vanderbilt University

CONDITIONAL SPENDING (with Thomas R. McCoy)

Lawrence M. Friedman
Professor of Law
Stanford University

LEGAL CULTURE

Robert Diderot Garcia
Professor of Law
University of California, Los Angeles

RACKETEER INFLUENCED AND CORRUPT
   ORGANIZATIONS ACT

Tom Gerety
President
Trinity College

RIGHT OF PRIVACY (UPDATE)

Michael J. Gerhardt
Associate Professor of Law
Marshall-Wythe School of Law, College of William
     and Mary

KENNEDY, ANTHONY M.

Stephen Gillers
Professor of Law
New York University

GOVERNMENT SECRECY

Ruth Bader Ginsberg
United States Circuit Judge
United States Court of Appeals, District of Columbia
     Circuit

McGOWAN, CARL

Michael J. Glennon
Professor of Law
University of California, Davis

SENATE AND FOREIGN POLICY

Robert D. Goldstein
Professor of Law
University of California, Los Angeles

BALANCED-BUDGET AMENDMENT
BLYEW V. UNITED STATES
CONFRONTATION, RIGHT OF (UPDATE)
DRUG TESTING

Robert A. Goldwin
Resident Scholar
American Enterprise Institute

GENDER RIGHTS

Gary Goodpaster
Professor of Law
University of California, Los Angeles

AUTOMOBILE SEARCH (UPDATE)
OPEN FIELDS DOCTRINE
RIGHTS OF THE CRIMINALLY ACCUSED
UNREASONABLE SEARCH (UPDATE)
VISAS

Joseph D. Grano
Professor of Law
Wayne State University

ABORTION AND THE CONSTITUTION (UPDATE 1B)

Erwin N. Griswold
Attorney at Law
Jones, Day, Reavis, & Pogue, Washington, D.C.

SUPREME COURT BAR

Walter Hellerstein
Professor of Law
University of Georgia

FRIENDLY, HENRY J.
STATE AND LOCAL GOVERNMENT TAXATION

Lawrence Herman
President's Club Professor of Law
Ohio State University

BODY SEARCH

A. E. Dick Howard
White Burkett Miller Professor of Law and Public
     Affairs
University of Virginia

STATE CONSTITUTIONS

Shirley Hufstedler
Hufstedler, Miller, Kaus, & Beardsley, Los Angeles

FEDERAL JUDICIAL APPOINTMENTS, TENURE, AND
     INDEPENDENCE

James Hutson
The Library of Congress

CONSTITUTIONAL CONVENTION, RECORDS OF

Gary J. Jacobsohn
Woodrow Wilson Professor of Government
Williams College

PRAGMATISM

John P. Kaminski
Professor of History and Director of the Center for the
     Study of the American Constitution
University of Wisconsin

FIRST CONGRESS

Kenneth L. Karst
  Professor of Law
  University of California, Los Angeles

  ARMED FORCES
  ATTORNEY GENERAL OF NEW YORK V. SOTO-LOPEZ
  BATSON V. KENTUCKY
  BOARD OF EDUCATION OF THE WESTSIDE
    COMMUNITY SCHOOLS V. MERGENS
  BOARD OF TRUSTEES OF STATE UNIVERSITY OF NEW
    YORK V. FOX
  DESHANEY V. WINNEBAGO COUNTY DEPARTMENT OF
    SOCIAL SERVICES
  EQUAL PROTECTION OF THE LAWS (UPDATE 1)
  HAZELWOOD SCHOOL DISTRICT V. KUHLMEIER
  HODGSON V. MINNESOTA
  LIBERALISM
  MERITOR SAVINGS BANK, FSB V. VINSON
  METRO BROADCASTING, INC. V. FCC
  MISSOURI V. JENKINS (1990)
  MISTRETTA V. UNITED STATES
  NIMMER, MELVILLE B.
  NONINTERPRETIVISM
  PATTERSON V. MCLEAN CREDIT UNION
  POSADAS DE PUERTO RICO ASSOCIATES V. TOURISM
    COMPANY OF PUERTO RICO
  RICHMOND (CITY OF) V. J. A. CROSON CO.
  SEXUAL ORIENTATION
  THORNBURGH V. AMERICAN COLLEGE OF
    OBSTETRICIANS AND GYNECOLOGISTS
  WASHINGTON V. HARPER
  WEBSTER V. REPRODUCTIVE HEALTH SERVICES
  WYGANT V. JACKSON BOARD OF EDUCATION

Evan J. Kemp, Jr.
  Chairman
  United States Equal Employment Opportunity
    Commission

  AMERICANS WITH DISABILITIES ACT

Randall Kennedy
  Professor of Law
  Harvard University

  MARSHALL, THURGOOD (UPDATE)

Charles R. Kesler
  Associate Professor of Government and Director of the
    Henry Salvatori Center for the Study of Freedom in
    the Modern World
  Claremont McKenna College

  REAGAN, RONALD (UPDATE)

Kit Kinports
  Associate Professor of Law
  University of Illinois

  BLACKMUN, HARRY A. (UPDATE 1)

Douglas W. Kmiec
  Professor of Law
  Notre Dame University

  ZONING (UPDATE)

Neil K. Komesar
  James E. & Ruth B. Doyle-Bascom Professor of Law
  University of Wisconsin

  POLITICS

Alex Kozinski
  United States Circuit Judge
  United States Court of Appeals, Ninth Circuit

  ADMINISTRATIVE SEARCH (UPDATE)

Seth F. Kreimer
  Associate Professor of Law
  University of Pennsylvania

  ENTITLEMENT

James E. Krier
  Earl Warren Deland Professor of Law
  University of Michigan

  EMINENT DOMAIN (UPDATE)

Philip B. Kurland
  Professor of Law
  University of Chicago

  IRAN-CONTRA AFFAIR

Philip A. Lacovara
  Managing Director & General Counsel
  Morgan, Stanley, & Co., Inc.

  INDEPENDENT COUNSEL

Wayne R. LaFave
  David C. Baum Professor of Law
  University of Illinois, Urbana-Champaign

  PLAIN VIEW DOCTRINE (UPDATE)
  REASONABLE EXPECTATION OF PRIVACY

Kenneth Lasson
Professor of Law
University of Baltimore

PATENT (UPDATE)

Michael Laurence
Washington, D.C.

CAPITAL PUNISHMENT (UPDATE 1) (with Franklin
　Zimring)

David W. Leebron
Professor of Law
Columbia University

COMPUTERS (with Rochelle C. Dreyfuss)

William E. Leuchtenberg
Professor of History
University of North Carolina, Chapel Hill

COURT-PACKING PLANS

Martin Lyon Levine
*UPS Professor of Law, Gerontology and Psychiatry,
　and the Behavioral Sciences*
University of Southern California

PSYCHIATRY AND CONSTITUTIONAL LAW

Sanford Levinson
Professor of Law
University of Texas, Austin

CONSTITUTION AS CIVIL RELIGION

Leonard W. Levy
*Andrew W. Mellon All-Claremont Professor of the
　Humanities, Emeritus*
Claremont Graduate School

ANNAPOLIS CONVENTION
BETHEL SCHOOL DISTRICT V. FRASER
BOLAND AMENDMENT
BOOTH V. MARYLAND
BOWEN V. KENDRICK
BOWSHER V. SYNAR
BRASWELL V. UNITED STATES
CALIFORNIA V. GREENWOOD
COLORADO V. CONNELLY
FLAG DESECRATION (UPDATE)
FORD V. WAINWRIGHT
FRAZEE V. ILLINOIS DEPARTMENT OF EMPLOYMENT
　SECURITY
HEATH V. ALABAMA

HUSTLER MAGAZINE AND LARRY FLYNT V. JERRY
　FALWELL
ILLINOIS V. PERKINS
ILLINOIS V. RODRIGUEZ
MARYLAND V. CRAIG
MCCLESKEY V. KEMP
MICHIGAN DEPARTMENT OF STATE POLICE V. SITZ
MILKOVICH V. LORAIN JOURNAL CO.
NATIONAL TREASURY EMPLOYEES UNION V. VON
　RAAB
PENRY V. LYNAUGH
RATIFIER INTENT
SALERNO, UNITED STATES V.
SKINNER V. RAILWAY LABOR EXECUTIVES
　ASSOCIATION
STANFORD V. KENTUCKY
TEXAS MONTHLY, INC. V. BULLOCK
TEXTUALISM
THOMPSON V. OKLAHOMA
UNENUMERATED RIGHTS

Hans A. Linde
Herman Phleger Visiting Professor of Law
Stanford University

SPENDING POWER

Christine A. Littleton
Professor of Law
University of California, Los Angeles

COMPARABLE WORTH
FEMINIST THEORY

Charles A. Lofgren
Crocker Professor of American Politics and History
Claremont McKenna College

VIETNAM WAR (UPDATE)
WAR POWERS (UPDATE 1)

Daniel H. Lowenstein
Professor of Law
University of California, Los Angeles

GERRYMANDER (UPDATE)
POLITICAL PARTIES, ELECTIONS, AND
　CONSTITUTIONAL LAW

Ira C. Lupu
Professor of Law
George Washington University

SEPARATION OF CHURCH AND STATE (UPDATE)

Stephen Macedo
Assistant Professor of Government
Harvard University

NEW RIGHT

Paul Marcus
Dean and Professor of Law
University of Arizona

CONSPIRACY LAW

John Marini
Professor of Political Science
University of Nevada, Reno

BUDGET PROCESS

Michael W. McConnell
Professor of Law
University of Chicago

RELIGIOUS LIBERTY (UPDATE 1)

Thomas R. McCoy
Professor of Law
Vanderbilt University

CONDITIONAL SPENDING (with Barry Friedman)

Frank I. Michelman
Professor of Law
Harvard University

PROPERTY RIGHTS
REPUBLICANISM AND MODERN CONSTITUTIONAL
    THEORY

Abner J. Mikva
United States Circuit Judge
United States Court of Appeals, District of Columbia
    Circuit

LEGISLATIVE PURPOSES AND MOTIVES

Martha Minow
Professor of Law
Harvard University

DISABILITIES, RIGHTS OF PERSONS WITH

Madeline Morris
Assistant Professor of Law
Duke University

ADVICE AND CONSENT TO SUPREME COURT
    NOMINATIONS (with Walter Dellinger)

Robert P. Mosteller
*Professor of Law and Senior Associate Dean for
    Academic Affairs*
Duke University

DOUBLE JEOPARDY (UPDATE 1)
SPEEDY TRIAL (UPDATE 1)

Paul L. Murphy
Professor of Law
University of Minnesota

WORLD WAR I

Gene R. Nichol
Dean and Professor of Law
University of Colorado

CIVIL LIBERTIES (UPDATE 1)
DAMAGES CLAIMS

Marlene Arnold Nicholson
Professor of Law
DePaul University

CAMPAIGN FINANCE (UPDATE 1)

John E. Nowak
Professor of Law
University of Illinois

POLICE INTERROGATION AND CONFESSIONS
    (UPDATE 1)

David M. O'Brien
Professor of Government and Graduate Advisor
University of Virginia

SUPREME COURT AT WORK

Phillip S. Paludan
Professor of History
University of Kansas

CIVIL WAR

Donald J. Pisani
Professor of History
Texas A & M University

ECONOMY
PROGRESSIVISM

Robert C. Post
Professor of Law
University of California, Berkeley

FEDERALISM AND CIVIL RIGHTS
PUBLIC FORUM (UPDATE 1)

L. A. Powe, Jr.
Professor of Law and Anne Regents Chair
University of Texas, Austin

BROADCASTING (UPDATE 1)
FREEDOM OF THE PRESS (UPDATE 1)

Jeremy Rabkin
Professor of Political Science
Cornell University

BUSH, GEORGE H. W.
RACIAL PREFERENCE

Jack N. Rakove
Professor of History
Stanford University

ORIGINAL INTENT

Norman Redlich
*Judge Weinfeld Professor of Law, Emeritus, and
    former Dean*
New York University Law School
Counsel
Wachtell, Lipton, Rosen, & Katz, New York City

RELIGIOUS SYMBOLS IN PUBLIC PLACES

Donald H. Regan
Professor of Law
University of Michigan

STATE REGULATION OF COMMERCE (UPDATE 1)

Judith Resnik
Orrin B. Evans Professor of Law
University of Southern California

PROCEDURAL DUE PROCESS OF LAW, CIVIL
    (UPDATE 1)

Donald A. Ritchie
Associate Historian
United States Senate

SENATE
SENATE SUBCOMMITTEE ON CONSTITUTIONAL RIGHTS

John P. Roche
*John M. Olin Distinguished Professor of American
    Civilization and Foreign Affairs*
Tufts University

LIBERAL CONSTITUTIONAL CONSTRUCTION

Ralph A. Rossum
President
Hampden-Sydney College

PRISONERS' RIGHTS (UPDATE 1)

Eugene V. Rostow
Sterling Professor of Law, Emeritus
Yale University and Distinguished Fellow, United
    States Institute of Peace

CONGRESS AND FOREIGN POLICY
EXECUTIVE POWER

Ronald D. Rotunda
Professor of Law
University of Illinois

WELFARE STATE

Lawrence G. Sager
Professor of Law
New York University

JURISDICTION, FEDERAL

Terrance Sandalow
Edison R. Sunderland Professor of Law
University of Michigan

LOCAL GOVERNMENT
MCCREE, WADE HAMPTON, JR.

Frederick Schauer
Frank Stanton Professor of the First Amendment
Harvard University

BORK NOMINATION
CHILDREN AND THE FIRST AMENDMENT

Harry N. Scheiber
Associate Dean and Professor of Law
University of California, Berkeley

NEW DEAL

Pierre Schlag
Professor of Law
University of Colorado

FIRST AMENDMENT (UPDATE 1)

Arthur M. Schlesinger, Jr.
Albert Schweitzer Chair in Humanities
City University of New York (Graduate School and
    University Center)

KENNEDY, ROBERT F. (UPDATE)

Peter H. Schuck
Simeon E. Baldwin Professor of Law
Yale University

CITIZENSHIP (UPDATE 1)
GOVERNMENT WRONGS

Stephen J. Schulhofer
Frank and Bernice J. Greenberg Professor of Law
University of Chicago

SENTENCING

Jeffrey D. Schultz
Georgetown University

JUDICIAL POWER AND LEGISLATIVE REMEDIES
MEESE COMMISSION

Gary T. Schwartz
Professor of Law
University of California, Los Angeles

PUNITIVE DAMAGES
WRIGHT, J. SKELLY

Herman Schwartz
Professor of Law
American University

CRIMINAL JUSTICE AND TECHNOLOGY

Martin Shapiro
Coffroth Professor of Law
University of California, Berkeley

BUREAUCRACY (UPDATE)

Suzanna Sherry
Professor of Law
University of Minnesota

O'CONNOR, SANDRA DAY (UPDATE 1)

Steven Shiffrin
Professor of Law
Cornell University

LOW-VALUE SPEECH
O'BRIEN FORMULA
PORNOGRAPHY AND FEMINISM

Larry G. Simon
*W. H. Armstrong Professor of Constitutional Law and
    Associate Dean of The Law Center*
University of Southern California

REHNQUIST COURT

David M. Skover
Professor of Law
University of Puget Sound

POLITICAL QUESTION DOCTRINE (UPDATE 1)
STATE ACTION (UPDATE 1)

Rogers M. Smith
Professor of Political Science
Yale University

CONSTITUTION AND CIVIC IDEALS
DECONSTRUCTION

Rodney A. Smolla
*James Gould Cutler Professor of Constitutional Law
    and Director of the Institute of Bill of Rights Law*
College of William and Mary

PRIVATE DISCRIMINATION

Aviam Soifer
Professor of Law
Boston University

CONSTITUTIONAL FICTIONS
COVER, ROBERT M.

Rayman L. Soloman
Associate Dean and Professor of Law
Northwestern University

SCALIA, ANTONIN

Frank J. Sorauf
Professor of Political Science
University of Minnesota

POLITICAL ACTION COMMITTEES

Theodore J. St. Antoine
Degan Professor of Law
University of Michigan

LABOR AND THE CONSTITUTION (UPDATE)

Kate Stith
Professor of Law
Yale University

SEARCH AND SEIZURE (UPDATE 1)
WHITE, BYRON R. (UPDATE 1)

Geoffrey R. Stone
Dean and Professor of Law
University of Chicago

BRENNAN, WILLIAM J., JR. (UPDATE 1)
FREEDOM OF SPEECH (UPDATE 1)

David A. Strauss
Professor of Law
University of Chicago

SOUTER, DAVID H.

Kathleen M. Sullivan
Professor of Law
Harvard University

AFFIRMATIVE ACTION (UPDATE 1)

James L. Sundquist
Senior Fellow, Emeritus
The Brookings Institution

CONSTITUTIONAL REFORM

Athan Theoharis
Professor of History
Marquette University

FEDERAL BUREAU OF INVESTIGATION

Phillip R. Trimble
Professor of Law
University of California, Los Angeles

EXECUTIVE PREROGATIVE
PRESIDENT AND THE TREATY POWER

Louise G. Trubek
Clinical Professor of Law
University of Wisconsin

PUBLIC INTEREST LAW

Mark Tushnet
Professor of Law
Georgetown University

CONSTITUTIONAL THEORY
CRITICAL LEGAL STUDIES
INTEREST GROUPS

Gerald F. Uelman
Dean and Professor of Law
Santa Clara University

CONTROLLED-SUBSTANCE ABUSE
ELECTED JUDICIARY

Melvin I. Urofsky
Professor of History
Virginia Commonwealth University

POPULISM
RECONSTRUCTION
WORLD WAR II

William W. Van Alstyne
William R. and Thomas S. Perkins Professor of Law
Duke University

FEDERALISM, CONTEMPORARY PRACTICE OF

Jonathan D. Varat
Professor of Law
University of California, Los Angeles

GOVERNMENT AS PROPRIETOR
STEVENS, JOHN PAUL (UPDATE 1)

Joseph Vining
Hawkins Professor of Law
University of Michigan

ADMINISTRATIVE AGENCIES
CRUEL AND UNUSUAL PUNISHMENT (UPDATE 1)

Silas Wasserstrom
Professor of Law
Georgetown University

TORTS (with Anne Woolhandler)

John G. West, Jr.
Ph.D. Candidate
Claremont Graduate School

ANTI-ABORTION MOVEMENT
BENDER V. WILLIAMSPORT
BOWERS V. HARDWICK
CHILD PORNOGRAPHY

COUNTY OF ALLEGHENY V. AMERICAN CIVIL
    LIBERTIES UNION
COY V. IOWA
CREATIONISM
DIAL-A-PORN
EMPLOYMENT DIVISION, DEPARTMENT OF HUMAN
    RESOURCES OF OREGON V. SMITH
EQUAL ACCESS
FREEDOM OF ASSOCIATION
FRISBY V. SCHULTZ
GOLDMAN V. WEINBERGER
JIMMY SWAGGART MINISTRIES V. BOARD OF
    EQUALIZATION OF CALIFORNIA
JOHNSON V. TRANSPORTATION AGENCY
LEMON TEST
LYNG V. NORTHWEST INDIAN CEMETERY
O'LONE V. ESTATE OF SHABAZZ
PARADISE, UNITED STATES V.
POLITICAL PHILOSOPHY OF THE CONSTITUTION
    (UPDATE)
RELIGIOUS FUNDAMENTALISM
RENTON (CITY OF) V. PLAYTIME THEATRES
RIGHT TO DIE
RUTAN V. REPUBLICAN PARTY OF ILLINOIS
SPECIAL PROSECUTOR
WITTERS V. WASHINGTON DEPARTMENT OF SERVICES
    FOR THE BLIND

James Boyd White
    Hart Wright Professor of Law and Professor of
    English
    University of Michigan

    CONSTITUTION AS LITERATURE

Charles H. Whitebread
    George T. Pfleger Professor of Law
    University of Southern California

    EYEWITNESS IDENTIFICATION

Christina Brooks Whitman
    Professor of Law
    University of Michigan

    SEX DISCRIMINATION (UPDATE 1)

Stephen F. Williams
    United States Circuit Judge
    United States Court of Appeals, District of Columbia
    Circuit

    LAW AND ECONOMICS THEORY

Ralph K. Winter
    United States Circuit Judge
    United States Court of Appeals, Second Circuit

    ORIGINALISM

Gordon S. Wood
    Professor of History
    Brown University

    AMERICAN REVOLUTION AND CONSTITUTIONAL
      THEORY
    REPUBLICANISM

Anne Woolhandler
    Georgetown University

    TORTS (with Silas Wasserstrom)

Mark G. Yudof
    Dean and James A. Elkins Centennial Chair in Law
    University of Texas, Austin

    EDUCATION AND THE CONSTITUTION (UPDATE)

Franklin Zimring
    Professor of Law and Director of the Earl Warren
    Legal Institute
    University of California, Berkeley
    Director of the Death Penalty Project
    American Civil Liberties Union of Northern California

    CAPITAL PUNISHMENT (UPDATE 1) (with Michael
      Laurence)

List of Contributors

(2000)

Kathryn Abrams
Professor of Law
Cornell University

GINSBURG, RUTH BADER

Norman Abrams
Vice Chancellor for Academic Personnel and Professor of Law
University of California, Los Angeles

FEDERAL CRIMINAL LAW (UPDATE)
LAW ENFORCEMENT AND FEDERAL–STATE RELATIONS (UPDATE)

Jeffrey Abramson
Louis Stulberg Chair in Law and Politics
Brandeis University

COMMUNITARIANISM

T. Alexander Aleinikoff
Professor of Law
Georgetown University

CITIZENSHIP (UPDATE 2)

Larry Alexander
Warren Distinguished Professor of Law
University of San Diego

NONJUDICIAL INTERPRETATION OF THE CONSTITUTION (UPDATE) (with Frederick Schauer)
STARE DECISIS (UPDATE)

Akhil Reed Amar
Southmayd Professor of Law
Yale University

BILL OF RIGHTS IN MODERN APPLICATION
FOURTEENTH AMENDMENT AS A NEW CONSTITUTION

Vikram D. Amar
Professor of Law
University of California, Hastings College of the Law, San Francisco

JURY DISCRIMINATION (UPDATE)
JURY SERVICE AS A POLITICAL RIGHT
JURY UNANIMITY (UPDATE)

Michael Asimow
Professor of Law
University of California, Los Angeles

ADMINISTRATIVE AGENCIES (UPDATE)

Ian Ayres
William K. Townsend Professor of Law
Yale University

ECONOMICS OF AFFIRMATIVE ACTION

Larry Catá Backer
Professor of Law
University of Tulsa

WELFARE RIGHTS (UPDATE)

Randy E. Barnett
Austin B. Fletcher Professor of Law
Boston University

NINTH AMENDMENT (UPDATE)

Hugh Baxter
Associate Professor of Law
Boston University

LEMON TEST (UPDATE)

Martin H. Belsky
Dean and Professor of Law
University of Tulsa

SCHWARTZ, BERNARD

Herman Belz
Professor of History
University of Maryland, College Park

LINCOLN AND CONSTITUTIONAL THEORY

Thomas C. Berg
Professor of Law
Samford University

LEE V. WEISMAN
RELIGIOUS LIBERTY (UPDATE 2)

Vivian Berger
Nash Professor of Law
Columbia University

CAPITAL PUNISHMENT (UPDATE 2)
PAYNE V. TENNESSEE

Richard B. Bernstein
Adjunct Professor of Law
New York University

TWENTY-SEVENTH AMENDMENT

G. Robert Blakey
William and Dorothy O'Neil Professor of Law
University of Notre Dame

FREE SPEECH AND RICO

Vincent Blasi
Corliss Lamont Professor of Civil Liberties
Columbia University
Massee Professor of Law
University of Virginia

BRANDEIS AND THE FIRST AMENDMENT
MILL AND FREEDOM OF EXPRESSION
MILTON AND FREEDOM OF EXPRESSION

Grace Ganz Blumberg
Professor of Law
University of California, Los Angeles

FOSTER FAMILIES

Scott R. Bowman
Assistant Professor of Political Science
California State University, Los Angeles

CORPORATE CITIZENSHIP

Lynn S. Branham
Visiting Professor of Law
University of Illinois, Urbana-Champaign

PRISONERS' RIGHTS (UPDATE 2)

Robert Brauneis
Associate Professor of Law
George Washington University

PROPERTY RIGHTS (UPDATE)

Kevin Brown
Professor of Law
Indiana University

AFROCENTRIC SCHOOLS

Rebecca L. Brown
Professor of Law
Vanderbilt University

POLITICAL QUESTION DOCTRINE (UPDATE 2)

Alan E. Brownstein
Professor of Law
University of California, Davis

ANTI-ABORTION MOVEMENT (UPDATE)

Victor Brudney
Weld Professor of Law, Emeritus
Harvard University

COMPELLED SPEECH

Dan L. Burk
Professor of Law
Seaton Hall University

DNA TESTING AND GENETIC PRIVACY

Robert A. Burt
Alexander M. Bickel Professor of Law
Yale University

RIGHT TO DIE (UPDATE)

Paul Butler
Associate Professor of Law
George Washington University

RACE AND CRIMINAL JUSTICE

Jay S. Bybee
Professor of Law
University of Nevada, Las Vegas

CHILD SUPPORT RECOVERY ACT
DOMESTIC VIOLENCE CLAUSE

Evan H. Caminker
Professor of Law
University of Michigan, Ann Arbor

BRENNAN, WILLIAM J., JR. (UPDATE 2)
GREGORY V. ASHCROFT
GUARANTEE CLAUSE (UPDATE)
NEW YORK V. UNITED STATES
SAENZ V. ROE
STATE IMMUNITY FROM FEDERAL LAW

Penelope Canan
Associate Professor of Sociology
University of Denver

STRATEGIC LAWSUITS AGAINST PUBLIC
PARTICIPATION IN GOVERNMENT (with George W.
Pring)

Devon W. Carbado
Acting Professor of Law
University of California, Los Angeles

RACE AND SEX IN ANTIDISCRIMINATION LAW

Mary M. Cheh
Elyce Zenoff Research Professor of Law
George Washington University

DRUG REGULATION (UPDATE 2)
DRUG TESTING (UPDATE)

Erwin Chemerinsky
*Sydney M. Irmas Professor of Public Interest Law,
Legal Ethics, and Political Science*
University of Southern California

ABSTENTION DOCTRINE (UPDATE)
FILIBUSTER (with Catherine L. Fisk)
LEBRON V. NATIONAL RAILROAD PASSENGER CORP.
STATE ACTION (UPDATE 2)

Ronald K. Chen
Associate Dean of Law
Rutgers University, Newark

SEX OFFENDER NOTIFICATION LAWS

Jesse H. Choper
Earl Warren Professor of Public Law
University of California, Berkeley

LOCKHART, WILLIAM B.
RELIGION CLAUSES IN INTERACTION

Morgan Cloud
Professor of Law
Emory University

SEARCH AND SEIZURE (UPDATE 2)

Dan T. Coenen
Associate Professor of Law
University of Georgia

DORMANT COMMERCE CLAUSE (UPDATE)

William Cohen
*C. Wendell and Edith M. Carlsmith Professor of Law,
Emeritus*
Stanford University

RIGHT TO TRAVEL (UPDATE)

David Cole
Professor of Law
Georgetown University

TERRORISM CONTROL AND THE CONSTITUTION

Ruth Colker
Heck-Faust Memorial Chair in Constitutional Law
Ohio State University

AMERICANS WITH DISABILITIES ACT (UPDATE)
DISABILITY DISCRIMINATION

Thomas F. Cotter
Associate Professor of Law
University of Florida

PRAGMATISM (UPDATE)

Kimberlé Crenshaw
Professor of Law
Columbia University

CRITICAL RACE THEORY (with Neil Gotanda, Gary
    Peller, and Kendall Thomas)

David B. Cruz
Associate Professor of Law
University of Southern California

SAME-SEX MARRIAGE, I
SEXUAL ORIENTATION (UPDATE)

Michael Kent Curtis
Professor of Law
Wake Forest University

SLAVERY AND CIVIL LIBERTIES

Barry Cushman
Professor of Law
University of Virginia

NEW DEAL (CONSTITUTIONAL SIGNIFICANCE)

Chandler Davidson
Professor of Sociology and Political Science
Rice University

RACE AND VOTING
VOTING RIGHTS ACT OF 1965 AND ITS AMENDMENTS
    (UPDATE)

Julie Davies
Professor of Law
University of the Pacific

CIVIL RIGHTS PRACTICE

Vine Deloria, Jr.
Professor of History
University of Colorado, Boulder

AMERICAN INDIANS AND THE CONSTITUTION
    (UPDATE)

Neal Devins
Goodrich Professor of Law
College of William and Mary

CLINTON, WILLIAM JEFFERSON

William S. Dodge
Associate Professor of Law
University of California, Hastings College of the Law,
    San Francisco

ALVAREZ-MACHAIN, UNITED STATES V.
EXTRATERRITORIALITY (UPDATE)
INTERNATIONAL LAW AND FEDERAL–STATE
    RELATIONS

Michael C. Dorf
Professor of Law
Columbia University

INCIDENTAL BURDENS ON CONSTITUTIONAL RIGHTS
KENNEDY, ANTHONY M. (UPDATE)

Davison M. Douglas
*Professor of Law and Director of the Institute of Bill
    of Rights Law*
College of William and Mary

MISSOURI V. JENKINS (1995)

Ellen Carol DuBois
Professor of History
University of California, Los Angeles

ANTHONY, SUSAN BROWNELL
SENECA FALLS CONVENTION
STANTON, ELIZABETH CADY
WOMAN SUFFRAGE MOVEMENT

Earl C. Dudley, Jr.
Professor of Law
University of Virginia

CONTEMPT POWER, JUDICIAL (UPDATE)

Lynne A. Dunn
Attorney at Law
Hiering, Dupignac, & Stanzione, Toms River, N.J.

POLICE PURSUITS AND CONSTITUTIONAL RIGHTS

Theodore Eisenberg
Henry Allen Mark Professor of Law
Cornell University

BRAY V. ALEXANDRIA WOMEN'S HEALTH CLINIC
COLLINS V. CITY OF HARKER HEIGHTS
CONSTITUTIONAL REMEDIES (UPDATE)
IMMUNITY OF PUBLIC OFFICIALS

Christopher L. Eisgruber
Professor of Law
New York University

BIRTHRIGHT CITIZENSHIP
NATIONAL UNITY, GROUP CONFLICT, AND THE
   CONSTITUTION
RATIONAL BASIS (UPDATE)
STEVENS, JOHN PAUL (UPDATE 2)

David E. Engdahl
Professor of Law
Seattle University

TAXING AND SPENDING POWERS (UPDATE)

Peter D. Enrich
*Associate Dean for Academic Affairs and Professor of
   Law*
Northeastern University

STATE TAX INCENTIVES AND SUBSIDIES TO BUSINESS

Richard A. Epstein
*James Parker Hall Distinguished Service Professor of
   Law*
University of Chicago

ANTIDISCRIMINATION LEGISLATION (UPDATE 2A)
REGULATORY TAKINGS

Cynthia L. Estlund
Professor of Law
Columbia University

EMPLOYEE SPEECH RIGHTS (PRIVATE)

Daniel A. Farber
Henry J. Fletcher Professor of Law
University of Minnesota

ECONOMIC REGULATION (UPDATE)

Katherine Hunt Federle
*Associate Professor of Law and Director of the Justice
   for Children Project*
Ohio State University

JUVENILE CURFEW LAWS

Louis Fisher
Senior Specialist in Separation of Powers
Congressional Research Service, The Library of
   Congress

CONSTITUTIONAL HISTORY, 1989–1999
LINE-ITEM VETO (UPDATE)
PRESIDENTIAL WAR POWERS

James S. Fishkin
Darrell K. Royal Regents Chair in Government
University of Texas, Austin

DELIBERATIVE DEMOCRACY

Catherine L. Fisk
Professor of Law
Loyola Law School, Los Angeles

FILIBUSTER (with Erwin Chemerinsky)

Owen M. Fiss
Sterling Professor of Law
Yale University

JUDICIAL INDEPENDENCE

Martin S. Flaherty
Visiting Professor of Law
China University of Political Science and Law, Beijing

HISTORY IN CONSTITUTIONAL ARGUMENTATION

William A. Fletcher
Richard W. Jennings Professor of Law
University of California, Berkeley

JURISDICTION, FEDERAL (UPDATE)
LUJAN V. DEFENDERS OF WILDLIFE
STANDING (UPDATE)

William E. Forbath
*Angus Wynne, Sr., Professor of Civil Jurisprudence
   and Professor of History*
University of Texas, Austin

CONSTITUTIONAL DUALISM

Maria Foscarinis
Executive Director
National Law Center on Homelessness and Poverty,
   Washington, D.C.

HOMELESSNESS AND THE CONSTITUTION

Jody Freeman
Acting Professor of Law
University of California, Los Angeles

ENVIRONMENTAL REGULATION AND THE
CONSTITUTION (UPDATE 2)

Steven I. Friedland
Professor of Law
Nova Southeastern University

SEXUAL PREDATOR LAWS

Barry Friedman
Professor of Law
Vanderbilt University

NEUTRAL PRINCIPLES

Joel Wm. Friedman
Professor of Law
Tulane University

WISDOM, JOHN MINOR

Lawrence M. Friedman
Marion Rice Kirkwood Professor of Law
Stanford University

HURST, J. WILLARD

Leon Friedman
*Joseph Kushner Distinguished Professor of Civil
    Liberties Law*
Hofstra University

EXECUTIVE PRIVILEGE (UPDATE)

Stephen Gardbaum
Professor of Law
University of California, Los Angeles

PREEMPTION (UPDATE)

Cliff Gardner
Attorney at Law
Gardner & Derham, San Francisco, Calif.

HABEAS CORPUS (UPDATE 2)

Elizabeth Garrett
Assistant Professor of Law
University of Chicago

TERM LIMITS

Michael J. Gerhardt
Professor of Law
College of William and Mary

CLINTON V. JONES
PRESIDENTIAL IMMUNITY

Howard Gillman
Associate Professor of Political Science
University of Southern California

LIVING CONSTITUTION

Michael J. Glennon
Professor of Law
University of California, Davis

SEPARATION OF POWERS (UPDATE)

Carole Goldberg
Professor of Law
University of California, Los Angeles

TRIBAL ECONOMIC DEVELOPMENT AND THE
CONSTITUTION

Joseph Goldstein
*Sterling Professor Emeritus of Law and Derald H.
    Ruttenberg Professorial Lecturer in Law*
Yale University

PUBLIC UNDERSTANDING OF SUPREME COURT
OPINIONS

Robert D. Goldstein
Professor of Law
University of California, Los Angeles

CHANDLER V. MILLER
PLANNED PARENTHOOD V. CASEY

Gary Goodpaster
Professor of Law
University of California, Davis

PROCEDURAL DUE PROCESS OF LAW, CIVIL
(UPDATE 2)

Joel M. Gora
Professor of Law
Brooklyn Law School

COMMUNICATIONS DECENCY ACT
"MUST CARRY" LAW
TURNER BROADCASTING SYSTEM, INC. V. FCC

Neil Gotanda
Professor of Law
Western State University

CRITICAL RACE THEORY (with Kimberlé Crenshaw,
  Gary Peller, and Kendall Thomas)

Mark A. Graber
Associate Professor of Government and Politics
University of Maryland, College Park

EMPLOYEE SPEECH RIGHTS (PUBLIC)
NATIONAL TREASURY EMPLOYEES UNION, UNITED
  STATES V.
WATERS V. CHURCHILL

Joseph D. Grano
Distinguished Professor of Law
Wayne State University

SCALIA, ANTONIN (UPDATE)

Linda Greenhouse
The New York Times
Washington, D.C.

JOURNALISTS AND THE SUPREME COURT

Bernard Grofman
Professor of Political Science
University of California, Irvine

ELECTORAL DISTRICTING, I
MILLER V. JOHNSON
SHAW V. RENO AND ITS PROGENY

Janet E. Halley
*Professor of Law and Robert E. Paradise Faculty
  Scholar*
Stanford University

ROMER V. EVANS
SEXUAL ORIENTATION AND THE ARMED FORCES

Marci A. Hamilton
Professor of Law
Yeshiva University

O'CONNOR, SANDRA DAY (UPDATE 2)

Ian F. Haney López
Acting Professor of Law
University of California, Berkeley

CIVIL RIGHTS ACT OF 1991
RACIAL DISCRIMINATION (UPDATE 2)

Bernard E. Harcourt
Associate Professor of Law
University of Arizona

CRUEL AND UNUSUAL PUNISHMENT (UPDATE 2)

Cheryl I. Harris
Professor of Law
University of California, Los Angeles

TRUTH, SOJOURNER

Erica Harris
Associate
Susman Godfrey, L.L.P., Houston, Texas

AGE DISCRIMINATION (UPDATE) (with Samuel
  Issacharoff)

John C. Harrison
Professor of Law and Class of 1966 Research Professor
University of Virginia

DEMOCRATIC THEORY AND CONSTITUTIONAL LAW

Hendrik Hartog
*Class of 1921 Bicentennial Chair in the History of
  American Law and Liberty*
Princeton University

RIGHTS ISSUES IN HISTORICAL PERSPECTIVE

Richard L. Hasen
Associate Professor of Law
Loyola Law School, Los Angeles

PATRONAGE
TIMMONS V. TWIN CITIES AREA NEW PARTY

Louis Henkin
University Professor, Emeritus
Columbia University

INTERNATIONAL HUMAN RIGHTS

Lawrence Herman
Professor of Law, Emeritus
Ohio State University

POLICE INTERROGATION AND CONFESSIONS
  (UPDATE 2)

Susan N. Herman
Professor of Law
Brooklyn Law School

DOUBLE JEOPARDY (UPDATE 2)
SPEEDY TRIAL (UPDATE 2)

Morton J. Horwitz
Charles Warren Professor of the History of American Law
Harvard University

TRANSFORMATION OF CONSTITUTIONAL LAW

Herbert Hovenkamp
Ben V. and Dorothy Willie Professor of Law and History
University of Iowa

LÓPEZ, UNITED STATES V.

A. E. Dick Howard
White Burkett Miller Professor of Law and Public Affairs
University of Virginia

INFLUENCE OF THE AMERICAN CONSTITUTION ABROAD (UPDATE)

Ruth-Arlene W. Howe
Professor of Law and Advisor to the Black Law Student Association and Third World Law Journal
Boston College

ADOPTION, RACE, AND THE CONSTITUTION

Dennis J. Hutchinson
Professor and Senior Lecturer in Law and editor of The Supreme Court Review
University of Chicago

KURLAND, PHILIP B.
WHITE, BYRON R. (UPDATE 2)

Keith N. Hylton
Professor of Law
Boston University

PROPERTY RIGHTS AND THE HUMAN BODY

Scott C. Idleman
Assistant Professor of Law
Marquette University

RELIGIOUS FREEDOM RESTORATION ACT

Samuel Issacharoff
Visiting Professor of Law
Columbia University

AGE DISCRIMINATION (UPDATE) (with Erica Harris)
CENSUS
ELECTORAL DISTRICTING, FAIRNESS, AND JUDICIAL REVIEW

Vicki C. Jackson
Professor of Law
Georgetown University

ELEVENTH AMENDMENT (UPDATE 2)
FEDERALISM
SOVEREIGN IMMUNITY (UPDATE)

Robert J. Kaczorowski
Professor of Law
Fordham University

MURPHY, PAUL L.

Elena Kagan
Visiting Professor of Law
Harvard University

LIBEL AND THE FIRST AMENDMENT (UPDATE)
MASSON V. NEW YORKER MAGAZINE, INC.

Jerry Kang
Acting Professor of Law
University of California, Los Angeles

ASIAN AMERICANS AND THE CONSTITUTION
INTERNET AND FREEDOM OF SPEECH

Daniel Kanstroom
Associate Professor of Law
Boston College

ANTITERRORISM AND EFFECTIVE DEATH PENALTY ACT

Kenneth L. Karst
David G. Price and Dallas P. Price Professor of Law
University of California, Los Angeles

CHURCH OF THE LUKUMI BABALU AYE, INC. V. CITY OF HIALEAH
EULE, JULIAN N.
FORSYTH COUNTY, GEORGIA V. NATIONALIST MOVEMENT
M. L. B. V. S. L. J.
NONMARITAL CHILDREN

Andrew L. Kaufman
Professor of Law
Harvard University

FREUND, PAUL A.
GRISWOLD, ERWIN N.

William K. Kelley
Associate Professor of Law
University of Notre Dame

AGOSTINI V. FELTON
BOARD OF EDUCATION OF KIRYAS JOEL VILLAGE
    SCHOOL DISTRICT V. GRUMET

Michael J. Klarman
*James Monroe Professor of Law and F. Palmer Weber
    Research Professor of Civil Liberties & Human
    Rights*
University of Virginia

CIVIL LIBERTIES (UPDATE 2)
SUBSTANTIVE DUE PROCESS (UPDATE 2)

Lisa A. Kloppenberg
Associate Professor of Law
University of Oregon

AVOIDANCE DOCTRINE

Andrew Koppelman
Assistant Professor of Law and Political Science
Northwestern University

BAEHR V. LEWIN

J. Morgan Kousser
Professor of History and Social Science
California Institute of Technology

REAPPORTIONMENT (UPDATE)
VOTING RIGHTS (UPDATE)

Candace Saari Kovacic-Fleischer
Professor of Law
American University

SEX DISCRIMINATION (UPDATE 2)
VIRGINIA, UNITED STATES V.

Harold J. Krent
Professor and Associate Dean
Chicago-Kent College of Law

UNITARY EXECUTIVE

Wayne R. LaFave
David C. Baum Professor of Law, Emeritus
University of Illinois, Urbana-Champaign

FOURTH AMENDMENT (UPDATE)

Kurt T. Lash
Professor of Law and W. Joseph Ford Fellow
Loyola Law School, Los Angeles

GOVERNMENT AID TO RELIGIOUS INSTITUTIONS
    (UPDATE 2)
RELIGION AND SECULARISM IN CONSTITUTIONAL
    INTERPRETATION AND DEMOCRATIC DEBATE
SCHOOL CHOICE

Stanley K. Laughlin, Jr.
*Professor of Law and Adjunct Professor of
    Anthropology*
Ohio State University

PUERTO RICO
TERRITORIES OF THE UNITED STATES

Frederick M. Lawrence
Professor of Law
Boston University

HATE CRIMES
R. A. V. V. CITY OF ST. PAUL
WISCONSIN V. MITCHELL

Evan Tsen Lee
Professor of Law
University of California, Hastings College of the Law,
    San Francisco

CONGRESSIONAL STANDING
MOOTNESS (UPDATE)
RIPENESS (UPDATE)

Andrew D. Leipold
Professor of Law
University of Illinois, Urbana-Champaign

JURY NULLIFICATION

Laurie L. Levenson
Professor of Law and William M. Rains Fellow
Loyola Law School, Los Angeles

FREE PRESS/FAIR TRIAL (UPDATE)

Sanford Levinson
*W. St. John Garwood and W. St. John Garwood, Jr.,
    Centennial Chair in Law and Professor of
    Government*
University of Texas, Austin

CONSTITUTIONAL THEORY (UPDATE)
GUN CONTROL

LUCAS v. SOUTH CAROLINA COASTAL COUNCIL
TAKING OF PROPERTY (UPDATE 2)

Charles J. McClain
*Vice Chair of the Jurisprudence and Social Policy
　Program*
University of California, Berkeley

ASIAN IMMIGRANTS AND CONSTITUTIONAL HISTORY

Michael W. McConnell
Presidential Professor of Law
University of Utah

ESTABLISHMENT CLAUSE (UPDATE)
LAMB'S CHAPEL v. CENTER MORICHES UNION FREE
　SCHOOL DISTRICT
LEE, REX EDWIN
RELIGION AND FREE SPEECH

John O. McGinnis
Professor of Law
Yeshiva University

SUPERMAJORITY RULES (with Michael B. Rappaport)

Elizabeth Mensch
Professor of Law
State University of New York, Buffalo

ABORTION AND THE CONSTITUTION (UPDATE 2A)

Douglas E. Mirell
Partner
Loeb & Loeb, Los Angeles

FREE SPEECH, MURDER MANUALS, AND INSTRUCTION
　OF VIOLENCE (with Robert N. Treiman)

Rachel F. Moran
Robert D. and Leslie-Kay Raven Professor of Law
University of California, Berkeley

"OFFICIAL ENGLISH" LAWS

Eric L. Muller
Associate Professor of Law
University of North Carolina, Chapel Hill

HARMLESS ERROR (UPDATE)

Gerald L. Neuman
Herbert Wechsler Professor of Federal Jurisprudence
Columbia University

ILLEGAL IMMIGRATION REFORM AND IMMIGRANT
　RESPONSIBILITY ACT

IMMIGRATION AND ALIENAGE (UPDATE 2)
IMMIGRATION REFORM AND CONTROL ACT

Roger K. Newman
Research Scholar
New York University

BREYER, STEPHEN G.

Gene R. Nichol
Dean and Burton Craige Professor of Law
University of North Carolina, Chapel Hill

PUBLIC LAW LITIGATION

Marlene Arnold Nicholson
Professor of Law
DePaul University

AUSTIN v. MICHIGAN CHAMBER OF COMMERCE AND
　THE "NEW CORRUPTION"

John T. Nockleby
Professor of Law
Loyola Law School, Los Angeles

HATE SPEECH

Dawn C. Nunziato
Associate Professor of Law
George Washington University

ANONYMOUS POLITICAL SPEECH (with David G. Post)

James L. Oakes
Senior Circuit Judge
United States Court of Appeals for the Second Circuit

JUDICIAL COLLEGIALITY

David M. O'Brien
*Leone Reaves and George W. Spicer Professor of
　Government and Foreign Affairs*
University of Virginia

REHNQUIST COURT (UPDATE)
SOUTER, DAVID H. (UPDATE)

James M. O'Fallon
*Associate Dean for Academics and Frank Nash
　Professor of Law*
University of Oregon

ATTORNEY SPEECH
FLORIDA BAR v. WENT FOR IT, INC.

Robert M. O'Neil
Director
Thomas Jefferson Center for the Protection of Free
Expression, Charlottesville, Virginia

COHEN V. COWLES MEDIA CO.
FOOD LION, INC. V. AMERICAN BROADCASTING CO.
(ABC)
JOURNALISTIC PRACTICES, TORT LIABILITY, AND THE
FREEDOM OF THE PRESS

Karen Orren
Professor of Political Science
University of California, Los Angeles

FEUDALISM AND THE CONSTITUTION

Joel R. Paul
Professor of Law
University of Connecticut

EXECUTIVE AGREEMENTS (UPDATE)

Michael Stokes Paulsen
Briggs and Morgan Professor of Law
University of Minnesota

IMPEACHMENT (UPDATE)

Anthony A. Peacock
Assistant Professor of Political Science
Utah State University

ELECTORAL DISTRICTING, II

Gary Peller
Professor of Law
Georgetown University

CIVIL RIGHTS (UPDATE 2)
CRITICAL RACE THEORY (with Kimberlé Crenshaw,
Neil Gotanda, and Kendall Thomas)

Robert V. Percival
*Robert Stanton Scholar, Professor of Law, and
Director of the Environmental Law Program*
University of Maryland, Baltimore

FEDERALISM AND ENVIRONMENTAL LAW

Cornelia T. L. Pillard
Associate Professor of Law
Georgetown University

RETROACTIVITY OF LEGISLATION (UPDATE)

David G. Post
Associate Professor of Law
Temple University

ANONYMOUS POLITICAL SPEECH (with Dawn C.
Nunziato)

Anne Bowen Poulin
Professor of Law
Villanova University

PLAIN FEEL DOCTRINE

Monroe E. Price
Professor of Law
Yeshiva University

COMMUNICATIONS AND COMMUNITY
COMMUNICATIONS AND DEMOCRACY

George W. Pring
Professor of Law
University of Denver

STRATEGIC LAWSUITS AGAINST PUBLIC
PARTICIPATION IN GOVERNMENT (with Penelope
Canan)

Jack N. Rakove
Professor of American History
Stanford University

MADISONIAN CONSTITUTION

Michael B. Rappaport
Professor of Law
University of San Diego

SUPERMAJORITY RULES (with John O. McGinnis)

Jamin Raskin
Professor of Constitutional Law
American University

ALIEN SUFFRAGE

Judith Resnik
Arthur Liman Professor of Law
Yale University

FEDERAL JUDICIAL ROLE
SINGLE-SEX EDUCATION

William L. Reynolds
Jacob A. France Professor of Judicial Process
University of Maryland

FULL FAITH AND CREDIT (UPDATE) (with William M. Richman)

William M. Richman
Distinguished University Professor of Law
University of Toledo

FULL FAITH AND CREDIT (UPDATE) (with William L. Reynolds)

Dorothy Roberts
Professor of Law
Northwestern University

RACE, REPRODUCTION, AND CONSTITUTIONAL LAW

Robert E. Rodes, Jr.
Professor of Law
University of Notre Dame

ABORTION AND THE CONSTITUTION (UPDATE 2B)

Daniel B. Rodriguez
Dean and Professor of Law
University of San Diego

LEGAL PROCESS

Gerald N. Rosenberg
Associate Professor of Political Science and Lecturer of Law
University of Chicago

COURTS AND SOCIAL CHANGE, I

Thomas D. Russell
Professor of Law and History
University of Texas, Austin

SLAVERY AND PROPERTY

David K. Ryden
Assistant Professor of Political Science and Towsley Research Scholar
Hope College

LOBBYING DISCLOSURE ACT
POLITICAL PARTIES (UPDATE)
PRIMARY ELECTION (UPDATE)

Austin Sarat
William Nelson Cromwell Professor of Jurisprudence and Political Science, President of the Law and Society Association, and Chair of the Working Group on Law, Culture, and the Humanities
Amherst College

SOCIAL SCIENCE RESEARCH AND CONSTITUTIONAL LAW

Frederick Schauer
Frank Stanton Professor of the First Amendment
John F. Kennedy School of Government, Harvard University

FREEDOM OF SPEECH (UPDATE 2)
NONJUDICIAL INTERPRETATION OF THE CONSTITUTION (UPDATE) (with Larry Alexander)

Harry N. Scheiber
Stefan Riesenfeld Professor of Law and History
University of California, Berkeley

DEVOLUTION AND FEDERALISM IN HISTORICAL PERSPECTIVE
DIRECT DEMOCRACY (UPDATE)
OCEAN LAW AND THE CONSTITUTION

Pierre Schlag
Byron R. White Professor of Law
University of Colorado, Boulder

POSTMODERNISM AND CONSTITUTIONAL INTERPRETATION

Gary T. Schwartz
William D. Warren Professor of Law
University of California, Los Angeles

PUNITIVE DAMAGES (UPDATE)

Maimon Schwarzschild
Professor of Law
University of San Diego
Barrister
Lincoln's Inn, London

ROSENBERGER V. RECTOR & VISITORS OF THE UNIVERSITY OF VIRGINIA
VALUE PLURALISM AND THE CONSTITUTION

Robert A. Sedler
Professor of Law
Wayne State University

ANTIDISCRIMINATION LEGISLATION (UPDATE 2B)
EQUAL PROTECTION OF THE LAWS (UPDATE 2)

Louis Michael Seidman
Professor of Law
Georgetown University

JUDICIAL ACTIVISM AND JUDICIAL RESTRAINT
(UPDATE)

Peter M. Shane
Professor of Law
University of Pittsburgh

JUDICIAL IMPEACHMENT
NIXON V. UNITED STATES

Gene R. Shreve
Richard S. Melvin Professor of Law
Indiana University, Bloomington

CHOICE OF LAW AND CONSTITUTIONAL RIGHTS

Mark Silverstein
Professor of Political Science
Boston University

CONFIRMATION PROCESS

David A. Sklansky
Acting Professor of Law
University of California, Los Angeles

BLACKMUN, HARRY A. (UPDATE 2)
CRACK COCAINE AND EQUAL PROTECTION
TRAFFIC STOPS

Bradley A. Smith
Professor of Law
Capital University

ELECTORAL PROCESS AND THE FIRST AMENDMENT

Christopher E. Smith
Professor of Criminal Justice
Michigan State University

THOMAS, CLARENCE

Steven D. Smith
Robert and Marion Short Professor of Law
University of Notre Dame

ACCOMMODATION OF RELIGION

Aviam Soifer
Professor of Law
Boston College

GROUPS AND THE CONSTITUTION

Clyde Spillenger
Professor of Law
University of California, Los Angeles

BRANDEIS AS PUBLIC INTEREST LAWYER

Kirk J. Stark
Acting Professor of Law
University of California, Los Angeles

STATE AND LOCAL GOVERNMENT TAXATION (UPDATE)

Maxwell L. Stearns
Professor of Law
George Mason University

ARTICLE III AND PUBLIC CHOICE THEORY

Carol S. Steiker
Professor of Law
Harvard University

CRIMINAL JUSTICE AND DUE PROCESS

Richard H. Steinberg
Acting Professor of Law
University of California, Los Angeles

NORTH AMERICAN FREE TRADE AGREEMENT

Geoffrey R. Stone
*Provost and Harry Kalven, Jr., Distinguished Service
   Professor of Law*
University of Chicago

CAPITOL SQUARE REVIEW AND ADVISORY BOARD V.
   PINETTE
FIRST AMENDMENT (UPDATE 2)
HURLEY V. IRISH-AMERICAN GAY, LESBIAN, AND
   BISEXUAL GROUP OF BOSTON
INTERNATIONAL SOCIETY FOR KRISHNA
   CONSCIOUSNESS V. LEE
PUBLIC FORUM (UPDATE 2)

Marcy Strauss
Professor of Law
Loyola Law School, Los Angeles

WITNESSES, JURORS, AND THE FREEDOM OF SPEECH

Kathleen M. Sullivan
*Dean, Richard E. Lang Professor of Law, and Stanley
   Morrison Professor of Law*
Stanford University

AMENDING PROCESS (UPDATE)

CORPORATE POWER, FREE SPEECH, AND DEMOCRACY
UNCONSTITUTIONAL CONDITIONS (UPDATE)

Kendall Thomas
Professor of Law
Columbia University

CRITICAL RACE THEORY (with Kimberlé Crenshaw,
Neil Golanda, and Gary Peller)

Amy L. Toro
Visiting Professor of Law
University of California, Davis

FAIRNESS DOCTRINE (HISTORICAL DEVELOPMENT
AND UPDATE)

Robert N. Treiman
Partner
Loeb & Loeb, Los Angeles

FREE SPEECH, MURDER MANUALS, AND INSTRUCTION
OF VIOLENCE (with Douglas E. Mirell)

Phillip R. Trimble
*Vice Provost for International Studies and Professor of
Law*
University of California, Los Angeles

FOREIGN AFFAIRS (UPDATE)
GULF WAR
MULTINATIONAL CORPORATIONS, GLOBAL MARKETS,
AND THE CONSTITUTION

Mark Tushnet
Carmack Waterhouse Professor of Constitutional Law
Georgetown University

COURTS AND SOCIAL CHANGE, II
PRIVATIZATION AND THE CONSTITUTION
STATE REGULATION OF COMMERCE (UPDATE 2)
WASTE, POLLUTION, AND THE CONSTITUTION

Melvin I. Urofsky
*Professor of History and Director of the Doctoral
Program in Public Policy & Administration*
Virginia Commonwealth University

ROOSEVELT COURT

William W. Van Alstyne
*William R. Perkins and Thomas C. Perkins Professor
of Law*
Duke University

COMMERCIAL SPEECH (UPDATE 2)
SECOND AMENDMENT (UPDATE)

Jon M. Van Dyke
Professor of Law
University of Hawai'i, Manoa

NATIVE HAWAIIAN SOVEREIGNTY MOVEMENTS

Michael Vitiello
*Director of the Appellate Advocacy Program and
Professor of Law*
University of the Pacific

CAREER CRIMINAL SENTENCING LAWS

Eugene Volokh
Professor of Law
University of California, Los Angeles

INTELLECTUAL PROPERTY LAW AND THE FIRST
AMENDMENT
WORKPLACE HARASSMENT AND THE FIRST
AMENDMENT, I

Lynn D. Wardle
Professor of Law
Brigham Young University

SAME-SEX MARRIAGE, II

Jonathan Weinberg
Professor of Law
Wayne State University

BROADCASTING (UPDATE 2)

James Weinstein
Amelia Lewis Professor of Constitutional Law
Arizona State University

NUDE DANCING

Robin West
Professor of Law
Georgetown University

CONSTITUTION AS ASPIRATION
DIFFERENCE AND CONSTITUTIONAL EQUALITY

G. Edward White
John B. Minor Professor of Law and History
University of Virginia

HOLMES AND FREE SPEECH

Keith E. Whittington
Assistant Professor of Politics
Princeton University

CONGRESSIONAL GOVERNMENT

David C. Williams
Professor of Law and the Charles L. Whistler Faculty Fellow
Indiana University, Bloomington

RADICAL POPULIST CONSTITUTIONAL INTERPRETATION
RIGHT OF REVOLUTION (UPDATE)

Adam Winkler
Ph.D. Candidate
University of California, Los Angeles

ARTICLES OF IMPEACHMENT OF WILLIAM J. CLINTON
BURDICK V. TAKUSHI

BURSON V. FREEMAN
CHICAGO V. MORALES
CLEBURNE (CITY OF) V. CLEBURNE LIVING CENTER, INC.
DISTRICT OF COLUMBIA (UPDATE)
HOPWOOD V. TEXAS
LADUE (CITY OF) V. GILLEO

John Yoo
Professor of Law
University of California, Berkeley

INDEPENDENT COUNSEL (UPDATE)

James B. Zagel
U.S. District Judge
Northern District of Illinois

PROSECUTORIAL DISCRETION AND ITS CONSTITUTIONAL LIMITS

A

ABBATE v. UNITED STATES

See: *Bartkus v. Illinois*

ABINGTON TOWNSHIP SCHOOL DISTRICT v. SCHEMPP
374 U.S. 203 (1963)

A Pennsylvania statute required that at least ten verses from the Holy Bible be read, without comment, at the opening of each public school day. A child might be excused from this exercise upon the written request of his parents or guardian.

In ENGEL V. VITALE (1962) the school prayer held unconstitutional had been written by state officials. The question in *Schempp* was whether this made a difference—there being no claim that Pennsylvania was implicated in the authorship of the holy scripture.

Justice TOM C. CLARK concluded that the Pennsylvania exercise suffered from an establishment-clause infirmity every bit as grave as that afflicting New York's prayer. Clark's opinion in *Schempp* was the first strict separationist opinion of the Court not written by Justice HUGO L. BLACK, and Clark formulated a test for establishment clause validity with a precision that had eluded Black. A state program touching upon religion or religious institutions must have a valid secular purpose and must not have the primary effect of advancing or inhibiting religion. The Pennsylvania Bible reading program failed the test on both counts.

Justices WILLIAM O. DOUGLAS and WILLIAM J. BRENNAN concurred separately in opinions reflecting an even

stricter separationism than Clark's. Justice ARTHUR J. GOLD-BERG also filed a brief concurring opinion.

Justice POTTER STEWART dissented, as he had in *Engel*, arguing that religious exercises as part of public ceremonies were permissible so long as children were not coerced to participate.

Schempp, along with *Murray v. Curlett* (decided the same day), settled whatever lingering question there may have been about the constitutionality of RELIGION IN PUBLIC SCHOOLS.

RICHARD E. MORGAN
(1986)

ABLEMAN v. BOOTH
21 Howard 506 (1859)

Ableman v. Booth, Chief Justice ROGER B. TANEY's last major opinion, was part of the dramatic confrontation between the Wisconsin Supreme Court, intent on judicial nullification of the FUGITIVE SLAVE ACTS, and the Supreme Court of the United States, seeking to protect the reach of that statute into the free states.

For his role in organizing a mob that freed Joshua Glover, an alleged fugitive, Sherman Booth was charged with violation of the Fugitive Slave Act of 1850. After trial and conviction, he was released by a writ of habeas corpus from the Wisconsin Supreme Court, which held the Fugitive Slave Act unconstitutional, the first instance in which a state court did so. The Wisconsin court instructed its clerk to make no return to a WRIT OF ERROR from the United States Supreme Court and no entry on the records of the court concerning that writ, thus defying the United States Supreme Court.

The Court took JURISDICTION despite the procedural irregularity. In a magisterial opinion for a unanimous Court, Taney condemned the obstruction of the Wisconsin court and reaffirmed federal JUDICIAL SUPREMACY under section 25 of the JUDICIARY ACT OF 1789. Because the state's sovereignty "is limited and restricted by the Constitution of the United States," no state court process, including habeas corpus, could interfere with the enforcement of federal law. Taney also delivered two significant dicta. He anticipated the later doctrine of DUAL SOVEREIGNTY, which was to hamper state and federal regulatory authority in the early twentieth century, when he wrote that though the powers of the state and federal governments are exercised within the same territorial limits, they "are yet separate and distinct sovereignties, acting separately and independently of each other, within their respective spheres." Taney concluded his opinion by declaring the Fugitive Slave Act of 1850 to be "in all of its provisions, fully authorized by the Constitution."

A reconstituted Wisconsin Supreme Court later conceded the validity of Taney's interpretation of section 25 and apologized to the United States Supreme Court, conceding that its earlier actions were "a breach of that comity, or good behavior, which should be maintained between the courts of the two governments."

WILLIAM M. WIECEK
(1986)

ABOLITIONIST CONSTITUTIONAL THEORY

American abolitionists developed comprehensive but conflicting theories about the place of slavery in the American constitution. Though these ideas did not positively influence political and legal debate until the 1850s, they exercised profound influence over subsequent constitutional development, merging with constitutional aspirations of nonabolitionist Republicans after the CIVIL WAR to provide the basis for what one writer has called the "Third Constitution": the THIRTEENTH through FIFTEENTH AMENDMENTS. From abolitionist constitutional ideals embedded in section 1 of the FOURTEENTH AMENDMENT, there emerged some principal trends of constitutional development in the century after the Civil War: SUBSTANTIVE DUE PROCESS, equality before the law, protection for the privileges of national and state CITIZENSHIP.

By the time abolitionists began systematically to expound constitutional ideas in the 1830s, the constitutional aspects of the controversy over slavery were well developed. Even before American independence, Quakers in

the Middle Colonies and some Puritan ministers in New England had attacked slavery on religio-ethical grounds. In SOMERSET'S CASE (1772) WILLIAM MURRAY (Lord Mansfield), Chief Justice of King's Bench, suggested that slavery could be established only by positive law and that, as a legal institution, it was "odious." The American Revolution witnessed the total abolition, exclusion, or disappearance of slavery in some northern jurisdictions (Vermont, Massachusetts and Maine, New Hampshire, the Northwest Territory) and its gradual abolition in the rest (Pennsylvania, New York, New Jersey, Connecticut, Rhode Island). Early antislavery groups, federated as the American Convention of Abolition Societies, worked in legal and paternalistic ways to protect freed blacks and provide them jobs and education. Yet these Revolutionary-era inhibitions on slavery were offset by gains slavery made in the drafting of the United States Constitution, in which ten clauses promoted slavery's security, most notably in the federal number clause (Article I, section 2, clause 3), the slave trade clause (Article I, section 9, clause 1), and the fugitive slave clause (Article IV, section 2, clause 3).

Constitutional controversy flared over slavery in several early episodes: the federal abolition of the international slave trade and its incidents, the Missouri crisis (1819–1821), the disputes over federal aid to colonization of free blacks, Denmark Vesey's slave revolt (Charleston, 1822), and the Negro Seamen's Acts of the southern coastal states (1822–1830). But not until the ideas of immediate abolition rejuvenated the antislavery movement did abolitionists begin a systematic constitutional assault on slavery. When they organized the American Anti-Slavery Society (AASS) in 1833, abolitionists, in a document drafted by WILLIAM LLOYD GARRISON, pledged themselves to tolerate the continued existence of slavery in the states and rejected the possibility that the federal government could abolish it there. But they insisted that slavery should be abolished immediately, that blacks should not suffer legal discrimination because of race, and that Congress should abolish the interstate slave trade, ban slavery in the DISTRICT OF COLUMBIA and the TERRITORIES, and refuse to admit new slave states.

The newly reorganized movement promptly encountered resistance that directed its thinking into constitutional modes. Federal efforts to suppress abolitionist mailings and to gag abolitionists' FREEDOM OF PETITION, together with mobbings throughout the northern states, diverted abolitionists briefly from the pursuit of freedom for blacks to a defense of CIVIL LIBERTIES of whites. At the same time, they assaulted slavery's incidents piecemeal, attempting to protect fugitive slaves from rendition, and seeking repeal of statutes that permitted sojourning masters to keep their slaves with them for limited periods of time in northern states. They secured enactment of PER-

SONAL LIBERTY LAWS: statutes that protected the freedom of black people in the northern states by providing them HABEAS CORPUS relief when seized as fugitives and by prohibiting state officials or public facilities from being used in the recapture of fugitives.

In 1839–1840, the unified antislavery movement split apart into three factions. Ironically, this organizational disaster stimulated abolitionists' systematic constitutional theorizing and broadcast their ideas widely outside the movement. Because of theological and tactical disagreements, the movement first broke into Garrisonian and political action wings, the Garrisonians condemning conventional electoral politics and the activists organizing a third party, the Liberty party, which ran its own presidential candidate in 1840 and 1844. The political action group subsequently split into those who believed slavery to be everywhere illegitimate and who therefore sought to have the federal government abolish slavery in the states, and those who continued to maintain the position of the original AASS Constitution, namely, that Congress lacked constitutional power to abolish slavery in the states. The Garrisonians, meanwhile, had concluded that the United States Constitution supported slavery and therefore called on northern states to secede from the Union and on individuals to disavow their allegiance to the Constitution.

Those who always maintained slavery's universal illegitimacy relied first on the DUE PROCESS clause of the Fifth Amendment, arguing that slaves were deprived of life, liberty, and property without legal justification, but they soon broadened their attack, ingeniously interpreting nearly a third of the Constitution's clauses, from the PREAMBLE to the TENTH AMENDMENT, to support their untenable thesis that slavery had usurped its preferred constitutional status. The 1840 publication of JAMES MADISON's notes of proceedings at the CONSTITUTIONAL CONVENTION OF 1787 was an embarrassment to them, disclosing as it did the concessions the Framers willingly made to the political power of slavery. Exponents of the universal-illegitimacy theory included Alvan Stewart, G. W. F. Mellen, Lysander Spooner, Joel Tiffany, and later, Gerrit Smith, JAMES G. BIRNEY, Lewis Tappan, and Frederick Douglass. Their principal contributions to later constitutional development included: their insistence on equality before the law irrespective of race; their vision of national citizenship protecting individuals' rights throughout the Union; their reliance on the PRIVILEGES AND IMMUNITIES clause (Article IV, section 2, clause 1) as a protection for persons of both races; and their uncompromising egalitarianism, which led them to condemn all forms of RACIAL DISCRIMINATION. They were scorned as extremists in their own time, even by fellow abolitionists, and modern scholars such as Robert Cover dismiss their ideas as "utopian."

Political action abolitionists who conceded the legality of slavery in the states remained closest to the mainstream of American politics and established a political alliance with like-minded men outside the abolitionist movement to create the Free Soil party in 1848. Their insistence that, as the federal government could not abolish slavery, neither could it establish it, led them to proclaim the doctrines of "divorce" and "freedom national." "Divorce" called for an immediate and absolute separation of the federal government from the support of slavery (for example, by abolishing the interstate slave trade and repealing the Fugitive Slave Act of 1793), coupled with an aggressive attack on the political bases of slavery's strength (repeal of the federal number clause, refusal to appoint slaveholders to federal posts). "Divorce" provided the doctrinal basis of the three-way Free Soil coalition of 1848, comprised of Conscience Whigs, Barnburner Democrats, and former Libertymen. Liberty leaders in the Free Soil group included SALMON P. CHASE (later Chief Justice of the United States), Gamaliel Bailey, STANLEY MATTHEWS (a future justice of the United States Supreme Court), Representative Owen Lovejoy, and Joshua Leavitt.

Stimulated by the widespread popularity of the WILMOT PROVISO (1846) in the north, which would have excluded slavery from all territories acquired as a result of the Mexican War, the abolitionist Free Soilers demanded "nonextension": the refusal to permit slavery in any American territories, and the nonadmission of new slave states. This became transformed into "freedom national," a constitutional doctrine holding that, under *Somerset*, freedom is the universal condition of humans, and slavery a local aberration created and continued only by local positive law. These ideas were cordially received by Whigs who formed a nucleus of the Republican party after the demise of the Free Soilers and the fragmentation of the regular parties as a result of the KANSAS-NEBRASKA ACT (1854): Joshua Giddings, CHARLES SUMNER, Charles Francis Adams, and Horace Mann. Other Republicans such as ABRAHAM LINCOLN and WILLIAM SEWARD refused to accept "divorce" but made nonextension the cornerstone of Republican policy. "Freedom national" even influenced anti-abolitionists such as Lewis Cass and then STEPHEN A. DOUGLAS, who promoted a modified version of it as the FREEPORT DOCTRINE of 1858.

Garrisonians dismissed the United States Constitution as the "covenant with death and agreement with hell" denounced by Isaiah, but they too influenced later constitutional development, principally through their insistence that the proslavery clauses of the Constitution would have to be repealed or nullified, and the federal government fumigated of its contamination with support of slavery. Though they included competent lawyers (Wendell Phillips, William I. Bowditch), the Garrisonians were distinguished chiefly by literary and polemical talent (Edmund

Quincy, Lydia Maria Child) and consequently made little contribution to systematic constitutional exposition.

The crises of the union in the 1850s, beginning with enactment of the Fugitive Slave Act in 1850, leading through the dramatic fugitive recaptures and rescues, the Kansas-Nebraska Act (1854) and "Bleeding Kansas," and culminating, constitutionally, in DRED SCOTT V. SANDFORD (1857), ABLEMAN V. BOOTH (1859), and the pending appeal of *People v. Lemmon* (1860), together with legislative activity (chiefly enactment of ever broader personal liberty laws, including Vermont's Freedom Act of 1858), enabled abolitionists to work together toward common goals, and to overcome or survive their sectarian quarrels of the 1840s. Though fragmented as a distinct movement, abolitionists permeated the press, parties, and the churches, diffusing their ideas widely among persons who had not been theretofore involved in the antislavery movement. Thus egalitarians like Sumner and THADDEUS STEVENS, conservative lawyers like JOHN BINGHAM and William Lawrence, and political leaders like WILLIAM PITT FESSENDEN and ROSCOE CONKLING were influenced by abolitionist constitutional ideas, appropriating them after the war and injecting them into the Constitution and its interpretation, both in cases and in statutes.

WILLIAM M. WIECEK
(1986)

Bibliography

DUMOND, DWIGHT L. 1961 *Antislavery.* Ann Arbor: University of Michigan Press.
FEHRENBACHER, DON 1978 *The Dred Scott Case: Its Significance in American Law and Politics.* New York: Oxford University Press.
GRAHAM, HOWARD J. 1968 *Everyman's Constitution.* Madison: State Historical Society of Wisconsin.
TEN BROEK, JACOBUS 1965 *Equal under Law.* New York: Collier Books.
WIECEK, WILLIAM M. 1977 *The Sources of Antislavery Constitutionalism in America, 1760–1848.* Ithaca, N.Y.: Cornell University Press.

ABOLITION OF SLAVERY

See: Slavery and the Constitution; Thirteenth Amendment

ABOOD v. DETROIT BOARD OF EDUCATION
431 U.S. 209 (1977)

Abood is one of the cases where union or agency shop agreements create speech and association problems, be-cause individuals must join unions in order to hold jobs and then must pay dues to support union activities with which the individuals may not agree. Here the union represented public employees. The Supreme Court has consistently held that there is no right *not* to associate in a labor union for the purposes of COLLECTIVE BARGAINING but that a union must develop methods of relieving a member of those portions of union dues devoted to union ideological activities to which he objects.

MARTIN SHAPIRO
(1986)

(SEE ALSO: *Freedom of Assembly and Association; Freedom of Speech; Labor and the Constitution.*)

ABORTION AND THE CONSTITUTION

The story of abortion and the Constitution is in part an episode in the saga of SUBSTANTIVE DUE PROCESS. During the period from the early 1900s to the mid-1930s, the Supreme Court employed the principle of substantive due process—the principle that governmental action abridging a person's life, liberty, or property interests must serve a legitimate governmental policy—to invalidate much state and federal legislation that offended the Court's views of legitimate policy, particularly socioeconomic policy. In the late 1930s and early 1940s, the Court, with a new majority composed in part of Justices appointed by President FRANKLIN D. ROOSEVELT, reacted to the perceived judicial excesses of the preceding generation by refusing to employ substantive due process to invalidate any state or federal legislation. During the next quarter century—the period between the demise of the "old" substantive due process and the birth of the "new"—the Court did not formally reject the principle of substantive due process; from time to time the Court inquired whether challenged legislation was consistent with the principle. But the Court's substantive due process review was so deferential to the legislation in question as to be largely inconsequential, as, for example, in WILLIAMSON V. LEE OPTICAL CO. (1955).

Then, in the mid-1960s, the Court changed direction. In GRISWOLD V. CONNECTICUT (1965) the Court relied on a constitutional RIGHT OF PRIVACY to rule that a state could not ban the use of contraceptives by married persons. In *Eisenstadt v. Baird* (1972), on EQUAL PROTECTION grounds, it ruled that a state may not ban the distribution of contraceptives to unmarried persons. Despite the rhetoric of the Court's opinions, there is no doubt that both were substantive due process decisions in the methodological (if not the rhetorical) sense: in each case the Court invalidated legislation that offended not any specific prohibition of the Constitution but simply the Court's views of the governmental policies asserted in justification of the states' regulations.

If any doubt remained about whether the Court had returned to substantive due process, that doubt could not survive the Court's decision in ROE V. WADE (1973), which employed substantive due process in both the rhetorical and the methodological senses. The Court ruled in *Roe* that the due process clause of the FOURTEENTH AMENDMENT prohibited a state from forbidding a woman to obtain an abortion in the period of pregnancy prior to the fetus's viability. Indeed, in *Roe* the Court applied a particularly strong version of the substantive-due-process requirement: because the criminal ban on abortion challenged in *Roe* abridged a "fundamental" liberty interest of the woman—specifically, her "privacy" interest in deciding whether to terminate her pregnancy—the Court insisted that the legislation not merely serve a legitimate governmental policy but that it be *necessary* to serve a COMPELLING STATE INTEREST. The Court concluded that only after viability was government's interest in protecting the life of the fetus sufficiently strong to permit it to ban abortion.

Obviously the written Constitution says nothing about abortion, and no plausible "interpretation" or "application" of any determinate value judgment fairly attributable to the framers of the Fourteenth Amendment prohibits state government from forbidding a woman to obtain an abortion. In that sense, the Supreme Court's decision in *Roe v. Wade* is an exemplar of JUDICIAL ACTIVISM. Thus, it was not surprising that the decision—the Court's constitutionalization of the matter of abortion—ignited one of those periodic explosions about the legitimacy of judicial activism in a democracy. (Earlier such explosions attended the Court's activism in the period from *Lochner v. New York* (1905) to the late 1930s and, more recently, the Court's decision in *Brown v. Board of Education* (1954) outlawing racially segregated public schooling.)

Many critics of the Court's decision in *Roe* complained about the judicial activism underlying the decision. In the view of most such critics, *Roe v. Wade* is simply a contemporary analogue of the almost universally discredited *Lochner v. New York* (1905), and no one who opposes the activist mode of judicial review exemplified by *Lochner* can consistently support the activist mode exemplified by *Roe*. Of course, the force of this argument depends on one's perception of what is wrong with *Lochner*: the activist mode of review exemplified by it or simply the Court's answer in *Lochner* to the question of economic liberty addressed there. There is no inconsistency in opposing *Lochner*'s doctrinal conclusions and supporting the activist mode of review exemplified by *Roe* (and by *Lochner*). In-

deed, one might support the activist mode of review exemplified by *Roe* and at the same time oppose *Roe*'s reasoning and result.

A second, distinct criticism of the Court's decision in *Roe* concerns not the legitimacy of judicial activism but the soundness of the Court's answer to the political-moral question it addressed. Because many persons believe, often on religious grounds, that the Court gave the wrong answer to the question whether state government should be permitted to ban abortion, there was, in the decade following *Roe*, a vigorous political movement to overrule *Roe* legislatively—either by taking away the Court's JURISDICTION to review state abortion laws, or by constitutional amendment or even simple congressional legislation to the effect that a fetus is a person within the meaning of the Fourteenth Amendment and that therefore state government may ban abortion to protect the life of the fetus. The proposals to limit the jurisdiction of the Court and to overrule *Roe* by simple congressional legislation, as opposed to constitutional amendment, became subjects of vigorous political and constitutional controversy.

The vigor of the political controversy over abortion cannot be fully comprehended—indeed, the Court's decision to constitutionalize the matter of abortion cannot be fully comprehended—without reference to an important development in American society that gained momentum in the 1970s and 1980s: a fundamental shift in attitudes toward the role of women in society. Many of those who opposed abortion and the "liberalization" of public policy regarding abortion did so as part of a larger agenda based on a "traditional" vision of woman's place and of the family. Many of those on the other side of the issue were seeking to implement a different vision—a feminist vision in which women are free to determine for themselves what shapes their lives will take, and therefore free to determine whether, and when, they will bear children.

Not surprisingly, this basic shift in attitudes toward women—from patriarchal to feminist—has been an occasion for deep division in American society. "Abortion politics" was merely one manifestation of that division (although an important one, to be sure). Thus, a controversy that sometimes seemed on the surface to consist mainly of a philosophical-theological dispute over the question, "When does 'life' begin?," actually involved much more. The complexity of the abortion controversy was dramatically evidenced by the fact that even within the Roman Catholic Church in the United States, which was the most powerful institutional opponent of abortion, attitudes toward abortion were deeply divided precisely because attitudes toward women were deeply divided.

As a consequence of its decision in *Roe v. Wade*, the Court has had to resolve many troublesome, controversial issues regarding abortion. For example, in PLANNED PAR-

ENTHOOD OF MISSOURI V. DANFORTH (1976) the Court ruled that a state may not require a woman to obtain the consent of her spouse before she terminates her pregnancy. The Court's rulings with respect to parental-consent and parental-notification requirements have not been a model of clarity, in part because the rulings have been fragmented. In *Bellotti v. Baird* (1979), for example, an 8–1 decision striking down the parental consent requirement, the majority split 4–4 as to the proper rationale. This much, however, is clear: state government may not require *every* minor, whatever her level of independence or maturity, to obtain parental consent before she terminates her pregnancy.

Undoubtedly the most controversial issue concerning abortion that the Court has addressed since *Roe v. Wade* involved abortion funding. In MAHER V. ROE (1977), the Court ruled that a state government that spends welfare funds to subsidize medical expenses incident to pregnancy and childbirth may decline to subsidize medical expenses incident to nontherapeutic abortion even if its sole reason for doing so is to discourage abortion. In a companion case, *Poelker v. Doe* (1977), the Court ruled that a public hospital that provides medical services relating to pregnancy and childbirth may decline to provide nontherapeutic abortions even if its sole reason for doing so is to discourage abortion. Three years later, in HARRIS V. MCRAE (1980), the Court sustained the HYDE AMENDMENT (to appropriations for the Medicaid program), which prohibited federal funding of abortion, including therapeutic abortion, even though the sole purpose of the amendment was to discourage abortion.

Some commentators have claimed that, notwithstanding the Court's arguments to the contrary, these abortion-funding cases cannot be reconciled with *Roe v. Wade*. They reason that the Court's decision in *Roe* can be satisfactorily explained only on the ground that government may not take action predicated on the view that abortion (in the pre-viability period) is morally objectionable, but that the governmental policies sustained in *Maher*, *Poelker*, and *McRae* were all manifestly predicated on just that view. There is probably no final explanation of the Court's decisions in the abortion-funding cases except in terms of judicial *Realpolitik*—that is, as an effort to retrench in the face of vigorous, often bitter, and widespread criticism of its decision in *Roe v. Wade* and threats to overrule *Roe* legislatively.

Its decision, in *Roe v. Wade*, to constitutionalize the deeply controversial issue of abortion represents one of the Supreme Court's most problematic ventures in recent times. Other moves by the Court were as controversial when initially taken—for example, the Court's choice in *Brown v. Board of Education* (1954) to begin to disestablish racially segregated public schooling—but few have been so persistently controversial. Whatever their eventual fate, *Roe* and its progeny have served as an occasion for some of the most fruitful thinking in this century on the proper role of the Supreme Court in American government.

MICHAEL J. PERRY
(1986)

(SEE ALSO: *Anti-abortion Movement; Reproductive Autonomy.*)

Bibliography

ELY, JOHN HART 1973 The Wages of Crying Wolf: A Comment on *Roe v. Wade. Yale Law Journal* 82:920.
PERRY, MICHAEL 1980 Why the Supreme Court was Plainly Wrong in the Hyde Amendment Case: A Brief Comment on *Harris v. McRae. Stanford Law Review* 32:1113–1128.
REGAN, DONALD 1979 Rewriting *Roe v. Wade. Michigan Law Review* 77:1569–1646.
TRIBE, LAURENCE H. 1978 *American Constitutional Law.* Pages 921–934. Mineola, N.Y.: Foundation Press.

ABORTION AND THE CONSTITUTION
(Update 1a)

Abortion LEGISLATION rarely, if ever, demonstrates concern for the well-being of women. It usually represents the state using coercive measures to persuade women to bear children rather than have abortions. As long as American society treats women and their reproductive capacity with disrespect by not funding prenatal care, postnatal care, paid pregnancy leave, effective and safe forms of BIRTH CONTROL, or child care, it is hard to imagine that a legislature that respects the well-being of women could enact restrictions on abortion. Thus, when we read abortion legislation or an abortion decision by the courts, we should ask ourselves whether that legislature or that court could have reached the decision that it reached if it fully respected the well-being of women. Under such a framework, we would have to conclude that the Missouri legislature that enacted the abortion legislation challenged in WEBSTER V. REPRODUCTIVE HEALTH SERVICES (1989) did not respect the well-being of women, especially poor or teenage women. Nevertheless, no member of the Supreme Court in *Webster*, including the dissenters, demonstrated a real grasp of the significance of the Missouri legislation on the lives and well-being of poor women and teenage women.

In *Webster*, the Supreme Court was asked to consider the constitutionality of a Missouri statute that contained four provisions arguably restricting a woman's ability to have an abortion. Two provisions received most of the

Court's attention: first, a requirement that a physician ascertain whether a fetus is viable prior to performing an abortion on any woman whom he or she has reason to believe is twenty or more weeks pregnant; and, second, a prohibition against using public employees or facilities to perform or assist an abortion not necessary to save the mother's life.

Chief Justice WILLIAM H. REHNQUIST wrote the opinion for the Court. His opinion was joined by four other Justices—BYRON R. WHITE, SANDRA DAY O'CONNOR, ANTONIN SCALIA, and ANTHONY M. KENNEDY—with respect to the second provision. Rehnquist's conclusion that this part of the statute was constitutional was an extension of the Court's earlier decisions in the Medicaid abortion-funding cases. Rather than apply the more stringent test that had been developed in ROE V. WADE (1973), Rehnquist applied the more lenient standard developed in HARRIS V. MCRAE (1980)—asking whether the state legislature had placed any obstacles in the path of a woman who chooses to terminate her pregnancy. Rehnquist concluded that the state's refusal to allow public employees to perform abortions in public hospitals leaves a pregnant woman with the same choices as if the state had chosen not to operate any public hospitals at all. As in *Harris v. McRae*, Rehnquist acknowledged that a state was permitted to make a value judgment favoring childbirth over abortion and to implement that judgment in allocating public funds and facilities.

Justice HARRY BLACKMUN's dissent, which was joined by Justices WILLIAM J. BRENNAN and THURGOOD MARSHALL, argued that Missouri's public facility provision could easily be distinguished from *Harris v. McRae* because of the sweeping scope of Missouri's definition of a public facility. (Justice JOHN PAUL STEVENS dissented separately.) Under Missouri's broad definition, any institution that was located on property owned, leased, or controlled by the government was considered to be public. Thus, the essentially private Truman Medical Center, which performed ninety-seven percent of abortions in the state after sixteen weeks of pregnancy, would be prohibited from performing abortions under the state statute. Even under the more lenient test developed by the Court in *Harris*, Justice Blackmun concluded that the funding provision should be held unconstitutional.

Justice Blackmun's discussion of the public facility provision comes only in a footnote and is not the primary focus of his decision. In order to understand the full impact of this provision on women's lives and health, it is useful to consider the AMICUS briefs filed on behalf of women of color and teenage women. These briefs noted that poor women and teenage women are more likely than other women to seek abortions at public health facilities because they do not have private physicians. They are also more likely to have second-trimester abortions because they delay having abortions until they save the necessary amount of money or find out how to get an abortion. When Blackmun noted that the health-care provider that performs nearly all of the second-trimester abortions will not be able to do so, he could have observed that poor women and teenagers would be disproportionately unable to procure legal abortions. Given the relationship between teenage pregnancy and the cycle of poverty, the inability to procure an abortion often has dramatic consequences in the life of a poor, teenage woman. Although Justice Blackmun was certainly correct to note that the public facility ban "leaves the pregnant woman with far fewer choices, or, for those too sick or too poor to travel, perhaps no choice at all," it would have been better if he had described the impact of this regulation in the race-, class-, and age-based way in which it is most likely to operate.

Justice Blackmun's discussion of the public facility provision skirted the question whether *Harris v. McRae* should be overturned. He tried to distinguish *Harris* from *Webster* rather than call for its reconsideration. The amicus brief submitted by women of color was not so subtle. They often used exactly the same information that they had provided the Supreme Court in *Harris* to argue that the well-being of poor women cannot be protected unless the government ensures that legal abortions are available to poor women on the same basis as middle-class women. A chart in an amicus brief submitted by an international women's health organization showed that the United States stands alone in the world in permitting abortion to be lawful but not funding any abortions for poor women unless their very lives are endangered. Although not all countries fund "abortion on demand" for poor women, all countries that make abortion lawful also fund therapeutic abortions for poor women. These comparative data show that the United States stands alone in the world in its disrespect for the lives and well-being of poor women. Unlike other Western countries, the United States fails to fund prenatal care, postnatal care, pregnancy leave, and child care but then tries to tell poor women that it "prefers" childbirth to abortion. The most logical explanation for this position of both the United States government and the state of Missouri is that government officials have not bothered to educate themselves on the impact that funding and public facility restrictions have on the lives of poor women. And, as long as poor women have virtually no political power, it seems unlikely that government officials will focus on their needs.

Both the majority and dissenting opinions in *Webster* did focus on the first provision of the Missouri statute. Chief Justice Rehnquist's discussion of this provision only received the support of Justices White and Kennedy, but the seperate concurrences of Justices O'Connor and Scalia made a majority for the conclusion that the provision was constitutional. The provision presented both technical and substantive difficulties. Technically, the provision appeared to require physicians to perform viability tests that were contrary to accepted medical practice, such as performing amniocentesis on a fetus that was under twenty-eight weeks old. If that had been the actual meaning of the statute, most of the Justices would have been compelled to find it unconstitutional even under the most lenient standard of review used by courts—the RATIONAL BASIS test—because the statute would have rationally served no public purpose. In order to avoid that conclusion, Rhenquist offered a somewhat strained interpretation of the statute so that a physician would have the discretion to perform only tests that were medically appropriate.

Having overcome this technical hurdle, Rehnquist then turned to the substantive difficulties posed by the provision. Under the Court's prior doctrine, as articulated in *Roe v. Wade*, a state was permitted to impose abortion restrictions to protect fetal life only in the third trimester of pregnancy. Because the viability-testing requirement took effect as early as twenty weeks, four weeks before the beginning of the third trimester, Rehnquist faced a seeming conflict with *Roe*.

Rehnquist concluded that the *Roe* trimester framework was too rigid and that if the state has an interest in preserving potential human life after viability, it also has an interest in preserving that potential life before viability. Although Rehnquist's statement about preserving potential human life might be read to mean that states could outlaw abortions before the twenty-fourth week and thereby overturn *Roe*, he refrained from reaching that conclusion, because that question was not before the Court.

A fourth vote for the majority position was cast by Justice Scalia. Scalia, unlike Rehnquist, concluded that *Roe* should be overturned and that states should be free to regulate or criminalize abortion at any stage of pregnancy.

The fifth vote for the majority position was cast by Justice O'Connor. Unlike the other members of the majority, she did not argue that *Roe* needed to be overturned, or even modified, to reach the conclusion that the viability provision was constitutional. O'Connor reinterpreted the Court's prior decisions to require that states "not impose an undue burden on a woman's abortion decision." Because she concluded that the viability tests could be performed without markedly increasing the cost of abortion, O'Connor concluded that the undue burden test had been satisfied. O'Connor's framework, unlike that of Rehnquist or Scalia, made it clear that states could not criminalize abortion as they had in the pre-*Roe* era because a criminal

penalty certainly would constitute an "undue burden." What other kinds of regulations would impose an undue burden, however, is unclear from O'Connor's opinion.

Justice Blackmun wrote a blistering opinion for the dissenters. He accused Justice Rhenquist of being deceptive in not acknowledging that he was really overturning *Roe*. Moreover, he chided Rhenquist for not giving the Court a usable framework to evaluate future abortion cases. Blackmun said that he feared "for the liberty and equality of the millions of women who have lived and come of age in the sixteen years since *Roe* was decided" and "for the integrity of, and public esteem for, this Court." Substantively, he accused the Court of offering no rationale for its rejection of the trimester framework, saying that the Court used an "it is so because we say so" jurisprudence. The trimester framework, he argued, does make sense because it reflects the developmental view that one is more entitled to the rights of CITIZENSHIP as one increases one's ability to feel pain, to experience pleasure, to survive, and to react to one's environment. Finally, he criticized the test purportedly used by the majority—whether the regulation "permissably furthers the State's interest in protecting potential human life"—as circular and meaningless. He argued that the standard of whether a regulation "permissably furthers" the state's interest was itself the *question* before the Court; it therefore could not be the *standard* that the Court applied in resolving the question.

Although Justice Blackmun wrote his dissent in strong language and even mentioned that the majority's opinion would have a dramatic effect on the "liberty and equality" of women's lives, there is no specific discussion of that effect. Blackmun spent most of his opinion explaining why there was no good reason to change the course of using the RIGHT OF PRIVACY on which the Court had commenced in his opinion in *Roe*.

One of the most disappointing parts of Blackmun's opinion is his conclusion that if the majority's technical interpretation of the provision were correct, he "would see little or no conflict with *Roe*." In other words, he appeared to agree with Justice O'Connor that such a provision would not constitute an undue burden on a woman's abortion decision. Blackmun dissented from the majority because he disagreed with its technical interpretation of the viability-testing provision, not because he fundamentally disagreed about the impact that requirement would have on women's lives and well-being.

If Justice Blackmun had truly considered the "liberty and equality" interests of sixteen million women, he would not have been so easily satisfied. As the briefs that were presented to the Court by women of color and teenage women dramatically showed, raising the cost of abortion, even marginally, has a marked impact on the ability of poor women to purchase abortions. And because women of color and teenage women are more likely to delay abortion decisions, they will be hit harder by the viability-testing requirement than are other women. For poor women, even the requirement that they pay for their own abortions is an undue burden on their reproductive decision making. Raising the cost of abortion presents an even greater— and even more undue—burden.

From the perspective of protecting the well-being of women, *Webster* is doubly discouraging. Not only did the majority of the Court not seem to understand the meaning of abortion regulations in women's lives, but even the dissenters did not display much understanding or sensitivity. They seemed more determined to protect the integrity of their prior decisions than to consider the reality of new abortion restrictions on women's lives.

RUTH COLKER
(1992)

(SEE ALSO: *Anti-abortion Movement; Feminist Theory; Reproductive Autonomy.*)

Bibliography

COLKER, RUTH   1989   Abortion and Dialogue. *Tulane Law Review* 63:1363–1403.

JAGGAR, ALISON   1974   Abortion and a Woman's Right to Decide. *Philosophical Forum* 5:347.

JUNG, PATRICIA BEATTIE and SHANNON, THOMAS A., eds. 1988 *Abortion and Catholicism: The American Debate.* New York: Crossroad Press.

MCDONNELL, KATHLEEN   1984   *Not An Easy Choice: A Feminist Re-examines Abortion.* Boston: South End Press.

ABORTION AND THE CONSTITUTION
(Update 1b)

With President RONALD REAGAN's elevation of Justice WILLIAM H. REHNQUIST to CHIEF JUSTICE and his appointment of Justices ANTONIN SCALIA and ANTHONY M. KENNEDY, many expected the Supreme Court to revisit its decision in ROE V. WADE (1973), which struck down laws against abortion. Tension mounted when the Supreme Court noted probable jurisdiction in WEBSTER V. REPRODUCTIVE HEALTH SERVICES (1989). Relying on *Roe*, the lower court in *Webster* had held unconstitutional several provisions of a Missouri statute regulating abortions, including a statement from its preamble that human life begins at conception, a requirement that the aborting physician perform a viability test when he or she has reason to believe the woman is at least twenty weeks' pregnant, and a prohibition on the use of public employees or public facilities to perform an abortion that is not necessary to save the mother's life. In its

appeal, Missouri, joined by the Department of Justice as AMICUS CURIAE, argued not only that the invalidated provisions should be upheld under *Roe* and the Court's subsequent abortion cases but, more significantly, that *Roe* itself should be overruled.

Without passing on the constitutional validity of all the statutory provisions that had been challenged, the Court, in a 5–4 decision, reversed the lower court and gave the prolife movement its first major legal victory since *Roe* was decided. Whether *Webster* will prove a truly significant victory for this movement, however, remains to be seen. First and most encouraging for prochoice advocates, the Court once again found no occasion to revisit *Roe's* controversial conclusion that the right to an abortion is protected by the Constitution's DUE PROCESS clauses. Second, although the Court's judgment of reversal garnered majority support, portions of Chief Justice Rehnquist's opinion did not obtain five votes. Particularly noteworthy was Justice SANDRA DAY O'CONNOR's refusal to join important sections of the opinion. Third, the extraordinary media publicity surrounding *Webster* may have contributed to exaggerated perceptions by both sides of what the Court actually held.

In upholding Missouri's restriction on the use of public employees or facilities to perform abortions, the *Webster* majority relied on the Court's previous abortion-funding cases. The Court emphasized, as it had done before, that as long as the states do not actually restrict the abortion decision, the Constitution allows them to make the value judgment that childbirth is preferable to abortion. In denying the use of public employees and facilities for abortions, Missouri did not place any obstacles in the path of women who choose to have an abortion; that is, Missouri's restriction left pregnant women with the same choices they would have had if the state had not chosen to operate public hospitals at all. In short, although the Constitution, as interpreted by *Roe*, may not allow the states to prohibit abortions, it does not give either doctors or women a right of access to public facilities for the performance of abortions.

Many prochoice commentators have criticized this aspect of the Court's holding in *Webster* because of its alleged effect on the availability of abortions for certain women. The Court's task, however, was to decide not whether Missouri made a wise or good policy choice but whether anything in the Constitution invalidated the choice that Missouri made through its democratic process. Viewed in this light, *Webster* and the previous abortion-funding cases are consistent with prevailing constitutional doctrine. Few would argue, for example, that because the state may not prohibit parents from sending their children to private schools, the state must fund private education for those parents who cannot afford it.

The statute's viability-testing requirement gave the Court more difficulty. The section of Chief Justice Rehnquist's opinion regarding this requirement, which was joined by only two other Justices, said that the constitutionality of the viability-testing requirement was called into doubt by the rigid trimester system established in *Roe* and followed in the Court's other abortion cases. The Chief Justice reached this conclusion because mandatory testing when the physician reasonably believes the pregnancy is at least in the twentieth week may impose burdens on second-trimester abortions involving fetuses who have not yet become viable. Taking the position that STARE DECISIS has less force in constitutional law than elsewhere, the plurality then abandoned *Roe's* trimester framework as unsound in principle and unworkable in practice.

The plurality emphasized that the concepts of trimesters and viability are not found in the Constitution's text or in any other place one might expect to find a constitutional principle, thus describing the Court's previous holdings as resembling an intricate code of regulations more than a body of constitutional doctrine. The plurality also questioned why the state's interest in protecting potential human life should come into existence only at the point of viability. Finally, eschewing STRICT SCRUTINY, the plurality upheld Missouri's testing requirement by concluding that it permissibly furthers the state's legitimate interest in protecting potential life. Without otherwise purporting to disturb *Roe*, the plurality thus modified and narrowed it.

Justice HARRY A. BLACKMUN, the author of *Roe*, wrote a stinging dissent contending that *Roe* could not survive the plurality's analysis. Justice Scalia wrote a concurring opinion agreeing with Justice Blackmun that the plurality's analysis effectively would overrule *Roe*, something he was prepared to do explicitly. Nevertheless, a majority of the Court did not accept Justice Scalia's invitation. Even assuming that the three Justices in the plurality share the view that their anlaysis is devastating to *Roe*—and it is not clear that they do—it requires five votes, not four, to overrule *Roe*. On the fundamental issue of whether *Roe* should be totally overruled, the still unresolved question is where Justice O'Connor stands.

Although she had strongly attacked the trimester system in her dissent in *Akron v. Akron Center for Reproductive Health Services* and had defended the position that the state's interest in protecting potential life exists throughout all the stages of pregnancy, Justice O'Connor did not join the plurality's rejection of the trimester system in *Webster*. Instead, she criticized the plurality for unnecessarily reaching out to modify *Roe*, and insisted that the viability-testing requirement was constitutional even when considered under the Court's previous cases. In her

view, the testing requirement did not unduly burden the woman's abortion decision, and only on this ground did she vote to sustain the testing requirement. Prochoice advocates thus may have reason to hope that Justice O'Connor has had a change of heart since *Akron*. In contrast, prolife advocates may take heart that Justice O'Connor indicated that she both continues to view the trimester framework as problematic and would find it appropriate to reexamine *Roe* in a case involving a statute whose constitutionality actually turned on its validity.

Because the plurality's reasoning in *Webster* tracks rather closely Justice O'Connor's dissent in *Akron*, it is fair to question, as Justices Blackmun and Scalia did, whether that reasoning, if explicitly endorsed in the future by a Court majority, would effectively overrule *Roe*. From the standpoint of logic, the position that *Webster* completely undermines *Roe* has considerable force. If the state's interest in protecting potential life exists equally at all stages of pregnancy, it would seem that the state should be able to prohibit abortions not simply in the third trimester, as *Roe* held, but throughout pregnancy. As Justice O'Connor stated in *Akron*, "potential life is no less potential in the first weeks of pregnancy than it is at viability or afterward." In Justice Blackmun's dissenting words, "if the Constitution permits a State to enact any statute that reasonably furthers its interest in potential life, and if that interest arises as of conception," then it is difficult to see why any statute that prohibits abortion is unconstitutional. The Court can escape the force of this reasoning only by repudiating the reasoning in the plurality's opinion in *Webster*.

It is curious that the future of *Roe* might turn on how a Court majority ultimately views the validity of the trimester framework. The fundamental jurisprudential issue in both *Roe* and *Webster*, as Justice Blackmun correctly recognized, is whether the Constitution protects an "unenumerated" general RIGHT OF PRIVACY or, at least, whether such an UNENUMERATED RIGHT properly includes the right to terminate a pregnancy. The Court rejected *Roe's* trimester framework in part because the concepts of trimesters and viability cannot be found in the Constitution's text, but this can equally be said of the right of privacy in general and of the right to terminate a pregnancy in particular. If the Constitution's text must be the source of constitutional rights, more than the trimester system is illegitimate about *Roe*. However, if the Court continues to adhere to the view that the Constitution can protect unenumerated rights and if one of these protected unenumerated rights is the right to terminate a pregnancy, Justice Blackmun would seem correct in finding it irrelevant that the Constitution does not refer to trimesters or viability. How could it, when it does not refer to abortion at all?

The debate about unenumerated rights is important because of its implications for the Court's proper role in constitutional interpretation. Viewed in these terms, the debate about *Roe* is a debate not about abortion as such but about the Court's role and the role of JUDICIAL REVIEW under the form of government established by the Constitution. Those who oppose the Court's use of unenumerated rights to invalidate statutes essentially argue that such action constitutes an abuse of authority, one that allows the Court to substitute its own value judgments for those of the politically accountable branches of government. Justice Scalia, who alone in *Webster* was prepared to overrule *Roe*, thus insisted that the Court in *Roe* had entered an area that, because of the Constitution's silence, demands political answers. He observed that both sides had engaged in street demonstrations and letter-writing campaigns to influence the Court's decision—the kind of activity, in his view, that should be directed at elected legislators rather than at judges who hold life tenure and who are sworn to uphold the Constitution even against majority will. From this perspective, *Roe* is no more defensible than the now infamous decision in LOCHNER V. NEW YORK (1905), which invalidated economic reform legislation on the basis of rights that could not be found in the Constitution's text.

Roe has been attacked even by some who defend the existence of unenumerated rights that the judiciary may enforce. One argument contends that *Roe* improperly rejected a natural law position with regard to human existence by permitting the state, through the device of law, to define human life in a way that excludes fetuses. Under this view, laws banning abortions are not simply constitutionally permissible but constitutionally required. Whatever the present Court does regarding the abortion issue, it does not seem prepared to embrace such an argument.

Shortly after deciding *Webster*, the Court agreed to decide cases raising issues concerning abortion statutes in other states. In these cases, the Court upheld parental notification without making further modifications of *Roe*. Whether or not the Court uses future cases to reexamine *Roe*, it is clear that a majority of the Court is now inclined to permit the states greater leeway in regulating abortions. How much additional regulation the states will enact, if so permitted, is not easy to predict. After *Webster*, abortion became a key issue in several political races, and the pro-choice side of the debate came away with some resounding political victories. Perhaps these elections have something to say to those who would substitute JUDICIAL ACTIVISM for the political process. At the least, the up-or-down choice presented by *Roe*'s constitutionalization of abortion seems to have precluded the various states from achieving through democratic means the political com-promises that many other societies have reached on the abortion question.

JOSEPH D. GRANO
(1992)

(SEE ALSO: *Abortion and the Constitution; Anti-Abortion Movement; Reproductive Autonomy.*)

Bibliography

BOPP, JAMES, JR. 1989 Will There Be a Constitutional Right to Abortion After Reconsideration of *Roe v. Wade? Journal of Contemporary Law* 15:131–173.

BORK, ROBERT J. 1989 *The Tempting of America*, pages 110–116. New York: Free Press.

FARBER, DANIEL 1989 Abortion After Webster. *Constitutional Commentary* 6:225–230.

GLENDON, MARY ANN 1987 *Abortion and Divorce in Western Law.* Cambridge, Mass.: Harvard University Press.

GRANO, JOSEPH 1981 Judicial Review and a Written Constitution in a Democratic Society. *Wayne Law Review* 28:1–75.

HIRSHMAN, LINDA 1988 Bronte, Bloom and Bork: An Essay on the Moral Education of Judges. *University of Pennsylvania Law Review* 137:177–231.

LOEWY, ARNOLD 1989 Why *Roe v. Wade* Should Be Overruled. *North Carolina Law Review* 67:939–948.

NOONAN, JOHN 1984 The Root and Branch of *Roe v. Wade, Nebraska Law Review* 63:668–679.

ABORTION AND THE CONSTITUTION
(Update 2a)

Politically and jurisprudentially, PLANNED PARENTHOOD V. CASEY (1992) is a complex case whose strengths are inextricably intertwined with its weaknesses. Those strengths include a political PRAGMATISM that helped to mute abortion conflict, combined with a PRECEDENT constrained and sensitively nuanced DUE PROCESS methodology rooted in COMMON LAW tradition and the legacy of the second Justice JOHN MARSHALL HARLAN. Weaknesses include the failure to articulate a clear, principled STANDARD OF REVIEW and a logically satisfying theory of abortion rights.

The decades prior to *Casey* had been marked by bitter abortion controversy. The promise of autonomy and gender equality implicit in abortion rights confronted a tradition-based insistence that the value of human life is not a subject appropriately open, relativistically, to unfettered personal choice. In 1973, ROE V. WADE had announced a fundamental RIGHT OF PRIVACY to choose abortion throughout the first two trimesters (protected by a STRICT SCRUTINY standard of review for restrictions during the first trimester, and allowing only restrictions rationally related to maternal health during the second). But *Roe* had exacerbated conflict, not molded consensus, and by 1992 many expected *Roe* to be OVERRULED. Only three Justices of the *Roe* Court remained on the bench, and two were *Roe* dissenters. Five sitting Justices were appointed by either President RONALD REAGAN or President GEORGE H. W. BUSH, both of whom ran on high-profile pro-life platforms. Meanwhile, in WEBSTER V. REPRODUCTIVE HEALTH SERVICES (1989), the Supreme Court had upheld not only a highly restrictive public facilities ban but also a viability test requirement effective at twenty weeks, thereby undercutting the trimester framework of *Roe*. Justices HARRY A. BLACKMUN and ANTONIN SCALIA (respectively, the author of *Roe* and the harshest critic of *Roe*) argued that *Webster* effectively overruled *Roe*, although a majority refused to take that step explicitly. Then the Court, in subsequent cases, upheld parental notification requirements and allowed a forty-eight–hour waiting period while still refusing to overrule *Roe*.

Justice SANDRA DAY O'CONNOR emerged as the pivotal figure in the Court's abortion law. O'Connor had consistently criticized the trimester framework of *Roe* and had argued that states could legitimately regulate abortion any time after conception so long as the resulting restrictions did not impose an "undue burden" on a woman's choice to abort before viability. O'Connor refused, however, to argue that *Roe* should be overruled, thereby inviting Scalia's scathing contempt.

In *Casey*, O'Connor's undue burden test became the definitive "middle ground" between those voting to uphold *Roe* in its purity (Blackmun and JOHN PAUL STEVENS) and those voting to overrule it (Scalia, WILLIAM H. REHNQUIST, BYRON R. WHITE, and CLARENCE THOMAS). Joined only by DAVID H. SOUTER and ANTHONY M. KENNEDY and denounced by both sides in the bitter abortion controversies, O'Connor's approach became controlling law and probably resonated with the moral ambivalence most Americans felt about abortion. At issue were five provisions of a Pennsylvania statute: informed consent, a twenty-four–hour waiting period with counseling, parental consent, spousal notification, and mandatory reports and records. Upholding all but the spousal notification provision, the joint opinion reaffirmed *Roe* by recognizing a constitutionally protected liberty interest in the choice to abort prior to viability, but also stated that this interest was balanced from the time of conception by the state's legitimate interest in the potential life of the unborn. As mediator between those two interests, the undue burden test meant the state could regulate abortions at any time after conception if the regulation did not have the "purpose or effect" of placing a "substantial obstacle in the path of a woman seeking an abortion prior to viability."

O'Connor's approach to *Roe* is characteristic of her methodology, paralleling, for example, her approach to ESTABLISHMENT CLAUSE jurisprudence in the contentious public display cases. It entails situating herself between two extreme approaches to controversial precedent— rigid application and complete overruling. She instead identifies a core purpose or meaning within the existing DOCTRINE which can be affirmed without categorical application of the prior rule. For *Roe*, that meant protecting a woman's ultimate choice, but not an unrestricted choice and not within the trimester framework.

This almost Llewellynesque common law approach to precedent—constrained but not mechanically bound— resonates with the SUBSTANTIVE DUE PROCESS jurisprudence of the second Justice Harlan, and Part II of the *Casey* joint opinion draws extensively on Harlan's DISSENTING OPINION in *Poe v. Ullman* (1961), probably the Court's most elegantly articulated defense of a tradition-guided conception of personal liberty. Harlan recognized a responsibility to give content to open-ended values like "liberty" yet at the same time stayed rooted in precedent and historical tradition—a tradition conceived not statically but as a "living process." The joint opinion in *Casey* effectively relocates reproductive rights within that substantive due process tradition, from which they had become disconnected given the absoluteness of the individual "privacy right" rationale of earlier decisions. Notably, while the substantive due process approach of *Casey* disappointed many by its failure to provide absolute protection, its nuanced contextualism opened space for a surprisingly sensitive judicial account of the actual effect of unwanted pregnancies, recognizing that the "liberty of the woman is at stake in a sense unique to the human condition and unique to the law."

While the joint opinion justified locating abortion within due process guarantees, the three Justices did not say *Roe* was correctly decided. The margin that keeps *Roe* intact is precedent, which provides not an "inexorable command" but important "prudential and pragmatic" constraints to guide courts. One constraint is reliance, and here the joint opinion almost lays out an equality argument, stating that after *Roe* women have shaped their thinking and choices with abortion as an option. "The ability of women to participate equally in the economic and social life of the nation has been facilitated by their ability to control their reproductive lives." The Court recognizes it cannot recapture 1973, as if *Roe* had never been part of the contentious reality of recent history. Instead, *Roe* had helped to form that reality, which included greater gender equality. Through the back door, so to speak, while discussing precedent, the joint opinion suggests gender quality as a foundation for abortion rights.

Refusing to find *Roe* in the same category as LOCHNER V. NEW YORK (1905) or PLESSY V. FERGUSON (1896), the three

Justices nevertheless proceed to reinterpret it, in the manner so typical of O'Connor, by separating out its core meaning from its more rigid (and, by implication, artificial) applications. *Roe* is now taken to mean only that the "ultimate" decision to abort is the woman's, so that states may regulate even when the "incidental effect is added difficulty or expense." A strength of this reinterpretation is its recognition that abortion is a serious moral question with a legitimately public dimension, a point *Roe* never conceded. Nevertheless, a woman's capacity to cope well with her own life is also at stake, and the actual context of a woman's life may in fact make a particular restriction "unduly burdensome" in a moral sense. *Casey* is an acknowledgement of that ethical complexity, as the contextual description of women facing domestic violence makes abundantly clear. Even for restrictions the Court upholds, further data are invited for reevaluation.

Nevertheless, facts cannot supply standards. The line between permissible and impermissible restriction presumably lies somewhere between "added difficulty or expense" and "undue burden" or "substantial obstacle." Which burdens are "undue"? Increased health risks? Economic hardships? How great must they be? Some courts, applying *Casey,* simply have resorted to surface analogies to the restrictions *Casey* upheld, justifying their treatment of similar restrictions in like manner. This mechanical approach to decisionmaking represents a failure to do the particularized factual analysis *Casey* requires; yet, the burden now on challengers to produce enough facts to satisfy this still-undefined standard is a heavy one.

Interpretation is further complicated by an uncertain standard of review for facial attacks, the norm in abortion cases. The joint opinion found the spousal notification provision unconstitutional because, to a "large fraction" of the cases to which it would be relevant, the restriction would impose a substantial obstacle. This was an unexplained departure from the more restrictive test for facial challenges that requires there be "no set of circumstances" under which the law could be applied constitutionally. Some courts, without clear Supreme Court guidance, have applied this restrictive test, making successful facial challenge almost impossible. Yet the more appropriate "large fraction" standard requires, like the undue burden test itself, an extensive factual record and a more nuanced consideration of the law's effect.

Scalia's dissent pointed to this lack of clarity in the novel undue burden test. He also pointed, sarcastically, to the vacuous phrases used to justify finding a liberty interest, such as the linking of abortion choice to one's "concept of existence, of meaning, of the universe, and of the mystery of human life." Empty phrases are cold comfort to those who think abortion is equivalent to murder—equally a statement about one's concept of existence and the mystery of human life—although arguably our traditional respect for freedom of conscience is not constitutionally irrelevant.

The joint opinion never meets Scalia's challenge. If the Court cannot resolve the value choices at the heart of the abortion controversy, why should it seize control from the democratic process? Conversely, too, if abortion is a legitimate choice, why should it be obstructed in ways that burden most heavily the young and the poor? At the core of *Casey* lies a still troubling lack of resolution. Nevertheless, faced with a moral, political, and constitutional question of extraordinary difficulty, the joint opinion at least represents a workable compromise and an invitation for further dialogue.

Since *Casey,* abortion controversy at the Supreme Court level has focussed on clinic violence and access problems caused by protestors in the ANTI-ABORTION MOVEMENT. For example, the Court has allowed application of federal racketeering law to an alleged conspiracy of anti-abortion activists and upheld a fifteen-foot fixed buffer zone around accesses to clinics while striking down a fifteen-foot floating buffer zone around persons and vehicles as too burdensome on FREEDOM OF SPEECH.

Meanwhile, many pro-life activists have focused energy on opposing so-called partial-birth abortions. In 1997 the U.S. SENATE passed a ban on partial-birth abortions only three votes short of a veto-proof majority. While President WILLIAM J. CLINTON vetoed the ban, he supported a defeated compromise bill banning all postviability abortions except in cases where a woman faces risk of death or "grievous injury" to health. Such laws have wide popular support. By January 1999, twenty-eight states had banned partial-birth abortions, although eighteen bans have been enjoined, chiefly on VAGUENESS grounds because language used to define the procedure (e.g., "partial vaginal delivery" of a "living" human infant) could be construed to apply to some constitutionally protected procedures, and even to medical help with spontaneous abortions. Notably, however, cases describing medical details of various abortion procedures for purposes of vagueness analysis make for grisly reading, a stark reminder of the key insight of *Casey*—abortion is, in fact, a complex ethical issue, which does not lend itself to clear and definitive legal resolution.

ELIZABETH MENSCH
(2000)

Bibliography

COLKER, RUTH 1992 *Abortion Dialogue: Pro-Choice, Pro-Life, and American Law.* Bloomington: University of Indiana Press.

CONDIT, CELESTE MICHELLE 1989 *Decoding Abortion Rhetoric: Communicating Social Change.* Urbana: University of Illinois Press.

DWORKIN, RONALD 1993 *Life's Dominion: An Argument About Abortion, Euthanasia, and Individual Freedom.* New York: Knopf.

GLENDON, MARY ANN 1989 *Abortion and Divorce in Western Law.* Cambridge, Mass.: Harvard University Press.

GRABER, MARK 1996 *Rethinking Abortion: Equal Choice, the Constitution, and Reproductive Politics.* Princeton, N.J.: Princeton University Press.

LUKER, KRISTIN 1984 *Abortion and the Politics of Motherhood.* Berkeley: University of California Press.

MENSCH, ELIZABETH and FREEMAN, ALAN 1993 *The Politics of Virtue: Is Abortion Debatable.* Durham, N.C.: Duke University Press.

TRIBE, LAURENCE 1990 *Abortion: The Clash of Absolutes.* New York: W. W. Norton.

ABORTION AND THE CONSTITUTION
(Update 2b)

The usual rationales for abortion may be characterized as the "Blob Theory" and the "Limpet Theory." According to the Blob Theory, the unborn child is a blob of tissue, an excrescence on the body of a woman. Her decision to excise it is nobody's business but her own. According to the Limpet Theory, the unborn child is a human being, but one inexplicably parasitic on a woman, who should be able to shed the burden if she chooses. The state can appropriate people's resources for the sustenance of other people, but appropriating their bodies goes too far. The Limpet Theory, being less subject to empirical refutation, has gradually gained ground over the Blob Theory since the early 1990s.

The shift is hinted at in some of the language of Justices SANDRA DAY O'CONNOR, ANTHONY M. KENNEDY, and DAVID H. SOUTER in their joint opinion in PLANNED PARENTHOOD V. CASEY (1992). They occasionally speak of "the life of the unborn" instead of mere "potential life," and at one point they say that the state may inform a woman of the "consequences to the fetus" if she has an abortion. In the end, though, like Justice HARRY A. BLACKMUN in ROE V. WADE (1973), they fix "viability" (i.e., ability to survive outside the womb) as the point at which the state can allow the child's interest in remaining alive to outweigh the mother's interest in ending the pregnancy.

Although only three Justices adopted the joint opinion in its entirety, it has become the last word from the Supreme Court on abortion, because the other opinions cancel each other out. So the prevailing doctrine is that the state can require a woman to retain a child in her womb only if the life of the child does not depend on her doing so. Until viability the state can place no "undue burden" on a woman's exercise of her right to an abortion, whereas after viability any restraint is acceptable if it does not endanger the woman's life or health.

The devil, of course, is in the details. There is not space here to cover all the nuances of the subject—parental permission, waiting periods, informed consent, and so on—that *Casey* touched upon but mainly left loose to rattle around a judicial system where most judges think either that no burden on abortion is undue or that any burden is.

The most important decision since *Casey* is *Women's Medical Professional Corporation v. Voinovich* (1997), in which the U.S. Court of Appeals for the Sixth Circuit struck down Ohio's attempt to limit postviability abortions in general and "partial-birth" abortions in particular. The court found three major defects in the statute. (1) It defined the partial-birth procedure in such a way as to inhibit a number of previability abortions. (2) Its restrictions on postviability abortions failed to include an exception for mental, as distinct from bodily, health. (3) It inhibited medical decisions regarding viability and health risk by subjecting such decisions to a requirement of reasonableness, and therefore of peer review. Having made these determinations, the court used a tendentious expansion of the concept of facial invalidity and an equally tendentious contraction of the principle of severability to invalidate the whole statute. There was also a provision for using whenever possible a procedure that would spare the life of a viable child. By holding the provisions of the statute not to be severable, the court made this provision inoperative without ever passing on it.

It is this last provision, passed over in silence, that seems most in keeping with the logic of *Casey*, such as it is. If there is doubt as to whether an unborn child can survive outside the womb, the obvious thing to do is to bring her out alive and let her try. Only in very rare cases will doing so pose more danger to a woman's health than bringing the child out in pieces. This is especially the case when the danger is to mental health. Generally, that danger comes not from the trauma of delivery but from the responsibility of parenthood. It continues at least through the child's late adolescence, and it affects the father as well as the mother.

Judge Danny Boggs, dissenting in *Voinovich*, likened legislators trying to comply with *Casey* to the comic character Charlie Brown, trying in vain to kick a football held by his friend Lucy:

> Charlie Brown keeps trying, but Lucy never fails to pull the football away at the last moment. Here, our court's judgment is that Ohio's legislators, like poor Charlie Brown, have fallen flat on their backs. I doubt that the lawyers and litigants will ever stop this game. Perhaps the Supreme Court will do so.

Judging by *Casey*, this hope in the Supreme Court is painfully misplaced. Note first that the two "prolife" opinions (by Chief Justice WILLIAM H. REHNQUIST and Justice ANTONIN SCALIA—each joining in the other's opinion, with Justices BYRON R. WHITE and CLARENCE THOMAS joining in both) do not reflect the moral claim of the life at stake. The Chief Justice says that a woman's interest in having an abortion is a liberty interest supported by the FOURTEENTH AMENDMENT, but is not strong enough to outweigh the state's interest in protecting the unborn. Nothing is said of the interest of the unborn in being protected. Scalia says that if reasonable people can disagree on an issue the courts should butt out unless there is a text inviting them in. He is probably right that the ultimate solution to such a question as this must be political, but his opinion is disappointing in its lack of moral focus.

The one morally serious opinion is Blackmun's, and it is dead wrong. He rightly accuses the Chief Justice of construing "personal-liberty cases as establishing only a laundry list of particular rights rather than a principled account." But he totally ignores the humanity of the unborn and regards all limitations on abortion as reducing women to production agents for the state.

Justice JOHN PAUL STEVENS goes along with much of the joint opinion, but objects to allowing the state "to inject into a woman's most personal deliberations its own view of what is best." (Contrast JOHN STUART MILL, *On Liberty* (1859): "Considerations to aid his judgment . . . may be offered to him, even obtruded on him, by others, but he himself is the final judge.")

The joint opinion is mainly notable for its innovative treatment of STARE DECISIS. It creates a special category of cases, those in which the Court "calls the contending sides of a national controversy to end their national division by accepting a common mandate rooted in the Constitution." It says that only a substantial change in surrounding circumstances would warrant overruling such a case. It appeals to two examples from the twentieth century (by limiting itself to this particular century, it conveniently avoids the overruling of DRED SCOTT V. SANDFORD (1857) at Appomattox): (1) the overruling of PLESSY V. FERGUSON (1896) allowing race SEGREGATION by BROWN V. BOARD OF EDUCATION (1954), and (2) the overruling of ADKINS V. CHILDREN'S HOSPITAL (1923) forbidding wage regulation by WEST COAST HOTEL V. PARRISH (1937). In both cases, the joint opinion gets the history wrong. These cases were not overruled because of changed circumstances. They were overruled because they were morally bankrupt when they came down, and were finally recognized to be so. That segregation was a badge of inferiority for Blacks was known at the time of *Plessy* by the first Justice JOHN MARSHALL HARLAN in dissent, by every Black person in the United States, and by every segregationist in the South.

The idea that it was first discovered in connection with *Brown* was characterized as a "dangerous myth" by Edmond Cahn, writing in 1955. The myth proved here how dangerous it was. *Adkins* and *Parrish* both dealt with whether the support of the working poor was a task of their employers or a task of the state. The economic conditions of the time had no effect whatever on the question. The four Justices from the *Adkins* majority who were still on the Court dissented in *Parrish* for the same reasons they voted with the majority in *Adkins*. Chief Justice CHARLES EVANS HUGHES, for the majority in *Parrish*, uttered the same condemnation of "sweating" employers that Chief Justice WILLIAM HOWARD TAFT, dissenting, had uttered in *Adkins*. The moral status of these cases had not changed between decision and overruling; what had changed was the membership of the Court. Those who see *Roe* as another example of moral bankruptcy can only wait for a comparable change.

ROBERT E. RODES, JR.
(2000)

ABRAMS v. UNITED STATES
250 U.S. 616 (1919)

In SCHENCK V. UNITED STATES (1919) Justice OLIVER WENDELL HOLMES introduced the CLEAR AND PRESENT DANGER test in upholding the conviction under the ESPIONAGE ACT of a defendant who had mailed circulars opposing military CONSCRIPTION. Only nine months later, in very similar circumstances, the Supreme Court upheld an Espionage Act conviction and Holmes and LOUIS D. BRANDEIS offered the danger test in dissent. *Abrams* is famous for Holmes's dissent which became a classic libertarian pronouncement.

Abrams and three others distributed revolutionary circulars that included calls for a general strike, special appeals to workers in ammunitions factories, and language suggesting armed disturbances as the best means of protecting the Russian revolution against American intervention. These circulars had appeared while the United States was still engaged against the Germans in WORLD WAR I. Their immediate occasion was the dispatch of an American expeditionary force to Russia at the time of the Russian revolution. The majority reasoned that, whatever their particular occasion, the circulars' purpose was that of hampering the general war effort. Having concluded that "the language of these circulars was obviously intended to provoke and to encourage resistance to the United States in the war" and that they urged munitions workers to strike for the purpose of curtailing the production of war materials, the opinion upheld the convictions without actually addressing any constitutional question. The majority obviously believed that the Espionage Act might constitutionally be applied to speech intended to obstruct the war effort.

Justice Holmes mixed a number of elements in his dissent, and the mixture has bedeviled subsequent commentary. Although it is not clear whether Holmes was focusing on the specific language of the Espionage Act or arguing a more general constitutional standard, his central argument was that speech may not be punished unless it constitutes an attempt at some unlawful act; an essential element in such an attempt must be a specific intent on the part of the speaker to bring about the unlawful act. He did not read the circulars in evidence or the actions of their publishers as showing the specific intent to interfere with the war effort against Germany that would be required to constitute a violation of the Espionage Act.

His *Abrams* opinion shows the extent to which Holmes's invention of the danger rule was a derivation of his thinking about the role of specific intent and surrounding circumstances in the law of attempts. For in the midst of his discussion of specific intent he wrote, "I do not doubt . . . that by the same reasoning that would justify punishing persuasion to murder, the United States constitutionally may punish speech that produces or is intended to produce a clear and imminent danger that it will bring about forthwith certain substantive evils that the United States constitutionally may seek to prevent. . . . It is only the present danger of immediate evil or an intent to bring it about that warrants Congress in setting a limit to the expression of opinion. . . ."

Over time, however, what has survived from Holmes's opinion is not so much the specific intent argument as the more general impression that the "poor and puny anonymities" of the circulars could not possibly have constituted a clear and present danger to the war effort. At least in contexts such as that presented in *Abrams*, the clear and present danger test seems to be a good means of unmasking and constitutionally invalidating prosecutions because of the ideas we hate, when the precautions are undertaken not because the ideas constitute any real danger to our security but simply because we hate them. Although the specific intent aspect of the *Abrams* opinion has subsequently been invoked in a number of cases, particularly those involving membership in the Communist party, the *Abrams* dissent has typically been cited along with *Schenck* as the basic authority for the more general version of the clear and present danger standard that became the dominant FREEDOM OF SPEECH doctrine during the 1940s and has since led a checkered career.

Justice Holmes also argued in *Abrams* that the common law of SEDITIOUS LIBEL has not survived in the United States; the Supreme Court finally adopted that position in NEW YORK TIMES V. SULLIVAN (1964).

The concluding paragraph of the *Abrams* dissent has often been invoked by those who wish to make of Holmes a patron saint of the libertarian movement:

> Persecution for the expression of opinions seems to me perfectly logical . . . but when men have realized that time has upset many fighting faiths, they may come to believe even more the very foundations of their own conduct that the ultimate good desired is better reached by free trade in ideas—that the best test of truth is the power of the thought to get itself accepted in the competition of the market, and that truth is the only ground upon which their wishes safely can be carried out. That at any rate is the theory of our Constitution. It is an experiment, as all life is an experiment. Every year if not every day we have to wager our salvation upon some prophecy based upon imperfect knowledge. While that experiment is part of our system I think that we should be eternally vigilant against attempts to check the expression of opinions that we loathe and believe to be fraught with death, unless they so imminently threaten immediate interference with the lawful and pressing purposes of the law that an immediate check is required to save the country. . . . Only the emergency that makes it immediately dangerous to leave the correction of evil counsels to time warrants making any exception to the sweeping command, "Congress shall make no law . . . abridging the freedom of speech."

Sensitized by the destructive powers of such "fighting faiths" as Fascism and communism, subsequent commentators have criticized the muscular, relativistic pragmatism of this pronouncement as at best an inadequate philosophic basis for the libertarian position and at worst an invitation to totalitarianism. The ultimate problem is, of course, what is to be done if a political faith that proposes the termination of freedom of speech momentarily wins the competition in the marketplace of ideas and then shuts down the market. Alternatively it has been argued that Holmes's clear and present danger approach in *Abrams* was basically conditioned by his perception of the ineffectualness of leftist revolutionary rhetoric in the American context of his day. In this view, he was saying no more than that deviant ideas must be tolerated until there is a substantial risk that a large number of Americans will listen to them. The clear and present danger test is often criticized for withdrawing protection of political speech at just the point when the speech threatens to become effective. Other commentators have argued that no matter how persuasive Holmes's comments may be in context, the clear and present danger approach ought not to be uncritically accepted as the single freedom of speech test, uniformly applied to speech situations quite different from those in *Abrams*. Perhaps the most telling criticism of the Holmes approach is that it vests enormous discretion in the judge, for ultimately it depends on the judge's prediction of what will happen rather than on findings of what has happened. Subsequent decisions such as that in FEINER V. NEW YORK

(1951) showed that judges less brave than Holmes or less contemptuously tolerant of dissident ideas, might be quicker to imagine danger.

MARTIN SHAPIRO
(1986)

Bibliography

CHAFEE, ZECHARIAH 1941 *Free Speech in the United States.* Cambridge, Mass.: Harvard University Press.

ABSOLUTISM
(Freedom of Speech and Press)

In the 1950s and 1960s, some Justices of the Supreme Court and some commentators on the Court's work debated an abstract issue of constitutional theory pressed on it by Justice HUGO L. BLACK: Is the FIRST AMENDMENT an "absolute," totally forbidding government restrictions on speech and the press that fall within the Amendment's scope, or is the FREEDOM OF SPEECH properly subject to BALANCING TESTS that weigh restrictions on speech against governmental interests asserted to justify them? With Black's retirement in 1971, the whole airy question simply collapsed.

The argument that the First Amendment "absolutely" guaranteed speech and press freedoms was first raised in the debate over the Sedition Act (1798) but did not become the focus of debate in Supreme Court opinions for another century and a half. The occasion was presented when the Court confronted a series of cases involving governmental restrictions on SUBVERSIVE ACTIVITIES. For ALEXANDER MEIKLEJOHN, First Amendment absolutism was built into the structure of a self-governing democracy. For Justice Black, it was grounded in the constitutional text.

Black argued that "the Constitution guarantees absolute freedom of speech"—he used the modern locution, including the press when he said "speech"—and, characteristically, he drew support from the First Amendment's words: "Congress shall make no law . . . abridging the freedom of speech, or of the press." He viewed all OBSCENITY and libel laws as unconstitutional; he argued, often supported by Justice WILLIAM O. DOUGLAS, that government could not constitutionally punish discussions of public affairs, even if they incited to illegal action. But Black never claimed that the First Amendment protected all communications, irrespective of context. He distinguished between speech, which was absolutely protected, and conduct, which was subject to reasonable regulation. So it was that the First Amendment absolutist, toward the end of his life, often voted to send marchers and other demonstrators to jail for expressing themselves in places where he said they had no right to be.

First Amendment absolutism fails more fundamentally, on its own terms. A witness who lies under oath surely has no constitutional immunity from prosecution, and yet her perjury is pure speech. Most observers, conceding the force of similar examples, have concluded that even Justice Black, a sophisticated analyst, must have viewed his absolutism as a debating point, not a rigid rule for decision. In the Cold War atmosphere of the 1950s, a debating point was sorely needed; there was truth to Black's charge that the Court was "balancing away the First Amendment." As Judge LEARNED HAND had argued many years previously, in times of stress judges need "a qualitative formula, hard, conventional, difficult to evade," if they are to protect unpopular political expression against hostile majorities. A "definitional" technique has its libertarian advantages. Yet it is also possible to "define away" the First Amendment, as the Court has demonstrated in its dealings with obscenity, FIGHTING WORDS, and some forms of libel and COMMERCIAL SPEECH.

Even when the Court is defining a category of speech out of the First Amendment's scope, it states its reasons. Thus, just as "balancers" must define what it is that they are balancing, "definers" must weigh interests in order to define the boundaries of protected speech. Since Justice Black's departure from the Court, First Amendment inquiry has blended definitional and interest-balancing techniques, focusing—as virtually all constitutional inquiry must ultimately focus—on the justifications asserted for governmental restrictions. Justice Black's enduring legacy to this process is not the theory of First Amendment absolutes, but his lively concern for the values of an open society.

KENNETH L. KARST
(1986)

Bibliography

KALVEN, HARRY, JR. 1967 Upon Rereading Mr. Justice Black on the First Amendment. *UCLA Law Review* 14:422–453.

ABSTENTION DOCTRINE

All the abstention doctrines refer to circumstances in which federal courts, having JURISDICTION over a case under a congressional enactment, nonetheless may defer to state tribunals as decision makers. Federal courts may not abstain simply because they believe that particular cases, on their facts, would more appropriately be heard in state courts; they have a general obligation to exercise jurisdiction in cases Congress has placed before them. Abstention is justified only in exceptional circumstances, and then only when it falls within a particular abstention doctrine.

There are several abstention doctrines; they differ in

their consequences and in their requirements. *Colorado River Water Conservation District v. United States* (1976) suggests a general doctrine that federal courts have power to defer in favor of ongoing state proceedings raising the same or closely related issues. This type of deference to ongoing proceedings often is not identified as abstention at all, and courts have not spelled out its requirements other than general discretion.

When a federal court does defer under this doctrine, it stays federal proceedings pending completion of the state proceedings. If the state does not proceed expeditiously, or if issues remain for decision, the federal court can reenter the case. When it does not abstain and both state and federal forums exercise their CONCURRENT JURISDICTION over a dispute, the JUDGMENT that controls is the first to become final. Federal courts deferring in favor of ongoing state proceedings avoid this wasteful race to judgment, but the price paid is that the federal plaintiff may lose the federal forum she has chosen and to which federal law entitles her.

In reconciling the competing interests, federal courts are much more likely to defer to prior state proceedings, in which the state plaintiff has won the race to the courthouse, than they are when the federal suit was first filed.

Deference, even to previously commenced state proceedings involving the same parties as the federal suit, is by no means automatic; it is discretionary—justified by the court's INHERENT POWER to control its docket in the interests of efficiency and fairness—and the Supreme Court has said that it is to be invoked sparingly. In *Colorado River Water Conservation District v. United States* the Court stated that the inherent problems in duplicative proceedings are not sufficient to justify deference to the state courts because of "the virtually unflagging obligation of the federal courts to exercise the jurisdiction given them."

This doctrine permitting deference serves as a backdrop to other doctrines that the Supreme Court more consistently calls "abstention." The most important of these today is the doctrine of YOUNGER V. HARRIS (1971). The doctrine started as a principle against enjoining state criminal prosecutions, but it has grown enormously. It has been expanded to bar not only suits for federal injunction but also suits for federal declaratory judgment concerning the constitutionality of an enactment involved in a pending prosecution; and today some believe it goes so far as to bar a federal damage action against state officials that might decide issues that would interfere with a state prosecution. Moreover, the doctrine has grown to protect state civil proceedings as well as criminal ones. Most remarkably, as the Court held in *Hicks v. Miranda* (1975), the doctrine now allows abstention even if the federal action is first filed, so long as the state commences prosecution

"before any proceedings of substance on the merits" have occurred in federal court. That rule effectively deters federal suit; a federal plaintiff who wins the race to the courthouse may simply provoke his own criminal prosecution. These developments together have turned *Younger* into a doctrine that permits federal courts to dismiss federal constitutional challenges to state criminal prosecution (or quasi-criminal) enactments whenever a state criminal prosecution (or other enforcement proceeding) provides a forum for the federal constitutional issue. The state forum in theory must be an adequate one, but courts applying the doctrine often overlook this aspect of the inquiry.

Courts abstaining under the *Younger* doctrine generally dismiss the federal suit rather than retaining jurisdiction. Federal plaintiffs who are left to defend state proceedings generally cannot return to federal court for adjudication of the federal or any other issues, and the state court's decision on the constitutional issue and others may control future litigation through collateral estoppel. Litigants do, of course, retain the possibility of Supreme Court review of the federal issues they raise in state court, but the chances that the Supreme Court will hear such cases are slim.

The *Younger* doctrine therefore often deprives the federal plaintiff of any federal forum—prior, concurrent, or subsequent to the state proceeding against him—for his CIVIL RIGHTS action against state officials. This contradicts the apparent purpose of SECTION 1983, TITLE 42, UNITED STATES CODE and its jurisdictional counterpart (section 1343, Title 28) that such a forum be available. Some of those convicted in state criminal prosecutions may later raise federal issues in federal HABEAS CORPUS proceedings, but ACCESS to habeas corpus is itself increasingly limited. (See STONE V. POWELL; WAINRIGHT V. SYKES.)

The *Younger* doctrine does have exceptions. If the federal court finds state courts inadequate on the facts of the particular case (because of what the Court in *Younger* termed "bad faith, harassment, or any other unusual circumstance that would call for equitable relief"), it will exercise its jurisdiction. But this approach turns around the usual rule that it takes exceptional circumstances to decline jurisdiction, not to justify its exercise. To avoid this conflict with the usual rules allowing Congress, not the courts, to determine the appropriate cases for federal jurisdiction, *Younger* abstention should be cut back, at least by limiting it to cases in which state proceedings began before the federal one. Such an approach would assimilate *Younger* abstention to the general doctrine of deference to ongoing state proceedings, discussed above.

In the meantime the expanded version of the *Younger* doctrine has largely displaced what had been the key form of abstention, formulated in RAILROAD COMMISSION OF TEXAS V. PULLMAN COMPANY (1941). *Pullman* abstention applies to cases involving federal constitutional challenges to state law. It allows (but does not require) federal judges to refrain from deciding highly uncertain questions of state law when resolution of the questions may avoid or affect the federal constitutional issue.

Pullman today is the only abstention doctrine in which deference to state courts is limited to state law issues. When the federal court abstains under the *Pullman* doctrine, it holds the case while the parties seek declaratory relief on the state law issues in state court. Unless the parties voluntarily submit federal along with state issues to the state court, they have a right to return to federal court after the state adjudication is completed, for decision of the federal issues and for federal factfinding. In this respect *Pullman* abstention is a narrower intrusion on federal court jurisdiction than the *Younger* doctrine is, although the cost of shuttling back and forth from state to federal court dissuades many federal plaintiffs from retaining their federal forum. *Pullman* also differs from *Younger* because the federal plaintiff generally initiates the proceedings in state court, and they are declaratory judgment proceedings rather than criminal prosecutions or civil enforcement proceedings.

As *Younger* has expanded to include some civil enforcement proceedings and to allow abstention in favor of later-filed state proceedings, it has reduced the area for *Pullman* abstention. Both doctrines typically apply to constitutional litigation against state officials. In many cases where *Pullman* abstention could be at issue, *Younger* is operative because a state enforcement proceeding against the federal plaintiff is a possibility as long as the federal plaintiff has violated the law she challenges. If, however, the federal plaintiff has not violated the enactment she challenges, *Younger* abstention cannot apply, for the state is unable to bring a prosecution or civil enforcement proceeding against her and thereby displace the federal forum. *Pullman*, therefore, is the applicable doctrine for pre-violation suits and for challenges to state enactments that do not involve state enforcement proceedings. Many of those cases, however, will be dismissed before abstention is considered; where the plaintiff has not violated the enactment she complains of, she may have trouble showing that her controversy is justiciable. (See RIPENESS.)

While *Pullman* abstention has therefore become less and less important, a new area has recently been created for a *Pullman*-like abstention. PENNHURST STATE SCHOOL V. HALDERMAN (1984), restricting federal courts' pendent jurisdiction, requires federal litigants in suits against state governments to use state courts to pursue any related state causes of action they do not wish to forfeit. *Pennhurst* thus creates the equivalent of a mandatory *Pullman* abstention category—where state courts must be given certain state law questions to adjudicate even while a federal court exercises jurisdiction over the rest of the case. This new category is not, however, dependent upon uncertainty in state law.

Another abstention doctrine, administrative abstention, was first articulated in *Burford v. Sun Oil Company* (1943). The *Burford* doctrine allows a federal court with jurisdiction of a case to dismiss in favor of state court adjudication, ongoing or not. Like *Younger* abstention, *Burford* abstention displaces federal jurisdiction; if abstention is ordered, state courts adjudicate all issues, subject only to Supreme Court review. The Court has never clearly explained which cases are eligible for administrative abstention. The doctrine is typically employed when a state administrative process has dealt with a controversy in the first instance and the litigant then asks a federal district court to exercise either its federal question or diversity jurisdiction to review that administrative interpretation. The federal court's ability to abstain under this doctrine may be limited to situations in which state statutes concentrate JUDICIAL REVIEW of the administrative process in a particular state court so that it becomes "an integral part of the regulatory process," as the Court said in *Alabama Public Service Commission v. Southern Railway* (1951), or to situations involving complex factual issues. There is no requirement that legal issues, state or federal, be unclear for this abstention to be ordered, or that the case contain any federal issues.

Burford abstention does not apply when state administrative remedies have been skipped altogether and the litigant has sued first in federal court. The only issue then is whether state administrative remedies must be exhausted. There is no overlap between *Burford* and the *Younger* or *Pullman* abstention doctrines, because exhaustion of administrative remedies has not been required in suits under section 1983, which today includes all constitutional litigation. The Court recently affirmed this exception to the exhaustion requirement in *Patsy v. Board of Regents* (1982). If the Court were to modify the section 1983 exception to the exhaustion requirement, retreat from the *Burford* doctrine would seem to follow. Otherwise, *Burford* would mandate state judicial review after deference to state administrative proceedings, so federal jurisdiction would be altogether unavailable in section 1983 cases whenever an administrative agency was available.

A final minor category of abstention, which seems to have been limited to EMINENT DOMAIN cases involving unclear state issues, is reflected in *Louisiana Light & Power Company v. Thibodaux* (1959). In contexts other than eminent domain, abstention is not proper simply to clarify difficult state law issues. (In states that provide for certification, however, a federal court without more can certify difficult state issues to the state supreme court.)

All these theories of abstention are judge-made rules, without any statutory authority; they avoid jurisdiction in cases where Congress has given it. By contrast, Congress itself has provided for deference to state processes in narrow categories of cases, most notably cases involving IN-JUNCTIONS against state rate orders and tax collections. And in the Anti-Injunction Act, Congress has generally prohibited federal injunctions against state proceedings. This prohibition is limited by explicit statutory exceptions, however, and by some judge-made exceptions, and since the area outside the prohibition also is limited, by the judge-made abstention doctrines, the statute apparently has little effect.

MARTHA A. FIELD
(1986)

Bibliography

FIELD, MARTHA A. 1974 Abstention in Constitutional Cases: The Scope of the Pullman Abstention Doctrine. *University of Pennsylvania Law Review* 122:1071–1087.
——— 1981 The Uncertain Nature of Federal Jurisdiction. *William & Mary Law Review* 22:683–724.
FISS, OWEN 1977 Dombrowksi. *Yale Law Journal* 86:1103–1164.
LAYCOCK, DOUGLAS 1977 Federal Interference with State Prosecutions: The Need for Prospective Relief. *Supreme Court Review* 1977:193–238.

ABSTENTION DOCTRINE
(Update)

In recent years, the Supreme Court has clarified three aspects of the abstention doctrines. First, *Quackenbush v. Allstate Insurance Co.* (1996) made it clear that abstention is not appropriate in suits for monetary damages, but rather only as to claims for injunctive or declaratory relief. The petitioner, Charles Quackenbush, the California Insurance Commissioner, sued Allstate Insurance Company in state court seeking money damages for breach of contract and torts. Allstate removed the matter to federal court based on DIVERSITY JURISDICTION.

The federal district court remanded the case to state court on the basis of *Burford v. Sun Oil Co.* (1942), which provides for federal court abstention when unified state proceedings are needed. The Supreme Court unanimously reversed. The Court concluded that "the power to dismiss under the *Burford* doctrine, as with other abstention doctrines, derives from the discretion historically enjoyed by courts of equity." Thus, abstention was inappropriate in the suit for money damages. Although the case dealt with only one type of abstention, it contained a broad statement that abstention is not appropriate in suits brought solely for money damages.

Second, in *Arizonans for Official English v. Arizona* (1997), the Court stressed the importance of federal courts' using state CERTIFICATION procedures when they are available. Many states have laws that allow a federal court to certify questions and send them to the state court for resolution. In a case involving a challenge to Arizona's English-only law, the Court said that certification should be used when there are "novel, unsettled questions" of state law. The Court said that "[t]aking advantage of certification made available by a State may greatly simplify an ultimate adjudication in federal court."

The Court indicated that federal courts should be more willing to abstain when certification procedures exist. The Court emphasized that certification does not involve the delays, expense, and procedural complexity that generally attend the abstention decision.

Finally, in *Wilton v. Seven Falls Co.* (1995) the Court ruled that in suits for DECLARATORY JUDGMENTS federal courts have discretion whether to defer to duplicative state proceedings. Wilton, an insurance underwriter, filed a suit for a declaratory judgment in federal court, seeking a ruling that it was not liable to Seven Falls Co. under insurance policies. Seven Falls then filed a suit in state court against Wilton and asked the federal court to dismiss or stay the state court proceedings. The district court granted the stay to avoid duplicative litigation and both the court of appeals and the U.S. Supreme Court affirmed.

Although the exceptional circumstances warranting abstention were not present, the Supreme Court unanimously concluded that the federal court had discretion to abstain under the federal Declaratory Judgment Act. The Court emphasized that the act is written in discretionary terms and that it has been understood to confer on federal courts unique and substantial discretion in deciding whether to declare the rights of litigants. The Court, however, offered little guidance as to the criteria that a federal court should apply in deciding whether to defer to state proceedings when there is a request for a federal declaratory judgment.

None of these decisions creates new abstention doctrines or dramatically changes existing ones. But each clarifies an important aspect of abstention doctrines.

ERWIN CHEMERINSKY
(2000)

Bibliography

REHNQUIST, JAMES C. 1994 Taking Comity Seriously: How to Neutralize the Abstention Doctrine. *Stanford Law Review* 46:1049–1114.
YOUNG, GORDON G. 1993 Federal Courts Abstention and State

Administrative Law from *Burford* to *Ankenbrandt*. *DePaul Law Review* 42:859–982.

ACADEMIC FREEDOM

Although academic freedom has become a FIRST AMENDMENT principle of special importance, its content and theoretical underpinnings have barely been defined. Most alleged violations of academic freedom can be sorted into three catagories: claims of individual professors against the state, claims of individual professors against the university administration or governing board, and claims of universities against the state. Judicial decisions have upheld claims in all three contexts.

The Supreme Court, however, has not developed a comprehensive theory of academic freedom comparable to its recent elaboration of freedom of association as a distinctive First Amendment DOCTRINE. The relationship between "individual" and "institutional" academic freedom has not been clarified. Nor has the Supreme Court decided whether academic freedom is a separate principle, with its own constitutional contours justified by the unique roles of professors and universities in society, or whether it highlights but is essentially coextensive with the general First Amendment rights of all citizens. Similarly unsettled is the applicability, if any, of academic freedom in primary and secondary schools. While acknowledging that teachers, unlike university professors, are expected to inculcate societal values in their students, the Supreme Court in BOARD OF EDUCATION V. PICO (1982) expressed concern about laws that "cast a pall of orthodoxy" over school as well as university classrooms. Student claims of academic freedom also remain unresolved.

This uncertainty about the constitutional definition of academic freedom contrasts with the internal understanding of the university community, which had elaborated its meaning before any court addressed its legal or constitutional significance. The modern American conception of academic freedom arose during the late nineteenth and early twentieth centuries, when the emerging research university eclipsed the religious college as the model institution of higher education. This structural change reflected an equally profound transformation of educational goals from conserving to searching for truth.

Academic freedom became associated with the search for truth and began to define the very idea of the university. Its content developed under the influence of Darwinism and the German university. The followers of Charles Darwin maintained that all beliefs are subject to the tests of inquiry and that apparent errors must be tolerated, and even expected, in the continuous search for truth. The German academic influence reinforced the growing secular tendencies in the United States. Many attributed the international preeminence of German universities to their traditions of academic freedom. As universities in the United States strove for similar excellence, they adapted these traditions.

This adaptation produced several major changes. The clear German differentiation between great freedom for faculty members within the university and little protection for any citizen outside it did not take hold in America. The ideal of FREEDOM OF SPEECH, including its constitutional expression in the First Amendment, and the philosophy of pragmatism, which encouraged the participation of all citizens in social and political life, prompted American professors to view academic freedom as an aspect of more general CIVIL LIBERTIES. The traditions of powerful administrators and lay boards of governors in American universities posed threats to academic freedom that did not exist in Germany, where universities were largely governed by their faculties. As a result, American professors sought freedom from university authorities as well as from external interference. And academic freedom, which in Germany encompassed freedom for both students and professors, became limited to professors in the United States.

The first major codification of the American conception of academic freedom was produced in 1915 by a committee of the nascent American Association of University Professors (AAUP). Subsequent revisions culminated in the 1940 *Statement of Principles on Academic Freedom and Tenure*, jointly sponsored by the AAUP and the Association of American Colleges, and currently endorsed by over 100 educational organizations. The 1940 *Statement* defines three aspects of academic freedom: freedom in research and publication, freedom in the classroom, and freedom from institutional censorship or discipline when a professor speaks or writes as a citizen. Many colleges and universities have incorporated the 1940 *Statement* into their governing documents. In cases involving the contractual relationship between professors and universities, courts have recently begun to cite it as the COMMON LAW of the academic profession. This contractual theory has provided substantial legal protection for academic freedom without the support of the First Amendment, whose applicability to private universities is limited by the doctrine of STATE ACTION.

The emergence of academic freedom as a constitutional principle did not begin until the McCarthy era of the 1950s, when public and university officials throughout the country challenged and investigated the loyalty of professors. Although earlier decisions had imposed some limitations on governmental intrusions into universities and schools, no Supreme Court opinion explicitly referred to academic freedom until Justice WILLIAM O. DOUGLAS, dissenting in ADLER V. BOARD OF EDUCATION (1952), claimed that it is contained within the First Amendment.

The Supreme Court endorsed this identification of academic freedom with the First Amendment in SWEEZY V. NEW HAMPSHIRE (1957), which reversed the contempt conviction of a Marxist scholar who had refused to answer questions from the state attorney general regarding his political opinions and the contents of his university lecture. A plurality of the Justices concluded that the state had invaded the lecturer's "liberties in the areas of academic freedom and political expression." Both the plurality and concurring opinions in *Sweezy* emphasized the importance to a free society of the search for knowledge within free universities and warned against governmental interference in university life. Justice FELIX FRANKFURTER's concurrence included a particularly influential reference to academic freedom that has often been cited in subsequent decisions. Quoting from a plea by South African scholars for open universities, Frankfurter identified "'the four essential freedoms of a university'—to determine for itself on academic grounds who may teach, what may be taught, how it shall be taught, and who may be admitted to study."

The opinions in *Sweezy* indicated that academic freedom and political expression are distinct yet related liberties, and that society benefits from the academic freedom of professors as individuals and of universities as institutions. Yet neither in *Sweezy* nor in subsequent decisions did the Supreme Court untangle and clarify these complex relationships. Throughout the 1950s, it alluded only intermittently to academic freedom in cases involving investigations of university professors, and reference to this term did not necessarily lead to protective results. Even the votes and reasoning of individual Justices fluctuated unpredictably. During this period, many within the academic community resisted the advocacy of academic freedom as a constitutional principle, fearing that a judicial definition might both weaken and preempt the one contained in the 1940 *Statement* and widely accepted throughout American universities.

Supreme Court opinions since the 1950s have emphasized that academic freedom is a "transcendent value" and "a special concern of the First Amendment," as the majority observed in KEYISHIAN V. BOARD OF REGENTS (1967). Justice LEWIS F. POWELL's opinion in REGENTS OF THE UNIVERSITY OF CALIFORNIA V. BAKKE (1978) reiterated the university's academic freedom to select its student body, but the Court has held in *Minnesota State Board for Community Colleges v. Knight* (1984) that academic freedom does not include the right of individual faculty members to participate in institutional governance. By eliminating the RIGHT-PRIVILEGE DISTINCTION, which had allowed dismissal of PUBLIC EMPLOYEES for speech otherwise protected by the First Amendment, the Supreme Court during the 1960s and 1970s dramatically expanded the rights of all public employees, including university professors, to speak in ways that criticize or offend their employers. Yet none of these decisions has refined the relationships between "individual" and "institutional" academic freedom or between "academic freedom" and "political expression," issues posed but not resolved in *Sweezy*. The Supreme Court's continuing reluctance even to recognize issues of academic freedom in cases decided on other grounds underlines the primitive constitutional definition of this term.

Cases since the early 1970s have raised novel issues of academic freedom. University administrators and governing boards have asserted the academic freedom of the university as an institution to resist JUDICIAL REVIEW of their internal policies and practices, which have been challenged by government agencies seeking to enforce CIVIL RIGHTS laws and other statutes of general applicability, by citizens claiming rights to freedom of expression on university property, and by professors maintaining that the university violated their own academic freedom or their statutory protection against employment discrimination. Faculty members have even begun to make contradictory claims of academic freedom against each other. Professors have relied on academic freedom to seek a constitutionally based privilege against compelled disclosure of their deliberations and votes on faculty committees to junior colleagues who want this information to determine whether they were denied reappointment or tenure for impermissible reasons, including reasons that might violate their academic freedom. These difficult issues may force the courts to address more directly the meaning and scope of academic freedom and to resolve many of the lingering ambiguities of previous decisions.

DAVID M. RABBAN
(1986)

(SEE ALSO: *Creationism; Tennessee v. Scopes.*)

Bibliography

HOFSTADTER, RICHARD and METZGER, WALTER 1955 *The Development of Academic Freedom in theUnited States.* New York: Columbia University Press.

LOVEJOY, ARTHUR 1937 Academic Freedom. In E. Seligman, ed., *Encyclopedia of the Social Sciences*, Vol. 1, pages 384–388. New York: Macmillan.

SYMPOSIUM 1963 Academic Freedom. *Law & Contemporary Problems* 28:429–671.

VAN ALSTYNE, WILLIAM 1972 The Specific Theory of Academic Freedom and the General Issue of Civil Liberty, In E. Pincoffs, ed., *The Concept of Academic Freedom*, pages 59–85. Austin: University of Texas Press.

ACCESS TO THE COURTS

Writing for the Supreme Court in BOUNDS V. SMITH (1977), Justice THURGOOD MARSHALL spoke confidently of "the fundamental constitutional right of access to the courts." In one sense, such a right has been a traditional and noncontroversial part of our constitutional law; barring unusual circumstances, anyone can bring a lawsuit, or be heard in his or her own defense. Justice Marshall, however, was referring to another kind of access. "Meaningful" access to the courts, *Bounds* held, gave state prisoners a right to legal assistance; the state must provide them either with law libraries or with law-trained persons to help them prepare petitions for HABEAS CORPUS or other legal papers. The modern constitutional law of access to the courts, in other words, is focused on the affirmative obligations of government to provide services to people who cannot afford to pay their costs. In this perspective, Justice Marshall's sweeping characterization goes far beyond the results of the decided cases.

The development began in the WARREN COURT era, with GRIFFIN V. ILLINOIS (1957) (state must provide free transcripts to convicted indigents when transcripts are required for effective APPEAL of their convictions) and DOUGLAS V. CALIFORNIA (1963) (state must provide appellate counsel for convicted indigents). GIDEON V. WAINWRIGHT (1963) interpreted the RIGHT TO COUNSEL to require state-appointed trial counsel in FELONY cases. The *Griffin* plurality had rested on both DUE PROCESS and EQUAL PROTECTION grounds, but by the time of *Douglas* equal protection had become the Court's preferred doctrine: the state, by refusing to pay for appellate counsel for some indigent defendants, had drawn "an unconstitutional line . . . between rich and poor." By the close of the Warren years, the Court seemed well on the way to a broad equal protection principle demanding strict judicial scrutiny of WEALTH DISCRIMINATIONS in the criminal justice system, including simple cases of inability to pay the costs of services needed for effective defense.

The Court remained sharply divided, however; the dissenters in *Griffin* and *Douglas* argued in forceful language that nothing in the Constitution required the states to take affirmative steps to relieve people from the effects of poverty. They saw no principled stopping-place for the majority's equality principle, and they objected to judicial intrusion into state budgetary processes. Even so, the same Justices found no difficulty in joining the 8–1 decision in BODDIE V. CONNECTICUT (1971), holding that a state could not constitutionally bar an indigent plaintiff from its divorce court for failure to pay a $60 filing fee. The *Boddie* majority, however, rested on a due process ground. The marriage relationship was "basic," and the state had monopolized the means for its dissolution; thus fundamental procedural fairness demanded access to the divorce court irrespective of ability to pay the fee.

From *Boddie* forward, the Court has dealt with constitutional claims of access to justice by emphasizing due process considerations of minimal fairness, and deemphasizing the equal protection notion that animated the Warren Court's decisions. At the same time, the Court has virtually ended the expansion of access rights. Thus ROSS V. MOFFIT (1974) pounced on language in *Douglas* about the "first appeal as of right," and refused to require state-appointed counsel to pursue discretionary appeals or Supreme Court review. And in *United States v. Kras* (1971) and *Ortwein v. Schwab* (1971) the Court, emphasizing the "monopoly" aspects of *Boddie*, upheld the application of filing fees to deny indigents access to a bankruptcy court and to judicial review of the denial of WELFARE BENEFITS. A similarly artificial line was drawn in the BURGER COURT's decisions on the right to counsel. The *Gideon* principle was extended, in ARGERSINGER V. HAMLIN (1972), to all prosecutions resulting in imprisonment. Yet in LASSITER V. DEPARTMENT OF SOCIAL SERVICES (1981) a 5–4 Court refused to hold that due process required a state to provide counsel for an indigent mother in a proceeding to terminate her parental rights, absent a showing of complexity or other special circumstances. Behind all these flimsy distinctions surely lay the same considerations urged from the beginning by the *Griffin* and *Douglas* dissenters: keep the "floodgates" closed; keep judges' hands off the allocation of public funds.

An access principle of minimal fairness is better than nothing. Yet in a great many contexts the essence of the access claim is an interest in equality itself. To have one's effective say is to be treated as a respected, participating member of the society. An effective hearing in court is more than a chance to influence a judge's decision; it is a vivid symbol of equal citizenship.

KENNETH L. KARST
(1986)

Bibliography

GOODPASTER, GARY 1970 The Integration of Equal Protection, Due Process Standards, and the Indigent's Right of Free Access to the Courts. *Iowa Law Review* 56:223–266.

MICHELMAN, FRANK I. 1973, 1974 The Supreme Court and Litigation Access Fees. Part 1, *Duke Law Journal* 1973:1153–1215; Part 2, *Duke Law Journal* 1974:527–570.

ACCOMMODATION OF RELIGION

In the seminal case of EVERSON V. BOARD OF EDUCATION (1947), the Supreme Court asserted that the FIRST AMENDMENT contains a principle of SEPARATION OF CHURCH AND STATE that in turn entails a prohibition on GOVERNMENTAL AID TO RELIGIOUS INSTITUTIONS. But the Justices have also cautioned that an excessive emphasis on separation might amount to public hostility, or "callous indifference," toward religion. This concern soon led the Court to qualify the "separation" theme by explaining that the First Amendment contemplates governmental "accommodation" of religion. In ZORACH V. CLAUSON (1952), for example, Justice WILLIAM O. DOUGLAS wrote for the Court that government "follows the best of our tradition" when it "respects the religious nature of our people and accommodates the public service to their spiritual needs." The early cases thus established the two poles that have shaped modern debate about RELIGIOUS LIBERTY, and around which opposing legions of "separationists" and "accommodationists" have aligned themselves.

A central difficulty has been to explain how mere accommodation differs from the "advancement" or "endorsement" of religion that the Court has declared impermissible. Thus far, neither judges nor legal scholars have managed a satisfactory account of this distinction. The Court has said that a law is a permissible accommodation if it merely lifts a government-created burden on religion without affirmatively assisting religion. But in an era of pervasive governmental regulation and subsidization, both direct and indirect, this line is difficult to discern. So, for example, the Court struck down a state provision exempting religious publications from sales tax—surely a government-imposed burden—on the ground that the exemption impermissibly advanced religion.

As an alternative, Justice SANDRA DAY O'CONNOR has suggested that the appropriate distinction is between those accommodations that "endorse" religion and those that do not. But of course some citizens will likely perceive almost any official accommodation of religion as an endorsement. Consequently, the application of O'Connor's test turns on highly artificial discussions of whether a hypothetical "reasonable" and properly, but not excessively, informed observer would perceive an endorsement.

Recently, some scholars have suggested that distinctions should be drawn in accordance with a policy of "substantive neutrality"—a position based on the premise that the constitutional objective is to prevent government from influencing people, pro or con, in matters of religion. In some contexts, this position would mean that religion should be treated in the same way that nonreligion is. So if government pays for students to attend secular public schools, for example, the same subsidy should be given to individuals who desire to attend religious schools. But where a government policy (a military conscription law, for example) would impose a special burden on some citizens' exercise of religion, substantive neutrality would require government to accommodate religious objectors by granting them a free-exercise exemption from the law unless there is a COMPELLING STATE INTEREST in requiring them to comply.

During the 1990s, the Court has moved in the direction of this substantive neutrality position in some respects. For example, the Court has held that a deaf student in a religious school is entitled to a state-supplied sign language interpreter that would be supplied under federal law for a deaf student in a public school. And the Court ruled that a Christian student newspaper at a state university could not be excluded from funding that nonreligious publications received. In other respects, however, the Court has moved away from the substantive neutrality position. Thus, in EMPLOYMENT DIVISION, DEPARTMENT OF HUMAN RESOURCES OF OREGON V. SMITH (1990), the Court repudiated the view that in some contexts religious objectors are constitutionally entitled to free-exercise exemptions from generally applicable laws.

Moreover, critics of the position argue that the label "substantive neutrality" is misleading. In a religiously diverse society, almost any controversial governmental action will correspond to some religious viewpoints and will conflict with other religious viewpoints. Hence, particular policies and outcomes can be made to seem neutral only by marginalizing or misrepresenting incompatible religious views.

The underlying problem, it seems, is that modern religion-clause jurisprudence has not developed any clear idea about why the baseline position that accommodation serves to qualify—the position, that is, of separation or no aid—is constitutionally required in the first place. Like the *Everson* Court, modern separationists typically take it for granted, on highly dubious historical grounds, that the First Amendment imposes a no aid principle. Consequently, they make little effort to articulate the rationale for that principle. Without a clear understanding of why government aid to religion is normally impermissible, however, it is difficult to consider why and when limited forms of government help should be treated as an exception to the general rule.

STEVEN D. SMITH
(2000)

ACT OF STATE DOCTRINE

Recognized by English courts as early as 1674, the act of state DOCTRINE prohibits United States courts from examining the validity of foreign acts of state. Chief Justice JOHN MARSHALL mentioned a doctrine of noninvolvement in 1808, but the Supreme Court did not accord it formal recognition until *Underhill v. Hernandez* (1897). Initially, the doctrine strongly resembled the doctrine of SOVEREIGN IMMUNITY which protects the person or acts of a sovereign. In fact, the act of state doctrine may have been invented to deal with technical deficiencies in sovereign immunity.

The act of state doctrine received renewed attention in *Banco Nacional de Cuba v. Sabbatino* (1964) where an 8–1 Supreme Court held that it applied even when the foreign state's sovereign act violated international law. Justice JOHN MARSHALL HARLAN's majority opinion rejected earlier assertions that the "inherent nature of sovereign authority" underlay the doctrine; instead it arose out of the SEPARATION OF POWERS. Justice BYRON R. WHITE, dissenting, read Harlan's opinion to declare "exclusive absolute [executive] control" of foreign relations. Acknowledging executive control, White claimed that "this is far from saying . . . that the validity of a foreign act of state is necessarily a POLITICAL QUESTION." The Court had, in fact, dismissed a specific executive branch request, contending that it need not be bound by executive determinations; the Court repeated this position in *Zschernig v. Miller* (1968) and unequivocally denied such executive control in *First National City Bank v. Banco Nacional de Cuba* (1972) (where two majority Justices joined four dissenters to so argue).

In an effort to harmonize the act of state doctrine with that of sovereign immunity, Justice White tried to create a commercial act exception to the act of state doctrine in *Alfred Dunhill of London, Inc. v. Cuba* (1976), but he failed to convince a majority on this issue. Because the case had involved no formal governmental decree, White would not have allowed the act of state defense. Even had an act of state been shown, White opposed the doctrine's extension to "purely commercial" acts of a sovereign or its commercial instrumentalities. He relied on the notion, accepted ever since *Bank of the United States v. Planters' Bank of Georgia* (1824), that a government's partnership in a commercial business does not confer sovereign status on that business.

Also in 1976, Congress passed the Foreign Sovereign Immunities Act which authorized American courts to determine foreign claims of sovereign immunity, thus approving judicial—as opposed to executive—decisions on the validity of such claims. Although the act established a general rule of immunity of foreign states from the jurisdiction of American courts, its "exceptions" were wideranging. Immunity is denied, for example, when the foreign state engages in commercial activity, or takes certain property rights in violation of international law, or is sued for damages for certain kinds of injury to person or property.

DAVID GORDON
(1986)

Bibliography

GORDON, DAVID 1977 The Origin and Development of the Act of State Doctrine. *Rutgers Law Journal* 8:595–616.

ADAIR v. UNITED STATES
208 U.S. 161 (1908)

After the Pullman strike, which paralyzed the nation's railroads, a federal commission blamed the antiunion activities of the railroads and recommended legislation which Congress enacted in 1898. The ERDMAN ACT sought to free INTERSTATE COMMERCE from railroad strikes by establishing a railroad labor board with arbitration powers and by protecting the right of railroad workers to organize in unions. This second objective was the subject of section ten of the act, which prohibited YELLOW DOG CONTRACTS, blacklisting union members, and discharging employees solely for belonging to a union. The act applied to carriers engaged in interstate commerce. Adair, a manager of a carrier, fired an employee solely because of his union membership; a federal court found Adair guilty of violating section ten. On appeal the Supreme Court, by a vote of 6–2, found section ten unconstitutional for violating the Fifth Amendment's DUE PROCESS clause and for exceeding the powers of Congress under the COMMERCE CLAUSE.

Justice JOHN MARSHALL HARLAN, who spoke for the Court, usually wrote broad commerce clause opinions, but this one was constricted. He could see "no legal or logical connection" between an employee's membership in a labor organization and the carrying on of interstate commerce. The Pullman strike, the federal commission, and Congress's finding that such a connection existed meant nothing to the Court. A week later the Court held, in LOEWE V. LAWLOR (1908), that members of a labor organization who boycotted a manufacturing firm, whose products were intended for interstate commerce, had restrained interstate commerce in violation of the SHERMAN ANTITRUST ACT. In *Adair*, however, the Court found no constitutional authority for Congress to legislate on the labor affairs of interstate railroads.

Most of Harlan's opinion dealt with the due process issue. He found section ten to be "an invasion of the personal liberty, as well as the right to property," guaranteed by the Fifth Amendment. It embraced the right of employers to contract for labor and the right of labor to contract for its services without government intervention. In his exposition of FREEDOM OF CONTRACT, which is a doctrine derived from SUBSTANTIVE DUE PROCESS, Harlan contended that "it is not within the functions of government . . . to compel any person, in the course of his business and against his will, to accept or retain the personal services of another. . . ." The right of the employee to quit, said Harlan, "is the same as the right of the employer, for whatever reason, to dispense with the services of such employee." The Court forgot the more realistic view it had expressed in HOLDEN V. HARDY (1898), and held that "any legislation" disturbing the "equality of right" arbitrarily interferes with "the liberty of contract which no government can legally justify in a free land." Justice JOSEPH MCKENNA dissented mainly on the ground that the Court "stretched to its extreme" the liberty of contract doctrine. The Court overruled *Adair* in 1949.

LEONARD W. LEVY
(1986)

Bibliography

LIEBERMAN, ELIAS 1950 *Unions Before the Bar.* Pages 44–55. New York: Harper & Row.

ADAMS, HENRY
(1838–1918)

Born to a family whose service to the Constitution was matched by a reverence for it "this side of idolatry," Henry Brooks Adams served the Constitution as a historian of the nation it established. His great *History of the United States during the Administrations of Jefferson and Madison* as well as his biographies of JOHN RANDOLPH and ALBERT GALLATIN and his *Documents Relating to New England Federalism* remain standard sources for the events and characters of the early republican years during which the Constitution was being worked out in practice. Among the highlights of these works are Adams's ironic account of THOMAS JEFFERSON's exercise of his constitutional powers in the face of his particularist scruples, the Republican hostility to the federal judiciary, and the fate of STATES' RIGHTS views. In reply to HERMANN VON HOLST's criticism of the Constitution, Adams wrote in 1876, "the Constitution has done its work. It has made a nation." Adams's own disillusion with this nation affected his writings. Like others of his generation, he became more determinist as he became less sanguine, and the *History* shows this shift in his view as the Constitution is described becoming an engine of American nationalism, democracy, expansion, and centralization. In his novels, historical theory, letters, and *The Education of Henry Adams*, he came to regard the Constitution as almost a figment of human intention in a

modern age—an age in which the kind of person it once was possible for an Adams to be has no role.

ROBERT DAWIDOFF
(1986)

Bibliography

SAMUELS, ERNEST 1948–1964 *Henry Adams.* 3 Vols. Cambridge, Mass: Harvard University Press.

ADAMS, JOHN
(1735–1826)

Massachusetts lawyer and revolutionary leader, first vice-president and second President of the United States, John Adams was also a distinguished political and constitutional theorist. Born in 1735, the descendant of three generations of hardy independent farmers in Braintree, Massachusetts, near Boston, he attended Harvard College and after graduation studied law for several years, gaining admission to the bar in 1758. The practice of a country lawyer held no charms for him. He took delight in the study of law and government, however, and this scholarly pursuit merged imperceptibly with the polemics of the revolutionary controversy, which probed the nature and history of the English constitution. Adams made his political debut in 1765 as the author of Braintree's protest against the Stamp Act. Increasingly, from the pressures of politics as well as of business, he was drawn to Boston, moving there with his young family in 1768. Unlike his cousin SAMUEL ADAMS, he was not an ardent revolutionist. He worried about the "mischievous democratic principles" churned up by the agitation; he braved the popular torrent to defend Captain Thomas Preston and the British soldiers accused of murder in the Boston Massacre. For several years he was torn between Boston and Braintree, and the different worlds they represented. Only in 1773 did he commit himself fully to the Revolution.

The next year, during the crisis produced by the Intolerable Acts, Adams was elected one of the Massachusetts delegates to the FIRST CONTINTENTAL CONGRESS, in Philadelphia. Events had shaken his lawyerlike stance on the issues, and he championed the patriots' appeal to "the law of nature," as well as to the English constitution and COLONIAL CHARTERS, in defense of American liberties. He wrote the crucial fourth article of the congress's declaration of rights denying the authority of Parliament to legislate for the colonies, though acquiescing in imperial regulation of trade as a matter of convenience. Back in Boston he expounded his views at length in the series of *Novanglus* letters in the press. TREASON and rebellion, he argued, were on the other side—the advocates of parliamentary supremacy abroad and the Tory oligarchy at home. He had no quarrel with George III, and he lauded the English constitution with its nice balance between king, lords, and commons and its distinctly republican character. Unfortunately, the constitution was not made for colonies. Denied REPRESENTATION in Parliament, they were deprived of the constitution's best feature. The proper relationship between the colonies and the mother country, Adams said, was the same as Scotland's before the Act of Union, that is, as an independent government owing allegiance to a common king. Had America been conquered, like Ireland, imperial rule would be warranted; but America was a discovered, not a conquered, country, and so the people possessed the NATURAL RIGHT to make their own laws as far as compatible with allegiance to the king.

In the Second Continental Congress Adams lost all hope of reconciliation on these terms, and he became a leading advocate of American independence. Although a member of the committee to draft the DECLARATION OF INDEPENDENCE, he made his greatest contribution when it came to the floor for debate. Before this he co-authored and championed the resolution—"a machine to fabricate independence" in opposition eyes—calling upon the colonies to form new governments. Nothing was more important to Adams than the making of new constitutions and the restoration of legitimate authority. He had read all the political theorists from Plato to Rousseau; now he reread them with a view to incorporating their best principles into the foundations of the polity. Government was "the divine science"—"the first in importance"—and American independence opened, in his eyes, a grand "age of political experiments." It was, he declared, "a time when the greatest lawgivers of antiquity would have wished to live. How few of the human race have ever enjoyed an opportunity of making an election of government—more than of air, soil, or climate—for themselves or their children!" To aid this work Adams sketched his ideas in an epistolary essay, *Thoughts on Government*, which was destined to have wide influence. Years later, in his autobiography, Adams said that he wrote to counteract the plan of government advanced by that "disastrous meteor" THOMAS PAINE in *Common Sense*. Paine's ideas, which gave shape to the new PENNSYLVANIA CONSTITUTION OF 1776, were "too democratical," mainly because they concentrated all power in a single representative assembly without mixture or balance. Adams, by contrast, proposed a "complex" government of representative assembly, council (or senate), and governor, each endowed with a negative on the others. The people would glide easily into such a government because of its close resemblance to the colonial governments they had known. It possessed additional merit for Adams as a thoroughly republican adaptation of the idealized balance of the English consti-

tution. Even as he challenged the work of constitution-making, however, Adams was assailed by doubts. The new governments might be too free to survive. The essence of republics was *virtue*, that is, selfless devotion to the common weal, but Adams, still a Puritan under his republican skin, clung to a theory of human nature that emphasized man's capacity for selfishness, ignorance, and vice. The POPULAR SOVEREIGNTY that was the basis of republican government possessed the power to destroy it.

In 1779, after returning to the United States from the first of two diplomatic missions abroad, Adams had the opportunity to amplify his constitutional theory, indeed to become the Solon of his native state. Massachusetts continued to be governed by a revolutionary body, the provincial congress, without legitimate constitutional authority. Only in the previous year the citizenry had rejected a constitution framed by the congress. Now they elected a CONSTITUTIONAL CONVENTION for the specific purpose of framing a FUNDAMENTAL LAW, which would then be referred back to them for approval. (When the process was completed in 1780, the MASSACHUSETTS CONSTITUTION exhibited, for the first time anywhere, all the means by which the theory of "constituent sovereignty," one of the foundations of the American republic, was put into practice.) Elected Braintree's delegate, Adams was assigned the task of preparing a draft constitution for consideration by the convention, and this became, after comparatively few changes, its final product. The preamble reiterated the contractual and consensual basis of government. It was followed by a declaration of rights, derivative of the Virginia model but much more elaborate. Adams was not responsible for Article III—the most disputed provision—making it the duty of the legislature, and thus in turn of the various towns and parishes, to support religion; yet this was consistent with the aim of the constitution as a whole to keep Massachusetts a Christian commonwealth. For Adams religion was as essential to virtue as virtue was to republicanism. Thus he proposed a RELIGIOUS TEST for all elected officials. (The delegates voted to confine the test to the office of governor.) The strength and independence of the executive was an unusual feature of the constitution. Reacting against monarchy, most of the new state constitutions weakened and shackled the governors; but Adams believed that a kingly executive was necessary to control the conflicting passions and interests in the legislature. Accordingly, he proposed to vest the Massachusetts governor with an absolute negative on legislation. The convention declined to follow him, however, conferring a suspensive veto only. Adams ever after felt that the trimming of the governor's legislative power was the one serious error of the convention. Otherwise, with respect to the legislature, his principles were fully embodied in the constitution. Representation in the lower house was based upon population, while representation in the upper house, being proportioned to the taxable wealth of the several senatorial districts, was based upon property. This system of giving representation to property as well as numbers had its principal source in the philosophy of James Harrington, whose axiom "power always follows property," Adams said, "is as infallible a maxim in politics as that action and reaction are equal in mechanics." Property was further joined to office by requiring wealth on an ascending scale of value to make representatives, senators, and governors eligible for their offices. Finally, the constitution retained the freehold qualification for the franchise. In these features it was a distinctly conservative document, and it would, Adams later complained, give him "the reputation of a man of high principles and strong notions in government, scarcely compatible with republicanism."

Adams was in France when the Massachusetts Constitution was ratified in 1780. After helping negotiate the treaty of peace, he was named by Congress the first minister of the United States to Great Britain. He did not return home until 1788. He had, therefore, no direct part in the formation of the United States Constitution. Of course, he took a keen interest in that event. Observing it from his station abroad, he was inevitably influenced by Europe's perception of the terrible weakness of the American confederation and by the tide of democratic revolution that, in his own perception, threatened to inundate the European continent.

Like many of the Americans who would attend the CONSTITUTIONAL CONVENTION OF 1787, Adams was alarmed by SHAY'S REBELLION in Massachusetts, and he took up his pen once again to show the way to constitutional salvation. His three-volume work, *Defence of the American Constitutions* (1787), was devoted to the classical proposition that the *"unum necessarium"* of republican government is the tripartite division of the legislative power, each of the branches embodying a distinctive principle and power—the one, the few, and the many, or monarchy, aristocracy, democracy—and the dynamics of the balance between them securing the equilibrium of the whole. The book's title was misleading. It was not actually a defense of the state constitutions, most of which Adams thought indefensible, but rather a defense of the true republican theory against the criticism of those constitutions by the French *philosophe* Robert Jacques Turgot and his school, who held that instead of collecting all authority at one center, as the logic of equality and popular sovereignty dictated, the American constitutions erred in dividing power among different social orders and principles of government in pale imitation of the English king, lords, and commons. Adams sought to demonstrate, of course, that this balanced government was founded in the law of reason and

nature. He ransacked European history, carving huge chunks from the writings of philosophers and historians—about eighty percent of the text—and adding his own argumentative comments to prove his point. All societies are divided between the few and the many, the rich and the poor, aristocrats and commoners; and these two orders, actuated by passion and ambition, are constantly at war with each other. The only escape, the only security, is through the tripartite balance. It involves, primarily, erecting a third power, a monarchical executive, to serve as a balance wheel and umpire between the democracy and the aristocracy. It involves also constituting these two great orders in insulated chambers, wherein each may flourish but neither may dominate or subvert the other. Vice, interest, and ambition are rendered useful when these two orders are made to control each other and a monarchical executive is installed as the presiding genius over the whole.

With the publication of the *Defence*, Adams's political thought hardened into a system that placed him at odds with democratic forces and opinion in both Europe and the United States. In 1789 the French National Assembly rejected his doctrine. At home he was alienated from many former political friends. The subject of his apostasy from republicanism became, it was said, "a kind of political phenomenon." He denied any apostasy, of course, and his use of such galvanizing abstractions as "monarchy" and "aristocracy" undoubtedly opened him to misrepresentation. Nevertheless, the character of his thought had changed. During his sojourn abroad Adams became the captive of Old World political fears, which he then transferred to the United States, where they did not belong. Here, as he sometimes recognized, all men were of one order. Yet for several years after his return to the United States, Adams did not disguise his belief that hereditary monarchy and aristocracy must eventually prove as necessary to the American republic as they had to every other. They were, he said, the only institutions that could preserve the laws and liberties of the people against discord, sedition, and civil war.

These beliefs did not prevent Adams's election as vice-president in 1788. Long a friend of a national government, he approved of the Constitution and even imagined the *Defence* had influenced it. He wished the executive were stronger and feared the recurrent shocks to the system from frequent elections and the factions, turbulence, and intrigue they bred. For a time he toyed with the idea of a second convention to overcome these weaknesses. His concern for the authority and dignity of the government led him to propose in the First Congress a high-sounding title ("His Most Benign Highness") for the President and splendid ceremonies of state in order to awe the people. He reiterated those views and continued the argument of the *Defence* in a series of articles (*Discourses on Davila*) in the *Gazette of the United States,* in Philadelphia. Since the articles also denounced the French Revolution, they were an American parallel to Edmund Burke's *Reflections on the Revolution in France.* When the doctrines were publicly labeled "political heresies" by Adams's old friend, THOMAS JEFFERSON, the secretary of state, the ideological division between them entered into the emerging party conflict. In this conflict Adams proved himself a loyal Federalist. Not wishing to cause further embarrassment to GEORGE WASHINGTON's administration, which the Republicans assailed as Anglican and monarchical, Adams put away his pen in 1791 and withdrew into the recesses of the vice-presidency.

Elected President in 1797, Adams at first sought political reconciliation with his Republican rival, Jefferson, but the effort foundered amidst intense partisanship and foreign crisis. The issue of war and peace with France absorbed his administration. Working to resolve it, Adams was handicapped both by the Republican opposition and by the High Federalists in his cabinet who took their orders from ALEXANDER HAMILTON. The collapse of negotiations with France was followed by frantic preparations for war in the spring of 1798. Adams favored naval defense—and the Navy Department was created. He distrusted Hamilton, who favored a large army, seeing in him a potential Caesar. When General Washington, called out of retirement to command the new army, demanded that the second place be given to Hamilton, Adams resisted, citing his prerogative as COMMANDER-IN-CHIEF, he but was finally forced to yield. He did not recommend and had no direct responsibility for the ALIEN AND SEDITION ACTS passed by Congress in July. Yet he contributed as much as anyone to the war hysteria that provoked this repressive legislation. In his public answers to the addresses of loyalty that poured into Philadelphia, Adams repeatedly condemned "the wild philosophy," "domestic treachery," and "spirit of party, which scruples not to go all lengths of profligacy, falsehood, and malignity in defaming our government." Thus branded disloyal by a President whose philosophy made no place for organized POLITICAL PARTIES, the Republican leaders became easy targets. Moreover, Adams cooperated in the enforcement of these laws. The Alien Law was not fully executed in a single instance, but Adams deserves little credit for this. He apparently approved the numerous prosecutions under the Sedition Law, and showed no mercy for its victims. In retrospect, when the impolicy of the laws was generally conceded, Adams still never doubted their constitutionality.

Despite the prescriptions of his political theory, Adams was not a strong President. Indeed, because of that theory, he continued to consider the office above party and politics, though the conception was already unworkable. In the end he asserted his authority and in one glorious act of statesmanship broke with the High Federalists and made peace with France. The domestic consequences were as important as the foreign. Adams sometimes said he made peace in order to squelch Hamilton and his designs for the army. Standing army, foreign adventurism, mounting debt and taxes—these dangers recalled to Adams the Whig doctrines of his youth. "All the declarations . . . of Trenchard and Gordon [see CATO'S LETTERS], Bolingbroke, Barnard and Walpole, Hume, Burgh, and Burke, rush upon my memory and frighten me out of my wits," he confessed. Patriotic, courageous, and wise, Adams's actions nevertheless split the Federalist party and paved the way for Jefferson's triumph in the election of 1800. Before he left office, Adams signed into law the JUDICIARY ACT OF 1801, creating many new federal courts and judgeships, which he proceeded to fill with faithful partisans. In the Republican view the Federalists retreated to the judiciary as a fortress from which to defeat every popular reform. Less noticed at the time but more important for the nation's constitutional development was the nomination and appointment of JOHN MASHALL as Chief Justice of the United States.

In retirement at Quincy, Adams slowly made peace with Jeffersonian Republicanism and watched his son JOHN QUINCY ADAMS, who broke with the Federalists in 1808, rise to become the sixth President of the United States. A compulsive and contentious reader, Adams never lost his enthusiasm for political speculation; and although he grew more and more hopeful about the American experiment, he continued to the end to warn the people against their own suicidal tendencies. In 1820 he attended the convention to revise the Massachusetts constitution he had drafted forty years before. When the reformers attacked the "aristocratical principle" of a senate bottomed on property, Adams spoke spiritedly in its defense. And, with most of the original constitution, it survived. The finest literary product of these years—one of the intellectual monuments of the age—was his correspondence with Thomas Jefferson, with whom he was reconciled in friendship in 1812. The correspondence traversed an immense field. In politics, the two men discoursed brilliantly on "natural aristocracy," further defining a fundamental issue of principle between them. Interestingly, Adams's political anxieties, unlike Jefferson's, never fixed upon the Constitution. He did not turn political questions into constitutional questions. He was a nationalist, of course, and spoke highly of the Union; but for all his work on constitutional government, Adams rarely uttered a complete thought on the United States Constitution. The amiability and learning, the candor and humor, with the occasional banter and abandon of his letters were all perfectly in character. In the often quoted observation of BENJAMIN FRANKLIN, John

Adams was "always an honest man, often a wise one, but sometimes, and in some things, absolutely out of his senses." He died, as did Jefferson, on the fiftieth anniversary of American independence, July 4, 1826.

MERRILL D. PETERSON
(1986)

Bibliography

ADAMS, CHARLES FRANCIS, ed. 1850–1856 *The Works of John Adams.* 10 Vols. Boston: Little, Brown.

BUTTERFIELD, LYMAN C., ed. 1961 *The Diary and Autobiography of John Adams.* 4 Vols. Cambridge, Mass.: Harvard University Press.

HARASZTI, ZOLTAN   1952   *John Adams and the Prophets of Progress.* Cambridge, Mass.: Harvard University Press.

HOWE, JOHN R., JR.   1966   *The Changing Political Thought of John Adams.* Princeton, N.J.: Princeton University Press.

KURTZ, STEPHEN G.   1957   *The Presidency of John Adams.* Philadelphia: University of Pennsylvania Press.

SMITH, PAGE   1962   *John Adams.* 2 Vols. Garden City, N.Y.: Doubleday.

ADAMS, JOHN QUINCY
(1767–1848)

John Quincy Adams served the nation in its earliest days, contributing as diplomat, secretary of state, President, and congressman to the development of constitutional government in America. Throughout his career he sought to be a "man of the whole nation," an ambition that earned him enemies in his native New England and in the South during a period of political sectionalism. As congressman from Massachusetts between 1831 and 1848, he played a decisive role in the development of the WHIG theory of the United States Constitution. His speeches in this period inspired a whole generation of Americans to resist the expansion of SLAVERY and to defend the Union.

Adams's political career began at the age of fifteen, when he went as private secretary to his father, JOHN ADAMS, on the diplomatic mission that negotiated the Treaty of Paris (1783). In 1801 he was elected United States senator. He angered Federalists by his support of THOMAS JEFFERSON's acquisition of Louisiana and by his cooperation with the administration's policy of countering English and French attacks on American shipping by economic means. This policy resulted in the Embargo (1807) and gave rise to a SECESSION movement in New England (culminating in the HARTFORD CONVENTION of 1814–1815). Eighteen months before his term ended, the legislature elected a replacement and Adams resigned his Senate seat. He returned to private practice of the law, supporting the Yazoo claimants before the Supreme Court in FLETCHER V. PECK (1809). In the same year, President JAMES MADISON appointed him minister to Russia. As secretary of state under JAMES MONROE (1816–1824), Adams secured American territorial claims to the Pacific Northwest and defended ANDREW JACKSON's conduct in Florida during the Seminole Wars. Adams was the principal author of the MONROE DOCTRINE, defending the Latin American republics from fresh incursions by European imperialism.

In 1824 Adams was elected President by the House of Representatives, none of the major candidates (Adams, Jackson, William Crawford, and HENRY CLAY) having achieved a majority in the ELECTORAL COLLEGE. The 1824 election created a political enmity between Adams and Jackson that seriously undermined Adams's presidency. Jackson had received a large plurality of popular votes, and the general's supporters portrayed Adams's election as an antidemocratic "corrupt bargain" between Adams and Clay, whom Adams appointed as secretary of state. In spite of Adams's strong disapproval of partisan politics, his administration gave rise to the second party system: Jacksonian Democrats versus Whigs.

In addition to the conflict between "plain republicans" and "aristocrats"—a popular division recalling the rhetoric of the Jeffersonians—another conflict arising from Adams's presidency was that between partisans of "BROAD CONSTRUCTION" and of "STRICT CONSTRUCTION" of the constitutional powers of the federal government. This division arose from Adams's call for a vigorous program of nationally funded INTERNAL IMPROVEMENTS—roads, canals, harbors, naval facilities, etcetera—a program that Henry Clay named the AMERICAN SYSTEM. But at bottom the division resulted from fundamental disagreements about the character of the Union.

Defeated for reelection in 1828, Adams seemed at the end of his career. In 1829 he wrote the least prudent, if most interesting, of his many essays and pamphlets, an account of the events leading up to the convening of the Hartford Convention, implicating many of New England's most famous men in TREASON. In writing this long essay (published posthumously as *Documents Relating to New England Federalism, 1801–1815*) he developed a THEORY OF THE UNION that constituted the burden of his speeches and public writings until his death in 1848, and that became the political gospel of the new Republican party and its greatest leader, ABRAHAM LINCOLN.

According to Adams, the Constitution was not a compact between sovereign states but was the organic law of the American nation, given by the American people to themselves in the exercise of their inalienable right to consent to the form of government over them. The state governments derived their existence from the same act of consent that created the federal government. They did not exist before the federal government, therefore, and could not have created it themselves by compact. What is more, the state governments, like the federal government, depended decisively on the truth of those first principles of politics enunciated in the DECLARATION OF INDEPENDENCE for their own legitimacy.

This Whig theory of the Constitution was politically provocative. By it slavery was a clear moral evil. Adams, like Lincoln after him, justified the compromise with slavery as necessary in the circumstances to the existence of a constitutional union in America, but Adams vehemently maintained the duty to prevent the spread of what was at best a necessary evil. While he advocated a scrupulous care for the legal rights of slavery where it was established, he insisted that the government of the United States must always speak as a free state in world affairs. He believed it to be a duty of the whole nation to set slavery, as Lincoln would later say, on the course of ultimate extinction.

This theory guided his words and deeds in the House of Representatives from 1831 until his death. For fourteen years he waged an almost single-handed war against the dominant Jacksonian Democratic majority in the House, a struggle focused on the GAG RULE. The gag rule was actually a series of standing rules adopted at every session of Congress from 1836 on. In its final form it read: "No petition, memorial, resolution, or other paper praying the abolition of slavery in the DISTRICT OF COLUMBIA or any State or Territory, or the slave trade between the States or Territories in which it now exists, shall be received by this House, or entertained in any way whatever."

The gag rule was part of a policy followed by the Democratic party in this period, on the advice of JOHN C. CALHOUN, among others, never in the least thing to admit the authority of Congress over slavery. Adams argued that the gag was a patent abrogation of the FIRST AMENDMENT's guarantee of FREEDOM OF PETITION. His speeches against the gag became a rallying point for the growing free-soil and abolition movements in the North, though Adams himself was cautious about endorsing the program of the radicals.

Through a long and varied career, Adams's statesmanship was guided by the twin principles of liberty and union. As a diplomat and architect of American foreign policy, Adams played a large part in the creation of a continental Republic. He believed that the westward expansion of the country was necessary if the United States was to minimize foreign interference in its domestic politics. Yet expansion brought the most powerful internal forces of disruption of the Union into play and prepared the way for the CIVIL WAR.

GEORGE FORSYTH
(1986)

Bibliography

BEMIS, SAMUEL F.   1949   *John Quincy Adams and the Foundations of American Foreign Policy*. New York: Knopf.

——— 1956   *John Quincy Adams and the Union*. New York: Knopf.

LIPSKY, GEORGE A.   1950   *John Quincy Adams: His Theories and Ideas*. New York: Crowell.

ADAMS, SAMUEL
(1722–1803)

Samuel Adams was one of the greatest leaders of the AMERICAN REVOLUTION whose career flourished during the long struggle with Great Britain. His strength was in Massachusetts state politics; he was less successful as a national politician. His speeches and writings influenced the shape of American constitutional thought.

Adams's political career began in 1764 when he wrote the instructions of the Boston town meeting to Boston's representatives in the legislature. These included the first formal denial of the right of Parliament to tax the colonists: "If taxes are laid upon us in any shape without our having a legal representation where they are laid, are we not reduced from the character of free subjects to the miserable state of tributary slaves?"

The next year he was elected to the legislature and assumed leadership of the radical popular opposition to the governing clique headed by THOMAS HUTCHINSON. Adams maintained that he was defending not only the rights of British colonists but also the NATURAL RIGHTS of all men: "The leading principles of the British Constitution have their foundation in the Laws of Nature and universal Reason. . . . British rights are in great measure the Rights of the Colonists, and of all men else." Adams led the opposition to the Stamp Act and the TOWNSHEND ACTS. He denounced these acts as unconstitutional, since they involved TAXATION WITHOUT REPRESENTATION.

In the MASSACHUSETTS CIRCULATION LETTER of 1768 Adams wrote of constitutions in general that they should be fixed and unalterable by ordinary legislation, and that under no constitution could subjects be deprived of their property except by their consent, given in person or by elected representatives. Of the British Constitution in particular he argued that, although Parliament might legislate on imperial matters, only the colonial assemblies could legislate on local matters or impose special taxes.

When the British government landed troops at Boston, Adams published a series of letters denouncing as unconstitutional the keeping of a standing army in peacetime without the consent of the people of the colony. "The Americans," he wrote, "as they were not and could not be represented in Parliament, were therefore suffering under military tyranny over which they were allowed to exercise no control."

In the early 1770s, Adams worked to create a network

of committees of correspondence. In November 1772, on behalf of the Boston Committee of Correspondence, he drafted a declaration of the rights of the colonists. In three sections it proclaimed the rights of Americans as men, as Christians, and as British subjects. A list of infringements of those rights followed, including the assumption by Parliament of the power to legislate for the colonies in all cases whatsoever and the grant of a royal salary to Governor Thomas Hutchinson and the judges in Massachusetts.

In January 1773 Hutchinson, addressing the legislature, argued for acceptance of the absolute supremacy of the British Parliament and asserted that there was no middle ground between unqualified submission and independence. Samuel Adams, along with JOHN ADAMS, drafted the reply of the Assembly, arguing anew that under the British Constitution the colonial legislature shared power with Parliament.

Samuel Adams was an early proponent of a Continental Congress, and in June 1774 he was elected to the First Continental Congress. There he played a key role in the adoption of the ASSOCIATION. In the Second Continental Congress he moved, in January 1776, for immediate independence and for a federation of the colonies. In July 1776, he signed the DECLARATION OF INDEPENDENCE.

Adams remained a member of the Continental Congress until 1781. He was a member of the original committee to draft the ARTICLES OF CONFEDERATION. Suspicious of any concentration of power, he opposed creation of the executive departments of finance, war, and foreign affairs. In 1779–1780 he was a delegate to the Massachusetts CONSTITUTIONAL CONVENTION, which produced the first of the Revolutionary state constitutions to be ratified by popular vote.

Throughout the Revolutionary period Adams was a staunch supporter of unified action. When, in 1783, a Massachusetts convention was held to plan resistance to congressional enactment of a pension for army officers, Adams, who had opposed the pension, defended Congress's right to pass it and spoke out against those who would dishonor the state's commitment to pay continental debts.

In 1787, after SHAYS' REBELLION had broken out, Adams, then president of the state senate, proposed to invoke the assistance of the United States as provided in the Articles of Confederation, but his motion failed in the lower house. Later, opposing the pardon of the rebels, he argued that there is a crucial difference between monarchy and self-government and that any "man who dares to rebel against the laws of a republic ought to suffer death."

Adams was not named a delegate to the CONSTITUTIONAL CONVENTION OF 1787, but he was influential at the Massachusetts ratifying convention: "I stumble at the threshold," he wrote to RICHARD HENRY LEE, "I meet with a national government, instead of a federal union of sovereign states." He was troubled by the division of powers in the proposed federal system, which constituted "*Imperia in Imperio* [supreme powers within a supreme power] justly deemed a Solecism in Politicks, highly dangerous, and destructive of the Peace Union and Safety of the Nation." Ironically, he echoed the argument of his old enemy Hutchinson that SOVEREIGNTY was indivisible. But, after a meeting of his constituents passed a resolution that "any vote of a delegate from Boston against adopting it would be contrary to the interests, feelings, and wishes of the tradesmen of the town," Adams altered his position. In the end he supported a plan whereby Massachusetts ratified the Constitution unconditionally but also proposed a series of amendments, including a BILL OF RIGHTS.

Adams was defeated by FISHER AMES for election to the first Congress. Thereafter, although he remained active in state politics as a legislator and governor (1794–1797), he never again sought or held national office under the Constitution.

DENNIS J. MAHONEY
(1986)

Bibliography

MAIER, PAULINE 1980 *The Old Revolutionaries: Political Lives in the Age of Samuel Adams.* New York: Knopf.

MILLER, JOHN C. 1936 *Sam Adams: Pioneer in Propaganda.* Boston: Little, Brown.

WELLS, WILLIAM V. 1865 *Life and Public Services of Samuel Adams . . . With Extracts from His Correspondence, State Papers, and Political Essays.* Boston: Little, Brown.

ADAMS v. TANNER
244 U.S. 590 (1917)

In a 5–4 decision, the Supreme Court declared unconstitutional a Washington state statute prohibiting individuals from paying employment agencies for their services. Although a loophole allowed prospective employers to pay the agencies' fees, Justice JAMES C. MCREYNOLDS nevertheless voided the law as a prohibition, not a regulation, of business. Citing ALLGEYER V. LOUISIANA (1897), McReynolds also declared the statute a violation of DUE PROCESS OF LAW. Justice LOUIS D. BRANDEIS dissented, joined by Justices OLIVER WENDELL HOLMES and JOHN H. CLARKE, demonstrating the "vast evils" that justified the legislature under STATE POLICE POWERS.

DAVID GORDON
(1986)

(SEE ALSO: *Olsen v. Nebraska ex rel. Reference & Bond Association; Ribnik v. McBride; Tyson & Brother v. Banton.*)

ADAMSON v. CALIFORNIA
332 U.S. 46 (1947)

By a 5–4 vote the Supreme Court, speaking through Justice STANLEY F. REED, sustained the constitutionality of provisions of California laws permitting the trial court and prosecutor to call the jury's attention to the accused's failure to explain or deny evidence against him. Adamson argued that the Fifth Amendment's RIGHT AGAINST SELF-INCRIMINATION is a fundamental national privilege protected against state abridgment by the FOURTEENTH AMENDMENT and that the same amendment's DUE PROCESS clause prevented comment on the accused's silence. Reed, relying on TWINING V. NEW JERSEY (1908) and PALKO V. CONNECTICUT (1937), ruled that the Fifth Amendment does not apply to the states and that even adverse comment on the right to silence does not deny due process.

The case is notable less for Reed's opinion, which GRIFFIN V. CALIFORNIA (1965) overruled, than for the classic debate between Justices FELIX FRANKFURTER, concurring, and HUGO L. BLACK, in dissent, on the INCORPORATION DOCTRINE. Joined by Justice WILLIAM O. DOUGLAS, Black read the history of the origins of the Fourteenth Amendment to mean that its framers and ratifiers intended to make the entire BILL OF RIGHTS applicable to the states, a position that Justice FRANK MURPHY, joined by Justice WILEY RUTLEDGE, surpassed by adding that the Fourteenth Amendment also protected unenumerated rights. Frankfurter, seeking to expose the inconsistency of the dissenters, suggested that they did not mean what they said. They would not fasten on the states the requirement of the SEVENTH AMENDMENT that civil cases involving more than $20 require a TRIAL BY JURY. They really intended only a "selective incorporation," Frankfurter declared, and consequently they offered "a merely subjective test." Black, in turn, purporting to be quite literal in his interpretation, ridiculed Frankfurter's subjective reliance on "civilized decency" to explain due process. History probably supports Frankfurter's argument on the original intent of the Fourteenth Amendment, but the Justices on both sides mangled the little historical evidence they knew to make it support preconceived positions.

LEONARD W. LEVY
(1986)

ADAMSON EIGHT-HOUR ACT
39 Stat. 721 (1916)

In 1916 major railway unions demanded an eight-hour working day and extra pay for overtime work. The railroads' refusal prompted a union call for a nationwide general strike. President WOODROW WILSON, fearing disastrous consequences, appealed to Congress for legislation to avert the strike and to protect "the life and interests of the nation." The Adamson Act mandated an eight-hour day for railroad workers engaged in INTERSTATE COMMERCE. The act also established a commission to report on the law's operation. Pending that report, the act prohibited reduction in pay rates for the shorter workday. Overtime would be recompensed at regular wages, not time and a half. Congress effectively constituted itself a labor arbitrator and vested its award with the force of law. The Supreme Court rejected the argument that Congress exceeded its constitutional authority in WILSON V. NEW (1917), sustaining the act. The Court distinguished LOCHNER V. NEW YORK (1905) by asserting that the Adamson Act did no more than supplement the rights of the contracting parties; the act did not interfere with the FREEDOM OF CONTRACT.

DAVID GORDON
(1986)

ADARAND CONSTRUCTORS, INC. v. PEÑA
505 U.S. 200 (1995)

Adarand Constructors, Inc. v. Peña, which was an AFFIRMATIVE ACTION case decided in 1995 by a five-Justice majority of the Supreme Court, held that "all racial classifications, imposed by whatever federal, state or local government actor, must be analyzed by a reviewing court under strict scrutiny. In other words, such classifications are constitutional only if they are narrowly tailored measures that further compelling governmental interests." In so holding, the Court OVERRULED its decision in METRO BROADCASTING, INC. V. FCC (1990) that "benign" racial classifications are subject only to intermediate scrutiny. The Court also eliminated the distinction drawn by its opinion in RICHMOND (CITY OF) V. J.A. CROSON CO. (1989) between state and local race-based affirmative action programs (which were held subject to STRICT SCRUTINY in *Croson*) and federal affirmative action programs.

In *Adarand,* a federal contractor passed over the low bid submitted by Adarand Constructors in favor of a higher-bidding minority-owned subcontractor, because federal highway regulations gave the contractor a financial bonus for selecting subcontractors owned by "socially and economically disadvantaged individuals." Members of enumerated minority groups and women were presumed by the regulations to be socially disadvantaged. The Court viewed the presumption of social disadvantage based on race and ethnicity as a facially race-based classification, subject to strict scrutiny.

Not all affirmative action is necessarily subject to strict

scrutiny under *Adarand*. The Court held in *Adarand* that affirmative action is subject to the same level of scrutiny as garden-variety discrimination. The level of scrutiny in ordinary discrimination cases has varied—strict scrutiny applies to discrimination on the basis of race, intermediate scrutiny to gender classifications, and rationality review to classifications not recognized as subject to special constitutional protection (for example, SEXUAL ORIENTATION and age). Under *Adarand,* the same variation in levels of scrutiny appears to apply to affirmative action.

In discussing strict scrutiny, the Court expressed the "wish to dispel the notion that strict scrutiny is 'strict in theory but fatal in fact.' " The example the Court gave of an affirmative action program that would survive strict scrutiny was a program set in place by a governmental body to remedy its own past discrimination. The Court did not indicate whether governmental affirmative action programs that are not remedial in this narrow sense (and most are not) would be permissible.

The Court remanded the *Adarand* case to the lower courts, allowing them the first opportunity to decide whether the highway regulations survive strict scrutiny. The trial court invalidated the affirmative action program, subjecting it to strict scrutiny. While the case was pending on appeal, Adarand Constructors itself applied for and received certification as a socially and economically disadvantaged business. Holding that Adarand no longer had STANDING to challenge a program from which it could now benefit, the U.S. Court of Appeals for the Tenth Circuit dismissed the case as moot and vacated the district court's opinion. Thus, whether the program at issue in *Adarand* is constitutional remains unsettled.

In response to *Adarand*, President WILLIAM J. CLINTON stated that his policy towards federal affirmative action was "mend it, don't end it," and ordered federal agencies to reexamine their affirmative action programs in that light.

DEBORAH C. MALAMUD
(2000)

Bibliography

MISHKIN, PAUL J. 1996 The Making of a Turning Point: *Metro* and *Adarand. California Law Review* 84:875–886.
U.S. DEPARTMENT OF JUSTICE 1996 Proposed Reforms to Affirmative Action in Federal Procurement. *Federal Register* 61: 26042.

ADDERLEY v. FLORIDA
385 U.S. 39 (1966)

A 5–4 Supreme Court, speaking through Justice HUGO L. BLACK, upheld TRESPASS convictions of CIVIL RIGHTS advocates demonstrating in a jail driveway, holding that where public property is devoted to a special use, FREEDOM OF SPEECH constitutionally may be limited in order to "preserve the property . . . for the use to which it is lawfully dedicated." This case signaled a new attention to the extent to which speakers have a right to carry their expressive activity onto private property and non-PUBLIC FORUM public property. It was also one of the first cases in which Justice Black exhibited the increasingly critical attitude toward demonstrations and other nontraditional forms of speech that marked his last years.

MARTIN SHAPIRO
(1986)

ADEQUATE STATE GROUNDS

Although most decisions of state courts falling within the Supreme Court's APPELLATE JURISDICTION involve questions of both state and federal law, the Supreme Court limits its review of such cases to the FEDERAL QUESTIONS. Moreover, the Court will not even decide the federal questions raised by such a case if the decision below rests on a ground of state law that is adequate to support the judgment and is independent of any federal issue. This rule applies to grounds based on both state substantive law and state procedures.

In its substantive-ground aspect, the rule not only protects the state courts' authority as the final arbiters of state law but also bolsters the principle forbidding federal courts to give ADVISORY OPINIONS. If the Supreme Court were to review the federal issues presented by a decision resting independently on an adequate state ground, the Court's pronouncements on the federal issues would be advisory only, having no effect on the resolution of the case. It has been assumed that ordinarily no federal policy dictates Supreme Court review of a decision resting on an independent state substantive ground; the winner in the state court typically is the same party who has asserted the federal claim. The point is exemplified by a state court decision invalidating a state statute on both state and federal constitutional grounds. This assumption, however, is a hindrance to Justices bent on contracting the reach of particular constitutional guarantees. In *Michigan v. Long* (1983) the BURGER COURT announced that when the independence of a state court's judgment from federal law is in doubt, the Court will assume that the judgment does not rest independently on state law. To insulate a decision from Supreme Court review now requires a plain statement by the state court of the independence of its state law ground.

Obviously, the highest state court retains considerable control over the reviewability of many of its decisions in the Supreme Court. If the state court chooses to rest decision only on grounds of federal law, as the California court did in REGENTS OF THE UNIVERSITY OF CALIFORNIA V. BAKKE (1978), the case is reviewable by the Supreme Court. Correspondingly, the state court can avoid review by the Supreme Court by resting solely on a state-law ground, or by explicitly resting on *both* a state and a federal ground. In the latter case, the state court's pronouncements on federal law are unreviewable. Recently, several state supreme courts (Alaska, California, Massachusetts, New Jersey, and Oregon) have used these devices to make important contributions to the development of both state and federal constitutional law.

When the state court's decision rests on a procedural ground, the usual effect is to cut off a party's right to claim a federal right, because of some procedural default. The Supreme Court generally insists that federal questions be raised in the state courts according to the dictates of state procedure. However, when the state procedural ground itself violates the federal Constitution (and thus is not "independent" of a federal claim), the Supreme Court will consider the federal issues in the case even though state procedure was not precisely followed. Another exception is exemplified in NAACP V. ALABAMA (1964). There the Court reviewed the NAACP's federal claims although the state court had refused to hear them on the transparently phony ground that they had been presented in a brief that departed from the prescribed format. The adequate state ground rule protects judicial federalism, not shamming designed to defeat the claims of federal right.

A similar rule limits the availability of federal HABEAS CORPUS relief for state prisoners. (See FAY V. NOIA; WAINWRIGHT V. SYKES.)

KENNETH L. KARST
(1986)

Bibliography

FALK, JEROME B., JR. 1973 The Supreme Court of California, 1971–1972—Foreword: The State Constitution: A More Than "Adequate" Nonfederal Ground. *California Law Review* 61:273–286.

ADKINS *v.* CHILDREN'S HOSPITAL
261 U.S. 525 (1923)

The *Adkins* case climaxed the assimilation of laissez-faire economics into constitutional law. At issue was the constitutionality of a congressional minimum wage law for women and children in the District of Columbia. (See DISTRICT OF COLUMBIA MINIMUM WAGE ACT.) The impact of the case was nationwide, affecting all similar state legislation. In the exercise of its police power over the District, Congress in 1918 established an administrative board with investigatory powers over wages and living standards for underprivileged, unorganized workers. After notice and hearing, the board could order wage increases by fixing minima for women and minors. The board followed a general standard set by the legislature: wages had to be reasonably sufficient to keep workers "in good health" and "protect their morals." A corporation maintaining a hospital in the District and a woman who had lost a job paying $35 a month and two meals daily claimed that the statute violated the Fifth Amendment's DUE PROCESS clause which protected their FREEDOM OF CONTRACT on terms mutually desirable.

The constitutionality of minimum wage legislation had come before the Court in STETTLER V. O'HARA (1917) but because Justice LOUIS D. BRANDEIS had disqualified himself, the Court had split evenly, settling nothing. In the same year, however, Professor FELIX FRANKFURTER won from the Court a decision sustaining the constitutionality of a state maximum hours law in BUNTING V. OREGON (1917). Although the Court sustained that law for men as well as for women and children, it neglected to overrule LOCHNER V. NEW YORK (1905). In that case the Court had held that minimum wage laws for bakers violated the freedom of contract protected by due process of law. Nevertheless, *Bunting* seemed to supersede *Lochner* and followed Justice OLIVER WENDELL HOLMES' *Lochner* dissent. The Court in *Bunting* presumed the constitutionality of the statute, disavowed examination of the legislature's wisdom in exercising its POLICE POWER, and asserted that the reasonableness of the legislation need not be proved; the burden of proving unreasonableness fell upon those opposed to the social measure.

Because *Bunting* superseded *Lochner* without overruling it, Frankfurter, who again defended the constitutionality of the statute, took no chances in *Adkins*. He relied on the principles of *Bunting*, the plenary powers of Congress over the District, and the overwhelmingly favorable state court precedents. In the main, however, he sought to show the reasonableness of the minimum wage law for women and children in order to rebut the freedom of contract DOCTRINE. In a BRANDEIS BRIEF, he proved the relation between the very low wages that had prevailed before the statute and the high incidences of child neglect, disease, broken homes, prostitution, and death.

A recent appointee, Justice GEORGE SUTHERLAND, spoke for the *Adkins* majority. Chief Justice WILLIAM HOWARD TAFT, joined by Justice EDWARD SANFORD, dissented also, separately. The vote was 5–3. Brandeis disqualified himself from participating because his daughter worked for the minimum wage board. Sutherland dismissed Frankfurter's brief with the comment that his facts were "interesting but only mildly persuasive." Such facts, said

Sutherland, were "proper enough for the consideration of lawmaking bodies, since their tendency is to establish the desirability or undesirability of the legislation; but they reflect no legitimate light upon the question of its validity, and that is what we are called upon to decide." The Court then found, on the basis of its own consideration of policy, that the statute was unwise and undesirable. Sutherland assumed that prostitution among the poor was unrelated to income. He claimed that the recently acquired right of women to vote had elevated them to the same status as men, stripping them of any legal protection based on sexual differences. That disposed of the 1908 ruling in MULLER V. OREGON. Consequently, women had the same right of freedom of contract as men, no more or less.

That freedom was not an absolute, Sutherland conceded, but this case did not fall into any of the exceptional categories of cases in which the government might reasonably restrict that freedom. Female elevator operators, scrubwomen, and dishwashers had a constitutional right to work for whatever they pleased, even if for less than a minimum prescribed by an administrative board. Employers had an equal right to pay what they pleased. If the board could fix minimum wages, employers might be forced to pay more than the value of the services rendered and might have to operate at a loss or even go out of business. By comparing the selling of labor with the selling of goods, Sutherland, ironically, supported the claim that capitalism regarded labor as a commodity on the open market. On such reasoning the Court found that the statute conflicted with the freedom of contract incorporated within the Fifth Amendment's due process clause. Paradoxically the Court distinguished away *Muller* and *Bunting* because they were maximum hours cases irrelevant to a case involving minimum wages, yet it relied heavily on *Lochner* as controlling, though it too was a maximum hours case. (See MAXIMUM HOURS AND MINIMUM WAGES.)

All this was too much for even that stalwart conservative, Chief Justice Taft, who felt bound by precedent to support the statute. Like Holmes, Taft perceived no difference in principle between a maximum hours law, which was valid, and a minimum wages law, which was not. Holmes went further. In addition to showing that both kinds of legislation interfered with freedom of contract to the same extent, he repudiated the freedom of conduct doctrine as he had in his famous *Lochner* dissent. He criticized the Court for expanding an unpretentious assertion of the liberty to follow one's calling into a far-reaching, rigid dogma. Like Taft, Holmes thought that *Bunting* had silently overruled *Lochner*. Both Taft and Holmes took notice of Frankfurter's evidence to make the point that the statute was not unreasonable. Holmes observed that it "does not compel anybody to pay anything. It simply forbids employment at rates below those fixed as the mini-

mum requirement of health and right living." Holmes also remarked that more than a women's suffrage amendment would be required to make him believe that "there are no differences between men and women, or that legislation cannot take those differences into account." Yet, the most caustic line in the dissenting opinions was Taft's: "it is not the function of this court to hold congressional acts invalid simply because they are passed to carry out economic views which the court believes to be unwise or unsound."

By this decision, the Court voided minimum wage laws throughout the country. Per curiam opinions based on *Adkins* disposed of state statutes whose supporters futilely sought to distinguish their administrative standards from the one before the Court in *Adkins*. Samuel Gompers, the leader of American trade unionism, bitterly remarked, "To buy the labor of a woman is not like buying pigs' feet in a butcher shop." A cartoon in the New York *World* showed Sutherland handing a copy of his opinion to a woman wage earner, saying, "This decision affirms your constitutional right to starve." By preventing minimum wage laws, the Court kept labor unprotected when the Depression struck. *Adkins* remained the law of the land controlling decisions as late as 1936; the Court did not overrule it until 1937. (See WEST COAST HOTEL V. PARRISH.)

LEONARD W. LEVY
(1986)

Bibliography

BERMAN, EDWARD 1923 The Supreme Court and the Minimum Wage. *Journal of Political Economy* 31:852–856.
POWELL, THOMAS REED 1924 The Judiciality of Minimum Wage Legislation. *Harvard Law Review* 37:545–573.

ADLER v. BOARD OF EDUCATION OF CITY OF NEW YORK
342 U.S. 485 (1952)

Adler was one of the cases in which state statutes barring members of "subversive" organizations from public school and other public employment were upheld against FIRST AMENDMENT attack on the basis that public employment is a privilege not a right. Most of these decisions were effectively overruled by KEYISHIAN V. BOARD OF REGENTS (1967).

MARTIN SHAPIRO
(1986)

(SEE ALSO: *Subversive Activity*.)

ADMINISTRATIVE AGENCIES

Administrative agencies, often called the "fourth branch," are entities of government that make decisions within particular substantive fields. Although these fields range over the full spectrum of public concern, the specificity of agencies' focus distinguishes them from other decision-making entities in the constitutional structure—the judiciary, the presidency, the Congress, indeed the individual citizen—each of which can be taken to have a scope of interest as broad as imagination will allow.

Agencies are perceived and known as such virtually without regard to their form or institutional location. They may be independent agencies—that is, not associated with any Article II executive department—which are generally administered by officials protected by law from the President's removal power. The Interstate Commerce Commission is such an agency, established over a century ago to decide entry, rates, and standards of service in the field of transportation. Alternatively, an agency may be found deep within an executive department, as the Food and Drug Administration is found within the Department of Health and Human Services. Or an agency may be identified with a cabinet officer in his or her capacity as administrator of a program. Agencies may have a handful of employees or they may have thousands. Large or small, they may speak through single individuals or through multimember collegial bodies, usually known as commissions.

The Administrative Procedure Act of 1946 serves as a second-level constitution for agencies of the federal government, specifying procedures and structural relations within and among them, and between them and other entities. But agencies are only presumptively subject to the Administrative Procedure Act—the Selective Service system, for example, has been exempted by Congress—and the act itself is in substantial part a restatement of the combination of COMMON LAW and constitutional law known as ADMINISTRATIVE LAW, which has been developing virtually since the beginning of the Republic in response to agencies' decision-making and enforcement activities.

Agencies have their origins as alternatives to Article III courts, making decisions in suits between individuals and to executive officials making decisions and seeking to enforce them in court suits. More recently agencies also have been seen as alternatives to decision making by legislative process through Congress and the President under Article I. Agencies have thus presented a difficulty for constitutional thinking under Articles I and III, arguably absorbing functions reserved to Congress, the President, and the judiciary. Agencies present a further difficulty under the due process clause of the Fifth Amendment when DUE PROCESS OF LAW is identified with legislative substance and court process.

The constitutional problem agencies pose has never reached any kind of closure. Instead, it has remained a tension in constitutional thought, unresolved because the creation and the maintenance of agencies have proceeded from inadequacies perceived in both legislative and judicial decision making.

Courts do not investigate or plan. Courts are not thought to display the resourcefulness of decision making committed to the achievement of a particular substantive end, such as workplace safety, nor the expertise of the specialists'. Courts other than the Supreme Court do not take initiative. There is widespread consensus, in fact, that courts should remain neutral and general. Moreover, the making of decisions in very large numbers of cases—those cases produced, for example, by disability benefit claims or the military draft—may be impeded by judicial process to the point that delay alone decides issues and legislated values are imperiled.

Congress also is not equipped to make any great number of particular decisions, and may be able to attend to a field of concern only at long intervals. Furthermore, where the unprecedented is faced, such as the discovery of radio waves or of nuclear energy, Congress often cannot do much more than define the field for decision. But legislators can foresee that failure to create a decision-making agency in the field effectively consigns the decisions of great public concern which will inevitably be made to individuals exercising powers under state laws of contract, property, and corporations.

Thus the existence and activity of agencies is rooted in felt necessity and is not the product of, or subject to, independent development of CONSTITUTIONAL THEORY. Nonetheless, SEPARATION OF POWERS, due process, and delegation concerns weave through determinations of internal agency structure and procedure made pursuant to statutes establishing particular agencies or under the Administrative Procedure Act. The same constitutional concerns underlie arrangement and rearrangement of the relations of the Judiciary, Congress, and the President to and through agencies. The concerns become acute and surface as explicit issues when Congress, seeking speed of decision or protection of an agency's initiative or planning, limits access to courts for review of agency decisions—partially or wholly precluding JUDICIAL REVIEW—or when the judiciary, for similar reasons, independently constricts STANDING to challenge an agency's action. The same concerns surface when Congress proves incapable of making even large choices of value within an agency's field of decision and again when the courts or Congress demand deference to agency choices of value—"deference," in this context, consisting of giving weight to what an agency says is the law because the agency says it. Constitutional questions constantly attend agency use of informal procedures in decision making. And constitutional questions both spark and restrain efforts by units within the office of the President, such as the OFFICE OF MANAGEMENT AND BUDGET, and by committees and individual members of Congress to intervene in an agency's consideration of issues. The LEGISLATIVE VETO, now disapproved on constitutional grounds, is only one of the means of congressional and executive involvement extending beyond formal participation in agency processes or the processes of judicial review.

The demands on agencies often press them to issue statements, characterized as rules, explicitly limiting the factors to be taken into account in a decision of a particular kind. These rules may govern decisions by the agency itself or by individuals and corporate bodies within the agency's field. In their formation some public participation may be allowed. Rule-making, if not peculiar to agencies, is characteristic of them, and agencies make rules whether or not explicitly authorized by statute to do so. But inasmuch as relevant factors for decision may then be excluded and decisions in particular cases may not be made on their full merits under the governing statutes, constitutional questions of due process are presented when individuals affected by such decisions challenge them. Here, too, justification is grounded in felt necessity, the acceptance of rough justice as preferable to the entire failure of justice. In addition, the crystallization of an agency rule is viewed as facilitating congressional reentry into a field through debate of defined issues leading to focused statutory amendments.

The demands on agencies to do what other governmental bodies are not equipped to do have also led to bureaucratic hierarchies within agencies. BUREAUCRACY raises the fundamental question of responsibility in decision making. The constitutional shadow is that of arbitrariness—the making of decisions by individuals within an agency who have not been delegated authority to make them or responsibility for them, and the enforcement of decisions that are not deliberately made but are rather the outcome of contending forces within and outside the agency. Congress and the courts have responded by establishing a body of administrative law judges, by requiring records of evidence and explanations of decisions, by requiring personal decision making (one constitutional formula is "the one who decides must hear"), and by prohibiting various kinds of EX PARTE contacts with agency decision makers. These responses to administrative bureaucracy have led in turn to fears that modern agencies may be overjudicialized as a result of attention to constitutional concerns.

The principal influence of administrative agencies on constitutional law is the impact of the form of legal thought they have generated, which has differed from conventional doctrine over a substantial period of American legal history. "Legality" in agency administration is not the correctness of an outcome but rather the proper taking of factors or values into account in the making of a decision.

There is little or no finality in administration: Decisions frequently remain open to revision and to justified reversal. There is no real distinction between agency action and agency inaction. The effects of agency decisions are examined and reexamined far beyond the bipolar limits of the judicial case. Values are routinely recognized—sometimes identified as noneconomic—to which no private claim can be made. In these respects, even though administrative law is evidently molded by constitutional concerns, administrative agencies may be considered seeds of anticonstitutional thought, for standard constitutional doctrine has maintained a markedly different structure of presuppositions and dichotomies. In judicial review of agencies the strong emphasis on the actualities of agency decision making, in contrast to acceptance of formal regularity in constitutional review of other decision-making bodies, contains further fundamental challenge. In large perspective, there is in administrative law a vision of agencies and courts joined with each other and with Congress in pursuit of evolving public values. This vision sits uneasily with an inherited vision, still alive in much constitutional thought, of government as invader of a private sphere of rights that it is the duty of courts to guard. The future of constitutional law will be guided in substantial part by the way these competing visions and modes of thought are integrated.

JOSEPH VINING
(1992)

(SEE ALSO: *Appointing and Removal Power, Presidential.*)

Bibliography

MASHAW, JERRY L. 1983 *Bureaucratic Justice.* New Haven, Conn.: Yale University Press.
STEWART, RICHARD B. and SUNSTEIN, CASS R. 1982 Public Programs and Private Rights. *Harvard Law Review* 95:1193–1322.
VINING, JOSEPH 1978 *Legal Identity: The Coming of Age of Public Law.* New Haven, Conn.: Yale University Press.

ADMINISTRATIVE AGENCIES
(Update)

Administrative agencies make government work. A statute that calls for government to provide benefits or to regulate the private sector will not achieve its goals unless a unit of government is given responsibility for implementing the statute. Such units are called administrative agencies. There are thousands of them in federal, state, and local governments.

Before undertaking to regulate the private sector, Congress or a state legislature must first determine that the problem is not being dealt with adequately by the market or through COMMON LAW litigation. Sometimes, regulation is the right answer—the private sector cannot handle certain problems (like deciding which of several applicants can telecast over Channel 4 or making sure that new drugs actually work or that doctors are qualified to practice medicine). But in other cases, private sector solutions work better than does government. Government bureaucracy can stifle initiative, and agencies can be captured by the bodies they are supposed to regulate. In those situations, we have recently seen a good deal of deregulation (for example, of railroad, trucking, and airline fares or stock brokerage fees).

A hypothetical regulatory statute will illustrate some of the choices that are available to policymakers. Suppose that Congress decides to regulate the naming of INTERNET sites because it finds that the problem is not being handled adequately by the private sector. It might enact a statute ("The Internet Act") containing various vague provisions on the problem of internet site names. Most important, the Internet Act will create the Internet Board to administer the statute and will define the board's powers.

The Internet Board might have a single agency head (as does the Food and Drug Administration (FDA)) or it might have several agency heads who must act collegially (as does the Securities and Exchange Commission (SEC)). The board would probably be organizationally located within an executive branch cabinet department, as the FDA is situated within the Department of Health and Human Services. A few agencies, such as the SEC, are independent, meaning that they are not within an executive branch department. Generally, the president cannot discharge the head of an independent agency without good cause.

What will the Internet Board actually do? The board might have several powers. It might be especially concerned with cybersquatters—people who register popular names for their website, such as IBM.com, hoping to sell the name to IBM once IBM discovers that the name is taken. Thus the board might investigate the problem of cybersquatters, either commissioning studies from experts or performing research itself. It might operate a registry of internet names (a task presently performed in the private sector). It might also have a staff of investigators and prosecutors to receive complaints about violations of the act and to investigate those complaints.

Next the board might adopt rules (or regulations—the two words mean the same thing). For example, the board might adopt a rule defining cybersquatting, providing that the board can strip a name from the squatter without compensating the squatter. If the Internet Act delegates rulemaking power to the Internet Board, the board's rules will have binding effect, just like statutes.

The Administrative Procedure Act (APA) requires all federal agencies to notify the general public and invite and consider their comments before adopting rules. The APA was passed in 1946. It is an important statute that governs all aspects of federal agency operations. All of the states have their own APAs, but generally local governments do not have APAs.

The hypothetical Internet Act may also delegate adjudicatory power to the Internet Board. Thus, if board investigators unearth a case of cybersquatting that violates its rules, it may take action against the squatter. For example, it may decide that Mary, who registered the name "IBM.com," is a cybersquatter and enter an order that strips her of that name without compensation and transfers it to IBM. In addition, it may penalize Mary by requiring her to pay a civil penalty either to IBM or to the government.

The Constitution provides that government cannot deprive anyone of life, liberty, or PROPERTY without DUE PROCESS OF LAW. The Fifth Amendment applies the due process clause to the federal government and the FOURTEENTH AMENDMENT applies it to state and local government. Due process would require the Internet Board to give notice and a fair trial-type hearing before it takes adjudicatory action against Mary. Thus she would be entitled to present witnesses and to the RIGHT OF CONFRONTATION of the witnesses against her. The APA supplements the requirements of due process; it contains detailed provisions that ensure impartial decisionmakers and fair administrative hearings.

The Internet Board's hearings probably would be conducted by administrative law judges (ALJs), board staff members whose only job would be to hear the board's cases and write proposed decisions. However, an ALJ would not make the final board decision; the head or heads of the board would make the final decision, based on the record of the hearing. They may agree or disagree with the ALJ's proposed decision.

JUDICIAL REVIEW OF ADMINISTRATIVE ACTS is important and extremely common. Courts scrutinize agency rules and orders to assure that they meet standards of legality, rationality, and fair procedure. Again, the APA provides the ground rules for judicial review.

One section of the APA is called the FREEDOM OF INFORMATION ACT (FOIA). It was first passed in 1966 and has been repeatedly amended. The most important part of FOIA is that any person has the right to demand that any agency give it any document in the agency's possession. FOIA has some narrowly defined exceptions, but most information possessed by government agencies must be disclosed on demand. FOIA is rigorously enforced by the federal courts.

Under our constitutional system, an administrative

agency shares power with each of the three branches. When it makes rules, it legislates in a way similar to enactments of laws by Congress. When it investigates and prosecutes violations of the rules, it enforces the law, much as would the President or a state governor. When it adjudicates cases, its actions resemble those of a court. For this reason, agencies are sometimes referred to as the fourth branch of government—a branch not provided for in the Constitution. Nevertheless, the Supreme Court long ago dispelled doubts about the power of Congress to delegate legislative and adjudicatory power to agencies. Administrative agencies are an essential element of modern government, which could not possibly function without them.

MICHAEL ASIMOW
(2000)

Bibliography

ASIMOW, MICHAEL; BONFIELD, ARTHUR EARL; and LEVIN, RONALD M. 1998 *State and Federal Administrative Law,* 2nd ed. St. Paul, Minn.: West Publishing Co.

DAVIS, KENNETH C. and PIERCE, RICHARD J. 1994 *Administrative Law Treatise,* 3rd ed. Boston, Mass.: Little Brown & Co.

STRAUSS, PETER L. 1981 *An Introduction to Administrative Justice in the United States.* Durham, N.C.: Carolina Academic Press.

ADMINISTRATIVE LAW

"Administrative law" describes the legal structure of much of the executive branch of government, particularly the quasi-independent agencies, and the procedural constraints under which they operate. Most of these constraints are statutory; those that do involve the Constitution flow chiefly from the doctrine of SEPARATION OF POWERS and the DUE PROCESS clause. To comprehend the effects of either of these on administrative law one must understand the growth of the administrative agency in the modern American state.

The early years of the twentieth century saw both a growth in the executive branch of the federal government and, perhaps more important, increased expectations about tasks it should perform. Some have seen these changes as a natural concomitant of industrialization; some as a growth in the power of a new professional class claiming to possess a nonpolitical expertise; some as the result of political pressure developed by farmers and small-town residents who looked to government to contain corporate juggernauts; some as the consequence of the desire of those very juggernauts to gain government sanction shielding them from the competitive forces of the marketplace. Whatever the causes, federal, state, and municipal governments took on new tasks in the closing decades of the nineteenth and the opening ones of the twentieth centuries.

Agencies such as the Interstate Commerce Commission, the Federal Trade Commission, the Food and Drug Administration, and the Federal Reserve Board bore witness to national perceptions that the existing economic and social mechanisms left something to be desired and that increased government intervention was the solution. At the local level the rise of social welfare agencies and zoning boards bespoke similar concerns.

With the coming of the Great Depression the federal government sought to revive the economy through numerous public programs designed both to coordinate sectors of the nation's industrial and commercial life (the WAGNER NATIONAL LABOR RELATIONS ACT, the AGRICULTURAL ADJUSTMENT ACT, the NATIONAL INDUSTRIAL RECOVERY ACT) and to create public jobs to reduce unemployment and increase consumer demand (the Civilian Conservation Corps, the Works Progress Administration, the Public Works Administration). Such agencies, generating regulations under the statutory umbrella of broad enabling legislation, came to be a standard feature on the American scene.

In a parallel development state governments created a number of agencies to coordinate and regulate everything from barbers to new car dealers, from avocado marketing to the licensing of physicians. Some of these boards appear to function chiefly as means of controlling entry into occupations and thereby shielding current practitioners from competition, but all function as branches of the government armed with at least some forms of regulatory power.

In some respects such state and national agencies represent not a new form of governmental power but a transfer to state and national levels of what had once been tasks of city government. The functioning of such municipal bureaucracies was, however, largely idiosyncratic and local—defined by the terms of the cities' charters and thus beyond the reach of national law. The migration of regulatory control from city to state and nation both enabled and necessitated the development of a new "administrative" law, which in America is almost entirely a creature of the twentieth century.

Most of that law is statutory, a function of the legislation that creates the board, agency, or commission and defines its tasks and powers. Citizens and enterprises wishing either to invoke or to challenge such powers use the statutorily specified procedures, which often involve both internal agency and external JUDICIAL REVIEW of administrative actions. At two points, however, the Constitution does speak to the structure and conduct of the agencies. In the formative years of the administrative state the Supreme Court expressed doubt about the place of the agency in the divided federal system of government. Since the NEW DEAL the constitutional focus has turned to the processes employed by administrative agencies, and the courts have regularly required agencies' procedures to conform to the due process clause.

The Constitution establishes three branches of the national government, and the courts early decided that no branch should exceed its own powers or intrude on areas designated as the province of another branch. This principle, known as the separation of powers, applies to numerous activities of the federal government, but it impinges particularly on the operation of administrative agencies charged with the formation and enforcement of broad federal policy.

Congress could not possibly specify just what tasks it wishes federal agencies to accomplish and also exactly how to perform them. At the opposite extreme it would just as obviously violate the separation of powers if Congress were to throw up its hands at the task of forming policy and instead direct the President to hit on whatever combination of revenue collection and expenditure he deemed best to fulfill the needs of the country. The concern is that Congress, if it asks an administrative agency not just to carry out defined tasks but also to participate in the formation of policy, has impermissibly given—delegated— its legislative power to the agency (a part of the executive branch).

That concern surfaced in a pair of Supreme Court decisions invalidating New Deal legislation. PANAMA REFINING CO. V. RYAN (1935) struck down a portion of the National Industrial Recovery Act that permitted the President to ban the interstate shipment of petroleum; the Court's ground was that Congress had provided no guidance as to when the President should do so or what aims were to justify the ban. A few months later, in SCHECHTER POULTRY CORP. V. UNITED STATES, the Court held unconstitutional another section of the same act; its DELEGATION OF POWER permitted the President to create codes of fair competition for various industries. Congress had defined neither the content of such codes nor the conditions for their proclamation, and some members of the Court evinced concern that the absence of standards could pave the way for what amounted to a governmentally sanctioned system of industrial cartels.

Since these two cases the Court has not invalidated a congressional delegation of power, but some have argued that the memory of these cases has induced the legislature to indicate more clearly the goals it intends the agency to accomplish, the means by which they are to be accomplished, and the processes that should accompany their implementation.

Even though an administrative agency does not perform tasks that constitutionally belong only to Congress,

it might nevertheless violate the constitutional structure of government by performing tasks belonging to the courts. The problem has several guises.

In some instances Congress in creating the agency has given it JURISDICTION that might otherwise have been exercised by the courts (for example, over maritime accidents). Did such congressional action, which could be viewed as a transfer of federal judicial jurisdiction to an agency, violate the constitutional structure of government or the rights of the parties? In *Crowell v. Benson* (1932) the Court concluded that if Congress established fair administrative procedures, the agency could hear and determine cases that might otherwise have been heard by the courts—with the saving proviso that the federal courts might review the agency's determination of questions of law.

That proviso pointed to another difficult question: the extent to which the courts might review agency decisions. Summarizing the history of this question, Louis Jaffe has said that we have moved from a nineteenth-century presumption of unreviewability to a twentieth-century presumption of reviewability. Such reviewability, however, flows from statutory interpretation rather than from constitutional compulsion: if Congress is sufficiently explicit, it can make an agency determination final and unreviewable—either because the statute explicitly says so or because it so clearly makes the decision in question a matter of agency discretion that there is no law to apply. For the most part, however, courts routinely scrutinize agency action for legality and at least minimal rationality and are prepared to give the agencies fairly great leeway in performing their tasks.

One measure of this leeway the agencies enjoy is the set of requirements imposed on litigants seeking to invoke federal judicial review of agency action. Such parties must satisfy the courts that they have STANDING (that is, actual injury caused by the agency action), that the dispute is ripe for judicial review (that is, that the case comes to the courts when it has sufficiently developed to render a judicial decision not merely abstract or hypothetical), and that they have exhausted their administrative remedies (that is, that they have sought such administrative redress as is available). Only the first two of these requirements— standing and RIPENESS—stem from the Constitution; all of them, however, condition the federal courts' exercise of judicial review.

Courts are prepared to grant such leeway, however, only to the extent that they are assured that the agency has complied with the requirements of due process in making its decisions. Due process plays two roles in administrative law. To the extent that agencies make rules only after extensive public participation in their deliberations, they address some of the concerns lying at the base of the delegation doctrine—ill-considered and hasty action. Due process also plays a second, more traditional role of assuring adjudicatory fairness. To the extent that agencies take action against those violating their rules, courts have often required that the agencies afford the violators various procedural protections.

Because an increasing number of Americans, from defense contractors and television broadcasters to mothers of dependent children and disabled veterans, depend on state and federal government for their livelihood, such protections have become increasingly important. In the second half of the twentieth century the courts have held many of those interests to be property, thus giving their holders the right to due process—sometimes including a FAIR HEARING—before suffering their deprivation. Thus state and federal agencies must give welfare recipients an opportunity to know and to contest factual findings before ending benefits; public schools and colleges have to supply students some form of NOTICE and process before suspending or expelling them; and public employers must grant tenured employees an opportunity to contest their dismissal. Courts have left the agencies some discretion as to the form of such procedures, which need not, for example, always include a hearing, but the process must suit the circumstances.

Because such protections flow from the due process clauses, they apply equally to state and to federal government; indeed, an important consequence of the constitutionalization of administrative process is that it has penetrated to state bureaucracies, some of which were perhaps less than exemplary in their concern for those affected by their actions. As a result both state courts and state legislatures have directed attention to the procedures of their agencies.

In a large sense, to understand the relationship of the administrative state to the Constitution, one has to spell constitution with a small "c," for the difficulties have been less with specific constitutional provisions than with the general picture of how executive action—especially action in new spheres—fits into received understandings of the world. That question is still debatable, but the debates, at least in the last half of the twentieth century, have taken place at the level of desirable policy, not of constitutional legality: so long as the agencies operate fairly, that much, apparently, is assured.

STEPHEN C. YEAZELL
(1986)

Bibliography

DAVIS, KENNETH C. 1978 *Administrative Law Treatise*. San Diego, Calif.: Davis.

JAFFE, LOUIS 1965 *Judicial Control of Administrative Action*. Boston: Little, Brown.

KOLKO, GABRIEL 1963 *The Triumph of Conservatism: A Reinterpretation of American History, 1900–1916*. New York: Free Press.

WIEBE, ROBERT 1967 *The Search for Order, 1877–1920*. New York: Hill & Wang.

ADMINISTRATIVE SEARCH

Safety inspections of dwellings by government officials, unlike police searches, are conducted to correct hazardous conditions rather than to secure EVIDENCE. Initially, therefore, the Supreme Court regarded such inspection as merely touching interests that were peripheral to the FOURTH AMENDMENT; the RIGHT OF PRIVACY of the householder must give way, even in the absence of a SEARCH WARRANT, to the interest in preserving a safe urban environment. *Frank v. Maryland* (1959) paradoxically granted greater protection under the Fourth Amendment to suspected criminals than to law-abiding citizens.

Later, the Court reversed itself in CAMARA V. MUNICIPAL COURT (1967), holding that the amendment was designed "to safeguard the privacy and security of individuals against arbitrary invasions by government officials," regardless of their purpose. However, because inspections would be crippled if the standard of proof needed for a warrant were the same as that required in a criminal case, the traditional PROBABLE CAUSE standard was discarded in favor of a flexible test based on the condition of the area and the time elapsed since the last inspection, rather than specific knowledge of the condition of the particular dwelling. After WYMAN V. JAMES (1971) WELFARE BENEFITS for support of a dependent child may be made conditional upon periodic visits to the home by a caseworker; a warrant is not required for such a visit.

The requirement of a warrant for inspections generally applies to business premises, as the Court held in *See v. City of Seattle* (1967). But in *Donovan v. Dewey* (1981) the Court held that coal mines, establishments dealing in guns and liquor, and other commercial properties that are comprehensively regulated by government may be inspected without a warrant, because an owner is obviously aware that his property will be subject to inspection.

JACOB W. LANDYNSKI
(1986)

Bibliography

LAFAVE, WAYNE R. 1967 Administrative Searches and the Fourth Amendment: The *Camara* and *See* Cases. *Supreme Court Review* 1967:2–38.

ADMINISTRATIVE SEARCH
(Update)

The Supreme Court has placed fewer checks on government searches pursuant to administrative schemes (health and safety inspections, for example) than it has placed on searches aimed at gathering evidence of criminal wrongdoing. Moreover, under current doctrine, government officials are less likely to need a SEARCH WARRANT for administrative searches of businesses than for similar searches of homes.

It is not at all obvious why this should be so. The FOURTH AMENDMENT, by its terms, protects people "in their persons, houses, papers, and effects, against unreasonable searches and seizures." The language of the amendment gives no indication that the reasonableness of a search should turn on whether the object of the search is evidence of a crime or of a safety code violation. Nor does it suggest that less protection is due papers and effects that are located in businesses rather than in homes. Nonetheless, the Supreme Court has shown a marked discomfort with the notions that safety inspections are to be subject to the same constitutional standard as criminal investigations and that businesses are entitled to the same protections as homes.

The Court first considered the administrative search in *Frank v. Maryland* (1959), holding that a homeowner could be arrested and fined for refusing a WARRANTLESS SEARCH of his home for health code violations. The majority made the remarkable assertion that the fundamental liberty interest at stake in the Fourth Amendment was the right to be free from searches for evidence to be used in criminal prosecutions, not a general RIGHT OF PRIVACY in one's home. The safety inspection, they said, touched "at most upon the peripery" of the interests protected by the Constitution. Justice WILLIAM O. DOUGLAS, writing for the four dissenters, argued that the Fourth Amendment was not designed to protect criminals only. He pointed out that, historically, much of the government action to which the Fourth Amendment was directed involved searches for violations of shipping regulations, not criminal investigations.

Justice Douglas was eventually vindicated, at least in part. CAMARA V. MUNICIPAL COURT (1967) held that Fourth Amendment protections do apply to administrative housing inspections and that such inspections require a warrant supported by PROBABLE CAUSE. While this is nominally the same standard as for criminal investigations, the Court explained that probable cause must itself depend upon a balancing of the need to search and the degree of invasion the search entails. To establish probable cause for administrative searches, government officials need satisfy only some reasonable legislative or administrative standard applicable to an entire area; they need not have specific information about a particular dwelling. The area warrant, as it is called, is thus based on a notion of probable cause very different from the traditional concept applicable in criminal cases. There is no probable cause for a search for evidence of a crime unless it is more likely than not that relevant evidence will be found at the specific dwelling searched. *See v. City of Seattle* (1967), the companion case to *Camara*, applied the area warrant requirement to the administrative inspection of businesses.

In arriving at its new balance for administrative searches, the *Camara* Court relied on three factors, none of which is wholly satisfactory. "First, [area inspections] have a long history of judicial and public acceptance." As an empirical matter, this statement was probably incorrect, as few of these cases had been to court, and none had previously made it to the Supreme Court. More important, the Court generally has found such historical justification insufficient to sustain government action that otherwise violates the Constitution.

"Second, the public interest demands that all dangerous conditions be prevented or abated, yet it is doubtful that any other canvassing technique would achieve acceptable results." Is the same not true of criminal law enforcement? Could government officials justify searching an entire block looking for a crack house on the theory that "[no] other canvassing technique would achieve acceptable results"? Surely not.

"Finally, because the inspections are neither personal in nature nor aimed at the discovery of evidence of crime, they involve a relatively limited invasion of the urban citizen's privacy." This reasoning has much in common with the majority's argument in *Frank*. Although the *Camara* language does support a more general right to privacy under the Fourth Amendment than *Frank* recognized, the Court apparently continues to see protection from unwarranted criminal investigation as more central to the amendment. Why this should be so remains a mystery; the individual's right to privacy and property protected by the Fourth Amendment should not vary according to the nature of the government's interest in the intrusion.

Another problem with the administrative search-criminal search distinction is that it is often difficult to tell one from the other. In many instances, health and safety regulations call for criminal penalties against offenders, and much administrative regulation of business is aimed at preventing criminal activity. A case in point is *New York v. Burger* (1987). When two police officers arrived to conduct an administrative inspection of Burger's automobile junkyard, Burger was unable to produce the required license and records. Proceeding without the traditional quantum of probable cause for a criminal investigation, the officers searched the yard and uncovered stolen vehicles, evidence used against Burger in a subsequent criminal prosecution. The Court held that the evidence could be used against Burger as the fruit of a valid administrative search, notwithstanding that the regulatory scheme was directed at deterring criminal behavior. By way of explanation, the Court offered a rather confusing distinction between administrative schemes, which set forth rules for the conduct of a business, on the one hand, and criminal laws, which punish individuals for specific acts of behavior, on the other.

The diminished safeguards applicable to administrative searches have been further eroded in cases involving businesses. Although *See* applied the area warrant requirement equally to searches of businesses and searches of homes, the Court has subsequently elaborated a distinction between the two. *Burger* is the present culmination of that line of cases. In *Burger*, not only was the search conducted with less than traditional probable cause, but the police officers did not have a warrant.

The Court began its move away from the *See* warrant requirement in *Colonnade Catering Corporation v. United States* (1970), where it upheld a conviction for turning away a warrantless inspection of a liquor storeroom. *United States v. Biswell* (1972) allowed a warrantless search of a gun dealer's storeroom. *Biswell* made it clear that the balancing approach of *Camara* and *See* would be applied not only in determining the quantum of probable cause necessary to support a warrant but also in deciding whether a warrant was necessary at all. In *Biswell* the Court argued that the effectiveness (and hence reasonableness) of the firearm inspection scheme depended on "unannounced, even frequent, inspections," which a warrant requirement could frustrate. No doubt we could reduce crime of all sorts if police were allowed to make "unannounced, even frequent, inspections" of everyone's home and business.

In addition to the familiar balancing approach, *Colonnade* and *Biswell* introduced another element into administrative search jurisprudence. The Court excused the warrant requirement, in part because those engaging in "closely regulated businesses," such as liquor vendors and firearms dealers, have a reduced expectation of privacy.

The Court at first seemed to limit the reach of *Colonnade* and *Biswell*, explaining in MARSHALL V. BARLOW'S, INC. (1978) that the closely regulated business exception to the warrant requirement was a narrow one. *Barlow's* established an area warrant requirement for searches pursuant to the federal Occupational Safety and Health Act, which applies to a wide range of businesses not necessarily subject to extensive government regulation.

The closely regulated exception returned, however, in *Donovan v. Dewey* (1981), which allowed warrantless inspection of mines pursuant to the federal Mine Safety and Health Act. The Court also returned to a balancing approach. Quoting *Biswell*, the Court stressed the need for unannounced and frequent inspection of mines, where "serious accidents and unhealthful working conditions" are "notorious."

In *Burger*, the most recent business search case, the Court summarized its case law and brought together the closely regulated and balancing approaches. Administrative searches of closely regulated businesses may be made without a warrant if three criteria are met: (1) there is a substantial government interest that informs the regulatory scheme; (2) warrantless inspections are necessary to further the regulatory scheme; and (3) the inspection program is of sufficient certainty and regularity as to limit the discretion of the inspecting officer and advise the business owner that the search is within the scope of the regulatory law.

Despite this latest attempt to refine the exception to the warrant requirement, the closely regulated distinction remains troubling. In essence, it is a form of implied consent theory: By voluntarily engaging in certain businesses, or seeking government licenses, business owners have agreed to give up a measure of their privacy. This line of reasoning is in apparent conflict with the doctrine of UN-CONSTITUTIONAL CONDITIONS, where the Court, in other cases, has frowned upon the conditioning of government privileges on the surrendering of a constitutional right. There is indeed something anomalous in the notion that the government, by its own intrusive actions, can create a reduced expectation of privacy.

ALEX KOZINSKI
(1992)

(SEE ALSO: *Reasonable Expectation of Privacy; Search and Seizure.*)

Bibliography

KRESS, JACK M. and IANNELLI, CAROLE D. 1986 Administrative Search and Seizure: Whither the Warrant? *Villanova Law Review* 31:705–832.

LAFAVE, WAYNE R. 1987 *Search and Seizure: A Treatise on the Fourth Amendment.* St. Paul, Minn.: West Publishing Co.

ADMIRALTY AND MARITIME JURISDICTION

In Article III of the Constitution, the JUDICIAL POWER OF THE UNITED STATES is made to extend "to all cases of admiralty and maritime jurisdiction." ALEXANDER HAMILTON says, in THE FEDERALIST #80, that "the most bigotted idolizers of State authority have not thus far shown a disposition to deny the national judiciary the cognizance of maritime causes." There is no reason not to believe him. The First Congress, in the JUDICIARY ACT OF 1789, gave this JURISDICTION to the UNITED STATES DISTRICT COURTS, which were to have "exclusive original cognizance of all civil causes of admiralty and maritime jurisdiction, saving to suitors, in all cases, the right of a COMMON LAW remedy, where the common law is competent to give it."

This language was verbally changed in the JUDICIAL CODE of 1948, but the change has had no effect, and was pretty surely not meant to have any, so that one may organize the subject (as it has, indeed, organized itself) around the two questions suggested by the original formula: (1) What is the content of the "exclusive cognizance" given the District Court? and (2) What is "saved" to suitors in the saving clause?

There is an admiralty jurisdiction in "prize"—a jurisdiction to condemn and sell, as lawful prize of war, enemy vessels and cargo. This jurisdiction was employed to effect a few condemnations after WORLD WAR II, but it has on the whole been very little used in this century. There is an admiralty jurisdiction over crime, but the admiralty clause serves in these cases solely as a firm theoretical foundation for American jurisdiction over certain crimes committed outside the country but on navigable waters; these cases are rarely thought of as "admiralty" cases, because INDICTMENT and trial are "according to the course of the common law," with such statutory and rule-based changes as affect all federal criminal proceedings. Normally, then, "admiralty jurisdiction" refers to jurisdiction over certain private-law concerns affecting the shipping industry—contracts to carry goods, charters of ships, marine insurance, ship collisions, seamen's or passengers' personal injuries, salvage, and so on.

The courts early followed the English rule limiting the jurisdiction to tidal waters, but a rather tortuous development around the middle of the nineteenth century extended this base to include first, the Great Lakes, then the Mississippi River, and at last all interior waters navigable in INTERSTATE or FOREIGN COMMERCE.

There was an early effort, moreover, to limit the jurisdiction to causes very strictly "arising" on these waters. Suits in marine insurance, for example, were thought to be outside the jurisdiction, because the contracts were made on land, and were to be performed (by payment) on land. On the other hand, some quite late cases extended the admiralty jurisdiction to events having no maritime flavor (e.g., an injury to a bather by a surfboard), on the basis of this same "locality" test. This "test," productive of ludicrous results, has often been abjured by the courts, but has a way of popping up again and again, in context after context.

The "saving clause" has been given an interpretation not at all of obvious correctness. The "common-law remedy" saved to suitors was held to comprise all IN PERSONAM causes of action. Thus, if a shipowner's ship is lost, and he claims indemnity from the insurance company, he is free to sue either in admiralty court or in a regular land-based court—and so on through the whole range of admiralty matters. What is *not* "saved to suitors," and is therefore really "exclusive" to the District Courts, is the suit IN REM, wherein a vessel, or other maritime property, is treated as the defendant party, and sued directly under its own name. In practice, this means that the plaintiff (or "libellant," as he used to be called) enjoys a high-priority security interest in the vessel, an interest called a "maritime lien."

The intricacies of admiralty procedure have been simplified in recent years. But one dominating peculiarity remains. Like EQUITY, admiralty (usually) does not use the jury. This fact is normally determinative of the plaintiff's choice, made under the "saving clause," between the admiralty forum and the land-bound court of law.

CHARLES L. BLACK, JR.
(1986)

Bibliography

GILMORE, GRANT and BLACK, CHARLES L., JR. 1975 *Admiralty*, 2nd ed. Mineola, N.Y.: Foundation Press.
ROBERTSON, DAVID W. 1970 *Admiralty and Federalism*. Mineola, N.Y.: Foundation Press.

ADOPTION, RACE, AND THE CONSTITUTION

Since Massachusetts enacted the first "modern" state adoption statute in 1851, adoption in the United States has been both a state judicial process and a child welfare service to promote the "best interests" of children in need of permanent homes. State law and adoption agency practices have traditionally tried to mirror biology; same-race placements simply were presumed to serve a child's "best interests."

The Supreme Court in MEYER V. NEBRASKA (1923) deemed the guarantee of liberty in the FOURTEENTH AMENDMENT to include the right "to marry, establish a home, and bring up children," and subsequently rendered decisions defining various elements of family relations as "fundamental interests." Yet, it has not recognized a fundamental interest in adopting children.

During the latter half of the twentieth century, legal access to ABORTION and lessening social stigma associated with NONMARITAL CHILDREN resulted in dramatically fewer voluntary relinquishments of white infants—what most prospective adopters initially seek. Instead, waiting children often had special needs, were older or minority children, or were part of large sibling groups who did not "match-up" with approved waiting families. A disproportionate number of these children were African American who remained in foster care longer periods of time than other children due to a shortage of approved African American homes.

Since the mid-1970s, two paradigm shifts in the adoption field set the stage for successful efforts in the 1990s to ban "same-race" placement preferences. First, the primary focus shifted from promoting the interests of children in need of homes to an emphasis on serving adults who seek to parent. Second, lawyers asserting rights of their clients to adopt any child were often the dominant professionals instead of social workers. Adoption was increasingly seen not solely as a specialized child-welfare service, but as a profitable business venture buoyed by a strong demand for babies of all colors. Legal scholars claimed that, in addition to frustrating the market for babies, statutory "same-race" placement preferences harmed African American children in violation of the EQUAL PROTECTION guarantee of the Fourteenth Amendment.

Because most forms of RACIAL DISCRIMINATION are unconstitutional and all racial criteria are subject to STRICT SCRUTINY, the question of what weight to give race in granting or denying adoption is a sensitive issue. According to Twila Perry, it has evoked acrimonious debate "between those who view transracial placements as positive for both the children and society as a whole and those who view them as injurious to Black children and Black communities." Some lower courts have held that using race as the sole factor in denying adoption or in placing children in foster homes violates the equal protection clause. Other courts, such as the District of Columbia Court of Appeals, in *Petition of R.M.G.* (1983), have ruled that race may be one of the relevant factors in a disputed adoption proceeding and that a court may consider how each contestant's race is likely to affect the child's development.

But the Supreme Court's 1984 decision in PALMORE V. SIDOTI (a suit by a white father seeking custody of his daughter because the custodial mother lived with and then married a black man) casts considerable doubt on the position taken in the *R.M.G.* case. In *Palmore* the Court recognized that racial and ethnic prejudices exist and might pose problems for a child living with a stepparent of a different race. Yet, the Court ruled that such problems could not justify a denial of constitutional rights nor the removal of the child from the custody of her mother. As Homer Clark, Jr., concluded, "fairly read, the opinion may be construed to say that the impact on a child caused by

living in a mixed race household . . . is not a factor which the Constitution permits the courts to take into account."

Ten years after *Palmore*, state court judicial challenges to "same-race" placement preference practices and aggressive lobbying of Congress resulted in federal legislation that eviscerates adoption's traditional emphasis on the "best interests" of the child in favor of race matching. Those dissatisfied with Senator Howard Metzenbaum's 1994 MultiEthnic Placement Act criticized the latitude given agencies and courts to consider cultural or racial identity needs of a child and a prospective foster or adoptive parent's ability to meet those needs. But those same people applauded the law's 1996 repeal by LEGISLATION that absolutely banned consideration of race in child placement decisionmaking.

Under the 1996 law, no state or other entity in a state receiving federal funds and involved in adoption or foster care may (1) deny any person the opportunity to become an adoptive or a foster parent; or (2) delay or deny the placement of a child for adoption or into foster care, on the basis of the race, color, or national origin of the adoptive or foster parent, or the child involved. Noncompliance is a violation of Title VI of the CIVIL RIGHTS ACT OF 1964, and financial penalties may result. Additionally, any individual aggrieved by a state's or other entity's violation may seek relief in any U.S. District Court.

Some view the claim that "same-race" placement preferences victimize the increasing numbers of African American children entering foster care as a diversionary "smokescreen" strategy. These observers emphasize the systemic barriers to meeting the needs of African American children, their families, and the African American community. They also point out that eliminating race from placement decisionmaking opens up a new source of infants to satisfy the demands of waiting white applicants, given the increasing numbers of voluntarily relinquished, biracial, nonmarital children (many with one black and one white parent) that historically have been assigned the racial designation of "Black."

RUTH-ARLENE W. HOWE
(2000)

Bibliography

BARTHOLET, ELIZABETH 1991 Where Do Black Children Belong? The Politics of Race Matching in Adoption. *University of Pennsylvania Law Review* 139:1163–1256.

CLARK, JR., HOMER H. 1988 Race and Religion in Adoption Placement. Pages 912–915 in *The Law of Domestic Relations in the United States*, 2nd ed. St. Paul, Minn.: West Publishing Co.

HOWE, RUTH-ARLENE W. 1995 Redefining the Transracial

Adoption Controversy. *Duke Journal of Gender Law & Policy* 2:131–164.

—— 1997 Transracial Adoption (TRA): Old Prejudices and Discrimination Float Under a New Halo. *Boston University Public Interest Law Journal* 6:409–472.

PERRY, TWILA L. 1993–1994 The Transracial Adoption Controversy: An Analysis of Discourse and Subordination. *New York University Review of Law & Social Change* 21:33–108.

ADVERSARY TRIAL

See: Rights of the Criminally Accused

ADVERTISING

See: Commercial Speech

ADVICE AND CONSENT

Under Article II, section 2, of the Constitution, the President's powers to make treaties and to appoint important public officials are to be exercised "by and with the advice and consent of the SENATE."

The formula "advice and consent" is an ancient one. It was used in British and American state papers and documents for over a thousand years prior to 1787. The use of these words in the Constitution was proposed by the Constitutional Convention's Committee on Remaining Matters, to which both the TREATY POWER and the APPOINTING POWER had been referred. The first proposal to associate the President and the Senate in the exercise of those powers was made by ALEXANDER HAMILTON, who wanted the Senate to act as a kind of PRIVY COUNCIL. In the debates over RATIFICATION OF THE CONSTITUTION opponents charged that the provision violated the principle of SEPARATION OF POWERS. But in THE FEDERALIST the practice was defended as an instance of CHECKS AND BALANCES and a means of involving the states in the making of important national policy.

In practice, the phrase "advice and consent" has come to have different meanings with respect to the two powers to which it is applied.

In the making of treaties, the advisory function has virtually disappeared. In August 1789, President GEORGE WASHINGTON sought to honor the letter of the Constitution by appearing in person before the Senate to ask its advice prior to negotiating an Indian treaty. When the Senate referred the matter to a committee, Washington walked out, and since that incident, no President has made such a formal request for advice in advance. The common modern practices by which Presidents include senators among American negotiators and consult with influential senators, the party leadership, and members of the Senate Foreign Relations Committee are better understood as political devices to improve the chances of obtaining consent than as deference to the constitutional mandate to obtain advice. In giving its consent to the President's making—or ratification—of a treaty, the Senate is not bound to accept or reject the whole document as submitted. The Senate may amend a treaty or attach reservations to it. Since either of these actions may compel renegotiation, they might be considered perverse forms of giving advice.

In the appointment of officers, the advisory function has become far more important. Nominees to the Supreme Court and to the most important executive and diplomatic posts are normally approved (or rejected) by the Senate on grounds of merit, integrity, and policy. In the case of other executive and judicial appointments, a practice known as "senatorial courtesy" has transformed the requirement for "advice and consent" into an instrument of senatorial control. Nominees cannot expect the Senate's consent to their appointment if it is not supported by senators of the President's party from their home states. If a federal appointee is to serve in a particular state, the senior senator of the President's party from that state (if there is one) customarily makes the actual selection.

DENNIS J. MAHONEY
(1986)

(SEE ALSO: *Advice and Consent to Supreme Court Nominations; Bork Nomination.*)

ADVICE AND CONSENT TO SUPREME COURT NOMINATIONS

The proper scope of the SENATE's role in confirming Supreme Court nominees has been the subject of recurring and often heated debate. The Constitution provides simply that the President "shall nominate, and by and with the advice and consent of the Senate, shall appoint ... Judges of the Supreme Court." Although the Senate also has the constitutional responsibility of advising on and consenting to presidential appointments of ambassadors, lower federal court judges, and many executive branch officials, debates over the nature of the Senate's role have generally arisen in the context of Supreme Court nominations.

The central issues of controversy have concerned the criteria the Senate should consider in making confirmation decisions and the appropriate range of questions that may be posed to and answered by a nominee. Debated points regarding appropriate criteria for confirmation have included the degree to which the Senate should defer to the President's preferred choice and whether it is appropriate to take a nominee's political views or judicial philosophy into account. The debate about the scope of questioning has centered on whether it is appropriate for senators to ask and nominees to answer questions about the nominee's political views and judicial philosophy and how these views and philosophy would apply to issues that may come before the Court.

Presidents and some members of the Senate have argued that selecting Justices is the President's prerogative and that, although the President may take a judicial prospect's philosophy into account, the Senate must limit its inquiry to whether the nominee has the basic qualifications for the job. These commentators maintain that the Senate should defer to the President's nomination of any person who is neither corrupt nor professionally incompetent. Others have contested this view and argued that the Senate, when it decides whether to consent to a nomination, is permitted to take into account the same range of considerations open to the President and to make its own independent determination of whether confirmation of a particular nominee is in the best interests of the country.

Presidents have often taken the position that the Senate should defer to the President's choice. President RICHARD M. NIXON, for example, claimed in 1971 that the President has "the constitutional responsibility to appoint members of the Court," a responsibility that should not be "frustrated by those who wish to substitute their own philosophy for that of the one person entrusted by the Constitution with the power of appointment." This view was echoed by President RONALD REAGAN, who asserted that the President has the "right" to "choose federal judges who share his judicial philosophy" and that the Senate should confirm Presidents' nominees "so long as they are qualified by character and competence."

Many of those who agree with Presidents Nixon and Reagan believe that the proper standard for Senate review of Supreme Court nominees is the deferential standard that the Senate has typically accorded to presidential nominations of executive officials, whose confirmation is generally expected unless the nominee is found to lack the character or competence necessary for the job. This analogy between executive and judicial appointments is not wholly apt. Whereas the President is entitled to have in the executive branch officials who share the President's philosophy and will carry out the chief executive's policies, judicial nominees are expected to exercise independent judgment. Those favoring a more active Senate role in the judicial confirmation process suggest that the proper analogy is to the Senate's role in ratifying or rejecting treaties or to the President's decision to sign or veto legislation—

instances in which an independent exercise of judgment by each branch is thought appropriate.

The consideration of the APPOINTMENTS CLAUSE by the CONSTITUTIONAL CONVENTION OF 1787 offers some support for the position that senators should exercise their own independent judgment about whether to confirm a nominee. The convention considered the issue of judicial appointments separately from its consideration of the appointment of executive officers. For much of the summer of 1787, the evolving drafts of the Constitution gave the Senate exclusive authority to appoint judges. Suggestions for giving the appointing authority to the President alone rather than to the Senate were soundly defeated.

On May 29, 1787, the convention began its work on the Constitution by taking up the VIRGINIA PLAN, which provided "that a National Judiciary be established . . . to be chosen by the National Legislature. . . ." Under this plan, the executive was to have no role at all in the selection of judges. When this provision came before the Convention on June 5, several members expressed concern that the whole legislature might be too numerous a body to select judges. JAMES WILSON's alternative providing that the President be given the power to choose judges found almost no support, however. JOHN RUTLEDGE of South Carolina stated that he "was by no means disposed to grant so great a power to any single person." JAMES MADISON agreed that the legislature was too large a body, but stated that "he was not satisfied with referring the appointment to the Executive." He was "rather inclined to give it to the Senatorial branch" as being "sufficiently stable and independent to follow their deliberate judgments."

One week later on June 13, Madison rendered his inclination into a formal motion that the power of appointing judges be given exclusively to the Senate rather than to the legislature as a whole. This motion was adopted without objection. On July 18 the convention reconsidered and reaffirmed its earlier decision to grant the Senate the exclusive power of appointing judges. James Wilson again moved "that the Judges be appointed by the Executive." His motion was defeated, six states to two, after delegates offered, as GUNNING BEDFORD of Delaware said, "solid reasons against leaving the appointment to the Executive." LUTHER MARTIN of Maryland, stating that he "was strenuous for an appointment by the 2nd branch," argued that "being taken from all the States [the Senate] would be the best informed of character and most capable of making a fit choice." ROGER SHERMAN of Connecticut concurred, "adding that the Judges ought to be diffused, which would be more likely to be attended to by the 2d branch, than by the Executive." NATHANIEL GORHAM of Massachusetts argued against exclusive appointment by the Senate, stating that "public bodies feel no personal responsibility, and give full play to intrigue and cabal." He offered what was to be the final compromise: appointment by the Executive "by and with the advice and consent" of the Senate. At this point in the convention, however, his motion failed on a tie vote.

The issue was considered once again on July 21. After a debate in which GEORGE MASON attacked the idea of executive appointment as a "dangerous prerogative [because] it might even give him an influence over the Judiciary department itself," the convention once again reaffirmed exclusive Senate appointment of judges of the Supreme Court. Thus the matter stood until the closing days of the convention. On September 4, less than two weeks before the convention's work was done, a committee of five reported out a new draft providing for the first time for a presidential role in the selection of judges: "The President . . . shall nominate and by and with the advice and consent of the Senate shall appoint Judges of the Supreme Court." Giving the President the power to nominate judges was not seen as tantamount to ousting the Senate from a central role. GOUVERNEUR MORRIS of Pennsylvania, a member of the Committee, paraphrased the new provision as one that retained in the Senate the power "to appoint Judges nominated to them by the President." With little discussion and without dissent, the Convention adopted this as the final language of the provision. Considering that the convention had repeatedly and decisively rejected any proposal to give the President exclusive power to select judges, it is unlikely that the drafters contemplated reducing the Senate's role to a ministerial one.

During the nineteenth century, the Senate took a broad view of the appropriate criteria to govern "advice and consent" decisions. During this period, the Senate rejected more than one of every four Supreme Court nominations. The Senate first rejected President GEORGE WASHINGTON's nomination of John Rutledge. The Senate went on to reject five of the nominees proposed by President JOHN TYLER and three of the four nominees put forward by President MILLARD FILLMORE. Since 1900, however, the rate of senatorial rejection of Supreme Court nominees has dropped sharply to a twentieth-century rejection rate of a mere one in thirteen.

Virtually all the parties to the twentieth-century debate on appropriate confirmation criteria agree on two threshold issues. The first is that it is appropriate for senators to consider "judicial fitness." No one contests that adequate judicial competence, ethics, and temperament are necessary conditions for confirmation and, therefore, appropriate criteria for senators to consider. The publicly stated bases of opposition to the nominations of LOUIS D. BRANDEIS, Judge Clement F. Haynsworth, and Judge George H. Carswell were presented in terms of these threshold, judicial-fitness criteria.

The unsuccessful opposition to Brandeis, nominated in 1916 by President WOODROW WILSON, based its public case against the nominee on alleged breaches of legal ethics. The successful opposition to confirmation of Judge Haynsworth, nominated to the Supreme Court by President Nixon in 1969, was articulated primarily in terms of charges that Haynsworth had violated canons of judicial ethics by sitting on cases involving corporations in which he had small financial interests. In addition to the ethics charges, some opponents raised objections to Haynsworth's CIVIL RIGHTS record. Two judicial-fitness objections formed the basis for the successful opposition to confirmation of Judge Carswell, nominated to the Supreme Court by President Nixon in 1970. The primary objection was that Carswell allegedly allowed racial prejudice to affect his judicial behavior. The second theme in the opposition to Carswell was that, as a matter of basic competence, he was at best a mediocre jurist.

Thus, in the Brandeis, Haynsworth, and Carswell nominations, opposition was presented as based on the judicial-fitness criteria of judicial temperament, ethics, and basic competence. In all three of these twentieth-century confirmation controversies, the acceptability of the judicialfitness criteria went unchallenged.

The second area of general agreement in the debate on appropriate criteria for confirmation decisions is that senators should not base their decisions on the nominee's predicted vote on a particular case or "single issue" likely to come before the Court. Supporters of the nomination of Judge John Parker, nominated to the Supreme Court by President HERBERT HOOVER in 1930, alleged that opposition to the nomination was based on a "single issue" of Parker's position on a particular labor-law question. Parker's opponents took pains to deny that their opposition was based on a single issue and argued that Parker's ruling in a previous case involving the question reflected Parker's own anti-union bias. This accusation—that, as a judge, Parker was biased in his rulings on such matters— was a way for the opponents of confirmation to frame their objection as one of judicial temperament and, thus, judicial fitness. The premise underlying the positions of both opponents and supporters of Parker was that a rejection based on a result-oriented single-issue criterion would be inappropriate.

Between the margins of agreement that judicial-fitness criteria are appropriate and that single-issue criteria are inappropriate lies the area of controversy. The debated issue is often framed as whether the nominee's "judicial philosophy" should be considered in the decision-making process. The term "judicial philosophy," when used in this context, refers to a range of concerns including the nominee's theory of judging (that is, the degree of judicial interference with legislative and executive decision making the nominee views as appropriate), the nominee's views on the level of generality at which constitutional provisions should be interpreted, and the nominee's interpretation of specific constitutional clauses or doctrines (such as the applicability of the EQUAL PROTECTION clause to women or the existence of a constitutional RIGHT OF PRIVACY).

The bases of opposition to President LYNDON B. JOHNSON's 1968 nomination of Justice ABE FORTAS (to be Chief Justice) and to President Reagan's nomination of Judge Robert Bork to the Supreme Court were framed largely in terms of these controversial "judicial philosophy" criteria. Consequently, the confirmation battles in these cases raged as much around the appropriateness of the criteria applied as around the merits of the nominees themselves.

The attack on Fortas's judicial philosophy was based on charges that he was a "judicial activist" (meaning that his theory of judging envisioned excessive intervention in the discretion of the elected branches) and that his substantive interpretations (of the First, Fifth, Sixth, and Fourteenth amendments) were flawed. Supporters of the Fortas nomination responded both on the merits—defending Fortas's theory of judging and his substantive interpretations—and by assailing the judicial philosophy criterion as inappropriate considerations for advice and consent decisions. (Although some ethics charges were raised during the confirmation proceedings, the very serious ethics charges that resulted in Fortas's resignation did not arise until the spring of 1969, during the Nixon presidency, many months after President Johnson had withdrawn his nomination of Justice Fortas to become Chief Justice.)

Like the Fortas nomination, the nomination of Judge Robert Bork to the Supreme Court was opposed largely on judicial philosophy grounds. (Although some critics raised ethics issues, including Bork's role in the "Saturday Night Massacre" in which the special prosecutor in the WATERGATE affair was fired, these issues did not form a primary basis of opposition.) Judge Bork's theory of judging was assailed as an inadequate conception of the proper role of the Supreme Court in protecting individual and "unenumerated" constitutional rights. Objections were also presented in terms of Bork's interpretations of specific constitutional clauses and doctrines, including his position on the existence of a constitutional right to privacy, his previous and contemporaneous interpretations of the equal protection clause as regards the protections afforded to women, his interpretations of the FIRST AMENDMENT's free speech clause, and his positions on civil rights. Much of the defense of Judge Bork took the form of challenging the acceptability of these controversial criteria.

The contours of the areas of agreement and disagreement on appropriate advice-and-consent criteria are not surprising. The debate on appropriate criteria follows from the constitutional provisions that structure the process of appointments to an independent, principle-oriented, countermajoritarian judiciary in a way that requires the consent of an elected, representative, majoritarian body. Senators' views about the proper role of the judiciary inform their positions on the relevance and propriety of each category of advice-and-consent criteria.

A foundational precept of the role of an independent judiciary is that judges must render decisions based on the rigorous application of principles, not their personal preferences, much less their biases. The broad agreement about this precept underlies and is reflected in the broad consensus that judicial fitness is an acceptable category of criteria for consent decisions. Competence in legal reasoning, high ethical standards, and unbiased judicious temperament are prerequisites to the consistent rendering of rigorously reasoned and principled decisions of law.

The same precept—that the essence of the judicial function is to render decisions based on principles—underlies the broad consensus that single-issue result-oriented criteria are unacceptable. Because of the principle-based nature of the judicial function, a judicial nominee must be evaluated on the basis of the anticipated process of his or her application of principles, regardless of whether that process will produce a senator's preferred outcome in any particular case. The ability of elected Presidents and elected senators to exert some general influence on the future course of the nation's jurisprudence is an appropriate (and appropriately limited) popular check on the exercise of the power of JUDICIAL REVIEW, without which this institution might not be acceptable in a constitutional democracy. Nonetheless, for Presidents or senators to demand that the judiciary not render decisions based on principle but, rather, act as an agent of the legislature furthering particular preferences, and for senators to enforce this demand by the threat or reality of nonconfirmation, would subvert the independence of the judiciary and violate the spirit of the SEPARATION OF POWERS.

Rather than a continued focus on the appropriate criteria for advice-and-consent decisions, a different aspect of the debate over the appropriate role of the Senate in the confirmation process came to the fore during consideration of the nomination of Justice DAVID H. SOUTER. Souter's views on controversial judicial and political issues were little known. The prominent questions during the Souter confirmation, therefore, were (1) where relatively little is known about the nominee's thinking, how may the Senate properly learn more about the nominee; and (2) what questions may properly be posed to the nominee during the confirmation hearings? These questions are not merely derivative of the larger question of what decision-making criteria are legitimate. The core objection to direct questions to the nominee—even on issues that might constitute legitimate decision-making criteria, such as substantive interpretation of particular constitutional clauses—is that, by offering an opinion on such issues, the nominee may thereafter feel bound to hold in subsequent cases in a manner consistent with the opinions stated during the confirmation hearings. Thus, the fear is that the nominee who opines on, say, the level of protection afforded to women by the equal protection clause during the confirmation hearing will, in effect, be "committed" to a certain outcome in future cases involving that issue.

But fear of judicial precommitment may be exaggerated. Surely there is no requirement that the individuals nominated to our highest court have never thought about—or reached tentative conclusions on—the important issues of law that face the country. So the only issue is whether sharing those thoughts with the senators during confirmation hearings would constitute a commitment not to change those views or not to be open to the arguments of parties litigating those issues in the future. There is no reason to believe that a statement of opinion during confirmation would constitute such a commitment. It would seem reasonable to suppose that an opinion mentioned during a confirmation hearing would be seen as not binding if it were generally understood that such statements are not binding. It would seem reasonable that a nominee might preface an opinion on such an issue with a statement that "these are my initial views on the issue, but they would certainly be open to change in the context of a case in which persuasive arguments were put forth by the parties." Justices would not be in any way committed to be "consistent" with their confirmation comments if it were understood that confirmation comments constitute nothing more and nothing less than frank statements by nominees of their best thinking on a particular issue to date.

MADELINE MORRIS
WALTER DELLINGER
(1992)

(SEE ALSO: *Appointing and Removal Power, Presidential; Bork Nomination.*)

Bibliography

MORRIS, MADELINE 1988–1989 The Grammar of Advice and Consent: Senate Confirmation of Supreme Court Nominees. *Drake Law Review* 38:863–887.

REES, GROVER, III 1983 Questions for Supreme Court Nominees at Confirmation Hearings: Excluding the Constitution. *Georgia Law Review* 17:913–967.

TRIBE, LAURENCE H. 1985 God Save This Honorable Court. New York: Mentor.

ADVISORY OPINION

Article III of the Constitution extends the JUDICIAL POWER OF THE UNITED STATES only to the decision of CASES OR CON-TROVERSIES. Since 1793, when the Supreme Court declined, in the absence of a concrete dispute, to give legal advice to President GEORGE WASHINGTON on the correct interpretation of treaties with France and Britain, the Court has refused steadfastly to issue advisory opinions, finding them inconsistent with Article III. This refusal is required whether the request seeks advice on interpretation of existing law or on the constitutionality of pending LEGISLATION or anticipated action. The Justices' view is that the federal courts function not as lawyers giving advice but as judges limited to deciding cases presented by adverse parties with a real, not a hypothetical, dispute, one that is subject to judicial resolution and the granting of meaningful relief. The Court held in *Aetna Life Insurance Co. v. Haworth* (1937) that the prohibition against advisory opinions does not preclude declaratory relief, but there must be a concrete controversy between parties of adverse legal positions which a DECLARATORY JUDGMENT can settle.

If doubts exist about the constitutionality of a proposed government policy or the legality of a contemplated application of current law, an advisory opinion could prevent the interim harm that adoption and application of law subsequently found invalid would cause. Moreover, advisory opinions could save time, money, and effort in deliberation and enforcement by clarifying legal limitations before invalid action is taken. Clearing away unlawful options could also contribute to the quality and focus of public debate and accountability.

The rule against advisory opinions responds to different considerations, however. It limits workload, but the dominant concerns involve judicial competence to decide issues in an advisory context and the place of the federal judiciary in a regime characterized by SEPARATION OF POWERS. Fear that decision before a dispute arises would be premature and unwise, that is, made without relevant facts stemming from application of law or other experience and without the benefit of perspectives presented by already affected parties, combined with concern that the advisory opinion may prejudge unfairly the decision of later concrete cases raising the same questions, induces judges to avoid making nonessential and potentially vulnerable decisions that might weaken judicial legitimacy. In addition, the prevailing belief views advisory opinions as likely to stifle rather than clarify the deliberative process, to distort the obligations of legislative or executive officials to evaluate legal questions independently, thereby blurring accountability, and to deprive experimental proposals of an opportunity to prove themselves before being reviewed for the legality of their actual effects.

JONATHON D. VARAT
(1986)

Bibliography

FRANKFURTER, FELIX 1924 Note on Advisory Opinions. *Harvard Law Review* 37:1002–1009.

AFFECTED WITH A PUBLIC INTEREST

The phrase "affected with a public interest," first used by the Supreme Court in *Munn v. Illinois* (1877), had a long and distinguished doctrinal lineage in the English COMMON LAW. The fountainhead of the modern development of that phrase was its formulation by Lord Chief Justice Matthew Hale, in his treatise *De Jure Maris,* written about 1670 and first published in 1787. In this work, Lord Hale discussed the basis for distinguishing property that was strictly private, property that was public in ownership, and an intermediate category of property (such as in navigable waters) that was private in ownership but subject to public use and hence a large measure of public control. In cases of business under a servitude to the public, such as wharves and cranes and ferries, according to Hale, it was legitimate for government to regulate in order to assure that the facilities would be available for "the common use" at rates that would be "reasonable and moderate." Once the public was invited to use such facilities, Hale wrote, "the wharf and the crane and other conveniences are affected with a publick interest, and they cease to be *juris privati* [a matter of private law] only." (See GRANGER CASES.)

When Chief Justice MORRISON R. WAITE, writing for the majority in *Munn,* cited Lord Hale, it was for the purpose of upholding rate regulation of grain elevators against a FOURTEENTH AMENDMENT defense that claimed that the elevator operator's vested property rights were being taken without JUST COMPENSATION. Explaining the *Munn* rule a year later, in his *Sinking Fund Cases* opinion, Justice JOSEPH P. BRADLEY pinned the "affectation" doctrine squarely to the concept of monopoly. The question in *Munn,* Bradley contended, was "the extent of the POLICE POWER in cases where the public interest is affected"; and the Court had concluded that regulation was valid when "an employment or business becomes a matter of such public interest and importance as to create a common charge or burden upon the citizens; in other words, when it becomes a practical monopoly, to which the citizen is compelled to resort. . . ."

In the period immediately following the decision in *Munn,* the Court erected a series of new doctrinal bulwarks for property interests. Among them were the concept of FREEDOM OF CONTRACT, the requirement that regulation must be "reasonable" as judged by the Court, and the notion of PUBLIC PURPOSE as a test for the validity of tax measures. As a result, the concept "affectation with a public interest" was pushed into the background, placing in abeyance such questions as whether only "monopoly" business came within its reach or whether instead it could be invoked to cover regulation of businesses that were not of this character.

In the decade of the 1920s, state legislation directly regulating prices and charges for service was challenged in federal courts and led to revitalization of the "affectation" doctrine by the Supreme Court. The issue, as the Court confronted it, had been set forth succinctly by Justice DAVID J. BREWER in an earlier opinion (*Cotting v. Kansas City Stockyards Co.,* 1901), upholding a state's regulation of stockyard charges on the ground that the business was affected with a public interest no less than a grain elevator or railroad or wharf. Yet the question must be posed, Brewer insisted, "To what extent may this regulation go?" Did any limits pertain, even in clear cases such as a stockyard's operation? Were the yards' owners left in a position, constitutionally, that they could be deprived "altogether of the ordinary privileges of others in mercantile business?"

In the hands of a property-minded, conservative Court the case-by-case development of the principle at issue, responding to Brewer's challenge, resulted in the creation of a closed legal category: only a business "affected with a public interest" might have prices or charges for service regulated; other, "ordinary," businesses were outside that closed category and therefore *not* subject to price or rate regulation. Chief Justice WILLIAM H. TAFT took on the challenge of defining more precisely the closed legal category in his opinion for the Court in WOLFF PACKING CO. V. COURT OF INDUSTRIAL RELATIONS OF KANSAS. Price and rate regulation were constitutional, Taft asserted, in regard to businesses that were public utilities (under an affirmative duty to render service to the public), businesses that historically had been subject to price regulation, and, finally, a rather baffling category, businesses that "though not public at their inception [historically] may be said to have risen to be such." Over strong objections of dissenters—most consistently Justices OLIVER WENDELL HOLMES and LOUIS D. BRANDEIS—the Court in subsequent years relied on this refined "affectation" doctrine to rule that even businesses subject to regulation in other respects could not be regulated as to rates of charge unless they met the criteria set down by Taft in *Wolff.* Mandated price minima or maxima were found unconstitutional with respect to theater ticket agencies, dairy vendors, gasoline retailers, and manufacturers and sellers of ice.

Dissenting Justices objected that the phrase "affected with a public interest" was so "vague and illusory" (as Justice HARLAN F. STONE charged in his dissent in *Tyson v. Banton,* 1927) as to amount to *carte blanche* for the Court to impose arbitrarily its policy preferences. Holmes was more direct: the concept, he stated in his own dissent in *Tyson,* was "little more than a fiction intended to beautify what is disagreeable to the sufferers." In Holmes's view, Lord Hale's language had been misapplied and had become a contrived limitation on the state's legitimate police power. "Subject to compensation when compensation is due," Holmes declared, "the legislature may forbid or restrict any business when it has a force of public opinion behind it."

Along with freedom of contract, the VESTED RIGHTS concept, the public purpose concept, and the doctrine of DUAL FEDERALISM, the "affectation" concept became emblematic of doctrinaire formalism mobilized by practitioners of JUDICIAL ACTIVISM. Such doctrines could undermine entirely, critics argued, the capacity of government to respond to changing objective social conditions or to emergency situations that required sweeping legislative intervention. Building on Justice Holmes's views, for example, the legal scholar WALTON H. HAMILTON wrote a widely noticed, wholesale attack on the Court in 1930. Although Hamilton was wrong in his view of the alleged novelty and obscurity of Lord Hale's treatise when Waite used it in *Munn*, he provided an eloquent argument for abandoning the notion of a closed category of businesses immune from price regulation. It was imperative, he argued, for the law to recognize the transformation of industrial structure and the competitive order in the previous half-century; the "affectation" doctrine was a conceptual straitjacket.

The advent of the Great Depression, along with the enactment of extraordinary legislation to deal with a great variety of emergency situations in a stricken society, lent additional weight to the realist argument that Holmes and commentators such as Hamilton and FELIX FRANKFURTER had set forth. Ruling on the constitutionality of an emergency milk price control law, enacted by New York State at the depth of the Depression spiral, the Supreme Court dramatically terminated the use of the "affectation" doctrine as a defense against price regulation: In NEBBIE V. NEW YORK (1934), the Court concluded that the phrase from Lord Hale meant simply "subject to the exercise of the police power." After *Nebbia*, so long as the procedural requirements of DUE PROCESS were met, the legislature was left "free to adopt whatever economic policy may reasonably be deemed to promote public welfare."

HARRY N. SCHEIBER
(1986)

Bibliography

HAMILTON, WALTON 1930 Affectation with a Public Interest. *Yale Law Journal* 34:1089–1112.

SCHEIBER, HARRY N. 1971 The Road to *Munn*: Eminent Domain and the Concept of Public Purpose in the State Courts. *Perspectives in American History* 5:327–402.

AFFIRMATIVE ACTION

The Supreme Court's momentous decisions in BROWN V. BOARD OF EDUCATION and BOLLING V. SHARPE (1954), and its subsequent implementation decision in *Brown II* (1955), were followed by a long string of rulings designed to render meaningful and effective the egalitarian promise inherent in the FOURTEENTH AMENDMENT. Compulsory racial SEGREGATION was at last no longer constitutionally permissible; the Fourteenth Amendment's guarantee of the EQUAL PROTECTION OF THE LAWS had become the effective law of the land for all levels of the public sector.

But in the judgment of a good many Americans, equality *qua* equality, even when conscientiously enforced with an even hand, would neither suffice to enable those previously deprived on racial grounds to realize the promises of equality of opportunity, nor would it atone, and provide redress, for the ravages wrought by two centuries of past discrimination. Consequently, as strongly urged by President LYNDON B. JOHNSON, programs were established in both the public and the private realms that were designed to go well beyond "mere" equality of opportunity and provide not only remedial but preferential compensatory action, especially in the worlds of EDUCATION and employment. Labeled "affirmative action"—as distinguished from "neutrality"—these programs were instituted to bring about increased minority employment opportunities, job promotions, and admissions to colleges and universities, among others. Understandably, affirmative action programs quickly became controversial because of their resort to RACIAL QUOTAS, also called euphemistically "goals" or "guidelines." Their proponents' justification has been that to provide an absolute measure of full equality of opportunity based upon individual merit does not suffice; that, given the injustices of the past, both preferential and compensatory treatment must be accorded through "affirmative action" that all but guarantees numerically targeted slots or posts based upon membership in racial groups or upon gender. Most critics of the policy's underlying philosophy have not necessarily objected to "affirmative action" policies such as aggressive recruiting, remedial training (no matter what the expense), and perhaps not even to what Justice LEWIS F. POWELL in REGENTS OF THE UNIVERSITY OF CALIFORNIA V. BAKKE (1978) termed a justifiable "plus" consideration of race along with other equitable factors. They do, however, object strenuously to policies that represent, or may be regarded as sanctioning, "reverse discrimination," generally characterized by the resort to such devices as the *numerus clausus*, that is, rigid quotas set aside to benefit identifiable racial groups, as in the controversial case of UNITED STEELWORKERS OF AMERICA V. WEBER (1979); to double standards in grading, ranking, and similar requirements on the employment, educational, and other relevant fronts of opportunity; and to "set aside" laws that guarantee specified percentages of contracts to minority groups, as in FULLILOVE V. KLUTZNICK (1980).

The basic issue, while philosophically replete with moral and ethical considerations, was ultimately bound to be fought out on the legal and constitutional front, thus engendering judicial decisions. Several provisions of the CIVIL RIGHTS ACT OF 1964, as amended—for example, Titles IV, VI, VII, and IX—seemed quite specifically not only to forbid racial, sexual, and other discrimination per se but also to proscribe the use of racial and related quotas. The Supreme Court rapidly confronted five major opportunities to address the issue; in each instance it found itself seriously divided. Each of the five decisions involved "affirmative action" and/or "reverse discrimination."

The first and second, DEFUNIS V. ODEGAARD (1974) and *Regents v. Bakke* (1978), dealt with preferential racial admissions quotas that by design advantaged nonwhite applicants and thereby ipso facto disadvantaged whites. In *De Funis* a five-member majority rendered a nondecision on the merits by ruling the case moot, because whatever the outcome of the case, Marco De Funis would be graduated by the University of Washington Law School. Justice WILLIAM O. DOUGLAS, dissenting from the MOOTNESS determination, warned that "the equal protection clause commands the elimination of racial barriers, not their creation in order to satisfy our theory as to how society ought to be organized." In *Bakke* the Court did reach the merits of the racial quota established by the University of California (Davis) medical school, ruling 5–4 (in two diverse lineups, each headed by Justice Powell) that whereas the latter's rigid quota violated Allan Bakke's rights under the Constitution and the CIVIL RIGHTS ACT OF 1964, the use of race as a "plus" along with other relevant considerations in admissions decisions did not. The third case, *United Steelworkers v. Weber*, concerned an employer-union craft-training plan that, on its face, directly violated Title VII of the Civil Rights Act of 1964, which clearly, indeed literally, interdicts racial quotas in employment. However, with Justices Powell and JOHN PAUL STEVENS disqualifying themselves from sitting in the cases, Justice WILLIAM J. BRENNAN, speaking for a majority of five, ruled that although the letter of the law appeared to forbid the arrangement, its purpose, as reflected in the legislative history, did not. The fourth case, *Fullilove v. Klutznick*, raised the fundamental question whether Congress, notwithstanding the Fourteenth Amendment's equal protection clause, could constitutionally legislate a ten percent set-aside plan for minority-owned construction companies desirous of obtaining government contracts. "Yes," held a 6–3 plurality—actually, the Court split 3–3–3—finding such legislation to be within the federal legislature's spending and regulatory powers under Article I of the Constitution. In his scathing DISSENTING OPINION, which he read in full from the bench on the day of the decision, Justice Stevens charged that the law represented a "per-

verse form of reparation," a "slapdash" law that rewards some who may not need rewarding and hurts others who may not deserve hurting. Suggesting that such a law could be used simply as a patronage tool by its authors—it had, in fact, been written on the floor of the House of Representatives without having gone to committee for hearings—he warned that it could breed more resentment and prejudice than it corrected. Echoing the first Justice JOHN MARSHALL HARLAN's memorable phrase in dissent in PLESSY V. FERGUSON (1896), namely, that "our Constitution is color-blind and neither knows nor tolerates classes among citizens," Stevens asked what percentage of "oriental blood or what degree of Spanish-speaking skill is required for membership in the preferred class?" With deep feelings, he suggested sarcastically that now the government must devise its version of the Nazi laws that defined who is a Jew, musing that "our statute books will once again have to contain laws that reflect the odious practice of delineating the qualities that make one person a Negro and make another white." The fifth case, *Memphis Fire Department v. Stotts*, seemed to draw a line (although only by the narrowest of margins, 5–4) when the Justice White-authored majority opinion held that duly established bona fide nondiscriminatory seniority systems supersede affirmative action plans.

Depending upon interpretation, one person's "affirmative action" may well constitute another's "reverse discrimination." Nonetheless, it is possible to essay distinctions. Thus, "affirmative action" may be regarded as encompassing the following five phenomena, all of which would appear to be both legal and constitutional: (1) both governmentally and privately sponsored activity designed to remedy the absence of needed educational preparation by special, even if costly, primary, and/or secondary school level preparatory programs or occupational skill development, always provided that access to these programs is not bottomed upon race or related group criteria or characteristics, but upon educational or economic need; (2) special classes or supplemental training, regardless of costs, on any level of education or training from the prenursery school bottom to the very top of the professional training ladder; (3) scrupulous enforcement of absolute standards of nondiscrimination on the basis of race, sex, religion, nationality, and age; (4) above-the-table special recruiting efforts to reach out to those members of heretofore underused, deprived, or discriminated-against segments of the citizenry; (5) provided the presence of explicit or implicit merit, of bona fide demonstrated or potential ability, the taking into account of an individual's race, gender, religion as an equitable consideration—the "plus" of which Justice Powell spoke in *Bakke*—but *only* if "all other things are equal."

"Reverse discrimination," on the other hand, which is

acceptable neither legally nor constitutionally, would constitute the following quartet: (1) adoption of a *numerus clausus*, the setting aside of quotas, be they rigid or semi-rigid, on behalf of the admission, recruitment, employment, or promotion of individuals and groups identified and classified by racial, religious, sexual, age, or nationality characteristics; such characteristics are *non sequiturs* on the fronts of individual merit and ability and may well be regarded as an insult to the dignity and intelligence of the quota beneficiaries; (2) slanting of what should be neutral qualification examinations or requirements; double standards in grading and rating; double standards in attendance, retention, and disciplinary requirements; (3) those "goals" and "guidelines" that allegedly differ from rigid quotas, and thus presumably pass legal and constitutional muster, but that, in application, are all but synonymous with enforced quotas; (4) legislative or executive "set aside" programs, such as the one at issue in the *Fullilove* case, that mandate percentage-quotas of awards and activities based upon racial, gender, and related classifications.

"Reverse discrimination" purports to justify itself as atonement for past discrimination. It sanctions the call to children to pay for the sins of their forebears; it embraces a policy that two wrongs make one right, that "temporary" discrimination is "benign" rather than "invidious" when it is designed to remedy past wrongs. Since the "temporary" all too often becomes the "permanent," temporary suspensions of fundamental rights are fraught with permanent dangers and represent prima facie denials of the equal protection of the laws guaranteed by the Fourteenth Amendment and the DUE PROCESS OF LAW guaranteed by the Fifth.

The line between "affirmative action" and "reverse discrimination" may be thin and vexatious, but it does not lie beyond recognition and establishment in our constitutional constellation.

HENRY J. ABRAHAM
(1986)

Bibliography

DWORKIN, RONALD 1977 *Taking Rights Seriously.* Cambridge, Mass.: Harvard University Press.
GLAZER, NATHAN 1976 *Affirmative Discrimination.* New York: Basic Books.
O'NEILL, ROBERT M. 1975 *Discriminating against Discrimination.* Bloomington: Indiana University Press.
ROCHE, GEORGE C., III 1974 *The Balancing Act: Quota Hiring in Higher Education.* La Salle, Ill.: Open Court.
ROSSUM, RALPH A. 1980 *Reverse Discrimination: The Constitutional Debate.* New York: Marcel Dekker.
SOWELL, THOMAS 1975 *Affirmative Action Reconsidered: Was It Necessary in Academia?* Washington, D.C.: American Enterprise Institute.

AFFIRMATIVE ACTION
(Update 1)

Do constitutional guarantees of EQUAL PROTECTION command that government must be "color-blind" or only that government may not subordinate any group on the basis of race? The Supreme Court's equal protection decisions have long straddled these two different principles. The color-blindness approach deems race morally irrelevant to governmental decision making under all circumstances. The antisubordination approach, by contrast, sees racial distinctions as illegitimate only when used by government as a deliberate basis for disadvantage. The two approaches divide sharply on the permissibility of affirmative action: advocates of color blindness condemn the use of racial distinctions even to benefit previously disadvantaged racial groups, whereas those who view equal protection solely as a ban on racial subordination see affirmative action as constitutionally benign.

Since 1985, the Supreme Court has continued to steer between these two approaches rather than unequivocally embrace either one. In earlier decisions, the Court had upheld a variety of RACIAL PREFERENCES, including the use of race as a factor in university admissions (as long as rigid RACIAL QUOTAS were not employed) in REGENTS OF UNIVERSITY OF CALIFORNIA V. BAKKE (1978), the set-aside of places for blacks in an industrial skills-training program in UNITED STEELWORKERS OF AMERICA V. WEBER (1979), and the set-aside of public works construction projects for minority business enterprises in FULLILOVE V. KLUTZNICK (1980). These cases made clear that affirmative action would not be struck down as readily as laws harming racial minorities, but neither would it be lightly tolerated. Governments could successfully defend affirmative action programs, but only with an especially strong justification.

The affirmative action cases since 1985 have bitterly divided the Court, and their outcomes have signaled a partial retrenchment for affirmative action. With the appointments of Justices SANDRA DAY O'CONNOR, ANTONIN SCALIA, and ANTHONY M. KENNEDY, the Court veered off its middle course and more sharply toward the color-blindness pole. Although the Court readily upheld affirmative action as a court-imposed remedy for RACIAL DISCRIMINATION against minorities, as in *Local 28, Sheet Metal Workers International Association v. EEOC* (1986), the Court struck down two municipalities' efforts to impose affirmative action on themselves. In WYGANT V. JACKSON BOARD OF EDUCATION (1986) the Court invalidated a school district's plan to protect minority teachers against layoffs ahead of more senior white teachers. And in RICHMOND (CITY OF) V. J. A. CROSON CO. (1989), the Court struck down a city's reservation of a percentage of public works construction for minority business enterprises—a set-aside modeled on the congressional program upheld in *Fullilove*. But METRO BROADCASTING v. FCC (1990), which upheld federal policies preferring minority broadcasters in the allocation of broadcast licenses, confounded those who thought *Croson* had sounded the death knell for affirmative action.

The central conflict in these cases was over what justification for affirmative action would suffice. Up until *Metro*, the Court accepted only narrowly remedial justifications. Affirmative action was upheld only as penance for particularized past sins of discrimination—not as atonement for "societal discrimination" as a whole. The Court treated affirmative action as a matter of corrective rather than distributive justice; minorities might be preferred for jobs, admissions, or contracts not to build a racially integrated future, but only to cure a racially discriminatory past.

The Court's account of affirmative action as a permissible remedy for past discrimination, however, left both sides unsatisfied. Opponents charged that affirmative action was a poor version of corrective justice because (1) unlike standard compensatory justice, affirmative action extends benefits beyond the specific victims of past discrimination; and (2) unlike standard retributive justice, affirmative action demands current sacrifice of persons who were not the actual perpetrators of past discrimination—persons the Court sometimes labels "innocent" whites. In the opponents' view, if affirmative action were truly remedial, neither would nonvictims benefit nor nonsinners pay. In contrast, advocates of affirmative action found the Court's requirements for proving remedial justification far too stringent. Governments are reluctant to confess to past sins of discrimination, advocates argued, and should be permitted to adopt affirmative action plans without official *mea culpas*.

Metro Broadcasting departed from the sin-based approach by accepting a nonremedial justification for the Federal Communications Commission's (FCC) minority-ownership preference policies: increased minority ownership would help diversify broadcast program content. A majority of the Court had never endorsed such a justification before, although Justice LEWIS F. POWELL's crucial *Bakke* opinion had defended racial preferences in university admissions as producing diversity in the classroom and Justice JOHN PAUL STEVENS had persistently advocated similar diversity-based justifications for affirmative action, for example, in his *Wygant* dissent. Such justifications implicitly adopt the antisubordination rather than the color-blindness approach: using racial distinctions to increase diversity is not a constitutional evil because it does not use race to impose disadvantage. As Justice Stevens wrote in his *Metro* concurrence, "[n]either the favored nor the disfavored class is stigmatized in any way."

When *Wygant*, *Croson*, and *Metro* are considered together, it appears that the Court's affirmative action decisions continue to steer between the color-blindness and antisubordination poles. *Wygant* and *Croson* should not be overstated as victories for color blindness because those decisions left open the possibility that other governments might do better than the Jackson school board or the Richmond city council at tailoring affirmative action narrowly to remedy demonstrable discrimination in their past. After *Wygant* and *Croson*, state and local affirmative action plans face a high but not insurmountable hurdle: the clearer the paper trail of past discrimination, the more flexible or waivable the target, the shorter the plan's duration, and the less entrenched the reliance interests of the displaced whites, the more likely such a plan will be upheld. However, *Metro* should not be overstated as a victory for the antisubordination view because this decision turned heavily on the Court's deference to its coequal branches (Congress and the FCC) and low valuation of broadcasters' rights—two factors especially appealing to Justice BYRON R. WHITE, who cast the decisive vote despite his earlier negative votes on affirmative action.

The dissenting opinions in *Metro Broadcasting* may well be more portentous for the future of affirmative action than Justice WILLIAM J. BRENNAN's majority opinion—the last opinion he wrote before retiring from the Court. The dissenters made thinly veiled reference to the backlash against affirmative action evident in national politics since the 1980 elections. Justice O'Connor's dissent, joined by Chief Justice WILLIAM H. REHNQUIST and Justices Scalia and Kennedy, spoke of affirmative action as "contributing to an escalation of racial hostility and conflict," and Justice Kennedy's dissent, joined by Justice Scalia, compared the FCC's policies with those of South Africa and suggested that affirmative action makes whites feel wrongfully stigmatized. Justice Scalia wrote similarly in his *Croson* concurrence that "[w]hen we depart from" pure meritocracy, "we play with fire, and much more than an occasional DeFunis, Johnson, or Croson burns." To the *Metro* majority, these objections appeared wildly overstated, and affirmative action readily distinguishable from the evils of apartheid or Jim Crow. Which view will prevail in the wake of Justice Brennan's departure from the Court remains to be seen.

KATHLEEN M. SULLIVAN
(1992)

(SEE ALSO: *Johnson v. Transportation Agency; Paradise, United States v.; Race-Consciousness.*)

Bibliography

SULLIVAN, KATHLEEN M.   1986   Sins of Discrimination: Last Term's Affirmative Action Cases. *Harvard Law Review* 100: 78–98.

WILLIAMS, PATRICIA J. 1990 Metro Broadcasting, Inc v. FCC: Regrouping in Singular Times. *Harvard Law Review* 104: 525–546.

AFFIRMATIVE ACTION
(Update 2)

There is no single definition of "affirmative action," either in American politics or in American constitutional law. The core of the debate over affirmative action concerns the consideration of race, ethnicity, or gender as a factor in selecting among applicants, with the aim of increasing the presence of traditionally disadvantaged groups among those selected. Where opponents of affirmative action see "quotas" or "preferences" or improper efforts to engineer "proportional representation" that result in the selection of "unqualified" applicants, supporters of affirmative action see race and gender as no more than a "plus factor" employed to assure "diversity" among fully qualified applicants. The debate rages in the courts, in electoral politics, and in the policymaking of public bodies.

In ADARAND CONSTRUCTORS, INC. V. PEÑA (1995), the Supreme Court held that all "racial classifications," however benign their intent, are subject to STRICT SCRUTINY by the courts. Post-*Adarand* affirmative action decisions in the federal courts of appeal have begun to determine which racially conscious programs constitute "racial classifications" and whether they survive strict scrutiny.

In the field of student admissions, the leading pre-*Adarand* case is REGENTS OF UNIVERSITY OF CALIFORNIA V. BAKKE (1978), in which the separate but governing opinion of Justice LEWIS F. POWELL, JR., endorsed the use of race as one factor among many to assure diversity in a student body. In HOPWOOD V. TEXAS (1996), the Fifth Circuit Court of Appeals declared that Powell's opinion was not binding PRECEDENT and struck down the University of Texas Law School's use of affirmative action in student admissions. That decision has been subject to much appropriate criticism. Powell's opinion is best understood as having applied strict scrutiny, and thus *Adarand* provides no basis for questioning *Bakke*'s authority. Even when *Bakke* is recognized as controlling authority, however, courts are now taking a hard look at whether affirmative action programs in education are in fact narrowly tailored to address legitimate diversity needs. For example, an affirmative action program at the high school level was rejected on narrow tailoring grounds (among others) by the First Circuit Court of Appeals in *Wessman v. Gittens* (1998).

In the field of government contracting, where *Adarand* is the Supreme Court's most recent decision, controversy exists over whether outreach and self-monitoring programs are "racial classifications" subject to strict scrutiny.

The Ninth Circuit Court of Appeals so held in *Monterey Mechanical Co. v. Wilson* (1998), which involved a California requirement that contractors make good faith efforts toward meeting minority hiring goals, a requirement that could be satisfied by a combination of outreach and data collection. The opinion triggered a vigorous dissent from several members of the court on a failed sua sponte request for rehearing en banc.

In the field of government employment, a plurality of the Supreme Court in WYGANT V. JACKSON BOARD OF EDUCATION (1986) rejected the use of race-based affirmative action in teacher layoffs. The plurality rejected two commonly asserted grounds for affirmative action in employment: the remedying of societal discrimination and the provision of minority role models. Consequently, and on the strength of the analogy between student admissions and teacher hiring, educational employers widely rely on "diversity" as their asserted COMPELLING STATE INTEREST in employment cases in which the employer has no demonstrable history of past discrimination. The availability of diversity as a constitutional justification may be weaker for noneducational employers, despite the wide popularity of affirmative action among businesses seeking to serve diverse domestic and global clienteles. Then again, the decision of the Seventh Circuit Court of Appeals in *Wittmer v. Peters* (1996) suggests that employers in one noneducational field—law enforcement and corrections—may be given especially broad leeway in experimenting with race-based hiring aimed at improving the ability of the state to diminish crime in minority communities.

As in the case of government contracting, the question of the applicability of strict scrutiny to outreach programs has received post-*Adarand* judicial attention in employment cases. In *Lutheran Church–Missouri Synod v. Federal Communications Commission* (1998), the District of Columbia Circuit Court of Appeals applied strict scrutiny to, and struck down, an FCC policy requiring radio stations to engage in outreach, to monitor the effects of their hiring practices on minorities and women, and to report the racial and gender composition of their workforces to the agency. The policy did not tie any penalty or benefit to the reported results. It was struck down nonetheless because, in the court's view, "[t]he entire scheme is built on the notion that stations should aspire to a workforce that attains, or at least approaches, proportional representation." As in *Monterey Mechanical*, several members of the court dissented from the denial of rehearing en banc, arguing that outreach and self-monitoring aimed at avoiding discrimination are not "racial classifications" subject to strict scrutiny under *Adarand*. In contrast, the Eleventh Circuit Court of Appeals, in *Allen v. Alabama State Board of Education* (1999), refused to see in *Adarand* grounds to challenge a CONSENT DECREE that required the Alabama

Board of Education to develop nondiscriminatory teacher certification tests using a methodology that required it to monitor the test items for disparate racial impact. Thus, the question of when permissible "race consciousness" crosses the border into suspect "racial classification" remains unsettled after *Adarand*.

In the current legal environment, trial courts may well engage in a searching analysis to determine which justifications for affirmative action are "compelling" in which settings and which forms of affirmative action, if any, are "narrowly tailored" to meet the government's goals. Between the use of strict scrutiny and federal courts' increasing scrutiny of scientific expert testimony in all types of cases pursuant to the Supreme Court's decision in *Daubert v. Merrell Dow Pharmaceuticals, Inc.* (1993), the next generation of defenses of affirmative action programs will need to be fact-based and sophisticated in proving the validity of the government's means and ends.

DEBORAH C. MALAMUD
(2000)

Bibliography

CHIN, GABRIEL, ed. 1998 *Affirmative Action and the Constitution*, 3 vols. New York: Garland.
SYMPOSIUM 1998 Twenty Years After *Bakke:* The Law and Social Science of Affirmative Action in Higher Education. *Ohio State Law Journal* 59:663–1067.

AFFIRMATIVE ACTION, ECONOMICS OF

See: Economics of Affirmative Action

AFROCENTRIC SCHOOLS

As long as private afrocentric schools allow all students the opportunity to attend their schools on a nonracial basis, they do not violate federal CIVIL RIGHTS laws. The constitutionality of a public school district that seeks to establish and operate an afrocentric school is a much more difficult question.

School districts that have established afrocentric schools normally have kept them formally open to any student who wishes to attend, on a racially neutral basis. Teachers and administrators are also normally selected on a racially neutral basis. Even though afrocentric schools involve conscious regard to race in establishing schools and organizing their educational programs, attendance at or employment in an afrocentric school is the result of individual choice, not government classification. School districts also continue to operate their ordinary schools. Students who do not choose to attend or are not admitted into an afrocentric school still receive a free public education.

The Supreme Court's 1995 opinion in MILLER V. JOHNSON made it clear that STRICT SCRUTINY is triggered when government classifies its citizens based on their race or ethnicity. But an afrocentric school set up on a nonracial basis does not require government to classify and treat its citizens as members of a racial or ethinic group. In addition, it may be that afrocentric schools set up on a nonracial basis do not produce discriminatory effects. Therefore, the operation and establishment of an afrocentric school—on a racially neutral basis—does not necessarily trigger strict scrutiny.

There are additional reasons why strict scrutiny should not be applied to afrocentric schools. In *United States v. Fordice* (1992), the Supreme Court addressed the obligation of Mississippi to eradicate the vestiges of a segregated school system within the state's universities. One of the issues was the continued viability of historically black colleges that had been established as part of an earlier effort to maintain SEGREGATION. In a CONCURRING OPINION Justice CLARENCE THOMAS indicated that although Mississippi was not constitutionally required to maintain historically black colleges, there may exist sound educational justifications for operating a historically black college that is open to all on a nonracial basis. If so, the establishment of an afrocentric school could be a legitimate exercise of the school district's power to make educational judgments and not an exercise in RACIAL DISCRIMINATION warranting strict scrutiny. It should be noted, however, that no other Justice joined Thomas's opinion in *Fordice* and there are tensions between it and Justice SANDRA DAY O'CONNOR'S OPINION FOR THE COURT.

If the decision to establish an afrocentric school triggers strict scrutiny, then the school will not likely survive a constitutional challenge. The Supreme Court has already rejected societal discrmination and the need for black students to have role models as COMPELLING STATE INTERESTS. The only compelling state interest that a majority of the Justices have accepted is remedying the effects of identified racial discrimination. Even if a compelling interest could be provided, there would still be the hurdle of narrow tailoring to overcome.

KEVIN BROWN
(2000)

Bibliography

ASANTE, MOLEFI KETE 1998 *The Afrocentric Idea*, revised and expanded edition. Philadelphia: Temple University Press.
BROWN, KEVIN 1993 Do African Americans Need Immersion Schools? The Paradoxes Created by the Conceptualization by Law of Race and Public Education. *Iowa Law Review* 78: 813–881.

AFROYIM v. RUSK
387 U.S. 253 (1967)

A section of the Nationality Act of 1940 stripped Americans of their CITIZENSHIP if they voted in a foreign political election. In PEREZ V. BROWNELL (1957) the Supreme Court upheld the constitutionality of this provision, 5–4. On the authority of *Perez*, the State Department refused a passport to Afroyim, a naturalized citizen, who had voted in an Israeli election. In *Afroyim*, however, a new five-Justice majority, speaking through Justice HUGO L. BLACK, overruled *Perez* and declared that the FOURTEENTH AMENDMENT's citizenship clause denied Congress authority to strip Americans of their citizenship without their consent. "Citizenship in this Nation is a part of a cooperative affair," Black wrote. "Its citizenry is the country and the country is its citizenry."

MICHAEL E. PARRISH
(1986)

AGE DISCRIMINATION

The racial CIVIL RIGHTS revolution of the 1950s and 1960s generated interest in constitutional protection for groups other than racial and religious minorities. Enhanced constitutional scrutiny of SEX DISCRIMINATION may be a consequence of the civil rights struggle.

Discrimination on the basis of age, however, has not become constitutionally suspect. In MASSACHUSETTS BOARD OF RETIREMENT V. MURGIA (1976) the Supreme Court held that some forms of age classification are not suspect and sustained against EQUAL PROTECTION attack a state statute requiring uniformed state police officers to retire at age fifty. In a PER CURIAM opinion, the Court concluded that the retirement did not affect a FUNDAMENTAL RIGHT, and characterized the affected class as uniformed police officers over age fifty. Perhaps intending to leave open heightened scrutiny of some age classifications, the Court stated that the requirement in *Murgia* did not discriminate against the elderly. In light of its findings with respect to the nature of the right and the relevant class, the Court held that mere rationality, rather than STRICT SCRUTINY, was the proper STANDARD OF REVIEW in determining whether the statute violated the equal protection clause. It found that the age classification was rationally related to furthering the state's interest of protecting the public by assuring physical preparedness of its uniformed state police.

In *Vance v. Bradley* (1979) the Court, in an opinion by Justice BYRON R. WHITE, again applied the RATIONAL BASIS test and held that Congress may require retirement at age sixty of federal employees covered by the Foreign Service retirement and disability system, even though it imposes no such limit on employees covered by the Civil Service retirement and disability system. In sustaining the mandatory retirement age, the Court emphasized Congress's special consideration of the needs of the Foreign Service. "Congress has legislated separately for the Foreign Service and has gone to great lengths to assure that those conducting our foreign relations will be sufficiently competent and reliable in all respects. If Congress attached special importance to high performance in these positions . . . it was quite rational to avoid the risks connected with having older employees in the Foreign Service but to tolerate those risks in the Civil Service."

But in the legislative arena, age discrimination did feel the effects of the constitutional egalitarian revolution. Section 715 of the CIVIL RIGHTS ACT OF 1964 required the secretary of labor to report to Congress on age discrimination in employment. In 1965 the secretary reported persistent arbitrary discrimination against older Americans. In 1967, upon the recommendation of President LYNDON B. JOHNSON, and relying on its powers under the COMMERCE CLAUSE, Congress passed the Age Discrimination in Employment Act (ADEA). The act, which has been amended several times, prohibits employment discrimination against persons between the ages of forty and seventy.

In EQUAL EMPLOYMENT OPPORTUNITY COMMISSION V. WYOMING (1983), prior to its OVERRULING of NATIONAL LEAGUE OF CITIES V. USERY (1976) in GARCIA V. SAN ANTONIO METROPOLITAN TRANSIT AUTHORITY (1985), the Court sustained against a TENTH AMENDMENT attack the constitutionality of Congress's 1974 extension of the ADEA to state and local governments. In a 5–4 decision, the Court found that applying the act's prohibition to a Wyoming mandatory retirement age for game wardens would not interfere with integral state functions because the state remained free to apply reasonable standards of fitness to game wardens.

Building on a provision in Title VII of the Civil Rights Act of 1964, the ADEA allows employers to take otherwise prohibited age-based action when age is a "bona fide occupational qualification reasonably necessary to the normal operation of the particular business." In its early interpretations of this provision, the Court has not given the defense an expansive reading. In *Western Air Lines, Inc. v. Criswell* (1985), in an opinion by Justice JOHN PAUL STEVENS, the Court held that Congress's "reasonably necessary" standard requires something more than a showing that an age-based requirement is rationally connected to the employer's business. Relying on the heightened standard, the Court therefore rejected an airline's defense of its requirement that flight engineers retire at age sixty. In *Johnson v. Mayor & City Council of Baltimore* (1985) the Court held that a federal statute generally requiring federal fire fighters to retire at age fifty-five does not establish that being under fifty-five is a bona fide occupational qualification under the ADEA for nonfederal fire fighters.

In the Age Discrimination Act of 1975 (ADA), following the racial antidiscrimination model of Title VI of the Civil Rights Act of 1964, Congress prohibited discrimination on the basis of age in programs or activities receiving federal financial assistance. The ADA thus joins Title IX of the EDUCATION AMENDMENTS OF 1972 and section 504 of the REHABILITATION ACT OF 1973, which prohibit, respectively, sex discrimination and discrimination against the handicapped in federally assisted programs. The ADA vests broad authority in the secretary of health and human services to promulgate regulations to effectuate the statute's antidiscrimination mandate. Like the ADEA, the ADA contains exceptions allowing discrimination on the basis of age when age is reasonably related to the program or activity. Other specific federal spending programs contain their own statutory prohibitions on age discrimination.

THEODORE EISENBERG
(1986)

Bibliography

SCHUCK, PETER H.   1979   The Graying of Civil Rights Law: The Age Discrimination Act of 1975. *Yale Law Journal* 89:27–93.

UNITED STATES DEPARTMENT OF LABOR   1965   *Report to the Congress on Age Discrimination in Employment under Section 715 of the Civil Rights Act of 1964.* Washington D.C.: Government Printing Office.

AGE DISCRIMINATION
(Update)

Unique among the first generation of ANTIDISCRIMINATION LEGISLATION, the Age Discrimination in Employment Act (ADEA) did not provide enhanced statutory protection for what would otherwise be a constitutionally protected category. As the Supreme Court held in MASSACHUSETTS BOARD OF RETIREMENT V. MURGIA (1976), "old age does not define a 'discrete and insular group' . . . in need of extra protection for the majoritarian process. Instead, it marks a stage that each of us will reach if we live out our normal life span."

The ADEA emerged from reports to Congress that older workers were being systematically excluded from the workplace based on age. As reported by the Secretary of Labor in 1967, for example, half of all private job openings were barred to applicants over fifty five, and a quarter forbade applicants over forty five. The act makes it illegal for an employer "to fail or refuse to hire or discharge any individual or otherwise discriminate against any individual . . . because of such individual's age." As presently for-

mulated, the act applies to all persons over forty years of age and its prohibitions now cover hiring practices and have essentially eliminated the practice of mandatory retirement.

Although the act was aimed at entry barriers to older employees, there is relatively little evidence of any success on that front. The ADEA's prohibitions did remove the formal barriers to entry for older employees. However, significant other barriers exist in the form of higher wages associated with the rising wage scales of American employment; the difficulty of assuming pension obligations; and the problems of superannuated skills in an evolving workplace. Thus, apart from issues of discrimination, the ADEA has had difficulty with the general trend that, as older workers age, they accumulate seniority, higher income level, and greater pension rights. All of these economic factors provide motivations for cost-conscious employers to avoid the employment of older workers. The Court considered the impact of economic factors correlated to age in *Hazen Paper Co. v. Biggins* (1993), but ruled that there is no age discrimination when the employer is motivated by some factor other than the employee's age—regardless of any correlation. This decision has produced considerable dissension among the lower courts, which must attempt to distinguish age-based motivations from age-related ones.

Instead of the initial focus on access to employment, the act became the primary tool for improving the position of older workers already in the workplace, particularly after the emergence of powerful lobbying agents such as the American Association of Retired Persons. Virtually all ADEA litigation now concerns end-of-career issues, oftentimes related to the availability of employee buyouts or the impact of reductions in force.

SAMUEL ISSACHAROFF
ERICA HARRIS
(2000)

Bibliography

ISSACHAROFF, SAMUEL and HARRIS, ERICA WORTH   1997   Is Age Discrimination Really Age Discrimination?: The ADEA's Unnatural Solution. *New York University Law Review* 72:780–840.

POSNER, RICHARD A.   1995   *Aging and Old Age.* Chicago: University of Chicago Press.

AGE DISCRIMINATION ACT
89 Stat. 728 (1975)

Enacted as Title III of the Older Americans Amendments of 1975, the Age Discrimination Act of 1975, like Title VI of the CIVIL RIGHTS ACT OF 1964 and other laws, links ANTIDISCRIMINATION LEGISLATION to Congress's spending power. Subject to important but ambiguous exceptions, the act prohibits exclusion on the basis of age from federally financed programs. In covered programs, the act affords greater protection against AGE DISCRIMINATION than the Supreme Court has held to be required under the EQUAL PROTECTION clause. In MASSACHUSETTS BOARD OF RETIREMENT V. MURGIA (1976), in upholding a statute requiring police officers to retire at age fifty, the Court found age not to be a SUSPECT CLASSIFICATION. The Age Discrimination in Employment Act, as well as some state laws, protect against age discrimination in employment.

THEODORE EISENBERG
(1986)

Bibliography

SCHUCK, PETER H. 1979 The Graying of Civil Rights Laws: The Age Discrimination Act of 1975. *Yale Law Journal* 89:27–93.

AGNELLO v. UNITED STATES
269 U.S. 20 (1925)

In *Agnello* the Supreme Court extended the scope of SEARCH INCIDENT TO ARREST from the person of the arrestee, previously authorized in WEEKS V. UNITED STATES (1914), to the premises on which the arrest was made. The precise extent of the allowable search was, however, not delineated; it became a matter of great judicial contention in later cases.

JACOB W. LANDYNSKI
(1986)

AGOSTINI v. FELTON
521 U.S. 203 (1997)

In *Agostini v. Felton*, the Supreme Court took the remarkable step of OVERRULING one of its own decisions in a later iteration of the very same litigation. In AGUILAR V. FELTON (1985), the Court held that the ESTABLISHMENT CLAUSE prohibited the City of New York from using funds provided by the federal government under Title I of the Elementary and Secondary Education Act of 1965 to provide special education services to disadvantaged students on the sites of private sectarian schools. Under the test set forth in LEMON V. KURTZMAN (1971), the *Aguilar* Court concluded that the program presented an unacceptable risk of entanglement between government and religion.

In the wake of *Aguilar*, the district court entered a permanent INJUNCTION barring the use of any public funds to conduct on-site education programs at religiously affiliated schools. New York estimated that the costs of complying with that injunction—for example, by establishing trailers near the schools in which the services could be provided—amounted to $100 million over ten years. After several subsequent decisions of the Court appeared to undermine the premise of *Aguilar* that the Constitution forbade any expenditure of public funds to provide on-site educational services at religiously affiliated schools, and after a majority of the Court (in separate opinions in different cases) had expressed the view that *Aguilar* should be reconsidered, New York filed a motion for relief from the judgment and injunction.

The Court, in an opinion by Justice SANDRA DAY O'CONNOR, agreed that decisions since *Aguilar*, particularly *Zobrest v. Catalina Foothills School District* (1993) and WITTERS V. WASHINGTON DEPARTMENT OF SERVICES FOR THE BLIND (1986), had established that participation in government aid programs by sectarian schools did not necessarily advance religion nor excessively entangle government with religion. On the contrary, a program that allocates benefits based on neutral, nonreligious criteria, and that provides the same level of benefits to religious and secular beneficiaries alike, does not threaten the unconstitutional ESTABLISHMENT OF RELIGION. O'Connor concluded that the decision in *Aguilar* was inconsistent with these subsequent cases, and that the doctrine of STARE DECISIS did not require *Aguilar* to be retained. After concluding that the conditions for relief from the prior injunction were met, the Court granted the city relief. The four dissenting Justices objected both to the Court's decision to allow the federal rules of procedure to be used to gain relief from an injunction in this context, and to the Court's substantive establishment clause analysis.

Apart from its practical significance, the decision in *Agostini* provides important doctrinal support for those defending voucher programs in which the government provides financial assistance to individuals that can be used to defray the costs of private education, including education at religious schools. Whether such programs are permissible promises to be one of the most hotly contested and important establishment clause questions to come before the Court in a generation.

WILLIAM K. KELLEY
(2000)

(SEE ALSO: *Government Aid to Religious Institutions; Religion in Public Schools; Religious Liberty; School Choice.*)

AGRICULTURAL ADJUSTMENT ACT OF 1933
48 Stat. 31

This act, the set piece of the NEW DEAL for agriculture, emphasized PRODUCTION controls in an effort to revive farming from its 1920s torpor. Stressing collective action, the act sought to boost farm prices. After WORLD WAR I ended, American farmers had found stiff new competition in the world market for the tremendously expanded U.S. farm output. As a result, surpluses ballooned and prices deflated. A modest recovery by 1923 had not taken firm hold, and the Depression in 1929 struck hard at farmers. Agricultural prices had dropped four times as far as industrial prices between 1929 and 1933. Shortly after FRANKLIN D. ROOSEVELT's inauguration in March 1933, his secretary of agriculture, Henry Wallace, met with farm leaders to formulate a relief plan. The resulting bill, drafted in part by JEROME FRANK, was ready in five days. To secure wide support, REXFORD TUGWELL and others recommended that this "farm relief" measure comprise elements of plans already proposed. As a result, it established parity prices—a price level that would allow the purchasing power of income from a commodity to equal its purchasing power in the base period, 1909–1914.

The act's avowed purpose, "to relieve the existing national economic emergency by increasing agricultural purchasing power," would be accomplished primarily by raising prices of seven basic commodities to parity levels. Control of production would be the means of achieving this goal. The secretary of agriculture could exert control by regulating benefit payments to farmers who voluntarily reduced production, by imposing marketing quotas, and by providing for government purchase of surpluses. The government would fund these efforts by imposing on the primary processors of agricultural goods an EXCISE TAX based on the difference between farm and parity prices. Benefit payments were designed to entice cooperation although participation was theoretically voluntary.

Senate opposition gave way to substantial public pressure for action and a lack of workable alternatives. The act also granted the secretary of agriculture power to make regulations to enforce the act (subject to presidential approval), assess penalties, and (with the secretary of the treasury) to have ultimate say in issues of payments to farmers. By late 1935 the act and a drought had provided much relief (net farm income rose 250 per cent), forecasting a profitable recovery for American agriculture. In January 1936, however, a 6–3 Supreme Court invalidated the statute in UNITED STATES V. BUTLER. A determined Congress passed a second AGRICULTURAL ADJUSTMENT ACT in 1938.

DAVID GORDON
(1986)

AGRICULTURAL ADJUSTMENT ACT OF 1938
50 Stat. 246

After the Supreme Court invalidated the AGRICULTURAL ADJUSTMENT ACT (AAA) OF 1933 in UNITED STATES V. BUTLER (1936), Congress passed a second AAA in 1938, citing the effect of farm PRODUCTION on INTERSTATE COMMERCE as the act's basis. Congress once again sought to achieve parity levels for principal commodities and maintain earlier soil conservation payments as well. The act retained voluntary participation and, acknowledging *Butler*, Congress now levied no processing taxes nor did it set up production quotas; instead the act inaugurated a system of marketing quotas. Such a quota applied only when two-thirds of a commodity's producers approved. Once a general quota was authorized, the secretary of agriculture could set specific quotas for individual farms and assess a penalty tax on violators. Moreover, approval of quotas made available special loans to help store surplus production. The 1938 act also provided means of increasing consumption to help alleviate surpluses, and created a Commodity Credit Corporation to make loans when income fell because of low prices, and a Federal Crop Insurance Corporation. The Supreme Court sustained the act in *Mulford v. Smith* (1939) and WICKARD V. FILBURN (1942).

DAVID GORDON
(1986)

AGRICULTURAL MARKETING AGREEMENT ACT
50 Stat. 246 (1937)

In 1933 the first AGRICULTURAL ADJUSTMENT ACT (AAA) developed programs for marketing various commodities. Congress strengthened that act two years later and, in 1937, reenacted many of the AAA provisions and amended others. The Agricultural Marketing Agreement Act stressed regulation of marketing, not of PRODUCTION. Responding to Supreme Court decisions that cast doubt on the marketing agreement provisions of the AAA, Congress now emphasized the separability of those sections. The act authorized the secretary of agriculture to set marketing quotas and price schedules and to sign voluntary agreements with producers. If fifty percent of the handlers and two-thirds of the producers of a commodity approved, the secretary could issue marketing orders. All such agreements were exempted from federal antitrust laws. The AAA's earlier effort to achieve parity prices (a level providing income with buying power equivalent to that for 1909–1914) by balancing production with consumption was now replaced by maintenance of "orderly marketing conditions for agricultural commodities in INTERSTATE COMMERCE." In addition, the 1937 act contained a broader definition of interstate and FOREIGN COMMERCE, declaring it to include any part of the "current" that is usual in the handling of a commodity. (See STREAM OF COMMERCE DOCTRINE.) The Supreme Court sustained the act in *United States v. Rock Royal Co-operative* (1939), finding that even a local transaction was "inextricably mingled with and directly affect[ed]" marketing in interstate commerce. The Court took similar action in WRIGHTWOOD DAIRY V. UNITED STATES (1942), even though that case involved purely INTRASTATE COMMERCE.

DAVID GORDON
(1986)

AGRICULTURE

See: *Butler, United States v.;* Subjects of Commerce; *Wickard v. Filburn*

AGUILAR v. FELTON
473 U.S. 402 (1985)

GRAND RAPIDS SCHOOL DISTRICT v. BALL
473 U.S. 373 (1985)

In COMPANION CASES a 5–4 Supreme Court held unconstitutional the assignment of public school teachers to parochial schools for special auxiliary services. In the Grand Rapids "shared time" case, Justice WILLIAM J. BRENNAN for the majority concerned himself only with the possibility that the teachers might advance religion by conforming their instruction to the environment of the private sectarian schools. The evidence did not validate his fear. In *Aguilar,* Brennan expressed the same fear but focused on the "excessive entanglement of church and state" which he asserted was present in New York City's program to implement the ELEMENTARY AND SECONDARY EDUCATION ACT passed by Congress in 1965. Advancing religion and excessive entanglement show violations of the FIRST AMENDMENT'S SEPARATION OF CHURCH AND STATE as construed by the Court in LEMON V. KURTZMAN (1971), where it devised a test to determine whether government has passed a law respecting an ESTABLISHMENT OF RELIGION.

The New York City program employed guidance counselors, psychologists, psychiatrists, social workers, and other specialists to teach remedial reading, mathematics, and English as a second language, and to provide guidance services. They worked part-time on parochial school premises, using only materials and equipment supplied by secular authorities; and, they acted under a ban against participation in religious activities. They worked under supervision similar to that which prevailed in public schools; the city monitored instruction by having supervisory personnel make unannounced "monthly" and "occasional" visits. Almost three-fourths of the educators in the program did not share the religious affiliation of any school in which they taught.

Brennan for the majority traveled a far path to find infirmities in the city's program. He expressed concern that the program might infringe the RELIGIOUS LIBERTY of its intended beneficiaries. He saw government "intrusion into sacred matters" and the necessity of an "ongoing inspection" to ensure the absence of inculcation of religion in the instruction. The need for "a permanent and pervasive State presence in the sectarian schools receiving aid" infringed values protected by the establishment clause.

Thus, if government fails to provide for surveillance to ward off inculcation, its aid unconstitutionally advances the religious mission of the church schools; if government does provide for monitoring, even if only periodically, it gets excessively entangled with religion. Justice SANDRA DAY O'CONNOR, dissenting, declared that the conclusion that the religious mission of the schools would be advanced by auxiliary services provided by the public was "not supported by the facts of this case." The nineteen-year record of the program showed not a single allegation of an attempt to indoctrinate religiously at public expense. The decision adversely affected disadvantaged parochial school children who needed special auxiliary services not provided by their parochial schools.

LEONARD W. LEVY
(1986)

AGUILAR v. TEXAS
378 U.S. 108 (1964)

The rule that an officer's affidavit supporting an application for a SEARCH WARRANT must contain more than the officer's "mere affirmation of suspicion" was established in *Nathanson v. United States* (1933). Probable cause requires a statement of "facts or circumstances" explaining the affiant's belief that criminal activity is afoot, thus allowing the magistrate to make an independent judgment. In *Aguilar* the same rule was applied to an affidavit based on information supplied by an informant.

The *Aguilar* affidavit stated that the officers "had received reliable information from a credible person" that narcotics were kept on the premises. Nothing in the affidavit allowed the magistrate to determine the accuracy of the informant's conclusion. Though hearsay information can satisfy PROBABLE CAUSE, said the Court, the affidavit must give EVIDENCE that the informant spoke from personal knowledge, and explain the circumstances that led the officer to conclude that he "was "credible' or his information "reliable." The *Aguilar* rule was discarded in ILLINOIS V. GATES (1983).

JACOB W. LANDYNSKI
(1986)

AKE v. OKLAHOMA
470 U.S. 68 (1985)

Following the PRECEDENTS of decisions holding that the RIGHT TO COUNSEL requires a state to provide a lawyer to an INDIGENT defendant, the Supreme Court held, 8–1, that the FOURTEENTH AMENDMENT's guarantee of PROCEDURAL DUE PROCESS requires a state to provide an indigent defendant access to such psychiatric examination and assistance necessary to prepare an effective defense based on the claim of insanity. Justice THURGOOD MARSHALL wrote the OPINION OF THE COURT. Chief Justice WARREN E. BURGER, in a CONCURRING OPINION, said that the decision was limited to capital cases. Justice WILLIAM H. REHNQUIST, dissenting, agreed that some such cases might require the state to provide psychiatric assistance, but argued that in this case, where the burden of proving insanity was on the defendant, the state had no such obligation.

KENNETH L. KARST
(1986)

AKRON v. AKRON CENTER FOR REPRODUCTIVE CHOICE

See: Reproductive Autonomy

A. L. A. SCHECHTER POULTRY CORP. v. UNITED STATES

See: *Schechter Poultry Corp. v. United States*

ALBANY PLAN

See: Franklin, Benjamin

ALBERTS v. CALIFORNIA

See: *Roth v. United States*

ALBERTSON v. SUBVERSIVE ACTIVITIES CONTROL BOARD
382 U.S. 70 (1965)

This was one of several cases in which the WARREN COURT, on self-incrimination grounds, struck down compulsory registration provisions aimed at individuals who were members of inherently suspect groups. (See MARCHETTI V. UNITED STATES.) The Communist party failed to register with the government as required by the SUBVERSIVE ACTIVITIES CONTROL BOARD. The Board's order obligated all members of the party to register. By refusing, Albertson made himself liable to criminal penalties; he offered numerous constitutional objections. The Supreme Court decided only his claim that the order violated his RIGHT AGAINST SELF-INCRIMINATION.

Justice WILLIAM J. BRENNAN for an 8–0 Court observed, "Such an admission of membership may be used to prosecute the registrant under the membership clause of the SMITH ACT . . . or under . . . the Subversive Activities Control Act. . . ." The government relied on an old decision requiring all taxpayers to file returns, but Brennan answered that tax regulations applied to the public, not to "a highly selective group inherently suspect of criminal activities." The government also argued that a grant of immunity from prosecution for registrants supplanted the right against self-incrimination. Relying on COUNSELMAN V. HITCHCOCK (1892), Brennan ruled that unless the government provided "absolute immunity" for all transactions relating to coerced admissions, it failed to supplant the right. In KASTIGAR V. UNITED STATES (1972) the Court switched from transactional to use immunity. (See IMMUNITY GRANTS.)

LEONARD W. LEVY
(1986)

ALCOHOL ABUSE

See: Punitive Damages

ALDERMAN v. UNITED STATES
394 U.S. 165 (1969)

During the 1960s, the government admitted it had engaged in illegal electronic surveillance. Criminal defendants overheard in such surveillance sought the transcripts of the conversations to determine whether their convictions had been based on illegal surveillance and were therefore reversible. The government tried to limit the right to challenge electronic surveillance to persons actually overheard and to restrict disclosure of the transcripts to the judge.

The Supreme Court ruled that (1) anyone overheard, or anyone on whose premises conversations were overheard, could challenge the legality of the surveillance, but no one else; and (2) a person found to have been illegally overheard was entitled to see the transcripts to determine whether his conviction was based on illegal surveillance.

HERMAN SCHWARTZ
(1986)

ALEXANDER, JAMES

See: Zenger's Case

ALEXANDER v. HOLMES COUNTY BOARD OF EDUCATION
396 U.S. 19 (1969)

Part of the "southern strategy" that helped elect President RICHARD M. NIXON had been an assertion that the Supreme Court had been too rigid in its treatment of school SEGREGATION. Thus it was no surprise when, on the eve of the opening of the fall 1969 school year, the Justice Department proposed that thirty-three Mississippi school boards be given an extension until December 1 to present DESEGREGATION plans. The UNITED STATES COURT OF APPEALS agreed, and the next day the plaintiffs sought an order from Justice HUGO L. BLACK staying this decision. Justice Black refused the stay but suggested that the case be brought to the whole Supreme Court for an early decision. The Court promptly granted CERTIORARI, heard the case in late October, and before month's end issued its order. The time for ALL DELIBERATE SPEED in school desegregation had run out; the school boards had an obligation "to terminate dual school systems at once." The BURGER COURT would not be a "Nixon Court" on this issue.

KENNETH L. KARST
(1986)

ALIEN

The status of aliens—persons who are not citizens of the United States—presented perplexing constitutional problems in this country only after the great waves of IMMIGRATION began in the nineteenth century. The question seems not to have troubled the Framers of the Constitution. JAMES MADISON, in THE FEDERALIST #42, defended the power of Congress to set a uniform rule of NATURALIZATION as a means for easing interstate friction. Absent such a congressional law, he argued, State A might grant CITIZEN-SHIP to an alien who, on moving to State B, would become entitled to most of the PRIVILEGES AND IMMUNITIES granted by State B to its citizens. Evidently it was assumed from the beginning that aliens were not protected by Article IV's privileges and immunities clause, and it is still the conventional wisdom—although not unchallenged—that aliens cannot claim "the privileges and immunities of citizens of the United States" guaranteed by the FOURTEENTH AMENDMENT.

Alienage has sometimes been treated as synonymous with dissent, or even disloyalty. The ALIEN AND SEDITION ACTS (1798), for example, were aimed not only at American citizens who opposed President JOHN ADAMS but also at their supporters among French and Irish immigrants. The PALMER RAIDS of 1919–1920 culminated in the DEPORTATION of hundreds of alien anarchists and others suspected of SUBVERSIVE ACTIVITIES. At the outbreak of WORLD WAR II, Attorney General FRANCIS BIDDLE was determined to avoid the mass internment of aliens; in the event, however, Biddle deferred to War Department pressure, and more than 100,000 persons of Japanese ancestry, alien and citizen alike, were removed from their West Coast homes and taken to camps in the interior. (See JAPANESE AMERICAN CASES, 1943–1944.)

When the KENTUCKY RESOLUTIONS (1798) protested against the Alien and Sedition Acts, they defended not so much the rights of aliens as STATES' RIGHTS. Indeed, the *rights* of aliens were not a major concern in the nation's early years. Even the federal courts' DIVERSITY JURISDICTION could be invoked in a case involving aliens only when citizens of a state were on the other side, as HODGSON V. BOWERBANK (1809) held. For this jurisdictional purpose, a "citizen" of a state still means a United States citizen who is also a state citizen. (An alien can sue another alien in a state court.) Thus, while a state can grant "state citizenship"—can allow aliens to vote, hold public office, or receive state benefits—that state citizenship does not qualify a person as a "citizen" within the meaning of the Constitution. Some states have previously allowed aliens to vote; even today, some states allow aliens to hold public office.

Most individual rights protected by the Constitution are not limited to "citizens" but extend to "people" or "persons," including aliens. An exception is the right to vote, protected by the FIFTEENTH, NINETEENTH, and TWENTY-SIXTH AMENDMENTS, which is limited to citizens. Aliens do not, of course, have the constitutional freedom of entry into the country that citizens have; aliens' stay here can be conditioned on conduct—for example, the retention of student status—that could not constitutionally be required of citizens. An alien, but not a citizen, can be deported for certain violations of law. In wartime, the property of enemy aliens can be confiscated. Yet aliens are subject to many of the obligations fastened on citizens: they pay taxes along with the rest of us, and, if Congress so disposes, they are as susceptible as citizens to CONSCRIPTION into the armed forces.

Congress, by authorizing the admission of some aliens for permanent residence, accepts those admittees as at least limited members of the national community. The CIVIL RIGHTS ACT OF 1866, for example, protects a resident alien against state legislation that interferes with the alien's earning a livelihood. The vitality of the PREEMPTION DOCTRINE in such cases no doubt rests on two assumptions: that the national government, not the states, has the primary responsibility for the nation's dealings with foreign countries, and that the regulation of another country's nationals is likely to affect those dealings.

Throughout our history, state laws have discriminated against aliens by disqualifying them from various forms of public and private employment, and from receiving public assistance benefits. Early decisions of the Supreme Court mostly upheld these laws, ignoring their evident tensions with congressional policy and rejecting claims based on the Fourteenth Amendment's EQUAL PROTECTION clause. Two decisions in 1948, OYAMA V. CALIFORNIA and TAKAHASHI V. FISH & GAME COMMISSION, undermined the earlier precedents, and in the 1970s the Court made a frontal assault on state discriminations against aliens.

A legislative classification based on the status of alienage, the Court announced in GRAHAM V. RICHARDSON (1971), was a SUSPECT CLASSIFICATION, analogous to a racial classification. Thus, justifications offered to support the classification must pass the test of STRICT SCRUTINY. State restrictions of WELFARE BENEFITS, on the basis of alienage, were accordingly invalidated. Two years later, this reasoning was extended to invalidate a law disqualifying aliens from a state's civil service, SUGARMAN V. DOUGALL (1973), and a law barring aliens from the practice of law, IN RE GRIFFITHS (1973). The string of invalidations of state laws continued with *Examining Board v. Flores de Otero* (1976) (disqualification to be a civil engineer) and *Nyquist v. Mauclet* (1977) (limiting eligibility for state scholarship aid).

In the *Sugarman* opinion, the Court had remarked that some state discriminations against aliens would not have to pass strict judicial scrutiny. The right to vote in state elections, or to hold high public office, might be limited to United States citizens on the theory that such rights are closely connected with the idea of membership in a political community. By the end of the decade, these words had become the foundation for a large exception to the principle of strict scrutiny of alienage classifications. The "political community" notion was extended to a broad category of public employees performing "government functions" requiring the exercise of discretion and re-

sponsibility. Disqualification of aliens from such jobs would be upheld if it was supported by a RATIONAL BASIS. FOLEY V. CONNELIE (1978) thus upheld a law disqualifying aliens to serve as state troopers, and AMBACH V. NORWICK (1979) upheld a law barring aliens from teaching in public schools unless they had shown an intent to become U.S. citizens. *Cabell v. Chavez-Salido* (1982) extended the same reasoning to state probation officers.

At the same time, the Court made clear that when Congress discriminated against aliens, nothing like strict judicial scrutiny was appropriate. *Mathews v. Diaz* (1976) announced an extremely deferential standard of review for such congressional laws, saying that the strong federal interest in regulating foreign affairs provided a close analogy to the doctrine of POLITICAL QUESTIONS—which suggests, of course, essentially no judicial scrutiny at all.

It was argued for a time that the preemption doctrine provides the most complete explanation of the Court's results in alienage cases. The early 1970s decisions, grounded on equal protection theory, instead might have been rested on congressional laws such as the 1866 act. The decisions on "governmental functions," seen in this light, would amount to a recognition that Congress has not admitted resident aliens to the "political community." On this theory, because Congress has not admitted "undocumented" aliens for any purpose at all, state laws regulating them would be viewed favorably. In PLYLER V. DOE (1982), the Supreme Court rejected this line of reasoning and held, 5–4, that Texas had denied equal protection by refusing free public education to children not lawfully admitted to the country while providing it for all other children. The majority, conceding that Congress might authorize some forms of state discrimination, discerned no such authorization in Congress's silence.

The preemption analysis, no less than an equal protection analysis, leaves the key term ("political community") for manipulation; on either theory, for example, the school teacher case seems wrongly decided. And the equal protection approach has one advantage that is undeniable: it focuses the judiciary on questions that bear some relation to life—substantive questions about degrees of discrimination and proffered justifications—rather than on the metaphysics of preemption.

KENNETH L. KARST
(1986)

Bibliography

NOTE 1975 Aliens' Right to Teach: Political Socialization and the Public Schools. *Yale Law Journal* 85:90–111.

—— 1979 A Dual Standard for State Discrimination Against Aliens. *Harvard Law Review* 92:1516–1537.

—— 1979 The Equal Treatment of Aliens: Preemption or Equal Protection? *Stanford Law Review* 31:1069–1091.

—— 1980 State Burdens on Resident Aliens: A New Preemption Analysis. *Yale Law Journal* 89:940–961.

PRESTON, WILLIAM, JR. 1963 *Aliens and Dissenters: Federal Suppression of Radicals, 1903–1933.* Cambridge, Mass.: Harvard University Press.

ROSBERG, GERALD M. 1977 The Protection of Aliens from Discriminatory Treatment by the National Government. *Supreme Court Review* 1977:275–339.

ALIENAGE

See: Immigration and Alienage

ALIEN AND SEDITION ACTS

Naturalization Act
1 Stat. 566 (1798)
Alien Act
1 Stat. 570 (1798)
Alien Enemies Act
1 Stat. 577 (1798)
Sedition Act
1 Stat. 596 (1798)

These acts were provoked by the war crisis with France in 1798. Three of the four acts concerned ALIENS. Federalist leaders feared the French and Irish, in particular, as a potentially subversive force and as an element of strength in the Republican party. The Naturalization Act increased the period of residence required for admission to CITIZENSHIP from five to fourteen years. The Alien Act authorized the President to deport any alien deemed dangerous to the peace and safety of the United States. The Alien Enemies Act authorized incarceration and banishment of aliens in time of war. The Sedition Act, aimed at "domestic traitors," made it a federal crime for anyone to conspire to impede governmental operations or to write or publish "any false, scandalous, and malicious writing" against the government, the Congress, or the President.

While Republicans conceded the constitutionality, though not the necessity, of the Naturalization and Alien Enemies acts, they assailed the others, not only as unnecessary and unconstitutional but as politically designed to cripple or destroy the opposition party under the pretense of foreign menace. The constitutional argument received authoritative statement in the VIRGINIA AND KENTUCKY RESOLUTIONS. In defense of the Alien Act, with its summary procedures, Federalists appealed to the inherent right of the government to protect itself. The same appeal was made for the Sedition Act. Federalists denied, further, that the act violated FIRST AMENDMENT guarantees of FREEDOM OF SPEECH and PRESS, which they interpreted as prohibitions of PRIOR RESTRAINT only. They also claimed that the federal government had JURISDICTION over COMMON LAW crimes, such as SEDITIOUS LIBEL, and so could prosecute without benefit of statute. The statute, they said, liberalized the common law by admitting truth as a defense and authorizing juries to return a general verdict.

Despite the zeal of President JOHN ADAMS' administration, no one was actually deported under the Alien Act. (War not having been declared, the Alien Enemies Act never came into operation.) The Sedition Act, on the other hand, was widely enforced. Twenty-five persons were arrested, fourteen indicted (plus three under common law), ten tried and convicted, all of them Republican printers and publicists. The most celebrated trials were those of Matthew Lyon, Republican congressman and newspaper editor in Vermont; Dr. Thomas Cooper, an English-born scientist and political refugee, in Philadelphia; and James T. Callender, another English refugee, who possessed a vitriolic pen, in Richmond. All were fined upward to $1,000 and imprisoned for as long as nine months. Before partisan judges and juries, in a climate of fear and suspicion, the boasted safeguards of the law proved of no value to the defendants, and all constitutional safeguards were rejected.

The repressive laws recoiled on their sponsors, contributing to the Republican victory in the election of 1800. The Sedition Act expired the day THOMAS JEFFERSON became President. He immediately voided actions pending under it and pardoned the victims. In 1802 the Alien Act expired and Congress returned the NATURALIZATION law to its old footing. Only the Alien Enemies Act remained on the statute book. Nothing like this legislation would be enacted again until the two world wars of the twentieth century.

MERRILL D. PETERSON
(1986)

Bibliography
SMITH, JAMES MORTON 1956 *Freedom's Fetters: The Alien and Sedition Laws and American Civil Liberties.* Ithaca, N.Y.: Cornell University Press.

ALIEN REGISTRATION ACT
54 Stat. 670 (1940)

This measure, popularly known as the Smith Act, was destined to become the most famous of the anticommunist measures of the Cold War, McCarthy period. The act required all ALIENS living in the United States to register with the government, be fingerprinted, carry identification cards, and report annually. Persons found to have ties to "subversive organizations" could be deported. The registration requirement was rescinded in 1982.

Such alien registration was only one of the various purposes of the act. It was directed primarily at SUBVERSIVE ACTIVITIES which were causing growing concerns on the eve of war, particularly communist-inspired strikes intended to injure American defense production. As the first federal peacetime SEDITION statute since 1798, the Smith Act in its most significant section made it a crime to "knowingly, or willfully, advocate, abet, advise, or teach the duty, necessity, desirability, or propriety of overthrowing or destroying any government in the United States by force and violence. . . ." Any attempts forcibly to overthrow the government of the United States by publication or display of printed matters, to teach, or to organize any group, or to become a "knowing" member of such an organization were forbidden. Section 3 forbade conspiracy to accomplish any of these ends. The act carried maximum criminal penalties of a $10,000 fine or ten years in prison or both; no one convicted under the law was to be eligible for federal employment during the five years following conviction.

The act, which did not mention the Communist party, attracted little attention at the time of its passage, and initial enforcement was spotty. Although five million aliens were registered and fingerprinted shortly following its passage, its antisubversive sections were not used until 1943, when a small group of Minneapolis Trotskyites were convicted. When the Cold War intensified, following 1947, the HARRY S. TRUMAN administration began a series of dramatic prosecutions of Communist party leaders. These and subsequent prosecutions eventually forced the Supreme Court to clarify the act's terms, starting with DENNIS V. UNITED STATES (1951), and extending through YATES V. UNITED STATES (1957), SCALES V. UNITED STATES (1961), and *Noto v. United States* (1961). As a result of these rulings, the measure's advocacy, organizing, and membership provisions were limited and made more precise.

PAUL L. MURPHY
(1986)

Bibliography

BELKNAP, MICHAEL R. 1977 *Cold War Political Justice: The Smith Act, the Communist Party, and American Civil Liberties.* Westport, Conn.: Greenwood Press.

ALIEN SUFFRAGE

CITIZENSHIP and voting are so closely linked in the modern political imagination that many Americans are shocked to learn that the United States once had a rich tradition of noncitizens' participating in local, state, and national elections. The practice first appeared in the colonies, which only required voters to be propertied white male residents—not British citizens. After the AMERICAN REVOLUTION and ratification of the Constitution, many of the states, like the Commonwealth of Virginia, continued to enfranchise propertied white male aliens in all state and therefore—under Article I of the Constitution—all federal elections. Congress also gave ALIENS the right to vote for representatives to their territorial legislatures when it reenacted the NORTHWEST ORDINANCE in 1789 and authorized the election of representatives to state constitutional conventions in Ohio, Indiana, Michigan, and Illinois. Although the War of 1812 upset alien suffrage in numerous states, the policy revived as the nation pressed westward in the 1840s and states such as Minnesota, Washington, Kansas, Nebraska, Nevada, Dakota, Wyoming, and Oklahoma tried hard to attract new residents by granting "declarant aliens"—those who had declared their intention to become citizens—VOTING RIGHTS and the symbolic standing they confer.

The CIVIL WAR polarized public sentiment around alien suffrage. Southerners attacked the political influence of immigrants, who generally arrived hostile to the institution of SLAVERY, while Northern states and politicians celebrated alien suffrage as a way to integrate newcomers to democratic life. The Union also drafted declarant aliens into the army on the theory that they were effectively state citizens, even if not yet citizens of the nation. Meanwhile, delegates to the Confederate constitutional convention in Montgomery, Alabama, wrote a blanket ban on alien voting into the CONFEDERATE CONSTITUTION. In the wake of Northern victory in the Civil War, thirteen new states adopted declarant alien suffrage, including Southern states now subject to RECONSTRUCTION governments eager to attract new blood and honor the valor of the many alien soldiers who fought for the Union. By the close of the nineteenth century, about half of the states and territories had experimented with giving aliens the right to vote alongside citizens.

The rise of anti-immigrant feeling at the turn of the twentieth century altered the political terrain that had nourished alien suffrage. Many states revised their constitutions and statutes by imposing a U.S. citizenship test for voting. By the time WORLD WAR I was over, the tide had shifted dramatically against alien suffrage, and the last state—Arkansas—gave it up in 1926. Thus, modern political nationalism and xenophobia displaced the natural rights logic that taxpaying aliens should be represented and the republican norm that communities benefit by participation of all members.

During the long history of alien suffrage, no court ever found noncitizen voting unconstitutional. On the contrary, state and lower federal courts consistently upheld the practice, and the Supreme Court repeatedly signaled its own acceptance of it. In 1874, in MINOR V. HAPPERSETT holding that women had no constitutionally protected right to vote, the Court invoked alien suffrage to prove that citizenship and suffrage are independent legal categories that do not necessarily imply one another. Again in 1904, in *Pope v. Williams*, the Court emphasized that states set voter qualifications themselves and have discretion to define persons who are not U.S. citizens as state and local citizens. As recently as 1973, the Court observed that U.S. citizenship is just a "permissible criterion" for voting rights, not a mandatory one. The Court's reading follows logically from the contrast between the Constitution's explicit U.S. citizenship requirements for service in Congress and its delegation of control over both state and federal qualifications for voting to the states themselves. Of course, alien suffrage is not constitutionally compelled—the Constitution's numerous suffrage provisions guarantee voting rights only to "citizens"—but it is clearly allowed, even today.

Whether alien suffrage has a vibrant future, as opposed to a past, remains to be seen. The practice survives as a remnant in numerous localities, and has found some renewed vitality in recent years. Both the New York and Chicago school systems permit noncitizens to vote in community school board elections. In 1992, the city of Takoma Park, Maryland, which borders Washington, D.C., conducted a referendum on whether to change its municipal charter to give all residents, regardless of citizenship status, the right to vote in city council, mayoral, and INITIATIVE elections. After rich debate on the subject, the measure passed and the City Council unanimously made the change. Proponents argued that immigrant populations are ignored by government if they lack votes, which are the hard currency of political power in democracy, and that noncitizen voting would become a pathway to full citizenship. They also invoked the pervasive European experience with noncitizen voting and the decision of the European Community to allow all citizens of member nations to vote in whatever local community they inhabit. It is possible that the disappearance of borders as barriers to capital investment and labor markets will increase the willingness of American communities to open up their political processes to new immigrants. But it is equally possible that globalization will make us cling harder to the twentieth century's nationalist marriage of voting with federal citizenship. At any rate, the issue of alien suffrage raises profound and interesting issues about the contested meanings of democracy, citizenship, and community membership.

JAMIN RASKIN
(2000)

Bibliography

NEUMAN, GERALD L. 1992 "We Are the People": Alien Suffrage in German and American Perspective. *Michigan Journal of International Law* 13:259–335.

RASKIN, JAMIN B. 1993 Legal Aliens, Local Citizens: The Historical, Constitutional and Theoretical Meanings of Alien Suffrage. *University of Pennsyluzuia Law Review* 141:1391–1470.
ROSBERG, GERALD M. 1977 Aliens and Equal Protection: Why Not the Right to Vote? *Michigan Law Review* 75:1092–1136.

ALL DELIBERATE SPEED

Chief Justice EARL WARREN achieved a unanimous decision in BROWN V. BOARD OF EDUCATION (1954) by assuring that enforcement of school DESEGREGATION would be gradual. Ordinarily, state officials found to be violating the Constitution are simply ordered to stop. *Brown II* (1955), however, instructed lower courts to insist only that offending school boards make "a prompt and reasonable start," proceeding toward full desegregation with "all deliberate speed."

This calculatedly elusive phrase was contributed by Justice FELIX FRANKFURTER, who had borrowed it from an old opinion by Justice OLIVER WENDELL HOLMES. Holmes attributed it to English EQUITY practice, but he may also have seen it in Francis Thompson's poem, "The Hound of Heaven." Whatever the phrase's origins, it was a thin cover for compromise. The objective presumably was to allow time for the white South to become accustomed to the end of SEGREGATION, in the hope of avoiding defiance of the courts and even violence. Robert Penn Warren, a southern man of letters who had not studied quantum mechanics, even tried to make gradualism in desegregation a historical necessity: "History, like nature, knows no jumps."

The South responded not with accommodation but with politically orchestrated defiance. A full decade after *Brown I*, two percent of southern black children were attending integrated schools. By 1969, the Supreme Court explicitly abandoned "all deliberate speed"; in ALEXANDER V. HOLMES COUNTY BOARD OF EDUCATION school boards were told to desegregate "at once."

No one pretends that the Supreme Court could have ended Jim Crow overnight, certainly not without support from Congress or the President. Yet the Court's decisions can command respect only when they are understood to rest on principle. *Brown* II, widely seen to be precisely the political accommodation it was intended to be, did not merely consign a generation of southern black school children to segregated schools. The decision weakened the Court's own moral authority in the very process gradualism was designed to aid.

KENNETH L. KARST
(1986)

Bibliography

WILKINSON, J. HARVIE, III 1979 *From Brown to Bakke*. New York: Oxford University Press.

ALLEN v. WRIGHT
468 U.S. 737 (1984)

The parents of black school children in districts that were undergoing DESEGREGATION brought suit against officials of the Internal Revenue Service (IRS). Alleging that the IRS had not adopted standards and procedures that would fulfill the agency's obligation to deny tax-exempt status to racially discriminatory private schools, the plaintiffs argued that the IRS in effect subsidized unconstitutional school SEGREGATION. The Supreme Court, 5–3, held that the plaintiffs lacked STANDING to raise this claim.

Justice SANDRA DAY O'CONNOR, for the majority, said that the plaintiffs' claim that they had been stigmatized by the IRS conduct was insufficient as a specification of injury, amounting to little more than a general claim that government must behave according to law. The parents' second claim of injury was that they had been denied the right to have their children attend school in a system that was not segregated. Here the asserted injury was sufficient, Justice O'Connor said, but the injury was not fairly traceable to IRS conduct. The Court thus reinforced the "causation" requirement for standing established in *Warth v. Seldin* (1975). The three dissenters made the familiar charge that the "causation" line of inquiry disguised a rejection of the plaintiffs' claim without really addressing the constitutional issue. As in *Warth*, the Court rejected the plaintiffs' claim of injury without giving them the chance to prove their case.

KENNETH L. KARST
(1986)

ALLEN-BRADLEY COMPANY v. LOCAL UNION #3
325 U.S. 797 (1945)

An 8–1 Supreme Court, dominated by appointees of FRANKLIN D. ROOSEVELT, held here that union actions that prompted nonlabor market control and business profits violated the SHERMAN ANTITRUST ACT. The union had obtained CLOSED SHOP agreements with New York City manufacturers of electrical equipment in return for a promise to strike or boycott any contractor who did not use the local manufacturers' equipment. Because out-of-city materials were cheaper, these agreements effectively restrained competition. Justice HUGO L. BLACK, for the Court, found that such action could be enjoined under the Sherman Act because neither the CLAYTON ACT nor the NORRIS-LAGUARDIA ACT protected union action not solely in its own interests.

DAVID GORDON
(1986)

ALLGEYER v. LOUISIANA
165 U.S. 578 (1897)

The Louisiana legislature sought to encourage local business by forbidding state citizens from buying marine insurance from out-of-state companies. Justice RUFUS PECKHAM, building on a long line of dissents by Justice STEPHEN J. FIELD, expounded a broad concept of "liberty" including the idea of FREEDOM OF CONTRACT. Liberty, said the Court, "is deemed to embrace the right of the citizen to be free in the enjoyment of all his faculties." In thus circumscribing state authority over interstate business, *Allgeyer* represents the first invalidation of a state act as a deprivation of freedom of contract without violating the FOURTEENTH AMENDMENT guarantee of DUE PROCESS OF LAW.

DAVID GORDON
(1986)

ALLIED STRUCTURAL STEEL COMPANY v. SPANNAUS
438 U.S. 234 (1978)

The modern revival of the CONTRACT CLAUSE began with UNITED STATES TRUST COMPANY V. NEW JERSEY (1977), a case in which the Supreme Court showed its willingness to make states live up to their own obligations as contracting parties. *Spannaus* carried the new doctrine further, imposing the contract clause as a significant limitation on the power of a state to regulate relations between private contracting parties.

Minnesota law required certain large employers, when they terminated pension plans or left the state, to provide for the funding of pensions for employees with ten years' service. Allied, in its pension plan, had reserved the right to terminate the plan and distribute the fund's assets to retired and current employees. On closing its Minnesota office, under the law Allied had to provide about $185,000 to fund pensions for its ten-year employees. The Supreme Court, 5–3, held the law unconstitutional as an impairment of the OBLIGATION OF CONTRACTS.

Justice POTTER STEWART wrote for the Court. Much of his opinion was devoted to distinguishing HOME BUILDING & LOAN ASSOCIATION V. BLAISDELL (1934). Here the law did not deal with a "broad, generalized economic or social problem" but focused narrowly, not on all employers or even all who left the state, but on those who previously had voluntarily established pension plans. The law did not merely temporarily alter contractual relationships but "worked a severe, permanent and immediate change in those relationships—irrevocably and retroactively." The law also "invaded an area never before subject to regulation by the State," thus invading reliance interests to a greater degree than would result from a more common (and hence foreseeable) type of regulation.

Justice WILLIAM J. BRENNAN, for the dissenters, correctly noted that the Court's opinion amounted to a major change in the judicial role in supervising state economic regulation, demanding STRICT SCRUTINY under the contract clause to protect contract-based expectations.

Spannaus seemed to invite businesses to challenge all manner of ECONOMIC REGULATIONS on the ground of excessive interference with contractual expectations. In *Exxon Corp. v. Eagerton* (1983), however, the Court sought to exorcise the ghost of FREEDOM OF CONTRACT. *Exxon* sharply limited the *Spannaus* principle to laws whose "sole effect" is "to alter contractual duties."

KENNETH L. KARST
(1986)

ALMEIDA-SANCHEZ v. UNITED STATES
413 U.S. 266 (1973)

A roving United States border patrol, without warrant or PROBABLE CAUSE, stopped and searched an automobile for illegal aliens twenty-five miles from the Mexican border. The Court ruled that while routine searches of persons and vehicles at the border are permissible, this search was conducted too far from the border to be reasonable under the FOURTH AMENDMENT.

JACOB W. LANDYNSKI
(1986)

ALVAREZ-MACHAIN, UNITED STATES v.
504 U.S. 655 (1992)

The Constitution requires the President to "take Care that the Laws be faithfully executed." Those laws include both TREATIES and customary INTERNATIONAL LAW. In *United States v. Alvarez-Machain* (1992), however, the executive branch effectively ignored the obligations of the United States under international law, and still it was upheld by the Supreme Court.

Humberto Alvarez-Machain, a Mexican citizen, was indicted for participating in the kidnapping, torture, and murder of a U.S. Drug Enforcement Administration agent. Rather than seek Alvarez-Machain's extradition, the United States offered a reward for his abduction and delivery to the United States. Mexico protested that the abduction violated its extradition treaty with the United States, which provided that neither nation was bound to deliver up its own nationals but that each would have discretion to do so upon the request of the other.

In a 6–3 decision, the Supreme Court concluded that the treaty did not "specify the only way in which one country may gain custody of a national of the other country for the purposes of prosecution" and that, in the absence of an express prohibition, forcible abduction did not violate the treaty. The Court, in a MAJORITY OPINION authored by Chief Justice WILLIAM H. REHNQUIST, acknowledged that such an abduction might still violate "general international law principles," but held that the district court retained JURISDICTION because under the venerable *Ker–Frisbie* rule "the power of a court to try a person for a crime is not impaired by the fact that he has been brought within the court's jurisdiction by reason of a 'forcible abduction.'"

Unfortunately, *Alvarez-Machain* is not the only case in which the executive branch's decision to ignore its treaty obligations has been upheld by the Court. In *Sale v. Haitian Centers Council* (1993), the executive took the position that the United Nations Convention Relating to the Status of Refugees, which forbade its signatories to "return . . . a refugee in any manner whatsoever" to a country where that refugee would suffer persecution, did not prohibit the U.S. Coast Guard from returning refugees intercepted at sea to Haiti. The Court agreed. In *Breard v. Greene* (1998), the United States effectively conceded that the Vienna Convention on Consular Relations had been violated because Virginia had not notified a Paraguayan citizen arrested for murder of his right to consular access. The executive branch argued, however, that the Paraguayan citizen had defaulted this claim by not raising it earlier and that Paraguay was not entitled to bring suit in federal court for a violation of the treaty. The Court agreed. Such cases cast doubt not only on the President's commitment to "take Care that the Laws be faithfully executed" but on the reliability of the United States as a treaty partner as well.

WILLIAM S. DODGE
(2000)

Bibliography

GLENNON, MICHAEL J. 1992 State-Sponsored Abduction: A Comment on *United States v. Alvarez-Machain*. *American Journal of International Law* 86:746–756.

HALBERSTAM, MALVINA 1992 In Defense of the Supreme Court Decision in *Alvarez-Machain*. *American Journal of International Law* 86:736–746.

MANN, F. A. 1989 Reflections on the Prosecution of Persons Abducted in Breach of International Law. Pages 407–421 in Yoram Dinstein, ed., *International Law at a Time of Perplexity*. Dordrecht, The Netherlands: Martinus Nijhoff Publishers.

VAGTS, DETLEV F. 1998 Taking Treaties Less Seriously. *American Journal of International Law* 92:458–462.

AMALGAMATED FOOD EMPLOYEES UNION v. LOGAN VALLEY PLAZA

See: Shopping Centers

AMBACH v. NORWICK
441 U.S. 68 (1979)

Ambach completed the process, begun in FOLEY V. CONNELIE (1978), of carving out a major exception to the principle that discrimination against ALIENS amounts to a SUSPECT CLASSIFICATION, triggering STRICT SCRUTINY of its justifications. New York forbade employment as public school teachers of aliens who had not shown an intention to seek U.S. CITIZENSHIP. The Supreme Court held, 5–4, that this discrimination did not deny its victims the EQUAL PROTECTION OF THE LAWS.

Justice LEWIS F. POWELL, for the majority, concluded that *Foley*, following OBITER DICTA in SUGARMAN V. DOUGALL (1973), implied the exception in question. Where "governmental functions" were involved, the state need show only that the exclusion of aliens had a RATIONAL BASIS. Public school teachers, like police officers, have great individual responsibility and discretion; part of a teacher's function is to transmit our society's values and prepare children to be participating citizens. Under the RATIONAL BASIS standard, the state need not show a close fit between its classification and its objectives; the standard is met if it is rational to conclude that citizens generally would be better able than aliens to transmit citizenship values.

Justice HARRY A. BLACKMUN, author of the *Sugarman* opinion, led the dissenters, pointing out the indiscriminate sweep of the disqualification of aliens, and its tenuous connection with educational goals. (Private schools, for example, were permitted to use alien teachers, even though they were charged with transmitting citizenship values to eighteen percent of New York's children.)

KENNETH L. KARST
(1986)

AMENDING PROCESS

Article V, which stipulates the methods by which the Constitution may be amended, reflects the Framers' attempt to reconcile the principles of the Revolution with their desire for stable government in the future. Early in the CONSTITUTIONAL CONVENTION OF 1787, GEORGE MASON, of Virginia suggested that inclusion in the Constitution of a specified mechanism for future amendments would help channel zeal for change into settled constitutional processes. "Amendments therefore will be necessary," he said, "and it will be better to provide for them, in an easy, regular and constitutional way than to trust to chance and violence." So viewed, the Article V amendment process is a somewhat conservative rendering of the revolutionary spirit that had claimed for the people an inalienable right to alter or abolish an inadequate government.

The Constitution sets out alternative methods both for proposing and for ratifying amendments. Amendments may be proposed by a two-thirds vote of both houses of Congress, or by a national constitutional convention. All of the amendments proposed thus far in our history have emanated from Congress. To become part of the Constitution, proposed amendments must gain the assent of three-fourths of the states. Article V gives Congress the power to choose whether proposed amendments (including any proposed by a constitutional convention) should be submitted to state legislatures or to state conventions for RATIFICATION. Congress has submitted every proposed amendment but one to the state legislatures.

Since 1789, over 5,000 bills proposing amendments to the Constitution have been introduced in Congress. Of these, only thirty-three received the necessary two-thirds vote of both houses of Congress and proceeded to the states for ratification. Twenty-six have been adopted; the remaining seven failed to be ratified. With only a few exceptions, the amendments proposed by Congress have come in clusters; virtually all of them arose during four brief periods.

The first of these periods ran from 1789 to 1804 and produced what may loosely be called the "Anti-Federalist amendments"—the BILL OF RIGHTS, the ELEVENTH AMENDMENT, and the TWELFTH AMENDMENT—each of which was, in part, a concession to Anti-Federalist or Jeffersonian interests. More than half a century passed before the Constitution was again amended. In 1865, sixty-one years after adoption of the Twelfth Amendment, Congress proposed and the states ratified the THIRTEENTH AMENDMENT, the first of the three RECONSTRUCTION amendments. The adoption of the FOURTEENTH AMENDMENT and the FIFTEENTH AMENDMENT followed in 1868 and 1870. A gap of almost another half-century intervened between the Reconstruction amendments and the next four amendments. These last grew out of the Populist and Progressive movements and provided for federal income taxation (the SIXTEENTH AMENDMENT, ratified in 1913), DIRECT ELECTION of senators (the SEVENTEENTH AMENDMENT, ratified in 1913), PROHIBITION (the EIGHTEENTH AMENDMENT, ratified in 1919), and WOMAN SUFFRAGE (the NINETEENTH AMENDMENT, ratified in 1920). A fifth Progressive amendment, the CHILD LABOR AMENDMENT, was proposed in 1924 but was not ratified.

Together, the first three periods accounted for all but three of the amendments adopted before 1960. (The only amendments that did not fall into one of these clusters were the TWENTIETH AMENDMENT, which limits the lame-duck session of Congress and was adopted in 1933; the TWENTY-FIRST AMENDMENT, which repealed prohibition and was adopted in 1933; and the TWENTY-SECOND AMENDMENT, which limits the President to two terms in office and was adopted in 1951). A fourth period of amendment activity lasted from 1961 to 1978. During these years, Congress proposed six amendments, four of which were adopted. The TWENTY-THIRD AMENDMENT gave the DISTRICT OF COLUMBIA three electoral votes in presidential elections. The TWENTY-FOURTH AMENDMENT abolished the POLL TAX for federal elections. The TWENTY-FIFTH AMENDMENT provided rules for presidential disability and PRESIDENTIAL SUCCESSION. The TWENTY-SIXTH AMENDMENT lowered the voting age to eighteen for both state and federal elections.

The fights over adoption of these twenty-six amendments, as well as battles over the proposed amendments that failed to be ratified, have produced conflicts over the proper procedures to be followed under the amendment article. The spare language of Article V leaves a number of questions unanswered. Between 1791 and 1931 the Supreme Court had occasion to address some of these issues. Arguments that there are implicit limits on the kind of amendments that may be adopted have not been accepted. In the *National Prohibition Cases* (1920) the Court rejected the argument that the Eighteenth Amendment (prohibition) was improper because of its interference with the states' exercise of their POLICE POWER. And in *Leser v. Garnett* (1922) the Court held that the Nineteenth Amendment's conferral of VOTING RIGHTS upon women was an appropriate exercise of the amendment power, rejecting the contention that "so great an addition to the electorate if made without the State's consent, destroys its autonomy as a political body."

In several decisions, the Court has given a broad reading to the power of Congress to propose amendments. In *Hollingsworth v. Virginia* (1798) the Court, sustaining the validity of the Eleventh Amendment, held that in spite of the veto clause of Article I, amendments proposed by Congress do not have to be submitted to the President for his signature. In the *National Prohibition Cases* (1920) the Court held that a two-thirds vote of a quorum of each house (rather than two-thirds of the entire membership) is sufficient to propose an amendment. In *Dillon v. Gloss* (1921) the Court held that Congress, when it proposes an amendment, has the power to set a reasonable time limit on ratification, and that seven years is a reasonable limit. The Court also rejected in *United States v. Sprague* (1931) the claim that amendments granting the federal government new, direct powers over the people may properly be

ratified only by the people themselves acting through state conventions, and held that the mode of ratification is completely dependent upon congressional discretion. And when Congress does choose to submit an amendment to state legislatures, those legislatures are exercising a federal function under Article V and are not subject to the control of state law. Thus, in *Hawke v. Smith* (1919) the Court held that a state may not make the legislature's ratification of an amendment dependent upon subsequent approval by a voter REFERENDUM.

From 1798 to 1931 the Supreme Court assumed in decisions such as *Hollingsworth, Hawke,* and *Dillon* that issues of constitutional law arising under Article V were to be determined by the Court in the ordinary course of JUDICIAL REVIEW. In COLEMAN V. MILLER (1939), however, the Court refused to address several challenges to Kansas's ratification of the proposed Child Labor Amendment. Issues such as the timeliness of a ratification and the effect of a state's prior rejection of the validity of its ratification were held to be nonjusticiable questions committed to "the ultimate authority in the Congress of its control over the promulgation of the amendment." The *Coleman* decision suggests that judicial review is precluded for all issues that might be considered and resolved by Congress when, at the end of the state ratification process, Congress decides whether or not to "promulgate" the amendment.

Critics of the *Coleman* decision have disputed the Court's conclusion that "congressional promulgation" should preclude the judiciary from resolving challenges to the constitutional validity of an amendment. Critics even question the very notion of "congressional promulgation" as final, necessary step in the amendment process. The text of Article V notes only two stages for the adoption of an amendment: proposal by Congress (or a convention) and ratification by the states. There is no mention of any further action for an amendment to become valid. The Court had expressly held in *Dillon v. Gloss* (1921) what the language of Article V implies: that a proposed amendment becomes part of the Constitution immediately upon ratification by the last necessary state legislature. No further "promulgation" by Congress (or anyone else) appears to be necessary under Article V.

The only occasion upon which Congress ever undertook, at the end of a ratification process, to "promulgate" the adoption of an amendment was during Reconstruction when Congress passed a resolution declaring the Fourteenth Amendment to have been validly adopted despite disputed ratifications from two states that had attempted to rescind. In deciding *Coleman,* the Supreme Court treated the isolated Reconstruction precedent as a settled feature of the amendment process and held that congressional promulgation of an amendment would be binding on the Courts. *Coleman* remains the Court's last word on how disputed amendment process issues are to be resolved. Unless *Coleman* is reconsidered, any challenges to the validity of the procedures used for amendment will be conclusively determined by the Congress sitting when the required number of ratifications are reported to have been received.

It is difficult to predict how unresolved questions concerning the amendment process might be answered. Among the more warmly disputed issues has been the question of whether a state that has ratified an amendment may validly rescind its ratification. The text of Article V is inconclusive; while it does not mention any right of rescission, such a right might be inferred from the right to ratify. However, most treatise writers and scholars of the nineteenth and twentieth centuries have assumed that ratification was final and rescission ineffective. OBITER DICTUM in *Coleman*, moreover, suggests that the Court might have affirmatively approved the decision of the Reconstruction Congress to ignore purported rescissions.

Arguments that rescission by a subsequent legislature ought to nullify a state's earlier ratification, or that ratifications should be considered valid only if they are sufficiently close in time to reflect a "contemporaneous consensus" among ratifying states, may reflect, in part, an unstated assumption that it ought to be very difficult to amend the Constitution. But even without a requirement that ratifications must remain unrescinded or must come within a confined period of time, an amendment will not become part of the Constitution as long as one chamber in thirteen of the fifty state legislatures simply does nothing. An amendment proposed by a supermajority of the national Congress, and formally accepted at some time by the legislatures of three-fourths of the states (even if some state legislatures also pass resolutions of "rescission"), has passed the tests Article V expressly requires. As JAMES MADISON noted in THE FEDERALIST #43, the amendment article was designed to guard "equally against that extreme facility, which would render the constitution too mutable; and that extreme difficulty which might perpetuate its discovered faults."

To insure that the full range of future constitutional changes would be a viable possibility, the Framers sought to provide some means of constitutional change free of the control of existing governmental institutions. The Framers therefore included alternative mechanisms both for proposing and for ratifying amendments. From the earliest days of the Constitutional Convention, the delegates sought to avoid giving Congress the sole authority to propose amendments. If the proposal of all amendments ultimately depended upon Congress, George Mason argued, "no amendments of the proper kind would ever be obtained by the people, if the Government should become oppressive, as he verily believed would be the case." Other

delegates, however, were apprehensive about the threat to national authority if state legislatures could effectively propose and ratify amendments without the involvement of some institution reflecting the national interest.

The solution to this dilemma was the "convention of the people." In addition to providing that amendments could be proposed by Congress, the final version of Article V provides that Congress must call "a Convention for proposing Amendments" whenever two-thirds of the state legislatures apply for one. Such a convention would be, like Congress, a deliberative body capable of assessing from a national perspective the need for constitutional change and capable of drafting proposed amendments for submission to the states for ratification. At the same time it would not be Congress itself, and therefore would not pose the threat of legislative self-interest's blocking needed reform of Congress.

No national convention for proposing amendments has ever been called. In recent years, however, a number of state legislatures have petitioned Congress to call a convention limited to proposing a particular amendment specified by the applying state legislatures. Some scholars consider these applications to be valid and argue that if similar applications are received from two-thirds of the state legislatures Congress should call the convention and seek to limit the convention to the particular amendment (or subject) specified in the state legislative applications. Others argue that such state applications are invalid because they erroneously assume that the agenda of the convention can properly be controlled by the applying state legislatures. These scholars argue that the only valid applications are those that recognize that a convention for proposing amendments is to be free to determine for itself what amendments should be proposed.

In addition to providing the alternative of a national convention for proposing amendments, Article V also provides an alternative method of ratifying amendments. For each amendment (whether proposed by Congress or by a national convention) Congress is free to choose whether to submit the amendment for ratification to state legislatures or to "conventions" in each state. By giving Congress this authority, Article V preserves the possibility of reforms restricting the power of state legislatures. The Constitution itself was submitted to ratifying conventions in each state, rather than to state legislatures. For thirty-two of the thirty-three proposed amendments Congress chose to submit its proposal to state legislatures. But the use of the convention method of ratification is not unprecedented: The Twenty-First Amendment repealing prohibition was submitted by Congress in 1933 to state conventions. Virtually every state chose to have delegates to its ratifying convention elected, and in every state the election of delegates was, for all practical purposes, a dispositive referendum on whether or not to ratify the amendment. In every state the voters' wishes were expeditiously carried out by the slate that had won election. In less than ten months from the time it was proposed by Congress, the amendment was ratified by elected conventions in three-fourths of the states.

The "convention of the people" was a familiar device in the eighteenth century. It now seems archaic, and the use of either a national convention for proposing amendments or state conventions for ratification are at present fraught with uncertainties. The convention device was nonetheless an imaginative effort to address a universal problem of constitution drafting: how to provide the means for future reform of governmental institutions when the only institutions readily available for proposing and approving changes are those already in existence, and possibly in need of reform themselves.

WALTER DELLINGER
(1986)

Bibliography

DELLINGER, WALTER   1984   The Legitimacy of Constitutional Change: Rethinking the Amendment Process. *Harvard Law Review* 97:386–432.

GRIMES, ALLEN P.   1978   *Democracy and the Amendments to the Constitution*. Lexington, Mass.: Lexington Books.

GUNTHER, GERALD   1979   The Convention Method of Amending the United States Constitution. *Georgia Law Review* 14: 1–25.

ORFIELD, LESTER BERNHARDT   1942   *The Amending of the Federal Constitution*. Ann Arbor: University of Michigan Press; Chicago: Callaghan & Co.

TRIBE, LAURENCE H.   1984   A *Constitution* We Are Amending: In Defense of a Restrained Judicial Role. *Harvard Law Review* 97:433–445.

AMENDING PROCESS
(Update)

Formal amendment of the U.S. Constitution under the procedural SUPERMAJORITY RULES set forth in Article V has been a remarkably rare occurrence. Of the many thousands of amendment proposals that have entered public discussion, only thirty-three have been proposed by Congress. Of those, only twenty-seven have been ratified by the states—with fully half of those consisting of the BILL OF RIGHTS and the RECONSTRUCTION amendments. And the states have never initiated a CONSTITUTIONAL CONVENTION. This experience contrasts sharply with the constitutional practice of the state governments, whose constitutions have been so frequently amended that they have taken on "the prolixity of a legal code"—a vice Chief Justice JOHN MARSHALL, in MCCULLOCH V. MARYLAND (1819), praised the federal Constitution for avoiding.

Several explanations may be offered for this sparing use of the power to amend the federal Constitution. First, Article V's requirements of supermajority approval in the Congress and wide geographical consensus among the states are, as intended, politically daunting as compared with enactment of ordinary LEGISLATION. Second, beyond these structural constraints, a political culture of self-restraint toward the founding document has developed from roots in the framing period. To be sure, Article V made amendment easier than it was under the ARTICLES OF CONFEDERATION, which required the consent of every state. Still, as JAMES MADISON, a principal architect of Article V, cautioned in FEDERALIST No. 49, the amendment power was to be used only "for certain great and extraordinary occasions." This culture of self-restraint has been reinforced by such modern events as the failure of PROHIBITION: the EIGHTEENTH AMENDMENT, which restricted the sale of alcoholic beverages, is the only amendment ever to be repealed, and that repeal, by the TWENTY-FIRST AMENDMENT, was so arduous and time-consuming as to discourage other amendment efforts for a generation.

Third, the Supreme Court has interpreted the original document and its formal amendments with considerable latitude, enabling adaptation to new circumstances and to changes in social understanding without formal amendment. Marshall's capacious interpretation of the powers of the national government may be one reason why the Constitution was amended only twice between the Bill of Rights and Reconstruction. And during the NEW DEAL, constitutional strictures on the powers of the federal and state governments to engage in economic redistribution were relaxed by revisions in judicial interpretation rather than by amendment—a course that some scholars suggest the administration of President FRANKLIN D. ROOSEVELT sought deliberately out of concern that an attempt at formal amendment would be politically untenable.

Against this backdrop of sparse constitutional amendment, the 1990s have witnessed two notable developments. First, although no newly proposed amendment has been adopted since the TWENTY-SIXTH AMENDMENT in 1971, an amendment first proposed by the FIRST CONGRESS in 1789, in language drafted by James Madison, became the TWENTY-SEVENTH AMENDMENT to the Constitution in 1992. This amendment, which delays the effect of any congressional pay raise until after the next election, lay dormant between its initial ratification by six states and the 1980s, when a wave of further state ratifications occurred. Michigan became the thirty-eighth state to ratify on May 7, 1992, providing the needed approval of three-fourths of the state legislatures. The National Archivist certified the amendment as part of the Constitution without congressional approval, and Congress voted thereafter to "accept" it. The apparent national consensus that the amendment was valid despite the two-century time lag between its first and last state ratification suggested that constitutional amendment does not depend on a contemporaneous expression of popular approval, but rather upon formal compliance with the procedures of Article V.

The second recent development is a striking and sudden proliferation of new constitutional amendment proposals that have gained serious consideration in Congress during the 1990s. This rash of constitutional amendment proposals represents the strongest concerted movement for constitutional change since the 1960s and 1970s, when over a dozen amendment proposals received serious consideration—including proposals to authorize SCHOOL PRAYERS, bar SCHOOL BUSING of students for purposes of racial integration, and outlaw ABORTION, none of which ultimately was enacted.

The amendment proposals that reached the floor of the U.S. HOUSE OF REPRESENTATIVES or the U.S. SENATE or both bodies during the 1990s included measures that would require congressional supermajority approval in order to depart from a BALANCED BUDGET; impose TERM LIMITS upon members of Congress; authorize the federal and state governments to punish FLAG DESECRATION; permit Congress greater latitude in regulating CAMPAIGN FINANCE; guarantee religious speech and participation in public programs; and require congressional supermajority approval of tax increases. Some of these amendment proposals, such as those on the balanced budget and flag desecration, failed by only one, two, or three votes in the Senate after passage in the House. Many other amendment proposals have received serious consideration in congressional committees, including measures that would guarantee victims' rights in criminal proceedings; give the President a LINE-ITEM VETO; and exclude the native-born children of illegal immigrants from CITIZENSHIP—as well as one that would amend the amendment process itself by making passage of amendments easier.

The recent amendment proposals have stirred debate between those who urge continued self-restraint and those who believe more frequent constitutional amendment appropriate. Opponents of ready resort to constitutional amendment argue that the function of the fundamental charter in providing NATIONAL UNITY and stability would be undermined if it were cluttered with expressions of momentary political bargains, responses to transient social concerns, or aspirational statements designed largely for symbolic effect—all of which would make it more difficult for the citizenry to distinguish between constitutional law and ordinary politics. On this view, needed constitutional change can be accomplished better through the deliberative process of judicial interpretation than through populist processes that are likely to give short shrift to the effect of amendments on future generations, on existing structural arrangements, and on the related body of constitutional law.

Those who favor readier constitutional amendment, by contrast, stress that the principle of POPULAR SOVEREIGNTY is at the core of American constitutionalism, and caution against idolatrous reverence for existing constitutional text, citing the admonition of THOMAS JEFFERSON against viewing the Constitution "like the ark of the covenant, too sacred to be touched." On this view, the elite and unelected body of the Supreme Court has no monopoly on constitutional wisdom, and its own interpretations merit correction by amendment when they deviate too far from popular will—as proponents of the flag desecration, campaign finance, or term limits amendments suggest the Court did in such decisions as *United States v. Eichman* (1990), BUCKLEY V. VALEO (1976), or *U.S. Term Limits v. Thornton* (1995).

The two camps agree that constitutional amendments ought not be used to solve problems that can be solved through ordinary legislation or the simple exercise of political will. They agree as well that constitutional amendments are sometimes appropriate to embody a compelling need for reform that responds to changed circumstances or consensus and is likely to be recognized as of abiding importance by future generations. They disagree on the scope of the amendment power on the continuum between these points.

KATHLEEN M. SULLIVAN
(2000)

(SEE ALSO: *Amendment Process (Outside Article V); Constitutional Dualism; Nonjudicial Interpretation of the Constitution; Transformation of Constitutional Law.*)

Bibliography
KYVIG, DAVID E.　1996　*Explicit and Authentic Acts: Amending the U.S. Constitution 1776–1995.* Lawrence: University of Kansas Press.

LEVINSON, SANFORD, ed.　1995　*Responding to Imperfection: The Theory and Practice of Constitutional Amendment.* Princeton, N.J.: Princeton University Press.

PAULSEN, MICHAEL STOKES　1993　A General Theory of Article V: The Constitutional Lessons of the Twenty-Seventh Amendment. *Yale Law Journal* 103:677–789.

SULLIVAN, KATHLEEN M.　1996　Constitutional Constancy: Why Congress Should Cure Itself of Amendment Fever. *Cardozo Law Review* 17:691–704.

AMENDMENT PROCESS (OUTSIDE ARTICLE V)

Few constitutional rules are as important as those regarding amendment because these rules define the conditions under which all other constitutional norms may be displaced. It is commonly believed that the words of Article V specify with precision the necessary and sufficient conditions for legitimate constitutional change:

> The Congress, whenever two thirds of both Houses shall deem it necessary, shall propose Amendments to this Constitution, or, on the Application of the Legislatures of two thirds of the several States, shall call a Convention for proposing Amendments, which, in either Case, shall be valid to all Intents and Purposes, as Part of this Constitution, when ratified by the Legislatures of three fourths of the several states, or by conventions in three fourths thereof, as the one or the other Mode of RATIFICATION may be proposed by the Congress; Provided that . . . no State, without its Consent, shall be deprived of its equal Suffrage in the SENATE.

Yet things are not so simple. First, the procedures seem far less precise than one might expect. Can Congress call for a CONSTITUTIONAL CONVENTION limited by subject matter? Does the President have any PRESENTMENT role? What voting rule must a convention follow? What apportionment ratio must it follow? Who sets the rules as to selection of delegates? The spare words of Article V are not very helpful in answering these and many other key questions. If determinate answers do exist, they lie outside of Article V: in other provisions of the Constitution, in the overall structure of the document, and in the history of its creation and amendment (and perhaps also the history of the creation and amendment of analogous legal documents, such as STATE CONSTITUTIONS).

Second, it is far from clear whether Article V lays down universally sufficient conditions for legitimate amendment. Could an amendment modify the rules of amendment themselves? (If so, the "equal suffrage" rules could easily be evaded by two successive "ordinary" amendments, the first of which repealed the "equal suffrage" rules of Article V and the second of which reapportioned the Senate.) Similarly, could a legitimate amendment generally purport to make itself (or any other random provision of the Constitution) immune from further amendment? But if not, what about an amendment that effectively entrenched itself from futher revision by, for instance, outlawing criticism of existing law? For answers, we must look beyond the words of Article V to the general structure of the Constitution and its overriding themes of POPULAR SOVEREIGNTY and republican government, which establish the preconditions for Article V itself. Thus, the rest of the document can help us distinguish between true constitutional amendments (changes within the preexisting deep structure of the document) and constitutional repudiations (which may formally seem to fit Article V, but in fact reject the Constitution's essence of deliberative popular sovereignty.)

Finally, it is also dubious whether Article V specifies universally necessary conditions for legitimate amendment. Two major theories of non-Article V amendment have recently emerged in legal scholarship. The first, championed by Professor Bruce Ackerman, begins by noting that the Philadelphia "Convention," which drafted Article V, was itself acting (in the name of "We, the People") in ways not expressly contemplated by the spare words of Article XIII of the ARTICLES OF CONFEDERATION. Like Article V, Article XIII at first seemed to specify absolutely necessary conditions for legitimate amendment, but Ackerman argues that the Philadelphia experience itself—the process by which our Constitution was framed and ratified—belies any such simplistic idea. And the same is true for Article V, especially given the Framers' self-referential use of the word "convention" in this article. Ackerman goes on to argue that the most important subsequent additions to our constitutional text, the Reconstruction Amendments, were not in fact adopted in strict compliance with Article V, and thus can only be legitimated if we properly recognize that "We, the People" may legitimately amend the Constitution by acting beyond the formal rules of Article V, but within the deep structure of popular sovereignty established by the document as a whole.

The second theory, propounded here, resembles Ackerman's, but differs in important respects. Whereas Ackerman focuses on Article XIII of the Articles of Confederation, this second theory begins by looking at state constitutions in effect in 1787. Virtually all the constitutions had amendment clauses similar to Article V, yet in none of these states was the federal Constitution ratified in strict conformity with the clauses. Like Article V, these clauses at first seemed to specify necessary conditions for amendment, but the events of 1787–89 belie such a simplistic reading. Subsequent developments in state constitutional law confirm the nonexclusivity of various amendment clauses; scores of amendments were adopted in the nineteenth century by means of popular ratification nowhere specified in the text of preexisting amendment clauses. These state clauses illuminate Article V. Like its state constitutional counterparts, Article V nowhere explicitly declares itself to be the only legitimate mechanism of constitutional amendment. Rather, Article V is best read as prescribing only the exclusive mechanism by which ordinary governmental entities—Congress and state legislatures—can amend the document that limits their powers. But Article V nowhere qualifies the right of the sovereign people themselves, acting outside of ordinary government in specially convened national conventions, to alter or abolish their governments at their pleasure. This reading of Article V draws support not only from the language of Article VII and the 1787–89 ratification process, but also from the specific words of, and the popular-sovereignty ideology underlying, the PREAMBLE ("We, the People"); the FIRST AMENDMENT ("right of the People [collectively] to assemble" in conventions); and the NINTH AMENDMENT and the TENTH AMENDMENT (reserving to "the People" collective right to alter and abolish government). Only if a current majority of deliberate citizens can, if they desire, amend our Constitution, can the document truly be said to derive from "We, the People of the United States," here and now, rather than from the hands of a small group of white men ruling us from their graves. Any contrary reading of Article V would violate the Preamble's promise that the Framers' "posterity" would continue to enjoy "the blessings of liberty"—most importantly, the liberty of popular self-government.

In the end, a narrow clause-bound approach is no more satisfying in the Article V context than elsewhere. The rest of the document and its subsequent history must always be consulted—sometimes with, at first, surprising results.

AKHIL REED AMAR
(1992)

Bibliography

ACKERMAN, BRUCE 1984 The Storrs Lectures: Discovering the Constitution. *Yale Law Journal* 93:1013–1072.

——— 1989 Constitutional Politics/Constitutional Law. *Yale Law Journal* 99:453–547.

AMAR, AKHIL REED 1987 Philadelphia Revisited: Amending the Constitution Outside Article V. *University of Chicago Law Review* 55:1043–1104.

BLACK, CHARLES 1963 The Proposed Amendment of Article V: A Threatened Disaster. *Yale Law Journal* 72:957–966.

——— 1972 Amending the Constitution: A Letter to a Congressman. *Yale Law Journal* 82:189–215.

CAPLAN, RUSSELL 1988 *Constitutional Brinksmanship.* New York: Oxford University Press.

DELLINGER, WALTER 1979 The Recurring Question of a "Limited" Constitutional Convention. *Yale Law Journal* 88:1623–1640.

——— 1983 The Legitimacy of Constitutional Change: Rethinking the Amendment Process. *Harvard Law Review* 97:386–432.

HALLETT, BENJAMIN FRANKLIN 1848 *Argument in the Rhode Island Causes on the Rights of the People.* Boston: Beale and Greene.

HOAR, ROGER SHERMAN 1917 *Constitutional Conventions.* Boston: Little, Brown.

JAMESON, JOHN ALEXANDER 1887 *A Treatise on Constitutional Conventions*, 4th ed. Chicago: Callaghan and Co.

VAN ALSTYNE, WILLIAM 1978 Does Article V Restrict the States to Calling Unlimited Conventions Only?—A Letter to a Colleague. *Duke Law Journal* 1978:1295–1306.

——— 1979 The Limited Constitutional Convention—The Recurring Answer. *Duke Law Journal* 1979:985–998.

WOOD, GORDON 1969 *The Creation of the American Republic, 1776–1789.* Chapel Hill: North Carolina Press.

AMERICAN CIVIL LIBERTIES UNION

The American Civil Liberties Union (ACLU) is the most important national organization dedicated to the protection of individual liberty. It was founded in 1920 by a distinguished group that included ROGER BALDWIN, Jane Addams, FELIX FRANKFURTER, Helen Keller, Scott Nearing, and Norman Thomas.

The principles of the ACLU are contained in the BILL OF RIGHTS: the right to free expression, above all, the freedom to dissent from the official view and majority opinion; the right to equal treatment regardless of race, sex, religion, national origin, or physical handicap; the right to DUE PROCESS in encounters with government institutions—courts, schools, police, bureaucracy—and with the repositories of great private power; the right to be let alone—to be secure from spying, from the unwarranted collection of personal information, and from interference in private lives.

The ACLU has participated in many controversial cases. It represented John Scopes when he was fired for teaching evolution; it fought for the rights of Sacco and Vanzetti; it defended the Scottsboro Boys, who were denied a FAIR TRIAL for alleged rape (see POWELL V. ALABAMA; NORRIS V. ALABAMA); it fought the Customs Bureau when it banned James Joyce's *Ulysses* (see UNITED STATES V. "ULYSSES"); it opposed the censorship of the Pentagon Papers (see NEW YORK TIMES V. UNITED STATES) and religious exercises in schools.

The ACLU has supported racial and religious minorities, the right of LABOR to organize, and equal treatment for women, and it has opposed arbitrary treatment of persons in closed institutions such as mental patients, prisoners, military personnel, and students.

The concept of CIVIL LIBERTIES, as understood by the ACLU, has developed over the years. For example, in the 1960s it declared that CAPITAL PUNISHMENT violated civil liberties because of the finality and randomness of executions; that military conscription, which substantially restricts individual autonomy, violated civil liberties except during war or national emergency; and that the undeclared VIETNAM WAR was illegal because of failure to abide by constitutional procedures for committing the country to hostilities.

On the other hand, while endorsing many legal protections for poor people, the ACLU has never held that poverty itself violated civil liberties. In addition, since a cardinal precept of the ACLU is political nonpartisanship, it does not endorse or oppose judicial nominees or candidates for public office.

The ACLU has been frequently attacked as subversive,

communistic, and even a "criminals' lobby." Its detractors have not recognized that by representing radicals and despised minorities the ACLU does not endorse their causes but rather the primacy and indivisibility of the Bill of Rights. This confusion cost the ACLU many members when in 1977 it secured the right of American Nazis to demonstrate peacefully in Skokie, Illinois.

The ACLU's national headquarters are in New York City; it maintains a legislative office in Washington, D.C., and regional offices in Atlanta and Denver. Its 250,000 members are organized in branches in all fifty states, which are tied to the national organization through revenue-sharing, participation in policy decisions, and united action on common goals. Each affiliate has its own board of directors and hires its own staff. The ACLU participates annually in thousands of court cases and administrative actions, legislative lobbying, and public education.

NORMAN DORSEN
(1986)

Bibliography

DORSEN, NORMAN 1984 The American Civil Liberties Union: An Institutional Analysis. *Tulane Lawyer* (Spring) 1984:6–14.

AMERICAN COMMUNICATIONS ASSOCIATION v. DOUDS
339 U.S. 382 (1950)

In one of the first cases in which the Supreme Court gave constitutional approval to the anticommunist crusade, Chief Justice FRED VINSON upheld provisions of the TAFT-HARTLEY ACT denying National Labor Relations Board services to unions whose officers had not filed affidavits stating they were not members of the Communist party and that they did "not believe in . . . the overthrow of the . . . Government by force or by any illegal or unconstitutional methods." The opinion of the Court became a model for denying FIRST AMENDMENT protections to alleged subversives through the use of a balancing technique. The Court argued that the statute touched only a few persons and that the only effect even upon them was that they must relinquish their union offices, not their beliefs. It argued that banning communists from NLRB-supported labor negotiations was reasonably related to the legitimate congressional end of protecting INTERSTATE COMMERCE, given the nature of the Communist party and the threat of political strikes. The Court concluded that "Considering the circumstances . . . the statute . . . did not unduly infringe freedoms protected by the First Amendment."

MARTIN SHAPIRO
(1986)

AMERICAN INDIANS AND THE CONSTITUTION

Indians are mentioned only three times in the Constitution. Yet the Supreme Court has developed a vast body of law defining the status of Indians and tribes in our federal system. This law makes use of constitutional sources but also draws heavily on the history between Indians and the federal government, including wars, conquest, treaties, and the assumption by the government of a protectorate relationship toward the tribes. It reveals that our government is not only, as is popularly believed, one of dual sovereigns, federal and state. There is also a third sovereign, consisting of Indian tribes, operating within a limited but distinct sphere.

The three references to Indians in the Constitution presage this body of law. Two of the three are found in Article I and the FOURTEENTH AMENDMENT, which exclude "Indians not taxed" from the counts for apportioning DIRECT TAXES and representatives to Congress among the states. The third reference is a grant of power to Congress in the COMMERCE CLAUSE of Article I to "regulate Commerce with . . . the Indian Tribes."

The phrase "Indians not taxed" was not a grant of tax exemption. Rather, it described the status of Indians at the time the Constitution was written. Indians were not taxed because generally they were treated as outside the American body politic. They were not United States citizens, and they were not governed by ordinary federal and state legislation. Tribal laws, treaties with the United States, and special federal Indian legislation governed their affairs. Only the few Indians who had severed their tribal relations and come to live in non-Indian communities were treated as appropriate for counting in the constitutionally mandated apportionment.

The phrase probably was chosen because the apportionment served partly to allocate tax burdens. That aspect of the apportionment has lost significance, however, since the SIXTEENTH AMENDMENT made it unnecessary for the federal government to apportion income taxes.

The exclusion of "Indians not taxed" from all aspects of apportionment has, in fact, been mooted by changes in the status of American Indians since ratification of the Fourteenth Amendment in 1868. Treaty-making with Indian tribes ended in 1871, and in 1924 all native-born Indians who had not already been made citizens by federal statute were naturalized. Indians were held subject to federal statutes, including tax laws, except where special Indian legislation or treaties offered exemptions. By 1940 the Department of the Interior officially recognized that there no longer were Indians who can properly be considered "Indians not taxed."

The commerce clause reference to Indians, by contrast, continues to have real force. Since the abandonment of federal treaty-making with Indian tribes in 1871, it has been the primary constitutional provision supporting exercises of federal power over Indians as such. Notwithstanding its reference to commerce "with the Indian Tribes," the clause also applies to transactions with individual tribal Indians, including some off-reservation transactions, and to non-Indians doing business on reservations. Congress's Article I power to regulate "the Territory or other Property belonging to the United States" supplements the treaty and Indian commerce clause powers. Most Indian lands are held in fee by the United States, subject to a beneficial tribal interest in reservations set aside by treaty or EXECUTIVE ORDER, and to the Indians' right of occupancy. Congress's power to make war was also invoked in the early years of dealing with the Indians.

This combination of powers, read together with the NECESSARY AND PROPER CLAUSE of Article I and the SUPREMACY CLAUSE of Article VI, has been the foundation of a complex structure of federal, state, and tribal relations. The federal government's power over Indian affairs is extensive and preemptive of state power. (See CHEROKEE INDIAN CASES, 1831–1832.) In the nineteenth century the courts called the federal power "plenary," and challenges to its exercise were labeled POLITICAL QUESTIONS. In fact this federal authority is a general POLICE POWER, comparable to Congress's power over the DISTRICT OF COLUMBIA and the TERRITORIES. In *Delaware Tribal Business Committee v. Weeks* (1977), the Court held that ordinary constitutional strictures apply to federal Indian legislation, and that, under the Fifth Amendment's DUE PROCESS CLAUSE in particular, such legislation must be reviewed to determine whether it is "tied rationally to the fulfillment of Congress's unique obligation toward the Indians." Even though this trust obligation has not prevented Congress from enacting laws contrary to the best interests of Indians, the Supreme Court now insists upon some determination that Indians will be protected when disadvantageous laws are passed. Thus, for example, Congress may not take Indian property for a non-Indian use without paying JUST COMPENSATION, and it may not arbitrarily give tribal assets to some tribal members but not others.

A law that satisfies the "tied rationally" test is not constitutionally defective under the EQUAL PROTECTION requirement of the Fifth Amendment's due process clause simply because it singles out Indians for special treatment. For example, Congress may establish a preference for employment of tribal Indians with the Bureau of Indian Affairs, or may subject Indians to harsher punishments than non-Indians would suffer in state court for doing the same acts. Such legislation is held not to constitute an otherwise forbidden racial classification, because of the separate status of Indians under the Constitution (i.e., their subjection to federal and tribal rather than state jurisdiction).

Although Congress has enacted laws governing a wide variety of activities on Indian reservations, there is no detailed code comparable to the District of Columbia's. In the absence of such federal legislation, states and Indian tribes have competed for control. The Supreme Court has repeatedly upheld tribal independence from state jurisdiction, basing its decisions on preemptive federal power over Indian affairs and the broad federal policy of setting aside lands for tribal self-government. Although in cases outside Indian law the Supreme Court has refused to apply the PREEMPTION DOCTRINE to exclude the operation of state law where congressional intent was doubtful, in Indian cases it has inferred preemptive intent from the general purposes of treaties and statutes to protect tribal resources and promote tribal sovereignty. Thus, absent clear and express congressional consent, states may not regulate non-Indian activities that affect tribal self-government. Despite their lack of authority over reservation Indians, states are prohibited by the Fourteenth Amendment from denying Indians rights available under state law.

Within their realm of authority, Indian tribes exercise powers of self-government, not because of any DELEGATION OF POWERS, but rather because of their original, unrelinquished tribal sovereignty. The Supreme Court recognized this sovereign status of Indian tribes in *United States v. Wheeler* (1978), which held that it would not constitute DOUBLE JEOPARDY to try an Indian in federal court after he had been convicted in tribal court because the court systems belong to separate sovereigns. The Constitution has never been invoked successfully to prevent Congress from abolishing tribal authority in whole or in part; but the Supreme Court has required a clear and specific expression of congressional intent before recognizing the termination of tribal powers. This canon of construction was established to implement the federal government's obligation to protect the Indian tribes. Some tribal powers were necessarily relinquished when the United States incorporated the tribes, such as the power to carry on foreign relations, the power to transfer Indian land without consent of the United States, and the power to prosecute non-Indians for crimes. These relinquished powers are few, however, and Congress could restore them if it chose.

Because the BILL OF RIGHTS limits only the federal government and the Fourteenth Amendment limits only the states, Indian tribes need not follow their dictates. However, in 1968, Congress enacted the Indian Civil Rights

Act, which conferred some but not all protections of the Bill of Rights on individuals subject to tribal authority.

CAROLE E. GOLDBERG-AMBROSE
(1986)

Bibliography

COHEN, F. 1982 *Handbook of Federal Indian Law.* Indianapolis: Bobbs-Merrill.
GETCHES, D. and WILKINSON, C. 1979 *Federal Indian Law: Cases and Materials.* St. Paul, Minn.: West Publishing Co.
PRICE, M. 1973 *Law and the American Indian: Readings, Notes and Cases.* Indianapolis: Bobbs-Merrill.

AMERICAN INDIANS AND THE CONSTITUTION
(Update)

American Indians are a casual part of the text of the Constitution. They are mentioned primarily in passing in the apportionment clause of section 2 and the COMMERCE CLAUSE of section 8 of Article I. The language of apportionment is again found in the FOURTEENTH AMENDMENT. In all three instances, the primary purpose was to define the powers of Congress and limitations on the states, not to provide a clear understanding of the relationship between the United States and the Indian tribes then living within and bordering the United States. Today, a large body of federal law governs relations among the federal government, the states, and the Indian tribes. The main constitutional foundations for these enactments are Congress's power to regulate commerce "with the Indian tribes" (construed to reach transactions with individual Indians), the NECESSARY AND PROPER CLAUSE, and the TREATY POWER.

In colonial times, the individual colonies dealt with Indians by royal authority or on their own initiative, and the power to deal with Indians on an individual state basis was preserved in the ARTICLES OF CONFEDERATION. Land purchases by states were permissible, but conducting war with Indian tribes required the consent of the CONTINENTAL CONGRESS. The English and French method for dealing with Indians had been the negotiation of treaties, and the United States continued the practice. The treaty clause of Article II, section 2 was employed to make treaties with Indian tribes, and the states were prohibited from making treaties by Article I, section 10. State treaties made with tribes before the Constitution was adopted remained valid, and in fact, some state treaties made before 1789 are still in force. While Indian treaty-making was a formal practice of the United States until 1871, Congress had been legislating concerning Indian affairs since the earliest days, beginning with the Non-Intercourse Act of 1793, which regulated trade with Indians.

In 1870, the SENATE JUDICIARY COMMITTEE issued a report that declared Indians to be subject to tribal JURISDICTION and to have allegiance to their own nations. The next year, however, the U.S. HOUSE OF REPRESENTATIVES insisted that the power of the President to recognize Indians for treaty-making purposes should be curtailed, and the U.S. SENATE agreed. Thereafter, agreements and contracts having the legal status of treaties were used to deal with Indians. More recently, congressional LEGISLATION has been used to resolve long-standing problems involving Indian rights and claims.

Two MARSHALL COURT decisions, *Cherokee Nation v. Georgia* (1831) and *Worcester v. Georgia* (1832), created the concept of the "domestic dependent nation" which was used to characterize the status of Indian tribes with respect to the federal government. *Johnson v. McIntosh* (1823) bolstered the idea that the United States had a special responsibility for the welfare of American Indians. This responsibility took both legal and political forms. On the legal side, *Delaware Tribal Business Committee v. Weeks* (1977) held that the DUE PROCESS clause of the Fifth Amendment required Congress, in enacting Indian legislation, to show that it bore a rational relation to fulfilling the United States' trust obligation. This trust responsibility also produced a legal obligation of federal ADMINISTRATIVE AGENCIES to protect tribal interests when those interests might be compromised by government action, such as the licensing of a dam with adverse environmental effects. On the political side, the idea of trust responsibility gradually blossomed into massive programs to assist Indians in adjusting to the economic and political institutions of the West. The Supreme Court confused the issue considerably in *United States v. Kagama* (1886) when it invoked this trust responsibility as a basis of congressional power, even as it ruled that the commerce clause did not justify the establishment of a CRIMINAL JUSTICE SYSTEM on an Indian reservation. In concluding that the trust responsibility gave the federal government such powers, the Court appeared to give Congress virtually unlimited power over Indians.

The Constitution did not, of its own force, limit the powers of tribal governments. In *Talton v. Mayes* (1896), the Court upheld the laws of the Cherokee Nation regarding GRAND JURY composition on the grounds that the Cherokees were self-governing, and had been so since before the adoption of the Constitution. Therefore, only the powers the Indian nation had specifically surrendered were to be subject to constitutional protection. This theory was reaffirmed sixty years later by a lower federal court in *Native American Church v. Navajo Tribal Council* (1959), laying the groundwork for modern tribal SOVEREIGNTY claims that tribes are separate political entities with a status higher than states.

The Indian Civil Rights Act of 1968 reduced this political isolation, imposing on tribes some of the guarantees of the federal Constitution in their dealings with individuals, including their own citizens. RELIGIOUS LIBERTY was the most notable constitutional guarantee not imposed on Indian tribes, because some of them were traditional theocracies. This law was enacted in response to a lower court ruling in 1965, *Colliflower v. Garland,* in which it was decided that an Indian could appeal a tribal court decision to a federal district court on the ground that the tribal court was partially a creation of the national government.

As a rule, constitutional guarantees have not been interpreted to protect American Indians directly. Although the THIRTEENTH AMENDMENT did away with SLAVERY, Congress had to pass a special act to prevent Navajo "peonage" and end the slave trade in captured children in the Southwest. *Elk v. Wilkins* (1884) ruled that even though Indians were born within the United States, they had to have a definite act by the United States to qualify as citizens and voters under the Fourteenth Amendment and the FIFTEENTH AMENDMENT; abandonment by the individual of tribal relations was insufficient by itself to sever his or her tribal membership. Neither the PROHIBITION amendment nor its repeal affected the sale of alcohol to American Indians, because treaties and federal statutes had already prohibited the activity.

The FIRST AMENDMENT guarantee of religious liberty has never been made effective for Indians. Church and state worked hand-in-hand to assimilate Indians, and for a long time missionaries were asked to provide educational opportunities that the federal government was bound to make available to the tribes. With the "peace policy" of President ULYSSES S. GRANT, churches were able to nominate Indian agents for the different reservations, eliminating any real distinction between state and church. In *Quick Bear v. Leupp* (1908), the Court ruled that it was permissible for the federal government to allocate tribal funds for sectarian education under the guise of granting religious freedom to the followers of certain Christian denominations. But the decision sought to circumvent federal statutory prohibitions on the use of public funds for religious education.

Persistent efforts were made to eliminate the use of peyote by Indians, beginning with congressional hearings in 1919 that sought to bring the cactus plant within prohibitions against alcoholic beverages. State courts were more reasonable in upholding the freedom of religion in the use of peyote until EMPLOYMENT DIVISION, DEPARTMENT OF HUMAN RESOURCES OF OREGON V. SMITH (1990), when the U.S. Supreme Court ruled that an Oregon anti-peyote statute could be applied constitutionally to the taking of peyote during Native American religious ceremonies. An earlier decision, *Lyng v. Northwest Indian Cemetery Protective Association* (1988), had found no violation of religious freedom in the federal government's authorization of a logging road through portions of a wilderness in California used by several tribes as vision quest and ceremonial sites. *Smith* and *Lyng,* considered together, constitute a serious impairment of American Indians' religious freedom. Recently, however, both Congress and some state legislatures have enacted laws that are more protective of Indian religious beliefs and practices.

Fifth Amendment protections of PROPERTY have also been impaired as a result of the complications introduced by treaties and land cessions of the late nineteenth century. One major problem has been to discover the primary role of the United States in these transactions. At the time of land cessions, did the government act as a purchaser or as the tribe's trustee? The Indian Claims Commission, in resolving long-standing land claims, had found that the Indians were paid unconscionably low sums for their lands. This conclusion led the courts to suggest, without clearly articulating the idea, that some land deals were in fact confiscations without JUST COMPENSATION. In *United States v. Sioux Nation of Indians* (1980), the Court reaffirmed that a transaction in which the United States acts as a "trustee," to advance a tribe's interests, is not subject to the just compensation clause of the Fifth Amendment. The Court made clear, however, that no presumption of congressional good faith could substitute for a careful judicial inquiry into that "factual" question. The cardinal rule in deciding these cases now seems to be that the government must identify which of two hats it will wear—trustee for the Indians or purchaser of land.

In the 1960s and 1970s, the trend in Indian affairs was to subcontract to tribal councils the administration of programs that the government would otherwise provide for reservation residents. A new line of thought, devised by the U.S. Bureau of Indian Affairs to slow the growth of this movement, has been to argue that either the APPOINTMENTS CLAUSE of Article II or a principle of nondelegation of powers prevents the federal government from surrendering any real decisionmaking to the tribes. Although this reasoning is contradicted by a century of administrative practices to the contrary, it illustrates the propensity of federal officials to rely on constitutional phrases to justify their positions.

In the early 1950s, Senator Patrick McCarran proposed a new constitutional amendment that would eliminate trade with Indian tribes from the commerce clause, but Congress rejected the amendment. His fellow legislators could not imagine another constitutional rubric under which the United States would have authority to deal with

Indian matters. The incident illustrates the extreme confusion and frustration involved in establishing a firm constitutional basis for treating Indians differently from other Americans. While the present structure of intergovernmental relations is based primarily on historical precedent, it is difficult to see how another structure, whether or not based on an amendment to the Constitution, could resolve the current conflicts of authority. One avenue would be to create a new property title for Indian lands, eliminating the so-called trust responsibility that rests on early international law and the doctrine of discovery. Indians as a group undoubtedly qualify for constitutional protection against state RACIAL DISCRIMINATION along the lines of BROWN V. BOARD OF EDUCATION (1954). Congressional discrimination presents more complicated issues; *Morton v. Mancari* (1974) upheld a hiring preference for qualified Indians in the federal Bureau of Indian Affairs.

VINE DELORIA, JR.
(2000)

(SEE ALSO: *Cherokee Indian Cases.*)

Bibliography

NEWTON, NELL JESSUP 1984 Federal Power Over Indians: Its Sources, Scope, and Limitations. *University of Pennsylvania Law Review* 132:195–288.

PEVAR, STEPHEN L. 1992 *The Rights of Indians and Tribes: The Basic ACLU Guide to Indian and Tribal Rights*, 2nd ed. Carbondale: Southern Illinois University Press.

STRICKLAND, RENNARD, ed. 1982 *Felix S. Cohen's Handbook of Federal Indian Law.* Charlottesville, Va.: Bobbs-Merrill.

WILKINSON, CHARLES F. 1987 *American Indians, Time, and the Law: Native Societies in a Modern Constitutional Democracy.* New Haven, Conn.: Yale University Press.

AMERICAN INSURANCE COMPANY v. CANTER
1 Peters 511 (1828)

Although the Constitution authorizes Congress to govern the TERRITORIES of the United States, it does not authorize the acquisition of territories. Consequently THOMAS JEFFERSON had constitutional qualms when he acquired the Louisiana Territory by treaty. This case settled the authority of the United States to acquire territory by the WAR POWERS or TREATY POWER, and sustained the power of Congress to establish LEGISLATIVE COURTS with JURISDICTION extending beyond the JUDICIAL POWER OF THE UNITED STATES as defined by Article III, section 2.

LEONARD W. LEVY
(1986)

AMERICAN JEWISH CONGRESS

Formed originally in 1918 as a temporary confederation of Jewish organizations to propose a postwar program by the Jewish people for presentation at the Versailles Peace Conference, the American Jewish Congress continued in existence and became fully organized under the chairmanship of Rabbi Stephen S. Wise in 1928. In the 1930s it emerged as a leading force in the anti-Nazi movement and in efforts to aid the victims of Hitlerism.

A new and still continuing chapter in its history was initiated in 1945 when, under the leadership of three socially minded lawyers, Alexander H. Pekelis, Will Maslow, and Leo Pfeffer, it established a Commission on Law and Social Action. The commission was based on two premises: that the security of American Jews is interdependent with that of all religions, races, and other national minorities, and that the security of all is dependent upon the integrity of the BILL OF RIGHTS and the EQUAL PROTECTION clause of the FOURTEENTH AMENDMENT.

Accordingly, the organization's legal staff have instituted litigation or submitted briefs AMICUS CURIAE in a wide variety of constitutional law cases, acquiring a status parallel to that of the AMERICAN CIVIL LIBERTIES UNION and the National Association for the Advancement of Colored People. Typical of these are suits challenging the constitutionality of the death penalty under the Eighth Amendment, racial SEGREGATION in public schools, anti-abortion legislation, racially RESTRICTIVE COVENANTS, LITERACY TESTS, for voters, disinheritance of illegitimate children, and denial of tax exemption to organizations advocating overthrow of government.

However, by far the majority of suits in which the organization has participated, either as amicus or as party, have involved either the establishment clause or the free exercise clause of the FIRST AMENDMENT, or the ban in Article VI of RELIGIOUS TESTS for public office. The commission's primacy in this arena is generally recognized among jurists, organizations, and scholars.

LEO PFEFFER
(1986)

Bibliography

PEKELIS, ALEXANDER H. 1950 *Law and Social Action.* Ithaca, N.Y.: Cornell University Press.

AMERICAN REVOLUTION AND CONSTITUTIONAL THEORY

The era of the American Revolution was one of the greatest and most creative periods of CONSTITUTIONALISM in modern history. The American revolutionaries virtually established the modern idea of a written constitution. There had, of course, been written constitutions before in Western history, but the Americans did something new and different. They made written constitutions a practical and everyday part of governmental life. They showed the world how written constitutions could be made truly fundamental and distinguishable from ordinary legislation and how such constitutions could be interpreted on a regular basis and altered when necessary. Further, they offered the world concrete and usable governmental institutions for carrying out these constitutional tasks.

Before the era of the American Revolution a constitution was rarely distinguished from the government and its operations. In the English tradition a constitution referred not only to FUNDAMENTAL RIGHTS but also to the way the government was put together or constituted. "By constitution," wrote Lord Bolingbroke in 1733, "we mean, whenever we speak with propriety and exactness, that assemblage of laws, institutions and customs, derived from certain fixed principles of reason, directed to certain fixed objects of public good, that compose the general system, according to which the community hath agreed to be governed." The English constitution, in other words, included both fundamental principles and rights and the existing arrangement of governmental laws, customs, and institutions.

By the end of the revolutionary era, however, the Americans' idea of a constitution had become very different from that of the English. A constitution was now seen to be no part of the government at all. A constitution was a written document distinct from, and superior to, all the operations of government. It was, as THOMAS PAINE said in 1791, "a thing *antecedent* to a government, and a government is only the creature of a constitution." And, said Paine, it was "not a thing in name only; but in fact." For the Americans a constitution was like a Bible, possessed by every family and every member of government. "It is the body of elements, to which you can refer, and quote article by article; and which contains . . . everything that relates to the complete organization of a civil government, and the principles on which it shall act, and by which it shall be bound." A constitution thus could never be an act of a legislature or of a government; it had to be the act of the people themselves, declared JAMES WILSON in 1790, one of the principal Framers of the federal Constitution in 1787; and "in their hands it is clay in the hands of a potter; they have the right to mould, to preserve, to improve, to refine, and furnish it as they please." If the English thought this new idea of a constitution resembled, as Arthur Young caustically suggested in 1792, "a pudding made by a recipe," the Americans had become convinced the English no longer had a constitution at all.

It was a momentous transformation of meaning in a short period of time. It involved not just a change in the Americans' political vocabulary but an upheaval in their whole political culture.

The colonists began the imperial crisis in the early 1760s thinking about constitutional issues in much the same way as their fellow Britons. Like the English at home, they believed that the principal threat to the people's rights and liberties had always been the prerogative powers of the king, those ancient but vague and discretionary rights of authority that the king possessed in order to carry out his responsibility for governing the realm. Indeed, the whole of English history was seen as a perennial struggle between these two conflicting rights—between a centralizing monarchy trying to fulfill its obligation to govern, on the one hand, and, on the other, local-minded nobles and people, in the House of Lords and the House of Commons, trying to protect their liberties. Each of the great political events of England's past, from the Norman Conquest to the Glorious Revolution, marked a moment defining the proper relationship between these two sets of conflicting rights—between power and liberty.

The eighteenth-century colonists had no reason to think about government much differently. Time and again they had been forced to defend their liberties against the intrusions of royal prerogative power. Relying for their defense on their colonial assemblies, their miniature counterparts to the House of Commons, they invoked their rights as Englishmen and what they called their ancient COLONIAL CHARTERS as devices guaranteeing the rights of the people against their royal governors. In fact, the entire English past was littered with such charters and other written documents to which the English people had repeatedly appealed in defense of their rights against the crown's power. All these documents, from MAGNA CARTA to the BILL OF RIGHTS of 1689, were merely written evidence of those "fixed principles of reason" from which Bolingbroke had said the English constitution was derived.

Although eighteenth-century Englishmen talked about the fixed principles and the fundamental law of the constitution, few of them doubted that Parliament, as the representative of the nobles and people and as the sovereign lawmaking body of the nation, was the supreme guarantor and interpreter of these fixed principles and FUNDAMENTAL LAW. Parliament was in fact the bulwark of the people's liberties against the crown's encroachments; it alone defended and confirmed the people's rights. The PETITION OF RIGHT, the HABEAS CORPUS ACT OF 1679, and the Bill of Rights were all acts of Parliament, mere statutes not different in form from other laws.

For Englishmen, therefore, as WILLIAM BLACKSTONE, the great eighteenth-century jurist, pointed out, there could be no distinction between the "constitution or frame or government" and "the system of laws." All were of a piece:

every act of Parliament was part of the English constitution and all law, customary and statute, was thus constitutional. "Therefore," concluded the British theorist William Paley, "the terms *constitutional* and *unconstitutional* mean *legal* and *illegal.*"

Nothing could be more strikingly different from what Americans came to believe. Indeed, it was precisely on this distinction between "legal" and "constitutional" that the American and British constitutional traditions most obviously diverged at the Revolution. During the 1760s and 1770s the colonists came to realize that although acts of Parliament, like the Stamp Act of 1765, might be legal, that is, in accord with the acceptable way of making law, such acts could not thereby be automatically considered constitutional, that is, in accord with the basic rights and principles of justice that made the English constitution the palladium of liberty that it was. It was true that the English Bill of Rights and the Act of Settlement in 1689 were only statutes of Parliament, but surely, the colonists insisted in astonishment, they were of "a nature more sacred than those which established a turnpike road." Under this pressure of events the Americans came to believe that the fundamental principles of the English constitution had to be lifted out of the lawmaking and other processes and institutions of government and set above them. "In all free States," said the revolutionary leader SAMUEL ADAMS in 1768, "the Constitution is fixed; and as the supreme Legislature derives its Powers and Authority from the Constitution, it cannot overleap the Bounds of it without destroying its own foundation." Thus, in 1776, when Americans came to frame their own constitutions for their newly independent states, they inevitably sought to make them fundamental and to write them out explicitly in documents.

It was one thing, however, to define a constitution as fundamental law, different from ordinary legislation and circumscribing the institutions of government; it was quite another to make such a distinction effective. In the years following the DECLARATION OF INDEPENDENCE, many Americans paid lip service to the fundamental character of their STATE CONSTITUTIONS, but, like eighteenth-century Britons, they continued to believe that their legislatures were the best instruments for interpreting and changing those constitutions. The state legislatures represented the people, and the people, it seemed, could scarcely tyrannize themselves. Thus, in the late 1770s and the early 1780s several state legislatures, acting on behalf of the people, set aside parts of their constitutions by statute and interpreted and altered them, as one American observed, "upon any Occasion to serve a purpose." Time and again, the legislatures interfered with the governor's designated powers, rejected judicial decisions, disregarded individual liberties and PROPERTY RIGHTS, and in general, as one victim complained, violated "those fundamental principles which first induced men to come into civil compact."

By the mid-1780s many American leaders had come to believe that the state assemblies, not the governors as they had thought in 1776, were the political authority to be most feared. Legislators were supposedly the representatives of the people who annually elected them; but "173 despots would surely be as oppressive as one," wrote THOMAS JEFFERSON. "An *elective despotism* was not the government we fought for." It increasingly seemed to many that the idea of a constitution as fundamental law had no practical meaning at all. "If it were possible it would be well to define the extent of the Legislative power," concluded a discouraged JAMES MADISON in 1785, "but the nature of it seems in many respects to be indefinite."

No one wrestled more persistently with this problem of distinguishing between statutory and fundamental law than Jefferson. By 1779, Jefferson had learned from experience that assemblies "elected by the people for the ordinary purposes of legislation only have no power to restrain the acts of succeeding assemblies." Thus, he realized that to declare his great VIRGINIA STATUTE OF RELIGIOUS LIBERTY to be "irrevocable would be of no effect in law; yet we are free," he wrote into the bill in frustration, "to declare, and do declare, that the rights hereby asserted are of the natural rights of mankind, and that if any act shall be hereafter passed to repeal the present or to narrow its operation, such act will be an infringement of natural right." But such a paper declaration was obviously not enough; he realized that something more was needed. By the 1780s, both he and Madison were eager "to form a real constitution" for Virginia; the existing one, enacted in 1776, was merely an "ordinance," with no higher authority than the other ordinances of the same session. They wanted a constitution that would be "perpetual" and "unalterable by other legislatures." But how? If the constitution were to be truly fundamental and immune from legislative tampering, somehow it would have to be created, as Jefferson put it, "by a power superior to that of the legislature."

By the time Jefferson came to write his *Notes on the State of Virginia* in the early 1780s, the answer had become clear: "To render a form of government unalterable by ordinary acts of assembly," said Jefferson, "the people must delegate persons with special powers. They have accordingly chosen special conventions to form and fix their governments." The conventions and congresses of 1775–1776 had been legally deficient legislatures made necessary by the refusal of the royal governors to call together the regular and legal representatives of the people. Now, however, these conventions were seen to be special alternative representations of the people temporarily given the exclusive authority to frame or amend constitutions. When

Massachusetts and New Hampshire wrote new constitutions in 1780 and 1784, the proper pattern of constitution making and altering was set: constitutions were formed or changed by specially elected conventions and then placed before the people for ratification. Thus, in 1787 those who wished to change the federal government knew precisely what to do: they called a CONSTITUTIONAL CONVENTION in Philadelphia and sent the resultant document to the states for approval. Even the French in their own revolution several years later followed the American pattern.

With the idea of a constitution as fundamental law immune from legislative encroachment more firmly in hand, some state judges during the 1780s began cautiously moving in isolated cases to impose restraints on what the assemblies were enacting as law. In effect, they said to the legislatures, as GEORGE WYTHE, judge of Virginia's highest court did in 1782, "Here is the limit of your authority; and hither shall you go, but no further." These were the hesitant beginnings of what would come to be called JUDICIAL REVIEW, that remarkable American practice by which judges in the ordinary courts of law have the authority to determine the constitutionality of acts of the state and federal legislatures.

In just these ways did Americans in the revolutionary era devise regular and everyday constitutional institutions both for controlling government and thereby protecting the rights of individuals and for changing the very framework by which the government operated.

GORDON S. WOOD
(1992)

(SEE ALSO: *Bill of Rights (United States); Constitutional Convention of 1787; Constitutional History Before 1776; Constitutional History, 1776–1789; Constitutionalism and the American Founding; Natural Rights and the Constitution; Social Compact Theory.*)

Bibliography

CORWIN, EDWARD S. 1955 *The "Higher Law" Background of American Constitutional Law.* Ithaca, N.Y.: Cornell University Press.

MCLAUGHLIN, ANDREW C. 1932 *Foundations of American Constitutionalism.* New York: Norton.

WOOD, GORDON S. 1969 *The Creation of the American Republic, 1776–1787.* Chapel Hill: University of North Carolina Press.

AMERICANS WITH DISABILITIES ACT
104 Stat. 327 (1990)

The Americans with Disabilities Act (ADA) of 1990 is the high-water mark in the expansion of CIVIL RIGHTS initiated by the CIVIL RIGHTS ACT OF 1964. The tactics, language, and libertarian aims of the disability rights movement note this debt, especially in the ADA's references to ending "segregation," "discrete and insular minority" status, and "political powerlessness." Brought about through a remarkable coalition of activists concerned about diverse disabilities, the personal involvement of President GEORGE BUSH, and overwhelming support in Congress, the ADA proclaims that "the Nation's proper goals regarding individuals with disabilities are to assure equality of opportunity, full participation, independent living, and economic self-sufficiency for such individuals" with disabilities.

The ADA defines disability as a "mental or physical impairment that substantially limits one or more of the major life activities." The legislation also covers those who have had a disability or are "regarded as having" a disability.

The four major titles of the ADA deal with employment, state and local governmental services (including public transportation), public accommodations, and telecommunications, respectively. The ADA requires that hearing or speech-impaired persons be able to communicate with hearing persons through a telephone relay system. New commercial buildings and alterations to existing ones must be designed and constructed to be fully accessible. However, only "readily achievable" alterations need be made to existing places of public accommodation. Public accommodations include facilities ranging from those specifically covered in the 1964 act, such as restaurants and hotels, to gymnasiums and bowling alleys. As a general rule, people with disabilities must have "the full and equal enjoyment of the goods, services, facilities, privileges, advantages, or accommodations of any place of public accommodation." New buses, trains, and other transportation facilities will also have to be accessible.

The most important provision of the ADA is Title I, which is the analogue of Title VII, the EMPLOYMENT DISCRIMINATION section of the 1964 Civil Rights Act. Enforced as well by the U.S. Equal Employment Opportunity Commission, Title I strikes down barriers to employment and promotion found in job qualifications, examinations, and classifications. Particularly noteworthy is the requirement that an employer provide "reasonable accommodation" to an "otherwise qualified" individual with a disability—thus enabling performance of the "essential functions" of the position. An employer cannot, however, be asked to bear an "undue hardship" in accommodating an otherwise qualified person with a disability.

Disputes over the ADA focused largely on the costs it would impose on covered entities and the definition of disability. Proponents argued that most of the required modifications are a minor financial burden, particularly in light of the estimated $169.4 billion spent annually on programs that primarily promote dependency. Supporters predicted that the productivity unleashed by individuals now able to work would cease their being dependent.

The ADA presents a striking interpretation of the equality of NATURAL RIGHTS on which the Constitution rests. It seeks to halt the slow march toward the nightmare world of perfectly classified types depicted in Aldous Huxley's *Brave New World*. The law relies on the FOURTEENTH AMENDMENT and the COMMERCE CLAUSE for its constitutional authority. But it not only affirms the equal civil rights of all persons, including those with severe mental and physical disabilities; it requires as well the elimination of both physical and attitudinal barriers. The enforcement of the ADA should not produce the quotas and preferences that have hitherto plagued civil rights enforcement. Individuals with disabilities need to be accommodated on an individual basis, not treated as a group. In seeking entry into the mainstream of American life the disability rights movement has fought ceaselessly against exactly this thoughtless group classification.

EVAN J. KEMP, JR.
(1992)

Bibliography

HUXLEY, ALDOUS 1932, 1969 *Brave New World*. New York: Harper & Row.
U.S. COMMISSION ON CIVIL RIGHTS 1983 *Accommodating the Spectrum of Individual Abilities*. Washington, D.C.: U.S. Government Printing Office.

AMERICANS WITH DISABILITIES ACT
42 U.S.C. 12101 (1990)
(Update)

The Americans with Disabilities Act (ADA) was signed into law on July 26, 1990, and became effective two years later. Title I of the statute prohibits EMPLOYMENT DISCRIMINATION on the basis of disability in the private sector, Title II prohibits discrimination in the provision of goods or services by public entities, and Title III prohibits discrimination in the provision of goods or services by PUBLIC ACCOMMODATIONS including a requirement of removal of barriers to access.

To justify the constitutionality of ADA, Congress invoked "the sweep of congressional authority, including the power to enforce the fourteenth amendment and to regulate commerce, in order to address the major areas of discrimination faced day-to-day by people with disabilities" in its statement of purpose. Consistent with that declaration, it defined an employer under Title I as a "person engaged in an industry affecting commerce." Similarly, it

defined a public accommodation in Title III as one of various entities like an inn or motel "if the operations of such entities affect commerce." Thus, Congress was careful to draft Titles I and III so that their constitutionality would be upheld under congressional power to regulate INTERSTATE COMMERCE.

Title II, however, could not be justified under the COMMERCE CLAUSE because it created a private right of action against state government. Because of the SOVEREIGN IMMUNITY of the states recognized by the ELEVENTH AMENDMENT, that kind of right can only be created pursuant to the FOURTEENTH AMENDMENT, SECTION 5 enforcement power. Hence, Congress also justified its authority for enacting ADA pursuant to the FOURTEENTH AMENDMENT.

Despite the care with which Congress drafted ADA to ensure its constitutionality, there have been numerous constitutional challenges to Title II of ADA. In each case, a state was sued by a private citizen under Title II and responded that the Eleventh Amendment barred suit for damages. The appellate courts rejected this argument, finding that Congress effectively abrogated states' Eleventh Amendment sovereign immunity from suits under ADA, pursuant to its Fourteenth Amendment enforcement power.

The Eleventh Amendment states: "The judicial power of the United States shall not be construed to extend to any suit in law or equity commenced or prosecuted against one of the United States by Citizens of another State, or by Citizens or Subjects of any Foreign State." This provision also prohibits suits brought against a state in federal court by its own citizens.

In *Seminole Tribe of Florida v. Florida* (1996), the Supreme Court held that the states' Eleventh Amendment sovereign immunity can only be overridden by Congress if it enacts LEGISLATION to regulate the states pursuant to its Fourteenth Amendment enforcement power. Further, the Court held that Congress must have intended to abrogate sovereign immunity by providing "a clear legislative statement" of its intent.

The federal circuit courts are in agreement that Congress has met this test with respect to ADA. Title II states explicitly that "A state shall not be immune under the eleventh amendment." Further, Congress specifically invoked its enforcement powers under the Fourteenth Amendment in enacting the statute. The remaining titles of ADA are readily justified by the commerce clause, and there have been no serious challenges to their constitutionality.

Nonetheless, the Court has recently strengthened the states' sovereign immunity recognized by the Eleventh Amendment. In the 1998–1999 term, the Court struck down three statutes that violated the states' sovereign immunity. None of these cases involved CIVIL RIGHTS statutes but they do raise some concerns about the constitutionality of such laws, including Title II of ADA. Moreover, at the time of this writing, the Court has agreed to hear argument in a case challenging the constitutionality of the Age Discrimination in Employment Act as violating state sovereign immunity in the 1999–2000 term. Thus, we can expect more activity from the Court in the area of sovereign immunity. It is possible that the Court will eventually side with the dissenting judges in the circuit courts, who have concluded that ADA Title II exceeds Congress's enforcement power under section 5 of the Fourteenth Amendment.

Outside the constitutional context, the Court has shown considerable interest in ADA. In the 1997–1998 term, it concluded that the term "individual with a disability" within ADA covers individuals who have HIV infection.

In the 1998–1999 term, it rendered decisions in five ADA cases. (The Court only rendered a total of seventy-five decisions by full opinion that term; so, five cases represented an unusual amount of attention by the Court for one statute.) In three of those cases, the Court accepted a narrow definition of the term "individual with a disability." Under that narrow definition, an individual is disabled (and thereby covered by ADA) if he or she has a physical or mental impairment that substantially limits that individual in one or more major life activities after the individual has had an opportunity to use mitigating measures such as medicines or prosthetic devices. Although the plaintiffs in those cases had hypertension and visual impairments, the Court's decisions raise the question whether individuals with mental illness, diabetes, or seizure disorders that are controllable with medication will be covered by ADA.

In another important case from the 1998–1999 term, the Court concluded that ADA Title II prohibits unnecessary institutional segregation so long as the state cannot show that, in the allocation of available resources, immediate integration for individuals with disabilities who live in institutional settings would be inequitable, given the responsibility the state has undertaken for the care and treatment of a large and diverse population of individuals with disabilities. This case is the equivalent of BROWN V. BOARD OF EDUCATION (1954) for the disability community. Nonetheless, its holding will not be sustainable if ADA Title II is struck down as unconstitutional.

RUTH COLKER
(2000)

AMERICAN SYSTEM

"American System" was the name given by HENRY CLAY (in the HOUSE OF REPRESENTATIVES, March 30–31, 1824) to the national program of economic policy that centered on the protective tariff for the encouragement of domestic manufactures. It assigned the general government a positive role in promoting balanced economic development within the "home market." Each of the great sections would concentrate on the productions for which it was best suited: the South on staples like cotton, the West on grains and livestock, the Northeast on manufacturing. The tariff would protect the market; INTERNAL IMPROVEMENTS would facilitate exchanges and bind the parts together; the national bank would furnish commercial credit and ensure a stable and uniform currency. These measures were implemented in varying degrees, but the system was overtaken by the disintegrating sectionalism of the 1820s and finally buried by Jacksonian Democracy. Constitutionally, the American System posited a broad view of federal powers. It was attacked as dangerously consolidating, indeed unconstitutional in all its leading measures. Although the opposition had other and deeper sources, it tended to become a constitutional opposition, culminating in South Carolina's NULLIFICATION of the tariff in 1832.

MERRILL D. PETERSON
(1986)

Bibliography

GOODRICH, CARTER, ed.   1967   *The Government and the Economy, 1783–1861.* Indianapolis: Bobbs-Merrill.

AMERICAN TOBACCO COMPANY, UNITED STATES v.

See: *Standard Oil Company v. United States*

AMES, FISHER
(1758–1808)

An extreme Federalist, Fisher Ames published his "Camillus" essays to promote the idea of the CONSTITUTIONAL CONVENTION OF 1787. The French Revolution inspired his suspicion of democracy—"only the dismal passport to a more dismal hereafter"—and led him to call for a government run by an "aristocracy of talent." Ames also opposed the BILL OF RIGHTS as unnecessary and unwise. Representing Massachusetts in Congress from 1789 to 1797, he vigorously defended JAY'S TREATY and the ALIEN AND SEDITION ACTS, but, by 1802, his radical partisanship left him an embittered STATES' RIGHTS advocate.

DAVID GORDON
(1986)

AMICUS CURIAE

(Latin: Friend of the Court.) The amicus curiae originally was a lawyer aiding the court. Today in American practice, the lawyers represent an organization, which is the amicus; the group's "friendship" to the court has become an artifice slightly disguising the fact that it is as much an advocate as any party. Although economic interests early employed the amicus brief, CIVIL LIBERTIES groups did not lag far behind. As early as 1904, a group representing Chinese immigrants participated in a Supreme Court case. By the 1940s, the activities of amici were extensive, well coordinated among sister organizations, and highly publicized. In the aftermath of several antisegregation decisions of the mid-1950s, southern legislators and other spokesmen criticized that participation as nonjudicial.

Prior to 1937 the Supreme Court had no formal rule governing amicus briefs. It was standard procedure first to seek consent of the parties to the filing of an amicus brief, but the Court almost invariably accepted an amicus brief irrespective of party consent. The 1937 rule required a request for party consent, but the same easy acceptance of participation continued. In 1949, in the face of criticism, the Court noted that consent of the parties would be expected; without such consent "such motions are not favored." For a decade thereafter denials exceeded granting of motions by a wide margin.

The rule has been retained in subsequent revisions. In practice, however, such motions are now virtually (though not quite) automatically granted, with or without party consent. It is rare for any amicus curiae other than the United States to be given leave to make an ORAL ARGUMENT.

The excitement over use of amicus briefs has died down. Most such presentations are well-coordinated with the main brief, serving chiefly to announce the positions of certain groups. The Court, however, seems well-served by broader sources of information, and some amicus briefs are more cogent or influential than the parties' briefs. Many potential amici curiae qualify for participation through intervention or CLASS ACTIONS. Critics of wider participation, therefore, concentrate their guns on those more significant targets.

SAMUEL KRISLOV
(1986)

(SEE ALSO: *Groups and the Constitution.*)

AMNESTY

Amnesty is the blanket forgiveness of a group of people for some offense, usually of a political nature. Although there is a technical distinction between an amnesty, which "forgets" the offense, and a pardon, which remits the penalty, historical practice and common usage have made the terms virtually interchangeable. In the United States, amnesty may be granted by the President (under the PARDONING POWER) or by Congress (as NECESSARY AND PROPER to the carrying out of any of several powers). Amnesty may be granted before or after conviction, and may be conditional or unconditional. But neither Congress nor the President may grant amnesty for offenses against state law.

The first instance of amnesty under the Constitution was extended in 1801 by President THOMAS JEFFERSON to persons convicted or charged under the ALIEN AND SEDITION ACTS. Between 1862 and 1868, Presidents ABRAHAM LINCOLN and ANDREW JOHNSON issued a series of six proclamations of conditional amnesty for southern rebels. Congress specifically authorized the first three but repealed the authorizing statute in 1867; President Johnson issued the last three on his own authority alone. In the TEST OATH CASES (1867), the Supreme Court struck down, as an unconstitutional interference with the pardoning power, an attempt by Congress to limit the effect of Johnson's amnesty. In 1872, exercising its power under section 3 of the FOURTEENTH AMENDMENT, Congress passed the Amnesty Act restoring the CIVIL RIGHTS of most rebels.

President GERALD R. FORD granted conditional amnesty in 1974 to military deserters and draft evaders of the VIETNAM WAR period. The terms of the amnesty required case-by-case determination by a special Presidential Clemency Board empowered to direct performance by applicants of alternative public service. Ford acted on his own authority after Congress failed to approve any of several amnesty proposals.

DENNIS J. MAHONEY
(1986)

ANCILLARY JURISDICTION

In some cases federal courts hear claims over which no statute confers federal JURISDICTION. Typically, this ancillary jurisdiction has been exercised in cases brought under the federal courts' DIVERSITY JURISDICTION. Suppose a California citizen sues an Arizona citizen in federal court, claiming a right to property. If another Californian claims the same property interest, no state court can take jurisdiction over the property under the federal court's control. It is thus necessary for the federal court to be able to hear that claim, even though the case of one Californian against another would not initially be within its jurisdiction. Similarly, a defendant sued in federal court can file a third-party claim against a co-citizen, which will be heard under the federal court's ancillary jurisdiction.

Ancillary jurisdiction is sometimes confused with PEN-DENT JURISDICTION, which permits a state *claim* to be heard in federal court along with a closely related FEDERAL QUES-TION. Ancillary jurisdiction results in the addition of a *party* who otherwise would not fall within the federal court's jurisdiction. The Supreme Court has not been hospitable to the suggestion that a federal court in a federal question case should take "pendent" jurisdiction over a closely related state law claim against a new party.

KENNETH L. KARST
(1986)

Bibliography

WRIGHT, CHARLES ALAN 1983 *The Law of Federal Courts*, 4th ed. Pages 28–32. St. Paul, Minn.: West Publishing Co.

ANNAPOLIS CONVENTION

In 1785 a few nationalists led by JAMES MADISON and AL-EXANDER HAMILTON sought desperately to preserve the Union of the states under the ARTICLES OF CONFEDERATION. Congress seemed inept and powerless. The chances that the United States might "Balkanize" seemed likely. As early as 1782 Hamilton had proposed a convention of the states to reassess their union. In 1785 delegates from Maryland and Virginia met in Alexandria to reconcile their mutual interests in Chesapeake Bay and the Potomac River. Madison promoted the plan of a convention of delegates from all of the states to consider augmenting the powers of Congress over commerce. Maryland and Virginia agreed on the call of such a convention in Annapolis in September 1786, and they invited all the states to send delegates.

When the Annapolis Convention met, only five states were in attendance. Undaunted, Hamilton and Madison made the best of the situation by framing a report, which those in attendance unanimously adopted, critical of the inadequacies of the Articles of Confederation and urging still another convention of all the states to assemble in Philadelphia in May 1787. The purpose of that convention would be to "take into consideration the situation of the United States, to devise such other provisions as shall appear to them necessary to render the constitution of the Federal Government adequate to the exigencies of the Union," and to report recommendations to Congress for confirmation by the states.

Thus, the Annapolis Convention was significant for calling the meeting that became the Philadelphia CONSTITU-TIONAL CONVENTION of 1787. SHAYS' REBELLION assisted the Confederation Congress in making up its mind to endorse the work of the Annapolis Convention. Confronted by the fact that the states were already electing delegates to the

Philadelphia Convention, Congress saved face by issuing its own call for that convention in the language used by the Annapolis Convention.

LEONARD W. LEVY
(1992)

ANNEXATION OF TEXAS

American settlers in the Mexican province of Texas revolted against the central government and established the independence of the Lone Star Republic in 1836. President ANDREW JACKSON was unable to effect annexation, however, because many feared war with Mexico and because abolitionists suspected a slaveholders' plot to increase the number of slave states. In 1842, President John Tyler revived annexationist efforts, abetted by a clique of proslavery expansionists, but an annexation treaty failed once again, due in part to the argument that the territories clause (Article IV, section 3) permitted annexation only of dependent TERRITORIES of other nations, not of independent nations themselves. Tyler then recommended annexation by JOINT RESOLUTION of Congress to obviate the constitutional requirement of a two-thirds Senate vote to ratify a treaty. This aroused further opposition, now including influential southern Whigs, who insisted that the issue involved grave foreign policy risks and hence was precisely the sort of question for which the Framers had required a super-majority. Despite this argument, congressional Democrats enacted a joint resolution in February 1845 declaring the Republic of Texas to be the twenty-eighth state.

WILLIAM M. WIECEK
(1986)

Bibliography

MERK, FREDERICK 1972 *Slavery and the Annexation of Texas.* New York: Knopf.

ANONYMOUS POLITICAL SPEECH

Political speech, the Supreme Court has often indicated, is at the core of the protection afforded by the FIRST AMENDMENT, given its central role in the democratic process. But it takes on a somewhat different cast when it is delivered anonymously—without any attribution of authorship (true anonymity) or with false or fictitious attribution of authorship (pseudonymity). On the one hand, anonymous or pseudonymous speech can function as a "shield from the tyranny of the majority." Requiring listeners to assess the value of speech on its own merits—that is, without regard to the speaker's popularity or unpopularity—allows voices that might otherwise be drowned out or dismissed to participate in and enrich the public debate. Moreover, insulating proponents of unpopular causes against retaliation encourages persecuted groups to speak without fear of reprisal. As the Court has noted on many occasions, anonymous political speech has a distinguished history in the political process of the United States, from colonial-era critics of the British Crown seeking protection from prosecution for SEDITIOUS LIBEL; to the authors of the eighty-five FEDERALIST essays (who published their contributions under the pseudonym "Publius"); to members of the National Association for the Advancement of Colored People protesting racial SEGREGATION in the 1950s. On the other hand, precisely because it is harder to trace the source of an anonymous or pseudonymous communication, distributors of false, fraudulent, or libelous information, or those seeking to use political contributions to corrupt the political process, might use anonymity as a shield to avoid accountability or public scrutiny.

The Court has had few opportunities to assess the constitutionality of government regulation of anonymous political speech. In *McIntyre v. Ohio Elections Commission* (1995), the Court made clear that such regulation was to be treated as a "content-based regulation . . . of pure speech" subject to the same "exacting scrutiny" as other attempts to regulate decisions concerning omissions or additions to the content of speech. As such, the Court will uphold regulation of this kind only where it is "narrowly tailored to serve an overriding state interest."

What is less clear from the limited PRECEDENT in this area is how the Court will strike the necessary balance so as to determine whether any particular state interest is sufficiently "overriding" to justify limitations on anonymous communication. In *McIntyre* itself the Court struck down Ohio's blanket ban on all anonymous campaign literature, finding the main interest asserted by the state— preventing the dissemination of fraudulent and libelous statements—insufficient to support so sweeping and "indiscriminate" a disclosure requirement. At the same time, the Court indicated that the state's interest might well justify a more limited identification requirement (although it gave no hint about what such a regulation would look like). At the same time, it strongly reaffirmed an earlier precedent—BUCKLEY V. VALEO (1976)— upholding disclosure requirements in the context of campaign contributions where the state interest in avoiding the appearance of corruption was served and the regulation was less intrusive on political self-expression.

DAVID G. POST
DAWN C. NUNZIATO
(2000)

(SEE ALSO: *Freedom of Speech.*)

Bibliography

FROOMKIN, A. MICHAEL 1996 Flood Control on the Information Ocean: Living With Anonymity, Digital Cash, and Distributed Databases. *Journal of Law & Commerce* 15:395–507.

POST, DAVID G. 1996 Pooling Intellectual Capital: Thoughts on Anonymity, Pseudonymity, and Limited Liability in Cyberspace. *University of Chicago Legal Forum* 1996:139–169.

ANTHONY, SUSAN BROWNELL
(1820–1906)

Susan B. Anthony was born in Adams, Massachusetts to a Quaker father and a Baptist mother. She never married and was a lifelong advocate of self-support for women. In 1850, she met ELIZABETH CADY STANTON, from whom she learned about women's rights, and became a passionate believer. Together they led the American women's rights movement for the next half-century. Their first goal was the establishment of basic economic rights for married women. Beginning in 1854, Anthony traveled across New York collecting petitions to the state legislature, which in 1860 passed a comprehensive Married Women's Property Act. Simultaneously, she was an organizer of the American Anti Slavery Society, and her women's rights and ABOLITIONIST sentiments were closely related.

After the Civil War and following the lead of the anti-slavery movement, Stanton and Anthony concentrated on equal citizenship and political rights for women. They tried but failed to get women included in the FOURTEENTH and FIFTEENTH AMENDMENTS, an effort which left them committed to a focus on political equality and the Constitution as the source of political rights. In 1869, they formed the National Woman Suffrage Association, precipitating a split with other women's rights activists not willing to criticize the Fifteenth Amendment or break with longtime abolitionist and Republican allies by doing so.

In the early 1870s, Anthony and Stanton advanced an innovative constitutional argument resting on the proposition that the Fourteenth Amendment included women when it established federal CITIZENSHIP. Inasmuch as the right to vote was patently the FUNDAMENTAL RIGHT of citizenship, they argued, woman suffrage was thus authorized by the Constitution. Accordingly, in November, 1872, Anthony took the most famous act of her life: she convinced Rochester, New York election officials to allow her to submit her ballot for President. For this she was found guilty of illegal voting in U.S. District Court, and fined $100, which she refused to pay. Two years later, the U.S. Supreme Court ruling on a related case, MINOR V. HAPPERSETT (1875), found decisively against the suffragists' constitutional construction.

From this point on, Anthony dedicated herself to securing a separate WOMAN SUFFRAGE amendment. In 1876, she presented a militant "Woman's Declaration of Rights" to the official Revolutionary Centennial in Philadelphia, condemning the refusal to extend the nation's democratic principles to women. In 1890, she oversaw the unification of the suffrage movement, and served as president of the newly created National American Woman Suffrage Association until 1900. Throughout the 1890s, Anthony, then in her seventies, traveled to California, Kansas, South Dakota, and Colorado to work for state suffrage REFERENDUMS and to England and France to organize suffragists internationally. In 1900, she retired and in 1906, she died. In 1920, her goal was finally realized with the ratification of the NINETEENTH AMENDMENT, known popularly as the Susan B. Anthony Amendment.

ELLEN CAROL DUBOIS
(2000)

(SEE ALSO: *Woman Suffrage Movement.*)

Bibliography

BARRY, KATHLEEN   1988   *Susan B. Anthony: A Biography of a Singular Feminist.* New York: Ballantine.

BUHLE, MARI JO and PAUL, eds.   1978   *Concise History of Woman Suffrage.* Urbana, Ill.: University of Illinois Press.

GORDON, ANN D., ed.   1997   *The Selected Papers of Elizabeth Cady Stanton and Susan B. Anthony.* Vol. 1. New Brunswick, N.J.: Rutgers University Press.

SHERR, LYNN   1995   *Failure is Impossible: Susan B. Anthony in Her Own Words.* New York: Times Books.

ANTI-ABORTION MOVEMENT

After ROE V. WADE (1973), opponents of ABORTION scrambled to find restrictions on abortion that the Supreme Court would uphold. These included laws requiring a short "cooling off" period between the request for an abortion and its performance; informed-consent laws requiring disclosure of the medical risks of abortion to women considering the procedure; medical regulations requiring that second-trimester abortions be performed in hospitals or establishing professional standards for those who perform abortions; viability regulations that would establish a uniform definition for viability or that required a doctor to determine whether the unborn child was viable before performing an abortion; and parental and spousal consent provisions. All were invariably struck down in the federal courts, leading law professor Lynn Wardle to conclude in 1981: "The courts have carried the doctrine of abortion privacy to incredible extremes. . . . The abortion industry . . . has wrapped itself in the robes of *Roe v. Wade*, [has] challenged many simple and ordinary state regulations (from record-keeping laws to parental notification requirements) and today claims constitutional immunity from many medical regulations."

Given the judiciary's effective ban on any local abortion regulation during the 1970s, the anti-abortion movement soon sought other methods to achieve its goals, including the constitutional-amendment process. Several constitutional amendments dealing with abortion were introduced in Congress after the Republicans gained control of the Senate in 1980. The first would have defined the term "person" in the Fifth Amendment and the FOURTEENTH AMENDMENT as encompassing "unborn offspring at every stage of development" and provided that "[n]o unborn person shall be deprived of life by any person." Another proposal, dubbed the "Human Life Federalism Amendment," provided that a "right to abortion is not secured by this Constitution" and that "Congress and the several states shall have the concurrent power to restrict and prohibit abortions." The intent of the latter amendment was to restore to the legislative branch the power to enact laws dealing with abortion. Many in the anti-abortion movement were critical of this approach, however, believing that it did not go far enough.

When it became clear that no constitutional amendment dealing with abortion could muster sufficient support, some sought to overturn *Roe* by congressional statute. The "Human Life Statute" was the result; it would have provided a congressional finding of fact that human life begins at conception; it also would have used congressional power to curtail the jurisdiction of the lower federal courts to deal with abortion. The Human Life Statute attracted a great deal of controversy while it lasted, and it received scorching criticism from many in the legal community as an unconstitutional attack on federal JUDICIAL POWER. The statute's defenders included law professors John T. Noonan, Jr. (now a federal appellate judge) and Joseph Witherspoon. Both argued that the right to life guaranteed by the Fourteenth Amendment ought to apply to children in the womb as a matter of proper constitutional interpretation; Witherspoon went to great lengths to show that the Fourteenth Amendment was enacted during a time when stricter abortion laws were sweeping the nation, indicating a general regard for unborn infants as persons with certain rights.

Despite a flurry of hearings and public debate, none of these measures ever had a serious prospect of passing. Once the Republicans lost control of the Senate, even the most zealous members of the anti-abortion movement realized this fact, and so attention turned to executive-branch action. By the late 1980s, many in the movement had decided that their best chance of overturning *Roe v. Wade* lay in new appointments to the Supreme Court. Hence, both RONALD REAGAN and GEORGE BUSH received widespread electoral support from abortion opponents, even though neither did much to promote anti-abortion legislation in Congress. Abortion opponents hoped Reagan and Bush would appoint Justices willing to undercut *Roe*. They did not hope in vain. In 1989 the Court finally upheld some minor abortion restrictions in WEBSTER V. REPRODUCTIVE HEALTH SERVICES, and Reagan-appointed Justices provided the decisive votes.

For many opponents of abortion, however, the change in the Court's direction came too late. Appalled by over fifteen million abortions since 1973 and alienated by a court system that they felt had disenfranchised them from the political system, a large segment of the anti-abortion movement turned from politics to mass CIVIL DISOBEDIENCE in the mid-1980s. Thousands became involved in a loose-knit organization known as "Operation Rescue," which staged nonviolent sit-ins to shut down abortion clinics. The magnitude of these protests is indicated by the number of protestors arrested, estimated at between twenty-eight and thirty-five thousand during one eighteen-month period. When tried for criminal trespass, members of Operation Rescue commonly invoke the necessity defense, arguing that they are compelled by a HIGHER LAW to engage in civil disobedience in order to save human life. A few courts have acquitted protestors on this basis, most notably one in Missouri that based its decision on a state law declaring that human life begins at conception.

As Operation Rescue protests have grown in size and number, some fairly drastic measures have been taken to stop the organization, including lawsuits based on the RACKETEER INFLUENCED AND CORRUPT ORGANIZATION ACT (RICO). Operation Rescue protestors have also encountered widespread police brutality. In Buffalo male protestors were handcuffed, beaten with clubs, and dragged face-down down a flight of stairs. In Dobbs Ferry, New York, women protestors were strip-searched and photographed nude by prison guards. In Los Angeles police broke a nonresisting man's arm twice, pounded the faces of other peaceful protestors into the asphalt, and repeatedly inflicted pain on protestors who were trying to comply with police requests. In several cities abusive police have removed their badges and name plates to prevent identification by both protestors and the news media. Reports of police brutality became so widespread that in late 1989 the United States Commission on Civil Rights voted to launch an investigation. William B. Allen, then chairman of the commission, declared: "It is imperative that we as a nation assert our commitment to equal treatment before the law. Nonviolent protestors should all be accorded the same treatment no matter what the subject of protest. To do less is to destroy the most prized achievement of the CIVIL RIGHTS MOVEMENT—the recognition of the rights of

everyone." The majority of public officials and members of the media, however, paid scant attention to the protestors' plight, and the brutality continued.

JOHN G. WEST, JR.
(1992)

(SEE ALSO: *Conservatism; Jurisdiction, Federal.*)

Bibliography

ALLEN, WILLIAM B. 1989 Police Brutality—But No Outrage. *The Wall Street Journal*, August 18.

SENATE COMMITTEE ON THE JUDICIARY 1982 *The Human Life Bill* (Hearings). 2 volumes. Washington, D.C.: U.S. Government Printing Office.

—— 1983 *Constitutional Amendments Relating to Abortion* (Hearings), 2 volumes. Washington, D.C.: U.S. Government Printing Office.

TERRY, RANDALL A. 1988 *Operation Rescue.* Springdale, Penn.: Whitaker House.

ANTI-ABORTION MOVEMENT
(Update)

In the 1980s and 1990s, protests by ABORTION opponents directed at clinics and physicians providing abortion services supplied a powerful impetus to doctrinal change in our understanding of the FIRST AMENDMENT. Anti-abortion activities ranged from "sidewalk counseling" of women seeking to enter clinics to residential picketing of the homes of abortion providers; aggressive expressive assaults against clinic patients and staff; mass protests; obstruction of clinic entrances; and threats and acts of violence. In response, clinics sought, and courts issued, injunctions creating protest-free buffer or bubble zones around the entrances of clinics. Local authorities enacted ordinances banning residential picketing or codifying clinic buffer zones. At the national level, Congress adopted the Freedom of Access to Clinic Entrances Act to protect clinic staff and patients from force, threats of force, and acts of obstruction.

As a general matter, expressive protests that do not involve unlawful conduct such as blocking entrances or assault are part of the robust debate on public policy issues that the First Amendment protects. Anti-abortion protests, however, raise special concerns that arguably justify more aggressive intervention and regulatory restrictions. While angry speech that causes anxiety and emotional distress does not lose its protected status, loud, accusatory demonstrations directed at the women seeking abortion services increase the medical risks of abortion procedures.

The state's interest in protecting the health of women

receiving abortion services was not the only justification offered for restricting anti-abortion protests. The line between protected, hurtful, and critical speech directed at individuals who do not want to hear a protestor's message and proscribable harassment has never been an easy one to draw, but at some point the following and badgering of patients and staff as they walk to and from clinics crosses that line and becomes subject to sanction. The state has a legitimate interest in enabling women to make medical choices free from harassment.

Moreover, a woman has a constitutional right to elect to have an abortion. When the exercise of rights comes into conflict, constitutional compromises sometimes have to be structured to allow sufficient "breathing room" for both protected interests. Courts and legislatures have attempted to take competing speech and privacy rights into account in regulating expressive activities outside of clinics.

Finally, the frequency and duration of anti-abortion protests have made them difficult to monitor and control. Unless police are stationed continually outside of clinics, harassment and obstruction can continue until police arrive, abate while authorities are present, and then resume after they depart. Regulations that have tried to prohibit only unprotected conduct, while permitting protestors to continue to engage in protected activities, have seemed easy to circumvent, and almost impossible to enforce effectively.

Lower courts and local authorities accepted many of these rationales in establishing buffer zones around clinics that prohibited protestors from engaging in virtually any expressive activity within a short radius of a clinic's entrance. The Supreme Court, however, focused almost exclusively on the enforcement justification in upholding the constitutionality of injunctions creating relatively narrow buffer zones in *Madsen v. Women's Health Center, Inc.* (1994) and *Pro-Choice Network of Western New York v. Schenck* (1997). To the Court, patients and staff were entitled to secure access to clinics. Accordingly, if lower court orders prohibiting obstruction and harassment were repeatedly violated by protestors, courts had the constitutional authority to issue more restrictive injunctions that precluded even nonobstructive expressive activities.

Injunctions that restricted anti-abortion protests beyond the narrow parameters of limited buffer zones, however, were held to violate the FREEDOM OF SPEECH. Moreover, the Court seemed to suggest that a pattern of prior obstruction and harassment by protestors was an essential precondition to the establishment of a buffer zone. Women's health concerns and RIGHT OF PRIVACY did not appear to be of sufficient weight to justify limits on the expressive activities of protestors.

ALAN E. BROWNSTEIN
(2000)

Bibliography

BROWNSTEIN, ALAN E. 1996 Rules of Engagement for Cultural Wars: Regulating Conduct, Unprotected Speech, and Protected Expression in Anti-Abortion Protests. *UC Davis Law Review* 29:1163–1216.

JACOBS, LESLIE GIELOW 1996 Nonviolent Abortion Clinic Protests: Reevaluating Some Current Assumptions about the Proper Scope of Government Regulations. *Tulane Law Review* 70:1359–1443.

WEINSTEIN, JAMES 1996 Free Speech, Abortion Access, and the Problem of Judicial Viewpoint Discrimination. *UC Davis Law Review* 29:471–543.

ANTIDISCRIMINATION LEGISLATION

From its inception, antidiscrimination legislation has shaped and been shaped by the Constitution. Antidiscrimination legislation's very existence is attributable to developments in constitutional law. Enactment of such legislation usually reflects a relatively favorable atmosphere for the promise of equality embodied in the THIRTEENTH, FOURTEENTH, and FIFTEENTH AMENDMENTS. When the values underlying these amendments are in decline, antidiscrimination legislation is not enacted, and often is not enforced.

Federal antidiscrimination laws have been enacted during two time periods. During the first period, which commenced near the end of the CIVIL WAR, Congress enacted the CIVIL RIGHTS ACT OF 1866, the Civil Rights Act of 1870, the FORCE ACT OF 1871, the Civil Rights Act of 1871, and the CIVIL RIGHTS ACT OF 1875. These early provisions, portions of which survive, exemplify two basic forms of antidiscrimination legislation. Some provisions, such as section 1 of the 1871 act (now section 1983) and section 3 of the 1866 act were purely remedial. They provided remedies for violations of federal rights but created no new substantive rights. Other provisions, such as section 1 of the 1866 act and section 16 of the 1870 act (now sections 1981 and 1982), were express efforts to change substantive law by fostering greater equality between black and white Americans.

The COMPROMISE OF 1877 marks the end of the first era during which antidiscrimination legislation flourished. Afterward, congressional and judicial developments favored neither enactment nor enforcement of antidiscrimination legislation. In the CIVIL RIGHTS REPEAL ACT of 1894 the first Democratic Congress since the Civil War repealed the few effective remnants of post-Civil War antidiscrimination legislation. A favorable climate for legislative implementation of the post-Civil War constitutional amendments did not reemerge until the late 1950s and early 1960s.

There were no significant antidiscrimination statutes in the intervening years.

As the constitutional amendments were given new vigor by the WARREN COURT, however, antidiscrimination legislation experienced a renaissance. Modern statutes, including the CIVIL RIGHTS ACTS OF 1957, 1960, 1964, and 1968, protect against discrimination in voting, employment, education, and housing. They represent a second era of federal antidiscrimination legislation, sometimes called part of the second reconstruction.

As in the case of earlier antidiscrimination statutes, the primary reason for enactment was to protect blacks from RACIAL DISCRIMINATION. Again, two kinds of provisions were enacted. Some provisions, such as the 1957 and 1960 Acts and Title VI of the 1964 act, are remedial in tone (though not always so interpreted) and do not purport to create new substantive rights. Others, such as Title VII of the 1964 act, which prohibits private discrimination in employment, confer new substantive rights.

Modern antidiscrimination legislation contains a recognizable subcategory that has been the fastest growing area of antidiscrimination law. Until about 1960 or 1970, antidiscrimination legislation could be equated with laws prohibiting one or more forms of racial discrimination. Subsequently, however, legislation prohibiting discrimination surfaced in many areas. For example, the AGE DISCRIMINATION ACT OF 1975, the Age Discrimination in Employment Act, the REHABILITATION ACT OF 1973, the DEVELOPMENTALLY DISABLED AND BILL OF RIGHTS ACT, the Education of Handicapped Children Acts, the Equal Pay Act, and the EDUCATION AMENDMENTS OF 1972 provide substantial protection to the aged, to the handicapped, and to women. Building on a technique first employed in Title VI of the 1964 act, most of these provisions apply only to programs or entities receiving federal financial assistance.

Although constitutional values can be viewed as the raison d'être of antidiscrimination legislation, the relationship between the Constitution and antidiscrimination laws runs much deeper. Their more complex relationship may be divided into two parts. First, antidiscrimination legislation has been the setting for judicial and congressional decisions concerning the scope of congressional power. One of the few universally agreed upon facts about the history of the Fourteenth Amendment is that it was meant to place the first major antidiscrimination statute, the Civil Rights Act of 1866, on firm constitutional footing. Before ratification of the Fourteenth Amendment, doubts were expressed about Congress's power under the Thirteenth Amendment to ban racially discriminatory state laws. Many believe that the Fourteenth Amendment was meant primarily to constitutionalize the 1866 Act's prohibitions. With the Fourteenth Amendment in place by 1868, Congress reaffirmed the 1866 Act's bans by reenacting them

as part of the Civil Rights Act of 1870. Some claim that the 1866 Act is so akin to a constitutional provision that its surviving remnants should be interpreted more like constitutional provisions than statutory ones.

Soon after this initial interplay between the Constitution and antidiscrimination laws, a foundation of constitutional interpretation grew out of litigation under antidiscrimination statutes. In a line of cases commencing with UNITED STATES V. CRUIKSHANK (1876) and culminating in UNITED STATES V. HARRIS (1883) and the CIVIL RIGHTS CASES (1883), the Court relied on what has come to be known as the STATE ACTION doctrine to invalidate antidiscrimination measures. The *Civil Rights Cases* invalidated the last piece of nineteenth-century civil rights legislation, the Civil Rights Act of 1875. In so doing the Court not only limited the Fourteenth Amendment to prohibiting state action but also rendered a narrow interpretation of the Thirteenth Amendment as a possible source of congressional power to enact antidiscrimination statutes.

The state action doctrine was not the only early limit on antidiscrimination legislation. In UNITED STATES V. REESE (1876) the Court found sections 3 and 4 of the Civil Rights Act of 1870, which prohibited certain interferences with voting, to be beyond Congress's power to enforce the Fifteenth Amendment because the sections were not limited to prohibiting racial discrimination. These limitations on antidiscrimination legislation carried over into the early twentieth century.

But some early antidiscrimination legislation survived constitutional attack and shifting political stances in Congress. For example, in EX PARTE YARBROUGH (1884) the Court sustained use of section 6 of the 1870 act (now section 241) to impose criminal sanctions against private individuals who used force to prevent blacks from voting in federal elections. And in *Ex parte Virginia* (1880), the Court sustained the federal prosecution of a state judge for excluding blacks from juries in violation of section 4 of the 1875 act. (See STRAUDER V. WEST VIRGINIA.)

The two lines of early constitutional interpretation of antidiscrimination laws have never been fully reconciled. As a result of the early limits on congressional power to enact antidiscrimination legislation, modern civil rights statutes have been drafted to reduce potential constitutional attacks. Thus, much of the Civil Rights Act of 1964 operates only on individuals and entities engaged in some form of INTERSTATE COMMERCE. Other portions of the 1964 act, and many other modern antidiscrimination laws, are based on Congress's TAXING AND SPENDING POWERS. By tying antidiscrimination legislation to the COMMERCE CLAUSE or the spending power, Congress hoped to avoid some of the constitutional problems that plagued early legislation enacted under the Thirteenth, Fourteenth, and Fifteenth Amendments.

A potential clash between the Court and Congress over the constitutionality of modern antidiscrimination legislation has not surfaced. The modern Court sustains antidiscrimination legislation even in the face of troublesome nineteenth-century precedents. In a landmark holding barely reconcilable with portions of the *Civil Rights Cases*, the Court in JONES V. ALFRED H. MAYER COMPANY (1968) found that Congress has power under the Thirteenth Amendment to ban private racial discrimination in housing. Later, in RUNYON V. MCCRARY (1976), the Court acknowledged Congress's power to outlaw racial discrimination in private contractual relations, including those relations involved in a child's attendance at a private segregated school. In GRIFFIN V. BRECKENRIDGE (1971) the Court relied on the Thirteenth Amendment to sustain a remnant of the 1871 act allowing for causes of action against private conspiracies to violate federal rights. The case undermined *United States v. Harris* and overruled an earlier contrary decision, *Collins v. Hardyman* (1948). Another antidiscrimination statute, the VOTING RIGHTS ACT OF 1965, provided the setting for important decisions in KATZENBACH V. MORGAN (1966) and SOUTH CAROLINA V. KATZENBACH (1966), which found Congress to have broad discretion to interpret and extend Fourteenth Amendment protection to situations which the judiciary had not found violative of the Fourteenth Amendment.

There is a second respect in which constitutional provisions and antidiscrimination legislation influence each other. From the beginning, their relationship has gone beyond one of merely testing the constitutionality of a particular antidiscrimination statute. Interpretation of one set of provisions has shaped the other. This interplay began with the Civil Rights Act of 1866. Soon after ratification of the Fourteenth Amendment, the question arose as to what constituted "the PRIVILEGES AND IMMUNITIES of citizens of the United States" referred to in the Fourteenth Amendment. In the SLAUGHTERHOUSE CASES (1873) the Court's first decision construing the Fourteenth Amendment, Justice STEPHEN J. FIELD argued in dissent that section 1 of the 1866 act provided Congress's interpretation of at least some of the privileges or immunities of United States citizens. Although Field's view did not prevail—the Court limited the privileges or immunities clause to a narrow class of rights—even the majority view of the privileges or immunities clause may have had a profound effect on subsequent development of antidiscrimination legislation.

This effect stems from the strong linguistic parallel between the Fourteenth Amendment's privileges or immunities clause and the rights listed as protected by many antidiscrimination laws. Sections 1983 and 242 protect persons against deprivations of their federal "rights, privileges or immunities." Section 1985(3) refers in part to "equal privileges and immunities." Section 241 refers to any federal "right or privilege." In subsequent cases brought under antidiscrimination statutes, federal courts, relying on the *Slaughterhouse Cases'* narrow interpretation of the Fourteenth Amendment's privileges or immunities clause, plausibly could render a similar narrow interpretation of the antidiscrimination statute. Not until MONROE V. PAPE (1961) did the Court settle that the rights, privileges, and immunities protected by section 1983 include at least all rights secured by the Fourteenth Amendment.

Just as CONSTITUTIONAL INTERPRETATION influenced early antidiscrimination laws and vice versa, modern antidiscrimination legislation influences constitutional interpretation. In GRIGGS V. DUKE POWER COMPANY (1971) the Court found that an employer's selection criteria with unintentional disparate effect on a minority could lead to a violation of Title VII of the Civil Rights Act of 1964. This and earlier Supreme Court cases generated pressure to find violative of the Fourteenth Amendment government action with uneven adverse effects on minorities. Not until WASHINGTON V. DAVIS (1976) and ARLINGTON HEIGHTS V. METROPOLITAN HOUSING DEVELOPMENT CORPORATION (1977) did the Court expressly reject the *Griggs* standard as a basis for constitutional interpretation. And in REGENTS OF THE UNIVERSITY OF CALIFORNIA V. BAKKE (1978), a major theme of the opinions is the relationship between the antidiscrimination standards embodied in Title VI of the Civil Rights Act of 1964 and those of the Fourteenth Amendment.

Judicial hostility to the RECONSTRUCTION civil rights program and subsequent congressional inaction left much of the civil rights field to the states. Early Massachusetts legislation covered school desegregation and PUBLIC ACCOMMODATIONS, but few other states enacted protective laws prior to 1883 and some laws that had been enacted by southern Reconstruction legislatures were repealed.

The *Civil Rights Cases'* invalidation of the Civil Rights Act of 1875 triggered the first major group of state antidiscrimination laws. Within two years of the decision, eleven states outlawed discrimination in public accommodations. Modest further legislative developments occurred before WORLD WAR II, including legislation aimed at violence generated by the Ku Klux Klan, some northern prohibitions on school segregation, and some categories of employment discrimination.

The next widespread state civil rights initiative, which covered employment discrimination, drew upon experience under the wartime Committee on Fair Employment Practices. New York's 1945 Law Against Discrimination, the first modern comprehensive fair employment law, established a commission to investigate and adjudicate complaints and became a model for other states' laws. Resort to administrative agencies, now possible in the vast majority of states, remains the primary state method of dealing with many categories of discrimination.

THEODORE EISENBERG
(1986)

Bibliography

BARDOLPH, RICHARD 1970 *The Civil Rights Record.* New York: Crowell.

KONVITZ, MILTON R. 1961 *A Century of Civil Rights.* New York: Columbia University Press.

MURRAY, PAULI 1961 *States' Laws on Race and Color.* New York: Woman's Division of Christian Service, The Methodist Church.

U.S. COMMISSION ON CIVIL RIGHTS 1970 *Federal Civil Rights Enforcement Effort.* Washington, D.C.: U.S. Government Printing Office.

ANTIDISCRIMINATION LEGISLATION
(Update 1)

Most antidiscrimination legislation forbids RACIAL DISCRIMINATION in such contexts as employment, housing, public accommodations, education, and voting. Similar legislation prohibits SEX DISCRIMINATION and, more recently, discrimination on the basis of age and handicap.

Enacted in response to racial unrest and mass civil protests, the CIVIL RIGHTS ACT OF 1964 was the first major federal antidiscrimination law in the modern era. Congress subsequently enacted the VOTING RIGHTS ACT OF 1965 and the Fair Housing Act of 1968. Each act has been amended several times.

The most ambitious titles of the 1964 Act—Title VII, prohibiting EMPLOYMENT DISCRIMINATION, and Title II, prohibiting discrimination in public accommodations—are now central features of the modern regulatory state. This legislation, however, initially faced stiff opposition. The opponents argued that the law represented undue federal intrusion into both the private sphere and state sovereignty and that the "law could not change what lies in the hearts of men." Modern antidiscrimination legislation rejects both these views. It effectively nationalizes nondiscrimination as a basic right of CITIZENSHIP, apparently laying to rest the post-Reconstruction view that the task of protecting CIVIL RIGHTS lay primarily within the powers of each state. Equally significant, the passage of antidiscrimination legislation seemed to embody a belief that law could significantly alter conduct and, eventually, "the hearts of men."

More recent developments suggest a fraying around the edges of antidiscrimination, both as national policy and as moral imperative. This fraying is suggested by debates over the status of antidiscrimination as a national priority, by judicial decisions limiting the reach of federal regulation, and by continuing racial hostilities that raise questions about the hearts of men and women.

Antidiscrimination law is not self-executing. Rather, its effectiveness is contingent upon the cooperation between the several branches of government and private citizens. Ideally, Congress creates the substantive protections and establishes the broad outlines of the enforcement framework, and the executive branch, ADMINISTRATIVE AGENCIES, and the judiciary elaborate these policies and apply them to specific contexts. The system works well when there is a general consensus about the importance of eliminating racial discrimination. In the last decade, however, the various governmental branches have been in conflict as to the scope, content, and priority of the antidiscrimination mandate. These conflicts not only reflect ideological differences with respect to race and racism, but hamper the development of a coherent and effective antidiscrimination law.

In the first seven years of the 1980s, the Civil Rights Division of the Justice Department opposed civil rights plaintiffs more often than it had in the previous two decades combined. A notable example is BOB JONES UNIVERSITY V. UNITED STATES (1982), in which the department, reversing the position of the administration of President JIMMY CARTER, argued against the decision of the Internal Revenue Service to deny tax exempt status to private colleges that practiced racial discrimination. Other evidence of a declining consensus concerning antidiscrimination policy is found in the increase of cases in which the Justice Department has sided against plaintiffs in antidiscrimination suits and others in which it has intervened to support reopening discrimination cases that were believed settled with AFFIRMATIVE ACTION consent decrees.

Legislative activity manifesting the growing conflict is represented by the frequency in which Congress has considered overturning Supreme Court decisions narrowing the scope of a number of civil rights acts. In 1982, Congress amended the Voting Rights Act and, in 1988, enacted the Civil Rights Restoration Act, both of which were to overturn Supreme Court decisions. The latter was enacted over a presidential veto. Another bill was introduced to provide a statutory basis for challenging the racially disproportionate distribution of the death penalty, in response to the Court's rejection of an EQUAL PROTECTION claim in MCCLESKEY V. KEMP (1987). Although this bill failed, Congress did strengthen the Fair Housing Act and is currently considering an omnibus bill to overturn several civil rights decisions of 1989.

The clearest evidence of the disintegrating consensus over antidiscrimination policy is apparent in these Supreme Court decisions. The Court's interpretive choices are often of critical importance in facilitating the effective enforcement of basic antidiscrimination principles. In the first decade after the Civil Rights Acts of 1964, the Court frequently interpreted ambiguous provisions in a manner that strengthened the substantive protection of civil rights legislation. Guided by a principle that eliminating racial discrimination "root and branch" was the highest priority, the Court upheld the constitutionality of civil rights legislation in the face of unfavorable precedent. In JONES V. ALFRED H. MAYER CO. (1968) and RUNYON V. MCCRARY (1976) the Court even resurrected Reconstruction civil rights laws long buried under an interpretation that placed most private discrimination outside the scope of antidiscrimination law.

Recently, however, the Court has been hesitant to take such broad interpretive positions and has even been willing to narrow the reach of antidiscrimination law. *Grove City College v. Bell* (1984) exemplifies this shift. Title IX of the 1972 amendments to Title VI of the 1964 act prohibited sex discrimination in any educational "program or activity" receiving federal financial assistance. President Carter's Justice Department read the words "program and activity" broadly to require a cutoff of funds to an entire institution whenever a single program or activity (for example, a college financial aid office) was in violation of the statute. In 1984, the Supreme Court in *Grove City* took a contrary view, limiting the cutoff of funds to the specific department rather than the entire institution.

PATTERSON V. MCLEAN CREDIT UNION (1989) reflects a similar shift away from expansive readings of the scope of antidiscrimination law. In one of his first opinions for the Court, Justice ANTHONY M. KENNEDY determined that a part of the CIVIL RIGHTS ACT OF 1866 (section 1981) prohibiting racial discrimination in the making and enforcement of contracts applied only to the formation of an employment contract and not to subsequent racial harassment by the employer. The dissenters argued that the Court created a false dichotomy between an employer who discloses discriminatory intentions at the time the contract is formed and the employer who conceals those discriminatory intentions until after the plaintiff has accepted the employment. *Patterson's* holding exemplifies a larger development: a partial deregulation of racial discrimination in employment.

Two primary reasons may explain the breakdown of the civil rights consensus and the increasing conflict over antidiscrimination law. First, the nature of radical discrimination in American society has changed. Antidiscrimination legislation has removed many formal barriers to full societal participation that previously excluded some groups. In one view, the removal of these barriers justifies a pre-

sumption of nondiscrimination; hence, claims of discrimination must overcome high burdens of proof. In this view, the removal of formal barriers also gives weight to competing interets, such as the seniority of other employees, STATES' RIGHTS, and freedom from governemental oversight. Others argue that antidiscrimination law must seek to eliminate practices that effectively discriminate against tradtionally excluded groups, whether such discrimination is formal and intentional or informal and inadvertant.

A second factor increasing the civil rights conflict reflects the relationship between antidiscrimination law and electoral politics. In eight years, President RONALD REAGAN not only presided over a major shift in Justice Department enforcement policy, but also appointed three conservative Supreme Court Justices SANDRA DAY O'CONNOR, ANTONIN SCALIA, and ANTHONY M. KENNEDY, and elevated the most conservative Justice, WILLIAM H. REHNQUIST, to Chief Justice. In addition, he appointed 370 judges to the federal bench, nearly half the federal judiciary. Many of these jurists interpret laws against a background preference for states' rights and employer autonomy, a preference that readily translates into decisions narrowing the reach of antidiscrimination laws. The demise of formal barriers and the ideological shifts within the judiciary and Justice Department have produced both a more restrictive antidiscrimination jurisprudence and a stagnated enforcement record.

For many critics, the Supreme Court's recent decisions raise the specter of an evisceration of antidiscrimination law comparable to the fate of laws enacted during the first Reconstruction. Congress may yet prevent the full eroding of the antidiscrimination law. However, the persistence of racial discrimination and the reemergence of analytical frameworks and values that have historically blunted the impact of civil rights laws suggest that antidiscrimination victories are, at best, provisional.

KIMBERLÉ CRENSHAW
(1992)

(SEE ALSO: *Capital Punishment and Race; Race-Consciousness; Racial Preference.*)

Bibliography

AMAKER, NORMAN C.   1988   *Civil Rights and the Reagan Administration.* Washington, D.C.: Urban Institute Press.
FREEMAN, ALAN   1990   Antidiscrimination Law: The View from 1989. *Tulane Law Review* 64:1407–1441.
KARST, KENNETH L.   1989   Private Discrimination and Public Responsibility: *Patterson* in Context. *The Supreme Court Review* 1989:1–51.

ANTIDISCRIMINATION LEGISLATION
(Update 2a)

The major piece of recent antidiscrimination legislation is the CIVIL RIGHTS ACT OF 1991. (The AMERICANS WITH DISABILITY ACT OF 1990 is outside the scope of this comment.) The 1991 act was passed chiefly in response to the decision of the Supreme Court in *Wards Cove Packing Co. v. Atonio* (1989). That decision undercut the disparate impact theories of discrimination (that is, those which look at the outcome of certain practices without regard to the employer's intention) that had been read into Title VII of the original CIVIL RIGHTS ACT OF 1964 in the Court's earlier decision in GRIGGS V. DUKE POWER COMPANY (1971). *Wards Cove* appeared to overturn the *Griggs* rule that employers could only escape disparate impact liability by showing a business necessity for a given practice. *Wards Cove* then allowed the employer to meet the lower standard of "reasonable business justification," transferring the burden of proof to the employee.

Wards Cove provoked a strong reaction from supporters of Title VII, who, after much negotiation and compromise, regained lost ground with the 1991 act. There Congress first found that *Wards Cove* "weakened the scope and effectiveness of Federal civil rights protections." In response, Congress added section 803(k)(1)(A) to the 1964 Civil Rights Act which provides that "a complaining party demonstrates that a respondent uses a particular employment practice that causes a disparate impact on the basis of race, color, religion, sex or national origin and the respondent fails to demonstrate that the challenged practice is job related for the position in question and consistent with business necessity." The 1991 act thus restores, perhaps in its entirety, the law on disparate impact as it was generally understood prior to *Wards Cove*, by reintroducing the notion of business necessity and by providing that both the burden of production and the burden of persuasion rest on the employer.

One issue left open by the 1991 act was the retroactive application of the 1991 act. That question was important because *Wards Cove* left in limbo disparate impact cases that were pending when the case was decided. If the 1991 act had applied retroactively, then employees in pending cases could have taken advantage of the 1991 act's provisions that allowed for compensatory and PUNITIVE DAMAGES provisions in a jury trial. These provisions represent a departure from Congress's decision in 1964 to ban punitive damages, cap damage awards to back-pay, and bar jury trials. In *Landgraf v. USI Film Products* (1994), the Court held, however, that the general RULE-OF-LAW presumption

against retroactive decisions had not been overcome because the 1991 act was silent on the question.

Even though the act is not retroactive, the modifications it contains have removed any doubts as to the statutory ground of the disparate impact test. No longer is it possible to attack the entire notion on the ground that the original 1964 act was limited to cases of intentional discrimination only. Today disparate impact theories have become an indisputable part of the civil rights law. Yet the 1991 act has done nothing to resolve the difficult questions of determining the appropriate occupational and geographical market that defines the boundaries of the labor pool against which any disparate impact claim should be litigated.

Seven years after the 1991 act, disparate impact cases appear to loom less large than before the passage of the act. In part, the relative quiet along the disparate impact front results from heightened emphasis on disputes over AFFIRMATIVE ACTION and SEX DISCRIMINATION in the form of WORKPLACE HARASSMENT. Yet, the change in legal terrain also results in part because employers since *Griggs* have been made aware of the serious exposure to disparate impact cases (which easily lend themselves to CLASS ACTIONS). They have thus taken, even before *Wards Cove*, key steps to bring their practices in alignment with *Griggs*. Their vigilance did not decrease with *Wards Cove*, because the campaign to overrule it legislatively began in earnest the day it was handed down. In one respect, however, the 1991 act did strengthen the position of employers. Section 703(k)(3) of the act provides that disparate impact theory shall not be used with respect to the rule that applies to testing or use of illegal drugs; in those cases, the employer may be held liable only if the rule is applied "with an intent to discriminate" on the familiar grounds outlawed under the 1964 act.

The 1991 act also ushered in a number of other important changes. Section 703(1) prohibited the practice of "race norming," which reported the percentile scores of individual applicants only with reference to the particular racial group of that applicant. Prior to the act, some employment services would report that an applicant was in the x percentile of those tested, without making it clear that the percentage was adjusted to the applicant's racial group. In this perspective, a black candidate would appear to fall within the higher percentage group than a white candidate who received an equal score. After 1991, employment services must report all scores in relationship to a nation-wide pool. In addition, the 1991 act clarifies in section 703(m) that a case of intentional discrimination can be made by showing that the forbidden ground was "a motivating factor" even if not the sole factor behind the employment decision—a rule that does not apply retroactively. Finally, again on a prospective basis, the act as noted expands the rights to compensatory and punitive damages in jury trials.

Antidiscrimination legislation has continued to expand in ways that go far beyond the contours of the original 1964 Civil Rights Act. This legislation has spilled over into such areas as family leave, health, and disability law. The obvious challenge in this growing area is to find rationales that justify the increased levels of intervention when by all measures the levels of institutional discrimination have declined sharply since the 1960s. This task is compounded especially when it becomes ever more difficult to attribute improvements in wages and employment conditions to the aggressive enforcement of civil rights laws, now that the obvious legislative targets have been overcome. It appears that free entry into competitive markets, now more than ever before, provides the strongest systematic defense against all forms of discrimination, without the immense regulatory drag of the current legal structure.

RICHARD A. EPSTEIN
(2000)

(SEE ALSO: *Retroactivity of Legislation.*)

Bibliography

EPSTEIN, RICHARD A. 1992 *Forbidden Grounds: The Case Against Employment Discrimination Laws.* Cambridge, Mass.: Harvard University Press.
KELMAN, MARK 1991 Concepts of Discrimination in "General Ability" Job Testing. *Harvard Law Review* 104:1158–1247.
SYMPOSIUM 1993 The Civil Rights Act of 1991: Unraveling the Controversy. *Rutgers Law Review* 45:887–1141.
—— 1993 The Civil Rights Act of 1991: Theory and Practice. *Notre Dame Law Review* 1993: 911–1164.

ANTIDISCRIMINATION LEGISLATION
(Update 2b)

Racial and gender EMPLOYMENT DISCRIMINATION has been a major factor in producing a condition of racial and gender inequality in the United States. Congress made a strong national commitment to bringing an end to racial and gender employment discrimination by the enactment of Title VII of the CIVIL RIGHTS ACT OF 1964. In the first two decades of its operation, the Supreme Court interpreted Title VII expansively in order to accomplish Congress's remedial purpose. The Court held that Title VII not only prohibited intentional discrimination, but also prohibited employment practices that were neutral in form, but that had a "disparate impact" on the employment opportunities of racial minorities and women. Under the rule of

GRIGGS V. DUKE POWER COMPANY (1971), whenever an employment practice had such an impact, it violated Title VII unless the employer could show that the practice was justified by "business necessity." At the same time the Court held that because the underlying purpose of Title VII was to increase employment opportunities for racial minorities and women in areas from which they had traditionally been excluded, Title VII permitted employers to give express preference to racial minorities and women in hiring and promotions—that is, AFFIRMATIVE ACTION—where minorities or women were manifestly underrepresented in a traditionally segregated job category of the employer's workforce. Under UNITED STEELWORKERS OF AMERICA V. WEBER (1979) and JOHNSON V. TRANSPORTATION AGENCY (1987), such preferences must be reasonable and must not "unfairly trammel" the interests of white or male employees.

In its 1988–1989 term, the Court rendered a series of decisions that were widely perceived as making it more difficult for racial minorities and women to establish Title VII discrimination claims against employers, particularly in regard to "disparate impact" claims. Congress responded by enacting the CIVIL RIGHTS ACT OF 1991, which overruled aspects of all these decisions, and added other provisions that expanded significantly the protections against employment discrimination afforded by federal law. In regard to "disparate impact" claims for example, the 1991 act provides that employment practices having an identifiable "disparate impact" are prohibited unless the employer can establish that the challenged practice "is job-related for the position in question and consistent with business necessity." At the same time, despite the heated debate over "affirmative action," Congress did not modify Title VII to prohibit the use of express employment preferences for racial minorities and women that the Court had held to be permissible. Although Title VII does not permit the use of "quotas" or require "proportionality," it does ensure that racial minorities and women will not suffer direct or indirect discrimination in their employment opportunities.

A pernicious form of "discrimination with respect to conditions of employment" under Title VII takes the form of sexual harassment. While the victims of sexual harassment are usually women, they can be men as well and, under the rule of *Oncale v. Sundowner Offshore Services* (1998), can be of the same sex as the perpetrator. The Court has defined more precisely when workplace behavior of a sexual nature can amount to "discrimination with respect to conditions of employment" and so be violative of Title VII. One situation is *quid pro quo* sexual harassment, which occurs when an employer or supervisor makes an employee's submission to sexual demands a condition for conferring or withholding employment benefits, and the employee either submits or suffers tangible employment harm because of the failure to do so. The other situation is *hostile environment* sexual harassment, which occurs when sexually objectionable behavior in the workplace is so "severe or pervasive as to alter the conditions of the victim's employment and create an abusive working environment."

In its 1998 term, the Supreme Court added some refinements to sexual harassment law. The employer is liable to the employee for a violation of Title VII whenever quid pro quo sexual harassment has been engaged in by an employer or a supervisor, and the employee has suffered tangible employment harm because of it. The employer is also liable for hostile environment sexual harassment engaged in by a supervisor, even though the employer had no knowledge of the behavior and was not negligent in employing the supervisor. However, the employer has a defense to such liability if (1) the employer exercised reasonable care to prevent and correct promptly any sexually harassing behavior and (2) the employee unreasonably failed to take advantage of any preventive or corrective opportunities provided by the employer. Thus, employers can protect themselves against Title VII liability for sexual harassment by establishing effective antiharassment policies and procedures, and communicating these policies and procedures to employees and supervisors. To the extent that employers establish and vigorously enforce effective antiharassment policies and procedures, there should be a significant decline in sexual harassment in the workplace.

ROBERT A. SEDLER
(2000)

(SEE ALSO: *Workplace Harassment.*)

Bibliography

ABRAMS, KATHRYN 1988 The New Jurisprudence of Sexual Harassment. *Cornell Law Review* 83:1169–1230.

BERNSTEIN, ANITA 1997 Treating Sexual Harassment with Respect. *Harvard Law Review* 111:445–527.

BROWNE, KINGSLEY R. 1993 The Civil Rights Act of 1991: A "Quota Bill," A Codification of *Griggs*, A Partial Return to *Wards's Cove*, or All of the Above. *Case Western University Law Review* 43:287–400.

FRANKE, KATHERINE M. 1997 What's Wrong with Sexual Harassment? *Stanford Law Review* 49:691–772.

GROVER, SUSAN S. 1996 The Business Necessity Defense in Disparate Impact Discrimination Cases. *Georgia Law Review* 30:387–430.

SEDLER, ROBERT A. 1992 Employment Equality, Affirmative Action, and the Constitutional Political Consensus. *Michigan Law Review* 90:1315–1337.

SPECIAL PROJECT 1995 Current Issues in Sexual Harassment Law. *Vanderbilt Law Review* 48:1009–1214.

SYMPOSIUM 1993 The Civil Rights Act of 1991: Theory and Practice. *Notre Dame Law Review* 68:911–1164.

ANTI-FEDERALIST CONSTITUTIONAL THOUGHT

The men who opposed the Constitution's unconditional RATIFICATION in 1787–1788 were called Anti-Federalists, although they claimed to be the true federalists and the true republicans. Contrary to common opinion, their major contribution to the American founding lies more in their critical examination of the new form of FEDERALISM and the new form of republican government than in their successful argument for a BILL OF RIGHTS.

The federalism issue was complicated by an ambiguity in usage during the Confederation period and by changes in both the Federalist and Anti-Federalist conceptions of federalism during the ratification debates. HERBERT J. STORING has explained the ambiguity by showing how "federal" referred to measures designed to strengthen the national authority, as opposed to state authority, but also to the principle of state supremacy. In the CONSTITUTIONAL CONVENTION, the federal principle meant congressional reliance on state requisitions for armies and taxes, in contrast to the national principle of direct governmental authority over individuals. The Anti-Federalists argued that the Constitution, which strengthened the national authority, went beyond the federal principle by moving away from requisitions and state equality in representation. Supporters of the Constitution were able to take, and keep, the name Federalists by treating any recognition of the state governments in the Constitution (for example, election, apportionment, ratification, amendment) as evidence of federalism, thereby redefining the term. JAMES MADISON, in THE FEDERALIST #39, consequently called the Constitution partly federal, partly national. For their part, the authors of the two best Anti-Federalist writings, who wrote under the pseudonyms Brutus and Federal Farmer, conceded the need for some direct governmental authority over individuals, thereby acknowledging the inadequacy of traditional federalism.

The Anti-Federalists emphasized the need to restrict the national power to what was absolutely necessary to preserve the union. They proposed limiting the national taxing power to imported goods, relying on requisitions if that source was insufficient. Moreover, Brutus proposed limiting standing armies in time of peace to what was necessary for defending the frontiers. If it became necessary to raise an army to repel an attack, he favored a two-thirds vote by both houses of Congress.

As part of their argument that a consolidation of power in the general government was incompatible with republicanism, the Anti-Federalists frequently cited Montesquieu for the proposition that republics must be small, lest the public good be sacrificed. But they agreed with the Federalists, against Montesquieu, that the first principle of republican government was the regulation and protection of individual rights, not the promotion of civic virtue. They also, with rare exceptions, assumed the necessity of representation, while Montesquieu mentioned it only in his discussion of England, not in his discussion of republics.

Defining republican government somewhere between a selfless dedication to the common good, on the one hand, and individualism plus the elective principle, on the other, the Anti-Federalists emphasized mildness in government as essential for public confidence. This mildness required a similarity "in manners, sentiments, and interests" between citizens and officials and among citizens themselves. This, in turn, made possible a genuine REPRESENTATION of the people. Federal Farmer called such representation and local jury trials "the essential parts of a free and good government."

When the Anti-Federalists examined the representation in Congress, they saw an emerging aristocracy. They claimed that the democratic class, especially the middle class or the yeomanry, would have little chance of gaining election against the aristocracy, the men of wealth and of political and professional prominence. Since the middle class was substantially represented in the state governments, the Anti-Federalists argued that the powers of Congress had to be restricted to produce a proper balance between the nation and the states.

The Anti-Federalist objections to the structure of the proposed government related either to federalism or to republicanism. As examples of the former, the Senate, despite state equality, did not satisfy federalism because the legislatures did not pay the senators and could not recall them, and because the voting was by individuals, not by state delegations. And Brutus, who viewed the JUDICIAL POWER as the vehicle of consolidation, objected to Congress's power to ordain and establish lower federal courts. He thought the state courts were adequate to handle every case arising under the Constitution in the first instance, and he favored a limited right of APPEAL to the Supreme Court. As examples of their republicanism, the Anti-Federalists feared the Senate, with its six-year term, plus reeligibility, and its substantial powers, especially regarding appointments and treaty-making, as a special source of aristocracy. The Anti-Federalists were only somewhat less critical of the executive. They favored the proposed mode of election but opposed reeligibility; they generally favored unity but wanted a separately elected council to participate in appointments; some supported and others opposed the qualified executive VETO POWER; and some ex-

pressed apprehension about the pardoning power and the COMMANDER-IN-CHIEF power. As for the judiciary, Brutus argued that the combination of tenure for GOOD BEHAVIOR plus a judicial power that extends to "all cases in law and EQUITY, arising under this Constitution," meant not only JUDICIAL REVIEW but JUDICIAL SUPREMACY. He preferred that the legislature interpret the Constitution, since the people could easily correct the errors of their lawmakers.

Finally, the Bill of Rights was as much a Federalist as an Anti-Federalist victory. The Anti-Federalists wanted a bill of rights to curb governmental power. When the Federalists denied the necessity of a federal bill of rights, on the ground that whatever power was not enumerated could not be claimed, the Anti-Federalists pointed to the Constitution's SUPREMACY CLAUSE and to the extensiveness of the enumeration of powers. Paradoxically, this decisive argument resulted in a bill of rights that confirmed the new federalism, with its extended republic. Neither the Anti-Federalist proposals to restrict the tax and WAR POWERS nor their proposal to restrict IMPLIED POWERS was accepted. Nevertheless, the Anti-Federalist concern about "big government" has continued to find occasional constitutional expression in the restrictive interpretation of the ENUMERATED POWERS, along with the TENTH AMENDMENT.

MURRAY DRY
(1986)

Bibliography
KENYON, CECELIA 1966 *The Antifederalists*. Indianapolis: Bobbs-Merrill.
STORING, HERBERT J. 1978 The Constitution and the Bill of Rights. Pages 32–48 in M. Judd Harmon, ed., *Essays on the Constitution of the United States*. Port Washington, N.Y.: Kennikat Press Corp.
——— 1981 *The Complete Anti-Federalist*. 7 Vols. Chicago: University of Chicago Press. (Volume 1 separately published in paperback as *What the Anti-Federalists Were For*.)

ANTIPEONAGE ACT OF 1867

See: Peonage

ANTITERRORISM AND EFFECTIVE DEATH PENALTY ACT
110 Stat. 1214 (1996)

On April 24, 1996, one year and five days after the Oklahoma City bombing, President WILLIAM J. CLINTON signed into law the Antiterrorism and Effective Death Penalty Act (AEDPA). The statute is extraordinarily far-ranging and implicates constitutional provisions from Article III to the suspension clause, the Fifth Amendment, and the FIRST AMENDMENT. AEDPA is also notoriously complex and not especially well-drafted. As Justice DAVID H. SOUTER put it in *Lindh v. Murphy* (1997), "in a world of silk purses and pigs' ears, the Act is not a silk purse of the art of statutory drafting."

The two most immediately effective features of AEDPA—drastic restriction of federal court HABEAS CORPUS review of criminal cases and broad expansion of the power to exclude and deport certain non-citizens— bore virtually no relation to the terrorist act committed by U.S. citizens which had spurred its passage and inspired its name. A more relevant but constitutionally dubious section prohibits the provision of "material support or resources" to groups designated "terrorist organizations." Other sections deal with victim assistance and restitution, JURISDICTION for lawsuits against "terrorist states," prohibitions on "assistance to terrorist states," nuclear, biological, and chemical weapons restrictions, plastic explosives restrictions, and various criminal law modifications relating to terrorism.

The restrictions on habeas corpus review in AEDPA were, in many respects, a codification of DOCTRINES already created by the Supreme Court and, as such, they are unlikely to be found unconstitutional in our era. However, AEDPA addresses issues such as delay, second and successive petitions, and finality with unprecedented rigidity and force and therefore implicates due process and other constitutional rights in new and often distressing ways. A sketch of AEDPA's main JUDICIAL REVIEW features includes (1) special court of appeals gate-keeping mechanisms and severe restrictions relating to second or subsequent habeas corpus petitions, (2) unprecedented deference to state court factual and legal findings, (3) strict new time limitations both on filing deadlines and federal court action on habeas corpus petitions, (4) limitations on evidentiary hearings in habeas corpus cases, and (5) special restrictions on habeas corpus petitions filed by certain state prisoners facing CAPITAL PUNISHMENT including a filing limitation of 180 days. To date, these provisions have generally withstood constitutional challenge although certain aspects of AEDPA have been interpreted narrowly to avoid constitutional issues.

In the IMMIGRATION arena, AEDPA (1) purported to eliminate judicial review of certain types of deportation orders, (2) severely restricted a venerable discretionary waiver of deportability—so-called "Section 212(c) relief"—that had permitted a long-term legal permanent resident who was convicted of a crime to avoid deportation after consideration of a variety of humanitarian and other factors, (3) expanded criminal grounds of deportation and expedited deportation procedures for certain types of cases, (4) created a new system for the "summary exclu-

sion" from the United States of certain asylum-seekers who lack proper documentation, with extremely limited judicial review, and (5) created a new type of radically streamlined "removal" proceeding— including the possibility of secret evidence—for noncitizens accused of "terrorist" activity. Some of these provisions were enhanced and many were superseded by the Illegal Immigration Reform and Immigrant Responsibility Act of 1996 (IIRAIRA).

Federal courts have grappled with difficult interpretive and constitutional problems raised by the immigration law sections of AEDPA. The main points of contention have been over RETROACTIVITY, DUE PROCESS, and the nature and scope of judicial review of administrative immigration decisions. Ultimately, many of these questions will likely be resolved by the Supreme Court.

DANIEL KANSTROOM
(2000)

Bibliography

BENSON, LENNI B. 1997 Back to the Future: Congress Attacks the Right to Judicial Review of Immigration Proceedings. *Connecticut Law Review* 29:1411–1494.

NOTE 1998 The Avoidance of Constitutional Questions and the Preservation of Judicial Review: Federal Court Treatment of the New Habeas Provisions. *Harvard Law Review* 111: 1578–1595.

SCAPERLANDA, MICHAEL 1996 Are We That Far Gone? Due Process and Secret Deportation Proceedings. *Stanford Law and Policy Review* 7:23–30.

TUSHNET, MARK and YACKLE, LARRY W. 1997 Symbolic Statutes and Real Laws: The Pathologies of the Antiterrorism and Effective Death Penalty Act and the Prison Litigation Reform Act. *Duke Law Journal* 47:1–86.

YACKLE, LARRY W. 1996 A Primer on the New Habeas Corpus Statute. *Buffalo Law Review* 44:381–449.

ANTITRUST LAW

Federal antitrust law comprises a set of acts of Congress, administrative regulations, and court decisions that attempt to regulate market structure and competitive behavior in the national ECONOMY. The substance of this law is found in the first two sections of the SHERMAN ACT (1890), which forbid concerted action in "restraint of trade" and acts that seek to "monopolize" any part of commerce. The COMMERCE CLAUSE is the nexus between antitrust law and constitutional law.

There are several persistent uncertainties concerning the proper meaning of these prohibitions: the extent to which they embody a particular concept of economic efficiency as a primary value; the degree to which they are designed to protect competition by valuing a market composed of a large number of small competitors rather than a few large units; and the extent to which they embody specific notions of consumer protection. Despite these disagreements, there is general consensus that the antitrust laws express a preference for free and open markets in which prices and production are set by competitive forces and in which neither restraint of trade nor monopolization determines important market conditions. The three most common forms of restraint of trade are competitor agreements to fix prices, to allocate customers and markets, and to exclude parties from the market by a boycott or group refusal to deal. Monopolization is behavior by a dominant firm in the relevant market designed to give the firm power to fix prices, set market conditions, and exclude potential competitors.

The antitrust laws have ancient roots in the English and American COMMON LAW. Most states have comparable laws which complement the congressional scheme with varying degrees of effectiveness. In addition, Congress has amended the original acts, most notably to deal with corporate mergers and consolidations and with price discrimination in the distribution of goods. After a generation of judicial interpretation of the Sherman Act's general prohibitions, Congress in 1914 adopted the CLAYTON ACT and FEDERAL TRADE COMMISSION ACT to supplement the Sherman Act with more specific prohibitions and to supplement judicial interpretation and enforcement with administrative agency rule-making and enforcement. Nonetheless, these additions are largely derivative; the Sherman Act's prohibitions of "restraints of trade" and "monopolization" remain the core of federal antitrust law.

Antitrust law bears a strong resemblance to constitutional law, both in the broad intentions and organic implications of its substantive law and in the methodology of its enforcement and interpretive growth. These laws have long been seen as more than simple statutes. The delphic demands of the Sherman Act are considered a structural imperative with social and political, as well as economic, implications. Justice HUGO L. BLACK summed up this perspective in *Northern Pacific Railroad v. United States* (1958): "The Sherman Act was designed to be a comprehensive charter of economic liberty aimed at preserving free and unfettered competition as the rule of trade. It rests on the premise that the unrestrained interaction of competitive forces will yield the best allocation of our economic resources, the lowest prices, the highest quality and the greatest material progress, while at the same time providing an environment conducive to the preservation of our democratic political and social institutions."

The Sherman Act was a political response to the threats presented by economic power associated with the industrial revolution in the late nineteenth century. Certainly farmers, industrial workers, and tradespersons suffered from the concentrated economic power of the new order. From their beginning, however, these laws also identified threats presented by concentrated economic power to the social and political fabric. The specifics of the Sherman Act are not demanded by the constitutional text, but they can be seen as the economic corollaries of a constitutional commitment to individual autonomy, free association, and the separation and division of power within society. The antitrust laws seek to prevent economic power from becoming so highly concentrated that political freedom is unworkable.

As units of economic organization have grown in size and markets have become more concentrated over the past century, the antitrust laws have provided one alternative to extensive and detailed governmental ECONOMIC REGULATION. In most of the world's political systems, industrialization has been matched by growing control of the economy by bureaucratic *dirigisme*. Although the American economy has hardly been free from governmental intervention, this involvement has been more modest as a result of the emphasis on private planning and control over enterprises through a competitive market regime. In this perspective, excessive bureaucratic control is seen as the enemy of both economic efficiency and individual liberty.

Not only do antitrust law and constitutional law share comparable legislative approaches; their interpretive processes also show strong similarities—a tendency reinforced by the degree to which the Supreme Court is given broad powers to articulate basic norms in both areas.

The antitrust laws present a uniquely varied set of enforcement procedures. In addition to the sanctions available under state law, the basic federal antitrust norms may be enforced by the Department of Justice in federal court either by criminal prosecution or by civil suit for INJUNCTION relief or DAMAGES. The Federal Trade Commission enforces the same basic norms by administrative CEASE AND DESIST ORDERS backed up by civil penalties. A third level of enforcement is available to any private party aggrieved through a damage action in federal court in which treble damages may be awarded. Finally, legislation enacted in 1976 permits state officials to bring damage actions in federal court on behalf of their citizens.

Antitrust cases may be instituted in any one of the federal district courts and be appealed to a court of appeals. Administrative proceedings may also be reviewed in any one of the courts of appeals. Thus, no single agency has policy control over the bringing of antitrust suits, nor is there any coordination of the often contradictory decisions by local courts and agencies below the level of the Supreme Court. To a degree familiar to constitutional lawyers but atypical in other areas of federal law, a question of antitrust law is not considered settled until the Supreme

Court decides it. The Court accepts only a few antitrust cases each year for decision, and the doctrinal impact of these decisions is profound.

Both constitutional and antitrust law generate the "big case," that peculiarly American form of political controversy in the form of litigation. Although there is reason to doubt the actual influence of antitrust law on the grand issues of national economic structure, the bringing of a major case is properly seen as an important political event. The investment of personnel and resources needed to accumulate the economic data necessary to prove a claim under these laws has long presented a major constraint to full enforcement. A big case is likely to exceed the natural lifespan of the national administration that institutes the suit, and may extend beyond the professional career span of government attorneys. As a consequence, charges of monopolization and other abuses of dominant market position are relatively rare. Cases charging specific acts in restraint of trade—particularly price fixing, production limits, and other cartelization—are more common because they are more susceptible to proof within the limits of a judicial trial.

The constraint of the big case produce two kinds of attempts to avoid full trial of cases. First, the great majority of antitrust cases are settled by consent decrees in which the government or private plaintiff is granted substantial relief. Concerned about the consistency of this practice with public interest, Congress in 1976 amended the law to require fuller judicial examination and public scrutiny of proposed settlements. Second, the problems of the big case have promoted the development of other enforcement techniques. The Federal Trade Commission Act of 1914 and the short-lived COMMERCE COURT represent two efforts to move both legislation and enforcement out of court and into specialized forums. The Federal Trade Commission (FTC) has broad power to proscribe unfair and anticompetitive behavior by rule, but the full potential of this technique has never been realized. Recently a hostile Congress has suspended many of the more important FTC trade rules.

The FTC and the Justice Department have also issued guidelines stating when the government will bring antitrust suits against proposed mergers or other changes in industry structure perceived to threaten overconcentration or monopoly. Because the confidence of securities markets is normally crucial to a successful merger, the threat of a suit often forecloses such a transaction.

The Constitution and the Sherman Act both use language drawn primarily from English common law sources to respond to dimly perceived new social needs that were expected to extend far into the future. In both cases the choice of operative terms served effectively to delegate to the Supreme Court power to pour meaning into common law terms. As few would suggest today that the full meaning of DUE PROCESS OF LAW is found in eighteenth-century common law sources, few would suggest that the meaning of "restraint of trade" is to be found in congressional understanding (actually, misunderstanding) of that common law term at the time the Sherman Act was enacted.

This protean aspect of the Sherman Act has always engendered the complaint that the act provides inadequate guidance to the economic decision makers who are subject to the law's commands. Despite three generations of attempts to contain the law in more specific statutory prohibitions and to delegate its enforcement to administrative experts, antitrust law retains its strong similarity to the process of constitutional adjudication by judicial decision. Even in those few areas of antitrust enforcement marked by heavy reliance on the specifics of the Clayton Act or administrative rules, the Sherman Act's general concepts of restraint of trade and monopolization retain their influence, broadening and reshaping the narrower rules.

As in constitutional litigation, the shifting tides of antitrust interpretation follow major changes in American economic and social thought. The conception of "restraint of trade," for example, has been modified by a RULE OF REASON, which exempts reasonable restraints of trade from the antitrust laws. Most contracts of any duration restrain the freedom of the parties to enter the market by obligating the parties to deal with each other. By the middle of the eighteenth century, the common law prohibition on contracts in restraint of trade had been made into a rule prohibiting only unreasonable restraints. This rule, of course, vastly expanded the potential power of judges, who decide what is reasonable.

When Congress enacted the Sherman Act it certainly had in mind this common law doctrine—although perhaps not the doctrine's specifics. The text declares all contracts in restraint of trade illegal. A persistent interpretive theme from the beginning has been the extent to which the Sherman Act incorporates a rule of reason. During periods when the dominant political thought is permissive of consolidations or economic power, the rule of reason tends to enlarge, thus increasing the power of the lower federal judiciary, who typically have been sympathetic to business interests. This development complicates the trial of cases, for defendants are permitted to enlarge the inquiry with evidence that their behavior, while generally of a prohibited sort, was reasonable under the circumstances. In contrast, during periods of vigorous antitrust enforcement the rule of reason recedes in favor of a per se rule of violation.

The earliest period of interpretation of the Sherman Act was marked by the dominance of a per se approach: competitor agreements fixing prices or allocating markets were per se offenses and could not be justified by evidence that the prices fixed were reasonable, or that conditions in the industry demanded efforts to stabilize market prices. The tone of majority opinions began to change with STANDARD OIL COMPANY V. UNITED STATES (1911), in which a general rule of reason standard was announced. Opposition to this vague standard during WOODROW WILSON's Democratic administration contributed to the enactment of the Clayton Act and the Federal Trade Commission Act. With the arrival of "normalcy" under President WARREN G. HARDING, a permissive rule of reason again flowered, and remained dominant for two decades.

Not until the late 1930s, when a new Supreme Court was in place and the NEW DEAL administration had turned away from unhappy experience with the *dirigisme* of the NATIONAL INDUSTRIAL RECOVERY ACT, did vigorous challenges to anticompetitive private market behavior again become popular. Per se rules forbidding a wide range of competitor collaboration and group refusals to deal were announced by the Court for the first time, or brought down from the attic in which they had lain since the Wilson era. This period lasted for a generation; toward its close in the late 1960s per se rules were extended beyond price fixing and competitor agreements to nonprice market allocations between manufacturers and distributors. The early 1970s brought changes in political climate and in the personnel of the Court, and again the course of antitrust doctrine changed. The new mood was apparent in a more restricted interpretation of merger policy, greater receptivity to distribution agreements, and the reassertion of the rule of reason in peripheral areas. As of the mid-1980s, however, the Court had not adopted the more radical shifts toward permissiveness urged by critics of the antitrust laws.

The Supreme Court's restrictive view of Congress's power under the commerce clause in the years following adoption of the Sherman Act produced an extremely narrow interpretation of the act in UNITED STATES V. E. C. KNIGHT COMPANY (1895). Manufacturing, said the Court, was not commerce; thus the act did not reach the stock transactions that gave one company almost complete control over sugar refining in the United States. Only "direct" restraints of interstate commerce itself were subject to the act, as the Court held in *Addyston Pipe & Steel Company v. United States* (1899). The "constitutional revolution" of the 1930s broadened not only the Court's conception of the commerce power but also its interpretation of the reach of the antitrust laws. By the time of SOUTH-EASTERN UNDERWRITERS ASSOCIATION V. UNITED STATES (1944), both changes were complete.

More recently, courts and commentators have noted a potential conflict between state authority to control alcoholic beverages under the TWENTY-FIRST AMENDMENT and claims that state regulatory authorities have participated in price fixing. This issue illustrates a more basic question:

does the Sherman Act decree a national free market, or may the states depart from competitive structures for economic activity otherwise within their regulatory power? The issue has arisen in connection with state utility regulation, control of the legal and medical professions, and agricultural marketing programs, all of which operate on a franchise or monopoly regulation model rather than a free market model. In general, the Supreme Court has held that state action regulating a market does not violate federal law and those complying with state law are not in violation of federal law.

The antitrust laws raise other constitutional questions. The vague language of the Sherman Act has given rise to claims of unconstitutionality when that act is the basis of a felony prosecution. The "big case" raises a variety of due process concerns, for it presses the judicial model to the outer limits of its capacity. The meaning of the right to TRIAL BY JURY, for example, requires clarification in cases presenting the complexity and gargantuan size found in many antitrust suits.

Perhaps the most puzzling set of constitutional concerns involves the connections between the Sherman Act's prohibitions on collective behavior (which it describes as contracts, combinations, and conspiracies in restraint of trade) and the associational rights protected by the FIRST AMENDMENT. An agreement among competitors seeking to exclude other potential competitors from the market is a conspiracy under the Sherman Act, even if the competitors enlist government agencies in their effort. On the other hand, an agreement among members of an industry to petition the government for legal relief from the economic threat of their competitors is constitutionally protected political activity. Supreme Court opinions "distinguishing" between these two kinds of activity have resorted to a pejorative label to explain their results, finding the political activity immune from antitrust claims unless it is a sham.

Comparable tensions exist between the Sherman Act's prohibitions of economic boycotts—which are seen as concerted refusals to deal—and political boycotts. To maintain this distinction requires a worldview in which economics and politics are unconnected spheres. Yet boycotts are per se offenses under the Sherman Act and some courts have held that political boycotts are a protected form of political protest.

A third tension is found in the case of permissible "natural monopolies"—for example, the owners of the railway terminal at the only point on a wide river suitable for a railway crossing. For three quarters of a century the Court has held that such holders of monopoly power are obligated to share it fairly with others. Several of these decisions treat this obligation as one resembling governmental power which carries along with it an obligation of "due process" procedural fairness. These decisions might be said to impose the constitutional obligation of government on those private accumulations of power that are found not to be prohibited outright by the Sherman Act. Together, the Constitution and the Sherman Act thus represent a total response to the problems of concentrated power in modern society: the Constitution controls governmental power, and the antitrust law controls concentrations of private economic power. At the seam between public and private organizations, the two bodies of law combine to limit the excesses of concentrated power.

ARTHUR ROSETT
(1986)

Bibliography

AREEDA, P. and TURNER, D.   1978–1980   *Antitrust Law: An Analysis of Antitrust Principles and their Application*, 5 vols. Boston: Little, Brown.

NEALE, A. D. and GOYDER, D. G.   1980   *The Antitrust Laws of the Usa*, 3rd ed. Cambridge: At the University Press.

SULLIVAN, L.   1977   *Antitrust*. St. Paul, Minn.: West Publishing Company.

APEX HOSIERY COMPANY v. LEADER
310 U.S. 469 (1940)

Destroying the effect of CORONADO COAL COMPANY V. UNITED MINE WORKERS (1925), although not overruling it, this opinion marked the shift toward a prolabor sentiment in the Supreme Court. The Court reaffirmed the application of the SHERMAN ANTITRUST ACT to unions but held that even a strike that effected a reduction of goods in INTERSTATE COMMERCE was no Sherman Act violation if it furthered legitimate union objectives. (See ALLEN-BRADLEY COMPANY V. LOCAL #3.) A particularly violent sit-down strike at the Apex plant reduced the volume of goods in commerce and resulted in extensive physical damage. Did the act forbid the union's actions? Justice HARLAN FISKE STONE, for a 6–3 Court, condemned the union's conduct, declaring that the company had a remedy under state law, but held that restraints not outlawed by the Sherman Act when accomplished peacefully could not be brought within the law's scope because they were accompanied by violence. The Court also denied that the resulting restraint of trade fell under the act. The union was not proceeding illegally by acting to eliminate nonunion or commercial competition in the market, even though a production halt must accompany a strike and lead to a temporary restraint. Only if the restraint led to a monopoly, price control, or discrimination among consumers would a violation occur. The Court thus substituted a test of restraint in the mar-

ketplace for the test of intent previously announced in BEDFORD CUT STONE V. JOURNEYMEN STONECUTTERS (1927). In dissent, Chief Justice CHARLES EVANS HUGHES, joined by Justices OWEN ROBERTS and JAMES C. MCREYNOLDS, insisted that the earlier decisions governed and that they had not confined the test of restraint to market control. The Court had abandoned its earlier approach; the next year it would supplement *Apex*, excluding both jurisdictional strikes and SECONDARY BOYCOTTS from Sherman Act coverage in *United States v. Hutcheson* (1941).

DAVID GORDON
(1986)

(SEE ALSO: *Antitrust Law*.)

APODACA v. OREGON

See: *Johnson v. Louisiana*

APPALACHIAN ELECTRIC POWER COMPANY v. UNITED STATES
311 U.S. 377 (1940)

Until this decision, federal authority over waterways extended only to those that were navigable. In this case the Supreme Court agreed to review the scope of federal power over completely nonnavigable waters. The Appalachian Electric Company asserted that the WATER POWER ACT of 1920 did not apply to the New River because its waters were not navigable; moreover, the act imposed conditions dealing with neither navigation nor its protection. Justice STANLEY F. REED, for a 6–2 Court, concluded that it was sufficient that the river might eventually be made navigable, thus broadening the earlier definition of federal authority. The COMMERCE CLAUSE was the constitutional provision involved and navigation was merely one of its parts. "Flood control, watershed development, recovery of the cost of improvements through utilization of power [also renders navigable waters subject] to national planning and control in the broad regulation of commerce granted the Federal Government." Justice OWEN ROBERTS, joined by Justice JAMES C. MCREYNOLDS, dissented from Reed's expansion of the test for navigability: "No authority is cited and I think none can be cited which countenances any such test."

DAVID GORDON
(1986)

APPEAL

An appeal is the invocation of the JURISDICTION of a higher court to reverse or modify a lower court's decision. Appeal from the decision of a federal district court, for example, is normally taken to a federal court of appeals. In earlier federal practice, an appeal was taken by way of a WRIT OF ERROR; today, the term "appeal" has replaced references to the former writ. In the Supreme Court, "appeal" is a term of art, referring to the Court's obligatory APPELLATE JURISDICTION. In this sense, filing an appeal is distinguished from petitioning for a WRIT OF CERTIORARI, which is the method of invoking the Court's discretionary jurisdiction.

In a case coming to the Supreme Court from a state court, appeal is the appropriate remedy when the highest state court has rejected one of two types of claims based on federal law: either the state court has upheld a state law, rejecting the claim that the law violates the federal Constitution or a federal statute or treaty, or it has held invalid a federal statute or treaty. In those two kinds of cases, the Supreme Court is, in theory, obliged to review state court decisions; in all other cases, only the discretionary remedy of certiorari is available. A similarly obligatory review, by way of appeal, is appropriate when a federal court of appeals holds a state statute invalid. However, the overwhelming majority of court of appeals decisions reviewed by the Supreme Court lie within the Court's discretionary review, on writ of certiorari.

Whether a case is or is not an appropriate case for an appeal lies to some extent within the control of counsel, who may be able to cast the case as a challenge to the constitutionality of a state law as applied to particular facts. Yet some cases lie outside counsel's power to characterize; thus, a claim that a valid statute is being applied in a discriminatory manner, in violation of the equal protection clause, is reviewable only on certiorari.

With each passing year the practical distinction between appeal and certiorari has lessened. The Supreme Court often dismisses an appeal "for want of a substantial federal question" under circumstances strongly indicating the Court's determination, on a discretionary basis, that the appeal is not worthy of being heard. Furthermore, the Court has had the power since 1925 to treat improperly filed appeal papers as if they were a petition for certiorari. The same "RULE OF FOUR" applies to both appeal and certiorari: the vote of four Justices is necessary for a case to be heard. With these factors in mind, commentators have persistently urged Congress to abolish the Supreme Court's appeal jurisdiction entirely, leaving the Court in full discretionary control over the cases it will hear.

KENNETH L. KARST
(1986)

Bibliography

STERN, ROBERT L. and GRESSMAN, EUGENE 1978 *Supreme Court Practice*, 5th ed. Chaps. 2–5. Washington, D.C.: Bureau of National Affairs.

APPELLATE JURISDICTION

A court's appellate jurisdiction is its power to review the actions of another body, usually a lower court. The appellate jurisdiction of our federal courts lies within the control of Congress. Article III of the Constitution, after establishing the Supreme Court's ORIGINAL JURISDICTION over certain cases, gives the Court appellate jurisdiction over all other types of cases within "the JUDICIAL POWER OF THE UNITED STATES" but empowers Congress to make "exceptions and regulations" governing that jurisdiction. In the JUDICIARY ACT OF 1789 Congress did not, formally, make exceptions to the Supreme Court's appellate jurisdiction; rather it purported to *grant* the Court jurisdiction to hear various types of cases on WRIT OF ERROR. The assumption has been that such an affirmative grant of appellate jurisdiction over specified types of cases is, by implication, an "exception," excluding the Court from taking appellate jurisdiction over cases not mentioned.

The Supreme Court itself accepted this line of reasoning in EX PARTE MCCARDLE (1869), stating that without a statutory grant of appellate jurisdiction it had no power to hear a case. Read broadly, this holding empowers Congress to undermine JUDICIAL REVIEW by withdrawing the Supreme Court's most important functions. Some commentators argue that Congress, in controlling the Supreme Court's appellate jurisdiction, is constitutionally bound to respect the Court's essential role in a system of SEPARATION OF POWERS. Other writers, however, reject this view, and the Supreme Court has been presented with no modern occasion to face the issue. (See JUDICIAL SYSTEM.)

Whatever the Constitution may ultimately require, Congress has acted on the assumption that it need not extend the Supreme Court's appellate jurisdiction to occupy the whole of the judicial power established by Article III. Until 1925, for example, the Court's appellate review of civil cases was limited by a requirement of a certain dollar amount in controversy. For the first century of the Court's existence, it had no general appellate jurisdiction over federal criminal cases, but reviewed such a case only on writ of HABEAS CORPUS or upon a lower court's certification of a division of opinion on an issue of law. Until 1914, the Supreme Court could review state court decisions only when they *denied* claims of federal right, not when they validated those claims. Although all these major limitations on the Court's appellate jurisdiction have now been eliminated, the halls of Congress perennially ring with calls for removing the Court's power over cases involving such emotion-charged subjects as SUBVERSIVE ACTIVITIES, school prayers, or ABORTION.

From the beginning the Supreme Court has reviewed cases coming from the lower federal courts and the state courts. The latter jurisdiction has been the source of political controversy, not only in its exercise but in its very existence. In a doctrinal sense, the power of Congress to establish the Court's appellate jurisdiction over state court decisions was settled early, in MARTIN V. HUNTER'S LESSEE (1816). In the realm of practical politics, the issue was settled when any serious thoughts of INTERPOSITION or NULLIFICATION were laid to rest by the outcome of the Civil War. (Ironically, the CONFEDERATE CONSTITUTION had provided a similar appellate jurisdiction for the Confederacy's own supreme court.) By the late 1950s, when the Court confronted intense opposition to school DESEGREGATION, its appellate jurisdiction was firmly entrenched; southern efforts to curb the Court failed miserably.

The Supreme Court's review of state court decisions is limited to issues of federal law. Even federal questions will not be decided by the Court if the state court's judgment rests on an ADEQUATE STATE GROUND. By congressional statute the Court is instructed to review only FINAL JUDGMENTS of state courts, but this limitation is now riddled with judge-made exceptions. The Court does, however, obey strictly its statutory instruction to review the decision of only the highest state court in which judgment is available in a given case. As *Thompson v. Louisville* (1960) shows, even a justice of the peace may constitute that "highest court" if state law provides no APPEAL from the justice's decision.

When the Supreme Court reviews a state court decision, all the jurisdictional limitations on the federal courts come into play. For example, although a state court may routinely confer STANDING on any state taxpayer to challenge state governmental action, the Supreme Court can take appellate jurisdiction only if the taxpayer satisfies the federal standards for standing.

Of the 4,000 cases brought to the Court in a typical year, only about 150 will be decided with full opinion. A large number of state criminal convictions raise substantial issues of federal constitutional law, but they largely go unreviewed in the Supreme Court. The WARREN COURT sought to provide a substitute federal remedy, facilitating access for state prisoners to federal habeas corpus. In the 1970s, however, the BURGER COURT drastically limited that access; in practical terms, a great many state convictions now escape review of their federal constitutional issues in any federal forum.

Final judgments of the federal district courts are normally reviewed in the courts of appeals, although direct appeal to the Supreme Court is available in a very few categories of cases. Usually, then, a case brought to the Supreme Court has already been the subject of one appeal. The Court thus can husband its resources for its main appellate functions: nourishing the development of a coherent body of federal law, and promoting that law's uniformity and supremacy.

For the Supreme Court's first century, its appellate jurisdiction was mostly obligatory; when Congress authorized a writ of error, the Court had no discretion to decline. The Court's second century has seen a progressive increase in the use of the discretionary WRIT OF CERTIORARI as a means of invoking Supreme Court review, with a corresponding decline in statutory entitlements to review on appeal. Today the Court has a high degree of discretion to choose which cases it will decide. Some observers think this discretion weakens the theoretical foundation of judicial review, expressed in MARBURY V. MADISON (1803). The Court there based its power to hold an act of Congress unconstitutional on the necessity to decide a case. If the Court has discretion whether to decide, the necessity disappears, and thus (so the argument goes) judicial review's legitimacy. Ultimately, that legitimacy may come to depend, both theoretically and politically, on the very power of congressional control so often seen as a threat to the Supreme Court's appellate jurisdiction.

KENNETH L. KARST
(1986)

Bibliography

BATOR, PAUL M.; MISHKIN, PAUL J.; SHAPIRO, DAVID L.; and WECHSLER, HERBERT, eds. 1973 *The Federal Courts and the Federal System*, 2nd ed. Chaps. 5, 11. Mineola, N.Y.: Foundation Press.

APPOINTING AND REMOVAL POWER, PRESIDENTIAL

Article II, section 2, clause 2, of the Constitution provides in part that the President "shall nominate, and by and with the ADVICE AND CONSENT of the Senate, he shall appoint, Ambassadors, other public Ministers and Consuls, Judges of the Supreme Court, and all other Officers of the United States, whose appointments are not herein otherwise provided for, and which shall be established by Law." It goes on to authorize Congress to provide for the appointment of "inferior officers" by the President, the courts, or the heads of departments. The only patent ambiguity is in the distinction between the appointment of "inferior officers" and those presidential appointments requiring advice and consent of the Senate. This problem has given little cause for concern, perhaps because Congress has erred on the side of requiring advice and consent appointments, so that even every officer in the armed forces receives such a presidential appointment.

The processes of the appointment power were canvassed by JOHN MARSHALL in MARBURY V. MADISON (1803), where he also addressed the question that has plagued the construction of Article II, section 2, clause 2, not the meaning of the appointment provisions but what meaning they have for the removal power. The language of the Constitution is silent about removal, except for impeachment and the life tenure it gives to judges. Marshall said:

> Where an officer is removable at the will of the executive, the circumstance which completes his appointment is of no concern; because the act is at any time revocable; and the commission may be arrested, if still in the office. But when the officer is not removable at the will of the executive, the appointment is not revocable, and cannot be annulled. It has conferred legal rights which cannot be resumed.
>
> The discretion of the executive is to be exercised until the appointment has been made. But having once made the appointment, his power over the office is terminated in all cases, where by law the officer is not removable by him. The right to the office is *then* in the person appointed, and he has the absolute, and unconditional power of accepting or rejecting it.
>
> Mr. Marbury, then, since his commission was signed by the president, and sealed by the secretary of state, was appointed; and as the law creating the office, gave the officer a right to hold for five years, independent of the executive, the appointment was not revocable, but vested in the officer legal rights, which are protected by the laws of his country.

Obviously, it was to Congress that Marshall ascribed the power to determine the length of the term, and the conditions for removal, except that all officers of the United States were removable by the process of IMPEACHMENT.

The question whether an appointment made by the President with the advice and consent of the Senate could be terminated by the executive without such senatorial approval was soon mooted. ALEXANDER HAMILTON had answered the question in THE FEDERALIST #77:

> It has been mentioned as one of the advantages to be expected from the cooperation of the Senate, in the business of appointments, that it would contribute to the stability of the administration. The consent of that body would be necessary to displace as well as to appoint. A change of the Chief Magistrate, therefore, would not occasion so violent or so general a revolution in the officers of the government as might be expected, if he were the sole disposer of offices. Where a man in any station had given satisfactory evidence of his fitness for it, a new President would be restrained from attempting a change in favor of a person more agreeable to him, by the apprehension that a discountenance of the Senate might frustrate the attempt, and bring some discredit upon himself. Those who can best estimate the value of a steady administration, will be most disposed to prize a provision which connects the official existence of public men with the approbation or disapprobation of that body, which from the greater permanence of its own composition, will in all probability

be less subject to inconsistency than any other member of the government.

Thus spake the founding father most given to support a strong presidency.

In the very first Congress, however, when it was concerned with the creation of the office of secretary of state, there was extensive debate about whether the removal power was inherently an executive function and therefore not to be encumbered by the necessity for senatorial approval. It was conceded that the appointment power, too, was intrinsically an executive power and, but for constitutional provision to the contrary, would have remained untrammeled by legislative authority. JAMES MADISON thus construed the provision in his lengthy argument in the House of Representatives: the President did not need the acquiescence of the Senate to remove an official who had been appointed with its consent. The impasse that developed in the House was resolved not by choosing one side or the other of the controversial question but rather by omission of any provision concerning the power of removal. Madison's position at the CONSTITUTIONAL CONVENTION OF 1787 had been that the President, like the king, should have the appointment power without condition. He failed to carry the Convention on that point. He sought in the legislature to protect the President's exclusive power of removal. He failed there, too, although the point was not taken definitively against him as it had been at the Convention. But if he failed in 1789, he was nevertheless to be vindicated in MYERS V. UNITED STATES (1926).

The issue had not remained moribund in the interim. In 1833, when ANDREW JACKSON removed two secretaries of the treasury for refusing to withdraw government deposits from the BANK OF THE UNITED STATES and put ROGER B. TANEY in their place, motions of censure were moved and passed in the Senate, supported by DANIEL WEBSTER, HENRY CLAY, and JOHN C. CALHOUN. But Jackson had his way, as he usually did. The issue reached proportions of a constitutional crisis in 1867, when President ANDREW JOHNSON was impeached, largely on the ground that he had violated the TENURE OF OFFICE ACT which forbade the removal of a cabinet officer before his successor had been nominated and approved by the Senate. Johnson escaped a guilty verdict in the Senate because the vote fell one shy of the two-thirds necessary for conviction. There were other instances in which the courts were called upon for construction of the removal power, and for the most part the decisions sided with the President, but usually by statutory rather than constitutional construction.

The controlling Supreme Court decision came in the *Myers* case in 1926, which arose out of the removal by the President of a local postmaster. Here Chief Justice WILLIAM HOWARD TAFT, after his experience as chief magistrate, was not prepared to tolerate the suggestion that a President could have foisted on his administration aides that he did not want, even if the aide were only a lowly postmaster. Perhaps Taft's first concern was that Congress would take over the execution of the laws by the creation of independent agencies over whose members the President would have no control at all if he could not exercise the power of removal. That was not the issue in *Myers*, but Taft wished to forestall future problems of independent agencies as well as to lay to rest the canard that the President could not remove those in the direct chain of command, such as a postmaster. He read the debates in the first Congress as establishing Madison's position rather than bypassing it. It took seventy pages of abuse of history to make Taft's point. The presidential power of removal thus became plenary. Justice OLIVER WENDELL HOLMES, in dissent, disposed of the Taft position in less than a page:

> We have to deal with an office that owes its existence to Congress and that Congress may abolish tomorrow. Its duration and the pay attached to it while it lasts depend on Congress alone. Congress alone confers on the President the power to appoint to it and at any time may transfer that power to other hands. With such power over its own creation, I have no more trouble in believing that Congress has power to prescribe a term of life for it free from any interference than I have in accepting the undoubted power of Congress to decree its end. I have equally little trouble in accepting its power to prolong the tenure of an incumbent until Congress or the Senate shall have assented to his removal. The duty of the President to see that the laws be executed is a duty that does not go beyond the laws or require him to achieve more than Congress sees fit to leave within his power.

History, however, has been on the side of Taft and Madison rather than on that of Hamilton, Marshall, and Holmes. An exception has been carved by the Court from the President's power of removal where the incumbent is charged with duties that may be called judicial, even if mixed with legislative and executive discretion, such as those involved in HUMPHREY'S EXECUTOR V. UNITED STATES (1935). Thus, Taft's championing of the presidential removal power has been sustained, except in the situation that bothered him most, the independent administrative agencies where legislative, executive, and judicial powers are all exercised by the incumbent.

PHILIP B. KURLAND
(1986)

Bibliography

CORWIN, EDWARD S. 1927 Tenure of Office and the Removal Power under the Constitution. *Columbia Law Review* 27: 353–399.

KURLAND, PHILIP B. 1978 *Watergate and the Constitution*, chap. 5. Chicago: University of Chicago Press.

MILLER, CHARLES A. 1969 *The Supreme Court and the Uses of History.* Chap. 4. Cambridge, Mass.: Harvard University Press.

APPOINTMENT OF SUPREME COURT JUSTICES

Under Article II, section 2, of the Constitution, Supreme Court Justices, like all other federal judges, are nominated and, with the ADVICE AND CONSENT of the SENATE, appointed by the President. No other textual mandate, either procedural or substantive, governs the Chief Executive's selection. However, section 1 of Article III—which deals exclusively with the judicial branch of the government—provides GOOD BEHAVIOR tenure for all federal judges; in effect, that means appointment for life. As additional security, that provision of the Constitution provides that the compensation of federal judges "shall not be diminished during their Continuance in Office." But neither the Constitution nor any federal statute provides any clue as to qualifications for office; neither a law degree nor any other proof of professional capability is formally required. But in practice none other than lawyers are appointable to the federal judiciary, in general, and the Supreme Court, in particular. All of the 102 individuals who sat on that highest tribunal through 1985 held degrees from a school of law or had been admitted to the bar via examination. Indeed, although all the Justices were members of the professional bar in good standing at the time of their appointment, it was not until 1922 that a majority of sitting Justices was composed of law school graduates, and not until 1957 that every Justice was a law school graduate. Once confirmed by the Senate, a Justice is removable only via IMPEACHMENT (by simple majority vote by the HOUSE OF REPRESENTATIVES) and subsequent conviction (by two-thirds vote of the Senate, there being a quorum on the floor). Only one Justice of the Supreme Court has been impeached by the House—Justice SAMUEL CHASE, by a 72–32 vote in 1804—but he was acquitted on all eight charges by the Senate in 1805. To all intents and purposes, once appointed, a Supreme Court Justice serves as long as he or she wishes—typically until illness or death intervenes.

Theoretically, the President has *carte blanche* in selecting his nominees to the Court. In practice, three facts of political life inform and limit his choices. The first is that it is not realistically feasible for the Chief Executive to designate a Justice and obtain confirmation by the Senate without the at least grudging approval by the two home state senators concerned, especially if the latter are members of the President's own political party. The time-honored practice of "Senatorial courtesy" is an omnipresent phenomenon, because of senatorial camaraderie and the "blue slip" approval system, under which the Judiciary Committee normally will not favorably report a nominee to the floor if an objecting home-state senator has failed to return that slip. (Senator Edward Kennedy, during his two-year tenure as head of the Committee, abandoned the system in 1979, but it was partly restored by his successor, Senator Strom Thurmond, in 1981.) Although nominations to the Supreme Court are regarded as a personal province of presidential choice far more than the appointment of other judges, the Senate's "advice and consent" is neither routine nor perfunctory, to which recent history amply attests. In 1968, despite a favorable Judiciary Committee vote, the Senate refused to consent to President Johnson's promotion of Justice ABE FORTAS to the Chief Justiceship; in 1969 it rejected President RICHARD M. NIXON's nomination of Judge Clement Haynsworth, Jr., by 55 to 45; and in 1970 it turned down that same President's selection of Judge G. Harrold Carswell by 51 to 45. Indeed, to date the Senate, for a variety of reasons, has refused to confirm twentyseven Supreme Court nominees out of the total of 139 sent to it for its "advice and consent" (twenty-one of these during the nineteenth century).

The second major factor to be taken into account by the President is the evaluative role played by the American Bar Association's fourteen-member Committee on the Federal Judiciary, which has been an unofficial part of the judicial appointments process since 1946. The committee scrutinizes the qualifications of all nominees to the federal bench and normally assigns one of four "grades": Exceptionally Well Qualified, Well Qualified, Qualified, and Not Qualified. In the rare instances of a vacancy on the Supreme Court, however, the committee has in recent years adopted a different, threefold, categorization: "High Standards of Integrity, Judicial Temperament, and Professional Competence"; "Not Opposed"; and "Not Qualified."

The third consideration incumbent upon the Chief Executive is the subtle but demonstrable one of the influence, however *sub rosa* and *sotto voce*, of sitting and retired jurists. Recent research points convincingly to that phenomenon, personified most prominently by Chief Justice WILLIAM HOWARD TAFT. If Taft did not exactly "appoint" colleagues to vacancies that occurred during his nine-year tenure (1921–1930), he assuredly vetoed those unacceptable to him. Among others also involved in advisory or lobbying roles, although on a lesser scale than Taft, were Chief Justices CHARLES EVANS HUGHES, HARLAN F. STONE, FRED VINSON, EARL WARREN, and WARREN E. BURGER and Associate Justices JOHN MARSHALL HARLAN I, SAMUEL F. MILLER, Willis Van Devanter, LOUIS D. BRANDEIS, and FELIX FRANKFURTER.

A composite portrait of the 101 men and one woman who have been Justices of the Supreme Court provides the following cross-section: native-born: 96; male: 101 (the first woman, SANDRA DAY O'CONNOR, was appointed by President RONALD REAGAN in the summer of 1981); white: 101 (the first black Justice, THURGOOD MARSHALL, was appointed by President LYNDON B. JOHNSON in 1967); predominantly Protestant: 91 (there have been six Roman Catholic and five Jewish Justices—the first in each category were ANDREW JACKSON's appointment of Chief Justice ROGER B. TANEY in 1836 and WOODROW WILSON's of Louis D. Brandeis in 1916, respectively); 50–55 years of age at time of appointment (the two youngest have been JOSEPH STORY, 33, in 1812 and WILLIAM O. DOUGLAS, 41, in 1939); of Anglo-Saxon ethnic stock (all except fifteen); from an upper middle to high social status (all except a handful); reared in a nonrural but not necessarily urban environment; member of a civic-minded, politically aware, economically comfortable family (all except a handful); holders of B.A. and, in this century, LL.B. or J.D. degrees (with one-third from "Ivy League" institutions); and a background of at least some type of public or community service (all except Justice GEORGE SHIRAS). Contemporary recognition of egalitarianism and "representativeness" may alter this profile, but it is not likely to change radically.

Only the President and his close advisers know the actual motivations for the choice of a particular Supreme Court appointee. But a perusal of the records of the thirty-five Presidents who nominated Justices (four—W. H. Harrison, ZACHARY TAYLOR, ANDREW JOHNSON, and JIMMY CARTER—had no opportunity to do so) points to several predominating criteria, most apparent of which have been: (1) objective merit; (2) personal friendship; (3) considerations of "representativeness"; (4) political ideological compatibility, what THEODORE ROOSEVELT referred to as a selectee's "real politics"; and (5) past judicial experience. Appropriate examples of (1) would be BENJAMIN N. CARDOZO (HERBERT HOOVER) and JOHN MARSHALL HARLAN (DWIGHT D. EISENHOWER); of (2) HAROLD H. BURTON (HARRY S. TRUMAN) and ABE FORTAS (LYNDON JOHNSON); of (4) HUGO BLACK (FRANKLIN D. ROOSEVELT) and WILLIAM HOWARD TAFT (WARREN G. HARDING); of (5) OLIVER WENDELL HOLMES (THEODORE ROOSEVELT) and DAVID J. BREWER (BENJAMIN HARRISON). Deservedly most contentious is motivation (3), under which Presidents have been moved to weigh such "equitable" factors as geography, religion, gender, race, and perhaps even age in order to provide a "representative" profile of the Court. Of uncertain justification, it is nonetheless a fact of life of the appointive process. Thus geography proved decisive in Franklin D. Roosevelt's selection of WILEY RUTLEDGE of Iowa ("Wiley, you have geography," Roosevelt told him) and ABRAHAM LINCOLN's selection of STEPHEN J. FIELD of California. But given the superb qualifications of Judge Cardozo, despite the presence of two other New Yorkers (Hughes and Stone), the former's selection was all but forced upon Hoover. The notion that there should be a "Roman Catholic" and "Jewish" seat has been present ever since the appointments of Taney and Brandeis. Although there have been periods without such "reserved" seats (for example, 1949–1956 in the former case and since 1965 in the latter), Presidents are aware of the insistent pressures for such "representation." These pressures have increased since the "establishment" of a "black" seat (Marshall in 1967, by Johnson) and a "woman's seat" (O'Connor, by Reagan, in 1981). It has become all but unthinkable that future Supreme Court lineups will not henceforth have "representatives" from such categories. That the Founding Fathers neither considered nor addressed any of these "representative" factors does not gainsay their presence and significance in the political process.

Whatever may be the merits of other criteria motivating presidential Supreme Court appointments, the key factor is the Chief Executive's perception of a candidate's "real" politics—for it is the nominee's likely voting pattern as a Justice that matters most to an incumbent President. To a greater or lesser extent, all Presidents have thus attempted to "pack" the bench. Court-packing has been most closely associated with Franklin D. Roosevelt. Failing a single opportunity to fill a Court vacancy during his first term (and five months of his second), and seeing his domestic programs consistently battered by "the Nine Old Men," Roosevelt moved to get his way in one fell swoop with his "Court Packing Bill" of 1937; however, it was reported unfavorably by the Senate Judiciary Committee and was interred by a decisive recommittal vote. Ultimately, the passage of time enabled him to fill nine vacancies between 1937 and 1943. Yet GEORGE WASHINGTON was able to nominate fourteen, of whom ten chose to serve, and his selectees were measured against a sextet of criteria: (1) support and advocacy of the Constitution; (2) distinguished service in the revolution; (3) active participation in the political life of the new nation; (4) prior judicial experience on lower tribunals; (5) either a "favorable reputation with his fellows" or personal ties with Washington himself; and (6) geographic "suitability." Whatever the specific predispositions may be, concern with a nominee's "real" politics has been and will continue to be crucial in presidential motivations. It even prompted Republican President Taft to award half of his six nominations to the Court to Democrats, who were kindred "real politics" souls (Horace H. Lurton, Edward D. White's promotion to Chief Justice, and JOSEPH R. LAMAR). In ten other instances the appointee came from a formal political affiliation other than that of the appointer, ranging from Whig President JOHN TYLER's appointment of Democrat SAMUEL NELSON in 1845 to Republican Richard M. Nixon's selection of Democrat LEWIS F. POWELL, JR. in 1971.

But to predict the ultimate voting pattern or behavior of a nominee is to lean upon a slender reed. In the characteristically blunt words of President Truman: "Packing the Supreme Court simply can't be done. ... I've tried and it won't work. ... Whenever you put a man on the Supreme Court he ceases to be your friend. I'm sure of that." There is indeed a considerable element of unpredictability in the judicial appointment process. To the question whether a judicial robe makes a person any different, Justice Frankfurter's sharp retort was always, "If he is any good, he does!" In ALEXANDER M. BICKEL's words, "You shoot an arrow into a far-distant future when you appoint a Justice and not the man himself can tell you what he will think about some of the problems that he will face." And late in 1969, reflecting upon his sixteen years as Chief Justice of the United States, Earl Warren pointed out that he, for one, did not "see how a man could be on the Court and not change his views substantially over a period of years ... for change you must if you are to do your duty on the Supreme Court." It is clear beyond doubt that the Supreme Court appointment process is fraught with imponderables and guesswork, notwithstanding the carefully composed constitutional obligations of President and Senate.

HENRY J. ABRAHAM
(1986)

(SEE ALSO: *Advise and Consent to Supreme Court Nominations*.)

Bibliography

ABRAHAM, HENRY J. 1985 *Justices and Presidents: A Political History of Appointments to the Supreme Court*, 2nd ed. New York: Oxford University Press.

—— 1986 The Judicial Process: An Introductory Analysis of the Courts of the United States, England and France, 5th ed. New York: Oxford University Press.

DANELSKI, DAVID J. 1964 *A Supreme Court Justice Is Appointed*. New York: Random House.

SCHMIDHAUSER, JOHN R. 1960 *The Supreme Court: Its Politics, Personalities and Procedures*. New York: Holt, Rinehart Winston.

—— 1979 *Judges and Justices: The Federal Appellate Judiciary*. Boston: Little, Brown.

APPOINTMENTS CLAUSE

Examining the debates of the CONSTITUTIONAL CONVENTION OF 1787, one finds that Article III, the Constitution's judicial component, proved to be its least controversial and the most readily draftable of all of its provisions. Delegates viewed the judiciary broadly as "the least dangerous branch," in the words of ALEXANDER HAMILTON, and such debate as did occur on the range and extent of the judiciary's power was predominantly concerned with the appointment of judges. Under EDMUND RANDOLPH'S VIRGINIA PLAN, the appointment power would have been granted to Congress as a whole, but the delegates yielded to JAMES MADISON's countersuggestion to vest it in the SENATE alone. Further debate moved the delegates toward vesting the appointment power solely with the President. To resolve the impasse, a special committee of eleven delegates was constituted in late August. Its compromise report, suggesting presidential appointment "by and with the ADVICE AND CONSENT of the Senate," was promptly adopted by the convention in early September, and it became part and parcel of Article III, section 2, paragraph two of the Constitution. Unamended, this provision governs today.

Under the terms of the appointments clause, Presidents have nominated and the Senate has confirmed, thousands of federal jurists. Although there have been some rejections of lower federal court nominees, by and large the Senate has been a willing partner in the confirmation process—arguably even playing a perfunctory role at this level. At the apex of the judicial ladder, the Supreme Court of the United States, senators have taken their role far more seriously, rejecting or refusing to take on one-fifth of all nominees to the high court. Thus, of 145 nominations made by thirty-five Presidents from 1789 through 1990, twenty-eight were formally rejected, purposely not acted on, indefinitely postponed, or were withdrawn by the President involved. (Presidents William H. Harrison, ZACHARY TAYLOR, and JIMMY CARTER had no opportunity to choose any nominee; ANDREW JOHNSON saw all of his rejected by a hostile Senate.) Of the twenty-eight rejections, all but five occurred in the nineteenth century.

The five rejections of the twentieth century—not counting the never acted on nominations of Homer Thornberry (LYNDON B. JOHNSON, 1968) and Douglas H. Ginsburg (RONALD REAGAN, 1987)—were lower federal court judges John J. Parker (HERBERT C. HOOVER, 1930); Clement F. Haynsworth, Jr. (RICHARD M. NIXON, 1969); G. Harrold Carswell (Nixon, 1970); the aborted promotion of Justice ABE FORTAS to CHIEF JUSTICE by President Johnson in 1968; and most recently, President Reagan's nomination of United States Court of Appeals Judge Robert H. Bork in 1987, which was rejected by the decisive vote of 58–42 (see BORK NOMINATION).

Inevitably, the Senate's role in judicial appointments has frequently given rise to the questioning of its authority to weigh factors other than pure "competence" in considering a nominee's qualifications. Is it entitled to examine, for instance, political, personal, and ideological factors, or anything else that it may deem appropriate along the road to its ultimate judgment? The answer is clearly "yes," no matter how distasteful certain aspects of the senatorial investigative role in individual cases may seem to both lay and professional observers. That "politics" indubitably plays a role may be regrettable, but it is also natural under our system. It plays a distinct role at both ends of the appointment process.

Although only incumbent Presidents really know why they selected nominees to the Court (or gave the nod to members of their administrations to do the basic selecting for them), history does identify four reasons or motivations governing the selection process: (1) objective merit; (2) personal and political friendship; (3) balancing "representation" or "representativeness" on the Court; and (4) "real" political and ideological compatibility. Obviously, more than just one of these factors may have been present in most nominations, and in some, all four played a role; yet it is not at all impossible to pinpoint one as the overriding motivation. And, more often than not, it has been the fourth reason listed, namely, concern with a nominee's *real*, as opposed to his or her *nominal*, politics. This concern prompted Republican President WILLIAM HOWARD TAFT to give half of his six appointments to Democrats who were kindred political soulmates; it prompted Republican Nixon to appoint Democrat LEWIS F. POWELL, Jr.; it spurred Democrat FRANKLIN D. ROOSEVELT to promote Republican HARLAN F. STONE to the Chief Justiceship; and it caused Democrat HARRY S. TRUMAN to appoint Republican HAROLD H. BURTON—to cite just a few illustrations. Yet, as history has also shown, there is no guarantee that what a President perceives as "real" politics will not fade like a mirage. Hence CHARLES WARREN, eminent chronicler of the judiciary in general and the Supreme Court in particular, properly observed that "nothing is more striking in the history of the Court than the manner in which the hopes of those who expected a judge to follow the political views of the President appointing him are disappointed."

So why has the Senate chosen to reject or failed to confirm twenty percent of the presidential nominees? The record points to eight reasons: (1) opposition to the nominating President, not necessarily the nominee (for example, all of Andrew Johnson's selectees); (2) opposition to the nominee's perceived jurisprudential or sociopolitical philosophy (for example, Hoover's choice of Parker); (3) opposition to the record of the incumbent court, which, rightly or wrongly, the nominee presumably supported (for example, ANDREW JACKSON's initial nomination of ROGER BROOKE TANEY as Associate Justice; (4) "senatorial courtesy," which is closely linked to the consultative nominating process (for example, GROVER CLEVELAND's back-to-back unsuccessful nominations of William B. Hornblower and Wheeler H. Peckham); (5) a nominee's perceived "political unreliability" on the part of the political party in power (for example, ULYSSES S. GRANT's selection of Caleb Cushing); (6) the evident lack of qualification or limited ability of the candidate (for example, Nixon's "I'll show the Senate" choice of Judge G. Harrold Carswell); (7) concerted, sustained opposition by interest and pressure groups (for example, the Hoover nomination of Parker and, most recently, Reagan's of Bork); and (8) the fear that the nominee would dramatically alter the Court's jurisprudential "line-up" (for example, the Bork nomination). Judge Bork's professional credentials were not in question; he lost overridingly because of his approach to constitutional law and CONSTITUTIONAL INTERPRETATION.

The appointments clause connotes a joint enterprise: informed by the Constitution's seminal provisions and providing for a SEPARATION OF POWERS and CHECKS AND BALANCES. The President selects; the Senate disposes. The Senate's role is second, but not secondary.

Arguably, Presidents' judicial appointments are their biggest "plums." Few if any other posts a President has the authority to fill possess the degree of influence, authority, and constitutionally built-in longevity that characterizes the judicial branch. But there are many other offices to be filled by presidential selection, including, by the language of Article II, section 2, paragraph two, "Ambassadors, other public Ministers and Consuls . . ., and all other Officers of the United States, whose appointments are not herein otherwise provided for and which shall be established by Law. . . ." All such others are to be appointed "by and with the Advice and Consent of the Senate," but the Constitution adds an important caveat: "Congress may by Law vest the Appointment of such inferior Officers, as they think proper, in the President alone, in the Courts of Law, or in the Heads of Departments."

The huge number of federal employees—some 3,500,000 as of mid-1990, not counting the military—has required Congress to provide for appointments as constitutionally authorized in the above-quoted ultimate sentence of the appointment power. In addition to all federal judicial nominations, Congress has retained full "advice and consent" authority over top positions of the military and the diplomatic services; over CABINET and top subordinate cabinet-level selections (it has drawn a line above a certain salary level for other high departmental and agency heads); and over specifically law-designated officials, such as independent regulatory commisioners. However, congress has vested appointive authority over huge numbers of nominations in the President alone—for example, the bulk of that cast army of civil service employees and almost all of the members of the ARMED FORCES (whose letters of appointment or draft are headed, "Greetings"—the butt of many jokes—are signed by the president in his role of chief executive). Moreover, again in line with the above-noted authority. Congress has seen fit to utilize its authority to vest the power at issue in the "Courts of Law."

The latter power became a hotly debated issue when Congress, in the Ethics of Government Act of 1978, created an INDEPENDENT COUNSEL to investigate high-ranking officials in the executive branch. In accordance with the statute's provisions, the ATTORNEY GENERAL must request an independent counsel unless he or she "finds that there are no reasonable grounds to believe that further investigation or prosecution is warranted." The request for an independent counsel must be directed to a panel of three federal judges, who are authorized to appoint the counsel (also called a SPECIAL PROSECUTOR) and to delineate the counsel's JURISDICTION. The act, which provides for removal of a court-appointed counsel by the attorney general only "for cause," was challenged by the President on sundry constitutional grounds, including the doctrine of the separation of powers (the chief executive's duty to see that laws are "faithfully executed") and the presidential APPOINTING AND REMOVAL POWERS. The controversy reached the Supreme Court in its 1987–88 term after a three-member panel of the U.S. Courts of Appeals for the District of Columbia had declared the statute unconstitutional by a 2–1 vote. In a dramatic 1988 opinion by Chief Justice WILLIAM H. REHNQUIST, for a 7–1 majority in *Morrison v. Olson*, the high tribunal reversed the lower court, ruling that the provisions of the challenged law vesting appointment of independent counsels in the judiciary do not violate the appointments clause, that the powers exercised by the counsel do not violate the judicial article of the Constitution, and that the law does not violate the separation of powers principle by impermissibly interfering with the functions of the executive branch. In a lengthy stinging solo dissent, Justice ANTONIN SCALIA charged his brethren with a misreading and gross violation of the separation of powers.

Aspects of the appointment power will continue to be controversial. It is a joint enterprise, even if the presidency can usually count on having its way. That there are major exceptions, however, was tellingly demonstrated by the Senate's dramatic rejections of President Reagan's Supreme Court nominee Robert H. Bork in 1987 and that by President GEORGE BUSH of John Tower to be his Secretary of Defense in 1989. Even if it is exercised infrequently, the Senate's potential check on the presidential prerogative is indeed real.

HENRY J. ABRAHAM
(1992)

(SEE ALSO: *Appointment of Supreme Court Justices.*)

Bibliography
ABRAHAM, HENRY J. 1985 *Justices Presidents*, 3rd ed. New York: Oxford University Press.

FARBER, DANIEL A. and SHERRY, SUZANNA 1990 *A History of the American Constitution.* St. Paul, Minn.: West Publishing Co.

HARRIS, JOSEPH P. 1953 *The Advice and Consent of the Senate.* Berkeley: University of California Press.

SCHMIDHAUSER, JOHN R. 1979 *Judges and Justices.* Boston: Little, Brown.

SEGAL, JEFFREY 1987 Senate Confirmation of Supreme Court Justices: Partisan and Institutional Politics. *The Journal of Politics* 49:998–1015.

TWENTIETH CENTURY FUND TASK FORCE ON JUDICIAL SELECTION 1988 *Judicial Roulette.* New York: Priority Press.

APPORTIONMENT

See: Reapportionment

APTHEKER v. SECRETARY OF STATE
378 U.S. 500 (1959)

Two top leaders of the Communist party appealed the revocation of their passports under section 6 of the Subversive Activities Control Act of 1950.

Justice ARTHUR J. GOLDBERG, in a plurality opinion for a 6–3 Supreme Court, held that that section "too broadly and indiscriminately restrict[ed] the RIGHT TO TRAVEL" and therefore abridged the liberty protected by the Fifth Amendment. The section was overly broad on its face because it did not discriminate between active and inactive members of subversive groups or among the various possible purposes for foreign travel.

Justices HUGO L. BLACK and WILLIAM O. DOUGLAS, concurring, would have held the entire act unconstitutional.

DENNIS J. MAHONEY
(1986)

ARGERSINGER v. HAMLIN
407 U.S. 25 (1972)

Argersinger culminated four decades of progression in RIGHT TO COUNSEL doctrine: from a DUE PROCESS requirement in CAPITAL PUNISHMENT cases, to application of the Sixth Amendment to the states in serious FELONIES, and finally, in *Argersinger,* to extension of the requirement to any case in which there is a sentence of imprisonment.

Argersinger, unrepresented by counsel, was convicted of a MISDEMEANOR and sentenced by a state court to ninety days in jail. The arguments in the Supreme Court were of an unusually practical rather than doctrinal nature. Much was made of the burden on state criminal justice systems that the extension of the right to counsel would cause. The state also argued that many misdemeanors, though carry-

ing potential jail sentences, are exceedingly straightforward cases that a layperson could handle by him- or herself. Moreover, it was argued that people who can afford lawyers often do not hire them for such simple cases because the cost is not worth what a lawyer could accomplish. The Court rejected all these contentions and established imprisonment as a clear test for requiring the appointment of counsel.

Seven years later, in *Scott v. Illinois* (1979), the Court held that the appointment of counsel was not required for a trial when imprisonment was a possibility but was not actually imposed. The anomalous result is that a judge must predict before the trial whether he will impose imprisonment in order to know whether to appoint counsel.

BARBARA ALLEN BABCOCK
(1986)

ARIZONANS FOR OFFICIAL ENGLISH v. ARIZONA

See: Mootness; "Official English" Laws

ARLINGTON HEIGHTS v. METROPOLITAN HOUSING DEVELOPMENT CORP.
429 U.S. 252 (1977)

This decision confirmed in another context the previous term's holding in WASHINGTON V. DAVIS (1976) that discriminatory purpose must be shown to establish race-based violations of the EQUAL PROTECTION clause. The Supreme Court declined to strike down a village's refusal to rezone land to allow multiple-family dwellings despite the refusal's racially discriminatory adverse effects. Writing for the Court, Justice LEWIS F. POWELL elaborated on the nature of the showing that must be made to satisfy the purpose requirement announced in *Washington v. Davis.* A plaintiff need not prove that challenged action rested solely on racially discriminatory purposes. Instead, proof that a discriminatory purpose was a motivating factor would require the offending party to prove that it would have taken the challenged action even in the absence of a discriminatory purpose. Powell noted the types of evidence that might lead to a finding of discriminatory purpose: egregious discriminatory effects, the historical background of the governmental action, departures from normal procedure, legislative and administrative history, and, in some instances, testimony by the decision makers themselves.

THEODORE EISENBERG
(1986)

ARMED FORCES

At the height of the Cold War, a doctor was drafted into the army; he was denied the commission usually afforded doctors because he refused to disclose whether he had been a member of any organization on the ATTORNEY GENERAL'S LIST of subversive organizations. Urging that he had a constitutional privilege to maintain the privacy of his associations, he sought a writ of HABEAS CORPUS in a federal court to compel the army either to discharge him or to award him a commission. The Supreme Court, in *Orloff v. Willoughby* (1953), first rejected his claim to a commission and then held that there was no right to JUDICIAL REVIEW "to revise duty orders as to one lawfully in the service." In discussing the latter point the Court remarked, almost as a throwaway line, "The military constitutes a specialized community governed by a separate discipline from that of the civilian."

The author of the *Orloff* opinion was Justice ROBERT H. JACKSON; one of his clerks that year, who would later become Chief Justice of the United States, was WILLIAM H. REHNQUIST. In PARKER V. LEVY (1974) and ROSTKER V. GOLDBERG (1981) Justice Rehnquist, writing for the Court, sought to make the "separate community" idea the foundation for a broad principle of deference—to military authorities and to Congress in military matters—that comes close to creating a "military exception" to the BILL OF RIGHTS.

Parker involved another drafted army doctor who was a bitter opponent of the VIETNAM WAR and who counseled enlisted men to refuse to go to Vietnam. He was convicted by a court-martial of "conduct unbecoming an officer" in violation of the Uniform Code of Military Justice (UCMJ). The court of appeals held this statutory language to be unconstitutionally vague in its application to speech, but the Supreme Court reversed. Parker's own speech was plainly beyond the pale, by any stretch of the FIRST AMENDMENT. The question was whether the VAGUENESS of the UCMJ entitled him to act, in effect, as a representative of officers not in court who might be deterred by the "conduct unbecoming" provision from engaging in speech that was constitutionally protected. Justice Rehnquist concluded that the answer was No; in applications of the UCMJ, the usual First Amendment standard of vagueness gave way to the looser standard for criminal laws regulating economic affairs. In discussing this issue he wrote at length on the theme of deference to the special needs of the military as a "separate community."

Rostker presented a quite different issue: whether Congress could constitutionally limit registration for the military draft to men, exempting women. Here too, Justice Rehnquist began by announcing an extreme form of deference—not to the judgment of military leadership or the President, both of whom had favored registering women as well as men, but to the judgment of Congress. Speaking of military affairs, Justice Rehnquist said, "perhaps in no other area has the Court accorded such deference to Congress." Furthermore, he said, courts have little competence in this area: "The complex, subtle, and professional decisions as to the composition, training, equipping, and control of a military force are essentially professional military judgments, subject always to civilian control of the Legislative and Executive branches." The rest followed easily for Rehnquist: any future draft would be designed to produce combat troops; women were ineligible for combat; therefore, women and men were "not similarly situated" and need not be treated equally.

Both of these decisions have had influence beyond their immediate concerns. *Parker v. Levy* has been cited in support of the military's power to impose much more far-reaching restrictions on First Amendment claims. Examples are *Greer v. Spock* (1976), holding that the streets of Fort Dix, although open to the public, could constitutionally be closed to a political speaker, and *Brown v. Glines* (1980), upholding an Air Force regulation requiring a service member to get a base commander's approval before circulating a petition on the base. *Rostker v. Goldberg* is routinely cited in political arguments supporting the services' continuing segregation of women to noncombat positions—to their severe disadvantage in the competition for promotion to high leadership positions. Furthermore, *Rostker* has been cited by some lower federal courts in support of service regulations purporting to bar the enlistment or commissioning of lesbians and gay men.

The Constitution explicitly recognizes the existence of a separate system of MILITARY JUSTICE. And no one contends that a private has a First Amendment right to debate with the lieutenant as to whether the platoon should assault an enemy gun emplacement. Plainly, the requirements of military discipline and the military mission demand significant attenuations of constitutional rights that would be protected in analogous civilian contexts. As either Justice Jackson or his clerk wrote in *Orloff*, "judges are not given the task of running the Army." But arguments for judicial abdication lose much of their force when the question is one of equal access to service membership for all citizens. When the issue is the SEGREGATION of the armed forces, the idea of a military exception to the Constitution is deeply offensive to the principle of equal CITIZENSHIP.

When the military services practice discrimination based on race or sex or SEXUAL ORIENTATION, they do not merely reflect patterns in the larger society; they reinforce those patterns in ways both instrumental and expressive. In the United States as in Europe, effective citizenship and eligibility for military service have gone hand in hand. Today the services are major educational institutions, serving as gateways to civilian employment and offering other educational benefits to veterans. Members and former members of the services are seen as having a special authority to speak on some of the most vital questions of national public policy. The services have historically performed a vital function in integrating into American life the members of diverse cultures. (In WORLD WAR I, for example, some twenty percent of draftees were foreign-born.) In short, the services not only shape the distribution of material and political advantages in our society; they are carriers of the flag, playing a special symbolic role in defining the nation.

Although President HARRY S. TRUMAN ordered the armed services (along with the federal civil service) to end racial segregation in 1948, the effective DESEGREGATION of the army was not accomplished until the KOREAN WAR—and then at the instance of battlefield commanders who recognized that their mission was jeopardized by the severe costs of segregation. Until that time, the army's leadership had resisted racial integration on two main grounds. First, they believed, as General George C. Marshall had put it in 1941, that "the level of intelligence and occupational skill of the Negro population is considerably below that of the white." Second, they believed that integration would be harmful to discipline, to morale, and to the mutual trust service members must have if they are to perform their missions successfully. In this view, blacks would make poor combat troops, and so whites would have little confidence in them. Korea proved otherwise; Vietnam proved otherwise. Today thirty percent of the army's enlisted personnel are black, and the army's General Colin Powell chairs the Joint Chiefs of Staff.

Still, the legacy of extreme judicial deference remains—attached not only to military judgments but to congressional judgments about military affairs, even when those judgments plainly are political, or sociological, or both. When the subject is discrimination, this sort of deference has no more justification than did judicial deference to the World War II orders that removed Japanese Americans from their West Coast homes and sent them to camps in the desert. Those orders, like today's discriminations against women and gays in the services, were advertised as a military necessity; the "military" judgment was summed up in the statement of General John DeWitt, who supervised the army's early administration of the program: "A Jap's a Jap."

Today the services have undertaken a massive educational program aimed at reducing racial and ethnic tensions. The myths of white supremacy have been discarded in a segment of American society that is crucial to the definition of equal citizenship. If and when the myths of masculinity are stripped away from the facts of service life and the services' missions in the 1990s, perhaps both Congress and the courts will recognize their responsibilities to end the services' continuing patterns of segregation by gender and sexual orientation. Until then, members of Congress and judges can ponder the comment of Justice HUGO L. BLACK, dissenting in *Orloff v. Willoughby*: "This whole episode appears to me to be one . . . to which Americans in a calmer future are not likely to point with much pride."

KENNETH L. KARST
(1992)

(SEE ALSO: *Sexual Orientation and the Armed Forces.*)

Bibliography
DALFIUME, RICHARD M. 1969 *Desegregation of the Armed Forces: Fighting on Two Fronts, 1939–1953.* Columbia: University of Missouri Press.

HIRSCHHORN, JAMES A. 1984 The Separate Community: Military Uniqueness and Servicemen's Constitutional Rights. *North Carolina Law Review* 62:177–254.

KARST, KENNETH L. 1991 The Pursuit of Manhood and the Desegregation of the Armed Forces. *UCLA Law Review* 38: 499–581.

KORNBLUM, LORI S. 1984 Women Warriors in a Men's World: The Combat Exclusion. *Journal of Law and Inequality* 2:351–445.

STIEHM, JUDITH HICKS 1989 *Arms and the Enlisted Woman.* Philadelphia: Temple University Press.

ZILLMAN, DONALD N. and IMWINKELRIED, EDWARD J. 1976 Constitutional Rights and Military Necessity: Reflections on the Society Apart. *Notre Dame Lawyer* 51:396–436.

ARMED FORCES AND SEXUAL ORIENTATION

See: Sexual Orientation and the Armed Forces

ARNETT v. KENNEDY
416 U.S. 134 (1974)

A fragmented Supreme Court held, 6–3, that a federal civil service employee had no PROCEDURAL DUE PROCESS right to a full hearing before being dismissed. Justice WILLIAM H. REHNQUIST, for three Justices, concluded that because the governing statute had provided for removal of an employee to "promote the efficiency of the service," the employee's "property" interest was conditioned by this limitation. Thus due process required no predismissal hearing. The other six Justices rejected this view, concluding that the Constitution itself defined the protection required, once the guarantee of procedural due process attached. However, three of the six found no right to a predismissal hearing in the protection defined by the Constitution. The dissenters, led by Justice WILLIAM J. BRENNAN, argued that GOLDBERG V. KELLY (1970) demanded a predismissal hearing, and commented that Justice Rehnquist's view would revive the "right-privilege" distinction that *Goldberg* had rejected. In BISHOP V. WOOD (1976) the Rehnquist position came to command a majority of the Court.

KENNETH L. KARST
(1986)

ARNOLD, THURMAN
(1891–1969)

Law professor, assistant attorney general, and federal judge, Thurman Arnold of Wyoming was a vigorous champion of both CIVIL LIBERTIES and ANTITRUST regulation. In 1930, when Arnold joined the Yale Law School faculty, which included WILLIAM O. DOUGLAS and WALTON HAMILTON, he had already developed a social and psychological approach to law. He had an extraordinary commitment to the concept of FAIR TRIAL in which he saw ritual significance, and, in *The Symbols of Government* (1935), Arnold described law as a mode of symbolic thinking that conditioned behavior. A witty and sarcastic writer, he described the interplay between CORPORATIONS and antitrust law in *The Folklore of Capitalism* (1937). The following year President FRANKLIN D. ROOSEVELT chose him to head the Antitrust Division of the Justice Department. Arnold was a zealous enforcer of antitrust legislation; he launched over 200 major investigations and saw his budget and personnel quadruple before his departure in 1943 to become a federal judge. Naturally unsuited for judicial office, he resigned within two years to enter private practice where ABE FORTAS soon joined him. Arnold welcomed controversial issues and represented defendants in loyalty cases of the late 1940s and the McCarthy era. Arnold was a spirited libertarian, and his career reflected his belief in the need to erase traditional intellectual boundaries and integrate disciplines and approaches.

DAVID GORDON
(1986)

Bibliography

KEARNY, EDWARD N. 1970 *Thurman Arnold, Social Critic.* Albuquerque: University of New Mexico Press.

ARREST

The constitutional law of arrest governs every occasion on which a government officer interferes with an individual's freedom, from full-scale custodial arrests at one end of the spectrum to momentary detentions at the other. Its essential principle is that a court, not a police officer or other executive official, shall ultimately decide whether a particular interference with the liberty of an individual is justified. The court may make this judgment either before an arrest, when the police seek a judicial warrant authorizing it, or shortly after an arrest without a warrant, in a hearing held expressly for that purpose. The law of arrest gives practical meaning to the ideal of the liberty of the individual, by defining the circumstances in which, and the degree to which, that liberty may be curtailed by the police or other officers of the government; it is thus a basic part of what we mean by the RULE OF LAW in the United States.

The principal constitutional standard governing arrest is the FOURTH AMENDMENT. This amendment is one article of the original BILL OF RIGHTS, which was held in BARRON V. BALTIMORE (1833) to apply only to the federal government. But in MAPP V. OHIO (1961) the Fourth Amendment was held to be among those provisions of the Bill of Rights that are "incorporated" in the FOURTEENTH AMENDMENT and is thus applicable to arrests by state as well as federal officers. (See INCORPORATION DOCTRINE.) Even without such a holding, of course, the Fourteenth Amendment, which regulates state interference with individual liberty, would have required the development of a body of law governing state arrests. The law so made might have been no less protective of the individual than the law actually made under the Fourth Amendment. As things are, however, the "unreasonableness" standard of the Fourth Amendment has been the basis of the constitutional law governing arrests by both federal and state officers.

What seizures are "unreasonable"? One obvious possibility is that seizures of the person should be held subject to the warrant clause, as searches are, and should accordingly be found "unreasonable" unless a proper warrant has been obtained or, by reason of emergency, excused. For many years the court flirted with such a rule, as in *Trupiano v. United States* (1948) and TERRY V. OHIO (1968), but it never flatly required a warrant for arrests, and in *United States v. Watson* (1976) it rejected that rule at least for FELONIES. This decision rested partly upon a historical English COMMON LAW rule excusing the warrant for felonies, but despite the similarities of language the analogy is not precise. In English law the term "felony" was reserved for offenses punishable by death and forfeiture, which give rise to a high probability of an attempt to flee; with us "felony" is usually defined by statute as an offense for which the possible punishment exceeds one year's imprisonment. The other basis for *Watson* was a combination of convenience and probability: because a warrant will in fact be excused on emergency grounds in a large class of cases, it is wise to dispense with the requirement entirely, and thus avoid the costs—improper arrests without warrants, delays to obtain unnecessary warrants—necessarily associated with close cases. The Court left open the possibility that arrest warrants may be required for MISDEMEANORS, at least (as at common law) for those not involving a BREACH OF THE PEACE nor committed in the presence of the arresting officer. This question is at present unresolved.

Somewhat more stable as a standard of reasonableness has been the substantive requirement that an arrest must be based upon PROBABLE CAUSE. This is not a term of scientific precision. It means essentially that an officer must demonstrate to a magistrate, before or after the arrest, that he has sufficient reason to believe in the guilt of the suspect to justify his arrest. Although probable cause is not susceptible of precise definition, the cases decided by the Court have gradually given it some content, especially where, as in SPINELLI V. UNITED STATES (1969), an officer's judgment rests on information received from another. In such cases the basic rule is that the officer must give the magistrate reason to trust the honesty of his informant, and reveal the grounds upon which the informant's charge rests—for example, that the informant saw a crime committed, or the suspect told him he had done it.

Probable cause is of course required only when there has been a "seizure" to which the Fourth Amendment speaks. The courts have found that term difficult to define as well, and difficult in ways that make the meaning of "probable cause" itself more uncertain. The world presents a wide range of police interferences with individual liberty, from minor detentions to full-scale incarceration, and it is widely agreed that some of these intrusions, at every level on the scale, are reasonable and appropriate and that others—again at every level—are inappropriate. Were every interference with liberty regarded as a "seizure" requiring demonstration of "probable cause," the Court would thus face a serious delemma: to hold minor intrusions invalid without a showing of traditional probable cause would outlaw an obviously important and generally accepted method of police work; but to permit them on probable cause grounds would water down the probable cause standard, greatly reducing the justification required to support a full-scale arrest. On the other hand, to hold that such intrusions were not "seizures" would seem to say that they are not regulated by the Fourth Amendment at all—nor under present doctrine, by the Fourteenth—and could therefore be inflicted upon a citizen at an officer's whim. In *Terry v. Ohio* the Court tried to deal with this problem by regarding some "seizures" (less than full-scale arrests) as not requiring "probable cause" but as nonetheless subject to the "reasonableness" requirement of the Fourth Amendment. *Terry* involved

the detention of persons an officer reasonably suspected to be planning an armed robbery, during which he asked them their identity and frisked them for weapons. The Court took great pains to make clear that it was not establishing a general right to detain on less than probable cause, and that the "reasonableness" of the seizure validated there was closely tied to the protective nature of the officer's measures and to his realistic apprehension of danger. The Court intimated that no detention beyond that necessarily involved in the frisk would be valid. But cases since *Terry* have undercut that position deeply. In *Adams v. Williams* (1972), for example, the Court explicitly talked about a right to detain on suspicion, and in *United States v. Mendenhall* (1980) a plurality of the Court held that there is no seizure when officers merely approach a person and ask him questions, even if they intend to arrest him, unless he can establish "objective grounds" upon which a reasonable person in his position would have believed he was not free to go. On the other hand, *Dunaway v. New York* (1979) expressly refused to adopt the view that increasingly lengthy detentions were permissible on increasingly good justification (which would effectively eliminate the idea that probable cause is required before "arrest," except in the technical sense of full-custody arrest); and *Delaware v. Prouse* (1979) held that a person driving a car may be stopped upon less than probable cause, but only if there is reasonable suspicion of a violation of law.

The precedents come to this: some confrontations between officers and citizens are not seizures at all; others are seizures that must be justified by a "reasonableness" requirement; still others are "arrests" for which probable cause is required. But there are no clear lines between the categories, and the Supreme Court has not given adequate attention to the ways in which a "seizure" can grow into an "arrest," thus defeating the basic aim of the probable cause requirement.

JAMES BOYD WHITE
(1986)

Bibliography

HALE, MATTHEW   (1685) 1972   *The Pleas of the Crown.* London: Professional Books.

LAFAVE, WAYNE R.   1978   *Search and Seizure: A Treatise on the Fourth Amendment.* Mineola, N.Y.: Foundation Press.

ARREST WARRANT

Under the FOURTH AMENDMENT, arrest warrants, like SEARCH WARRANTS, may be issued only upon PROBABLE CAUSE, supported by oath or affirmation, and particularly describing the person to be seized. Much of the constitutional doctrine governing search warrants is therefore applicable by analogy to arrest warrants.

At English COMMON LAW, a law enforcement officer was authorized to make a warrantless arrest when he had reasonable grounds to believe that a FELONY had been committed and that the person to be arrested was the perpetrator. A warrantless misdemeanor arrest, however, was permitted only when the misdemeanor was committed in the officer's presence. Consistent with this rule, Congress and almost all states have permitted warrantless arrests in public places since the beginning of the nation.

In view of this history, the Supreme Court held in *United States v. Watson* (1976) that the Fourth Amendment does not require a law enforcement officer to obtain a warrant for a felony arrest made in a public place even though there may be ample opportunity to obtain the warrant. Although recognizing that the preference for a neutral and detached magistrate applies to the issuance of arrest warrants, the Court reasoned that this judicial preference was insufficient to justify a departure from the common law at the time of the adoption of the Fourth Amendment and from the judgment of Congress and the states.

It may be argued that the preference for a warrant for searches should apply with equal, if not greater, force to arrests because of the significant infringement of personal liberty involved. Unless history is to be regarded as irrelevant in constitutional interpretation, however, the result in *Watson* is correct in view of the unambiguous history relating to warrantless arrests in public places. Moreover, the Court in *Gerstein v. Pugh* (1975) recognized that after a warrantless arrest a timely judicial determination of probable cause is a prerequisite to detention.

The Court has distinguished between arrests made in public places and those made in private homes. Because of, among other things, the historical importance attached to one's privacy at home and the uncertainty in the common law over warrantless arrests in private homes, a law enforcement officer may not enter a person's home to make an arrest without first obtaining a warrant. The distinction has been made in such cases as PAYTON V. NEW YORK (1980) and STEAGALD V. UNITED STATES (1981).

Probable cause in the context of arrest warrants means probable cause to believe that a crime was committed and that the person to be arrested committed it. Unlike a search warrant, an arrest warrant may be issued on the basis of a grand jury INDICTMENT, provided that the GRAND JURY is "properly constituted" and the indictment is "fair upon its face." The Court's willingness to let a grand jury's judgment substitute for that of a neutral and detached magistrate is attributable to that grand jury's relationship to the courts and its historical role in protecting individ-

uals from unjust prosecution. An INFORMATION filed by a prosecutor, by contrast, will not justify the issuance of an arrest warrant, for the prosecutor's role is inconsistent with that of a neutral and detached magistrate.

The particularity requirement, expressly applied to arrest warrants by the warrant clause, mandates that the warrant contain sufficient information to identify the person to be arrested. It is intended to preclude the use of a general or "dragnet" arrest warrant.

If a person is illegally arrested without a warrant, such an arrest will not prevent the person from being tried or invalidate his conviction. Any EVIDENCE obtained as a result of the arrest, however, including statements made by the person arrested, may be excluded under the FRUIT OF THE POISONOUS TREE DOCTRINE as applied in WONG SUN V. UNITED STATES (1963).

JAMES R. ASPERGER
(1986)

Bibliography

LAFAVE, WAYNE R. 1978 *Search and Seizure: A Treatise on the Fourth Amendment.* Vol. 2:215–260. St. Paul, Minn.: West Publishing Co.

ARTHUR, CHESTER A.
(1830–1886)

A New York lawyer and politician, Chester Alan Arthur was nominated for vice-president in 1880 to placate the ULYSSES S. GRANT or "stalwart" branch of the Republican party. In September 1881 Arthur became President when President JAMES GARFIELD was assassinated. Although his previous political activities had revolved around the New York customs house and the distribution of Republican patronage, as President Arthur supported civil service reform and opposed unnecessary federal expenditures. He was denied the Republican nomination in 1884 by a combination of reformers, who did not trust him, and by party members opposed to any reforms.

PAUL FINKELMAN
(1986)

Bibliography

DUENECKE, JUSTIN D. 1981 *The Presidencies of James A. Garfield and Chester A. Arthur.* Lawrence: Regents Press of Kansas.

ARTICLE III

See: Judicial Power

ARTICLE III AND PUBLIC CHOICE THEORY

Article III of the Constitution limits federal JUDICIAL POWER to deciding actual CASES AND CONTROVERSIES. The Supreme Court has construed these terms to require that federal court claims be ripe and not moot, that litigants who seek relief have STANDING, and that the cases neither call for ADVISORY OPINIONS nor present POLITICAL QUESTIONS. Beginning in the early 1970s, with the BURGER COURT, and continuing throughout the REHNQUIST COURT, the standing barrier has proved the most significant—and elusive—of these JUSTICIABILITY barriers.

Under the guise of standing, the Court has prevented litigants from raising the claims of others, claims that are diffuse, and claims that present an attenuated causal linkage between allegedly unconstitutional government action and harm to plaintiff. The Court has fashioned three constitutional prerequisites to Article III standing, all drawn from the COMMON LAW of tort: injury in fact, causation, and redressability. In doing so, the Court has drawn criticism for applying the concept of injury in a seemingly inconsistent manner. In REGENTS OF THE UNIVERSITY OF CALIFORNIA V. BAKKE (1978), for example, the Court conferred standing upon a medical school applicant who challenged a state AFFIRMATIVE ACTION program by characterizing his claimed injury as the opportunity to compete, even though he might have been rejected had the program not been in place. In contrast, by focusing on the attenuated causal linkage between the law challenged and the desired outcome, the Court in ALLEN V. WRIGHT (1984) denied standing to the parents of African American public-school children who challenged an Internal Revenue Service tax policy, which, they alleged, subsidized "white flight." Had the *Bakke* Court embraced the *Allen* Court's causal linkage analysis, it could have denied standing, and had the *Allen* Court embraced the *Bakke* Court's opportunity-injury analysis, it could have conferred standing.

Public choice theory (and specifically social choice) provides a basis for modeling standing and the closely related DOCTRINE of STARE DECISIS. As the following cases illustrate, under certain conditions, the preferences of Supreme Court Justices are prone to the anomaly that public choice theorists call "cycling." In *Washington v. Seattle School District No. 1* (1982), the Court struck down a Washington statewide ballot INITIATIVE limiting the circumstances under which local school boards could order racially integrative SCHOOL BUSING. In CRAWFORD V. BOARD OF EDUCATION (1982), decided on the same day, the Court upheld a California constitutional amendment limiting the circumstances under which state courts could order racially integrative busing. Despite these divided outcomes, five Justices, who split on the results of the two cases, formed an overlapping majority that viewed the cases as indistinguishable. If we assume strict adherence to PRECEDENT, when judicial preferences cycle as in these cases, the order—or path—in which cases are decided becomes critical to the substantive evolution of legal doctrine. Thus, had these two cases been decided a year apart, rather than on the same day, the outcomes in both would have depended on which case arose first, assuming that the Justices vote sincerely, meaning that they place precedent ahead of doctrinal preferences. While stare decisis thus renders legal doctrine "path dependent," that consequence is inevitable in a regime seeking stable doctrine. The greater problem, however, is the incentive among interest group litigants to try to manipulate the path of cases to influence doctrinal evolution.

The standing ground rules ameliorate the incentives to manipulate case orders as the vehicle to exert a disproportionate influence over doctrine, which is created by stare decisis. Each of the standing rules, and most notably the proscription on a third-party and diffuse-harm standing, can be translated into a presumptive requirement that the litigant be directly affected by a set of facts beyond his or her control as a precondition to litigating in federal court. *Bakke* and *Allen* are best understood as cases in which the Justices intuited whether factors commonly associated with path manipulation, or with traditional dispute resolution, predominated. While the standing ground rules do not prevent path dependency, an inevitable byproduct of stare decisis, they do ground the critical path of case decisions in fortuitous historical facts presumptively beyond the control of the litigants themselves. In an historical period when the Court's members were most prone to possessing cyclical preferences, the Court transformed its standing doctrine in a manner that substantially raised the cost to INTEREST GROUPS of attempting to manipulate the order of case decisions in an effort to exert disproportionate influence on the evolution of constitutional doctrine.

MAXWELL L. STEARNS
(2000)

Bibliography

FLETCHER, WILLIAM A. 1988 The Structure of Standing. *Yale Law Journal* 98:221–291.
STEARNS, MAXWELL L. 1995 Standing and Social Choice: Historical Evidence. *Univeristy of Pennsylvania Law Review* 144:309–462.
——— 1995 Standing Back from the Forest: Justiciability and Social Choice. *California Law Review* 83:1309–1413.
——— 2000 *Constitutional Process: A Social Choice Analysis of Supreme Court Decision Making.* Ann Arbor: University of Michigan Press.
WINTER, STEVEN L. 1988 The Metaphor of Standing and the

Problem of Self Governance. *Stanford Law Review* 40:1371–1516.

ARTICLE III COURTS

See: Constitutional Court

ARTICLE V CONVENTIONS CLAUSE

Article V provides for two methods of proposing amendments to the Constitution. Congress may propose amendments by a two-thirds vote of both houses or "on the Application of the Legislatures of two thirds of the several States, shall call a Convention for proposing Amendments." Any amendments proposed by a CONSTITUTIONAL CONVENTION, like those proposed by Congress, become part of the Constitution upon RATIFICATION by three-fourths of the states. No such convention has been called since the adoption of the Constitution. In the 1980s, however, more than thirty state legislatures applied to Congress for the calling of a "limited" convention restricted to proposing a BALANCED BUDGET AMENDMENT to the Constitution. Proponents claimed to be only a few states short of the thirty-four applications necessary to trigger such a constitutional convention. Other states have in recent years submitted applications for constitutional conventions limited to other single subjects, including ABORTION, SCHOOL PRAYER, and term limitations for members of Congress.

The issue of the validity of these applications has been a subject of sharp debate. Do the state legislatures have the power to control the agenda of a constitutional convention by limiting the convention to considering only one precise amendment or one defined subject? If the state legislatures do not have the authority to limit the convention to a single subject or a particular amendment, should state applications that contemplate a "limited" convention be treated as valid application for a more general convention? Some light is shed on these questions by the debates over the AMENDING PROCESS at the CONSTITUTIONAL CONVENTION OF 1787.

The drafters of the Constitution were generally in agreement that some provision should be made for future amendments and that Congress should be empowered to propose amendments. There was also agreement that Congress should not be the only body empowered to propose amendments. As GEORGE MASON of Virginia noted, exclusive congressional authority to propose amendments would pose a problem if Congress itself were in need of CONSTITUTIONAL REFORM. One alternative—allowing state legislatures to propose amendments—was rejected after

ALEXANDER HAMILTON warned that "[t]he State Legislatures will not apply for alterations but with a view to increase their own powers." If state legislatures had the power to propose amendments that would then be returned to those same state legislatures for ratification, those legislatures could enhance their power at the expense of the national government without the active participation of any national forum.

The constitutional convention device created by Article V provided an institution in addition to Congress empowered to propose constitutional amendments. Such a convention would be, like Congress, a deliberative body capable of assessing, from a national perspective, the need for constitutional change and drafting proposals for submission to the states for ratification. At the same time it would *not* be Congress and therefore could not pose the threat of legislative self-interest blocking needed reform of Congress itself.

The essential characteristic of the constitutional convention is that it is free of the control of the existing institutions of government. The convention mode of proposing amendments was seen as avoiding both the problem of congressional obstruction of needed amendments and the problem posed by state legislative self-interest. To be sure, such a convention can be held only upon the petition of state legislatures; once properly convened, however, such a convention, in the view of many scholars, may properly determine its own agenda and submit for ratification the amendments it deems appropriate.

The most contentious question concerning constitutional conventions under Article V is whether state requests for a convention are valid applications if they presume to limit the convention to a single amendment specified in the application. Many of the applications submitted in the 1980s, for example, called for a convention for "the sole and exclusive purpose" of proposing an amendment requiring a balanced federal budget.

Some scholars and members of Congress argued that such "limited" applications were valid and that if a sufficient number of legislatures applied in this fashion Congress should call a "limited" convention. Some of those who consider the applications valid would have Congress limit the convention to the exact wording proposed by the state legislatures; others would have Congress broaden the subject matter to the "federal budget," for example, and limit the convention to this more general subject.

There is a substantial argument, however, that applications for a "limited" convention are simply invalid. The debates of the Framers suggest that any convention was to be free of controlling limits imposed either by Congress or by the state legislatures. Although the applying state legislatures are free, of course, to suggest amendments they desire a convention to consider, the convention itself would have the final authority to determine what kinds of amendments to propose. If the state legislatures were to possess, in addition to the right to summon a convention into existence and to ratify any proposed amendments, the added power to control the convention's deliberations by specifying the amendment to be proposed, state legislatures would be given more authority over constitutional revision than the Framers contemplated.

The argument that state legislatures lack the power to control a convention's proposals does not preclude an applying state legislature from suggesting the amendment it desires the convention to consider or even from submitting a suggested draft, as long as the application is premised on an understanding that the convention has final control over the decision of what amendments to propose. Many state legislatures that applied in the 1980s made it clear that they opposed the calling of a convention if the convention could not be limited, and some explicitly deemed their applications "null and void" unless "the convention is limited to the subject matter of this Resolution." If it is the case that a "Convention for proposing Amendments" has the final authority under the Constitution to determine what amendments to propose, then state resolutions requesting a convention only if the convention is restricted by constraints that cannot constitutionally be imposed are not valid.

WALTER DELLINGER
(1992)

(SEE ALSO: *Amendment Process (Outside Article V).*)

Bibliography

CAPLAN, RUSSELL L. 1988 *Constitutional Brinkmanship: Amending the Constitution by National Convention.* New York: Oxford University Press.

DELLINGER, WALTER 1979 The Recurring Question of the "Limited" Constitutional Convention. *Yale Law Journal* 88: 1623–1640.

——— 1984 The Legitimacy of Constitutional Change: Rethinking the Amendment Process. *Harvard Law Review* 97: 386–432.

GUNTHER, GERALD 1979 The Convention Method of Amending the United States Constitution. *Georgia Law Review* 14: 1–25.

VAN ALSTYNE, WILLIAM W. 1979 The Limited Constitutional Convention—The Recurring Answer. *Duke Law Journal* 1979:985–998.

ARTICLES OF CONFEDERATION

On March 1, 1781, Congress proclaimed ratification of the constitution for a confederation named "the United States of America." People celebrated with fireworks and toasts, and a Philadelphia newspaper predicted that the day would forever be memorialized "in the annals of America. . . ." Another newspaper gave thanks because the states had at last made perpetual a union begun by the necessities of war.

The war was only three months old when BENJAMIN FRANKLIN proposed the first continental constitution. He called it "Articles of Confederation and Perpetual Union," a name that stuck. Because the war was then being fought to achieve a reconciliation with England on American terms, Congress would not even consider Franklin's plan. But a year later, when Congress appointed a committee to frame a DECLARATION OF INDEPENDENCE, it also appointed a committee, consisting of one member from each state, to prepare "the form of a confederation to be entered into by these colonies." JOHN DICKINSON of Pennsylvania, whom the committee entrusted to draft the document, borrowed heavily from Franklin's plan and seems not to have been influenced by other committee members. One complained that Dickinson's plan involved "the Idea of destroying all Provincial Distinctions and making every thing of the most minute kind bend to what they call the good of the whole."

Dickinson was a "nationalist" in the sense that he believed that a strong central government was needed to build a union that could effectively manage its own affairs and compete with other nations. Congress, which was directing the war, became the hub of the Confederation. It was a unicameral house in which each state delegation had a single vote, making the states equal, and Dickinson proposed no change. Franklin, by contrast, had recommended that REPRESENTATION in Congress be apportioned on the basis of population, with each delegate having one vote. Dickinson carried over Franklin's generous allocation of powers to Congress, except for a power over "general commerce." Neither Franklin nor Dickinson recommended a general tax power. Congress requisitioned monies from each state for a common treasury, leaving each state to raise its share by taxation. Congress had exclusive powers over war and peace, armies and navies, foreign affairs, the decision of disputes between states, admiralty and prize courts, the coinage of money and its value, borrowing money on the credit of the United States, Indian affairs, the western boundaries of the states claiming lands to the Pacific, the acquisition of new territory and the creation of new states, standards of weights and measures, and the post office. Dickinson also recommended a "council of state" or permanent executive agency that would enforce congressional measures and administer financial, diplomatic, and military matters. Dickinson proposed many limitations on state power, mainly to secure effective control over matters delegated to Congress. The states could not, for example, levy IMPOSTS or duties that violated treaties of the United States. Even the sovereign power of the states over their internal concerns was limited by the qualification in Article III, the crux of the Dickinson draft: "Each colony [Dickinson always referred to "colony" and not "state"] shall retain and enjoy as much of its present Laws, Rights and Customs, as it may think fit, and reserves to itself the sole and exclusive Regulation and Government of its internal police, in all matters that shall not interfere with the Articles of Confederation." Clearly Dickinson envisioned a confederation in which the states did not master the central government.

Nationalists who supported the Dickinson draft in Congress argued, as did JOHN ADAMS, that the purpose of the confederation was to meld the states into "one common mass. We shall no longer retain our separate individuality" on matters delegated to Congress. The four New England states had the same relation to Congress that "four counties bore to a single state," Adams declared. The states could build roads and enact poor laws but "they have no right to touch upon continental subjects." JAMES WILSON, another centralist, contended that the Congress should represent all the people, not the states, because "As to those matters which are referred to Congress, we are not so many states, we are one large state." Few Congressmen were nationalists, however, and few nationalists were consistent. Congressmen from Virginia, the largest state, rejected state equality in favor of proportional representation in Congress with each delegate voting; but because Virginia claimed a western boundary on the Pacific, it rejected the nationalist contention that Congress had succeeded to British SOVEREIGNTY with respect to the West and should govern it for the benefit of all. Congressmen from Maryland, a small state without western claims, adamantly held to that nationalist position but argued for state equality—one state, one vote—on the issue of representation. How requisitions should be determined also provoked dissension based on little principle other than self-interest.

The disputes over representation, western lands, and the basis for requisitions deadlocked the Congress in 1776. The next year, however, state supremacists who feared centralization won a series of victories that decisively altered the character of the confederation proposed by Dickinson and championed by Franklin, Adams, and Wilson. Dickinson's Article III was replaced by a declaration that "Each State retains its sovereignty, freedom, and independence, and every power, jurisdiction, and right, which is not by this confederation expressly delegated to the United States, in Congress assembled." Thus, colonial control over internal police became state sovereignty over all reserved powers, and the central government received only "expressly delegated" powers rather than implied powers to control even internal police in-

volving matters of continental concern. State supremacists also restricted the power of Congress to make commercial treaties: no treaty could prohibit imports or exports, and no treaty could prevent a state from imposing retaliatory imposts. The revised Articles also scrapped Dickinson's executive branch, accepted the state sovereignty principle that each state cast an equal vote, modified Congress's judicial authority to decide all intercolonial disputes, and denied the power of Congress to fix the western boundaries of states.

Maryland, however, refused to accept the decision on the boundary issue. Although Congress completed the Articles in November 1777, unanimous ratification by state legislatures came hard. By the beginning of 1779, however, Maryland stood alone, the only state that had not ratified, and Maryland was unmovable. As unanimity was necessary, Maryland had the advantage as well as a great cause, the creation of a national domain. In 1780 New York and Connecticut ceded their western lands to the United States. Congress then adopted a report recommending the cession of western claims by other states, and in October 1780, Congress yielded to Maryland by resolving that ceded lands should be disposed of for the common benefit of the United States and be formed into "republican states, which shall become members of the federal union" on equal terms with the original states. Virginia's acceptance in January 1781 was decisive. Maryland ratified.

When Congress had submitted the Articles for ratification its accompanying letter accurately stated that its plan was the best possible under the circumstances; combining "in one general system" the conflicting interests of "a continent divided into so many sovereign . . . communities" was a "difficulty." The Articles were the product of the AMERICAN REVOLUTION and constituted an extraordinary achievement. Congress had framed the first written constitution that established a federal system of government in which the sovereign powers were distributed between the central and local governments. Those powers that unquestionably belonged to Parliament were delegated to the United States. Under the Articles Congress possessed neither tax nor commerce powers, the two powers that Americans in the final stages of the controversy with Britain refused to recognize in Parliament. Americans were fighting largely because a central government claimed those powers, which Americans demanded for their provincial legislatures. Given the widespread identification of liberty with local autonomy, the commitment to limited government, and the hostility to centralization, the states yielded as much as could be expected at the time. Because Congress represented the states and the people of the states, to deny Congress the power to tax was not logical, but the opposition to centralized powers of taxation was so fierce that even nationalists supported the requisition system. "It takes time," as JOHN JAY remarked, "to make sovereigns of subjects."

The sovereignty claimed by the states existed—within a limited sphere of authority. The Articles made the United States sovereign, too, within its sphere of authority: it possessed "sole and exclusive" power over fundamental matters such as foreign affairs, war and peace, western lands, and Indian affairs. The reservation of some sovereign powers in the states meant the surrender of other sovereign powers to the central government. Americans believed that sovereignty was divisible and divided it. In part, FEDERALISM is a system of divided sovereign powers. The Articles had many defects, the greatest of which was that the United States acted on the states rather than the people and had no way of making the states or anyone but soldiers obey. The failure to create executive and judicial branches, the requirement for unanimity for amendments, and the refusal to concede to Congress what had been denied to Parliament resulted in the eventual breakdown of the Articles. They were, nevertheless, a necessary stage in the evolution of the Constitution of 1787 and contained many provisions that were carried over into that document. (See CONSTITUTIONAL HISTORY, 1776–1789.)

LEONARD W. LEVY
(1986)

Bibliography

HENDERSON, H. JAMES   1974   Party Politics in the Continental Congress. New York: McGraw-Hill.

JENSEN, MERRILL   1963 (1940)   Articles of Confederation: An Interpretation of the Social-Constitutional History of the American Revolution. Madison: University of Wisconsin Press.

RAKOVE, JACK N.   1979   The Beginnings of National Politics: An Interpretive History of the Continental Congress. New York: Knopf.

ARTICLES OF IMPEACHMENT OF ANDREW JOHNSON
(1868)

Eleven articles of IMPEACHMENT of President ANDREW JOHNSON were voted by the HOUSE OF REPRESENTATIVES in March 1868. The impeachment was largely a product of partisan dissatisfaction with Johnson's approach to RECONSTRUCTION of the South.

Nine of the articles concerned Johnson's attempt to remove Secretary of War EDWIN M. STANTON, supposedly in defiance of the TENURE OF OFFICE ACT of 1867—although, by its letter, the act did not apply to Stanton, who had been appointed by ABRAHAM LINCOLN. The charges ranged from simple violation of the act to conspiracy to seize the property of the War Department and to gain control over its expenditures. However far-fetched, each of the nine articles alleged a specific illegal or criminal act.

The last two articles were overtly political and reflected a different notion of the concept of impeachable offense. Based on accounts of Johnson's speeches, the articles charged that he ridiculed and abused Congress and had questioned the constitutional legitimacy of the Thirty-Ninth Congress.

The impeachment was tried to the SENATE which, in May 1868, failed by one vote to give a two-thirds vote for conviction of any of the articles, and so acquitted Johnson.

DENNIS J. MAHONEY
(1986)

Bibliography

BENEDICT, MICHAEL LES   1973   The Impeachment and Trial of Andrew Johnson. New York: W. W. Norton.

ARTICLES OF IMPEACHMENT OF RICHARD M. NIXON
(1974)

Three articles of IMPEACHMENT of President RICHARD M. NIXON were voted by the Committee on the Judiciary of the HOUSE OF REPRESENTATIVES between July 27 and July 30, 1974. The vote on the articles followed an extended investigation of the so-called WATERGATE affair, the President's knowledge of an involvement in that affair, and a prolonged controversy concerning what constitutes an "impeachable offense." All three articles, as voted, had reference to Watergate, and all charged breach of the oath of office.

The first article charged Nixon with having "prevented, obstructed, and impeded the administration of justice" by withholding evidence and participating in the "cover-up" of the Watergate affair. The nine specifications included making false statements to investigators, approving of others giving false testimony, condoning the payment of "hush money" to potential witnesses, and interfering with the conduct of the investigation.

The second article charged Nixon with misusing the powers of his office and with "repeated conduct violating the constitutional rights of citizens." Five specifications included misusing the Internal Revenue Service, Federal Bureau of Investigation, and Central Intelligence Agency; attempting to prejudice the right to a FAIR TRIAL (of one Daniel Ellsberg); and failing to act against subordinates who engaged in illegal activities.

The third article charged Nixon with disobeying subpoenas issued by the committee itself in the course of its investigation. This article was approved only narrowly since some committee members argued that a good faith assertion of EXECUTIVE PRIVILEGE was not a constitutionally impeachable offense. Two other articles were defeated in the committee vote.

The articles of impeachment never came to a vote in the full House of Representatives. On August 9, 1974, facing the virtual certainty of impeachment and of conviction by the SENATE, Richard M. Nixon became the first president ever to resign.

DENNIS J. MAHONEY
(1986)

Bibliography

UNITED STATES HOUSE OF REPRESENTATIVES, COMMITTEE ON THE JUDICIARY 1974 *Impeachment of Richard Nixon, President of the United States*. Washington, D.C.: Government Printing Office.

ARTICLES OF IMPEACHMENT OF WILLIAM J. CLINTON
(1998)

On December 19, 1998, the U.S. HOUSE OF REPRESENTATIVES voted two articles of IMPEACHMENT against President WILLIAM J. CLINTON. The House charged Clinton with perjury and obstruction of justice arising from the President's concealment of an intimate relationship with a White House intern, Monica Lewinsky.

The first article, approved by a vote of 228–205, accused Clinton of violating "his constitutional oath faithfully to execute the office of President" by "willfully [providing] perjurious, false and misleading testimony" to a federal GRAND JURY about his relationship with Lewinsky and his efforts to cover it up. The grand jury had been empaneled by the INDEPENDENT COUNSEL, Kenneth Starr, who as part of his wide-ranging (and, to many, partisan) investigation of Clinton was looking into allegations that Clinton lied and suborned perjury in a civil sexual harassment lawsuit.

The second article, approved by a 221–212 margin, charged Clinton with obstruction of justice in the civil lawsuit and in the grand jury proceedings. Among its seven specifications, the article accused Clinton of encouraging witnesses (Lewinsky and Betty Curry, the President's secretary) to commit perjury, securing job assistance for a witness (Lewinsky) to corruptly influence her testimony, and allowing his attorney (Robert Bennett) to make false statements to a federal judge.

Two additional articles were approved by the House Judiciary Committee but rejected by the full House.

The impeachment trial in the U.S. SENATE lasted five weeks. Neither article of impeachment garnered the two-thirds SUPERMAJORITY required to remove the President from office.

ADAM WINKLER
(2000)

ARVER v. UNITED STATES

See: Selective Draft Law Cases

ASH, UNITED STATES v.
413 U.S. 300 (1973)

The RIGHT TO COUNSEL did not apply when the prosecutor showed eyewitnesses to a crime an array of photographs, including that of the indicted accused. The photographic showing was merely a part of the prosecutor's trial preparation (that is, done in order to refresh recollection) and neither the defendant's nor his lawyer's presence was constitutionally required.

BARBARA ALLEN BABCOCK
(1986)

ASHTON v. CAMERON COUNTY WATER IMPROVEMENT DISTRICT
298 U.S. 513 (1936)

This is one of the several cases of the period whose decision gave the impression that the United States was constitutionally incapable of combating the Great Depression. Over 2,000 governmental units ranging from big cities to small school districts had defaulted, and the CONTRACT CLAUSE prevented the states from relieving their subdivisions. Congress, responding to pressure from states and creditors, passed the Municipal Bankruptcy Act of 1934, authorizing state subdivisions to apply to federal bankruptcy courts to get their debts scaled down. In accordance with the statute, a Texas water district, supported by state law, applied for a bankruptcy plan that would make possible a final settlement of fifty cents on the dollar, the payment financed by a federal loan. The federal bankruptcy court controlled the bankruptcy plan, which could not be enforced unless approved by creditors holding at least two-thirds of the debt, as required by the statute.

The Supreme Court held the Municipal Bankruptcy Act to be an unconstitutional exercise of Congress's delegated BANKRUPTCY POWER. For a five-member majority, Justice JAMES C. MCREYNOLDS declared that that power was subject to state sovereignty, which cannot be surrendered or impaired by legislation. Congress had violated the TENTH AMENDMENT by infringing on state control over the fiscal affairs of state subdivisions. That the act required state consent, here eagerly given, was irrelevant to the Court. Thus the Court protected the states and even creditors against their will. Justice BENJAMIN N. CARDOZO, for the dissenters, characterizing the majority opinion as "divorced from the realities of life," argued that Congress had framed the statute with sedulous regard for state sovereignty and the structure of the federal system. The Court retreated in *United States v. Bekins* (1938).

LEONARD W. LEVY
(1986)

ASHWANDER v. TENNESSEE VALLEY AUTHORITY
297 U.S. 288 (1936)

Ashwander was part of a protracted litigation over the constitutionality of the Tennessee Valley Authority (TVA), a government development corporation established by the NEW DEAL. (See CONSTITUTIONAL HISTORY, 1933–1945; TENNESSEE VALLEY AUTHORITY ACT.) TVA was organized to develop the economy of a river valley by improving navigation and flood control and especially by generating cheap electric power for homes, farms, and industry. In *Ashwander* preferred shareholders in an existing power company sued in federal court to enjoin the company and TVA from carrying out a contract under which TVA would purchase much of the company's property and equipment, and TVA would allocate areas for the sale of power. The plaintiffs attacked the whole TVA program as exceeding the scope of congressional power. The district court granted the INJUNCTION, but the court of appeals reversed, upholding the contract. The Supreme Court, 8–1, affirmed the court of appeals.

Chief Justice CHARLES EVANS HUGHES, for the majority, concluded that Wilson Dam, where TVA was generating power, had been built in 1916 to provide power for national defense needs, including the operation of nitrate plants used in the making of munitions, and to improve navigation—both objectives concededly within the powers of Congress. If excess electricity were generated at the dam, Hughes said, Congress had the power to sell it, as it might sell any other property owned by the United States. Justice JAMES C. MCREYNOLDS, dissenting alone on the constitutional merits, pointed out the transparency of the majority's doctrinal clothing: TVA was in the power-generating business for its own sake, not as an adjunct to some military program long since abandoned.

Justice LOUIS D. BRANDEIS, dissenting in part, agreed with the majority's views on congressional power but argued that the plaintiffs' complaint should have been dismissed for want of STANDING. As preferred shareholders,

they could show no injury to themselves from the contract. Brandeis went on, in *Ashwander*'s most famous passages, to discuss a series of "rules" under which the Supreme Court had "avoided passing upon a large part of all the constitutional questions pressed upon it for decision." Some of the "rules" flow from Article III of the Constitution, including the standing requirement Brandeis sought to effectuate in *Ashwander* itself. Others, however, express policies of preference for nonconstitutional grounds for decision, for formulating the narrowest possible constitutional grounds, for construing federal statutes to avoid constitutional questions, and the like.

Some modern commentators have read the Brandeis opinion in *Ashwander* to stand for a broad policy of judicial discretion to avoid deciding cases that might place the Court in awkward political positions. Brandeis himself, a stickler for principled application of the Court's jurisdictional requirements, surely had no such generalized discretion in mind. Nonetheless, some of his successors have found it convenient to cite his comments in *Ashwander* in support of far less principled avoidance techniques. (See POE V. ULLMAN.)

KENNETH L. KARST
(1986)

ASIAN AMERICANS AND THE CONSTITUTION

Asians first arrived in the United States in substantial numbers in the mid-nineteenth century. Initially tolerated, these Chinese laborers were soon vilified, especially when the economy soured. By 1882, Congress enacted the CHINESE EXCLUSION ACT, the first federal race-based restriction on IMMIGRATION. Frustrated with what were viewed as loopholes, Congress passed the Scott Act in 1888, which retroactively denied reentry of tens of thousands of Chinese, even those who held official certificates guaranteeing their right to return. In CHAE CHAN PING V. UNITED STATES (1889) (the Chinese Exclusion Case), the Supreme Court explained that the DUE PROCESS rights of these Chinese were not violated. As an incident to SOVEREIGNTY, Congress could defend America against an "Oriental invasion" by revoking at will whatever residency permission previously granted.

In 1892, Congress took another drastic step by passing the Geary Act, which created a registration requirement for all Chinese laborers. Those found without proper papers could be summarily deported unless they could prove their legal residence through "at least one credible white witness." In *Fong Yue Ting v. United States* (1893), the Court upheld this act and emphasized that Congress's inherent power to exclude ALIENS—made clear in *Chae*

Chan Ping—also included the power to deport. In these and two other cases involving Asians, *Nishimura Ekiu v. United States* (1892) and *Yamataya v. Fisher* (1903), the Court established Congress's plenary power over immigration, the exercise of which remains subject to cursory JUDICIAL REVIEW.

Exclusion of Asian Americans reached beyond the physical border to the political border of CITIZENSHIP. The first naturalization statute, passed in 1790, restricted naturalization to "free white persons," and was amended after the CIVIL WAR to include persons of African descent. In *Ozawa v. United States* (1922), a person of Japanese ancestry argued that he should be eligible for citizenship because "white" was a catch-all category excluding only blacks and AMERICAN INDIANS. The Court rejected this argument and explained that white meant Caucasian, an equivalence "so well established" that it could not be disturbed.

The next year, an Asian Indian argued that under prevailing ethnological theories, he was in fact Caucasian and thus eligible for citizenship. In *United States v. Thind* (1923), the Court backed away from the equivalence it had drawn just one year before. Instead of interpreting "white" as Caucasian (considered to be a technical term of art), the Court now opted to interpret "white" in its popular sense. On this view, "white" meant people who looked Northwest European, who were "bone of their bone and flesh of their flesh." Thus, "white" would not include "Hindus" who would retain "indefinitely the clear evidence of their ancestry."

The one bright spot in the Court's immigration jurisprudence for Asian Americans is WONG KIM ARK V. UNITED STATES (1898). There, the Court first recognized that the FOURTEENTH AMENDMENT granted citizenship to all persons born on American soil—even to the unpopular Chinese.

The prejudices that fueled physical and political exclusion also burdened Asian Americans' daily lives. In the 1880s, for example, San Francisco manipulated facially neutral ordinances to close Chinese laundries while keeping White laundries open. Surprisingly, in YICK WO V. HOPKINS (1886), the Court held that this biased exercise of discretion violated the Fourteenth Amendment's EQUAL PROTECTION clause. This victory, however, was exceptional. Consider, for instance, the initial upholding of the alien land laws. Threatened by Japanese competition in farming, white agricultural interests persuaded Western state governments to forbid "aliens ineligible for citizenship" (the code phrase for Asians) from owning land. In *Terrace v. Thompson* (1923) and *Porterfield v. Webb* (1923), the Court concluded that these laws did not amount to RACIAL DISCRIMINATION and that states could limit PROPERTY ownership to citizens. Eventually, after WORLD WAR II and the related internment of Japanese Americans, the Court be-

gan to express doubts about the continuing constitutionality of alien land laws in OYAMA V. CALIFORNIA (1948) and of related laws barring "aliens ineligible for citizenship" from certain lines of work (such as fishing) in TAKAHASHI V. FISH AND GAME COMMISSION (1948). Following the Court's cues, various state supreme courts and legislatures removed these laws in the 1950s and 1960s.

As another example, consider how Asian Americans were often subject to educational SEGREGATION. When challenged on equal protection grounds, the Court held in GONG LUM V. RICE (1927) that a Chinese American girl could be forced to attend the "colored" school. On the authority of PLESSY V. FERGUSON (1896), separate was deemed equal for Asians as it was for blacks.

The Constitution's most tragic failure of Asian Americans occurred just one-half century ago with the internment of approximately 120,000 persons of Japanese descent. Over two-thirds were American citizens, mostly young children born on American soil. Blinded by prejudice, America could not distinguish between the enemy Japan and Americans who happened to be of Japanese descent.

The internment plan, which comprised curfew, evacuation, and detention orders, was challenged in the JAPANESE AMERICAN CASES. In *Hirabayashi v. United States* (1943) and *Yasui v. United States* (1943), the Court addressed only the narrow question of curfews and concluded that "[r]easonably prudent men" had "ample ground" and "[s]ubstantial basis" to believe that Japanese Americans might "aid a threatened enemy invasion." In KOREMATSU V. UNITED STATES (1943), the Court again refused to address the constitutionality of the total internment plan and addressed only the evacuation orders. The Court introduced what would evolve into the SUSPECT CLASSIFICATIONS doctrine of equal protection law, that "all legal restrictions which curtail the civil rights of any single racial group are immediately suspect." Despite this suggestion of heightened scrutiny, the Court deferred to the government's claims of military necessity. The majority insisted that Korematsu was evacuated not "because of hostility to him or his race . . . but because we are at war with the Japanese Empire." Perhaps the Court's misstep was caused by the government's suppression of exculpatory evidence, uncovered four decades later. On the other hand, even without such evidence, Justice FRANK MURPHY knew enough to call the MAJORITY OPINION a fall into "the ugly abyss of racism."

Only in the final case, *Endo v. United States* (1943), did the Court confront the issue of indefinite detention of concededly loyal Americans of Japanese descent. But even here, the Court avoided striking down such detention as unconstitutional. Instead, it decided the case on statutory grounds and declared that the War Relocation Authority, which managed the internment camps, had gone beyond its delegated powers. In other words, indefinite detention was the work of rogue bureaucrats, not President FRANKLIN D. ROOSEVELT or the Congress. In sum, the Constitution has been an unreliable ally in the Asian American struggle for CIVIL RIGHTS.

JERRY KANG
(2000)

Bibliography

KIM, HYUNG-CHAN, ed. 1992 *Asian Americans and the Supreme Court.* New York: Greenwood Press.
McCLAIN, CHARLES, ed. 1994 *Asian Americans and the Law.* New York: Garland Publishing.

ASIAN IMMIGRANTS AND CONSTITUTIONAL HISTORY

Most Americans are aware that Asian immigrants have been the victims of racial prejudice and the objects of racially discriminatory laws repeatedly throughout our history. Less widely appreciated is the fact that they have been vigorous in challenging these laws in the courts and that these cases have contributed in important ways to the shaping of the American constitutional order.

Large numbers of Chinese immigrated to the Pacific coastal states, mainly California, during the second half of the nineteenth century. Their presence soon aroused intense racial antagonism, which in turn led to the enactment of numerous state laws and local ordinances designed to make their lives difficult and discourage them from staying. The Chinese tested many of these laws in state or federal court and were successful in having many of them overturned, either on the grounds that they conflicted with the Constitution, with federal CIVIL RIGHTS legislation, or with federal treaties.

In *Ho Ah Kow v. Nunan* (1879), Supreme Court Justice STEPHEN J. FIELD, sitting as a CIRCUIT COURT judge, nullified a San Francisco ordinance requiring all prisoners in the county jail to have their heads shaved to an inch of the scalp. The ordinance was aimed at humiliating Chinese prisoners who wore their hair in a long braided queue. Field ruled that the ordinance violated the Civil Rights Act of 1870, which forbade differential punishments based on race, and the EQUAL PROTECTION clause of the FOURTEENTH AMENDMENT, which, he declared, the Chinese, though ALIENS, were entitled to invoke. In the landmark case of YICK WO V. HOPKINS (1886), a San Francisco ordinance had required anyone operating a laundry in a wooden building to obtain the approval of the Board of Supervisors. Some two hundred Chinese laundry proprietors applied for permission but all were refused. Many

continued to operate and were arrested, while some eighty Caucasians who did not have permits continued to operate laundries in wooden buildings with impunity. Two arrested Chinese laundrymen, with the support of the Chinese Laundrymen's League, brought separate actions in state and federal court attacking the constitutionality of the ordinance. The Supreme Court ruled that the ordinance as applied contravened the Constitution. The ordinance was suspect, the Court said, because it vested uncontrolled discretion in the supervisors. Such discretion was subject to abuse and here was an example of such abuse. From the evidence one could not help but conclude that the ordinance, though neutral in wording, was being applied in a racially discriminatory manner ("with an evil eye and an unequal hand") and this violated the equal protection clause. It was the first instance in which the Court affirmed that resident aliens, as well as citizens, were protected by the Fourteenth Amendment. Its provisions, the Court declared, applied "to all persons within the territorial jurisdiction, without regard to any differences of race, of color, or of nationality."

In 1882 Congress passed the first of several CHINESE EXCLUSION ACTS. These acts suspended the coming of Chinese laborers into the country and regulated the rights of laborers already here. The Chinese mounted several legal challenges to these acts that reached the Supreme Court. Among the most noteworthy are CHAE CHAN PING V. UNITED STATES (the Chinese Exclusion Case) (1889) and *Fong Yue Ting v. United States* (1893).

In *Chae Chan Ping*, the Chinese plaintiffs challenged a feature of the 1888 act that had the effect of denying entry into the country of Chinese whose right to enter had been guaranteed by an 1880 treaty with China. But the Court held that the United States had plenary and virtually unconstrained power over IMMIGRATION, that Congress could abrogate the provisions of a treaty by a later law, and that any rights created under the treaty could similarly be cancelled by later LEGISLATION. In *Fong Yue Ting*, the Chinese plaintiffs successfully attacked many features of the 1892 exclusion act, including a section requiring all resident Chinese laborers to apply for and carry identity cards. The Court held that just as the federal government had unconstrained power to exclude foreigners seeking to enter the country it had "absolute" and "unqualified" power to control the residence of those already here. The federal government could set up a system of identification and registration and provide the most summary procedures for deportation. (In subsequent cases, some brought by Chinese immigrants, the Court has backed off somewhat from this extreme position.)

The first Chinese Exclusion Act forbade any state or federal court from granting NATURALIZATION to any person of Chinese ancestry. It remained unclear whether children born in the United States to Chinese parents were citizens under the Fourteenth Amendment. According to section 1 of the amendment "all persons born or naturalized in the United States, and subject to the jurisdiction thereof, are citizens of the United States." In *United States v. Wong Kim Ark* (1896), the Court, relying heavily on COMMON LAW understandings of CITIZENSHIP, concluded that, save for the children of diplomats, children of whatever ethnicity born in the United States were American citizens.

By 1900 the Chinese population on the West Coast of the United States had diminished substantially, and the Chinese were ceasing to be the flash point for hostility. Attention shifted to another Asian immigrant group, the Japanese, whose numbers were increasing.

Many Japanese gained a foothold in farming. In response California and other Western states passed the Alien Land Laws, limiting the right to own or lease agricultural land to citizens and aliens eligible for citizenship. Japanese would-be purchasers and Caucasian would-be sellers challenged these laws, but in a pair of decisions handed down in 1923—*Terrace v. Thompson* and *Porterfield v. Webb*—the Court validated them all. It held that the states, absent a treaty, could legislate against ownership of real PROPERTY by foreigners and that they could differentiate between classes of foreigners in determining eligibility for ownership rights without violating the equal protection clause.

The most important twentieth-century cases involving Asians, and some of the most important cases in the history of American constitutional law, arose out of the forcible relocation and internment of over 100,000 Japanese Americans during WORLD WAR II. In the wake of the declaration of war on Japan military authorities on the West Coast, with the approval of President FRANKLIN D. ROOSEVELT and Congress, issued a series of orders, among other things, imposing a curfew on persons of Japanese ancestry, forbidding them to leave certain designated areas, and ordering them into assembly centers for removal to detention camps. The legitimacy of the orders was attacked in a series of cases brought by American citizens of Japanese ancestry. These tested, as perhaps never before or since, the power of the national government to curtail individual CIVIL LIBERTIES.

In *Hirabayashi v. United States* (1943), the Court upheld the curfew as a valid exercise of the federal government's broad discretion under the WAR POWER. In the exercise of that power, the government could infringe radically on civil liberties during wartime and could even do so on a racial basis so long as it could offer a rational justification for the decision. While acknowledging that racial distinctions were by their nature odious to a free people, the Court emphasized that the judiciary was not competent to second-guess the military's judgment.

In KOREMATSU V. UNITED STATES (1944), the Court affirmed the conviction of a Japanese American for remaining in a designated area against military orders. Korematsu argued that the order was part of an overall plan of forcible removal to detention camps, but the MAJORITY OPINION of Justice HUGO L. BLACK, over three dissents, refused to address that issue. (Justice FRANK MURPHY, noting the racial stereotyping that ran through the government's justification of its actions, characterized them as falling into the "ugly abyss of racism.") Significantly, the Court did say that racially discriminatory laws were "suspect," subject to "the most rigid [judicial] scrutiny," and could be justified only by "pressing public necessity." This statement implied clearly that the federal government was bound by the equal protection principle even if not, literally, by the Fourteenth Amendment equal protection clause itself. (It may be doubted whether the Court applied its own test in the *Korematsu* case.) In *Ex parte Endo* (1944), decided the same day, the Court, while again refusing to rule on the validity of the use of detention camps, held that the military could not continue to detain a Japanese American woman whose loyalty it had conceded.

Two cases involving the rights of Asian citizens or residents decided in the immediate post–World War II period deserve discussion. In *Oyama v. California* (1948), the Court revisited the Alien Land Laws. A Japanese national living in California had paid the purchase price for agricultural land and put title in the name of his U.S. citizen son. Under California law this transaction created a presumption that the purchase had been consummated with the intention of evading the Alien Land Law, and the state Attorney General began proceedings to forfeit the land. The Court ruled that the provision violated the equal protection rights of the citizen son. It refused, however, to invalidate the law itself.

A few months later the Court struck down another piece of anti-Japanese legislation. In TAKAHASHI V. FISH AND GAME COMMISSION (1948), the Court nullified a California law denying commercial fishing licenses to resident aliens ineligible for citizenship. (By this time virtually all other Asians had been made eligible for naturalization; thus, the law in practice affected only Japanese fishermen.) Aliens lawfully present in a state had the right to equal legal privileges with all citizens, the Court held. These legal privileges included the right to work for a living, and this right trumped the state's asserted interest in conserving fish within its territorial waters for the benefit of its citizens.

Cases brought by nineteenth-century Chinese immigrants helped establish several important and enduring Fourteenth Amendment principles, among them: (1) that persons born in the United States of alien parents are citizens of the United States, (2) that persons resident in the United States, whether citizens or not, are entitled to DUE

PROCESS OF LAW and the equal protection of the laws, making them immune from state-sponsored discrimination at least in most areas of life, and (3) that laws equal on their face can violate the equal protection clause if administered in a discriminatory manner. The Chinese Exclusion Act cases, as noted above, are the fundament on which the modern constitutional law of immigration was built.

The postwar and wartime JAPANESE AMERICAN CASES are significant milestones in the evolution of the modern constitutional order. *Oyama* and *Takahashi* extended Fourteenth Amendment equal protection analysis into areas of state regulation previously thought free from such scrutiny and are harbingers of the robust presence the equal protection clause was beginning to assume in constitutional law. The Japanese American curfew and relocation cases, on their face so inhospitable to the nondiscrimination principle, contributed in their own ironic way to the growth of that principle. Both *Hirabayashi* and *Korematsu* recognized that racial distinctions were odious. And in *Korematsu,* Justice Black, even while approving one of the most racially invidious classification schemes in our history, articulated a test that would eventually prove to be fatal when applied to racial classification schemes, whether sanctioned by the state or federal government.

CHARLES J. McCLAIN
(2000)

(SEE ALSO: *Asian Americans and the Constitution; Racial Discrimination.*)

Bibliography
DANIELS, ROGER   1977   *The Politics of Prejudice: The Anti-Japanese Movement in California and the Struggle for Japanese Exclusion.* Berkeley, Calif.: University of California Press.
IRONS, PETER   1983   *Justice at War.* New York: Oxford University Press.
KIM, HYUNG-CHAN, ed.   1992   *Asian Americans and the Supreme Court: A Documentary History.* New York: Greenwood Press.
McCLAIN, CHARLES J.   1994   *In Search of Equality: the Chinese Struggle Against Discrimination in Nineteenth-Century America.* Berkeley: University of California Press.
———, ed.   1994   *Asian Americans and the Law: Historical and Contemporary Perspectives,* 4 vols. New York: Garland Publishing.
SALYER, LUCY E.   1995   *Law Harsh as Tigers: Chinese Immigrants and the Shaping of Modern Immigration Law.* Chapel Hill: University of North Carolina Press.

ASSISTANCE, WRIT OF

The term "writ of assistance" is applied to several distinct types of legal documents. Of greatest significance to American constitutional history was the writ of assistance issued to customs inspectors by the English Court of the Exchequer authorizing the search of all houses suspected of containing contraband. Such writs were first used no later than 1621, and their form was codified in 1662. They are still used regularly in Britain and in many nations of the British Commonwealth.

In colonial America, writs of assistance were used as GENERAL SEARCH WARRANTS and were authorized by a statute of the British Parliament. In a famous Massachusetts case, PAXTON'S CASE (1761), JAMES OTIS argued that the statute authorizing writs of assistance should be held invalid because it was contrary to MAGNA CARTA and the COMMON LAW; but his argument was rejected. The colonial experience with writs of assistance led to the requirement in the FOURTH AMENDMENT that SEARCH WARRANTS particularly describe the place to be searched and the object of the search.

WILLIAM J. CUDDIHY
(1986)

Bibliography
SMITH, M. H.   1978   *The Writs of Assistance Case.* Berkeley: University of California Press.

ASSOCIATED PRESS CO. v. NLRB

See: Wagner Act Cases

ASSOCIATION, THE

The Continental Association was created by the First Continental Congress on October 18, 1774. It was "a non-importation, non-consumption, and non-exportation agreement" undertaken to obtain redress of American grievances against the British Crown and Parliament. The Articles of Association were signed on October 20 by the representatives of twelve colonies, solemnly binding themselves and their constituents to its terms.

The articles listed the most pressing American grievances (TAXATION WITHOUT REPRESENTATION, extension of admiralty court jurisdiction, denial of TRIAL BY JURY in tax cases), enumerated the measures to be taken (cessation of commercial ties to Britain), prescribed the penalty for noncompliance (a total breaking off of communication with offenders), and established the machinery for enforcement (through committees of correspondence).

The Association was a major step toward the creation of a federal union of American states. It was the first prescriptive act of a national Congress to be binding directly on individuals, and the efforts at enforcement of or compliance with its terms certainly contributed to the formation of a national identity. With but little exaggeration the historian RICHARD HILDRETH wrote: "The signature of the Association may be considered as the commencement of the American union."

DENNIS J. MAHONEY
(1986)

ATASCADERO STATE HOSPITAL v. SCANLON
473 U.S. 234 (1985)

The opinions in this case made clear that PENNHURST STATE SCHOOL AND HOSPITAL V. HALDERMAN (1981) was a watershed in the Supreme Court's modern treatment of the ELEVENTH AMENDMENT. By the same 5–4 division as in *Pennhurst*, the Court here held that an individual could not obtain relief against a state agency in federal court for harm caused by the agency's violation of the federal REHABILITATION ACT of 1973. In an opinion by Justice LEWIS F. POWELL, the majority concluded that California had not waived its SOVEREIGN IMMUNITY under that amendment, and that Congress, in the act, had not lifted the state's immunity to suit by individual plaintiffs. The latter point carried the Court's restrictive reading of the Eleventh Amendment a step beyond even the *Pennhurst* opinion: a congressional purpose to lift state immunity, the majority said, cannot be found by implication from a statute's purposes, but only in an explicit statement in the statute itself.

The four dissenters, speaking primarily through Justice WILLIAM J. BRENNAN, made a vigorous and broad-ranging attack on the majority's recent approach to Eleventh Amendment issues. Justice Brennan, as before, accused the majority of misconceiving the purposes of the Framers in writing Article III, misreading the text and the purposes of the Eleventh Amendment, and generally twisting the fundamental premises of American FEDERALISM to "put the federal judiciary in the unseemly position of exempting the states from compliance with laws that bind every other legal actor in our nation."

It seems clear that the shock of *Pennhurst* persuaded some of the *Scanlon* dissenters to join Justice Brennan's campaign for a fundamental reorientation of Eleventh Amendment jurisprudence. Four Justices agreed that the recent majority's doctrine "intrudes on the ideal of liberty under law by protecting the States from the consequences of their illegal conduct."

KENNETH L. KARST
(1986)

ATOMIC ENERGY ACT
68 Stat 919 (1954)

The initial Atomic Energy Act (1946) had created an independent five-person Atomic Energy Commission (AEC) to exercise complete civilian control over the production of atomic energy and associated research programs. By the early 1950s, criticism of the statute mounted because it limited the role of private enterprise in the atomic energy field, overemphasized military phases, and created unwarranted secrecy, precluding the dissemination of technical information to other nations.

The 1954 Amendment addressed these concerns. Its overriding policy objective, strongly supported by President DWIGHT D. EISENHOWER, was to facilitate the commercial development and exploitation of nuclear power by private industry. The key provisions were: private ownership of nuclear facilities; private use of fissionable material (though the AEC still retained title, until revision in 1964); liberalized patenting rights; industrial access to needed technical information; and a program for international cooperation in developing peaceful applications of nuclear energy, particularly nuclear power. The principal focus of the act was to make the nuclear industry economically independent and internally competitive.

Regulatory provisions of the 1954 act authorized the AEC to license facilities and operators producing or using radioactive materials. This licensing process, subject to judicial review by the terms of the act, was to protect the public health, safety, life, and property. Little guidance or standards for licensure was provided, and the question of safety hazards from nuclear technology was not considered. Thus the AEC's administration of the act was slowly hammered out through the regulatory process; that situation continued after the Commission was folded into the Department of Energy in 1974.

PAUL L. MURPHY
(1986)

Bibliography
ROLPH, ELIZABETH S. 1979 *Nuclear Power and the Public Safety*. Lexington, Mass.: Lexington Books.

ATTAINDER, BILL OF

See: Bill of Attainder

ATTAINDER OF TREASON

Upon conviction of and sentencing for TREASON, a person is attainted: he loses all claim to the protection of the law.

Under English law attainder of treason worked "corruption of blood," depriving the traitor's descendants of the right to inherit property from or through him. The second clause of Article III, section 2, of the Constitution virtually abolishes attainder of treason. Because of that clause, ABRAHAM LINCOLN insisted that the forfeiture of ex-Confederates' property under the CONFISCATION ACT of 1862 be only for the lifetime of the owner. Construing the act and the constitutional provision in *Wallach v. Van Riswick* (1872), the Supreme Court held that the limitation on attainder of treason was solely for the benefit of the heirs.

DENNIS J. MAHONEY
(1986)

ATTORNEY GENERAL AND DEPARTMENT OF JUSTICE

The job of attorney general for the United States, as it was then called, was created by the JUDICIARY ACT OF 1789. The last sentence of that remarkable statute called for the appointment (presumably by the President) of "a meet person, learned in the law, ... whose duty it shall be to prosecute and conduct all suits in the Supreme Court in which the United States shall be concerned, and to give his advice and opinion upon questions of law when required by the President of the United States, or when requested by the heads of any of the departments, touching any matters that may concern their departments, and [who] shall receive such compensation for his services as shall by law be provided." The first attorney general was EDMUND RANDOLPH, and his salary was $1,500. He had no office or staff provided by his government.

There have been seventy-three attorneys general between Randolph's tenure and that of William French Smith (1981–1985), counting JOHN J. CRITTENDEN twice. From the beginning they have been members of the President's cabinet—fourth in rank after the secretaries of state, treasury, and war (now defense). Since 1870 the attorney general has also been head of the Department of Justice. For the most part, the attorneys general have been citizens of outstanding achievement and public service, although not necessarily of extraordinary professional and intellectual ability; the latter qualities have traditionally been associated with the SOLICITOR GENERAL. Nine attorneys general subsequently sat on the Supreme Court of the United States, two as Chief Justice (ROGER B. TANEY, 1831–1833, and HARLAN F. STONE, 1924–1925); three were nominated to that bench but never confirmed; one was confirmed but never took his seat (EDWIN M. STANTON, 1860–1861); and at least two turned down nominations to the Court (Charles Lee, 1795–1801, as Chief Justice, and LEVI LINCOLN, 1801–1805). Only three attorneys general

have had their careers seriously eroded by personal and professional misconduct (Harry M. Daugherty, 1921–1924; John N. Mitchell, 1969–1972; and Richard G. Kleindienst, 1972–1974). Of these, Daugherty was acquitted of charges of attempting to defraud the United States in the Teapot Dome scandal, Mitchell served a prison term for a conspiracy to obstruct justice in connection with the WATERGATE affair, and Kleindienst entered a plea bargain of guilty to a MISDEMEANOR involving his veracity in congressional testimony.

The Department of Justice grew with government after 1870, but at an increasingly accelerated rate, expanding enormously in the 1970s and early 1980s. The budget of the Department for fiscal year 1984 was over three billion dollars; it had increased by almost fifty percent since the beginning of 1981. In addition to the attorney general, top officials now include one deputy attorney general, five deputy associate attorneys general, one associate attorney general, five deputy associate attorneys general, the solicitor general, ten assistant attorneys general, and ninety-four United States attorneys (with coordinate United States marshals), all appointed by the President and all bearing responsibility of some sort in the litigation and advice-giving functions of the Department. These officers are backed by the vast investigative resources of the FEDERAL BUREAU OF INVESTIGATION (FBI). In addition, the Department runs the Immigration and Naturalization Service, the Federal Bureau of Prisons, the Drug Enforcement Agency, and various research and public policy arms.

Public perception of the department as a major instrument of public policy, with a significant effect on the quality of American society, started roughly with the JOHN F. KENNEDY administration in the 1960s, when ROBERT F. KENNEDY (1961–1964) was appointed attorney general by his brother. Before that, the department mostly functioned as a professional law office charged with enforcing the few federal criminal statutes that existed, representing the government in other litigation, and giving advice to the President, especially on questions requiring construction of the Constitution. There had been sporadic periods, however, during which the department temporarily emerged as an important arm of federal government.

The department was established by Congress primarily as the instrument of government to work with the FREEDMEN'S BUREAU in implementing the CIVIL RIGHTS statutes that accompanied the passage of the Civil War amendments. The first attorneys general to run the Department—Amos T. Akerman (1870–1872) and George Henry Williams (1872–1875)—were accordingly deeply engaged in the temporary and unsuccessful efforts then to protect the ideal of racial equality through law. Charles J. Bonaparte (1906–1909), both under President THEODORE ROOSEVELT and in his professional life after that, was also active in the cause of racial justice, using in part the technique of AMICUS CURIAE briefs. Bonaparte also actively enforced the SHERMAN ANTITRUST ACT of 1890, following the traditions of his immediate predecessors, PHILANDER C. KNOX (1901–1904) and WILLIAM H. MOODY (1904–1906). On the darker side, A. MITCHELL PALMER (1919–1921) brought the department into public controversy in the stunning PALMER RAIDS of 1919, in which more than 5,000 persons were taken into custody, their names apparently culled from lists of over 60,000 put together by the agency that became the FBI. No federal criminal charges were lodged against any of them, proposals for federal laws against peacetime SEDITION having failed to pass Congress, and the affair remains a moment of disgrace in the department's history.

The inescapable intertwining of law enforcement priorities and public policy has caused debate over the qualifications that attorneys general should meet. On the one hand, there is the tradition of the even-handed, objective, nonpolitical rule of law, implemented by an impartial Department of Justice. The department's own slogan exemplifies this strand of its work: "The United States wins its case whenever justice is done one of its citizens in the courts." Yet it is not possible to run the department without making choices that have wide public impact; not surprisingly, those choices reflect the political goals of the President. Since the mid-1950s the department's political role has been especially visible in civil rights matters, but it has been marked in antitrust policy, for example, since the passage of the Sherman Act of 1890. Even the work of the Lands Division, which is now also responsible for laws affecting ENVIRONMENTAL REGULATION and the use of natural resources, has strong political effects. The Criminal Division has devoted major energies to the control of organized crime as the result of new policy initiatives of the Kennedy administration in the early 1960s. The FBI, since the death of J. EDGAR HOOVER, has changed not only its direction—away from a concentration on perceived threats to internal security, for one part, and automobile thefts, for another—but also its techniques and training programs, by the initiation of elaborate undercover investigations called "scams."

In the mid-1970s, White House manipulation of the department during the Watergate scandal led Senator Sam J. Ervin of North Carolina seriously to examine, in a series of hearings, the possibility of separating the Department of Justice from presidential control. There were substantial constitutional objections to his plan, stemming from the undoubted constitutional power of the President to run the executive branch with people of his own choosing, at least in policymaking positions. The proposed legislation failed, partly for that reason, and partly because of principled opposition from many lawyers and former

government officials who believed it not only inevitable but also appropriate that law enforcement priorities and policies be part of a presidential candidate's platform and a presidential program. No one, however, supported a presidential right to corruption, and Congress did create the office of a special prosecutor to be filled from time to time by appointment triggered by nonfrivolous charges against any presidential appointee or personal staff member. Such a special prosecutor is, by law, immunized against political accountability to the attorney general or the White House.

The creation of a statutory special prosecutor, in place of the ad hoc use of such a position at the time of Teapot Dome and Watergate, did not, of course, end discussion of the qualifications required of an attorney general. Robert F. Kennedy (1961–1964), John N. Mitchell (1969–1972), and Edwin Meese (1985–) had been campaign managers for the Presidents who appointed them, and Herbert Brownell (1953–1957), Griffin B. Bell (1977–1979), and William French Smith (1981–1985) were closely associated with their Presidents' political careers. The argument that close political associates should be disqualified from appointment as the nation's chief law enforcement officer is not borne out by the public careers of these men. Only one, Mitchell, was connected with corruption or scandal. Robert Kennedy, professionally the least qualified of all at the time of his appointment, was a spectacularly successful leader of the department; his tenure was marked by policy innovation and attention to career professionals, and scrupulously devoid of political favoritism. In short, it is difficult to generalize, from the record, on what background is best. A full commitment to the rule of law, an ability to command professional respect, the administrative skill to run a large and diverse bureaucracy, a constitutional regard for an independent judiciary, and the political habit of appropriate deference to the place of Congress in the constitutional scheme are the traits that the Senate must look for in giving its advice and consent. None of these qualifications is necessarily associated with any particular background.

There is implicit in the periodic debate about what qualifications are needed for an attorney general an ambivalence about the identification of his (or her) client. The legal profession has come to realize that the client-lawyer relationship imagined in lawyers' codes of professional responsibility does not fit the corporate-bureaucratic world. Lawyers who are used to concern about whether they represent the managers of a corporation, or some abstract corporate entity, or other financial interests find the problem even more acute in government service. The attorney general is the lawyer for the President, but he is also the lawyer for the United States, which includes the Congress, and which is governed by a Constitution. The conflicts inherent in this multifaceted responsibility have been reflected, for example, in the department's use of WIRETAPPING and electronic surveillance. Both originated with ambiguous presidential approval, though neither was authorized by Congress nor controlled by explicit legislation. When the Supreme Court applied the exclusionary rule to surveillance by TRESPASS, and then to the product of taps, the response of the department was to confine the use of those devices to investigative work; they were not to be used as EVIDENCE in court. The combining of constitutional constraints on law enforcement behavior, legislative policy, and presidential direction did not take place until decades after the process started. Similar problems of ambiguity of duty are reflected whenever the Congress enacts legislation, or the Supreme Court announces constitutional rules, that the President wants to avoid.

The emergence, in the years since mid-century, of the federal role in ending racial discrimination is largely a product of Justice Department policymaking, mostly with, but sometimes ahead of, the approval of the President. Until recently, the department was consistently in advance of congressional policy. In 1939, without any statutory authority, Attorney General FRANK MURPHY (1939–1940) set up a Civil Rights Section in the Criminal Division to enforce the criminal code's civil rights provisions, which had not been used for years. For the first time, the FBI was thereby drawn, against its will, into the investigation of civil rights violations, particularly in police brutality cases. The section had no authority in civil matters, but its creation immediately created a focus inside the executive branch for the emerging civil rights constituency. The resulting tie between Justice Department policy and the civil rights movement lasted, with some erosion in the early 1970s, until 1981.

In 1948, under TOM C. CLARK (1945–1949), the department initiated a consistent practice of supporting civil rights groups through amicus curiae briefs in private litigation in the Supreme Court. The case was SHELLEY V. KRAEMER (1948), which held racially RESTRICTIVE COVENANTS to be unenforceable in state courts. The solicitor general filed important briefs thereafter in BROWN V. BOARD OF EDUCATION (1954) and its progeny, even though it was far from clear that President DWIGHT D. EISENHOWER supported the positions taken, and it was certain that a majority of Congress did not. In 1960 the department went a step further, although in a technically ambiguous fashion, when it urged reversal in one of the first SIT-IN cases to reach the Court, *Boynton v. Virginia* (1960). A total of twenty-five amicus curiae briefs were filed between 1955 and 1961. In the meantime, the department took the lead in persuading Congress to give it limited litigation authority in VOTING RIGHTS cases, through the CIVIL RIGHTS ACTS OF 1957 and 1960. It seems clear that the 1957 statute at least was drafted and steered through the Congress

without the participation, and perhaps without the full understanding, of the President.

Under Robert Kennedy (1961–1964), the department increased its activity in the civil rights field, filing nine amicus curiae briefs in the Supreme Court in 1961, nineteen in 1962, and twenty-eight in 1963. The department at the same time drastically increased not only its own litigation in the lower federal courts in voting rights cases but also its intervention as a party in private suits. In one unusual case, despite the general duty of the attorney general to defend federal legislation, the department attacked the constitutionality of a federal statute that contemplated racially separate hospitals. Civil Rights Division lawyers effectively took over the litigation in crucial cases involving schools in New Orleans, Birmingham, and Montgomery; the University of Mississippi at Oxford in 1962; and the University of Alabama in Huntsville and Tuscaloosa in 1963. They also initiated an INJUNCTION suit to protect the Freedom Riders in 1961, and, following that incident, sought to persuade the Interstate Commerce Commission to require the immediate DESEGREGATION of all interstate bus and rail facilities. All these actions were taken with the approval of the President, but despite congressional refusal to authorize Department of Justice initiatives outside the voting area.

The comprehensive CIVIL RIGHTS ACT OF 1964 finally legitimated the kind of litigating activism the department had undertaken, and the VOTING RIGHTS ACT OF 1965 authorized massive federal intervention, outside the judicial system, into areas where racial discrimination in registration or voting persisted. In the meantime, the department was forced, on its own, to seek to protect the physical security of civil rights workers operating in severely hostile territories. The problem was never quite solved. United States marshals and special temporary deputies volunteering from other branches of the department, especially the Immigration and Naturalization Service, and on one occasion the Bureau of Prisons, served at the direction of the attorney general as ad hoc peace-keeping forces. The FBI, a natural source of manpower for such purposes, never let its people be used for police duty. Several times, starting with Little Rock in 1957, troops were required, with the authorization of the President. At such moments, the department was converted from a law office to a crisis-management center, with consequences for its public responsibility that still persist.

If the Department of Justice is free to participate actively in promoting one direction in the formulation of government policy, and of constitutional rule-making in the courts, it can also undertake to move in the opposite direction. Starting in 1981, the department did just that. In the area of civil rights, it opposed positions previously advocated by the government in school, employment, and voting rights matters, both in its own litigation and through amicus curiae briefs. The civil rights organizations thus found themselves in legal combat with their national government. Further, the department moved far outside the scope of its mandated law enforcement function, filing briefs in constitutional litigation opposing assertions by private citizens of their RIGHT OF PRIVACY in abortion decisions in one line of cases, for example, and their rights under the religion clause of the FIRST AMENDMENT in another. The department's earlier role in civil rights matters had been different, because it had reflected not only the policies of several administrations but also the will of the nation as expressed in the RULE OF LAW, under the Reconstruction amendments, especially the EQUAL PROTECTION clause.

The department's new social mission, announced as official policy by Attorney General Smith in a speech in 1981, fortified the Senate in its questioning of what kind of attorney general is appropriate for a Department of Justice possessing the enormous power it now does. Whether the department should be confined to a traditional role of impartial law enforcement or should continue to press for shifts in social and legal policy is an issue that may never be cleanly and finally resolved. Yet the issue is important in a nation where, in the oft-quoted words of ALEXIS DE TOCQUEVILLE, "scarcely any political question arises . . . that is not resolved, sooner or later, into a judicial question."

BURKE MARSHALL
(1986)

Bibliography

BIDDLE, FRANCIS BEVERLEY 1962 *In Brief Authority.* Garden City, N.Y.: Doubleday.

CARR, ROBERT K. (1947) 1964 *Federal Protection of Civil Rights.* Ithaca, N.Y.: Cornell University Press.

CUMMINGS, HOMER STILLE and MCFARLAND, CARL 1937 *Federal Justice.* New York: Macmillan.

DEPARTMENT OF JUSTICE 1980 *Attorney General of the United States.* Washington, D.C.: Department of Justice.

HUSTON, LUTHER A. 1968 *The Department of Justice.* New York: Praeger.

HUSTON, LUTHER A.; MILLER, ARTHUR SELWYN; KRISLOV, SAMUEL; and DIXON, ROBERT G., JR. 1968 *Roles of the Attorney General of the United States.* Washington, D.C.: American Enterprise Institute for Public Policy Research.

NAVASKY, VICTOR S. 1971 *Kennedy Justice.* New York: Atheneum.

ATTORNEY GENERAL OF NEW YORK v. SOTO-LOPEZ
476 U.S. 898 (1986)

The fragmentation of the Supreme Court in this case offered one more proof of the doctrinal disarray of the RIGHT TO TRAVEL. The Court, 6–3, held invalid a New York law giving military veterans a preference in hiring by the state civil service, but limiting the preference to veterans who had been New York residents when they entered the service. Justice WILLIAM J. BRENNAN, for four Justices, concluded that the law was a "penalty" on the right to free interstate migration and thus subject to the test of STRICT SCRUTINY; under this test, the law failed. Chief Justice WARREN E. BURGER and Justice BYRON R. WHITE each concurred separately, following the EQUAL PROTECTION rationale of *Zobel v. Williams* (1982) and concluding that the law's discrimination lacked a RATIONAL BASIS.

Justice SANDRA DAY O'CONNOR, for the three dissenters, argued as she had in *Zobel* that there is no "free-floating right to migrate" and that the proper question was whether the law violated the PRIVILEGES AND IMMUNITIES clause of Article IV. She answered this question in the negative. The law offered only a one-time preference to a relatively small number of applicants, who were treated the same as the vast majority of New Yorkers in seeking state jobs; the preference was not absolute, but added points to examination scores. Thus, the interest at stake could not be considered "fundamental" to interstate harmony. Addressing Justice Brennan's argument on its own terms, she said the same considerations showed that the discrimination was not a "penalty" on interstate travel.

The Brennan and O'Connor views each have a threshold test that requires some importance for the interest lost when a state prefers its own residents. Once past this threshold, however, Justice O'Connor would measure the law's validity against the privileges and immunities rhetoric of intermediate scrutiny rather than the rhetoric of strict scrutiny. Given that no Justice under eighty years of age joined Justice Brennan's opinion and that three members of the *Soto-Lopez* majority have retired from the Court, Justice O'Connor's view appears to be ascending. There is the embarrassment that the text of the privileges and immunities clause prohibits a state's discrimination, not against its own citizens, but against citizens of another state; however, the Court has confronted more serious textual embarrassments in the past, with only a trace of a blush.

KENNETH L. KARST
(1992)

ATTORNEY GENERAL'S COMMISSION ON PORNOGRAPHY

See: Meese Commission

ATTORNEY GENERAL'S LIST

President HARRY S. TRUMAN's Executive Order 9835 inaugurated a comprehensive investigation of all federal employees and made any negative information a potential basis for a security dismissal. A list of subversive organizations was to be prepared by the attorney general, and membership in any listed group was a ground for REASONABLE DOUBT as to an employee's loyalty. The only guidelines the order provided were that any designated organization must be "totalitarian, Fascist, Communist, or subversive," or one "approving the commission of acts of force or violence to deny to others their constitutional rights." During the first year under the order, the attorney general so designated 123 organizations. Over time, and frequently as a result of protests, certain organizations were deleted; new ones were also added. By November 1950, 197 organizations had been so listed, eleven of which were labeled subversive, twelve as seeking to overthrow the government by unconstitutional means, and 132 as communist or communist front.

Critics questioned the constitutionality of the list's compilation and use, on FIRST AMENDMENT grounds, as an "executive BILL OF ATTAINDER" and as involving unfair procedures violating the DUE PROCESS CLAUSE of the Fifth Amendment. The Supreme Court in JOINT ANTI-FASCIST REFUGEE COMMITTEE V. MCGRATH (1951) raised serious questions regarding the fairness of the compilation procedure, and demands grew for suitable hearings to be granted organizations before their inclusion. No procedural changes were instituted in the Truman years, however, and the list continued to be used under the Eisenhower loyalty program. (See LOYALTY-SECURITY PROGRAMS.)

PAUL L. MURPHY
(1986)

Bibliography

BONTECOU, ELEANOR 1953 *The Federal Loyalty-Security Program.* Ithaca, N.Y.: Cornell University Press.

ATTORNEY SPEECH

Restraints on communication have long been a central feature of the regulation of professional activities. The ancient offense of barratry, aimed at one who stirred up quarrels and suits, carried forward into modern regulation of lawyer conduct, including restrictions on advertising and other forms of solicitation of business. Justifications for the restraints cited the need to protect uninformed and vulnerable people from unscrupulous practitioners, as well as the need to preserve the professional character of legal practice. A common element of the notion of professionalism is the idea that the practice is driven, at least in part, by other than commercial values. Advertising of services was widely considered by bar associations that regulate the practice of law to elevate the commercial over the professional dimensions of the practice.

Prohibitions on lawyer advertising and solicitation were protected from constitutional attack so long as the Supreme Court generally adhered to the position that COMMERCIAL SPEECH was outside the ambit of FIRST AMENDMENT protection. However, when the Court abandoned that position in VIRGINIA STATE BOARD OF PHARMACY V. VIRGINIA CONSUMER COUNCIL (1976), it was soon confronted with claims that restrictions on advertising and solicitation by attorneys were unconstitutional. In BATES V. STATE BAR OF ARIZONA (1977), the Court concluded that newspaper advertising of prices associated with routine legal matters, such as uncontested divorces and simple personal bankruptcies, was constitutionally protected. The Court rejected the argument that the state's concern for the professionalism of the bar was adequate to justify prohibition on price advertising, as well as the claim that price advertising was inherently misleading because of the unpredictability of complicating factors in even the most mundane of legal matters. At the same time, the Court acknowledged that some regulation of lawyer advertising might be warranted, and so refused to articulate a broadly protective constitutional rule.

Regulation of client solicitation was presented by two cases decided in 1978. *Ohralik v. Ohio State Bar* (1978) involved the in-person solicitation of business from an accident victim. *Ohralik* displays an ambivalence about the protection of commercial speech that pervades doctrinal development of the subject. Commercial speech regulation brings together speech regulation, which is generally highly suspect, and commercial regulation, which is generally permissible on a showing that public ends are reasonably served. In *Bates*, the Court had emphasized the educational value of the advertising, and characterized the regulation as seeking to accomplish a legitimate end through the device of forcing ignorance on the consumer—kinds of arguments that are associated with standard speech-protective doctrine. In *Ohralik*, the Court emphasized the business regulation aspect of the ban on in-person solicitation, with a focus on the specific harms associated with the practice. It made clear that the move to bring commercial speech under the protection of the First Amendment did not place it on the same plane of importance as, for example, political speech. At least with regard to speech that was primarily concerned to propose a commercial transaction, the high degree of judicial scrutiny associated with core First Amendment values was not warranted.

In re Primus (1978) involved solicitation by letter of a woman who had been sterilized as a condition of receiving medical assistance from the state. The attorney was working with the AMERICAN CIVIL LIBERTIES UNION, and thus presented the Court with the special circumstances of ideological advocacy, where lawsuits are motivated by political considerations rather than pecuniary gain. The Court appeared to find the relation to traditional forms of protected speech controlling, though the effort to distinguish court-awarded fees from client-paid fees demonstrated the difficulty in maintaining a clean distinction between commercial and noncommercial forms of expression.

A few years after *Primus* and *Ohralik,* the Court set out a general approach for testing the regulation of commercial speech, in CENTRAL HUDSON GAS AND ELECTRIC COMPANY V. PUBLIC SERVICE COMMISSION (1980), requiring that regulations of nonmisleading commercial speech regarding legal activities serve a substantial governmental interest in a direct and narrowly focused way. Using the analytical framework established in *Central Hudson,* the Court struck down prohibitions on direct mail advertising, and advertising of special qualifications. More recently, in FLORIDA BAR V. WENT FOR IT, INC. (1995), the Court sustained a prohibition on direct mail solicitation of personal injury and wrongful death clients within thirty days of the event that was the basis for the claim. The Court was persuaded that protecting the sensibilities of accident victims and their families, and the reputation of the legal profession, were interests of sufficient importance to outweigh the attenuated First Amendment value of the interdicted communication.

The organized legal profession has reached an accommodation with the infusion of overt commercialism that followed from *Bates.* Nice questions regarding the balance between commercial and professional values may remain to be resolved, but it is unlikely that they will much alter the regime of lawyer advertising with which we have become familiar.

JAMES M. O'FALLON
(2000)

AUSTIN v. MICHIGAN CHAMBER OF COMMERCE AND THE "NEW CORRUPTION"

The Supreme Court's lack of consistent doctrinal analysis in its treatment of the constitutionality of CAMPAIGN FINANCE regulation was dramatically illustrated in *Austin v. Michigan Chamber of Commerce* (1990). Justice THURGOOD MARSHALL, writing for the majority, upheld the application to the Michigan chamber of commerce of a ban on corporate political expenditures from treasury funds in candidate elections. The Michigan statute permitted such expenditures only when the funds used came from voluntary contributions to political committees (PACs). Articulating a rationale that Justice ANTONIN SCALIA in dissent scoffingly dubbed the "new corruption," the majority concluded that Michigan's purpose was compelling and that the statutory means were narrowly tailored.

Beginning with the seminal campaign finance case BUCKLEY V. VALEO (1976), the only interest the Court had found sufficient to support limits on campaign funding was preventing "corruption" and "improper influence." In subsequent cases the Court interpreted these terms quite narrowly, seemingly limiting their meaning to quid pro quo transactions with candidates. However, in *Austin,* Marshall explained that the statute prevented "a different type of corruption in the political arena: the corrosive and distorting effect of immense aggregations of wealth that are accumulated with the help of the corporate form and that have little or no correlation to the public's support for the corporation's political ideas."

A deviation from the Court's narrow definition of corruption had first been seen several years before *Austin* in *Federal Election Commission v. Massachusetts Citizens for Life (MCFL)* (1986). In that case the Court had invalidated the application of a federal restriction like that in *Austin* when applied to a nonprofit, purely ideological corporation, but suggested in *dicta* that the statute could be constitutionally applied to most other corporations. Quoting from *MCFL,* in *Austin* Marshall explained that corporate " 'resources amassed in the economic marketplace' . . . [permit corporations] to obtain 'an unfair advantage in the political marketplace.' "

The *Austin* majority emphasized that the act was not an "attempt 'to equalize the relative influence of speakers on elections,' " as Justice ANTHONY M. KENNEDY charged in his dissent. The equalization rationale had been consistently rejected by the Court as a basis for contribution and expenditure limitations since *Buckley.* Instead, Marshall explained that the act "ensures that expenditures reflect actual public support for the political ideas espoused by corporations." Such support cannot be assumed when corporate treasury funds rather than voluntary political committee funds are used, unless the corporation is formed purely for ideological purposes. Although the chamber of commerce was in part an ideological corporation, it also performed services for its members. Furthermore, many chamber members were business corporations rather than individuals; thus the chamber could serve as a conduit for corporate expenditures from other corporate treasuries.

By focusing on a lack of actual public support for corporate expression as a necessary element in its determination that the political influence caused by corporate political expenditures is "unfair," the majority in *Austin* seemingly assumed that unequal contributions or expenditures in political races are fair if they reflect inequality of support, but not if they reflect inequality in resources between supporters of candidates. However, the Court had at least implicitly rejected this assumption in previous cases when it invalidated restrictions on individual expenditures on behalf of candidates, amounts candidates could spend on their own behalf, and limits on contributions in ballot measure elections.

Apparently recognizing that their "unfairness" rationale was not consistent with precedent, the *Austin* majority added another element to its doctrinal structure. Marshall explained "that the mere fact that corporations may accumulate large amounts of wealth is not the justification. . . rather [it is] the unique state-conferred corporate structure that facilitates the amassing of large treasuries." He described these advantages as "limited liability, perpetual life, and favorable treatment of the accumulations and distributions of assets."

The Court's attempt to limit the fairness rationale to corporations has been severely criticized. As the dissenting Justices pointed out, wealth accumulated by individuals and by unincorporated associations may also be facilitated by government actions. Furthermore, the Court had ignored the argument that receipt of government benefits justifies restrictions on corporate political expenditures when it invalidated bans on corporate expenditures in ballot measure elections in FIRST NATIONAL BANK OF BOSTON V. BELLOTTI (1978). Indeed, the majority and concurring opinions in *Austin* closely resemble the analyses of the *Bellotti* dissents.

Because the ban in *Bellotti* was significantly more restrictive than the requirement of using a political committee for expenditures, *Austin* is distinguishable. Nevertheless, the general themes of the majorities in both *Bellotti* and *Buckley* are strikingly inconsistent with the doctrinal structure created in *Austin*.

MARLENE ARNOLD NICHOLSON
(2000)

(SEE ALSO: *Corporations and the Constitution; Corporate Citizenship; Corporate Power, Free Speech, and Democracy.*)

Bibliography

EULE, JULIAN N. 1990 Promoting Speaker Diversity: *Austin* and *Metro Broadcasting. Supreme Court Review* 1990:105–130.

WINKLER, ADAM 1998 Beyond *Bellotti. Loyola of Los Angeles Law Review* 32:133–220.

AUTOMOBILE SEARCH

Automobile searches constitute a recognized exception to the FOURTH AMENDMENT's requirement of a SEARCH WARRANT. When police have PROBABLE CAUSE to believe an automobile is transporting contraband, they may, under CARROLL V. UNITED STATES (1925) and BRINEGAR V. UNITED STATES (1941), conduct a WARRANTLESS SEARCH of the vehicle lest it disappear before a warrant can be obtained. Under CHAMBERS V. MARONEY (1970) the search may be delayed until the vehicle has been removed to a police station, though the emergency that attends a search on the road has dissipated. The rules governing automobile searches apply also to mobile homes, according to *California v. Carney* (1985).

Early cases stressed the vehicle's mobility as justification for a warrantless search, but most recent cases have also emphasized an individual's reduced expectation of privacy in an automobile. In contrast to a dwelling, an automobile usually does not serve as a repository of one's belongings; its interior is plainly visible from the outside; and it is commonly stopped by police enforcing inspection and licensing laws. Nonetheless, as the court held in COOLIDGE V. NEW HAMPSHIRE (1971), a car parked on private property may not be searched without a warrant.

Systematic stopping of automobiles at checkpoints for license and registration checks is permitted, but under the Court's decision in *Delaware v. Prouse* (1979), their random stopping is forbidden absent suspicious circumstances. And under *Opperman v. South Dakota* (1976) a lawfully impounded vehicle may be subjected to a warrantless inventory search to safeguard the owner's possessions and protect police from false property claims.

The scope of the warrantless automobile search is as broad as one a magistrate could authorize with a warrant. As the Court held in UNITED STATES V. ROSS (1982), the search may encompass "every part of the vehicle that might contain the object of the search," including the trunk, glove compartment, and closed containers. Furthermore, the Court has applied lenient standards in automobile search cases as to the EVIDENCE needed to establish probable cause. Justice JOHN MARSHALL HARLAN, dissenting in UNITED STATES V. HARRIS (1971), accurately remarked that the problem of automobile searches "has typically been treated as *sui generis* by this Court."

JACOB W. LANDYNSKI
(1986)

Bibliography

LAFAVE, WAYNE R. 1978 *Search and Seizure: A Treatise on the Fourth Amendment*, Vol. 2:508–544, 565–581. St. Paul, Minn.: West Publishing Co.

LANDYNSKI, JACOB W. 1971 The Supreme Court's Search for Fourth Amendment Standards: The Warrantless Search. *Connecticut Bar Journal* 45:30–39.

AUTOMOBILE SEARCH
(Update)

The Supreme Court has interpreted the FOURTH AMENDMENT, which protects persons, houses, papers and effects from unreasonable governmental SEARCH AND SEIZURE, to mean that governments may not conduct unwarranted searches where people have a REASONABLE EXPECTATION OF PRIVACY. In general, to conduct a search invading protected privacy, governmental authorities must obtain a SEARCH WARRANT from a judicial officer, issued after showing there is PROBABLE CAUSE to conclude that EVIDENCE of a crime is discoverable at a certain place. There are some exceptions to this general rule requiring search warrants to conduct a search, and automobile searches constitute one of them.

Obtaining a warrant takes time, and the delay might permit an automobile to leave the JURISDICTION before a warrant was issued or police executed it. All mobile vehicles, including mobile homes capable of ready movement, thus present fleeting search targets. The Supreme Court has also concluded—not without substantial criticism—that because of automobile uses and pervasive governmental regulation of them, persons have a lesser expectation of privacy in automobiles than in homes or offices. Consequently, because of an automobile's mobility and the lesser privacy accorded it, where police have probable cause to believe an automobile is, or contains, evidence of a crime, they may stop it and seize it, or, in the latter case, search it, without a warrant.

Police retain this WARRANTLESS SEARCH authority even when the automobile is not immediately mobile or even likely to be moved. Furthermore, although an automobile is immobilized once seized, thus allowing time to obtain a warrant, the Supreme Court—reasoning that delayed vehicle searches involve no greater privacy invasion than immediate search at the scene—has permitted warrantless automobile searches after immobilization. A rule requiring warrants for delayed searches would incline police to conduct on-scene searches, causing traffic problems or creating other difficulties for the police, particularly in arrest cases involving prisoner transportation. Consequently, when police have probable cause to search an automobile, they may search it immediately on seizure or subsequently.

The nature of the probable cause, and the evidence the police seek, determine the legitimacy and the proper scope of an automobile search. For example, probable cause to believe that a suitcase in a car trunk encloses evidence of crime justifies stopping the car and seizing the suitcase from the trunk, but not a more general car search. By contrast, probable cause to think that an automobile contains marijuana may justify a close search of the entire automobile, including door panels, upholstery, and any containers within the car. Police may thus search any vehicle parts or containers—whether locked, hidden, or generally inaccessible—that may contain the evidence they have probable cause to seek.

Police may stop and search a car when they have probable cause to believe it contains evidence of a crime, whether or not they have probable cause to arrest the driver or passengers. They may also stop a car to arrest the driver or passengers, but probable cause to arrest does not necessarily give rise to probable cause to search the car for evidence of a crime. Arresting automobile occupants for a just-completed convenience-store robbery undoubtedly justifies an extensive search of their car for evidence related to the robbery. Arresting a driver for an outstanding traffic warrant, however, does not justify an automobile search, for the offense is not one involving evidence that might be in the car.

A separate rule governing SEARCHES INCIDENT TO AN ARREST, however, comes into play in automobile cases. To protect themselves and others from harm and to prevent the destruction of evidence, officers may, on taking persons into custody upon ARREST, search them and any areas the arrestees may immediately reach. In arresting automobile drivers or occupants officers may, at least when those arrested are in or near the automobile, search them and any place in the car they may reach. Generally speaking, this rule authorizes a search of any area within the passenger compartment or open to it.

Police may also search vehicles after impounding them. Police sometimes impound an automobile on arrest of the driver or when the vehicle is found unsafe, illegally parked, or abandoned. To protect the owner's property, and the police from property claims, police may, pursuant to standardized procedures, conduct warrantless inventory searches of impounded vehicles and secure the items found within them. The standardized-procedures requirement is designed to ensure that police do not use their inventory search authority as a pretext to search vehicles when they lack probable cause.

GARY GOODPASTER
(1992)

Bibliography

LAFAVE, WAYNE R. 1987 *Search and Seizure: A Treatise on the Fourth Amendment.* St. Paul, Minn.: West Publishing Co.

AUTOMOBILE SEARCH AND TRAFFIC STOPS

See: Traffic Stops

AVERY v. MIDLAND COUNTY
390 U.S. 474 (1968)

In this case, the Supreme Court held that the ONE PERSON, ONE VOTE rule required equal districts in a Texas county commissioners' court election. The decision, in effect, extended the rule's sway from the fifty states to such of the 81,304 units of government as possessed "general responsibility and power for local affairs." Justices JOHN M. HARLAN, ABE FORTAS, and POTTER STEWART dissented, arguing that the Court had overreached its APPELLATE JURISDICTION; that a rigidly uniform one person, one vote rule ignored the special needs functions of most local governments; and that it would discourage joint activity by metropolitan units, thereby undermining the practical benefits of state-level reapportionment.

WARD E. Y. ELLIOTT
(1986)

AVOIDANCE DOCTRINE

The avoidance doctrine is a group of judicially created techniques employed to avoid CONSTITUTIONAL INTERPRETATION. The Supreme Court developed this special approach to JUDICIAL REVIEW to restrain federal courts from developing constitutional law unnecessarily. The avoidance theme dates back to the earliest days of the Court, when the Court identified the Article III judicial review power. Justice LOUIS D. BRANDEIS set out the modern avoidance doctrine in ASHWANDER V. TENNESSEE VALLEY AUTHORITY (1936). Avoidance is predicated on SEPARATION OF POWERS concerns; FEDERALISM concerns; the continued political viability of courts staffed with unelected, life-tenured judges; the final and delicate nature of judicial review; and the paramount importance of constitutional adjudication.

The avoidance doctrine consists of a series of seven rules that are closely related to other restraints on federal courts. Several of the rules mirror the constitutional and prudential aspects of the Court's heightened modern JUSTICIABILITY standards. One important avoidance rule encourages courts to look for nonconstitutional grounds to dispose of a lawsuit, even if jurisdiction exists.

Obviously, federal courts do render constitutional decisions. When they do so, another avoidance technique urges them to rule no more broadly than the precise facts require. Avoidance suggests using measured constitutional steps and narrowly framed relief. Avoidance cautions against general legal advice or broad rules to guide future conduct.

The Court's use of the avoidance doctrine has been inconsistent and at times politically driven. For example,

Brandeis and Justice FELIX FRANKFURTER deemed the avoidance doctrine essential to promote deference to the NEW DEAL Congress and executive branch. These Justices were responding to the JUDICIAL ACTIVISM of the conservative Court during the *Lochner* era, which frequently struck down state and federal legislative and executive programs. One year prior to the COURT-PACKING plan of President FRANKLIN D. ROOSEVELT, Brandeis in *Ashwander* warned that fallible judges should use judicial review sparingly. As the liberal majority of the WARREN COURT recognized new constitutional rights, conservative judges and scholars praised avoidance as a foundational rule of judicial restraint.

Although avoidance techniques prove sound on occasion, sometimes avoidance fails to protect constitutional rights sufficiently. Avoidance can engender great delay and increased expense for securing rights. Narrowed rulings provide little guidance, so that constitutional rights are not protected uniformly. Some avoidance measures actually fail to promote deference to other decisionmakers by disguising the role of courts in interpreting the Constitution.

Additionally, the avoidance doctrine is a flexible approach to judicial review. Judges must determine when reaching a constitutional question is necessary. Courts invoke avoidance techniques more frequently in cases involving sensitive social issues such as RACIAL DISCRIMINATION or ABORTION, and in cases in which the Court's countermajoritarian role is an important protection against the more politically responsive areas of government. For example, the avoidance doctrine counsels that judges should interpret statutes to avoid constitutional problems. During the era of MCCARTHYISM the Court refused to clearly define FIRST AMENDMENT rights. Instead, it eventually used the avoidance doctrine to interpret narrowly a congressional act prohibiting SEDITION, concluding that Congress did not intend to prohibit mere words of Communist proponents. Although this avoided a direct collision with Congress, the Court was not deferential to congressional intent. Moreover, it did not offer speech constitutional protection, thus leaving open possibilities for future political targeting of unpopular speakers.

To protect themselves from charges of antidemocratic judicial activism, federal judges must take the avoidance doctrine seriously. But avoidance entails costs and it should be scrutinized carefully. When federal judges fail to exercise the power of judicial review in politically sensitive cases, they can abdicate their constitutional responsibility to protect enduring rights against temporal repressive majorities. And when judges use avoidance techniques inconsistently, they do not provide justice evenhandedly.

LISA A. KLOPPENBERG
(2000)

Bibliography

BICKEL, ALEXANDER M. 1986 *The Least Dangerous Branch: The Supreme Court at the Bar of Politics,* 2nd. ed. New Haven, Conn.: Yale University Press.

GINSBURG, RUTH BADER 1992 Speaking in a Judicial Voice. *New York University Law Review* 67:1185–1209.

GUNTHER, GERALD 1964 The Subtle Vices of the "Passive Virtues"—A Comment on Principle and Expediency in Judicial Review. *Columbia Law Review* 64:1–25.

KLOPPENBERG, LISA A. 1996 Avoiding Serious Constitutional Doubts: The Supreme Court's Construction of Statutes Raising Free Speech Concerns. *UC Davis Law Review* 30:1–93.

SCHAUER, FREDERICK 1996 *Ashwander* Revisited. *Supreme Court Review* 1995:71–98.

B

BACKUS, ISAAC
(1724–1806)

A Baptist minister in Massachusetts from 1756, Isaac Backus gained increasing recognition as an agent, chief spokesman, and campaigner for RELIGIOUS LIBERTY for his New England co-religionists, who were harassed by hostile local officials' narrow interpretation and restrictive implementation of laws exempting Baptists from contributing to the support of Congregational churches. In pamphlets and newspapers, in an appearance before the Massachusetts delegation to the First Continental Congress, and in promoting civil disobedience by encouraging Baptists not to comply with statutes dealing with support of churches, he struggled unsuccessfully to abolish public tax support for religion.

More pietist than civil libertarian, Backus sought religious freedom primarily to prevent state interference with the church. He supported his arguments by citing the Massachusetts Charter's grant of religious liberty to all Protestants and by pointing up the contrast between local oppression of Baptists and New Englanders' charges of English tyranny. By 1780, however, he had come to affirm religious liberty as a NATURAL RIGHT.

As a delegate to the Massachusetts ratifying convention, Backus supported the federal Constitution, convinced that its prohibition against tests precluded any ESTABLISHMENT OF RELIGION. He showed little or no interest in the passage of the FIRST AMENDMENT. Backus equated religious liberty almost entirely with voluntary choice of churches and voluntary support of ministers. He perceived America as a Christian country, did not object to Sabbath laws or to public days of prayer, and approved a Massachusetts law requiring legislators to profess Christianity. Such views typified contemporary evangelical opinion.

THOMAS CURRY
(1986)

Bibliography

McLAUGHLIN, WILLIAM G. 1967 *Isaac Backus and the American Pietistic Tradition.* Boston: Little, Brown.
———, ed. 1968 *Isaac Backus on Church, State, and Calvinism: Pamphlets, 1754–1789.* Cambridge, Mass.: Harvard University Press.

BADGES OF SERVITUDE

There was truth in the claim of SLAVERY's defenders that many a northern "wage slave" worked under conditions less favorable than those of his enslaved counterpart down South. The evil of slavery was not primarily its imposition of hard work but its treatment of a person as if he or she were a thing. The laws governing slaves carried out this basic theme by systematically imposing a wide range of legal disabilities on slaves, preventing them not only from entering into the public life of the community (by voting, being members of juries, or speaking in public meetings) but also from owning property, making contracts, or even learning to read and write. All these disabilities were designed not merely to preserve a system of bondage to service, but to serve as badges of servitude, symbolizing the slaves' degraded status. In a moment of racist candor, Chief Justice ROGER B. TANEY extended this view of the stigmatized status of slaves to all black persons, slave or free. His opinion for the Supreme Court in DRED SCOTT V. SANDFORD (1857) spoke of blacks as "a subordinate and inferior class of beings," upon whom had been impressed "deep and enduring marks of inferiority and degradation."

Although slaves were often physically branded, the "marks" of which Taney spoke were metaphorical; they were the aggregate of legal restrictions imposed on slaves. When slavery was abolished by the THIRTEENTH AMENDMENT (1865), those marks did not disappear. The amendment, however, did not stop with the abolition of slavery and involuntary servitude; it also empowered Congress to enforce the abolition. From an early time it was argued that the amendment authorized Congress to enact laws to eradicate not only slavery itself but the "badges of servitude" as well. This view was at first accepted in principle by the Supreme Court, and then rejected in the early twentieth century. However, in JONES V. ALFRED H. MAYER CO. (1968), the Court reverted to the earlier interpretation, concluding that RACIAL DISCRIMINATION was the sort of "badge of servitude" that Congress could prohibit.

In the meanwhile, a parallel doctrinal development has become apparent. The CIVIL RIGHTS ACT OF 1866 and the FOURTEENTH AMENDMENT both recognized the CITIZENSHIP of the freed slaves. Both were designed to end the notion of superior and inferior classes of persons and to replace a system of sociopolitical subordination with the status of equal citizenship. (See EQUAL PROTECTION OF THE LAWS.) Because the principle of equal citizenship protects against the imposition of stigma, it often operates in the same symbolic universe that produced badges of servitude. To give full effect to the symbol and substance of equal citizenship is one of the major challenges of the nation's third century.

KENNETH L. KARST
(1986)

Bibliography

KINOY, ARTHUR   1967   The Constitutional Right of Negro Freedom. *Rutgers Law Review* 21:387–441.

BAD TENDENCY TEST

In 1920 New York convicted Benjamin Gitlow of violating its statute prohibiting "advocating, advising or teaching the doctrine that organized government should be overthrown by force." Gitlow had published in the journal *Revolutionary Age* a "Left Wing Manifesto," thirty-four pages of Marxist rhetoric calling for class struggle leading to revolution and the dictatorship of the proletariat.

In GITLOW V. NEW YORK (1925) Gitlow's counsel argued in the Supreme Court that since the manifesto contained no direct INCITEMENT to criminal action, Gitlow must have been convicted under the "bad tendency test." That test was borrowed from the eighteenth-century English law of SEDITIOUS LIBEL which made criticism of government criminal because such criticism might tend to contribute to government's eventual collapse.

This bad tendency test ran counter to the CLEAR AND PRESENT DANGER test of SCHENCK V. UNITED STATES (1919). In *Gitlow* Justice EDWARD SANFORD virtually adopted the bad tendency test for instances in which a legislature had decided that a particular variety of speech created a sufficient danger. Even though there was no evidence of any effect resulting from the Manifesto's publication, the Court stressed that its language constituted advocacy of

mass action which shall progressively foment industrial disturbances, and, through . . . mass action, overthrow . . . government. . . . The immediate danger is none the less real and substantial because the effect of a given utterance cannot be accurately foreseen. . . . A single revolutionary spark may kindle a fire that, smoldering for a time, may burst into a sweeping and destructive conflagration. . . . [The State] cannot reasonably be required to defer the adoption of measures for its own peace and safety until the revolutionary utterances lead to . . . imminent and immediate danger of its own destruction.

Justices OLIVER WENDELL HOLMES and LOUIS D. BRANDEIS dissented in *Gitlow*, invoking the clear and present danger test. When that test came to dominate the Court's FIRST AMENDMENT opinions in the 1930s and early 1940s, the bad tendency test seemed to be overthrown.

Nevertheless much of Sanford's approach survived. Judge LEARNED HAND's "discounting formula" as adopted in DENNIS V. UNITED STATES (1951) allows speech to be suppressed "where the gravity of the evil, discounted by its improbability" justifies suppression. As *Dennis* itself illustrates, if the danger is painted as sufficiently grave, speech may be suppressed even if there is a very low probability that the evil will occur or that the particular speech in question will contribute to that occurrence. In *Dennis* the Court replaced the present danger test with the requirement that where an organized subversive group exists, the group intends to bring about overthrow "as speedily as the circumstances would permit." Such an approach echoed Sanford's plea that the government need not wait until the danger of revolution is imminent.

MARTIN SHAPIRO
(1986)

(SEE ALSO: *Freedom of Speech; Subversive Activity.*)

Bibliography

CHAFEE, ZECHARIAH, JR.   (1941) 1969   *Free Speech in the United States.* New York: Atheneum.

LINDE, HANS   1970   "Clear and Present Danger" Reexamined:

Dissonance in the Brandenburg Concerto. *Stanford Law Review* 22:1163–1186.

BAEHR v. LEWIN
852 P.2d 44 (Hawai'i 1993)

Three same-sex couples claimed that Hawai'i had violated their rights by denying them MARRIAGE licenses. The Hawai'i Supreme Court agreed, holding that denying marriage licenses to same-sex couples is unconstitutional unless the state can show a compelling reason to do so. The court's argument rested on the EQUAL PROTECTION clause of the Hawai'i state constitution, which prohibits SEX DISCRIMINATION. The court held that the marriage statute imposed a sex-based classification, because it "restricts the marital relation to a male and a female." The court therefore held that the statute would be unconstitutional unless the state could show that this classification was necessary to some COMPELLING STATE INTEREST and remanded the case for a trial on that question. (Because the decision was based on the state constitution and raised no federal issues, it could not be appealed to the U.S. Supreme Court.)

In 1996, as expected, the state lost at trial. It appealed the case once more to the Hawai'i Supreme Court. While the appeal was pending, the INJUNCTION was stayed, so that SAME-SEX MARRIAGE continued to be effectively prohibited in Hawai'i. In November 1998, the Hawai'i electorate ratified an amendment to the state constitution providing that the legislature has the power to reserve marriage to opposite-sex couples. There was disagreement about whether the result in the case would be affected by the amendment absent new legislation, but in December 1999, the court held that the statute was now valid. The court did not, however, retract the analysis set forth in its earlier opinion.

The argument that persuaded the court is unfamiliar but clear. If Lucy is permitted to marry Fred, but Ricky may not marry Fred, then Ricky is being discriminated against on the basis of his sex. This argument, however, had always lost in court before *Baehr*. (The Hawai'i plaintiffs did not even bother to make it, and the court had to come up with the argument by itself.) One counterargument had always been made by courts in other states: if lesbians and gay men are equally discriminated against, then there is no sex discrimination. This counterargument continued to persuade the one dissenting judge in *Baehr*. The legal innovation in *Baehr* was that the court noticed that this counterargument was the same one the U.S. Supreme Court had rejected in LOVING V. VIRGINIA, the 1967 case in which it struck down a law forbidding interracial marriage. Virginia had defended its MISCEGENATION law

with the argument that, although it was true that blacks were forbidden to marry whites, whites were equally forbidden to marry blacks. The U.S. Supreme Court firmly rejected this argument; if prohibited conduct is defined by reference to a characteristic, then the prohibition is not neutral with respect to that characteristic. If this argument is accepted in the same-sex marriage context, then it has important implications for federal constitutional law, for classifications based on sex require an "exceedingly persuasive justification" to be upheld. The principles established in *Baehr* thus imply presumptive invalidity for all laws that discriminate on the basis of SEXUAL ORIENTATION.

ANDREW KOPPELMAN
(2000)

BAIL

Bail is the prevailing method by which American law has dealt with a puzzling problem: what to do with a person accused of crime during the time between arrest and trial? Imprisonment imposed before trial subjects one who has not been and may never be convicted to disabilities that have all the attributes of punishment, disrupts employment and family ties, hampers the preparation of a defense, increases pressures to plead guilty, and, compared with bailed defendants, may prejudice trial outcomes and lead to more severe sentences. The development of the institution of bail over centuries of English history and its acceptance and liberalization in colonial America was an attempt to mitigate these handicaps and, by affording an opportunity for pretrial release, to emphasize the values underlying the presumption of innocence while also minimizing the risk that an accused who was not jailed would flee and evade justice. Thus bail makes possible pretrial release if the accused can provide financial security, which is subject to forfeiture if the conditions of the bond are violated.

Traditionally, the amount of security is set in an amount deemed by the court to be sufficient to deter flight and enforce compliance with the court's orders. The defendant's own money or property may be put up for this purpose, but in modern times the prevalent method of providing the required security is the purchase by the defendant of a commercial bail bond for a premium, usually about ten percent of the prescribed security. Conditional release on bail may also be available at later stages of the criminal process, for example, pending APPEAL after conviction or pending a hearing on parole or probation revocation, but the predominant use of bail and the most difficult questions raised by its administration relate to the pretrial period.

A "right to bail" is not a right to pretrial release but

merely a right to have a court set the amount of the security to be required. A majority of criminal defendants have little or no financial ability to provide security. Furthermore, bondsmen can and often do refuse to bond those they regard as poor risks even if the amount of the premium is tendered. Thus a high rate of pretrial detention of those unable to provide bail has long been a characteristic feature of American criminal justice. Since the early 1960s a widespread bail reform movement has introduced procedures designed to reduce the dependence of the traditional system on the requirement of financial security, but these changes have supplemented rather than replaced money bail, which remains a dominant feature of the system.

The only direct reference to bail in the Constitution is the brief clause in the Eighth Amendment that "excessive bail shall not be required." There are serious problems in the interpretation of the scope of this limited clause and its application under modern conditions. On its face the language is only a restriction of the amount of security which a judge can require, and poses no constitutional barrier to legislative or judicial denial of bail. Alternatively, the clause has been read as necessarily implying a right to bail, as otherwise the clause is left with little significance.

There is no easy resolution of this problem. To infer from the clause a right to bail that is protected from legislative abrogation reads into it words that are not there and necessarily leaves the scope of such a right uncertain. But a literal interpretation renders the clause superfluous, as PROCEDURAL DUE PROCESS OF LAW would protect against judicial abuse of a legislatively granted right to bail. A narrow reading also takes no account of the long history of what the Supreme court in *Stack v. Boyle* (1951) called the "traditional right to freedom before conviction . . . secured only after centuries of struggle," and leaves in a constitutional vacuum a critical stage of the criminal process which has significant impact on the implementation of other constitutionally protected rights of defendants. For nearly two centuries the question has remained unresolved, for two main reasons. First, the transitory nature of detention and the poverty of most defendants unable to raise bail pose barriers to appellate review. Second, until 1984 federal statutory law and the constitutions or laws of most states guaranteed a pretrial right to bail in all but some capital cases, thereby rendering it unnecessary to reach the constitutional issue. Little direct evidence of what was intended by the framers of the clause can be found in the sparse and inconclusive legislative history of the Eighth Amendment's proposal by the First Congress. At the same time that Representative JAMES MADISON introduced the amendment in the House, a Senate committee was preparing the JUDICIARY ACT OF 1789, which included a right to bail in all but capital cases. Both bail

provisions were uncontroversial and undebated, and both went their separate ways to enactment. There is no indication that anyone in Congress recognized the anomaly of incorporating the basic right governing pretrial practice in a statute while enshrining in the Constitution the derivative protection against judicial abuse of that right. The anomaly is compounded by Madison's insistence, in the House debates on the BILL OF RIGHTS, that whereas England's Bill of Rights raised a barrier only against the power of the Crown, "a different opinion prevails in the United States," where protection against abuse "must be levelled against the Legislative" branch. What we do know, however, about the origin of the clause and the context in which it arose sheds some light relevant to its interpretation.

The words of the bail clause were taken verbatim from the revolutionary VIRGINIA DECLARATION OF RIGHTS of 1776, drafted by GEORGE MASON, and by him taken, with the substitution of "shall" for "ought," from the 1689 English Bill of Rights. Mason states that his purpose in drafting the Virginia Declaration was to provide effectual securities for the essential rights of CIVIL LIBERTY, and it is difficult to believe that he intended to deal with the issue of pretrial liberty by words that, literally construed, offer no security against its denial. Although steeped in English constitutional history, Mason was not a lawyer, may not have understood the complexity of the English law, and may have thought that the clause encapsulated the whole subject. In its English context, however, the excessive bail clause in the 1689 Bill of Rights was the culmination of a chain of events that went back to MAGNA CARTA and of a long succession of detailed statutes that established the scope of the right to bail.

This development was climaxed in the seventeenth century by three important acts of Parliament which had been provoked by abuses in the administration of bail law. In 1628, by the PETITION OF RIGHT, the provision of Magna Carta that "no freeman shall be . . . detained in prison . . . unless by the law of the land" was made applicable to pretrial detention and thus was not limited, as the Crown had maintained in *Darnell's Case* (1627), to imprisonment only after conviction. Next, the HABEAS CORPUS ACT OF 1679, after referring to prolonged detentions caused by the inability of detainees to get any judge to set and take bail, mandated a speedy procedure for this purpose. Finally, the Bill of Rights of 1689 sought to curb the judicial abuse of requiring excessive bail. Thus the English structure was tripartite, and protection against denial of pretrial release through the prohibition of excessive bail must be read in the context not only of the extraordinary procedure provided by HABEAS CORPUS but also with reference to the long history of parliamentary bail statutes. Habeas corpus, of course, was included in the body of the American constitution, but the substantive right to bail was omitted. The argument that this omission seems to have been inadvertent at a time when the Framers were preoccupied with other, more immediately pressing issues, and that such a substantive right must have been the intent of the clause, is the core of the historical case for a broad interpretation.

Beginning with the MASSACHUSETTS BODY OF LIBERTIES in 1641, most of the American colonies reduced the number of capital offenses and otherwise liberalized the English law of bail, and in 1682 Pennsylvania extended the right to bail to those charged with all offenses except those capital cases "where the proof is evident or the presumption great," language that was widely copied in state constitutions after Independence. Besides the Judiciary Act of 1789, the closest contemporary record reflecting what seems to have been a widespread political approach to the right to bail, at the time that the Bill of Rights was before the First Congress, was the enactment two years earlier by the CONTINENTAL CONGRESS of the NORTHWEST ORDINANCE for the governance of the territories beyond the Appalachians. In substantially the same language as that used in Pennsylvania nearly a century earlier, the ordinance made bailable as of right those charged with any except capital offenses.

Given the widespread right to bail that had been provided by federal statute and state law, it is not surprising that until recent years there has been a dearth of litigation asserting an Eighth Amendment constitutional right to pretrial bail. The few occasions on which the Supreme Court has dealt with the subject have not required a resolution of the issue, but there are inconclusive and inconsistent OBITER DICTA in some of the cases. On the one hand, in *Schilb v. Kuebel* (1971), which upheld a bail reform statute, the Court said that "Bail, of course, is basic to our system of law," and earlier a unanimous Court in *Stack v. Boyle* had stressed the importance of providing for pretrial release lest "the presumption of innocence, secured only after centuries of struggle, would lose its meaning." But in *Carlson v. Landon*, decided in the same term as *Stack*, a 5–4 Court held that alien communists were not entitled to bail pending adjudication of DEPORTATION charges against them. Most of the *Carlson* majority's long opinion concerned the limited rights of ALIENS, the classification of deportation as a noncriminal proceeding, and the validity and exercise of the attorney general's discretionary delegated power to bail aliens; but it also included six sentences implying that even in criminal proceedings the Eighth Amendment does not afford a right to bail. Although frequently cited, considering the noncriminal emphasis in the case and the brevity and superficiality of the Eighth Amendment analysis, the *Carlson* obiter dictum warrants little weight. Probably more significant is SCHALL The Court stressed the noncriminal classification of the

proceeding; it noted the limited rights of juveniles compared with adults and the detention's very limited duration; and it observed that there is no historical tradition of a right to juvenile pretrial release and that the detention practice that was upheld has existed throughout the country. Despite all these distinguishing characteristics, the weight given to the importance of preventing pretrial crime and to the possibility of its prediction is suggestive of how the Court might deal with parallel questions in an adult denial-of-bail criminal case.

A number of other controversial issues in pretrial bail law will remain whether or not the Supreme Court infers some form of a right to bail from the Eighth Amendment. The 1984 federal Bail Reform Act and some state constitutional or statutory amendments permit preventive detention of those charged with noncapital offenses if a court finds that pretrial release would pose a danger of future criminal activity. Besides extending the traditional practice which has denied the right to bail only in some capital cases, these enactments also breach long-standing PRECEDENT that only the risk of failure to appear for trial or other limited conduct directly impairing the court's processes, such as threats against witnesses, is relevant to the bail decision. Although the change is in some sense more theoretical than real, direct authorization for judges to explore the uncharted waters of predictions of future dangerousness will in practice undermine the values that gave rise to bail and result in further increases in the proportion of defendants jailed pending trial.

Bail is not constitutionally excessive if the amount does not exceed that normally required for the charged offense. These normal amounts are sufficient to result in very high rates of detention and to mask the existence of de facto preventive detention for those unable to post bond. It was a concern for more equal justice in criminal law administration and a reaction against this discrimination against the poor that gave rise to the bail reform movement of the 1960s and the widespread introduction of other incentives and sanctions as substitute deterrents for money bail. Although this reform, unevenly and incompletely implemented, has had some success, the number of those detained has remained high and is growing. The issue of blatant WEALTH DISCRIMINATION in bail law administration remains to be resolved.

CALEB FOOTE
(1986)

Bibliography

FLEMMING, ROY B. 1982 *Punishment before Trial: An Organizational Perspective of Felony Bail Processes.* New York: Longman's.

FOOTE, CALEB 1985 The Coming Constitutional Crisis in Bail.

University of Pennsylvania Law Review 113:959–999, 1125–1185.

FREED, DANIEL J. and WALD, PATRICIA M. 1964 *Bail in the United States, 1964.* Washington, D.C.: U.S. Department of Justice.

TRIBE, LAURENCE H. 1970 An Ounce of Detention. *Virginia Law Review* 56:371–407.

BAIL
(Update)

In 1986, when the *Encyclopedia of the American Constitution* was first published, some scholars maintained that the Eighth Amendment's prohibition of "excessive bail" implied a right to bail in all noncapital cases. Others argued that the clause afforded no right to bail in any case. According to this second group, the Eighth Amendment imposed no limitation on Congress's power to deny bail; it governed only the amount of bail when bail was permitted.

Strongly supported by the language of the Supreme Court in *Stack v. Boyle* (1951), many scholars also maintained that the only legitimate purpose of bail under the Eighth Amendment (and of detention when an accused could not secure his or her pretrial release) was to prevent flight or else to protect the integrity of the trial process in other ways (notably, by preventing the intimidation of witnesses). Other scholars contended that a court also could lawfully consider the risk that a defendant would commit crimes during the pretrial period in setting bail and, perhaps, in denying pretrial release altogether. The principal unresolved issues posed by the Eighth Amendment were whether the amendment implied a right to bail and what standards, criteria, or objectives a court could consider in determining whether bail was "excessive."

The Supreme Court addressed these issues and the due process issues posed by pretrial PREVENTIVE DETENTION in UNITED STATES V. SALERNO (1987). *Salerno* upheld the constitutionality of the Federal Bail Reform Act of 1984, which permits detention without bond in some federal cases when neither bail nor other conditions of release "will reasonably assure . . . the safety of any other person and the community."

Holding that the Eighth Amendment does not afford a right to bail in all noncapital cases, the Court quoted the suggestion of *Carlson v. Landon* (1952) that the amendment does not create a right to bail in any case. Finding it unnecessary to resolve this issue, however, the Court indicated that the amendment might create a right to bail in some cases and not others, depending on the strength of the government's reasons for denying bail. The defendants had argued that a denial of bail could be regarded as "infinite" bail, and the Court did not reject this conten-

tion. It held, however, that infinite bail was not always excessive. The Court also concluded that dangerousness, as well as the risk of flight, could be considered in judging the propriety of pretrial detention.

The Supreme Court resolved the Fifth Amendment due process issues in *Salerno* through the sort of cost-benefit analysis that has characterized much of its recent constitutional jurisprudence. The Court's opinion noted "the individual's strong interest in liberty" and declared that this interest was both "important" and "fundamental." The opinion concluded, however, that "the government's interest in community safety can . . . outweigh an individual's liberty interest."

The phrase "liberty interest" first appeared in a Supreme Court opinion in 1972. Its author, Justice WILLIAM H. REHNQUIST, later became chief justice and wrote the Salerno opinion. Use of the phrase "liberty interest," which seems to mark liberty as the appropriate subject of a utilitarian trade, has increased greatly in recent years.

Critics of the Supreme Court's cost-benefit analysis suggest that even the most brutal governmental actions may advance "compelling" interests and that some governmental impositions cannot be justified by countervailing public gains. For example, if psychologists developed the capacity to predict future criminality with substantial accuracy, the detention of people who, unlike the defendants in *Salerno*, had not been charged with any crime might be justified through the same analysis that the Supreme Court used to justify the preventive detention in Salerno. The liberty interests of the people detained for failing the psychologists' predictive tests would not differ from the liberty interests of the people detained under current law, and the governmental interest in preventing future crime would also be identical.

An analysis that balances the burdens imposed by a governmental action against the public gain produced by this action seems to omit traditional considerations of individual responsibility and opportunity. This analysis also departs from a tradition-based "fundamental fairness" approach to the due process clause—an approach that might have been more likely to invalidate the detention in *Salerno*. For more than 300 years following the Pennsylvania Frame of Government in 1682, Americans withheld bail only in capital cases and then only when the proof of guilt was "evident and the presumption great." These Americans apparently chose to run greater risks than cost-benefit analysis could have justified.

The Supreme Court recognized that its cost-benefit analysis would not have justified the detention in *Salerno* if this detention had qualified as punishment. However strong the government's interest in imposing criminal punishment, the Constitution precludes it unless the accused has been afforded a trial at which the government must establish his or her guilt beyond a REASONABLE DOUBT and must comply with other constitutional requirements. Examining Congress's intent, the Court concluded that the objective of the Bail Reform Act was to "prevent danger to the community" and that this objective was "regulatory, not penal."

The Court did suggest that "detention in a particular case might become excessively prolonged, and therefore punitive." It is difficult to envision how Congress's motive could change from regulatory to punitive at some moment in a case of prolonged detention, and the Court offered no hint of when this metamorphosis of LEGISLATIVE INTENT might occur. The Bail Reform Act itself imposes no limit on the length of preventive pretrial detention, and the deadlines of the Federal Speedy Trial Act are flexible. In one recent case, an appellate court declined to find a sixteen-month period of pretrial preventive detention unlawful per se. The Supreme Court's view of retrospectively changing legislative motive may be difficult to understand, but it is likely to save some defendants from detention for a year or more without trial.

Federal courts have made extensive use of the preventive detention provisions of the Bail Reform Act, and both the percentage of defendants detained before trial and the populations of federal pretrial detention facilities have increased substantially. Although many states have enacted preventive detention measures as well, judges and prosecutors appear to have used these state statutes less frequently. One reason may be that the state statutes typically lack a significant provision of the federal act: "The judicial officer may not impose a financial condition that results in the pretrial detention of the person." In state courts, judges and prosecutors may find it easier to set high bail and thereby accomplish preventive detention sub rosa than to comply with the procedural requirements of local preventive detention legislation.

Since the 1960s, bail reform has proceeded from two directions. Judges have released more defendants on recognizance and on nonfinancial conditions, and, especially in the federal courts, judges have detained more defendants without the option of posting bond. Both reforms have made the wealth of defendants less important in determining the probability of their pretrial incarceration, and even the opponents of preventive detention might agree that dangerousness is a less offensive basis for detention than poverty. Both currents of reform move the United States closer to the patterns of pretrial release and detention found in European nations, where bail either is not authorized or has fallen into disuse.

ALBERT W. ALSCHULER
(1992)

(SEE ALSO: *Compelling State Interest; Pennsylvania Colonial Charters; Procedural Due Process of Law, Criminal.*)

Bibliography

ALSCHULER, ALBERT W. 1986 Preventive Pretrial Detention and the Failure of Interest-Balancing Approaches to Due Process. *Michigan Law Review* 85:510–569.

UNITED STATES DEPARTMENT OF JUSTICE, BUREAU OF JUSTICE STATISTICS 1988 *Pretrial Release and Detention: The Bail Reform Act of 1984.* Washington, D.C.: U.S. Department of Justice.

BAILEY v. ALABAMA
219 U.S. 219 (1911)

After the demise of the BLACK CODES some southern states resorted to other devices to insure a steady supply of labor. One Alabama statute effectively converted civil breach of contract into the crime of fraud by making it *prima facie* EVIDENCE of intent to defraud that a worker accept an advance on wages and then neither repay the advance nor perform the work contracted for.

In *Bailey* the Supreme Court held (7–2) that the Alabama law constituted a system of PEONAGE in violation of the THIRTEENTH AMENDMENT's prohibition of involuntary servitude. Justice CHARLES EVANS HUGHES, for the majority, argued that involuntary servitude was a broader concept than SLAVERY and included schemes for enforced labor.

Justice OLIVER WENDELL HOLMES, dissenting, argued that Alabama was acting within its power to define crimes and their punishments.

DENNIS J. MAHONEY
(1986)

BAILEY v. DREXEL FURNITURE CO.
(Child Labor Tax Case)
259 U.S. 20 (1922)

Following the decision invalidating the KEATING-OWEN CHILD LABOR ACT in HAMMER V. DAGENHART (1918), Congress passed a new law in 1919, this time based on its TAXING POWER. The statute levied a ten percent tax on the net profits of mines or factories that employed underage children. Congress had previously used the tax power for social and economic purposes, and the Supreme Court consistently had upheld such enactments, notably in VEAZIE BANK V. FENNO (1869) and MCCRAY V. UNITED STATES (1904).

When the Child Labor Tax Case was decided in 1922, only Justice JOHN H. CLARKE dissented, without opinion, from Chief Justice WILLIAM HOWARD TAFT's opinion for the Court. Taft concluded that the obvious regulatory effect of the law infringed on state JURISDICTION over PRODUCTION and that *Hammer v. Dagenhart* was controlling. Congress, he said, had imposed a tax that was really a penalty for the purpose of reaching a local subject. Like the Justices in *Hammer*, Taft feared the destruction of federalism. "To give such magic to the word "tax," he said, would remove all constitutional limitations upon Congress and abolish "the sovereignty of the States." He distinguished the Court's earlier rulings upholding federal taxes on state bank notes, oleomargarine, and narcotics by insisting that they had involved regulations or prohibitions that were "reasonably adapted to the collection of the tax." Taft, in fact, advanced the unhistorical proposition that the regulatory purposes of the taxes in those cases were only "incidental" to a primary motive of raising revenue.

The Child Labor Tax Case was favorably cited in UNITED STATES V. BUTLER (1936), but a year later, in SONZINSKY V. UNITED STATES, the Court upheld a federal licensing tax on firearms dealers. Justice HARLAN FISKE STONE's opinion sharply repudiated Taft's, contending that the incidental effect of regulation was irrelevant. Courts, he said, were incompetent to question congressional motives; specifically, they should not measure a tax's regulatory effect and use it to argue that Congress had exercised another power denied by the Constitution. Similar arguments were registered in UNITED STATES V. KAHRIGER (1953) when the Court sustained a federal tax on gambling businesses.

STANLEY I. KUTLER
(1986)

Bibliography

WOOD, STEPHEN 1968 *Constitutional Politics in the Progressive Era: Child Labor and the Law.* Chicago: University of Chicago Press.

BAKER v. CARR
369 U.S. 186 (1962)

Chief Justice EARL WARREN considered *Baker v. Carr* the most important case decided by the Warren Court. Its holding was cryptic: "the right [to equal districts in the Tennessee legislature] is within the reach of judicial protection under the FOURTEENTH AMENDMENT." Many people expected REAPPORTIONMENT under *Baker* to vitalize American democracy. Others feared that it would snare the judiciary in unresolvable questions of political REPRESENTATION, outside the proper bounds of its constitutional authority.

Tennesseans, like others, had moved from countryside to urban and suburban districts, but no redistricting had taken place since 1901. Supporters of reapportionment claimed that the resulting swollen districts made "second-class citizens" of city voters; they blamed "malapportionment" for urban woes and legislative apathy. Finding little

legislative sympathy for these claims, they turned to the courts.

But they had several hurdles to clear. The framers of the Fourteenth Amendment had repeatedly denied that it protected the right to vote. Perhaps it protected rights of representation, but the Court had found such rights too cloudy, too sensitive, and too "political" to settle judicially. (See POLITICAL QUESTIONS.)

The central hurdle was the "standards problem" expounded by Justice FELIX FRANKFURTER in COLEGROVE V. GREEN (1946) and in his *Baker* dissent. How could the Court tell lower courts and legislatures the difference between good representation and bad, lacking clear constitutional guidance? The Constitution was a complex blend of competing and countervailing principles, not a mandate for equal districts. "What is actually asked of the Court . . . is to choose among competing bases of representation—ultimately, really, among competing theories of philosophy—in order to establish an appropriate form of government for . . . the states. . . ." Frankfurter accused the Court of sending the lower courts into a "mathematical quagmire."

Writing for the majority, Justice WILLIAM J. BRENNAN argued that the *Colegrove* court had not found apportionment a political question but had declined to hear it using EQUITY discretion. But he did not answer Frankfurter's challenge to lay down workable standards, nor Justice JOHN MARSHALL HARLAN's objection, later reasserted in REYNOLDS V. SIMS (1964), that nothing in the Constitution conveyed a right to equal districts. Brennan merely claimed that "judicial standards under the EQUAL PROTECTION CLAUSE are well developed and familiar," and that "the right asserted is within the reach of judicial protection under the Fourteenth Amendment."

The concurring Justices, WILLIAM O. DOUGLAS and TOM C. CLARK, were not so cautious. Clark felt that "rational" departures from equal districts, such as districts approved by popular referendum, should be permitted. Douglas emphasized that the standards would be flexible (though he would later vote for rigid standards).

These opinions, and *Baker*'s place in history, make sense only in the context of Solicitor General Archibald Cox's AMICUS CURIAE brief supporting intervention. To take on a cause that could, and later did, jeopardize the seats of most of the legislators in the country, and invite formidable political reprisals, the Justices had to move with caution. Cox's brief reassured them that the JOHN F. KENNEDY administration, like its predecessor, favored intervention. The executive support probably swayed the votes of at least two Justices, Clark and POTTER STEWART. Had these voted against intervention, the Court would have divided 4–4, leaving intact the lower court's decision not to hear the case.

Moreover, Cox's brief did address Harlan's and Frankfurter's challenges. As with BROWN V. BOARD OF EDUCATION (1954), he argued, constitutional authority could be demonstrated from social need, as perceived by social scientists, incorporated into a spacious reading of the Fourteenth Amendment. As for standards, there were two possibilities: an absolute, individual right to vote, perhaps grounded on the equal protection clause, and a loose, group right to equal representation, perhaps grounded on the DUE PROCESS CLAUSE. Of the two, Cox seemed to favor the looser one, forbidding "egregious cases" of "gross discrimination." He even showed how such a standard might be drawn on a map of Tennessee. Because he was explicit, Brennan could afford to be cryptic and let the Cox brief draw most of Frankfurter's and Harlan's fire.

Within two years the Court announced in *Reynolds v. Sims* that equal representation for equal numbers was the "fundamental goal" of the Constitution and laid down standards so strict that every state but one, Oregon, was compelled to reapportion. Compliance with *Baker* was widespread and quick. Opposition was strong but late. By 1967 the states had come within a few votes of the two-thirds needed to call a CONSTITUTIONAL CONVENTION to strip courts of redistricting power, but by then reapportionment was largely completed, and the movement died.

Reapportionment added many urban and suburban seats to legislatures, replacing rural ones, but there is little evidence that it produced any of the liberalizing, vitalizing policies its proponents had predicted. What it did bring was a plague of GERRYMANDERING, renewed after each census, because it forced legislators to redistrict without forcing them to be nonpartisan. The Court since *Baker* has been powerless to control gerrymanders. Packing or diluting a group in a district can strengthen or weaken the group, or do both at once. There is no way short of commanding PROPORTIONAL REPRESENTATION to equalize everyone's representation. Nor is there a workable way to equalize representation in the ELECTORAL COLLEGE, the Senate, the national party conventions, party committees, runoff elections, executive appointments, or MULTIMEMBER DISTRICTS. The Court opened these doors when it announced that representation was the fundamental goal of the Constitution, but it closed them when it found that they raised the standards problem too plainly to permit intervention, exactly as Frankfurter had warned.

Baker has left us two legacies. The good one is equalizing district size. The bad one is rhetorical indirection, constitutional fabrication, and a penchant for overriding the wishes of people and their representatives, as for example, in *Lucas v. Forty-fourth General Assembly* (1964). Whether the good legacy is worth the bad, and whether it even added on balance to equal representation, can be told only with reference to the full breadth

of representation which was too complicated for the Court to touch.

WARD E. Y. ELLIOTT
(1986)

Bibliography

COX, ARCHIBALD 1967 *The Warren Court: Constitutional Decision as an Instrument of Reform.* Cambridge, Mass.: Harvard University Press.

DIXON, ROBERT G., JR. 1968 *Democratic Representation: Reapportionment in Law and Politics.* New York: Oxford University Press.

ELLIOTT, WARD E. Y. 1975 *The Rise of Guardian Democracy: The Supreme Court's Role in Voting Rights Disputes, 1845–1969.* Cambridge, Mass.: Harvard University Press.

NAVASKY, VICTOR 1971 *Kennedy Justice.* New York: Atheneum.

BALANCED-BUDGET AMENDMENT

Since one was first introduced in 1936, various versions of a balanced-budget amendment to the United States Constitution have been proposed in Congress. Such proposals have been introduced regularly since the 1970s. Moreover, since 1975, such an amendment has been the subject of applications (approximately thirty-two by 1990) by state legislatures for a CONSTITUTIONAL CONVENTION. All such proposals seek to encourage or mandate the adoption of a balanced BUDGET. Some of them have additional goals and would more accurately be denominated "balanced-budget and tax limitation," "deficit limitation," or "federal government limitation" amendments.

The only such proposed amendment to have passed either house is S.J. Res. 58, adopted by the Senate in 1982. It provided that Congress must annually adopt (and may subsequently amend as needed) a prospective statement in which anticipated total outlays (other than principal payments) do not exceed anticipated total receipts (other than borrowing), unless such an anticipated deficit is authorized by three-fifths of the whole number of each house. It charged Congress and the President with assuring that actual outlays do not exceed the anticipated outlays provided in the statement, although they may exceed actual receipts. It limited each year's rate of growth of planned receipts to the previous year's rate of growth in the national income, unless otherwise authorized by a majority of the whole number of each house. It also fixed the deficit as of the date of ratification, subject to enlargement by a vote of three-fifths of the whole number of each house. In wartime these requirements could be suspended by a simple majority.

Enforcement of such an amendment could affect the SEPARATION OF POWERS. It could enhance presidential power by justifying the IMPOUNDMENT OF FUNDS, for example, or involve the judiciary in overseeing the BUDGET PROCESS, an area heretofore at the very center of majoritarian decision making. Whether current doctrines of STANDING, JUSTICIABILITY, and POLITICAL QUESTION would preclude this judicial supervision is uncertain, and was left uncertain in the congressional debates.

Quoting Justice OLIVER WENDELL HOLMES, JR.'s dissent in LOCHNER V. NEW YORK (1905) to the effect that "a constitution is not intended to embody a particular economic theory. . . . It is made for people of fundamentally differing views," critics argue that the proposed amendment does not belong in the Constitution. That charter can endure the ages by defining structures of power within a regime of ordered liberty, rather than by specifying temporary and highly controversial economic policies, especially amendments, such as this one, with profound distributional effects. Moreover, they fear that such an amendment would weaken constitutional government. If effective, it could create paralyzing supermajority hurdles to daily governance. In contrast, the few other constitutional provisions requiring supermajorities (other than the veto override) do not risk interfering with the ongoing functions of government; even a DECLARATION OF WAR requires only a simple majority. Alternatively, critics argue that if the amendment proved a nullity by being either suspended or ignored, the Constitution's authority as positive law could be undermined. A suspension clause is a rarity in the United States Constitution, in contrast to those of other countries with a lesser tradition of CONSTITUTIONALISM. Even if such an amendment were not formally suspended, Congress might evade the amendment through such devices as off-budget federal agencies and CORPORATIONS and costly regulation of the private and state sectors in lieu of spending programs. For example, states with a balanced-budget requirement have resorted to splitting their budgets into a balanced operating budget and a capital budget financed by borrowing.

In response, supporters argue that current deficits are economically, politically, and morally ruinous, and are destructive of the country's future. Further, they contend that such proposed amendments seek not only to enact a particular economic theory but also to cure a flaw, identified by public choice theory, in the constitutional structure. Because of the nature of "concentrated benefits and dispersed costs," no effective constituency exists to oppose spending decisions. In the absence of a mandatory balanced budget, Congress has ceased to be a deliberative body that resolves and transcends factions' competing demands, because deficits allow representatives to respond to their constituents' multiple spending demands without regard to taxing decisions. This structural defect did not appear before 1960, the proponents explain, because an

unwritten constitutional principle favoring peacetime balanced budgets and the reduction of debt had prevailed since 1789. But in the past few decades, Keynesian theory and theories of the WELFARE STATE have undermined this principle; and the institutions that had enforced the principle, POLITICAL PARTIES with strong local ties and the congressional seniority system, have been weakened. Moreover, Supreme Court decisions broadly interpreting Congress's ENUMERATED POWERS have eliminated other constitutional restraints that limited spending. It should be noted that this explanation does not account for the President's major role in enlarging and perpetuating deficits.

ROBERT D. GOLDSTEIN
(1992)

Bibliography

CONGRESSIONAL BUDGET OFFICE 1982 *Balancing the Federal Budget and Limiting Federal Spending: Constitutional and Statutory Approaches.* Washington, D.C.: Government Printing Office.

MOORE, W. S. and PENNER, RUDOLPH G. 1980 *The Constitution and the Budget.* Washington, D.C.: American Enterprise Institute.

WHITE, JOSEPH and WILDAVSKY, AARON 1989 *The Deficit and the Public Interest: The Search for Responsible Budgeting in the 1980's.* Berkeley and Los Angeles: University of California Press.

BALANCING TEST

Although the intellectual origins of the balancing of interests formula lie in ROSCOE POUND's sociological jurisprudence, the formula was introduced into constitutional law as a means of implementing the Supreme Court's oft-repeated announcement that FIRST AMENDMENT rights are not absolute. In determining when infringement on speech may be justified constitutionally, the Court may balance the interest in FREEDOM OF SPEECH against the interest that the infringing statute seeks to protect. Thus the Court may conclude that the interests in NATIONAL SECURITY protected by the Smith Act outweigh the interests in speech of those who advocate forcible overthrow of the government, or that the free speech interests of pamphleteers outweigh the interest in clean streets protected by an antilittering ordinance forbidding the distribution of handbills.

The 1950s campaign against alleged subversives brought two interlocking problems to the Supreme Court. The dominant free speech DOCTRINES of the Court were PREFERRED FREEDOMS and the CLEAR AND PRESENT DANGER TEST. Because alleged subversives were exercising preferred speech rights and the government was unprepared to offer evidence that their speech did constitute a present danger of violent overthrow of the government, the Court found it difficult under the existing formulas to uphold government anticommunist action. Because established First Amendment doctrine appeared to be on a collision course with an anticommunist crusade that appeared to enjoy overwhelming popular support, free speech provided the crucial arena for the penultimate crisis of the judicial self-restraint movement. (The ultimate crisis came in BROWN V. BOARD OF EDUCATION, 1954.) Although the logical implication of that movement suggested that the Court ought never declare an act of Congress unconstitutional as a violation of the BILL OF RIGHTS, the Court was not prepared to go so far. The Justices' dilemma was that they were the inheritors of pro-freedom of speech doctrines but wished to uphold infringements upon speech without openly abdicating their constitutional authority.

The way out of this dilemma was the balancing formula. It allowed the Court to vindicate legislative and executive anticommunist measures case by case without ever flatly announcing that the Court had gone out of the business of enforcing the First Amendment. LEARNED HAND's "clear and probable" or "discounting" formula adopted by the Supreme Court in DENNIS V. UNITED STATES (1951) was the vital bridge in moving from a clear and present danger test that impels judicial action to a balancing test that veils judicial withdrawal. For Hand's test permits conversion of the danger test from an exception to freedom of speech invoked when speech creates an immediate danger of violent crime to a general formula for outweighing speech claims whenever the goals espoused in the speech are sufficiently antithetical to those of the majority. Justice FELIX FRANKFURTER's concurrence in *Dennis* and the majority opinion in BARENBLATT V. UNITED STATES (1959) not only made the antispeech potential of the balancing doctrine clear but also exhibited its great potential for absolute judicial deference to coordinate branches. For if constitutional judgments are ultimately a matter of balancing interests, in a democratic society who is the ultimate balancer? Necessarily, it is the Congress in which all the competing interests are represented. Thus the Court deferred to Congress's judgment that the needs of national security outweighed the speech rights of the enemies of that security.

Proponents of the balancing doctrine argue that no one is really willing to give any constitutional right absolute sway and that the act of judging always involves a weighing of competing claims. Certainly when constitutional rights such as free speech and FAIR TRIAL come into conflict, balancing of the two appears inevitable. The opponents of balancing argue for "principled" versus "ad hoc" or case-by-case balancing. If judges are left free to balance the particular interests in each particular case, they are always free to decide any case for or against the rights claimed by the way they state the interests. Opponents of ad hoc balancing insist that whatever balancing must be done should be done in the course of creating constitutional rules that will then be applied even-handedly in all cases. Thus, if fair trial and free speech values conflict, we may want a rule that upholds the constitutionality of banning prosecutors from pretrial release of confessions, but we do not want the kind of ad hoc balancing in which judges are free to find that in some cases such bans are constitutional and in others they are not.

Balancing has remained a principal doctrine in the freedom of speech area and has spread to other constitutional areas such as PRIVACY. Its capacity as a vehicle for judicial discretion is illustrated by BUCKLEY V. VALEO (1976), in which the Court used the balancing doctrine to march through the complex CAMPAIGN FINANCE ACT, striking down some provisions and upholding others in what was effectively a total legislative redrafting, and by the ABORTION cases (see ROE V. WADE, 1973) in which the Court used the balancing doctrine to invest with constitutional authority the "trimester" scheme it invented.

In GIBSON V. FLORIDA LEGISLATIVE INVESTIGATING COMMITTEE (1963) the Court held that government might infringe upon a First Amendment right only when it could show a COMPELLING STATE INTEREST. This formula may be viewed as weighting the balance of interests in favor of constitutional rights, but any government interests can be stated in such a way as to appear compelling. The Court's employment of the balancing test always leaves us uncertain whether any legislative infringement of free speech or other rights, no matter how direct or how open, will be declared unconstitutional, for the Court may always be prepared to find some state interest sufficiently weighty to justify the infringement.

MARTIN SHAPIRO
(1986)

(SEE ALSO: *Absolutism; Judicial Activism and Judicial Restraint.*)

Bibliography

FRANTZ, LAURENT B. 1963 Is the First Amendment Law? *California Law Review* 51:729–754.

HAND, LEARNED 1958 *The Bill of Rights.* Cambridge, Mass.: Harvard University Press.

MENDELSON, WALLACE 1962 On the Meaning of the First Amendment: Absolutes in the Balance. *California Law Review* 50:821–828.

BALDWIN, ABRAHAM
(1754–1807)

Abraham Baldwin represented Georgia at the CONSTITUTIONAL CONVENTION OF 1787 and signed the Constitution.

He served on the Committee on Representation, and, although personally opposed to equal representation of states in the SENATE, the Connecticut-born Baldwin played a key role in securing the GREAT COMPROMISE. He later spent eighteen years in Congress.

DENNIS J. MAHONEY
(1986)

BALDWIN, HENRY
(1780–1844)

Henry Baldwin of Pittsburgh was appointed to the Supreme Court on January 4, 1830, by ANDREW JACKSON. After graduating from Yale College in 1797, he studied law with ALEXANDER J. DALLAS and began his practice in Pittsburgh where he joined the bar in 1801. Law spilled over naturally into politics for Baldwin, and from 1816 to 1822 he served in Congress, where he gained a reputation as an economic nationalist. He also defended Andrew Jackson from charges of misconduct in Spanish Florida and later supported him for President—efforts that won him a seat on the Supreme Court.

Though an unknown judicial quantity, Baldwin was acceptable to the still-dominant JOSEPH STORY-JOHN MARSHALL wing of the Court because of his reputation as a "sound" man and talented lawyer—and because he was not JOHN BANNISTER GIBSON, whom conservatives feared would get the appointment. Baldwin's supporters were soon disappointed, then shocked. Almost immediately the new Justice was out of phase with the Court's nationalism and at odds with several of its members, especially Story, whose scholarly, didactic style Baldwin found offensive and threatening. After serving less than a year on the Court, he wanted off. Worse still, his collapse in 1833 (which caused him to miss that term of the Court) signaled the onset of a mental condition that progressively incapacitated him. Occasionally he rose to the level of his early promise, as for example in *United States v. Arredondo* (1832) where the principle was established that land claims resting on acts of foreign governments (which in the Spanish and Mexican cessions amounted to millions of acres) were presumed valid unless the United States could prove otherwise. Another solid effort was *Holmes v. Jennison* (1840) where he upheld the right of a state to surrender fugitives to a foreign country even though such a power cut into the policymaking authority of the national government in FOREIGN AFFAIRS. His circuit efforts were also well received at first and deservedly so, judging from such opinions as *McGill v. Brown* (1833) where he handled a complicated question of charitable bequests with considerable sophistication.

Baldwin's constitutional philosophy, so far as it can be detected, was set forth in his *General View of the Origin and Nature of the Constitution and Government of the United States*, a rambling, unconvincing treatise published in 1837 (mainly, it would seem, to rescue him from pressing debts). Baldwin presumed to stake out a middle constitutional ground for himself between extreme STATES' RIGHTS constitutional doctrine and the broad nationalism of Marshall and Story which he explicitly condemned as unfounded and usurpatory. He took particular pains to refute the thesis in Story's *Commentaries on the Constitution* (1833) that SOVEREIGNTY devolved on the whole people after 1776. Baldwin's final position on the matter appeared to be little more than a reductionist version of JOHN C. CALHOUN's theories.

The states' rights theory set forth in *General View* was consistent with Baldwin's *Jennison* opinion and his preference for STATE POLICE POWER as stated in the slavery case of GROVES V. SLAUGHTER (1841). On the other hand, in *McCracken v. Hayward* (1844), he did not hesitate to strike down an Illinois stay law that impaired contractual rights. His unpublished opinion in BANK OF AUGUSTA V. EARLE (1839) took the extremely nationalist position that a foreign corporation's right to do business in a state was protected by the PRIVILEGES AND IMMUNITIES clause of Article IV, section 2, of the Constitution.

To say where Baldwin really stood is difficult. He wrote less than forty majority opinions during his fourteen years on the Court. Of those, few were important and fewer still were coherent expositions of constitutional DOCTRINE. He withdrew more and more into paranoiac isolation, carping at his colleagues, criticizing reporter Richard Peters, and pondering his rapidly deteriorating financial situation. He dissented more and more (thirty-some times counting unwritten dissents) and with less and less purpose. That a number of his separate opinions were delivered too late to be included in the reports suggests that his impact in the Court's CONFERENCE was peripheral at best. His effectiveness on the circuit declined, too, if one credits the growing complaints of district judge Joseph Hopkinson who sat with him in Pennsylvania. Baldwin died in 1844, deeply in debt, without friends and with no prospect of being remembered favorably. Illness had taken a heavy toll. His influence on American law was negligible and his presence on the Supreme Court was probably counterproductive.

R. KENT NEWMYER
(1986)

Bibliography

BALDWIN, HENRY 1837 *A General View of the Origin and Nature of the Constitution and Government of the United States.* . . . Philadelphia: John C. Clark.

GATELL, FRANK O. 1969 Henry Baldwin. In Leon Friedman

and Fred L. Israel (eds.), *The Justices of the United States Supreme Court, 1789–1969*, Vol. 1, pages 571–598. New York: Chelsea House.

BALDWIN, ROGER N.
(1884–1981)

Until the United States entered WORLD WAR I, Roger Nash Baldwin was a social worker and a leading expert on juvenile courts. A pacifist who feared that the war might cause repression of individual rights, Baldwin helped to found the National Civil Liberties Bureau in 1917. The Bureau defended CONSCIENTIOUS OBJECTORS and those prosecuted for allegedly antiwar speeches and publications. Reorganized in 1920 by Baldwin and others as the AMERICAN CIVIL LIBERTIES UNION, it expanded its efforts to include among its many clients leaders of the International Workers of the World and other labor organizations; John T. Scopes, who violated Tennessee's anti-evolution law in 1925 and was prosecuted in the infamous "monkey trial"; the Jehovah's Witnesses; and even those, such as the Ku Klux Klan and the German American Bund, who opposed FREEDOM OF SPEECH for all but themselves. Baldwin was also committed to efforts on behalf of human rights abroad; despite his sympathy for radical causes, his investigation of the Soviet Union led him to oppose communism. In 1940, at his urging, the ACLU adopted a loyalty resolution barring supporters of totalitarian dictatorships from membership, only to find later that the government LOYALTY OATHS, which it fought in court, were based on its own resolution. Baldwin served as director of the ACLU until 1950, as its chairman from 1950 to 1955, and as its international work adviser until his death. After WORLD WAR II, Baldwin was counselor on CIVIL LIBERTIES in the reconstruction of the governments of Japan, Korea, and Germany.

RICHARD B. BERNSTEIN
(1986)

Bibliography

LAMSON, PEGGY 1976 *Roger Baldwin, Founder of the American Civil Liberties Union: A Portrait*. Boston: Houghton Mifflin.

BALDWIN v. FISH & GAME COMMISSION
436 U.S. 371 (1978)

The Supreme Court, 6–3, sustained Montana's exaction of a substantially higher elk-hunting license fee for nonresidents than for residents. Temporarily abandoning the approach of TOOMER V. WITSELL (1948), the Court said that the PRIVILEGES AND IMMUNITIES clause of Article IV of the Constitution protected citizens of other states only as to fundamental rights, a category that did not include the "sport" of killing elk. *Toomer*'s approach returned four weeks later in HICKLIN V. ORBECK (1978), but the Court in Hicklin neither overruled nor distinguished *Baldwin*. (See RESIDENCE REQUIREMENTS.)

KENNETH L. KARST
(1986)

BALDWIN v. NEW YORK
399 U.S. 66 (1970)

When DUNCAN V. LOUISIANA extended the SIXTH AMENDMENT'S TRIAL BY JURY provision to the states in 1968, the Court said that MISDEMEANORS, crimes punishable by imprisonment for less than six months, may be tried without a jury. Petty offenses have always been exempt from the amendment's guarantee of trial by jury in "all criminal prosecutions." Baldwin, having been sentenced to a year in jail for pickpocketing, claimed on APPEAL that New York City had deprived him of his right to a trial by jury. The Court held that the Constitution requires a trial by jury if an offense can be punished by imprisonment for more than six months. Justice BYRON R. WHITE, for a plurality, found decisive the fact that one city alone in the nation denied trial by jury when the possible punishment exceeded six months. Justices HUGO L. BLACK and WILLIAM O. DOUGLAS, concurring separately, would have ruled that the Constitution requires a jury for all accused persons without exception.

LEONARD W. LEVY
(1986)

BALLARD, UNITED STATES v.

See: Postal Power; Religion and Fraud

BALLEW v. GEORGIA
435 U.S. 223 (1978)

In *Ballew v. Georgia*, the Supreme Court unanimously held that a five-person jury in a nonpetty criminal case does not satisfy the right to TRIAL BY JURY under the Sixth Amendment as applied to the states through the FOURTEENTH AMENDMENT. *Ballew* involved a misdemeanor conviction for exhibiting an obscene motion picture.

Although all the Justices agreed upon the result, four separate opinions were written on the five-person jury issue. Justice HARRY A. BLACKMUN joined by Justice JOHN PAUL STEVENS relied heavily on SOCIAL SCIENCE RESEARCH in concluding that there was substantial doubt that a five-person jury functioned effectively, was likely to reach accurate results, or truly represented the community. Justice BYRON R. WHITE concluded that a jury of less than six would fail to represent the sense of the community. Justice LEWIS F. POWELL joined by Chief Justice WARREN E. BURGER and Justice WILLIAM H. REHNQUIST agreed that five-person juries raised "grave questions of fairness" indicating that "a line has to be drawn somewhere if the substance of jury trial is to be preserved." Since an earlier case, WILLIAMS V. FLORIDA (1970), had upheld the constitutionality of six-person juries, the effect of *Ballew* was to draw the constitutional line between five and six.

NORMAN ABRAMS
(1986)

(SEE ALSO: *Jury Size.*)

BALLOT ACCESS

Throughout most of the nineteenth century, voters were required to bring their own ballots to the polling places. Usually, ballots were preprinted by the POLITICAL PARTIES and contained straight party tickets. When the secret ballot was introduced around the turn of the century, states had to print ballots and decide which parties and candidates should be listed. Until 1968, criteria for ballot access were controlled entirely by the states.

In that year, George Wallace enjoyed significant support in his independent challenge to the major party nominees for the presidency, RICHARD M. NIXON and HUBERT H. HUMPHREY. Wallace met the requirements for ballot listing in every state but Ohio, where he satisfied the 15 percent signature requirement but was unable to do so by the early deadline of February 7. In *Williams v. Rhodes* (1968), the Supreme Court ordered Ohio to list Wallace. Although the state had an interest in seeking to assure that the eventual winner would receive a majority of the votes, it could not pursue that objective by shielding the two established parties from competition. Three years later, in *Jenness v. Fortson* (1971), the Court upheld Georgia ballot access requirements that had prevented most but not all independent candidates and new parties from reaching the ballot.

Some critics have complained that the Court's standard for evaluating ballot access requirements in *Williams, Jenness,* and several subsequent decisions has been too vague. In *Williams* the Court said such requirements must be justified by a COMPELLING STATE INTEREST, but in *Anderson v. Celebrezze* (1983) the Court moved toward a more general BALANCING TEST, denying that there was a "litmuspaper test" for identifying invalid regulations. Despite the

criticisms of those who favor neat doctrinal formulations, the pattern of results in ballot access cases has been reasonably clear. The Court has struck down requirements that bar truly competitive candidates and parties, while upholding other requirements, even those that work harshly against typical third parties and independent candidates who have no prospect of winning more than a small percentage of votes.

One exception is that the Court has struck down mandatory filing fees for ballot listing even when, as in *Lubin v. Panish* (1974), the fee was low enough that it could not realistically have blocked a seriously competitive candidacy. Another is that the Court has upheld restrictions intended to prevent losing factions in primaries from carrying over their intraparty disputes into general elections. For example, in *Storer v. Brown* (1974), the Court upheld a California statute barring members of a party from running as independent candidates.

The ballot access cases have also been criticized more substantively on the ground that they permit states to adopt overly restrictive requirements. Justice THURGOOD MARSHALL, dissenting in *Munro v. Socialist Workers Party* (1986), criticized the majority for presuming "that minorparty candidates seek only to get elected." Instead, he pointed out, their candidacies serve "to expand and affect political debate." Those who believe that carrying out the function of choosing officers to run the government ought to be the main consideration in designing electoral procedures are likely to take a more favorable view of the ballot access decisions.

DANIEL H. LOWENSTEIN
(2000)

Bibliography

SMITH, BRADLEY A. 1991 Note, Judicial Protection of Ballot-Access Rights: Third Parties Need Not Apply. *Harvard Journal on Legislation* 28:167–217.

WINGER, RICHARD 1996 How Ballot Access Laws Affect the U.S. Party System. *American Review of Politics* 16:321–340.

BALLOT INITIATIVE

See: Direct Democracy; Initiative; Referendum

BALTIMORE CITY DEPARTMENT OF SOCIAL SERVICES v. BOUKNIGHT

See: Freedom of Association

BANCROFT, GEORGE
(1800–1891)

A liberal Democrat from Massachusetts, Bancroft served as JAMES POLK's secretary of the navy and acting secretary of war, as ANDREW JOHNSON's adviser, and as minister to Great Britain and to Germany. He was also the most popular, influential, and respected American historian of the nineteenth century. His twelve-volume epic on American liberty, the *History of the United States from the Discovery of the Continent,* written over half a century, contains 1,700,000 words. The last two volumes, a *History of the Formation of the Constitution of the United States* (1882), covered 1782–1789. The work benefited from Bancroft's notes of his interview with JAMES MADISON in 1836; Madison also opened his private archives to him. Bancroft was an indefatigable researcher. His chronological narrative of the origins, framing, and RATIFICATION OF THE CONSTITUTION was based on manuscript letters as well as public records. He included over 300 pages of letters, many printed for the first time.

Bancroft wrote in a grand style that is today considered florid. His essentially political interpretation remained the standard work of its kind until superseded in 1928 by CHARLES WARREN's *The Making of the Constitution,* although ANDREW C. MCLAUGHLIN's *Confederation and Constitution* (1908) exceeded both in judicious analysis. Bancroft's work is remarkably fair, although Madisonian in approach. He viewed the Constitution as a bundle of compromises between nationalists and states' rightists, North and South, large states and small ones. The epigraph to his work was William Gladstone's judgment that "the American Constitution is the most wonderful work ever struck off at a given time by the brain and purpose of man." CHARLES BEARD made Bancroft one of his prime targets because of Bancroft's belief that the Framers were principled patriots who gave their loyalty to a concept of national interest that transcended purse and status without compromising republican ideals.

LEONARD W. LEVY
(1986)

Bibliography

NYE, RUSSELL 1964 *George Bancroft.* New York: Washington Square Press.

BANK HOLIDAY OF 1933

See: Emergency Bank Act

BANK OF AUGUSTA v. EARLE
13 Peters 519 (1839)

This case was vitally important to CORPORATIONS because it raised the question whether a corporation chartered in one state could do business in another. Justice JOHN MCKINLEY on circuit duty ruled against corporations, provoking Justice JOSEPH STORY to say that McKinley's opinion frightened "all the corporations of the country out of their proprieties. He has held that a corporation created in one State has no power to contract or even to act in any other State. . . . So, banks, insurance companies, manufacturing companies, etc. have no capacity to take or discount notes in another State, or to underwrite policies, or to buy or sell goods." McKinley's decision seemed a death sentence to all interstate corporate business. On APPEAL, DANIEL WEBSTER, representing corporate interests, argued that corporations were citizens entitled to the same rights, under the COMITY CLAUSE in Article IV, section 2, of the Constitution, as natural persons to do business. With only McKinley dissenting, Chief Justice ROGER B. TANEY for the Court steered a middle way between the extremes of McKinley and Webster. He ruled that a corporation, acting through its agents, could do business in other states if they did not expressly prohibit it from doing so. In the absence of such a state prohibition, the Court would presume, from the principle of comity, that out-of-state corporations were invited to transact business. Thus a state might exclude such corporations or admit them conditionally; but the Court overruled McKinley's decision, and corporations as well as WHIGS, like Webster and Story, rejoiced.

LEONARD W. LEVY
(1986)

(SEE ALSO: *Citizenship; Privileges and Immunities.*)

BANK OF THE UNITED STATES ACTS
1 Stat. 191 (1791)
3 Stat. 266 (1816)

The first Bank of the United States (1791–1811) was chartered by Congress on a plan submitted by Secretary of the Treasury ALEXANDER HAMILTON as part of his financial system. Modeled on the century-old Bank of England, the national bank harnessed private interest and profit for public purposes. It received an exclusive twenty-year charter. It was capitalized at $10,000,000, of which the government subscribed one-fifth and private investors the remainder, one-fourth in specie and three-fourths in government stock. Located at Philadelphia and authorized to establish branches, it was to be the financial arm of government (a ready lender, a keeper and tranferrer of funds); through its powers to mount a large paper circulation and advance commercial credit, the bank would also augment the active capital of the country and stimulate enterprise. JAMES MADISON had opposed the bank bill in Congress entirely on constitutional grounds. His arguments, turning on the absence of congressional power and invasion of the reserved rights of the states, were repeated in opinions submitted to President GEORGE WASHINGTON by Attorney General EDMUND RANDOLPH and Secretary of State THOMAS JEFFERSON. They were answered, convincingly in Washington's mind, by Hamilton's argument on the doctrine of IMPLIED POWERS.

The Second Bank of the United States (1816–1836) was an enlarged and revised version of the first. Republican constitutional objections had finally prevailed when Congress refused to recharter the first bank in 1811. But the disorganization of the country's finances during the War of 1812 led the Madison administration to propose a national bank. After several false starts, a plan was agreed upon by Congress in 1816. In 1791, there had been three state-chartered banks; in 1816 there were 260, and Congress acted to recover its abandoned power to regulate the currency. As the constitutional issue receded, controversy shifted to practical and technical questions of banking policy. Inept management, state bank jealousy, and severe financial pressure in 1818–1819 produced demands for revocation of the bank's charter. Aided by the Supreme Court's decision in MCCULLOCH V. MARYLAND (1819), the bank weathered this storm and under the efficient direction of Nicholas Biddle not only prospered but gained widespread public support in the 1820s. Nevertheless, President ANDREW JACKSON attacked the bank on financial, political, and constitutional grounds. Biddle and his political friends decided to make the bank the leading issue in the 1832 presidential election by seeking immediate renewal of the charter not due to expire until 1836. Congress obliged, and Jackson vetoed the recharter bill with a powerful indictment of the bank as a privileged moneyed institution that trampled on the Constitution. (See JACKSON'S VETO OF THE BANK BILL.)Asserting the independence of the three branches of government in the interpretation of the Constitution, he declared, "The opinion of the judges has no more authority over Congress than the opinion of Congress has over the judges, and on that point the President is independent of both." After Jackson's reelection, the ties between the government and the bank were quickly severed.

MERRILL D. PETERSON
(1986)

Bibliography

HAMMOND, BRAY 1957 *Banks and Politics in America from the Revolution to the Civil War.* Princeton, N.J.: Princeton University Press.

BANKRUPTCY ACT
52 Stat. 883 (1938)

The Bankruptcy Act of 1938, known as the Chandler Act, represented Congress's first comprehensive revision of the Bankruptcy Act of 1898. (See BANKRUPTCY POWER.) Under the financial strain caused by the Depression, the nation needed supplementary bankruptcy legislation. In a series of measures from 1933 through 1937, Congress sought to foster rehabilitation and reorganization of financially distressed debtors' nonexempt assets. The measures covered individual workers, railroads, farmers, nonrailroad CORPORATIONS, and municipalities. The Chandler Act both revised the basic bankruptcy provisions of the 1898 act and restructured and refined the Depression-era amendments. It segregated the rehabilitation and reorganization provisions into separate chapters, a structure adhered to in the Bankruptcy Reform Act of 1978. But the 1938 act neither sought nor achieved organic changes in bankruptcy law.

THEODORE EISENBERG
(1986)

Bibliography

WARREN, CHARLES 1935 *Bankruptcy in United States History.* Cambridge, Mass.: Harvard University Press.

BANKRUPTCY POWER

Article I, section 8, of the Constitution authorizes Congress to establish "uniform Laws on the subject of Bankruptcies throughout the United States." As interpreted in the CIRCUIT COURT decision in *In re Klein* (1843), this clause empowers Congress to enact laws covering all aspects of the distribution of a debtor's property and the discharge of his debts. Contrary to some early arguments, Congress's bankruptcy power is not limited to legislating only for the trader class. Commencing in 1800, Congress repeatedly exercised its bankruptcy power during periods of depression or financial unrest, but all early bankruptcy laws were repealed whenever unrest subsided. Since 1898, however, the United States continuously has had a comprehensive bankruptcy law, one completely revised by the BANKRUPTCY REFORM ACT of 1978.

Article I expressly requires bankruptcy legislation to be uniform. As interpreted in *Hanover National Bank v.*

Moyses (1902), the uniformity limitation does not prevent incorporation of state law into federal bankruptcy provisions. Bankruptcy law, the Court held in that case, is uniform "when the trustee takes in each state whatever would have been available to the creditor if the bankrupt law had not been passed. The general operation of the law is uniform although it may result in certain particulars differently in different states." And under the *Regional Rail Reorganization Act Cases* (1974) a bankruptcy statute may confine its operations to a single region where all covered bankrupt entities happen to be located. *Railway Executives' Association v. Gibbons* (1982), the only Supreme Court case to invalidate a bankruptcy law for lack of uniformity, struck down the Rock Island Transition and Employee Assistance Act because it covered only one of several railroads then in reorganization.

However many other theoretical limitations restrict Congress's bankruptcy power, only a few have led to invalidation of bankruptcy legislation. As interpreted in reorganization cases, the Fifth Amendment's DUE PROCESS CLAUSE limits Congress's bankruptcy power to alter or interfere with the rights of secured creditors. In LOUISVILLE JOINT STOCK LAND BANK V. RADFORD (1934) the Court found the original FRAZIER-LEMKE ACT unconstitutional because it too drastically interfered with a mortgagee's interest in property. But within months Congress enacted the second Frazier-Lemke Act, with scaled down interference, which the Court upheld in WRIGHT V. VINTON BRANCH OF MOUNTAIN TRUST BANK OF ROANOKE (1937). And in *Continental Illinois National Bank and Trust Co. v. Chicago, Rock Island and Pacific Railway Company* (1935) the Court held that secured creditors could at least temporarily be enjoined from selling their security. *Van Huffel v. Harkelrode* (1931) allows property to be sold free of a mortage holder's encumbrance where his or her rights are transferred to the proceeds of the sale. The *Regional Rail Reorganization Act Cases* found no constitutional flaw in the government's refusal to permit liquidation of an unsuccessful business where the Tucker Act permitted a suit for damages in the COURT OF CLAIMS.

For a brief period, there was doubt about Congress's authority to regulate municipal bankruptcies. In ASHTON V. CAMERON COUNTY WATER IMPROVEMENT DISTRICT (1937) the Supreme Court invalidated, as an interference with state sovereignty, a 1934 municipal bankruptcy law. But in *United States v. Bekins* (1938), in a shift that may be attributable to changes in Court personnel, the Court sustained a similar law. The Bankruptcy Reform Act of 1978 contains an updated municipal bankruptcy law.

Under STURGES V. CROWNINSHIELD (1819), when no national bankruptcy laws are in effect, states may regulate insolvency. Their effectiveness in doing so is limited by the requirement that states not impair the OBLIGATION OF CONTRACTS. When national bankruptcy legislation is in effect, *Stellwagen v. Clum* (1918) and other cases indicate that state laws are abrogated only to the extent that they undermine federal law.

THEODORE EISENBERG
(1986)

Bibliography

WARREN, CHARLES 1935 *Bankruptcy in United States History.* Cambridge, Mass.: Harvard University Press.

BANKRUPTCY REFORM ACT
92 Stat. 2549 (1978)

The Bankruptcy Reform Act of 1978 was the first comprehensive revision of federal bankruptcy law since 1938 and the first completely new bankruptcy law since 1898. (See BANKRUPTCY POWER.) Although the 1978 act made many substantive changes in bankruptcy law, its most controversial changes concern the organization of the bankruptcy system. The act expanded the bankruptcy court's authority to include JURISDICTION over virtually all matters relating to the bankrupt and the bankrupt's assets. This expansion, combined with Congress's failure to staff the new bankruptcy courts with life-tenured judges, led the Supreme Court in NORTHERN PIPELINE CONSTRUCTION CO. V. MARATHON PIPE LINE CO. (1982) to invalidate portions of the act's jurisdictional scheme. (See JUDICIAL POWER OF THE UNITED STATES.) In an effort to upgrade the bankruptcy courts, the act, in selected pilot districts, creates a system of United States trustees to administer and supervise bankruptcy cases, leaving courts free to perform more traditional adjudicatory functions. One of the statute's most significant changes is to consolidate into a single reorganization proceeding what had been three different methods for reorganizing financially distressed CORPORATIONS.

THEODORE EISENBERG
(1986)

Bibliography

Selected Articles on the Bankruptcy Reform Act of 1978 1979 *St. Mary's Law Journal* 11:247–501.

BANTAM BOOKS, INC. v. SULLIVAN
372 U.S. 58 (1963)

In *Bantam Books v. Sullivan* the Supreme Court struck down a state system of informal censorship, holding that the regulation of OBSCENITY must meet rigorous procedural safeguards to guard against the repression of constitutionally protected FREEDOM OF SPEECH. Rhode Island had created a commission to educate the public concerning books unsuitable to youths. The commission informed book and magazine distributors that certain publications were "objectionable" for distribution to youths under eighteen years of age and threatened legal sanctions should a distributor fail to "cooperate." Distributors, rather than risk prosecution, had removed books from public circulation, resulting in the suppression of publications the state conceded were not obscene.

KIM MCLANE WARDLAW
(1986)

BARBOUR, PHILIP P.
(1783–1841)

Philip P. Barbour was appointed to the Supreme Court by ANDREW JACKSON in December 1835 to fill the seat vacated by GABRIEL DUVALL. Born into Virginia's slaveholding plantation elite, Barbour held constitutional values that promoted the interest of that class. His law was largely self-taught, though he attended the College of William and Mary briefly in 1802 before beginning full-time practice in Orange County, Virginia. Beginning in 1812, Barbour served two years in the Virginia Assembly, following which he was elected to Congress where he served until 1825 and then again for two years beginning in 1827. For a brief time he was a Judge of the General Court of Virginia, and in 1830 he was appointed to the federal district court for Eastern Virginia, where he remained until assuming his Supreme Court duties in 1836.

Barbour's views on the Constitution were essentially those of the Richmond Junto of which he was a member. As a STATES' RIGHTS constitutionalist, he was opposed to federally sponsored INTERNAL IMPROVEMENTS, the protective tariff, and the second BANK OF THE UNITED STATES, an institution he viewed as a private CORPORATION whose stock the government should not own. He defended SLAVERY vigorously during the Missouri debates and, at the Virginia Constitutional Convention of 1829–1830, voted consistently with tidewater slaveholders against the democratic forces of the West. Barbour also supported the court-curbing plan of Senator Richard Johnson of Kentucky, prompted by the Court's decision in COHENS V. VIRGINIA (1821), and in 1827 he himself sponsored a measure that would have required a majority of five of seven Justices to hold a law unconstitutional.

Four years on the Court gave Barbour little chance to translate his states' rights philosophy and theory of judicial power into law. He wrote only a handful of opinions, and only in MAYOR OF NEW YORK V. MILN (1837) did he speak for the majority in an important case. There he upheld a New York regulation of immigrants as a STATE POLICE POWER measure, but his exposition of doctrine was inchoate at best and did little to influence future decisions. States' rights thinking also informed his vote in CHARLES RIVER BRIDGE V. WARREN BRIDGE (1837) (where he joined the new Jacksonian majority in refusing to extend by implication the 1819 ruling in DARTMOUTH COLLEGE V. WOODWARD) and in BRISCOE V. BANK OF KENTUCKY, also in 1837 (where the new majority refused to invalidate state bank notes on the ground that they were not BILLS OF CREDIT prohibited by Article I, section 10, of the Constitution).

Although he was a consistent advocate of states' rights, Barbour was not, as JOHN QUINCY ADAMS charged, a "shallow-pated wild-cat" bent on destroying the Union. Indeed, compared to the states' rights views of PETER DANIEL who succeeded him, Barbour's appear moderate and restrained. Even DANIEL WEBSTER conceded that he was "honest and conscientious," and Justice JOSEPH STORY, for all his objection to Barbour's constitutional notions, thought him a "perspicacious" and "vigorous" judge.

R. KENT NEWMYER
(1986)

Bibliography

CYNN, P. P. 1913 Philip Pendleton Barbour. *The John P. Branch Historical Papers* (Randolph Macon College) 4:67–77.
GATELL, FRANK O. 1969 Philip Pendleton Barbour. In Leon Friedman and Fred L. Israel (eds.), *The Justices of the United States Supreme Court, 1789–1969*, Vol. 1, pages 717–734. New York: Chelsea House.

BAREFOOT v. ESTELLE
463 U.S. 880 (1983)

In *Barefoot v. Estelle* the Supreme Court gave its approval to expedited federal collateral review of CAPITAL PUNISHMENT cases. In a 6–3 decision the Court approved the consolidation of hearings on procedural and substantive motions, the separate arguing of which had frustrated imposition of the death penalty even when the claims supporting the appeal were without merit. The opinion by Justice BYRON R. WHITE declared that no constitutional right of the convict was impaired by the one-step appeals process.

DENNIS J. MAHONEY
(1986)

BARENBLATT v. UNITED STATES
360 U.S. 109 (1959)

In a 5–4 decision, Justice JOHN MARSHALL HARLAN writing for the majority, the Supreme Court upheld Barenblatt's conviction for contempt of Congress based on his refusal to answer questions of the HOUSE COMMITTEE ON UN-AMERICAN ACTIVITIES about his membership in the Communist party. He argued that such questions violated his rights of FREEDOM OF SPEECH and association by publically exposing his political beliefs. In an earlier decision, WATKINS V. UNITED STATES (1957), the Court had offered some procedural protections to witnesses before such committees and held out hope that it would offer even greater protections in the future. *Barenblatt* ended that hope.

The Court did follow the *Watkins* approach of denouncing "exposure for the exposure's sake" and requiring that Congress have a legislative purpose for its investigations. But it presumed that Congress did have such a purpose, refusing to look at the actual congressional motives behind the investigation.

Barenblatt is the classic case of a FIRST AMENDMENT ad hoc BALANCING TEST. The Court held that the First Amendment protected individuals from compelled disclosure of their political associations. But Justice Harlan went on to say, "Where First Amendment rights are asserted to bar governmental interrogation, resolution of the issue always involved a balancing by the Courts of the competing private and public interest at stake in the circumstances shown." Then he balanced Barenblatt's interest in not answering questions about his communist associations against Congress's interest in frustrating the international communist conspiracy to overthrow the United States government. The interests thus defined, the Court had no trouble striking the balance in favor of the government. More than any other decision, *Barenblatt* establishes that the freedom of speech may be restricted by government if, in the Court's view, the government's interest in committing the infringement is sufficiently compelling.

MARTIN SHAPIRO
(1986)

BARKER v. WINGO
407 U.S. 514 (1972)

The SPEEDY TRIAL right protects a defendant from undue delay between the time charges are filed and trial. When a defendant is deprived of that right, the only remedy is dismissal with prejudice of the charges pending against him. In *Barker*, the leading speedy trial decision, the Supreme Court discussed the criteria by which the speedy trial right is to be judged. The Court adopted a BALANCING TEST involving four factors to be weighed in each case where the issue arises. They are: (1) the length of the delay; (2) the reasons for the delay; (3) the defendant's assertion of his right; and (4) prejudice to the defendant, such as pretrial incarceration and inability to prepare a

defense. In reaching its decision the Court noted that the speedy trial right is unique inasmuch as it protects societal rights as well as those of the accused. In many instances, delayed trials benefit a defendant because witnesses disappear or memories fade. The balancing takes into consideration the varied interests protected by that right.

WENDY E. LEVY
(1986)

BARNES v. GLEN THEATRE

See: First Amendment; Freedom of Speech; Nude Dancing

BARRON v. CITY OF BALTIMORE
7 Peters 243 (1833)

When JAMES MADISON proposed to the First Congress the amendments that became the BILL OF RIGHTS, he included a provision that no state shall violate FREEDOM OF RELIGION, FREEDOM OF PRESS, or TRIAL BY JURY in criminal cases; the proposal to restrict the states was defeated. The amendments constituting a Bill of Rights were understood to be a bill of restraints upon the United States only. In *Barron*, Chief Justice JOHN MARSHALL for a unanimous Supreme Court ruled in conformance with the clear history of the matter. *Barron* invoked against Baltimore the clause of the Fifth Amendment prohibiting the taking of private property without JUST COMPENSATION. The "fifth amendment," the Court held, "must be understood as restraining the power of the general government, not as applicable to the states."

LEONARD W. LEVY
(1986)

BARROWS v. JACKSON
346 U.S. 249 (1953)

Following the decision in SHELLEY V. KRAEMER (1948), state courts could no longer constitutionally enforce racially RESTRICTIVE COVENANTS by INJUNCTION. The question remained whether the covenants could be enforced indirectly, in actions for damages. In *Barrows*, white neighbors sued for damages against co-covenantors who had sold a home to black buyers in disregard of a racial covenant. The Supreme Court held that the sellers had STANDING to raise the EQUAL PROTECTION claims on behalf of the black buyers, who were not in court, and went on to hold that the FOURTEENTH AMENDMENT barred damages as well as injunctive relief to enforce racial covenants. Chief Justice FRED M. VINSON, who had written the *Shelley* opinion, dissented, saying the covenant itself, "standing alone," was valid, in the absence of judicial ejectment of black occupants.

KENNETH L. KARST
(1986)

BARTKUS v. ILLINOIS
359 U.S. 121 (1959)

ABBATE v. UNITED STATES
359 U.S. 187 (1959)

A 5–4 Supreme Court held in *Bartkus v. Illinois* that close cooperation between state and federal officials did not violate the DOUBLE JEOPARDY clause when Illinois tried (and convicted) Bartkus for a robbery of which a federal court had acquitted him. Justice FELIX FRANKFURTER's majority opinion de-emphasized the connection between the prosecutions. Despite "substantially identical" INDICTMENTS and although the Federal Bureau of Investigation had given all its EVIDENCE to state authorities, Frankfurter could find no basis for the claim that Illinois was "merely a tool of the federal authorities" or that the Illinois prosecution violated the DUE PROCESS CLAUSE of the FOURTEENTH AMENDMENT. He rejected the assertion that the Fourteenth Amendment was a "short-hand incorporation" of the BILL OF RIGHTS and also cited the test of PALKO V. CONNECTICUT (1937) with approval.

Justice HUGO L. BLACK, joined by Chief Justice EARL WARREN and Justice WILLIAM O. DOUGLAS, dissented. Black found such prosecutions "so contrary to the spirit of our free country that they violate even the prevailing view of the Fourteenth Amendment." Justice WILLIAM J. BRENNAN, dissenting separately, presented convincing evidence that federal officers solicited, instigated, guided, and prepared the Illinois case, amounting to a second federal prosecution "in the guise of a state prosecution."

Justice Brennan joined the *Bartkus* majority in *Abbate v. United States*, decided the same day. The defendants here were indicted and convicted in both state and federal courts for the same act, the federal prosecution following the state conviction. Brennan, for the majority, relied squarely on UNITED STATES V. LANZA (1922), concluding that "the efficiency of federal law enforcement must suffer if the Double Jeopardy Clause prevents successive state and federal prosecutions." Black, for the same minority, relied on his *Bartkus* dissent and the distinction "that a State and the Nation can [not] be considered two wholly separate sovereignties for the purpose of allowing them to do together what, generally, neither can do separately."

DAVID GORDON
(1986)

BASSETT, RICHARD
(1745–1815)

Richard Bassett represented Delaware at the CONSTITUTIONAL CONVENTION OF 1787 and signed the Constitution. Although there is no record of his speaking at the Convention, he was a leader in securing Delaware's ratification. He went on to become governor and chief justice of Delaware, and a United States senator.

DENNIS J. MAHONEY
(1986)

BATES, EDWARD
(1793–1869)

A St. Louis attorney and WHIG leader, Edward Bates, a moderate on SLAVERY, opposed the LECOMPTON CONSTITUTION and repeal of the MISSOURI COMPROMISE. In 1860 he sought the Republican presidential nomination, and from 1861 to 1864 he was President ABRAHAM LINCOLN's ATTORNEY GENERAL and most conservative adviser. In response to EX PARTE MERRYMAN (1861) he defended Lincoln's suspension of HABEAS CORPUS on the weak rationale that the three branches of government were co-equal and that Chief Justice ROGER B. TANEY therefore could not order Lincoln to act. Bates personally disliked the suspension but thought it preferable to martial law. The CONFISCATION ACTS undermined Bates's sense of property rights, and his department rarely supported these acts. Bates strongly supported the EMANCIPATION PROCLAMATION, but he insisted it be limited to areas still under rebel control. He believed that free blacks could be United States citizens because he narrowly construed DRED SCOTT V. SANDFORD (1857) to apply only to Negroes "of *African* descent" suing in Missouri. Bates supplied legal opinions to support the legal tender statutes, but he opposed the admission of West Virginia on constitutional grounds. He also opposed the use of black troops and retaliation for atrocities by Confederates committed on black prisoners of war. Nevertheless, he urged Lincoln to give Negro soldiers equal pay once they were enlisted. Bates consistently urged Lincoln to assert his constitutional role as COMMANDER-IN-CHIEF when Union generalship was poor. Bates had a broad view of his office and exerted a greater control over the United States district attorneys than his predecessors.

PAUL FINKELMAN
(1986)

Bibliography

CAIN, MARVIN E.   1965   *Lincoln's Attorney General: Edward Bates of Missouri.* Columbia: University of Missouri Press.

BATES v. STATE BAR OF ARIZONA
433 U.S. 350 (1977)

In 1976 two Phoenix lawyers ran newspaper advertisements offering "routine" legal services for "very reasonable" prices. A 5–4 Supreme Court declared here that the FIRST AMENDMENT protected this form of COMMERCIAL SPEECH. The majority rejected a number of "countervailing state interests" urged against the FREEDOM OF SPEECH protection, relying on VIRGINIA STATE BOARD OF PHARMACY V. VIRGINIA CITIZENS' CONSUMER COUNCIL (1976). The dissenters strenuously objected to the majority's equating intangible services—which they found impossible to standardize and rarely "routine"—with "prepackaged prescription drugs." The Court rejected, 9–0, a contention that the SHERMAN ANTITRUST ACT barred any restraint on such advertising.

DAVID GORDON
(1986)

BATSON v. KENTUCKY
476 U.S. 79 (1986)

This decision made a major change in the law of JURY DISCRIMINATION. In SWAIN V. ALABAMA (1965) the Supreme Court had held that systematic exclusions of black people from criminal trial juries in a series of cases would be a prima facie showing of RACIAL DISCRIMINATION in violation of the EQUAL PROTECTION clause of the FOURTEENTH AMENDMENT. The Court said, however, that a prosecutor's use of PEREMPTORY CHALLENGES to keep all potential black jurors from serving in a particular case would not be such a showing. In *Batson* the Court, 7–2, overruled *Swain* on the latter point and set out standards for finding an equal protection violation based on a prosecutor's use of peremptory challenges in a single case.

In a Kentucky state court James Batson had been convicted of burglary and receipt of stolen goods. After the trial judge had ruled on challenges of potential jurors for cause, the prosecutor had used peremptory challenges—challenges that need not be justified by a showing of potential bias—to keep all four black members of the jury panel from serving on the trial jury. The Kentucky courts denied the defendant's claims that this use of peremptory challenges violated his Sixth Amendment right to TRIAL BY JURY and his right to equal protection of the laws.

In reversing this decision, the Supreme Court's majority spoke through Justice LEWIS F. POWELL. The equal protection clause barred a prosecutor from challenging potential jurors solely on account of their race. *Swain's* narrow evidentiary standard would allow deliberate racial discrimination to go unremedied. Accordingly, the majority ruled that a defendant establishes a prima facie case of racial discrimination by showing that the prosecutor has used peremptory challenges to keep potential jurors of the defendant's race from serving and that the circumstances raise an inference that the prosecutor did so on account of the defendant's race. If the trial court makes these findings, the burden shifts to the prosecution to offer a race-neutral explanation for the challenges. The judge must then decide whether the defendant has established purposeful discrimination. Plainly, *Batson's* evidentiary standard leaves much to the trial judge's discretion.

Justice THURGOOD MARSHALL concurred, but said he would hold all peremptory challenges unconstitutional because of their potential for discriminatory use. Justices BYRON R. WHITE and SANDRA DAY O'CONNOR concurred separately, stating that the new evidentiary standard should be applied only prospectively. Chief Justice WARREN E. BURGER dissented, stating that the longstanding practice of peremptory challenges served the state's interest in jury impartiality and arguing that such challenges were typically made for reasons that could not be articulated on nonarbitrary grounds. Justice WILLIAM H. REHNQUIST also dissented, defending the legitimacy of peremptory challenges even when they are based on crude stereotypes.

Peremptory challenges have, indeed, long been based on group stereotypes. If the Supreme Court were to apply the standard to challenges of other groups, the law would be, in practice, much as Justice Marshall said it should be. Even if the new standard is limited to cases of racial discrimination, if trial judges apply it zealously, prosecutors will likely confine their challenges of potential black jurors in cases involving black defendants to challenges for cause.

In *Holland v. Illinois* (1990) the Court rejected, 5–4, a white defendant's claim that the prosecutor's use of peremptory challenges to keep blacks off the trial jury violated the Sixth Amendment right to a jury drawn from a fair cross-section of the community. A majority of the Justices, however, expressed the view that *Batson's* equal protection principle, which in this case the defendant had not raised, would extend to such a case. That view became law in *Powers v. Ohio* (1991).

KENNETH L. KARST
(1992)

BAYARD v. SINGLETON
1 Martin (N. Car.) 42 (1787)

This was the first reported American state case in which a court held a legislative enactment unconstitutional. This and the TEN POUND ACT CASES are the only authentic examples of the exercise of JUDICIAL REVIEW carried to its furthest limit before the circuit work of the Justices of the Supreme Court of the United States in the 1790s. During the Revolution, North Carolina had confiscated and sold Tory estates; to protect the new owners, the legislature enacted that in any action to recover confiscated land, the courts must grant a motion to dismiss the suit. Bayard brought such a suit, and Singleton made a motion for dismissal. Instead of granting the motion, the high court of the state delayed decision and recommended a jury trial to settle the issue of ownership. The court seemed to be seeking a way to avoid holding the act unconstitutional and hoped that the legislature might revise it. The legislature summoned the judges before it to determine whether they were guilty of malpractice in office by disregarding a statute. The legislature found no basis for IMPEACHMENT but refused to revise the statute. On a renewed motion to dismiss, the court held the act void, on the ground that "by the constitution every citizen had undoubtedly a right to a decision of his property by TRIAL BY JURY." In defense of judicial review, the court reasoned that no statute could alter or repeal the state constitution, which was FUNDAMENTAL LAW. The court then submitted the case to a jury. The committee of the legislature that had heard the charges against the judges included RICHARD DOBBS SPAIGHT, a vehement antagonist of judicial review, and William R. Davie, co-counsel for Bayard; shortly after, both men represented North Carolina at the CONSTITUTIONAL CONVENTION OF 1787. James Iredell, later one of the first Justices of the Supreme Court of the United States, also represented Bayard. Iredell published an address, "To the Public," in 1786, anticipating the doctrine of *Bayard v. Singleton,* and his correspondence with Spaight on judicial review best reflects the arguments at that time for and against the power of courts to hold enactments unconstitutional. Spaight's position, that such a power was a "usurpation" by the judiciary, accorded with the then prevailing theory and practice of legislative supremacy.

LEONARD W. LEVY
(1986)

BEACON THEATRES, INC. v. WESTOVER
359 U.S. 500 (1964)

Fox West Coast Theatres, Inc., contending that it was being harassed and that its business was being impeded by the threats of a competitor, Beacon Theatres, Inc., to bring an ANTITRUST suit, brought an action for DECLARATORY JUDGMENT in the U.S. District Court. Beacon, in a countersuit, alleged conspiracy in restraint of trade, and asked treble damages under the SHERMAN ANTITRUST ACT.

Judge Westover, exercising his discretion under the Declaratory Judgment Act and the FEDERAL RULES OF CIVIL PROCEDURE, decided to hear first the declaratory judgment suit, which, as an action in EQUITY did not require a jury. Only if that suit were decided in favor of Beacon would the antitrust suit be tried.

The Supreme Court, in an opinion by Justice HUGO L. BLACK, held (5–3) that Westover's decision deprived Beacon of its right to TRIAL BY JURY in a civil case. Because trial by jury is a constitutional right, judicial discretion must be used to preserve it unless there is a showing that irreparable harm would result from the delay. "Only under the most imperative circumstances," Black wrote, ". . . can the right to a jury trial of legal issues be lost through prior determination of equitable claims."

DENNIS J. MAHONEY
(1986)

BEARD, CHARLES A.
(1874–1948)

Charles Austin Beard, more than any other historian, shaped the way twentieth-century Americans look at the framing of the Constitution. He thus occupied, as he said a historian should, "the position of a statesman dealing with public affairs."

After being graduated at de Pauw and Columbia Universities, Beard continued his studies in Europe. His early writings reflect a theory of strict economic determinism; in *The Rise of American Civilization* (1927) he argued that the CIVIL WAR was less a struggle between SLAVERY and freedom than an epiphenomenon of emerging industrialism. Throughout his career as a teacher at Columbia University and the New School for Social Research and as a writer he maintained that historians cannot discover or describe the past as it actually was, but must instead reinterpret the past in order to shape their own times and the future.

Beard's most influential work was his *Economic Interpretation of the Constitution.* First published in 1913, the book was part of the Progressive movement's assault on such "undemocratic" constitutional obstacles to reform as the CHECKS AND BALANCES, and FEDERALISM. The work was republished, with a new introduction, in 1935, when the forms of CONSTITUTIONALISM again seemed to frustrate attempts at reform legislation. The thesis of the book is that the Constitution was framed by large holders of personal property and capital (especially government securities) in order to further their own economic interests and to frustrate the majority will. The effect of the book at the time of each publication was to undermine the legitimacy of the Constitution in the public mind by ascribing base motives to its authors. Beard's assumptions about the amounts and types of property owned by the Framers have been thoroughly discredited; yet his thesis about the origin of the Constitution became the standard version taught in universities and public schools. Even his opponents have adopted Beard's analytical framework.

Besides the *Economic Interpretation,* Beard, alone or with his wife, Mary Ritter Beard, was author of some two dozen books on politics and history. He was also president both of the American Historical Association and of the American Political Science Association.

DENNIS J. MAHONEY
(1986)

Bibliography

BROWN, ROBERT E. 1956 *Charles Beard and the Constitution.* Princeton, N.J.: Princeton University Press.

BEAUHARNAIS v. ILLINOIS
343 U.S. 250 (1952)

The Supreme Court upheld, 5–4, an Illinois GROUP LIBEL statute that forbade publications depicting a racial or religious group as depraved or lacking in virtue. Justice FELIX FRANKFURTER first argued that certain categories of speech including LIBEL had traditionally been excluded from FIRST AMENDMENT protection, and he then deferred to the legislative judgment redefining libel to include defamation of groups as well as individuals. By mixing excluded-categories arguments with arguments for judicial deference to legislative judgments for which there is a RATIONAL BASIS, the opinion moves toward a position in which the relative merits of a particular speech are weighed against the social interests protected by the statute, with the ultimate constitutional balance heavily weighted in favor of whatever balance the legislature has struck. Although *Beauharnais* has not been overruled, its continued validity is doubtful after NEW YORK TIMES V. SULLIVAN (1964).

MARTIN SHAPIRO
(1986)

(SEE ALSO: *Freedom of Speech.*)

BECKER AMENDMENT
(1964)

The public indignation aroused by the Supreme Court's decisions on school prayer and Bible reading (ENGEL V. VITALE, 1962; ABINGTON TOWNSHIP V. SCHEMPP, 1963) provoked the introduction in Congress of over 160 proposals to amend the Constitution. When Chairman Emmanuel Celler, who opposed the amendments, bottled them up in his House Judiciary Committee, the proponents united behind a compromise measure drafted by Representative Frank J. Becker of New York.

The Becker Amendment was worded as a guide to interpretation of existing constitutional provisions rather than as new law. It had three parts. The first two provided that nothing in the Constitution should be deemed to prohibit voluntary prayer or scripture reading in schools or public institutions or the invocation of divine assistance in government documents or ceremonies or on coins or currency. The third part declared: "Nothing in this article shall constitute an ESTABLISHMENT OF RELIGION."

Under pressure of parliamentary maneuvering, Celler conducted hearings in 1964—at which many denominational leaders and constitutional scholars expressed opposition to the Becker Amendment—but his committee never reported any proposal to the House. Amendments similar to Becker's have been introduced in subsequent Congresses, but none has come close to the majority votes needed for submission to the states.

DENNIS J. MAHONEY
(1986)

BEDFORD, GUNNING, JR.
(1747–1812)

Gunning Bedford, Jr., represented Delaware at the CONSTITUTIONAL CONVENTION OF 1787 and signed the Constitution. A spokesman for small-state positions, he vigorously advocated equal representation of the states in Congress; he also argued for easy removal of the president and against the VETO POWER. He was a delegate to Delaware's ratifying convention.

DENNIS J. MAHONEY
(1986)

BEDFORD CUT STONE COMPANY v. JOURNEYMEN STONE CUTTERS ASSOCIATION
273 U.S. 37 (1927)

The company sought to destroy the union. The union's national membership of 5,000 men then refused to work on buildings made of the stone quarried by the company, which sought an INJUNCTION on the ground that the union's activities restrained INTERSTATE COMMERCE in violation of the ANTITRUST laws. Lower federal courts refused to enjoin the union. The Supreme Court commanded the injunction. The dissenting opinion of Justices LOUIS D. BRANDEIS and OLIVER WENDELL HOLMES revealed the significance of the case. When, Brandeis observed, capitalists combined to control major industries, the Court ruled that their restraints on commerce were "reasonable" and not violations of the antitrust acts. When, however, a small union, as its only means of self-protection, refused to work on products of an antiunion company, the Court forgot its RULE OF REASON and discovered unreasonable restraint. Brandeis might have added that the Court had made "antitrust" a synonym for "antilabor."

LEONARD W. LEVY
(1986)

BELL v. MARYLAND
378 U.S. 226 (1964)

This case was the last SIT-IN case decided before the PUBLIC ACCOMMODATIONS provisions of the CIVIL RIGHTS ACT OF 1964 took effect. Twelve black students were convicted of criminal trespass for their participation in a sit-in demonstration in Baltimore. The Supreme Court reversed their conviction and remanded to the Maryland courts for clarification of state law. Six Justices, however, addressed the larger constitutional question that had been presented to the Court in case after case in the early 1960s: whether the FOURTEENTH AMENDMENT, in the absence of congressional legislation, provided a right to service in places of public accommodation. These six Justices divided 3–3.

Justices WILLIAM O. DOUGLAS and ARTHUR J. GOLDBERG, concurring in the reversal of the convictions, argued that racial SEGREGATION in public accommodations imposed a caste system that was inconsistent with the abolition of slavery and with the Fourteenth Amendment's establishment of CITIZENSHIP. The refusal to serve blacks, Douglas said, did not reflect any interest in the proprietor's associational RIGHT OF PRIVACY, but rather was aimed at promoting business. Because the restaurant was "property that is serving the public," it had a constitutional obligation not to exclude a portion of the public on racial grounds. Chief Justice EARL WARREN joined Goldberg's opinion, which focused on the rights of citizenship.

Justice HUGO L. BLACK dissented, joined by Justices JOHN MARSHALL HARLAN and BYRON R. WHITE. He indicated strongly his view that Congress, in enforcing the Fourteenth Amendment, could provide a right of access to public accommodations. In the absence of such a law, however, Black was unwilling to find in the Fourteenth Amendment a right to enter on the property of another against the owner's will. (At the ORAL ARGUMENT of the *Bell* case, Justice Black had observed, "But this was *private property*.") The state was entitled to protect the owner's decision by the ordinary processes of law without con-

verting the owner's personal prejudices into state policy, and thus STATE ACTION.

KENNETH L. KARST
(1986)

BELL v. WOLFISH

See: Right of Privacy

BELMONT, UNITED STATES v.
301 U.S. 324 (1937)

Belmont arose in the wake of President FRANKLIN D. ROOSEVELT's formal recognition of the Soviet Union in 1933 pursuant to an EXECUTIVE AGREEMENT between the two countries. In conjunction with this act of recognition, Soviet claims to assets located in the United States and nationalized by the Soviet Union in 1918 were assigned to the United States under a collateral agreement known as the "Litvinov Assignment." When the federal government sought to enforce these claims in the state of New York, however, the New York courts dismissed the suit, holding that to allow the federal government to enforce the assignment would contradict New York public policy against confiscation of private property.

The Supreme Court unanimously reversed, holding that the Litvinov Assignment, as part of the process of recognition, not only created international obligations but also superseded any conflicting state law or policy. In so holding, the Court affirmed the President's constitutional authority to speak "as the sole organ" of the national government in formally recognizing another nation and to take all steps necessary to effect such recognition. The Court stated that all acts of recognition unite as one transaction (here, in an "international compact" or executive agreement) which, unlike a formal TREATY, becomes a part of the "supreme Law of the Land" without requiring the ADVICE AND CONSENT of the Senate.

BURNS H. WESTON
(1986)

(SEE ALSO: *Foreign Affairs; Pink, United States v.*)

Bibliography

HENKIN, LOUIS   1972   *Foreign Affairs and the Constitution.* Mineola, N.Y.: Foundation Press.

BENDER v. WILLIAMSPORT
475 U.S. 534 (1986)

High school students in Pennsylvania sought permission to meet together at school for prayer and Bible study during extracurricular periods. School authorities refused permission on the basis of the ESTABLISHMENT CLAUSE, despite the fact that the school allowed a wide variety of other student groups to meet on school premises. The students filed suit, claiming violation of their FIRST AMENDMENT right to FREEDOM OF SPEECH.

The district court sided with the students, invoking the doctrine of EQUAL ACCESS enunciated by the Court in WIDMAR V. VINCENT (1981). However, the appeals court reversed, claiming that allowing the students to meet would violate the establishment clause. The Supreme Court granted certiorari to decide the question, which it subsequently declined to do. A bare majority of the Court's Justices side-stepped the constitutional controversy altogether by holding that the party who appealed the district court ruling lacked STANDING.

The four dissenters would have reached the merits of the case and extended the analysis of *Widmar* to secondary schools. According to the dissenters, not only did the establishment clause not forbid religious student groups from meeting on school premises, but schools had an affirmative duty under the First Amendment to allow such groups access to school facilities on the same basis as other groups.

The decision in *Bender* allowed the Court to put off indefinitely the question of whether the Constitution requires equal access in secondary schools. While *Bender* was still in litigation, Congress guaranteed equal access by statute, thus reducing pressure on the Court to resolve the free-speech question.

JOHN G. WEST, JR.
(1992)

(SEE ALSO: *Board of Education of the Westside Community Schools v. Mergens; Religious Fundamentalism.*)

BENIGN RACIAL CLASSIFICATION

Although race must always be regarded as a SUSPECT CLASSIFICATION, there are circumstances in which official RACIAL DISCRIMINATION may be constitutionally permissible because the purpose is "benign and ameliorative." In *United States v. Montgomery County Board of Education* (1969), for example, the Supreme Court upheld a system of RACIAL QUOTAS for teachers imposed by a federal judge as part of a desegregation program. In REGENTS OF UNIVERSITY OF CALIFORNIA V. BAKKE (1978) the Court invalidated quotas but indicated that preferential treatment of minority applicants would be acceptable. The question remains whether the government can sponsor AFFIRMATIVE ACTION without denying any person EQUAL PROTECTION OF THE LAWS.

DENNIS J. MAHONEY
(1986)

BENTON, THOMAS HART
(1782–1858)

A Missouri attorney, senator (1821–1851), and congressman (1853–1855), Thomas Hart Benton was an avid Jacksonian Democrat who led the opposition, on constitutional and economic grounds, to rechartering the second BANK OF THE UNITED STATES. A hard-money man, nicknamed "Old Bullion," Benton supported President ANDREW JACKSON's "specie circular" despite its adverse effects on his cherished goal of westward expansion. Benton opposed NULLIFICATION, and was ever after an enemy of JOHN C. CALHOUN and state sovereignty, allegedly saying in 1850 that Calhoun "died with TREASON in his heart and on his lips." Benton opposed extension of and agitation over SLAVERY, and he personally favored gradual emancipation. Thus, Benton opposed the ANNEXATION OF TEXAS, bellicose agitation over Oregon, war with Mexico (although he ultimately voted for the war), the WILMOT PROVISO, and HENRY CLAY's "Omnibus Bill" because all of these issues would impede western expansion and California statehood by involving them with slavery extension. Benton ultimately voted for some of the compromise measures in 1850, including the extension of slavery into some of the territories, but he opposed the new fugitive slave law. His opposition led to proslavery backlash and his defeat for reelection in 1850. In 1854 Benton published his senatorial memoirs, *Thirty Years View*, and in 1856–1857 *An Abridgement of the Debates of Congress*. While on his death bed, Benton wrote a long tract on DRED SCOTT V. SANDFORD in which he argued for the constitutionality of the MISSOURI COMPROMISE and savaged Chief Justice ROGER B. TANEY's opinion, which Benton believed was legally, historically, and constitutionally invalid, blatantly proslavery, and antiunion.

PAUL FINKELMAN
(1986)

Bibliography
CHAMBERS, WILLIAM W. 1956 *Old Bullion Benton: Senator from the New West.* Boston: Little, Brown.

BENTON v. MARYLAND
395 U.S. 784 (1969)

This decision, one of the last of the WARREN COURT, extended the DOUBLE JEOPARDY provision of the Fifth

Amendment to the states. (See INCORPORATION DOCTRINE.) A Maryland prisoner, having been acquitted on a larceny charge, successfully appealed his burglary conviction, only to be reindicted and convicted on both counts. A 7–2 Supreme Court, speaking through Justice THURGOOD MARSHALL, overruled PALKO V. CONNECTICUT (1937) and, relying on DUNCAN V. LOUISIANA (1968), declared that the Fifth Amendment guarantee "represents a fundamental ideal" which must be applied. Dissenting, Justices JOHN MARSHALL HARLAN and POTTER STEWART reiterated their opposition to incorporation, concluding that the WRIT OF CERTIORARI had been improvidently granted. In OBITER DICTUM they added that retrial here violated even the *Palko* standards.

DAVID GORDON
(1986)

BEREA COLLEGE v. KENTUCKY
211 U.S. 45 (1908)

Berea College, founded half a century earlier by abolitionists, was fined $1,000 under a Kentucky statute forbidding the operation of racially integrated schools. The Supreme Court affirmed the conviction, 7–2, sustaining the law as an exercise of state power to govern CORPORATIONS. Justice JOHN MARSHALL HARLAN, a Kentuckian personally acquainted with the college, dissented, arguing that the law unconstitutionally deprived the school of liberty and property without DUE PROCESS OF LAW. His denunciation of state-enforced SEGREGATION also echoed his dissent in PLESSY V. FERGUSON (1896). The majority addressed neither issue.

KENNETH L. KARST
(1986)

BERGER v. NEW YORK
388 U.S. 41 (1967)

A New York statute authorized electronic surveillance by police under certain circumstances. A conviction for conspiring to bribe a state official based on such surveillance was set aside because the statute did not meet FOURTH AMENDMENT requirements: (1) it did not require the police to describe in detail the place to be searched or the conversation to be seized, or to specify the particular crime being investigated; (2) it did not adequately limit the period of the intrusion; (3) it did not provide for adequate notice of the eavesdropping to the people overheard. These requirements were later incorporated in the OMNIBUS CRIME CONTROL AND SAFE STREETS ACT (1968).

HERMAN SCHWARTZ
(1986)

BERMAN v. PARKER

See: Eminent Domain; Public Use; Taking of Property

BETHEL SCHOOL DISTRICT v. FRASER
478 U.S. 675 (1986)

The Supreme Court had previously held that the FIRST AMENDMENT's protection of FREEDOM OF SPEECH does not stop at school doors. In this case the Court held that a student's freedom of speech is not coextensive with an adult's because school authorities may rightly punish a student for making indecent remarks in a school assembly, which disrupt the educational process. School authorities might constitutionally teach civility and appropriateness of language by disciplining the offensive student. Justice THURGOOD MARSHALL agreed with the majority on the obligation of the school to safeguard its educational mission, but believed that the authorities failed to prove that the speech was offensive. Justice JOHN PAUL STEVENS, also dissenting, claimed that the speech was not offensive. The case is significant as a diminution of free speech by students; they cannot say what can be said constitutionally outside a school.

LEONARD W. LEVY
(1992)

BETTS v. BRADY
316 U.S. 455 (1942)

In *Betts* an INDIGENT defendant was convicted of robbery after his request for appointed counsel was denied. The Court held that the DUE PROCESS clause of the FOURTEENTH AMENDMENT required states to furnish counsel only when special circumstances showed that otherwise the trial would be fundamentally unfair. Here, because the defendant was of "ordinary intelligence" and not "wholly unfamiliar" with CRIMINAL PROCEDURE, the Court found no special circumstances.

Over the next two decades, *Betts* was consistently undermined by expansion of the "special circumstances" exception, resulting in the appointment of counsel in most FELONY cases, until it was finally overruled in GIDEON V. WAINWRIGHT (1963).

BARBARA ALLEN BABCOCK
(1986)

(SEE ALSO: *Right to Counsel.*)

BEVERIDGE, ALBERT J.
(1862–1927)

Albert Jeremiah Beveridge of Indiana, a lawyer and orator of extraordinary talent and overweening ambition, served two terms in the United States SENATE (1899–1911) as a Republican. He advocated imperialism to open new markets for American industry and favored permanent annexation of the insular TERRITORIES gained in the Spanish American War, without extension of constitutional protections and self-government, for which their non-Anglo-Saxon inhabitants were unfit. An economic nationalist, Beveridge favored repeal of the SHERMAN ANTITRUST ACT, believing that trusts should not be broken up but regulated in the national interest. Defeated for reelection, Beveridge joined THEODORE ROOSEVELT's Progressive Party and was its candidate for governor in 1912. Defeated again, he turned to writing a long-planned biography of Chief Justice JOHN MARSHALL. The four-volume work, completed in 1919, won a Pulitzer Prize for biography. In the book Beveridge presents Marshall as the statesman who molded the Constitution to meet the needs of a vigorous, commercial nation, over the objections of petty agrarians and disunionists like THOMAS JEFFERSON.

DENNIS J. MAHONEY
(1986)

Bibliography

BOWERS, CLAUDE G.   1932   *Beveridge and the Progressive Era.* New York: Literary Guild.

BIBB v. NAVAJO FREIGHT LINES, INC.
359 U.S. 520 (1959)

A unanimous Supreme Court here voided a state highway safety regulation because the state failed to demonstrate sufficient justification to balance the burden it imposed on INTERSTATE COMMERCE. An Illinois statute required trucks using its highways to employ a particular mudguard, outlawed in Arkansas and distinct from those allowed elsewhere. The Court said that cost and safety problems alone were insufficient reason for invalidation, given the "strong presumption of validity" owing to the statute. But, by creating a conflicting standard, the Illinois statute had seriously interfered with and imposed a "massive" burden on interstate commerce.

DAVID GORDON
(1986)

(SEE ALSO: *State Regulation of Commerce.*)

BIBLE READING

See: Religion in Public Schools

BICAMERALISM

Bicameralism, the principle of CONSTITUTIONALISM that requires the legislature to be composed of two chambers (or houses), is a feature of the United States Constitution and of the constitution of every state except Nebraska. Bicameralism is supposed to guarantee deliberation in the exercise of the LEGISLATIVE POWER, by requiring that measures be debated in and approved by two different bodies before becoming law. It is also one of those "auxiliary precautions" by which constitutional democracy is protected from the mischiefs latent in popular self-government.

Bicameralism is not distinctively American; there were bicameral legislatures in the ancient republics of Greece and Rome, and there are bicameral legislatures in most countries of the world today. Bicameralism is found in the constitutions of nondemocratic countries (such as the Soviet Union) as well as of democratic countries. And, despite historical association with disparities of social class, both legislative chambers in democratic countries—emphatically including the United States—are typically chosen in popular elections; in countries where one house is chosen other than by election, that house is significantly less powerful than the elective house. Moreover, although it is the practice of most federal nations (such as Australia, Switzerland, and the Federal Republic of Germany) to reflect the constituent SOVEREIGNTY of the states in one house of the legislature, there are bicameral legislatures in countries where FEDERALISM is unknown.

The American colonists came originally from Britain and were familiar with the BRITISH CONSTITUTION. In Parliament, as the Framers knew it, there were two houses with equal power, reflecting two orders of society: the House of Lords comprising the hereditary aristocracy of England (together with representatives of the Scots nobility and the ecclesiastical hierarchy), and the House of Commons representing the freeholders of the counties and the chartered cities. Seats in the House of Commons were apportioned according to the status of the constituency (five seats per county, two per city), not according to population.

The local lawmaking bodies in the colonies were originally unicameral. Bicameralism was introduced in Massachusetts in 1644, in Maryland in 1650, and (in a unique form) in Pennsylvania in 1682; but in each case the "upper house" was identical with the governor's council, and so performed both legislative and executive functions. In the eighteenth century, all of the colonial legislatures but one were bicameral, with a lower house elected by the freeholders and an upper house generally comprising representatives of the wealthier classes. At the same time the upper houses (although retaining the name "council") became distinctly legislative bodies.

When the newly independent states began constructing constitutions after 1776, all but Pennsylvania and Georgia provided for bicameral legislatures. Typically, the upper house was elected separately from the lower and had higher qualifications for membership, but it was elected from districts apportioned on the same basis and by electorates with the same qualifications. In two states, Maryland and South Carolina, the upper houses were elected indirectly.

The CONTINENTAL CONGRESS, although it conducted a war, negotiated a peace, and directed the collective business of the United States, was never in form a national legislature. Even after its status was regularized by the ARTICLES OF CONFEDERATION, the Congress was a body composed of delegates selected by the state governments and responsible to them. A bicameral Congress was neither desirable nor feasible until Congress became the legislative branch of a national government.

The delegates to the CONSTITUTIONAL CONVENTION OF 1787 agreed at the outset on a bicameral national legislature. In the VIRGINIA PLAN, membership in the first house of Congress would have been apportioned according to the population of the states, and the second house would have been elected by the first. The GREAT COMPROMISE produced the Congress as we know it, with the HOUSE OF REPRESENTATIVES apportioned by population (described by JAMES MADISON in THE FEDERALIST #39 as a "national" feature of the Constitution) and with equal REPRESENTATION of the states in the SENATE (a "federal" feature), so that Congress itself reflects the compound character of American government.

The two principles of apportionment serve to insure that different points of view are brought to bear on deliberations in the two houses. That consideration is also advanced by having different terms for members of the two houses; a shorter term bringing legislators into more frequent contact with public opinion, a longer term permitting legislators to take a more extended view of the public interest. The priority of the House of Representatives with respect to revenue (taxing) measures and the association of the Senate with the executive in the exercise of the TREATY POWER and the APPOINTING POWER also tend to introduce different points of view into legislative deliberations. Until abolished by the SEVENTEENTH AMENDMENT, the election of senators by the state legislatures also contributed to the formation of different viewpoints.

The principal justification for bicameralism is that it increases and improves the deliberation on public measures. But bicameralism is also a device to protect constitutional government against the peculiar evils inherent in democratic government. One must guard against equating democracy, or even majority rule, with the immediate satisfaction of the short-term demands of transient majorities. As *The Federalist* #10 points out, a faction—a group whose aims are at odds with the rights of other citizens or with permanent and aggregate interests of the whole country—may at any given time amount to a majority of the population. Although no mechanical device can guarantee that a majority faction will not prevail, the bicameral structure of Congress operates to make such a result less likely than it might otherwise be.

The Supreme Court cited the importance of bicameralism in the American constitutional system as one reason for striking down the LEGISLATIVE VETO in IMMIGRATION AND NATURALIZATION SERVICE V. CHADHA (1983). According to Chief Justice WARREN E. BURGER, that device permitted public policy to be altered by either house of Congress, contravening the belief of the Framers "that legislation should not be enacted unless it has been carefully and fully considered" lest special interests "be favored at the expense of public needs."

Bicameralism is also a principle of American constitutionalism at the state level. At one time representation of the lesser political units, typically the counties, was the rule for state upper houses. In REYNOLDS V. SIMS (1964), however, the Supreme Court held that such schemes of representation resulted in the overvaluation of the votes of rural citizens relative to those of urban and suburban citizens and that they therefore denied the latter the EQUAL PROTECTION OF THE LAWS in violation of the FOURTEENTH AMENDMENT. Some commentators, both scholars and politicians, predicted that imposition of the ONE PERSON, ONE VOTE standard would spell the doom of bicameralism at the state level. However, no state has changed to a unicameral system since the *Reynolds* decision.

Even more than to the innate reluctance of politicians to abolish any public office, this fact is testimony to the independent vitality of bicameralism as a constitutional principle. Even when territoriality is removed as a rationale, the desirability of having a second opinion on proposals before they become law cannot be gainsaid. Hence there is a tendency in the states to find ways of giving their upper houses a distinct perspective. The ordinary differentiation is by the size of the chambers and the length of the terms of office. Some states have tried, with the Supreme Court's approval, to preserve the territorial basis of the upper house by creating MULTIMEMBER DISTRICTS in the more populous territorial units.

The meaning of constitutionalism in a democratic polity is that the short-term interests of the majority will not be allowed to prevail if they are contrary to the rights of the minority or to the permanent and aggregate interests of the whole. The permanent and aggregate interests are not represented by any person or group of people, but they are protected by a constitutional system that requires prudent deliberation in the conduct of lawmaking. Bicameralism is an important constitutional principle because, and to the extent that, it institutionalizes such deliberation.

DENNIS J. MAHONEY
(1986)

Bibliography

EIDELBERG, PAUL 1968 *The Political Philosophy of the American Constitution.* New York: Free Press.

WHEARE, KENNETH C. 1963 *Legislatures.* New York: Oxford University Press.

BICKEL, ALEXANDER M.
(1925–1974)

Alexander Bickel was a professor at Yale Law School from 1956 to 1974 and a prolific writer on law and politics. He became the most influential academic critic of the progressive liberal jurisprudence of his time, although he at first made only sympathetic refinements of that doctrine. Having served as a clerk for Justice FELIX FRANKFURTER and edited some unpublished judicial opinions of Justice LOUIS D. BRANDEIS, he, like they, rejected the old CONSTITUTIONALISM of private rights and unchanging FUNDAMENTAL LAW in favor of a living law, evolving with social conditions and with a progressive consciousness. His first important book, *The Least Dangerous Branch* (1962), advanced a variation of Frankfurter's prescription of judicial restraint. Bickel elaborated ways, such as avoiding a constitutional question, by which the SUPREME COURT might accommodate political democracy while enforcing the "principled goals" of a more open, humane, and free society.

In *The Supreme Court and the Idea of Progress* (1970), however, Bickel departed sharply from his role of political tactician for the rule of Supreme Court principle. He attacked the WARREN COURT's principles as themselves impolitic. In Bickel's view, the Court, confident that progress required nationalizing and leveling constitutional limits on the electoral process and an extension of desegregation to racial balancing, had imposed an egalitarianism that was subjective and arbitrary. As a result, Bickel argued, the Court had bred a legalistic authoritarianism and threatened the quality of public schools and distinctive communities.

The Morality of Consent (1975) was published posthumously. It examined the turmoil attending the VIETNAM WAR, student revolt, and WATERGATE, extended Bickel's critique, and attempted a reconstruction. Bickel portrayed the entire American order as under siege and ill-defended. He saw universities as well as governments and corporations endangered by two extremes of theory—a committed moralism, which tended to a dictatorship of the self-righteous, and a permissive relativism, which would defend nothing and eroded the moral and social fabric. Bickel recurred to Edmund Burke's critique of the French Declaration of the Rights of Man, and then painstakingly set forth his own morality of consent, a morality to sustain not individual claims but the social process of communicating and governing.

ROBERT K. FAULKNER
(1986)

Bibliography

FAULKNER, ROBERT K. 1978 Bickel's Constitution: The Problem of Moderate Liberalism. *American Political Science Review* 72:925–940.

BIDDLE, FRANCIS
(1886–1968)

Born to wealth and social position, Francis Biddle of Pennsylvania was graduated from Harvard College and Harvard Law School and became a law clerk to Justice OLIVER WENDELL HOLMES. He entered public service in 1934 as FRANKLIN D. ROOSEVELT's chairman of the National Labor Relations Board. He also served as counsel for the congressional investigation of the Tennessee Valley Authority (1938); as a judge on the United States Court of Appeals for the Third Circuit (1939–1940); as solicitor general (1940–1941); and as attorney general (1941–1945). Biddle stoutly championed CIVIL LIBERTIES and, albeit unsuccessfully, opposed the evacuation of Japanese Americans from the West Coast. He also served on the International Military Tribunal at Nuremberg, which tried the major German war criminals (1945–1946). Thereafter, Biddle retired to a life of writing and leisure. His chief books were *Fear of Freedom* (1951), an assault on McCarthyism; *Justice Holmes, Natural Law, and the Supreme Court* (1961); and *In Brief Authority* (1962), a record of his public service.

HENRY J. ABRAHAM
(1986)

Bibliography

BIDDLE, FRANCIS 1962 *In Brief Authority: From the Years with Roosevelt to the Nürenberg Trial.* Garden City, N.Y.: Doubleday.

BILL OF ATTAINDER

In American constitutional law, a bill of attainder is any legislative act that inflicts punishment on designated individuals without a judicial trial. The term includes both the original English bill of attainder, which condemned a person to death for treason or felony and confiscated his property, and the bill of pains and penalties, used for lesser offenses and punishments. The first bill of attainder was passed by Parliament in 1459. They were common during the Tudor and Stuart reigns, and Cromwell's and William and Mary's parliaments also resorted to them. During the Revolutionary period, several state legislatures used bills of attainder to condemn Tories and to confiscate their property. THOMAS JEFFERSON in 1778 drafted, and the Virginia legislature passed, a bill of attainder against Josiah Philips, a notorious Tory brigand. The abuse of the procedure in English and American history foreshadowed the possibility of even greater abuse in the future. The bill of attainder, with its disregard of DUE PROCESS OF LAW, could be a potent weapon for the vengeful and covetous.

At the CONSTITUTIONAL CONVENTION OF 1787, ELBRIDGE GERRY, proposed a prohibition against bills of attainder. The measure passed unanimously; it appears in Article I, section 9, as a limitation on Congress, and in Article I, section 10, as a limitation on the states. That the prohibition was meant to extend to all legislative punishments may be seen from a congressional debate in 1794. When Federalist Representative THOMAS FITZSIMONS introduced a resolution to censure the Jeffersonian Democratic Societies and to accuse them of fomenting the WHISKEY REBELLION, JAMES MADISON, denounced it as a bill of attainder.

The Supreme Court first spoke to the question in the TEST OATH CASES (1867). The Court held unconstitutional both a Missouri requirement that practitioners of certain professions swear that they had not aided the Confederate cause and a federal requirement that lawyers take such an oath to practice before federal courts. Since former rebels could not take the oaths, they were effectively deprived of their livelihoods. The Missouri legislature and the Congress had therefore passed bills imposing punishment on the ex-Confederates without judicial trial or conviction of any crime.

No other federal law was held to violate the ban on bills of attainder until UNITED STATES V. LOVETT (1946). In that case the Court held unconstitutional a rider to an appropriations bill which prohibited any payment to three named PUBLIC EMPLOYEES, previously identified as subversives before a congressional committee, unless they were first discharged and reappointed. In *Lovett* the Court expanded on the definition it had given in the *Test Oath Cases*, making clear that all legislative acts were covered, "no matter what their form."

In recent judicial interpretation of the bills-of-attainder clause a law prohibiting Communist party members from holding labor union office was declared unconstitutional (see UNITED STATES V. BROWN); but a law requiring subversive organizations to register with a government agency, and another commandeering the records of a disgraced ex-President were upheld.

DENNIS J. MAHONEY
(1986)

(SEE ALSO: *Communist Party v. Subversive Activities Control Board; Nixon v. Administrator of General Services.*)

Bibliography
CHAFEE, ZECHARIAH 1956 *Three Human Rights in the Constitution of 1787.* Lawrence: University of Kansas Press.

BILL OF CREDIT

A bill of credit is a promissory note issued by a government on its own credit and intended to circulate as money. Under Article I, section 10, of the Constitution the states are prohibited from emitting bills of credit. The prohibition was regarded as essential by the Framers of the Constitution, and it was included without significant debate or dissent by the CONSTITUTIONAL CONVENTION OF 1787.

Bills of credit are, in fact, unsecured paper currency. Both ALEXANDER HAMILTON and JAMES MADISON, referring to the prohibition in THE FEDERALIST (#44 and #80), wrote of a prohibition on "paper money." In the years immediately preceding the adoption of the Constitution, many states had issued unsecured currency in a deliberately inflationary policy intended to benefit borrowers. As long as local politicians had the power to stimulate inflation, there could be no stable economy. The "more perfect union" required that money have essentially the same purchasing power in every state and region.

The MARSHALL COURT, in CRAIG V. MISSOURI (1830), held that a state issue of certificates acceptable for tax payments violated the prohibition on bills of credit, since they were "paper intended to circulate through the community for its ordinary purposes, as money." But the TANEY COURT held that notes issued by a state-chartered bank—of which the state was the sole stockholder—did not violate the prohibition, since they were not issued "on the faith of the state." (See BRISCOE V. BANK OF KENTUCKY.)

DENNIS J. MAHONEY
(1986)

BILL OF RIGHTS (ENGLISH)
(December 16, 1689)

During the controversy with Great Britain, from 1763 to 1776, American editors frequently reprinted the English

Bill of Rights, and American leaders hailed it as "the second MAGNA CARTA." After the DECLARATION OF INDEPENDENCE, Americans framing their first state constitutions drew upon the Bill of Rights; certain clauses of the national Constitution and our own BILL OF RIGHTS, the first ten amendments, can also be traced to the English statute of 1689. Its formal title was, "An act for declaring the rights and liberties of the subject, and settling the succession of the crown." Like Magna Carta, the PETITION OF RIGHT, and other constitutional documents safeguarding "liberties of the subject," the Bill of Rights imposed limitations on the crown only. Indeed, the document capped the Glorious Revolution of 1688–1689 by which England hamstrung the royal prerogative and made the crown subservient to Parliament, which remained unrestrained by any constitutional document. In effect the Bill of Rights ratified parliamentary supremacy, which is the antithesis of the American concept of a bill of rights as a bill of restraints upon the government generally. Notwithstanding its inflated reputation as a precursor of the American Bill of Rights, the English bill was quite narrow in the range of its protections even against the crown. In fact it established no new principles, except, perhaps, for the provision against standing armies in time of peace without parliamentary approval. Sir William S. Holdsworth, the great historian of English law, declared, "We look in vain for any statement of constitutional principle in the Bill of Rights," a judgment that is too severe.

The Bill of Rights confirmed several old principles of major significance. No TAXATION WITHOUT REPRESENTATION, which became the American formulation, here was limited to the assertion that levying money by royal prerogative "without grant of parliament" was illegal. The FREEDOM OF PETITION, protected by our FIRST AMENDMENT, and indirectly the FREEDOM OF ASSEMBLY go back to time immemorial, as the British say, but were here enshrined as part of the FUNDAMENTAL LAW. Article I, section 6, of the Constitution, protecting freedom of speech for members of Congress, derives from a clause in the Bill of Rights confirming a principle fought for by Parliament for a century and a half. Our Eighth Amendment follows closely the language of another provision of the Bill of Rights, which declares, "That excessive BAIL ought not to be required, no excessive fines imposed, nor CRUEL AND UNUSUAL PUNISHMENTS inflicted." The guarantee against excessive bail made the writ of HABEAS CORPUS effective by plugging the one loophole in the HABEAS CORPUS ACT OF 1679; the crown's judges had defeated that act's purpose by fixing steep bail that prisoners could not afford. The ACT OF TOLERATION OF 1689 preceded the Bill of Rights by a few months and is equally part of the constitutional inheritance of the Glorious Revolution.

The foremost significance of the English Bill of Rights, so called because it began as a declaration and ended as a bill enacted into law, probably lies in the symbolism of the name, conveying far more than the document itself actually protects. As an antecedent of the American Bill of Rights of 1791, the act of 1689 is a frail affair, though it achieved its purpose of cataloguing most of the rights that the Stuarts had breached. As a symbol of fundamental law and the RULE OF LAW it was a mighty precursor of the fuller catalogues of rights developed by the American states and in the Constitution.

LEONARD W. LEVY
(1986)

Bibliography

SCHWOERER, LOIS G. 1981 *The Declaration of Rights, 1689.* Baltimore: Johns Hopkins University Press.

BILL OF RIGHTS (UNITED STATES)

On September 12, 1787, the only major task of the CONSTITUTIONAL CONVENTION OF 1787 was to adopt, engross, and sign the finished document reported by the Committee on Style. The weary delegates, after a hot summer's work in Philadelphia, were eager to return home. At that point GEORGE MASON remarked that he "wished the plan had been prefaced by a Bill of Rights," because it would quiet public fears. Mason made no stirring speech for CIVIL LIBERTIES; he did not even argue the need for a bill of rights or move the adoption of one, though he offered to second a motion if one were made. ELBRIDGE GERRY moved for a committee to prepare a bill, Mason seconded, and without debate the delegates, voting by states, defeated the motion 10–0. A motion to endorse FREEDOM OF THE PRESS was also defeated, after ROGER SHERMAN declared, "It is unnecessary. The power of Congress does not extend to the Press."

Not a delegate to the convention opposed a bill of rights in principle. The overwhelming majority believed "It is unnecessary." Although they were recommending a strong national government that could regulate individuals directly, Congress could exercise only ENUMERATED POWERS or powers necessary to carry out those enumerated. A bill of rights would restrain national powers, but, as Hamilton asked, "Why declare that things shall not be done which there is no power to do?" Congress had no power to regulate the press or religion.

Civil liberties, supporters of the Constitution believed, faced danger from the possibility of repressive state action, but that was a matter to be guarded against by state bills of rights. Some states had none, and no state had a comprehensive list of guarantees. That fact provided the supporters of ratification with another argument: if a bill were framed omitting some rights, the omissions might justify their infringement. The great VIRGINIA DECLARATION OF RIGHTS had omitted the FREEDOMS OF SPEECH, assembly, and petition; the right to the writ of HABEAS CORPUS; the right to GRAND JURY proceedings; the RIGHT TO COUNSEL; and freedom from DOUBLE JEOPARDY, BILLS OF ATTAINDER, and EX POST FACTO laws. Twelve states, including Vermont, had framed constitutions, and the only right secured by all was TRIAL BY JURY in criminal cases; although all protected religious liberty, too, five either permitted or provided for ESTABLISHMENTS OF RELIGION. Two passed over a free press guarantee. Four neglected to ban excessive fines, excessive BAIL, compulsory self-incrimination, and general SEARCH WARRANTS. Five ignored protections for the rights of assembly, petition, counsel, and trial by jury in civil cases. Seven omitted a prohibition on ex post facto laws. Nine failed to provide for grand jury proceedings, and nine failed to condemn bills of attainder. Ten said nothing about freedom of speech, while eleven were silent on double jeopardy. Omissions in a national bill of rights raised dangers that would be avoided if the Constitution simply left the rights of Americans uncatalogued. The Framers also tended to be skeptical about the value of "parchment barriers" against "overbearing majorities," as JAMES MADISON said. As realists they understood that the constitutional protection of rights would mean little during times of popular hysteria or war; any framer could cite examples of gross abridgments of civil liberties in states that had bills of rights.

The lack of a bill of rights proved to be the strongest argument of the opponents of ratification. The usually masterful politicians who dominated the Constitutional Convention had made a serious political error. Their arguments against including a bill of rights were neither politic nor convincing. A bill of rights could do no harm, and, as THOMAS JEFFERSON pointed out in letters persuading Madison to switch positions, might do some good. Moreover, the contention that listing some rights might jeopardize others not mentioned was inconsistent and easily answered. The inconsistency derived from the fact that the Constitution as proposed included some rights: no RELIGIOUS TEST for office; jury trials in criminal cases; the writ of habeas corpus; a tight definition of TREASON; and bans on ex post facto laws and bills of attainder. The argument that to include some rights would exclude others boomeranged; every right excluded seemed in jeopardy. Enumerated powers could be abused; the power to tax, opponents argued, might be used against the press or religion. Moreover, the argument that a bill of rights was unnecessary could not possibly apply to the rights of the criminally accused or to personal liberties of a procedural nature. The new national government would act directly on the people and be buttressed by an undefined executive power and a national judiciary to enforce laws made by Congress; and Congress had the authority to define crimes and prescribe penalties for violations of its laws. PATRICK HENRY contended that the proposed Constitution empowered the United States to torture citizens into confessing their violations of congressional enactments.

Mason's point that a bill of rights would quiet the fears of the people was unanswerable. Alienating him and his followers was bad politics and blunderingly handed them a stirring cause around which they could muster opposition to ratification. No rational argument—and the lack of a bill of rights created an extremely emotional issue not amenable to rational argument—could possibly allay the fears generated by demagogues like Henry and principled opponents like Mason.

In Pennsylvania, the second state to ratify, the minority demanded a comprehensive bill of rights. Massachusetts, the sixth state to ratify, was the first to do so with recommended amendments, although only two—jury trial in civil suits and grand jury INDICTMENT—belonged in a bill of rights. But Massachusetts led the way toward recommended amendments, and the last four states to ratify recommended comprehensive bills of rights. Every right that became part of the ten amendments known as the Bill of Rights was included in state recommendations, with the exception of JUST COMPENSATION for property taken.

Some Federalists—above all Madison, whose political position in Virginia deteriorated because of his opposition to a bill of rights—finally realized that statecraft and political expediency dictated a switch in position. In states where ratification was in doubt, especially New York, Virginia, and North Carolina, Federalists pledged themselves to subsequent amendments to protect civil liberties, as soon as the new government went into operation.

In the first Congress, Representative Madison sought to fulfill his pledge. His accomplishment in the face of opposition and apathy entitles him to be remembered as "father of the Bill of Rights" even more than as "father of the Constitution." Many Federalists thought that the house had more important tasks, like the passage of tonnage duties. The opposition party, which had capitalized on the lack of a bill of rights in the Constitution, hoped for either a second convention or amendments that would cripple the substantive powers of the government. They had used the bill of rights issue as a smokescreen for objections to the Constitution's provisions on DIRECT TAXES, the judicial power, and the commerce power; these objections could not be dramatically popularized, and now the Anti-Federalists sought to scuttle Madison's proposals. They began by stalling, then tried to annex amendments aggrandizing state powers, and finally depreciated the importance of the very protections of individual liberty that they had formerly demanded. Madison meant to prove that the new government was a friend of liberty, and he understood that his amendments, if adopted, would make extremely difficult the passage of genuinely Anti-Federalist proposals. He would not be put off; he was insistent, compelling, unyielding, and, finally, triumphant.

On June 8, 1789, he made his long masterful speech before an apathetic House, introducing amendments culled mainly from state constitutions and state ratification proposals. All power, he argued, is subject to abuse and should be guarded against by constitutional provisions securing "the great rights of mankind." The government had only limited powers, but it might, unless prohibited, use general warrants in the enforcement of its revenue laws. In Great Britain, bills of rights merely erected barriers against the powers of the crown, leaving the powers of Parliament "altogether indefinite," and in Great Britain, the constitution left unguarded the "choicest" rights of the press and of conscience. The great objective he had in mind, Madison declared, was to limit the powers of government, thus preventing legislative as well as executive abuse, and above all preventing abuses of power by "the body of the people, operating by the majority against the minority." Mere "paper barriers" might fail, but they raised a standard that might educate the majority against acts to which they might be inclined. To the argument that a bill of rights was not necessary because the states constitutionally protected freedom, Madison had two responses. One was that some states had no bills of rights, others "very defective ones." The states constituted a greater danger to liberty than the new national government. The other was that the Constitution should, therefore, include an amendment that "No State shall violate the equal rights of conscience, or the freedom of the press, or the trial by jury in criminal cases." This, Madison declared, was "the most valuable amendment in the whole list." To the contention that an enumeration of rights would disparage those not in the list, Madison replied that the danger could be guarded against by adopting a proposal of his composition that became the NINTH AMENDMENT. If his amendments were "incorporated" into the constitution, Madison said, using another argument borrowed from Jefferson, "independent tribunals of justice will consider themselves in a peculiar manner the guardians of those rights; they will be an impenetrable bulwark against every assumption of power in the legislative or executive; they will be naturally led to resist every encroachment upon rights expressly stipulated for in the constitution. . . ."

Supporters of Madison informed him that Anti-Federalists did not really want a bill of rights and that his proposals "confounded the Anties exceedingly. . . ." Madison's proposals went to a select committee, of which he was a member, though its chairman, John Vining of Delaware, thought the House had "more important business." The committee added freedom of speech to the recommended prohibitions on the states, made some stylistic changes, and urged the amendments, which the House adopted. Madison, however, had proposed to "incorporate" the amendments within the text of the Constitution at appropriate points. He did not, that is, recommend their adoption as a separate "bill of rights." Members objected that to incorporate the amendments would give the impression that the Framers of the Constitution had signed a document that included provisions not of their composition. Another argument for lumping the amendments together was that the matter of form was so "trifling" that the House should not squander its time debating the placement of the various amendments. Indeed, Aedanus Burke of South Carolina, an Anti-Federalist, thought the amendments were "not those solid and substantial amendments which the people expect; they are little better than whip-syllabub, frothy and full of wind . . . it will be better to drop the subject." Men of Burke's views in the Senate managed to kill the proposed restrictions on the states, and the Senate sought to cripple the clause against establishments of religion. A conference committee of the two houses, which included Madison, accepted the Senate's joining together several amendments but agreed to Madison's phrasing of the proposal that became the FIRST AMENDMENT. The House accepted the conference report on September 24, 1789, the Senate a day later. Virginia's senators, William Grayson and RICHARD HENRY LEE, both Anti-Federalists, opposed the amendments because they left "the great points of the Judiciary, direct taxation, &c to stand as they are. . . ." Lee informed Patrick Henry that they had erred in their strategy of accepting ratification on the promise of subsequent amendments. Grayson reported to Henry that the amendments adopted by the Senate "are good for nothing. . . ."

Within six months of the time the amendments, or Bill of Rights, were submitted to the states for approval, nine states ratified. Connecticut and Georgia refused to ratify on the ground that the Bill of Rights was unnecessary; they belatedly ratified on the sesquicentennial anniversary of the ratification of the Constitution in 1939. (Massachusetts ratified in 1939, too, although both houses of its legislature in 1790 had adopted most of the amendments, but they had failed to send official notice of ratification.) The admission of Vermont to the union in 1791 made necessary ratification by eleven states. Vermont's ratification of the amendments in November 1791 made Virginia's approval indispensable as the eleventh state. The battle there was stalled in the state senate, where the Anti-Federalists were in control. They first sought to sabotage the Bill of Rights and then, having failed in their chief objective to abolish the power of Congress to enact direct taxes, they irresolutely acquiesced two years later. Virginia finally ratified on December 15, 1791, making the Bill of Rights part of the Constitution.

The history of the framing and ratification of the Bill of Rights is sparse. We know almost nothing about what the state legislatures thought concerning the meanings of the various amendments, and the press was perfunctory in its reports, if not altogether silent. But for Madison's persistence the amendments would have died in Congress. Our precious Bill of Rights was in the main the result of the political necessity for certain reluctant Federalists to make their own a cause that had been originated, in vain, by the Anti-Federalists to vote down the Constitution. The party that had first opposed a Bill of Rights inadvertently wound up with the responsibility for its framing and ratification, while the party that had first professed to want it discovered too late that it was not only embarrassing but politically disastrous for ulterior party purposes.

LEONARD W. LEVY
(1986)

Bibliography

BRANT, IRVING 1965 *The Bill of Rights: Its Origin and Meanings.* Indianapolis: Bobbs-Merrill.

DUMBAULD, EDWARD 1957 *The Bill of Rights and What It Means Today.* Norman: University of Oklahoma Press.

RUTLAND, ROBERT A. 1955 *The Birth of the Bill of Rights, 1776–1791.* Chapel Hill: University of North Carolina Press.

SCHWARTZ, BERNARD 1977 *The Great Rights of Mankind: A History of the American Bill of Rights.* New York: Oxford University Press.

BILL OF RIGHTS IN MODERN APPLICATION

Modern law and theory about the BILL OF RIGHTS reflects the contributions of eighteenth-century Framers, nineteenth-century Reconstructors, and twentieth-century judges. The most central juridical event in the development has been the "incorporation" of the Bill of Rights against state and local governments, a once controversial but now widely accepted judicial DOCTRINE that draws strong support from the text and ORIGINAL INTENT of the FOURTEENTH AMENDMENT.

The standard story about the Bill of Rights focuses on the Founding era in general and JAMES MADISON in particular, but this story ignores all the ways in which the RECONSTRUCTION generation breathed new life into an old bill. A separate Bill of Rights was no part of Madison's carefully conceived original plan at Philadelphia. And many lawmakers in the First Congress were relatively un-

interested in the Bill, finding it a "nauseous" distraction. By contrast, Ohio Congressman JOHN A. BINGHAM, the father of the Fourteenth Amendment in the Reconstruction era, placed the Bill of Rights at the center of his thinking about constitutionalism. His speeches in the Thirty-Ninth Congress are far more inspired, and perhaps more inspiring, than Madison's in the First.

The Bill of Rights that emerged in the 1790s was a creature of its time. In the afterglow of a Revolutionary War waged by local governments against an imperial center, the bill of the 1790s affirmed various rights against Congress, but none against the states, as the Supreme Court properly held in BARRON V. CITY OF BALTIMORE (1833). And the rights that the original bill did affirm sounded more in FEDERALISM than in libertarianism. Congress could not establish a national church, but neither could it disestablish state churches. The FIRST AMENDMENT was thus less anti-establishment than it was pro-STATES' RIGHTS; religious policy would be decided locally, not nationally, in the American equivalent of the European Peace at Augsburg and Treaty of Westphalia. The SECOND AMENDMENT celebrated local militias (the heroes of the AMERICAN REVOLUTION), and the THIRD AMENDMENT likewise reflected uneasiness about a central standing army. Much of the rest of the bill reinforced the powers of local juries. (The Fifth Amendment safeguarded GRAND JURIES; the Sixth Amendment, criminal PETIT JURIES; and the SEVENTH AMENDMENT, civil juries. Beyond these specific clauses, many other parts of the original bill also championed the role of juries—who would protect popular publishers like John Peter Zenger in First Amendment cases, would hold abusive government officials liable for UNREASONABLE SEARCHES in FOURTH AMENDMENT cases, and would help assess JUST COMPENSATION in Fifth Amendment cases.) The only amendment endorsed by every state convention demanding a Bill of Rights was the TENTH AMENDMENT, which emphatically affirmed states' rights. Madison wanted more—a bill championing individual rights, and protecting them against states, too—but in 1791, he was struggling against the tide. His proposed amendment requiring states to respect speech, press, conscience, and juries passed the U.S. HOUSE OF REPRESENTATIVES (as the presciently numbered Fourteenth Amendment) but died in a U.S. SENATE that championed states' rights. Only after a CIVIL WAR dramatized the need to limit abusive states would a new Fourteenth Amendment and distinctly modern view of the bill emerge—a bill celebrating individual rights and preventing states from abridging fundamental freedoms.

In retrospect, we can see that the process of incorporation began in the late nineteenth century, when the Court in CHICAGO BURLINGTON & QUINCY RAILWAY V. CHICAGO (1897) applied the principles of the TAKINGS clause to states. The incorporation of First Amendment FREEDOM

OF SPEECH rights began in earnest in 1925 (GITLOW V. NEW YORK), and the religion clauses were first brought to bear against states in 1940 (CANTWELL V. CONNECTICUT, decided under the free exercise clause), and in 1947 (EVERSON V. BOARD OF EDUCATION, decided under the ESTABLISHMENT CLAUSE). Later in the 1940s, the Court incorporated the Fourth Amendment (initially, without the EXCLUSIONARY RULE); and in the early 1960s, with Justice FELIX FRANKFURTER's departure from the Court, the logjam broke, and the Court made virtually all the rest of the bill applicable against states and local governments. The vehicle for this transformation was Justice WILLIAM J. BRENNAN, JR.'s brainchild—a theory of "selective incorporation" that in theory steered midway between Justice HUGO BLACK's insistence on total incorporation and critics' condemnation of the very idea of incorporation. In practice, Brennan's and the WARREN COURT's application of this doctrine came very close to the results advocated by Black. Today, only the Second and Seventh Amendments, and the Fifth Amendment's grand jury clause, have not been incorporated.

Mid-twentieth-century critics of the idea of incorporation—like Frankfurter and the second Justice JOHN M. HARLAN—argued that applying the Bill of Rights against state and local governments would ultimately weaken American liberty. If judges were to use the bill against states, the argument went, these judges would be tempted to water the bill down to take account of the considerable diversity of state practice; and then in turn, these judges would hold the federal government to only this watered-down version. But as Black and his fellow incorporationsts anticipated, extension of the Bill of Rights against the states has, in general, dramatically strengthened the bill, not weakened it, in both legal doctrine and popular consciousness. Unused muscles atrophy, while those that are regularly put to use grow strong. Before the Civil War, the Bill of Rights played a surprisingly trivial role. Only once was it used by the Court before 1866 to invalidate federal action, and that one use was DRED SCOTT V. SANDFORD (1857)—which easily accepted the highly implausible claim that the Fifth Amendment DUE PROCESS clause invalidated free-soil territory laws like the NORTHWEST ORDINANCE and the MISSOURI COMPROMISE. In a review of newspapers published in 1841, a recent scholar could find not even one fiftieth anniversary celebration of the Bill of Rights.

In area after area, incorporation enabled judges first to invalidate state and local laws, and then, with this doctrinal base thus built up, judges could begin to keep Congress in check. The First Amendment is illustrative. Before 1925, when the Court began in earnest the process of First Amendment incorporation, free speech had never prevailed against a repressive statute in the U.S. Supreme Court. (And although no case ever reached the Court, no lower federal court in the 1790s ever invalidated the infamous SEDITION ACT of 1798.) Within a few years of incorporation, however, freedom of expression and religion began to win in the High Court in landmark cases involving states, like STROMBERG V. CALIFORNIA and NEAR V. MINNESOTA EX REL. OLSON in 1931 protecting free speech and FREEDOM OF THE PRESS, and *Cantwell v. Connecticut* in 1940 protecting RELIGIOUS LIBERTY. These and other cases began to build up a First Amendment tradition, in and out of court, and that tradition could then be used against even federal officials. Not until 1965 did the Court strike down an act of Congress on First Amendment grounds, and when it did so (in LAMONT V. POSTMASTER GENERAL), it relied squarely on doctrine built up in earlier cases involving states. Consider also the FLAG-DESECRATION cases of *Texas v. Johnson* (1989) and *United States v. Eichman* (1990). In the first case, the Justices defined the basic First Amendment principles to strike down a state statute and then, in the second case, the Court stood its ground on this platform to strike down an act of Congress.

The large body of modern legal doctrine concerning the Bill of Rights has rolled out of courtrooms and into the vocabulary and vision of law students, journalists, activists, and ultimately the citizenry at large. But without incorporation, and the steady flow of cases created by state and local laws, the Supreme Court would have had far fewer opportunities to be part of the ongoing American conversation about liberty. Here, too, we see that the central role of the Bill of Rights today owes at least as much to the Reconstruction as to the Founding.

Perhaps nowhere has the importance of incorporation in shaping American jurisprudence been more evident than in the field of constitutional CRIMINAL PROCEDURE. The overwhelming majority of criminal cases are prosecuted by state governments under state law; only after the incorporation of the Fourth, Fifth, Sixth, and Eighth Amendments did federal courts develop a robust and highly elaborate—if also highly controversial and perhaps mistaken—jurisprudence of constitutional criminal procedure. The centrality of race to modern conceptions of CIVIL RIGHTS and CIVIL LIBERTIES further confirms the significance of Reconstruction. Sometimes the role of the Fourteenth Amendment is explicitly acknowledged—as when the Court in BOLLING V. SHARPE (1954) read the Framers' Fifth Amendment due process clause in light of the Reconstructors' EQUAL PROTECTION clause. Other times, the influence of the Fourteenth Amendment on the jurisprudence of the Bill of Rights has been almost unconscious, as in the landmark 1964 case of NEW YORK TIMES V. SULLIVAN. The facts of this case—involving an all-white local jury from an ex- Confederate state trying to shut down the speech of a Yankee newspaper and a national CIVIL RIGHTS MOVEMENT led by a black preacher—obviously call to mind images of Reconstruction, but the Court tried to tell a Founding-era story starring Madison and Zenger rather than a Reconstruction tale touting Bingham and Frederick Douglass. But only the Reconstruction can explain why—contra ZENGER'S CASE—local juries are not always to be trusted to protect free expression.

The modern notion of a self-contained federal bill of rights also derives at least as much from Reconstruction as from the Founding. The federal Constitution contains no explicit caption introducing a "Bill of Rights"—unlike many early state constitutions, which feature a self-styled "declaration of rights" preceding an explicit "frame of government." And because the first ten federal amendments ultimately came in as appendices rather than as a preface, still-later amendments had the effect of pushing early amendments to the middle—ten early postscripts before later post-postscripts. It was Bingham's generation that in effect added a closing parenthesis after the first eight (or nine or ten) amendments, distinguishing these amendments from all others. As a result, Americans today can lay claim to a federal *"Bill* of Rights" set apart from everything else, and symbolically first even if textually middling.

Bingham and others also insisted that the early amendments were largely a "Bill of *Rights"*—of persons, not states. Today's conventional wisdom sharply distinguishes between structural issues and rights issues. Here too, this distinction is attributed to the Framers—their Constitution delineated structure; their bill delineated rights. But once again this conventional account misreads the Founding and misses the Reconstruction. Structure and rights tightly intertwined in the original Constitution and in the original Bill of Rights, which themselves tightly intertwined. The basic need to separate rights from structure comes from the Fourteenth Amendment itself—from the need for a suitable filter that enables incorporation to mine and refine rights from the mixed ore in which these rights were initially embedded in the Framers' quarry.

What, in the end, are we to make of the pervasive ways in which our stock stories have exaggerated the Founding and diminished the Reconstruction? Perhaps many of us are guilty of a kind of curiously selective ancestor worship—one that gives too much credit to Madison and not enough to Bingham, that celebrates THOMAS JEFFERSON and PATRICK HENRY but slights Harriet Beecher Stowe and Frederick Douglass. Great as Madison and Jefferson were, they lived and died as slaveholders, and their Bill of Rights was tainted by its quiet complicity with the original sin of SLAVERY. Even as we celebrate the Framers, we must ponder the sobering words of CHARLES PINCKNEY in the 1788 South Carolina ratification debates: "Another reason weighed particularly, with the members of this state, against the insertion of a bill of rights. Such bills generally begin with declaring that all men are by nature free. Now, we should make that declaration with very bad grace, when a large part of our property consists in men who are actually born slaves."

But the Fourteenth Amendment did begin with an affirmation of the freedom—and citizenship—of all. The midwives of this new birth of freedom were women alongside men, blacks alongside whites. As twentieth-century judges have begun to realize, because of these nineteenth-century men and women, our eighteenth-century Bill of Rights has taken on new life and meaning.

AKHIL REED AMAR
(2000)

(SEE ALSO: *Fourteenth Amendment as a New Constitution; Incorporation Doctrine.*)

Bibliography

AMAR, AKHIL REED   1997   *The Constitution and Criminal Procedure: First Principles.* New Haven, Conn.: Yale University Press.
———   1998   *The Bill of Rights: Creation and Reconstruction.* New Haven, Conn.: Yale University Press.
CURTIS, MICHAEL KENT   1986   *No State Shall Abridge: The Fourteenth Amendment and the Bill of Rights.* Durham, N.C.: Duke University Press.

BINGHAM, JOHN A.
(1815–1900)

An Ohio attorney, John Armor Bingham was a congressman (1855–1863, 1865–1873), Army judge advocate (1864–1865), solicitor of the COURT OF CLAIMS (1864–1865), and ambassador to Japan (1873–1885). After President ABRAHAM LINCOLN's assassination, President ANDREW JOHNSON appointed Bingham as a special judge advocate (prosecutor) to the military commission trying the accused assassination conspirators. Bingham was particularly effective in answering defense objections during the trials and in justifying the constitutionality of trying the civilian defendants in military courts.

From 1865 to 1867 Bingham served on the JOINT COMMITTEE ON RECONSTRUCTION. As a Republican moderate Bingham supported congressional reconstruction but demanded strict adherence to the Constitution and favored early readmission of the ex-Confederate states. He offered numerous amendments to moderate the CIVIL RIGHTS ACT OF 1866, and although these passed he still voted against the bill, because he believed Congress lacked the authority to protect freedmen in this manner. Bingham wanted very much to protect them, and during the debates over the civil rights bill he argued that a new constitutional amendment was the answer. Bingham believed that the results of the war—including the death of both SLAVERY and state SOVEREIGNTY, as well as the protection of CIVIL LIBERTIES for blacks—could be secured only by an amendment that would nationalize the BILL OF RIGHTS. By working to apply the Fifth and FIRST AMENDMENTS to the states Bingham linked the antislavery arguments of the antebellum period to postbellum conditions.

In 1865 Bingham suggested an amendment that would empower Congress "to secure to all persons in every State of the Union equal protection in their rights, life, liberty, and property." Bingham believed the THIRTEENTH AMENDMENT had not only freed blacks but also made them citizens. As citizens of the United States they were among "the People of the United States" referred to in the PREAMBLE to the Constitution and protected by the Fifth Amendment. However, Bingham was unsure whether the enforcement provision of the Thirteenth Amendment allowed Congress to guarantee and protect CIVIL RIGHTS. Johnson's veto of the 1866 Civil Rights bill only increased Bingham's determination to place such protection beyond the reach of a presidential veto or repeal by a future Congress. Bingham therefore drafted what became section 1 of the FOURTEENTH AMENDMENT, protecting the freedmen by explicitly making them citizens, prohibiting states from abridging their PRIVILEGES AND IMMUNITIES as United States citizens, and guaranteeing all persons DUE PROCESS and EQUAL PROTECTION of the law. In 1871 Bingham reaffirmed his belief that the amendment was designed to protect those privileges and immunities "chiefly defined in the first eight amendments to the Constitution of the United States." Thus, as Bingham saw it, the ABOLITIONIST CONSTITUTIONAL THEORY of the antebellum period became part of the Constitution.

By 1867 Bingham was at least temporarily a Radical Republican. He supported THADDEUS STEVENS's bill for military reconstruction after the ex-Confederate states refused to ratify the Fourteenth Amendment and after numerous outrages had been perpetrated against freedom. Initially opposed to IMPEACHMENT, he was elected to the impeachment committee and was made chairman after threatening to resign unless given that position. Bingham vigorously pursued the prosecution of Johnson, and after it failed he attempted to investigate the seven Republican senators who voted against impeachment.

Bingham had initially opposed linking black suffrage to readmission to the Union, and opposed efforts by Stevens to create such a linkage. He argued that Congress lacked the constitutional authority to do this. But by 1870 he supported the FIFTEENTH AMENDMENT and sought to extend the franchise even further, by prohibiting religious, property, or nationality limitations on the ballot. In 1871, with the three new amendments legitimizing congressional ac-

tion, Bingham supported the three "force bills," which prohibited states and individuals from violating the newly acquired constitutional rights of the freedmen, gave the federal government supervisory powers over national elections, and made numerous acts federal crimes under the Ku Klux Klan Act. (See FORCE ACTS.) Bingham, the careful constitutionalist and moderate Republican leader, defended these acts because they were a response to the terror being inflicted against blacks, and because they were now constitutional.

PAUL FINKELMAN
(1986)

Bibliography

HYMAN, HAROLD M. and WIECEK, WILLIAM M. 1982 *Equal Justice under Law: Constitutional Development, 1835–1875.* New York: Harper & Row.

SWIFT, DONALD C. 1968 John A. Bingham and Reconstruction: The Dilemma of a Moderate. *Ohio History* 77:76–94.

BINNEY, HORACE
(1780–1875)

A leading Philadelphia attorney, Horace Binney edited six volumes of the Pennsylvania Supreme Court's decisions, covering the years 1799–1814. In 1862 Binney published two pamphlets entitled *The Privilege of the Writ of Habeas Corpus under the Constitution,* in which he defended President ABRAHAM LINCOLN's suspension of the writ. Binney argued that the President, and not Congress, had the power to suspend HABEAS CORPUS, and that each branch of the government had the right to interpret the Constitution independently. In 1865 Binney answered the many critics of his earlier work with a third pamphlet of the same title.

PAUL FINKELMAN
(1986)

Bibliography

BINNEY, CHARLES CHAUNCEY 1903 *The Life of Horace Binney, with Selections from His Letters.* Philadelphia: Lippincott.

BIRNEY, JAMES G.
(1792–1857)

A slaveholder, James Gillespie Birney studied law under ALEXANDER DALLAS, was a mildly antislavery politician in Kentucky and Alabama, and was a spokesman for the American Colonization Society. In 1834 he freed his remaining slaves, abandoned colonization, and formed the Kentucky Anti-Slavery Society. Finding Kentucky too dangerous for an abolitionist, Birney moved to Cincinnati, and in 1836 began publishing an antislavery newspaper, *The Philanthropist*. Unlike WILLIAM LLOYD GARRISON, whom he bitterly opposed, Birney believed that the United States Constitution could be a useful tool for abolitionists. He also argued for abolitionist political activity. In 1840 he was the Liberty party candidate for the presidency, but he drew only 7,069 votes. Four years later he won 62,300 votes, helping set the stage for more successful antislavery parties.

Birney was involved in three legal cases that helped develop his antislavery constitutionalism. In 1836 an anti-abolitionist mob in Cincinnati destroyed his press. Birney hired SALMON P. CHASE in a successful suit against the mob leaders for damages to the press. In 1837 Birney sheltered and hired a runaway slave named Matilda, and when she was captured, Chase and Birney defended her on the ground that having voluntarily been brought to Ohio, she therefore was not a fugitive slave; they also made the dubious argument that slaves who escaped from Kentucky into Ohio could not be recaptured, because the NORTH-WEST ORDINANCE provided only for the return of slaves who escaped from the "original states." Matilda was returned south, but Chase and Birney were more successful in appealing Birney's conviction for harboring slaves, which the Ohio Supreme Court overturned. (See ABOLITIONIST CONSTITUTIONAL THEORY.)

PAUL FINKELMAN
(1986)

Bibliography

FLADELAND, BETTY L.   1955   *James Gillespie Birney: Slaveholder to Abolitionist*. Ithaca, N.Y.: Cornell University Press.

BIRTH CONTROL

The American birth control movement began in the early twentieth century as a campaign to achieve a right of REPRODUCTIVE AUTONOMY in the face of hostile legislation in many states. By the time that campaign succeeded in getting the Supreme Court to espouse a constitutional RIGHT OF PRIVACY which allowed married couples to practice contraception, there was not a single state in which an anticontraception law was being enforced against private medical advice or against drugstore sales. GRISWOLD V. CONNECTICUT (1965) and its successor decisions thus did not create the effective right of choice; they recognized and legitimized the right, by subjecting restrictive legislation to strict judicial scrutiny and finding justifications wanting. (See FUNDAMENTAL INTERESTS.)

Contraception is only the most widely practiced method of birth control; others (apart from abstinence) are STERILIZATION and abortion. The Supreme Court, partly on the precedent of *Griswold*, recognized in ROE V. WADE (1973) a woman's constitutional right to have an abortion, qualified by the state's power to forbid abortion during the latter stages of pregnancy. The Court has had no occasion to recognize a person's right to choose to be sterilized, because the states have not sought to restrict that freedom. In any event the birth control movement has now won its most important constitutional battles; both married and single persons are free, both in fact and in constitutional theory, to choose not to beget or bear children.

"Birth control," however, has another potential meaning that is the antithesis of reproductive choice. The state may seek to coerce persons to refrain from procreating, either through compulsory sterilization or by other sanctions aimed at restricting family size. On present constitutional doctrine, the decision to procreate is "fundamental," requiring some COMPELLING STATE INTEREST to justify its limitation. (See SKINNER V. OKLAHOMA.) Although judicial recognition of such an interest is not inconceivable in some future condition of acute overpopulation, no such decision is presently foreseeable.

The constitutional right to choose whether to have a child or be a parent is properly rested today on SUBSTANTIVE DUE PROCESS grounds; "liberty" is precisely the point. Yet the interest in equality has also played a significant role in the development of these rights of choice. Justice BYRON R. WHITE, concurring in *Griswold*, pointed out how enforcement of an anticontraceptives law against birth control clinics worked to deny the disadvantaged from obtaining help in controlling family size. The well-to-do needed no clinics. And once *Griswold* recognized the right of married persons to practice contraception, the Supreme Court saw that EQUAL PROTECTION principles demanded extension of the right to be unmarried. (See EISENSTADT V. BAIRD; CAREY V. POPULATION SERVICES INTERNATIONAL.) Finally, judicial recognition of rights of reproductive choice has followed the progress of the women's movement. The breakdown of the traditional sexual "double standard" and the opening of new opportunities for women outside the "housewife marriage" have gone together, both socially and in constitutional development. No longer is the "erring woman" to be punished with unwanted pregnancy or parenthood. In 1920 Margaret Sanger wrote, "Birth control is woman's problem." Half a century later, the Supreme Court heard that message.

KENNETH L. KARST
(1986)

Bibliography

CHARLES, ALAN F.   1980   Abortion and Family Planning: Law and the Moral Issue. Pages 331–356 in Ruth Roemer and

George McKray (eds.), *Legal Aspects of Health Policy: Issues and Trends.* Westport, Conn.: Greenwood Press.

GREENAWALT, KENT 1971 Criminal Law and Population Control. *Vanderbilt Law Review* 24:465–494.

NOTE 1971 Legal Analysis and Population Control: The Problem of Coercion. *Harvard Law Review* 84:1856–1911.

BIRTHRIGHT CITIZENSHIP

The FOURTEENTH AMENDMENT provides, "All persons born or naturalized in the United States, and subject to the jurisdiction thereof, are citizens of the United States and of the State wherein they reside." Congress has expanded the range of persons who can claim birthright CITIZENSHIP. For example, children born to American couples abroad receive birthright citizenship under statutory law.

Interpretive controversies have arisen over the Fourteenth Amendment's "jurisdictional proviso," which requires that persons be "subject to the JURISDICTION" of the United States in order to claim constitutional birthright citizenship. It is widely agreed that the proviso was intended to carve out an exception for children born to foreign diplomats or invading armies. The crucial question is whether the proviso has other applications.

Late in the nineteenth century, the Supreme Court held in *Elk v. Wilkins* (1884) that AMERICAN INDIANS born on reservations had not been born subject to the jurisdiction of the United States. *Elk* has never been overruled, but, for practical purposes, it no longer matters; by 1940, Congress had granted birthright citizenship to all Native Americans born in the United States.

In recent decades, the major controversy about the Constitution's citizenship rule has concerned its application to the children of ALIENS who enter the country unlawfully. The Fourteenth Amendment draws no distinctions based on the nationality of a child's parents, and the Court has added none. On the contrary, the Court has asserted that the native-born children of all aliens automatically acquire citizenship by virtue of the Fourteenth Amendment's rule. That assertion appeared in a footnote to PLYLER V. DOE (1982); it was dictum, but it is consistent with the way in which federal IMMIGRATION officials have interpreted the amendment.

During the 1980s, two Yale professors, Rogers Smith and Peter Schuck, maintained that the Fourteenth Amendment's jurisdictional proviso excluded the native-born children of aliens who enter the country illegally. Schuck and Smith reasoned that by their unlawful entry, the aliens refuse to submit to the jurisdiction of American law. Schuck and Smith buttressed this textual argument with a theoretical one. Communities, they said, should be founded on consent; for that reason, foreigners and their children should not be allowed to obtain American citizenship without getting permission from those who already had it.

Schuck and Smith were not hostile to immigration; indeed, they favored increasing the flow of legal immigrants into the United States. During the 1990s, however, anti-immigrant politicians mounted their own assault on the rule granting citizenship to the native-born children of aliens who are unlawfully in the country. Some embraced the interpretive argument advanced by Schuck and Smith; others, including California Governor Pete Wilson, called for a constitutional amendment.

It is hard to deny the appeal of a purely consensual political community, in which every member is present through his or her own free choice, and in which no member is present without the approval of his or her compatriots. It is equally hard, however, to apply this ideal to modern nation states. For example, a child born to immigrant parents and raised in the United States will find her identity and opportunities comprehensively shaped by American political power. American law will govern her education, her encounters with the police, her economic circumstances, her claim to health care, and more. By what right does the United States exercise such pervasive authority over the child? Perhaps the parents consented to having it exercised over them when they entered the country. The child, however, never had any meaningful opportunity to consent.

Consent is an impossibly demanding requirement against which to evaluate citizenship rules. The Fourteenth Amendment's rule incorporates a more realistic norm, one based on reciprocity. Because the United States claims authority to regulate pervasively the lives of the children born within its borders, the United States must permit those children to share in the benefits that flow from that exercise of power. It must admit them to the political community, so that power is exercised for them rather than merely upon them.

Without this principle, the United States might develop a permanent class of laborers, descendants of illegal aliens who would go from cradle to grave in the United States without sharing in its political life. Other Americans might get substantial benefits by exploiting such a workforce. Indeed, some sectors of the American agricultural community have routinely relied on aliens who are subject to deportation; the vulnerability of these workers makes them a ready source of cheap labor.

A permanent workforce of second-class persons would replicate some aspects of slave labor. It is no accident that the Fourteenth Amendment's citizenship rule stands in the way of such a system. The rule was adopted to enfranchise American slaves and their descendants, and, more specifically, to overrule DRED SCOTT V. SANDFORD (1857). In *Scott*, Chief Justice ROGER BROOKE TANEY concluded that no person descended from slaves could become a citizen of the United States. In dissent, Justices BENJAMIN R. CURTIS and JOHN MCLEAN repudiated Taney's position. McLean simply asserted that any free person who had been born in the United States was an American citizen. Curtis offered a more elaborate argument. He analogized the states to foreign sovereigns, and argued that the power to define citizenship was an essential incident of SOVEREIGNTY. Therefore, Curtis concluded, birthright citizenship depended on state law.

The Fourteenth Amendment rejected not only Taney's theory, but also Curtis's, which had been widely accepted by lawyers before the CIVIL WAR. After the Fourteenth Amendment, states no longer had the power to say who was entitled to membership in their political community. The issue was settled by national law, and state citizenship was reduced to an incident of residence. The states had lost a traditional indicator of sovereign status. This development reflects how deeply the Civil War changed American FEDERALISM.

CHRISTOPHER L. EISGRUBER
(2000)

Bibliography

CARENS, JOSEPH H. 1987 Who Belongs? Theoretical and Legal Questions About Birthright Citizenship in the United States. *University of Toronto Law Journal* 37:413–443.

EISGRUBER, CHRISTOPHER L. 1997 Birthright Citizenship and the Constitution. *New York University Law Review* 72:54–96.

KARST, KENNETH L. 1989 *Belonging to America: Equal Citizenship and the Constitution.* New Haven, Conn: Yale University Press.

KETTNER, JAMES H. 1978 *The Development of American Citizenship 1608–1870.* Chapel Hill: University of North Carolina Press.

NEUMAN, GERALD L. 1996 *Strangers to the Constitution: Immigrants, Borders, and Fundamental Law.* Princeton, N.J.: Princeton University Press.

NOTE 1994 The Birthright Citizenship Amendment: A Threat to Equality. *Harvard Law Review* 107:1026–1043.

SCHUCK, PETER H. and SMITH, ROGERS M. 1985 *Citizenship Without Consent: Illegal Aliens in the American Polity.* New Haven, Conn.: Yale University Press.

BISHOP v. WOOD
426 U.S. 341 (1976)

Bishop worked a major change in the modern law of PROCEDURAL DUE PROCESS, enshrining in the law the view Justice WILLIAM H. REHNQUIST had unsuccessfully urged in ARNETT V. KENNEDY (1974): the due process right of a holder of a statutory "entitlement" is defined by positive law, not by the Constitution itself.

Here, a city ordinance that classified a police officer as a "permanent employee" was nonetheless interpreted by the lower federal courts to give an officer employment only "at the will and pleasure of the city." The Supreme Court held, 5–4, that this ordinance created no "property" interest in the officer's employment, and that, absent public disclosure of the reasons for his termination, he had suffered no stigma that impaired a "liberty" interest. The key to the majority's decision presumably lay in this sentence: "The federal court is not the appropriate forum in which to review the multitude of personnel decisions that are made daily by public agencies."

In dissent, Justice WILLIAM J. BRENNAN accurately commented that the Court had resurrected the "right/privilege" distinction, discredited in GOLDBERG V. KELLY (1970),and insisted that there was a federal constitutional dimension to the idea of "property" interests, not limited by state law and offering the protections of due process to legitimate expectations raised by government.

KENNETH L. KARST
(1986)

BITUMINOUS COAL ACT
50 Stat. 72 (1937)

After CARTER V. CARTER COAL COMPANY (1936), Congress restored regulation of bituminous coal in INTERSTATE COMMERCE. The new act, designed to control the interstate sale and distribution of soft coal and to protect interstate commerce, levied a nineteen and one-half percent tax on all producers but remitted payment to those who accepted the new code. Price-fixing provisions constituted the crux of the act; Congress did not reenact any labor provisions, although it encouraged free COLLECTIVE BARGAINING.

The act established a National Bituminous Coal Commission to supervise an elaborate procedure for setting minimum prices. Unfair competition or sales below established prices violated the code. The act provided extensive PROCEDURAL DUE PROCESS and several means of enforcement, including CEASE-AND-DESIST ORDERS and private suits carrying treble damage awards for injured competitors.

An 8–1 Supreme Court sustained the act in *Sunshine Anthracite Coal Company v. Adkins* (1940). Conceding the tax was "a sanction to enforce the regulatory provisions of the Act," the majority held that Congress might nevertheless "impose penalties in aid of the exercise of any of its ENUMERATED POWERS." The Court thus upheld the act under the COMMERCE CLAUSE, declaring that the method of regulation was for legislative determination.

DAVID GORDON
(1986)

BIVENS v. SIX UNKNOWN NAMED AGENTS OF THE FEDERAL BUREAU OF NARCOTICS
403 U.S. 388 (1971)

This is the leading case concerning IMPLIED RIGHTS OF ACTION under the Constitution. Federal agents conducted an unconstitutional search of Webster Bivens's apartment. Bivens brought an action in federal court seeking damages for a FOURTH AMENDMENT violation. Although no federal statute supplied Bivens with a cause of action, the Supreme Court, in an opinion by Justice WILLIAM J. BRENNAN, held that Bivens could maintain that action.

Two central factors led to the decision. First, violations of constitutional rights ought not go unremedied. The traditional remedy, enjoining unconstitutional behavior, plainly was inadequate for Bivens. And the Court was unwilling to leave Bivens to the uncertainties of state tort law, his principal alternative source of action. Second, the implied constitutional cause of action makes federal officials as vulnerable as state officials for constitutional misbehavior. Prior to *Bivens*, state officials were subject to suits under SECTION 1983, TITLE 42, UNITED STATES CODE, for violating individuals' constitutional rights. An action against federal officials had to be inferred in *Bivens* only because section 1983 is inapplicable to federal officials.

Both factors emerged again in later cases. DAVIS V. PASSMAN (1979) recognized an implied constitutional cause of action for claims brought under the Fifth Amendment, and *Carlson v. Green* (1980) extended *Bivens* to other constitutional rights. BUTZ V. ECONOMOU (1978) extended to federal officials the good faith defense that state officials enjoy under section 1983.

Bivens raises important questions about the scope of federal JUDICIAL POWER. Chief Justice WARREN E. BURGER and Justices HUGO L. BLACK and HARRY BLACKMUN dissented on the ground that Congress alone may authorize damages against federal officials. The majority, and Justice JOHN MARSHALL HARLAN in a concurring opinion, required no congressional authorization. But they left open the possibility that Congress might have the last word in the area through express legislation.

THEODORE EISENBERG
(1986)

BLACK, HUGO L.
(1886–1971)

When Hugo LaFayette Black was appointed to the Supreme Court in 1937, the basic tenets of his mature judicial philosophy had already been formed. Born in the Alabama hill country in 1886, Black received his law degree from the University of Alabama in 1906. He practiced law, largely handling personal injury cases, in Birmingham during the next twenty years and served brief terms as police court judge and county prosecutor. In 1926 he was elected to the United States Senate; after reelection in 1932 he became an outspoken advocate of the NEW DEAL and a tenacious investigator. Throughout his career he read extensively in history, philosophy, and literary classics. From THOMAS JEFFERSON he took his view of the FIRST AMENDMENT. Aristotle, his "favorite author," and JOHN LOCKE offered appealing theoretical perspectives on the nature of government and society.

Coming to the bench in the aftermath of President FRANKLIN D. ROOSEVELT'S COURT-PACKING plan, which he vigorously espoused, Black searched for a jurisprudence of certainty, seeking clear, precise standards that would limit judicial discretion, protect individual rights, and give government room to operate. He saw the Constitution as a set of unambiguous commands designed to prevent the recurrence of historic evils. In its text and the intent of its Framers he found the authority for applying some provisions virtually open-ended, and others rather more strictly. All constitutional questions he considered open until he dealt with them; but when he came to a conclusion, he maintained it with single-minded devotion. His opinions never suggested that he entertained any doubts.

Black's Senate years left an indelible impression on his performance as Justice. Each of the popular branches must be left to carry out its duties according to the original constitutional understanding. Congress makes the laws, he noted in YOUNGSTOWN SHEET & TUBE COMPANY V. SAWYER (1952); the President's functions are limited to the recommending and vetoing of bills. Congress, Black believed, had the power to regulate whatever affected commerce. Likewise, unless states discriminated against INTERSTATE COMMERCE, they had the power to regulate in the absence of contrary congressional direction. Nor, under the DUE PROCESS clause of the FOURTEENTH AMENDMENT, might courts consider the appropriateness of legislation. In *Lincoln Federal Labor Union v. Northwestern Iron & Metal Company* (1949), he observed that the Court had rejected "the *Allgeyer-Lochner-Adair-Coppage* constitutional doctrine"; the states had power to legislate "so long as their laws do not run afoul of some specific federal constitutional provision, or of some valid federal law."

Black's adamant refusal to expand judicial power through the due process clause forced him to develop an alternative theory to protect the rights enumerated in the BILL OF RIGHTS. He had to overcome his initial "grave doubts" about the validity of JUDICIAL REVIEW. CHAMBERS V. FLORIDA (1940) was an early milestone. Courts, he stated in that case, "stand against any winds that blow as havens of refuge for those who might otherwise suffer because they are helpless, weak, outnumbered, or because they are non-conforming victims of prejudice and public excitement." Finally, in *Adamson v. California* (1947), he laid down the formulation that guided him for the rest of his career:

> My study of the historical events that culminated in the Fourteenth Amendment . . . persuades me that one of the chief objects that the provisions of the Amendment's first section, separately, and as a whole, were intended to accomplish was to make the Bill of Rights applicable to the States. . . . I fear to see the consequences of the Court's practices of substituting its own concepts of decency and fundamental justice for the language of the Bill of Rights as its point of departure in interpreting and enforcing that Bill of Rights. . . . To hold that his Court can determine what, if any, provisions of the Bill of Rights will be enforced, and if so to what degree, is to frustrate the great design of a written Constitution.

Only by limiting judges' discretion, and demanding that they enforce the textual guarantees, could the protection of these rights be ensured. Black feared that the "shock the conscience" test, which Justice FELIX FRANKFURTER employed for the Court in *Rochin v. California* (1952), with its "accordion-like qualities" and "nebulous" and "evanescent standards," "must inevitably imperil all the individual liberty safeguards specifically enumerated in the Bill of Rights."

Black applied his INCORPORATION DOCTRINE in scores of cases. From his early days as a public official he hated coerced confessions, and he viewed POLICE INTERROGATIONS without counsel as secret inquisitions in flat violation of the FIFTH AMENDMENT's guarantee of the RIGHT AGAINST SELF-INCRIMINATION. "From the time government begins to move against a man," he said when the Court considered MIRANDA V. ARIZONA (1966), "when they take him into custody, his rights attach." He led the Court in expanding the RIGHT TO COUNSEL from his first term, when he held in JOHNSON V. ZERBST (1938) that in a federal prosecution counsel must be appointed to represent a defendant who cannot afford to hire an attorney. To his supreme satisfaction he wrote the opinion in GIDEON V. WAINWRIGHT (1963), overruling BETTS V. BRADY (1942) and making similar assistance mandatory in state FELONY trials. More of his dissents eventually became law than those of any other Justice.

Given his approach of allowing free play to the spirit of the Constitution while resting his justifications largely on its words, the generalities of the EQUAL PROTECTION clause presented problems of interpretation for Black. In his view, Article I conferred on qualified voters the rights to vote and to have their votes counted in congressional elections. Dissenting in COLEGROVE V. GREEN (1946), he argued

that both Article I and the equal protection clause required that congressional district lines be drawn "to give approximately equal weight to each vote cast." Black formally buried *Colegrove* in WESBERRY V. SANDERS (1963). In every REAPPORTIONMENT case, as in every case involving an INDIGENT prosecuted for crime, he supported the equal protection claim. He shared in the widespread agreement that the Fourteenth Amendment had been designed primarily to end RACIAL DISCRIMINATION, and made the first explicit reference to race as a SUSPECT CLASSIFICATION which must be subjected to the "most rigid scrutiny." Ironically, this came in one of the JAPANESE AMERICAN CASES (1943), in which he upheld, over biting dissents, a conviction for violating a military order during WORLD WAR II excluding all persons of Japanese ancestry from the West Coast. But as the Court moved beyond race in applying the equal protection clause, Black refused to follow. Classifications based on wealth or poverty were not "suspect"; and even though the claims in VOTING RIGHTS cases were essential for the democratic process to reach its full potential, he denied them.

During the first twenty-five years of his tenure, Black's opinions had remarkable constancy as he unflaggingly pursued his goal of human advancement within the bounds of constitutional interpretation. But new issues confronted the Court and the country in the 1960s. Black was fighting old age, and Court work, he admitted, was harder. Because of cataract operations he did not read nearly so much as he had. References in his opinions to books and articles became infrequent, and the cases he cited were often his old ones as he repeatedly accused his colleagues of going beyond their province. No longer was he reading the words of the Constitution expansively; his interpretations were restraining and cramped; and his categories of permissible legal action narrowed. Increasingly, he had trouble adjusting to a world that was changing. His opinions took on an essay-like quality, with a new structure and tone, and a note of anger crept into them.

From the beginning Black consistently interpreted the FOURTH AMENDMENT as restrictively as any Justice in the Court's modern history. Refusing to examine the term "unreasonable" in SEARCH AND SEIZURE cases, he generally accepted law enforcement actions. Almost invariably he validated WARRANTLESS SEARCHES including SEARCHES INCIDENT TO ARREST. His Fourth Amendment opinions emphasized the guilt of the accused, often starting with detailed descriptions of the crime; and, oddly, he ignored the amendment's rich history. After calling the EXCLUSIONARY RULE "an extraordinary sanction, judicially imposed," in *United States v. Wallace & Tiernan Company* (1949), he changed his mind: by linking the Fourth and Fifth Amendments in MAPP V. OHIO (1961), he found that "a constitutional basis emerges which not only justifies but actually requires" the rule. But his enthusiasm waned as the Court enlarged the FOURTH AMENDMENT's scope. In his last search and seizure case, COOLIDGE V. NEW HAMPSHIRE (1971), he converted this limitation on government into a grant of power: "The Fourth Amendment provides a constitutional means by which the Government can act to obtain EVIDENCE to be used in criminal prosecutions. The people are obliged to yield to a proper exercise of authority under that Amendment."

By the time the RIGHT OF PRIVACY matured as an issue, Black had tied himself to the text as a mode of constitutional interpretation. Two heated dissents indicated his narrow conception of the Fourth Amendment. Seemingly oblivious to the dangers of WIRETAPPING, he wrote in BERGER V. NEW YORK (1967): "Had the framers of this amendment desired to prohibit the use in court of evidence secured by an unreasonable search and seizure, they would have used plain appropriate language to say that conversations can be searched and words seized. . . ." Finding no mention of privacy in the Constitution, he dismissed it as a "vague judge-made goal" and denigrated it: "the 'right of privacy' . . . , like a chameleon, has a different color for every turning," he wrote in *Berger*. He accurately viewed its elevation to separate constitutional status in GRISWOLD V. CONNECTICUT (1965) as the revival of SUBSTANTIVE DUE PROCESS. "Use of any such broad, unbounded judicial authority would make of this Court's members a day-to-day constitutional convention." Black rejected the idea of a living Constitution. His *Adamson* dissent not only had expanded horizons but had set limits.

Black was most famous for his views on the First Amendment. In *Milk Wagon Drivers Union v. Meadowmoor Diaries* (1941), his initial opinion on the subject, he said, "Freedom to speak and write about public questions . . . is the heart of our government. If that be weakened, the result is debilitation; if it be stilled, the result is death." He ceaselessly implored the Court to expand the amendment's protections, and embellished his opinions with moving libertarian rhetoric. But as in other areas during his last half-dozen years or so, Black narrowed his construction and retreated from many of his previous positions.

He subscribed fully to the "preferred position" doctrine of the First Amendment. He used, and reworked, the CLEAR AND PRESENT DANGER test in BRIDGES V. CALIFORNIA (1941), adding words that he repeated often: "the First Amendment does not speak equivocally. It prohibits any law 'abridging the freedom of speech, or of the press.' It must be taken as a command of the broadest scope that explicit language . . . will allow." But slowly "clear and present danger," with its inherent balancing of disparate interests, disillusioned Black. The First Amendment "forbids compromise" in matters of conscience, he argued in

AMERICAN COMMUNICATIONS ASSOCIATION V. DOUDS (1950). The "basic constitutional precept" is that "penalties should be imposed only for a person's own conduct, not for his beliefs or for the conduct of those with whom he may associate"; those "who commit overt acts in violation of valid laws can and should be punished."

A new word began to appear as his opinions, invariably in dissent, grew more shrill and strident. "I think the First Amendment, with the Fourteenth, 'absolutely' forbids such laws without any 'ifs' or 'buts' or whereases," he wrote when the Court upheld a GROUP LIBEL statute in BEAUHARNAIS V. ILLINOIS (1952). The First Amendment "grants an absolute right to believe in any governmental system, discuss all governmental affairs, and argue for desired changes in the existing order," he proclaimed in *Carlson v. Landon* (1952)—"whether or not such discussion incites to action, legal or illegal," he added in YATES V. UNITED STATES (1957). He refined this speech-conduct distinction in BARENBLATT V. UNITED STATES (1959). Some laws "directly," while others "indirectly," affect speech; when in the latter cases the speech and action were intertwined, Black was willing to use a BALANCING TEST weighing "the effect on speech . . . in relation to the need for control of the conduct."

For many years Black voted to invalidate statutes as direct abridgments of First Amendment rights. He opposed such governmental actions as prescribing LOYALTY OATHS in WIEMAN V. UPDEGRAFF (1952); promulgating lists of "subversive" organizations in JOINT ANTI-FASCIST REFUGEE COMMITTEE V. MCGRATH (1952); demanding organizations' membership lists in GIBSON V. FLORIDA LEGISLATIVE INVESTIGATION COMMITTEE (1963); conducting LEGISLATIVE INVESTIGATIONS of suspected subversives in BARENBLATT V. UNITED STATES or prosecuting for subversive advocacy in DENNIS V. UNITED STATES (1951); and imposing penalties for Communist party membership in APTHEKER V. SECRETARY OF STATE (1965). Under his standard, OBSCENITY and LIBEL laws as well as the state's conditioning admission to the bar on an applicant's beliefs were unconstitutional. In cases of direct abridgment of speech, Black charged in UPHAUS V. WYMAN (1960), any balancing test substituted "elastic concepts" such as "arbitrary" and "unreasonable" for the Constitution's plain language, reducing the document's "absolute commands to mere admonitions." "Liberty, to be secure for any," he wrote in *Braden v. United States* (1961), "must be secure for all—even for the most miserable merchants of hated and unpopular ideas." The framers had ensured that liberty by doing all the balancing that was necessary.

Black was equally outspoken in RELIGIOUS LIBERTY cases, and played a key role in the development of the First Amendment's religious guarantees. He wrote the Court's opinion in EVERSON V. BOARD OF EDUCATION (1947), the first case declaring that the establishment clause applied to the states. After listing the clause's standards and stating that it was intended to erect, in Jefferson's words, "a wall of separation between Church and State," Black noted that government cannot "contribute tax-raised funds to the support of an institution which teaches the tenets and faith of any church." But for the state to pay the bus fares of all pupils, including those in parochial schools, served a secular purpose, and did not violate the establishment clause. In MCCOLLUM V. BOARD OF EDUCATION (1948), writing for the Court, he held unconstitutional a RELEASED TIME program in which religious instruction took place in a public school. In the school prayer case of ENGEL V. VITALE (1962), of all his opinions the one that produced the most vocal opposition, Black concluded that a state-sponsored "non-denominational" prayer was "wholly inconsistent" with the establishment clause. The clause prohibited any laws that "establish an official religion whether [they] operate directly to coerce non-observing individuals or not." Religion, he wrote, "is too personal, too sacred, too holy, to permit its 'unhallowed perversion' by a civil magistrate."

The direct action cases in the mid-1960s tested Black's First Amendment philosophy. He expounded the limitations that TRESPASS and BREACH OF THE PEACE statutes placed on FREEDOM OF SPEECH. Earlier, he had held, in GIBONEY V. EMPIRE STORAGE AND ICE COMPANY (1949), that legislatures could regulate PICKETING, but in *Barenblatt* he noted that they could not abridge "views peacefully expressed in a place where the speaker had a right to be." "Picketing," he now wrote in *Cox v. Louisiana* (1965), "though it may be utilized to communicate ideas, is not speech, and therefore is not of itself protected by the First Amendment." This was a very different Black from the one who in FEINER V. NEW YORK (1951) labeled the Court's decision sanctioning police action to silence a speaker as "a long step toward totalitarian authority."

New emphases emerged. The ownership of property became pivotal. A property owner, governmental or private, was under no obligation to provide a forum for speech; if owners could not control their property, Black feared, the result would be mob violence. The RULE OF LAW now took precedence over encouraging public discourse and protest. Focusing on maintaining "tranquility and order" in cases like *Gregory v. Chicago* (1969), Black deprecated protesters who "think they have been mistreated or . . . have actually been mistreated," and their supporters, who "do no service" to "their cause, or their country." Gone was much of his former admiration of dissenters, toleration of the unorthodox, and receptivity toward new ideas.

Nonetheless, Black remained uncompromising in protecting FREEDOM OF THE PRESS. In his view the people had

the right to read any books or see any movies, regardless of content. In his final case, NEW YORK TIMES V. UNITED STATES (1971), he reexpressed his faith:

> Both the history and language of the First Amendment support the view that the press must be left to publish news, whatever the source, without censorship, INJUNCTIONS, or PRIOR RESTRAINTS.
>
> In the First Amendment the Founding Fathers gave the free press the protection it must have to fulfill its essential role in our democracy. The press was to serve the governed, not the governors. . . . The press was protected so that it could bare the secrets of government and inform the people. Only a free and unrestrained press can effectively expose deception in government. And paramount among the responsibilities of a free press is the duty to prevent any part of the government from deceiving the people and sending them off to distant lands to die of foreign fevers and foreign shot and shell.

Three months later he was dead.

Black is one of the handful of great judges in American history, second only to JOHN MARSHALL in his impact on the Constitution. Certain of his premises, and convinced that he and history were at one, he was a tireless, evangelical, constitutional populist. If the Court did not accept his most sweeping doctrines whole, it accepted them piece by piece. Incorporation stands as his monument, but equally enduring is his preeminence in sensitizing a whole generation to the value of the great freedoms contained in the Bill of Rights.

ROGER K. NEWMAN
(1986)

Bibliography

FRANK, JOHN P.   1977   Hugo L. Black: Free Speech and the Declaration of Independence. *University of Illinois Law Forum* 2:577–620.

LANDYNSKI, JACOB W.   1976   In Search of Justice Black's Fourth Amendment. *Fordham Law Review* 45:453–496.

REICH, CHARLES A.   1963   Mr. Justice Black and the Living Constitution. *Harvard Law Review* 76:673–754.

SNOWISS, SYLVIA   1973   The Legacy of Justice Black. *Supreme Court Review* 1973:187–252.

SYMPOSIUM   1967   Mr. Justice Black: Thirty Years in Retrospect. *UCLA Law Review* 14:397–552.

BLACK, JEREMIAH S.
(1810–1883)

Jeremiah S. Black served on the Pennsylvania Supreme Court (1851–1857), as U.S. Attorney General (1857–1860), U.S. Secretary of State (1860–1861), and U.S. Supreme Court reporter (1861–1862). He advised ANDREW JOHNSON during the early phase of his IMPEACHMENT, and defended Samuel Tilden's claim to the presidency in the disputed election of 1876. A lifelong Democrat, Black was particularly antagonistic to abolitionists. During the winter of 1860–1861 Black opposed SECESSION and urged President JAMES BUCHANAN to reinforce federal military bases in the South. Buchanan appointed Black to the Supreme Court of the United States, but the SENATE refused to confirm him.

PAUL FINKELMAN
(1986)

Bibliography

BRIGANCE, WILLIAM N. 1934 *Jeremiah Sullivan Black, a Defender of the Constitution and the Ten Commandments*. Philadelphia: University of Pennsylvania Press.

BLACK CODES

In 1865–1866, the former slave states enacted statutes, collectively known as the "Black Codes," regulating the legal and constitutional status of black people. The Black Codes attempted to accomplish two objectives: (1) to enumerate the legal rights essential to the status of freedom of blacks; and (2) to provide a special criminal code for blacks. The latter objective reflected the two purposes of the antebellum law of slavery: race control and labor discipline.

In the view of white Southerners, emancipation did not of its own force create a civil status or capacity for freedmen. The southern state legislatures accordingly specified the incidents of this free status: the right to buy, sell, own, and bequeath property; the right to make contracts; the right to contract valid marriages, including so-called common-law marriages, and to enjoy a legally recognized parent-child relationship; the right to locomotion and personal liberty; the right to sue and be sued, and to testify in court, but only in cases involving black parties.

But the Codes also reenacted elements of the law of slavery. They provided detailed lists of civil disabilities by recreating the race-control features of the slave codes. They defined racial status; forbade blacks from pursuing certain occupations or professions; prohibited blacks from owning firearms or other weapons; controlled the movement of blacks by systems of passes; required proof of residence; prohibited the congregation of groups of blacks; restricted blacks from residing in certain areas; and specified an etiquette of deference to whites, such as by prohibiting blacks from directing insulting words at whites. The Codes forbade racial intermarriage and provided the death penalty for blacks raping white women, while omitting special provisions for whites raping black women. (See MISCEGENATION.) They excluded blacks from

jury duty, public office, and voting. Some Black Codes required racial SEGREGATION in public transportation or created Jim Crow schools. Most Codes authorized whipping and the pillory as punishment for freedmen's offenses.

The Codes salvaged the labor-discipline elements of slave law in master-and-servant statutes, VAGRANCY and pauper provisions, apprenticeship regulations, and elaborate labor contract statutes, especially those pertaining to farm labor. Other provisions permitted magistrates to hire out offenders unable to pay fines. These statutes provided a basis for subsequent efforts, extending well into the twentieth century, to provide a legal and paralegal structure forcing blacks to work, restricting their occupational mobility, and providing harsh systems of forced black labor, sometimes verging on PEONAGE.

The Black Codes profoundly offended the northern ideal of equality before the law. Northerners lost whatever sympathies they might have entertained for the plight of southern whites trying to make the revolutionary transition from a slave society, based on a legal regime of status, to a free, capitalist society based on will and contract. Northerners determined to force the former slave states to create new structures of racial equality. Consequently, the Black Codes were repealed or left unenforced during the congressional phase of Reconstruction. Later Redeemer and Conservative state legislatures reenacted the Jim Crow provisions and labor contract statutes to provide the statutory component of the twilight zone of semifreedom that characterized the legal status of southern blacks through WORLD WAR I.

WILLIAM M. WIECEK
(1986)

Bibliography

WILSON, THEODORE B. 1965 *The Black Codes of the South*. University: University of Alabama Press.

BLACKMUN, HARRY A.
(1908–   )

Nothing in Harry A. Blackmun's background presaged that within three years of his appointment he would write the most controversial Supreme Court opinion of his time— ROE V. WADE (1972)—providing significant constitutional protection to women and their doctors in the area of abortion.

After graduating from public school in St. Paul, Minnesota, where he and WARREN E. BURGER were elementary school classmates, young Blackmun attended Harvard College, having graduated in 1929 *summa cum laude*, and Harvard Law School, being graduated in 1932. He practiced law in St. Paul and then as resident counsel at the

Mayo Clinic in Rochester, Minnesota. In 1959 President DWIGHT D. EISENHOWER appointed him to the Eighth Circuit, where he served for eleven unremarkable years until, in 1970, President RICHARD M. NIXON selected him to fill the vacancy on the Supreme Court created by the resignation of Justice ABE FORTAS.

Blackmun's early years on the Supreme Court did little to disturb his image as a judicial clone of his boyhood friend Warren Burger, at whose wedding he had served as best man. The two voted together so often that the press dubbed them the Minnesota Twins.

Blackmun's voting patterns shifted over the years until by the mid-1980s he was more likely to vote with Justices WILLIAM J. BRENNAN and THURGOOD MARSHALL in defense of a broad vision of constitutional rights than with Burger. When asked whether his views have changed, Blackmun asserts that he has remained constant while the Court has shifted, causing his recent opinions merely to appear more libertarian. If, however, one compares early and late Blackmun opinions, it is difficult to accept Blackmun's protestation that nothing has changed in his legal universe except the backdrop.

One widely held hypothesis seeking to explain Blackmun's apparent shift in views is linked to the stormy public reaction that greeted what is undoubtedly his most significant Supreme Court opinion—*Roe v. Wade.* In *Roe,* drawing on his years at the Mayo Clinic, Blackmun brought a medical perspective to the controversy over the constitutionality of state laws prohibiting abortion. In a now familiar construct, he divided pregnancy into trimesters, holding that the state had no compelling interest in preserving fetal life during the first two trimesters, but that the interest in viable fetal life became compelling in the final trimester. In the years following *Roe,* Blackmun vigorously defended the right of a pregnant woman, in consultation with her doctor, to decide freely whether to undergo an abortion, writing a series of opinions striking down state statutes designed to place obstacles in a woman's path and vigorously dissenting from the Court's willingness to uphold a ban on federal funds to poor women seeking abortions.

Public reaction to Blackmun's abortion decisions was intense. He was subjected to vigorous personal criticism by individuals who believe deeply in a moral imperative of preserving fetal life from the moment of conception. Critics called his opinion in *Roe* a classic example of judicial overreaching and even compared it to Chief Justice ROGER B. TANEY's infamous opi1857nion in DRED SCOTT V. SANDFORD 1857.

Subjected to sustained personal and professional criticism after *Roe,* Blackmun was forced, according to one view, to confront fundamental questions about his role as a Supreme Court Justice. From the crucible of the personal and professional pressures generated by his abortion decisions, many believe that there emerged a Justice with a heightened commitment to the use of judicial power to protect individual freedom.

In fact, the linkage between Blackmun's defense of a woman's right to choose to undergo an abortion and his other major doctrinal innovation—the COMMERCIAL SPEECH doctrine—is a direct one. In *Bigelow v. Virginia* (1975) Blackmun wrote for the Court invalidating a ban on advertisements by abortion clinics and suggesting for the first time that a consumer's right to know might justify First Amendment protection for speech that merely proposed a commercial transaction. One year later, in VIRGINIA STATE BOARD OF PHARMACY V. VIRGINIA CITIZENS CONSUMER COUNCIL (1976) and BATES V. STATE BAR OF ARIZONA (1976), he struck down bans on advertising by pharmacists and lawyers, explicitly granting First Amendment protection for the first time to commercial speech. In his more recent commercial speech opinions, Blackmun's First Amendment analysis has become more trenchant, with his concurrence in CENTRAL HUDSON GAS & ELECTRIC CO. V. PUBLIC SERVICE COMMISSION (1980) ranking as a milestone in Supreme Court First Amendment theory.

Blackmun's third principal contribution to constitutional DOCTRINE—the defense of ALIENS—precedes his abortion decisions. In GRAHAM V. RICHARDSON, one of Blackmun's early majority opinions, he wrote the opinion that outlawed discrimination against resident aliens in granting WELFARE BENEFITS, holding that aliens, as a politically powerless group, were entitled to heightened judicial protection under the EQUAL PROTECTION clause. In later years, his majority opinions invalidated attempts to exclude aliens from all civil service jobs and from state-funded college scholarships; and, although he concurred in the Court's decision upholding the exclusion of aliens from the state police, he vigorously dissented from decisions upholding bans on alien public school teachers and deputy probation officers.

Blackmun's most significant FEDERALISM opinion dramatically illustrates his evolution on the Court. In 1976 he provided the crucial fifth vote for Justice WILLIAM H. REHNQUIST's opinion in NATIONAL LEAGUE OF CITIES V. USERY, invalidating congressional minimum wage protection for municipal employees as a violation of state SOVEREIGNTY. A decade later, however, Blackmun changed his mind and, abandoning the Rehnquist-Burger position, wrote the Court's opinion in GARCIA V. SAN ANTONIO METROPOLITAN TRANSPORTATION AUTHORITY (1985), rejecting their view of state sovereignty and overruling *Usery.*

The hypothesis that Blackmun's apparent drift toward the Brennan-Marshall wing of the Court is linked to the controversy over his abortion decisions is not wholly persuasive. It does not explain Justice Blackmun's pre-*Roe* decisions protecting aliens and it overlooks the fact that as a little known judge of the Eighth Circuit, Blackmun was among the first federal judges to declare prison conditions violative of the Eighth Amendment. Furthermore, it does not explain why, in the criminal law and CRIMINAL PROCEDURE area, Blackmun's post-*Roe* jurisprudence continues to construe Fourth, Fifth, and Sixth Amendment protections narrowly.

A more fruitful approach to Blackmun's voting patterns is to take seriously his protestation that a consistent judicial philosophy underlies his Supreme Court career. The task is difficult, for Blackmun's judicial philosophy defies easy categorization in terms of fashionable labels. He is "liberal" in cases involving racial minorities and aliens, but "conservative" in the criminal procedure area. His abortion decision in *Roe* has been called the most "activist" in the Court's history, but his *Garcia* federalism opinion counsels "judicial restraint." His commercial speech opinions are rigorously "libertarian," but his tax, antitrust law, and securities law opinions champion vigorous government intervention. Not surprisingly, therefore, attempts to evaluate Blackmun's work using currently fashionable yardsticks often lead to a critical judgment that he is doctrinally inconsistent. In fact, Blackmun's Supreme Court work appears linked by a unifying thread—a reluctance to permit preoccupation with doctrinal considerations to force him into the resolution of an actual case on terms that fail to do intuitive justice to the parties before the Court.

Blackmun's commitment to a jurisprudence of just deserts is reflected in three characteristic motifs that pervade his opinions. First, he is openly mistrustful of rigidly doctrinaire analyses that force him into unfair or unreasonable resolutions of cases. In rejecting the Court's two-tier equal protection analysis in favor of a more "flexible" doctrine, or expressing skepticism about prophylactic EXCLUSIONARY RULES in the criminal process, or searching for a federalism compromise based more on pragmatism than on theory, or rejecting automatic use of the OVERBREADTH DOCTRINE in FIRST AMENDMENT cases, Justice Blackmun refuses to allow doctrine to force him into dispute resolutions that seem intuitively unfair or that give an unjust windfall to one of the parties before the Court.

Second, his opinions are fact-oriented, canvassing both adjudicative and LEGISLATIVE FACTS in an attempt to place the dispute before the Court in a realistic context. In his more recent opinions, he frequently scolds the Court for slighting a case's factual context, often complaining that the Court's desire to announce law has taken it beyond the actual dispute before the Court.

Finally, he insists upon results that accord with his view of the "real" world. His decisions have tended to support efforts to undo the consequences of RACIAL DISCRIMINATION and have demonstrated an increasing empathy for the plight of the powerless, while demonstrating little sympathy for lawbreakers. Such a personal vision of "reality" must ultimately inject a dose of subjectivism into the decision-making process. Yet Justice Blackmun's qualities of mind and heart serve to remind the Court that a doctrinaire, intellectualized jurisprudence needs to be balanced by a jurisprudence grounded in intuitive fairness to the parties, human warmth, and pragmatic realism.

BURT NEUBORNE
(1986)

Bibliography

FUQUA, DAVID 1980 Justice Harry A. Blackmun: The Abortion Decisions. *Arkansas Law Review* 34:276–296.
NOTE 1983 The Changing Social Vision of Justice Blackmun. *Harvard Law Review* 96:717–736.
SCHLESSINGER, STEVEN R. 1980 Justice Harry Blackmun and Empirical Jurisprudence. *American University Law Review* 29:405–437.
SYMPOSIUM 1985 Dedication to Justice Harry A. Blackmun— Biography; Tributes. *Hamline Law Review* 8:1–149.

BLACKMUN, HARRY A.
(1908–   )
(Update 1)

Harry Andrew Blackmun was born in the small town of Nashville, Illinois, on November 12, 1908, but spent most of his childhood in St. Paul, Minnesota. He attended Harvard College on a scholarship, graduating summa cum laude in 1929 with a major in mathematics. Torn between medicine and law, he chose the latter route and attended Harvard Law School, from which he graduated in 1932.

Immediately after graduation Blackmun served as a law clerk to Judge John B. Sanborn of the UNITED STATES COURT OF APPEALS for the Eighth Circuit. He then joined the Minneapolis law firm of Dorsey, Coleman, Barker, Scott, and Barber, where he specialized in tax, civil litigation, and estates. Blackmun left the firm in 1950 to become resident counsel at the Mayo Clinic in Rochester, Minnesota, where he says he enjoyed "the happiest years of my professional experience," with "a foot in both camps, law and medicine."

In 1959 President DWIGHT D. EISENHOWER nominated Blackmun to replace his former employer, Judge Sanborn, on the Eighth Circuit. Blackmun served on that court for eleven years, and then, after the Senate refused to confirm Clement F. Haynsworth, Jr., and G. Harrold Carswell for ABE FORTAS's seat on the Supreme Court, President RICHARD M. NIXON nominated Blackmun, thus accounting for the nickname that Blackmun uses to refer to himself:

"Old No. 3." Blackmun was unanimously confirmed by the Senate and was sworn in as the Supreme Court's ninety-ninth Justice on May 12, 1970.

In appointing Blackmun, Nixon was looking for a judge who shared his philosophy of judicial restraint and would work to reverse the liberal, activist rulings of the WARREN COURT. Nixon's hopes for his new appointee, coupled with Blackmun's long-term friendship with Chief Justice WARREN E. BURGER, who had known Blackmun since childhood and had asked Blackmun to serve as the best man at his wedding, led the media to refer to Burger and Blackmun as the "Minnesota Twins." The two Justices' similar voting patterns during Blackmun's early years on the Court lent credence to the epithet.

Although Blackmun has generally lived up to Nixon's expectations in criminal procedure cases, he increasingly sided with Justice WILLIAM J. BRENNAN, JR., in other controversial cases and is now considered part of the Court's liberal wing. For his part, Blackmun puts little stock in such labels, noting shortly after being nominated to the Supreme Court, "I've been called a liberal and a conservative. Labels are deceiving." He claims that his views have not changed over the years, but that "it's the Court that's changed under me."

Whatever the truth on this issue, Blackmun will likely be best remembered for his controversial and groundbreaking opinion in ROE V. WADE (1973). *Roe* held that the constitutional RIGHT OF PRIVACY protected a woman's right to an ABORTION, thereby in effect invalidating abortion statutes in forty-six states.

Blackmun has continued to advocate the constitutional right to abortion. He wrote the Court's opinions in PLANNED PARENTHOOD OF CENTRAL MISSOURI V. DANFORTH (1976), invalidating requirements of spousal and parental consent, and in *Akron v. Akron Center for Reproductive Health, Inc.* (1983) and *Thornburgh v. American College of Obstetricians and Gynecologists* (1986), striking down various efforts to impose procedural restrictions limiting the availability of abortions.

More recently, however, Blackmun has found himself in dissent on the abortion issue. In *Webster v. Reproductive Health Services* (1989), Chief Justice WILLIAM H. REHNQUIST, joined by Justices BYRON R. WHITE and ANTHONY M. KENNEDY, observed that *Roe's* "rigid trimester analysis" had proven "unsound in principle and unworkable in practice." Although they did not believe the case required the Court to reconsider the validity of *Roe's* holding, Justice ANTONIN SCALIA's concurrence indicated that he was ready to overrule *Roe*. Responding in a passionate dissent, Blackmun voiced his "fear for the liberty and equality of the millions of women who have lived and come of age in the 16 years since *Roe* was decided" and concluded that "for today, at least, . . . the women of this Nation still retain the liberty to control their destinies. But the signs are evident and very ominous, and a chill wind blows."

Although Blackmun's position on abortion has remained constant, in other areas he has demonstrated an admirable willingness to reconsider his views. His open-mindedness reflects his belief that the law is "not a rigid animal or a rigid profession," but rather a "constant search for truth," as well as his perception that a Supreme Court Justice "grows constitutionally" while on the bench.

One illustration of Blackmun's evolution is his increased tolerance of nontraditional lifestyles. Dissenting in COHEN V. CALIFORNIA (1971), Blackmun argued that the "absurd and immature antic" of wearing a jacket in court bearing the words "Fuck the draft" was not constitutionally protected. He likewise dissented in *Smith v. Goguen* (1974), concluding that the states may constitutionally prosecute those who "harm the physical integrity of the flag by wearing it affixed to the seats of [their] pants." More recently, however, he joined the controversial majority opinions in *Texas v. Johnson* (1989) and *United States v. Eichman* (1990), which held that the FIRST AMENDMENT prohibited prosecution of defendants who had burned the American flag during political protests.

Blackmun's growing tolerance of diversity is also obvious in his dissent in BOWERS V. HARDWICK (1986), which upheld the criminalization of sodomy. His stinging dissent observed that "a necessary corollary of giving individuals freedom to choose how to conduct their lives is acceptance of the fact that different individuals will make different choices" and that "depriving individuals of the right to choose for themselves how to conduct their intimate relationships poses a far greater threat to the values most deeply rooted in our Nation's history than tolerance of nonconformity could ever do."

As he has become more accepting of the unconventional, Blackmun has also become more suspicious of institutions. During his early years on the Court, he tended to defer to institutional prerogatives, believing that a judicial policy of noninterference would leave institutions free to exercise their discretion in the public interest. In his first majority opinion, WYMAN V. JAMES (1971), Blackmun rejected a welfare recipient's FOURTH AMENDMENT challenge to home visits from the welfare department caseworker, whom Blackmun described as "not a sleuth but rather . . . a friend to one in need." He dissented in BIVENS V. SIX UNKNOWN NAMED AGENTS (1971) because he feared that creating a tort remedy for Fourth Amendment violations by federal agents would "open] the door for another avalanche of new federal cases," thereby tending "to stultify proper law enforcement and to make the day's labor for the honest and conscientious officer even more onerous."

More recently, however, Blackmun has become less

trusting of public officials and institutions. In *United States v. Bailey* (1980), for example, his recognition of the "atrocities and inhuman conditions of prison life in America" led him to support a broader duress defense in prison escape cases than the majority was willing to recognize. The picture he painted of prison officials was not a sympathetic one: he described them as indifferent to prisoners' health and safety needs and even as active participants in "the brutalization of inmates."

Given his growing distrust of public officials, Blackmun has increasingly minimized the concerns about the federal courts' caseload expressed in his *Bivens* dissent and instead has opposed limitations on ACCESS TO THE COURTS. He believes that statutes authorizing federal CIVIL RIGHTS suits represent "the commitment of our society to be governed by law and to protect the rights of those without power against oppression at the hands of the powerful." Accordingly, in *Allen v. McCurry* (1980) he dissented from the Court's holding that federal courts must give preclusive effect to prior state court adjudications in civil rights suits; in *Rose v. Lundy* (1982) he opposed the strict exhaustion requirement the majority imposed on HABEAS CORPUS petitioners; and in ATASCADERO STATE HOSPITAL V. SCANLON (1985) he joined Justice Brennan's dissent, which would have prohibited the states from invoking the ELEVENTH AMENDMENT to bar FEDERAL QUESTION suits in federal court.

Another manifestation of Blackmun's increased suspicion of institutions has been his endorsement of more rigorous judicial scrutiny of social and economic legislation under the EQUAL PROTECTION clause. Such legislation is upheld so long as it meets the RATIONAL BASIS test—that is, so long as the legislative means are rationally related to a legitimate governmental purpose. Over the years, the Court has given conflicting signals as to how deferential the rational basis test is. In *United States Railroad Retirement Board v. Fritz* (1980) the Court held that the test was satisfied if a judge could think of some plausible, hypothetical reason for the statutory scheme; whether this hypothetical justification bore any relationship to the legislature's actual purpose was, the Court said, "constitutionally irrelevant." Less than three months later, however, Blackmun's majority opinion in *Schweiker v. Wilson* (1981) observed that the rational basis test is "not a toothless one," and upheld the Medicaid provision at issue there only after finding that the statutory classification represented "Congress' deliberate, considered choice." Similarly, in his separate opinion in *Logan v. Zimmerman Brush Company* (1982), Blackmun found a legislative classification irrational, explaining that the justification for statutory classifications "must be something more than the exercise of a strained imagination."

The limitations imposed by FEDERALISM on the federal government's powers provide a second illustration of Blackmun's willingness to rethink his views. Blackmun represented the decisive fifth vote in NATIONAL LEAGUE OF CITIES V. USERY (1976), where the Court concluded that the TENTH AMENDMENT prohibited Congress from regulating the wages and hours of state employees. His brief concurring opinion interpreted the majority opinion as adopting a balancing approach that sought to accommodate competing federal and state concerns and that would permit federal regulation in areas where the federal interest was "demonstrably greater." Although this interpretation may have represented wishful thinking on Blackmun's part, he did join the majority opinion in full.

After deserting the other Justices from the *National League of Cities* majority in both *Federal Energy Regulatory Commission v. Mississippi* (1982) and EQUAL EMPLOYMENT OPPORTUNITY COMMISSION V. WYOMING (1983), Blackmun ultimately wrote the opinion overruling *National League of Cities* in GARCIA V. SAN ANTONIO METROPOLITAN TRANSIT AUTHORITY (1985). Blackmun explained

that the *National League of Cities* approach had proven unworkable because it had been unable to identify a principled way of defining those integral state functions deserving of Tenth Amendment protection. He likewise renounced his own balancing approach because it, too, had not provided a coherent standard capable of consistent application by the lower courts.

Though he ultimately rejected a balancing approach in the Tenth Amendment context, one of Blackmun's judicial trademarks has been his tendency to reach decisions by balancing conflicting interests. He believes that "complex constitutional issues cannot be decided by resort to inflexible rules or predetermined categories." Consequently, he pays close attention to the facts of a case and often makes decisions on a case-by-case basis, rather than a sweeping doctrinal one.

Illustrative of Blackmun's balancing approach are his majority opinions in *Bigelow v. Virginia* (1975), VIRGINIA STATE BOARD OF PHARMACY V. VIRGINIA CONSUMERS COUNCIL (1976), and BATES V. STATE BAR OF ARIZONA (1977), which provided the framework for the Court's modern approach to First Amendment cases involving COMMERCIAL SPEECH. Prior to these decisions, the Court considered commercial speech outside the realm of constitutional protection. In each of these three cases, however, Blackmun balanced the First Amendment interests of the advertisers against the public interests served by regulating commercial speech, because, as he explained in *Virginia State Board of Pharmacy*, "the free flow of commercial information is indispensable . . . to the proper allocation of resources in a free enterprise system, . . . [and] to the formation of intelligent opinions as to how that system ought to be regulated or altered." Applying this BALANCING TEST in each case, Blackmun struck down statutes banning advertisements of abortions, prescription drug prices, and legal fees. In each instance, he decided only the narrow issue confronting the Court, expressly declining to consider the extent to which commercial speech might be regulated in other contexts.

Blackmun's commercial speech opinions also illustrate another characteristic of his judicial philosophy—an interest in the real-world impact of the Court's decisions. His opinions often express concern that the Supreme Court operates too frequently from an "ivory tower." In his separate opinion in REGENTS OF UNIVERSITY OF CALIFORNIA V. BAKKE (1978), for example, Blackmun urged his colleagues to "get down the road toward accepting and being a part of the real world, and not shutting it out and away from us." The balancing approach Blackmun adopted in the commercial speech cases likewise avoided abstract generalizations and focused the Court's attention on the concrete results of each case—in *Virginia State Board of Pharmacy*, for example, on the fact that "those whom the suppression of prescription price information hits the hardest are the poor, the sick, and particularly the aged."

Blackmun has written a series of majority opinions in cases discussing the constitutionality of state efforts to tax interstate and foreign commerce that similarly emphasizes the real-world impact of the state tax at issue in each case. In *Complete Auto Transit, Inc. v. Brady* (1977) his opinion overruled prior Supreme Court precedent that held state taxes on the privilege of doing business within the state per se unconstitutional as applied to INTERSTATE COMMERCE, and instead adopted a four-part test that stressed the practical effect of the state tax. He followed the same approach in *Department of Revenue v. Association of Washington Stevedoring Companies* (1978) and then in *Japan Line, Ltd. v. County of Los Angeles* (1979), where he adapted the *Complete Auto Transit* test to state taxation of foreign commerce.

Blackmun's emphasis on real-world concerns has often been directed more specifically to the effect of the Court's decisions on the powerless, less fortunate members of society. He strives to do justice to the parties in each case, remarking in one interview, "To me, every case involves people. . . . If we forget the humanity of the litigants before us, . . . we're in trouble, no matter how great our supposed legal philosophy can be." This concern is evident in Blackmun's opinions as well. He concurred only in the result in *O'Bannon v. Town Court Nursing Center* (1980) because he found the majority's approach "heartless." His dissent in *Ford Motor Company v. Equal Employment Opportunity Commission* (1982), an employment discrimination case, criticized the majority's reliance on "abstract and technical concerns" that bore "little resemblance to those that actually motivated" the injured employees or anyone "living in the real world."

Aliens are perhaps the disadvantaged group for whom Blackmun has spoken most forcefully and consistently. In a series of majority opinions during the 1970s beginning with GRAHAM V. RICHARDSON (1971), which held that WELFARE BENEFITS could not be conditioned on citizenship or duration of residence in this country, Blackmun urged that alienage be treated as a suspect classification. His more recent statements on behalf of aliens have come in dissent. In *Cabell v. Chavez-Salido* (1982), which upheld a statute that denied aliens employment in any "peace officer" position, Blackmun's dissent focused on the majority's failure to consider the practical impact of its holding. He objected that the Court's abandonment of strict scrutiny was more than an academic matter; in *Cabell,* for example, the majority's permissive standard of review might permit the state to exlude aliens from more than seventy jobs, including toll takers, furniture and bedding inspectors, and volunteer fire wardens.

Blackmun has also focused on the impact of the Court's decisions on the poor. Although one of his early opinions, *United States v. Kras* (1973), upheld a fifty-dollar filing fee in bankruptcy cases in part because paying the fee in installments would result in weekly payments "less than the price of a movie and little more than the cost of a pack or two of cigarettes," Blackmun recently has exhibited more understanding of the plight of the poor. In addition to the concerns articulated in the commercial speech cases, he dissented from the Court's decision in *Beal v. Doe* (1977) to approve a ban on the use of Medicaid funds for nontherapeutic abortions, characterizing the majority's assumption that alternative funding sources for abortions are available to indigent women as "disingenuous and alarming, almost reminiscent of: "Let them eat cake." Again, he contrasted the actual impact of the Court's ruling with its abstract, formalistic approach: "There is another world 'out there,' the existence of which the Court, I suspect, either chooses to ignore or fears to recognize."

Finally, Blackmun has spoken on behalf of racial minorities and the institutionalized. He has consistently voted to uphold AFFIRMATIVE ACTION plans, concluding in his seperate opinion in *Bakke* that " in order to get beyond racism, we must first take account of race." In *Youngberg v. Romeo* (1982) his concurring opinion argued that involuntarily commited retarded persons are entitled to treatment as well as care. "For many mentally retarded people," he reasoned, "the difference between the capacity to do things for themselves within an institution and total dependence on the institution for all their needs is as much liberty as they ever will know." His dissent in *Bailey* criticized the majority's "impeccable exercise in undisputed general principles and technical legalism" and argued that the scope of the duress defense available in prison escape cases must instead be evaluated in light of the "stark truth" of the "shocking" conditions of prison life.

Although history may best remember Blackmun as the author of *Roe v. Wade*, his contribution to the Court has in fact been much broader. He has thoughtfully balanced conflicting policies, conscientiously and thoroughly digesting the details of each case without reaching out to make decisions based on broad, sweeping generalizations. He has been concerned about the actual impact of the Court's decisions, refusing to permit his place on the Court to allow him to lose compassion for the "little people." He has been receptive to new ideas and exhibited a capacity for growth, in keeping with his recognition that "there is no room in the law for arrogance" and his sense that he, as well as the Supreme Court, has "human limitations and fallibility."

KIT KINPORTS
(1992)

(SEE ALSO: *Flag Desecration; Judicial Activism and Judicial Restraint.*)

Bibliography

KOBYLKA, JOSEPH F. 1985 The Court, Justice Blackmun, and Federalism: A Subtle Movement with Potentially Great Ramifications. *Creighton Law Review* 19:9–49.

NOTE 1983 The Changing Social Vision of Justice Blackmun. *Harvard Law Review* 96:717–736.

SYMPOSIUM 1985 Dedication to Justice Harry A. Blackmun— Biography; Tributes; Articles. *Hamline Law Review* 8:1–149.

—— 1987 Justice Harry A. Blackmun: The Supreme Court and the Limits of Medical Privacy. *American Journal of Law and Medicine* 13:153–525.

WASBY, STEPHEN L. 1988 Justice Harry A. Blackmun in the Burger Court. *Hamline Law Review* 11:183–245.

BLACKMUN, HARRY A.
(1908–1999)
(Update 2)

Justice Harry A. Blackmun retired from the Supreme Court in June 1994. The opinions he wrote during his last years on the Court continued to reflect the "real world" PRAGMATISM, the deepening sympathy for the powerless, and the strong commitment to pluralism that had marked his previous writings.

As earlier, Blackmun's pragmatism often led him to favor fact-intensive determinations over the application of hard-and-fast rules. Typical was Blackmun's opinion for the Court in MISTRETTA V. UNITED STATES (1989), in which he rejected SEPARATION OF POWERS objections to the federal SENTENCING guidelines, because he concluded that neither the guidelines nor the commission that promulgated them realistically threatened the constitutional scheme of CHECKS AND BALANCES. Similarly, in *International Union, UMWA v. Bagwell* (1994), Blackmun's final constitutional opinion for the Court, he refused to adopt any firm rule regarding when fines for violating civil CONTEMPT OF COURT orders should count as criminal sanctions for purposes of the Sixth Amendment right to TRIAL BY JURY. Instead, he reasoned that the determination of any given case should turn on the degree to which the circumstances implicate the need for the protection. He took an equally functional approach in his opinion for the Court in *Pacific Mutual Life Insurance Company v. Haslip* (1991), rejecting any "mathematical bright line rule" for determining when PUNITIVE DAMAGES violate DUE PROCESS. Blackmun remained particularly opposed to rigid doctrinal analysis when he believed it blocked justice for the weak. He decried, for example, the "sterile formalism" of the Court's decision in DESHANEY V. WINNEBAGO COUNTY DEPARTMENT OF SOCIAL SERVICES (1989), which found the due process clause of the FOURTEENTH AMENDMENT inapplicable to the failure of county officials to protect a four-year-old boy from his violently abusive father.

In contrast, Blackmun continued to champion strict and often expansive application of rules promoting pluralism and protecting minorities. A prime example was the rule of BATSON V. KENTUCKY (1986), barring prosecutors from exercising PEREMPTORY JURY CHALLENGES based on race. Blackmun wrote for the Court when it extended *Batson* to invalidate race-based peremptory challenges by criminal defendants in *Georgia v. McCollum* (1992), and gender-based peremptory challenges in *J. E. B. v. Alabama* (1994), in both cases stressing the message of hostility and exclusion sent when members of a group historically blocked from full participation in American self-government are systematically ejected from the jury box. Blackmun tended to be similarly uncompromising when applying the FIRST AMENDMENT. His opinion for the Court in FORSYTH COUNTY V. NATIONALIST MOVEMENT (1992) voided an ordinance that capped parade permit fees at $1,000 but let a county administrator set the fee partly based on the group seeking the permit. "A tax based on the content of speech," Blackmun explained, "does not become more constitutional because it is a small fee." To protect RELIGIOUS DIVERSITY he favored strict application of the ESTABLISHMENT CLAUSE and generous accommodation of minority faiths under the free exercise clause. He thus dissented sharply from the Court's determination in EMPLOYMENT DIVISION, DEPARTMENT OF HUMAN RESOURCES OF OREGON V. SMITH (1990) that the free exercise clause provides no protection against neutral laws that only incidentally prohibit religious practices.

Blackmun remained strongly committed to the right to ABORTION recognized in his opinion for the Court in ROE V. WADE (1973), all the more so as attacks on that ruling escalated both inside and outside the Court. He dissented strenuously in *Ohio v. Akron Center for Reproductive Health* (1990), when the Court upheld a parental notification requirement for abortions performed on minors, and in RUST V. SULLIVAN (1991), when the Court upheld the "gag rules" barring federally funded family-planning services from providing information about abortion. His opinions in these cases focused on the effects the challenged rules would have on women seeking abortions, and highlighted, as had Blackmun's earlier opinions in THORNBURGH V. AMERICAN COLLEGE OF OBSTETRICIANS AND GYNECOLOGISTS (1986) and WEBSTER V. REPRODUCTIVE HEALTH SERVICES (1989), the degree to which Blackmun had come to view *Roe* as principally about a woman's right to self-determination. When a bare majority of the Court reaffirmed the central holding of *Roe* in PLANNED PARENTHOOD V. CASEY (1992), Blackmun commended the PLURALITY OPINION as "an act of personal courage and constitutional principle," but pointedly warned that his own tenure on the Court was drawing to a close.

Ultimately, however, Blackmun's sharpest and most revealing split with the REHNQUIST COURT came not over abortion but over CAPITAL PUNISHMENT. Blackmun's early opinions on the U.S. Court of Appeals for the Eighth Circuit and on the Supreme Court had made clear that, although he believed the death penalty was constitutional, he was personally opposed to executions and found cases challenging them "excruciating." Over time he grew increasingly uncomfortable with the Supreme Court's handling of capital cases. Finally, in an extraordinary DISSENTING OPINION from the denial of CERTIORARI in *Callins v. Collins* (1994), Blackmun announced his conclusion that the death penalty was unconstitutional. He explained that experience had shown it impossible to administer capital punishment in a manner free from RACIAL DISCRIMINATION and caprice, and yet sensitive to the requirements of individualized fairness. Moreover, he charged, the Court had stopped even trying to address that challenge.

Callins was in several respects a fitting capstone to Blackmun's service on the Court. It reflected both his constant attention to the practical operation of the principles announced by the Court and his long-standing concern for the law's treatment of outcasts. It also illustrated his willingness to reconsider his earlier views in light of further experience, a willingness rooted in his open acknowledgement of the difficulty of constitutional adjudication.

Although Justice FELIX FRANKFURTER famously described his version of judicial restraint as "judicial humil-

ity," its most vocal supporters, Frankfurter included, have not been judges renowned for their modesty. Blackmun, in *Callins* and throughout his career, exemplified a different, more straightforward kind of judicial humility. He had a keen awareness of the limits of human certainty, and hence of the possibility that he himself might be mistaken. Nevertheless he was steadfast in defending the Constitution as he understood it, particularly when he understood it to protect those most needing protection. The model he provided of humane judging—openly provisional yet resolutely compassionate—is perhaps his greatest legacy.

DAVID A. SKLANSKY
(2000)

Bibliography

COYNE, RANDALL   1995   Marking the Progress of a Humane Justice: Harry Blackmun's Death Penalty Epiphany. *University of Kansas Law Review* 43:367–416.

KARLAN, PAMELA S.   1993   Bringing Compassion Into the Province of Judging: Justice Blackmun and Outsiders. *Dickinson Law Review* 97:527–540.

———   1994   From Logic to Experience. *Georgetown Law Review* 83:1–4.

KOH, HAROLD HONGJU   1994   The Justice Who Grew. *Journal of Supreme Court History* 1994:5–8.

BLACKSTONE, WILLIAM
(1723–1780)

The influence of Sir William Blackstone's *Commentaries on the Laws of England*, first published at Oxford between 1765 and 1769, was pervasive in American jurisprudence for much of the nineteenth century, although the work affected constitutional thought more in the realm of philosophy rather than that of specific legal doctrine. The appeal of this four-volume summation of the COMMON LAW, in the beginning of the American federal system, may be explained in part by its highly readable style and its function as a ready reference for many lawyers and jurists whose professional preparation was often indifferent. The practical need for a comprehensive and coherent view of the parent stock more than offset a tentative effort to make the new nation entirely independent of English legal institutions; and after the first American annotations to Blackstone by ST. GEORGE TUCKER in 1804, the importing of successive English editions and the periodic publication of fresh American editions by jurists like THOMAS M. COOLEY of Michigan and scholars like William Draper Lewis of the University of Pennsylvania made the *Commentaries* a standard reference for more than a hundred years.

The almost instant appeal of Blackstone to the English New World colonies—soon to be arguing their entitlements to the "rights of Englishmen" which they finally concluded could be secured only through independence of England itself—lay not only in its comprehensiveness but also in its epitomizing of the creative mercantilist jurisprudence of Blackstone's friend and contemporary, WILLIAM MURRAY (Lord Mansfield), which demonstrated the adaptability of the common law to "modern" economic objectives. The colonial elite, who had devoted the last generation before independence to "Americanization" of the English law, had economic views substantially similar to the scions of the English ruling classes to whom Blackstone delivered his Oxford lectures as Vinerian professor of English law. It was not surprising, therefore, that the *Commentaries*—to be followed in the post-Revolutionary period by the published reports of Mansfield—should appeal to the ruling element in the new nation, which was eager to continue the rules of an ordered economy.

These American leaders, Edmund Burke reminded his listeners in his 1775 "Speech on Conciliation," had a sophisticated legal knowledge, and the proof was in the fact that at that date almost as many copies of the *Commentaries* had been sold in the colonies as in England. JOHN MARSHALL's father was a subscriber to the first Philadelphia printing of 1771–1772, and both the future Chief Justice and his great antagonist, THOMAS JEFFERSON, read assiduously in the volumes. Jefferson wrote that Blackstone's work was "the most elegant and best digested" of any English treatise, "rightfully taking [its] place by the side of the Justinian institutes." While he considered that its continuing popularity in the new nation encouraged a too-slavish reliance on English precedent, he applauded St. George Tucker's plan to bring out an edition with American annotations.

In constitutional thought, the obvious differences in the structure of British and American government stimulated Tucker and succeeding American editors to prepare elaborate essays distinguishing between the frames, although not necessarily the philosophies, of the two constitutional systems. Parliamentary supremacy, which Blackstone endorsed, was in one sense emulated in the organization of the legislative departments as provided in both state and national constitutions. The recent memory of arbitrary and preemptive authority exercised by royal governors led Tucker to make the "popular" branch dominant over the executive. Ironically, Chief Justice Marshall, however congenial he found Blackstone's definition of law in general, was to embody the general principles of the *Commentaries* into a judicial definition of American FEDERALISM which made the judicial an equal branch. Nevertheless, a succession of influential nineteenth-century jurists after Marshall converted the Blackstonian conservatism into the *laissez-faire* principles that dominated American constitutional law until the 1930s.

The Tucker interpretation of the *Commentaries* led, through his sons, NATHANIEL BEVERLEY TUCKER and HENRY ST. GEORGE TUCKER, to a strict constructionist or "STATES' RIGHTS" school of constitutional thought, which was brought to its zenith in the speeches and writings of Henry's son, John Randolph Tucker. His 1877 Saratoga Springs lecture on state-federal relations as affected by the post-CIVIL WAR amendments to the Federal Constitution culminated in his posthumously published *Commentaries on the Constitution* (1899). This view, merging with Cooley's edition of 1870, kept the conservative jurisprudence of Blackstone in a position of influence until the revolution in American constitutional doctrine in the NEW DEAL crisis of the 1930s.

WILLIAM F. SWINDLER
(1986)

Bibliography

BOORSTIN, DANIEL J. (1941) 1973 *The Mysterious Science of the Law: An Essay on Blackstone's Commentaries.* Cambridge, Mass.: Harvard University Press; reprint, Gloucester, Mass.: Peter Smith.
KATZ, STANLEY M., ed. [William Blackstone] 1979 *Commentaries on the Laws of England: A Facsimile of the First Edition.* Chicago: University of Chicago Press.
KENNEDY, DUNCAN 1979 The Structure of Blackstone's Commentaries. *Buffalo Law Review* 28:205–382.

BLAINE AMENDMENT
(1875)

Representative James G. Blaine of Maine, with the support of President ULYSSES S. GRANT, introduced, in December 1875, a proposed constitutional amendment to prohibit state financial support of sectarian schools. The amendment was intended to prevent public support of the Roman Catholic schools which educated a large percentage of the children of European immigrants.

The first clause of the proposed amendment provided that "no State shall make any laws respecting an ESTABLISHMENT OF RELIGION or prohibiting the free exercise thereof." This is an indication that Congress did not believe that the FOURTEENTH AMENDMENT incorporated the religion clauses of the FIRST AMENDMENT. (See INCORPORATION DOCTRINE.)

The second clause would have prohibited the use or control by a religious sect or denomination of any tax money or land devoted to public education. Together with the first clause this prohibition suggests the connection between support of church-related schools and establishment of religion recognized in twentieth-century Supreme Court opinions beginning with EVERSON V. BOARD OF EDUCATION (1947).

The Blaine Amendment was approved by the HOUSE OF REPRESENTATIVES, 180–7; but even a heavily amended version failed to carry two-thirds of the SENATE, and so the proposal died.

DENNIS J. MAHONEY
(1986)

(SEE ALSO: *Government Aid to Religious Institutions.*)

BLAIR, JOHN
(1732–1800)

John Blair was a member of the Virginia House of Burgesses when the AMERICAN REVOLUTION began. In 1776, as a delegate to the state CONSTITUTIONAL CONVENTION, he served on the committee that drafted the VIRGINIA DECLARATION OF RIGHTS and the VIRGINIA CONSTITUTION. In 1777 he was appointed a judge, and in 1780 he became chancellor of Virginia. As a justice of the Court of Appeals he joined in deciding COMMONWEALTH V. CATON (1782). He was a delegate to both the CONSTITUTIONAL CONVENTION OF 1787—at which he never made a speech—and the Virginia ratifying convention. In 1789 President GEORGE WASHINGTON appointed him one of the original Justices of the Supreme Court of the United States. He served on the Supreme Court until 1796, a period during which the Court handed down few important decisions. In the most noteworthy, *Chisholm v. Georgia* (1793), Blair joined in the decision to hear a case brought against a state by a citizen of another state, arguing that to refuse to do so would be to "renounce part of the authority conferred, and, consequently, part of the duty imposed by the Constitution."

DENNIS J. MAHONEY
(1986)

Bibliography

ROSSITER, CLINTON   1966   *1787: The Grand Convention.* New York: Macmillan.

BLASPHEMY

Defaming religion by any words expressing scorn, ridicule, or vilification of God, Jesus Christ, the Holy Ghost, the doctrine of the Trinity, the Old or New Testament, or Christianity, constitutes the offense of blasphemy. In the leading American case, *Commonwealth v. Kneeland* (1838), Chief Justice LEMUEL SHAW of Massachusetts repelled arguments based on FREEDOM OF THE PRESS and on RELIGIOUS LIBERTY when he sustained a state law against blasphemy and upheld the conviction of a pantheist who

simply denied belief in God, Christ, and miracles. In all the American decisions, the courts maintained the fiction that the criminality of the words consisted of maliciousness or the intent to insult rather than mere difference of opinion.

The Supreme Court has never decided a blasphemy case. In BURSTYN, INC. V. WILSON (1951) the Court relied on FREEDOM OF SPEECH to void a New York statute authorizing the censorship of "sacrilegious" films. Justice FELIX FRANKFURTER, concurring, observed that blasphemy was a far vaguer term than sacrilege because it meant "criticism of whatever the ruling authority of the moment established as the orthodox religious doctrine." In 1968, when the last prosecution of blasphemy occurred in the United States, an appellate court of Maryland held that the prosecution violated the First Amendment's ban on ESTABLISHMENT OF RELIGION and its protection of freedom of religion. Should a blasphemy case ever reach the Supreme Court, that Court would surely reach a similar result.

LEONARD W. LEVY
(1986)

Bibliography

LEVY, LEONARD W.   1981   *Treason Against God: A History of the Offense of Blasphemy.* New York: Schocken Books.

BLATCHFORD, SAMUEL
(1820–1893)

Samuel Blatchford had been a federal judge for fifteen years when CHESTER A. ARTHUR appointed him to the Supreme Court in 1882. Like Horace Gray, Arthur's other appointee, Blatchford had initially made his mark on the profession as a reporter. Beginning in 1852, he published a volume of admiralty cases decided in the Southern District of New York, a volume of CIVIL WAR prize cases from the same JURISDICTION, and twenty-four volumes of Second Circuit decisions. He continued to report Second Circuit opinions following his appointment as district judge (1867), circuit judge (1872), and circuit justice. Blatchford's expertise in admiralty, PATENT, and construction of the national banking acts made him the Supreme Court's workhorse; he wrote 435 majority opinions during his eleven-year tenure, almost twenty percent more than his proportional share.

Two personal characteristics shaped Blatchford's modest contributions to American constitutional development. He was singularly uninterested in questions of statecraft, political economy, and philosophy; he was so committed to a collective conception of the judicial function that he dissented less frequently then any Justice since the era of JOHN MARSHALL. These attitudes, coupled with Chief

Justice MORRISON R. WAITE's disinclination to assign him cases involving CONSTITUTIONAL INTERPRETATION, kept Blatchford out of the limelight during his first eight years on the Court. But his compromising tendency prompted MELVILLE W. FULLER, Waite's successor, to regard him as the logical spokesman for narrow, unstable majorities in two controversial FOURTEENTH AMENDMENT cases. Blatchford's lackluster performances in CHICAGO, MILWAUKEE AND ST. PAUL RAILWAY V. MINNESOTA (1890) and *Budd v. New York* (1892) underscored his stolid approach to constitutional law.

At issue in the *Chicago, Milwaukee* case was the validity of an 1887 Minnesota statute establishing a railroad commission authorized to set maximum rate schedules that would be "final and conclusive." Because this scheme left no role for courts in reviewing railroad rates, the briefs focused on two previous statements by Chief Justice Waite. In *Munn v. Illinois* (1877) Waite had explained that "the controlling fact" in rate controversies was "the power to regulate at all." And he had added that "for protection against abuses by legislatures the people must resort to the polls, not the courts." In the *Railroad Commission Cases* (1886), however, Justice STANLEY MATTHEWS had persuaded Waite to acknowledge that "under the pretense of regulating fares and freights, the State cannot require a railroad corporation to carry persons or property without reward; neither can it do that which in law amounts to a taking of private property for PUBLIC USE without JUST COMPENSATION, or without DUE PROCESS OF LAW." Speaking for a 6–3 majority, Blatchford concluded that Waite's majority opinion in the Railroad Commission Cases presupposed at least some role for the courts; it followed that the Minnesota law could not be sustained. At one point Blatchford came very close to equating due process with judicial process, but he cautiously retreated and ultimately said nothing about either the scope of JUDICIAL REVIEW or its rationale, which went beyond Waite's enigmatic OBITER DICTUM. Only the dissent by JOSEPH P. BRADLEY forthrightly summarized what seemed to be the majority's premise. "In effect," he complained, the Court had now held "that the judiciary, and not the legislature, is the final arbiter in the regulation of fares and freights."

Budd brought both of the central issues in *Munn* back to the Court for reconsideration. Speaking again for a majority of six, Blatchford reiterated the Court's conclusion that bulk storage and handling of grain was a "business AFFECTED WITH A PUBLIC INTEREST. Consequently rates of charge for these services might be regulated by state governments. But what of *Chicago, Milwaukee*, which Bradley had described as "practically overrul[ing]" *Munn?* The two cases were "quite distinguishable," Blatchford insisted, "for in this instance the rate of charges is fixed directly by the legislature." Blatchford apparently regarded this formulation as an appropriate means of reconciling all previous decisions on the subject. But the distinction between legislative and commission regulation was so artificial that Justice JOHN MARSHALL HARLAN simply ignored it in his characteristically robust opinion for the Court in SMYTH V. AMES (1898). Seymour D. Thompson, editor of the *American Law Review*, was less gracious. "It was no great disparagement of him," Thompson remarked in a critical appraisal of Blatchford's constitutional law opinions, "to say that he was probably a better reporter than Judge."

CHARLES W. MCCURDY
(1986)

Bibliography
PAUL, ARNOLD 1969 Samuel Blatchford. Pages 1401–1414 in Leon Friedman and Fred L. Israel, eds., *The Justices of the United States Supreme Court, 1789–1969: Their Lives and Major Opinions.* New York: Chelsea House.

BLOCK GRANTS

See: Federal Grants-in-Aid; Revenue Sharing

BLOOD SAMPLES

See: Testimonial and Nontestimonial Compulsion

BLOUNT, WILLIAM
(1749–1800)

William Blount was a delegate to the CONSTITUTIONAL CONVENTION OF 1787 from North Carolina and a signer of the Constitution. Blount did not speak at the Convention and, disliking the result, signed the Constitution only to attest to the fact that it was consented to by all of the states represented.

DENNIS J. MAHONEY
(1986)

BLUE RIBBON JURY

Under the laws of some states, cases of unusual importance or complexity may be tried to special juries chosen from a venire with qualifications higher than those for the ordinary jury panel. Such juries are commonly called "blue ribbon juries." In *Fay v. New York* (1947) the Supreme Court affirmed (5–4) the constitutionality of using a blue ribbon jury in a criminal prosecution. Whether such juries would meet the contemporary standard of being drawn from a source fairly representative of the community is uncertain. (See JURY DISCRIMINATION; TAYLOR V. LOUISIANA.) In any event, blue ribbon juries have fallen into disuse.

DENNIS J. MAHONEY
(1986)

BLUM v. YARETSKY
457 U.S. 991 (1982)
RENDELL-BAKER v. KOHN
457 U.S. 830 (1982)

Following the Supreme Court's decision in BURTON V. WILMINGTON PARKING AUTHORITY (1961), commentators and lower courts began to ask whether a significant state subsidy to a private institution might make that institution's conduct into STATE ACTION, subject to the limitations of the Fourteenth Amendment. *Blum* and *Rendell-Baker* ended two decades of speculation; by 7–2 votes, the Court answered "No."

In *Blum* patients in private nursing homes complained that they had been transferred to facilities offering lesser care without notice or hearing, in violation of their rights to PROCEDURAL DUE PROCESS. Through the Medicaid program, the state paid the medical expenses of ninety percent of the patients; the state also subsidized the costs of the homes and extensively regulated their operation through a licensing scheme. The Court rejected each of these connections, one by one, as an argument for finding state action. The Constitution governed private conduct only when the state was "responsible" for that conduct; normally, such responsibility was to be found in state coercion or significant encouragement; these features were missing here.

In *Rendell-Baker* employees of a private school complained that they had been discharged for exercising their rights of FREEDOM OF SPEECH, and fired without adequate procedural protections. The Court reached neither issue, because it concluded that the action of the school did not amount to state action. Although the school depended on public funding, no state policy—no coercion or encouragement—influenced the employees' discharge.

Dissents in the two cases were written by Justices WILLIAM J. BRENNAN and THURGOOD MARSHALL, respectively. They argued that a consideration of all the interconnections between the institutions and the states, including the heavy subsidies, amounted to the kind of "significant state involvement" found in *Burton*. But considering the totality of circumstances in order to find state action is precisely what a majority of the BURGER COURT has been unwilling to do.

KENNETH L. KARST
(1986)

BLYEW v. UNITED STATES
80 U.S. 581 (1872)

The Supreme Court first interpreted the CIVIL RIGHTS ACT OF 1866 in April 1872 in *Blyew v. United States*. That case narrowly construed a jurisdictional provision, in the act's Section 3, that granted JURISDICTION to federal trial courts over criminal and civil "causes" that "affect[ed]" persons who "are denied or cannot enforce" in state court the rights of equality secured by the act's Section 1.

The case arose following the ax murder of a black family in rural Kentucky. Because a state statute precluded the testimony by a black person against a white defendant, it appeared probable that a state court would have excluded the dying declaration of the family's teenage son identifying the perpetrators as John Blyew and George Kennard. The federal attorney for Kentucky, Benjamin Bristow (who would soon argue this case as the first SOLICITOR GENERAL of the United States), obtained a federal INDICTMENT for the state-law crime of murder against Blyew and Kennard and prosecuted them in federal court. To establish jurisdiction under the 1866 act, the indictment asserted that the defendants' victims were denied or could not enforce the same right to testify in state court as white persons enjoy. This was only one among many criminal and civil cases brought in the Kentucky federal court on such a theory.

Convicted and sentenced to death, the defendants appealed. Exercised by this federal interference with its state courts, Kentucky hired (and the Supreme Court permitted) Judge Jeremiah Black to represent Kentucky at ORAL ARGUMENT.

The Court, through Justice WILLIAM STRONG, held that in a criminal trial only the government and the defendant, but not the victim, are persons "affected" within the meaning of the 1866 act. Because neither of these parties had been denied rights under Section 1, the federal court lacked jurisdiction.

With its narrow construction of the "affecting" jurisdiction, the Court avoided the constitutional question of whether Congress can enforce the FOURTEENTH AMENDMENT by granting federal court jurisdiction over state-law causes of action to avoid the risk of a biased state forum. The Court partially resolved this question in *Strauder v. West Virginia* (1880), which upheld the 1866 act's removal jurisdiction. But by then Congress had eliminated the narrowly interpreted "affecting" jurisdiction in its 1874 codification of United States statutes.

By its HOLDING, the Court eliminated the important CIVIL RIGHTS remedial tool of providing a nondiscriminatory federal forum to enforce the COMMON LAW of crimes and torts (including common law duties of nondiscrimination). Since *Blyew*, the model for federal civil rights criminal enforcement has primarily involved the adoption of a substantive federal criminal statute, with the attendant constitutional and practical difficulties of defining federal rights under both the SLAUGHTERHOUSE CASES (1873) and the CIVIL RIGHTS CASES (1883). Effective civil rights enforcement has been hobbled by this limitation, among others, ever since. Moreover, without the counterexample of the "affecting" jurisdiction, the Court has more plausibly developed doctrines restraining federal court intrusion on discriminatory state enforcement of state law.

The *Blyew* decision permits identifying the Supreme Court's hostility to federal civil rights enactments as early as the end of the first administration of ULYSSES S. GRANT. It also suggests that by the time the Court rendered the *Slaughterhouse* decision, it understood the implications that decision would have for federal civil rights enforcement. This precludes treating the Court's subsequent decisions limiting civil rights legislation as merely expressing a consensus of the political branches reached in the waning days of RECONSTRUCTION.

Blyew is also noteworthy because Justice JOSEPH P. BRADLEY, in dissent, first put forward a theory of a group right to the adequate protection of the law and the "badges and incidents" theory of the THIRTEENTH AMENDMENT found in the *Civil Rights Cases.*

The Court's failure to appreciate a class's cognizable interest in the effective protection of the law continues to the present. *Blyew,* for example, anticipated *Linda R. S. v. Richard D.* (1973) a century later, in which the Court held that a crime victim lacked standing to challenge a prosecutorial decision, because it directly affected only the state and defendant.

ROBERT D. GOLDSTEIN
(1992)

Bibliography
GOLDSTEIN, ROBERT D. 1989 *Blyew:* Variations on a Jurisdictional Theme. *Stanford Law Review* 41:469–566.
KAZCOROWSKI, ROBERT 1985 *The Politics of Judicial Interpretation: The Federal Courts, Department of Justice and Civil Rights, 1866–1876.* New York: Oceana.

BOARD OF CURATORS v. HOROWITZ
435 U.S. 78 (1979)

A state university medical student was dismissed during her final year of study for failure to meet academic standards. The Supreme Court unanimously held that she had not been deprived of her PROCEDURAL DUE PROCESS rights, but divided 5–4 on the reasons for that conclusion. For a majority, Justice WILLIAM H. REHNQUIST commented that

the student had not asserted any "property" interest, and strongly hinted that she had not been deprived of a "liberty" interest. Nevertheless, assuming the existence of an interest entitled to due process protections, Rehnquist said that a dismissal for academic rather than disciplinary reasons required no hearing or opportunity to respond. Four concurring Justices disagreed with the remarkable conclusion that due process required a fair procedure for the ten-day suspension of an elementary school pupil in GOSS V. LOPEZ (1975) but not for the academic dismissal of a medical student. Here, however, the four Justices agreed that the student had been given a sufficient hearing.

Horowitz illustrates the artificiality of the Court's recent narrowing of the "liberty" or "property" interests to which the guarantee of procedural due process attaches. A student's interest in avoiding academic termination fits awkwardly into those categories, in their recent restrictive definitions. Yet the student plainly deserves protection against termination procedures that are arbitrary. The specter of judges' having to read examination papers is no more than a specter. The concern of procedural due process is not the fairness of a particular student's termination, but the fairness of the procedural system for depriving a person of an important interest.

KENNETH L. KARST
(1986)

BOARD OF DIRECTORS OF ROTARY INTERNATIONAL v. ROTARY CLUB

See: Freedom of Association

BOARD OF EDUCATION v. ALLEN
392 U.S. 236 (1968)

New York authorized the loan of state-purchased textbooks to students in nonpublic schools. Justice BYRON R. WHITE, speaking for the Supreme Court, relied heavily on the "pupil benefit theory" which he purportedly derived from EVERSON V. BOARD OF EDUCATION (1947). If the beneficiaries of the governmental program were principally the children, and not the religious institutions, the program could be sustained.

Justice HUGO L. BLACK, the author of *Everson,* dissented. *Everson,* he recalled, held that transportation of students to church-related schools went "to the very verge" of what was permissible under the establishment clause. Justices WILLIAM O. DOUGLAS and ABE FORTAS also dissented.

Allen stimulated efforts to aid church-related schools in many state legislatures. Later opinions of the Court, invalidating many such aid programs, have limited *Allen's* precedential force to cases involving textbook loans.

RICHARD E. MORGAN
(1986)

(SEE ALSO: *Government Aid to Religious Institutions.*)

BOARD OF EDUCATION v. PICO
457 U.S. 853 (1982)

Six students sued a school board in federal court, claiming that the board had violated their FIRST AMENDMENT rights by removing certain books from the high school and junior high school libraries. The board had responded to lists of "objectionable" and "inappropriate" books circulated at a conference of conservative parents. A fragmented Supreme Court, voting 5–4, remanded the case for trial.

Four Justices concluded that it would be unconstitutional for the school board to remove the books from the libraries for the purpose of suppressing ideas. Four others argued for wide discretion by local officials in selecting school materials, including library books. One Justice would await the outcome of a trial before addressing the constitutional issues. Thus, although the decision attracted national attention, it did little to solve the intractable constitutional puzzle of GOVERNMENT SPEECH.

KENNETH L. KARST
(1986)

BOARD OF EDUCATION OF KIRYAS JOEL VILLAGE SCHOOL DISTRICT v. GRUMET
512 U.S. 687 (1994)

New York State passed a statute creating a public school district that was coterminous with the boundaries of the Village of Kiryas Joel. Kiryas Joel's entire population consisted of adherents of the Satmar Hasidim, a traditional and insular sect of orthodox Judaism. Most Satmar children attended private religious schools. The public school district was established to meet the needs of Satmar children with disabilities that entitled them to publicly funded special education. The Supreme Court held that the creation of the school district under these circumstances violated the FIRST AMENDMENT prohibition on the ESTABLISHMENT OF RELIGION.

Justice DAVID H. SOUTER's opinion (for a majority of the Court on some issues and only a plurality on others) held that New York impermissibly favored religion over nonreligion, and one religious group over others, by drawing district lines explicitly to include members of the Satmar, and only them. New York could not constitutionally establish a separate school district to allow the Satmars to avoid educating their children among those who did not share their cultural practices, especially considering that there was no assurance in New York law that other culturally or religiously identifiable groups would be afforded a similar ACCOMMODATION OF RELIGION in the future. Justice ANTHONY M. KENNEDY concurred in the judgment. For him the constitutional infirmity in New York's creation of the school district was that it impermissibly drew the political boundaries defining the district on the basis of the religion of those who lived within it.

Justice ANTONIN SCALIA, joined by two other Justices, forcefully dissented, arguing that the establishment clause was not implicated by the state's accommodation of the Satmars' cultural insularity. None of the sect's religious practices contributed to the village's desire not to educate Satmar children among nonadherents. The fact that those holding public authority happen to hold certain religious beliefs does not establish that they hold that authority because of those beliefs. To Scalia it was clear that the cultural insularity of the Satmars, and not their religious beliefs, had led to the accommodation. The dissenters also objected to the notion that, in order to justify a current accommodation, the state must somehow give assurances that it will provide similar accommodations in unknown future circumstances. In the wake of this decision, New York passed general laws permitting incorporation of school districts; although the matter is not without doubt, it appears likely that a new school district formed pursuant to the amended law will pass muster with a majority of the Supreme Court.

The situation leading up to the creation of the Kiryas Joel school district was the product of the Court's decision in AGUILAR V. FELTON (1985), which held that it was unconstitutional for the state to fund special education for handicapped children in sectarian schools. The Satmar children with special education needs, who theretofore had attended programs at an annex to their religious school, were thus forced to attend programs with nonadherents, a situation that they and the other students found disruptive. In response, the state created the Kiryas Joel school district. The rule in *Aguilar* proved unenduring, however, as the Court OVERRULED that decision in AGOSTINI V. FELTON (1997). If *Aguilar* had been decided correctly in the first place, the entire saga of Kiryas Joel would have been avoided. For the future, the annex alternative is likely once again available.

WILLIAM K. KELLEY
(2000)

(SEE ALSO: *Government Aid to Religious Institutions.*)

BOARD OF EDUCATION OF THE WESTSIDE COMMUNITY SCHOOLS v. MERGENS
496 U.S. 226 (1990)

In WIDMAR V. VINCENT (1981) the Supreme Court held that a state university had denied a student religious group's FREEDOM OF SPEECH by barring the group from holding a worship meeting on campus. Concluding that the university had created a limited PUBLIC FORUM, the Court rejected the university's argument that allowing the meeting would amount to an unconstitutional ESTABLISHMENT OF RELIGION. In 1984, Congress adopted the Equal Access Act, prohibiting a public high school that receives federal aid from denying religious, philosophical, or political student groups access to its facilities if it allows access by other "noncurriculum related" student groups. The lower federal courts disagreed about the law's constitutionality, and some commentators expected the Supreme Court's resolution of the conflict to illuminate the future path of ESTABLISHMENT CLAUSE jurisprudence. In the event, the light failed.

In *Mergens* the Supreme Court upheld the act, 8–1, against an establishment clause challenge. Justice SANDRA DAY O'CONNOR, writing for herself and three other Justices, found the case closely similar to *Widmar*—as far as the establishment clause question was concerned—and applied the three-part LEMON TEST. First, Congress had a secular purpose of preventing discrimination against religious speech. Second, the primary effect of the law was not to advance religion. Neither Congress nor the school district had endorsed or sponsored any religious group's speech. Furthermore, the act had forbidden school officials to participate in religious groups' meetings and required that any such meetings be held during noninstructional time. Third, the school's requirement of a faculty sponsor did not amount to excessive entanglement of the school with religion.

Justice ANTHONY M. KENNEDY, joined by Justice ANTONIN SCALIA, concurred. Following his opinion in COUNTY OF ALLEGHENY V. AMERICAN CIVIL LIBERTIES UNION (1989), Kennedy rejected the "endorsement" gloss on the LEMON TEST. He would uphold a law against an establishment clause challenge if it did not directly benefit religion to the degree of establishing a state religion, or coerce someone into participating in a religious activity. Here, Congress and the school board had done neither.

Justice THURGOOD MARSHALL, joined by Justice WILLIAM J. BRENNAN, also concurred. For him, the law raised more serious establishment clause problems than had *Widmar;* the school had not simply opened a forum, but had treated its after-school clubs as serving educational functions. He

concurred on the assumption that the school would be required to redefine its club program to negate the appearance of sponsorship. Justice JOHN PAUL STEVENS dissented on statutory grounds, arguing that the school's existing club program was "curriculum related," so that the act did not require access for a religious group.

KENNETH L. KARST
(1992)

(SEE ALSO: *Bender v. Williamsport; Equal Access; Religious Fundamentalism.*)

BOARD OF REGENTS v. ROTH
408 U.S. 564 (1972)

A nontenured state college teacher, hired for a one-year term, was told he would not be rehired for the following year. The Supreme Court held, 5–3, that he had not been deprived of PROCEDURAL DUE PROCESS. Justice POTTER STEWART, for the majority, announced a restrictive view of the nature of the interests protected by the due process guarantee. Henceforth the Court would look for an impact on some "liberty" or "property" interest, rather than examine the importance of the deprivation imposed by the state. Here the teacher had no "property" interest beyond his one-year contract, and his nonrenewal required no hearing.

In a companion case, *Perry v. Sindermann* (1972), the Court found a "property" interest in an unwritten policy that was the equivalent of tenure for a state junior college teacher. Furthermore, the teacher had alleged that his contract had not been renewed because of his exercise of FIRST AMENDMENT freedoms—a "liberty" claim that did not depend on his tenured status.

KENNETH L. KARST
(1986)

BOARD OF TRUSTEES OF STATE UNIVERSITY OF NEW YORK v. FOX
492 U.S. 469 (1989)

This decision significantly altered the doctrinal formula governing COMMERCIAL SPEECH. In CENTRAL HUDSON GAS AND ELECTRIC CORP. V. PUBLIC SERVICE COMMISSION (1980) the Supreme Court had held that a state's regulation of commercial speech must be "no more extensive than necessary" to achieve the regulation's purposes. In *Fox*, a 6–3 majority explicitly disavowed the idea that a state was limited to the LEAST RESTRICTIVE MEANS in regulating commercial advertising. Justice ANTONIN SCALIA wrote for the Court.

A state-university regulation of on-campus business activity effectively prevented a seller of household goods from holding "Tupperware parties" in the dormitories. Although the company's representatives not only sold goods but also made presentations on home economics, the Court concluded that the speech was commercial. The transactions proposed were lawful, and the advertising was not misleading; thus, the interest-balancing part of the *Central Hudson Gas* formula came into play. Here the university had important interests in preserving a noncommercial atmosphere on campus and tranquillity in the dormitories. Although the regulation did directly advance these interests, other means, less restrictive on speech, would arguably have served just as well. Justice Scalia noted that previous opinions had suggested that regulations of advertising must pass a "least restrictive means" test, but decided that such a formulation was too burdensome on the states. Rather, what is required is "a fit [between means and ends] that is not necessarily perfect, but reasonable; that represents not necessarily the single best disposition but one whose scope is 'in proportion to the interest served'" (quoting from *In re R.M.J.*, dealing with lawyer advertising).

Justice HARRY A. BLACKMUN, who had written the Court's early opinions admitting commercial speech into the shelter of the FIRST AMENDMENT, wrote for the three dissenters. He argued that the statute was invalid for OVERBREADTH, and said he need not discuss the least-restrictive-means question.

KENNETH L. KARST
(1992)

BOB JONES UNIVERSITY v. UNITED STATES
461 U.S. 574 (1983)

The Internal Revenue Service adopted a policy in 1969 of denying federal income tax exemption, available by statute to educational and religious institutions, to schools that practiced racial discrimination. Bob Jones University, an institution that had a multiracial student body but restricted interracial socializing, and Goldsboro Christian Schools, which practiced racial SEGREGATION on the basis of religious conviction, sought to have their tax-exempt status reinstated. In an opinion by Chief Justice WARREN E. BURGER, the Supreme Court held, 8–1, that the Internal Revenue Service had the power, even without explicit statutory authorization, to enforce by its regulations a "settled public policy" against racial discrimination in education. None of the Justices accepted the schools' claim that the regulations infringed on the First Amendment's guarantee of religious liberty, but Justice WILLIAM H. REHNQUIST, dissenting, warned of the danger of abrogating the SEPARATION OF POWERS.

DENNIS J. MAHONEY
(1986)

BOB-LO EXCURSION COMPANY v. MICHIGAN
333 U.S. 28 (1948)

Although this decision unsettled interpretations of the COMMERCE CLAUSE, it nevertheless dealt SEGREGATION another blow. A Detroit steamship company violated a state CIVIL RIGHTS statute by refusing to transport a black girl to a local, though Canadian, destination. Justice WILEY RUTLEDGE's majority opinion distinguished MORGAN V. VIRGINIA (1946) and stressed the local nature of transportation in upholding the statute. Justices WILLIAM O. DOUGLAS and HUGO L. BLACK thought the law should be sustained because there could be no conflict with a congressional law; Chief Justice FRED M. VINSON and Justice ROBERT H. JACKSON dissented, arguing that *Morgan* and HALL V. DECUIR (1878) governed.

DAVID GORDON
(1986)

BODDIE v. CONNECTICUT
401 U.S. 371 (1971)

An INDIGENT sought to file for divorce in a state court but was unable to pay the $60 filing fee. The Supreme Court held, 8–1, that the state had unconstitutionally limited the plaintiff's ACCESS TO THE COURTS. For a majority, Justice JOHN MARSHALL HARLAN rested decision on a PROCEDURAL DUE PROCESS theory. The marriage relationship was "basic" in our society, and the state had monopolized the means for legally dissolving the relationship. Justice WILLIAM O. DOUGLAS, concurring, would have rested decision on an EQUAL PROTECTION theory.

Two subsequent 5–4 decisions, *United States v. Kras* (1971) and *Ortwein v. Schwab* (1971), made clear that *Boddie* had not implied a general right of access in all civil cases. *Boddie*'s due process approach, rather than equal protection, has guided the Court's subsequent dealings with WEALTH DISCRIMINATION in the civil litigation process.

KENNETH L. KARST
(1986)

BODY SEARCH

The term "body search" is limited to strip searches (forcing a suspect to disrobe to enable an officer to observe the naked body), body cavity searches (inserting a finger or instrument into the rectum or vagina), and other penetrations of the body, such as extracting blood. Body searches do not violate the RIGHT AGAINST SELF-INCRIMINATION, because, as held in SCHMERBER V. CALIFORNIA (1966), they do not result in TESTIMONIAL COMPULSION. Nor do they violate DUE PROCESS OF LAW unless conducted in a shocking manner. The FOURTH AMENDMENT is the principal restriction on body searches.

The Supreme Court has, in recent years, balanced competing interests in determining whether a search violates the Fourth Amendment. This approach, which usually results in upholding the search, has been used by courts with devastating effect in situations such as BORDER SEARCHES and prison searches; in the context of both, body searches may occur.

A person who enters the United States may be searched without a SEARCH WARRANT, without PROBABLE CAUSE, and without even reasonable suspicion. This rule applies to a search of a suspect's outer garments and luggage or other containers. If a border search is more intrusive, it may be governed by more stringent standards. The Supreme Court has never reviewed a strip search case that arose at the border. Although lower courts require neither a warrant nor probable cause for such a search, they do require some justification, often expressed as "real suspicion." This standard approximates the "reasonable suspicion" standard that TERRY V. OHIO (1968) used to justify a STOP-AND-FRISK. Although a strip search is far more intrusive than a stop-and-frisk, its occurrence at the border is said to justify the *Terry* standard.

The Supreme Court has never reviewed a body cavity search case that arose at the border. Lower courts do not require a warrant. Nor do they require probable cause, most choosing a "reasonable suspicion" standard. These are dubious positions. Given the lack of EXIGENT CIRCUMSTANCES and the indignity of an exploration of body cavities, it would be appropriate to require both a warrant and probable cause. Even if constitutional at its inception, a body cavity search might be unreasonable and therefore unconstitutional in its execution. Relevant factors include the place in which the examination occurs, the person making the examination, and the manner in which the examination is made.

The Supreme Court held in *Hudson v. Palmer* that, as a result of the needs of prison security and discipline, "society is not prepared to recognize as legitimate any subjective expectation of privacy that a prisoner might have in his prison cell." This means that a prison cell may be searched without a warrant, probable cause, or even reasonable suspicion. It probably also means that prisoners' outer garments may be searched routinely. *Hudson* does not directly deal with strip searches or body cavity searches.

Five years before *Hudson*, in *Bell v. Wolfish* (1979), a highly debatable 5–4 decision, the Supreme Court relied on the interest in prison security to uphold the strip-searching of inmates of a pretrial detention facility whenever they had a contact visit with an outsider. As part of the search, the prisoner had to expose body cavities to visual inspection. The Court required neither probable cause nor reasonable suspicion. *Bell* does not explicitly authorize routine strip searches, however. Nor does it deal with the digital or instrumental exploration of body cavities.

Lower courts have disagreed about the scope of *Hudson* and *Bell*. Most courts wisely have not interpreted these cases to withdraw all Fourth Amendment protection from prison inmates. Although they do not require a warrant or probable cause, these lower courts authorize strip searches and body cavity searches only on reasonable suspicion or after the occurrence of some event such as a contact visit or the leaving and reentering of the prison. These lower courts also recognize that even if a strip search or body cavity search is justified at its inception, its execution may offend the Fourth Amendment. For example, in *Bonitz v. Fair* (1986) the United States Court of Appeals for the Second Circuit held that body cavity searches of female prisoners were unconstitutional when conducted by nonmedical personnel in an unhygienic manner and in the view of male officers.

Courts apply higher standards when the person searched is a prison employee or visitor.

Body searches occur in settings other than the border and prisons, and the Supreme Court has decided several relevant cases. In *Schmerber*, the Court held that the Fourth Amendment did not require a police officer to obtain a warrant before ordering a doctor to withdraw blood from an apparently drunk driver. The alcoholic content of blood is evanescent and might disappear or change in the time it would take to obtain a warrant. If evidence is not evanescent, however, a warrant might well be required unless the officer is entitled to act routinely, as in fingerprinting all arrestees, for example. Even though it did not require a warrant, *Schmerber* did require a "clear indication" that the driver's blood would disclose intoxication. The Court probably meant to require more than probable cause to justify the subcutaneous intrusion, but in subsequent cases it suggested that "clear indication" means no more than probable cause and may mean less.

In *Winston v. Lee* (1985) the Court prohibited the surgical removal of a bullet from a robbery suspect's body. The removal had been ordered by a state court on probable cause to believe that the bullet, fired from the victim's gun, would identify the suspect as the robber. The Supreme Court balanced the state's need for the evidence against the intrusion of surgery under a general anesthetic. It found that the state already had substantial identification evidence and that the operation posed significant risks. *Winston* is one of the rare cases in which the Court has used the balancing approach to increase, rather than lower, the protections of the Fourth Amendment.

LAWRENCE HERMAN
(1992)

(SEE ALSO: *Prisoners' Rights; Right of Privacy.*)

Bibliography

LAFAVE, WAYNE R.   1987   *Search and Seizure,* 2nd ed. St. Paul, Minn.: West Publishing Co.

WHITEBREAD, CHARLES H. and SLOBOGIN, CHRISTOPHER   1986   *Criminal Procedure,* 2nd ed. Mineola, N.Y.: Foundation Press.

BOERNE (CITY OF) v. FLORES

See: Religious Freedom Restoration Act

BOLAND AMENDMENT

The Boland Amendment featured in the IRAN-CONTRA AFFAIR and implicated President RONALD REAGAN in a failure to perform his constitutional duty to execute the laws faithfully.

From 1982 through 1986, Congress annually enacted the Boland Amendment as a rider to Defense Department appropriations. The amendment prohibited military assistance to the Contras, the armed opposition to Nicaragua's communist government. The amendment applied to any agency or entity of the United States "involved in intelligence activities." The President signed the amendment annually, although opposing it on policy grounds. Reagan never intimated his belief that its restrictions were unconstitutional or did not apply to him, to any of his executive officers, or to the National Security Council (NSC). When the Iran-Contra Affair became public, the President made inconsistent statements; only then did his administration take the position that the Boland Amendment did not extend to the NSC.

While the amendment was operative, however, the administration, including the director of the NSC, had consistently declared that it complied with the amendment in letter and spirit. In fact, executive officers in the White House had covertly aided the Contras. Furthermore, all involved acknowledged that the amendment prohibited solicitation of funds from other countries. Yet, while the amendment was operative, funds were solicited from Saudi Arabia and Taiwan for military assistance to the Contras, and monies from Iran were used for the same purpose.

The power to appropriate conditionally would be an empty one if the President could command his subordinates to violate an act of Congress that he had signed. Funds raised by the government must, under Article I, section 9, go through the federal Treasury and be in accord with laws passed by Congress. Otherwise, Congress's power over the purse would be debilitated if not meaningless. President Reagan either failed in his constitutional duty to "take care that the laws be faithfully executed" or participated along with high-ranking subordinates in the clandestine violation of law.

LEONARD W. LEVY
(1992)

(SEE ALSO: *Constitutional History, 1980–1989.*)

Bibliography

UNITED STATES: PRESIDENT'S SPECIAL REVIEW BOARD   1987   *Tower Commisson Report.* New York: Bantam-Times Books.

BOLLING v. SHARPE
347 U.S. 497 (1954)

In the four cases now known as BROWN V. BOARD OF EDUCATION (1954), the Supreme Court held that racial SEGREGATION of children in state public schools violated the FOURTEENTH AMENDMENT's guarantee of the EQUAL PROTECTION OF THE LAWS. *Bolling,* a companion case to *Brown,* involved a challenge to school segregation in the DISTRICT OF COLUMBIA. The equal protection clause applies only to the states. However, in previous cases (including the JAPANESE AMERICAN CASES, 1943–1944) the Court had assumed, at least for argument, that the Fifth Amendment's guarantee of DUE PROCESS OF LAW prohibited arbitrary discrimination by the federal government.

The Court in *Bolling* also drew on OBITER DICTA in the Japanese American Cases stating that racial classifications were suspect, requiring exacting judicial scrutiny. Because school segregation was "not reasonably related to any proper governmental objective," the District's practice deprived the segregated black children of liberty without due process. Chief Justice EARL WARREN wrote for a unanimous Court.

The Court concluded its Fifth Amendment discussion

by remarking that because *Brown* had prohibited school segregation by the states, "it would be unthinkable that the same Constitution would impose a lesser duty on the Federal Government." Critics have suggested that what was "unthinkable" was the political implication of a contrary decision. But the notions of liberty and equality have long been understood to overlap. The idea of national CITIZENSHIP implies a measure of equal treatment by the national government, and the "liberty" protected by the Fifth Amendment's due process clause implies a measure of equal liberties. Doctrinally as well as politically, a contrary decision in *Bolling* would have been unthinkable.

KENNETH L. KARST
(1986)

BOLLMAN, EX PARTE, v. SWARTWOUT
4 Cranch 75 (1807)

The Supreme Court discharged the prisoners, confederates in AARON BURR's conspiracy, from an INDICTMENT for TREASON. The indictment specified their treason as levying war against the United States. Chief Justice JOHN MARSHALL, for the Court, distinguished treason from a conspiracy to commit it. He sought to prevent the crime of treason from being "extended by construction to doubtful cases." To complete the crime of treason or levying war, Marshall said, a body of men must be "actually assembled for the purpose of effecting by force a treasonable purpose," in which everyone involved, to any degree and however remote from the scene of action, is guilty of treason. But the levying of war does not exist short of the actual assemblage of armed men. Congress had the power to punish crimes short of treason, but the Constitution protected Americans from a charge of treason for a crime short of it.

Bollman is also an important precedent in the law of federal JURISDICTION. In OBITER DICTUM, Marshall stated that a federal court's power to issue a WRIT OF HABEAS CORPUS "must be given by written law," denying by inference that the courts have any inherent power to grant habeas corpus relief, apart from congressional authorization. (See EX PARTE MCCARDLE; JUDICIAL SYSTEM.)

LEONARD W. LEVY
(1986)

BOND, HUGH LENNOX
(1828–1893)

President ULYSSES S. GRANT on July 13, 1870, commissioned Hugh Lennox Bond judge of the newly created Fourth Circuit Court, a position he filled until his death. The Maryland judge was immediately called upon to hold court in an eleven-county section of South Carolina that had been plagued by the Ku Klux Klan's reign of terror. The judge fearlessly restored the rights of freedmen in South Carolina, but he did so in the belief that the states retained responsibility for preserving most CIVIL RIGHTS. Congress, he insisted, could only impede the traditional power of the states over the franchise when there was evidence of direct STATE ACTION resulting in discrimination based on race, color, or previous condition of servitude. Bond rejected the view that the CIVIL WAR amendments incorporated rights deriving from natural law; the protection of such rights, he concluded, remained squarely within state discretion.

He refused to allow the concept of dual CITIZENSHIP to erect an absolute bar to FEDERAL PROTECTION. In *United States v. Petersburg Judges of Elections* (1874), election officials were charged with preventing voting by freedmen without any overt act of RACIAL DISCRIMINATION. Bond acknowledged that under the concept of dual citizenship the states could take away certain rights, such as the franchise. He held, however, that so long as states continued to grant those rights, the federal government could protect freedmen by inferring discriminatory intent from acts depriving them of the rights that had been granted.

Bond insisted on the supremacy of the national government in its proper sphere. In 1876 he ordered the release of the Board of Canvassers of South Carolina who had been imprisoned by the state supreme court for attempting to report election returns favorable to RUTHERFORD B. HAYES. Bond held that Article I, section 2, protected the Canvassers in their capacity as federal officials.

During RECONSTRUCTION Bond courageously extended federal judicial protection to freedmen. Yet even this most vigorous champion in the circuit courts of freedmen's civil rights eschewed the Radical Republicans' CONSTITUTIONAL INTERPRETATION of the Civil War amendments.

KERMIT L. HALL
(1986)

Bibliography

HALL, KERMIT L. 1984 Political Power and Constitutional Legitimacy: The South Carolina Ku Klux Klan Trials, 1871–1872. *Emory Law Journal* 33:921–951.

BONHAM'S CASE
8 Coke 113b (1610)

Although the issue in *Bonham's Case* concerned the power of the Royal College of Physicians to discipline nonmembers, its importance principally derives from its subsequent use as a precedent for JUDICIAL REVIEW and the subordination of LEGISLATION to a higher, constitutional law. Thomas Bonham, holder of a doctorate from Cambridge University, continued to practice in London after being refused permission by the College. Acting under powers conferred by royal charter and parliamentary statutes, the college authorities accordingly fined Bonham and secured his incarceration, thus triggering his suit for false imprisonment before the Court of Common Pleas.

Chief Justice Sir EDWARD COKE ruled in Bonham's favor. Although most of his numerous grounds were technical, Coke also criticized the statutory power of the college to be the original judge in a case to which it had itself been a party and concluded that the COMMON LAW courts could "control" and render void those acts of Parliament that were "against Common Right, and Reason, or repugnant, or impossible to be performed."

Coke, nevertheless, invoked no judicial power to invalidate legislation or measure its constitutionality. He advised only that the statute be construed strictly, not nullified, thus prescribing a rule of statutory construction rather than a doctrine of constitutional superintendence. Coke assumed, moreover, that the defect in the law inhered not in UNCONSTITUTIONALITY but in want of reasonableness and in impossibility of performance. The common law court intervened here as the handmaiden, not the antagonistic overseer, of Parliament, a brother court, and only for the purpose of recapturing a reasonableness that permeated the immutable laws sought by bench and Parliament alike.

Coke's use of evidence was also defective. Coke misquoted, for example, a major precedent, *Tregor's Case* (1334), by infusing into it language that it actually lacked to secure the desired result.

Two antagonistic streams of interpretation devolve from *Bonham's Case.* The Glorious Revolution of 1688 signaled the dominance of Parliament over court as well as crown and, thus, the demise of the spacious judicial interpretation of legislation advocated by Coke. In 1765 WILLIAM BLACKSTONE definitively stated that no power could control unreasonable statutes, for such control subverted all government by setting the judiciary over the legislature. Although Coke's opinion in *Bonham* retained wide currency in the seventeenth century, its erosion began almost immediately and accelerated in the following century. In *The Duchess of Hamilton's Case* (1712), for example, Sir Thomas Powys insisted that judges must "strain hard" to avoid interpretations of statutes that would nullify them.

As the American Revolution approached, however, *Bonham's Case* evolved in the American colonies in the opposite direction as a fixed constitutional barrier against Parliament. Thus, in PAXTON'S CASE (1761) JAMES OTIS urged

the Massachusetts Superior Court to impose a disabling interpretation on the British statute of 1662 that had codified WRITS OF ASSISTANCE. Although only private parties, not bench and Parliament, had directly clashed in *Bonham's Case,* Otis advanced it as a firm precedent for judicial evisceration of legislation. Coke questioned only the reasonableness of a statute; Otis and his followers challenged a law's constitutionality.

WILLIAM J. CUDDIHY
(1986)

Bibliography

CORWIN, EDWARD S.   1929   *The "Higher Law" Background of American Constitutional Law.* Ithaca, N.Y.: Cornell University Press.

THORNE, SAMUEL   1938   The Constitution and the Courts: A Reexamination of the Famous Case of Dr. Bonham. Pages 15–24 in Conyers Read (ed.), *The Constitution Reconsidered.* New York: Columbia University Press.

BONUS BILL

See: Internal Improvements

BOOTH v. MARYLAND
482 U.S. 496 (1987)

Conflicting views on CAPITAL PUNISHMENT emerged in this case dealing with the constitutionality of victim impact statements (VIS). In conformance with state law, the prosecution introduced VIS at the SENTENCING phase of a capital trial. Those statements described the effects of the crime on the victims and their families. Naturally, they were intensely emotional and, according to the majority of the Court, had the effect of prejudicing the sentencing jury. Dividing 5–4, the Court ruled that the VIS provided information irrelevant to a capital-sentencing decision and that the admission of such statements created a constitutionally unacceptable risk that the jury might impose the death penalty arbitrarily or capriciously. Therefore, according to the Court, the VIS conflicted with the Eighth Amendment's CRUEL AND UNUSUAL PUNISHMENT clause. How the murderer could have been exposed to cruel and unusual punishment by the jurors' having listened to statements describing the impact of his crime is mystifying.

Justice BYRON R. WHITE, for the dissenters, believed that VIS are appropriate evidence in capitalsentencing hearings. Punishment can be increased in noncapital cases on the basis of the harm caused and so might be increased in capital cases. VIS reminded the jurors that just as the murderer ought to be regarded as an individual, so too should the victim whose death constituted a unique loss to his family and the community. Justice ANTONIN SCALIA, for the same dissenters, contended that the Court's opinion wrongly rested on the principle that the death sentence should be inflicted solely on the basis of moral guilt. He thought the harm done was also relevant. Many people believed that criminal trials favored the accused too much if they did not consider the harm inflicted on the victim and the victim's family. The Court's previous opinions required that all mitigating factors must be placed before the capital-sentencing jury; yet the Court here required the suppression of the suffering caused by the defendant. This muted one side of the debate on the appropriateness of capital punishment.

LEONARD W. LEVY
(1992)

BORDER SEARCH

A search at an international boundary of a person, a vehicle, or goods entering the United States may be carried out without a SEARCH WARRANT and in the absence of PROBABLE CAUSE or even suspicion. In *United States v. Ramsey* (1977) the Supreme Court said that this extraordinary power, which also allows the government to open international mail entering the United States, "is grounded in the recognized right of the sovereign to control . . . who and what may enter the country." The First Congress, in 1789, authorized WARRANTLESS SEARCHES of vessels suspected of carrying goods on which customs duty had been evaded, and similar provisions have been enacted subsequently. As the Court held in ALMEIDA-SANCHEZ V. UNITED STATES (1973), such a search may be conducted not only at the border itself but also at its "functional equivalent," such as "an established station near the border," or "a point marking the confluence of two or more roads that extend from the border," or an airplane arriving on a nonstop flight from abroad.

Under *United States v. Brignoni-Ponce* (1975) an automobile may not be stopped by a roving patrol car miles from the border (in an area that is not its legal equivalent) to determine whether the occupants are illegal aliens unless there is reasonable suspicion. Under *United States v. Martinez-Fuerte* (1976) automobiles may be stopped for this purpose at fixed checkpoints; in these circumstances the opportunity of officers to act arbitrarily is limited.

JACOB W. LANDYNSKI
(1986)

Bibliography

LAFAVE, WAYNE R. 1978 *Search and Seizure: A Treatise on the Fourth Amendment.* Vol. 3:275–327. St. Paul, Minn.: West Publishing Co.

BORK NOMINATION

On June 26, 1987, Justice LEWIS F. POWELL retired from the Supreme Court for reasons of health and age. On July 1, 1987, President RONALD REAGAN nominated Judge Robert H. Bork of the United States Court of Appeals for the District of Columbia Circuit, former Solicitor General of the United States and Professor of Law at the Yale Law School, to replace Justice Powell. The nomination was rejected by the Senate on October 23, 1987 by a vote of forty-two for and fifty-eight against. Although any Senate rejection of a presidential nominee for the Supreme Court is noteworthy, the proceedings surrounding the Bork nomination were uniquely important in providing what turned out to be virtually a public referendum on the deepest questions of constitutional theory. The outcome of this referendum is likely to have long-term effects not only on future nominations, but also on the practice of CONSTITUTIONAL INTERPRETATION.

As a prominent academic, public official, and judge with a firmly established reputation as a political and judicial conservative, Judge Bork had been thought of as a potential nominee for some years. When he was nominated in 1987, opposition crystallized immediately, led by groups such as Common Cause, People for the American Way, Planned Parenthood, and the AMERICAN CIVIL LIBERTIES UNION, the last of whose opposition to the nomination represented a departure from longstanding practice. This opposition, reflected first in the divided and only qualified endorsement of the American Bar Association Standing Committee on the Federal Judiciary, was manifested in newspaper and television advertisements, extensive lobbying efforts, organization of letter-writing campaigns directed primarily at members of the SENATE JUDICIARY COMMITTEE, and in elaborately orchestrated testimony before this Committee (chaired by Senator Joseph Biden of Delaware), testimony featuring a significant number of prominent law school professors.

The public debate and the televised proceedings before the Judiciary Committee focused on five issues, four of which turned out to be much less important than the fifth. First was Judge Bork's role as solicitor general during the administration of President RICHARD M. NIXON and, in particular, his role as the one who as acting attorney general finally implemented the President's order to remove Archibald Cox as SPECIAL PROSECUTOR after both the attorney general (Elliott Richardson) and the deputy attorney general (William Ruckleshaus) had refused. Testimony at the hearings, however, including testimony from Richardson supporting the nomination, established the political and moral plausibility, if not the ultimate correctness, of Bork's action, and quickly removed this issue from center stage.

Second, Judge Bork's writings on ANTITRUST LAW generated some objections based on the possibility that he would be insufficiently supportive of vigorous enforcement of the antitrust laws. Little came of this, however, in part because of the comparative infrequency of antitrust cases in the Supreme Court and, in larger part, because it became clear that Judge Bork's writings in this area, although controversial, were widely respected and well within the mainstream of academic and professional debate.

Third was Bork's view about FREEDOM OF SPEECH and FREEDOM OF THE PRESS under the FIRST AMENDMENT, in particular the position articulated in a 1971 article, "Neutral Principles and Some First Amendment Problems," in the *Indiana Law Journal*. In this article, Bork argued that only explicitly political speech and not art or literature or anything else not directly relating to political argument was protected by the First Amendment. Although this view represented a substantial departure from both the existing case law and the bulk of academic commentary, Bork's testimony before the Judiciary Committee, conjoined with opinions he had written while on the Court of Appeals, like *Ollman v. Evans* (1984), established that he no longer held this view, at least to such an extent, and the issue turned out to be less important than was first expected.

Fourth, Judge Bork had objected both to the Supreme Court's opinion in SHELLEY V. KRAEMER (1948) striking down judicial enforcement of racially restrictive covenants as unconstitutional state action and to the public-accommodation provisions of the CIVIL RIGHTS ACT OF 1964, calling the latter at the time an act of "unsurpassed ugliness." At the hearings, however, Judge Bork made it clear that he was an unqualified supporter of BROWN V. BOARD OF EDUCATION (1954) and many other Supreme Court decisions outlawing racial SEGREGATION and that he no longer held the views he had set forth in 1963. Moreover, his record on the Court of Appeals and as solicitor general, although hardly aggressive on questions of discrimination on the basis of race and gender, confirmed that Judge Bork no longer held views as hostile to civil rights as might have been inferred solely from some of his earlier writings. This issue never disappeared from the hearings and represented a significant reason for the opposition of numerous civil rights organizations, but in the final analysis, like Bork's views on the First Amendment, it played a somewhat smaller role than had earlier been anticipated.

Fifth and most important were Judge Bork's views about constitutional interpretation and constitutional theory, particularly as they related to questions about the use of ORIGINAL INTENT and about the existence of UNENUMERATED RIGHTS in general and the RIGHT OF PRIVACY in particular. In this context, Judge Bork's views were more consistent over time, as shown in cases like *Dronenburg*

v. Zech (1984), representing a view pursuant to which constitutional interpretation was legitimate according to Bork only if restricted to provisions explicitly set forth in the constitutional text, with textual indeterminacies to be resolved by exclusive reference to the original intent of the drafters.

The import of this position was that Judge Bork viewed these Supreme Court decisions finding unenumerated rights in the Constitution as illegitimate judicial usurpation of legislative or majoritarian authority. The discussion of this issue focused largely on the right of privacy, whose recognition Judge Bork viewed as beyond the proper province of the Supreme Court, and on the Supreme Court decisions in ROE V. WADE (1973) on ABORTION and GRISWOLD V. CONNECTICUT (1965) on contraception, both of which were based on principles of enforcement of unenumerated rights or Fourteenth Amendment SUBSTANTIVE DUE PROCESS that Judge Bork found impermissible.

Although Judge Bork's views in this regard were often characterized during the hearings as outside of the academic or professional mainstream, his skepticism about substantive due process, unenumerated rights, and the right to privacy reflected a commonly articulated academic position throughout the 1970s and early 1980s and a position often articulated by academics whose personal political views would have been sympathetic to the enforcement of privacy and abortion rights as a matter of legislative or political policy. In this regard, the charge that Bork's views were widely divergent from the so-called mainstream was simply factually inaccurate.

That Bork's views did not represent some alledged radical right-wing view (see Ronald Dworkin, "The Bork Nomination," *The New York Review of Books*, August 13, 1987), however, does not entail the conclusion that these views could not permissibly be taken into account by the President in nominating him or by the Senate in deciding whether to give their advice and consent to the nomination. From this perspective one of the lessons of the entire process was that a prospective Justice's views about questions of constitutional interpretation and substantive constitutional law became more permissible part of senatorial inquiry than they had previously been. Although the rhetoric at the time inaccurately stressed the "out of the mainstream" character of these views, it does not follow that the senators are obliged to give their ADVICE AND CONSENT to every nominee whose views are within the mainstream. The rejection of the Bork nomination represents a change in practice (in part confirmed in subsequent nominations) toward a process in which senators feel more comfortable about critically inquiring into substansive questons about consitiutional law than they had in the past.

The rejection of the nomination can therefore also be

taken as a virtual public referendum on the right to privacy and perhaps also on the authority of the Supreme Court to enforce unenumerated rights. Although opposition to the abortion decisions was taken to be less "extreme," Bork's opposition to *Griswold* was the focus of the controversy. In their testimony, Bork and his supporters stressed the distinction between the desirability of a right and its existence or historical embodiment in the Constitution, arguing that the desirability of a right, including the right to privacy, was not a sufficient condition for its judicial recognition under a view that recognized majoritarian supremacy and the limited role of JUDICIAL REVIEW. And in opposition, Bork's adversaries before the Judiciary Committee focused on the intrinsic desirability of a right to privacy, on the social obsolescence of the contraception prohibition struck down in *Griswold*, on a Lockean tradition of NATURAL RIGHTS, on the NINTH AMENDMENT, and on a relatively long history of Supreme Court use of substantive due process to encompass unenumerated rights and to invalidate state and federal legislation inconsistent with them.

The final committee vote of five to nine against the nomination (October 6, 1987), as well as the Senate vote consistent with this negative recommendation (both of which included negative votes by Republicans), may well represent a public and legislative endorsement of the authority of the Supreme Court both to interpret the Constitution by use of sources not limited to the original intentions of the Framers and to identify and to enforce rights not explicitly enumerated in the text of the document. Although other factors played a role in the defeat of the nomination, including Bork's views on CIVIL RIGHTS and freedom of speech and a personal style more academic than publicly engaging, the centrality of the privacy-unenumerated rights issue has been confirmed by subsequent nominations. During the proceedings leading to the confirmation of Justice DAVID H. SOUTER, he consistently avoided expressing his views about *Roe v. Wade*, but made clear that he believed both that it was permissible for the Court to identify and enforce unenumerated rights and that the right to privacy was one of them. Insofar as these statements manifest a shift such that it is no longer plausible for a Supreme Court Justice (or nominee) to deny the existence of unenumerated rights or the right to privacy, the rejection of the Bork nomination must be considered not only as the rejection of a particular nominee, but also and more significantly, as the punctuation mark on a longer term constitutional transformation.

FREDRICK SCHAUER
(1992)

(SEE ALSO: *Conservatism.*)

Bibliography
ACKERMAN, BRUCE 1990 Robert Bork's Grand Inquisition. *Yale Law Journal* 99:1419–1439.
BORK, ROBERT H. 1990 *The Tempting of America: The Political Seduction of the Law.* New York: Macmillan.
BRONNER, ETHAN 1989 *Battle for Justice: How the Bork Nomination Shook America.* New York: W. W. Norton.
NAGEL, ROBERT F. 1990 Meeting the Enemy. *University of Chicago Law Review* 57:633–656.
PERTSCHUK, MICHAEL and SCHAETZEL, WENDY 1989 *The People Rising: The Campaign Against the Bork Nomination.* New York: Thunder's Mouth Press.
SANDALOW, TERRANCE 1990 The Supreme Court in Politics. *Michigan Law Review* 88:1300–1325.
SYMPOSIUM 1987 The Bork Nomination. *The Cardozo Law Review* 9:1–530.

BORROWING POWER

Congress, under Article I, section 8, of the Constitution, may "borrow money on the credit of the United States." This power is ordinarily exercised through the sale of bonds or the issuance of BILLS OF CREDIT. The latter, sometimes called "treasury notes" or "greenbacks," are intended to circulate as currency and thus, in effect, to require the public to lend money to the government. In the GOLD CLAUSE CASES (1935) the Supreme Court held that the government, in borrowing, is bound by the terms of its contracts, but Congress, by invoking SOVEREIGN IMMUNITY, denied its creditors any legal remedy.

DENNIS J. MAHONEY
(1986)

BOSTON BEER COMPANY v. MASSACHUSETTS
97 U.S. 25 (1878)

This case introduced the doctrine of INALIENABLE POLICE POWER, which weakened the CONTRACT CLAUSE's protections of property. The company's charter authorized it to manufacture beer subject to a reserved power of the legislature to alter, amend, or repeal the charter. The state subsequently enacted a prohibition statute. The RESERVED POLICE POWER should have been sufficient ground for the holding by the Court that the prohibition statute did not impair the company's chartered right to do business. However, Justice JOSEPH P. BRADLEY, in an opinion for a unanimous Court, found another and "equally decisive" reason for rejecting the argument that the company had a contract to manufacture and sell beer "forever." The company held its rights subject to the POLICE POWER of the state to promote the public safety and morals. "The Legislature,"

Bradley declared, "cannot, by any contract, devest itself of the power to provide for these objects." Accordingly the enactment of a statute prohibiting the manufacture and sale of intoxicating liquors did not violate the contract clause. Decisions such as this, by which the police power prevailed over chartered rights, produced a doctrinal response: the development of SUBSTANTIVE DUE PROCESS to protect property.

LEONARD W. LEVY
(1986)

BOUDIN, LOUIS B.
(1874–1952)

Louis Boudianoff Boudin was a prominent New York attorney and the author of books and articles on constitutional law, jurisprudence, and government regulation of the economy. His most significant work was *Government by Judiciary* (2 vols., 1932), a massive, iconoclastic history of the doctrine of JUDICIAL REVIEW. Boudin argued that, beginning in 1803 with JOHN MARSHALL's opinion in MARBURY V. MADISON, the federal judiciary had gradually expanded its powers and authority at the expense of the legislative and executive branches, culminating in a "government by judiciary" hostile to the basic principles of the Constitution established by its Framers and to the tenets of democratic government. While Boudin's admirers praised his erudition and accepted his exposure of the weaknesses of the historical case for judicial review, his critics questioned his tendency to write as an advocate rather than as a historian and charged that his conclusions were not supported by an impartial examination of the historical evidence.

RICHARD B. BERNSTEIN
(1986)

BOUNDS v. SMITH
430 U.S. 817 (1977)

Several state prisoners sued North Carolina prison authorities in federal court, claiming they had been denied legal research facilities in violation of their FOURTEENTH AMENDMENT rights. The Supreme Court, 6–3, upheld this claim in an opinion by Justice THURGOOD MARSHALL.

For the first time the Court explicitly recognized a "fundamental constitutional right of ACCESS TO THE COURTS." This right imposed on prison authorities the affirmative duty to provide either adequate law libraries or the assistance of law-trained persons, so that prisoners might prepare HABEAS CORPUS petitions and other legal papers. The three dissenters each wrote an opinion. Justice

WILLIAM H. REHNQUIST complained that the majority had neither defined the content of "meaningful" access nor specified the source of the Fourteenth Amendment right; an EQUAL PROTECTION right, he pointed out, would conflict with ROSS V. MOFFITT (1974).

KENNETH L. KARST
(1986)

BOWEN v. KENDRICK
487 U.S. 589 (1988)

In this case the Court sustained the facial constitutionality of Congress's 1981 Adolescent Family Life Act against a claim that it violated the ESTABLISHMENT CLAUSE of the FIRST AMENDMENT. The statute authorized federal funds for services, publicly or privately administered, that related to adolescent sexuality and pregnancy. A federal district court found that the statute, on its face and as administered, advanced religion by subsidizing and allowing sectarian organizations to preach their message to adolescents; the statute also unduly entangled the government with religion, by requiring official monitoring to ensure that religiously affiliated grantees did not promote their religious missions. The Court, by a 5–4 vote, reversed and remanded the case for a determination whether it was unconstitutionally applied.

Chief Justice WILLIAM H. REHNQUIST, for the majority, observed that the statute neither required grantees to be religiously affiliated nor suggested that religious institutions were specially qualified to provide the services subsidized by the government. Congress merely assumed that religious organizations as well as nonreligious ones could influence adolescent behavior. Congress impartially made the monies available to achieve secular objectives, regardless whether the funds went to sectarian or secular institutions. This was not a case in which the federal subsidies flowed primarily to pervasively sectarian institutions; moreover, the services provided to adolescents, such as pregnancy testing or child care, were not religious in nature. The majority also held that the government monitoring required by the statute did not necessarily entangle it excessively with sectarianism. Conceding, however, that the act could be administered in such a way as to violate the establishment clause, the Court returned the case to the district court for a factual finding on that issue.

The four dissenters, speaking through Justice HARRY A. BLACKMUN, may have been influenced by the fact that the statute banned grants to institutions that advocated ABORTION. Blackmun, as devoid of doubts as was Rehnquist, confidently deplored a decision that breached the LEMON TEST by providing federal monies to religious organizations, thereby enabling them to promote their religious missions in ways that were pervasively sectarian and, contradictorily, requiring intrusive oversight by the government to prevent that objective. The majority, Blackmun reasoned, distorted the Court's precedents and engaged in doctrinal missteps to reach their conclusion, by treating the case as if it merely subsidized a neutral function such as dispensing food or shelter instead of pedagogical services that impermissibly fostered religious beliefs.

LEONARD W. LEVY
(1992)

BOWEN v. OWENS

See: Sex Discrimination

BOWERS v. HARDWICK
478 U.S. 186 (1986)

Hardwick was charged with engaging in homosexual sodomy in violation of a Georgia statute, but after a preliminary hearing the prosecutor declined to pursue the case. Despite the fact that Hardwick was not going to be prosecuted, he brought suit in federal court to have the Georgia sodomy statute declared unconstitutional. The court of appeals held that the Georgia statute violated Hardwick's FUNDAMENTAL RIGHTS because homosexual activity is protected by the NINTH AMENDMENT and the DUE PROCESS clause of the FOURTEENTH AMENDMENT.

The Supreme Court disagreed, holding 5–4 that the statue did not violate any fundamental rights protected by the Consitution—in particular, that the act did not violate the RIGHT OF PRIVACY announced by the court in previous cases.

Writing for the majority, Justice BYRON R. WHITE contended that previous rulings delineating a constitutional right of privacy could not be used to strike down a law against sodomy. Previous precedents in this field focused on "family, marriage or procreation," said White, and neither Hardwick nor the court of appeals had demonstrated a connection between homosexual activity and these areas. In making his argument from precedent, White explicitly denied that the Court had ever announced a general right of private sexual conduct. Precedent aside, White argued that if the Court itself is to remain constitutionally legitimate, it must be wary of creating new rights that have little or no basis in the text or design of the Constitution. Such rights can be adopted by the Court only if they are so implicit in the concept of ordered liberty or so rooted in the nation's history that they mandate protection; homosexual sodomy meets neither requirement. Given White's framework of analysis, the other arguments marshaled by

Harwick also had to fail. The argument that since his conduct took place in the privacy of his home it must be protected fails because one has no right to engage in criminal conduct within one's home. And the argument that the law has no RATIONAL BASIS because it was based solely on the moral views of its supporters fails because "law . . . is constantly based on notions of morality."

Writing for the dissenters, Justice HARRY A. BLACKMUN declared what the majority denied—that a general constitutional right of private sexual conduct (or "intimate association") exists. Blackmun thereby shifted the burden of proof from Hardwick to the government. Because intimate association is generally protected by the Constitution, the government must prove that any regulations in this area are valid. Georgia did not do so; hence, the statute was invalid.

The Court's ruling in *Bowers* engendered a great deal of controversy. Many had wanted the Court to use the case to place discrimination on the basis of SEXUAL ORIENTATION in the same category as racial or gender discrimination. Yet it is understandable why the Court did not do so. Gender and race are not clearly analogous to sexual orientation, for neither is defined by conduct in the way that sexual orientation is. Homosexual sodomy has faced public disapproval for centuries because it is *behavior* that society has judged destructive for a variety of reasons, including its effects on public health, safety, and morality. Whether this judgment is correct or not may be debated, but the Court did not wish to resolve the debate by imposition of its own will in the matter.

JOHN G. WEST, JR.
(1992)

(SEE ALSO: *Freedom of Intimate Association; Sexual Orientation; Sexual Preference and the Constitution.*)

Bibliography

WELLER, CHRISTOPHER W. 1986 *Bowers v. Hardwick:* Balancing the Interests of the Moral Order and Individual Liberty. *Cumberland Law Review* 16:555–592.

BOWMAN v. CHICAGO & NORTHWESTERN RAILWAY COMPANY
125 U.S. 465 (1888)

The Supreme Court, by a vote of 6–3, held that a state statute prohibiting common carriers from importing intoxicating liquors into the state, except under conditions laid down by the state, violated the COMMERCE CLAUSE, because interstate transportation required a single regulatory system; the absence of congressional action made no difference.

LEONARD W. LEVY
(1986)

(SEE ALSO: *State Regulation of Commerce.*)

BOWSHER v. SYNAR
478 U.S. 714 (1986)

A 7–2 Supreme Court held that a basic provision of a major act of Congress unconstitutionally violated the principle of SEPARATION OF POWERS because Congress had vested executive authority in an official responsible to Congress. The Balanced Budget and Emergency Deficit Control Act of 1985 (GRAMM-RUDMAN-HOLLINGS) empowered the comptroller general, who is appointed by the President but removable by JOINT RESOLUTION of Congress, to perform executive powers in the enforcement of the statute. In the event of a federal budget deficit, the act requires across-the-board cuts in federal spending. The comptroller general made the final recommendations to the President on how to make the budget cuts.

Five members of the Court, speaking through Chief Justice WARREN E. BURGER, applied a severely formalistic view of separation of powers. They sharply distinguished EXECUTIVE POWER from LEGISLATIVE POWER. The comptroller general was removable only at the initiative of Congress for "transgressions of the legislative will." Congress regarded the official as an officer of the legislative branch, and persons holding the office had so regarded themselves. But the powers exercised by the comptroller general were executive in nature, preparing reports on projected federal revenues and expenditures and specifying the reductions necessary to reach target deficit levels. Because the comptroller general was "Congress's man" and was removable by Congress, the assignment of executive powers to the office gave Congress a direct role in the execution of the laws, contrary to the constitutional structure of the government.

Justice JOHN PAUL STEVENS, joined by Justice THURGOOD MARSHALL, agreed that the Gramm-Rudman-Hollings provision was unconstitutional, but for wholly different reasons. Stevens too described the comptroller general as a legislative officer, but believed that the removal power was irrelevant. Gramm-Rudman-Hollings was defective because by vesting the officer with important legislative powers over the budget, it subverted the legislative procedures provided by the Constitution. Money matters require consideration and voting by both houses of Congress; this body cannot constitutionally delegate so great a legislative power to an agent.

Justice BYRON R. WHITE, dissenting, believed that the threat to separation of powers conjured up by the seven-member majority was "wholly chimerical." He believed that the NECESSARY AND PROPER CLAUSE supported vesting some executive authority in the comptroller general. This officer exercised no powers that deprived the President of authority; the official chosen by Congress to implement its policy was nonpartisan and independent. He or she could not be removed by Congress by joint resolution except with the President's approval.

The concurring Justices and the dissenters understood that the Constitution's separation of powers does not make each branch wholly autonomous; each depends on others and exercises the powers of others to a degree. The Constitution mixes powers as well as separates them. The three branches are separate, but their powers are not. Gramm-Rudman-Hollings reflected the modern administrative state. The majority Justices, who could not even agree among themselves whether the comptroller general exercised executive or legislative powers, lacked the flexibility to understand they did not have to choose between labels. The Court, which quoted MONTESQUIEU and misapplied THE FEDERALIST, ignored #47 and #48, which warned only against "too great a mixture of powers," but approved of a sharing of powers. Currently, money bills originate in the White House and its Bureau of the Budget, despite the provision in Article I, section 7. The First Congress established the President's CABINET and required the secretary of treasury to report to Congress, and all of ALEXANDER HAMILTON's great reports on the economy were made to Congress, not the President. No Court that cared a fig for ORIGINAL INTENT or that understood the realities of policymaking today would have delivered such simplistic textbookish opinions.

LEONARD W. LEVY
(1992)

BOYCOTT

A boycott is a group refusal to deal. Such concerted action is an effective way for society's less powerful members, such as unorganized workers or racial minorities, to seek fair treatment in employment, public accommodations, and public services. But as the Supreme Court recognized in *Eastern States Retail Lumber Dealers' Association v. United States* (1914): "An act harmless when done by one may become a public wrong when done by many acting in concert, for it then takes on the form of a conspiracy."

Boycotts by private entrepreneurs were illegal at common law as unreasonable restraints on commercial competition. The Sherman Act of 1890 made it a federal offense to form a "combination . . . in restraint of trade."

The Supreme Court has interpreted that prohibition as covering almost every type of concerted refusal by business people to trade with others. The constitutionality of outlawing commercial boycotts has never seriously been questioned.

Employee boycotts may be either "primary" or "secondary." A primary boycott involves direct action against a principal party to a dispute. A union seeking to organize a company's work force may call for a strike, a concerted refusal to work, by the company's employees. A secondary boycott involves action against a so-called neutral or secondary party that is doing business with the primary party. The union seeking to organize a manufacturing company might appeal to the employees of a retailer to strike the retailer in order to force the retailer to stop handling the manufacturer's products.

Although early American law regarded most strikes as criminal conspiracies, modern statutes like the WAGNER NATIONAL LABOR RELATIONS ACT (NLRA) treat primary strikes in the private sector as "protected" activity, immune from employer reprisals. Even so, the Supreme Court has never held there is a constitutional right to strike. Furthermore, the Court sustained the constitutionality of statutory bans on secondary boycott strikes or related picketing in *Electrical Workers Local 501 v. NLRB* (1951). The use of group pressure to enmesh neutrals in the disputes of others was sufficient to enable government to declare such activity illegal.

Consumer boycotts present the hardest constitutional questions. Here group pressure may not operate directly, as in the case of a strike. Instead, the union or other protest group asks individual customers, typically acting on their own, not to patronize the subject firm. Yet if the appeal is to customers of a retailer not to shop there so long as the retailer stocks a certain manufacturer's goods, a neutral party is the target. The NLRA forbids union PICKETING to induce such a secondary consumer boycott. The Supreme Court held this limited prohibition constitutional in NLRB V. RETAIL CLERKS LOCAL 1001 (1980), although there was no majority rationale. A plurality cited precedent concerning secondary employee boycotts, ignoring the differences between individual and group responses.

On the other hand, when a civil rights organization conducted a damaging boycott against white merchants to compel them to support demands upon elected officials for racial equality, the Supreme Court declared in NAACP V. CLAIBORNE HARDWARE CO. (1982) that a state's right "to regulate economic activity could not justify a complete prohibition against a nonviolent, politically motivated boycott designed to force governmental and economic change and to effectuate rights guaranteed by the Constitution itself." The Court relied on the FIRST AMENDMENT rights of FREEDOM OF ASSEMBLY AND ASSOCIATION, and FREEDOM OF

PETITION. The emphasis on the right to petition government raises the possibility of a different result if the merchants themselves, rather than the public officials, had been the primary target of the boycott. But that would appear incongruous. The Court needs to refine its constitutional analysis of consumer boycotts.

THEODORE J. ST. ANTOINE
(1986)

Bibliography

HARPER, MICHAEL C. 1984 The Consumer's Emerging Right to Boycott: *NAACP v. Claiborne Hardware* and Its Implications for American Labor Law. *Yale Law Journal* 93:409–454.

KENNEDY, RONALD E. 1982 Political Boycotts, the Sherman Act, and the First Amendment: An Accommodation of Competing Interests. *Southern California Law Review* 55:983–1030.

BOYD v. UNITED STATES
116 U.S. 616 (1886)

Justice LOUIS D. BRANDEIS believed that *Boyd* will be remembered "as long as civil liberty lives in the United States." The noble sentiments expressed in JOSEPH P. BRADLEY's opinion for the Court merit that estimate, but like many another historic opinion, this one was not convincingly reasoned. To this day, however, members of the Court return to *Boyd* to grace their opinions with its authority or with an imperishable line from Bradley's.

Boyd was the first important SEARCH AND SEIZURE case as well as the first important case on the RIGHT AGAINST SELF-INCRIMINATION. It arose not from a criminal prosecution but from a civil action by the United States for the forfeiture of goods imported in violation of customs revenue laws. In such cases an 1874 act of Congress required the importer to produce in court all pertinent records tending to prove the charges against him or suffer the penalty of being taken "as confessed." The Court held the act unconstitutional as a violation of both the FOURTH and FIFTH AMENDMENTS. The penalty made the production of the records compulsory. That compulsion, said Bradley, raised "a very grave question of constitutional law, involving the personal security and PRIVILEGES AND IMMUNITIES of the citizen. . . ." But did the case involve a search or a seizure, and if so was it "unreasonable," and did it force the importer to be a witness against himself in a criminal case?

Bradley conceded that there was no search and seizure as in the forcible entry into a man's house and examination of his papers. Indeed, there was no search here for evidence of crime. The compulsion was to produce records that the government required importers to keep; no private papers were at issue. Moreover, no property was confiscated as in the case of contraband like smuggled goods. The importer, who was not subject to a search, had merely to produce the needed records in court; he kept custody of them. But the Court treated those records as if they were private papers, which could be used as EVIDENCE against him, resulting in the forfeiture of his property, or to establish a criminal charge. Though the proceeding was a civil one, a different section of the same statute did provide criminal penalties for fraud.

Bradley made a remarkable linkage between the right against UNREASONABLE SEARCH and seizure and the right against self-incrimination. The "fourth and fifth amendments," he declared, "almost run into each other." That they were different amendments, protected different interests, had separate histories, and reflected different policies was of no consequence to Bradley. He was on sound ground when he found that the forcible production of private papers to convict a man of crime or to forfeit his property violated the Fifth Amendment and was "contrary to the principles of a free government." He was on slippery ground when he found that such a compulsory disclosure was "the equivalent of a search and seizure—and an unreasonable search and seizure—within the meaning of the fourth amendment." His reasoning was that though the case did not fall within the "literal terms" of either amendment, each should be broadly construed in terms of the other. Unreasonable searches and seizures "are almost always made for the purpose of compelling a man to give evidence against himself," and compulsion of such evidence "throws light on the question as to what is an 'unreasonable search and seizure.'. . ." In support of his reasoning Bradley quoted at length from Lord Camden's opinion (see CHARLES PRATT) in *Entick v. Carrington* (1765). Camden, however, spoke of a fishing expedition under GENERAL WARRANTS issued by an executive officer without authorization by Parliament. There was no warrant in this case, and there was authorization by Congress for a court to compel production of the specific records required by law to be kept for government inspection, concerning FOREIGN COMMERCE which Congress may regulate. In this case, however, Bradley thought meticulous analysis was out of place. He feared that unconstitutional practices got their footing in "slight deviations" from proper procedures, and the best remedy was the rule that constitutional protections "for the security of person and property should be liberally construed." Close construction, he declared, deprived these protections of their efficacy.

Justice SAMUEL F. MILLER, joined by Chief Justice MORRISON R. WAITE, concurred in the judgment that that offensive section of the act of Congress was unconstitutional. Miller found no search and seizure, let alone an unreasonable one. He agreed, however, that Congress had

breached the right against self-incrimination, which he thought should be the sole ground of the opinion.

The modern Court no longer assumes that the Fifth Amendment is a source of the Fourth's EXCLUSIONARY RULE or that the Fourth prohibits searches for MERE EVIDENCE. Moreover, the production of private papers may be compelled in certain cases, as when the Internal Revenue Service subpoenas records in the hands of one's lawyer or accountant.

LEONARD W. LEVY
(1986)

Bibliography

GERSTEIN, ROBERT S. 1979 The Demise of Boyd: Self-Incrimination and Private Papers in the Burger Court. *UCLA Law Review* 27:343–397.

LANDYNSKI, JACOB W. 1966 *Search and Seizure and the Supreme Court.* Pages 49–61. Baltimore: Johns Hopkins University Press.

BRADLEY, JOSEPH P.
(1813–1892)

Joseph P. Bradley's appointment to the Supreme Court in 1870 by President ULYSSES S. GRANT was seen as part of Grant's supposed court-packing scheme. But whatever shadow that event cast on Bradley's reputation rapidly disappeared. For more than two decades on the bench, he commanded almost unrivaled respect from colleagues, lawyers, and legal commentators, and over time he consistently has been ranked as one of the most influential jurists in the Court's history.

When Bradley was appointed he already was a prominent railroad lawyer and Republican activist. Indeed, friends had been advocating his appointment to the Court nearly a year before his appointment. Shortly after Grant's inauguration in 1869, the Republicans increased the size of the court from eight to nine. While Grant and Congress haggled over the selection of a new Justice, the Court decided, 4–3, that the legal tender laws were unconstitutional. Justice ROBERT C. GRIER clearly was senile, and after he cast his vote against the laws his colleagues persuaded him to resign. That gave Grant two appointments and, on February 7, 1870, he nominated WILLIAM STRONG and Bradley—and the Court almost simultaneously announced its legal tender decision.

Within a year, Bradley and Strong led a new majority to sustain the constitutionality of greenbacks (unsecured paper currency). In his CONCURRING OPINION, Bradley saw the power to emit BILLS OF CREDIT as the essential issue in the case, and from that he contended that "the incidental power of giving such bills the quality of legal tender follows almost as matter of course." Bradley also emphasized the government's right to maintain its existence. He insisted it would be a "great wrong" to deny Congress the asserted power, "a power to be seldom exercised, certainly; but one, the possession of which is so essential, and as it seems to me, so undoubted." (See LEGAL TENDER CASES.)

Three months after his appointment, Bradley conducted circuit court hearings in New Orleans where he encountered the SLAUGHTERHOUSE CASES. He held unconstitutional the Louisiana statute authorizing a monopoly for slaughtering operations. Three years later, when the case reached the Supreme Court on appeal, Bradley dissented as the majority sustained the regulation. With Justice STEPHEN J. FIELD, Bradley believed that the creation of the monopoly and the impairment of existing businesses violated the PRIVILEGES AND IMMUNITIES clause of the FOURTEENTH AMENDMENT. Such privileges, Bradley had said earlier in his circuit court opinion, included a citizen's right to "lawful industrial pursuit—not injurious to the community—as he may see fit, without unreasonable regulation or molestation."

The antiregulatory views that Bradley advanced in *Slaughterhouse* did not persist as the major theme of his judicial career, as they did for Justice Field. JUDICIAL REVIEW and judicial superintendence of DUE PROCESS OF LAW could be maintained, he said, in *Davidson v. New Orleans* (1878), "without interfering with that large discretion which every legislative power has of making wide modifications in the forms of procedure." A year earlier, Bradley had vividly demonstrated his differences with Field when he provided Chief Justice MORRISON R. WAITE with the key historical sources and principles for the public interest doctrine laid down in *Munn v. Illinois* (1877). (See AFFECTATION WITH A PUBLIC INTEREST.)

The Court largely gutted the *Munn* ruling when it held in Wabash, St. Louis, and *Pacific Railway v. Illinois* (1886) that states could not regulate interstate rates, even in the absence of congressional action. Bradley vigorously dissented, protesting that some form of regulation was necessary and that the Court had wrongly repudiated the public interest doctrine of the GRANGER CASES. Ironically, Bradley, the old railroad lawyer, found himself almost totally isolated when he dissented from the Court's finding that the judiciary, not legislatively authorized expert commissions, had the right to decide the reasonableness of railroad rates. That decision, in *Chicago, Milwaukee and St. Paul Railway Co. v. Minnesota,* (1890), marked the triumph of Field's dissenting views in *Munn;* yet Bradley steadfastly insisted that rate regulation "is a legislative prerogative and not a judicial one."

Bradley insisted on responsibility and accountability from the railroads in numerous ways. In *New York Central R.R. v. Lockwood* (1873) he wrote that railroads could not,

by contract, exempt themselves from liability for negligence. "The carrier and his customer do not stand on a footing of equality," he said. In *Railroad Company v. Maryland* (1875) he agreed that Maryland could compel a railroad to return one-fifth of its revenue in exchange for a right of way without compromising congressional control over commerce. But Bradley found clear lines of distinction between federally chartered and state chartered railroads. When the Court, in *Railroad Company v. Peniston* (1873), approved Nebraska's tax of a congressionally chartered railroad, Bradley disagreed, arguing that the carrier was a federal GOVERNMENT INSTRUMENTALITY; similarly, he joined Field in dissent in the SINKING FUND CASES (1879), arguing that Congress's requirement that the Union Pacific deposit some of its earnings to repay its debt to the federal government was tantamount to the "repudiation of government obligations."

Bradley generally advocated a broad nationalist view of the COMMERCE CLAUSE. He wrote, for example, the opinion of the Court in *Robbins v. Shelby Taxing District* (1887), one of the most famous of the "drummer" cases of the period, holding that discriminatory state taxation of out-of-state salesmen unduly burdened interstate commerce. He also maintained that states could not tax the gross receipts of steamship companies or telegraph messages sent across state lines. Yet he steadfastly resisted the attempts of business to avoid their fair share of tax burdens, and he ruled that neither goods destined for another state nor goods that arrived at a final destination after crossing state lines were exempt from state taxing. (See STATE TAXATION OF COMMERCE.)

Despite Bradley's broad reading of the Fourteenth Amendment in the *Slaughterhouse Cases*, he voted with the Court majority that failed in various cases to sustain national protection of the rights of blacks. He ruled against the constitutionality of the FORCE ACT of 1870 while on circuit, and the Court sustained his ruling in UNITED STATES V. CRUIKSHANK (1876). He acquiesced in UNITED STATES V. REESE (1876), crippling enforcement of the FIFTEENTH AMENDMENT, and in HALL V. DECUIR (1878) he agreed that a Louisiana law prohibiting racial segregation on railroads burdened interstate commerce. Unlike that of most of his colleagues, Bradley's interpretation of the commerce power was consistent, for he dissented with JOHN M. HARLAN when the Court in 1890 approved a state law requiring segregated railroad cars.

Bradley's most famous statement on racial matters came in the CIVIL RIGHTS CASES (1883). Speaking for all his colleagues save Harlan, Bradley held unconstitutional the CIVIL RIGHTS ACT OF 1875. He limited the scope of the Fourteenth Amendment when he wrote that it forbade only STATE ACTION and not private RACIAL DISCRIMINATION. Bradley eloquently—if unfortunately—captured the national mood when he declared: "When a man has emerged from slavery, and by the aid of beneficient legislation has shaken off the inseparable concomitants of that state, there must be some stage in the progress of his elevation when he takes the rank of a mere citizen and ceases to be the special favorite of the laws. . . ." Bradley concurred in BRADWELL V. ILLINOIS (1873), in which the Court held that Illinois had not violated the EQUAL PROTECTION clause of the Fourteenth Amendment when it refused to admit a woman to the bar. He stated that a woman's "natural and proper timidity" left her unprepared for many occupations, and he concluded that "the paramount destiny and mission of woman are to fulfill the noble and benign offices of wife and mother." Clearly, there were limits to the liberty that Bradley had so passionately advocated in the *Slaughterhouse Cases.*

The variety of significant opinions by Bradley demonstrates his enormous range and influence. In BOYD V. UNITED STATES (1886) he established the modern FOURTH AMENDMENT standard for SEARCH AND SEIZURE questions, advocating a narrow scope for governmental power: "It is the duty of courts to be watchful for the constitutional rights of the citizen, and against any stealthy encroachments thereon." In COLLECTOR V. DAY (1871) he dissented when the Court held that state officials were exempt from federal income taxes, and nearly sixty years later the Court adopted his position. He spoke for the Court in CHURCH OF JESUS CHRIST OF LATTER-DAY SAINTS V. UNITED STATES (1890), stipulating that forfeited Mormon property be applied to charitable uses, including the building of common schools in Utah. Finally, he helped resolve the Court's difficulties over the exercise of recently enacted JURISDICTION legislation and sustained the right of federal CORPORATIONS to remove their causes from state to federal courts. That opinion made possible a staggering number of new tort and corporate cases in the federal courts.

Bradley played a decisive role in the outcome of the disputed election of 1877 as he supported Rutherford B. Hayes's claims. He was the fifteenth member chosen on the Electoral Commission whose other members included seven Democrats and seven Republicans. Thus, Hayes and the Compromise of 1877 owed much to Bradley's vote.

Bradley, Field, Harlan, and SAMUEL F. MILLER are the dominant figures of late nineteenth-century judicial history. Field's reputation rests on his forceful advocacy of a conservative ideology that the Court embraced but eventually repudiated. Harlan's claims center on his CIVIL RIGHTS views. Miller's notions of judicial restraint continue to have vitality. But Bradley's range of expertise, his high technical competency, and the continuing relevance of his work arguably place him above those distinguished contemporaries. Indeed, a mere handful of Supreme Court Justices have had a comparable impact.

STANLEY I. KUTLER
(1986)

Bibliography

FAIRMAN, CHARLES   1950   What Makes a Great Justice? *Boston University Law Review* 30:49–102.
MAGRATH, C. PETER   1963   *Morrison R. Waite: The Triumph of Character.* New York: Macmillan.

BRADWELL v. ILLINOIS
16 Wallace 130 (1873)

Bradwell is the earliest FOURTEENTH AMENDMENT case in which the Supreme Court endorsed sex discrimination. Mrs. Myra Bradwell, the editor of the *Chicago Legal News*, was certified by a board of legal examiners as qualified to be a member of the state bar. An Illinois statute permitted the state supreme court to make rules for admission to the bar. That court denied Mrs. Bradwell's application for admission solely on the ground of sex, although the fact that the applicant was married also counted against her: a married woman at that time was incapable of making binding contracts without her husband's consent, thus disabling her from performing all the duties of an attorney. She argued that the PRIVILEGES AND IMMUNITIES clause of the Fourteenth Amendment protected her CIVIL RIGHT as a citizen of the United States to be admitted to the bar, if she qualified.

Justice SAMUEL F. MILLER, speaking for the Court, declared that the right to be admitted to the practice of law in a state court was not a privilege of national CITIZENSHIP protected by the Fourteenth Amendment. Justice JOSEPH P. BRADLEY, joined by Justices NOAH SWAYNE and STEPHEN J. FIELD, concurred in the JUDGMENT affirming the state court, but offered additional reasons. History, nature, COMMON LAW, and the civil law supported the majority's reading of the privileges and immunities clause, according to Bradley. The "spheres and destinies" of the sexes were widely different, man being woman's protector; her "timidity and delicacy" unfit her for many occupations, including the law. Unlike Myra Bradwell, an unmarried woman might make contracts, but such a woman was an exception to the rule. "The paramount destiny and mission of woman are to fulfill the noble and benign offices of wife and mother. This is the law of the Creator." Society's rules, Bradley added, ought not be based on exceptions. Chief Justice SALMON P. CHASE dissented alone, without opinion, missing a chance to advocate the cause of SEX EQUALITY, at least in the legal profession.

LEONARD W. LEVY
(1986)

BRANCH v. TEXAS

See: Capital Punishment Cases of 1972

BRANDEIS, LOUIS D.
(1856–1941)

The appointment of Louis D. Brandeis to the United States Supreme Court was not merely the crowning glory of an extraordinary career as a practicing lawyer and social activist. It was also the inauguration of an equally extraordinary career on the bench. In twenty-three years as a Justice, Brandeis acquired a stature and influence that few—before or since—could match. In part, this achievement reflected the fact that he was already a public figure when he ascended to the Court. But his skills as a jurist provided the principal explanation. He mastered details of procedure, remained diligent in researching the facts and law of the case, and, whatever the subject, devoted untold hours to make his opinions clear and logical. Perhaps the highest compliment came from colleagues who disagreed with his conclusions. "My, how I detest that man's ideas," Associate Justice GEORGE SUTHERLAND once observed. "But he is one of the greatest technical lawyers I have ever known."

Brandeis's opinions and votes on the Court were very much a product of his environment and experience. Born in Louisville, Kentucky, shortly before the CIVIL WAR, he grew up in a family that provided him with love and security. That background probably helped him in establishing skills as a tenacious lawyer in Boston, where he opened his office one year after graduating from Harvard Law School first in his class. Brandeis attained local and then national fame when he used his formidable talents to effect reform at the height of the Progressive movement in the early 1900s. He fought the establishment of a privately owned subway monopoly in Boston, was instrumental in developing a savings bank life insurance system to prevent exploitation of industrial workers by large insurance companies, developed the famed BRANDEIS BRIEF—a detailed compilation of facts and statistics—in defense of Oregon's maximum hour law for women, and even took on the legendary J. P. Morgan when the corporate magnate tried to monopolize New England's rail and steamship lines. Brandeis's renown as "the people's attorney" spread across the country when, in 1910, he led a team of lawyers in challenging Richard A. Ballinger's stewardship of the nation's natural resources as secretary of the interior in the administration of President WILLIAM HOWARD TAFT.

Because of Brandeis's well-known credentials as a lawyer who had single-handedly taken on the "trusts," WOODROW WILSON turned to him for advice in the presidential campaign of 1912. The relationship ripened, and after his election to the White House Wilson repeatedly called upon Brandeis for help in solving many difficult problems. Through these interactions Wilson came to appreciate Brandeis's keen intelligence and dedication to the public welfare. In January 1916 he nominated the Boston attorney to the Supreme Court. Brandeis was confirmed by the United States Senate almost six months later after a grueling and bitter fight.

For Brandeis, law was essentially a mechanism to shape man's social, economic, and political relations. In fulfilling that function, he believed, the law had to account for two basic principles: first, that the individual was the key force in society, and second, that individuals—no matter what their talents and aspirations—had only limited capabilities. As he explained to HAROLD LASKI, "Progress must proceed from the aggregate of the performances of individual men" and society should adjust its institutions "to the wee size of man and thus render possible his growth and development." At the same time, Brandeis did not want people coddled because of inherent limitations. Quite the contrary. People had to stretch themselves to fulfill their individual potentials.

In this context Brandeis abhorred what he often called "the curse of bigness." People, he felt, could not fully develop themselves if they did not have control of their lives. Individual control, however, was virtually impossible in a large institutional setting—whether it be a union, a CORPORATION, the government, or even a town. From this perspective, Brandeis remained convinced that democracy could be maintained only if citizens—and especially the most talented—returned to small communities in the hinterland and learned to manage their own affairs.

This commitment to individual development led Brandeis to assume a leadership position in the Zionist Movement in 1914 and retain it after he went on the Court. In Palestine, Brandeis believed, an individual could control his life in a way that would not be possible in the United States.

This theme—the need for individuals and local communities to control their own affairs—also threads the vast majority of Brandeis's major opinions on the Court. Some of the most controversial of Brandeis's early opinions concerned labor unions. Long before his appointment to the Court he had viewed unions as a necessary element in the nation's economy. Without them large CORPORATIONS would be able to exploit workers and prevent them from acquiring the financial independence needed for individual control. Brandeis made his views known on this matter in HITCHMAN COAL & COKE COMPANY V. MITCHELL (1917). That case concerned the United Mine Workers' efforts to unionize the workers in West Virginia. As a condition of employment the mine owner forced his employees to sign a pledge not to join a union. A majority of the Court held that UMW officials had acted illegally in trying to induce the workers to violate that pledge.

Brandeis dissented. He could not accept the majority's conclusion that a union agreement would deprive the workers and mine owner of their DUE PROCESS rights under the FOURTEENTH AMENDMENT to FREEDOM OF CONTRACT. "Every agreement curtails the liberty of those who enter into it," Brandeis responded. "The test of legality is not whether an agreement curtails liberty, but whether the parties have agreed upon some thing which the law prohibits. . . ." Brandeis also saw no merit in the majority's concern with the UMW's pressure on workers to join the union. The plaintiff company's lawsuit was premised "upon agreements secured under similar pressure of economic necessity or disadvantage," he observed. "If it is coercion to threaten to strike unless plaintiff consents to a closed union shop, it is coercion also to threaten not to give one employment unless the applicant will consent to a closed non-union shop."

Brandeis adhered to these views in other labor cases that came before the Court. Eventually, the Court came around to Brandeis's belief that unions had a right to engage in peaceful efforts to push for a CLOSED SHOP. Brandeis himself added a finishing touch in an opinion he delivered in *Senn v. Tile Layers Union* (1937), where he upheld a state law restricting the use of INJUNCTIONS against PICKETING.

While concern for the plight of labor was vital to his vision of society, nothing concerned Brandeis more than the right of a state or community to shape its own environment. For this reason he voted to uphold almost every piece of social legislation that came before the Court. Indeed, he wanted to reduce federal JURISDICTION in part because, as he told FELIX FRANKFURTER, "in no case practically should the appellate federal courts have to pass on the construction of state statutes." Therefore, if the state wanted to regulate the practices of employment agencies, expand the disability protection to stevedores who worked the docks, or take other social actions, he would not stand in the way. As he explained for the Court in *O'Gorman & Young v. Hartford Insurance Company* (1931), "the presumption of constitutionality must prevail in the absence of some factual foundation of record for overthrowing the statute." This meant that the Court must abide by the legislature's judgment even if the Court found the law to be of doubtful utility.

Only a few months after *O'Gorman* Brandeis applied this principle in NEW STATE ICE COMPANY V. LIEBMANN (1932). The Oklahoma Legislature had passed a law that prohibited anyone from entering the ice business without first getting a certificate from a state corporation commission showing that there was a public need for the new business. A majority of the Court struck the law down because the ice business was not so AFFECTED WITH A PUBLIC INTEREST to justify a measure that would, in effect, restrict competition.

Brandeis was all for competition. He had long believed that large corporations were dangerous because they often eliminated competition and with it the right of individuals

to control their lives, a proposition he examined in detail in *Liggett Company v. Lee* (1933). Whatever misgivings he had about the merits of the Oklahoma law, Brandeis had no trouble accepting the state's right to make its own decisions, especially at a time when the nation was grappling with the problems of the Depression. "It is one of the happy incidents of the federal system," he wrote in dissent, "that a single courageous State may, if its citizens choose, serve as a laboratory; and try novel social and economic experiments without risk to the rest of the country. This Court has the power to prevent an experiment. . . . But in the exercise of this high power, we must be ever on our guard, lest we erect our prejudices into legal principles."

The Tennessee case was an exception to Brandeis's general inclination to protect the states' right to legislate. In fact, he was so devoted to states' rights that he once openly disregarded one of his most-oft stated juridical principles—never decide constitutional matters that can be avoided. Brandeis relied on this principle when he refused to join the Court's opinion in ASHWANDER V. TENNESSEE VALLEY AUTHORITY (1936) upholding the constitutionality of federal legislation establishing the TVA. In a CONCURRING OPINION he argued that they should have dismissed the case without deciding the constitutional issue because the plaintiffs had no STANDING to bring the lawsuit.

Brandeis was willing to ignore the teachings of his TVA opinion, however, when Chief Justice CHARLES EVANS HUGHES asked the aging Justice to write the Court's opinion in ERIE RAILROAD V. TOMPKINS (1938). The Court had voted to overrule SWIFT V. TYSON (1842), a decision that concerned cases arising under DIVERSITY JURISDICTION. Specifically, *Swift* allowed federal courts to ignore the laws of the states in which they were located and instead to apply FEDERAL COMMON LAW. *Swift* thus enabled litigants in certain cases to shop for the best forum in filing a lawsuit, for a federal court under *Swift* could and often did follow substantive law different from that applied by local courts.

Brandeis had long found *Swift* offensive. Not only did it mean that different courts in the same state could come to different conclusions on the same question; of greater importance, *Swift* undermined the ability of the state to control its own affairs. He was no doubt delighted when Hughes gave him the chance to bury *Swift;* and he wanted to make sure there could be no resurrection by a later Court or Congress. He therefore wrote an opinion holding that *Swift* violated the Constitution because it allowed federal courts to assume powers reserved to the states. The constitutional basis for the opinion was startling for two reasons: first, Brandeis could have just as easily overturned *Swift* through a revised construction of the JUDICIARY ACT OF 1789; and second, none of the parties had even raised the constitutional issue, let alone briefed it.

Brandeis would depart from his ready endorsement of state legislation if the law violated FUNDAMENTAL FREE-DOMS and individual rights. It was not only a matter of constitutional construction. The BILL OF RIGHTS played a significant role in the individual's, and ultimately the community's, right to control the future. Brandeis knew, for example, that, without FIRST AMENDMENT protections, he never could have achieved much success as "the people's attorney" in battling vested interests. In those earlier times he had sloughed off personal attacks of the bitterest kind to pursue his goals. He knew that, in many instances, he would have been silenced if his right of speech had depended on majority approval. And he expressed great concern when citizens were punished—even during wartime—for saying or writing things someone found objectionable. "The constitutional right of free speech has been declared to be the same in peace and in war," he wrote in dissent in *Schaeffer v. United States* (1920). "In peace, too, men may differ widely as to what loyalty to our country demands; and an intolerant majority, swayed by passion or fear, may be prone in the future, as it has often been in the past, to stamp as disloyal opinions with which it disagrees." This point was later amplified in his concurring opinion in WHITNEY V. CALIFORNIA (1927). The Founding Fathers, Brandeis wrote, recognized "that fear breeds repression; that repression breeds hate; that hate menaces stable government; that the path of safety lies in the opportunity to discuss freely supposed grievances and proposed remedies; and that the fitting remedy for evil counsels is good ones."

Brandeis, then, often brought clear and deepseated convictions to the conference table. He was not one, however, to twist arms and engage in the lobbying that other Justices found so successful. "I could have had my views prevail in cases of public importance if I had been willing to play politics," he once told Frankfurter. "But I made up my mind I wouldn't—I would have had to sin against my light, and I would have hated myself. And I decided that the price was too large for the doubtful gain to the country's welfare."

Brandeis therefore tried to use established procedures to persuade his colleagues. To that end he would often anticipate important cases and distribute his views as a "memorandum" even before the majority opinion was written. In OLMSTEAD V. UNITED STATES (1928), for example, he tried to convince the Court that the federal government should not be allowed to use EVIDENCE in a criminal case that its agents had obtained by WIRETAPPING. The eavesdropping had been done without a judicial warrant and in violation of a state statute. Brandeis circulated a memorandum reflecting views that had not been debated at conference. The government should not be able to profit by its own wrongdoing, he said—especially when, as here, it impinged on the individual's RIGHT TO PRIVACY

(a right he had examined as a lawyer in a seminal article in the *Harvard Law Review*). The memorandum could not command a majority, and Brandeis later issued an eloquent dissent that focused on the contention that warrantless wiretaps violated the FOURTH AMENDMENT's protection against UNREASONABLE SEARCHES and seizures.

At other times Brandeis would use the Saturday conferences to urge a view upon his colleagues. On one occasion—involving *Southwestern Bell Telephone Company v. Public Service Commission* (1923)—an entire day was devoted to a seminar conducted by Brandeis to explain why a utility's rate of return should be based on prudent investment and not on the reproduction cost of its facilities. Few, if any, Justices shared Brandeis's grasp of rate-making principles. Hence, it took more than two decades of experience and debate before the Court—without Brandeis—accepted the validity of his position.

Brandeis took his losses philosophically. He knew that progress in a democracy comes slowly, and he was prepared to accept temporary setbacks along the way. But he rarely faded in his determination to correct the result. If his brethren remained impervious to his reasoning, he was willing to use other resources. He peppered Frankfurter and others with suggestions on articles for the *Harvard Law Review*. He also turned to the numerous congressmen and senators who frequently dined with him. Were they interested in introducing legislation to restrict federal jurisdiction or some other objective? If the answer was affirmative, Brandeis often volunteered the services of Frankfurter (whose expenses in public interest matters were generally assumed by Brandeis).

Few of these extrajudicial activities produced concrete results. Brandeis was apparently pleased, consequently, when Hughes became Chief Justice in 1930. Brandeis felt that the former secretary of state had a better command of the law than did Taft, the preceding Chief Justice, and would be able to use that knowledge to expedite the disposition of the Court's growing caseload. Of greater significance, Hughes and some other new members of the Court had views that closely coincided with Brandeis's. In fact, in 1937, BENJAMIN N. CARDOZO, HARLAN FISKE STONE, and Brandeis—the so-called liberal Justices—began to caucus in Brandeis's apartment on Friday nights to go over the cases for the Saturday conference.

With this kind of working relationship, plus the change in the times, Brandeis was able to join a majority in upholding New Deal legislation (he voted against only three New Deal measures). He also lived to see many of his earlier dissents become HOLDINGS of the Court, particularly in cases concerning labor and the right of states to adopt social legislation. After his death, many other dissents—including his First Amendment views and his contention that warrantless wiretaps were unconstitutional—would also become the law of the land. But Brandeis's overriding ambition—the desire to establish a legal framework in which individuals and communities could control their affairs—was frustrated by developments that would not yield to even the most incisive judicial opinion. Unions, like corporations and even government, continued to grow like Topsy. Almost everyone, it seemed, became dependent on a large organization. Brandeis, a shrewd realist, surely recognized the inexorable social, economic, and political forces that impeded the realization of his dreams for America. None of that, however, would have deterred him from pursuing his goals. As he once explained to his brother, the "future has many good things in store for those who can wait, . . . have patience and exercise good judgment."

LEWIS J. PAPER
(1986)

Bibliography

BICKEL, ALEXANDER M.   1957   *The Unpublished Opinions of Mr. Justice Brandeis: The Supreme Court at Work.* Cambridge, Mass.: Harvard University Press.

FRANKFURTER, FELIX, ed. 1932 *Mr. Justice Brandeis.* New Haven, Conn.: Yale University Press.

FREUND, PAUL   1964   Mr. Justice Brandeis. In Allison Dunham and Philip B. Kurland, eds., *Mr. Justice.* Chicago: University of Chicago Press.

KONEFSKY, SAMUEL J.   1956   *The Legacy of Holmes and Brandeis: A Study in the Influence of Ideas.* New York: Macmillan.

MASON, ALPHEUS T.   1946   *Brandeis: A Free Man's Life.* New York: Viking Press.

PAPER, LEWIS J.   1983   *Brandeis.* Englewood Cliffs, N.J.: Prentice-Hall.

BRANDEIS AND THE FIRST AMENDMENT

Justice LOUIS D. BRANDEIS served on the Supreme Court from 1916 until 1939 following a legendary career as a practicing attorney. During that lengthy tenure he had several occasions to consider the meaning of the FIRST AMENDMENT guarantee of FREEDOM OF SPEECH, including a number of cases involving critics of the nation's entry into WORLD WAR I. It is, however, a single CONCURRING OPINION he wrote in 1927 that accounts for Brandeis's reputation as arguably our greatest First Amendment judge.

WHITNEY V. CALIFORNIA (1927) grew out of the prosecution of a middle-aged woman for being a member of an organization that advocated changes in government and industrial ownership by means of force or violence. Anita Whitney did not herself advocate or favor the use of force for these purposes, but she attended a convention of a party that voted down her proposed resolution endorsing peaceful methods of change and thereafter remained an active member of the organization. She was prosecuted, convicted, and sent to prison for her association with the group.

She appealed her conviction to the Supreme Court, claiming that the First Amendment protects the political association in which she had engaged. A majority of the Court rejected her contention and affirmed the conviction. Brandeis, joined by Justice OLIVER WENDELL HOLMES, JR., concurred separately. He found a procedural barrier to considering her First Amendment defense and thus he voted to affirm her conviction. Brandeis nevertheless objected strenuously to the majority's rejection of Whitney's claim on the merits. He reiterated the view, previously expressed by Holmes in opinions Brandeis had joined, that under the First Amendment speech can be regulated only when it creates a CLEAR AND PRESENT DANGER of harm. On this occasion, Brandeis even tightened that test, concluding that the only harms that can justify regulation must amount to a "serious injury to the state." It is not, however, his refinement of the clear-and-present danger test that accounts for the extraordinary stature of the *Whitney* opinion. It is Brandeis's exploration of the philosophical foundations of the commitment to free speech that makes the opinion such an important document, and Brandeis such a pivotal figure in the First Amendment tradition.

Brandeis begins his treatment of the subject by ascribing two key tenets to "[t]hose who won our independence." First, they "believed that the final end of the state was to make men free to develop their faculties." Second, they believed that in the conduct of government "the deliberative forces should prevail over the arbitrary." Brandeis perceived an important connection between these two ideas. He says the founders of the American republic "valued liberty both as an end and as a means." To Brandeis, liberty entails much more than being left alone to make self-regarding hedonistic choices or to form arbitrary or self-serving beliefs. Although the American revolutionaries "believed liberty to be the secret of happiness," they also believed "courage to be the secret of liberty." Here Brandeis echoes the great funeral oration of Pericles in Thucydides's *History of the Peloponnesian War*, one of Brandeis's favorite books. Courage is a demanding virtue. Persons who develop their faculties of self-discipline, independence, and strength of character, according to Pericles and Brandeis, not only achieve a meaningful and enduring type of personal happiness but also make the best citizens and contribute the most to the polity. In this way, Brandeis links individual liberty with collective self-government.

That linkage lies at the heart of his high regard for the freedom of speech. He considered the decision to repress unorthodox, threatening speech to be a self-defeating capitulation to fear. "Fear of serious injury cannot alone justify suppression of free speech and assembly," he states. "Men feared witches and burnt women. It is the function of speech to free men from the bondage of irrational fears." Brandeis worried greatly about the adverse effect on the character of a political community that follows from getting caught up in the cycle of distrust and resentment that the regulation of speech both manifests and fuels. "[F]ear breeds repression," he says, and "repression breeds hate." Such "hate menaces stable government." The more productive response to threatening ideas, Brandeis believed, is to display a form of civic courage: "the path of safety lies in the opportunity to discuss freely supposed grievances and proposed remedies . . . the fitting remedy for evil counsels is good ones."

There can be little doubt that Brandeis's faith in the power of "more speech" was informed by his general attitude toward change. "Those who won our independence by revolution were not cowards," he says. "They did not fear political change. They did not exalt order at the cost of liberty." To him, the choice between repression and toleration represents a fundamental test of character. To fail to trust the power of more speech is to "discourage thought, hope, and imagination." The consequences of such a course, Brandeis believed, are deadly: "the greatest menace to freedom is an inert people."

VINCENT BLASI
(2000)

(SEE ALSO: *Brandeis as Public Interest Lawyer.*)

Bibliography

BLASI, VINCENT   1988   The First Amendment and the Ideal of Civic Courage: The Brandeis Opinion in *Whitney v. California. William and Mary Law Review* 29:653–697.

LAHAV, PNINA   1988   Holmes and Brandeis: Libertarian and Republican Justifications for Free Speech. *Journal of Law and Politics* 4:451–482.

STRUM, PHILIPPA   1993   *Brandeis: Beyond Progressivism,* chapter 6. Lawrence: University Press of Kansas.

BRANDEIS AS PUBLIC INTEREST LAWYER

Had he never been appointed to the U.S. Supreme Court, LOUIS D. BRANDEIS's place in the history of American public law would nonetheless be secure. His reform work as the "people's attorney" inspired two generations of PUBLIC INTEREST LAWYERS and plays a continuing role in debates over the figure and function of the "good lawyer."

Brandeis gave little evidence of his intense interest in using law in the public arena until the 1890s, when he had been in practice in Boston for over a decade. During the 1880s, in partnership with his law school classmate Samuel Warren, Brandeis had developed a steady and lucrative clientele, largely small- to medium-sized manufacturers and entrepreneurs drawn to Brandeis's burgeoning reputation for energy, judgment, and financial acumen. His experience with this clientele—Brandeis, as a Jew and non-native of New England, was largely excluded from REPRESENTATION of Boston's wealthiest and most prestigious financial institutions—helped form Brandeis's hostility to concentrations of economic and political power.

Perhaps the most impressive of Brandeis's many lawyering skills was his remarkable understanding of the business as well as the legal aspects of his clients' enterprises. In one of his best-known letters, to a young lawyer at his firm, he wrote: "Your law may be perfect, your ability to apply it great, and yet you cannot be a successful adviser unless your advice is followed; it will not be followed unless you can satisfy clients, unless you impress them with your superior knowledge, and that you cannot do unless you know their affairs better than they do because you see them from a fullness of knowledge." Partly through his involvement in railroad reorganization matters in the 1890s, he developed an understanding of corporate finance far in advance of that held by most of his lawyer contemporaries.

It was Brandeis's discovery that "business corrupts politics," as well as his restless pursuit of a more publicly meaningful professional life, that led to his first forays into public interest lawyering. He became seriously involved in municipal politics when he opposed the efforts of the Boston Elevated Railway Company to obtain extensive franchise rights and, ultimately, monopoly control over transportation in the notoriously congested Boston area. In the course of fighting the Elevated, Brandeis breathed political life into two reform-minded but genteel citizens' groups, the Public Franchise League and the Associated Board of Trade. These same groups later combined to oppose the proposed capitalization of eight consolidated gas companies who had obtained major concessions from the Massachusetts legislature. With characteristic ingenuity and independence, Brandeis departed from the views of several of his erstwhile reform colleagues and pushed through a compromise plan, according to which the Consolidated Gas Company could increase dividends to shareholders only upon a corresponding reduction in rates charged to consumers.

Brandeis's services as a lawyer–reformer, many of them rendered to clients without fee, eventually spread to the state, regional, and national levels. In his 1905 speech "The Opportunity in the Law" he urged lawyers to take up a position between the CORPORATIONS and the people, beholden to neither. Probably his most ambitious, and easily his most bitterly fought, battle involved the efforts of the New Haven Railroad, whose interests were controlled by J. P. Morgan, to obtain monopoly leverage over transportation in New England by merging with the Boston & Maine Railroad. In his nine years of jousting with the New Haven, Brandeis scored as many defeats as victories, and some historians now question the economic wisdom of his relentless assault on the merger. But his efforts at understanding and exposing the serpentine financial maneuverings of the New Haven—as he would do with respect to the "Money Trust" in his 1914 muckraking classic, *Other People's Money, and How the Bankers Use It*—justifiably made him a hero to fellow reformers.

Brandeis infused many of his nominally private legal representations with public purpose. His commitment to adjusting the disputes of labor and capital led him to counsel his business clients to avoid taking intransigent positions in their relations with their employees. Among his clients were the Filene brothers, with whom he collaborated in devising innovative plans for employee management and governance in their well-known Boston department store. His reputation for both creativity and fairmindedness led to his selection to mediate and broker the "Protocol of Peace" in the New York garment trades in 1910. Although the Protocol did not survive the continuing warfare between garment workers and employers, it remained a landmark in LABOR mediation that inspired advocates of industrial justice for many years.

Brandeis gave his name to one of the signal developments in constitutional advocacy in the 1908 Supreme Court case of MULLER V. OREGON. He was asked by labor reformers to represent the state of Oregon in defense of its maximum-hours law for women, which had been assaulted as unconstitutional. Before a Court that had emphatically declared its hostility to such protective labor LEGISLATION in LOCHNER V. NEW YORK (1905), Brandeis presented a BRIEF consisting of two pages of legal argument followed by more than one hundred pages of excerpts from SOCIAL SCIENCE studies purporting to demonstrate the evil effects of overwork on women and, hence, on society. This "BRANDEIS BRIEF", despite what now appear to be the gender paternalism of its arguments and the crudities of its social science, confirmed Brandeis's brilliance as a public law advocate. For he attained a victory for his client by giving the Court a means of distinguishing *Lochner,* and in the process helped establish a new form of legal argument informed by social realities. Brandeis's approach in *Muller* became one of the rallying cries of the new SOCIOLOGICAL JURISPRUDENCE that would ripen into the LEGAL REALISM movement of the 1920s.

When Brandeis was nominated for the Supreme Court in 1916, his enemies, some of whom nursed wounds from old legal battles or who opposed the appointment on political grounds, claimed that Brandeis had acted unethi-

cally in a number of episodes from his law practice. Most of the accusations proved groundless. They did reveal, however, that Brandeis assumed some risks in his daring use of the lawyer–client relation as a medium for promoting the public good. More than most lawyers, Brandeis was directive rather than reactive in his representations; he took such cases as appealed to his sense of justice and policy, largely avoided the constraining hand of clients, and generally seemed to view himself as "counsel to the situation" (a phrase he made famous). At times, representation of a client became a formality that enabled him to advocate his preferred solution to a pressing question of public policy. This extraordinary autonomy strained the limits of traditional notions of representation and implicitly rejected their emphasis on unblinking loyalty to the client's goals. For this reason Brandeis remains a continuing inspiration for those who see in lawyering the possibilities for the exercise of "moral activism," in legal scholar David Luban's phrase. He also remains an apt symbol for the ambiguities and controversies that attend the role of the "public interest lawyer" in a changing world.

CLYDE SPILLENGER
(2000)

Bibliography

ABRAMS, RICHARD M. 1962 Brandeis and the New Haven–Boston & Maine Merger Revisited. *Business History Review* 36:408–430.

BRANDEIS, LOUIS D. 1914 *Business—A Profession.* Boston: Small, Maynard.

—— 1914 *Other People's Money, and How the Bankers Use It.* New York: F. A. Stokes.

BRANDEIS, LOUIS D. and GOLDMARK, JOSEPHINE 1969 *Women in Industry.* New York: Arno.

FRANK, JOHN P. 1965 The Legal Ethics of Louis D. Brandeis. *Stanford Law Review* 17:683–709.

LEVY, DAVID W. 1969 The Lawyer as Judge: Brandeis' View of the Legal Profession. *Oklahoma Law Review* 22:374–395.

LUBAN, DAVID 1988 *Lawyers and Justice: An Ethical Study.* Princeton, N.J.: Princeton University Press.

MASON, ALPHEUS T. 1946 *Brandeis: A Free Man's Life.* New York: Viking Press.

SIMON, WILLIAM H. 1985 Babbitt v. Brandeis. *Stanford Law Review* 37:565–587.

SPILLENGER, CLYDE 1996 Elusive Advocate: Reconsidering Brandeis as People's Lawyer. *Yale Law Journal* 105:1445–1535.

STRUM, PHILIPPA 1994 The Legacy of Louis Dembitz Brandeis, People's Attorney. *American Jewish History* 81:406–427.

UROFSKY, MELVIN I. 1971 *A Mind of One Piece: Brandeis and American Reform.* New York: Scribner.

BRANDEIS BRIEF

The opinion of the Supreme Court in MULLER V. OREGON (1908) began with an unusual acknowledgment: the Court had found useful a brief by LOUIS D. BRANDEIS, supporting Oregon's law regulating women's working hours. The brief had presented the views of doctors and social workers, the conclusions of various public committees that had investigated the conditions of women's labor, and an outline of similar legislation in the United States and overseas. The Court said that although these materials "may not be, technically speaking, authorities," they were "significant of a widespread belief that woman's physical structure, and the functions she performs in consequence thereof, justify special legislation." Its intimations of female dependency aside, this comment marked an important event: the Court's recognition of the utility of briefing and argument addressed to the factual basis for legislation.

Underlying the *Muller* opinion's comment lay a deeper change in the judiciary's conception of its proper role. Since around the time of the Civil War, lawyers and judges had commonly believed that the development of legal (including constitutional) doctrine was a pursuit of truth. In this view, there were answers to be found in authoritative documents such as laws and constitutions. The *Muller* opinion signaled a recognition that judges had a creative, legislative role, that they were properly concerned with the evaluation of the factual basis for legislation. This development, which sometimes bore the name of SOCIOLOGICAL JURISPRUDENCE and which culminated in the LEGAL REALISM of the 1920s and 1930s, represented a major shift in judicial attitudes. Judges came to see themselves as active participants in adapting the law to the needs of society. The technique of the Brandeis brief came to serve not only in cases involving ECONOMIC REGULATION but also in other constitutional contexts far removed. A famous modern example is BROWN V. BOARD OF EDUCATION (1954), in which an AMICUS CURIAE brief detailed the views of social scientists on the educational harm of racial SEGREGATION in schools.

It is possible to present such factual material as EVIDENCE in the trial of a constitutional case, and today it is not unusual for counsel to do so. However, the Brandeis brief has become a common technique in the Supreme Court and other appellate courts. In the *Muller* case, the Brandeis brief aimed at demonstrating that the Oregon legislature reasonably could have believed that certain evils existed and that a limit on women's working hours would mitigate them. Brandeis himself argued no more than that. The assumption was that the law was valid if there was a RATIONAL BASIS for the legislature's assumptions. Evidence on the other side of the factual questions would, in theory, be irrelevant. When the presumption of constitutionality is weaker—that is, when the state must justify its legislation by reference to a COMPELLING STATE INTEREST or some other heightened STANDARD OF REVIEW—

the Brandeis brief technique may recommend itself to either side of the argument.

KENNETH L. KARST
(1986)

(SEE ALSO: *Legislative Facts.*)

Bibliography

FREUND, PAUL A. 1951 *On Understanding the Supreme Court.* Chap. 3. Boston: Little, Brown.

BRANDENBURG v. OHIO
395 U.S. 444 (1969)

Libertarian critics of the CLEAR AND PRESENT DANGER test had always contended that it provided insufficient protection for speech because it depended ultimately on judicial guesses about the consequences of speech. Judges inimical to the content of a particular speech could always foresee the worst. Thus, to the extent that the test did protect speech, its crucial element was the imminence requirement, that speech was punishable only when it was so closely brigaded in time with unlawful action as to constitute an attempt to commit, or incitement of, unlawful action. When the Supreme Court converted clear and present danger to clear and probable danger in DENNIS V. UNITED STATES (1951) it actually converted the clear and present danger test into a BALANCING TEST that allowed judges who believed in judicial self-restraint to avoid enforcing the FIRST AMENDMENT by striking every balance in favor of the nonspeech interest that the government sought to protect by suppressing speech. The *Dennis* conversion, however, was even more damaging to the clear and present danger rule than a flat rejection and open replacement by the balancing standard would have been. A flat rejection would have left clear and present danger as a temporarily defeated libertarian rival to a temporarily triumphant antilibertarian balancing standard. The conversion to probable danger not only defeated the danger test but also discredited it among libertarians by removing the imminence requirement that had been its strongest protection for dissident speakers. Accordingly commentators, both libertarian and advocates of judicial self-restraint, were pleased to announce that *Dennis* had buried the clear and present danger test.

Some critics of the danger test had supported LEARNED HAND's approach in MASSES PUBLISHING CO. V. PATTEN (1917), which had focused on the advocacy content of the speech itself, thus avoiding judicial predictions about what the speech plus the surrounding circumstances would bring. *Masses* left two problems, however: the "Marc Antony" speech which on the surface seems innocuous but in the circumstances really is an incitement, and the speech preaching violence in circumstances in which it is harmless. OLIVER WENDELL HOLMES himself had injected a specific intent standard alongside the danger rule, arguing that government might punish a speaker only if it could prove his specific intent to bring about an unlawful act.

Eighteen years after *Dennis*, carefully avoiding the words of the clear and present danger test itself, the Supreme Court brought together these various strands of thought in *Brandenburg v. Ohio*, a PER CURIAM holding that "the constitutional guarantees of free speech . . . do not permit a state to forbid or proscribe advocacy of the use of force or law violation except where such advocacy is directed to inciting or producing imminent lawless action and is likely to incite or produce such action." In a footnote the Court interpreted *Dennis* and YATES V. UNITED STATES (1957) as upholding this standard. The decision itself struck down the Ohio Criminal Syndicalism Act which proscribed advocacy of violence as a means of accomplishing social reform. The Court overruled WHITNEY V. CALIFORNIA (1927).

MARTIN SHAPIRO
(1986)

BRANT, IRVING
(1885–1976)

Irving Newton Brant was a journalist, biographer, and constitutional historian. A strong supporter of President FRANKLIN D. ROOSEVELT, Brant published *Storm over the Constitution* in 1936; a vigorous defense of the constitutionality of the New Deal, it strongly influenced Roosevelt's later attempt to enlarge the membership of the Supreme Court. Brant's concentration in this book on the intent of the Framers of the Constitution led him to begin a biography of JAMES MADISON. Now regarded as definitive, his six-volume biography (1941–1961) had two aims: the rehabilitation of Madison's reputation as constitutional theorist and political leader, and the refutation of the STATES' RIGHTS interpretation of American history (which denied that the Revolutionary generation considered the newly created United States to be one nation). Brant's other works include *The Bill of Rights* (1965), a history championing the absolutist interpretation of the BILL OF RIGHTS espoused by Justices HUGO L. BLACK and WILLIAM O. DOUGLAS, and *Impeachment: Trials and Errors* (1972).

RICHARD B. BERNSTEIN
(1986)

BRANTI v. FINKEL
445 U.S. 507 (1980)

Branti v. Finkel tightened the FIRST AMENDMENT restrictions on the use of PATRONAGE in public employment first established in *Elrod v. Burns* (1976). Justice JOHN PAUL STEVEN'S MAJORITY OPINION held that upon taking office a public defender could not constitutionally dismiss two assistants solely because they were affiliated with a different political party. The 6–3 majority held that these dismissals denied the employees' freedoms of belief and association. The employer had failed to show a sufficient connection between party loyalty and effective job performance.

Justice POTTER STEWART dissented, analogizing the public defender's office to private law practice. Justice LEWIS F. POWELL, joined by Justice WILLIAM H. REHNQUIST, also dissented, reiterating his dissenting view in *Elrod* that patronage plays an honorable, traditional role in American politics.

AVIAM SOIFER
(1986)

BRANZBURG v. HAYES
408 U.S. 665 (1972)

Branzburg v. Hayes combined several cases in which reporters claimed a FIRST AMENDMENT privilege either not to appear or not to testify before grand juries, although they had witnessed criminal activity or had information relevant to the commission of crimes. The reporters' chief contention was that they should not be required to testify unless a GRAND JURY showed that a reporter possessed information relevant to criminal activity, that similar information could not be obtained from sources outside the press, and that the need for the information was sufficiently compelling to override the First Amendment interest in preserving confidential news sources.

Justice BYRON R. WHITE's opinion for the Court not only rejected these showings but also denied the very existence of a First Amendment testimonial privilege. Despite the asserted lack of any First Amendment privilege, the White opinion allowed that "news gathering" was not "without its First Amendment protections" and suggested that such protections would bar a grand jury from issuing SUBPOENAS to reporters "other than in good faith" or "to disrupt a reporter's relationship with his news sources." White rejected any requirement for a stronger showing of relevance, of alternative sources, or of balancing the need for the information against the First Amendment interest.

Nevertheless, Justice LEWIS F. POWELL, who signed White's 5–4 OPINION OF THE COURT, attached an ambiguous CONCURRING OPINION stating that a claim to privilege "should be judged on its facts by the striking of a proper balance between FREEDOM OF THE PRESS" and the government interest. Most lower courts have read the majority opinion through the eyes of Justice Powell. An opinion that emphatically denied a First Amendment privilege at various points seems to have created one after all.

STEVEN SHIFFRIN
(1986)

(SEE ALSO: *Reporter's Privilege.*)

BRASWELL v. UNITED STATES
487 U.S. 99 (1988)

Because the Fifth Amendment's RIGHT AGAINST SELF-INCRIMINATION is a personal one that can be exercised only by natural persons, the custodian of a CORPORATION's records may not invoke this right. The contents of corporate records are not privileged either. In this case, however, Braswell, who had been subpoenaed to produce the corporation's records, was its sole shareholder. He claimed that the production of the records, under compulsion, forced him to incriminate himself. Had he been the sole proprietor of a business, the Court would have agreed. But because he had incorporated, he lost the protection of the Fifth Amendment.

Four dissenters strongly maintained that the Court majority, by splitting hairs, had ignored realities. The Court used the fiction that the government did not seek the personal incrimination of Braswell, when it forced him as the head of his solely owned corporation to produce the records. This had the effect of giving the government the evidence needed to convict him. The majority openly conceded that to hold otherwise would hurt the government's efforts to prosecute white collar crime.

LEONARD W. LEVY
(1992)

BRAUNFELD v. BROWN

See: Sunday Closing Laws

BRAY v. ALEXANDRIA WOMEN'S HEALTH CLINIC
506 U.S. 263 (1993)

Abortion rights supporters invoked the anticonspiracy provision of 42 U.S.C. § 1985(3) to attempt to enjoin organized anti-abortion demonstrators from protesting at abortion clinics. The statute had been interpreted in GRIFFIN V. BRECKENRIDGE (1971) to require a "class-based, invidiously discriminatory animus" before covering the action of conspirators. The plaintiffs claimed that the demonstrators had the requisite animus against women. The Supreme Court, in an opinion by Justice ANTONIN

SCALIA, and over the full or partial dissents of four Justices, held that the demonstrations were "not directed specifically at women, but are intended to protect the victims of abortion." The animus alleged by the plaintiffs was not established, for want of the requisite focus on women as a class. The Court also found that the plaintiffs failed to allege a right protected against private encroachment, as required by the statute. The RIGHT TO TRAVEL allegedly interfered with was not the target of the demonstrations.

THEODORE EISENBERG
(2000)

(SEE ALSO: *Abortion and the Constitution; Anti-abortion Movement.*)

BREACH OF THE PEACE

Breach of the peace statutes are today popularly called disorderly conduct statutes. The wording of breach of the peace or disorderly conduct statutes varies significantly from one city or state to another. Generally, such statutes are violated if a person commits acts or makes statements likely to promote violence or disturb "good order" in a public place. Under modern statutes, as under the older COMMON LAW, it is possible to be guilty of committing a breach of the peace solely through the use of words likely to produce violence or disorder.

When a person is prosecuted for breach of the peace for his or her physical actions there is no significant FIRST AMENDMENT issue. Thus, if a person commits a breach of the peace by punching or shoving other persons in public no First Amendment issue arises. However, if a mixture of expression and physical activity forms the basis for the prosecution, the court must ask whether the person is being punished for the physical activity alone. Thus, a person might be convicted of a breach of the peace for using SOUNDTRUCKS OR AMPLIFIERS if the statute punished any use of a sound amplification device, regardless of the message communicated.

When a person is accused of committing a breach of the peace by speaking to others, a court must determine whether the guarantees of FREEDOM OF SPEECH and assembly have been violated. In addition, the court must determine whether the statute is tailored to avoid punishing constitutionally protected speech.

Although the Supreme Court has held that the First Amendment does not prohibit the punishment of FIGHTING WORDS, it has upheld few convictions for breach of the peace based solely upon verbal conduct. A considerable number of breach of the peace and disorderly conduct statutes have been held unconstitutional under the doctrine of VAGUENESS and OVERBREADTH.

A breach of the peace or disorderly conduct statute that

can be constitutionally applied to persons who physically interfere with police officers engaged in police functions cannot constitutionally serve as the basis for punishing the use of insulting or annoying language to a police officer, short of actual interference with the officer's ability to perform police functions.

A person engaged in lawful speech in a public place may sometimes be confronted by a HOSTILE AUDIENCE. In such a situation the police must attempt to protect the individual speaker, or disperse the crowd, before ordering the speaker to cease his or her advocacy of the unpopular message. If it appears that the officers cannot otherwise prevent violence, they may order the speaker or speakers to cease their speech or assembly, and a refusal to comply can constitutionally be punished as disorderly conduct. Breach of the peace statutes may also be applied as consistent with the First Amendment to prohibit conduct that would interfere with the use of government property not traditionally open to speech. Thus, the state might prohibit activities near jails or school buildings if those activities interfere with the government's ability to operate the school or jail.

JOHN E. NOWAK
(1986)

Bibliography

MONAGHAN, HENRY P. 1981 Overbreadth. *The Supreme Court Review* 1981:1–40.

NOWAK, JOHN E.; ROTUND, RONALD D.; and YOUNG, J. NELSON 1983 *Constitutional Law.* Pages 954–958, 973–987. St. Paul, Minn.: West Publishing Co.

BREARLY, DAVID
(1745–1790)

David Brearly represented New Jersey at the CONSTITUTIONAL CONVENTION OF 1787 and signed the Constitution. He was a spokesman for the small states, favoring equal representation of the states in Congress. He served on the Committee of Eleven on remaining matters, and delivered its reports to the Convention. He was later president of New Jersey's ratifying convention.

DENNIS J. MAHONEY
(1986)

BRECKINRIDGE, JOHN
(1760–1806)

John Breckinridge studied law under Virginia's GEORGE WYTHE, then moved to Kentucky, serving as state attorney general (1795–1797), state representative (1798–1800), United States senator (1801–1805), and United States at-torney general (1805–1806). During the ALIEN AND SEDITION ACT crisis Breckinridge traveled to Virginia, where he convinced THOMAS JEFFERSON, through an intermediary, that the vice-president's resolutions condemning the acts should be introduced in Kentucky, and not North Carolina, Jefferson's initial choice. Breckinridge revised Jefferson's draft by deleting the term NULLIFICATION, thus allowing Kentucky to condemn the acts and declare them unconstitutional without actually defying the federal government. Breckinridge then guided the resolutions through the Kentucky legislature while hiding Jefferson's authorship. In 1802 Breckinridge drafted and shepherded through the Senate an act to repeal the JUDICIARY ACT OF 1801—that eleventh-hour creation of the Federalists under JOHN ADAMS which allowed the outgoing President to appoint additional federal judges. Breckinridge argued that the repeal was constitutional, because if Congress had the power to create inferior courts, then Congress could also abolish them. He also contended against a judicial power to hold unconstitutional acts of Congress or of the President. Breckinridge initially doubted the constitutionality of the LOUISIANA PURCHASE, but in 1803 he introduced the Breckinridge Act which created territorial government for Louisiana. Like the Kentucky Resolutions, this act was secretly written by Jefferson.

PAUL FINKELMAN
(1986)

(SEE ALSO: *Virginia and Kentucky Resolutions.*)

Bibliography

HARRISON, LOWELL H. 1969 *John Breckinridge: Jeffersonian Republican.* Louisville, Ky.: Filson Club.

BREEDLOVE v. SUTTLES
302 U.S. 277 (1937)

Georgia levied an annual POLL TAX of one dollar on every inhabitant between ages twenty-one and sixty except blind persons and women who did not register to vote. Voting registration was conditioned on payment of accrued poll taxes. A white male, denied registration for failure to pay poll taxes, challenged this scheme as a violation of the EQUAL PROTECTION and PRIVILEGES AND IMMUNITIES clauses of the FOURTEENTH AMENDMENT, and of the NINETEENTH AMENDMENT as well. In an opinion by Justice PIERCE BUTLER, a unanimous Supreme Court summarily rejected all these challenges and upheld the law. *Breedlove* was overruled in HARPER V. VIRGINIA BOARD OF ELECTIONS (1966).

KENNETH L. KARST
(1986)

BREITHAUPT v. ABRAM
352 U.S. 432 (1957)

The taking of blood from an unconscious person to prove his intoxication and therefore his guilt for involuntary manslaughter was not conduct that "shocks the conscience" within the meaning of ROCHIN V. CALIFORNIA (1952), nor was it coercing a confession; accordingly the Supreme Court, in a 6–3 opinion by Justice TOM C. CLARK, found no violation of DUE PROCESS OF LAW.

LEONARD W. LEVY
(1986)

BRENNAN, WILLIAM J., JR.
(1906–   )

William Joseph Brennan, Jr., was appointed an Associate Justice of the United States Supreme Court in October 1956. He quickly became, in both an intellectual and statistical sense, the center of gravity of what commentators have come to call the WARREN COURT, dissenting less than any other Justice, and fashioning many of that Court's most important opinions.

He came to the Court with more past judicial experience than any of his colleagues. For seven years he had been a New Jersey state judge, beginning his career at the trial level and rapidly advancing to the New Jersey Supreme Court. He had also been prominent in the movement to reform the antiquated New Jersey court system. He understood and cared about the practical workings of the justice system, and this concern was to prove important in the development of his constitutional perspective.

Brennan was a committed civil libertarian who believed in "providing freedom and equality of rights and opportunities, in a realistic and not merely formal sense, to all the people of this nation." He considered courts to be the particular guardians of constitutional rights. "[T]he soul of a government of laws," he once wrote, "is the judicial function, and that function can only exist if adjudication is understood by our people to be, as it is, the essentially disinterested, rational and deliberate element of our society." For Brennan, the judicial function demanded a continual effort to translate constitutional values into general doctrinal formulations. This emphasis on DOCTRINE distinguished Brennan from his colleague WILLIAM O. DOUGLAS, who was an equally committed civil libertarian.

Brennan viewed courts as the last resort of the politically disfranchised and the politically powerless. Constitutional litigation was for him "a form of political expression"; it was often, he wrote in NAACP V. BUTTON (1963), "the sole practicable avenue open to a minority to petition for redress of grievances." Litigation was thus an alternative, perhaps the only alternative, to social violence.

For these reasons he seized every opportunity to enlarge litigants' access to federal courts. Exemplary is his opinion in BAKER V. CARR (1962), which held that the issue of unequal legislative representation was justiciable in federal court, and which Chief Justice EARL WARREN called "the most important case that we decided in my time." In opinion after opinion Brennan worked to open the doors of the federal courthouse, and to make available such federal judicial remedies for violations of the Constitution as HABEAS CORPUS, INJUNCTIONS, DECLARATORY JUDGMENTS, and DAMAGES. In later years Brennan dissented vigorously as many of these opinions were cut back by the BURGER COURT.

Because he believed that "the ultimate protection of individual freedom is found in judicial enforcement" of constitutional rights, Brennan did not flinch from the exercise of JUDICIAL POWER. When the time came, for example, to accelerate the ALL DELIBERATE SPEED with which BROWN V. BOARD OF EDUCATION (1955) had ordered the nation's public schools to be desegregated, Brennan, in GREEN V. NEW KENT COUNTY SCHOOL BOARD (1968), shattered the facade of southern "freedom-of-choice" plans and wrote that racial discrimination must end "*now*" and "be eliminated root and branch." In KEYES V. SCHOOL DISTRICT #1 OF DENVER (1973) Brennan took the lead in applying the requirement of *Brown* to northern school districts, and in cases like FRONTIERO V. RICHARDSON (1973) and CRAIG V. BOREN (1976) he played a major role in causing gender classifications to be subjected to substantial scrutiny under the EQUAL PROTECTION clause of the FOURTEENTH AMENDMENT.

Brennan was a nationalist. He believed in the power of Congress to define and protect CIVIL RIGHTS and to govern the national economy unrestrained by concerns of state SOVEREIGNTY. He disapproved of state regulations that interfered with interstate commerce. He favored the judicial imposition of national, constitutional values onto local decision-making processes. He believed, for example, that federal courts should fully incorporate almost all the guarantees of the BILL OF RIGHTS into the Fourteenth Amendment, and enforce them against the states. He dissented often and forcefully against the "federalist" leanings of the Burger Court. To Brennan the primary purpose of "the federal system's diffusion of governmental power" was to secure "individual freedom."

In his most enduring opinions, Brennan brought a unique and characteristic analysis to bear on the question of constitutional rights. Instead of inquiring into the power of government to regulate rights, he would instead focus on the manner in which the government's regulation actually functioned. The implications of this shift in focus were profound. They are perhaps most visible in the area of FIRST AMENDMENT adjudication.

To appreciate Brennan's contribution to First Amendment jurisprudence, it must be remembered that the Court to which Brennan was appointed was still reverberating from the effects of the constitutional crisis of the 1930s. It was, for example, groping for a means of reconciling judicial protection of First Amendment freedoms with the deep respect for majoritarian decision making that was the legacy of the Court's confrontation with President FRANKLIN D. ROOSEVELT's New Deal. At the time Brennan joined the Court, the Justices were embroiled in a vigorous but ultimately unproductive debate as to whether First Amendment freedoms were "absolutes" or whether they should be "weighed" against competing government interests in regulation. (See ABSOLUTISM; BALANCING TESTS.) Both sides of the debate viewed government interests and individual rights as locked in an indissoluble and paralyzing conflict. Brennan's lasting contribution was to push the Court beyond this debate and to create a form of analysis in which this conflict receded from view. The essence of Brennan's approach was a precise and persistent focus on the processes and procedures through which government sought to regulate First Amendment freedoms.

Justice Brennan first used this approach in his second term on the Court in the modest but seminal case of SPEISER V. RANDALL (1958). The case involved a California law which denied certain tax exemptions to those who refused to execute an oath stating that they did "not advocate the overthrow of the United States or of the State of California by force of violence or other unlawful means." Significantly, Brennan did not approach the case in terms of an "absolute" right to engage in such advocacy. Nor did he inquire into California's "interests" in controlling such speech; he was willing to assume that California could deny tax exemptions to those who had engaged in proscribed speech.

Brennan focused his analysis instead on the procedures used to determine which taxpayers to penalize. He interpreted the California scheme as placing on taxpayers the burden of demonstrating that they had not engaged in unlawful speech. This procedure was unconstitutional, Brennan concluded, because it created too great a danger that lawful speech would be adversely affected. "The vice of the present procedure is that, where particular speech falls close to the line separating the lawful and the unlawful, the possibility of mistaken factfinding—inherent in all litigation—will create the danger that the legitimate utterance will be penalized. The man who knows that he must bring forth proof and persuade another of the lawfulness of his conduct necessarily must steer far wider of the unlawful zone than if the State must bear these burdens."

By focusing on the manner in which California had regulated speech, rather than on its power to do so, Brennan was led to inquire into the actual, practical effects of the regulatory scheme. He thus shifted the focus of judicial inquiry away from the particular speech of the litigant, and toward the impact of the legislation, as concretely embedded in its procedural setting, on concededly legitimate speech. This change in focus was central to Brennan's First Amendment jurisprudence, and it was the foundation of many of the Warren Court's innovations in this area. It had, for example, obvious relevance for the procedures used by government to regulate unprotected forms of speech like OBSCENITY. Brennan spelled out these implications in a series of influential obscenity decisions that demonstrated the substantive impact of such nominally procedural isses as BURDEN OF PROOF and the nature and timing of judicial HEARINGS.

Brennan's form of inquiry also led to a careful scrutiny of the VAGUENESS of government regulations of speech. Prior to *Speiser* the issue of "vagueness" was primarily conceived in terms of the rather weak NOTICE requirements of the DUE PROCESS clause. But Brennan's analysis offered a strict, new, and specifically First Amendment rationale for the doctrine. As Brennan explained in KEYISHIAN V. BOARD OF REGENTS (1967), a case involving a New York law prohibiting public school teachers from uttering "seditious" words, "[w]hen one must guess what conduct or utterance may lose him his position, one necessarily will 'steer far wider of the unlawful zone.'"

Brennan's focus on the practical impact of regulation also led him to the conclusion that the separation of legitimate from illegitimate speech had to be accomplished with "precision" and by legislation incapable of application to legitimate speech. As Brennan wrote in *Button*, First Amendment freedoms are "delicate and vulnerable," and "the threat of sanctions may deter their exercise almost as potently as the actual application of sanctions." In *Button* Brennan coined the term OVERBREADTH to capture this requirement that First Amendment regulations be narrowly tailored, and the term and the requirement have since become doctrinal instruments of major significance.

The framework of analysis developed by Brennan not only dominated the First Amendment jurisprudence of the Warren Court; it remained influential with the Burger Court that succeeded it. Its prominence was in large measure due to its apparent accommodation of government interests in regulation, if only the government could formulate its regulation more narrowly or more precisely. This accommodation, however, was in some respects illusory. The exact degree of constitutionally mandated precision or clarity was never specified, and the psychological assumptions that underlay the approach were not susceptible to empirical verification. As a result the requirements of clarity and precision could without explicit justification be loosened to uphold some government regulations, or tightened to strike down others. The indirection at the heart of this approach thus left it vulnerable to manipulation.

The approach was at its most compelling, therefore, when it was fused with an underlying substantive vision of the First Amendment. An illustration is the opinion which is Brennan's masterpiece, NEW YORK TIMES COMPANY V. SULLIVAN (1964). At issue in *Sullivan* was the Alabama law of LIBEL, which permitted a public official to recover damages for defamatory statements unless the speaker could prove that the statements were true. With reasoning similar to that in *Speiser* and *Button*, Brennan concluded that Alabama's allocation of the burden of proof was unconstitutional, because it "dampens the vigor and limits the variety of public debate" by inducing "self-censorship."

In *Sullivan*, however, Brennan took the unusual and penetrating step of lifting this analysis from its procedural setting and applying it to the substantive standards required by the First Amendment. Noting that the central purpose of the First Amendment was "the principle that debate on public issues should be uninhibited, robust, and wide-open," Brennan concluded that this purpose would be undermined if those who criticized public officials were subject to "any test of truth." He noted that an "erroneous statement is inevitable in free debate, and [it] must be protected if the freedoms of expression are to have the 'breathing space' that they 'need . . . to survive.' The need for "breathing space" led Brennan to conclude that speech about public officials had to be constitutionally protected unless uttered with "actual malice"; that is, uttered "with knowledge that it was false or with reckless disregard of whether it was false or not." The actual malice standard thus incorporated into the substantive law of the First Amendment the insights Brennan had accumulated as a result of his prior focus on the process of regulation. The result, as ALEXANDER MEIKLEJOHN was moved to proclaim, was "an occasion for dancing in the streets."

Although Brennan's focus on process rather than power is most apparent in First Amendment opinions, it also pervades his entire approach to constitutional law. In *Speiser*, for example, California had argued that since a tax exemption was not a right but a privilege bestowed at the pleasure of the state, it could also be withdrawn by the state for any reason. The so-called RIGHT-PRIVILEGE DISTINCTION had a venerable judicial pedigree, and was supported by Supreme Court precedents as recent as *Barsky v. Board of Regents* (1954). Brennan, however, brought a fresh perspective to bear on this argument, for he was concerned not with California's power to withdraw the privilege but with the manner in which it did so. From this perspective the right-privilege distinction was beside the point.

Brennan repeatedly attacked the right-privilege distinction, and many of his most important opinions, contributing to or originating major lines of doctrinal development, were predicated upon its rejection. Examples include SHERBERT V. VERNER (1963), which resuscitated the doctrine of "unconstitutional conditions" as applied to the denial of unemployment compensation; SHAPIRO V. THOMPSON (1969), which created the FUNDAMENTAL RIGHTS strand of equal protection analysis and applied it to durational RESIDENCY REQUIREMENTS for welfare recipients; and GOLDBERG V. KELLY (1970), which for the first time applied the protections of PROCEDURAL DUE PROCESS to the recipients of government entitlements such as WELFARE BENEFITS.

Brennan's focus on process deeply influenced both the Warren and the Burger courts. As the welfare state increased in complexity, Brennan's approach provided the basis for flexible yet far-reaching judicial review of government action. We can recognize the consequences of this approach in the shape of modern constitutional inquiry, with its characteristic scrutiny into whether government has acted through appropriate procedures and in a manner not unduly burdening the exercise of constitutional rights.

It is noteworthy that the results of this scrutiny depend upon an apprehension of the actual impact of government action. In later years Brennan's views on this subject were informed by a compassion and empathy that were not always shared by his colleagues. With the advent of the Burger Court, Brennan increasingly became a dissenter. His dissents, like his majority opinions, tended to be careful and lawyerly, without the eloquence or sting that mark the most memorable examples of the genre. Often, however, both Brennan and the majority were writing within doctrinal frameworks that Brennan himself had helped to create. His success in redefining the major questions of constitutional law is the measure of his achievement.

ROBERT C. POST
(1986)

Bibliography

BRENNAN, WILLIAM JOSEPH, JR. 1969 Convocation Address. *Notre Dame Lawyer* 44:1029–1033.

—— 1981 Justice Thurgood Marshall: Advocate for Human Need in American Jurisprudence. *Maryland Law Review* 40: 390–397.

HECK, EDWARD V. 1980 Justice Brennan and the Heyday of Warren Court Liberalism. *Santa Clara Law Review* 20:841–887.

HUTCHINSON, DENNIS J. 1983 Hail to the Chief: Earl Warren and the Supreme Court. *Michigan Law Review* 81:922–930.

KALVEN, HARRY, JR. 1964 The New York Times Case: A Note on "The Central Meaning of the First Amendment." *Supreme Court Review* 1964:191–221.

LEVY, LEONARD W., ed. 1972 *The Supreme Court under Earl Warren.* New York: Quadrangle Books.

BRENNAN, WILLIAM J., JR.
(1906–   )
(Update 1)

After graduating near the top of his Harvard Law School class, William Brennan returned to his hometown, Newark, New Jersey, where he joined a prominent law firm and specialized in labor law. As his practice grew, Brennan, a devoted family man, resented the demands it made on his time and accepted an appointment to the New Jersey Superior Court in order to lessen his work load. Brennan attracted attention as an efficient and fair-minded judge and was elevated to the New Jersey Supreme Court in 1952. President DWIGHT D. EISENHOWER, appointed him to the Supreme Court of the United States in 1956. The appointment was criticized at the time as "political," on the ground that the nomination of a Catholic Democrat on the eve of the 1956 presidential election was intended to win votes for the Republican ticket.

Once on the Court, Brennan firmly established himself as a leader of the "liberal" wing. Often credited with providing critical behind-the-scenes leadership during the WARREN COURT years, Brennan fashioned many of that Court's most important decisions. He continued to play a significant role—although more often as a dissenter, lamenting what he believed to be the evisceration of Warren Court precedents—as the ideological complexion of the Court changed in the 1970s and 1980s.

Brennan was a committed civil libertarian who believed that the Constitution guarantees "freedom and equality of rights and opportunities . . . to all people of this nation." For Brennan, courts were the last resort of the politically disfranchised and the politically powerless, and constitutional litigation was often "the sole practicable avenue open to a minority to petition for redress of grievances." Thus, in Brennan's view, the courts played an indispensable role in the enforcement, interpretation, and implementation of the most cherished guarantees of the United States Constitution. As Brennan observed, the Constitution's "broadly phrased guarantees ensure that [it] need never become an anachronism: The Constitution will endure as a vital charter of human liberty as long as there are those with the courage to defend it, the vision to interpret it, and the fidelity to live by it."

Brennan had an especially influential impact in the areas of EQUAL PROTECTION OF THE LAWS, DUE PROCESS, FREEDOM OF SPEECH, and CRIMINAL PROCEDURE. In his interpretation of the equal protection clause, Brennan evinced little tolerance for INVIDIOUS DISCRIMINATION by

the government. When Brennan joined the Court in 1956, the equal protection clause was high on the Court's agenda, for the Court had just handed down its explosive decisions in BROWN V. BOARD OF EDUCATION (1954, 1955). Despite these decisions, and to the Court's mounting frustration, SEGREGATION of southern schools remained largely intact more than a decade after *Brown.* In GREEN V. COUNTY SCHOOL BOARD OF NEW KENT (1968), however, Brennan's opinion for the Court finally dismantled the last serious barriers to DESEGREGATION by invalidating the "freedom of choice" plans that had been used to forestall desegregation in the rural South. Putting aside the ALL DELIBERATE SPEED formula, Brennan emphatically expressed his own and the Court's impatience at the pace of desegregation: "The burden on a school board today is to come forward with a plan that promises realistically to work, and promises realistically to work *now.*"

When the Court first considered the lawfulness of school segregation in a city that had never expressly mandated racially segregated education by statute, it was again Brennan, writing for a closely divided Court in KEYES V. SCHOOL DISTRICT NO. 1 OF DENVER (1973), who took a strong stand on the issue: "A finding of intentionally segregative school board action in a meaningful portion of a school system . . . creates a presumption that other segregated schooling within the system is not adventitious [and] shifts to school authorities the burden of proving that other segregated schools within the system are not also the result of intentionally segregative actions."

Although Brennan naturally assumed a leadership role in condemning RACIAL DISCRIMINATION, he sharply distinguished such discrimination from race-conscious AFFIRMATIVE ACTION programs designed to protect racial minorities. Brennan explained the distinction in his separate opinion in REGENTS OF UNIVERSITY OF CALIFORNIA V. BAKKE (1978): "Against the background of our history, claims that law must be 'color-blind' or that the datum of race is no longer relevant to public policy must be seen as aspiration rather than as description of reality. [We] cannot . . . let color blindness become myopia which masks the reality that many 'created equal' have been treated within our lifetimes as inferior both by law and by their fellow citizens." Brennan therefore concluded that the purpose of "remedying the effects of past societal discrimination is . . . sufficiently important to justify the use of race-conscious" affirmative action programs "where there is a sound basis for concluding that minority representation is substantial and chronic and that the handicap of past discrimination is impeding access of minorities to the [field]."

Brennan also played a pivotal role in the evolution of equal protection doctrine in the area of SEX DISCRIMINATION. In FRONTIERO V. RICHARDSON (1973) Brennan, writing a PLURALITY OPINION for four Justices, argued that classifications based on sex are inherently suspect and, like racial classifications, must be subjected to STRICT SCRUTINY. Taking a strong stand on the issue, Brennan explained that "our Nation has had a long and unfortunate history of sex discrimination" and that history has traditionally been "rationalized by an attitude of 'romantic paternalism' which, in practical effect, put women, not on a pedestal, but in a cage." Although Brennan never garnered the crucial fifth vote for this position, he did gain a decisive victory in CRAIG V. BOREN (1976), in which he wrote for the Court that gender-based classifications must be subjected to intermediate scrutiny and that "to withstand constitutional analysis" such classifications "must serve important governmental objectives and must be substantially related to achievement of those objectives."

Brennan also opened the door to the Court's REAPPORTIONMENT revolution. Prior to 1962, the Court had consistently declined to consider claims that state laws prescribing legislative districts that were not approximately equal in population violated the Constitution. As Justice Frankfurter explained in COLEGROVE V. GREEN (1946), such controversies concern "matters that bring courts into immediate and active relations with party contests," and "courts ought not to enter this political thicket." In BAKER V. CARR (1962) Brennan rejected this reasoning and held that a claim that the apportionment of the Tennessee General Assembly violated the appellants' rights under the equal protection clause "by virtue of the debasement of their votes" stated "a justiciable cause of action." Brennan explained that "the question here is the consistency of STATE ACTION with the Federal Constitution," and such claims are not nonjusticiable merely "because they touch matters of state governmental organization." Brennan's opinion for the Court in *Baker* led the way to REYNOLDS V. SIMS (1964), and its progeny, which articulated and enforced the constitutional principle of ONE PERSON, ONE VOTE.

Closely related to the Court's reapportionment decisions was the equal protection doctrine of implied FUNDAMENTAL RIGHTS. Prior to 1969, the Court had hinted on several occasions that the RATIONAL BASIS standard of review might not be applicable to classifications that penalize the exercise of such rights. Building upon these intimations, Brennan held in SHAPIRO V. THOMPSON (1969) that a law that denied WELFARE BENEFITS to residents who had not resided within the JURISDICTION for at least one year immediately prior to their application for assistance penalized the right to interstate travel by denying newcomers "welfare aid upon which may depend the ability of families to subsist." Brennan concluded that because the classification penalized an implied fundamental right it amounted to unconstitutional "invidious discrimination" unless it was "necessary to promote a compelling governmental interest." Brennan's opinion in *Shapiro* crystallized

the implied fundamental rights doctrine and thus opened the door to a series of subsequent decisions invalidating classifications that unequally affected VOTING RIGHTS, the right to be listed on the ballot, the RIGHT TO TRAVEL, and the right to use contraceptives.

Although Brennan played a central role in shaping equal protection doctrine in the 1960s, by the 1970s and 1980s he often found himself fighting rearguard actions in an effort to protect his earlier equal protection decisions, particularly in the areas of reapportionment and implied fundamental rights. Occasionally, however, he won a hard-earned victory. In PLYLER V. DOE (1982), for example, Brennan mustered a five-Justice majority to invalidate a Texas statute that denied free public education to children who had not been legally admitted into the United States. Although conceding that education is not a fundamental right, Brennan nonetheless persuaded four of his brethren that intermediate scrutiny was appropriate because the statute imposed "a lifetime hardship on the discrete class of children not accountable for their disabling status."

As these decisions suggest, Brennan was consistently ready and willing to assert judicial authority to enforce the Constitution's guarantee of "the equal protection of the laws." This same activism was evident in Brennan's due process opinions. GOLDBERG V. KELLY (1970) is perhaps the best example. Traditionally, the Court had defined the "liberty" and "property" interests protected by the due process clause by reference to the COMMON LAW. The Court held that if government took someone's property or invaded his bodily integrity, the due process clause required some kind of hearing; but the Court deemed the clause inapplicable if government denied an individual some public benefit to which he had no common law right, such as public employment, a license, or welfare. This doctrine seemed increasingly formalistic with the twentieth-century expansion of governmental benefit programs and governmental participation in the economy, for while more and more individuals grew increasingly dependent upon government, prevailing doctrine gave no constitutional protection against even the most arbitrary withdrawal of governmental benefits.

In *Goldberg*, Brennan dramatically redefined the scope of the interests protected by the due process clause. Brennan explained that "much of the existing wealth in this country takes the form of rights that do not fall within traditional common law concepts of property," and it is "realistic today to regard welfare entitlements as more like property than a 'gratuity.'" This being so, Brennan held, a state could not constitutionally terminate public assistance benefits without affording the recipient the opportunity for an evidential hearing prior to termination. In this opinion, Brennan launched a new era in the extension of due process rights, and in subsequent decisions, the Court, building upon *Goldberg*, held that the suspension of drivers' licenses, the termination of public employment, the revocation of parole, the termination of food stamps, and similar matters must be undertaken in accordance with the demands of due process.

Despite his extraordinary contributions to the governing principles of American equal protection and due process jurisprudence, Brennan's greatest legacy may be in the area of free expression. When Brennan joined the Court, the country was in the throes of its efforts to suppress communism, and this undoubtedly affected Brennan's views on free expression. Brennan's influence on the Court in this area of the law was felt almost immediately. Two years before Brennan's appointment, the Court, in *Barsky v. Board of Regents* (1954), reaffirmed the RIGHT-PRIVILEGE DISTINCTION in upholding the suspension of a physician's medical license because of events arising out of his communist affiliations. Four years later, in SPEISER V. RANDALL (1958), Brennan's opinion for the Court explicitly rejected the right privilege distinction. *Speiser* involved a California law that established a special property tax exemption for veterans, but denied the exemption to any veteran who advocated the violent overthrow of the government. Brennan rejected the state's argument that the disqualification was lawful because it merely withheld a "privilege": "To deny an exemption to claimants who engage in certain forms of speech is in effect to penalize them for such speech. Its deterrent effect is the same as if the State were to fine them for this speech. The appellees are plainly mistaken in their argument that, because a tax exemption is a 'privilege' . . . , its denial may not infringe speech."

Brennan's rejection of the rightprivilege distinction in *Speiser* was a critical step in the evolution of FIRST AMENDMENT doctrine. It did not, however, end the case, and Brennan proceeded to articulate a second—and equally important—principle of First Amendment doctrine. Turning to the procedure mandated by the California law, Brennan held that the law violated the First Amendment because it required the applicant to prove that he had not advocated the violent overthrow of government. Brennan explained that "the vice of the present procedure is that, where particular speech falls close to the line separating the lawful and the unlawful, the possibility of mistaken factfinding—inherent in all litigation—will create the danger that the legitimate utterance will be penalized." Moreover, "the man who knows that he must bring forth proof and persuade another of the lawfulness of his conduct must steer far wider of the unlawful zone than if the State must bear these burdens."

This emphasis on the procedure by which government regulates expression was a hallmark of Brennan's First Amendment jurisprudence. Indeed, Brennan was the principal architect of both the First Amendment VAGUENESS principle and the OVERBREADTH doctrine. Brennan's first full articulation of the vagueness principle came in KEYISHIAN V. BOARD OF REGENTS (1967), which invalidated a New York law prohibiting schoolteachers from uttering "seditious" words. Building upon his opinion in *Speiser*, Brennan grounded the vagueness principle in his observation that "when one must guess what conduct or utterance may lose him his position, one necessarily will 'steer far wider of the unlawful zone.'"

Brennan coined the term "overbreadth" in NAACP V. BUTTON (1963), and he first fully explained the rationale of the doctrine in *Gooding v. Wilson* (1972): "The transcendent value to all society of constitutionally protected expression is deemed to justify allowing 'attacks on overly broad statutes with no requirement that the person making the attack demonstrate that his own conduct could not be regulated by a statute drawn with the requisite narrow specificity.' . . . This is deemed necessary because persons whose expression is constitutionally protected may well refrain from exercising their rights for fear of criminal sanctions provided by a statute susceptible of application to protected expression."

Brennan's views on free expression were influenced not only by governmental efforts to suppress communism but by the CIVIL RIGHTS MOVEMENT. In *NAACP v. Button* (1963), for example, Brennan held that a Virginia law prohibiting any organization to retain a lawyer in connection with litigation to which it was not a party was unconstitutional as applied to the activities of the NAACP and the NAACP LEGAL DEFENSE & EDUCATIONAL FUND. Brennan explained that "in the context of NAACP objectives, litigation is not a technique of resolving private differences; it is a means for [achieving] equality of treatment [for] the members of the Negro Community." In such circumstances, litigation "is a form of political expression," and "groups which find themselves unable to achieve their objectives through the ballot frequently turn to the courts." Indeed, for the group the NAACP "assists, litigation may be the most effective form of political association." By bringing litigation within the ambit of First Amendment protection, Brennan's opinion for the Court in *Button* both highlighted the central role of courts as effective instruments of political and social change and empowered organizations like the NAACP to pursue aggressively the vindication of constitutional rights without obstruction from often hostile state governments.

Perhaps Brennan's most important First Amendment opinion, NEW YORK TIMES V. SULLIVAN (1964), also grew out of the civil rights movement. At issue in *Sullivan* was the Alabama law of libel, which permitted a public official to recover damages for defamatory statements unless the accuser could prove that the statements were true. The case was brought by a Montgomery city commissioner on the basis of several inaccurate statements contained in an advertisement that described the civil rights movement and concluded with an appeal for funds. An Alabama jury found in favor of the commissioner and awarded him damages in the amount of $500,000.

Prior to *Sullivan* it was settled doctrine that libelous utterances were unprotected by the First Amendment and could be regulated without raising "any constitutional problem." With a sensitivity to the history of SEDITIOUS LIBEL and an awareness of the dangers even civil libel actions pose to free and open debate in cases like *Sullivan*, Brennan rejected settled doctrine and held that "libel can claim no talismanic immunity from constitutional limitations." To the contrary, libel "must be measured by standards that satisfy the First Amendment." Moreover, considering the case "against the background of a profound national commitment to the principle that debate on public issues should be uninhibited, robust, and wide-open," Brennan maintained that the "advertisement, as an expression of grievance and protest on one of the major public issues of our time, would seem clearly to qualify for constitutional protection." Balancing the competing interests, Brennan concluded that because "erroneous statement is inevitable in free debate" and "must be protected if the freedoms of expression are to have the 'breathing space' that they 'need . . . to survive,'" the First Amendment must be understood to prohibit any public official to recover damages for libel unless "he proves that the statement was made with 'actual malice'—that is, with knowledge that it was false or with reckless disregard of whether it was false or not."

Brennan also played a central role in the evolution of the law of OBSCENITY. In ROTH V. UNITED STATES (1957), the Court's first confrontation with the obscenity issue, Brennan wrote for the Court that obscenity is "utterly without redeeming social importance" and is thus "not within the area of constitutionally protected speech." Characteristically, however, Brennan emphasized that "sex and obscenity are not synonymous" and that it is "vital that the standards for judging obscenity safeguard the protection of . . . material which does not treat sex in a manner appealing to prurient interest." Sixteen years later, after struggling without success satisfactorily to define "obscenity," Brennan came to the conclusion that the very concept is so inherently vague that it is impossible to "bring stability to this area of the law without jeopardizing fundamental First Amendment values." Brennan therefore concluded in his dissenting opinion in *Paris Adult Theatre I v. Slaton* (1973) that "at least in the absence of distribution to juveniles or obtrusive exposure to unconsenting adults," the First Amendment prohibits the suppression of "sexually oriented materials on the basis of their alleg-

edly 'obscene' contents." Not surprisingly, this analysis once again revealed the essential touchstones of Brennan's First Amendment jurisprudence—a recognition of the need for precision of regulation and a sensitivity to the practical dynamics of governmental efforts to limit expression. As Brennan cautioned in *Paris Adult Theatre*, "in the absence of some very substantial interest" in suppressing even LOW-VALUE SPEECH, "we can hardly condone the ill effects that seem to flow inevitably from the effort."

As in the equal protection area, and as suggested in *Paris Adult Theatre*, Brennan spent most of his energies in free speech cases in the 1970s and 1980s in dissent. This was especially true in cases involving content-neutral regulations of expression, such as HEFFRON V. INTERNATIONAL SOCIETY FOR KRISHNA CONSCIOUSNESS, INC. (1981), and cases involving the regulation of sexually oriented expression, such as FEDERAL COMMUNICATIONS COMMISSION V. PACIFICA FOUNDATION (1978). As in the equal protection area, however, Brennan won a few notable victories. In *Elrod v. Burns* (1976), for example, Brennan wrote a plurality opinion holding the patronage practice of dismissing public employees on a partisan basis violative of the First Amendment; in BOARD OF EDUCATION V. PICO (1982) he wrote a plurality opinion holding unconstitutional the removal of books from a public school library; and in *Texas v. Johnson* (1989) he wrote the opinion of the Court holding that an individual who burned the American flag as a form of political protest had engaged in constitutionally protected conduct that could not be prohibited under a state FLAG DESECRATION statute.

Brennan's opinions in the realm of criminal procedure followed a similar pattern—landmark opinions expanding CIVIL LIBERTIES during the Warren Court, vigorous and often bitter dissents during the BURGER COURT and the REHNQUIST COURT. Brennan's earlier opinions are illustrated by FAY V. NOIA (1963), *Davis v. Mississippi* (1969), and UNITED STATES V. WADE (1967). In *Fay*, Brennan significantly expanded the availability of federal HABEAS CORPUS, holding the writ available not only to persons challenging the jurisdiction of the convicting court but to any individual who was convicted in a proceeding that was "so fundamentally defective as to make imprisonment . . . constitutionally intolerable." In *Davis*, Brennan limited the use of dragnet investigations and invalidated as an unreasonable SEARCH AND SEIZURE the detention of twenty-five black youths for questioning and fingerprinting in connection with a rape investigation where there were no reasonable grounds to believe that any particular individual was the assailant. And in *Wade*, Brennan held that courtroom identifications of an accused must be excluded from evidence where the accused was exhibited to witnesses before trial at a postindictment LINEUP without notice to the accused's counsel. The common theme of these and other Brennan opinions in the area of criminal procedure was that judges must be especially vigilant to protect those individuals whose rights to fair, decent, and equal treatment in the CRIMINAL JUSTICE SYSTEM might too easily be lost to intolerance, indifference, ignorance, or haste.

Brennan also adopted a consistently firm stand against the constitutionality of CAPITAL PUNISHMENT. In *Furman v. Georgia*, Brennan maintained that the CRUEL AND UNUSUAL PUNISHMENT clause "must draw its meaning from the evolving standards of decency that mark the progress of a maturing society" and that a punishment is cruel and unusual "if it does not comport with human dignity." Noting that the "uniqueness" of capital punishment is evident in its "pain, in its finality, and in its enormity," Brennan concluded that the death penalty "stands condemned as fatally offensive to human dignity" because it is "degrading" to the individual, "arbitrarily" inflicted, "excessive," and unacceptable to "contemporary society." Although he did not persuade a majority to this point of view, he adhered to this position as a matter of unshakable principle throughout his career.

At the time of his appointment to the Supreme Court, much was made of Brennan's Catholicism. It was thought by many, for better or worse, that he would narrowly represent the interests of a Catholic constituency. Brennan did not meet those expectations. To the contrary, guided by his constitutional philosophy rather than his religion, Brennan frequently angered Catholics on such controversial issues as SCHOOL PRAYER, Bible readings, moments of silence, GOVERNMENT AID TO RELIGIOUS INSTITUTIONS (including parochial schools), public displays of the crèche, BIRTH CONTROL, and ABORTION. In this way, as in others, Brennan no doubt surprised many of those who were most responsible for his appointment to the Court.

After serving more than three decades as an Associate Justice, Brennan resigned from the Supreme Court in 1990. He will be remembered as one of the most influential Justices in the history of the Court. Throughout his long and distinguished tenure, Brennan unflinchingly championed the rights of the poor, the unrepresented, and the powerless. There were, of course, those who rejected Brennan's vision of the Constitution and who maintained that he too readily mistook his own preferences for the demands of the Constitution, but there can be no doubt that Brennan expressed his unique and powerful vision of the Constitution as "a vital charter of human liberty" with rare eloquence, intelligence, clarity, and courage.

GEOFFREY R. STONE
(1992)

Bibliography

BERGER, RAOUL 1988 Justice Brennan vs. the Constitution. *Boston College Law Review* 29:787–801.

BLASI, V. 1982 *The Burger Court: The Counter-Revolution That Wasn't.* New Haven, Conn.: Yale University Press.

BRENNAN, WILLIAM J., JR. 1977 State Constitutions and the Protection of Individual Rights. *Harvard Law Review* 90:489–504.

———— 1988 Reason, Passion, and the Progress of the Law. *Cardozo Law Review* 10:23–24.

KALVEN, HARRY, JR. 1988 *A Worthy Tradition: Freedom of Speech in America.* New York: Harper & Row.

LEEDS, J. 1986 A Life on the Court. *New York Times Magazine,* October 5, pp. 24–80.

SCHWARTZ, H. 1987 *The Burger Years: Rights and Wrongs in the Supreme Court, 1969–1986.* New York: Viking.

STONE, GEOFFREY R.; SEIDMAN, LOUIS M.; SUNSTEIN, CASS R.; and TUSHNET, MARK V. 1986 *Constitutional Law.* Boston: Little, Brown.

BRENNAN, WILLIAM J., JR.
(1906–1997)
(Update 2)

William Joseph Brennan, Jr., was born to Irish immigrant parents in Newark, New Jersey in 1906. He was graduated near the top of his class at Harvard Law School in 1931, without taking the sole constitutional law course offered at that time. After practicing labor law for a hometown firm, Brennan accepted an appointment to the New Jersey Superior Court in 1949 and was elevated three years later to the state Supreme Court. In October 1956, President DWIGHT D. EISENHOWER offered Brennan a recess appointment to the U.S. Supreme Court, partly because the two men shared a concern about the practical workings of the justice system, and partly because Eisenhower thought appointment of a Catholic Democrat would aid his reelection campaign that year. Brennan served as an Associate Justice until July 20, 1990, a period just shy of thirty-four years spanning parts of five different decades. During this period Brennan wrote over 500 MAJORITY OPINIONS articulating the law of the land.

Generally regarded today as among the handful of greatest jurists ever to grace the Court, Brennan had an almost unparalleled impact on our constitutional jurisprudence. His influence is partly attributable to his lengthy service during a period of tremendous political, social, and cultural transformation; as OLIVER WENDELL HOLMES, JR., once said, "A great man represents . . . a strategic point in the campaign of history, and part of his greatness consists in his being there." But it takes a great and focused man to seize the moment and make his mark. Brennan did so in two ways. First, through opinions both voluminous and visionary, he significantly reconstructed the architecture of constitutional DOCTRINE respecting political and CIVIL RIGHTS. Second, he developed and sustained a progressive methodological approach to interpreting the grand rights-protective phrases of the Constitution, an approach which, although criticized and contested, must be grappled with by subsequent Justices and serious students of the Constitution.

One testament to the doctrinal and social significance of Brennan's jurisprudence is that he often gave differing answers when asked to identify his most important constitutional decision. Perhaps most frequently, he would cite BAKER V. CARR (1962) and its legacy for legislative REAPPORTIONMENT. Previously, the Court had refused to consider claims that unequally populated legislative voting districts violate the Constitution. As Justice FELIX FRANKFURTER had explained in COLEGROVE V. GREEN (1946), such controversies concern "matters that bring courts into immediate and active relations with party contests," and "courts ought not to enter this political thicket." In *Baker*, however, Brennan rejected this reasoning and recognized the JUSTICIABILITY of a claim that the malapportionment of the Tennessee General Assembly violated the rights of voters to EQUAL PROTECTION OF THE LAWS "by virtue of the debasement of their votes." Brennan's opinion for the Court paved the way for REYNOLDS V. SIMS (1964) and its progeny, articulating the now-familiar constitutional principle of ONE PERSON, ONE VOTE, which some claim revolutionized politics in various parts of the country. This principle became a constitutional axiom of democratic governance; spawned further judicial protections against more subtle forms of racial or political vote-dilution; and helped to energize Congress to protect VOTING RIGHTS through federal LEGISLATION.

At other times, Brennan would identify NEW YORK TIMES V. SULLIVAN (1964) as his most significant judicial contribution. At issue in *Sullivan* was Alabama's LIBEL law, which permitted a public official to recover damages for defamatory statements unless the speaker could prove that her pronouncements were true. According to existing case law, libelous statements lacked FIRST AMENDMENT protection and were therefore subject to plenary state regulation. But Brennan rejected this settled doctrine and held that "libel can claim no talismanic immunity from constitutional limitations." For Brennan, the First Amendment reflected a "profound national commitment to the principle that the debate on public issues should be uninhibited, robust, and wide-open," and this commitment was undermined by holding persons who criticize public officials to a rigorous "test of truth." Brennan observed that "erroneous statement is inevitable in free debate, and must be protected if the freedoms of expression are to have the 'breathing space' that they 'need . . . to survive.'" Even false speech about public officials, Brennan concluded, should be immune from libel claims for damages unless uttered "with knowledge that it was false or with

reckless disregard of whether it was false or not." Application of this so-called "actual malice" standard for libel has since been broadened to protect an array of speakers contributing to a rich public debate on matters of public import.

On still other occasions, Brennan would identify GOLDBERG V. KELLY (1970) as his signature achievement on the Court. Previously, the Court had defined the "liberty" and "property" interests protected by the DUE PROCESS clauses by reference to COMMON LAW principles. If government took someone's PROPERTY or invaded her liberty as defined by the common law, due process required some sort of hearing; but no hearing was required for deprivations of public benefits, such as public employment, a license, or welfare. This doctrine seemed increasingly formalistic with the twentieth-century expansion of government employment and largesse. While more and more people grew increasingly dependent on such forms of "new property," prevailing doctrine did not protect against even the most arbitrary withdrawal of governmental benefits. But *Goldberg* dramatically redefined the scope of the interests protected by the due process clauses. Apparently moved by the tragedy of a family incorrectly cut off from its lifeline, Brennan recognized that "much of the existing wealth in this country takes the form of rights that do not fall within traditional common law concepts of property"; so, it is "realistic today to regard welfare entitlements as more like property than a 'gratuity.'" As a result, *Goldberg* held, a state may not terminate public assistance benefits without affording the recipient an evidentiary hearing prior to termination. Brennan's opinion, which envisioned a humanization of bureaucracy, launched a new era in the extension of due process rights. In subsequent decisions the Court extended *Goldberg* to grant due process protection to the termination of public employment, the termination of food stamps, the revocation of parole, the suspension of drivers' licenses, and many similar governmental actions.

Brennan wrote landmark opinions for the Court on many other important issues as well. With respect to equal protection rights, Brennan was heavily involved in the post–BROWN V. BOARD OF EDUCATION (1954) efforts to enforce integrationist remedies to combat entrenched racial school SEGREGATION. For example, in GREEN V. COUNTY SCHOOL BOARD (1968), Brennan rejected the "freedom of choice" plans used to forestall desegregation in the South; in KEYES V. SCHOOL DISTRICT NO. 1 OF DENVER (1973), he articulated a doctrinal rule more relevant for northern school systems establishing a rebuttable presumption that intentional segregation in part of a system infects the whole; and in COOPER V. AARON (1958), he drafted the PER CURIAM opinion proclaiming JUDICIAL SUPREMACY in CONSTITUTIONAL INTERPRETATION and denouncing Southern political resistance to the dictates of *Brown*. Brennan laid the foundation for two decades of ardent support for AFFIRMATIVE ACTION programs in his PLURALITY OPINION in REGENTS OF UNIVERSITY OF CALIFORNIA V. BAKKE (1978), culminating in his short-lived decision in METRO BROADCASTING V. FCC (1990) holding that federal affirmative action programs need not be subjected to the strictest judicial scrutiny. In FRONTIERO V. RICHARDSON (1973) and CRAIG V. BOREN (1976), Brennan led the Court to subject sex-based classifications to a demanding form of "intermediate" judicial scrutiny. With respect to First Amendment rights, Brennan was the architect of the modern OVERBREADTH doctrine in NAACP V. BUTTON (1963) and the modern VAGUENESS doctrine in KEYISHIAN V. BOARD OF REGENTS (1967). At the end of his career he preserved the core meaning of the First Amendment by authoring the controversial 5–4 decisions in *Texas v. Johnson* (1989) and *United States v. Eichman* (1990), which extended constitutional protection to FLAG DESECRATION as an act of political protest. In the realm of criminal justice, Brennan's doctrinal legacy includes not only individually important decisions such as FAY V. NOIA (1963) concerning the scope of the writ of HABEAS CORPUS, but also his successful drive for "selective" INCORPORATION DOCTRINE that made most of the BILL OF RIGHTS applicable to the states, and consequently part of our national political consciousness. Other landmark cases protecting an array of individual's rights include SHERBERT V. VERNER (1963) (RELIGIOUS LIBERTY), KATZENBACH V. MORGAN (1966) (Congress's FOURTEENTH AMENDMENT, SECTION 5 power), SHAPIRO V. THOMPSON (1969) (RIGHT TO TRAVEL), IN RE WINSHIP (1970) (beyond reasonable doubt requirement), BIVENS V. SIX UNKNOWN NAMED AGENTS (1971) (CONSTITUTIONAL REMEDIES), and PENN CENTRAL TRANSPORTATION CO. V. NEW YORK CITY (1978) (REGULATORY TAKINGS). Brennan was also instrumental in drafting the per curiam opinions in BRANDENBURG V. OHIO (1969) (FREEDOM OF SPEECH), and BUCKLEY V. VALEO (1976) (CAMPAIGN FINANCE reform).

These opinions exemplify Brennan's wide-ranging influence over the contemporary constitutional landscape not only for their discrete holdings, but for their articulation of sophisticated doctrinal frameworks that inevitably shaped the presentation and consideration of later cases. Once described as a "virtuoso of doctrine," Brennan carefully crafted tests, rules, and STANDARDS OF REVIEW, and embedded them through repetition to the point where, as Justice DAVID H. SOUTER foretold when he eulogized Brennan, future Justices "in subject after subject of the national law . . . will either accept the inheritance of his thinking, or . . . will have to face him squarely and make good on [their] challenge to him."

Brennan's doctrinal architecture is all the more impressive and formidable because it reflects a coherent and heart-felt substantive vision of the Constitution's grand design: the protection of human dignity. Brennan himself explained that, "As augmented by the Bill of Rights and the Civil War Amendments, this [constitutional] text is a sparkling vision of the supremacy of the human dignity of every individual." This vision explains Brennan's appreciation of *Baker* and its progeny's insistence on fair and participatory governance; he observed that "[r]ecognition of the principle of 'one person, one vote' as a constitutional principle redeems the promise of self-governance by affirming the essential dignity of every citizen in the right to equal participation in the democratic process." Dignity also requires that governments treat individuals with regularity, decency, and respect; these themes emerged throughout Brennan's opinions regarding equality, due process, and criminal justice. Perhaps moved by his own experiences with oppressed laborers and the poor during the Great Depression, Brennan wrote eloquently about the Constitution's proper concern with marginalized individuals for whom the promise of America had yet to be redeemed. And when he finally retired from judicial service, he explained, "It is my hope that the Court during my years of service has built a legacy of interpreting the Constitution and federal laws to make them responsive to the needs of the people whom they were intended to benefit and protect."

One reason for Brennan's remarkable success at translating his substantive visions into constitutional law was his ability to forge case-specific majority coalitions comprised of Justices with differing ideological and methodological views. Brennan was a pragmatic visionary, strategically determining in each case just how far to push his view of the law. He deployed his Irish charm, wit, and winning personality to establish relationships of mutual enjoyment and respect with his associates. But people-skills alone cannot account for his success at forging consensus among colleagues, who themselves were too strong-minded and independent to be cajoled in important cases. Rather, Brennan frequently bridged differences among his colleagues through careful foresight, drafting opinions tactically to accommodate their expected and expressed concerns. As Brennan vividly illustrated to every new set of law clerks by waggling his hand with five fingers extended, he constantly focused on the fact that it takes five agreeing Justices to make PRECEDENT. Thus he was frequently willing to compromise his own views somewhat in order to preserve an opinion of the Court, securing the optimal from within the possible.

This accommodationist strategy was rarely needed during the WARREN COURT era, particularly between 1962 when Justice Felix Frankfurter was replaced by Justice ARTHUR J. GOLDBERG and 1969 when Chief Justice EARL WARREN retired. While the Warren Court's product was shaped by several minds, Brennan frequently crafted the language and rules that transformed principles into law. During the subsequent BURGER COURT era, Brennan became the leader of a fluctuating group of Justices, never a secure majority, who struggled on an issue-by-issue basis to maintain and sometimes even extend the Warren Court legacy. During this period, and even later on the more conservative REHNQUIST COURT, Brennan's savvy coalition-building efforts led to some surprising liberal victories. These ranged from PLYLER V. DOE (1982), a 5–4 decision invalidating a Texas law denying a free public education to children of illegal immigrants, to *Metro Broadcasting*, Brennan's final majority opinion before retirement, a 5–4 decision upholding a race-conscious affirmative action program designed to enhance speaker diversity in BROADCASTING. Moreover, Brennan also worked hard behind the scenes to influence the opinions of his colleagues in cases of enduring significance. For example, in GRISWOLD V. CONNECTICUT (1965), he convinced Justice WILLIAM O. DOUGLAS to rest the invalidation of a law restricting access to BIRTH CONTROL on more expansive RIGHT OF PRIVACY grounds rather than narrower FREEDOM OF ASSOCIATION grounds. And in *Bakke*, he influenced Justice LEWIS F. POWELL to include in his controlling separate opinion an affirmance of RACE-CONSCIOUSNESS as one nondispositive factor in higher education admissions. Thus Brennan used his considerable powers of persuasion, as well as strategic sensitivity, to control outcomes and shape doctrines even on a divided and oft-divisive Court.

In several areas of the law, Brennan was unable to halt the step-by-step dismantling by the Burger and Rehnquist Courts of his earlier doctrinal structures. For example, in cases such as WAINWRIGHT V. SYKES (1977) and *Teague v. Lane* (1989), the Court severely restricted the availability of the writ of habeas corpus as a means of challenging state criminal procedures. In cases such as MCCLESKEY V. KEMP (1987), the Court began to retreat from its earlier promises of stringent judicial enforcement of racial equality. And in *Gregg v. Georgia* (1976) and its progeny, the Court definitively rejected Brennan's claim that CAPITAL PUNISHMENT necessarily constitutes CRUEL AND UNUSUAL PUNISHMENT. In these realms, when Brennan's efforts to form and maintain coalitions failed, he frequently resorted to rigorous and spirited dissent calculated variously to chide his colleagues, prompt congressional reactions, embolden lower courts, and plant the seeds for a future Court turnabout. Indeed, in the death penalty context he eschewed his general accommodationist stance and, along with Justice THURGOOD MARSHALL, stubbornly adhered to his "view that the death penalty is in all circumstances cruel and unusual punishment," well after the Court had rejected this extreme position. Brennan marginalized himself in this line of cases, and some have suggested that his

refusal to wield his consensus-building skills cost him the opportunity to temper the Court's systematic rollback of procedural protections to death-sentenced defendants over the last decade of his tenure.

Brennan's impact on modern constitutional discourse extends beyond the substantive to the methodological. Brennan developed, practiced, and claimed legitimacy for the interpretive principle of a "LIVING CONSTITUTION." This principle entails two commitments. First, constitutional interpretation involves a purposive or functional inquiry: A judge should reflect on the values and ideals underlying the constitutional text; consider how those ideals interact with the practical world; and shape doctrine to best attain those values. Second, given this purposive inquiry, the Constitution's operationalized meaning should change as the needs and demands of society change. As Brennan once explained: "The burden of judicial interpretation is to translate the majestic generalities of the Bill of Rights, conceived as part of the pattern of liberal government in the eighteenth century, into concrete restraints on officials dealing with the problems of the twentieth century. . . . For the genius of the Constitution rests not in any static meaning it might have had in a world that is dead and gone, but in the adaptability of its great principles to cope with current problems and current needs. What the constitutional fundamentals meant to the wisdom of other times cannot be the measure to the vision of our time." For judges to make up new constitutional principles is illegitimate, he conceded, but for judges to adapt old principles to changing conditions is both appropriate and necessary.

Brennan's methodological approach has generated significant controversy, in part because of the apparent subjectivity in this distinction between making up new principles and adapting old ones. The commonplace charge of JUDICIAL ACTIVISM is misplaced; as evidenced by the Rehnquist Court's recent rulings concerning state SOVEREIGNTY and affirmative action, Justices with very different interpretive commitments frequently trump democratic decisions as well. The more serious charge is that, in the process of discerning the values underlying the Constitution's grand structure and vague rights-protective provisions, Brennan inevitably read his own personal values and ideals into the text. While conceding that constitutional interpretation can never be a mechanical enterprise, Brennan's critics accused him of straying too far from the anchors of textual plain meaning and the ORIGINAL INTENT of the Framers such that he essentially remade the Constitution in his own image. As Justice ANTONIN SCALIA has proclaimed, Brennan's approach would measure the validity of democratic decisions "against each Justice's assessment of what is fair and just." Brennan did not shy from such a charge. He candidly defended the importance and indeed necessity of operationalizing the Constitution's broad purposes and ideals in a contemporary context, although he recognized that this translation was necessarily a somewhat subjective exercise. He vehemently denied, however, that his jurisprudence merely imposed his personal value judgments into the Constitution; he viewed himself as interpreting through the lens of modern context the judgments already embedded there. Whether this view is accurate and, more generally, whether implementation of a "living Constitution" fulfills or ignores the duty of fidelity to the design of the Framers are the methodological questions that frame the central controversy in constitutional jurisprudence today. Brennan is thus the archetype of a compelling conception of judging in a modern constitutional democracy.

Upon his retirement, Brennan was at ease with the possibility that many of his specific contributions to constitutional law would be supplanted in the future. The commitments he articulated and rules he crafted were, to his mind, the best possible answers to the particular questions of his time. But given changing societal conditions, technologies, and bureaucratic structures, and his belief that society's view of human dignity "will never cease to evolve," he expected that both the questions and answers of tomorrow would leave those of today behind. Thus, while many of his doctrines will surely survive and influence legal dispositions for generations, others will just as surely be overruled or become irrelevant. But upon his death in 1997 he would have been proud enough of his legacy if future Justices would embrace his commitment to the evolving nature of constitutional meaning, and agree with his view that "the progress of the law depends on a dialogue between heart and head."

EVAN H. CAMINKER
(2000)

(SEE ALSO: *Constitutional History, 1945–1961; Constitutional History, 1961–1977; Constitutional History, 1977–1985; Constitutional History, 1980–1989.*)

Bibliography

BLASI, VINCENT 1982 *The Burger Court: The Counter-Revolution That Wasn't.* New Haven, Conn.: Yale University Press.

BRENNAN, WILLIAM J., JR. 1986 The Constitution of the United States: Contemporary Ratification. *South Texas Law Review* 27:433–445.

——— 1988 Reason, Passion, and "The Progress of the Law." *Cardozo Law Review* 10:3–23.

CLARK, HUNTER R. 1995 *Justice Brennan: The Great Conciliator.* New York: Birch Lane Press.

ROSENKRANZ, E. JOSHUA and SCHWARTZ, BERNARD, eds. 1997 *Reason and Passion: Justice Brennan's Enduring Influence.* New York: W. W. Norton & Company.

SCHWARTZ, BERNARD 1994 "Brennan vs. Rehnquist"—Mirror

Images in Constitutional Construction. *Oklahoma City University Law Review* 19:213–250.

SYMPOSIUM 1990 A Tribute to Justice William J. Brennan, Jr. *Harvard Law Review* 104:1–39.

——— 1997 In Memoriam: William J. Brennan, Jr. *Harvard Law Review* 111:1–50.

BREWER, DAVID J.
(1837–1910)

David Josiah Brewer forged conservative socioeconomic beliefs into constitutional DOCTRINE. From the time he assumed his seat on the Supreme Court in December 1889, Brewer unabashedly relied on judicial power to protect private property rights from the supposed incursions of state and federal legislatures. Through more than 200 DISSENTING OPINIONS, most of which came during his last ten years on the bench, Brewer emerged as the conservative counterpart of the liberal "Great Dissenter," JOHN MARSHALL HARLAN.

Like his uncle, Justice STEPHEN J. FIELD, Brewer moved from moderate liberalism as a state judge to strident conservatism on the federal bench. Increasing doubts about the power of the Kansas legislature to regulate the manufacture and sale of alcohol punctuated his twelve-year career on the state supreme court. Brewer refrained from directly challenging a constitutional amendment that destroyed the livelihood of distillers without compensation, although, in *State v. Mugler* (1883), he expressed serious reservations about it. After President CHESTER A. ARTHUR appointed him to the Eighth Circuit in 1884, Brewer adopted a more aggressive position. He held that Kansas distillers deserved JUST COMPENSATION for losses suffered because of PROHIBITION, a position that the Supreme Court subsequently rejected in MUGLER V. KANSAS (1887).

Brewer's CIRCUIT COURT opinions on railroad rate regulation proved more prophetic. He ignored the Supreme Court's HOLDING in *Munn v. Illinois* (1877) that state legislatures could best judge the reasonableness of rates. (See GRANGER CASES.) Instead, Brewer asserted that judges had to inquire broadly into the reasonableness of rates and to overturn LEGISLATION that failed to yield a FAIR RETURN ON FAIR VALUE of investment.

These views persuaded President BENJAMIN HARRISON to appoint Brewer the fifty-first Justice of the Supreme Court. The new Justice immediately lived up to expectations by contributing to the emerging doctrine of SUBSTANTIVE DUE PROCESS OF LAW. Brewer advocated use of the Fifth Amendment and the FOURTEENTH AMENDMENT to shelter corporate property rights from federal and state legislation. Three months after his appointment he joined the majority in the important case of CHICAGO, MILWAUKEE

AND ST. PAUL RAILWAY COMPANY V. MINNESOTA (1890) in striking down a state statute that did not provide for JUDICIAL REVIEW of rates established by an independent commission. More than other members of the Court, Brewer sought to expand the limits of substantive due process. Two years later, when the Court reaffirmed its *Munn* holding in *Budd v. New York* (1893), Brewer complained in dissent that the public interest doctrine granted too much discretion to the legislature. The Court ultimately accepted his position. In REAGAN V. FARMERS' LOAN AND TRUST COMPANY (1894) he spoke for a unanimous Court in holding that a state legislature could not force a railroad to carry persons or freight without a guarantee of sufficient profit. Brewer dramatically expanded the range of issues that the legislature had to consider when determining profitability, and, in so doing, he broadened the grounds for judicial intervention.

Brewer also applied judicial review to congressional acts. He joined the Court's majority in UNITED STATES V. E. C. KNIGHT COMPANY (1895) in narrowing Congress's power under the COMMERCE CLAUSE. He silently joined the same year with Chief Justice MELVILLE W. FULLER in POLLOCK V. FARMERS' LOAN AND TRUST COMPANY . . . decision that obliterated more than one hundred years of PRECEDENT in favor of a federal income tax.

Brewer's important decision in IN RE DEBS (1895) coupled judicial power and property rights with a sweeping assertion of national power. The *Debs* case stemmed from the actions of the militant American Railway Union and its leader, Eugene V. Debs, in the Pullman strike of 1894. Debs had refused to obey an INJUNCTION granted by a lower federal court in Chicago that ordered the strikers to end their BOYCOTT of Pullman cars. President GROVER CLEVELAND dispatched troops to restore the passage of INTERSTATE COMMERCE and of the mails. The lower federal court then found Debs and other union members in contempt of court and imprisoned them. Debs petitioned the Supreme Court for a writ of HABEAS CORPUS on the ground that the lower court had exceeded its EQUITY power in issuing the injunction and that the subsequent EX PARTE contempt proceedings had resulted in conviction of a criminal offense without benefit of the procedural guarantees of the criminal law.

Brewer brushed aside Debs's claims with an opinion that blended morality, national supremacy, and the sanctity of private property. In JOHN MARSHALL-like strokes he concluded that the Constitution granted Congress ample power to oversee interstate commerce and the delivery of the mails. The President had acted properly in dispatching federal troops to quell the strikers, because the Constitution had pledged the power of the national government to preserve the social and economic order. The courts, Brewer concluded, had to protect property rights and this included the use of the CONTEMPT POWER to punish persons who refused to abide by injunctions. He disingenuously admonished Debs to seek social change through the ballot box.

Brewer in the post-*Debs* era retreated into STRICT CONSTRUCTION. This narrowing of his constitutional jurisprudence occurred at a time when most of the other Justices embraced the moderate middle class reformist ethos of the Progressive movement. Brewer, Chief Justice Fuller, and Justice RUFUS PECKHAM emerged as the conservative right wing of the Court.

Brewer disparaged Congress's resort to ENUMERATED POWERS to accomplish purposes not originally contemplated by the Framers. This contrasted sharply with his opinion in *Debs*. He dissented with Chief Justice Fuller in CHAMPION V. AMES (1903) on the ground that an act of Congress regulating interstate sale of lottery tickets threatened to destroy the TENTH AMENDMENT. More than issues of FEDERALISM troubled Brewer; his opinion reflected a socioeconomic agenda aimed at protecting property rights. In *South Carolina v. United States* (1905) he spoke for the Court in holding that the federal government could place an internal revenue tax on persons selling liquor, even though those persons acted merely as agents for the state. Brewer argued that state involvement, free from the federal TAXING POWER, in private business would lead inexorably to public ownership of important segments of the economy.

Brewer championed the concept of FREEDOM OF CONTRACT. He first articulated it for the Court in *Frisbie v. United States* (1895), and he joined with the majority two years later in ALLGEYER V. LOUISIANA when it struck down a Louisiana law affecting out-of-state insurance sales. Although the Court subsequently applied the concept unevenly, Brewer dogmatically clung to it. Between HOLDEN V. HARDY (1898) and *McLean v. Arkansas* (1909), Brewer routinely opposed state and federal laws designed to regulate labor. The single exception was MULLER V. OREGON (1908), and Brewer's opinion for a unanimous Court in that case ironically contributed to the new liberalism of the Progressive era.

LOUIS D. BRANDEIS in *Muller* submitted a massive brief based on extensive documentary evidence about the health and safety of women workers. It openly appealed to judicial discretion, and Brewer took the opportunity to infuse his long-held views of the dependent condition of women into constitutional doctrine. He denied an absolute right of liberty of contract; instead he concluded that under particular circumstances state legislatures might intervene in the workplace. The supposed physical disabilities of women provided the mitigating circumstances that made the Oregon ten-hour law constitutional. He emphatically argued that the Court had not retreated from substantive due process. Nevertheless, the *Muller* decision and the BRANDEIS BRIEF encouraged constitutional litigation that three decades later shattered Brewer's most cherished conservative values.

The son of a Congregationalist minister and missionary, Brewer never lost touch with his Puritan sense of character and obligation. His jurisprudence forcefully, although naively, proclaimed that material wealth and human progress went hand in hand.

KERMIT L. HALL
(1986)

Bibliography

CRAMER, RALPH E. 1965 Justice Brewer and Substantive Due Process: A Conservative Court Revisited. *Vanderbilt Law Review* 18:61–96.

PAUL, ARNOLD M. 1969 David J. Brewer. Pages 1515–1549 in Leon Friedman and Fred L. Israel, eds., *The Justices of the Supreme Court, 1789–1969.* New York: Chelsea House.

BREWER v. WILLIAMS
430 U.S. 378 (1977)

This highly publicized case produced three concurring and three dissenting opinions and Justice POTTER STEWART's opinion for a 5–4 majority. Williams, who had kidnapped and murdered a child, was being transported by police who had read the MIRANDA RULES to him. But the police played on his religious beliefs. Although they had agreed not to interrogate him and he had declared that he wanted the assistance of counsel and would tell his story on seeing his counsel, a detective convinced him to show where he had buried the body so that the child could have a Christian burial. The Court reversed his conviction, ruling that the use of EVIDENCE relating to or resulting from his incriminating statements violated his RIGHT OF COUNSEL once adversary proceedings against him had begun, and he had not waived his right. (See NIX V. WILLIAMS.)

LEONARD W. LEVY
(1986)

BREWSTER v. UNITED STATES
408 U.S. 501 (1972)

A 6–3 Supreme Court held that the SPEECH OR DEBATE CLAUSE does not protect a United States senator from prosecution for accepting a bribe in return for a vote on pending legislation. The clause, said Chief Justice WARREN E. BURGER, only forbids inquiry into legislative acts or the motives behind those acts. Justices WILLIAM J. BRENNAN and WILLIAM O. DOUGLAS attacked the majority's distinction between money-taking and voting and joined Justice BYRON R. WHITE who contended that the only issue was the proper forum for the trial.

DAVID GORDON
(1986)

BREYER, STEPHEN G.
(1938–   )

Stephen G. Breyer came to the Supreme Court in 1994 with a well-developed judicial philosophy. It was not a completely formed constitutional philosophy, for his career had largely been spent outside the constitutional field.

Born in San Francisco in 1938, Breyer was graduated from Stanford University in 1959 and spent two years as a Marshall scholar at Oxford University. He was graduated from Harvard Law School in 1964, after which he clerked for Justice ARTHUR J. GOLDBERG and spent two years in the ANTITRUST division of the U.S. Department of Justice. From 1967 to 1980 he taught at Harvard Law School, specializing in antitrust and administrative law. Breyer also served as a prosecutor on the WATERGATE special prosecution in 1973 and, in 1974, as special counsel to the U.S. SENATE subcommittee on administrative practice and procedures, chaired by Senator Edward M. Kennedy. As chief counsel to the SENATE JUDICIARY COMMITTEE in 1979 he crafted the LEGISLATION that led to the deregulation of the airline industry.

In 1980 Breyer was appointed to the U.S. Court of Appeals for the First Circuit; he became its chief judge in 1990. Sitting on the federal judicial moon, he necessarily reflected the sun of Supreme Court PRECEDENT. Breyer deferred to ADMINISTRATIVE AGENCY decisions and tended to interpret statutory provisions narrowly. He was one of the original members of the United States Sentencing Commission that in 1987 promulgated controversial federal SENTENCING guidelines. Breyer conceived the idea of a numerical framework that all federal judges would have to apply.

In 1994 President WILLIAM J. CLINTON nominated Breyer to replace the retiring Justice HARRY A. BLACKMUN. The Senate easily confirmed him, and on August 11, 1994, Breyer took his seat as the nation's 108th Supreme Court Justice. He joined a Court that generally supported both FREEDOM OF SPEECH claims and STATES' RIGHTS. It was more skeptical of federal authority than any Court in recent history. At the same time it believed more in neutrality than in equality, particularly in RACIAL DISCRIMINATION and AFFIRMATIVE ACTION cases.

He dissented from the Court's opinion in UNITED STATES V. LÓPEZ (1995), invalidating the Gun-Free School Zone

Act of 1990 on the ground that Congress failed to show that the possession of a gun in school "substantially affects" INTERSTATE COMMERCE. Breyer agreed that Congress must have evidence that "gun- related violence near the classroom poses a serious economic threat" to interstate commerce. "The Constitution requires us to judge the connection between a regulated activity and interstate commerce," but "at one remove." In a lengthy appendix Breyer listed reports and studies from which Congress "could reasonably have found the empirical connection that its law, implicitly or explicitly, asserts."

Breyer has aptly been called "a skeptical friend of government regulation." In his 1993 book, *Breaking the Vicious Cycle*, he charged that the regulatory process wasted both government and private resources and also diverted attention away from true health and environmental concerns. Breyer called for the establishment of a corps of elite civil servants that would have broad discretion to make "common-sense" decisions about regulation. In *Kumho Tire Co. v. Carmichael* (1999), he expanded the trial judge's general "gate-keeping" obligation set forth in *Daubert v. Merrell Dow Pharmaceuticals I* (1993) to apply to testimony "based on 'technical' and 'other specialized' knowledge."

Denver Area Education Telecommunications Consortium v. FCC (1996) is Breyer's major FIRST AMENDMENT effort to date. Writing for the Court, he explicitly refused to select a definitive level of scrutiny or category of cases in which to place free speech regulations of indecent material on cable television. He based this refusal on the dynamic nature of telecommunications and BROADCASTING technology. Any decision, Breyer concluded, would likely be based on assumptions that further innovation would quickly render obsolete.

Questions of EXECUTIVE POWER have been prominent during Breyer's tenure. In his concurrence in CLINTON V. JONES (1997), which verges on a qualified dissent, he agreed with the Court that the Constitution does not automatically grant the President immunity from civil suits based on his private conduct. But Breyer noted that once a trial of the President is scheduled, it can only be held when it does not "interfere with the President's discharge of his public duties." The LINE-ITEM VETO law did not violate any SEPARATION OF POWERS issue, Breyer wrote in dissent in *Clinton v. New York* (1998). It was an "experiment" of "representative government" that did not "threaten the liberties of individual citizens."

Breyer's opinions flow easily, frequently stating the issue or the relevant statute or regulation at the outset. In 1982 he stopped using footnotes, returning to an older style that incorporates all sources into the text. His opinions do not evince an overall view of human nature. Suspicious of overarching theories, Breyer decides the case

at hand, giving some guidance for the future while declining to reach out to embrace broader principles. He takes a more lenient view than the majority's as to the JUSTICIABILITY requirement. Dissenting in *Raines v. Byrd* (1997), he would have narrowed the inquiry to whether the plaintiffs' status as members of Congress brought an otherwise justiciable controversy outside the scope of Article III.

Breyer has written in several cases involving prisoners. In *Richardson v. McKnight* (1997) he wrote for the Court that prison guards who are employees of a private prison management company are not entitled to qualified immunity from suits by prisoners. Dissenting from the Court's upholding, in *Kansas v. Hendricks* (1997), a law providing for the involuntary commitment of violent sexual predators, Breyer emphasized the law's concern for treatment as the most relevant factor in distinguishing a punitive from a nonpunitive purpose. He urged the Court, in a sole dissent from a denial of certiorari in *Elledge v. Florida* (1998), to hear the appeal of a prisoner who spent more than twenty-three years in prison on death row. The prisoner's claim, "argue[d] forcefully," is "a serious one," given the Eighth Amendment's prohibition against CRUEL AND UNUSUAL PUNISHMENTS, Breyer wrote.

Befitting his background, Breyer has long criticized the "textual" approach to STATUTORY INTERPRETATION championed by Justice ANTONIN SCALIA. Judges, he said in 1984, should interpret a statute "in light of what its purpose must have been," and legislative history must be used to determine this. As he opened his concurring– dissenting opinion in *Schenck v. Pro Choice Network* (1997), "Words take on meaning in context."

"Economics alone," Breyer has written, "cannot prescribe how much a society should spend." Shortly before he went on the Court, he stated his philosophy of judging: "The law is supposed to fit together in a way that makes the human life of people a little bit better."

ROGER K. NEWMAN
(2000)

BRICKER AMENDMENT
(1952)

Senator John Bricker of Ohio in 1952 introduced a proposed constitutional amendment designed to limit the TREATY POWER and the President's power to make EXECUTIVE AGREEMENTS. The proposal was an outgrowth of widespread isolationist sentiment following the KOREAN WAR, and of fear of the possible consequences of the DOCTRINE of MISSOURI V. HOLLAND (1920) when combined with the United Nations Charter or the so-called Universal Declaration of Human Rights. The amendment, as introduced, would have declared that "a provision of a treaty or other international agreement which conflicts with this Constitution shall not be of any force or effect," and would have prohibited "self-executing" treaties by requiring separate, independently valid congressional action before a treaty could have force as "internal law."

President DWIGHT D. EISENHOWER opposed the Bricker Amendment, arguing that it would make effective conduct of FOREIGN AFFAIRS impossible and deprive the President "of his historic position as the spokesman for the nation." In February 1954, the Senate defeated the Bricker Amendment, and later it failed by one vote to give the required two-thirds approval to a weaker version written by Senator Walter F. George.

DENNIS J. MAHONEY
(1986)

BRIDGES v. CALIFORNIA
TIMES-MIRROR CO. v. CALIFORNIA
314 U.S. 252 (1941)

In these two companion cases, handed down by the Supreme Court on the same day, a bare majority of five Justices overturned exercises of the CONTEMPT POWER against Harry Bridges, a left-wing union leader, and the *Los Angeles Times*, then a bastion of the state's conservative business establishment, for their out-of-court remarks concerning pending cases. Bridges had been found in contempt for a telegram that predicted a longshoreman's strike in the event of a judicial decree hostile to his union; the *Times* had been punished for an editorial that threatened a judge with political reprisals if he showed leniency toward convicted labor racketeers.

Justice HUGO L. BLACK's majority opinion, joined by Justices WILLIAM O. DOUGLAS, FRANK MURPHY, STANLEY F. REED, and ROBERT H. JACKSON, held that both the telegram and the editorial had been protected by the FIRST AMENDMENT via the DUE PROCESS clause of the FOURTEENTH AMENDMENT against abridgment by the states; neither pronouncement constituted a CLEAR AND PRESENT DANGER to the administration of criminal justice in California courts. Justice FELIX FRANKFURTER, writing for himself and three others, dissented.

Frankfurter's dissent represented the original majority view when the cases were first argued in the spring of 1941. But the defection of Justice Murphy over the summer and the later addition of Justice Jackson produced a new majority for Black by October when the two cases were reargued.

MICHAEL E. PARRISH
(1986)

BRIEF

Although the term may refer to a number of different kinds of legal documents, in American usage a "brief" ordinarily is a written summary of arguments presented by counsel to a court, and particularly to an appellate court. In the Supreme Court, counsel file briefs only after the Court has granted review of the case. Counsel's first opportunity to acquaint the Court with arguments in the case thus comes in the filing of a petition for a WRIT OF CERTIORARI (or, in the case of an APPEAL, a "jurisdictional statement"), and the papers opposing such a petition. By rule the Court prescribes the length and form of briefs, requires that they be printed (unless a party is permitted to proceed IN FORMA PAUPERIS, as one who cannot afford certain costs), and sets the number of copies to be filed. By the time of ORAL ARGUMENT, the Justices normally have had full opportunity to read and analyze the briefs (including reply briefs) of counsel for the parties and also for any AMICI CURIAE. At or after the argument, the Court may ask counsel to file supplemental briefs on certain issues.

KENNETH L. KARST
(1986)

(SEE ALSO: *Brandeis Brief.*)

Bibliography

STERN, ROBERT L. and GRESSMAN, EUGENE 1978 *Supreme Court Practice*, 5th ed. Chaps. 6–7. Washington, D.C.: Bureau of National Affairs.

BRINEGAR v. UNITED STATES
338 U.S. 160 (1949)

In *Brinegar* the Supreme Court reaffirmed and broadened the rule in CARROLL V. UNITED STATES (1925) authorizing search of an automobile on the road where PROBABLE CAUSE exists to believe it contains contraband. The Court ignored the lack of congressional authorization for the WARRANTLESS SEARCH, a factor present, and emphasized, in *Carroll*.

JACOB W. LANDYNSKI
(1986)

BRISCOE v. BANK OF
COMMONWEALTH OF KENTUCKY
11 Peters 257 (1837)

This is one of the cases decided by the Supreme Court during the first term that ROGER B. TANEY was Chief Justice, and the decision panicked conservatives into the belief that the constitutional restraints which the MARSHALL COURT imposed on the states no longer counted. The case was decided during a depression year when an acute shortage of currency existed. Kentucky authorized a bank, which was state-owned and -operated, to issue notes that circulated as currency. Justice JOSEPH STORY made a powerful argument that the state notes violated the constitutional injunction against state BILLS OF CREDIT, but he spoke in lonely dissent. The Court, by a 6–1 vote, sustained the act authorizing the state bank notes. Justice JOHN MCLEAN, for the majority, assumed that the clause prohibiting bills of credit did not apply to notes not issued on the faith of a state by a CORPORATION chartered by the state. McLean's weak argument was dictated by the practical need for an expansion of the circulating medium. Economics rather than law governed the case.

LEONARD W. LEVY
(1986)

BRITISH CONSTITUTION

Most eighteenth-century Englishmen believed that they were the freest people in the world. Foreign observers, such as MONTESQUIEU and Voltaire from France or Jean-Louis De Lolme from Geneva, concurred. Great Britain had somehow created and protected a unique heritage—a CONSTITUTION—that combined liberty with stability. This constitution was no single document nor even a collection of basic texts, although MAGNA CARTA, the BILL OF RIGHTS of 1689, and other prominent documents were fundamental to the tradition. It depended as much upon a series of informal understandings within the ruling class as upon the written word. And it worked. It "insures, not only the liberty, but the general satisfaction in all respects, of those who are subject to it," affirmed De Lolme. This "consideration alone affords sufficient ground to conclude without looking farther," he believed, "that it is also much more likely to be preserved from ruin." Not everyone agreed. English radicals insisted by the 1770s that only electoral reform and a reduction of royal patronage could preserve British liberty much longer. A vigorous press, the most open in Europe, subjected ministers to constant and often scathing criticism, which a literate and growing public thoroughly enjoyed. Yet until late in the prerevolutionary crisis of 1763–1775, North Americans shared the general awe for the British constitution and frequently insisted that their provincial governments displayed the same virtues.

Apologists explained Britain's constitutional achievement in both legal and humanistic terms. The role of "mixed government" in preserving liberty appealed to a broad audience. Even lawyers used this theme to organize a bewildering mass of otherwise disparate information drawn from the COMMON LAW, parliamentary statutes, and administrative practice. "And herein indeed consists the true excellence of the English government, that all parts of it form a mutual check upon each other," proclaimed Britain's foremost jurist, Sir WILLIAM BLACKSTONE, in 1765. "In the legislature, the people are a check upon the nobility, and the nobility a check upon the people; . . . while the king is a check upon both, which preserves the executive power from encroachment. And this very executive power is again checked, and kept within due bounds by the two houses. . . ."

To work properly, mixed government (or a "mixed and balanced constitution") had to embody the basic elements of the social order: the crown, consisting not just of the monarch but of the army and navy, the law courts, and all other officeholders with royal appointments; the titled aristocracy with its numerous retainers and clients; and land-holding commoners. Each had deep social roots, a fixed place in government, and the power to protect itself from the others. United as king, lords, and commons (or as the one, the few, and the many of classical thought), they became a sovereign power beyond which there was no appeal except to revolution, as American colonists reluctantly admitted by 1775.

Although the king could do no wrong, his ministers could. Every royal act had to be implemented by a minister who could be held legally accountable for what he did. Into the early eighteenth century, this principle generated frequent IMPEACHMENTS, a cumbersome device for attempting to achieve responsible government. By mid-century, impeachment, like the royal veto, had fallen into disuse. Crown patronage had become so extensive that a parliamentary majority hostile to the government almost never occurred in the century after the Hanoverian Succession of 1714. When it did, or even when it merely seemed inevitable, as against Sir Robert Walpole in 1742 and Lord North in 1782, the minister usually resigned, eliminating the need for more drastic measures. When William Pitt the Younger refused to resign in the face of an implacably hostile commons majority in 1783–1784, his pertinacity alarmed many contemporaries. It seemed to portend a major crisis of the constitution until Pitt vindicated himself with a crushing victory in the general election of 1784.

British CONSTITUTIONALISM took for granted a thoroughly aristocratic society. Mixed government theory rested upon the recognition of distinct social orders, linked in countless ways through patron-client relationships. Its boast, that it provided a government of laws and not of men, had real merit, which an independent judiciary assiduously sustained. In like manner the House of Commons really did check the ambitions of the crown.

The quest for responsible ministers still had not reached its nineteenth-century pattern of cabinet government, but it had moved a long way from the seventeenth-century reliance upon impeachment.

The Revolution converted American patriots from warm admirers to critics of British constitutionalism. Some, such as Carter Braxton of Virginia, hoped to change the British model as little as possible. Others, especially THOMAS PAINE, denounced the entire system of mixed government as decadent and corrupt, fit only for repudiation. Most Americans fell between these extremes. They agreed that they needed formal written constitutions. In drafting them, they discovered the necessity for other innovations. Lacking fixed social orders, they simply could not sustain a mixed government. Patron-client relations were also much weaker among the Americans, who had come to regard most crown patronage as inevitably corrupt, a sign of the decay of English liberty. Americans built governments with no organic roots in European social orders. In nearly every state, they separated the government into distinct branches—legislative, executive, and judicial—to keep each behaving legally and correctly. The SEPARATION OF POWERS thus became the American answer to the mixed and balanced constitution. This rejection of government by king, lords and commons led inexorably to a redefinition of SOVEREIGNTY as well. Americans removed sovereignty from government and lodged it with the people instead. To give this distinction substance, they invented the CONSTITUTIONAL CONVENTION and the process of popular ratification. This transformation made true FEDERALISM possible. So long as sovereignty remained an attribute of government, it had to belong to one level or the other— to Parliament or the colonial legislatures. But once it rested with the people, they became free to grant some powers to the states and others to a central government. In 1787–1788, they finally took that step.

JOHN M. MURRIN
(1986)

Bibliography

BLACKSTONE, WILLIAM   (1765–1769) 1979   *Commentaries on the Laws of England,* ed. by Stanley N. Katz et al. Chicago: University of Chicago Press.

BREWER, JOHN   1976   *Party Ideology and Popular Politics at the Accession of George III.* Cambridge: At the University Press.

DE LOLME, J. L.   1775   The Constitution of England, or An Account of the English Government; In which it is compared with the Republican Form of Government, and occasionally with the other Monarchies in Europe. London: T. Spilsbury for G. Kearsley.

POCOCK, J. G. A.   1975   *The Machiavellian Moment: Florentine Political Thought and the Atlantic Republican Tradition.* Princeton, N.J.: Princeton University Press.

ROBERTS, CLAYTON   1966   *The Growth of Responsible Government in Stuart England.* Cambridge: At the University Press.

BROADCASTING

Broadcasting is the electronic transmission of sounds or images from a single transmitter to all those who have the appropriate receiving equipment. It is thus a powerful medium for communicating ideas, information, opinions, and entertainment. In many countries broadcasting has become an arm of government. In the United States, however, Congress established the Federal Radio Commission in 1927 and then the Federal Communications Commission (FCC) in 1934 to award broadcasting licenses to private parties. Although a number of licenses were also designated for "public broadcasting," most were allocated to qualified applicants who promised to serve the public interest by acting as public trustees of the airwaves.

The asserted basis for government intervention in the United States was, initially, to eliminate the interference created when many different parties broadcast over the same frequency in the same area. Yet this chaos could have been eliminated with a mere registration requirement and the application of property rights concepts, allocating broadcast licenses by deed, as land is allocated. Instead, the potential interference was used to justify a complex and comprehensive regulatory scheme, embodied in the COMMUNICATIONS ACT of 1934.

In 1952, the FCC established a pattern of allocating television licenses to ensure that the maximum number of local communities would be served by their own local broadcast stations, a departure from the more centralized broadcasting systems of most other countries. Although this decision has added additional voices of local news in many communities, most local television stations affiliated with national networks to share the cost of producing programs of higher technical quality. Thus, while broadcast regulation always has been premised on the primacy of these local outlets, much of it has focused on the relationship between local stations and the powerful national broadcasting networks.

Government regulation of broadcasting obviously presents dangers to the FREEDOM OF SPEECH. Notwithstanding a statutory prohibition on censorship in the Communications Act, the existence of the licensing scheme has significantly influenced the content of programs. Holders of valuable licenses are careful not to offend the FCC, lest they jeopardize their chances of a license renewal. Raised eyebrows and stated concerns about aspects of content prevent station management from acting as freely as newspapers or magazines do. (See FAIRNESS DOCTRINE.) Indeed, only in the last quarter-century have broadcasters come to understand the dominant role that they can play in the distribution of news and information in the United States.

Until recently, the distinct constitutional status of broadcast regulation was premised on the assumption that only a limited number of broadcasting frequencies existed and on the right of the federal government to insure that this scarce commodity was used in the public interest. But recent technological developments have belied this basis for special intervention. Clearly, policy and not physics created the scarcity of frequencies, and now that economic conditions have made alternative media practical, the FCC has begun to open the broadcasting spectrum to new entrants, such as direct broadcast satellites, low-power television, and microwave frequencies.

Nevertheless, in FCC v. PACIFICA FOUNDATION (1978) the Supreme Court suggested that the extraordinary impact of broadcasting on society is itself a possible basis for special rules, at least during hours when children are likely to be listening and watching. This rationale appears to be the only remaining basis for giving broadcasting special constitutional treatment. Technology is rendering obsolete all other distinctions between broadcasting and printed material. For the receiver of ideas at a home console, all manner of data—words and hard copy and soft images—will come through the atmosphere, or over cables, or both. Distinctions based on the mode of delivery of information will have less and less validity. FCC efforts to repeal broadcast regulations, however, have often met with congressional disapproval.

MONROE E. PRICE
(1986)

(SEE ALSO: *Columbia Broadcasting System, Inc. v. Federal Communications Commission.*)

Bibliography

COASE, R. H. 1959 The Federal Communications Commission. *Journal of Law & Economics* 2:1–40.

BROADCASTING
(Update 1)

From its inception in the early days of commercial radio, federal regulation of the broadcast industry has rested on three policies that are not always compatible: (1) competition among broadcasters; (2) a fiduciary duty to serve the public interest; and (3) the promotion of local needs and interests. From the FAIRNESS DOCTRINE to the allocation of television licenses, broadcast regulation represented a conscious effort to maximize the public welfare by providing essential information and to encourage national diversity through the celebration of local uniqueness. In the name of the public interest standard of the COMMUNICATIONS ACT of 1934, broadcasters have been characterized as owing fiduciary obligations to their audiences—with the Federal Communications Commission (FCC) and then the courts as appropriate bodies to enforce the trust. The goal of assuring local, public-interest programming, however, is built on theoretical foundations that weaken significantly when it must confront the economic forces and consumer choices that underlie the policy of relying on competition.

The linchpin of broadcast regulation is limited entry by government license, reinforcing an idea of scarcity that has convinced decision makers that broadcasting is so different from the print media that it may be regulated in ways that would be unconstitutional if applied to a newspaper. From *NBC v. United States* (1943) to RED LION BROADCASTING CO. V. FCC (1969), to COLUMBIA BROADCASTING SYSTEM, INC. V. FEDERAL COMMUNICATIONS COMMISSION (1981), the Supreme Court has concluded that the broadcast spectrum is an inherently limited resource. Because this conclusion justifies distinguishing broadcasting from print, the Court must implicitly conclude that newsprint, printing presses, and therefore the print media in general, are not inherently limited. Thus, the Court has noted that more people want broadcast licenses than can have them, without ever pausing to note that the reason for excess demand is that broadcast licenses are highly valuable yet given away free. If the facilities for publishing major newspapers were given away free, there would also be more individuals who wish them than could have them. Essentially the Court has seen broadcasters as competing only against other local broadcasters providing the same service, but print outlets as competing against every other print possibility in the world. After being the last bastion for the belief in broadcast scarcity, the Court signaled in *FCC v. League of Women Voters of California* (1984) that if Congress or the FCC would say that broadcasting was no longer scarce, it, too, would agree.

As notions of scarcity were losing their former intellectual force, the FCC ceased a variety of policies that limited direct competition with broadcasting. Beginning with a deregulatory period in the late 1970s, policies brought broadcasters under increasing competition, not only from UHF stations that had been marginal but, more important, from two other sources: (1) an unshackled cable industry that was able to exceed fifty percent household penetration by the late 1980s; and (2) videocassette recorders, which, being outside the jurisdiction of the FCC, rapidly became standard household items in the 1980s. Because of increased competition, broadcasters could no longer assume they could reap monopoly profits and then assert that they would use some of the excess revenues to air the sort of public-interest programming that appeals far more to the FCC than to local audiences. These changes in the marketplace brought many of the key assumptions about broadcasting into question. Nowhere was this more apparent than with the fairness doctrine, the talisman of broadcaster as fiduciary.

The fairness doctrine mandates that broadcasters give adequate coverage to significant public issues and ensure that such coverage fairly presents conflicting views on those issues. Held constitutional in *Red Lion*, the fairness doctrine encapsulates a journalistic code of ethics to which most reporters and publishers in all media profess allegiance. Nevertheless, as the Court unanimously held in MIAMI HERALD PUBLISHING COMPANY V. TORNILLO (1974), in all other media the idea of fairness is enforced internally rather than by the legal system. For the nonbroadcast media the FIRST AMENDMENT mandates that the government leave issues of fairness to editors and readers, not to judges.

The fairness doctrine allows legal challenges to broadcasters who present controversial programming. Even if the challenges ultimately fail, the questioning of editorial decisions (where the law mandates that the editor answer) not only imposes time and legal costs but also carries the dim possibility of loss of license. There are no similar costs for avoiding controversy, and everyone agrees that is what some broadcasters do. This is precisely the behavior that the CHILLING EFFECT doctrine would predict. *Red Lion* had denied the existence of a chilling effect because the fairness doctrine fit so perfectly within the premises of broadcast regulation, but in the years following *Red Lion*, accented by President RICHARD M. NIXON's attitudes toward the networks as the most visible example of the hated media establishment, the chill became so obvious that it was a major part of the FCC's decision to repeal the doctrine in 1985.

The FCC's repeal was attacked on two fronts. Congress passed legislation codifying the fairness doctrine, but President RONALD REAGAN's veto, on constitutional grounds, was sustained. Similarly the District of Columbia Circuit Court of Appeals, relying on the alternative that the fairness doctrine no longer served the public interest, affirmed the repeal and the Supreme Court denied CERTIORARI in early 1990. Congressional Democrats, however, remain wedded to the fairness doctrine because they confuse its name with its effects and are pressured by constituency groups that view the potential of acquiring airtime as overriding any adverse effects the doctrine might have. As long as the majority party in Congress holds this position, it is likely that the fairness doctrine will be imposed legislatively and the Supreme Court will be forced to settle the constitutional question.

It is conceivable, although unlikely, that the Supreme Court could cling to scarcity as the explanation for the constitutional distinction between print and broadcasting. More likely, however, the Court would either concede there are no relevant constitutional distinctions or fashion a new one, as it did to sustain the regulation of indecency in FEDERAL COMMUNICATIONS COMMISSION V. PACIFICA FOUNDATION (1978). *Pacifica* concluded that broadcasting could be regulated differently because its unique pervasiveness made it an uninvited intruder in the home and in any event it was uniquely accessible to children. Pervasiveness could be the Court's echo of the more common, if unexplained, conclusion that broadcasting is too powerful a force not to be regulated. Although this explanation is antithetical to the First Amendment because of its similarities to the rationale for regulating the press under the English COMMON LAW, power is nevertheless the most likely surviving rationale for treating broadcasting differently. The rationale might be made more platable by a suggestion that broadcasting had obtained its power because of its privileged monopoly status under federal law, so that continued regulation would be both essential and constitutional.

Whatever may be the answer to the constitutional question of the status of over-the-air broadcasting, the answer's importance, if and when it is given, may be largely historical, given the increasing dominance and penetration of cable with its more numerous viewing options. Once a poor stepchild whose growth was hindered by the FCC to benefit broadcasters, by the 1980s cable had become a major force in communications policy. The Cable Communications Policy Act of 1983, a compromise between the cable industry and the National League of Cities, has set the terms of the current debate by allowing cities to select their own (typically monopolistic) franchisees, but freeing cable from most regulations, especially rate regulation, to which it had formerly been subject. The result has been a predictable escalation in the price for cable service, which too often is accompanied by poor service. This combination has led to increasing calls for reregulation. This development places legislative compromises back at issue and makes it increasingly likely that the Court will have to decide where cable fits into the constitutional scheme of FREEDOM OF THE PRESS.

Franchising is the key issue in cable. Almost every city has preferred to grant an exclusive franchise to the operator of its choice, which thereafter enjoys a monopoly. Initially perceived as in the cities' interest by guaranteeing service (and as a patronage plum), the monopoly franchise is increasingly recognized as having the attributes of monopolies everywhere: a poor product at an excessive price. Yet fears remain that allowing unlimited entry may allow a cable company to skim the cream from the best areas (typically high-density residential areas with customers who can pay), leaving other areas of the city with little or no service.

The answer to exclusive franchises and to subsidiary issues such as rate regulation or requiring a cable system to dedicate a fixed number of no-user-cost access channels over which it has no program control will probably turn on how the Supreme Court chooses to conceptualize cable. In *Los Angeles v. Preferred Communications* (1986), the Court ducked a constitutional decision on exclusive franchising, but three options seem dominant: the broadcast model, the print model, and a hybrid of the two. The last, in keeping with recent jurisprudence that every medium is "a law unto itself," would allow the Court to make up rules that strike a majority as sensible as each case arises. The Court's confidence in its ability to tailor constitutional doctrine to the needs and attributes of a new medium of mass communication harkens back to similar ill-fated hopes for its constitutional treatment of broadcasting.

L. A. POWE, JR.
(1992)

Bibliography

KRATTENMAKER, THOMAS G. 1985 The Fairness Doctrine Today. *Duke Law Journal* 1985:151–176.

POWE, LUCAS A., JR. 1987 *American Broadcasting and the First Amendment.* Berkeley: University of California Press.

SPITZER, MATTHEW 1989 The Constitutionality of Broadcast Licensing. *New York University Law Review* 64:990–1071.

BROADCASTING
(Update 2)

The contours of modern U.S. broadcast regulation were set in RED LION BROADCASTING CO. V. FCC (1969), in which the Supreme Court upheld the FAIRNESS DOCTRINE, which required licensees to cover controversial issues of public importance and provide a reasonable opportunity for the presentation of opposing points of view. The Court explained that in order to avoid interference on the airwaves, a government agency had to limit the number of broadcast speakers. Because only a lucky few could be licensed to broadcast, the government could require those few to act as trustees or fiduciaries on behalf of the larger excluded community, and obligate them to present views, representative of the community, that otherwise would have no broadcasting outlet. Where it received mutually exclusive applications for a single initial broadcast license, the Federal Communications Commission (FCC) held comparative hearings to ensure that it selected the applicant that would best serve the "public interest."

Congress, the courts, and the FCC have moved away from the *Red Lion* model in important respects. The FCC repealed the fairness doctrine in 1987. It held its last comparative hearing in 1994; since 1998, it has resolved those conflicts by auctions.

Yet it remains plain that broadcasting today is not governed by the same FIRST AMENDMENT rules as print. Congress reemphasized in the Telecommunications Act of 1996 that broadcasters retain an obligation—not shared by speakers in other media—to serve the public interest, convenience, and necessity. The FCC has given that obligation life in its children's programming rules. President WILLIAM J. CLINTON appointed a blue-chip advisory body to explore the public-interest obligations that might be imposed on digital broadcasters—which is to say, all television broadcasters after the year 2006. Congress has required direct satellite broadcasters providing video programming to reserve a portion of their channel capacity for noncommercial educational or information programming. None of this is remotely consistent with the print model for regulation of speech. The Court, however, has shown little interest in reexamining broadcasting's special regulatory status.

Regulatory arrangements for cable television, by contrast, have come under sharp constitutional attack. Lower courts have split over whether franchising authorities may, consistently with the First Amendment, require cable operators to provide public, educational, and governmental access channels, or to satisfy technical requirements such as channel capacity or quality of service. The Court has been bedeviled by its cable television docket. *Denver Area Educational Tele-Communications Consortium v. FCC* (1996), examining provisions relating to the broadcast of indecent programming on cable public-access channels, yielded six opinions and no majority. In TURNER BROADCASTING SYSTEM V. FCC (1994) and *Turner Broadcasting System v. FCC* (1997), which upheld statutory provisions requiring cable television systems to transmit the signals of local broadcast stations—so-called "MUST CARRY" LAWS—the Justices found themselves sharply divided over basic principles.

It may be, though, that both Title III of the Communications Act (applying one regulatory scheme to over-the-air broadcast) and Title VI (applying another to cable television) rely on outmoded categories. The explosive growth of the INTERNET—together with the more general trend toward packet-switched transmission of digitized content—is breaking down old regulatory boundaries. Audio and video programming can be transmitted over the Internet in defiance of traditional regulatory models. In *Reno v. ACLU* (1997), the Court—stating that the Internet gives every person "a voice that resounds farther than it could from any soapbox"—indicated that governmental restrictions on Internet speech should be subject to stringent review. As video, voice, and text increasingly shift to the Internet, new forms of electronic content delivery will develop outside of the broadcast and cable regulatory regimes. Current distinctions among different transport modes may come to seem increasingly artificial. In such a circumstance, current justifications for different constitutional treatment of those transport modes will seem increasingly artificial as well.

JONATHAN WEINBERG
(2000)

Bibliography

CHEN, JIM   1996   The Last Picture Show. *Minnesota Law Review* 80:1415–1510.

KRATTENMAKER, THOMAS and POWE, LUCAS A.   1994   *Regulating Broadcast Programming*. Cambridge, Mass.: MIT Press.

LEVI, LILI   1996   Not With A Bang But A Whimper: Broadcast License Renewal and the Telecommunications Act of 1996. *Connecticut Law Review* 29:243–287.

ROBINSON, GLEN O.   1998   The Electronic First Amendment: An Essay for the New Age. *Duke Law Journal* 47:899–970.

WEINBERG, JONATHAN   1993   Broadcasting and Speech. *California Law Review* 81:1101–1206.

BROAD CONSTRUCTION

Broad construction, sometimes called "loose construction," is an approach to CONSTITUTIONAL INTERPRETATION emphasizing a permissive and flexible reading of the Constitution, and especially of the powers of the federal government. Like its opposite, STRICT CONSTRUCTION, the phrase has political, rather than technical or legal, significance.

ALEXANDER HAMILTON advocated broad construction in his 1791 controversy with THOMAS JEFFERSON over the constitutionality of the bill to establish the Bank of the United States. The essence of Hamilton's position, which was accepted by President GEORGE WASHINGTON and endorsed by the Supreme Court in MCCULLOCH V. MARYLAND (1819), was the doctrine of IMPLIED POWERS: that the delegated powers implied the power to enact legislation useful in carrying out those powers. The broad constructionists also argued that the NECESSARY AND PROPER CLAUSE empowered Congress to make any law convenient for the execution of any delegated power. Similarly, broad construction justified enactment of the ALIEN AND SEDITION ACTS and expenditures for INTERNAL IMPROVEMENTS.

In his Report on Manufactures (1792) Hamilton advocated a broad construction of the TAXING AND SPENDING POWER that would authorize Congress to spend federal tax money for any purpose connected with the GENERAL WELFARE, whether or not the subject of the appropriation was within Congress's ordinary LEGISLATIVE POWER. Broad construction of the COMMERCE CLAUSE and of the taxing and spending power now forms the constitutional basis for federal regulation of the lives and activities of citizens. Proponents of broad construction argue that the Constitution must be adapted to changing times and conditions. However, a thoroughgoing broad construction is clearly incompatible with the ideas of LIMITED GOVERNMENT and CONSTITUTIONALISM.

The Constitution both grants power to the government and imposes limitations on the exercise of governmental power. Consistent usage would describe the expansive reading of either, and not just of the former, as broad construction. Indeed, President RICHARD M. NIXON frequently criticized the WARREN COURT for its "broad construction" of constitutional provisions guaranteeing the procedural rights of criminal defendants. The more common usage, however, reserves the term for constitutional interpretation permitting a wider scope for governmental activity.

In the late 1970s and the 1980s, broad construction was largely displaced by a new theory of constitutional jurisprudence called "noninterpretivism." Unlike broad construction, which depends upon a relationship between government action and some particular clause of the Constitution, noninterpretivism justifies government action on the basis of values presumed to underlie the constitutional text and to be superior to the actual words in the document.

DENNIS J. MAHONEY
(1986)

Bibliography

AGRESTO, JOHN   1984   *The Supreme Court and Constitutional Democracy*. Ithaca, N.Y.: Cornell University Press.

BROADRICK v. OKLAHOMA
413 U.S. 601 (1973)

The FIRST AMENDMENT doctrine of OVERBREADTH, developed by the WARREN COURT in the 1960s, came under increasing criticism from within the Supreme Court. In *Broadrick*, that criticism culminated in the invention of a "substantial overbreadth" DOCTRINE.

Oklahoma law restricted the political activities of state civil servants; such employees were forbidden to "take part in the management or affairs of any political party or in any political campaign," except to vote or express opinions privately. Three civil servants sued in a federal district court for a declaration that the law was unconstitutional for VAGUENESS and overbreadth. The district court upheld the law, and on direct review the Supreme Court affirmed, 5–4.

Justice BYRON R. WHITE, for the majority, concluded that the overbreadth doctrine should not be used to invalidate a statute regulating conduct (as opposed to the expression of particular messages or viewpoints) unless the law's overbreadth is "substantial, . . . judged in relation to the statute's plainly legitimate sweep." Although Oklahoma's law was theoretically capable of constitutionally impermissible application to some activities (the use of political buttons or bumper stickers were arguable examples), it was not substantially overbroad—not likely to be applied to a substantial number of cases of constitutionally protected expression. Thus the law's overbreadth did not threaten a significant CHILLING EFFECT on protected speech, and could be cured through "case-by-case analysis" rather than invalidation on its face. Appellants had conceded that their own conduct (campaigning for a superior state official) could be prohibited under a narrowly drawn statute.

Justice WILLIAM J. BRENNAN, for three dissenters, called the decision "a wholly unjustified retreat" from established principles requiring facial invalidation of laws capable of applications to prohibit constitutionally protected speech. Justice WILLIAM O. DOUGLAS, dissenting, generally attacked the validity of laws restricting public employees' political activity.

On the same day the Court reaffirmed, 6–3, the validity of the HATCH ACT, which similarly restricts federal civil servants, in *Civil Service Commission v. National Association of Letter Carriers* (1973).

KENNETH L. KARST
(1986)

BROCKETT v. SPOKANE ARCADES, INC.
472 U.S. 491 (1985)

The *Brockett* opinion refined the DOCTRINE of OVERBREADTH in FIRST AMENDMENT cases. A Washington statute provided both civil and criminal sanctions against "moral nuisances"—businesses purveying "lewd" matter. Various purveyors of sexually oriented books and films sued in federal district court for a DECLARATORY JUDGMENT that the law was unconstitutional and an INJUNCTION against its enforcement. That court denied relief, but the court of appeals held the law INVALID ON ITS FACE. The defect, the court said, was the law's definition of "lewd" matter, which followed the Supreme Court's formula defining OBSCENITY, but defined the term "prurient" to include material that "incites lasciviousness or lust." That definition was substantially overbroad, the court said, because it included material that aroused only a normal, healthy interest in sex.

A 6–2 Supreme Court reversed, in an opinion by Justice BYRON R. WHITE. The Court agreed that, under MILLER V. CALIFORNIA (1973), a work could not be held ob-

scene if its only appeal were to "normal sexual reactions" and accepted the lower court's interpretation that "lust" would embrace such a work. However, Justice White said, these plaintiffs were not entitled to a facial invalidation of the law. They had alleged that their own films and books were not obscene, but were constitutionally protected. In such a case, there is "no want of a proper party to challenge the statute, no concern that an attack on the statute will be unduly delayed or protected speech discouraged." The proper course would be to declare the statute's partial invalidity—here, to declare that the law would be invalid in application to material appealing to "normal . . . sexual appetites." In contrast, when the state seeks to enforce such a partially invalid statute against a person whose own speech or conduct is constitutionally *unprotected*, the proper course, assuming the law's substantial overbreadth, is to invalidate the law entirely. The result is ironic, but explainable. In the latter case, if the court did not hold the law invalid on its face, there would be a serious risk of a CHILLING EFFECT on the potential protected speech of others who were not in court.

The propriety of partial invalidation depended on the SEVERABILITY of the Washington statute, but that issue was easily resolved: the law contained a severability clause, and surely the legislature would not have abandoned the statute just because it could not be applied to material appealing to normal sexual interests.

Justice SANDRA DAY O'CONNOR joined the OPINION OF THE COURT but argued separately, joined by Chief Justice WARREN E. BURGER and Justice WILLIAM H. REHNQUIST, that the case was appropriate for federal court ABSTENTION, awaiting guidance from the state courts on the statutory meaning of "lust." Justice WILLIAM J. BRENNAN, joined by Justice THURGOOD MARSHALL, dissented, agreeing with the court of appeals.

KENNETH L. KARST
(1986)

BRONSON v. KINZIE
1 Howard 311 (1843)

As a result of the depression of 1837 many states passed debtors' relief legislation to assist property holders who were losing their farms and homes by foreclosure. Illinois, for example, provided that foreclosed property could not be sold at auction unless it brought two-thirds of its appraised value, and that the property sold at foreclosure might be repurchased by the debtor within one year at the purchase price plus ten percent. Such legislation, which operated retroactively on existing contracts, did not directly affect their obligation, the duties of the contracting parties toward each other; it affected their remedies, the means by which the OBLIGATION OF CONTRACTS can be enforced.

By a vote of 7–1 the Supreme Court held the Illinois statutes unconstitutional on the ground that they violated the CONTRACT CLAUSE. The opinion of Chief Justice ROGER B. TANEY remained the leading one on the subject for ninety years, until distinguished away by HOME BUILDING LOAN ASSOCIATION V. BLAISDELL (1934). Taney conceded that the states have power to change the remedies available to creditors confronted by defaulting debtors, on condition that the changed remedy does not impair the obligation of existing contracts. "But if that effect is produced, it is immaterial whether it is done by acting on the remedy or directly on the contract itself." Taney reasoned that the rights of a contracting party could be "seriously impaired by binding the proceedings with new conditions and restrictions, so as to make the remedy hardly worth pursuing." In this case he found that if the state could allow the debtor to repurchase his lost property within a year, it might allow still more time, making difficult a determination of how much time the state might allow. Taney did not say why one year was too long, or why the Court could not fix a rule. He did say that the state requirement fixing two-thirds of the value as the minimum purchasing price "would frequently render any sale altogether impossible." He offered no test by which the state could know whether a change in the remedy adversely affected the obligation of a contract. Justice JOSEPH STORY privately wrote, "There are times when the Court is called upon to support every sound constitutional doctrine in support of the rights of property and of creditors."

LEONARD W. LEVY
(1986)

BROOM, JACOB
(1752–1810)

Jacob Broom, a member of the CONSTITUTIONAL CONVENTION OF 1787 from Delaware, was a signer of the Constitution. He spoke briefly several times, exhibiting a desire to protect small-state interests and a distrust of a strong executive. When some delegates wanted to dissolve the Convention over the issue of REPRESENTATION, Broom argued against them.

DENNIS J. MAHONEY
(1986)

BROWN, HENRY BILLINGS
(1836–1913)

Henry Billings Brown served on the Supreme Court from 1890 to 1906. During that period, he wrote more than 450 majority opinions and dissenting or CONCURRING OPINIONS in some fifty other cases, many of which had contemporary and historical significance. Justice Brown's jurisprudence revealed some hesitance, some ambivalence, even contradiction as he struggled to perform the judicial function.

The glorification of private property and free competition reflected one dimension of Brown's thought. He considered the right of private property "the first step in the emergence of the civilized man from the condition of the utter savage," and he joined the majority in LOCHNER V. NEW YORK (1905), striking down a state law that limited the hours of bakery workers to a maximum of sixty per week or ten per day. Yet Brown usually construed the STATE POLICE POWER broadly and sanctioned legislative modification of laissez faire principles. In HOLDEN V. HARDY (1898) Brown upheld Utah's maximum hours act for miners, rejecting arguments that the state had violated the CONTRACT CLAUSE and denied property without DUE PROCESS. He looked realistically at the disparity in bargaining position between employer and employee, recognizing that fear of losing their jobs prompted laborers to perform work detrimental to their health. Concern for public health and inequality of bargaining power justified the state regulation.

POLLOCK V. FARMERS' LOAN & TRUST CO. (1895) also revealed Brown's willingness to permit legislative regulation of private property. When the Court struck down a congressional tax on incomes, Brown eloquently dissented, protesting that the decision ignored a century of "consistent and undeviating" precedent and represented "a surrender of the TAXING POWER to the moneyed class." Although opponents of the tax had raised the specter of socialism to dissuade Congress from raising funds, Brown construed *Pollock* as "the first step toward the submergence of the liberties of the people in a sordid despotism of wealth."

Brown supported the gradual development of federal power as a necessary concomitant to a modern industrial economy. He also wrote many of the Court's ADMIRALTY opinions, broadly interpreting federal JURISDICTION and the scope of federal maritime law. Brown similarly endorsed an expansive federal power under the COMMERCE CLAUSE, joining, for example, Justice OLIVER WENDELL HOLMES' classic statement of the STREAM OF COMMERCE doctrine in SWIFT & CO. V. UNITED STATES (1905).

Brown's CRIMINAL PROCEDURE and CIVIL LIBERTIES opinions reflected the general attitude of late nineteenth-, early twentieth-century America toward criminals, blacks, and women. In BROWN V. WALKER (1896) he held that the Fifth Amendment RIGHT AGAINST SELF-INCRIMINATION was not violated if the state coerced testimony and afforded IMMUNITY from criminal prosecution. Social disgrace and ridicule might result from invoking the Fifth Amendment, but a "self-confessed criminal" did not deserve protection from his neighbors' negative judgment.

Brown's callousness to CIVIL RIGHTS is manifest in one of the most infamous decisions of the nineteenth century—PLESSY V. FERGUSON (1896). For the Court, Brown upheld a Louisiana statute requiring railroads to provide "equal but separate accommodations" for "white" and "colored" patrons. In a remarkably disingenuous opinion, he reasoned that the statute had "no tendency to destroy the legal equality of the two races" and did "not necessarily imply the inferiority of either race to the other." Brown rejected a Fourteenth Amendment EQUAL PROTECTION challenge, citing as precedent state cases decided prior to passage of the FOURTEENTH AMENDMENT. To Brown the Louisiana law was a reasonable legislative decision consistent with "the established usages, customs and traditions of the people." In other words, Brown conceived civil rights as adequately protected in the legislative process; he did not envision civil rights as enforceable by a minority against the majority. *Plessy* mirrored the late nineteenth-century's belief in physical and social differences between the races. Contemporary scientific and social science thought considered the Negro and Caucasian races as biologically separate and the Caucasian race as superior. In *Plessy*, Brown constitutionalized the prevailing prejudices of his era.

ROBERT JEROME GLENNON
(1986)

Bibliography

GLENNON, ROBERT JEROME 1973 Justice Henry Billings Brown: Values in Tension. *University of Colorado Law Review* 44: 553–604.

BROWN v. ALLEN
344 U.S. 443 (1953)

In *Brown v. Allen* the Supreme Court rejected the claim that North Carolina practiced unconstitutional JURY DISCRIMINATION. Speaking through Justice STANLEY F. REED, the Court held that the state did not deny EQUAL PROTECTION to blacks by randomly selecting jury panels from lists of property taxpayers, even though there was still a significantly smaller proportion of black jurors than black citizens. The Court declined to consider whether selecting for jury duty those with the most property constituted WEALTH DISCRIMINATION. Justices HUGO L. BLACK, FELIX FRANKFURTER, and WILLIAM O. DOUGLAS, dissenting, argued that the tax-list selection technique was not a "complete neutralization of RACIAL DISCRIMINATION."

DENNIS J. MAHONEY
(1986)

BROWN v. BOARD OF EDUCATION
347 U.S. 483 (1954)
349 U.S. 294 (1955)

In the dual perspectives of politics and constitutional development, *Brown v. Board of Education* was the Supreme Court's most important decision of the twentieth century. In four cases consolidated for decision, the Court held that racial SEGREGATION of public school children, commanded or authorized by state law, violated the FOURTEENTH AMENDMENT's guarantee of the EQUAL PROTECTION OF THE LAWS. A companion decision, BOLLING V. SHARPE (1954), held that school segregation in the DISTRICT OF COLUMBIA violated the Fifth Amendment's guarantee of DUE PROCESS OF LAW.

Brown illustrates how pivotal historical events, viewed in retrospect, can take on the look of inevitability. To the actors involved, however, the decision was anything but a foregone conclusion. The principal judicial precedent, after all, was PLESSY V. FERGUSON (1896), which had upheld the racial segregation of railroad passengers, partly on the basis of an earlier Massachusetts decision upholding school segregation. More recent Supreme Court decisions had invalidated various forms of segregation in higher education without deciding whether *Plessy* should be overruled. Just a few months before the first *Brown* decision, Robert Leflar and Wylie Davis outlined eleven different courses open to the Supreme Court in the cases before it.

The four cases we now call *Brown* were the culmination of a twenty-year litigation strategy of the NAACP, aimed at the ultimate invalidation of segregation in education. (See SEPARATE BUT EQUAL DOCTRINE.) Part of that strategy had already succeeded; the Supreme Court had ordered the admission of black applicants to state university law schools, and had invalidated a state university's segregation of a black graduate student. The opinions in those cases had emphasized intangible elements of educational quality, particularly the opportunity to associate with persons of other races. (See SWEATT V. PAINTER.) The doctrinal ground was thus prepared for the Court to strike down the segregation of elementary and secondary schools—if the Court was ready to occupy that ground.

The Justices were sensitive to the political repercussions their decision might have. The cases were argued in December 1952, and in the ordinary course would have been decided by the close of the Court's term in the following June or July. Instead of deciding, however, the Court set the five cases for reargument in the following term and proposed a series of questions to be argued, centering on the history of the adoption of the Fourteenth Amendment and on potential remedies if the Court should rule against segregation. The available evidence suggests that the Court was divided on the principal issue in the cases—the constitutionality of separate but equal public schools—and that Justice FELIX FRANKFURTER played a critical role in persuading his brethren to put the case over so that the incoming administration of President DWIGHT D. EISENHOWER might present its views as AMICUS CURIAE. It is clear that the discussion at the Court's CONFERENCE on the cases had dealt not only with the merits of the black children's claims but also with the possible reaction of the white South to a decision overturning school segregation. Proposing questions for the reargument, Justice Frankfurter touched on the same concern in a memorandum to his colleagues: ". . . for me the ultimate crucial factor in the problem presented by these cases is psychological—the adjustment of men's minds and actions to the unfamiliar and the unpleasant."

When Justice Frankfurter wrote of "the adjustment of men's minds," he had whites in mind. For blacks, Jim Crow was an unpleasant reality that was all too familiar. It is not surprising that the Justices centered their political concerns on the white South; lynchings of blacks would have been a vivid memory for any Justice who had come to maturity before 1930. In any event the Court handled the *Brown* cases from beginning to end with an eye on potential disorder and violence among southern whites.

Chief Justice FRED M. VINSON, who had written the opinions invalidating segregation in higher education, appeared to some of his brethren to oppose extending the reasoning of those opinions to segregation in the public schools. Late in the summer of 1953, five weeks before the scheduled reargument of *Brown*, Vinson died suddenly from a heart attack. With *Brown* in mind, Justice Frankfurter said, in a private remark that has since become glaringly public, "This is the first indication I have ever had that there is a God."

Vinson's replacement was the governor of California, EARL WARREN. At the *Brown* reargument, which was put off until December, he did not say much. In conference, however, Warren made clear his view that the separate but equal doctrine must be abandoned and the cases decided in favor of the black children's equal protection claim. At the same time, he though the Court should avoid "precipitous action that would inflame more than necessary." The conference disclosed an apparent majority for the Chief Justice's position, but in a case of such political magnitude, a unanimous decision was devoutly to be wished. The vote was thus postponed, while the Chief Justice and Justice Frankfurter sought for ways to unite the Court. Near-unanimity seems to have been achieved by agreement on a gradual enforcement of the Court's decision. A vote of 8–1 emerged late in the winter, with Justice ROBERT H. JACKSON preparing to file a separate concurrence. When

Jackson suffered a heart attack, the likelihood of his pursuing an independent doctrinal course diminished. The Chief Justice circulated a draft opinion in early May, and at last Justice STANLEY F. REED was persuaded of the importance of avoiding division in the Court. On May 17, 1954, the Court announced its decision. Justice Jackson joined his brethren at the bench, to symbolize the Court's unanimity.

The opinion of the Court, by Chief Justice Warren, was calculatedly limited in scope, unilluminating as to doctrinal implications, and bland in tone. The South was not lectured, and no broad pronouncements were made concerning the fate of Jim Crow. *Plessy* was not even overruled—not then. Instead, the opinion highlighted two points of distinction: the change in the status of black persons in the years since *Plessy*, and the present-day importance of public education for the individual and for American society. Borrowing from the opinion of the lower court in the Kansas case (*Brown* itself), the Chief Justice concluded that school segregation produced feelings of inferiority in black children, and thus interfered with their motivation to learn; as in the graduate education cases, such intangibles were critical in evaluating the equality of the educational opportunity offered to blacks. In *Plessy*, the Court had brushed aside the argument that segregation stamped blacks with a mark of inferiority; the *Brown* opinion, on the contrary, stated that modern psychological knowledge verified the argument, and in a supporting footnote cited a number of social science authorities. (See LEGISLATIVE FACTS.) Segregated education was inherently unequal; the separate but equal doctrine thus had no place in education.

In the ordinary equal protection case, a finding of state-imposed inequality is only part of the inquiry; the Court goes on to examine into justifications offered by the state for treating people unequally. In these cases the southern states had argued that segregation promoted the quality of education, the health of pupils, and the tranquillity of schools. The *Brown* opinion omitted entirely any reference to these asserted justifications. By looking only to the question of inequality, the Court followed the pattern set in earlier cases applying the separate but equal doctrine. However, in its opinion in the companion case from the District of Columbia, the Court added this remark: "Segregation in public education is not reasonably related to any proper governmental objective. . . ." With those conclusory words, the Court announced that further inquiry into justifications for school segregation was foreclosed.

The *Brown* opinion thus presented a near-minimum political target, one that could have been reduced only by the elimination of its social science citations. Everyone understood the importance of educational opportunity. Nothing was intimated about segregation in PUBLIC ACCOM-

MODATIONS or state courthouses, hospitals, or prisons. Most important of all, the Court issued no orders to the defendant school boards, but set the cases for yet another argument at the next term on questions of remedy: should segregation be ended at once, or gradually? Should the Supreme Court itself frame the decrees, or leave that task to the lower courts or a SPECIAL MASTER?

A full year passed before the Court issued its remedial opinion. *Brown II*, as that opinion is sometimes called, not only declined to order an immediate end to segregation but also failed to set deadlines. Instead, the Court told the lower courts to require the school boards to "make a prompt and reasonable start" towart "compliance at the earliest practicable date," taking into account such factors as buildings, transportation systems, personnel, and redrawing of attendance district lines. The lower courts should issue decrees to the end of admitting the plaintiff children to the schools "on a racially nondiscriminatory basis with ALL DELIBERATE SPEED. . . ."

This language looked like—and was—a political compromise; something of the sort had been contemplated from the beginning by Chief Justice Warren. Despite the Court's statement that constitutional principles could not yield to disagreement, the white South was told, in effect, that it might go on denying blacks their constitutional rights for an indefinite time, while it got used to the idea of stopping. Unquestionably, whatever the Court determined in 1954 or 1955, it would take time to build the sense of interracial community in the South and elsewhere. But in *Brown II* the Court sacrificed an important part of its one legitimate claim to political and moral authority: the defense of principle. A southern intransigent might say: after all, if *Brown* really did stand for a national principle, surely the principle would not be parceled out for separate negotiation in thousands of school districts over an indefinite time. The chief responses of the white South to the Court's gradualism were defiance and evasion. (See DESEGREGATION.) In 1956 a "Southern Manifesto," signed by nineteen Senators and 82 members of the House of Representatives, denounced *Brown* as resting on "personal political and social ideas" rather than the Constitution. One Mississippi senator, seeking to capitalize on the country's recent anticommunist fervor, called racial integration "a radical, pro-Communist political movement." President Eisenhower gave the decision no political support, promising only to carry out the law of the land.

Criticism of another sort came from Herbert Wechsler, a Columbia law professor with impressive credentials as a CIVIL RIGHTS advocate. Wechsler argued that the Supreme Court had not offered a principled explanation of the *Brown* decision—had not supported its repeated assertion that segregation harmed black school children.

Charles L. Black, Jr., a Texan and a Yale professor who had worked on the NAACP briefs in *Brown*, replied that all Southerners knew that Jim Crow was designed to maintain white supremacy. School segregation, as part of that system, must fall before a constitutional principle forbidding states deliberately to disadvantage a racial group. This defense of the *Brown* decision is irrefutable. But the *Brown* opinion had not tied school segregation to the system of Jim Crow, because Chief Justice Warren's strategy had been to avoid sweeping pronouncements in the interest of obtaining a unanimous Court and minimizing southern defiance and violence.

Within a few years, however, in a series of PER CURIAM orders consisting only of citations to *Brown*, the Court had invalidated state-supported segregation in all its forms. In one case *Plessy* was implicitly overruled. Jim Crow was thus buried without ceremony. Yet the intensity of the southern resistance to *Brown* shows that no one had been deceived into thinking that the decision was limited to education. Not only did the occasion deserve a clear statement of the unconstitutionality of the system of racial segregation; political practicalities also called for such a statement. The Supreme Court's ability to command respect for its decisions depends on its candid enunciation of the principles underlying those decisions.

Both *Brown* opinions, then, were evasions. Even so, *Brown* was a great decision, a personal triumph for a great Chief Justice. For if *Brown* was a culmination, it was also a beginning. The decision was the catalyst for a political movement that permanently altered race relations in America. (See SIT-IN; CIVIL RIGHTS ACT OF 1964; VOTING RIGHTS ACT OF 1965.) The success of the civil rights movement encouraged challenges to other systems of domination and dependency: systems affecting women, ALIENS, illegitimate children, the handicapped, homosexuals. Claims to racial equality forced a reexamination of a wide range of institutional arrangements throughout American society. In constitutionaldoctrinal terms, *Brown* was the critical event in the modern development of the equal protection clause as an effective guarantee of equal CITIZENSHIP, a development that led in turn to the rebirth of SUBSTANTIVE DUE PROCESS as a guarantee of fundamental personal liberties. After *Brown*, the federal judiciary saw itself in a new light, and all Americans could see themselves as members of a national community.

KENNETH L. KARST
(1986)

Bibliography

BELL, DERRICK 1980 *Brown v. Board of Education* and the Interest-Convergence Dilemma. *Harvard Law Review* 93: 518–533.

BLACK, CHARLES L., JR.   1960   The Lawfulness of the Segregation Decisions. *Yale Law Journal* 69:421–430.

KLUGER, RICHARD   1975   *Simple Justice.* New York: Knopf.

LEFLAR, ROBERT A. and DAVIS, WYLIE H.   1954   Segregation in the Public Schools—1953. *Harvard Law Review* 67:377–435.

WECHSLER, HERBERT   1959   Toward Neutral Principles of Constitutional Law. *Harvard Law Review* 73:1–35.

WILKINSON, J. HARVIE, III   1979   *From Brown to Bakke.* New York: Oxford University Press.

BROWN v. MARYLAND
12 Wheat. 419 (1827)

The Court, over the sole dissent of Justice SMITH THOMPSON, held unconstitutional a state act imposing an annual license tax of $50 on all importers of foreign merchandise. Since the state charged only $8 for a retailer's license, the Court could have found that the license tax on wholesalers of imported goods discriminated against FOREIGN COMMERCE, but Chief Justice JOHN MARSHALL, for the Court, expressly declined to give an opinion on the discrimination issue. Marshall rested his opinion partly on a finding that the license tax constituted a state IMPOST or customs duty on imports, contrary to the IMPORT-EXPORT CLAUSE of Article I, section 16, clause 2, of the Constitution. The sale of an import, Marshall reasoned, is inseparably related to bringing it into the country under congressional tariff acts and paying the duty on it.

Marshall had still greater interests to protect. He turned this simple case of a prohibited state impost, or of a state discrimination against foreign commerce, into an opportunity to lay down a rule explaining when federal authority over foreign commerce ceased and the state power to tax its internal commerce began: as long as the importer retained the property in his possession in the "original package" in which he imported it, federal authority remained exclusive; but when the importer broke the package and mixed the merchandise with other property, it became subject to STATE TAXATION. Marshall therefore found that the state act was a violation of the COMMERCE CLAUSE interpreted as vesting an exclusive national power, as well as a violation of the import-export clause, and Marshall added, "we suppose the principles laid down in this case, to apply equally to importations from a sister State."

In the time of Chief Justice ROGER B. TANEY (who represented the state in *Brown*), the Court rejected that supposition and still later ruled that the ORIGINAL PACKAGE DOCTRINE applies only to foreign commerce. Although many imports, like crude oil and natural gas, no longer come in "packages," making the doctrine inapplicable, a state tax on foreign commerce still in transit remains an unconstitutional impost. But little remains today of the original package doctrine. In MICHELIN TIRE CORP. V. WAGES (1976) the Court abandoned the doctrine in cases involving nondiscriminatory *ad valorem* property taxes, ruling that such taxes, even on goods imported from abroad and remaining in their original packages, do not fall within the constitutional prohibition against state taxation of imports.

LEONARD W. LEVY
(1986)

BROWN v. MISSISSIPPI
297 U.S. 278 (1936)

In this landmark decision, the Court for the first time held unconstitutional on DUE PROCESS grounds the use of a coerced confession in a state criminal proceeding. In a unanimous opinion reflecting outrage at the judicial system of Mississippi as well as at its law enforcement officers, Chief Justice CHARLES EVANS HUGHES found difficult to imagine methods "more revolting to the sense of justice" than those used by the state in this case. The record showed that prolonged "physical torture" of black suspects extorted their confessions; they were tried in a rush without adequate defense, were convicted solely on the basis of the confessions which they repudiated, and were quickly sentenced to death. The transcript read "like pages torn from some medieval account. . . ."

Yet the state supreme court, over dissenting opinions, had sustained the convictions on the basis of arguments later used by the state before the Supreme Court: under TWINING V. JERSEY (1908) the Constitution did not protect against compulsory self-incrimination in state courts, and counsel for the prisoners had not made a timely motion for exclusion of the confessions after proving coercion. To these arguments, Hughes replied, first, "Compulsion by torture to extort a confession is a different matter. . . . The rack and torture chamber may not be substituted for the witness stand" except by a denial of due process of law. The state could regulate its own CRIMINAL PROCEDURE only on condition that it observed the fundamental principles of liberty and justice. Second, Hughes regarded counsel's technical error as irrelevant compared to the fact that the wrong committed by the state was so fundamental that it made the whole proceeding a "mere pretense of a trial" and rendered the convictions void.

Brown did not revolutionize state criminal procedure or abolish third-degree methods. But it proved to be the foundation for thirty years of decisions on POLICE INTERROGATION AND CONFESSIONS, finally resulting in an overruling of *Twining* and a constitutional law intended by the FOURTEENTH AMENDMENT.

LEONARD W. LEVY
(1986)

BROWN v. SOCIALIST WORKERS '74 CAMPAIGN COMMITTEE
459 U.S. 87 (1982)

In BUCKLEY V. VALEO (1976) the Supreme Court refused to recognize a blanket FIRST AMENDMENT right of minor political parties to keep their contributors and their disbursements confidential. The Court said, however, that such a right would be recognized in particular cases when parties could show that political privacy was essential to their exercise of First Amendment rights. *Brown* was such a case. The party had shown a "reasonable probability of threats, harassment, or reprisals" in the event of disclosure. The Court thus held, unanimously, that Ohio could not compel the disclosure of contributions to the party, and held, 6–3, that the same logic protected against compulsory disclosure of the party's expenditures, such as wages or reimbursements paid to party members and supporters.

KENNETH L. KARST
(1986)

BROWN v. UNITED STATES
381 U.S. 437 (1965)

This decision revitalized the Constitution's prohibitions on BILLS OF ATTAINDER. The TAFT-HARTLEY ACT had made it a crime for a member of the Communist party to be a labor union officer. Brown, convicted under this law, argued that it violated the FIRST AMENDMENT, the Fifth Amendment's DUE PROCESS clause, and Article I, section 9, which forbids Congress to pass a bill of attainder. A 5–4 Supreme Court agreed with the latter argument. Citing CUMMINGS V. MISSOURI (1867), EX PARTE GARLAND (1867), and UNITED STATES V. LOVETT (1946), Chief Justice EARL WARREN said that the law amounted to legislative punishment of a specifically designated group. Congress might weed dangerous persons out of the labor movement, but it must use rules of general applicability, leaving adjudication to other tribunals. (See also IRREBUTTABLE PRESUMPTIONS.) Justice BYRON R. WHITE, for the dissenters, argued that Congress had shown no punitive purpose, but had intended to prevent future political strikes.

KENNETH L. KARST
(1986)

BROWN v. WALKER
161 U.S. 591 (1896)

After COUNSELMAN V. HITCHCOCK (1892) Congress authorized transactional immunity to compel the testimony of anyone invoking the RIGHT AGAINST SELF-INCRIMINATION in a federal proceeding. Appellant, despite a grant of immunity, refused to testify before a GRAND JURY investigating criminal violations of federal law. He argued that Congress could not supersede a constitutional provision by a mere statute and that the statute did not immunize him from all liabilities that might ensue from incriminating admissions. The Supreme Court, by a 5–4 majority, held that the act provided an immunity commensurate with the scope of the Fifth Amendment right and therefore constitutionally supplanted it.

Justice HENRY B. BROWN, for the Court, declared that if the compulsory disclosures could not possibly expose the witness to criminal jeopardy, the demand of the Fifth Amendment was satisfied. The statute did not have to protect him from every possible detriment that might result from his evidence, as long as it exempted the witness from prosecution for any crime to which he testified under compulsion. If his testimony "operates as a complete pardon for the offense to which it relates,—a statute absolutely securing to him such immunity from prosecution would satisfy the demands of the clause of question." But he could be compelled to be a witness against himself if a statute of limitations barred prosecution, if his evidence merely brought him into public disgrace, or if he had already received a pardon or absolute immunity and thus stood with respect to such offense "as if it had never been committed."

The dissenters argued that the act was unconstitutional because the amendment protected the witness from compulsory testimony that would expose him to INFAMY even in the absence of a prosecution. They added that the act also exposed the witness to a possible prosecution for perjury, which could not possibly be imputed if he did not have to testify. (See IMMUNITY GRANTS.)

LEONARD W. LEVY
(1986)

BROWNING-FERRIS INDUSTRIES, INC. v. KELCO DISPOSAL, INC.

See: Punitive Damages

BRYCE, JAMES
(1838–1922)

Educated at Oxford University and called to the bar at Lincoln's Inn, James Bryce was Regius Professor of Civil Law at Oxford from 1870 until 1893. A member of the Liberal party, he served in the House of Commons (1874–1906) and was a member of four cabinets. His writings on American government and politics were influential both in America and abroad and he was even elected president of the American Political Science Association.

Bryce's most noted work on America was *The American Commonwealth* (1888; last revised, 1910). Rejecting the model of ALEXIS DE TOCQUEVILLE's *Democracy in America*, Bryce set out to describe the American experience without deriving from it any general theories about democracy. A well-educated and widely traveled British politician, Bryce was most impressed by the very constitutional principles Americans frequently take for granted: JUDICIAL REVIEW, and a fixed, written FUNDAMENTAL LAW beyond the amending power of the legislature. He thought the diffusion and limitation of governmental power in America were valuable safeguards against despotism, and that bicameralism and separation of powers provided the opportunity for full discussion of important measures; but he saw two great defects: the possibility that deadlock would prevent prompt action and the difficulty of fixing personal responsibility for policies and actions.

One of Bryce's important contributions as an empirical political scientist was his treatment of the POLITICAL PARTIES. The parties, he observed, constituted "a sort of second and unofficial government" directing the affairs of the legally constituted institutions. The party system counteracted the effects of federalism and separation of powers by linking the interests of legislative and executive officers and by making the results of local elections dependent upon national issues.

Bryce published thirteen other books, including *Studies in History and Jurisprudence* (1901) and *Modern Democracies* (1921), which present American government in comparative perspective, and numerous articles. He was the British ambassador to the United States from 1907 until 1913, and upon his retirement was elevated to the peerage as Viscount Bryce.

DENNIS J. MAHONEY
(1986)

Bibliography

IONS, EDMUND S. 1970 *James Bryce and American Democracy, 1870–1920*. New York: Humanities Press.

BUCHANAN, JAMES
(1791–1868)

A Pennsylvania attorney, James Buchanan was a congressman (1821–1831), minister to Russia and Britain (1832–1834, 1853–1856), senator (1834–1845), secretary of state (1845–1849), and President (1856–1861). In 1831 Buchanan thwarted a repeal of the Supreme Court's APPELLATE JURISDICTION under section 25 of the JUDICIARY ACT OF 1789. The rest of his prepresidential career reflected his

Democratic party regularity and support of STATES' RIGHTS. He attacked Chief Justice ROGER B. TANEY's nationalistic opinion in *Holmes v. Jennison* (1840), denounced the HOLDING in MCCULLOCH V. MARYLAND (1819), and urged a reduction in the number of Supreme Court Justices. In 1844 he declined an appointment to the Court. A close friend of many Southerners, Buchanan hated ABOLITIONISTS, always supported constitutional and congressional protection for slavery, and was the archetypal doughface—the northern man with southern principles. This outlook continued to his presidency and helped undermine it.

Before his inaugural address, Buchanan conversed with Chief Justice Taney while the audience looked on. In his address Buchanan observed that the question of SLAVERY IN THE TERRITORIES was of "little practical importance," in part because it was a "judicial question, which legitimately belongs to the Supreme Court of the United States, before whom it is now pending, and will, it is understood, be speedily and finally settled. To their decision, in common with all good citizens, I shall cheerfully submit. . . ." Two days later the decision was announced in DRED SCOTT V. SANDFORD (1857), and it appeared to many that Taney improperly had informed Buchanan of what the pending decision would hold. For over a month before the decision Buchanan had communicated with Justice JOHN CATRON of Tennessee and ROBERT C. GRIER of Pennsylvania about the case, successfully urging them to support Taney's position that the MISSOURI COMPROMISE was unconstitutional. Two years later, in his "House Divided Speech," ABRAHAM LINCOLN would accuse Buchanan of conspiring with Taney, President FRANKLIN PIERCE, and Senator STEPHEN A. DOUGLAS to force slavery into the territories. Although there was no conspiracy on this issue, Buchanan promoted slavery in the territories. In 1858 he unsuccessfully attempted to bring Kansas into the Union under the proslavery LECOMPTON CONSTITUTION. His support of slavery and southern Democrats helped split the party in 1860 over Douglas's nomination.

After Lincoln's election Buchanan presided over the disintegration of the Union, failing to act in any meaningful way. In December 1860 he blamed the crisis on the "long-continued and intemperate interference of the Northern people with the question of slavery in the Southern States. . . ." He asserted the Union "was intended to be perpetual," and that SECESSION "is revolution," but he also concluded that neither Congress nor the President had any constitutional authority "to coerce a State into submission which is attempting to withdraw" from the Union. The Union, he declared, rested "on public opinion." Buchanan spent his last few months in office vainly seeking a compromise which the South no longer wanted and whose terms the North found unacceptable. During these months Buchanan failed to protect military positions in the South, preserve national authority there, or prepare the nation for the impending war. Buchanan bequeathed to Lincoln a Union from which seven states had departed.

PAUL FINKELMAN
(1986)

Bibliography

SMITH, ELBERT B. 1975 *The Presidency of James Buchanan.* Lawrence: University of Kansas Press.

BUCHANAN v. WARLEY
245 U.S. 60 (1917)

Buchanan was the most important race relations case between PLESSY V. FERGUSON (1896) and SHELLEY V. KRAEMER (1948). A number of southern border cities had adopted residential SEGREGATION ordinances. NAACP attorneys constructed a TEST CASE challenging the constitutionality of Louisville's ordinance, which forbade a "colored" person to move into a house on a block in which a majority of residences were occupied by whites, and vice versa. A black agreed to buy from a white a house on a majority-white block, provided that the buyer had the legal right to occupy the house. The seller sued to compel performance of the contract; the buyer defended on the basis of the ordinance. The Kentucky courts upheld the ordinance. In the Supreme Court, both sides focused the argument on the constitutionality of neighborhood segregation. An unusual number of AMICUS CURIAE briefs attested to the case's importance.

A unanimous Supreme Court reversed, holding the ordinance invalid. Justice WILLIAM R. DAY's opinion discussed at length the rights to racial equality and the "dignity of citizenship" established in the THIRTEENTH and FOURTEENTH AMENDMENTS, as well as the rights to purchase and hold property, established by the CIVIL RIGHTS ACT OF 1866. He lamely distinguished *Plessy* as a case in which no one had been denied the use of his property. Ultimately, however, he rested decision on a theory of SUBSTANTIVE DUE PROCESS: the ordinance unconstitutionally interfered with property rights.

Day's curious opinion may have aimed at persuading two of his brethren. Justice JAMES C. MCREYNOLDS generally attached greater weight to claims of constitutional property rights than to claims to racial equality. And Justice OLIVER WENDELL HOLMES had prepared a draft DISSENTING OPINION that was not delivered, arguing that the white seller lacked STANDING to assert the constitutional right of blacks.

Despite the ground for decision, *Buchanan* was seen by the press as a major CIVIL RIGHTS victory for blacks. And when the Supreme Court faced ZONING in a nonracial context, it upheld an ordinance in VILLAGE OF EUCLID V. AMBLER REALTY CO. (1926). *Buchanan* plainly was more than a property rights decision.

KENNETH L. KARST
(1986)

Bibliography

SCHMIDT, BENNO C., JR. 1982 Principle and Prejudice: The Supreme Court and Race in the Progressive Era. Part 1: The Heyday of Jim Crow. *Columbia Law Review* 82:444, 498–523.

BUCK v. BELL
274 U.S. 200 (1927)

In *Buck* the Supreme Court upheld, 8–1, a Virginia law authorizing the STERILIZATION of institutionalized mental defectives without their consent. Justice OLIVER WENDELL HOLMES, for the Court, wrote an opinion notable for epigram and insensitivity. Virginia's courts had ordered the sterilization of a "feeble minded" woman, whose mother and child were similarly afflicted, finding that she was "the probable potential parent of socially inadequate offspring," and that sterilization would promote both her welfare and society's. Holmes, the Civil War veteran, remarked that public welfare might "call upon the best citizens for their lives"; these "lesser sacrifices" were justified to prevent future crime and starvation. There was no violation of SUBSTANTIVE DUE PROCESS. Citing JACOBSON V. MASSACHUSETTS (1905), he said, "The principle that sustains compulsory VACCINATION is broad enough to cover cutting the Fallopian tubes. . . . Three generations of imbeciles are enough."

Turning to EQUAL PROTECTION, which he called "the usual last resort of constitutional arguments," Holmes saw no violation in the law's reaching only institutionalized mental defectives and not others: "the law does all that is needed when it does all that it can." Justice PIERCE BUTLER noted his dissent.

Although *Buck* continues to be cited, its current authority as precedent is doubtful. (See SKINNER V. OKLAHOMA.)

KENNETH L. KARST
(1986)

Bibliography

CYNKAR, ROBERT J. 1981 Buck v. Bell: "Felt Necessities" v. Fundamental Values? *Columbia Law Review* 81:1418–1461.
GOULD, STEPHEN JAY 1984 Carrie Buck's Daughter. *Natural History* July:14–18.
LOMBARDO, PAUL A. 1985 Three Generations, No Imbeciles:

New Light on *Buck v. Bell. New York University Law Review* 60:30–62.

BUCKLEY v. VALEO
424 U.S. 1 (1976)

In *Buckley* the Supreme Court dealt with a number of constitutional challenges to the complex provisions of the FEDERAL ELECTIONS CAMPAIGN ACT. The act provided for a Federal Elections Commission, members of which were to be appointed variously by the President and certain congressional leaders. The Court held the congressional appointment unconstitutional; Article 2, section 2, prescribes a process for appointing all officers who carry out executive and quasi-judicial duties: appointment by the President, with confirmation by the Senate. Congress subsequently amended the statute to meet the Court's objections.

Rejecting both FIRST AMENDMENT and EQUAL PROTECTION challenges, the Court upheld, 7–2, the provision of public funds for presidential campaigns in amounts that favored major parties over minor parties.

The Court used a BALANCING TEST in considering First Amendment challenges to the provisions limiting expenditures by candidates and contributions to candidates in congressional elections. For both expenditures and contributions the Court defined the government's interest as preventing corruption and appearance of corruption.

The Court placed the interest of the candidate in FREEDOM OF SPEECH on the other side of the balance in striking down the expenditure provisions. Limiting expenditure limited the amount of speech a candidate might make. The Court rejected the argument that another legitimate purpose of the statute was to equalize the campaign opportunities of rich and poor candidates. The PER CURIAM opinion said that the government might not seek to equalize speech by leveling down the rights of rich speakers. High expenditures by rich candidates created no risk of corruption. Indeed, the opinion demonstrated that such a candidate was not dependent on others' money.

In upholding the contribution limits, the Court characterized the First Amendment interest of contributors not as freedom of speech but freedom of association. It reasoned that the initial contribution of $1,000 allowed by the statute completed the act of association and that further contributions did not significantly enhance the association. Further contributions did, however, increase the risk of corruption.

The statute's requirement that all contributions over $100 be a matter of public record were challenged as violating the right to anonymous political association previously recognized in NAACP V. ALABAMA (1958). The Court upheld the reporting provisions but said that individual applications to contributors to small unpopular parties might be unconstitutional.

MARTIN SHAPIRO
(1986)

Bibliography

POLSBY, DANIEL D.   1976   Buckley v. Valeo: The Special Nature of Political Speech. *Supreme Court Review* 1976:1–44.

BUDGET

The federal budget is the comprehensive annual program of income and expenditure of the federal government. The budget is not a constitutional requirement, nor does it answer to either the "appropriations made by law" or the "regular statement of account" of Article I, section 9, of the Constitution. Rather the budget is a legislatively created device to regularize the exercise of the TAXING AND SPENDING POWER.

In the nineteenth century there was no overall annual spending program. Appropriations bills were formulated by various congressional committees, which thereby exercised considerable control over the executive departments. A national budget process was first recommended by the Commission on Economy and Efficiency, appointed by President WILLIAM HOWARD TAFT in 1908; and the BUDGET AND ACCOUNTING ACT, which governed the budget process for over half a century, was enacted in 1921.

Because expenditure is an executive function, the President, as chief executive, was given authority to prepare and submit the budget. This represented a major shift of power within the government in favor of the executive branch. President FRANKLIN D. ROOSEVELT further consolidated presidential authority in 1939 by transferring the Bureau of the Budget (created by the 1921 act) from the Treasury Department to the Executive Office of the President. In 1969, President RICHARD M. NIXON restyled the bureau OFFICE OF MANAGEMENT AND BUDGET and increased its control over the operations of executive departments and agencies.

Congress reasserted its role in fiscal policymaking by the CONGRESSIONAL BUDGET AND IMPOUNDMENT CONTROL ACT (1974). The act created a permanent budget committee in each house of Congress, established the Congressional Budget Office to provide independent evaluation of executive economic planning, and prescribed a timetable for each phase of the budget and appropriations process. Even after passage of this act, however, the budget process is necessarily dominated by the chief executive.

DENNIS J. MAHONEY
(1986)

(SEE ALSO: *Balanced-Budget Amendment; Budget Process.*)

Bibliography

BORCHERDING, THOMAS E., ed. 1977 *Budgets and Bureaucrats: The Sources of Government Growth.* Durham, N.C.: Duke University Press.

MARINI, JOHN 1978 The Politics of Budget Control: An Analysis of the Impact of Centralized Administration on the Separation of Powers. Unpublished Ph.D. dissertation, Claremont Graduate School.

BUDGET AND ACCOUNTING ACT
42 Stat. 20 (1921)

Among the aims of the reform movement of the early twentieth century was the creation of neutral processes and agencies to perform public functions, substituting administration for politics in the delivery of government services. One key reform was the introduction of the federal BUDGET. Proposed by President WILLIAM HOWARD TAFT's Commission on Economy and Efficiency, enactment of a federal budget law was delayed by WORLD WAR I. When Congress finally passed a bill in 1920, President WOODROW WILSON, although a longtime advocate of a budget system, vetoed it rather than submit to its limitation of his REMOVAL POWER. A virtually identical bill was passed the following year and signed into law by President Warren Harding, who called it "the greatest reformation in governmental practice since the beginning of the Republic."

Under the act, the President alone was responsible for submitting to Congress each year a statement of the condition of the treasury, the estimated revenues and expenditures of the government for the year, and proposals for meeting revenue needs. The act created the Bureau of the Budget, to receive, compile, and criticize the estimates and requests of the various departments, and the General Accounting Office, to audit the government's fiscal activities.

The Budget and Accounting Act caused a major change in the balance of power within the government, giving the President, rather than Congress, effective control over government spending. The act provided the machinery through which, during the middle third of the twentieth century, the national executive managed the whole economy.

DENNIS J. MAHONEY
(1986)

(SEE ALSO: *Budget Process.*)

Bibliography

MARINI, JOHN 1978 The Politics of Budget Control: An Analysis of the Impact of Centralized Administration on the Separation of Powers. Unpublished Ph.D. dissertation, Claremont Graduate School.

BUDGET PROCESS

Budgeting moved to center stage in American politics in the last quarter of the twentieth century. The budget process, with the TAXING AND SPENDING POWER, has become the focal point of the administrative state. It is the place where political institutions have sought to accommodate the various interests seeking a share of the national wealth. The growth of the public sector, which has accompanied the increase in size of both federal and state budgets, has obscured the distinction between the public and private spheres. At one time, governments controlled expenditures, and budgets provided the means of limiting claims on available resources. Budget conflict was contained because of fundamental agreement concerning the ends of government. With the growth of the bureaucratic state, the consensus in support of LIMITED GOVERNMENT has weakened, as has support for limited—or balanced—budgets. The problem of budget control is exacerbated by a failure of the parties and institutions of government to achieve a new consensus, or political realignment, concerning the purposes of public spending. The Constitution, which separates the powers of government, has provided the conditions for budget strife.

The budget, as a formal plan of government in a fiscal year, is a centralizing device, one that presupposes a conception of the state as an active mechanism pursuing positive purposes in the interest of the people it is created to serve. The modern budget system is the concomitant of the administrative state, which, in principle, is an unlimited government. In America the administrative state traces its origins to the Progressive movement. The national executive budget system was among the political reforms demanded by the Progressives. In their view, the presidential budget, along with party reform, would give activist Presidents the ability to pursue the interests of a national majority. The United States was the last modern industrial nation to adopt an executive budget system. Congress was reluctant to give Presidents the power to formulate budgets, because its members thought such authority would undermine the SEPARATION OF POWERS.

The growth of federal expenditures during WORLD WAR I convinced national leaders—including those in Congress—that the legislative body was incapable of effective management of public resources. Thus, in 1921 an executive budget system was established through the BUDGET AND ACCOUNTING ACT. The President was given the power to formulate a budget and oversee its implementation. At its inception the executive budget was not considered a means of aggrandizing presidential power but a neutral mechanism to ensure economy and efficiency.

In 1939 President FRANKLIN D. ROOSEVELT reorganized the executive branch and placed the Bureau of the Budget at the center of the newly created Executive Office of the President. Roosevelt had become aware of the planning and management capabilities of the budget office. Furthermore, increased government expenditures during the Great Depression and the economic theories of John Maynard Keynes provided the conditions for using the budget to implement federal fiscal policy. The federal budget became an important tool in the presidential attempt to manage the economy. As long as Presidents and Congress agreed on national priorities, there were few unmanageable conflicts concerning economic policy or budget control.

The centralization of administration in Washington during the 1960s and early 1970s began to erode the consensus forged during the NEW DEAL. The new regulatory bureaucracy created during the Great Society tended to polarize society as well as the political institutions. The divergence between the parties led to heightened conflict between the political branches of government. The Democratic Party, which dominated the legislative branch, was committed to the maintenance of an administrative state. The Republican party, increasingly able to capture the executive branch, sought to limit the size of government. The 1972 reelection of RICHARD M. NIXON produced a crisis in the budget process that led to fundamental reform. In Nixon's view, Congress had become so wedded to the interests of the bureaucratic state that it could no longer control its appetite for increased public expenditures. Nixon sought to limit public spending by impounding expenditures that broke the executive budget. Without control of the budget, the Democratic majority in Congress was unable to challenge the President's authority in formulating economic policy or in establishing national priorities. The 1974 CONGRESSIONAL BUDGET AND IMPOUNDMENT CONTROL ACT gave Congress the technical capability and institutional means of controlling the amounts of money spent. Congress was at once a dominant force in the formulation of fiscal policy and a major force in setting the priorities of the nation.

Congress succeeded in challenging presidential control of the budget, but the price of success was an institutional inability to reach agreement on expenditures, except at ever higher levels. The reforms in Congress during the 1970s, which accommodated the growth of the administrative state, had weakened congressional leadership and empowered individual members. Power moved from committee chairs to subcommittee chairs. The links between Congress and the permanent bureaucracy undermined presidential attempts to manage the executive branch.

The budget process was dominated by those interests in Congress and the bureaucracy that supported the priorities of the administrative state. The growth of the federal government could not be seriously challenged without control of the levers of public spending.

The election of RONALD REAGAN proved to be a serious threat to those committed to the growth of the administrative state. Reagan used the budget process to establish his own priorities, which included a reduction in the size of government. He took advantage of the reconciliation procedure of the Budget Act to force reductions in expenditures, but at the same time reduced tax rates. However, the 1982 recession, coupled with the rapid collapse of inflation, prevented a reduction of expenditures. Instead, the growth of the defense budget and the maintenance of social spending led to an explosion of deficit financing and increased the national debt. Further, the budget process could no longer limit expenditures without fundamental changes in the laws. Nearly half of all federal expenditures now take the form of direct transfer payments to individuals, called ENTITLEMENTS. The political difficulty of raising new revenues, coupled with a mistrust of presidential power, led Congress to attempt to reduce the deficit by procedural devices such as the GRAMM-RUDMAN-HOLLINGS ACT. Congress lacked the will to act, but refused to trust Republican Presidents with the power to cut the few remaining controllable portions of the budget. The result has been stalemate and budget gimmickry.

Until recently, the Constitution of the United States was considered "the instrument and symbol" of politics in America. The Constitution authorized and legitimized the limited charecter of government and symbolized the notion of a HIGHER LAW. The law was seen to be dictated by the nature and reason—not merely legislative majorities—and was the source of legitimate authority. It provided the means by which the various institutions of government and the rights and powers of majorities could be reconciled. It is presupported a structure of government in which the characteristic activity of government—lawmaking by legislative majorites—could culminate in reasonable public law in interest of all. The primary virtue of the legislative branch is the capapcity for such deliberation, or public reasoning. It is by means of such deliberation and reconciliation that the various private intersts could be made compatible with the common good.

But Congress no longer functions primarily as a deliberative body, and the constitutional order has readjusted itself accordingly. The courts are now routinely involved in general policymaking, and Congress is excessively concerned with the details of executive administration. Moreover, Congress is less effective today in reconciling particular interests in light of the general interest. Congress has delegated much of its lawmaking authority to administrative bodies, and its primary role has become one of administrative oversight. Since the late 1960s, Congress has maintained an administrative apparatus whose task it is to solve—in a technically rational way, using the methods of science and social science—the social and political problems of industrial or postindustrial society.

The federal budget is in the process of replacing the Constitution as the "instrument and symbol" of American politics. Whereas the powers of government were once thought to be limited, now only resources are limited. The budget is the instrument by which the bureaucratic state is fueled; it is the symbol of the centralization of administration that is the dominant political reality of the American regime. The most important political questions are no longer questions of principle or public right but of money and finance. The Constitution was the embodiment of the principles of republican government. The budget has become the symbol of American pluralism at best and redistributionist politics at worst. The Constitution was concerned with institutions, law, and the common good. The budget is the embodiment of the administrative state. It reflects a concern with administrative detail rather than principle, rulemaking rather than lawmaking, and the attempt to placate every private interest, rather than pursuance of a common good.

JOHN MARINI
(1992)

(SEE ALSO: *Balanced-Budget Amendment; Impoundment of Funds; Progressive Constitutional Thought; Progressivism.*)

Bibliography

SCHICK, ALLEN   1980   *Congress and Money.* Washington, D.C.: Urban Institute.
SHUMAN, HOWARD E.   1984   *Politics and the Budget.* Englewood Cliffs, N.J.: Prentice-Hall.
WILDAVSKY, AARON   1988   *The New Politics of the Budgetary Process.* Glenview, Ill.: Scott, Foresman.

BUNTING v. OREGON
243 U.S. 426 (1917)

This decision upheld maximum hour legislation and approved state regulations of overtime wages as a proper exception to the prevailing constitutional standards of FREEDOM OF CONTRACT. A 1913 Oregon law prescribed a ten-hour day for men and women alike, thus expanding the law regulating women's hours which had been upheld in MULLER V. OREGON (1908). In addition, the measure required time and a half wages for overtime up to three hours per day. Justice JOSEPH MCKENNA's opinion for the 5–3 majority (there was no written dissent) assumed the va-

lidity of the working hours regulations, thus ignoring LOCHNER V. NEW YORK (1905) as well as Justice DAVID J. BREWER's careful distinction in *Muller* that the status of women required special legislative concern. Lawyers for Bunting had attacked the law for its wage-fixing provisions and had invoked *Lochner* and *Muller* to demonstrate that the Oregon statute had no reasonable relation to the preservation of public health. McKenna, focusing on the overtime provision, denied that it was a regulation of wages. The statute, he contended, was designed as an hours law, and the Court was reluctant to consider it as a "disguise" for illegal purposes. Somewhat ingenuously, McKenna argued that the overtime provision was permissive and that its purpose was to burden and deter employers from using workers for more than ten hours. He admitted that the requirement for overtime might not attain that end, "but its insufficiency cannot change its character from penalty to permission." The Oregon Supreme Court had construed the overtime provision as reflecting a legislative desire to make the ten-hour day standard; beyond that, McKenna and his colleagues were not willing to inquire into legislative motive.

Bunting provided frail support in behalf of wage legislation. A few weeks later, the Court split 4–4 on Oregon's minimum wage law (STETTLER V. O'HARA), but in 1923 the Court struck down such legislation in ADKINS V. CHILDREN's HOSPITAL.

STANLEY I. KUTLER
(1986)

Bibliography

MASON, ALPHEUS T.   1946   *Brandeis: A Free Man's Life.* New York: Viking Press.

BURBANK v. LOCKHEED AIR TERMINAL
411 U.S. 624 (1973)

The Supreme Court, in a 5–4 vote, struck down a city ordinance regulating air traffic as a violation of the SUPREMACY CLAUSE. The ordinance prohibited jets from taking off between 11 p.m. and 7 a.m. and also forbade the airport operator from allowing such flights. The Court, speaking through Justice WILLIAM O. DOUGLAS, applied the PREEMPTION DOCTRINE and found the ordinance in conflict with two federal statutes which provided for the regulation of navigable airspace. Justice WILLIAM H. REHNQUIST, for the dissenters, contended that these statutes did not supersede the STATE POLICE POWER.

DAVID GORDON
(1986)

BURCH v. LOUISIANA
441 U.S. 130 (1979)

In *Burch v. Louisiana*, the Supreme Court held that conviction by a 5–1 vote of a six-person jury in a state prosecution for a nonpetty offense violates the accused's right to TRIAL BY JURY under the SIXTH and FOURTEENTH AMENDMENTS. *Burch* involved a prosecution for exhibiting two obscene motion pictures.

In two earlier cases, APODACA V. OREGON (1972) and JOHNSON V. LOUISIANA (1972), the Court had sustained 10–2 and 9–3 verdicts, and it had also previously ruled in BALLEW V. GEORGIA (1978) that juries of less than six persons were unconstitutional. In *Burch*, the Court concluded that "having already departed from the strictly historical requirements of jury trial, it is inevitable that lines must be drawn somewhere if the substance of the jury trial right is to be preserved." It relied mainly upon "the same reasons that led us in *Ballew* to decide that use of a five person jury threatened the fairness of the proceeding and the proper role of the jury." *Burch* did not resolve the constitutionality of different majority verdict systems for juries composed of seven through eleven members or majorities of 8–4 or 7–5 on a jury of twelve.

NORMAN ABRAMS
(1986)

(SEE ALSO: *Jury Size; Jury Unanimity.*)

BURDEN OF PROOF

Although the Constitution does not mention burden of proof, certain principles are widely accepted as having constitutional status. The first and most significant of these is the rule that in a criminal case the government must prove its case "beyond a REASONABLE DOUBT." This is the universal COMMON LAW rule, and was said by the Supreme Court in IN RE WINSHIP (1970) to be an element of DUE PROCESS. This standard is commonly contrasted with proof "by a preponderance of the evidence" or "by clear and convincing evidence." The standard of proof is in practice not easily susceptible to further clarification or elaboration.

To what matters does the burden apply? The *Winship* Court said it extended to "every fact necessary to constitute the crime with which [a defendant] is charged." The government must prove its case beyond a reasonable doubt. But suppose the defendant raises a defense of AL-IBI, insanity, duress, or diplomatic immunity? With respect to such defenses the usual rule is that the defendant may be required to produce some evidence supporting his claim; if he does not, that defense will not be considered by the jury. By what standard should the jury be instructed to evaluate such a defense? Should they deny the defense unless they are persuaded by a preponderance of the evidence that the defendant has established it? Or does the "burden of persuasion" on the issue raised by the defendant remain on the government, so that the jury must acquit unless persuaded beyond a reasonable doubt that the defense falls? On this complicated question there is no settled view. The answer should probably vary with the kind of defense: alibi, for example, is not really an affirmative defense but a denial of facts charged. Such a defense as diplomatic immunity, however, might be regarded as one upon which the defendant should bear the burden of proof.

The foregoing structure is complicated by the existence of "presumptions," that is, legislative or judicial statements to the effect that if one fact is proved—say, possession of marijuana—another fact essential to conviction may be "presumed"—say, that the marijuana was illegally imported. The Supreme Court has held such a legislative presumption valid when the proved fact makes the ultimate fact more likely than not.

The burden of proof beyond a reasonable doubt is a critical element of due process. Like the requirements that laws be public and their prohibitions comprehensible and prospective, that trials be public and by jury, and that the defendant have counsel, the burden of proof limits the power of the government to impose arbitrary or oppressive punishments. It reinforces the rights of the defendant not to be a witness against himself nor to take the stand, for it imposes upon the government the task of proving its whole case on its own. A lower standard of proof would pressure defendants to involve themselves in the process of their own condemnation.

In civil cases, the rule is simply stated: the legislature may decide upon the burden of proof as it wishes, usually choosing the "preponderance of the evidence" test. In specialized proceedings, such as motions to suppress evidence for criminal trials, special rules have evolved. (See STANDARDS OF REVIEW.)

JAMES BOYD WHITE
(1986)

Bibliography
MCCORMICK, CHARLES 1954 *Handbook of the Law of Evidence.* Chap. 6. St. Paul, Minn.: West Publishing Co.

BURDICK v. TAKUSHI
504 U.S. 428 (1992)

Write-in voting, whereby the voter unsatisfied with the official candidates listed on the ballot card can write in the name of any person she would like to be elected, has been a staple of elections since the adoption of the state-printed—or "Australian"—ballot at the end of the nineteenth century. In *Burdick v. Takushi*, however, the Supreme Court, in a 6–3 decision, held that write-in voting was not a constitutionally mandated mechanism for exercising the right to vote, upholding Hawai'i's ban on write-in voting in state and federal elections.

Alan Burdick, a Hawai'i citizen, argued that the ban impermissibly infringed on his FREEDOM OF SPEECH, FREEDOM OF ASSOCIATION, and right to vote under the FIRST AMENDMENT and the FOURTEENTH AMENDMENT. Although recognizing an impairment of Burdick's choice on election day, the Court, per Justice BYRON R. WHITE, explained that all election laws governing BALLOT ACCESS, such as registration and qualification requirements, "invariably impose some burden upon individual voters." Because Hawai'i provided "easy access" to the primary ballot—requiring candidates to obtain only fifteen to twenty-five signatures depending on the office— the ban on write-in voting posed a "very limited" burden on voter choice that was justified by the state's interest in an efficient and orderly ELECTORAL PROCESS.

In his DISSENTING OPINION, Justice ANTHONY M. KENNEDY disagreed with the majority's conclusion that the burden on VOTING RIGHTS was insignificant. The very ballot access rules that the majority found to be liberal, Kennedy concluded were onerous, resulting in unopposed races in over one-third of state House of Representative elections and high numbers of blank, uncast ballots. Citizens who objected to the single candidate listed on the state-printed ballot in a given election had "no way to cast a meaningful vote."

ADAM WINKLER
(2000)

BUREAUCRACY

The Constitution creates an executive branch that neatly fits into the SEPARATION OF POWERS and CHECKS AND BALANCES system that the Framers devised. But the Constitution does not explicitly provide for the kind of administrative branch, or bureaucracy, that evolved beginning in the late nineteenth century. Congress created both independent commissions, such as the Interstate Commerce Commission (established in 1887), and other executive agencies that regulated a wide range of economic activities, and delegated to those bodies the authority both to make law through rule-making and to adjudicate cases arising under their JURISDICTION.

The Framers of the Constitution understandably did not foresee the development of an executive branch that would be a dominant force in lawmaking and adjudication, functions that they expected to be carried out by Congress and the courts. They conceived of "administration" as the "mere execution" of "executive details," to use ALEXANDER HAMILTON's description in THE FEDERALIST #72. Article II makes the President chief executive by giving him the responsibility to "take care that the laws be faithfully executed." He has the authority to appoint public ministers and other executive branch officials designated by Congress, subject to the ADVICE AND CONSENT of the Senate. He may "require the opinion in writing, of the principal officer in each of the executive departments, upon any subject relating to the duties of their respective offices. . . ." Hamilton concluded in *The Federalist* #72: "The persons, therefore, to whose immediate management the different administrative matters are committed ought to be considered as assistants or deputies of the Chief Magistrate and, on this account, they ought to derive their offices from his appointment, at least from his nomination, and ought to be subject to his superintendence."

Hamilton thought, as did most of the Framers, that the President would be, to use Clinton Rossiter's characterization in *The American Presidency* (1956), chief administrator. From a Hamiltonian perspective—one that later turned up in the presidential supremacy school of thought in public administration, reflected in the Report of the President's Committee on Administrative Management in 1937—the President is constitutionally responsible for the administrative branch.

Whatever may have been the intent of the Framers, the Constitution they designed allows and even requires both congressional and judicial intrusion into executive branch affairs. Two factors help to explain the constitutional ambiguities surrounding executive branch accountability. First, the system of separation of powers and checks and balances purposely gives Congress both the motivation and the authority to share with the President control over the executive branch. Congress jealously guards its position and powers, and its constitutional incentive to check the President encourages legislators to design an executive branch that will, in many respects, be independent of the White House. Other political incentives support those of the Constitution in encouraging Congress to hold the reins of the bureaucracy. Political pluralism has fragmented congressional politics into policy arenas controlled by committees. They form political "iron triangles" with agencies and special interests for their mutual benefit. The resulting executive branch pluralism is a major barrier to presidential control.

Agency performance of quasi-legislative and quasi-judicial functions is the second factor complicating the Hamiltonian prescription for the President to be chief administrator. From the standpoint of constitutional theory,

Congress and the courts are the primary legislative and judicial branches, respectively. Each has a responsibility to oversee administrative activities that fall within their spheres. Congressional, not presidential, intent should guide agency rule-making. Moreover, the constitutional system, as it was soon to be interpreted by the Supreme Court, gave to the judiciary sweeping authority to exercise JUDICIAL REVIEW over Congress and, by implication, over the President and the bureaucracy as well. Chief Justice JOHN MARSHALL stated in MARBURY V. MADISON (1803): "It is emphatically the province and duty of the Judicial Department to say what the law is. Those who apply the rule to particular cases must, of necessity, expound and interpret that rule." In concrete CASES AND CONTROVERSIES, where administrative action is appropriately challenged by injured parties, courts interpret and apply both statutory and constitutional law.

The hybrid character of the bureaucracy confuses the picture of its place in the governmental scheme. Constitutional prescriptions apply to the bureaucracy as they do to other branches. The bureaucracy must conform to the norms of separation of powers and checks and balances, PROCEDURAL DUE PROCESS, and democratic participation. The formal provisions of the Constitution and the broader politics of the system have shaped the administrative branch in various ways, limiting and controlling its powers.

Ironically, although the President alone is to be chief executive, Congress actually has more constitutional authority over the bureaucracy than does the White House as the result of its extensive enumerated powers under Article I. These do not mention the executive branch explicitly but by application of the doctrine of IMPLIED POWERS give the legislature the authority to create administrative departments and agencies and determine their course of action. Under the TAXING AND SPENDING POWER, the commerce power, and the WAR POWERS, Congress has authorized the creation of a vast array of agencies to carry out its responsibilities. The Legislative Reorganization Act of 1946 mandated Congress to establish oversight committees to supervise the bureaucracy and see to it that agencies were carrying out legislative intent. More important than legislative oversight, a responsibility most committee chairmen eschew because of its limited vote-getting value, is the appropriations and authorization process carried out by dozens of separate committees on Capitol Hill. Committee chairmen and their staffs indirectly sway administrative policymaking through committee hearings and informal contact with administrators who know that Congress strongly influences agency budgets.

The President's executive powers under Article II mean little unless Congress acquiesces in their exercise and buttresses the President's position in relation to the bureaucracy. It is congressional DELEGATION OF POWER to the President as much as, if not more than, the Constitution that determines to what extent he will be chief administrator. But the bureaucracy is always a pawn in the executive-legislative power struggle. Congressional willingness to strengthen presidential authority over the executive branch depends upon political forces that dictate the balance of power between Capitol Hill and the White House. Presidents have valiantly struggled but only intermittently succeeded in obtaining from Congress the powers they have requested to give them dominance over the bureaucracy.

From the NEW DEAL of FRANKLIN D. ROOSEVELT through the Great Society of LYNDON B. JOHNSON, Congress often agreed to requests for increased powers over the bureaucracy. During Roosevelt's administration, Congress for the first time gave the President authority to reorganize the executive Branch, subject to LEGISLATIVE VETO by a majority vote of either the House or the Senate. Roosevelt issued a historic EXECUTIVE ORDER in 1939 creating the presidential bureaucracy—the Executive Office of the President—to help him carry out his executive responsibilities. Laws granting the President reorganization authority were periodically renewed and acted upon until 1973 when Congress, in reaction to the WATERGATE revelations and concern over the "imperial presidency," allowed the reorganization act to expire. Although Congress renewed the reorganization law during the subsequent administration of President GERALD FORD, presidential authority over the bureaucracy had been impaired by the CONGRESSIONAL BUDGET AND IMPOUNDMENT CONTROL ACT of 1974 and other laws. Under the Congressional Budget Act the President could no longer permanently impound funds appropriated by Congress, as President RICHARD M. NIXON had done on over forty separate occasions. The law prevented the President from interfering with administrative implementation of legislative programs.

The courts, too, have claimed administrative turf, by exercising judicial review. Most of the statutes of individual agencies as well as the Administrative Procedure Act of 1946 set forth broad standards of procedural due process that administrators must follow when their decisions directly affect private rights, interests, and obligations. The courts not only interpret these statutory requirements but also apply to the administrative realm constitutional criteria for procedural fairness. For example, the Supreme Court held, in *Wong Yang Sung v. McGrath* (1950), that the Fifth Amendment's DUE PROCESS clause requires the Immigration Service to hold a full hearing with an independent judge presiding, before ordering the DEPORTATION of an illegal ALIEN whose life and liberty might be threatened if he were forced to return to his native land.

Involvement of the three original branches of government in the operations of the bureaucracy does not by itself solve the problem administrative agencies pose to the constitutional theory and practice of the separation of powers. Agencies performing regulatory functions combine in the same hands executive, legislative, and judicial powers. The Administrative Procedure Act of 1946 required a certain degree of separation of functions within agencies by creating an independent class of ADMINISTRATIVE LAW judges who initially decide formal rule-making and adjudicatory cases, which are those that by statute require trial-type hearings. Administrative judges must make their decisions on the record; *ex parte* consultations outside of the agency are forbidden entirely and, within the agency, can be made only in rule-making proceedings. Attempts to impose a judicial model on the administrative process, however, have not solved the constitutional dilemma posed by the fusion of powers within the bureaucracy. Commissions, boards, and agency heads have virtually unlimited discretion to overturn, on the basis of policy considerations, the decisions made by administrative law judges. Courts have supported the imposition of a judicial model on lower-level administrative rule-making and adjudicatory decisions, but have recognized the need for the heads of agencies to have discretion in interpreting legislative intent and flexibility in implementing statutory policy.

Another problem that the bureaucracy poses to the constitutional system is that of democratic control and accountability. An unelected, semi-autonomous administrative branch with the authority to make law arguably threatens to undermine the principles of representative government by removing lawmaking powers from Congress. The solution, in this view, is to restore the delegation of powers doctrine expressed by the Supreme Court in SCHECHTER POULTRY CORPORATION V. UNITED STATES (1935), holding that the primary legislative authority resides in Congress and cannot be delegated to the administrative branch. The *Schechter* rule was never strictly followed, and executive branch lawmaking increased and was even supported by the courts after that decision. However, judges did require that legislative intent be fairly clearly expressed, and they encouraged Congress to tighten agency procedural requirements to guarantee both fairness and compilation of records sufficient to permit effective judicial review.

Administrative discretion in lawmaking and adjudication remains a reality regardless of the intricate network of presidential, congressional, and judicial controls over the bureaucracy. But administrative agencies are not conspiracies to undermine individual liberties and rights, nor to subvert democratic government, a view that conservatives and liberals alike have of the enormous power of the executive branch. Political demands have led to the creation of executive departments and agencies that continue

to be responsive to the interests in their political constituencies, a democratic accountability that is narrow but, nevertheless, an important part of the system of administrative responsibility.

The bureaucracy performs vital governmental functions that the three original branches cannot easily carry out. Essential to any modern government is a relatively large and complex administrative branch capable of implementing the wide array of the programs democratic demands produce. American bureaucracy has added an important new dimension to the constitutional system. Because it is so profoundly shaped by the separation of powers, by the process of checks and balances, and by democratic political forces, it does fit, although imperfectly, into the system of constitutional democracy the Framers desired.

PETER WOLL
(1986)

Bibliography

FRIENDLY, HENRY J. 1962 *The Federal Administrative Agencies.* Cambridge, Mass.: Harvard University Press.
LANDIS, JAMES M. 1938 *The Administrative Process.* New Haven, Conn.: Yale University Press.
WOLL, PETER 1977 *American Bureaucracy.* New York: Norton.

BUREAUCRACY
(Update)

The Constitution fails to provide for the largest and one of the most important components of American government, the bureaucracy. The Framers understood that the presidency could not function without a group of persons comparable to the English servants of the crown. The Constitution does provide one specific reference to at least the top level of the bureaucracy: "The President . . . may require the Opinion in writing, of the principal officer in each of the executive Departments" (Article II, section 2). The Constitution also specifies how government officers are to be appointed—some by the President with the ADVICE AND CONSENT of the Senate and some by the President alone. It prohibits members of Congress from holding executive office, thus preventing the creation of cabinet government of the European kind. It specifically authorizes Congress to establish an army, navy, and post office. The Framers could also have specified what other departments, such as Treasury and State, should exist. Indeed, they could have provided a complete organization chart of the whole executive branch. But they did not. Instead, they appear to have deliberately left further evolution of the executive branch to Congress and to the President.

The Supreme Court has on occasion played a major role

in shaping the CONSTITUTIONAL THEORY of bureaucracy. From early in the Republic there have been two rival views of the bureaucracy. One, associated with ALEXANDER HAMILTON and later the Progressives, stresses the need for neutrality and expertise. The other emphasizes democratic responsibility. Jacksonian notions of "rotation in office" and "the spoils system" were the expression of this democratic theme. To prevent a gap between the governors and the governed, ordinary citizens were to take their turns in office and then return to private life. The partisans of the party that won one election were to be given government jobs and then turned out in favor of the partisans of whatever party won the next. Such arrangements undercut any vision of an expert bureaucracy reaching "correct" decisions. The Progressive view was eventually embodied in a series of state and federal civil service statutes that gradually incorporated more and more government workers into a system of entry and promotion by technical examinations and GOOD BEHAVIOR tenure.

The Hatch Act of 1939 prohibited federal civil servants from making contributions to, or participating in, election campaigns, in order to protect them from pressure by the President or their politically appointed superiors to actively support the President's party. The Hatch Act was challenged as a violation of the civil servants' FIRST AMENDMENT political participation rights. In *U.S. Civil Service Commission v. National Association of Letter Carriers* (1973) the Supreme Court decisively supported the Progressive theory of bureaucracy by holding that the compelling interest in an expert neutral career civil service outweighed the First Amendment claims at issue.

In a subsequent case, the Court directly confronted one of the last true "rotation in office" systems in the United States. Cook County, Illinois, prosecutors were political appointees. Whenever party control of the elected county executive changed, prosecutors of the winning party replaced those of the losing party. In *Elrod v. Burns* (1979) the prosecutors of the losing party argued that their First Amendment rights were being violated since they were being fired solely because of their political beliefs. Although the Court acknowledged the American tradition of the spoils system, it concentrated on the First Amendment issues and held for the fired prosecutors. Historically, whenever civil service protections were extended to a further category of government positions, those currently holding the positions, even though they owed their appointments to political favor rather than expert qualifications, were "blanketed in"—that is, allowed to keep their jobs. In the Cook County case, the Court in effect blanketed in all the remaining spoils appointees in the United States. The theory of a neutral bureaucracy free of party control has become part of the Constitution, not as a distinct provision but by judicial interpretation of the free speech clause.

The simple schema of the first three articles of the Constitution—Article I, Congress; Article II, presidency; and Article III, judiciary—would seem to place the executive department under the President, who is constitutionally endowed with "the executive power of the United States." Particularly since the NEW DEAL, many commentators have stressed the need for presidential control over the ever-growing and increasingly complex federal bureaucracy. In spite of what would appear to be the clear structure of the Constitution, the federal departments are as much, or more, the creatures of Congress as they are the servants of the President. Precisely because Article II does not itemize the executive departments or specify their organization, they have no independent constitutional status. Instead, every executive agency must be crafted by congressional statute, and all of its powers, programs, and expenditures also must be authorized by statute. Congress may further specify by statute the details of agency organization and procedure.

Beginning in the mid-1970s, with the presidency increasingly in the hands of one party and Congress in that of the other, more attention was given to the potential contradictions between the legal basis of the executive departments as congressional creations and the position of the President as chief executive. Agencies live between the duties imposed on them by statute and the executive authority wielded by the President. Recent Presidents have sought to give substantive content to their constitutional authority to "take care that the Laws be faithfully executed" and to assert that whatever discretion the executive agencies wield in the administration of law ultimately belongs to the President. The President's opponents respond by stressing the degree to which the agencies are bound by statutory duties imposed by Congress and the obligation of the President to obey those statutes. Typically these issues arise in the context of broadly worded or incomplete regulatory statutes that must be fleshed out by agency enacted rules. Because they involve ADMINISTRATIVE LAW and statutory interpretation, these issues often escape the attention of constitutional law specialists. The regulatory statute may be conceived as expressing, however vaguely and incompletely, a single, definite government policy that the agency must discover and embody correctly in its rules. Or such a statute may be seen as setting general goals and outer limits and then delegating to the agency an element of lawmaking discretion in fashioning detailed rules. In this view, although some rules are clearly foreclosed by the statute, the agency is free to choose from among a number of alternatives within the boundaries set by the statute. Agency choice will, and should, vary, depending on the policy views of the President and political appointees to the agencies. The former view tends to isolate the agency from presidential control, and the latter, to maximize such control.

Most immediately the issue is one of the relative policymaking power of the career agency bureaucracy and the politically appointed agency executives. The more we conceive of a single correct rule that most closely corresponds to the dictates of the statute, the greater must be the policy authority of the bureaucracy; it is the administrators who have long experience in dealing with the statute and great expertise in the factual data on which the correctness of a rule must depend. The more the statute is conceived as delegating lawmaking authority to the agency—that is, the discretion to choose from among alternative, equally valid rules—the greater policy authority should be vested in the President and his appointees, for if rule making really is discretionary lawmaking, then it should be done by those held accountable by the electoral process—not by a nonelected technocracy.

When courts reviewing the lawfulness of agency rules choose one of these visions or the other, the judges are deciding the degree to which the agencies belong to Congress or to the President. Depending on the statutory language, the circumstances, and the underlying constitutional theory of the judge, individual decisions go in one direction or the other. The collective impact of these decisions over time will move the federal bureaucracy more toward Article I or toward Article II and thus determine a fundamental aspect of constitutional law, even though those cases do not overtly raise constitutional questions. Such recent Supreme Court decisions as *Chevron U.S.A. v. Natural Resources Defense Council* (1984) and *Motor Vehicle Manufacturers Institute v. State Farm Mutual* (1983) keep both visions alive.

In a series of decisions on more explicitly constitutional SEPARATION OF POWERS issues, some Justices have sometimes sought to draw bright lines between congressional and presidential control over the bureaucracy. The Court's basic position, however, appears to be that it will seek to maintain a balance between the two without creating a firm boundary. This estimate seems confirmed in such cases as IMMIGRATION AND NATURALIZATION SERVICE V. CHADHA (1983), NIXON V. ADMINISTRATOR OF GENERAL SERVICES (1977), BOWSHER V. SYNAR (1986), and *Morrison v. Olson* (1988). One of these cases, *Chadha*, raises the specter of bureaucratic escape from both Congress and the presidency. Congress often passes statutes that vest great lawmaking authority in the agencies. If the bureaucrats in the agencies can use a theory of statutory duty to shield themselves from presidential control, then the agencies may float free of both Article I and Article II and become

a "fourth branch" of government unless Congress exercises some continuing control over the agencies after it has made broad delegations of power to them. One congressional attempt to exercise such poststatutory enactment control is the LEGISLATIVE VETO. In some of its delegatory statutes Congress has provided that before an agency promulgates a rule, it must submit the rule for Congress's approval. The Supreme Court ruled the legislative veto unconstitutional in *Chadha*. Congress has a number of other important weapons of administrative oversight, the most important being its appropriation control. It always retains the power to amend the statutes so as to preclude agency action of which it disapproves and ultimately the power to pass new statutes fundamentally altering the programmatic mandates and the organization or even existence of an agency that displeases it. Yet Congress frequently makes broad, vague, or contradictory delegations to the agencies precisely because it cannot muster the political will to specify what it wants. In such circumstances, it also may not muster the will to control the agency's exercise of the lawmaking power delegated to it. Therein lies the appeal to some of enhancing the power over the agencies of another elected official, the President. These grave constitutional questions work themselves out less in major Supreme Court cases than in the detailed language of statutes and the day-to-day practices of such presidential arms as the OFFICE OF MANAGEMENT AND BUDGET.

MARTIN SHAPIRO
(1992)

(SEE ALSO: *Administrative Agencies; Appointing and Removal Power, Presidential; Appointments Clause; Freedom of Speech; Hatch Act; Regulatory Agencies.*)

Bibliography
FISHER, LOUIS 1988 *Constitutional Dialogues*. Princeton, N.J.: Princeton University Press.
SHAPIRO, MARTIN 1988 *Who Guards the Guardians*. Athens, Ga.: University of Georgia Press.
WOLL, PETER 1963 *American Bureaucracy*. New York: Norton.

BURFORD v. SUN OIL COMPANY

See: Abstention Doctrine

BURGER, WARREN E.
(1907–1995)

Warren Earl Burger was born in St. Paul, Minnesota. He attended the University of Minnesota and, in 1931, received a law degree from St. Paul College of Law (today known as the William Mitchell College of Law). After practicing law in St. Paul for several years, he became the assistant attorney general in charge of the Civil Division of the Department of Justice during the administration of DWIGHT D. EISENHOWER. In 1955, Burger was appointed a judge on the United States Court of Appeals for the District of Columbia Circuit. He served in that capacity until 1969, when he became the Chief Justice of the United States, having been nominated for that position by RICHARD M. NIXON.

In the years of his tenure as Chief Justice, the Supreme Court has been marked publicly as having a majority of Justices who hold a generally conservative orientation toward constitutional issues. Burger himself is widely viewed as a primary proponent of this conservative judicial posture and, at least during the early years of the BURGER COURT, he was expected to lead the other conservative Justices in a major, if one-sided, battle to undo as much as could be undone of the pathbreaking work of its predecessor, the quite distinctly liberal WARREN COURT.

To the surprise of many the record of the Burger Court has been extraordinarily complicated, or uneven, when viewed against both of its commonly assumed objectives of overturning Warren Court decisions and of achieving what is often called a "nonactivist" judicial posture toward new claims for constitutional rights. Although it is true that a few Warren Court innovations have been openly discarded (for example, the recognition of a FIRST AMENDMENT right to speak in the context of privately owned SHOPPING CENTERS was overturned) and several other doctrines significantly curtailed (for example, the well-known 1966 ruling in MIRANDA V. ARIZONA has been narrowed as new cases have arisen), it is also true that many Warren Court holdings have been vigorously applied and even extended (for example, the principle of SEPARATION OF CHURCH AND STATE has been forcefully, if still confusingly, applied). What is perhaps most surprising of all, whole new areas of constitutional jurisprudence have been opened up. The foremost example here, of course, is the Court's highly controversial decision in ROE V. WADE (1973), which recognized a woman's constitutional right to have an abortion—subject to a set of conditions that rivaled in their legislation-like refinement the Warren Court's greatly maligned rules for the *Miranda* warnings. Against this history of overrulings, modifications, extensions, and new creations in the tapestry of decisions of its predecessor Courts, it is difficult to characterize the constitutional course steered by the modern Supreme Court under the stewardship of Warren Burger.

The same difficulty arises if one focuses more specifically on the constitutional thought of Burger himself. Burger may properly be regarded as one of the Court's most conservative members. In the field of criminal justice, he has tended to support police and prosecutors. He has joined in a large number of decisions limiting would-be litigants' access to the federal courts. Although he played an important role in the Court's recognition of constitutional rights in areas such as SEX DISCRIMINATION, discrimination against ALIENS, and SCHOOL BUSING, in each of these areas he has resisted extension of the rights initially recognized. Nonetheless, he has been inclined to accept the validity of congressional CIVIL RIGHTS legislation, and to read those laws generously. And he has been a strong supporter of claims of RELIGIOUS LIBERTY. Generally, he has joined the majority as it has pursued this surprisingly labyrinthine constitutional course. The starting point, therefore, for thinking about the constitutional thought of Warren Burger (just as it is for the Court as a whole during his tenure) is the realization that his opinions do not reflect an especially coherent vision of the Constitution and its contemporary significance.

But to say that the decisions and opinions of Burger, taken together, do not add up to a coherent whole does not mean that there are no important themes working their way through them. It is in fact quite possible to locate several distinct threads of thought: for example, a desire to return greater political power to the states in the federal system and to give greater protection to property interests is frequently reflected in Burger's constitutional opinions. But perhaps the most important characteristic of Warren Burger's opinions while Chief Justice is to be found in the area of individual rights and freedoms. It is there that one feels the strongest tension between a commitment to constitutional standards that control and limit the legislative process and a desire to maintain legislative control over the moral and intellectual climate of the community. It is in the resolution of that tension that one is able to determine what is most distinctive about Burger's constitutional jurisprudence.

Burger has frequently displayed a willingness to protect individual freedom at the expense of the interests of the state. His opinion for the Court in *Reed v. Reed* (1971), for example, was the first to subject gender classifications to more rigorous EQUAL PROTECTION scrutiny than had theretofore been the case. But, that said, it is also critical to an understanding of Burger's approach to the BILL OF RIGHTS to see that the depth of his commitment to individual liberties has been limited by a seemingly equal reluctance to extend constitutional protection to individuals or groups whose challenged behavior has gone beyond what may be called the customary norms of good behavior.

Two areas of First Amendment decisions are revealing here. In WISCONSIN V. YODER (1972), for example, Burger wrote an opinion for the Court upholding the right of members of an Amish religious community to refuse, on religious grounds, to comply with the Wisconsin compulsory school-attendance law. In his opinion Burger repeatedly emphasized the fact that the Amish had adopted a traditional lifestyle, saying at one point how "the Amish communities singularly parallel and reflect many of the virtues of THOMAS JEFFERSON's ideal of the "sturdy yeoman." On the other hand, in every case in which a speaker who used indecent language has sought the protection of the First Amendment, Burger has rejected the claim (though in these cases, usually in dissent) and, in doing so, has stressed the importance of maintaining community norms about proper and improper behavior.

In Burger's opinions, therefore, the protection of a specific liberty is often tied to his assessment of the respectability of the behavior. Sometimes this underlying attitude for a decision has been misinterpreted for other motivations. For example, in COLUMBIA BROADCASTING SYSTEM, INC. V. DEMOCRATIC NATIONAL COMMITTEE (1973), a major decision rejecting the claim that individuals and groups have a constitutional and statutory right to purchase airtime from broadcast stations in order to discuss public issues, Burger emphasized the importance of preserving the "journalistic autonomy" or "editorial discretion" of broadcasters, a theme reported in the press accounts of the case at the time. But this suggestion that the decision rested on a heightened respect for editorial freedom, and a preparedness to live with the consequent risks of bad editorial behavior, was considerably undermined by an additional thought Burger expressed. Freedom for broadcast journalists was to be preferred, he said, because broadcasters were regulated and therefore "accountable," while "[n]o such accountability attaches to the private individual, whose only qualifications for using the broadcast facility may be abundant funds and a point of view."

It is a noteworthy feature of Burger's constitutional work that in the area of FREEDOM OF THE PRESS he has written many of the Court's most prominent decisions upholding claims of the print media for protection against various forms of government regulation. Burger wrote for the Court in MIAMI HERALD PUBLISHING CO. V. TORNILLO (1974), holding that states could not require a newspaper to provide access to political candidates who had been criticized in the newspaper's columns; in NEBRASKA PRESS ASSOCIATION V. STUART (1976), holding that courts could not enjoin the media from publishing in advance of trial purported confessions and other evidence "implicative" of an accused individual; and in RICHMOND NEWSPAPERS, INC. V. VIRGINIA (1980), holding that courts could not follow a course of generally excluding the media from attending and observing criminal trials.

Yet, despite this strong record of extending constitutional protection to the press, the Burger Court, and especially Burger himself, has been strongly criticized by various segments of the press for retreating from earlier precedents and for being generally hostile to press claims. Burger, it is true, has sometimes voted along with a majority to reject press claims, as, for example, in BRANZBURG V. HAYES (1972), when the press urged the Court to recognize a limited constitutional privilege for journalists against being compelled to give testimony to grand juries, or in GERTZ V. ROBERT WELCH, INC. (1974), when the press sought to extend the "actual malice" standard in libel actions to all discussions of public issues, not just to those discussions concerning public officials and PUBLIC FIGURES. But an objective assessment of the holdings of the Burger Court does not seem to warrant the general accusation of its hostility to the press. It is too easy to lose sight of the basic truth that in virtually every case that involved significant issues of press freedom Burger has supported the press, and in many of them has written the majority opinions.

Is it possible to account for this discrepancy between criticism and performance? Here again the best explanation is to be found in Burger's disinclination to extend constitutional protection to activity judged as falling below conventional standards of good behavior. But in the area of freedom of the press this disinclination has manifested itself less in the actual results Burger has reached in particular cases and more in the craftsmanship and the tone of his judicial opinions.

The contrast between the opinions of the Warren Court and of Burger in the freedom of press area is remarkable. With Warren Court opinions the tone struck is almost uniformly that of praise for the role performed by the press in the American democratic political system. They extol the virtues of an open and free press. Although the same theme is to be found in Burger's judicial work, one often encounters rather sharp criticism of the press as well. Burger has actively used the forum of the Supreme Court judicial opinion to ventilate his feelings about the condition of the American press, and not everything he has had to say in that forum has been complimentary. One should consider in this regard one of the major cases in the free press area just mentioned, *Miami Herald Publishing Co. v. Tornillo*. In that case Burger's opinion for the Court begins with a lengthy and detailed description of the argument advanced by the state of Florida in support of its statute, which guaranteed limited access for political candidates to the columns of newspapers. The press has grown monopolized and excessively powerful, the state contended: "Chains of newspapers, national newspapers, national wire and news services, and one-newspaper towns, are the dominant features of a press that has become noncompetitive and enormously powerful and influential in its capacity to manipulate popular opinion and change the course of events. . . . Such national news organizations provide syndicated 'interpretive reporting' as well as syndicated features and commentary, all of which can serve as part of the new school of 'journalism.' " While ultimately rejecting the legal conclusion that the state sought to draw from this assumed social reality, Burger's opinion nevertheless strongly intimates sympathy with the general portrait of the press which the state's argument had painted. Thus, while the press may have had an ally in the constitutional result, it did not in the battle for public opinion generally.

Although Warren Burger retired from the Supreme Court at the end of the 1985–1986 term, what the lasting impact of his constitutional thought will be is of course impossible to tell. For the moment the most appropriate general assessment is that Burger's constitutional work displays a general disunity of character, while suggesting a responsiveness to generally conservative instincts, even when he is on the liberal side.

LEE C. BOLLINGER
(1986)

Bibliography

BLASI, VINCENT, ed.   1983   *The Burger Court.* New Haven, Conn.: Yale University Press.
BOLLINGER, LEE C.   1986   *The Tolerant Society: Freedom of Speech and Extremist Speech in America.* New York: Oxford University Press.
CHOPER, JESSE   1980   *Judicial Review and the National Political Process.* Chicago: University of Chicago Press.
SYMPOSIUM   1980   The Burger Court: Reflections on the First Decade. *Law and Contemporary Problems* 43:1.

BURGER COURT
(1969–1986)

The roots of the Burger Court lie in the JUDICIAL ACTIVISM of the WARREN COURT. The social vision of the Supreme Court under EARL WARREN was manifested on many fronts—dismantling racial barriers, requiring that legislative apportionment be based upon population, and vastly expanding the range of rights for criminal defendants, among others. At the height of its activity, during the 1960s, the Warren Court became a forum to which many of the great social issues of the time were taken.

Such activism provoked sharp attacks on the Court. Some of the criticism came from the ranks of the academy, other complaints from political quarters. In the 1968 presidential campaign, RICHARD M. NIXON objected in particular to the Court's CRIMINAL PROCEDURE decisions—rulings which, he said, favored the country's "criminal forces" against its "peace forces."

During his first term as President, Nixon put four Justices on the Supreme Court—WARREN E. BURGER, HARRY A. BLACKMUN, LEWIS F. POWELL, JR., and WILLIAM H. REHNQUIST. Rarely has a President been given the opportunity to fill so many vacancies on the Court in so short a time. Moreover, Nixon was explicit about the ideological basis for his appointments; he saw himself as redeeming his campaign pledge "to nominate to the Supreme Court individuals who share my judicial philosophy, which is basically a conservative philosophy."

Thus was born the Burger Court. For a time, pundits, at least those of liberal persuasion, took to calling it "the Nixon Court." Reviewing the 1971 term, *The New Republic* lamented that the "single-mindedness of the Nixon team threatens the image of the Court as an independent institution."

Inevitably, the work of the Burger Court was compared with that of its predecessor, the Warren Court. During the early Burger years, there was evidence that, with Nixon's four appointees on the bench, a new, and more conservative, majority was indeed in the making on the Court.

By the summer of 1976, a conservative Burger Court seemed to have come of age. For example, near the end of the 1975 term the Court closed the doors of federal courts to large numbers of state prisoners by holding that a prisoner who has had a full and fair opportunity to raise a FOURTH AMENDMENT question in the state courts cannot relitigate that question in a federal HABEAS CORPUS proceeding. In other criminal justice decisions, the Court whittled away at the rights of defendants, showing particular disfavor for claims seeking to curb police practices.

Decisions in areas other than criminal justice likewise showed a conservative flavor. For example, in the same term the Court used the TENTH AMENDMENT to place limits on Congress's commerce power, rejected the argument that claims of AGE DISCRIMINATION ought to trigger the higher level of JUDICIAL REVIEW associated with SUSPECT CLASSIFICATIONS (such as race), and refused to hold that CAPITAL PUNISHMENT is inherently unconstitutional.

By the mid-1970s, a student of the Court might have summarized the Burger Court, in contrast with the Warren Court, as being less egalitarian, more sensitive to FEDERALISM, more skeptical about the competence of judges to solve society's problems, more inclined to trust the governmental system, and, in general, more inclined to defer to legislative and political processes. By the end of the 1970s, however, such generalizations might have been thought premature—or, at least, have to be tempered. As the years passed, it became increasingly more difficult to draw clean distinctions between the years of Earl Warren and those of Warren Burger.

Cases involving claims of SEX DISCRIMINATION furnish an example. In 1973 four Justices (WILLIAM J. BRENNAN, WILLIAM O. DOUGLAS, BRYON R. WHITE, and THURGOOD MARSHALL) who had been on the Court in the Warren era sought to have the Court rule that classifications based on sex, like those based on race, should be viewed as "inherently suspect" and hence subject to STRICT SCRUTINY. The four Nixon appointees (together with Justice POTTER STEWART) joined in resisting such a standard. Yet, overall, the Burger Court's record in sex discrimination cases proved to be one of relative activism, even though the Court applied an intermediate STANDARD OF REVIEW in those cases, rather than one of strict scrutiny. In the 1978 term, for example, there were eight cases that in one way or another involved claims of sex discrimination; in six of the eight cases the Justices voted favorably to the claim, either on the merits or on procedural grounds.

In the early 1980s, with the Burger Court in its second decade, there was evidence that a working majority, conservative in bent, was taking hold. Two more Justices from the Warren era (William O. Douglas and Potter Stewart) had retired. Taking their place were appointees of Republican presidents—JOHN PAUL STEVENS (appointed by President GERALD R. FORD) and SANDRA DAY O'CONNOR (named by President RONALD REAGAN). While Stevens tended to vote with the more liberal Justices, O'Connor appeared to provide a dependable vote for the more conservative bloc on the Court.

In the 1983 term the conservatives appeared to have firm control. The Court recognized a "public safety" exception to the MIRANDA RULES and a "good faith" exception to the EXCLUSIONARY RULE in Fourth Amendment cases. The Justices upheld a New York law providing for the PREVENTIVE DETENTION of juveniles and sustained the Reagan administration's curb on travel to Cuba. As one commentator put it, "Whenever the rights of the individual confronted the authority of government this term, government nearly always won." The AMERICAN CIVIL LIBERTIES UNION's legal director called it "a genuinely appalling term," one in which the Court behaved as a "cheerleader for the government."

No sooner had such dire conclusions been drawn than the Burger Court once again confounded the Court-watchers. The very next term saw the Court return to the mainstream of its jurisprudence of the 1970s. The Court's religion cases are an example. Between 1980 and 1984 the Court appeared to be moving in the direction of allowing government to "accommodate" religion, thus relaxing the barriers the FIRST AMENDMENT erects between church and state. The Court rebuffed challenges to Nebraska's paying a legislative chaplain and Pawtucket, Rhode Island's displaying a Christmas crèche. Yet in the 1984 term the Court resumed a separationist stance, invalidating major programs (both federal and state) found to channel public aid to church schools, invalidating an Alabama statute providing for a "moment of silence or prayer" in public schools,

and striking down a Connecticut law making it illegal for an employer to require an employee to work on the employee's chosen Sabbath. The Reagan administration had filed briefs in support of the challenged laws in all four cases, and in each of the four cases a majority of the Justices ruled against the program.

Even so brief a sketch of the Burger Court's evolution conveys something of the dialectical nature of those years on the Court. In reading Burger Court opinions, one is sometimes struck by their conservative thrust, sometimes by a liberal result. Here the Burger Court is activist, there it defers to other branches or bodies. There is continuity with the Warren years, but discontinuity as well. One is struck, above all, by the way in which the Court in the Burger era has become a battleground on which fundamental jurisprudential issues are fought out.

No simple portrait of the Burger Court is possible. Some measure of the Burger years may be had, however, by touching upon certain themes that characterize the Burger Court—the questions which observers of the Court have tended to ask and the issues around which decision making on the Court has tended to revolve.

At the outset of the Burger era, many observers thought that a more conservative tribunal would undo much of the work of the Warren Court. This prophecy has been unfulfilled. The landmarks of the Warren Court remain essentially intact. Among those landmarks are BROWN V. BOARD OF EDUCATION (1954) (school desegregation), REYNOLDS V. SIMS (1964) (legislative REAPPORTIONMENT), and the decisions applying nearly all of the procedural protection of the BILL OF RIGHTS in criminal trials to the states.

In all of these areas, there have been, to be sure, important adjustments to Warren Court doctrine. Sometimes, a majority of the Burger Court's Justices have shown a marked distaste for the ethos underlying those precedents. Thus, while leaving such precedents as MIRANDA V. ARIZONA (1956) and MAPP V. OHIO (1961) standing, the Burger Court has frequently confined those precedents or carved out exceptions. Yet, despite criticisms, on and off the bench, of the INCORPORATION DOCTRINE, there has been no wholesale attempt to turn the clock back to the pre-Warren era.

In school cases, while the Burger Court has rebuffed efforts to provide remedies for de facto SEGREGATION, where de jure segregation is proved the Court has been generous in permitting federal judges to fashion effective remedies (it was an opinion of Chief Justice Burger, in SWANN V. CHARLOTTE-MECKLENBURG BOARD OF EDUCATION (1971) that first explicitly upheld lower courts' use of busing as a remedy in school cases). In legislative apportionment cases, the Burger Court has permitted some deviation from strict conformity to a population basis in drawing state and local government legislative districts, but the essential requirement remains that REPRESENTA-TION must be based on population.

A common complaint against the Warren Court was that it was too "activist"—that it was too quick to substitute its judgment for decisions of legislative bodies or other elected officials. In opinions written during the Burger years, it is common to find the rhetoric of judicial restraint, of calls for deference to policy judgments of legislatures and the political process generally.

Some Burger Court decisions reflect a stated preference for leaving difficult social issues to other forums than the courts. In rejecting an attack of Texas's system of financing public schools through heavy reliance on local property taxes, Justice Powell argued against judges' being too ready to interfere with "informed judgments made at the state and local levels."

Overall, however, the record of the Burger Court is one of activism. One of the hallmarks of activism is the enunciation by the Court of new rights. By that standard, no judicial decision could be more activist than the Burger Court's decision in ROE V. WADE (1973). There Justice Blackmun drew upon the vague contours of the FOUR-TEENTH AMENDMENT'S DUE PROCESS clause to decide that the RIGHT TO PRIVACY (itself a right not spelled out in the Constitution) implies a woman's right to have an ABORTION.

In the modern Supreme Court, the Fourteenth Amendment's due process and EQUAL PROTECTION clauses have been the most conspicuous vehicles for judicial activism. The Warren Court's favorite was the equal protection clause—the so-called new equal protection which, through strict scrutiny and other such tests, produced such decisions as *Reynolds v. Sims*. With the advent of the Burger Court came the renaissance of SUBSTANTIVE DUE PROCESS.

An example of the Burger Court's use of substantive due process is Justice Powell's plurality opinion in MOORE V. EAST CLEVELAND (1977). There the Court effectively extended strict scrutiny to a local ordinance impinging on the "extended family." Powell sought to confine the ambit of substantive due process by offering the "teachings of history" and the "basic values that underlie our society" as guides for judging. It is interesting to recall that, only a few years before *Roe* and *Moore*, even as activist a Justice as Douglas had been uncomfortable with using substantive due process (hence his peculiar "emanations from a penumbra" opinion in GRISWOLD V. CONNECTICUT, 1965). The Burger Court, in opinions such as *Roe* and *Moore*, openly reestablished substantive due process as a means to limit governmental power.

Another index of judicial activism in the Supreme Court is the Court's willingness to declare an act of Congress unconstitutional. Striking down a state or local action in order to enforce the Constitution or federal law is com-

mon, but invalidation of congressional actions is rarer. The Warren Court struck down, on average, barely over one federal statute per term; the Burger Court has invalidated provisions of federal law at about twice that rate. More revealing is the significance of the congressional policies overturned in Burger Court decisions. Among them have been campaign finance (BUCKLEY V. VALEO, 1976), the eighteen-year-old vote in state elections (OREGON V. MITCH-ELL, 1970), special bankruptcy courts (NORTHERN PIPELINE CONSTRUCTION CO. V. MARATHON PIPE LINE CO., 1982), and the LEGISLATIVE VETO (IMMIGRATION AND NATURALIZATION SERVICE V. CHADHA, 1983).

Yet another measure of judicial activism is the Court's oversight of the behavior of coordinate branches of the federal government, apart from the substantive results of legislative or executive actions. The Burger Court thrust itself directly into the WATERGATE crisis, during Nixon's presidency. Even as the IMPEACHMENT process was underway in Congress, the Supreme Court, bypassing the Court of Appeals, expedited its hearing of the question whether Nixon must turn over the Watergate tapes. Denying Nixon's claim of EXECUTIVE PRIVILEGE, the Court set in motion the dénouement of the crisis, resulting in Nixon's resignation. The Burger Court has similarly been willing to pass on the ambit of Congress's proper sphere of conduct. For example, the Court's narrow view of what activity is protected by the Constitution's SPEECH OR DEBATE CLAUSE would have surprised WOODROW WILSON, who placed great emphasis on Congress's role in informing the nation.

Closely related to the question of judicial activism is the breadth and scope of the Court's business—the range of issues which the Court chooses to address. Justice FELIX FRANKFURTER used to warn against the Court's plunging into "political thickets" and was distressed when the Warren Court chose to treat legislative apportionment as appropriate for judicial resolution.

Reviewing the record of the Burger Court, one is struck by the new ground it has plowed. Areas that were rarely entered or went untouched altogether in the Warren years have since 1969 become a staple of the Court's docket. In the 1960s Justice ARTHUR J. GOLDBERG sought in vain to have the Justices debate the merits of capital punishment, but the Court would not even grant CERTIORARI. By contrast, not only did the Burger Court, in *Furman v. Georgia* (1972), rule that capital statutes as then administered were unconstitutional, but also death cases have appeared on the Court's calendar with regularity. (See CAPITAL PUNISH-MENT CASES OF 1972, 1976.)

Sex discrimination is another area that, because of Burger Court decisions, has become a staple on the Justices' table. In *Hoyt v. Florida* (1961) the Warren Court took a quite relaxed view of claims of sex discrimination in a decision upholding a Florida law making jury service for women, but not for men, completely voluntary. By the time Warren Burger became Chief Justice, in 1969, the women's movement had become a visible aspect of the American scene, and since that time the Burger Court has fashioned a considerable body of law on women's rights.

The Burger Court has carried forward—or has been carried along with—the "judicialization" or "constitutionalization" of American life. The victories won by blacks in court in the heyday of the CIVIL RIGHTS movement have inspired others to emulate their example. Prisoners, voters victimized by malapportionment, women, juveniles, inmates of mental institutions—virtually any group or individual failing to get results from the legislative or political process or from government bureaucracies has turned to the courts for relief. And federal judges have woven remedies for a variety of ills.

The Burger Court might have been expected to resist the process of constitutionalization. On some fronts, the Justices have slowed the process. SAN ANTONIO INDEPENDENT SCHOOL DISTRICT V. RODRIGUEZ (1973) represents a victory for a hands-off approach to SCHOOL FINANCE (although it is undercut somewhat by the Court's subsequent decision in *Plyler v. Doe*, 1982). But such decisions seem to be only pauses in the expansion of areas in which the judiciary is willing to inquire.

The Burger Court may sometimes reach a "liberal" result, sometimes a "conservative" one. In some cases the Justices may lay a restraining hand on the EQUITY powers of federal judges, and in some they may be more permissive. All the while, however, the scope of the Supreme Court's docket expands to include wider terrain. In constitutional litigation, there seems to be a kind of ratchet effect: once judges enter an area, they rarely depart. This pattern characterizes the Burger era as much as it does that of Warren.

Even in areas that seemed well developed in the Warren Court, the Burger Court has added new glosses. It was long thought that COMMERCIAL SPEECH fell outside the protection of the First Amendment; the Burger Court brought it inside. It was Burger Court opinions that enlarged press rights under the First Amendment to include, at least in some circumstances, a right of access to criminal trials. The jurisprudence by which government aid to sectarian schools is tested is almost entirely of Burger Court making. Most of the case law sketching out the contours of personal autonomy in such areas as abortion, BIRTH CONTROL, and other intimate sexual and family relations dates from the Burger era. If idle hands are the devil's workshop, the Burger Court is a temple of virtue.

The contour of rights consists not only of substantive doctrine; it also includes jurisdiction and procedure. Who shall have access to the federal forum, when, and for the resolution of what rights—these have been battlegrounds in the Burger Court. If a case may be made that the Burger Court has achieved a retrenchment in rights, it may be that the case is the strongest as regards the Court's shaping of procedural devices.

Warren Court decisions reflected a mistrust in state courts as forums for the vindication of federal rights. Burger Court decisions, by contrast, are more likely to speak of the COMITY owed to state courts. Thus, in a line of decisions beginning with YOUNGER V. HARRIS (1971), the Burger Court has put significant limitations on the power of federal judges to interfere with proceedings (especially criminal) in state courts. The Court also has sharply curtailed the opportunity for state prisoners to seek federal habeas corpus review of state court decisions.

Technical barriers such as STANDING have been used in a number of cases to prevent plaintiffs' access to federal courts. For example, in *Warth v. Selden* (1976) black residents of Rochester were denied standing to challenge exclusionary ZONING in the city's suburbs. Similarly, in SIMON V. EASTERN KENTUCKY WELFARE RIGHTS ORGANIZATION (1976) poor residents of Appalachia were held not to have standing to challenge federal tax advantages granted to private hospitals that refused to serve the INDIGENT.

By no means, however, are Burger Court decisions invariable in restricting access to federal courts or in limiting remedies for the violation of federal law. Some of the Court's interpretations of SECTION 1983, TITLE 42, UNITED STATES CODE (a civil rights statute dating back to 1871) have made that statute a veritable font of litigation. The Warren Court had ruled, in 1961, that Congress, in enacting section 1983, had not intended that municipalities be among the "persons" subject to suit under the statute; in 1978, the Burger Court undertook a "fresh analysis" of the statute and concluded that municipalities are subject to suit thereunder.

Going further, the Court ruled, in 1980, that municipalities sued under section 1983 may not plead as a defense that the governmental official who was involved in the alleged wrong had acted in "good faith"; the majority disregarded the four dissenters' complaint that "ruinous judgments under the statute could imperil local governments." And in another 1980 decision the Court held that plaintiffs could use section 1983 to redress claims based on federal law generally, thus overturning a long-standing assumption that section 1983's reference to federal "laws" was to equal rights legislation. The Burger Court's section 1983 rulings have been a major factor in the "litigation explosion" which in recent years has been the subject of so much legal and popular commentary.

The reach of federal courts' equity powers has been another hotly debated issue in the Burger Court. CLASS ACTIONS seeking to reform practices in schools, prisons, jails, and other public institutions have made INSTITU-

TIONAL LITIGATION a commonplace. Such suits go far beyond the judge's declaring that a right has been violated; they draw the judge into ongoing supervision of state or local institutions (recalling the quip that in the 1960s federal district judge Frank Johnson was the real governor of Alabama). Institutional litigation in federal courts raises serious questions about federalism and often blurs the line between adjudication, legislation, and administration.

Some Burger Court decisions have attempted to curb federal judges' equity power in institutional cases. For example, in RIZZO V. GOODE (1976) Justice Rehnquist, for the majority, reversed a lower court's order to the Philadelphia police department to institute reforms responding to allegations of police brutality; Rehnquist admonished the judge to refrain from interfering in the affairs of local government. Similarly, in prison cases, the Burger Court has emphasized the importance of federal judges' deference to state prison officials' judgment about questions of prison security and administration.

In important respects, however, the Burger Court has done little to place notable limits on federal courts' equity powers. Especially is this true in school DESEGREGATION cases. A wide range of remedies has been approved, including busing, redrawing of attendance zones, and other devices. Although the Court has maintained the distinction between DE FACTO AND DE JURE segregation (thus requiring evidence of purposeful segregation as part of a plaintiff's prima facie case), decisions such as those from Columbus and Dayton (both in 1979) show great deference to findings of lower courts used to support remedial orders against local school districts.

Painting a coherent portrait of the Burger Court is no easy task. An effort to describe the Court in terms of general themes, such as the Justices' attitude to judicial activism, founders on conflicting remarks in the Court's opinions. Likewise, an attempt to generalize about the Burger Court's behavior in any given area encounters difficulties.

Consider, for example, the expectation—understandable in light of President Nixon's explicit concern about the Warren Court's rulings in criminal justice cases—that the Burger Court would be a "law and order" tribunal. In the early years of the Burger Court (until about 1976), the Court, especially in its rulings on police practices, seemed bent on undermining the protections accorded in decisions of the Warren years. The majority showed their attitude to the exclusionary rule by referring to it as a "judicially created remedy," one whose benefits were to be balanced against its costs (such as to the functioning of a GRAND JURY). In the late 1970s, the Court seemed more sympathetic to *Miranda* and to other devices meant to limit police practices. But in the early 1980s, especially in

SEARCH AND SEIZURE cases, the Court seemed once again markedly sympathetic to law enforcement.

Or consider the Court's attitudes to federalism. In some decisions, the Burger Court has seemed sympathetic to the interests of states and localities. In limiting state prisoners' access to federal writs of habeas corpus, the Court shows respect for state courts. In rebuffing attacks on inequalities in the financing of a state's public schools, the Court gives breathing room to local judgments about running those schools. In limiting federal court intervention in prison affairs, the Court gives scope for state judgments about how to run a prison.

Yet many Burger Court decisions are decidedly adverse to state and local governments' interests. The Court's section 1983 rulings have exposed municipalities to expensive damage awards. The Burger Court has been more active than the Warren Court in using the dormant COMMERCE CLAUSE to restrict state laws and regulations found to impinge upon national interests. And in the highly controversial decision of GARCIA V. SAN ANTONIO METROPOLITAN TRANSIT AUTHORITY (1985) the Court said that, if the states have Tenth Amendment concerns about acts of Congress, they should seek relief from Congress, not from the courts (in so ruling, the Court in *Garcia* overturned NATIONAL LEAGUE OF CITIES V. USERY, 1976, itself a Burger Court decision).

How does one account for such a mixed record, replete with conflicting signals about basic jurisprudential values? The temperament and habits of the Justices of the Burger Court play a part. Pundits often imagine the Justices coming to the Court's conference table with "shopping lists," looking for cases on which to hang doctrinal innovations. For most (although not necessarily all) of the Justices, this picture is not accurate. By and large, the Justices tend to take the cases as they come. This tendency is reinforced by the Court's workload pressures. Far more cases come to the Burger Court than came to the Warren Court. Complaints by the Chief Justice about the burden thus placed on the Court are frequent, and in 1975 it was reported that at least five Justices had gone on record as favoring the concept of a National Court of Appeals to ease the Supreme Court's workload.

The Burger years on the Court have lacked the larger-than-life figures of the Warren era, Justices like HUGO L. BLACK and Felix Frankfurter, around whom issues tended to polarize. Those were judges who framed grand designs, a jurisprudence of judging. Through their fully evolved doctrines, and their arm-twisting, they put pressure on their colleagues to think about cases in doctrinal terms. Since the departure of the great ideologues, the Justices have been under less pressure to fit individual cases into doctrinal tableaux. Ad hoc results become the order of the day.

The Burger Court has been a somewhat less ideological bench than was the Warren Court. Many of the Court's most important decisions have turned upon the vote of the centrists on the bench. It is not unusual to find, especially in 5–4 decisions, that Justice Powell has cast the deciding vote. Powell came to the bench inclined to think in the pragmatic way of the practicing lawyer; as a Justice he soon came to be identified with "balancing" competing interests to arrive at a decision. The Burger Court's pragmatism, its tendency to gravitate to the center, blurs ideological lines and makes its jurisprudence often seem to lack any unifying theme or principle.

A Burger Court decision—more often, a line of decisions—often has something for everyone. In *Roe v. Wade* the Court upheld the right of a woman to make and effectuate a decision to have an abortion. Yet, while invalidating state laws found to burden the abortion decision directly, the Court has permitted state and federal governments to deny funding for even therapeutic abortions while funding other medical procedures. In REGENTS OF THE UNIVERSITY OF CALIFORNIA V. BAKKE (1978) a majority of the Justices ruled against RACIAL QUOTAS in a state university's admissions process, but a university, consistent with *Bakke*, may use race as a factor among other factors in the admissions process.

Burger Court decisions show a distaste for categorical values. The Warren Court's fondness for prophylactic rules, such as *Miranda* or the Fourth Amendment exclusionary rule, is not echoed in the Burger Court. The Burger bench may not have jettisoned those rules outright, but most Justices of this era show a preference for fact-oriented adjudication rather than for sweeping formulae.

Burger Court opinions are less likely than those of the Warren Court to ring with moral imperatives. Even when resolving so fundamental a controversy as that over abortion, a Burger Court opinion is apt to resemble a legislative committee report more nearly than a tract in political theory. A comparison of such Warren Court opinions as *Brown v. Board of Education* and *Reynolds v. Sims* and a Burger Court opinion such as *Roe v. Wade* is instructive. Warren Court opinions often read as if their authors intended them to have tutorial value (Justice Goldberg once called the Supreme Court "the nation's schoolmaster"); Burger Court opinions are more likely to read like an exercise in problem solving.

For most of its existence, the Burger Court has been characterized by a lack of cohesive voting blocs. For much of its history, the Burger years have seen a 2–5–2 voting pattern—Burger and Rehnquist in one wing, Brennan and Marshall in the other wing, the remaining five Justices tending to take more central ground. Justice Stewart's re-

placement by Justice O'Connor (a more conservative Justice) tended to reinforce the Burger-Rehnquist wing, while Justice Stevens gravitated more and more to the Brennan-Marshall camp. Even so, the Burger Court was a long way from the sharp ideological alignments of the Warren years.

The Court's personalities and dynamics aside, the nature of the issues coming before the Burger Court help account for the mixed character of the Court's record. The Warren Court is well remembered for decisions laying down broad principles; *Brown, Mapp, Miranda,* and *Reynolds* are examples. The task of implementing much of what the Warren Court began fell to the Burger Court. Implementation, by its nature, draws courts into closer judgment calls. It is one thing to lay down the principle that public schools should not be segregated by race, but quite another to pick one's way through the thicket of de facto-de jure distinctions, interdistrict remedies, and shifting demographics. Had the Warren Court survived into the 1970s, it might have found implementation as difficult and splintering as has the Burger Court.

If the Warren Court embodied the heritage of progressivism and the optimistic expectations of post-World War II America, the Burger years parallel a period of doubt and uncertainty about solutions to social problems in the years after the Great Society, the VIETNAM WAR, and Watergate. In a time when the American people might have less confidence in government's capacity in other spheres, the Supreme Court might well intuitively be less bold in imposing its own solutions. At the same time, there appeared, in the Burger years, to be no turning back the clock on the expectations of lawyers and laity alike as to the place of an activist judiciary in public life. Debate over the proper role of the judiciary in a democracy is not insulated from debate over the role of government generally in a society aspiring to ORDERED LIBERTY. Judgments about the record of the Burger Court, therefore, tend to mirror contemporary American ideals and values.

A. E. DICK HOWARD
(1986)

Bibliography

BLASI, VINCENT, ed. 1983 *The Burger Court: The Counter-Revolution That Wasn't.* New Haven, Conn.: Yale University Press.

FUNSTON, RICHARD Y. 1977 *Constitutional Counterrevolution?: The Warren Court and the Burger Court: Judicial Policy Making in Modern America.* Cambridge, Mass.: Schenkman.

LEVY, LEONARD W. 1974 *Against the Law: The Nixon Court and Criminal Justice.* New York: Harper & Row.

MASON, ALPHEUS T. 1979 *The Supreme Court from Taft to Burger,* 3rd ed. Baton Rouge: Louisiana State University Press.

WOODWARD, BOB and ARMSTRONG, SCOTT   1979   *The Brethren: Inside the Supreme Court.* New York: Simon & Schuster.

EMERSON, THOMAS I.   1980   First Amendment Doctrine and the Burger Court. *California Law Review* 68:422–481.

HOWARD, A. E. DICK   1972   Mr. Justice Powell and the Emerging Nixon Majority. *Michigan Law Review* 70:445–468.

REHNQUIST, WILLIAM H.   1980   The Notion of a Living Constitution. *Texas Law Review* 54:693–706.

SALTZBERG, STEPHEN A.   1980   Foreword: The Flow and Ebb of Constitutional Criminal Procedure in the Warren and Burger Courts. *Georgetown Law Journal* 69:151–209.

BURGESS, JOHN W.
(1842–1931)

John W. Burgess was professor of political science and constitutional law at Columbia University (1876–1912) where he founded America's first graduate department of political science. Trained in Germany, Burgess sought to develop an American political science based on historical determinism rather than the NATURAL RIGHTS assumptions of the DECLARATION OF INDEPENDENCE. He saw the CIVIL WAR as a necessary step in the process by which FEDERALISM gave way to nationalism. He understood the Constitution as creating the two spheres of government and liberty, and as granting rights to individuals rather than protecting preexisting rights. His most important book was *Political Science and Comparative Constitutional Law* (1890).

DENNIS J. MAHONEY
(1986)

BURKE-WADSWORTH SELECTIVE TRAINING AND SERVICE ACT

See: Selective Service Acts

BURNS BAKING COMPANY v. BRYAN
264 U.S. 504 (1924)

The Supreme Court, speaking through Justice PIERCE BUTLER, declared unconstitutional a Nebraska statute that prohibited short-weighting as well as overweighting of bread as a violation of DUE PROCESS and an arbitrary interference with private business. Justice LOUIS D. BRANDEIS dissented, joined by OLIVER WENDELL HOLMES, decrying the decision as "an exercise of the powers of a super-legislature," and urging deference to the legislature's basis for state action.

DAVID GORDON
(1986)

BURR, AARON
(1756–1836)

Aaron Burr of New York served as a Continental Army officer during the Revolutionary War and later practiced law in Albany and New York City. He was elected four times to the legislature and was for two years state attorney general before serving a term in the United States SENATE (1791–1797). He organized the New York Republican party and was the first person to use the Tammany Society for political purposes.

In 1800 Burr was nominated for vice-president on the Republican ticket. Under the ELECTORAL COLLEGE system as it then existed, Burr received the same number of votes as his party's presidential nominee, THOMAS JEFFERSON. The HOUSE OF REPRESENTATIVES took thirty-six ballots to break the tie and elect Jefferson President, and did so only after ALEXANDER HAMILTON interceded with Federalist congressmen.

After his term as vice-president ended in 1805, Burr became involved in a bizarre intrigue, generally supposed to have had as its object the creation of a separate nation southwest of the Appalachian Mountains. His expedition was thwarted, and Burr and several of his confederates were tried for TREASON. President Jefferson personally directed the prosecution and publicly proclaimed the conspirators guilty. In EX PARTE BOLLMAN AND SWARTOUT (1807) the Supreme Court released two of Burr's lieutenants on a writ of HABEAS CORPUS, refusing to extend the constitutional definition of treason to include conspiracy to commit the offense. A few months later Burr himself was tried before JOHN MARSHALL, sitting as circuit judge, and was acquitted on procedural grounds. The acquittal was the occasion of a renewed Jeffersonian assault against Marshall and the independence of the judiciary.

Burr spent the five years following his trial in European exile, and he never returned to public life.

DENNIS J. MAHONEY
(1986)

Bibliography

LOMASK, MILTON   1979   *Aaron Burr: The Years from Princeton to Vice President, 1756–1805.* New York: Farrar, Straus & Giroux.

——— 1982   *Aaron Burr: The Conspiracy and Years of Exile, 1805–1836.* New York: Farrar, Straus & Giroux.

BURSON v. FREEMAN
504 U.S. 191 (1992)

There is no speech more important for a democracy than political speech pertaining to elections. Nevertheless, all fifty states prohibit political speech in and around polling places on election day. In *Burson v. Freeman*, the Supreme Court, in a 5–3 decision, held that a ban on political speech within 100 feet of the entrance to polling places on election day was not an unconstitutional infringement of the FREEDOM OF SPEECH.

The PLURALITY OPINION of Justice HARRY A. BLACKMUN reasoned that the impairment of core FIRST AMENDMENT rights was justified by the COMPELLING STATE INTEREST in avoiding voter intimidation and election fraud. Despite the OVERBREADTH of the ban—not all prohibited speech would intimidate voters or threaten fraud—the Court was swayed by the fact that every state has long-standing "campaign-free" zones around polling places and by the fear that other measures to preserve electoral integrity might involve unwelcome police presence at the polls.

Justice JOHN PAUL STEVENS, in dissent, agreed that the state's interests were compelling, but argued that smaller campaign-free zones, perhaps no larger than 50 feet, were adequate to insure free access to the polls. Moreover, the ban's application to ordinary campaign-related speech, such as posters and signs, was content-discriminatory and bore no relationship to the prevention of fraud or intimidation.

ADAM WINKLER
(2000)

BURSTYN, INC. v. WILSON
343 U.S. 495 (1952)

The Supreme Court in this case unanimously overruled a 1915 decision that movies are a business "pure and simple," not entitled to constitutional protection as a medium for the communication of ideas. Justice TOM C. CLARK, for the *Burstyn* Court, ruled that expression by means of movies is included within the free speech and free press clauses of the FIRST AMENDMENT and protected against state abridgment by the FOURTEENTH. In this case New York authorized a state censor to refuse a license for the showing of any film deemed "sacrilegious," a standard that permitted unfettered and unprejudiced discretion. (See VAGUENESS DOCTRINE.) The state, Clark declared, had no legitimate interest in protecting any religion from offensive views. Justice FELIX FRANKFURTER, concurring, emphasized the danger to the creative process and to RELIGIOUS LIBERTY from a standard so vague that it could be confused with BLASPHEMY.

LEONARD W. LEVY
(1986)

BURTON, HAROLD
(1888–1964)

Probably no member of the United States Supreme Court enjoyed greater affection from his colleagues on the bench than Justice Harold Burton, whom FELIX FRANKFURTER once described as having "a kind of a boy scout temperament," and whom others praised for his kindness, reasonableness, and unfailing integrity. "There is no man on the bench now who has less pride of opinion," Frankfurter noted, ". . . or is more ready to change positions, if his mind can be convinced. And no vanity guards admission to his mind." Burton, a former mayor of Cleveland and United States senator from Ohio, enjoyed several other distinctions as well. Named to the Court in 1945, he was the only Republican appointed between 1933 and 1953; he also proved to be the most liberal of HARRY S. TRUMAN's four appointees, which, considering the nature of the competition, did not demand much liberalism.

Although dubbed by the press as one member of Truman's law firm, which also included FRED M. VINSON, TOM C. CLARK, and SHERMAN MINTON, Burton broke ranks with the President on the most crucial test of executive power during his tenure, when he joined Justice HUGO L. BLACK's opinion in YOUNGSTOWN SHEET & TUBE CO. V. SAWYER (1952), which declared Truman's seizure of the nation's steel mills illegal in the absence of congressional legislation.

With the notable exception of JOINT ANTI-FASCIST REFUGEE COMMITTEE V. McGRATH (1951), however, Burton routinely upheld the Truman administration's efforts to destroy the American Communist party and to purge from the federal government suspected subversives during the high tide of the post-1945 Red Scare. He voted with the majority, for instance, in AMERICAN COMMUNICATIONS ASSOCIATION V. DOUDS (1950), in DENNIS V. UNITED STATES (1951), and in *Bailey v. Richardson* (1951), in which the VINSON COURT sustained the noncommunist oath provisions of the TAFT-HARTLEY ACT, the conviction of eleven top Communist party leaders under the Smith Act, and the federal government's LOYALTY AND SECURITY PROGRAM.

Apart from Minton and STANLEY F. REED, Burton became the most virulent antiradical on the bench during the 1950s. In *Slochower v. Board of Education* (1956) he dissented against Clark's opinion voiding the dismissal of a professor who had invoked his right AGAINST SELF-INCRIMINATION during an investigation into his official conduct. He also dissented in SWEEZY V. NEW HAMPSHIRE (1957), when the Court reversed the conviction of another professor for refusing to answer questions about his classes posed by the state's attorney general. And he, Minton, and Reed were the only dissenters in PENNSYLVANIA V. NELSON

(1956), when the Court invalidated the SEDITION law of that state and, by implication, similar statutes in other states.

Generally, Burton followed an equally conservative standard with respect to criminal justice issues. Here, too, he usually endorsed the claims of government rather than those of the individual. In *Bute v. Illinois* (1948) he wrote for a majority of five that reaffirmed the rule of BETTS V. BRADY (1942), which permitted the states to prosecute noncapital felonies without appointing counsel for indigent defendants. He also tolerated forms of police conduct that offended even Frankfurter's conception of DUE PROCESS. (See RIGHT TO COUNSEL.)

Moments of compassion and insight redeemed Burton's otherwise lackluster record in CIVIL LIBERTIES cases. In *Louisiana ex rel. Francis v. Resweber* (1947), perhaps his most famous opinion, he rebelled against Louisiana's efforts to execute a convicted murderer after the first grisly attempt failed because of low voltage in the electric chair. He also joined Black and Frankfurter in their futile efforts to secure a full hearing before the Supreme Court for Julius and Ethel Rosenberg, who were convicted of espionage at the depths of the cold war with the Soviet Union.

By the conclusion of his judicial career in 1956, moreover, he had emerged as one of the Court's most outspoken foes of racial SEGREGATION, despite an unpromising beginning in MORGAN V. VIRGINIA (1946), where he had been the lone dissenter against Black's opinion invalidating the application of that state's Jim Crow law to interstate buses. Four years before BROWN V. BOARD OF EDUCATION, Burton had been prepared to overrule the SEPARATE BUT EQUAL DOCTRINE in *Henderson v. United States* (1950). Reluctantly, he bowed to the preference of several colleagues for invoking the COMMERCE CLAUSE to topple segregation on southern railroads in that case, but he joined Chief Justice EARL WARREN's opinion eagerly in *Brown*. Suffering from a debilitating illness that later claimed his life, Burton retired from the Court in 1958.

MICHAEL E. PARRISH
(1986)

Bibliography

BERRY, MARY F.   1978   *Stability, Security, and Continuity: Mr. Justice Burton and Decision-Making in the Supreme Court, 1945–1958*. Westport, Conn.: Greenwood Press.

BURTON v. WILMINGTON PARKING AUTHORITY
365 U.S. 715 (1961)

Burton exemplifies the interest-balancing approach to the STATE ACTION limitation of the FOURTEENTH AMENDMENT used by the Supreme Court during the Chief Justiceship of EARL WARREN. A private restaurant, leasing space in a publicly owned parking structure, refused to serve Burton because he was black. In a state court action, Burton sought declaratory and injunctive relief, claiming that the restaurant's refusal amounted to state action denying him the EQUAL PROTECTION OF THE LAWS. The state courts denied relief, but the Supreme Court reversed, 7–2, holding the Fourteenth Amendment applicable to the restaurant's conduct.

Public agencies owned the land and the building, had floated bonds, were collecting revenues to pay for the building's construction and maintenance, and received rent payments from the restaurant. The restaurant could expect to draw customers from persons parking in the structure; correspondingly, some might park there because of the restaurant's convenience. Profits earned from the restaurant's RACIAL DISCRIMINATION, the Court said, were indispensable elements in an integral financial plan. All these interrelated mutual benefits taken together amounted to significant involvement of the state in the private racial discrimination. Justice TOM C. CLARK, for the majority, disclaimed any pretensions of establishing a general rule about state aid to private discrimination, or even for the leasing of state property. Under "the peculiar facts or circumstances" here, the state action limitation was satisfied.

Justice POTTER STEWART, concurring, said simply that a state statute permitting a restaurant's proprietor to refuse service to persons offensive to a majority of patrons amounted to official authorization of private discrimination—a theme explored later in REITMAN V. MULKEY (1967). Justice JOHN MARSHALL HARLAN dissented, joined by Justice CHARLES E. WHITTAKER. Harlan complained that the majority had offered no guidance for determining when the state action limitation would be satisfied. Rather than pursue this inquiry, he urged a REMAND to the state courts for further illumination of the "authorization" question raised by Justice Stewart.

KENNETH L. KARST
(1986)

BUSH, GEORGE H. W.
(1924–   )

George Bush served two terms as vice-president during the presidency of RONALD REAGAN, who had been his rival for the Republican presidential nomination in 1980. With Reagan's support, Bush was then elected President in 1988. Bush was thus the first President since 1836 to be elected from the vice-presidency, an office that does not usually provide much prominence or stature to its incumbent. Bush was also one of the few Presidents in this century to have reached the White House without having previously won a single statewide election (he was defeated in bids to become U.S. senator from Texas in 1966 and 1970). With the exception of the popular leader DWIGHT D. EISENHOWER, all the others in this category— WILLIAM HOWARD TAFT, HERBERT C. HOOVER, and GERALD R. FORD—proved to be one-term Presidents.

Apart from serving two terms in the U.S. HOUSE OF REPRESENTATIVES (1966–1970), Bush owed his political experience before 1980 to a succession of presidential appointments in the administrations of RICHARD M. NIXON and Gerald Ford. He served successively as U.S. ambassador to the United Nations (1971–1973), chief of the U.S. Liaison Office (that is, de facto ambassador) in the People's Republic of China (1974–1975), and director of the Central Intelligence Agency (1976). His performance in these posts made no enemies but also did little to define his political character or to win him a broad popular following.

In the 1988 presidential campaign, Bush courted the conservative constituencies of Ronald Reagan. He attacked his opponent for his affiliation with the AMERICAN CIVIL LIBERTIES UNION and expressed sympathy with several key conservative complaints against the constitutional rulings of both the WARREN COURT and the BURGER COURT. He thus expressed support for constitutional amendments to prohibit ABORTION and to reauthorize SCHOOL PRAYER. He also supported a constitutional amendment to require a BALANCED BUDGET. As President, he urged a constitutional amendment to overturn the Supreme Court's ruling that FLAG DESECRATION is protected by the FIRST AMENDMENT. None of these amendments was pushed with any sustained energy or intensity by the Bush administration, however, and none found majority support in Congress.

Bush's first choice for the Supreme Court when the retirement of Justice WILLIAM J. BRENNAN opened a vacancy in the summer of 1990 was characteristic of his nonconfrontational style as President. DAVID H. SOUTER, an almost totally unknown New Hampshire state supreme court justice, proved to have taken few public stands on constitutional controversies, and President Bush announced that he, himself, had neither questioned Souter nor learned from others what Souter's views might be on abortion or on other controversial subjects. Bush did, however, emphasize his expectation that Souter would fairly interpret the Constitution instead of "legislating" his own policy preferences. The President was prepared to indicate in general terms that he thought recent Supreme Court Justices had not always properly observed this distinction, but he did not single out any particular decisions for such criticism.

In general, during his first two years in office, President Bush adopted a conciliatory stance toward a Congress dominated by the opposition party. He did assert presidential prerogatives in vetoing congressional measures he thought overly restrictive of the presidency or of the constitutional duties of the executive branch, but he did not make this a major theme either. He conceded before his election that the so-called IRAN-CONTRA AFFAIR in the Reagan administration may have involved significant departures from the law and pledged to observe legal constraints with complete devotion. He did make efforts to consult congressional leaders when he committed U.S. forces to conflict in Panama in 1989 and in the Middle East in 1990, and both efforts generally received broad support in Congress. Like his predecessors, however, President Bush did not acknowledge that he was bound by the 1974 War Powers Resolution; he submitted required reports to Congress, but presented these as voluntary measures of cooperation rather than compliance with binding law.

In the conflict over Iraq's conquest of neighboring Kuwait, President Bush pursued active diplomatic efforts, culminating in a United Nations Security Council Resolution authorizing the use of force to liberate Kuwait. After sending almost half a million American troops to Saudi Arabia, President Bush did finally seek and receive direct congressional authorization for the use of force in this conflict. U.S. air strikes followed within days of this vote in accord with a deadline established in both the U.N. resolution and the congressional resolution. Though the congressional resolution received only a bare majority in the Senate in a largely partisan vote, it was widely accepted as the constitutional equivalent of a DECLARATION OF WAR and essentially put an end to further legal debate about the U.S. military role in the war against Iraq. With the onset of decisive military operations, support for he President in the country rose to record levels.

JEREMY RABKIN
(1992)

Bibliography

BUSH, GEORGE with DOUGLAS WEAD 1988 *Man of Integrity.* Eugene, Ore.: Harvest House.

BUSH, GEORGE 1989 Statement on Signing the Treasury, Postal Service and General Government Act, 1990 (November 3, 1989) in *Public Papers of the Presidents, Administration of George Bush, 1989.* Washington, D.C.: U.S. Government Printing Office.

BUSH, GEORGE H. W.
(1924–)
(Update)

George Herbert Walker Bush was the forty-first President of the United States. The son of a prominent businessman and U.S. senator, Bush was born in Milton, Massachusetts on June 12, 1924, but spent almost all of his childhood in Greenwich, Connecticut. Upon his graduation from prep school, Bush entered the Navy in 1942. For the remainder of WORLD WAR II he served as a naval aviator and was awarded the Distinguished Flying Cross. After the end of the war, Bush entered Yale University, where he was graduated Phi Beta Kappa with honors in 1948.

Subsequently, Bush moved to Texas, where he became cofounder and half-owner of an oil drilling company in 1950. In 1967 he sold the oil drilling company and thereafter concentrated on politics and public service. He was a member of the U.S. HOUSE OF REPRESENTATIVES from 1967 to 1971, Ambassador to the UNITED NATIONS from 1971 to 1973, Chairman of the Republican National Committee from 1973 to 1974, Chief Liaison Officer to China from 1975 to 1976, and Director of the Central Intelligence Agency from 1976 to 1977. Bush unsuccessfully sought the Republican nomination for President in 1980. However, RONALD REAGAN, who obtained the nomination, chose Bush as his running mate. Reagan won the election, and Bush served two terms as Vice-President.

In 1988, with Reagan's support, Bush was chosen as the Republican nominee for President. He then defeated Democrat Michael Dukakis in the general election. However, after serving a single term as President, Bush was defeated in his reelection bid by Democrat WILLIAM J. CLINTON in 1992.

The most important potential constitutional crisis of the Bush presidency arose in connection with the American response to Iraq's invasion of Kuwait in 1990. Bush quickly rallied international support for a massive, United States–led military operation designed to expel the Iraqis. The plan included a ground assault on the nation of Iraq. Many questioned whether the armed forces of the United States could be committed to such an operation without a formal DECLARATION OF WAR by Congress. Although no such declaration was forthcoming, Bush was successful in obtaining a resolution from Congress that supported military intervention against Iraq. Ultimately, the quick, spectacular success of Operation Desert Storm, as it was called, muted the legal critics of Bush's actions.

Constitutional arguments were also deeply intertwined with domestic politics during the Bush administration. For example, Bush publicly supported the pro-life position on ABORTION and voiced strong opposition to race-based AFFIRMATIVE ACTION; moreover, his administration also vigorously pressed these views in the federal courts. However, the most significant constitutional legacy of the Bush presidency lay not in its approach to any specific issue, but rather in presidential appointments to the federal courts.

Like Reagan before him, Bush generally sought out conservative appointees at all levels, thereby continuing the erosion of judicial support for liberal constitutionalism. His appointment of CLARENCE THOMAS to the Supreme Court epitomized this trend; after his narrow success in a bitter struggle over confirmation, Thomas has become perhaps the most conservative Justice of the post–WARREN COURT era. By contrast, DAVID H. SOUTER—Bush's other appointee to the Court—has proven to be far more sympathetic to liberal positions. Thus, while Bush's appointees clearly moved the balance of judicial power to the right, he was not entirely successful in his effort to assure the preeminence of conservative legal thought on the Supreme Court.

EARL M. MALTZ
(2000)

Bibliography

MERVIN, DAVID   1996   *George Bush and the Guardian Presidency.* New York: St. Martin's Press.
PARMENT, HERBERT S.   1997   *George Bush: The Life of a Lone Star Yankee.* New York: Scribner.

BUSHELL'S CASE
6 State Trials 999 (1670)

A unanimous decision of the Court of Common Pleas, *Bushell's Case* stands for the proposition that a jury may not be punished for returning a verdict contrary to a court's direction. In medieval England, bribery and intimidation were commonly accepted methods of insuring "correct" verdicts, but the Privy Council and the Star Chamber had eliminated those practices by the sixteenth century. Nevertheless, the Star Chamber often handled as corrupt any acquittal that it felt contradicted the evidence. The popular view increasingly opposed punishment for jurors unless they returned a clearly corrupt verdict, and the House of Commons endorsed that position in 1667. The decision in *Bushell's Case* brought the law into line.

When jurors in a case against William Penn and other Quakers persisted in finding the defendants innocent—despite three days of starvation—Bushell and the other jurors were fined and imprisoned. Bushell obtained a writ of HABEAS CORPUS in the Court of Common Pleas and was subsequently discharged. Chief Justice John Vaughan delivered a powerful opinion distinguishing between the "ministerial" (administrative) and judicial functions of jurors. Violations of the former were finable but a verdict was judicial and therefore not subject to penalty. The Court only judged the law. The jury was obliged to deduce the facts from the evidence, and the court could not penalize them for disagreeing with its deductions and directions. Seventeenth-century jurors were expected and required to utilize their own knowledge of a case, private knowledge a judge likely did not have. Only by handpicking jurors could the Crown insure favorable verdicts.

DAVID GORDON
(1986)

BUSING, SCHOOL

See: School Busing

BUTCHER'S UNION SLAUGHTERHOUSE v. CRESCENT CITY SLAUGHTERHOUSE
111 U.S. 746 (1884)

In this case the INALIENABLE POLICE POWER doctrine again defeated a VESTED RIGHTS claim based on the CONTRACT CLAUSE. Louisiana revoked a charter of monopoly privileges, which the Supreme Court had sustained in the first of the SLAUGHTERHOUSE CASES (1873). Although the contract was supposedly irrepealable for a period of twenty-five years, the Court, in an opinion by Justice SAMUEL F. MILLER, maintained that one legislature cannot bind its successors on a matter involving the GENERAL WELFARE, specifically the public health. No legislature can contract away the state's inalienable power to govern slaughterhouses, which affect the public health. Four Justices, concurring separately, argued that the original monopoly was unconstitutional and its charter revocable, because it violated the liberty and property of competing butchers; the four employed SUBSTANTIVE DUE PROCESS in construing the FOURTEENTH AMENDMENT.

LEONARD W. LEVY
(1986)

BUTLER, BENJAMIN F.
(1818–1893)

A Massachusetts labor lawyer and Democratic politician, Benjamin Franklin Butler became a Union general in 1861. Butler declared that runaway slaves were "contrabands of war," and used them as noncombatants, refusing to return them to their masters. Later he supported the use of Negro soldiers and in 1864 forced the Confederacy to treat black Union prisoners of war according to the rules of war by retaliating against Confederate prisoners. In 1862 Butler directed the occupation of New Orleans, where his strict application of martial law kept a hostile population under control with virtually no violence. In 1865 Butler advocated that black veterans be given con-

fiscated land and the franchise. After entering Congress in 1867, Butler was a manager of President ANDREW JOHNSON'S IMPEACHMENT. Butler approached the trial as if he were prosecuting a horse thief. Butler's lack of dignity in presenting EVIDENCE probably contributed to Johnson's acquittal.

PAUL FINKELMAN
(1986)

Bibliography

HOLZMAN, ROBERT S.   1978   *Stormy Ben Butler.* New York: Octagon Books.

BUTLER, PIERCE
(1744–1822)

Irish-born Pierce Butler represented South Carolina at the CONSTITUTIONAL CONVENTION OF 1787 and signed the Constitution. It was Butler who first proposed the Convention's secrecy rule. A frequent speaker, he favored a weak central government and championed the interests of slaveholders. He was later a United States senator.

DENNIS J. MAHONEY
(1986)

BUTLER, PIERCE
(1866–1939)

President WARREN G. HARDING appointed Pierce Butler to the Supreme Court in 1922 in part because Harding wanted to name a conservative Democrat. He also preferred a Roman Catholic. As with other Harding judicial appointments, Chief Justice WILLIAM HOWARD TAFT had an influential role. Before his appointment, Butler had gained some fame as a railroad attorney, particularly for his defense of the carriers in the MINNESOTA RATE CASES (1913) and for his actions as a regent of the University of Minnesota, which led to the dismissal of faculty members who opposed WORLD WAR I or who were socialists.

Progressive senators opposed Butler's confirmation, but marshaled only eight votes against him. The *New York Times* said that Butler's antagonists favored only judges who supported labor unions and opposed CORPORATIONS; the *St. Louis Post-Dispatch* countered that Butler's chief qualities were "bigotry, intolerance, narrowness, and partisanism." Taft predictably praised the appointment as "a most fortunate one." Until his death in 1939, Butler consistently followed the ideological direction friends and foes had anticipated.

Butler maintained his hostility to political dissenters while on the bench. He supported the majority in upholding a New York criminal anarchy law in GITLOW V. NEW YORK (1925). In UNITED STATES V. SCHWIMMER (1929) he sustained the government's denial of CITIZENSHIP to a sixty-year-old pacifist woman. In 1931 he broke with the majority in STROMBERG V. CALIFORNIA and in NEAR V. MINNESOTA to favor a state conviction of a woman who had displayed a red flag and a state court INJUNCTION against a newspaper editor who had harshly criticized public officials. In the *Near* case, Butler contended that FREEDOM OF THE PRESS should not protect an "insolent publisher who may have purpose and sufficient capacity to contrive and put into effect a scheme or program for oppression, blackmail, or extortion." Six years later Butler joined three others to protest the Court's revival of Justice OLIVER WENDELL HOLMES'S CLEAR AND PRESENT DANGER doctrine in HERNDON V. LOWRY (1937). In one of his final statements, in *Kessler v. Strecker* (1939), he approved the DEPORTATION of an ALIEN who had once joined the Communist party but had never paid dues and long since had left the organization.

A Justice's views rarely are monolithic. In the area of CIVIL RIGHTS, for example, Butler stood alone in opposing state STERILIZATION of mental "defectives" in BUCK V. BELL (1927). Perhaps Butler's Catholicism motivated his vote; in any event, a half century later it was discovered that the sterilized woman had never been an imbecile, as Justice Holmes had callously characterized her. Butler also had strong views on the sanctity of the FOURTH AMENDMENT. In OLMSTEAD V. UNITED STATES (1928) he dissented from Taft's opinion upholding the use of WIRETAPPING for gaining evidence, and in another PROHIBITION case Butler insisted that the Fourth Amendment's prohibition of UNREASONABLE SEARCHES should be construed liberally. "Security against unlawful searches is more likely to be attained by resort to SEARCH WARRANTS than by reliance upon the caution and sagacity of petty officers," he wrote in *United States v. Lefkowitz* (1932).

His concern for the criminally accused, however, was not reflected in POWELL V. ALABAMA (1932), as he dissented with Justice JAMES C. MCREYNOLDS when the Court held that the "Scottsboro Boys" had been denied their RIGHT TO COUNSEL. He consistently opposed black claimants. For example, he dissented when the Court invalidated the Texas all-white primary election in NIXON V. CONDON (1932); he asserted in BREEDLOVE V. SUTTLES (1937) that payment of a POLL TAX as a condition to exercise VOTING RIGHTS did not violate the FOURTEENTH AMENDMENT; and he dissented when the Court first successfully attacked the SEPARATE BUT EQUAL DOCTRINE in MISSOURI EX REL. GAINES V. CANADA (1938). He also sustained state laws that prevented aliens from owning farm land in *Porterfield v. Webb* (1923).

Throughout the 1920s, Butler found the Court receptive to his conservative economic views. He was an aggressive spokesman for the claims of utilities, particularly in rate and valuation cases. He insisted on judicial prerogatives in such cases, relying on DUE PROCESS OF LAW to justify a court's determination of both law and facts. In general, Butler favored valuing utility property at reproduction costs in order to determine rate structures. He led the Court in striking down a state statute forbidding use of unsterilized material in the manufacture of mattresses in *Weaver v. Palmer Bros. Co.* (1924); and, in EUCLID V. AMBLER REALTY COMPANY (1926), he dissented when the Court, led by his fellow conservative, Justice GEORGE H. SUTHERLAND, sustained local zoning laws.

In the tumultuous NEW DEAL years, Butler was one of the conservative "Four Horsemen," along with McReynolds, Sutherland, and WILLIS VAN DEVANTER. He opposed every New Deal measure that came before the Court. Butler rarely spoke in these cases, but before the Court reorganization battle he wrote the majority opinion narrowly invalidating a New York minimum wage law. Echoing LOCHNER V. NEW YORK (1905) and invoking ADKINS V. CHILDREN'S HOSPITAL (1923), Butler declared in MOREHEAD V. NEW YORK EX REL. TIPALDO (1936) that the state act violated the FOURTEENTH AMENDMENT's due process clause. Less than a year later, the *Tipaldo* decision was overturned. Thereafter, Butler and his fellow conservatives found themselves at odds with the new majority. To the end, however, they all resolutely kept the faith.

STANLEY I. KUTLER
(1986)

Bibliography

BROWN, FRANCIS JOSEPH 1945 *The Social and Economic Philosophy of Pierce Butler.* Washington: Catholic University Press.

DANIELSKI, DAVID J. 1964 *A Supreme Court Justice Is Appointed.* New York: Random House.

BUTLER, UNITED STATES v.
297 U.S. 1 (1936)

In this historic and monumentally inept opinion, the Supreme Court ruled that the United States has no power to regulate the agrarian sector of the ECONOMY. The AGRICULTURAL ADJUSTMENT ACT OF 1933 (AAA) sought to increase the purchasing power and living standards of farmers by subsidizing the curtailment of farm PRODUCTION and thus boosting farm prices. Congress raised the money for the subsidies by levying an EXCISE TAX on the primary processors of each crop, in this case a cotton mill, which passed on to the consumer the cost of the tax. AAA was the agricultural equivalent of a protective tariff. By a vote of 6–3 the Court held, in an opinion by Justice OWEN ROBERTS, that the statute unconstitutionally invaded the powers reserved to the states by the TENTH AMENDMENT. "It is a statutory plan," Roberts declared, "to regulate and control agricultural production, a matter beyond the powers delegated to the federal government. The tax, the appropriation of the funds raised, and the direction for their disbursement, are but parts of the plan. They are but means to an unconstitutional end." Roberts reached his DOCTRINE of DUAL FEDERALISM by simplistic MECHANICAL JURISPRUDENCE. He sought to match the statute with the Constitution and, finding that they did not square, seriously limited the TAXING AND SPENDING POWER.

Roberts did not question the power of Congress to levy an excise tax on the processing of agricultural products; he also conceded that "the power of Congress to authorize expenditures of public moneys for public purposes is not limited by the direct grants of legislative power found in the Constitution." He did not even deny that aiding the agrarian sector of the economy benefited the GENERAL WELFARE, in accord with the first clause of Article I, section 8; rather he reasoned that the Court did not need to decide whether an appropriation in aid of agriculture fell within the clause. He simply found that the Constitution did not vest in the government a power to regulate agricultural production. He ruled, too, that the tax was not really a tax, because Congress had not levied it for the benefit of the government; it expropriated money from processors to give to farmers. The tax power cannot, Roberts declared, be used as an instrument to enforce a regulation of matters belonging to the exclusive realm of the states, nor can the tax power be used to coerce a compliance which Congress has no power to command.

Despite Roberts's insistence on calling the crop curtailment program "coercive," it was in fact voluntary; a minority of farmers elected not to restrict production, foregoing subsidies. But Roberts added that even a voluntary plan would be unconstitutional as a "federal regulation of a subject reserved to the states." He added: "It does not help to declare that local conditions throughout the nation have created a situation of national concern; for that is but to say that whenever there is a widespread similarity of local conditions, Congress may ignore constitutional limitations upon its own powers and usurp those reserved to the states."

Justice HARLAN FISKE STONE, joined by Justices LOUIS D. BRANDEIS and BENJAMIN N. CARDOZO, wrote a scathing, imperishable dissent, one of the most famous in the Court's history. Strongly defending the constitutionality of the AAA on the basis of the power to tax and spend, Stone lambasted Roberts's opinion as hardly rising "to the dignity of an argument" and as a "tortured construction of the Constitution." Stone's opinion confirmed President FRANKLIN D. ROOSEVELT's belief that it was the Court, not the Constitution, that stood in the way of recovery. The

AAA decision helped provoke the constitutional crisis of 1937.

LEONARD W. LEVY
(1986)

Bibliography

HART, HENRY M. 1936 Processing Taxes and Protective Tariffs. *Harvard Law Review* 49:610–618.
MURPHY, PAUL L. 1955 The New Deal Agricultural Program and the Constitution. *Agricultural History* 29:160–169.

BUTLER v. MICHIGAN
352 U.S. 380 (1957)

Michigan convicted Butler for selling to an adult an "obscene" book that might corrupt the morals of a minor. The Supreme Court unanimously reversed, in an opinion by Justice FELIX FRANKFURTER, who declared that the statute was not restricted to the evil with which it dealt; it reduced adults "to reading only what is fit for children," thereby curtailing their FIRST AMENDMENT rights as protected by the DUE PROCESS clause of the FOURTEENTH AMENDMENT.

LEONARD W. LEVY
(1986)

BUTZ v. ECONOMOU
438 U.S. 478 (1978)

In an action against the Department of Agriculture and individual department officials for alleged constitutional violations, the Court united two previously separate doctrinal strands governing official liability. *Butz* indicated that immunity from personal liability of federal executive officials in direct actions under the Constitution would be available only under circumstances in which state executive officials would be immune from analogous constitutional actions under SECTION 1983, TITLE 42, UNITED STATES CODE. *Butz* also extended absolute immunity to judicial and prosecutorial officials within an ADMINISTRATIVE AGENCY.

THEODORE EISENBERG
(1986)

(SEE ALSO: *Executive Immunity; Judicial Immunity.*)

BYRNES, JAMES F.
(1879–1972)

Few members of the United States Supreme Court in this century have led more varied political lives than James F. Byrnes of South Carolina, who served as congressman,

United States senator, and governor of his state, czar of production during WORLD WAR II, and secretary of state. In these other roles, Byrnes left a larger historical legacy than he did on the Court, where he remained for only the October 1941 term.

He wrote sixteen opinions for the Court, never dissented, and did not write a CONCURRING OPINION. As a Justice, he is remembered chiefly for his opinion in EDWARDS V. CALIFORNIA (1942), where he and four others invalidated as a burden on INTERSTATE COMMERCE a California "anti-Okie" law that made it a MISDEMEANOR to bring into the state indigent nonresidents. Initially, Byrnes had been inclined to strike down the law as a violation of the PRIVILEGES AND IMMUNITIES clause of the FOURTEENTH AMENDMENT (a position held by four other Justices), but he finally rejected this approach under pressure from Chief Justice HARLAN FISKE STONE and Justice FELIX FRANKFURTER. Although he also wrote for the Court in *Taylor v. Georgia* (1942), where the Justices voided that state's debt-peonage law, Byrnes did not usually exhibit great sensitivity to the claims of CIVIL LIBERTIES, or to the complaints of convicted felons and working-class people.

MICHAEL E. PARRISH
(1986)

Bibliography

BYRNES, JAMES 1958 *All in One Lifetime.* New York: Harper & Row.

CABELL v. CHAVEZ-SALIDO

See: Alien

CABINET

Whether or not the President should have a cabinet or council was a leading issue at the CONSTITUTIONAL CONVENTION. Such bodies were prevalent in the colonial governments and in the states that succeeded them. Another key element of the cabinet that also crystallized in the preconstitutional period was the concept of the department. Under the ARTICLES OF CONFEDERATION, Congress established four executive offices in 1781: a secretary of FOREIGN AFFAIRS, a secretary of war, a superintendent of finance, and a secretary of marine.

At the Philadelphia Convention, GOUVERNEUR MORRIS proposed that there be a Council of State, consisting of the Chief Justice of the Supreme Court and the heads of departments or secretaries, of which there should be five, appointed by the President and holding office at his pleasure. The President should be empowered to submit any matter to the council for discussion and to require the written opinion of any one or more of its members. The President would be free to exercise his own judgment, regardless of the counsel he received. Morris's proposal was rejected in the late-hour efforts of the Committee of Eleven to complete the draft of the Constitution. Instead, the Committee made two principal provisions for advice for the President. Its draft specified that "The President, by and with the ADVICE AND CONSENT of the Senate, shall appoint ambassadors, and other public ministers, judges of the Supreme Court, and all other officers of the United States, whose appointments are not herein provided for." This provision is attributed to the New York state constitution in which the governor shared the appointment power with the Senate. The draft by the Committee of Eleven also provided that the President "may require the opinion, in writing, of the principal officer of each of the Executive Departments upon any subject relating to the duties of their respective offices."

GEORGE MASON resisted this plan, declaring that omission of a council for the President was an experiment that even the most despotic government would not undertake. Mason proposed an executive council composed of six members, two from the eastern, two from the middle, and two from the southern states. BENJAMIN FRANKLIN seconded the proposal, observing that a council would check a bad President and be a relief to a good one. Gouverneur Morris objected that the President might induce such a council to acquiesce in his wrong measures and thereby provide protection for them. Morris's view prevailed and Mason's plan was defeated. Doubtless a potent factor in the outcome was the expectation that the venerated GEORGE WASHINGTON would become the first President and that a council of some power might impede his functioning. CHARLES PINCKNEY, who once had advocated a council, now argued that it might "thwart" the President.

With the Constitution's prescriptions so sparse, it remained for Washington's presidency to amplify the concept of the cabinet. Congress in 1789 created three departments (State, War, and Treasury) and an attorney general who was not endowed with a department. Washington's appointees—THOMAS JEFFERSON as secretary of state, ALEXANDER HAMILTON as secretary of treasury, Major

General Henry Knox as secretary of war, and EDMUND RANDOLPH as attorney general—reflected Mason's emphasis on geographic representation, for they were drawn from the three principal sections of the country. Washington frequently requested the written opinions of his secretaries on important issues and asked them for suggestions for the annual address to Congress.

In 1793, the diplomatic crisis arising from the war between Britain and France caused the cabinet to take firmer shape as an institution. Washington and his secretaries gathered in a series of meetings, including a notable one of April 19 at which the issuance of the PROCLAMATION OF NEUTRALITY was agreed upon. Jefferson recorded that the meetings occurred "almost every day." Because the crisis persisted throughout 1793, the collegial character of the cabinet became well established. Jefferson, Randolph, and Madison referred to the assembled secretaries as the "cabinet," but Washington did not employ the term. Although "cabinet" was long employed in congressional discussion, it did not appear in statutes until the General Appropriation Act of 1907.

The Constitution's meager provisions left Washington largely free to tailor the cabinet to his own preferences. He selected his secretaries on the basis of their individual talents, without regard to their political or policy predispositions. This procedure proved costly, leading to continuous dispute between Hamilton and Jefferson that required a remaking of the cabinet. Washington then resolved not to recruit appointees strongly opposed to his policies. Presidents have applied this principle in constituting their cabinets ever since.

Washington did not consider himself limited by the Constitution to seeking advice only from his department heads. Congressman JAMES MADISON was a frequent adviser on Anglo-American diplomatic issues, on executive appointments, and on the President's reply to the formal addresses of the two houses of Congress. Chief Justice JOHN JAY provided counsel on diplomatic questions, addresses to Congress, and on the political aspects of a presidential tour of the New England states.

Washington was less successful in seeking counsel from the Senate and the Supreme Court. He visited the Senate to discuss issues arising from an Indian treaty under negotiation, and was rebuffed when legislators made clear that his presence constrained their deliberations. The SUPREME COURT, equally self-protective, declined to render ADVISORY OPINIONS.

Washington set the pattern for future presidencies in reaffirming the constitutional arrangement of a strong, independent, single executive, and in rejecting any division of responsibility between the President and the cabinet. Ever since, the view has prevailed that the Constitution confers upon the President the ultimate executive authority and responsibility, which he does not share with the department heads individually or collectively.

Like the President, the cabinet is subject to such basic principles as SEPARATION OF POWERS and CHECKS AND BALANCES, on which the Constitution was constructed. Consequently, both the cabinet and the President are susceptible to the influence of the other two branches. The paucity of constitutional provision and the circumstances of the cabinet's beginning in Washington's administration, together with its continuous presence in all succeeding administrations, cause the cabinet's institutional status to rest upon custom. Since its founding in 1793, the cabinet, as Richard F. Fenno, Jr., has written, has continued to be "an extra-legal creation, functioning in the interstices of the law, surviving in accordance with tradition, and institutionalized by usage alone." Its influence and, to a large degree, its form rest on the will of the President of the moment.

Not surprisingly, given its acute dependence on the President, the cabinet has varied widely in its functions and its importance. Jefferson recruited a cabinet of supportive fellow partisans, but JOHN QUINCY ADAMS drew into his cabinet representatives of his party's great factions who had contested his rise to the Presidency. JAMES MONROE used his cabinet for the arduous crafting of the MONROE DOCTRINE, but ABRAHAM LINCOLN is one of many Presidents who used his cabinet sparingly. ANDREW JACKSON preferred the counsel of his "kitchen cabinet," an informal, unofficial body of friends who did not hold high position. JOHN TYLER rejected the request of his Whig cabinet that matters be decided by majority vote, with each secretary and the President having but one vote. ANDREW JOHNSON added fuel to the flames of his IMPEACHMENT when he removed Secretary of War EDWIN M. STANTON. Johnson's congressional foes contended that he violated the TENURE OF OFFICE ACT of 1867, which purported to deny the President the right to remove civil officials, including members of his cabinet, without senatorial consent.

The twentieth century, too, has seen wide variation in the demeanors of Presidents toward their cabinets, from WARREN G. HARDING, who considered it his duty to build a cabinet comprised of the "best minds" in the nation, to WOODROW WILSON and JOHN F. KENNEDY, who used their cabinets little and chafed under extended group discussion. DWIGHT D. EISENHOWER endeavored to make the cabinet a central force in his administration through innovations to enhance its operating effectiveness. He created the post of secretary of the cabinet, empowered to arrange an agenda for cabinet meetings and to oversee the preparation of "cabinet papers" by the departments and agencies presenting proposals for cabinet deliberation and presidential decision. The results of cabinet discussions were recorded, responsibilities for implementation were allotted among the departments and agencies, and a system of follow-up was installed to check on accomplishment.

RICHARD M. NIXON designated four members of his cabinet counselors to the President and empowered them to supervise clusters of activity in several or more departments and agencies. With his popularity dropping and an election looming, JIMMY CARTER reshuffled his administration on an unprecedented scale in 1979 by ejecting discordant cabinet secretaries and replacing them with more supportive appointees. RONALD REAGAN instituted a structure of cabinet councils for broad policy areas with memberships of department secretaries and White House staff, supported by subcabinet working groups.

The cabinet's lack of specific delineation in the Constitution contributes to its weakness in coordinating the far-flung activities of the executive branch and in producing innovative policy on the scale and at the pace the President requires. These shortcomings have caused the cabinet to be overshadowed by more recent institutions of the modern presidency that assist in policy development and coordination. These are largely concentrated in the Executive Office of the President, which includes, among other units, the White House Office, the OFFICE OF MANAGEMENT AND BUDGET, the National Security Council, and the Council of Economic Advisers.

The cabinet's frail constitutional base has made the development of the departments susceptible to forces inimical to the cohesiveness that the concept of a "cabinet" implies. Often departments, such as Labor, Agriculture, and Commerce, were brought into being more by the pressures of their client groups than by the President's preference, and without a clear concept of what a department should be. Frequently alliances are formed between the client groups, the department's bureaus, and congressional committees with jurisdiction over the department. These alliances' combined strength has often exceeded the President's and frustrated his will. Even department heads have sometimes proved more responsive to their alliances than to the President.

Because the doctrines of separation of powers and checks and balances bring the cabinet and its departments within reach of the courts and Congress, those branches too have shaped those executive institutions. The Supreme Court, for example, in *Kendall v. United States* (1838), circumscribed the President's discretionary power over the department head when it upheld a lower court decision ordering the postmaster general to pay a complainant money owed by the United States. The payment was a MINISTERIAL ACT which gave the President "no other control over the officer than to see that he acts honestly, with proper motives." Despite the silence of the Constitution concerning the power of removal, Presidents have long removed department heads for any cause they see fit, and in MYERS V. UNITED STATES (1926) the Court upheld an order of the postmaster general to remove a first-class postmaster despite a statute requiring that the removal be by the advice and consent of the Senate.

The cabinet departments depend on Congress for money, personnel, and other resources necessary to function. In effect, department secretaries look to Congress for the means of survival, sometimes straining their ties with the President. Much of the substance of cabinet rank is provided by Congress: salary, title, membership in bodies such as the National Security Council, place in the line of presidential succession. Members of Congress often assert that department heads, notwithstanding their relation with the President, have responsibilities to the legislators. The powers and functions of the department head are conferred by acts of Congress. Although Congress respects the cabinet secretary's advisory role to the President, he is not solely the President's aide in his extra-cabinet functions, but performs in a shadow area of joint executive-legislative responsibility, and struggles with the resulting dilemmas. It is virtually indispensable that a department secretary attract the confidence of Congress as well as that of the President.

The cabinet's few moorings in the Constitution make its relationships with the POLITICAL PARTIES uncertain and fluctuating. Wilson once conceived of the cabinet as a potential link between the President and his party in Congress. He subsequently abandoned this view and like many other Presidents emphasized loyalty and competence in cabinet selection. JOHN QUINCY ADAMS, Warren G. Harding, HARRY S. TRUMAN, and other Presidents used the cabinet to diminish intraparty factionalism, chiefly by appointing their rivals for the presidential nomination to cabinet posts. Eisenhower allotted several posts to persons with ties to his rival, ROBERT A. TAFT. Parties, however, have considerably less influence on the cabinet than the chief executive or Congress.

LOUIS W. KOENIG
(1986)

Bibliography

FENNO, RICHARD F., JR. 1959 *The President's Cabinet.* Cambridge, Mass.: Harvard University Press.
HINSDALE, MARY 1911 *A History of the President's Cabinet.* Ann Arbor: University of Michigan Press.
HORN, STEPHEN 1960 *The Cabinet and Congress.* New York: Columbia University Press.

CABLE TELEVISION

See: Broadcasting

CAHN, EDMOND
(1906–1964)

Edmond Cahn's civil libertarianism emphasized the importance of a written Constitution and the role of the judiciary in upholding the guarantees of the BILL OF RIGHTS. Judicial review is a historically "legitimate" device, he believed, for "converting promises on parchment into living liberties," and the Supreme Court is "the nation's exemplar and disseminator of democratic values." "The firstness of the FIRST AMENDMENT" ensures "the indefinitely continuing right to be exposed to an ideological variety." SEPARATION OF CHURCH AND STATE strengthens both entities and places sovereignty of choice in the populace. The First Amendment, by securing the basis for participation in the democratic process, provides an indispensable moral link between the governed and the governors.

Cahn's fact-skepticism, continually questioning factual assumptions, led him to indict CAPITAL PUNISHMENT, because a mistake-laden legal system should not impose an irreversible penalty. He insisted that the morally neutral social sciences occupy a subordinate place in judicial decisions and that "a judge untethered by a text is a dangerous instrument." He shared much in common with his friend, Justice HUGO L. BLACK, whose off-Court advocacy of First Amendment ABSOLUTISM he did not explicitly adopt. Cahn, a professor of law at New York University, had great confidence in the democratic citizen, freed from false certainties and protected by the mandates of the Bill of Rights, to prevent or repair injustice.

ROGER K. NEWMAN
(1986)

CALANDRA, UNITED STATES v.
414 U.S. 338 (1974)

In *Calandra* the Court refused to apply the EXCLUSIONARY RULE to bar a GRAND JURY from questioning a witness on the basis of unlawfully seized EVIDENCE. The Court pointed out that although grand juries are subject to certain constitutional limitations, they are not bound by the restrictive procedures that govern trials. Since the exclusionary rule is not a constitutional right that redresses an invasion of privacy, but rather a deterrent against future police misconduct, its application should be restricted to situations where it will be most effective as a remedy. Exclusion at the grand jury level would deter only those searches in which evidence is intended solely for grand jury use; if the evidence should be presented at a subsequent trial, it would be excluded.

JACOB W. LANDYNSKI
(1986)

CALDER v. BULL
3 Dallas 386 (1798)

Calder is the leading case on the meaning of the constitutional injunction against EX POST FACTO LAWS. Connecticut had passed an act setting aside a court decree refusing to probate a will, and the plaintiff argued that the act constituted an ex post facto law. In the Court's main opinion Justice SAMUEL CHASE ruled that although all ex post facto laws are necessarily "retrospective," retrospective laws adversely affecting the citizen in his private right of property or contracts are not ex post facto laws. The prohibition against the latter extended only to criminal, not civil, cases. An ex post facto law comprehends any retrospective penal legislation, such as making criminal an act that was not criminal when committed, or aggravating the act into a greater crime than at the time it was committed, or applying increased penalties for the act, or altering the rules of EVIDENCE to increase the chances of conviction.

The case is also significant in constitutional history because by closing the door on the ex post facto route in civil cases, it encouraged the opening of another door and thus influenced the course of the DOCTRINE of VESTED RIGHTS. The CONTRACT CLAUSE probably would not have attained its importance in our constitutional history, nor perhaps the DUE PROCESS clause substantively construed, if the Court had extended the ex post facto clause to civil cases. In *Calder*, Chase endorsed the judicial doctrine of vested rights drawn from the HIGHER LAW, as announced by Justice WILLIAM PATERSON in VAN HORNE'S LESSEE V. DORRANCE (1795). Drawing on "the very nature of our free Republican governments" and "the great first principles of the social compact," Chase declared that the legislative power, even if not expressly restrained by a written CONSTITUTION, could not constitutionally violate the right of an antecedent and lawful private contract or the right of private property. To assert otherwise, he maintained, would "be a political heresy," inadmissible to the genius and spirit of our governmental system.

Justice JAMES IREDELL concurred in the judgment as well as the definition of ex post facto laws but maintained that judges should not hold an act void "merely because it is, in their judgment, contrary to the principles of natural justice," which he thought undefinable by fixed standards. (See FUNDAMENTAL LAW; SUBSTANTIVE DUE PROCESS.)

LEONARD W. LEVY
(1986)

CALHOUN, JOHN C.
(1782–1850)

John C. Calhoun, foremost southern statesman of his time, was a product of the great Scots-Irish migration that took possession of the southern backcountry before the AMERICAN REVOLUTION. Born near Abbeville, South Carolina, young Calhoun received a smattering of education at a local academy and in his twentieth year went "straight from the backwoods" to Yale College. He excelled by force of intellect and zeal. In 1805, not long after graduating, he attended Litchfield Law School. This New England Federalist education left a permanent impression on Calhoun's mind, though all his political associations were Jeffersonian. Returning to South Carolina, he was admitted to the bar and hung out his shingle in Abbeville. But Calhoun did not take to the law. After making it the steppingstone to the political career he desperately wanted, he gave it up altogether. In 1807 he was elected to the legislature, taking the seat once held by his father. Sometime later he married Floride Bonneau Colhoun, who belonged to the wealthy lowcountry branch of the family, and brought her to the plantation he had acquired above the Savannah River. After two sessions at Columbia, Calhoun won election to the Twelfth Congress. He took his place with the "war hawks" and upon a brilliant maiden speech was hailed as "one of the master-spirits who stamp their name upon the age in which they live."

Calhoun's major biographer has conveniently divided his career into three phases: nationalist, nullifier, sectionalist. During the first, which ended in 1828, Calhoun was successively congressman, secretary of war, and vice-president. As a nationalist, he was the chief congressional architect of the Second Bank of the United States; he supported the tariff of 1816, including its most protective feature, the minimum duty on cheap cotton cloth; and he was a prominent advocate of INTERNAL IMPROVEMENTS. Many Republicans, headed by President JAMES MADISON, believed a constitutional amendment was necessary to sanction federally funded internal improvements. But Calhoun, speaking for his Bonus Bill to create a permanent fund for this purpose, declared that he "was no advocate for refined arguments on the Constitution. The instrument was not intended as a thesis for the logician to exercise his ingenuity on. It ought to be construed with plain, good sense. . . ." He held that the GENERAL WELFARE clause was a distinct power; to those who balked at that, he cited the ENUMERATED POWER to establish post roads. Deeply committed to a system of roads and canals and other improvements to strengthen the Union and secure its defenses, Calhoun, like Hamilton before him, viewed the Constitution as the starting-point for creative statesmanship. Later, when advocating internal improvements as secretary of war, he passed over the constitutional question in silence, thereby avoiding conflict with his chief, JAMES MONROE, who inherited Madison's scruples on the subject.

Calhoun made his first bid for the presidency in 1824

as an unabashed nationalist who professed "to be above all sectional or party feelings and to be devoted to the great interests of the country." He had to settle for the vice-presidency, however; and in that office he seized the first occasion to join the Jacksonian coalition against the National Republican administration of JOHN QUINCY ADAMS. Meanwhile, economic distress revolutionized the politics of South Carolina, driving Calhoun's friends off the nationalist platform and onto the platform of STATES' RIGHTS and STRICT CONSTRUCTION occupied for the past decade by his inveterate enemies. Calhoun was not a leader but a follower—a late one at that—in this movement. By 1827 he, too, had turned against the tariff as the great engine of "consolidation." It was unconstitutional, exploitative of the South, and, with other nationalist measures, it threatened "to make two of one nation." After the "tariff of abominations" the next year, Calhoun, at the request of a committee of the state legislature, secretly penned a lengthy argument against the tariff, showing its unconstitutionality, and expounded the theory of NULLIFICATION as the rightful remedy. (See EXPOSITION AND PROTEST.) The theory was speciously laid in the VIRGINIA AND KENTUCKY RESOLUTIONS. They, of course, were devised to secure the rule of the majority; Calhoun's theory, on the other hand, was intended to protect an aggrieved minority. Moreover, he was precise where those famous resolutions were ambiguous; and, unlike them, he invoked the constitution-making authority of three-fourths of the states. That authority might grant by way of amendment a federal power, such as the protection of manufactures, denied by any one of the states. Calhoun believed that the power of nullification in a single state would act as a healthy restraint on the lawmaking power of Congress; if not, and nullification occurred, the issue would be referred to a convention for decision. Each state being sovereign under this theory, SECESSION was always a last resort; but Calhoun argued that the Union would be strengthened, not weakened or dissolved, under the operation of nullification. Indeed, the Union could be preserved only on the condition of state sovereignty and strict construction—an exact reversal of his earlier nationalist position. The legislature published the *South Carolina Exposition* in December 1828. Although Calhoun's authorship was kept secret for several years, he had become the philosopher-statesman of a movement.

Calhoun hoped for reform from the new administration of ANDREW JACKSON, in which he was, again, the vice-president. But he was quickly disappointed. Personal differences, perhaps more than differences of principle or policy, caused his break with Jackson, completed early in 1831. Laying aside his presidential ambitions—he had hoped to be Jackson's successor—Calhoun issued his Fort Hill Address in July, publicly placing himself at the head of the nullification party in South Carolina. Named for the plantation near Pendleton that was ever after Calhoun's home, the address elaborated the theory set forth in the *Exposition*. When in the following year South Carolina nullified the tariff, it did so in strict conformity with the theory. Calhoun resigned the vice-presidency and was elected to the Senate to lead the state's cause in Washington. He denounced the President's FORCE BILL as a proposition to make war on a sovereign state. In a notable debate with DANIEL WEBSTER, he expounded the theory of the Union as a terminable compact of sovereign states and within that theory vindicated the constitutionality of nullification. (See UNION, THEORIES OF.) But Calhoun backed away from confrontation. He seized the olive branch of tariff reform HENRY CLAY dangled before him. The crisis was resolved peacefully. The nullifiers declared a victory, of course; and Calhoun vaunted himself on the basis of this illusion.

Henceforth, Calhoun abandoned nullification as a remedy and associated his constitutional theory with varying stratagems of sectional resistance to the alleged corruptions and majority tyranny of the general government. The idea of the "concurrent majority," in which the great geographical sections provided the balancing mechanism of estates or classes in classical republican theory, held a more and more important place in his thought. He came to believe that the government of South Carolina, with the balance of legislative power between lowcountry and upcountry established by "the compromise of 1808," embodied this theory. Slavery, of course, was at the bottom of the sectional interest for which Calhoun sought protection. In 1835 he proposed an ingenious solution to the problem of abolitionist agitation through the United States mail. Direct intervention, as Jackson proposed, was unconstitutional, Calhoun said; but the general government could cooperate in the enforcement of state laws that barred "incendiary publications." He thus invented the doctrine of "federal reenforcement" of state laws; and though his bill was defeated, his object was attained by administrative action. Calhoun led the fight in the Senate against the reception of petitions for the abolition of slavery in the DISTRICT OF COLUMBIA. He denied that there was an indefeasible right of petition. Regarding the attack on slavery in the District as an attack on "the outworks" of slavery in the states, he held that the mere reception of the petitions, even if they were immediately tabled, as would become the practice, amounted to an admission of constitutional authority over slavery everywhere. The fight was, therefore, the southern Thermopylae. In 1838, indulging his penchant for metaphysical solutions, Calhoun introduced in the Senate a series of six resolutions which, in principle, would throw a constitutional barricade around slavery wherever it existed—in the states, in the District, and in the territories (Florida then being the only territory). In an allusion to Texas, one resolution declared that refusal to annex territory lest it expand slavery violated the compact of equal sovereign states. This last resolution was dropped, others were modified, and as finally passed the resolutions advanced Calhoun's position by inches rather than yards.

Calhoun never naïvely believed that abolitionism constituted the chief danger to the South. The chief danger was from consolidation, from spoilsmen, from banks and other privileged interests fattening themselves at the public trough, and from the attendant corruption that undermined republican virtue and constitutional safeguards. The only remedy was to strip the government of its excessive revenues, powers, and patronage, and return to the Constitution as it came from the hand of the Framers. For a time, seeing Jackson as the immediate enemy, Calhoun worked with the Whigs; in 1840 he returned to the Democratic fold. He had become convinced that the Democratic party offered better prospects of security for the South. In addition, he hoped to realize his presidential ambition in succession to his old enemy, MARTIN VAN BUREN, in 1844. This was not to be.

The year 1844 found Calhoun secretary of state, engineering the ANNEXATION OF TEXAS, in the shattered administration of John Tyler. Returning to the Senate the following year, he lent his powerful voice to the Oregon settlement, opposed the Mexican War, then became the foremost champion of slavery in the new territories. He set forth his position in resolutions countering the WILMOT PROVISO in 1847: the territories are common property of the states; the general government, as the agent of the states, cannot discriminate against the citizens or institutions of any one in legislating for the territories; the restriction of slavery would be discriminatory; and finally, the people of the territories have the right to form state governments without condition as to slavery. Before long Calhoun repudiated the MISSOURI COMPROMISE and called for the positive protection of SLAVERY IN THE TERRITORIES. The leader of an increasingly militant South, he nevertheless acted, as in the past, to restrain disunionist forces. Secession was never an acceptable solution in his eyes.

The senator's last major speech—he was too ill to deliver it himself—occurred in March 1850 in response to Henry Clay's compromise plan. Calhoun did not so much oppose the measures of this plan as consider them inadequate. The balanced, confederate government of the Constitution had degenerated into a consolidated democracy before which the minority South was helpless. Only by restoring the sectional balance could the Union be saved, and he vaguely suggested a constitutional amendment for this purpose. Within the month he was dead. Two posthumous publications were his political testament. The *Disquisition on Government* contained his political theory, including the key idea of the concurrent majority. The *Discourse on the Constitution* specifically applied the theory to the American polity. After recommending various reforms, such as repeal of the 25th section of the JUDICIARY ACT OF 1789, the *Discourse* concluded with a proposal for radical constitutional change: a dual executive, elected by North and South, each chief vested with the VETO POWER. This was a metaphysical solution indeed! Yet it was one that epitomized Calhoun's paradoxical relationship to the Constitution. Although he made a fetish of the Constitution, he could never accept its workings and repeatedly advocated fundamental reforms. Although he proclaimed his love of the Union, his embrace was like the kiss of death. And while exalting liberty, he based his ideal republic on slavery and rejected majority rule as incompatible with constitutional government.

MERRILL D. PETERSON
(1986)

Bibliography

CRALLE, RICHARD K., ed.   1853–1857   *The Works of John C. Calhoun.* 6 Vols. New York: D. Appleton & Co.

MERIWETHER, ROBERT L.; HEMPHILL, W. EDWIN; WILSON, CLYDE N.; and others, eds.   1959–1980   *The Papers of John C. Calhoun.* 8 Vols. to date. Columbia: University of South Carolina Press.

WILTSE, CHARLES M.   1944   *John C. Calhoun: Nationalist, 1782–1828.* Indianapolis: Bobbs-Merrill.

——   1949   *John C. Calhoun: Nullifier, 1829–1839.* Indianapolis: Bobbs-Merrill.

——   1951   *John C. Calhoun: Sectionalist, 1840–1850.* Indianapolis: Bobbs-Merrill.

CALIFANO v. GOLDFARB
430 U.S. 199 (1977)

CALIFANO v. WEBSTER
430 U.S. 313 (1977)

These decisions illustrated the delicacy of distinguishing between "benign" gender classifications and unconstitutional ones. *Goldfarb* invalidated, 5–4, a SOCIAL SECURITY ACT provision giving survivor's benefits to any widow but only to a widower who actually had received half his support from his wife. *Webster,* decided three weeks later, unanimously upheld the same law's grant of a higher level of old age benefits to women than to men.

In *Goldfarb* four Justices, led by Justice WILLIAM J. BRENNAN, saw the law as a discrimination against women workers, whose surviving families received less protection. The provision had not been adopted to compensate widows for economic disadvantage but to provide generally for survivors; Congress had simply assumed that wives are usually dependent. Saving the cost of individualized determinations of dependency was also insufficient to justify the discrimination. Four other Justices, led by Justice WILLIAM H. REHNQUIST, saw the law as a discrimination against male survivors; because the discrimination was not invidious, implying male inferiority or burdening a disadvantaged minority, it should be upheld as "benign." Justice JOHN PAUL STEVENS agreed with Justice Rehnquist that the discrimination ran against men; however, it was only "the accidental byproduct of a traditional way of thinking about females." Lacking more substantial justifications, it was invalid. (See Justice Stevens's concurrence in CRAIG V. BOREN).

All the Justices in *Webster* agreed that the gender discrimination was not the product of "archaic and overbroad generalizations" about women's dependency but was designed to compensate for women's economic disadvantages. The *Goldfarb* dissenters, concurring separately in *Webster,* suggested that the fine distinction between the two results would produce uncertainty in the law.

KENNETH L. KARST
(1986)

(SEE ALSO: *Sex Discrimination.*)

CALIFANO v. WEBSTER

See: *Califano v. Goldfarb*

CALIFANO v. WESTCOTT
443 U.S. 76 (1979)

The Supreme Court unanimously found unconstitutional SEX DISCRIMINATION in a federal law providing WELFARE BENEFITS to families whose children were dependent because fathers (but not mothers) were unemployed. The discrimination was based on sexual stereotyping that assumed fathers were breadwinners and mothers homemakers, and was not substantially related to the goal of providing for dependent children. Four Justices would have invalidated the benefits granted by the statute. A majority of five, speaking through Justice HARRY A. BLACKMUN, instead construed the statute to extend benefits to children of unemployed mothers as well as fathers.

KENNETH L. KARST
(1986)

CALIFORNIA v. GREENWOOD
486 U.S. 35 (1988)

A person's trash if subjected to public scrutiny might reveal intimate matters that could be embarrassing and even expose one to blackmail or criminal prosecution. But anyone throwing away household trash takes the risk of exposure, even if the trash is disposed of in an opaque plastic bag that is sealed. This was the Supreme Court's announcement in this case.

Justice BYRON R. WHITE, for a 6–2 Court, held that the FOURTH AMENDMENT's prohibition against UNREASONABLE SEARCHES and seizures does not apply to those who leave their sealed trash outside their curtilage for collection by the trash collector. In this case, an observant policewoman, suspecting Greenwood of dealing in narcotics, obtained the trash collector's cooperation and found enough incriminating EVIDENCE to establish PROBABLE CAUSE for a search of the residence. This evidence was used to convict him. The question was whether the initial WARRANTLESS SEARCH of the trash violated the Fourth Amendment. The Court ruled that those discarding their trash by placing it on the street for collection abandoned any REASONABLE EXPECTATION OF PRIVACY they might otherwise have. The two dissenters believed that the warrantless investigation of the trash constituted an appalling invasion of privacy.

LEONARD W. LEVY
(1992)

CALIFORNIA FEDERAL SAVINGS AND LOAN v. GUERRA

See: Sex Discrimination

CALVIN'S CASE
2 Howell's State Trials 559 (1608)

The assumption of the English throne by King James VI of Scotland in 1603 raised the question of what rights accrued in England to Scotsmen born subsequently (the *post-nati*). The English House of Commons wrecked James's plan for a union of the two kingdoms by refusing to permit the NATURALIZATION of Scotsmen dwelling in England and thereby their right to acquire property as native-born Englishmen did. In *Calvin's Case*, however, Lord Chancellor Ellesmere, speaking for the Courts of Chancery and King's Bench, held that the COMMON LAW conferred such naturalization and, thereby, the rights to inherit, sue, and purchase property. In the final stage of the controversy with Parliament that led to the AMERICAN REVOLUTION, Americans relied on *Calvin's case* when claiming that they owed allegiance only to George III personally and were not subject to the authority of Parliament.

WILLIAM J. CUDDIHY
(1986)

CAMARA v. MUNICIPAL COURT
387 U.S. 523 (1967)

In *Camara* the Supreme Court held that the householder may resist warrantless ADMINISTRATIVE SEARCHES of dwellings by inspectors implementing fire, health, housing, and similar municipal codes. However, because the inspection is not a criminal investigation, PROBABLE CAUSE for a warrant may be found without information about the individual dwelling, on the basis of such factors as the date of the last inspection and the condition of the area. Similar protection was accorded to commercial premises in *See v. Seattle* (1967).

JACOB W. LANDYNSKI
(1986)

CAMDEN, LORD

See: Pratt, Charles

CAMINETTI v. UNITED STATES

See: *Hoke v. United States*

CAMPAIGN FINANCE

Enlargement of the electorate and development of modern communications have heightened the importance of campaign funds for communicating with voters, a purpose less patently wicked or easily regulated than vote-buying and bribery, which have long been illegal.

Modern attempts to regulate campaign financing, which raise sweeping constitutional issues, have been largely centered on the FEDERAL ELECTION CAMPAIGN ACT of 1971 and its various amendments. Federal law has developed along six identifiable lines: prohibitions of bribery and corrupt practices; disclosures of campaign contributions and expenditures; limits on the amount of contributions from individuals and groups; prohibitions against contributions from certain sources, such as corporate or union treasuries; limits on total expenditures; and public financing.

Although the regulation of bribery and corrupt practices does not generally raise significant constitutional issues, all of the other elements of the Federal Election Campaign Act and of comparable state laws do. In BUCKLEY V. VALEO (1976), the landmark case on the constitutionality of political finance regulations, the Supreme Court held that expenditures to advocate the election or defeat of candidates are constitutionally protected speech and may not be limited. Subsequent decisions have held that no limit may be imposed on expenditures in REFERENDUM or INITIATIVE campaigns. And in *Common Cause v. Schmitt* (1982) an evenly divided Court sustained a lower court ruling that limits on expenditures by groups or individuals, acting independently, were impermissible, even when the candidate has agreed to limits as a condition for obtaining campaign public subsidies.

Campaign contributions embody a lesser element of constitutionally protected speech, but they are also an exercise of FREEDOM OF ASSEMBLY AND ASSOCIATION guaranteed in the FIRST AMENDMENT. Contributions may be limited to achieve COMPELLING STATE INTERESTS, such as avoidance of "the actuality and appearance of corruption." The Supreme Court has not yet identified any other compelling interest that justifies limits on campaign contributions. Hence, in *Buckley* the Court voided limits on a candidate's contributions to his own campaign and, in *Citizens Against Rent Control v. Berkeley* (1981), invalidated limits on contributions in referendum campaigns, because in neither case did the contributions pose a danger of corrupting candidates.

The rule against expenditures by and contributions from CORPORATIONS, labor unions, and other specified sources has not yet been tested in court, but its justification is largely undermined by FIRST NATIONAL BANK OF BOSTON V. BELLOTTI (1978), which struck down limits on referendum expenditures by corporations because First Amendment speech rights extend to corporations. Presumably the speech and association rights inherent in making contributions attach to corporations, unions, and other associations, and only limits necessary to avoid the actuality or appearance of corruption could be applied.

Public subsidies of campaigns and parties have been adopted by Congress and several states. In *Buckley* the Court held that such expenditures are within the ambit of the spending power of the general welfare clause. The Court also sustained a limit on expenditures for candidates who voluntarily accept public subsidies. No unconstitutional discrimination was found in limiting eligibility for subsidies to parties that had received a specified percentage of the vote in a prior election.

The Court has acknowledged that some persons may be deterred from making contributions and others may be subject to harassment if they exercise their constitutional right to make contributions, but substantial governmental interests warrant disclosure because it assists voters to evaluate candidates, deters corruption, and facilitates enforcement of contribution limits. Minor parties and independent candidates, however, because they have only a modest likelihood of coming to power and because they are often unpopular, need show only "a reasonable probability that compelled disclosure . . . of contributors will subject them to threats, harassment, or reprisals" in order to obtain relief from the disclosure requirements. Minor-party expenditures were also held exempt from disclosure, in BROWN V. SOCIALIST WORKERS '74 CAMPAIGN COMMITTEE (1982), to protect First Amendment political activity.

Equality and liberty, both values rooted in the Constitution, come into conflict in regulation of political finance. Limitations on contributions and expenditures have been justified as efforts to equalize the influence of citizens and groups in the political process. Money and the control of technology, especially communications media, pose special problems of scale; the magnitude of potential inequality between citizens far exceeds that which occurs in traditional or conventional political participation.

In balancing First Amendment liberties and the concern for political equality, the Supreme Court has, in the area of campaign finance, consistently given preference to speech and association rights, with little reference to the inequality this may produce between citizens. The Court has sustained limits on contributions only to avoid corruption, not to achieve equality. Similarly, the Court has permitted public subsidies, which equalize funds available to candidates, and expenditure limits attached to such subsidies, which create an equal ceiling on spending. But equality is not the controlling principle; the Court has made clear that candidate participation in public subsidy- and limitation schemes must be voluntary and that such schemes do not impose ceilings on expenditures by persons acting independently of candidates.

Although equality in the political process has constitutional imprimatur in voting, contemporary constitutional doctrines relating to campaign finance neither acknowledge the validity of equality interests nor provide means for effecting them.

DAVID ADAMANY
(1986)

Bibliography

NICHOLSON, MARLENE 1977 *Buckley v. Valeo*: The Constitutionality of the Federal Election Campaign Act Amendments of 1974. *Wisconsin Law Review* 1977:323–374.

CAMPAIGN FINANCE
(Update 1)

Criticism of political-funding practices and calls for further reforms increased in the latter half of the 1980s as the cost of campaigns continued to escalate and repeated fundraising scandals were publicized. Turnover of congressional seats reached an all-time low, in part because challengers found it difficult to compete in expensive media campaigns. The growing number of POLITICAL ACTION COMMITTEES contributed most heavily to congressional incumbents, particularly to those in the majority party, and both parties exploited the loopholes found in the federal funding restrictions.

During this period the Supreme Court again considered the constitutionality of existing campaign-finance restrictions, continuing to grapple with the conflict between FIRST AMENDMENT liberties and the concern for political equality, a conflict inherent in attempts to regulate political funding. In the mid-1980s, the Court reiterated and even strengthened principles previously established in BUCKLEY V. VALEO (1976), including the rejection of equalization of political influence as an appropriate rationale for funding restrictions. However, at the end of the 1980s, a majority of the Court for the first time explicitly resolved the conflict by giving preference to equality rather than liberty, possibly signaling that they would view further legislative reforms with greater favor than in the past.

In *Federal Election Commission v. National Conservative Political Action Committee* (1985) the Court invalidated a federal statute that limited independent expenditures by political committees supporting presidential candidates who accepted public subsidies. Writing for the majority, WILLIAM H. REHNQUIST, then an Associate Justice, asserted that "the only legitimate and compelling government interests thus far identified" were preventing the appearance and reality of corruption. Defining the term "corruption" more explicitly than in previous cases, Justice Rehnquist made clear that he was referring to "quid pro quo" arrangements with office holders.

One year later, in *Federal Election Commission v. Massachusetts Citizens for Life* (*MCFL*) (1986), the Court held that the federal requirement that independent expenditures by CORPORATIONS in federal elections be made through voluntary funds given to political committees was unconstitutional as applied to MCFL. However, a change in the premises of a majority of the Justices was evident in Justice

WILLIAM J. BRENNAN's opinion both from the narrowness of the HOLDING and from the lengthy explanation, quite unnecessary to the decision, as to why the restriction could be constitutionally applied to most other corporations.

The dicta from *MCFL* became a holding when the Court, in AUSTIN V. MICHIGAN CHAMBER OF COMMERCE (1990), upheld the application of a state statute similar to the one at issue in *MCFL*. According to Justice THURGOOD MARSHALL's majority opinion, the Chamber was not the kind of ideological corporation that was entitled to First Amendment protection under the reasoning of *MCFL* because its assets did not necessarily reflect support for its political expression.

The majority in *Austin* asserted that the compelling interest served by the statute was preventing "a different type of corruption in the political arena: the corrosive and distorting effect of immense aggregations of wealth that are accumulated with the help of the corporate form and that have little or no correlation to the public's support for the corporation's political ideas." In dissent, Justice ANTONIN SCALIA scoffingly referred to the majority's rationale as "the New Corruption" and accused them of adopting the approach of "one man, one minute." Indeed, the distinction between the compelling interest found in *Austin* and the interest in equalization of political influence, which had been rejected in *Buckley* and other cases, is not easy to discern.

By limiting the rationale to situations in which the wealth used for expression "was accumulated with the help of the corporate form," the majority purported to avoid a clash with PRECEDENT. Stressing that the state gives corporations the advantages of perpetual life and freedom from personal liability, the Court concluded that it was appropriate to prevent the use of funds amassed with the help of these benefits from unfairly influencing the electoral process. However, Justice ANTHONY M. KENNEDY pointed out in dissent that the majority's analysis was inconsistent with the reasoning in FIRST NATIONAL BANK OF BOSTON V. BELLOTTI (1978), in which the Court had invalidated bans on corporate expenditures in ballot-measure elections. Indeed, the shift in the majority's approach in *MCFL* and *Austin* is illustrated by the fact that the Court's opinions in these cases strongly resemble the DISSENTING OPINIONS in *Bellotti*. Although *Bellotti* is distinguishable from *MCFL* and *Austin* because the burdens on corporate expression were more severe, the broad principles articulated in *Bellotti* are clearly at odds with the basic premises of *Austin*.

The dichotomy between the majority and the dissents in *Austin* is a classic formulation of the tension between equality and liberty that lies behind all the cases in this area. Because *Austin* and *MCFL* represent a shift toward greater attention to political equality, these decisions could open up new possibilities for reform as legislatures in the 1990s struggle with the problems caused by the ever spiraling costs of political campaigns.

MARLENE ARNOLD NICHOLSON
(1992)

Bibliography

MUTCH, ROBERT E. 1988 *Campaigns, Congress and Courts: The Making of Federal Campaign Law.* Westport, Conn.: Greenwood Press.

NICHOLSON, MARLENE A. 1987 The Supreme Court's Meandering Path in Campaign Finance Regulation and What It Portends for Future Reform. *Journal of Law and Politics* 3: 509–565.

CAMPAIGN FINANCE
(Update 2)

"Criticism of political-funding practices and calls for further reforms increased in the latter half of the 1980s as the cost of campaigns continued to escalate and repeated fundraising scandals were publicized." So began the "campaign finance" update for the first supplement to the *Encyclopedia of the American Constitution.* Change "1980s" to "1990s" and the same introduction will serve for this, the second update. Chances are a similar date change will suffice for the third.

The elaborate structure of constitutional doctrine established to govern campaign finance regulation in BUCKLEY V. VALEO and subsequent cases has been based in large part on three dichotomies. First, the Supreme Court distinguishes between limits on campaign expenditures and limits on campaign contributions. The latter are much more likely to be upheld than the former, because the Court regards limits on contributions as more directly targeted at conflict of interest, while limits on expenditures more directly restrict speech.

Second, because the Court sees prevention of corruption as the main legitimate goal of campaign finance regulation, it is more likely to uphold restrictions in campaigns for elective office than in campaigns on ballot measures. Finally, the Court is more likely to uphold restrictions on campaign finance activities of business CORPORATIONS than of individuals and other entities, primarily because the financial resources accumulated by corporations reflect their business success rather than any support for their political views.

Guided by these dichotomies, the Court has laid down rules for what sorts of campaign finance regulation are permissible under the FIRST AMENDMENT, but no one claims there is a consistent pattern to these rules. The Court's logically fragile doctrinal structure has come under increasing pressure in the 1990s from outside critics, from political events, and from within the Court itself. Yet paradoxically, the pressure on the *Buckley* superstructure may assure its survival, as demands for change come from opposite directions.

In Congress, every session features serious debate on campaign finance regulation, but partisan differences, combined perhaps with a reluctance on the part of many members to tamper with a system that has served them well, have prevented any significant amendments to federal campaign law since 1979. On the other hand, new forms of campaign finance regulation have been enacted at the state level, especially but not exclusively in states with the INITIATIVE process. The new forms of regulation are already being challenged in the lower courts. By the early 2000s, the Court will have to decide the validity of restrictions that do not fit neatly within the *Buckley* doctrinal structure, such as contribution limits considerably lower than those upheld in *Buckley,* and inducements for candidates to agree to spending limits consisting not of money or other forms of campaign assistance, but of liberalized contribution limits.

Limits on campaign spending, declared unconstitutional in *Buckley,* have long been the most popular form of campaign regulation. In the 1990s, many reformers who previously supported public financing of campaigns began to demand spending limits, as they gave up on the political feasibility of public funding. Many prominent law professors and a few political scientists have called for overturning *Buckley's* proscription of spending limits. Other scholars, perhaps fewer in number, argue for the extension of *Buckley,* to render invalid all or most forms of regulation other than disclosure.

Both the uneasiness with *Buckley* and the difficulty of replacing it were apparent in the only major campaign finance decision of the Court in the mid-1990s, *Colorado Republican Federal Campaign Committee v. Federal Election Commission* (1996). Federal law imposes limits on party contributions to candidates, limits considerably higher than those applicable to other contributors. At the same time, it has been generally understood that a party is so intrinsically united with its nominees that it is incapable of making independent expenditures, which under *Buckley* cannot be regulated at all. In *Colorado Republican,* Justice STEPHEN G. BREYER, speaking for a three-member plurality, ruled that if as a factual matter the party acts independently of the candidate, the party has the same right as any other speaker to engage in unlimited independent spending.

Though Breyer's logic may be sound, his result creates a perverse incentive for parties and their candidates to make sure that their campaign efforts are uncoordinated, a result that is hard to justify under any imaginable view of democratic politics. Perhaps for this reason, the remaining six Justices refused to be bound by the *Buckley* logic. Justice JOHN PAUL STEVENS, writing for two Justices, would have permitted the government the right to ban independent spending by parties. In a more dramatic departure from *Buckley,* Stevens conceded the government "an important interest in leveling the electoral playing field by constraining the costs of federal campaigns."

Justices ANTHONY M. KENNEDY and CLARENCE THOMAS, each speaking for himself and the remaining two Justices, would have departed from *Buckley* in the opposite direction by protecting campaign expenditures by parties from regulation, even if the party's activities were coordinated with the candidate. Since *Buckley,* coordinated expenditures have been treated as contributions and thus subject to limitation. Thomas, speaking only for himself, would have overruled *Buckley* in one respect by declaring all limits on campaign contributions unconstitutional.

On and off the Court, the efforts of campaign finance regulators and deregulators continue to offset each other. However shaky, the *Buckley* regime appears to have plenty of life left in it.

DANIEL H. LOWENSTEIN
(2000)

Bibliography

COMMENTARY ON CAMPAIGN FINANCE REFORM 1998 *Connecticut Law Review* 30:775–910.

LOWENSTEIN, DANIEL HAYS 1995 *Election Law: Cases and Materials.* Durham, N.C.: Carolina Academic Press.

SULLIVAN, KATHLEEN M. 1997 Political Money and Freedom of Speech. *UC Davis Law Review* 30:663–690.

SYMPOSIUM 1992 Comparative Political Expression and the First Amendment. *Capital University Law Review* 21:381–609.

——— 1994 Campaign Finance Reform. *Columbia Law Review* 94:1125–1414.

CAMPBELL, JOHN A.
(1811–1889)

John Archibald Campbell was the TANEY COURT's most thoughtful advocate of STATES' RIGHTS and, with the exception of JOSEPH STORY, its most penetrating legal scholar. Although never a constitutional doctrinaire like PETER V. DANIEL, Campbell rooted his constitutional jurisprudence in a southern exceptionalism antagonistic to corporate and federal judicial power. Appointed by President FRANKLIN PIERCE in March 1853, Campbell served until April 1861 when he resigned to return to Alabama and eventual support for the Confederacy.

Campbell analyzed constitutional disputes as clashes between sovereign entities. He dissented from successful efforts by the majority to expand federal ADMIRALTY JURISDICTION to river waters above the ebb and flow of the tide. In *Jackson v. Steamboat Magnolia* (1858) he ridiculed these efforts as factually incorrect, historically superficial, and purposefully intended to diminish state SOVEREIGNTY. Campbell only once won acceptance for his narrow view of federal admiralty jurisdiction when he persuaded a bare majority in *Taylor v. Carry* (1858) that, where claims against a vessel rested on conflicting state and federal JURISDICTION, the claimants had to proceed under the former.

Justice Campbell's most important decisions involved CORPORATIONS. The Taney Court recognized corporations as citizens, a status that enabled them to seek relief from unfavorable state legislative and judicial action through federal DIVERSITY JURISDICTION. Campbell in 1853 dissented when the Court reaffirmed this position in *Marshall v. Baltimore and Ohio Railroad.* He charged that the majority perverted the meaning of CITIZENSHIP and crippled state economic regulation.

Campbell also dissented from the majority's view that corporate charters, even when narrowly construed, were contracts in perpetuity. In PIQUA BRANCH BANK V. KNOOP (1854) and DODGE V. WOOLSEY (1856) he insisted, respectively, that state legislatures and CONSTITUTIONAL CONVENTIONS could alter tax-exemption provisions of previously granted charters. The states, Campbell argued, had to retain sovereign power to tax corporations in order to promote the public interest. A political and economic agenda informed Campbell's thinking about corporate CITIZENSHIP and the CONTRACT CLAUSE: federal judicial protection of interstate corporations tilted the balance of national power in favor of northern manufacturing.

Campbell eased the dichotomy between state and federal sovereignty only on questions involving SLAVERY. In DRED SCOTT V. SANDFORD (1857) he concluded that the federal judiciary had a constitutional responsibility to protect slave property. He reiterated the primacy of federal judicial power in cases in the Fifth Circuit involving enforcement of the slave trade and neutrality laws. Like northern federal judges, who enforced the Fugitive Slave Acts, Campbell charged southern federal juries to adhere to a national RULE OF LAW.

During the post-CIVIL WAR era Campbell made his most lasting contribution to constitutional jurisprudence as an attorney for the corporations he once attacked. The Supreme Court in the SLAUGHTERHOUSE CASES (1873) narrowly rejected his arguments in behalf of the rights of corporate citizenship and SUBSTANTIVE DUE PROCESS under the FOURTEENTH AMENDMENT, but two decades later the Justices embraced them.

KERMIT L. HALL
(1986)

Bibliography

SCHMIDHAUSER, JOHN R. 1958 Jeremy Bentham, the Contract Clause, and Justice John Archibald Campbell. *Vanderbilt Law Review* 11:801–820.

CANTWELL v. CONNECTICUT
310 U.S. 296 (1940)

Newton Cantwell and his sons, Jesse and Russell, were arrested in New Haven, Connecticut. As Jehovah's Witnesses and, by definition, ordained ministers, they were engaged in street solicitation. They distributed pamphlets, made statements critical of the Roman Catholic Church, and offered to play for passers-by a phonograph record including an attack on the Roman Catholic religion. The Cantwells were convicted of violating a Connecticut statute that prohibited persons soliciting money for any cause without a certificate issued by the state secretary of the Public Welfare Council. Jesse Cantwell was also convicted of the COMMON LAW offense of inciting a BREACH OF THE PEACE.

Justice OWEN J. ROBERTS delivered the opinion of a unanimous Court: although Connecticut had a legitimate interest in regulating the use of its streets for solicitation, the means the state had chosen infringed upon the RELIGIOUS FREEDOM of solicitors. The secretary appeared to have unlimited discretion to determine the legitimacy of a religious applicant and either issue or withhold the certificate. If issuance had been a "matter of course," the requirement could have been maintained, but so wide an official discretion to restrict activity protected by the free exercise clause was unacceptable. (See PRIOR RESTRAINT.)

The conviction of Jesse Cantwell for inciting breach of the peace was also constitutionally defective. Justice Roberts noted that the open-endedness of the common law concept of breach of the peace offered wide discretion to law enforcement officials. When such a criminal provision was applied to persons engaging in FIRST AMENDMENT-protected speech or exercise of religion there must be a showing of a CLEAR AND PRESENT DANGER of violence or disorder. Although Cantwell's speech was offensive to his listeners, it had not created such a danger.

As a religious freedom precedent, *Cantwell* is important in two ways: first, it made clear that the free exercise clause of the First Amendment applied to the states through the DUE PROCESS clause of the FOURTEENTH AMENDMENT; second, it suggested (in contrast to previous case law, for example, REYNOLDS V. UNITED STATES, 1879) that the free exercise clause protected not only beliefs but also some actions. The protection of belief was absolute, Roberts wrote, but the protection of action was not; it must give way in appropriate cases to legitimate government regulation. The implication was that at least some government regulations of religion-based conduct would be impermissible.

RICHARD E. MORGAN
(1986)

CAPITAL PUNISHMENT

In 1971, the year before the Supreme Court began its long and tortured experiment in constitutional regulation of the death penalty, Justice JOHN MARSHALL HARLAN issued an ominous warning. In *McGautha v. California* he said that because of the irreducible moral complexity and subjectivity of capital punishment, any effort to impose formal legal rationality on the choice between life and death for a criminal defendant would prove futile: "To identify before the fact those characteristics of criminal homicides and their perpetrators which call for the death penalty, and to express these characteristics in language which can be fairly understood and applied by the sentencing authority, appear to be tasks which are beyond present human ability."

A constitutional interpreter who accepted Justice Harlan's pronouncement could draw one of at least two possible implications from it. She could conclude that in the face of this moral uncertainty, courts cannot interfere in legislative decisions about capital punishment, for judges have no objective principles to correct legislators. On the other hand, she could conclude that capital punishment must be constitutionally forbidden, because this moral uncertainty means that legislators cannot make the death penalty process conform to the minimal constitutional principles of the RULE OF LAW. But a constitutional interpreter might also conclude that Justice Harlan was unnecessarily cynical, and that an enlightened judicial effort might achieve an acceptable moral and instrumental rationality in the administration of the death penalty. The erratic constitutional history of capital punishment both before and after *McGautha* reflects the stubborn difficulty of these questions. That history reveals a complex, often confused experiment in lawmaking. It also illuminates the fundamental, recurring dilemma that Justice Harlan described, and lends sobering support to his pronouncement.

The Fifth Amendment says that no person "shall be deprived of life . . . without DUE PROCESS OF LAW." Thus, a strict textual reader would easily conclude that the Constitution does not forbid capital punishment per se. And indeed in early America, execution was the automatic penalty for anyone convicted of murder or any of several other felonies. Well into the nineteenth century, a jury that believed a defendant to be guilty of murder had no legal power to save him from death. As the states began to draw distinctions among degrees of murder, a prosecutor had to win a conviction on an aggravated or first-degree murder charge to ensure execution, but, after conviction, the death penalty still lay beyond the legal discretion of the jury.

One potential constitutional restraint on the death penalty lay in the Eighth Amendment prohibition of CRUEL AND UNUSUAL PUNISHMENT. But at least in the Supreme Court's contemporary historical interpretation, *Gregg v. Georgia* (1976), the authors of the cruel and unusual punishment clause did not intend to forbid conventional capital punishment for serious crimes. Rather, the Eighth Amendment, drawing on the English BILL OF RIGHTS of 1689, was intended merely to prohibit any punishments not officially authorized by statute or not lying within the sentencing court's jurisdiction, and any torture or brutal, gratuitously painful methods of execution.

For most of the nineteenth century, American courts placed virtually no constitutional restrictions on capital punishment. Nevertheless, the state legislatures gradually rejected the automatic death penalty scheme. Some legislators may have believed that the automatic death laws were too harsh, and that at least some murderers merited legal mercy. Others, paradoxically, may have felt that the automatic death penalty law actually proved too lenient. A jury that believed a defendant was guilty of first-degree murder, but did not believe he deserved execution, could engage in "JURY NULLIFICATION"—it could act subversively by acquitting the defendant of the murder charge.

In any event, by the early twentieth century most of the states had adopted an entirely new type of death penalty law that gave juries implicit, unreviewable legal discretion in the choice between life and death sentences. The jury was instructed that if it found the defendant guilty of the capital crime, it must then decide between life and death. The jury had no legal guidance in this decision. Moreover, the jury rarely received any general information about the defendant's background, character, or previous criminal record that might be relevant to sentence; it only had the evidence proffered on the guilt issue. Although a few states eliminated capital punishment entirely late in the nineteenth century or early in the twentieth century, the new unguided discretion statute was essentially the model American death penalty law until 1972.

Executions of murderers and rapists were fairly frequent in the United States until the 1960s, though the rate of execution peaked at about 200 per year during the Depression and then dropped during WORLD WAR II. By the 1960s, however, the long-standing practice of death sentencing through unguided jury discretion began to face increasing moral and political opposition. Beyond any fundamental change in moral attitudes toward state killing itself, the opposition sounded essentially three themes. First, early empirical studies by social scientists cast grave doubt on the major instrumental justification for the death penalty—its general deterrent power over murderers. Second, even informal data on the patterns of execution under the unguided discretion laws suggested that the criminal justice system in general, and sentencing juries in particular, acted randomly and capriciously in selecting defendants for capital punishment. The process did not treat like cases alike, and no rational principle emerged to explain why some defendants were executed and others of similar crimes or character were not.

Third, to the extent that any pattern emerged at all, it was the unacceptable pattern of race. Critics of the death penalty offered empirical evidence that the race of the defendant was an important factor in a jury's choice between life and death, and that the race of the victim was potentially a still greater factor. Blacks were sentenced to death more often than whites, and people who committed crimes against whites were executed far more often than those who committed crimes against blacks. The racial pattern was absolutely overwhelming in the instance of rape, where virtually all executed rapists were black men convicted of raping white women, but the pattern was powerfully suggestive for murder as well.

As these themes emerged in academic commentary, legal argument, and even public opinion in the late 1960s, the courts faced increasing pressure to impose some legal restraint on the death penalty. In the most important and most enigmatic decision on capital punishment in American history, *Furman v. Georgia* (1972), a muddled consensus of the Supreme Court ignored Justice Harlan's warning and accepted the challenge, if not the ultimate conclusion, of the arguments against capital punishment. All nine Justices wrote separate opinions in *Furman*, and by a vote of 5–4 the Court reversed the death sentences before them. But the five opinions for reversal achieved at best a vague, thematic consensus about the problems with the death penalty, and no majority position on the solution.

Justices WILLIAM J. BRENNAN and THURGOOD MARSHALL alone were clearly persuaded that the death penalty was categorically unconstitutional in all cases. Responding to the powerful textualist argument that the authors of the Constitution and the Bill of Rights contemplated a legal death penalty, the Justices chose to read the Eighth Amendment's cruel and unusual punishments clause as a flexible instrument that could adjust constitutional law to American society's moral development. Thus, "evolving standards of decency," reflected in public opinion, jury behavior, and legislative attitudes, had come to condemn the death penalty. Moreover, the Eighth Amendment authorized judges to examine the moral and instrumental justification for capital punishment, and neither retribution nor general deterrence withstood scrutiny. Retribution was an unworthy moral principle, and general deterrence had no empirical support.

But the *Furman* majority hinged on the more cautious and cryptic views of Justices WILLIAM O. DOUGLAS, BYRON R. WHITE, and POTTER STEWART. They avoided the question of whether capital punishment had become an absolutely forbidden penalty, and instead seemed to conclude that, as administered under the unguided discretion laws, capital punishment had achieved impermissibly random or racially discriminatory effects. Thus, the official signal from *Furman* seemed to be that the states could try yet again to develop sound capital punishment laws that would resolve the dilemma between legal guidance and discretion, though the Court certainly suggested no particular formula for doing so. (See CAPITAL PUNISHMENT CASES OF 1972.)

The immediate effect of *Furman* was to suspend all executions for a few years while about three-fourths of the state legislatures prepared their responses. The responses took two statutory forms. Ironically, a few states "solved" the problem of unguided discretion by completely eliminating discretion. Essentially, they returned to the early nineteenth-century model of the automatic death penalty, at least for those convicted of the most serious aggravated murders. Most of the states that restored the death penalty, however, chose a subtler, compromise approach, which might be called the "guided discretion" statute. A rough common denominator of these guided discretion statutes is a separate hearing on the question of penalty after a defendant is convicted of first degree murder. This hearing is a novel cross between the traditional discretionary sentencing hearing conducted by a trial judge in noncapital cases, and a formal, if abbreviated, criminal trial. In most states, the jury decides the penalty, though in a few states the judge either decides the penalty alone or has power to override a jury recommendation on penalty.

The matters at issue in this hearing consist of aggravating and mitigating factors which the two sides may establish. These factors partly overlap with the issues that would be resolved at the guilt trial, but comprehend new information about the defendant's character or background, which would normally be legally irrelevant at the guilt trial. Thus, the prosecution may establish that the defendant committed the murder in an especially heinous or sadistic way; that the victim was a specially protected person such as a police officer; that the murder was for hire or for some other form of pecuniary gain; that the murder was committed in the course of a rape, robbery, or burglary; or that the defendant had a substantial record of earlier violent crimes. Conversely, the defense may introduce evidence that the defendant, though unable to prove legal insanity, was emotionally impaired or under the influence of drugs at the time of the crime; that he was young, or had no serious criminal record; that he had suffered serious abuse or neglect as a child; or that since arrest he had demonstrated remorse and model prison behavior.

The sentencing judge or jury hears these factors and orders execution only if, according to some statutory formula, the aggravating circumstances outweigh the mitigating. Most of the statutes expressly enumerated these factors, and in addition provided for automatic appellate review of the death sentence. Many also required the state appellate court to conduct periodic "proportionality reviews" of death and life sentences in comparable murder cases, to ensure that the new system avoided the problem of caprice denounced in *Furman*.

In 1976 the states returned to the Supreme Court to learn whether they had properly met the obscure challenge of *Furman*. In a cluster of five cases handed down the same day, the Court once again failed to produce a majority opinion. Justices Brennan and Marshall would have struck down both types of statutes. Chief Justice WARREN E. BURGER and Justices HARRY A. BLACKMUN, BYRON R. WHITE, and WILLIAM H. REHNQUIST would have upheld both types of statutes. The swing plurality of Justices Potter Stewart, LEWIS F. POWELL, and JOHN PAUL STEVENS thus decided the constitutional fate of capital punishment, and the outcome, at least, of the 1976 cases was clear: the automatic death penalty statutes fell and the new guided discretion statutes survived.

First, in *Woodson v. North Carolina*, the plurality rejected the new automatic death laws as misguided solutions to the problem of discretion. These statutes were too rigid to capture the quality of individualized mercy required in death sentencing, and only revived the problem of "jury nullification" that had plagued the old automatic sentencing more than a century earlier. Second, in the key opinion in *Gregg v. Georgia* (1976) the plurality upheld the new guided discretion statutes as the proper solution to the complex of problems discerned in *Furman*. To do so, of course, the plurality had to reject the categorical arguments against the death penalty made by Justices Marshall and Brennan in *Furman*, and so it squarely held that the death penalty does not inevitably violate the BILL OF RIGHTS. The plurality opinion accepted retribution as a justifiable basis for execution, in particular because state-enacted revenge on murderers might prevent the more socially disruptive risk of private revenge. The plurality also found the empirical evidence of the general deterrent power of capital punishment to be equivocal, and declared that in the face of equivocal evidence, judges had to defer to popular and legislative judgments. Thus, the simple fact that three-fourths of the state legislatures had chosen to reenact the death penalty after *Furman* became a primary ground for the general constitutional legitimacy of capital punishment. The plurality relied on the curious principle that the state legislatures, which are supposedly subject to the Eighth Amendment, had become a major source of the evolving moral consensus that could determine the meaning of the Eighth Amendment.

The plurality then examined the Georgia guided discretion statute, as well as the statutes of Florida and Texas, in *Proffitt v. Florida* and *Jurek v. Texas.* It concluded that the substantive and procedural elements of the new concept of the penalty hearing, combined with the promise of strict appellate review, indicated that these statutes, on their face, were constitutionally sufficient to prevent the random and racist effects of the old unguided discretion laws. (See CAPITAL PUNISHMENT CASES OF 1976).

A year later, with the execution of Gary Gilmore in Utah, capital punishment was effectively restored in America. But because of the uncertain meaning of *Gregg,* the rate of execution, compared to the rate of death sentencing, remained very low for several years thereafter. While *Gregg* probably foreclosed any argument that capital punishment was fundamentally unconstitutional, it confirmed that the operation of the death penalty laws remained subject to very strict due process-style constraints. Thus, the death penalty defense bar quickly found numerous legal arguments for challenging particular death sentences or particular elements of the new state statutes. Some of the new legal claims involved state law issues: The new aggravating circumstances that entered the law of homicide after *Furman* had made state substantive criminal law doctrine far more complex than before.

Most of the new claims, however, were constitutional. In one series of cases, the court extended "Eighth Amendment due process" by imposing a sort of revived WARREN COURT criminal procedure jurisprudence on the state death penalty hearing. It gave capital defendants a CONFRONTATION right to rebut aggravating evidence in *Gardner v. Florida* (1977), and a COMPULSORY PROCESS right to present hearsay mitigating evidence in *Green v. Georgia* (1979); it applied the due process "void-for-vagueness" principle to aggravating factors in *Godfrey v. Georgia* (1980) and the RIGHT AGAINST SELF-INCRIMINATION and RIGHT TO COUNSEL to penalty phase investigation in ESTELLE V. SMITH (1981); and it applied the principles of DOUBLE JEOPARDY to penalty phase determination in *Bullington v. Missouri* (1981). As the Court extended "Eighth Amendment due process," the defense bar pushed the lower courts still further to shape the penalty hearing into a formal criminal trial. It claimed, for example, that the Sixth and Eighth Amendments guaranteed the capital defen-

dant a jury trial at the penalty phase, and that the jury had to apply the reasonable doubt standard to any choice of death over life.

At the same time, though it had foreclosed categorical arguments against the death penalty as a punishment for murder, the Court drew another line of decisions effectively limiting the death penalty to the crime of aggravated murder. In COKER V. GEORGIA (1977) the Court held that the death penalty was categorically disproportionate as a punishment for rape of adult women—and, by implication, for any nonhomicidal crime. In so holding, it noted that the great majority of states had repealed the death penalty for rape, and thus continued the method of legislation—counting as a form of constitutional jurisprudence. Yet the Court also engaged in its own moral balancing of the severity of the crime of rape and the severity of the sentence of death, claiming under the Eighth Amendment some independent power to determine when a punishment was so disproportionate as to be "cruel and unusual." The Court further applied this jurisprudence of legislative consensus finding and moral reasoning in ENMUND V. FLORIDA (1982). There, the Court forbade the death penalty as punishment for certain attenuated forms of unintentional felony murder.

After the Court had refined the new constitutional law of the death penalty, the process of appellate litigation in the state supreme courts—and even more so in federal district courts on HABEAS CORPUS petitions—became increasingly complex. It also became increasingly prolonged: the vast majority of defendants sentenced to death under the new laws were likely never to suffer execution, and for those that did, the time between original sentence and execution was often as long as ten years. Meanwhile, the Supreme Court encountered an ever increasing caseload of death penalty cases, in which it was continually asked to fine-tune still further the new constitutional regulation of capital punishment. But the Court's effort at formal legal regulation began to seem self-perpetuating, endlessly creating new grounds for reversible error. The appellate and habeas corpus courts were increasingly overwhelmed with death cases.

The Court recognized that it had exacerbated, not resolved, the inescapable tension between rational legal constraint and subjective jury discretion in the administration of capital punishment, and it began an effort to change course. The result, however, was that it was soon moving confusingly in both directions at once as it faced the fundamental—and perennial—legal issue: the feasibility of strict statutory rules, rather than open-ended discretionary standards, in choosing which defendants should die.

Ironically, perhaps the key decision in explaining the apparent unraveling of the Court's effort at constitutional regulation in the death penalty was a great defense victory—*Lockett v. Ohio* (1978). There, the Court held that the state must permit the sentencing judge or jury to give independent consideration to any mitigating factors about the defendant's character, crime, or record that the defense could reasonably proffer, even if those factors fell outside the state statute's carefully enumerated list of mitigating factors. The Court took the view that the moral principles of individualized sentencing demanded a degree of jury discretion that no formal statutory list could capture. The echo of Justice Harlan's 1971 warning was obvious. The Court faced the argument that *Lockett* had, ironically, revived all the problems of unguided jury discretion it had denounced in *Furman* and purported to resolve in *Gregg*.

The defense bar quickly lent support to this view, inundating the lower courts with *Lockett* claims that exploited the vast moral relativism of the concept of mitigation. Defendants sought to introduce evidence unrelated to technical criminal responsibility yet vaguely related to their moral deserts, such as evidence of upright, citizenlike conduct in prison while awaiting trial, or of late-found literary promise. The proffered mitigating evidence sometimes was not about the defendant's character at all: a defendant had a loving family that would suffer terribly if he died young; or, however culpable the defendant was, he had an equally culpable accomplice who had managed to gain a plea to a noncapital charge. Other defendants argued that a jury could not make a sound normative judgment about penalty unless it heard detailed evidence about the gruesome physical facts of execution. Still others read *Lockett* as mandating that a jury must receive an explicit instruction that it had full legal power to exercise mercy. It could spare a defendant after consulting its subjective assessment of his moral deserts, regardless of the technical outcome of its measurement of formal aggravating and mitigating factors.

A few years after *Lockett*, facing the complaint that it had revived, at least on the defendant's side, the very unguided discretion that *Furman* purported to prohibit, the Court arrived at a crudely symmetrical solution. In a bizarrely obscure pair of decisions, *Zant v. Stephens* and *Barclay v. Florida* (1983), the Court held that the state, in effect, had its own *Lockett* rights: so long as the sentencing judge or jury established at least one statutorily defined aggravating factor, it could also take account of aggravating factors about the defendant's crime or character that did not appear on the statute's enumerated list. Having taken an important, if ambivalent, step toward regulating capital punishment, the Court, perhaps reflecting simply its own weariness at the overload of death cases before it, had embarked on deregulation. Along with *Zant* and *Barclay*, the Court began, in *California v. Ramos* (1983) and *Pulley v. Harris* (1984), to remove most formal restrictions on such things as prosecution closing argument in the penalty phase and state appellate proportionality review. In *Spaziano v. Florida* (1984) the Court made clear that the apparent trial-like formality of the penalty phase did not create any defense right to jury sentencing. Once again, Justice Harlan echoed ominously.

In any event, partly because the Court has begun to narrow the grounds on which capital defendants can claim legal error, the execution rate has begun a slow but steady increase, with the number of post-*Furman* executions passing fifty in 1985. For the foreseeable future, a tired and conservative Court is not likely to entertain many dramatic procedural or substantive attacks on the death penalty, and so capital punishment has achieved political, if not intellectual, stability.

A remarkable irony, though, lies in one remaining possibility for a very broad attack on the death penalty. In the years since *Furman*, social scientists have conducted more sophisticated empirical studies of patterns of death sentencing and have uncovered evidence of random and racially disparate effects similar to the evidence that helped bring down the old unguided discretion laws in *Furman*. Most important, studies using multiple regression analysis have found significant evidence that, holding all other legitimate factors constant, murderers of whites are far more likely to suffer the death sentence than murderers of blacks.

One of the obvious implications of this evidence is that though the new guided discretion statutes reviewed in *Gregg* at first looked like they would meet the demands of *Furman*, they now may have proved failures. If so, there is no reason not to declare capital punishment unconstitutional yet again. It would seem politically unrealistic to think that the court would now accept this implication. But it is nevertheless important to consider how one might reconcile this evidence with the modern constitutional doctrine of capital punishment.

One could finesse the issue by taking the view that no system can be perfect and that the statistical discrepancy is insignificant. Or one could acknowledge that the discrepancy is significant and disturbing, but still ascribe it to the inevitable, often unconscious prejudices of jurors, rather than to any deliberate racist conduct by legislators or prosecutors. If so, one might conclude that the Constitution requires the states to do only what is morally possible, not what is morally perfect. To put the matter in doctrinal terms, one could engage in some mildly revisionist history of *Furman* and *Gregg*. That is, one could say that *Furman* only required the state legislatures to make their best efforts to devise rational, neutral death penalty laws, that *Gregg* had upheld the new guided discretion statutes on their face as proof that the state legislatures had made that effort successfully, and that constitutional law has no more to say about capital punishment. Whatever the conclusion, capital punishment has given constitutional doctrine making one of its most vexing challenges.

ROBERT WEISBERG
(1986)

(SEE ALSO: *Barefoot v. Estelle.*)

Bibliography

BEDAU, HUGO ADAM (1967) 1982 *The Death Penalty in America.* Oxford: Oxford University Press.

BERNS, WALTER 1979 *For Capital Punishment.* New York: Basic Books.

BOWERS, WILLIAM J., with PIERCE, GLENN L. 1984 *Legal Homicide: Death as Punishment in America, 1864–1982.* Boston: Northeastern University Press.

DEATH PENALTY SYMPOSIUM 1985 *U.C. Davis Law Review* 18: 865–1480.

GRANUCCI, ANTHONY F. 1969 Nor Cruel and Unusual Punishments Inflicted: The Original Meaning. *California Law Review* 57:839–865.

GROSS, SAMUEL R. and MAURO, ROBERT 1985 Patterns of Death: An Analysis of Racial Disparities in Capital Sentencing and Homicide Victimization. *Stanford Law Review* 37:27–153.

LEMPERT, RICHARD 1981 Desert and Deterrence: An Assessment of the Moral Bases of the Case for Capital Punishment. *Michigan Law Review* 79:1177–1231.

WEISBERG, ROBERT 1983 Deregulating Death. *Supreme Court Review* 1983:304–395.

CAPITAL PUNISHMENT
(Update 1)

During the 1980s, a majority of Justices on the Supreme Court struggled without success to disengage the Court from playing an intimate role in the day-to-day administration of capital punishment. As early as 1984, an article on the evolving jurisprudence of capital punishment in the Court could plausibly be titled "Deregulating Death," and the Court continued to reject major challenges to state systems of capital punishment for the rest of the decade. In the wake of *McCleskey v. Kemp,* decided in 1987, scholars could conclude that "nothing appears left of the abolitionist campaign in the courts—nothing but the possibility of small-scale tinkering" (Burt, p. 1741).

Yet conflicts about capital punishment have been a persistent and growing problem for the Court through the 1980s, and there are no indications that the burden will lessen soon. The number of capital cases producing opinions increased during the decade from about five per term in the early 1980s to about ten per term in the late 1980s.

Moreover, the level of dispute among the Justices has substantially increased during the course of the decade. In the early 1980s, most challenges to capital punishment were rejected by substantial majorities of the Justices, with a 7–2 vote being the most common outcome during the 1982, 1983, and 1984 terms. Only three of seventeen opinions issued during these three terms were decided by 5–4 margins. Justices WILLIAM J. BRENNAN and THURGOOD MARSHALL were the isolated dissenters in most of these early cases.

By contrast, in the four terms after October 1985, the Court has been sharply and closely divided. Of the twenty-seven cases decided over this span, fourteen produced 5–4 divisions, with Justices JOHN PAUL STEVENS and HARRY A. BLACKMUN usually joining Justices Brennan and Marshall in opposition to the deregulatory thrust of the Court majority. We know of no other body of the Supreme Court doctrine in which the majority of cases divide the Court 5–4.

With the Court divided almost to the point of a mathematical law of maximal disagreement, both JURISPRUDENCE and decorum have suffered. Few would suggest that the Court's decisions of the past decade cumulate into a body of doctrine that is even minimally coherent. And close decisions on questions that are literally matters of life and death do not promote good manners among Justices locked in conflict. It is thus no surprise that Court decorum has been put at some risk by the sustained contentiousness of the death penalty cases.

Close and acrimonious division of the Justices may also undermine the degree to which the Supreme Court's decisions confer legitimacy on the practice of execution in the 1990s. Confidence in the fairness of the system is not bolstered when four of nine Justices publicly proclaim that the race of the victim has a discriminatory influence on whether defendants receive death sentences. The result is that the consistent but slim majority support on the Court may not provide much momentum for public acceptance of the equity of capital punishment, much as the Court's leadership toward abolition was undermined by a slim and divided majority on the Court in *Furman v. Georgia* (1972). A 5–4 majority may lack the institutional credibility to help make executions an accepted part of a modern American governmental system.

One other pattern is of special significance when discussing capital punishment in the Supreme Court during the 1980s: The transition from theory to practice of executions has not yet occurred in most of the United States. Despite the Court's attempts to withdraw from close supervision of death cases, the backlog of death cases has increased substantially, and the lower federal courts continue to play an important role in stopping executions. Indeed, over half of federal court of appeals decisions in death penalty cases result in overturning the death sentence.

As of January 1990, although thirty-seven states have legislation authorizing capital punishment (and thirty-four of these have prisoners under death sentence), only thirteen states have executed since the reauthorization of the capital punishment in *Gregg v. Georgia*, in 1976. Nine of the thirteen states with a recent execution are located in the South; only one new state resumed executions during the last four years of the 1980s.

The number of executions has also stayed low throughout the 1980s, with a high of twenty-seven in 1987 and an annual average of about twenty for the last five years of the 1980s. But, although the level of executions remained low and eighty percent of these are clustered in four southern states, the number of prisoners under death sentence had increased by the end of 1989 to about 2,400, a more than one-hundred-year supply at the prevailing rates of execution.

Thus, by the end of the 1980s, the withdrawal of the Supreme Court from regulation of the administration of the death penalty had not yet produced a substantial increase in the number of executing states or the number of executions. But the long involvement of the federal courts had helped produce a death row population four times as great as that which cast a shadow on the Court when *Furman v. Georgia* was decided in 1972.

Against this backdrop, an ad hoc committee chaired by retired Justice LEWIS F. POWELL diagnosed the problem that generated these numbers as the delay produced by repetitive and multiple federal APPEALS. The committee suggested the enactment of new statutory procedures for handling death penalty cases in the federal court, which, by and large, would eliminate the filing of successor federal petitions. Under the new procedures, if the state has provided counsel to those sentenced to death through the state appeal and HABEAS CORPUS process, absent extraordinary circumstances, a federal court would lack the power to stay an execution of the condemned person upon the filing of a successor federal petition.

Should such procedures be enacted and actually reduce federal appeal time more than they increase state appeal time, further pressure toward increasing numbers of executions will occur just when large numbers of cases will be exhausting currently available federal reviews.

But even if the Powell committee recommendations were to maintain delay at current levels, but shift more of the total procedural load onto state courts, this result might serve one significant objection that motivated the exercise—it would reduce the extent to which the federal courts could be blamed for delay in execution. A persistent

fact of American government is that even among institutions and actors that believe twenty-five executions a year is more appropriate in the United States than 250, there is constant pressure to avoid appearing to be responsible for restricting the scale of executions. The politics of capital punishment at all levels in the United States involves passing the apparent responsibility for preventing executions to other actors or institutions. And the Powell committee's work can be understood in part as a public-relations gesture in this tradition of passing the buck away from the federal court system.

In 1989 and 1990, the Supreme Court, by the familiar 5–4 vote, responded to the considerations that had moved the Powell committee. Now, with few exceptions, a federal habeas corpus petition must be denied when it rests on a claim of a "new right"—one that had not yet been recognized by the Supreme Court when the appeals ended in the state courts. Not only has the Court specifically applied this new bar to death penalty cases, but it has also read the idea of a "new right" broadly enough to bar all but a very few claims.

What would be the impact of true federal court withdrawal from restrictions on execution? The potential number of executions that could result is quite high, two or three times as many as the 199 executions that were to date the twentieth-century high recorded in 1935. How many state governors or state court systems would compensate and to what degree remains to be seen. Practices like executive clemency that used to be a statistically important factor in restricting executions atrophied during the twenty-five years of primary federal court intervention in the capital-punishment process. Whether these processes would reappear under the pressure of large numbers of pending executions in northern industrial states cannot be predicted, nor is it possible to project a likely national number of executions that could represent a new level of equilibrium.

The one certainty is that the U.S. Supreme Court will play a central day-to-day role in any substantial increase in executions. Whatever its doctrinal intentions or public-relations ambitions, the Supreme Court will be for the mass media and the public the court of last resort for every scheduled execution in the United States for the foreseeable future. If executions climb to 100 or 150 per year, the continuing role of the Court as the last stop before the gallows will be that element of the Court's work most sharply etched in the public mind. For an institution narrowly divided on fundamental questions, this case-by-case process could increase both the labor and the acrimony of the Court's involvement with capital punishment. To escape this role would call for more than a shift in procedure or court personnel; it would require a different country.

Under these circumstances, will the hands-off doctrine the Court has so recently constructed continue as executions multiply? In the short run, any major shift in doctrine would be regarded as a surprise. This is a matter more of personnel than of precedent. STARE DECISIS has not often been a reliable guide to Supreme Court pronouncements in capital punishment. Instead, doctrine seems more the servant of policy than its master in this field, and this is equally the case for *Gregg v. Georgia* as for *Furman v. Georgia.* But the current majority is apparently firm and includes the four youngest Justices.

In the long run, if the United States is to join the community of Western nations that has abolished capital punishment, the U.S. Supreme Court is the most likely agency of abolition in the national government. The principal flaws in the system of capital punishment are the same as they have been throughout the twentieth century. The doctrinal foundations for reacting to these matters are easily found in the Court's prior work.

No matter the course of the Court's future pronouncements, capital punishment will remain an area of inevitable judicial activism in one important respect: Whatever the substance of American policy toward executions, the U.S. Supreme Court will continue to be the dominant institutional influence of national government on executions in the United States.

FRANKLIN ZIMRING
MICHAEL LAURENCE
(1992)

(SEE ALSO: *Capital Punishment and Race; Capital Punishment Cases of 1972; Capital Punishment Cases of 1976.*)

Bibliography

AD HOC COMMITTEE ON FEDERAL HABEAS CORPUS IN CAPITAL CASES 1989 *Committee Report and Proposal.* Washington, D.C.: Judicial Conference of the United States.

BURT, ROBERT A. 1987 Disorder in the Court: The Death Penalty and the Constitution. *Michigan Law Review* 85:1741–1819.

WEISBERG, ROBERT 1983 Deregulating Death. In Philip J. Kurland, Gerhard Gasper, and Dennis J. Hutchinson, eds., *Supreme Court Review,* pp. 305–396. Chicago: University of Chicago Press.

ZIMRING, FRANKLIN E. and HAWKINS, GORDON 1986 *Capital Punishment and the American Agenda.* New York: Cambridge University Press.

CAPITAL PUNISHMENT
(Update 2)

The mid-1990s have witnessed an end to what one scholar described in the early 1980s as "a roller coaster system of capital justice, in which large numbers of people are constantly spilling into and out of death row, but virtually no executions take place." Executions averaged forty-five a year from 1992–1997, peaking in 1997 at seventy-one. Although death row continues to grow (at the end of 1997, it exceeded 3,300 inmates), one can anticipate a time in which more people are executed in a year than are added to the capital prison population.

A major reason for this dismal trend is the continued retreat of the Supreme Court from active monitoring of the death penalty. While defendants still chalk up occasional victories, these are mainly in cases affecting relatively small numbers of prisoners. Indeed, death penalty opponents have not generally mounted broad-based claims in the 1990s. With the Court's sanction in the late 1980s of capital punishment for the mentally retarded, PENRY V. LYNAUGH (1989), for perpetrators as young as sixteen, STANFORD V. KENTUCKY (1989), for felony murderers who did not intentionally kill, *Tison v. Arizona* (1987), and for persons sentenced in systems tainted by RACIAL DISCRIMINATION, MCCLESKEY V. KEMP (1987), it appears that few if any systemic challenges remain.

Justice HARRY A. BLACKMUN voiced his disgust with the majority's performance in this area. "From this day forward," he announced in *Callins v. Collins* (1994), "I no longer shall tinker with the machinery of death." He had concluded that the twin goals of modern death penalty jurisprudence under the Eighth Amendment, eliminating arbitrariness and ensuring individualized sentencing, stood in irreconcilable tension: advancing the one jeopardized the other. Worse yet, he noted, the Court was retreating from both of these principles.

Blackmun's criticism was well-founded. The Court continued a trend begun in the mid-1980s, tolerating laws and practices that detracted from the goal of nonarbitrariness. In addition, it showed increased willingness to compromise the aim that it had pursued more faithfully until the 1990s—individualized sentencing. For example, it affirmed a death sentence even though the jurors were not permitted to give the defendant's youth full mitigating effect in *Johnson v. Texas* (1993), and upheld a trial court's sentencing instructions that failed to mention mitigation in *Buchanan v. Angelone* (1998).

Arguably the most important setbacks for capital defendants occurred in the field of HABEAS CORPUS, rather than the Eighth Amendment. Since the 1970s, and increasingly over the following two decades, the Court has been narrowing access to federal court review by death-sentenced prisoners—the most avid consumers of the writ.

Throughout this period, the Court has demanded procedural punctilio of habeas petitioners. Slight missteps by defense counsel, in either state or federal forums, barred federal review of the merits of the prisoner's contentions unless he was able to demonstrate "cause" for, and "prejudice" from, the procedural default or, in the alternative, actual innocence. At the same time, the Court has declined to recognize innocence as a freestanding constitutional claim under the Eighth or FOURTEENTH AMENDMENTS for inmates seeking to avoid execution by presenting new evidence of innocence. In denying habeas applicants hearings on their claims, the Justices relied heavily on law precluding habeas courts from declarating or applying "new rules" favoring defendants. While most of the decisions in this area purported to interpret the statutes governing habeas, some dealt with issues implicating constitutional principles—for example, the doctrine that the Court cannot review decisions resting on an independent and adequate state law ground.

Congress echoed the Court's anti-habeas sentiment, enacting the ANTI-TERRORISM AND EFFECTIVE DEATH PENALTY ACT OF 1996 (AEDPA). Among other things, it drastically limited second or successive habeas petitions, imposed a statute of limitations on habeas filings, and arguably established a deferential STANDARD OF REVIEW of state decisions on questions of law or mixed questions of law and fact.

In addition to issues of STATUTORY INTERPRETATION, these provisions give rise to constitutional questions—such as whether the law amounts to a suspension of the writ, violates DUE PROCESS, or infringes on Article III's requirement of an independent judiciary—that the Court will have to resolve. In 1996, the Justices upheld one of its restrictions against a suspension clause attack. Other cases are percolating in the lower courts and will surely afford the Justices many opportunities to construe the statute's meaning and validity.

What does the future hold for capital punishment and the Court? Aside from habeas, it appears for the moment that the Court will likely continue to "tinker" with minor aspects of the doctrine. The newest Justices, RUTH BADER GINSBURG and STEPHEN G. BREYER, moderate liberals on capital punishment, replaced a liberal—Justice Blackmun—and a conservative—Justice BYRON R. WHITE; therefore, not very much has changed. Changes in the Court's jurisprudence regarding the death penalty will probably have more to do with changes in the Court's personnel than with paradigm shifts in ideology.

VIVIAN BERGER
(2000)

(SEE ALSO: *Cruel and Unusual Punishment; Procedural Due Process of Law, Criminal.*)

Bibliography

BERGER, VIVIAN 1991 Black Box Decisions on Life or Death—If They're Arbitrary, Don't Blame the Jury: A Reply to Judge Patrick Higginbottom. *Case Western Reserve Law Review* 41: 1067–1092.

—— 1994 *Herrera v. Collins:* The Gateway of Innocence for Death-Sentenced Prisoners Leads Nowhere. *William and Mary Law Review* 35:943–1023.

GREENBERG, JACK 1982 Capital Punishment as a System. *Yale Law Journal* 91:908–936.

STEIKER, CAROL S. and STEIKER, JORDAN M. 1995 Sober Second Thoughts: Reflections on Two Decades of Constitutional Regulation of Capital Punishment. *Harvard Law Review* 109: 355–438.

SUNDBY, SCOTT 1991 The *Lockett* Paradox: Reconciling Guided Discretion and Unguided Mitigation in Capital Sentencing. *UCLA Law Review* 38:1147–1208.

CAPITAL PUNISHMENT AND RACE

In MCCLESKEY V. KEMP (1987), the Supreme Court grappled with the difficult issue of race and CAPITAL PUNISHMENT. Confronted with statistical studies that indicated potential RACIAL DISCRIMINATION in the assignment of death sentences in the state of Georgia, the Court considered Eighth Amendment and EQUAL PROTECTION challenges to the application of the Georgia death penalty statute. Whereas no significant disparities existed with respect to the race of defendants, statistical evidence, using sophisticated regression analysis, indicated that blacks were 4.3 times more likely to receive death sentences when they killed whites than when they killed blacks.

McCleskey, a black, had killed a white police officer during an armed robbery. The fact that the race of the victim made it more likely that he would receive the death penalty was, McCleskey argued, a violation of equal protection guarantees and the Eighth Amendment's ban on CRUEL AND UNUSUAL PUNISHMENT. The Court, although expressing some reservations about both the credibility and the relevance of the statistical evidence, nevertheless assumed their validity in order to reach the constitutional questions.

Speaking through Justice LEWIS F. POWELL, the Court's majority of five refused to break new ground in its equal protection jurisprudence. Powell began by noting that it was a settled principle that "a defendant who alleges an equal protection violation has the burden of proving 'the existence of purposeful discrimination'" and that the purposeful discrimination had "a discriminatory effect on him." Therefore, "McCleskey must prove that the decisionmakers in *his* case acted with discriminatory purpose." Statistical inference, the Court ruled, could at best indicate only that there was a risk that racial discrimination had been a factor in McCleskey's sentencing. The Court has in certain contexts—selection of jury venire and Title VII—accepted statistics as prima facie proof of discrimination. Moreover, the statistics (particularly in the jury cases) do not have to present a "stark" pattern in order to be accepted as sole evidence of discriminatory intent.

Yet the Court in *McCleskey* distinguished capital sentencing cases as less amenable to statistical proof because of the "uniqueness" of each capital case and the consequent difficulty of aggregating data. Each jury is unique and "the Constitution requires that its decision rest on consideration of innumerable factors that vary according to the characteristics of the individual defendant and the facts of the particular capital offense." In contrast, the jury-selection and Title VII cases are concerned only with limited ranges of circumstances and are thus more amenable to statistical analysis.

The Court therefore held that for McCleskey's claim of purposeful discrimination to prevail, he "would have to prove that the Georgia Legislature enacted or maintained the death penalty statute *because* of an anticipated racially discriminatory effect." But, as the Court laconically notes, this was a claim that was rejected in *Gregg v. Georgia* (1976). Thus, the Court concluded that "absent far stronger proof, . . . a legitimate and unchallenged explanation" for McCleskey's sentence "is apparent from the record: McCleskey committed an act for which the United States Constitution and Georgia laws permit imposition of the death penalty."

McCleskey also sought to use statistics to support his Eighth Amendment claim that the discretion given to sentencers in the Georgia criminal justice system makes it inevitable that any assignment of the death penalty will be "arbitrary and capricious." The Court has interpreted Eighth Amendment requirements to mean that sentencers must be governed by state laws that contain carefully defined standards that narrow the discretion to impose the death penalty. That is, sentencers must exercise only "guided discretion." But there can be no limits with respect to the sentencer's discretion not to impose the death penalty.

As the Court stated in *Lockett v. Ohio* (1978), "the sentencer" cannot be "precluded from considering, as a mitigating factor, any aspect of a defendant's character or record and any of the circumstances of the offense that the defendant proffers as a basis for a sentence less than death." Discretion that ensures the treatment of all persons as "uniquely individual human beings" is thus an essential ingredient of Eighth Amendment jurisprudence. The Court has ruled that mandatory death sentences are unconstitutional because the "respect for humanity underlying the Eighth Amendment requires consideration of the character and record of the individual offender and the circumstances of the particular offense as a constitutionally indispensable part of the process of inflicting the penalty of death."

The presence of such discretion, however, makes it impossible for actual decisions to result in racial proportionality. And to stipulate racial proportionality as a requirement either of equal protection or the Eighth Amendment would mean that the sentencer's discretion would have to be limited or extinguished. Proportionality requirements also present the daunting prospect that blacks who are convicted of killing blacks will have to receive the death penalty at an accelerated rate. Of course, proponents of the use of statistics as a measure of equal protection and Eighth Amendment rights do not expect any such result. Rather, their ultimate purpose is to abolish capital punishment under the guise that it is impossible to mete out death sentences in any rational or otherwise nonarbitrary manner. The Court, however, remains unwilling to accept statistical evidence as a sufficient proof of capriciousness and irrationality.

Because the existence of discretion will always produce statistical disparities, the "constitutional measure of an unacceptable risk of racial prejudice influencing capital sentencing decisions" cannot be defined in statistical terms. Rather, the constitutional risk must be addressed in terms of the procedural safeguards designed to minimize the influence of racial prejudice in the criminal justice system as a whole. After a thorough review of the Georgia system in *Gregg*, the Court concluded that procedural safeguards against racial discrimination were constitutionally adequate. As the Court rightly said, "where the discretion that is fundamental to our criminal process is involved, we decline to assume that what is unexplained is invidious."

The Eighth Amendment is not limited to capital sentencing but extends to all criminal penalties. Thus, a racial proportionality requirement for capital sentencing would open the possibility that all sentences could be challenged not only on the grounds of race but on the grounds of any irrelevant factor that showed enough of a statistical disparity to indicate that the sentencing was "irrational" or "capricious." Some cynics have described this as a kind of AFFIRMATIVE ACTION for sentencing decisions. Such a situation not only would prove unworkable but, by limiting the discretion that remains at the heart of the criminal justice system, would also prove to be unjust. The vast majority of convicted murderers, for example, do not receive death sentences, because the discretionary element of the system spares them. The small percentage who do receive death sentences have thorough and exhaustive procedural protections. Under these circumstances, it would be impossible to argue that statistical disparities based on race indicate systemic racism in the CRIMINAL JUSTICE SYSTEM or that the statistical disparities indicate a fundamentally unjust system.

Moreover, some scholars have questioned the validity of the statistics used in the *McCleskey* case. Interracial murders are more likely to involve aggravating circumstances (e.g., armed robbery, kidnapping, rape, torture, or murder to silence a witness to a crime) than same-race murders, which involve more mitigating factors (e.g., quarrels between friends and relatives). Given the relative rarity of blacks being murdered by whites, the statistics are bound to be skewed, but they do not necessarily prove or even indicate racial discrimination.

Taking into account the different levels of aggravating and mitigating circumstances, one recent study of Georgia sentencing practices concluded that evidence "supports the thesis that blacks who kill whites merit more serious punishment and are not themselves the victims of racial discrimination. By the same token, the same evidence suggests that blacks who kill blacks deserve less punishment and are not being patronized by a criminal justice system because it places less value on a black life."

Given the controversial nature of the statistical evidence proffered in the *McCleskey* case and the doctrine that equal protection and Eighth Amendment rights belong to "uniquely individual human beings" rather than racial groups, the Supreme Court was wise to reject abstract statistical disparities as proof of individual injury.

EDWARD J. ERLER
(1992)

Bibliography

HEILBRUN, ALFRED B., JR.; FOSTER, ALLISON; and GOLDEN, JILL 1989 The Death Sentence in Georgia, 1974–1987. *Criminal Justice and Behavior* 16:139–154.

KENNEDY, RANDALL L. 1988 *McCleskey v. Kemp:* Race, Capital Punishment, and the Supreme Court. *Harvard Law Review* 101:1388–1443.

CAPITAL PUNISHMENT CASES OF 1972

Furman v. Georgia
Jackson v. Georgia
Branch v. Texas
408 U.S. 238 (1972)

The Eighth Amendment clearly and expressly forbids the infliction of CRUEL AND UNUSUAL PUNISHMENTS (a prohibition that since 1947 has applied to the states as well as to the national government), and opponents of CAPITAL PUNISHMENT have long argued that to execute a convicted criminal, whatever his crime, is such a punishment. It was obviously not so regarded by the persons who wrote and ratified the BILL OF RIGHTS. They acknowledged the legitimacy of the death penalty when, in the Fifth Amendment, they provided that no person "shall be held to answer for a capital . . . crime, unless on a PRESENTMENT or INDICTMENT of a GRAND JURY," and when in the same amendment they provided that no one shall, for the same offense, "be twice put in jeopardy of life or limb," and when they forbade not the taking of life as such but the taking of life "without DUE PROCESS OF LAW" (a formulation repeated in the FOURTEENTH AMENDMENT). The question of the original understanding of "cruel and unusual" is put beyond any doubt by the fact that the same First Congress that proposed the Eighth Amendment also provided for the death penalty in the first Crimes Act. In 1958, however, the Supreme Court, in the course of holding deprivation of CITIZENSHIP to be a cruel and unusual punishment, accepted the argument that the meaning of cruel and unusual is relative to time and place; the Eighth Amendment, the Court said in TROP V. DULLES (1958), "must draw its meaning from the evolving standards of decency that mark the progress of a maturing society." Implicit in this statement is the opinion that society, as it matures, becomes gentler, and as it becomes gentler, it is more disposed to regard the death penalty as cruel and unusual. According to one member of the five-man majority in the 1972 cases, that point had been reached: "capital punishment," wrote Justice THURGOOD MARSHALL, "is morally unacceptable to the people of the United States at this time in their history."

This assessment of the public's opinion could not reasonably provide the basis of the Court's judgment in these cases; contrary to Marshall, the polls showed a majority in favor of the death penalty and, more to the point, there were at that time some 600 persons on death row, which is to say, some 600 persons on whom the American people, acting through their federal and state courts, had imposed death sentences. Marshall's assessment was also belied by the reaction to the Court's decision: Congress and thirty-five states promptly enacted new death penalty statutes, and it is fair to assume that they did so with the consent of their respective popular majorities. The states remained authorized, or at least not forbidden, to do so, because the Court did not declare the death penalty as such to be a cruel and unusual punishment; only two members of the 1972 majority adopted that position. Justice WILLIAM J. BRENNAN said that the death penalty, for whatever crime imposed, "does not comport with human dignity." Marshall, in addition to finding it to be morally unacceptable, said its only possible justification was not that it was an effective deterrent (he accepted Thorsten Sellin's evidence that it was not) but as a form of retribution, a way to pay criminals back, and, he said, the Eighth Amendment forbade "retribution for its own sake." The other majority Justices found the death penalty to be cruel and unusual only insofar as the statutes permitted it to be imposed discriminatorily (WILLIAM O. DOUGLAS), or arbitrarily and capriciously (POTTER STEWART), or (because it is imposed infrequently) pointlessly or needlessly (BYRON R. WHITE).

That the death penalty has historically been imposed, if not capriciously, then at least in a racially and socially discriminatory fashion seems to be borne out by the statistics. Of the 3,859 persons executed in the United States during the years 1930–1967, when, for a time, executions ceased, 2,066, or fifty-four percent, were black. Georgia alone executed 366 persons, of whom 298 were black. Although American juries have shown increasing reluctance to impose the death penalty (despite the majority sentiment in favor of it in principle), they have been less reluctant to impose it on certain offenders, offenders characterized not by their criminality but by their race or class. "One searches our chronicles in vain for the execution of any members of the affluent strata in this society," said Douglas. "The Leopolds and Loebs are given prison terms, not sentenced to death." The three cases decided in 1972 illustrate his argument. The statutes (two from Georgia, one from Texas) empowered the juries to choose between death and imprisonment for the crimes committed (murder in the one case and rape in the other two), and in each case the jury chose death. As crimes go, however, those committed here were not especially heinous. In the *Furman* case, for example, the offender entered a private home at about 2 a.m. intending to burglarize it. He was carrying a gun. When heard by the head of the household, William Micke, a father of five children, Furman attempted to flee the house. He tripped and his gun discharged, hitting Micke through a closed door and killing him. Furman was quickly apprehended, and in due course tried and convicted. The salient facts would appear to be these: the offender was black and the victim was white, which was also true in the other two cases decided that day.

By holding that the death penalty, as it has been administered in this country, is a cruel and unusual punishment, the Supreme Court challenged the Congress and the state legislatures, if they insisted on punishing by executing, to devise statutes calculated to prevent the arbitrary or discriminatory imposition of the penalty.

WALTER BERNS
(1986)

Bibliography

BERNS, WALTER 1979 *For Capital Punishment: Crime and the Morality of the Death Penalty.* New York: Basic Books.
BLACK, CHARLES L., JR. 1974 *Capital Punishment: The Inevitability of Caprice and Mistake.* New York: Norton.
LEVY, LEONARD 1974 *Against the Law: The Nixon Court and Criminal Justice.* Pages 383–420. New York: Harper & Row.
SELLIN, THORSTEN 1980 *The Penalty of Death.* Beverly Hills, Calif.: Sage Publications.
VAN DEN HAAG, ERNEST 1975 *Punishing Criminals: Concerning a Very Old and Painful Question.* Pages 225–228. New York: Basic Books.

CAPITAL PUNISHMENT CASES OF 1976

Gregg v. Georgia, 428 U.S. 153
Jurek v. Texas, 428 U.S. 262
Proffitt v. Florida, 428 U.S. 242
Woodson v. North Carolina, 428 U.S. 280
Roberts v. Louisiana, 428 U.S. 325
Green v. Oklahoma, 428 U.S. 907

Writing for the Supreme Court in *McGautha v. California* (1971), only a year before the CAPITAL PUNISHMENT CASES OF 1972, Justice JOHN MARSHALL HARLAN said, "To identify before the fact those characteristics of criminal homicides and their perpetrators which call for the death penalty, and to express these characteristics in language which can fairly be understood and applied by the sentencing authority, appear to be tasks which are beyond present human ability." Yet, in *Furman v. Georgia* (1972), by declaring unconstitutional statutes that permitted arbitrary, capricious, or discriminatory imposition of the death penalty, the Court challenged the Congress and the various state legislatures to write new statutes that did express in advance the characteristics that would allow the sentencing authorities to distinguish between what is properly a capital and what is properly a noncapital case. The statutes involved in the 1976 cases were drafted in the attempt to meet these requirements.

Three states (North Carolina, Louisiana, Oklahoma) attempted to meet them by making death the mandatory sentence in all first-degree murder cases, thereby depriving juries of all discretion, at least in the sentencing process. By the narrowest of margins, the Court found these mandatory sentencing laws unconstitutional. Justices WILLIAM J. BRENNAN and THURGOOD MARSHALL held to their views expressed in the 1972 cases that the death penalty is unconstitutional per se. In the 1976 cases they were joined by Justices POTTER STEWART, LEWIS F. POWELL, and JOHN PAUL STEVENS (new on the Court since the 1972 decisions) who held, in part, that it was cruel and unusual to treat alike all persons convicted of a designated offense. Their view was that no discretion is as cruel as unguided discretion.

The three statutes upheld in 1976 (those from Georgia, Texas, and Florida) permitted jury sentencing discretion but attempted to reduce the likelihood of abuse to a tolerable minimum. All three statutes, and especially the one from Georgia, embodied procedures intended to impress on judge and jury the gravity of the judgment they are asked to make in capital cases. For example, all three required the sentencing decision to be separated from the decision as to guilt or innocence. In one way or another, all three implied that a sentence of death must be regarded as an extraordinary punishment not to be imposed in an ordinary case, even an ordinary case of first-degree murder. For example, the Georgia law required (except in a case of treason or aircraft hijacking) a finding beyond a REASONABLE DOUBT of the presence of at least one of the aggravating circumstances specified in the statute (for example, that the murder "was outrageously and wantonly vile, horrible and inhuman"), and required the sentencing authority to specify the circumstance found. In addition, the trial judge was required to instruct the jury to consider "any mitigating circumstances" (an element that was to play an important role in the 1978 capital punishment cases). Finally, Georgia required or permitted an expedited APPEAL to or review by the state supreme court, directing that court to determine whether, for example, "the sentence of death was imposed under the influence of passion, prejudice, or any other arbitrary factor," or was "excessive or disproportionate to the penalty imposed in similar cases, considering both the crime and the defendant."

These statutes went to great lengths to do what Harlan in *McGautha* had said could not be done but which, in effect, the Court in 1972 had said must be done: to characterize in advance the cases in which death is an appropriate punishment, or in which the sentencing authority (whether judge or jury) is entitled to decide that the death penalty is appropriate. With only Brennan and Marshall dissenting, the Court agreed that all three statutes met the constitutional requirements imposed four years earlier.

From the 1976 decisions emerged the following rules: the death penalty in and of itself is not a cruel and unusual punishment; a death sentence may not be carried out unless the sentencing authority is guided by reasonably clear statutory standards; in imposing the penalty, the sentencing authority must consider the characteristics of the offender and the circumstances of his offense; mandatory death sentences for murder (and presumably for all other offenses) are unconstitutional; the punishment must not be inflicted in a way that causes unnecessary pain; finally, the death penalty may not be imposed except for heinous crimes ("the punishment must not be grossly out of proportion to the severity of the crime").

The Court's decisions were a bitter disappointment not only to the hundreds of persons on death row who now seemingly faced the real prospect of being executed but also to the equally large number of persons who had devoted their time, talent, and in some cases their professional careers to the cause of abolishing the death penalty.

They had been making progress toward that end. In other Western countries, including Britain, Canada, and France, the death penalty had either been abolished by statute or been allowed to pass into desuetude; in the United States almost a decade had passed since the last legal execution. In this context it was easy for the opponents of capital punishment to see the Supreme Court's 1972 decision as a step along the path leading inevitably to complete and final abolition of the death penalty. This hope was dashed, at least temporarily, in 1976.

Not only did the Court for the first time squarely hold that "the punishment of death does not invariably violate the Constitution" but it also gave explicit support to the popular principle that punishment must fit the crime and that, in making this calculation, the community may pay back the worst of its criminals with death. Prior to 1976, the capital punishment debate had focused on the deterrence issue, and a major effort had been made by social scientists to demonstrate the absence of evidence showing the death penalty to be a more effective deterrent than, for example, life imprisonment. This opinion was challenged in 1975 by University of Chicago econometrician Isaac Ehrlich. Employing multiple regression analysis, Ehrlich concluded that each execution might have had the effect of deterring as many as eight murders. His findings were made available to the Court in an AMICUS CURIAE brief filed in a 1975 case by the solicitor general of the United States. In the 1976 opinion announcing the judgment of the Court, Stewart cited the Ehrlich study, acknowledged that it had provoked "a great deal of debate" in the scholarly journals, but nevertheless concluded that, at least for some potential murderers, "the death penalty undoubtedly is a significant deterrent." If this conclusion remains undisturbed, the focus of the capital punishment debate will shift to the issue of human dignity or the propriety of retribution. Thus, Stewart's statement on paying criminals back takes on added significance. With the concurrence of six Justices, he said, "the decision that capital punishment may be the appropriate sanction in extreme cases is an expression of the community's belief that certain crimes are themselves so grievous an affront to humanity that the only adequate response may be the penalty of death."

This sanctioning of the retributive principle especially disturbed Marshall, one of the two dissenters. Along with many opponents of the death penalty, he would be willing to allow executions if they could be shown to serve some useful purpose—for example, deterring others from committing capital crimes—but to execute a criminal simply because society demands its pound of flesh is, he said, to deny him his "dignity and worth." Why it would not deprive a person of dignity and worth to use him (by executing him) in order to influence the behavior of other persons, Marshall did not say; apparently he would be willing to accept society's calculations but not its moral judgments.

An unwillingness to accept society's moral judgments best characterizes the opposition to capital punishment, a fact reflected in the differences between popular and sophisticated opinion on the subject. Sophisticated opinion holds that the death penalty does not comport with human dignity because, as Brennan (the other dissenter) said, it treats "members of the human race as nonhumans, as objects to be toyed with and discarded." Popular opinion holds that to punish criminals, even to execute them, is to acknowledge their humanity, insofar as it regards them, as it does not regard other creatures, as responsible moral beings. Sophisticated opinion agrees with ABE FORTAS who, after he left the Supreme Court, argued that the "essential value" of our civilization is the "pervasive, unqualified respect for life"; this respect for life forbids the taking of even a murderer's life. Popular opinion holds that what matters is not *that* one lives but *how* one lives, and that society rightly praises its heroes, who sacrifice their lives for their fellow citizens, and rightly condemns the worst of its criminals who prey upon them.

In 1976, seven members of the Supreme Court agreed that society is justified in making this severe moral judgment, but this agreement on the principle may prove to be less significant than the Justices' inability to join in a common opinion of the Court. Embodied in that inability were differences in the extent to which the Justices were committed to the principle, and it could have been predicted that, in future cases, some of them would find reason not to apply it.

WALTER BERNS
(1986)

Bibliography

BERNS, WALTER 1979 *For Capital Punishment: Crime and the Morality of the Death Penalty.* New York: Basic Books.

DAVIS, PEGGY C.; WOLFGANG, MARVIN E.; GIBBS, JACK P.; VAN DEN HAAG, ERNEST; and NAKELL, BARRY 1978 Capital Punishment in the United States: A Symposium. *Criminal Law Bulletin* 14:5–80.

EHRLICH, ISAAC 1975 The Deterrent Effect of Capital Punishment. *American Economic Review* 65:397–417.

ENGLAND, JANE C. 1977 Capital Punishment in the Light of Constitutional Evolution: An Analysis of Distinctions Between *Furman* and *Gregg*. *Notre Dame Lawyer* 52:596–610.

GILLERS, STEPHEN 1980 Deciding Who Dies. *University of Pennsylvania Law Review* 129:1–124.

LEMPERT, RICHARD O. 1981 Desert and Deterrence: An Assessment of the Moral Bases for Capital Punishment. *Michigan Law Review* 79:1177–1231.

CAPITATION TAXES

A capitation tax, or POLL TAX, is a tax levied on persons. A capitation tax takes a fixed amount for each person subject to it, without regard to income or property. Under Article I, section 9, any federal capitation tax must be apportioned among the states according to population, a restriction originally intended to prevent Congress from taxing states out of existence.

In the twentieth century some states made payment of capitation taxes a qualification for voting, usually in order to reduce the number of black voters. The TWENTY-FOURTH AMENDMENT and HARPER V. VIRGINIA BOARD OF ELECTIONS (1966) ended this practice.

DENNIS J. MAHONEY
(1986)

(SEE ALSO: *Direct and Indirect Taxes; Excise Tax.*)

CAPITOL SQUARE REVIEW AND ADVISORY BOARD v. PINETTE
515 U.S. 753 (1995)

In this decision, the Supreme Court invalidated an administrative decision that denied permission to the Ku Klux Klan to erect a large, unattended cross in Capitol Square, a PUBLIC FORUM located in front of the Ohio Statehouse. The administrators had determined that observers might conclude that the state endorsed the religious beliefs embodied in the cross. The Court reasoned that excluding the cross would be consistent with the FREEDOM OF SPEECH guarantee of the FIRST AMENDMENT only if a decision to allow the cross would itself violate the ESTABLISHMENT OF RELIGION clause. The central question was therefore whether the board could constitutionally have permitted the cross to be erected. On this issue, the Court was sharply divided.

In a PLURALITY OPINION, Justice ANTONIN SCALIA, writing for four Justices, argued that the establishment clause is violated in these circumstances only if the government engages in religious expression itself or discriminates in favor of religious expression. Thus, in his view, if the board had "neutrally" permitted all speakers to erect such displays, without regard to their message, its decision to permit a cross as part of that policy would not have violated the establishment clause.

In CONCURRING OPINIONS, Justices SANDRA DAY O'CONNOR, DAVID H. SOUTER, and STEPHEN G. BREYER disagreed with Scalia that the establishment clause could not be violated by "neutral policies that happen to benefit religion." In their view, even neutral policies could violate the establishment clause if the circumstances are such "that the community would think that the [State] was endorsing religion." As applied to this case, however, these Justices concluded that this problem was not present because "the reasonable observer" would be "able to read and understand an adequate disclaimer."

Justice JOHN PAUL STEVENS dissented on the ground that the establishment clause "prohibits government from allowing [unattended] displays that take a position on a religious issue [in] front of the seat of government," for "viewers reasonably will assume that [government] approves of them." Justice RUTH BADER GINSBURG also dissented.

GEOFFREY R. STONE
(2000)

CAPTIVE AUDIENCE

The Supreme Court has encountered conflicts between FREEDOM OF SPEECH and PRIVACY. In some cases speech conflicts with a nonspeech interest, such as a claimed right to preserve one's peace and quiet. In other cases speech interests may be discerned on both sides; the listener objects to having to hear an uncongenial message. The notion of "captive audience" refers to both types of case. The right not to be compelled to listen to unwelcome messages may be viewed as a corollary to the right not to be compelled to profess what one does not believe, announced in WEST VIRGINIA BOARD OF EDUCATION V. BARNETTE (1943).

Justice WILLIAM O. DOUGLAS first argued the rights of captive auditors in a dissent in *Public Utilities Commission v. Pollak* (1952). His views reemerged in *Lehman v. Shaker Heights* (1974). There a city-owned transit system devoted transit advertising space solely to commercial and public service messages, refusing space to a political candidate. Four Justices held that placard space in city-owned buses and street cars did not constitute a PUBLIC FORUM because the space was incidental to a commercial transportation venture. Admitting, however, that city ownership implicated STATE ACTION, the four agreed that the transit system's advertising policies must not be "arbitrary, capricious, or invidious." The ban on political advertising was a reasonable means "to minimize chances of abuse, the appearance of favoritism and the risk of imposing upon a captive audience."

Justice Douglas concurred. His main point was that commuters, forced onto public transit as a economic necessity, should not be made a captive audience to placard advertising they cannot "turn off." They have a right to be protected from political messages that they are totally without freedom of choice to receive or reject.

The dissenters argued that, whether or not buses and streetcars were special-purpose publically owned property

that could be denied public forum status, the city could not constitutionally discriminate among placard messages on the basis of their content.

A finding that a public forum did exist would likely be decisive for the captive audience issue. Surely there is only the most attenuated "right not to receive" when one enters a public forum whose very definition is that it is open to all senders; those who do not wish to receive a particular visual message are expected to turn away their eyes. *Lehman* and COHEN V. CALIFORNIA (1971) illustrate this tension between the public forum and captive audience concepts.

MARTIN SHAPIRO
(1986)

Bibliography

BLACK, CHARLES 1953 He Cannot Choose but Hear: The Plight of the Captive Auditor. *Columbia Law Review* 53:960–974.

CAHILL, SHEILA M. 1975 The Public Forum: Minimum Access, Equal Access and the First Amendment. *Stanford Law Review* 28:117–148.

CARDOZO, BENJAMIN N.
(1870–1938)

The towering professional and public reputation that OLIVER WENDELL HOLMES enjoyed when he retired from the Supreme Court in 1932 contributed to President HERBERT HOOVER'S selection of Benjamin Nathan Cardozo as his successor despite the fact that there were already two New Yorkers and one Jew on the Supreme Court. Cardozo was one of the very few lawyers in the country whose reputation resembled that of Holmes. A series of famous opinions, his extrajudicial writings, especially *The Nature of the Judicial Process*, his position as chief judge of an able New York Court of Appeals, and his almost saintlike demeanor propelled him into prominence and combined with the usual exigencies of fate and political calculation to put him onto the Supreme Court.

During his five and one-half terms on the Supreme Court from 1932 to 1938, one of Cardozo's major contributions was his demonstration of the utility of COMMON LAW techniques to elaboration of the FOURTEENTH AMENDMENT. Ever since the passage of that amendment, a substantial body of constitutional thought has sought to prevent, or at least to limit, the substantive interpretation of its open-ended provisions. The line stretches from the SLAUGHTERHOUSE CASES (1873) through LEARNED HAND to the current day. The arguments in the 1980s are considerably more complex and theoretical than they were in the nineteenth century and in the 1920s and 1930s. Yet the underlying theme remains essentially the same: the inappropriateness in a democratic society of a nonelected court giving substantive content to broad constitutional phrases such as DUE PROCESS OF LAW and EQUAL PROTECTION OF THE LAWS because of the lack of appropriate sources of judicial law for such an endeavor. The controversies in Cardozo's day revolved around the use of the due process clauses and the equal protection clause to test both the economic legislation that marked an increasingly regulatory society and the numerous infringements by government of individual rights. Although Cardozo's political and social outlook differed somewhat from those of his predecessors on the Court, Holmes, LOUIS D. BRANDEIS, and HARLAN FISKE STONE, he shared the general substantive constitutional outlook that they had espoused for many years: great deference to legislative judgments in economic matters but a more careful scrutiny to constitutional claims of governmental violation of CIVIL RIGHTS in noneconomic matters.

Thus Cardozo was consistently to be found joining those members of the Court, especially Brandeis and Stone, who voted to uphold ECONOMIC REGULATION against attack on COMMERCE CLAUSE, due process, and equal protection grounds. He wrote some of the more eloquent dissents, *Liggett v. Lee* (1933) (Florida chain store tax), PANAMA REFINING COMPANY V. RYAN (1935) (the "hot oil" provision of the NATIONAL INDUSTRIAL RECOVERY ACT), *Stewart Dry Goods Company v. Lewis* (1935) (graduated taxes on gross sales), and CARTER V. CARTER COAL COMPANY (1936) (The Guffey-Snyder Act), and two of the major Court opinions after the Court reversed itself and adopted the constitutional views of the former dissenters. In STEWARD MACHINE COMPANY V. DAVIS (1937) and HELVERING V. DAVIS (1937) Cardozo's opinions upholding the SOCIAL SECURITY ACT expounded Congress's power under the TAXING AND SPENDING clause of the Constitution and provided the theoretical basis for upholding major legislative policies in a way that complemented the parallel recognition of expansive congressional power under the commerce clause. He also viewed the commerce clause as imposing broad limits on the power of individual states to solve their economic problems at the expense of their neighbors (*Baldwin v. Seelig*, 1935), although he recognized at the same time that state financial needs required some tempering of those views (*Henneford v. Silas Mason Co.*, 1937).

Cardozo's special contribution lay in his discussion of the methodological approach to substantive results. Long before joining the Supreme Court, he had considered the appropriate factors that shape decision making for a judge, and although his primary experience was in the common law, he had considered the issue with respect to constitutional law as well. Many would sharply curtail the judiciary's role in constitutional, in contrast to common law, adjudication because of the legislature's inability to overturn most constitutional decisions, but Cardozo viewed

the process of judicial decision making as unitary. In *The Nature of the Judicial Process* he had proposed a fourfold division of the forces that shape the growth of legal principles: logic or analogy (the method of philosophy); history (the historical or evolutionary method); custom (the method of tradition); and justice, morals, and social welfare (the method of sociology).

Those who have attacked the common law approach to Fourteenth Amendment adjudication have perceived the specter of subjectivism in employment of all these methods, but especially in the last. Cardozo saw "justice, morals, and social welfare," which he also labeled as "accepted standards of right conduct," as especially relevant in constitutional adjudication. He struggled to find an acceptable formula for deriving those standards, finally settling on "the principle and practice of the men and women of the community whom the social mind would rank as intelligent and virtuous."

Cardozo never directly met the charge of subjectivism, especially subjectivism in Fourteenth Amendment adjudication, for his message about judging was aimed at a different target: the regressive results produced by too slavish adherence to the so-called objective factors of precedent and logic. But he clearly did not believe that all was "subjective" or that complete reliance on "objective" factors was possible either. One did the best one could to avoid judging on the basis of purely personal values. "History or custom or social utility or some compelling sentiment of justice or sometimes perhaps a semi-intuitive apprehension of the pervading spirit of our law must come to the rescue of the anxious judge, and tell him where to go."

Cardozo brought these ideas with him to the Supreme Court and applied them to a number of notable issues. From its earliest days and notwithstanding bad experience with SUBSTANTIVE DUE PROCESS of law, epitomized by DRED SCOTT V. SANDFORD (1857) and LOCHNER V. NEW YORK (1905), the Court had become committed, in different guises and formulations, to the notion that various rights, liberties, privileges, or immunities existed that were not spelled out in the Constitution. Although there had been occasional discussion since the end of the nineteenth century of the question whether the Fourteenth Amendment "incorporated" specific provisions of the BILL OF RIGHTS (see INCORPORATION DOCTRINE), most major decisions in the twentieth century had used the due process clause on its own to assess whether a particular "liberty" had been denied. As the attack on the Court's use of the due process clause to strike down economic regulation increased throughout the 1930s, the Court began to refocus the issue of protection of noneconomic rights more in terms of incorporation of particular provisions of the Bill of Rights into the Fourteenth Amendment.

The classic reformulation was rendered by Cardozo in PALKO V. CONNECTICUT (1937). To be incorporated the claimed right must be "fundamental"; or one without which "neither liberty nor justice would exist"; or it must "be implicit in the concept of ORDERED LIBERTY." Without pursuing all the ramifications of the debate over "selective incorporation," as the *Palko* DOCTRINE came to be known, we should note that in the midst of the most severe attack on the Court's interpretation of the Fourteenth Amendment, Cardozo and the whole Court never questioned the notion that the amendment had a substantive content. The approach they chose, the selective incorporation doctrine, required the weighing of factors and building up of precedents in a common law fashion with only the general language of the Fourteenth Amendment as a starting point.

Two Fourteenth Amendment cases suffice to demonstrate specific attempts to apply a "common law" method of judging. In *Snyder v. Massachusetts* (1934) Cardozo wrote an opinion holding that due process was not violated when the defendant was not permitted to be present at a jury view of the scene of an alleged crime. After recognizing that the Fourteenth Amendment protected privileges "fundamental" to a FAIR TRIAL, he considered history, which showed that a view of the scene by a jury was not considered part of the "trial"; current practice in other states, which generally permitted the defendant to be present; and potential prejudice to defendant, which he found to be remote. The balance of these factors led him to conclude that there was nothing fundamental, on the facts of Snyder's case, about the right being asserted.

In GROSJEAN V. AMERICAN PRESS COMPANY (1936), Cardozo wrote an opinion, never published, concerning a Louisiana statute that placed a tax on newspapers that carried advertising and had a circulation over 20,000. The majority had originally agreed to hold the statute unconstitutional on equal protection grounds. After Cardozo wrote an opinion concurring on grounds of violation of FREEDOM OF THE PRESS, Justice GEORGE SUTHERLAND substituted a new opinion for a unanimous Court adopting the free press rationale, although in an ambiguous formulation that suggests unconstitutional motivation as at least one of its rationales. The opinion that Cardozo then withdrew is one of his best, and it discusses his methodology and substantive rationale quite clearly. What is a law "abridging the freedom of the press" may be somewhat more specific than the question whether a law denies liberty without due process of law (or denies a PRIVILEGE OR IMMUNITY of national CITIZENSHIP), but it was not much more of a specific starting point for the Court in the context of the Louisiana statute.

Cardozo's draft opinion considered exhaustively the English use first of licenses and then of taxation to control the press as part of the history that led to adoption of the FIRST AMENDMENT. That history led him to conclude that the tax involved was a modern counterpart of those repressive tactics. But he also recognized the financial needs of government. He thus concluded unambiguously—and innovatively—that while the press was not immune from taxation and while classifications were normally a matter of legislative discretion, freedom of the press could be safeguarded only if the press was not subjected to discriminatory taxation vis-à-vis other occupations and through use of internal classifications. The opinion is a splendid example of the use of history and reason combined with a sympathetic appreciation of the setting in which the press functions and of modern needs to assure its "freedom."

Another interesting substantive view was his analysis, before coming to the Supreme Court, of three due process cases that have become increasingly important to modern constitutional theory: MEYER V. NEBRASKA (1923) and *Bartel v. Iowa* (1923) (state laws forbidding teaching of foreign languages to young children held unconstitutional) and PIERCE V. SOCIETY OF SISTERS (1928) (state requirement that all children attend public school through eighth grade held unconstitutional). In *The Paradoxes of Legal Science* he characterized the unconstitutional legislation and the nature of the "liberty" that was upheld in the following prophetic language. "Restraints such as these are encroachments upon the free development of personality in a society that is organized on the basis of family." This emphasis on "free development of personality" and "family" is a stunning extrapolation of a second level of generalization from the constitutional principle of "liberty"; it places Cardozo a half century ahead of his time, for such a conception of the "liberty" protected by the Fourteenth Amendment did not resurface until GRISWOLD V. CONNECTICUT (1965) and ROE V. WADE (1973); and it is a graphic (and controversial) example of the operation of the "method of sociology" in CONSTITUTIONAL INTERPRETATION.

Cardozo was a judge for twenty-four years and he thought hard about what he did. If he was not wholly successful in making a useful statement that would clarify the basis for the creative leap of judgment that enabled him to value certain arguments more than others and thus to reach a conclusion, no one in the half century that followed has been more successful. More important, he provided assistance in his extrajudicial writings and in the reasoning of his opinions for the position, which continues to have considerable support among constitutional theorists and especially among judges, that asserts the validity of applying techniques of common law adjudication to the elaboration of Fourteenth Amendment doctrine. Finally and perhaps even more controversially, he demonstrated that an able, conscientious judge who believed that substantive Fourteenth Amendment adjudication was different from legislating might so comport himself on the bench as to offer hope to his successors a half century later that that position is desirable and capable of achievement.

ANDREW L. KAUFMAN
(1986)

Bibliography

Collected essays on Cardozo in joint 1939 issues of *Columbia Law Review*, 39, #1; *Harvard Law Review*, 52, #3; *Yale Law Journal*, 48, #3; and *Cardozo Law Review*, 1, #1.

KAUFMAN, ANDREW L. 1969 Benjamin Cardozo. In Leon Friedman and Fred L. Israel, eds., *The Justices of the Supreme Court of the United States, 1789–1969*, 3:2287–2307. New York: Chelsea House.

——— 1979 Cardozo's Appointment to the Supreme Court. *Cardozo Law Review* 1:23–53.

CAREER CRIMINAL SENTENCING LAWS

As a response to concern about violent crime, career criminal sentencing laws—commonly known as "three-strikes" laws—became popular with state legislatures and Congress during the mid-1990s. Like habitual offender statutes that have existed in this country since its inception, three-strikes laws dramatically increase the punishment for various repeat offenders. These statutes may limit parole eligibility and impose extremely long sentences, usually life in prison, even for offenders whose final "strike" is a nonviolent crime.

Three-strikes laws are subject to significant criticisms: (1) they were enacted when violent crime rates were already declining; (2) they rely on a questionable assumption that incarceration reduces crime significantly; and (3) they allocate prison resources poorly because they result in long prison sentences for nonviolent offenders and for aging felons past their peak crime years.

Despite the questionable use of resources, three-strikes laws are almost certainly constitutional. Offenders have raised two significant constitutional challenges to habitual offender statutes: (1) they violate the DOUBLE JEOPARDY clause of the Fifth Amendment; and (2) at least some sentences are grossly disproportionate, in violation of the Eighth Amendment's prohibition against CRUEL AND UNUSUAL PUNISHMENT.

Because the Supreme Court has held that the double jeopardy clause protects against multiple punishments for the same offense, offenders have argued that recidivist sentencing statutes punish defendants for their earlier, previously punished crimes. However, courts have repeatedly reaffirmed the holding of *Moore v. Missouri* (1895), which upheld enhanced punishment under such a statute

against a double jeopardy challenge. Among other reasons, courts reject the double jeopardy claim because the enhanced sentence is for a current offense and because the offender is more culpable in light of his continued criminal activity.

Only once has the Court found a term of imprisonment to be a violation of the Eighth Amendment's prohibition against cruel and unusual punishment: in SOLEM V. HELM (1983), wherein the defendant received a term of life imprisonment without benefit of parole although his record involved only nonviolent felonies. In *Harmelin v. Michigan* (1991), a divided Court failed to overrule *Helm*, but limited *Helm*'s application to sentences for minor, nonviolent crimes. Many three-strikes laws avoid the limited protection afforded by *Helm* either by providing a statutory minimum sentence that allows parole eligibility, distinguishing it from the sentence imposed in *Helm*, or by imposing a life sentence only on an offender with a criminal history involving violence, which brings it within *Harmelin*.

MICHAEL VITIELLO
(2000)

Bibliography

DONZIGER, STEVEN R., ed. 1996 *The Real War on Crime: The Report of the National Criminal Justice Commission.* New York: HarperPerennial.

DUBBER, MARKUS D. 1995 Recidivist Statutes as Arational Punishment. *Buffalo Law Review* 43:689–724.

VITIELLO, MICHAEL 1997 Three Strikes: Can We Return to Rationality? *The Journal of Criminal Law and Criminology* 87:395–481.

CAREY v. POPULATION SERVICES INTERNATIONAL
431 U.S. 678 (1977)

By a 7–2 vote the Supreme Court in *Carey* invalidated three New York laws restricting the advertisement and sale of BIRTH CONTROL devices. Justice WILLIAM J. BRENNAN wrote for a majority concerning two of the laws. First, he read GRISWOLD V. CONNECTICUT (1965) and ROE V. WADE (1973) to require STRICT SCRUTINY of laws touching the "fundamental" decision "whether to bear or beget a child." New York had limited the distribution of contraceptives to licensed pharmacists, and had not offered a sufficiently compelling justification. Second, he read the FIRST AMENDMENT to forbid a law prohibiting the advertising or display of contraceptives. (See COMMERCIAL SPEECH.)

The Court was fragmented in striking down the third law, which forbade distribution of contraceptives to minors under sixteen except under medical prescription.

Justice Brennan, for himself and three other Justices, conceded that children's constitutional rights may not be the equivalent of adults' rights. Yet he found insufficient justification for the law in the state's policy of discouraging sexual activity among young people. He doubted that a limit on access to contraceptives would discourage such activity, and in any case the state could not delegate to doctors the right to decide which minors should be discouraged. Three concurring Justices expressed less enthusiasm for minors' constitutional rights to sexual freedom but found other paths to the conclusion that the New York law as written was invalid.

Chief Justice WARREN E. BURGER dissented without opinion, and Justice WILLIAM H. REHNQUIST filed a short dissent that was unusually caustic, even by his high standard for the genre.

Carey was not the last word on the troublesome problem of minors' rights concerning REPRODUCTIVE AUTONOMY; the Court has repeatedly returned to the issue in the ABORTION context. Yet *Carey's* opinion invalidating the law limiting contraceptives sales to pharmacists was important for its recognition that *Griswold v. Connecticut* stood not merely for a right of marital PRIVACY but also for a broad FREEDOM OF INTIMATE ASSOCIATION.

KENNETH L. KARST
(1986)

CAROLENE PRODUCTS COMPANY, UNITED STATES v.
Footnote Four
304 U.S. 144 (1938)

Footnote four to Justice HARLAN F. STONE's opinion in UNITED STATES V. CAROLENE PRODUCTS CO. (1938) undoubtedly is the best known, most controversial footnote in constitutional law. Stone used it to suggest categories in which a general presumption in favor of the constitutionality of legislation might be inappropriate. The issue of if and when particular constitutional claims warrant special judicial scrutiny has been a core concern in constitutional theory for nearly fifty years since Stone's three-paragraph footnote was appended to an otherwise obscure 1938 opinion.

The *Carolene Products* decision, handed down the same day as ERIE RAILROAD V. TOMPKINS (1938), itself reflected a new perception of the proper role for federal courts. It articulated a position of great judicial deference in reviewing most legislation. In his majority opinion, Stone sought to consolidate developing restraints on judicial intervention in economic matters, symbolized by WEST COAST HOTEL CO. V. PARRISH (1937). But in footnote four Stone also went on to suggest that legislation, if challenged with certain types of constitutional claims, might not merit the same deference most legislation should enjoy.

Stone's opinion upheld a 1923 federal ban on the interstate shipment of filled milk. The Court thus reversed a lower federal court and, indirectly, the Illinois Supreme Court, in holding that Congress had power to label as adulterated a form of skimmed milk in which butterfat was replaced by coconut milk. Today the decision seems unremarkable; at the time, however, not only was the result in *Carolene Products* controversial but the theory of variable judicial scrutiny suggested by its footnote four was new and perhaps daring.

Actually, only three other Justices joined that part of Stone's opinion which contained the famous footnote, though that illustrious trio consisted of Chief Justice CHARLES EVANS HUGHES, Justice LOUIS D. BRANDEIS, and Justice OWEN J. ROBERTS. Justice HUGO L. BLACK refused to agree to the part of Stone's opinion with the footnote because Black wished to go further than Stone in proclaiming deference to legislative judgments. Justice PIERCE BUTLER concurred only in the result; Justice JAMES C. MCREYNOLDS dissented; and Justices BENJAMIN N. CARDOZO and STANLEY F. REED did not take part.

In fact, the renowned footnote does no more than tentatively mention the possibility of active review in certain realms. The footnote is nonetheless considered a paradigm for special judicial scrutiny of laws discriminating against certain rights or groups. The first paragraph, added at the suggestion of Chief Justice Hughes, is the least controversial. The paragraph hints at special judicial concern when rights explicitly mentioned in the text of the Constitution are at issue. This rights-oriented, interpretivist position involves less of a judicial leap than the possibility, suggested in the rest of the footnote, of additional grounds for judicial refusal or reluctance to defer to judgments of other governmental branches.

The footnote's second paragraph speaks of possible special scrutiny of interference with "those political processes which can ordinarily be expected to bring about repeal of undesirable legislation." To illustrate the ways in which clogged political channels might be grounds for exacting judicial review, Stone cites decisions invalidating restrictions on the right to vote, the dissemination of information, freedom of political association, and peaceable assembly.

The footnote's third and final paragraph has been the most vigorously debated. It suggests that prejudice directed against DISCRETE AND INSULAR MINORITIES may also call for "more searching judicial inquiry." For this proposition Stone cites two commerce clause decisions, MCCULLOCH V. MARYLAND (1819) and *South Carolina State Highway Dept. v. Barnwell Bros.* (1938), as well as FIRST

AMENDMENT and FOURTEENTH AMENDMENT decisions invalidating discriminatory laws based on religion, national origin, or race. Judicial and scholarly disagreement since 1938 has focused mainly on two questions. First, even if the category "discrete and insular minorities" seems clearly to include blacks, should any other groups be included? Second, does paragraph three essentially overlap with paragraph two, or does it go beyond protecting groups who suffer particular political disadvantage? The question whether discrimination against particular groups or burdens on certain rights should trigger special judicial sensitivity is a basic problem in constitutional law to this day.

Footnote four thus symbolizes the Court's struggle since the late 1930s to confine an earlier, free-wheeling tradition of judicial intervention premised on FREEDOM OF CONTRACT and SUBSTANTIVE DUE PROCESS, on the one hand, while trying, on the other, to create an acceptable basis for active intervention when judges perceive political disadvantages or racial or other invidious discrimination.

Dozens of Supreme Court decisions and thousands of pages of scholarly commentary since *Carolene Products* have explored this problem. In EQUAL PROTECTION analysis, for example, the approach introduced in footnote four helped produce a two-tiered model of judicial review. Within this model, legislation involving social and economic matters would be sustained if any RATIONAL BASIS for the law could be found, or sometimes even conceived of, by a judge. In sharp contrast, STRICT SCRUTINY applied to classifications based on race, national origin, and, sometimes, alienage. Similarly, judicial identification of a limited number of FUNDAMENTAL RIGHTS, such as VOTING RIGHTS, sometimes seemed to trigger a strict scrutiny described accurately by Gerald Gunther as " 'strict' in theory and fatal in fact."

Though this two-tiered approach prevailed in many decisions of the WARREN COURT, inevitably the system became more flexible. "Intermediate scrutiny" is now explicitly used in SEX DISCRIMINATION cases, for example. The Court continues to wrestle with the problem suggested in footnote four cases involving constitutional claims of discrimination against whites, discrimination against illegitimate children, and total exclusion of some from important benefits such as public education. Parallel with footnote four, the argument today centers on the question whether it is an appropriate constitutional response to relegate individuals who claim discrimination at the hands of the majority to their remedies within the political process. Yet, as new groups claim discriminatory treatment in new legal realms, the meaning of "discrete and insular minorities" grows more problematic. Undeniably, however, the categories suggested in footnote four still channel the debate.

A good example is John Hart Ely's *Democracy and Distrust* (1980), an influential book that expands upon footnote four's theme of political participation.

Justice LEWIS H. POWELL recently stated that footnote four contains "perhaps the most far-sighted dictum in our modern judicial heritage." Yet Powell also stressed that, in his view, it is important to remember that footnote four was merely OBITER DICTUM and was intended to be no more. Even so, the tentative words of footnote four must be credited with helping to initiate and to define a new era of constitutional development. The questions raised by footnote four remain central to constitutional thought; controversy premised on this famous footnote shows no sign of abating.

AVIAM SOIFER
(1986)

Bibliography

BALL, MILNER S. 1981 Don't Die Don Quixote: A Response and Alternative to Tushnet, Bobbitt, and the Revised Texas Version of Constitutional Law. *Texas Law Review* 59:787–813.

ELY, JOHN HART 1980 *Democracy and Distrust*. Cambridge, Mass.: Harvard University Press.

LUSKY, LOUIS 1982 Footnote Redux: A *Carolene Products* Reminiscence. *Columbia Law Review* 82:1093–1105.

POWELL, LEWIS F., JR. 1982 *Carolene Products* Revisited. *Columbia Law Review* 82:1087–1092.

CARPENTER, MATTHEW H.
(1824–1881)

A Wisconsin lawyer and senator (1869–1875, 1879–1881), Matthew Hale Carpenter was a vigorous Douglas Democrat who favored compromise to prevent SECESSION. Nevertheless, believing secession treasonous, Carpenter supported the war and became a Republican. During RECONSTRUCTION Carpenter successfully argued *Ex Parte Garland* (1867) which held the FEDERAL TEST ACT of 1865 unconstitutional. (See TEST OATH CASES.) Subsequently General ULYSSES S. GRANT hired Carpenter as counsel for the Army in EX PARTE MCCARDLE (1868). Carpenter's successful defense of the Army and of the right of Congress to limit Supreme Court JURISDICTION led to his election to the SENATE in 1869. There he was generally a strong supporter of Grant's administration, but he only mildly supported CIVIL RIGHTS. In 1872 Carpenter vigorously opposed federal legislation mandating integrated schools and juries because, among other reasons, the statute would violate STATES' RIGHTS. Similarly, as defense counsel he successfully argued for a narrow reading of the FOUR-

TEENTH AMENDMENT in the SLAUGHTERHOUSE CASES (1873). As a former railroad lawyer, however, Carpenter was a leader in protecting business interests. He led the debates supporting the JURISDICTION ACT of 1875, which greatly expanded the JURISDICTION OF FEDERAL COURTS to hear cases in which CORPORATIONS might claim constitutional rights. In 1876 he successfully defended Secretary of War William Belknap in his IMPEACHMENT trial. In 1877 Carpenter unsuccessfully represented Samuel Tilden before the presidential electoral commission. He was defeated for reelection in 1875 because of his connection with Grant administration scandals, but was reelected to the Senate in 1879, serving until his death.

PAUL FINKELMAN
(1986)

Bibliography

THOMPSON, EDWING BRUCE 1954 *Matthew Hale Carpenter: Webster of the West.* Madison: State Historical Society of Wisconsin.

CARR, ROBERT K.
(1908–1979)

Robert Kenneth Carr was an educator and political scientist; he taught at Dartmouth College (1937–1959) and was president of Oberlin College (1960–1970). In 1947 Carr served as Executive Secretary of the President's Committee on Civil Rights appointed by HARRY S. TRUMAN and played a leading role in framing its report, *To Secure These Rights* (1947); this report's detailed presentation of the legal and social disabilities imposed on America's black population sparked nationwide controversy. Carr's own book on the subject, *Federal Protection of Civil Rights: Quest for a Sword* (1947), set forth the history of federal civil rights laws and their enforcement and demonstrated their inadequacy in theory and practice. In *The House Committee on Un-American Activities, 1946–1950* (1952), Carr argued that the carelessness and irresponsibility displayed by members and staff of the HOUSE COMMITTEE ON UN-AMERICAN ACTIVITIES outweighed the benefits of alerting the public to the dangers posed by communism at home and abroad; he concluded that the committee's record argued strongly for its own abolition. Carr also wrote two books on the Supreme Court for general readers, *Democracy and the Supreme Court* (1936) and *The Supreme Court and Judicial Review* (1942), and several other books on education and American government.

RICHARD B. BERSTEIN
(1986)

CARROLL, DANIEL
(1730–1796)

Daniel Carroll, a wealthy, European-educated Roman Catholic from Maryland, was a signer of both the ARTICLES OF CONFEDERATION and the Constitution. Carroll, who favored a strong national government, spoke often and served on three committees. He was subsequently elected to the first HOUSE OF REPRESENTATIVES.

DENNIS J. MAHONEY
(1986)

CARROLL v. PRESIDENT AND COMMISSIONERS OF PRINCESS ANNE
393 U.S. 175 (1968)

After a meeting of a "white supremacist" group at which "aggressively and militantly racist" speeches were made to a racially mixed crowd, the group announced another rally for the next night. Local officials obtained an EX PARTE order enjoining the group from holding a rally for ten days. The Supreme Court, reviewing this order two years later, held that the case fell within an exception to the doctrine of MOOTNESS: rights should not be defeated by short-term orders "capable of repetition, yet evading review."

A unanimous Court held that the *ex parte* order violated the FIRST AMENDMENT. An INJUNCTION against expressive activity requires NOTICE to the persons restrained and a chance to be heard, absent a showing that it is impossible to give them notice and a hearing.

KENNETH L. KARST
(1986)

CARROLL v. UNITED STATES
267 U.S. 132 (1925)

In *Carroll* the Supreme Court held that an officer can stop and search an automobile without a warrant if there is PROBABLE CAUSE to believe the vehicle contains contraband.

The Court noted that national legislation had routinely authorized WARRANTLESS SEARCHES of vessels suspected of carrying goods on which duty had been evaded. The analogy was shaky; Congress's complete control over international boundaries would justify searching any imports even without probable cause. The Court also approved this warrantless search on a dubious interpretation of the National Prohibition Act. But the Court had independent grounds beyond history and congressional intent for its decision: the search was justified as an implied exception to the FOURTH AMENDMENT's warrant requirement, because the vehicle might be driven away before a warrant could be obtained. Given these EXIGENT CIRCUMSTANCES, probable cause rather than a warrant satisfied the constitutional test of reasonableness. Indeed, legislative approval was not considered in the later AUTOMOBILE SEARCH cases.

JACOB W. LANDYNSKI
(1986)

CARTER, JAMES COOLIDGE
(1827–1905)

One of the preeminent legal philosophers of his time, James Coolidge Carter frequently appeared before the Supreme Court. Stressing that the FREEDOM OF CONTRACT limited the commerce power, Carter lost two 5–4 decisions in ANTITRUST cases: UNITED STATES V. TRANS-MISSOURI FREIGHT ASSOCIATION (1897) and *United States v. Joint Traffic* (1898). He also defended the constitutionality of the income tax in POLLOCK V. FARMERS' LOAN & TRUST COMPANY (1895). The clearest exposition of his views appears in *Law: Its Origin, Growth and Function* (1905) where he contended that law must harmonize with customary beliefs.

DAVID GORDON
(1986)

CARTER, JIMMY
(1924–   )

As the first President elected after the WATERGATE scandal, Jimmy Carter was strongly oriented toward moral duties, Christian ethics, faith, trust, and personal rectitude. The "nobility of ideas" theme evoked in his inaugural address ranged broadly from human rights to the elimination of nuclear weapons. Missing from this pantheon of principles, however, was an understanding of the constitutional system and the mechanics of government needed to translate abstract visions into concrete accomplishments.

Carter considered himself an activist President and wanted to use the power of his office to correct social, economic, and political inequities. Some of his contributions to the legal system were long-lasting, such as the large number of women and persons from minority groups he placed on the federal courts. But comprehensive reforms for welfare, taxation, health, and energy became mired in Congress because of Carter's inability to articulate his beliefs and mobilize public opinion. He and his associates wrongly assumed that institutional resistance

from Congress and the executive branch could be overcome simply by appealing to the people through the media.

Carter's congressional relations staff started off poorly and never recovered. By campaigning both against Congress and the bureaucracy, Carter had alienated the very centers of power he needed to govern effectively. He advocated "cabinet government" until the impression of departmental autonomy suggested weak presidential leadership. A major shake-up in July 1979 led to the firing or resignation of five cabinet secretaries, all with a history of friction with certain members of the White House staff. The abrupt nature of these departures cast doubt on Carter's judgment and stability, implying that in any contest between personal loyalty and professional competence, loyalty would prevail.

In foreign policy, the Camp David accord in 1978 marked a high point for Carter when he produced a "framework for peace" between Israeli Prime Minister Menachem Begin and Egyptian President Anwar Sadat. The ratification of the PANAMA CANAL TREATIES also marked a personal triumph, although Carter required last-minute assistance from several senators. His recognition of the People's Republic of China seriously damaged his relations with a number of members of Congress, who were offended by his lack of consultation and the breach of faith with Taiwan. When some of the congressional opponents challenged the termination of the defense treaty with Taiwan, however, the Supreme Court in GOLDWATER V. CARTER (1979) ordered the case dismissed for lack of JUSTICIABILITY. The Iranian revolution and the seizure of the American Embassy in Teheran produced a bitter fourteen months of "America held hostage." This development, including the abortive rescue attempt in 1980, exacerbated Carter's problems of weak leadership and perceived helplessness.

Carter and his associates from Georgia arrived in office with the reputation of amateurs, an image they would never dispel. Carter had campaigned as an outsider, treating that title as a virtue that would set him apart from politicians tainted by the "establishment." He came as a stranger and remained estranged. Having carefully dissociated himself he could not form associations. Throughout his four years he demonstrated little understanding of or interest in legislative strategy, the levers of power, or political leadership.

LOUIS FISHER
(1986)

Bibliography

JOHNSON, HAYNES   1980   *In the Absence of Power: Governing America.* New York: Viking.

CARTER v. CARTER COAL CO.
298 U.S. 238 (1936)

This was the NEW DEAL's strongest case yet to come before the Supreme Court, and it lost. At issue was the constitutionality of the BITUMINOUS COAL ACT, which regulated the trade practices, prices, and labor relations of the nation's single most important source of energy, the bituminous industry in twenty-seven states. No industry was the subject of greater federal concern or of as many federal investigations. After the Court killed the NATIONAL INDUSTRIAL RECOVERY ACT (NIRA) and with it the bituminous code, Congress enacted a "Little NIRA" for bituminous coal. Although the statute contained no provision limiting the amount of bituminous that could be mined, the Court held it unconstitutional as a regulation of PRODUCTION.

The statute had two basic provisions, wholly separable and administered separately by independent administrative agencies. One agency supervised the price and trade-practices section of the statute; the other the labor section, dealing with MAXIMUM HOURS AND MINIMUM WAGES, and COLLECTIVE BARGAINING. In NEBBIA V. NEW YORK (1934) the Court had sustained against a due process attack the principle of price-fixing in the broadest language. The labor sections seemed constitutional, because strikes had crippled INTERSTATE COMMERCE and the national economy on numerous occasions and four times required federal troops to quell disorders. The federal courts had often enjoined the activities of the United Mine Workers as restraining interstate commerce.

The Court voted 6–3 to invalidate the labor provisions and then voted 5–4 to invalidate the entire statute. Justice GEORGE SUTHERLAND for the majority did not decide on the merits of the price-fixing provisions. Had he attacked them, he might have lost Justice OWEN J. ROBERTS, who had written the *Nebbia* opinion. The strategy was to hold the price provisions inseparable from the labor provisions, which were unconstitutional, thereby bringing down the whole act, despite the fact that its two sections were separable.

Sutherland relied mainly on the stunted version of the COMMERCE CLAUSE that had dominated the Court's opinions in UNITED STATES V. E. C. KNIGHT CO. (1895) and more recently in the NIRA and AGRICULTURAL ADJUSTMENT ACT cases: production is local; labor is part of production; therefore the TENTH AMENDMENT reserves all labor matters to the states. That the major coal-producing states, disavowing STATES' RIGHTS, had supported the congressional enactment and emphasized the futility of STATE REGULATION OF COMMERCE meant nothing to the majority. Sutherland rejected the proposition that "the power of the federal government inherently extends to purposes affecting the nation as a whole with which the states severally cannot deal." In fact the government had relied on the commerce power, not INHERENT POWERS. But Sutherland stated that "the local character of mining, of manufacturing, and of crop growing is a fact, whatever may be done with the products." All labor matters—he enumerated them—were part of production. That labor disputes might catastrophically affect interstate commerce was undeniable but irrelevant, Sutherland reasoned, because their effect on interstate commerce must always be indirect and thus beyond congressional control. The effect was indirect because production intervened between a strike and interstate commerce. All the evils, he asserted, "are local evils over which the federal government has no legislative control." (See EFFECTS ON COMMERCE.)

Chief Justice CHARLES EVANS HUGHES dissented on the question whether the price-fixing provisions of the statute were separable. Justice BENJAMIN N. CARDOZO, supported by Justices LOUIS D. BRANDEIS and HARLAN F. STONE, dissented on the same ground, adding a full argument as to the constitutionality of the price-fixing section. He contended too that the issue on the labor section was not ripe for decision, because Carter asked for a decree to restrain the statute's operation before it went into operation. Cardozo's broad view of the commerce power confirmed the Roosevelt administration's belief that the majority's anti-labor, anti-New Deal bias, rather than an unconstitutional taint on the statute, explained the decision.

LEONARD W. LEVY
(1986)

Bibliography

STERN, ROBERT L. 1946 The Commerce Clause and the National Economy, 1933–1946. *Harvard Law Review* 49:664–674.

CARY, JOHN W.
(1817–1895)

As the general counsel of the Chicago, Milwaukee & St. Paul Railway, John W. Cary was involved in some of the most important court cases on ECONOMIC REGULATION in the late 1800s. In briefs submitted in the GRANGER CASES (1877), Cary went beyond the doctrine of VESTED RIGHTS and the guarantee of JUST COMPENSATION relied on by other railroad attorneys such as WILLIAM EVARTS. Cary contended that state fixing of prices (including railroad rates) deprived stockholders not only of their property but also of their *liberty*, that is their freedom to use and control their property. A legislative power to fix prices, he argued, would be "in conflict with the whole structure and theory of our government, hostile to liberty. . . ."

In *Chicago, Milwaukee & St. Paul Railway v. Minnesota* (1890), Cary, along with WILLIAM C. GOUDY, successfully argued that the reasonableness of state-fixed rates was subject to JUDICIAL REVIEW.

DENNIS J. MAHONEY
(1986)

CASES AND CONTROVERSIES

Article III of the Constitution vests the JUDICIAL POWER OF THE UNITED STATES in one constitutionally mandated Supreme Court and such subordinate federal courts as Congress may choose to establish. Federal judges are appointed for life with salaries that cannot be diminished, but they may exercise their independent and politically unaccountable power only to resolve "cases" and "controversies" of the kinds designated by Article III, the most important of which are cases arising under the Constitution and other federal law. The scope of the federal judicial power thus depends in large measure on the Supreme Court's interpretations of the "case" and "controversy" limitation applicable to the Court itself and to other Article III tribunals.

That limitation not only inhibits Article III courts from arrogating too much power unto themselves; it also prevents Congress from compelling or authorizing decisions by federal courts in nonjudicial proceedings and precludes Supreme Court review of state court decisions in proceedings that are not considered "cases" or "controversies" under Article III. The limitation thus simultaneously confines federal judges and reinforces their ability to resist nonjudicial tasks pressed on them by others.

The linkage between independence and circumscribed power is a continuously important theme in "case" or "controversy" jurisprudence, as is the connection between "case" or "controversy" jurisprudence and the power of JUDICIAL REVIEW of government acts for constitutionality— a power that MARBURY V. MADISON (1803) justified primarily by the need to apply the Constitution as relevant law to decide a "case." During the CONSTITUTIONAL CONVENTION OF 1787, EDMUND RANDOLPH, proposed that the President and members of the federal judiciary be joined in a council of revision to veto legislative excesses. The presidential VETO POWER was adopted instead, partly to keep the judiciary out of the legislative process and partly to insure that the judges would decide cases independently, without bias in favor of legislation they had helped to formulate. Similar concerns led the convention to reject CHARLES PINCKNEY's proposal to have the Supreme Court provide ADVISORY OPINIONS at the request of Congress or the President. Finally, in response to JAMES MADISON's doubts about extending the federal judicial power to expound the Con-

stitution too broadly, the Convention made explicit its understanding that the power extended only to "cases of a Judiciary nature." The Framers understood that the judicial power of constitutional governance would expand if the concept of "case" or "controversy" did.

What constitutes an Article III "case," of a "judiciary nature," is hardly self-evident. No definition was articulated when the language was adopted, but only an apparent intent to circumscribe the federal judicial function, and to insure that it be performed independently of the other branches. In this century, Justice FELIX FRANKFURTER suggested that Article III precluded federal courts from deciding legal questions except in the kinds of proceedings entertained by the English and colonial courts at the time of the Constitution's adoption. But the willingness of English courts to give advisory opinions then—a practice clearly inconsistent with convention history and the Court's steadfast policy since 1793—refutes the suggestion. Moreover, from the outset the SEPARATION OF POWERS aspect of the "case" or "controversy" limitation has differentiated CONSTITUTIONAL COURTS (courts constituted under Article III) from others. Most fundamentally, however, the indeterminate historical contours of "cases" or "controversies" inevitably had to accommodate changes in the forms of litigation authorized by Congress, in the legal and social environment that accompanied the nation's industrial growth and the rise of the regulatory and welfare state, and in the place of the federal judiciary in our national life.

After two centuries of elaboration, the essential characteristics of Article III controversies remain imprecise and subject to change. Yet underlying the various manifestations of "case" or "controversy" doctrine are three core requirements: affected parties standing in an adverse relationship to each other, actual or threatened events that provoke a live legal dispute, and the courts' ability to render final and meaningful judgments. These criteria—concerning, respectively, the litigants, the facts, and judicial efficacy—have both independent and interrelated significance.

As to litigants, only parties injured by a defendant's behavior have constitutional STANDING to sue. COLLUSIVE SUITS are barred because the parties' interests are not adverse.

As to extant factual circumstances, advisory opinions are banned. This limitation not only bars direct requests for legal rulings on hypothetical facts but also requires dismissal of unripe or moot cases, because, respectively, they are not yet live, or they once were but have ceased to be by virtue of subsequent events. The parties' future or past adversariness cannot substitute for actual, current adversariness. Disputes that have not yet begun or have already ended are treated as having no more present need for decision than purely hypothetical disputes. (See RIPENESS; MOOTNESS).

The desire to preserve federal judicial power as an independent, effective, and binding force of legal obligation is reflected both in the finality rule, which bars decision if the judgment rendered would be subject to revision by another branch of government, and in the rule denying standing unless a judgment would likely redress the plaintiff's injury. These two rules are the clearest instances of judicial self-limitation to insure that when the federal courts do act, their judgments will be potent. To exercise judicial power ineffectively or as merely a preliminary gesture would risk undermining compliance with court decrees generally or lessening official and public acceptance of the binding nature of judicial decisions, especially unpopular constitutional judgments. Here the link between the limitations on judicial power and that power's independence and effectiveness is at its strongest.

Historically, congressional attempts to expand the use of Article III judicial power have caused the greatest difficulty, largely because the federal courts are charged simultaneously with enforcing valid federal law as an arm of the national government and with restraining unconstitutional behavior of the coequal branches of that government. The enforcement role induces judicial receptivity to extensive congressional use of the federal courts, especially in a time of expansion of both the federal government's functions and the use of litigation to resolve public disputes. The courts' checking function, however, cautions judicial resistance to congressional efforts to enlarge the scope of "cases" or "controversies" for fear of losing the strength, independence, or finality needed to resist unconstitutional action by the political branches.

The early emphasis of "case" or "controversy" jurisprudence was on consolidating the judiciary's independence and effective power. The Supreme Court's refusal in 1793 to give President GEORGE WASHINGTON legal advice on the interpretation of treaties with France—the founding precedent for the ban on advisory opinions—rested largely on the desire to preserve the federal judiciary as a check on Congress and the executive when actual disputes arose. Similarly, HAYBURN'S CASE (1792) established that federal courts would not determine which Revolutionary War veterans were entitled to disability pensions so long as the secretary of war had the final say on their entitlement: Congress could employ the federal judicial power only if the decisions of federal courts had binding effect. In the mid-nineteenth century the concern for maintaining judicial efficacy went beyond finality of substantive judgment to finality of remedy. The Supreme Court refused to accept appeals from the Court of Claims, which Congress had established to hear monetary claims against the United States, because the statutory scheme forbade pay-

ment until the Court certified its judgments to the treasury secretary for presentation to Congress, which would then have to appropriate funds. The Court concluded that Congress could not invoke Article III judicial power if the judges lacked independent authority to enforce their judgments as well as render them.

Preserving judicial authority remains an important desideratum in the twentieth century, but the growing pervasiveness of federal law as a means of government regulation—often accompanied by litigant and congressional pressure to increase access to the federal courts—inevitably has accentuated the law-declaring enforcement role of the federal judiciary and tended to expand the "case" or "controversy" realm. MUSKRAT V. UNITED STATES (1911) cited the courts' inability to execute a judgment as a reason to reject Congress's authorization of a TEST CASE to secure a ruling on the constitutionality of specific statutes it had passed. Similarly, the Court initially doubted the federal courts' power to give DECLARATORY JUDGMENTS. Yet, by the late 1930s, the Supreme Court had upheld both its own power to review state declaratory judgment actions and the federal DECLARATORY JUDGMENT ACT of 1934. The declaratory judgment remedy authorizes federal courts to decide controversies before legal rights are actually violated. The judge normally enters no coercive order, but confines the remedy to a binding declaration of rights. So long as the controversy is a live one, between adverse parties, and the decision to afford a binding remedy rests wholly with the judiciary, the advisory opinion and finality objections pose no obstacles. A controversy brought to court too early may fail Article III ripeness criteria, but the declaratory remedy itself does not preclude the existence of a "case" or "controversy."

Congress has succeeded in expanding the reach of federal judicial power not only by creating new remedies for the federal courts to administer but also by creating new substantive rights for them to enforce. The Supreme Court maintains as a fundamental "case" or "controversy" requirement that a suing party, to have standing, must have suffered some distinctive "injury in fact." The injury must be particularized, not diffuse; citizen or taxpayer frustration with alleged government illegality is insufficient by itself. In theory, Congress cannot dispense with this requirement and authorize suits by individuals who are not injured. Congress may, however, increase the potential for an injury that will satisfy Article III, simply by legislating protection of new rights, the violation of which amounts to a constitutional "injury in fact." For example, *Trafficante v. Metropolitan Life Insurance Company* (1972) held that a federal CIVIL RIGHTS ban on housing discrimination could be enforced not only by persons refused housing but also by current tenants claiming loss of desired interracial associations; the Court interpreted the statute to create a legally protected interest in integrated housing. To a point, then, Article III "cases" or "controversies" expand correspondingly with the need to enforce new federal legislation. Yet the scope of congressional power to transform diffuse harm into cognizable Article III injury remains uncertain and apparently stops short of providing everyone a judicially enforceable generalized right to be free of illegal governmental behavior, without regard to more individualized effects.

The historically approved image is that federal judges decide politically significant public law issues only to resolve controversies taking the form of private litigation. Over the years, however, this picture has had to accommodate not only congressional creation of enforceable rights and remedies but also the modern realities of public forms of litigation such as the CLASS ACTION, the participation of organized public interest lawyers, and lawsuits aimed at reforming government structures and practices. (See INSTITUTIONAL LITIGATION.) Public law adjudication, especially constitutional adjudication, is certainly the most important function of the federal courts. The inclination to stretch the boundaries of "cases" or "controversies" to provide desired legal guidance on important social problems, although it has varied among federal judges and courts of different eras, increases in response to congressional authorization and the perception of social need. Offsetting that impulse, however, are two countervailing considerations. First, the judges realize that the more public the issues raised, the more democratically appropriate is a political rather than a judicial resolution. Second, they understand the importance of a litigation context that does not threaten judicial credibility, finality, or independence; that presents a realistic need for decision; and that provides adequate information and legal standards for confident, well-advised decision making. These competing considerations will continue to shape the meaning of "cases" and "controversies," setting the limits of the federal judicial function in ways that preserve the courts' checking and enforcement roles in the face of changes in the forms and objectives of litigation, in the dimensions of federal law, and in the expectations of government officials and members of the public.

JONATHAN D. VARAT
(1986)

Bibliography

BRILMAYER, LEA 1979 The Jurisprudence of Article III: Perspectives on the "Case or Controversy" Requirement. *Harvard Law Review* 93:297–321.

MONAGHAN, HENRY P. 1973 Constitutional Adjudication: The Who and When. *Yale Law Journal* 82:1363–1397.

RADCLIFFE, JAMES E. 1978 *The Case-or-Controversy Provision.* University Park: Pennsylvania State University Press.

TUSHNET, MARK V. 1980 The Sociology of Article III: A Response to Professor Brilmayer. *Harvard Law Review* 93: 1698–1733.

CATEGORICAL GRANTS-IN-AID

See: Federal Grants-in-Aid

CATO'S LETTERS

Between 1720 and 1723 John Trenchard and Thomas Gordon, collaborating under the pseudonym of "Cato," published weekly essays in the London newspapers, popularizing the ideas of English libertarians, especially JOHN LOCKE. Gordon collected 138 essays in four volumes which went through six editions between 1733 and 1755 under the title, *Cato's Letters: Essays on Liberty, Civil and Religious.* CLINTON ROSSITER, who rediscovered "Cato," wrote, "no one can spend any time in the newspapers, library inventories, and pamphlets of colonial America without realizing that *Cato's Letters* rather than Locke's *Civil Government* was the most popular, quotable, esteemed source of political ideas in the colonial period." The essays bore titles such as "Of Freedom of Speech . . . inseparable from publick Liberty," "The Right and Capacity of the People to judge of Government," "Liberty proved to be the unalienable Right of all Mankind," "All Government proved to be instituted by Men," "How free Governments are to be framed to last," "Civil Liberty produces all Civil Blessings," and "Of the Restraints which ought to be laid upon publick Rulers." Almost every colonial newspaper from Boston to Savannah anthologized *Cato's Letters,* and the four volumes were imported from England in enormous quantities. The most famous of the letters were those on the FREEDOM OF SPEECH and FREEDOM OF THE PRESS. Cato conceded that freedom posed risks, because people might express themselves irreligiously or seditiously, but restraints on expression resulted in injustice, tyranny, and ignorance. "Cato" would not prosecute criminal libels because prosecution was more dangerous to liberty than the expression of hateful opinions. The sixth edition is available in an American reprint of 1971.

LEONARD W. LEVY
(1986)

Bibliography

JACOBSON, DAVID L. 1965 Introduction to *The English Libertarian Heritage.* Indianapolis: Bobbs-Merrill.

CATRON, JOHN
(c.1786–1865)

President ANDREW JACKSON appointed John Catron, his fellow Tennessean and political disciple, to the Supreme Court in 1837. A man who reflected Jackson's own views, Catron had been chief justice of Tennessee. While on the state bench, Catron had undoubtedly endeared himself to Jackson by opposing the BANK OF THE UNITED STATES and challenging JOHN MARSHALL'S *Worcester v. Georgia* (1832) opinion on Indian rights. Jackson's appointment of Catron filled one of two new positions created by the Judiciary Act of 1837. JOHN MCKINLEY of Alabama received the other appointment. The two decisively altered the geographic complexion of the Court, because five of the nine justices represented slaveholding circuits.

Catron's constitutional law decisions illustrated the judicial search for a balance between national and state power in the antebellum period. For example, in the LICENSE CASES (1847) Catron emphatically held that the commerce power could be exercised by Congress "at pleasure," but that absent such legislation, states might regulate INTERSTATE COMMERCE within their own boundaries. In the PASSENGER CASES (1849) he voted to strike down state taxes on immigrants because Congress had exercised its authority over foreign commerce.

Catron's opinions on the rights and powers of CORPORATIONS varied widely. He concurred in Chief Justice ROGER B. TANEY's opinion in BANK OF AUGUSTA V. EARLE (1839), holding that states could exclude foreign corporations, and he also agreed when the Court expanded federal court JURISDICTION over corporate activities in *Louisville Railroad Co. v. Letson* (1844). Except as a party to a diversity suit, however, a corporation, Catron insisted, was not a citizen within the sense of the Constitution. Catron resisted the TANEY COURT's accommodation with corporate interests in the Ohio bank cases of the 1850s. In PIQUA BRANCH BANK V. KNOOP (1854) he vigorously opposed the use of the CONTRACT CLAUSE to protect state legislative tax exemptions in corporate charters. In a companion case, Catron saw the burgeoning power of corporations as threatening to subvert the state governments that had created them. He believed that the community rights doctrine of CHARLES RIVER BRIDGE V. WARREN BRIDGE COMPANY (1837) had become "illusory and nearly useless, as almost any beneficial privilege, property, or exemption, claimed by corporations" might be construed into a contract to the corporation's advantage. He also protested when the Court, in DODGE V. WOOLSEY (1856), invalidated Ohio's constitutional amendment repealing corporate tax exemptions.

Catron's role in DRED SCOTT V. SANDFORD (1857) was more prominent for his extrajudicial activities than for his opinion. Before the decision, he wrote several letters to President-elect JAMES BUCHANAN, notifying him of the Court's resolution to "decide and settle a controversy which has so long and seriously agitated the country, and which *must* ultimately be decided by the Supreme Court." He also urged Buchanan to pressure his fellow Pennsylvanian, Justice ROBERT GRIER, to join in the effort to decide the constitutional question of congressional control over SLAVERY IN THE TERRITORIES. Catron's political maneuverings have overshadowed his opinion which deviated in some significant respects from Taney's. For example, he did not think that the Court could review the plea in abatement and he thought Taney's discussion of black CITIZENSHIP unnecessary. He also differed from the Chief Justice on the scope of congressional power over the TERRITORIES, acknowledging that it was plenary, save for a few exceptions, such as slavery.

Catron closed his long career with some measure of distinction. Unlike his colleague, Justice JOHN CAMPBELL, who resigned, or Taney, who bitterly opposed the Union's war efforts and President ABRAHAM LINCOLN's conduct of the war, Catron clung to a Jacksonian faith in the Union. He carried out his circuit duties in Tennessee, Kentucky, and Missouri, often at great personal risk. He lost much of his property in Nashville when he failed to respond to a local demand that he resign. Although he opposed Lincoln's blockade policy when he dissented in the PRIZE CASES (1863), on circuit he upheld the confiscation laws and the government's suspension of the writ of HABEAS CORPUS. "I have to punish Treason, will," Catron wrote. With that expression, and through his judicial decisions, Catron faithfully reflected the spirit of his patron, Andrew Jackson.

STANLEY I. KUTLER
(1986)

Bibliography

GATTELL, FRANK OTTO 1969 John Catron. In Leon Friedman and Fred L. Israel, eds., *The Justices of the Supreme Court*, Vol. 1:737–768. New York: Chelsea House.

SWISHER, CARL B. 1935 *Roger B. Taney.* New York: Macmillan.

CEASE AND DESIST ORDER

In ADMINISTRATIVE LAW, cease and desist orders require the cessation of specific violations of law or government regulations. The power to issue such orders may be granted to REGULATORY COMMISSIONS by Congress. Cease and desist orders are issued only after FAIR HEARING and are subject to review in the federal courts.

DENNIS J. MAHONEY
(1986)

CENSORSHIP

See: Prior Restraint and Censorship

CENSUS

Article I of the Constitution requires a decennial census of the population in order to apportion congressional REPRESENTATION among the states. In the landmark REAPPORTIONMENT cases of the 1960s, the census assumed a central role not only in apportionment but in the process of ELECTORAL DISTRICTING as well. Following the command of JAMES MADISON in FEDERALIST No. 54 that "numbers are the only proper scale of representation," the Supreme Court in REYNOLDS V. SIMS (1964) decreed that "[p]opulation is, of necessity, the starting point for consideration and the controlling criterion for judgment in legislative apportionment controversies." Reliance on the census was indispensable for the Court's willingness to confront the "political thicket" of redistricting and representation.

First, numerical standards from the census provided unassailable empirical data and thereby stemmed charges of the judiciary's making impermissible political decisions. Second, the census provided the denominator for the ONE PERSON, ONE VOTE rule, which emerged as the most successful JUSTICIABLE standard for overseeing politics. Third, the imposition of objective apportionment constraints furthered the efforts to control GERRYMANDERING and helped realize the Court's 1969 command that "each resident citizen has, as far as is possible, an equal voice in the selections [of public officials]."

Since the 1960s, the hope that the census could bring constitutional order to the reapportionment process has faded. Despite its apparent simplicity, the one person, one vote rule engendered considerable litigation and conflicting rules of tolerable deviations for federal and state redistricting. Rather than defeat gerrymanders, the one person, one vote standard spawned a burgeoning industry of computer-aided redistricting that in turn allowed clever partisan manipulations. Even the Court admitted in 1983 that "the rapid advances in computer technology and education during the last two decades make it relatively simple to draw contiguous districts of equal population and at the same time to further whatever secondary goals the State has."

The increased constitutional role occupied by the census also raised the pressure on the decennial enumeration. For all its appearance of objective neutrality, the census involves difficult demographic decisions resulting from a large and mobile population. The census requires "attribution" and "correction" of residence for persons not found during the actual enumeration, for college students, for overseas citizens, for military personnel stationed abroad, for individuals who maintain two homes, and for homeless individuals, among others. In addition, beginning in 1950, the U.S. Bureau of the Census began a post-enumeration survey of the population to check against systematic undercounts. Among the discoveries was that racial and ethnic minorities were significantly more likely to be missed in the enumeration, a problem that persists to this day. Because the resolution for these technical issues has immediate consequences for apportionment, for in-state districting, and for eligibility for federal matching funds, it is not surprising that the census itself is increasingly the subject of litigation.

One source of litigation concerns apportionment decisions between the states. In *Department of Commerce v. Montana* (1992), for example, a state sued over the mechanism for apportioning the fractional remainder when the census numbers were divided by the 435 seats in Congress. *Franklin v. Massachusetts* (1992) challenged the manner in which overseas federal employees were counted, on the ground that an apparently disproportionate number selected states without income taxes as their official residences. In each case, the Supreme Court, using a generous RATIONAL BASIS STANDARD OF REVIEW, granted the federal government wide discretion in implementing the census and in apportioning congressional seats.

Far more contentious has been the persistent undercount of minorities that, critics argue, would be alleviated by using more sophisticated statistical adjustments of the census—as opposed to the elusive attempt to count each and every American. In *Wisconsin v. New York* (1996), however, the Court again applied rational basis review to hold that the decision by the U.S. Secretary of Commerce not to adjust the census statistically to compensate for the minority undercount was within the broad discretion of the executive branch.

More recently, the Court, in *Department of Commerce v. United States House of Representatives* (1999), ruled that the census cannot be statistically adjusted for the purpose of congressional apportionment. The decision was premised exclusively on whether the Census Act, as a matter of STATUTORY INTERPRETATION, itself prevents using sampling in the congressional apportionment context. Because the Court did not reach any constitutional issues, the decision left unresolved whether the Constitution permits statistical sampling in other contexts, such as redistricting and allocation of federal funds to the states, as well as whether a statutory amendment to the Census Act to permit sampling for congressional apportionment would be constitutional.

SAMUEL ISSACHAROFF
(2000)

Bibliography

ISSACHAROFF, SAMUEL and LICHTMAN, ALLAN J. 1993 The Census Undercount and Minority Representation: The Constitutional Obligation of the States to Guarantee Equal Representation. *Review of Litigation* 13:1–29.

CENTRAL HUDSON GAS & ELECTRIC CORP. v. PUBLIC SERVICE COMMISSION
447 U.S. 557 (1980)

Central Hudson is the leading decision establishing ground rules for the Supreme Court's modern protection of COMMERCIAL SPEECH under the FIRST AMENDMENT. New York's Public Service Commission (PSC), in the interest of conserving energy, forbade electrical utilities to engage in promotional advertising. The Supreme Court held, 8–1, that this prohibition was unconstitutional.

Justice LEWIS F. POWELL, for the Court, used an analytical approach to commercial speech that combined a TWO-LEVEL THEORY with a BALANCING TEST. First, he wrote, it must be determined whether the speech in question is protected by the First Amendment. The answer to that question is affirmative unless the speech is "misleading" or it is "related to illegal activity" (for example, by proposing an unlawful transaction). Second, if the speech falls within the zone of First Amendment protection, the speech can be regulated only if government satisfies all the elements of a three-part interest-balancing formula: the asserted governmental interest must be "substantial"; the regulation must "directly advance" that interest; and the regulation must not be "more extensive than is necessary to serve that interest."

This intermediate STANDARD OF REVIEW seems loosely patterned after the standard used under the EQUAL PROTECTION clause in cases involving SEX DISCRIMINATION. In those cases, the Court typically accepts that the governmental interest is important; when a statute is invalidated, the Court typically regards gender discrimination as an inappropriate means for achieving the governmental interest. The *Central Hudson* opinion followed this pattern: the promotional advertising was protected speech, and the state's interest in conservation was substantial and directly advanced by the PSC's regulation. However, prohibiting all promotional advertising, including statements that would not increase net energy use, was not the LEAST RESTRICTIVE MEANS for achieving conservation.

Concurring opinions by Justices HARRY A. BLACKMUN and JOHN PAUL STEVENS, both joined by Justice WILLIAM J. BRENNAN, adopted more speech-protective doctrinal positions. Justice WILLIAM H. REHNQUIST, in lone dissent, argued that the PSC's regulation was only an ECONOMIC REGULATION of a state-regulated monopoly, raising no important First Amendment issue.

KENNETH L. KARST
(1986)

CENTRAL PACIFIC RAILROAD CO. v. GALLATIN

See: Sinking Fund Cases

CERTIFICATION

Certification may refer to a broad range of acts of government officials high and low: a clerk may certify the accuracy of a copy of a document; the Federal Power Commission may issue a certificate that a natural gas pipeline will serve "public convenience and necessity." In federal courts, however, certification has a narrower meaning. A court may certify questions of law to another court for authoritative decision.

The UNITED STATES COURTS OF APPEALS are authorized by Congress to certify "distinct and definite" questions of law for decision by the Supreme Court. The practice has been criticized for influencing the Supreme Court to decide issues in the abstract, without a complete factual record, and for weakening the Court's control over the questions it will decide. Partly for these reasons, this form of certification is rarely used.

More frequently, federal district courts certify doubtful questions of state law for decision by state courts. About half the states expressly authorize their courts to answer such certified questions, and the Supreme Court has applauded the technique. This form of certification is merely a variant form of abstention.

KENNETH L. KARST
(1986)

Bibliography
BATOR, PAUL M.; MISHKIN, PAUL J.; SHAPIRO, DAVID L.; and WECHSLER, HERBERT, eds. 1973 *Hart and Wechsler's The Federal Courts and the Federal System*, 2nd ed. Pages 1582–1586. Mineola, N.Y.: Foundation Press.

CERTIORARI, WRIT OF

A writ of certiorari is an order from a higher court directing a lower court to transmit the record of a case for review in the higher court. The writ was in use in England and America before the Revolution. Unlike the WRIT OF ERROR, which was used routinely to review final judgments of lower courts, certiorari was a discretionary form of review that might be granted even before the lower court had given judgment.

When Congress established the circuit courts of appeals in 1891, it expressly authorized the Supreme Court to review certain of these courts' decisions, otherwise declared to be "final," by issuing the writ of certiorari, which remained discretionary. In 1925, Congress expanded the

Court's certiorari JURISDICTION and reduced the availability of the writ of error (renamed APPEAL). Certiorari is today the chief mode of the Supreme Court's exercise of APPELLATE JURISDICTION. Proposals to abolish the Court's theoretically obligatory jurisdiction over appeals would leave appellate review entirely to certiorari, and thus to the Court's discretion.

By statute the Court is authorized to grant certiorari in any case that is "in" a federal court of appeals. Thus in an appropriate case the Court can bypass the court of appeals and directly review the action of the district court, as it did in the celebrated case of UNITED STATES V. NIXON (1974).

The Supreme Court's rules have long stated some considerations governing the Court's discretionary grant or denial of certiorari. Three factors are emphasized: (1) conflicts among the highest courts of the states or the federal courts of appeals; (2) the resolution of important unsettled issues of federal law; and (3) the correction of error. These factors do not exhaust but only illustrate the considerations influencing the Court's certiorari policy.

KENNETH L. KARST
(1986)

Bibliography

LINZER, PETER 1979 The Meaning of Certiorari Denials. *Columbia Law Review* 79:1227–1305.

CHAE CHAN PING v. UNITED STATES
(Chinese Exclusion Case)
130 U.S. 581 (1889)

The CHINESE EXCLUSION ACT of 1882 authorized the issuance of certificates to Chinese ALIENS, guaranteeing their right to reenter the United States after leaving. In 1888 Congress amended that act to prohibit reentry by voiding all outstanding certificates, destroying the right of Chinese to land. Justice STEPHEN J. FIELD, for a unanimous Supreme Court, admitted that this act "is in contravention of express stipulations of the Treaty of 1868 (and other agreements) . . . but it is not on that account invalid or to be restricted in its enforcement. The treaties were of no greater legal obligation than the Act of Congress." He asserted that the treaties were equivalent to federal statutes and they might thus be "repealed or modified at the pleasure of Congress." Because "no paramount authority is given to one over the other" the government could constitutionally exclude aliens from the United States as "an incident of SOVEREIGNTY."

DAVID GORDON
(1986)

CHAFEE, ZECHARIAH, JR.
(1885–1957)

Modern scholarship in the area of free speech is indelibly stamped with the ideas of Zechariah Chafee, Jr., a distinguished professor of law and University Professor at Harvard, and a CIVIL LIBERTIES activist.

Chafee, scion of a comfortable business-oriented New England family, left the family's iron business to enter Harvard Law School, returning there in 1916 to teach. Inheriting ROSCOE POUND's third-year EQUITY course, in which Pound dealt with INJUNCTIONS against libel, Chafee, uncertain as to the meaning of FREEDOM OF SPEECH, read all pre-1916 cases on the subject. He concluded that the few existing decisions reached results unsatisfactory to one seeking precedents for free speech protection. This realization, coupled with stringent new wartime espionage and SEDITION laws, and their often arbitrary enforcement, persuaded him of the importance of developing a modern law of free speech. Starting with articles in the *New Republic* and the *Harvard Law Review*, and a 1920 book, *Freedom of Speech*, Chafee attempted workable delineations between liberty, which he felt must be safeguarded carefully, and the restraints that emergency situations might warrant. Unhappy with the insensitivity of OLIVER WENDELL HOLMES' initial CLEAR AND PRESENT DANGER construct in SCHENCK V. UNITED STATES (1919), Chafee, with the assistance of Judge LEARNED HAND, set out to persuade Holmes that the test for speech should consider not only the individual's interest in freedom but also the social desirability of injecting provocative thought into the marketplace. "Tolerance of adverse opinion is not a matter of generosity, but of political prudence," Chafee argued. Holmes embraced this position in his dissent in ABRAMS V. UNITED STATES (1919), having been newly convinced that the FIRST AMENDMENT established a national policy favoring a search for truth, while balancing social interests and individual interests. Contemporary traditionalists reacted negatively with a move to oust Chafee from Harvard Law School. Such action was thwarted when Harvard President A. Lawrence Lowell rallied to Chafee's defense.

Chafee, as one of the nation's leading civil libertarians in the 1920s became involved with a number of vital issues. He served on commissions to probe owner autocracy and brutality in the mining regions of the East, and he spoke out publicly against excessive use of the labor injunction to curtail legitimate union activities. In 1929 he headed a subcommittee of the Wickersham Commission which looked into police use of the "third degree" and improper trial procedures. He played a prominent role in the American Bar Association's Commission on the BILL OF RIGHTS in the late 1930s, and in the 1940s served on the

Commission on Freedom of the Press, afterward performing similar duties for the United Nations.

Chafee maintained a deep commitment to legal education. He personally regarded as his principal professional accomplishment the Federal Interpleader Act of 1936, a statute creating federal court JURISDICTION when persons in different states make conflicting claims to the same shares of stock or the same bank accounts. His chief influence can be seen, however, in the work of generations of attorneys and judges, nurtured on his free speech and civil liberties view, who have rewritten First Amendment doctrine along Chafee's lines.

PAUL L. MURPHY
(1986)

Bibliography

MURPHY, PAUL L. 1979 *World War I and the Origin of Civil Liberties in the United States.* New York: Norton.

CHAMBERS v. FLORIDA
309 U.S. 227 (1940)

Chambers was the first coerced confession case to come before the Court since the landmark decision in BROWN V. MISSISSIPPI (1936). In *Brown,* the physical torture being uncontested, the state had relied mainly on the point that the RIGHT AGAINST SELF-INCRIMINATION did not apply to state proceedings. In *Chambers,* before the state supreme court finally affirmed the convictions it had twice reversed so that juries could determine whether the confessions had been freely and voluntarily made, and the record showed no physical coercion. Moreover, the state contested the JURISDICTION of the Supreme Court to review the judgments, arguing that there was no question of federal law to be denied. However, the Supreme Court, in an eloquent opinion by Justice HUGO L. BLACK, unanimously asserted jurisdiction and reversed the state court.

Black rejected the state's jurisdictional argument, declaring that the Supreme Court could determine for itself whether the confessions had been obtained by means that violated the constitutional guarantee of DUE PROCESS OF LAW. Reviewing the facts Black found that the black prisoners, having been arrested on suspicion without warrant, had been imprisoned in a mob-dominated environment, held incommunicado, and interrogated over five days and through a night until they abandoned their disclaimers of guilt and "confessed." POLICE INTERROGATION had continued until the prosecutor got what he wanted. On the basis of these facts Black wrote a stirring explanation of the relation between due process and free government, concluding that courts in our constitutional system stand "as havens of refuge for those who might otherwise suffer be-

cause they are helpless, weak, outnumbered, or because they are non-conforming victims of prejudice. . . ." Applying the exclusionary rule of *Brown,* the Court held that psychological as well as physical torture violated due process.

LEONARD W. LEVY
(1986)

CHAMBERS v. MARONEY
399 U.S. 42 (1970)

In this important FOURTH AMENDMENT case involving the automobile exception to the SEARCH WARRANT clause, the police had seized a car without a warrant and had searched it later, without a warrant, after having driven it to the police station, where they impounded it. Justice BYRON R. WHITE for the Supreme Court acknowledged that the search could not be justified as having been conducted as a SEARCH INCIDENT TO ARREST; nor could he find EXIGENT CIRCUMSTANCES that justified the WARRANTLESS SEARCH.

White simply fudged the facts. He declared that there was "no difference between on the one hand seizing and holding a car before presenting the PROBABLE CAUSE issue to a magistrate and on the other hand carrying out an immediate search without a warrant." Either course was "reasonable under the Fourth Amendment," but the police had followed neither course in this case. Probable cause for the search had existed at the time of the search, and White declared without explanation that probable cause still existed later when the police made the search at the station, when the felons were in custody. However, the possibility that they might drive off in the car did not exist; that possibility had alone occasioned the automobile exception in the first place. Absent a risk that the culprits might use the vehicle to escape with the fruits of their crime, the constitutional distinction between houses and cars did not matter. White saw no difference in the practical consequences of choosing between an immediate search without a warrant, when probable cause existed, and "the car's immobilization until a warrant is obtained." That logic was irrefutable and irrelevant, because the failure of the police to obtain the warrant gave rise to the case. Only Justice JOHN MARSHALL HARLAN dissented from this line of reasoning.

Until this case mere probable cause for a search, as judged only by a police officer, did not by itself justify a warrantless search; the case is significant, too, because of its implied rule that exigent circumstances need not justify the warrantless search of a car. Following *Chambers,* the Court almost routinely assumed that if a search might have been made at the time of arrest, any warrantless search conducted later, when the vehicle was impounded, was a valid one.

LEONARD W. LEVY
(1986)

CHAMPION v. AMES
188 U.S. 321 (1903)

As the twentieth century opened, the Supreme Court began to sustain use of the COMMERCE CLAUSE as an instrument to remedy various social and economic ills. (See NATIONAL POLICE POWER.) In 1895 Congress forbade interstate transportation of lottery tickets, seeking to safeguard public morals. Opponents challenged the act on three grounds: the tickets themselves were not SUBJECTS OF COMMERCE, Congress's power to regulate INTERSTATE COMMERCE did not extend to outright prohibition, and such a power would violate the TENTH AMENDMENT's reservation of certain powers to the states.

A 5–4 Court sustained the act, emphasizing Congress's plenary power over commerce. Because the tickets indicated a cash prize might be won, they were items liable to be bought or sold—thus, subjects of commerce and so subject to regulation. Citing the complete prohibition on FOREIGN COMMERCE in the EMBARGO ACT OF 1807, Justice JOHN MARSHALL HARLAN asserted that the power of regulation necessarily included the power of prohibition. Although he rejected the contention that "Congress may arbitrarily exclude from commerce among the states any article . . . it may choose," Harlan justified the ban on transporting lottery tickets on the ground that Congress alone had power to suppress "an evil of such appalling character," thus propounding the NOXIOUS PRODUCTS DOCTRINE. Harlan dismissed the Tenth Amendment objection: that provision was no bar to a power that had been "expressly delegated to Congress."

Chief Justice MELVILLE W. FULLER led Justices DAVID BREWER, Rufus Peckham, and GEORGE SHIRAS in dissent. Fuller noted that the motive underlying the legislation was to suppress gambling, not to regulate commerce. He feared the disruption of distinct spheres of authority and the "creation of a centralized government." He also challenged Harlan's assertion that the commerce power included the right of prohibition. The Court, citing *Champion*, however, would soon uphold the PURE FOOD AND DRUG ACT (in HIPOLITE EGG COMPANY V. UNITED STATES, 1911), the MANN ACT (in HOKE V. UNITED STATES, 1913), and others, relying on its expansive view of the commerce clause.

DAVID GORDON
(1986)

(SEE ALSO: *Darby Lumber Company, United States v.; Hammer v. Dagenhart.*)

CHAMPION AND DICKASON v. CASEY
Cir. Ct., Rhode Island (1792)

Reported widely in newspapers in June 1792, this was the first case in which a federal court held a state act unconstitutional as a violation of the CONTRACT CLAUSE. Rhode Island had passed a stay law, postponing by three years the time for a debtor to pay his creditors.

The Circuit Court for the district, presided over by Chief Justice JOHN JAY, ruled that the stay law impaired the OBLIGATION OF CONTRACTS contrary to Article I, section 10.

LEONARD W. LEVY
(1986)

CHANDLER v. FLORIDA
449 U.S. 560 (1981)

The Supreme Court here distinguished away ESTES V. TEXAS (1965), in which it had held that the televising of a criminal trial violated DUE PROCESS OF LAW because of the inherently prejudicial impact on criminal defendants. In *Chandler* an 8–0 Court ruled that the prejudicial effect must be actually shown by the facts of the particular case; Florida's statute, at issue here, imposed adequate safeguards on the use of electronic media in court, thereby insuring due process of law. Presumably the decision promoted FREEDOM OF THE PRESS and the principle of a PUBLIC TRIAL.

LEONARD W. LEVY
(1986)

(SEE ALSO: *Free Press/Fair Trial.*)

CHANDLER v. MILLER
620 U.S. 305 (1997)

In *Chandler v. Miller*, the Supreme Court, in a MAJORITY OPINION by Justice RUTH BADER GINSBURG, struck down a Georgia statute requiring candidates for certain state offices (including judges, legislators, and executive officials) to certify that they had taken and passed a urinalysis test for illegal drugs within thirty days prior to qualifying for nomination or election. The Court characterized this requirement as an UNREASONABLE SEARCH under the FOURTH AMENDMENT. Following PRECEDENT, the Court indicated that a reasonable search must normally be based on "individualized suspicion of wrongdoing" unless a "particularized exception" applies. Such an exception can only be justified if, first, the court finds "special needs" for the search "beyond the normal need for law enforcement" or "crime detection"; and, second, if pursuant to a "context specific inquiry" that balances the "competing private and public interests," a court finds that the privacy interests are "minimal" and that substantial enough governmental interests would be "placed in jeopardy by a requirement of individualized suspicion." Unlike the evidence of drug use by railway employees in SKINNER V. RAILWAY LABOR EXECUTIVES' ASSOCIATION (1989) and by students in *Vernonia School District 47J v. Acton* (1995), the record did not contain evidence that the danger of drug use by candidates was "concrete" or "real," or that the public safety was at immediate risk. Unlike the record in NATIONAL TREASURY EMPLOYEES UNION V. VON RAAB (1989), the record in this case did not show that criminal investigation would be inadequate. Nor did it show that DRUG TESTING (the timing of which was in the candidate's control) would effectively deter drug use. Georgia's real interest, the Court concluded, was not "special" but "symbolic," namely, the "image the State seeks to project." Accordingly, the Court found that the risk to public safety was not "substantial" or "important" enough to override the candidate's privacy. The Court explicitly did not reach the Fourth Amendment questions involved in requiring candidates to undergo and disclose the results of a general medical exam or to make a financial disclosure.

The lone dissenter, Chief Justice WILLIAM H. REHNQUIST, showed that the Court could easily have reached the opposite conclusion under the malleable special-needs DOCTRINE, which had been fashioned during his tenure as CHIEF JUSTICE and had moved Fourth Amendment debate away from PROBABLE CAUSE and warrants and toward whether suspicion is necessary at all.

In this case involving a search of judges, the Court appeared at last to be troubled by its ever-decreasing protection of privacy as it cast about for some ground on which to limit the potent special-needs doctrine to only a few exceptional cases (like airport searches) where privacy interests are minimal and there is substantial evidence that public safety is in jeopardy. But in striking down the statute, the Court devised no clear or effective limits on this doctrine and questioned no earlier opinion applying it. Alternatively, given the unique facts of this case, perhaps the Court was troubled not by a concern for privacy but for the potential constraints on public discourse and electoral campaigns that may result if, for purely symbolic purposes, a previously elected legislature can compel, through intrusive investigations, newly contending candidates for office to acquiesce in its policies and thereby obtain their implicit acceptance of policies that should instead be subject to debate.

ROBERT D. GOLDSTEIN
(2000)

(SEE ALSO: *Drug Regulation; Search and Seizure.*)

CHANDLER ACT

See: Bankruptcy Act

CHAPLINSKY v. NEW HAMPSHIRE
315 U.S. 568 (1941)

In *Chaplinsky,* Justice FRANK MURPHY, writing for a unanimous Supreme Court, introduced into FIRST AMENDMENT jurisprudence the TWO-LEVEL THEORY that "There are certain well-defined and narrowly limited classes of speech, the prevention and punishment of which have never been thought to raise any constitutional problem. These include the lewd and obscene, the profane, the libelous, and the insulting or "FIGHTING WORDS"—those which by their very utterance inflict injury or tend to incite an immediate breach of the peace." *Chaplinsky* itself arose under a "fighting words" statute, which the state court had interpreted to punish "words likely to cause an average addressee to fight." In this narrow context the decision can be seen as an application of the CLEAR AND PRESENT DANGER test. COHEN V. CALIFORNIA (1971), emphasizing this rationale, offered protection to an OBSCENITY that created no danger of violence.

In its broader conception of categories of speech excluded from First Amendment protection, the case served as an important doctrinal source for many later obscenity and libel decisions.

MARTIN SHAPIRO
(1986)

CHAPMAN v. CALIFORNIA

See: Harmless Error

CHARLES RIVER BRIDGE v. WARREN BRIDGE COMPANY
11 Peters 420 (1837)

The Charles River Bridge case reflected the tension within ALEXIS DE TOCQUEVILLE's proposition that the American people desired a government that would allow them "to acquire the things they covet and which [would] . . . not debar them from the peaceful enjoyment of those possessions which they have already acquired." A metaphor for the legal strains that accompanied technological change, the case spoke more to the emerging questions of railroad development than to the immediate problem of competing bridges over the Charles River.

Following the Revolution, some investors petitioned the Massachusetts legislature for a charter to build a bridge over the Charles River, linking Boston and Charlestown. Commercial interests in both cities supported the proposal, and the state issued the grant in 1785. The charter authorized the proprietors to charge a variety of tolls for passage, pay an annual fee to Harvard College for the loss of its exclusive ferry service across the river, and then, after forty years, return the bridge to the state in "good repair."

Construction of the bridge began immediately, and in 1786, it was open to traffic, benefiting the proprietors, the communities, and the back country. The land route from Medford to Boston, for example, was cut from thirteen to five miles, and trade dramatically increased as the bridge linked the area-wide market. Success invited imitation, and other communities petitioned the legislature for bridge charters. When the state authorized the West Boston Bridge to Cambridge in 1792, the Charles River Bridge proprietors asked for compensation for the revenue losses they anticipated, and the state extended their charter from forty to seventy years. Ironically, that extension provided the basis for future political and legal assaults against the Charles River Bridge. Other bridges followed and no compensation was offered. The state specifically refuted any monopoly claims and the Charles River Bridge proprietors refrained from claiming any.

Increasing prosperity and population raised the collection of tolls to nearly $20,000 annually in 1805; the share values had increased over 300 percent in value. The toll rates having remained constant since 1786, profits multiplied. Swollen profits stimulated community criticism and animated a long-standing hostility toward monopolies. Opportunity was the watchword and special privilege its bane.

Beginning in 1823, Charlestown merchants launched a five-year effort to build a competing "free" bridge over the Charles. They argued that the existing facility was inadequate, overcrowded, and dangerous; but basically, they appealed for public support on the grounds that the tolls on the Charles River Bridge were "burdensome, vexatious, and odious." The proprietors, defending the bridge's utility, offered to expand and improve it. They consistently maintained that the legislature could not grant a new bridge franchise in the vicinity without compensating them for the loss of tolls. But the political climate persuaded legislators to support the new bridge, and in 1828, after rejecting various schemes for compensation, the legislature approved the Warren Bridge charter. The act established the bridge's termini at 915 feet from the existing bridge on the Boston side, and at 260 feet from it on the Charlestown side. The new bridge was given the same toll schedule as the Charles River Bridge, but the state provided that after the builders recovered their investment and five per cent interest, the bridge would revert to the commonwealth. In any event, the term for tolls could not exceed six years. Governor LEVI LINCOLN had previously vetoed similar legislation, but in 1828 he quietly acquiesced.

The new bridge, completed in six months, was an instant success—but at the expense of the Charles River Bridge. During the first six months of the Warren Bridge's operations, receipts for the old bridge rapidly declined. Net income for the Warren Bridge in the early 1830s consistently was twice that for the Charles River Bridge.

Counsel for the old bridge proprietors wasted little time in carrying their arguments to the courts. After DANIEL WEBSTER and LEMUEL SHAW failed to gain an INJUNCTION to prevent construction of the new bridge, they appeared in the state supreme court to argue the merits of the charter in 1829, nearly one year after the bridge's completion. Shaw and Webster contended that the Charles River Bridge proprietors were successors to the Harvard ferry's exclusive franchise. In addition, they argued that the tolls represented the substance of the 1785 charter. Although the charter for the new bridge did not take away the plaintiffs' franchise, the 1828 act effectively destroyed the tolls—the essence and only tangible property of the franchise. The lawyers thus contended that the new bridge charter violated the CONTRACT CLAUSE and the state constitutional prohibition against expropriation of private property without compensation. The Warren Bridge defendants denied the old bridge's monopoly claims and emphasized that the state had not deprived the Charles River Bridge proprietors' continued right to take tolls. They also maintained that the old bridge proprietors had waived exclusivity when they accepted an extension of their franchise in 1792 after the state had chartered the West Boston Bridge.

The state supreme court, dividing equally, dismissed the complaint to facilitate a WRIT OF ERROR to the United States Supreme Court. The Jacksonian Democrats on the state court supported the state and their Whig brethren opposed it. The former rejected monopoly claims and berated the Charles River Bridge proprietors for their failure to secure an explicit monopoly grant. Chief Justice Isaac Parker, acknowledging that the 1785 grant was not exclusive, agreed that the state could damage existing property interests for the community's benefit without compensation. But he insisted that "immutable principles of justice" demanded compensation when the forms of property were indistinguishable. He conceded that canals and railroads might legitimately destroy the value of a turnpike; but when the state chartered a similar franchise, then operators of the existing property could claim an indemnity.

The United States Supreme Court first heard arguments in the case in March 1831. Although absences and disagreements prevented any decision before JOHN MARSHALL's death in 1835, the Court's records offer good circumstantial evidence that he had supported the new bridge. Following several new appointments and ROGER B. TANEY's confirmation as Chief Justice, the Court heard reargument in January 1837. Webster again appeared for the plaintiffs; defendants engaged Simon Greenleaf of Harvard, a close associate of JOSEPH STORY and JAMES KENT. Both sides essentially continued the arguments advanced in the state court. Finally, in February 1837, after nearly nine years of litigation, the Court decisively ruled in behalf of the state's right to charter the new bridge.

Taney's opinion sought to balance property rights against community needs by strictly construing the old bridge charter. He rejected the proprietors' exclusivity claim, contending that nothing would pass by implication. "The charter . . . is a written instrument which must speak for itself," he wrote, "and be interpreted by its own terms." He confidently asserted that the "rule" of STRICT CONSTRUCTION was well settled and he particularly invoked Marshall's 1830 PROVIDENCE BANK V. BILLINGS opinion, rejecting a bank's claim to implied tax immunity. Like Marshall, Taney concluded that the implications of exclusivity constituted a derogation of community rights. He argued that the community's "interests" would be adversely affected if the state surrendered control of a line of travel for profit. Taney neatly combined old Federalist doctrines of governmental power with the leaven of Jacksonian rhetoric: "The continued existence of a government would be of no great value," he believed, "if by implications and presumptions, it was disarmed of the powers necessary to accomplish the ends of its creations; and the functions it was designed to perform, transferred to the hands of privileged CORPORATIONS."

But the touchstone of Taney's opinion was its practical response to the contemporary reality of public policy needs. Taking note of technological changes and improvements, such as the substitution of railroad traffic for that of turnpikes and canals, Taney argued that the law must be a spur, not an impediment, to change. If the Charles River Bridge proprietors could thwart such change, he feared that the courts would be inundated with suits seeking to protect established property forms. Turnpike companies, for example, "awakening from their sleep," would call upon courts to halt improvements which had taken their place. Railroad and canal properties would be jeopardized and venture capital would be discouraged. The Supreme Court, he concluded, would not "sanction principles" that would prevent states from enjoying the advances of science and technology. Taney thus cast the law with the new entrepreneurs and risk-takers as the preferred agents for material progress.

In his dissent Justice Story rejected Taney's reliance upon strict construction and advanced an imposing line of precedents demonstrating that private grants had been construed in favor of the grantees. "It would be a dishonour of the government," Story said, "that it should pocket a fair consideration, and then quibble as to the obscurities and implications of its own contract." But Story's dissent was not merely a defense of VESTED RIGHTS. Like Taney, he, too, was concerned with progress and public policy. But whereas Taney emphasized opportunity, Story maintained that security of title and the full enjoyment of existing property was a necessary inducement for private investment in public improvements. Story insisted that the proprietors were entitled to compensation. He thus discounted the potentially staggering social and economic costs implicit in a universal principle requiring JUST COMPENSATION when new improvement projects diminished the value of existing franchises.

Story's position reflected immediate reality. Several years earlier, the state's behavior in the bridge controversy had discouraged stock sales for the proposed Boston and Worcester Railroad. Lagging investment finally had forced the legislature to grant the railroad a thirty-year guarantee of exclusive privileges on the line of travel.

Given the materialism of the American people, Taney's arguments had the greater appeal and endurance. He allied the law with broadened entrepreneurial opportunities at the expense of past assets. Nothing threatened the economic aspirations of Americans more than the scarcity of capital; nothing, therefore, required greater legal encouragement than venture capital, subject only to the risks of the marketplace. These were the concerns that took a local dispute over a free bridge out of its provincial setting and thrust it into the larger debate about political economy. In a society that placed a premium on "progress" and on the release of creative human energy to propel that progress, the decision was inevitable. And throughout American economic development, the Charles River Bridge case has fostered the process that Joseph Schumpeter called "creative destruction," whereby new forms of property destroy old ones in the name of progress.

STANLEY I. KUTLER
(1986)

Bibliography

KUTLER, STANLEY I.   (1971) 1977   *Privilege and Creative Destruction: The Charles River Bridge Case*, rev. ed. New York: Norton.

CHARTERS, COLONIAL

See: Colonial Charters

CHASE, SALMON P.
(1808–1873)

Born in New Hampshire, Salmon Portland Chase enjoyed an elite education as a private pupil of his uncle, Episcopal Bishop Philander Chase of Ohio, as a Dartmouth student (graduating 1826), and as an apprentice lawyer (1827–1830) to United States Attorney General WILLIAM WIRT. Subsequently, Chase rose quickly as a Cincinnati attorney, beginning also his numerous, seemingly opportunistic, successive changes in political party affiliations. Abandoning Whig, then Democratic ties, Chase became in turn a member of the Liberty party and of the Republican organizations, winning elections to the United States Senate (1848–1855, 1860–1861), and to Ohio's governorship (1856–1860). He was an unsuccessful candidate for the Republican presidential nomination in 1860. ABRAHAM LINCOLN appointed Chase secretary of the treasury (1861–1864), and Chief Justice of the United States (1864–1873). Yet in 1864 Chase tried to thwart Lincoln's second term, in 1868 he maneuvered for the Democratic presidential nomination, and in 1872 he participated in the "Liberal Republican" schism against ULYSSES S. GRANT.

Such oscillations reflected more than Chase's large personal ambitions. Constitutional, legal, and moral concerns gave his public life coherence and purpose. These concerns derived from Chase's early conviction that men and society were easily corrupted, that SLAVERY was America's primary spoiling agent, and that political corruption was a close second. Although Chase, observing Wirt in the *Antelope* litigation (1825), found the doctrine in SOMERSET'S CASE (1772) an acceptable reconciliation of slavery and the Constitution as of that year, later events, especially those attending fugitive slave recaptures, unpunished assaults on abolitionists, and increases in slave areas due especially to the Mexican War and the treaties that closed it off, brought him to accept ABOLITIONIST CONSTITUTIONAL THEORY. Chase concluded that slavery's expansion beyond existing limits would demoralize white labor.

The first steps on this ultimately abolitionist road came from Chase's association with and brave defenses of Ohio antislavery activists, including JAMES BIRNEY, and of fugitive slaves; such defenses won Chase the nickname "attorney general for runaway negroes." A merely opportunistic Cincinnati lawyer would have had easier routes to success than this. Defending runaways and their abettors, Chase abjured HIGHER LAW pleadings popular among abolitionists; he focused instead on technical procedures and on a carefully developed restatement of state-centered FEDERALISM in which he insisted that nonslave jurisdictions also enjoyed STATES' RIGHTS. Slave states were able to export their recapture laws into free states via the federal FUGITIVE SLAVERY statutes. Chase argued that residents of free states also deserved to have the laws of their states concerning the status of citizens enjoy reciprocal effect and respect within slavery jurisdictions. Such a traffic of free state laws and customs across the federal system was impossible (and was to remain so until Appomattox). Chase insisted that residents of free states possessed at least the right to protect their co-residents of any race within those states from being reduced to servitude without DUE PROCESS.

Chase's evolving ideas culminated in a "freedom national" position, a general program for resolving the dilemma that slavery posed to a federal society based on assumptions of legal remedies, CIVIL RIGHTS, and CIVIL LIBERTIES. In his thinking, free labor was more than a marketplace phenomenon. It was a moral imperative, a complex of ethical relationships that the nation, under the Constitution, must nurture. Reformed, corruption-free two-party politics, with even blacks voting, was the way Chase discerned finally to nationalize freedom, a nationalization based upon acceptance of the DECLARATION OF INDEPENDENCE and the BILL OF RIGHTS as minimum definitions of the nation's interest in private rights adversely affected by state wrongs or private inequities.

The CIVIL WAR and the wartime and post-Appomattox RECONSTRUCTION of the southern states were the contexts in which Chase refined his thinking about individuals' rights and the nation's duty to protect them. Lincoln found a place in his cabinet for every one of the major competitors for the Republican presidential nomination in 1860, and Chase became secretary of the treasury. Once the war started, Chase had responsibility to provide an adequate circulating medium for the suddenly ballooning marketplace needs of the government, of the banking and commercial communities of the Union states, and of the millions of urban and rural entrepreneurs who rushed to expand production. Chase helped key congressmen to shape the historic wartime laws on national banking, income taxation, and legal tender (the legitimacy of the last of which Chase himself was to question as Chief Justice, in the LEGAL TENDER CASES).

The most outspoken abolitionist in Lincoln's cabinet, Chase also carved out a role for Treasury officials, who were responsible for administering rebels' confiscated property, in the Army's coastal experiments for abandoned, runaway, or otherwise freed blacks. He applauded the CONFISCATION ACTS, the EMANCIPATION PROCLAMATION, the major elements in Lincoln's MILITARY RECONSTRUCTION, the FREEDMEN'S BUREAU statute, and the THIRTEENTH AMENDMENT. Upon ROGER B. TANEY's death in late 1864, Lincoln, well aware of Chase's antipathy to the decision in DRED SCOTT V. SANDFORD (1857) and his commitment to irreversible emancipation, both of which the President shared, named the Ohioan to be Chief Justice.

After Appomattox, Chase, for his first years as Chief Justice, found that the work of the Court was almost exclusively with white men's rights rather than with the momentous, race-centered public questions that faced the Congress and the new President, ANDREW JOHNSON. On circuit, however, Chase's *In re Turner* opinion sustained broadly, in favor of a black female claimant, the provisions of the 1866 CIVIL RIGHTS ACT for enforcing the Thirteenth Amendment. In his opinion, Chase insisted that federal rights against servitude were defendable in national courts as against both state or private action or inaction, and he emphasized that a state's standard of right could serve as an adequate federal standard so long as the state did not discriminate racially.

Some contemporaries applauded *In re Turner* as an articulation of the new, nationalized federal system of rights that the Thirteenth Amendment appeared to have won. Chase's other circuit opinions did not, therefore, disturb race egalitarians, and generally won favor in professional legal and commercial media. These opinions dealt with numerous litigations concerning private relationships such as marriage licenses, trusts and inheritances, business contracts, and insurance policies made under rebel state dispensation. Chase recognized the validity of these legal arrangements. His decisions helped greatly to stabilize commerce and family relationships in the South.

The course of post-Appomattox Reconstruction as controlled both by President Johnson and by Congress, troubled Chase deeply. He knew, from his work in Lincoln's cabinet, how narrowly the Union had escaped defeat and tended, therefore, to sustain wartime measures. Yet he revered both the CHECKS AND BALANCES of the national government and the state-centered qualities of the federal system reflected in the Constitution. Therefore, in EX PARTE MILLIGAN (1866), Chase, still new on the Court, joined in the unanimous statement that Milligan, who had been tried by a military court, should preferably have been prosecuted in a civilian court for his offenses. But Chase, with three other Justices, dissented from the majority's sweeping condemnation of any federal military authority over civilians in a nonseceded state. The dissenters insisted instead that Congress possessed adequate WAR POWER to authorize military courts.

Chase again dissented from the 5–4 decision in the TEST OATH CASES (1867). Though privately detesting oath tests, Chase held to a public position that legislators, not judges, bore the responsibility to prescribe professional qualifications and licensing standards. By this time Congress had decided on Military Reconstruction. Mississippi officials, appointed earlier by Johnson, asked the Court for an INJUNCTION against the President's enforcing Congress's reconstruction law, and for a ruling that it was unconstitutional. For an unanimous Court, Chase refused to honor the petition (MISSISSIPPI V. JOHNSON, 1867), relying on the POLITICAL QUESTION doctrine. He agreed with his colleagues also in *Georgia v. Stanton* (1867) in refusing to allow the Court to intrude into political questions involving enforcement of the Reconstruction statutes. Mississippians again tried to enlist the Court against Congress. In early 1868 EX PARTE MCCARDLE raised *Milligan*-like issues of military trials of civilians, and of the Court's jurisdiction to hear such matters under the HABEAS CORPUS ACT OF 1867. Congress thereupon diminished the Court's APPELLATE JURISDICTION under that statute. Chase, for the Court, acquiesced in the diminution, though pointing out that all other habeas jurisdiction remained in the Court.

He supported Congress's Military Reconstruction as a statutory base for both state restorations and black suffrage, but he was offended by the Third Reconstruction Act (July 1867), providing that military decisions would control civil judgments in the South. The IMPEACHMENT of Andrew Johnson, with Chase presiding over the Senate trial, seemed to threaten the destruction of tripartite checks and balances. Chase drifted back toward his old Democratic states' rights position, a drift signaled by his advocacy of universal amnesty for ex-rebels and universal suffrage. He had tried, unsuccessfully, to have the FOURTEENTH AMENDMENT provide for both. His enhanced or renewed respect for states' rights was evident in *United States v. DeWitt* (1869), in which the Court declared a federal law forbidding the transit or sale of dangerous naphtha-adulterated kerosene, to be an excessive diminution of STATE POLICE POWERS.

This decision, the first in which the Court denied Congress a capacity to act for regulatory purposes under the COMMERCE CLAUSE, like the decisions on Reconstruction issues, suggests how far the CHASE COURT engaged in JUDICIAL ACTIVISM. Striking in this regard were the Legal Tender Cases. The first of these, *Hepburn v. Griswold* (1870), resulted in a 4–3 decision that the 1862 law authorizing greenbacks as legal tender was invalid as applied to contracts made before passage of the statute. Chase, for the thin majority, insisted that the statute violated the Fifth Amendment's due process clause, concluding that the spirit of the CONTRACT CLAUSE, though by its terms restraining only the states, applied also to the federal government. The trio of dissenters—all, like Chase, Republican appointees—saw the money and war powers as adequate authority for the statute.

Then, later in 1870, President ULYSSES S. GRANT named two new Justices to the Court: JOSEPH P. BRADLEY and WILLIAM STRONG. The new appointees created, in *Knox v. Lee* (1871), the second Legal Tender Case decision, a majority that overruled *Hepburn*. The new majority now upheld the nation's authority to make paper money legal tender for contracts entered into either before or after enactment of the statute, an authority not pinned necessarily to the war power.

Chase was in the minority in the SLAUGHTERHOUSE CASES (1873) in which the majority found no violation of the Thirteenth or Fourteenth Amendments in a state's assignment of a skilled-trade monopoly to private parties. The doctrine of *Slaughterhouse*, that the privileges of United States citizenship did not protect basic civil rights, signaled a sharp retreat from Chase's own *In Re Turner* position, and was a fateful step by the Court toward what was to become a general retreat from Reconstruction.

Slaughterhouse, along with Chase's anti-Grant position in 1872, closed off Chase's long and tumultuous career; he died in 1873. His career was consistent in its anticorruption positions and in its infusions of moral and ethical ideas into constitutional, legal, and political issues. Party-jumping was incidental to Chase's ends of a moral democracy, federally arranged in a perpetual union of perpetual states; he gave this concept effective expression in TEXAS V. WHITE (1869).

To be sure, neither Chase nor "his" Court created novel legal doctrines. But he, and it, helped greatly to reclaim for the Court a significant role in determining the limits of certain vital public policies, both national and state. In the tumults of Reconstruction, while avoiding unwinnable clashes with Congress, Chase bravely insisted that effective governmental power and individual rights could co-exist. He and his fellow Justices advanced novel constitutional doctrines drawn from the prohibitions against ex post facto laws and BILLS OF ATTAINDER, and from the commerce and money powers. In retrospect, such experiments with doctrine take on the quality of interim defenses of judicial authority between prewar reliance on the contract clause, as example, and the post-Chase development of the due process clause of the Fourteenth Amendment.

At the same time, Chase tried to focus the Court's attention on individuals' rights as redefined first by the Thirteenth and then by the Fourteenth Amendment, as against both private and public wrongs. As one who for years had observed at first hand the capacity of nation and states and private persons to wrong individuals, Chase, as Chief Justice, brought a particular sense of urgency to the goal fo protecting individual rights. He failed to convert a majority of his brethren to this task. Instead, America deferred its constitutional commitments. (See CONSTITUTIONAL HISTORY, 1865–1877.)

HAROLD M. HYMAN
(1986)

Bibliography
FAIRMAN, CHARLES 1971 *History of the Supreme Court of the United States: Reconstruction and Reunion, 1864–1888.* New York: Macmillan.

HUGHES, DAVID 1965 Salmon P. Chase: Chief Justice. *Vanderbilt Law Review* 18:569–614.

HYMAN, HAROLD M. and WIECEK, WILLIAM M. 1982 *Equal Justice under Law: Constitutional Development 1835–1875.* Chaps. 11–13. New York: Harper & Row.

WALKER, PETER F. 1978 *Moral Choices.* Chaps. 13–14. Baton Rouge: Louisiana State University Press.

CHASE, SAMUEL
(1741–1811)

Samuel Chase was one of the most significant and controversial members of America's revolutionary generation. Irascible and difficult, but also extremely capable, he played a central role in Maryland politics during the 1760s and 1770s, signed the DECLARATION OF INDEPENDENCE, and was a member of the Continental Congress from 1775 to 1778. In the latter year ALEXANDER HAMILTON denounced him for using confidential information to speculate in the flour market. During the 1780s Chase pursued various business interests, practiced law, rebuilt his political reputation, and became an important anti-Federalist leader. After the adoption of the Constitution, for reasons that remain unclear, he became an ardent Federalist.

In 1795 he was nominated for a position on the federal bench. President GEORGE WASHINGTON was at first wary of recommending him, but when he had trouble filling a vacancy on the United States Supreme Court, he offered the position to Chase, who accepted in 1796. As one of the better legal minds in the early republic, Chase delivered several of the Court's most important decisions in the pre-Marshall period. In WARE V. HYLTON (1796) he provided one of the strongest statements ever issued on the supremacy of national treaties over state laws. The decision invalidated a Virginia statute of 1777 that placed obstacles in the way of recovery of debts owed by Americans to British creditors, a law in clear violation of a specific provision of the treaty of peace with Great Britain (1783). In HYLTON V. UNITED STATES (1796) Chase and the Supreme Court for the first time passed upon the constitutionality of an act of Congress, upholding the carriage tax of 1794. Chase concluded that only CAPITATION TAXES were direct taxes subject to the constitutional requirement of apportionment among the states according to population. In CALDER V. BULL (1798), where the Supreme Court held that the prohibition against EX POST FACTO LAWS in the Constitution extended only to criminal, not civil, laws, Chase addressed the issue of constitutionality in natural law terms, presaging those late-nineteenth-century jurists who, in furthering the concept of SUBSTANTIVE DUE PROCESS, were to argue that the Supreme Court could properly hold laws invalid for reasons lying outside the explicit prohibitions of the constitutional text. Riding circuit, he ruled in *United States v. Worrall* (1798) that the federal courts had no jurisdiction over crimes defined by COMMON LAW. This position, which Chase abandoned, was adopted by the Supreme Court in *United States v. Hudson and Goodwin* (1812). (See FEDERAL COMMON LAW OF CRIMES.)

A fierce partisan, Chase refused to recognize the legitimacy of the Jeffersonian opposition in the party struggles of the late 1790s. He used his position on the bench to make speeches for the Federalists and he supported the passage of the ALIEN AND SEDITION ACTS in 1798. Riding circuit, he enforced the law with a vengeance when he presided over the trials of John Fries of Pennsylvania for TREASON and John Callendar of Virginia for SEDITION, sentencing the former to death (Fries was eventually pardoned by President JOHN ADAMS) and the latter to a stiff fine and a prison sentence. When THOMAS JEFFERSON and the Republicans came to power in 1801 and repealed the JUDICIARY ACT OF 1801, Chase vigorously campaigned behind the scenes for the Supreme Court to declare the repeal law unconstitutional, but the other Justices did not go along with him. Chase, however, remained adamant in his opposition to the Jeffersonians, refusing to alter his partisan behavior. "Things," he argued, "must take their natural course, from *bad* to *worse*." In May 1803, in an intemperate charge to a GRAND JURY in Baltimore, he launched yet another attack on the Republican party and its principles.

Shortly thereafter, President Jefferson urged that Chase be removed from office. The House of Representatives voted for his IMPEACHMENT, and he came to trial before the United States Senate. The Constitution authorizes impeachment and conviction of federal government officers for "Treason, Bribery, or other high Crimes and Misdemeanors." Many of the more militant Republicans, unhappy with Federalist control of the judiciary, favored an expansive view of what should constitute an impeachable offense. As one put it: "Removal by impeachment was nothing more than a declaration by Congress to this effect: You held dangerous opinions and if you are suffered to carry them into effect, you will work the destruction of the Union. We want your offices for the purpose of giving them to men who will fill them better." Others, including a number of Republicans, favored a narrow definition: impeachment was permitted only for a clearly indictable offense.

Chase proved to be a formidable opponent. Aided by a prestigious group of Federalist trial lawyers, he put up a strong defense, denying that any of his actions were indictable offenses under either statute or common law. His attorneys raised various complicated and even moot legal questions such as the binding quality of local custom; the reciprocal rights and duties of the judge, jury, and defense counsel; the legality of bad manners in a court room; the rules of submitting EVIDENCE; and the problems involved in proving criminal intent. The prosecution was led by JOHN RANDOLPH, an extreme Republican and highly emotional man who badly botched the legal part of his argument. Chase was acquitted on all counts, even though most senators disliked him and believed his conduct on the bench had been improper. The final result was not so much a vote for Chase as it was against a broad definition of the impeachment clause—a definition that might be used to remove other judges, perhaps even to dismantle the federal judiciary altogether. Even Jefferson appears to have come around to this point of view; he made no attempt to enforce party unity when the Senate voted, and he was not unhappy with the outcome of the trial.

Although Chase served on the Supreme Court for the rest of his life, he no longer played an important role. JOHN MARSHALL had begun his ascendancy, and although Marshall was a staunch nationalist, he was less overtly partisan than Chase and less inclined to provoke confrontations with the Jeffersonians.

RICHARD E. ELLIS
(1986)

Bibliography

ELLIS, RICHARD E. 1981 The Impeachment of Samuel Chase. Pages 57–78 in Michal Belknap, ed., *American Political Trials*. Westport, Conn.: Greenwood Press.

HAW, JAMES et al. 1981 *Stormy Patriot: The Life of Samuel Chase*. Baltimore: Johns Hopkins University Press.

CHASE COURT
(1864–1873)

The decade of SALMON P. CHASE's tenure as CHIEF JUSTICE of the United States was one of the more turbulent in the history of the Supreme Court. Laboring under the cloud of hostility engendered by DRED SCOTT V. SANDFORD (1857), hurt by partisan attacks from without and divisions within, staggering under loads of new business, the Chase Court nevertheless managed to absorb and consolidate sweeping new jurisdictional grants to the federal courts and to render some momentous decisions.

The Chase Court displayed an unusual continuity of personnel, which was offset by political and ideological heterogeneity. Of the nine men Chase joined on his accession (the Court in 1864 was composed of ten members), seven served throughout all or nearly all his brief tenure. But this largely continuous body was divided within itself by party and ideological differences. JOHN CATRON, who died in 1865, JAMES M. WAYNE, who died in 1867, and ROBERT C. GRIER, who suffered a deterioration in his faculties that caused his brethren to force him to resign in 1870, were Democrats. NATHAN CLIFFORD, an appointee of President JAMES BUCHANAN, and STEPHEN J. FIELD were also Democrats, the latter a War Democrat. SAMUEL F. MILLER, DAVID DAVIS, and JOSEPH P. BRADLEY were Republicans. Chase himself was an ex-Democrat who had helped form the Republican party in 1854, but he drifted back to the Democratic party after the war and coveted its presidential nomination. WILLIAM STRONG, Grier's replacement, and NOAH SWAYNE were also Democrats who turned Republican before the war. Like the Chief Justice, Davis never successfully shook off political ambitions; he accepted and then rejected the Labor Reform party's nomination for the presidency in 1872. From 1870, Republicans dominated the Court, which had long been controlled by Democrats.

The work of the Supreme Court changed greatly during Chase's tenure. In 1862 and 1866, Congress realigned the federal circuits, so as to reduce the influence of the southern states, which under the Judiciary Act of 1837 had five of the nine circuits. Under the Judiciary Act of 1866, the southern circuits were reduced to two. By the same statute, Congress reduced the size of the Court from ten to seven members, mainly to enhance the efficiency of its work, not to punish the Court or deprive President ANDREW JOHNSON of appointments to it. In 1869, Congress again raised the size of the Court to nine, where it has remained ever since. More significantly, the business of the Court expanded. By 1871, the number of cases docketed had doubled in comparison to the war years. This increase resulted in some measure from an extraordinary string of statutes enacted between 1863 and 1867 expanding the JURISDICTION OF THE FEDERAL COURTS in such matters as REMOVAL OF CASES from state to federal courts, HABEAS CORPUS, claims against the United States, and BANKRUPTCY.

The Chase Court was not a mere passive, inert repository of augmented jurisdiction: it expanded its powers of JUDICIAL REVIEW to an extent unknown to earlier Courts. During Chase's brief tenure, the Court held eight federal statutes unconstitutional (as compared with only two in its entire prior history), and struck down state statutes in thirty-six cases (as compared with thirty-eight in its prior history). The attitude that produced this JUDICIAL ACTIVISM was expressed in private correspondence by Justice Davis, when he noted with satisfaction that the Court in EX PARTE MILLIGAN (1866) had not "toadied to the prevalent idea, that the legislative department of the government can override everything." This judicial activism not only presaged the Court's involvement in policy during the coming heyday of SUBSTANTIVE DUE PROCESS; it also plunged the Chase Court into some of the most hotly contested matters of its own time, especially those connected with RECONSTRUCTION. The Court also attracted the public eye because of the activities of two of its members: Chase's and Davis's availability as presidential candidates, and Chase's firm, impartial service in presiding over the United States SENATE as a court of IMPEACHMENT in the trial of Andrew Johnson.

The Chase Court is memorable for its decisions in four areas: Reconstruction, federal power (in matters not directly related to Reconstruction), state regulatory and tax power, and the impact of the FOURTEENTH AMENDMENT.

Nearly all the cases in which the Supreme Court disposed of Reconstruction issues were decided during Chase's tenure. The first issue to come up was the role of military commissions. In EX PARTE VALLANDIGHAM, decided in February 1864 (ten months before Chase's nomination), the Court refused to review the proceedings of a military commission, because the commission is not a court. But that did not settle the issue of the constitutional authority of military commissions. The matter came up again, at an inopportune time, in *Ex parte Milligan*, decided in December 1866. Milligan had been arrested, tried, convicted, and sentenced to be hanged by a military commission in Indiana in 1864 for paramilitary activities on behalf of the Confederacy. The Court unanimously ruled that his conviction was illegal because Indiana was not in a theater of war, because the civil courts were functioning and competent to try Milligan for TREASON, and because he was held in violation of the provisions of the HABEAS CORPUS ACT OF 1863. But the Court split, 5–4, over an OBITER DICTUM in Justice Davis's MAJORITY OPINION stating that the Congress could never authorize military commissions in areas outside the theater of operations where the civil courts were functioning. The Chief Justice, writing for the minority, declared that Congress did have the power to authorize commissions, based on the several WAR POWERS clauses of Article I, section 8, but that it had not done so; hence Milligan's trial was unauthorized.

Milligan created a furor in Congress and deeply implicated the Court in the politics of Reconstruction. Assuming that military commissions were essential to the conduct of Reconstruction, Democrats taunted Republicans that *Milligan* implied that they were unconstitutional, and hence that proposed Republican measures providing for military trials in the CIVIL RIGHTS ACT OF 1866 and FREEDMEN'S BUREAU Act violated the Constitution. Taken together with subsequent decisions, *Milligan* caused Republicans some anxiety. But, as Justice Davis noted in private correspondence and as Illinois Republican LYMAN TRUMBULL stated on the floor of the Senate, the decision in reality had no application to the constitutional anomaly of Reconstruction in the South.

The Court next seemed to challenge congressional Reconstruction in the TEST OATH CASES, *Ex parte Garland* and *Cummings v. Missouri*, both 1867. The court, by 5–4 decisions, voided federal and state statutes requiring a candidate for public office or one of the professions to swear that he had never participated or assisted in the rebellion. The Court's holding, that they constituted BILLS OF ATTAINDER and EX POST FACTO LAWS, seemingly threatened programs of disfranchisement and oath qualification, another part of proposed Reconstruction measures. Then, in February 1868, the Court announced that it would hear arguments in EX PARTE MCCARDLE, another challenge to military commissions. William McCardle had been convicted by a military commission for publishing inflammatory articles. A federal circuit court denied his petition for a writ of habeas corpus under the HABEAS CORPUS ACT OF 1867, a measure that had broadened the scope of the writ, and he appealed the denial to the Supreme Court. Alarmed, congressional Republicans enacted a narrowly drawn statute known as the McCardle repealer, denying the Supreme Court appellate jurisdiction in habeas petitions brought under the 1867 act. In 1869, the Court accepted the constitutionality of the repealer, because Article III, section 2, made the Court's APPELLATE JURISDICTION subject to "such Exceptions . . . as the Congress shall make." But Chief Justice Chase pointedly reminded the bar that all the rest of the Court's habeas appellate authority was left intact. This broad hint bore fruit in *Ex parte Yerger* (1869), where the Court accepted jurisdiction of a habeas appeal under the JUDICIARY ACT OF 1789. Chief Justice Chase chastised Congress for the McCardle repealer and reaffirmed the scope of the Great Writ.

In the meantime, the Court had turned to other Reconstruction issues. As soon as Congress enacted the MILITARY RECONSTRUCTION ACTS of 1867, southern attorneys sought to enjoin federal officials, including the President and the secretary of war, from enforcing them. In MISSISSIPPI V. JOHNSON (1867), the Court unanimously rejected this petition. Chief Justice Chase drew on a distinction, originally suggested by his predecessor Chief Justice JOHN

MARSHALL in MARBURY V. MADISON (1803), between ministerial and discretionary responsibilities of the President, stating that the latter were not subject to the Court's injunctive powers. In *Georgia v. Stanton* (1867), the Court similarly dismissed a petition directed at the secretary of war and General ULYSSES S. GRANT, holding that the petition presented POLITICAL QUESTIONS resolvable only by the political branches of the government. But the words of Justice Nelson's opinion seemed to suggest that if the petition had alleged a threat to private property (rather than the state's property), there might be a basis for providing relief. In May 1867, Mississippi's attorneys moved to amend their petition to specify such a threat. The Court, in a 4–4 order (Justice Grier being absent), rejected the motion. This minor, unnoticed proceeding was probably the truest index to the attitudes of individual Justices on the substantive policy questions of Reconstruction.

The Court's final involvement with Reconstruction came with TEXAS V. WHITE (1869) and *White v. Hart* (1872). In the former case, decided on the same day that the Supreme Court acknowledged the validity of the McCardle repealer, the postwar government of Texas sought to recover some bonds that the Confederate state government had sold to defray military costs. Because a state was a party, this was an action within the ORIGINAL JURISDICTION of the Supreme Court. But one of the defendants challenged the jurisdictional basis of the action, claiming that Texas was not a state in the constitutional sense at the time the action was brought (February 1867). This challenge directly raised important questions about the validity of SECESSION and Reconstruction. Chief Justice Chase, writing for the six-man majority (Grier, Swayne, Miller, dissenting) met the issue head on. He first held that secession had been a nullity. The Union was "indissoluble," "an indestructible Union, composed of indestructible States" in Chase's resonant, memorable phrasing. But, he went on, though the relations of individual Texans to the United States could not be severed, secession had deranged the status of the state within the Union. In language suggestive of the "forfeited-rights" theory of Reconstruction propounded by Ohio congressman Samuel Shellabarger which had provided a conceptual basis for Republican Reconstruction, Chase stated that the rights of the state had been "suspended" by secession and war. Congress was responsible for restoring the proper relationship, in wartime because of its authority under the military and militia clauses of Article I, section 8, and in peacetime under the guarantee of a REPUBLICAN FORM OF GOVERNMENT in Article IV, section 4. This was preponderantly a question to be resolved by Congress rather than the President, and hence the Lincoln and Johnson governments in power before enactment of the Military Reconstruction Acts were "provisional." Congress enjoyed wide latitude in working out details of Reconstruction policy. The sweeping language of Chase's opinion strongly implied the constitutionality of military Reconstruction. The majority opinion also offered a useful distinction between legitimate acts of the Confederate government of Texas, such as those designed to preserve the peace, and invalid ones in support of the rebellion.

In *White v. Hart* (1872) the Court reaffirmed its general position in *Texas v. White* and emphasized that the relationship of states in the union was a political question for the political branches to resolve. At the same time, the Court disposed of two lingering issues from the war in ways that reaffirmed the doctrine of *Texas v. White*. In *Virginia v. West Virginia* (1870) it accepted the creation of the daughter state, shutting its eyes to the obvious irregularities surrounding the Pierpont government's consent to the separation, and insisting that there had been a "valid agreement between the two States." And in *Miller v. United States* (1871), echoing the PRIZE CASES (1863), a six-man majority upheld the constitutionality of the confiscation provisions of the Second Confiscation Act of 1862 on the basis of the Union's status as a belligerent.

The Chase Court decisions dealing with secession, war, and Reconstruction have stood well the test of time. *Milligan* and the *Test Oath Cases* remain valuable defenses of individual liberty against arbitrary government. The *McCardle* decision was a realistic and valid recognition of an explicit congressional power, while its sequel, *Yerger*, reaffirmed the libertarian implications of *Milligan*. The Court's position in the cases seeking to enjoin executive officials from enforcing Reconstruction was inevitable: it would have been hopeless for the Court to attempt to thwart congressional Reconstruction, or to accede to the Johnson/Democratic demand for immediate readmission of the seceded states. *Texas v. White* and *White v. Hart* drew on a sound prewar precedent, LUTHER V. BORDEN (1849), to validate actions by the dominant political branch in what was clearly a pure political question. Taken together, the Reconstruction cases evince a high order of judicial statesmanship.

The Chase Court made only tentative beginnings in issues of federal and state regulatory power, but those beginnings were significant. The first federal regulatory question to come up involved the currency. In VEAZIE BANK V. FENNO (1869) the Court sustained the constitutionality of sections of the Internal Revenue Acts of 1865 and 1866 that imposed a ten percent tax on state bank notes for the purpose of driving them out of circulation. Chase first held that the tax was not a DIRECT TAX (which would have had to be apportioned among the states) and then upheld Congress's power to issue paper money and create a uniform national currency by eliminating state paper.

The LEGAL TENDER CASES were more controversial. As secretary of the treasury, Chase had reluctantly acquiesced in the issuance of federal paper money. But when the issue came before the Court in the First Legal Tender Case (*Hepburn v. Griswold*, 1870), Chase, speaking for a 4–3 majority, held the Legal Tender Act of 1862 unconstitutional because it made greenbacks legal tender for preexisting debts. The division on the court was partisan: all the majority Justices were Democrats (Chase by this time had reverted to his Democratic antecedents), all the dissenters Republicans. Chase's reasoning was precipitate and unsatisfactory. He asserted that the act violated the OBLIGATION OF CONTRACTS, but the CONTRACT CLAUSE limited only the states. To this Chase responded that the act was contrary to the "spirit of the Constitution." He also broadly implied that the statute violated the Fifth Amendment's guarantee of DUE PROCESS.

An enlarged Court in 1871 reversed *Hepburn*, upholding the constitutionality of the 1862 statute in the Second Legal Tender Cases, with the two new appointees, Bradley and Strong, joining the three dissenters of the first case. Justice Strong for the majority averred that "every contract for the payment of money, simply, is necessarily subject to the constitutional power of the government over the currency." The Court's turnabout suggested to contemporaries that President Grant had packed the Court to obtain a reversal of the first decision. Grant was opposed to the decision, and he knew that Bradley and Strong were also opposed; but he did not secure from them any commitments on the subject, and he did not base his appointments solely on the single issue of legal tender.

Other Chase Court decisions involving federal power were not so controversial. In *United States v. Dewitt* (1870) Chase for the Court invalidated an exercise of what would come to be called the NATIONAL POLICE POWER, in this case a provision in a revenue statute prohibiting the mixing of illuminating oil with naphtha (a highly flammable mixture). Chase held that the COMMERCE CLAUSE conferred no federal power over the internal affairs of the states, and that the subject matter was remote from the topic of raising revenue. He simply assumed that there was no inherent national police power. In COLLECTOR V. DAY (1871) Justice Nelson for a divided Court held that federal revenue acts taxing income could not reach the salary of a state judge. Justice Bradley's dissent, maintaining the necessity of federal power to reach sources of income that included some functions of state government, was vindicated in GRAVES V. NEW YORK EX REL. O'KEEFE (1939), which overruled *Day*. In contrast to the foregoing cases, *The Daniel Ball* (1871) upheld the power of Congress to regulate commerce on navigable waterways, even where these were wholly intrastate.

The Chase Court decisions passing on the regulatory and taxing authority of the states caused less controversy.

These cases are significant principally as evidence that the Court continued unabated its prewar responsibility of monitoring the functioning of the federal system, inhibiting incursions by the states on national authority and the national market, while at the same time preserving their scope of regulation and their sources of revenue intact. The first case of this sort, GELPCKE V. DUBUQUE (1864), involved a suit on bonds, issued by a city to encourage railroad building, which the city was trying to repudiate. The state courts had reversed their prior decisions and held that citizens could not be taxed to assist a private enterprise such as a railroad. The Supreme Court, in an opinion by Justice Swayne, reversed the result below, thus upholding the validity of the bonds. Swayne intemperately declared that "We shall never immolate truth, justice, and the law, because a state tribunal has erected the altar and decreed the sacrifice." The decision was welcomed in financial circles, particularly European ones, and presaged a Court attitude sympathetic to investors and hostile to repudiation, especially by a public agency.

The Court displayed less passion in other cases. In *Crandall v. Nevada* (1868), it struck down a state CAPITATION tax on passengers of public conveyances leaving the state as an unconstitutional interference with the right of persons to move about the country. The commerce clause aspects of the case were left to be decided later. Another case involving personal liberty, *Tarble's Case* (1872), vindicated the Court's earlier position in ABLEMAN V. BOOTH (1859) by holding that a state court in a habeas corpus proceeding could not release an individual held in federal custody (here, an allegedly deserting army volunteer).

But most cases testing the scope of state regulatory power dealt with commerce. In PAUL V. VIRGINIA (1869) the Court, through Chase, held that the negotiation of insurance contracts did not constitute commerce within the meaning of the commerce clause, and hence that a state was free to regulate the conduct of insurance companies as it pleased. This doctrine lasted until 1944. But one aspect of Justice Field's concurring opinion in *Paul* had momentous consequences. He asserted that, for purposes of the PRIVILEGES AND IMMUNITIES clause of Article IV, CORPORATIONS could not be considered "citizens," and were thus not entitled to the privileges and immunities of natural PERSONS. This caused attorneys to look to other sources, such as the due process clause (with its term "person") as a source of protection for corporations. During the same term, in WOODRUFF V. PARHAM (1868), the Chase Court upheld a municipal sales tax applied to goods brought into the state in INTERSTATE COMMERCE even though they were still in their original package, thus limiting Marshall's ORIGINAL PACKAGE DOCTRINE announced in BROWN V. MARYLAND (1827) to imports from other nations.

Three 1873 cases demonstrated the Court carefully adjusting the federal balance. In the State Freight Tax Case the Court struck down a state tax on freight carried out of the state. But in the *Case of the State Tax on Railway Gross Receipts* the Court upheld a state tax on a corporation's gross receipts, even when the taxpayer was a carrier and the tax fell on interstate business. And in the *Case of the State Tax on Foreign-Held Bonds* the Court struck down a tax on interest on bonds as applied to the securities of out-of-state bondholders.

The last category of major Chase Court cases dealt with the scope of the Reconstruction Amendments, and the extent to which they would alter the prewar balances of the federal system. One of Chase's circuit court decisions, *In re Turner* (1867), suggested that this potential might be broad. Chase there held a Maryland BLACK CODE's apprenticeship provision unconstitutional on the ground that it imposed a condition of involuntary servitude in violation of the THIRTEENTH AMENDMENT. This decision might have been the prelude to extensive federal involvement in matters that before the war would have been considered exclusively within the STATE POLICE POWER. But this possibility was drastically narrowed in the SLAUGHTERHOUSE CASES (1873), the last major decision of the Chase Court and one of the enduring monuments of American constitutional law. Justice Miller for the majority held that "the one pervading purpose" of the Reconstruction Amendments was the liberation of black people, not an extension of the privileges and rights of whites. Miller construed the privileges and immunities, due process, and EQUAL PROTECTION clauses of the Fourteenth Amendment in light of this assumption, holding that none of them had deranged the traditional balance of the federal system. The states still remained the source of most substantive privileges and immunities, and the states remained primarily responsible for securing them to individuals. This ruling effectively relegated the definition and protection of freedmen's rights to precisely those governments—Redeemer-dominated southern states—least likely to provide that protection. Because "we do not see in those [Reconstruction] amendments any purpose to destroy the main features of the general system," Miller rejected a substantive interpretation of the new due process clause and restricted the equal protection clause to cases of "discrimination against the negroes as a class."

The future belonged to the *Slaughterhouse* dissenters, Justices Bradley and Field. Bradley articulated the doctrine of substantive due process, arguing that the right to pursue a lawful occupation is a property right which the state may not interfere with arbitrarily or selectively. Field, in a dissent in which Chase joined (Swayne dissented in a separate opinion) relied on the privileges and immunities clause of the Fourteenth Amendment, seeing in it a guarantee of "the fundamental rights" of free men, which cannot be destroyed by state legislation. His insistence on an "equality of right, with exemption from all disparaging and partial enactments, in the lawful pursuits of life" foreshadowed the doctrine of FREEDOM OF CONTRACT.

Yet Field's and Bradley's insistence on the right to follow a chosen occupation, free of arbitrary discrimination, did not avail Myra Bradwell in her effort to secure admission to the Illinois bar (BRADWELL V. ILLINOIS, 1873). Justice Miller for the majority (Chase being the lone dissenter) refused to overturn a decision of the Illinois Supreme Court denying her admission to the bar solely on the ground of her gender. "The paramount mission and destiny of woman are to fulfill the noble and benign offices of wife and mother. This is the law of the Creator," Bradley wrote in a concurrence. "And the rules of civil society . . . cannot be based upon exceptional cases." The emergent scope of the due process, equal protection, and privileges and immunities clauses were to have a differential application as a result of the *Slaughterhouse* dissents and *Bradwell* ruling, securing the rights of corporations and men in their economic roles, while proving ineffectual to protect others from discrimination based on race and gender. (See RACIAL DISCRIMINATION; SEX EQUALITY.)

During its brief span, the Chase Court made enduring contributions to American constitutional development. It handled the unprecedented issues of Reconstruction with balance and a due recognition of the anomalous nature of issues coming before it. Yet in those decisions, Chase and his colleagues managed to preserve protection for individual rights while at the same time permitting the victorious section, majority, and party to assure a constitutional resolution of the war consonant with its military results. In non-Reconstruction cases, the Chase court continued the traditional function of the Supreme Court in monitoring and adjusting the allocation of powers between nation and states. It was more activist than its predecessors in striking down federal legislation, while it displayed the same nicely balanced concern for state regulatory power and protection of the national market that was a characteristic of the TANEY COURT.

WILLIAM M. WIECEK
(1986)

Bibliography

FAIRMAN, CHARLES   1939   *Mr. Justice Miller and the Supreme Court, 1862–1890.* Cambridge, Mass.: Harvard University Press.

———   1971   *Reconstruction and Reunion, 1864–88, Part One* (vol. VI of the Oliver Wendell Holmes Devise *History of the Supreme Court of the United States*). New York: Macmillan.

HYMAN, HAROLD M. and WIECEK, WILLIAM M.   1982   *Equal Justice Under Law: Constitutional Development 1835–1875.* New York: Harper & Row.

KUTLER, STANLEY I.   1968   *Judicial Power and Reconstruction Politics.* Chicago: University of Chicago Press.

SILVER, DAVID M.   1957   *Lincoln's Supreme Court.* Urbana: University of Illinois Press.

SWISHER, CARL B.   1930   *Stephen J. Field: Craftsman of the Law.* Washington, D.C.: Brookings Institution.

WARREN, CHARLES   1937   *The Supreme Court in United States History*, rev. ed. Boston: Little, Brown.

CHATHAM, LORD

See: Pitt, William

CHECKS AND BALANCES

In its precise meaning, "checks and balances" is not synonymous with SEPARATION OF POWERS; it refers instead to a system of rules and practices designed to maintain the separation of powers. The executive VETO POWER is considered part of this system, along with the power of JUDICIAL REVIEW, the IMPEACHMENT power, and other powers available to any of the branches of government for combating the encroachments of the others.

JAMES MADISON formulated the American theory of checks and balances in response to the ANTI-FEDERALIST charge that the proposed Constitution would contain an overlap of governmental functions, violating the principle of separated powers. Expressing a pessimistic view of human nature, he argued in THE FEDERALIST #10 that the way to avoid majority tyranny lay in creating a large national community of diverse and numerous economic interests, not in statesmanship or in religious and moral constraints. In *The Federalist* #47–49 Madison went on to argue that neither sharply drawn institutional boundaries nor appeals to the electorate could be relied upon to maintain the separation of powers. Both methods presupposed the virtues of official lawfulness and electoral nonpartisanship, virtues whose unreliability was attested by experience. Because such "external checks" were ineffective, said Madison in *The Federalist* #51, maintaining the separation of powers would require "internal checks" that linked the officeholders' personal ambitions to their duties. Officials would defend their constitutional prerogatives if they felt that doing so were a means to furthering their personal ambitions. "[A]mbition checking ambition"—not virtue—was the key to constitutional maintenance. And effective checks required each branch to have a hand in the others' functions. For example, the veto is the President's hand in the legislative function.

Madison knew, however, that this partial blending of

power did not go far enough. Power might still be concentrated if all these branches were united in one interest or animated by the same spirit. Thinkers from Aristotle to MONTESQUIEU had taught that constitutions could be maintained at least partly through a balance of social groups such as estates or economic classes. But theorists with democratic pretensions could not institutionalize such social divisions. The problem for the Framers was to prevent a single interest from predominating in a society that had few official distinctions of status and class. Their answer was to rely on the different institutional psychologies of governmental branches whose personnel would represent the different constituencies and perspectives of a large and diverse society. Thus, Madison argued in *The Federalist* #62–63 that because of differences in age, period of CITIZENSHIP, tenure of office, constituency, and, to a lesser degree, legislative function, members of the House of Representatives and Senate would pursue different policies with different consequences for the long term and varying impact on local, national, and international opinion. ALEXANDER HAMILTON wrote in *The Federalist* #70–71 that presidential types would be likely to seek the acclaim that attends success in difficult tasks, especially tasks requiring leaders to stand against and change public opinion. Such differences in institutional psychology, compounded by the federal features of the electoral system and the pluralism of an essentially democratic, secular, and commercial society, were expected to impede the formation of political parties disciplined enough to overcome the moderating influence of separated institutions.

The American system of checks and balances envisions strong executive and judicial branches. Experience had taught the Framers that popular legislatures were a greater threat to the separation of powers than were executives or courts. Accordingly, *The Federalist* #51 rationalized the bicameralism of Congress and the independence of the executive and judicial branches as means of weakening the naturally strongest branch and strengthening the weaker ones. This positive feature of the system complements its negative function of preventing concentrations of power. The Framers thus sought to achieve separation of governmental institutions without sacrificing the capacity for coordinated leadership when times demanded.

The system of checks and balances has worked well in some respects, but not in all. It has discouraged concentrations of power through centralized and disciplined political parties. Although government is fragmented in normal times, the system does permit central leadership in times of crisis, as the presidencies of THOMAS JEFFERSON, ABRAHAM LINCOLN, and FRANKLIN D. ROOSEVELT attest. It has also helped to create a remarkable degree of judicial independence without producing a judiciary seriously at

odds with public opinion on any given issue for too long. The system has not worked so well in the case of Congress, which has undermined its own position by a practice of broad DELEGATION OF POWER to the executive and independent agencies. Many such delegations are necessitated by the problems and complexities that have brought the triumph of the administrative state. But far too many delegations are little more than acts of political buckpassing explained by the perception that the way to reelection does not lie in clear positions on controversial questions, but in constituency services and publicity that is politically safe. After the Great Depression and before the Supreme Court's decision in IMMIGRATION AND NATURALIZATION SERVICE V. CHADHA (1983), Congress compounded avoidable offense to the separation of powers when it tried to straddle the question of legislative responsibility, limiting many of its buckpassing delegations of power with various versions of the LEGISLATIVE VETO.

Congress's experience shows that there is a limit to the ability of the system to maintain a constitutional arrangement through reliance on personal ambition. Personal ambition sometimes dictates surrendering institutional prerogatives. The same can be said when Presidents compromise firmness in anticipation of elections and when judges propose "judicial self-restraint" in response to threats like court-packing and withdrawals of JURISDICTION. Despite the Framers' theory of checks and balances, officials must at some point respect constitutional duty as something other than mere means to personal ambition.

SOTIRIOS A. BARBER
(1986)

Bibliography

FISHER, LOUIS 1978 *The Constitution Between Friends: Congress, the President, and the Law.* New York: St. Martin's Press.
SHARP, MALCOLM 1938 The Classical American Doctrine of "the Separation of Powers." In Association of American Law Schools, *Selected Essays on Constitutional Law.* Vol. 4:168–194. Chicago: Foundation Press.
VILE, M. J. C. 1967 *Constitutionalism and the Separation of Powers.* Oxford: Clarendon Press.

CHEROKEE INDIAN CASES
Cherokee Nation v. Georgia
5 Peters 1 (1831)
Worcester v. Georgia
6 Peters 515 (1832)

The Cherokee Indian Cases prompted a constitutional crisis marked by successful state defiance of the Supreme Court, the Constitution, and federal treaties. The United

States had made treaties with the Georgia Cherokee, as if they were a sovereign power, and pledged to secure their lands. Later, in 1802, the United States pledged to Georgia that in return for its relinquishment of the Yazoo lands (see FLETCHER V. PECK) the United States would extinguish the Cherokee land claims in Georgia. The Cherokee, however, refused to leave Georgia voluntarily in return for wild lands west of the Mississippi. In 1824 Georgia claimed LEGISLATIVE JURISDICTION over all the Indian lands within its boundaries. The Cherokee, who had a written language and a plantation economy, then adopted a CONSTITUTION and declared their sovereign independence. Georgia, which denied that the United States had authority to bind the state by an Indian treaty, retaliated against the Cherokee by a series of statutes that nullified all Indian laws and land claims and divided Cherokee lands into counties subject to state governance. President ANDREW JACKSON supported the state against the Indians, and Congress, too, recognizing that the Indians could not maintain a separate sovereignty within the state, urged them to settle on federally granted land in the west or, if remaining in Georgia, to submit to state laws.

The Cherokee turned next to the Supreme Court. Claiming to be a foreign state within the meaning of Article III, section 2, of the Constitution, the Indians invoked the Court's ORIGINAL JURISDICTION in a case to which a state was a party and sought an INJUNCTION that would restrain Georgia from enforcing any of its laws within Cherokee territory recognized by federal treaties. By scheduling a hearing the Court exposed itself to Georgia's wrath. Without the support of the political branches of the national government, the Court faced the prospect of being unable to enforce its own decree or defend the supremacy of federal treaties against state violation.

The case of Corn Tassel, which suddenly intervened, exposed the Court's vulnerability. He was a Cherokee whom Georgia tried and convicted for the murder of a fellow tribesman, though he objected that a federal treaty recognized the exclusive right of his own nation to try him. On Tassel's application Chief Justice JOHN MARSHALL issued a WRIT OF ERROR to the state trial court and directed the governor of the state to send its counsel to appear before the Supreme Court. Georgia's governor and legislature contemptuously declared that they would resist execution of the Court's writ with all necessary force, denounced the Court's infringement of state SOVEREIGNTY, and hanged Corn Tassel. Justice JOSEPH STORY spoke of "practical NULLIFICATION." Newspapers and politicians throughout the nation took sides in the dispute between the Court and the state, and Congress in 1831 debated a bill to repeal section 25 of the JUDICIARY ACT OF 1789. Although the House defeated the repeal bill, Whigs despondently predicted that the President would not support the Court if it decided the *Cherokee Nation* case contrary to his view of the matter.

The Court wisely decided, 4–2, to deny jurisdiction on the ground that the Cherokee were not a foreign state in the sense of Article III's use of that term. Although Marshall for the Court declared that the Cherokee were a "distinct political society" capable of self-government and endorsed their right to their lands, he candidly acknowledged that the Court could not restrain the government of Georgia "and its physical force." That, Marshall observed, "savors too much of the exercise of political power" and that was what the bill for an injunction asked of the Court.

A year later, however, the Court switched its strategy. At issue in *Worcester* was the constitutionality of a Georgia statute that prohibited white people from residing in Cherokee territory without a state license. Many missionaries, including Samuel Worcester, defied the act in order to bring a TEST CASE before the Supreme Court, in the hope that the Court would endorse Cherokee sovereignty and void the state's Cherokee legislation. Worcester and another, having been sentenced to four years' hard labor, were the only missionaries to decline a pardon; they applied to the Court for a writ of error, which Marshall issued. Georgia sent the records of the case but again refused to appear before a Court that engaged in a "usurpation" of state sovereignty. The state legislature resolved that a reversal of the state court would be deemed "unconstitutional" and empowered the governor to employ all force to resist the "invasion" of the state's administration of its laws. The case was sensationally debated in the nation's press, and nearly sixty members of Congress left their seats to hear the argument before the Supreme Court.

In an opinion by Marshall, with Justice HENRY BALDWIN dissenting, the Court reaffirmed its jurisdiction under section 25, upheld the exclusive power of the United States in Indian matters, endorsed the authority of the Cherokee Nation within boundaries recognized by federal treaties, declared that the laws of Georgia had no force within these boundaries, and held that the "acts of Georgia are repugnant to the Constitution, laws, and treaties of the United States." The Court also reversed the judgment of the Georgia court and commanded the release of Worcester.

Why did the Court deliberately decide on the broadest possible grounds and challenge Georgia? In a private letter, Justice Story, noting that the state was enraged and violent, expected defiance of the Court's writ and no support from the President. "The Court," he wrote, "has done its duty. Let the nation do theirs. If we have a government let its commands be obeyed; if we have not it is as well to know it. . . ." Georgia did resist and Jackson did nothing. He might have made the famous remark, "John Marshall has made his decision; now let him enforce it." But Jackson knew Marshall's reputation for political craftiness, knew that a majority of Congress resisted all efforts to curb the Court, and knew that public opinion favored the Court and revered its Chief as the nation's preeminent Unionist. Jackson did nothing because he did not yet have to act. The state must first refuse execution of the Court's writ before the Court could order a federal marshal to free Worcester, and it could not issue an order to the marshal without a record of the state court's refusal to obey the writ. Not until the next term of the Court could it decide whether it had a course of action that would force the President either to execute the law of the land or disobey his oath of office. Marshall believed that public opinion would compel Jackson to execute the law. In the fall of 1832, however, Marshall pessimistically wrote that "our Constitution cannot last. . . . The Union has been prolonged thus far by miracles. I fear they cannot continue."

A miracle did occur, making the Court's cause the President's before the Court's next term; the SOUTH CAROLINA ORDINANCE OF NULLIFICATION intervened, forcing Jackson to censure state nullification of federal law. Georgia supported Jackson against South Carolina, and he convinced Georgia's governor that the way to dissociate Georgia from nullification was to free Worcester. The governor pardoned him. Worcester, having won the Supreme Court's invalidation of the Georgia Cherokee legislation, accepted the pardon. The lawyers for the Cherokee persuaded them to desist from further litigation in order to preserve a Unionist coalition against nullificationists. In 1838, long after the crisis had passed, the Cherokees were forcibly removed from their lands. The Court could not save them. It never could. It had, however, saved its integrity ("The Court has done its duty") by defending the supreme law of the land at considerable risk.

LEONARD W. LEVY
(1986)

Bibliography

BURKE, JOSEPH C. 1969 The Cherokee Cases: A Study of Law, Politics, and Morality. *Stanford Law Review* 21:500–531.

WARREN, CHARLES 1923 *The Supreme Court in United States History*, 3 vols. Vol. 2:189–229. Boston: Little, Brown.

CHEROKEE NATION v. GEORGIA

See: Cherokee Indian Cases

CHICAGO v. MORALES
527 U.S. 41 (1999)

During the 1980s and 1990s, cities experienced a marked increase in organized gang activity, often linked to the street sale of drugs. Cities and states, frustrated by the inability of ordinary criminal prohibitions to eliminate gangs, sought new ways to control the presence of gangs in urban areas.

Chicago, in an effort to crack down on—as described in its brief to the Supreme Court—"obviously brazen, insistent and lawless gang members and hangers-on on the public ways" who "intimidate residents" and "destabilize" neighborhoods, authorized its police to arrest anyone milling about "without any apparent purpose" in the company of a suspected gang member. Under the law, police could order any loiterers to disperse and, if they refused, arrest them, even absent any evidence of criminal wrongdoing.

In a 6–3 decision, the Supreme Court declared Chicago's ordinance unconstitutional because of its VAGUENESS. The majority, in an opinion authored by Justice JOHN PAUL STEVENS, explained that the law failed to give the ordinary citizen "adequate notice of what is forbidden and what is permitted" when using the public streets. Moreover, the majority held that "the freedom to loiter for innocent purposes is part of the 'liberty'" protected by the FOURTEENTH AMENDMENT guarantee of DUE PROCESS OF LAW.

In dissent, Justice ANTONIN SCALIA, Justice CLARENCE THOMAS, and Chief Justice WILLIAM H. REHNQUIST accused the majority of improperly crafting a "constitutional right to loiter," despite a long history of anti-loitering laws in every state.

In fact, the MAJORITY OPINION comports with sixty years of PRECEDENT—dating back to *Lanzetta v. United States* (1939)—invalidating vague and standardless laws that target vagrants, suspected criminals, or their associates by criminalizing innocent activity in public. *Morales* serves notice on cities that they cannot sacrifice CIVIL LIBERTIES in their quest to eradicate street gangs.

ADAM WINKLER
(2000)

(SEE ALSO: *Procedural Due Process of Law, Criminal; Vagrancy Laws.*)

CHICAGO, BURLINGTON & QUINCY RAILROAD CO. v. CHICAGO
166 U.S. 226 (1897)

A 7–1 Supreme Court here sustained a $1 award as JUST COMPENSATION for a TAKING OF PROPERTY, holding that the SEVENTH AMENDMENT precluded it from reexamining facts, decided by a jury, which dictated that amount. Although due process required compensation, a nominal sum did not deprive the railroad of either due process or EQUAL PROTECTION. The Court required a "fair and full equivalent for the thing taken by the public" and stressed the necessity for understanding the spirit of due process. "In determining what is DUE PROCESS OF LAW, regard must be had to substance, not to form."

DAVID GORDON
(1986)

CHICAGO, BURLINGTON & QUINCY RAILROAD CO. v. IOWA

See: Granger Cases

CHICAGO, MILWAUKEE & ST. PAUL RAILROAD CO. v. ACKLEY

See: Granger Cases

CHICAGO, MILWAUKEE & ST. PAUL RAILWAY CO. v. MINNESOTA
134 U.S. 418 (1890)

This decision, making the courts arbiters of the reasonableness of railroad rates, presaged the Supreme Court's final acceptance of SUBSTANTIVE DUE PROCESS ten years later. The Minnesota legislature had established a commission to inspect rail rates and alter those it deemed unreasonable. A 6–3 Court struck down the statute as a violation of both substantive and PROCEDURAL DUE PROCESS. Justice SAMUEL BLATCHFORD found that the statute neglected to provide procedural due process: railroads received no notice that the reasonableness of their rate was being considered, and the commission provided no hearing or other chance for the railroads to defend their rates. Moreover, Blatchford said that a rate's reasonableness "is eminently a question for judicial investigation, requiring due process of law for its determination." A company, denied the authority to charge reasonable rates and unable to turn to any judicial mechanism for review (procedural due process) would necessarily be deprived "of the lawful use of its property, and thus, in substance, and effect, of the property itself, without due process of law" (substantive due process). In dissent, Justice JOSEPH P. BRADLEY declared that the majority had effectively overruled MUNN V. ILLINOIS (1877). Bradley's opinion explicitly rejected the assertion that reasonableness was a question for judicial determination; it is, he said, "pre-eminently a legislative one, involving considerations of policy as well as of remuneration." If the legislature could fix rates (as precedent had shown), why could it make no such delegation of power to a commission? Indeed, the Court's next step, in REAGAN V. FARMERS' LOAN & TRUST COMPANY (1894), would

be the claim of power to void statutes by which the legislature itself directly set rates, and, in SMYTH V. AMES (1898), the Court would reach the zenith, actually striking down a state act for that reason.

DAVID GORDON
(1986)

CHIEF JUSTICE, ROLE OF THE

The title "Chief Justice" appears only once in the Constitution. That mention occurs not in Article III, the judicial article, but in connection with the Chief Justice's role as presiding officer of the SENATE during an IMPEACHMENT trial of the President. With such a meager delineation of powers and duties in the Constitution, the importance of the office was hardly obvious during the early days of the Republic. Despite President GEORGE WASHINGTON's great expectations for the post, his first appointee, JOHN JAY, left disillusioned and convinced that neither the Supreme Court nor the chief justiceship would amount to anything. Yet, a little over a century later, President WILLIAM HOWARD TAFT stated that he would prefer the office to his own. During that intervening century, an office of considerable power and prestige had emerged from the constitutional vacuum. Since then, the Chief Justice's role has continued to evolve. Today, the office is the product of both the personalities and the priorities of its incumbents and of the institutional forces which have become stronger as the Supreme Court's role in our government has expanded and matured.

Like the other Justices of the Supreme Court, the Chief Justice of the United States is appointed by the President with the ADVICE AND CONSENT of the Senate. He enjoys, along with all other full members of the federal judiciary, life tenure "during his GOOD BEHAVIOR." With respect to the judicial work of the Court, he has traditionally been referred to as *primus inter pares*—first among equals. He has the same vote as each Associate Justice of the Court. His judicial duties differ only in that he presides over the sessions of the Court and over the Court's private CONFERENCE at which the cases are discussed and eventually decided. When in the majority, he assigns the writing of the OPINION OF THE COURT. Like an Associate Justice, the Chief Justice also performs the duties of a circuit Justice. A circuit Justice must pass upon various applications for temporary relief and BAIL from his circuit and participate, at least in a liaison or advisory capacity, in the judicial administration of that circuit. By tradition, the Chief Justice is circuit Justice for the Fourth and District of Columbia Circuits.

In addition to his judicial duties, the Chief Justice has, by statute, responsibility for the general administration of the Supreme Court. While the senior officers of the Court are appointed by the entire Court, they perform their daily duties under his general supervision. Other employees of the Court must be approved by the Chief Justice.

The Chief Justice also serves as presiding officer of the JUDICIAL CONFERENCE OF THE UNITED STATES. The Conference, composed of the chief judge and a district judge from each circuit, has the statutory responsibility for making comprehensive surveys of the business of the federal courts and for undertaking a continuous study of the rules of practice and procedure. The Chief Justice, as presiding officer, must appoint the various committees of the Conference which undertake the studies necessary for the achievement of those statutory objectives. He must also submit to the Congress an annual report of the proceedings of the Conference and a report as to its legislative recommendations. Other areas of court administration also occupy the Chief Justice's attention regularly. He has the authority to assign, temporarily, judges of the lower federal courts to courts other than their own and for service on the Panel on Multidistrict Litigation. He is also the permanent Chairman of the Board of the Federal Judicial Center which develops and recommends improvements in the area of judicial administration to the Judicial Conference.

From time to time, Congress has also assigned by statute other duties to the Chief Justice. Some are related to the judiciary; others are not. For instance, he must appoint some of the members of the Commission on Executive, Legislative, and Judicial Salaries; the Advisory Corrections Council; the Federal Records Council; and the National Study Commission on Records and Documents of Federal Officials. He also serves as Chancellor of the Smithsonian Institution and as a member of the Board of Trustees of both the National Gallery of Art and the Joseph H. Hirshhorn Museum and Sculpture Garden.

In addition to these formal duties, the Chief Justice is considered the titular head of the legal profession in the United States. He traditionally addresses the American Bar Association on the state of the judiciary and delivers the opening address at the annual meeting of the American Law Institute. He is regularly invited to other ceremonial and substantive meetings of the bar. Finally, as head of the judicial branch, he regularly participates in national observances and state ceremonies honoring foreign dignitaries.

The foregoing catalog of duties, while describing a burdensome role, does not fully indicate the impact of the Chief Justice on the Supreme Court's work. For instance, with respect to his judicial duties, the Chief Justice, while nominally only "first among equals," may exercise a significant influence on the Court's decision-making process and, consequently, on its final judicial work product. His most obvious opportunity to influence that process is while presiding at the Court's conference. He presents each case initially and is the first to give his views. Thus, he has the opportunity to take the initiative by directing the Court's inquiry to those aspects of the case he believes are crucial. Moreover, although the Justices discuss cases in descending order of seniority, they vote in the opposite order. Therefore, while speaking first, the "Chief," as he is referred to by his colleagues, votes last and commits himself, even preliminarily, only after all of the associates have explained their positions and cast their votes. If he votes with the majority, he may retain the opinion for himself or assign it to a colleague whose views are most compatible with his own. In cases where there is significant indecision among the Justices, it falls to the "Chief" to take the initiative with respect to the Court's further consideration of the case. He may, for instance, suggest that further discussion be deferred until argument of other related cases or he may request that several Justices set forth their views in writing in the hope that such a memorandum might form the basis of a later opinion.

There are also more indirect but highly significant ways by which the "Chief" can influence the decision-making process. As presiding officer during open session, he sets a "tone" which can make ORAL ARGUMENT either a formal, stilted affair or a disciplined but relaxed, productive dialogue between the Court and counsel. Even the Chief Justice's "administrative" duties within the Court can have a subtle influence on the Court's decision-making processes. The efficient administration of the Court's support services as well as the employment of adequate staff personnel can nurture an ambiance conducive to harmonious decision making.

While occupancy of the Court's center chair no doubt gives the incumbent an enhanced capacity to influence jurisprudential developments, there are clear limitations on the exercise of that power. The Court is a collegial institution; disagreement on important issues is a natural phenomenon. In such a context, as Justice WILLIAM H. REHNQUIST put it in a 1976 article: "The power to calm such naturally troubled waters is usually beyond the capacity of any mortal chief justice. He presides over a conference not of eight subordinates, whom he may direct or instruct, but of eight associates who, like him, have tenure during good behavior, and who are as independent as hogs on ice. He may at most persuade or cajole them." Political acumen is often as important as intellectual brilliance. Whatever the Chief's view of his power, he must remember that, in the eyes of the associates, "the Chief Justice is not entitled to a presumption that he knows more law than other members of the Court . . . ," as Justice Rehnquist said in chambers in *Clements v. Logan* (1981). Other institutional concerns further constrain the Chief's ability to guide the Court's decisions. All Chief Justices have recognized, although to varying degrees, a responsibility to see not only that the Court gets its business done but also that it does so in a manner which maintains the country's confidence. Sometimes, those objectives require that the Chief refrain from taking a strong ideological stance and act as a mediator in the formation of a majority. Similarly, while the assignment power can be a powerful tool, it must be exercised to ensure a majority opinion that advances, not retards, growth in the law. Even the prerogative of presiding over the conference has a price. The Chief Justice must spend significant additional time reviewing all the petitions filed with the Court. As the performance of Chief Justice CHARLES EVANS HUGHES demonstrated, perceiving those areas of ambiguity and conflict that are most troublesome in the administration of justice is essential to leading effectively the discussion of the conference. For the same reason, the Chief must take the time to master the intricacies of the Court's procedure.

The extrajudicial responsibilities of the Chief Justice can also place him at a distinct disadvantage in influencing the Court's jurisprudential direction. The internal decision-making process of the Court is essentially competitive. There is nothing so humble as a draft opinion with four votes and nothing so arrogant as one with six. Such a process does not easily take into account that one participant must regularly divert his attention because of other official responsibilities. Moreover, there is a special intellectual and physical cost in shifting constantly between the abstract world of the appellate judge and the pragmatic one of the administrator. A Chief Justice who takes all his responsibilities seriously must experience the fatiguing tension that inevitably results from such bifurcation of responsibilities. Here, however, there may be compensating considerations. Whatever advantage the Chief may lose in the judicial bargaining because of administrative distractions may well be partially recovered by the prestige gained by his accomplishments beyond the Court. The Court has benefited from a strong Chief Justice's defense against specific political threats such as President FRANKLIN D. ROOSEVELT's Court-packing plan. It has also benefited when the Chief's efforts have resulted in legislation making its own workload more manageable. Chief Justice Taft's support of the JUDICIARY ACT OF 1925, for instance, gave the Court more control over its own docket and, consequently, increased capacity to address, selectively, the most pressing issues. In modern times, the tremors of the litigation explosion that has engulfed the lower courts have been felt on the Supreme Court. The accomplishments of a Chief Justice in alleviating these problems cannot be overlooked by his associates.

Certainly, with respect to nonjudicial matters, a Chief Justice's special responsibility for institutional concerns has commanded respect from the associates. Even such greats as Justice LOUIS D. BRANDEIS regularly consulted the Chief on matters that might have an impact on the reputation of the Court as an institution. This same identification of the Chief Justice with the Supreme Court as an institution has made some Chief Justices the acknowledged spokesperson for both the Supreme Court and the lower federal courts before the other branches of government and, indeed, before the public.

With no specific constitutional mandate to fulfill, early Chief Justices, most especially JOHN MARSHALL, molded the office in which they served just as they molded the courts over which they presided. In those formative periods, the dominance of personal factors was understandable. Today, however, significant institutional forces also shape the office. In addition to the extrajudicial duties imposed by Congress, the Court, now a mature institution of American government, exerts through its traditions a powerful influence over every new incumbent of its bench—including the person in the center chair.

KENNETH F. RIPPLE
(1986)

Bibliography

FRANKFURTER, FELIX 1953 Chief Justices I Have Known. *Virginia Law Review* 39:883–905.
FREUND, PAUL A. 1967 Charles Evans Hughes as Chief Justice. *Harvard Law Review* 81:4–43.
REHNQUIST, WILLIAM H. 1976 Chief Justices I Never Knew. *Hastings Constitutional Law Quarterly* 3:637–655.
SWINDLER, WILLIAM F. 1971 The Chief Justice and Law Reform. *The Supreme Court Review* 1971:241–264.

CHILD BENEFIT THEORY

Protagonists of aid to religious schools have sought to justify the practice constitutionally through what has become known as the child benefit theory. The establishment clause, they urge, forbids aid to the schools but not to the children who attend them. Recognizing that the schools themselves benefit from the action, they argue that the benefit is secondary to that received by the pupils, and note that the courts have long upheld governmental assistance to children as an aspect of the POLICE POWER.

The recognition is at least implicit in Supreme Court decisions through BOARD OF EDUCATION V. ALLEN (1968). Thus, in *Bradfield v. Roberts* (1899), the Court upheld the validity under the establishment clause of a grant of federal funds to finance the erection of a hospital in the DISTRICT OF COLUMBIA, to be maintained and operated by an order of nuns. The Court reasoned that the hospital corporation was a legal entity separate from its incorporators, and concluded that the aid was for a secular purpose.

Later court decisions ignored this fiction, consistently upholding grants to religious organizations, corporate or noncorporate, to finance hospitals that, though owned and operated by churches, nevertheless were nonsectarian in their admission policies, and generally benefited the patients.

In EVERSON V. BOARD OF EDUCATION (1947) the Court upheld use of tax-raised funds to finance transportation to religious schools, in part because the program had the secular purpose to enable children to avoid the risks of traffic or hitchhiking in going to school. In COCHRAN V. LOUISIANA STATE BOARD OF EDUCATION (1930) and *Board of Education v. Allen* (1968) the Court similarly sustained laws financing the purchase of secular textbooks for use in parochial schools. The beneficiaries of the laws, the Court asserted, were not the schools but the children who attended them.

More recent decisions, however, manifest a weakening of the theory. In *Board of Education v. Nyquist* (1973) the Court refused to uphold a law to finance costs of maintenance and repair in religious schools, notwithstanding a provision that the program's purpose was to insure the health, welfare, and safety of the school children.

Two years later, in *Meek v. Pittenger,* the Court refused to extend *Allen* to encompass the loan of instructional materials to church-related schools, even though the materials benefited nonpublic school children and were provided for public school children. Finally, in WOLMAN V. WALTER (1977) the Court, unwilling to overrule either *Everson* or *Allen*, nevertheless refused to extend them to encompass educational field trip transportation to governmental, industrial, cultural, and scientific centers.

In these later cases, the Court has rejected the argument that if public funds were not used for these support services, many parents economically unable to pay for them would have to transfer their children to the public schools in violation of their own and of their children's religious conscience.

LEO PFEFFER
(1986)

(SEE ALSO: *Establishment of Religion; Separation of Church and State.*)

Bibliography

DRINAN, ROBERT F., S. J. 1963 *Religion, the Courts, and Public Policy.* Chap. 5. New York: McGraw-Hill.
PFEFFER, LEO 1967 *Church, State and Freedom,* rev. ed. Chap. 14. Boston: Beacon Press.

CHILD LABOR AMENDMENT

Two years after BAILEY V. DREXEL FURNITURE CO. (1922) when for the second time the Supreme Court invalidated a federal child labor law, Congress approved a constitutional amendment empowering it to regulate on the subject. But from 1924 until 1938, the amendment languished in state legislatures, with only twenty-eight of the requisite thirty-six having ratified it by 1938.

Led by the National Association of Manufacturers, critics contended that the proposed amendment endangered traditional state powers and local control of PRODUCTION. The Granges also lobbied in agricultural states in the South and Midwest, arguing that such congressional power would threaten the use of children on family farms. Religious groups maintained that the amendment would lead to federal control of education and increase the costs of educating children. Newspapers overwhelmingly opposed the amendment on the grounds that they would be deprived of delivery boys.

The Court's decision in the WAGNER ACT CASES (1937) renewed interest in congressional legislation. The FAIR LABOR STANDARDS ACT in 1938 outlawed child labor, and in UNITED STATES V. DARBY (1941), the Court sustained the legislation and overturned its own precedents. The new law and the *Darby* decision combined to make the amendment unnecessary.

The lengthy ratification process prompted Congress to impose time limits on many subsequent amendments. The child labor amendment also raised a knotty constitutional problem when one state reversed its position (in a disputed vote) and approved ratification. That action was challenged in COLEMAN V. MILLER (1939), but the Court sidestepped the issue as a POLITICAL QUESTION and left its resolution to Congress.

STANLEY I. KUTLER
(1986)

Bibliography

WOOD, STEPHEN 1968 *Constitutional Politics in the Progressive Era: Child Labor and the Law.* Chicago: University of Chicago Press.

CHILD LABOR CASE

See: *Hammer v. Dagenhart*

CHILD LABOR TAX ACT
40 Stat. 1138 (1918)

In HAMMER V. DAGENHART (1918), a 5–4 Supreme Court voided the Child Labor Act of 1916, which had forbidden carriers from transporting the products of child labor in INTERSTATE COMMERCE, as a prohibition, not a regulation, of commerce. This distinction had been thought rejected as early as CHAMPION V. AMES (1903). Progressive reformers, intent on abolishing child labor, had shifted the basis of their efforts from the COMMERCE CLAUSE to the TAXING POWER, thus invoking a new set of powerful precedents, notably MCCRAY V. UNITED STATES (1904).

In late 1918 Congress passed a Revenue Act to which had been added an amendment known as the Child Labor Tax Act. A ten percent EXCISE TAX was imposed on the net profits from the sale of child labor-produced items. This tax extended to any factory, mine, or mill employing children under fourteen, or to the age of sixteen under certain circumstances. Congressmen from the major cotton textile manufacturing states, southern Democrats, cast nearly all the negative votes.

In BAILEY V. DREXEL FURNITURE CO. (1922) an 8–1 Court invalidated the act, *McCray* and UNITED STATES V. DOREMUS (1919) notwithstanding, as a violation of the powers reserved to the states by the TENTH AMENDMENT.

DAVID GORDON
(1986)

Bibliography

WOOD, STEPHEN B. 1968 *Constitutional Politics in the Progressive Era: Child Labor and the Law.* Chicago: University of Chicago Press.

CHILD LABOR TAX CASE

See: *Bailey v. Drexel Furniture Co.*

CHILD PORNOGRAPHY

Every year, thousands of children are compelled to engage in pornographic acts for the production of films and photographs. Child pornography is one of the most insidious forms of child abuse because the victimization does not stop with the physical acts of abuse. In the words of Justice BYRON R. WHITE, "the pornography's continued existence causes the child victims continuing harm by haunting the children in years to come." Because child pornography is child abuse, the Supreme Court has held that it is not protected by the FIRST AMENDMENT. In NEW YORK V. FERBER (1982) the Court ruled that the production and distribution of child pornography can be prosecuted even if the material does not meet the legal test for OBSCENITY because, even if it is not legally obscene, it is still the product of child abuse and, hence, a proper object of state regulation.

In *Osborne v. Ohio* (1990) the Court extended the doctrine of *Ferber* to cover the private possession of child pornography. Ohio prosecuted Osborne for possessing child pornography in violation of a state statute. Osborne

contended that the First Amendment prohibited the state from proscribing private possession, but the Supreme Court disagreed by a vote of 6–3. (Osborne's conviction was nevertheless overturned on procedural grounds.) The Court noted that much of the production and sale of child pornography has gone underground and is therefore difficult to prosecute. The only effective way to stop the child abuse by pornographers is by banning possession of the material outright.

Writing for the dissenters, Justice WILLIAM J. BRENNAN argued that the Ohio statute suffered from OVERBREADTH because of its loose definition of what constituted child pornography. Even if the statute had not been overbroad, however, Brennan would have invalidated it. Recalling the words of STANLEY V. GEORGIA (1969), Brennan said that "if the First Amendment means anything, it means that the State has no business telling a man, sitting alone in his own house, what book he may read or what films he may watch."

Brennan's analysis was inapposite to the case at hand, however. No adult has the right to compel a child to appear in a pornographic film or photo; hence, it stretches the imagination to claim that someone else has the right to possess (and derive pleasure from) what the pornographer had no right to produce in the first place. Laws against the possession of child pornography not only help to stop the abuse of children through the production of the pornography; they also protect the child victims' right to privacy after the unlawful photographs or films have been produced.

JOHN G. WEST, JR.
(1992)

Bibliography

ATTORNEY GENERAL'S COMMISSION ON PORNOGRAPHY 1981 *Attorney General's Commission on Pornography, Final Report,* part II, chapter 7. Washington, D.C.: U.S. Government Printing Office.

CHILDREN AND THE FIRST AMENDMENT

Because many conceptions of the FIRST AMENDMENT's protection of speech and press are premised on a model of human rationality and human choice and because traditional views about children take them to be incapable of having the rationality and exercising the capacity of choice assumed for adults, issues about the free speech rights of children have always been problematic. Indeed, the need to protect children from harmful ideas they may be incapable of evaluating has been explicitly a part of the free speech tradition since JOHN STUART MILL's *On Liberty.*

Treating minors as different for free speech purposes has been a recurring feature of OBSCENITY law. Although the Supreme Court reaffirmed in *Pinkus v. United States* (1978) that it is impermissible to judge the obscenity of material directed primarily to adults on the basis of its possible effect on children, the Court has also held in *Ginsberg v. New York* (1968) that where sexually explicit material is directed at juvenile readers or viewers it is permissible to apply the test for obscenity in light of a juvenile rather than an adult audience. In addition, the Court in NEW YORK V. FERBER (1982) relied on the importance of protecting juvenile performers in allowing CHILD PORNOGRAPHY prosecution for the distribution of material not legally obscene, although it is clear that analogous justifications for restrictions on publications remain impermissible with respect to adult participants. Still, the Court has been sensitive to the likely overuse of children-protecting rationales for restricting speech, and although in FEDERAL COMMUNICATIONS COMMISSION V. PACIFICA FOUNDATION (1978) it relied on a protection of children rationale in upholding restrictions on the times during which sexually explicit or offensive radio programs might be broadcast, in *Sable Communications of California, Inc. v. FCC* (1989) it unanimously struck down a federal law restricting "indecent" telephone communications because of an insufficient showing that a restriction of this magnitude was necessary to protect children. *Sable* thus continued a tradition going back at least to BUTLER V. MICHIGAN (1957), in which Justice FELIX FRANKFURTER made clear that a law reducing the adult population to reading only what was fit for children would be an impermissible encroachment on First Amendment freedoms.

More commonly, the issue has arisen in the context of restrictions on speech in the public schools. Although it is so obvious as never to have generated a Supreme Court case that children as speakers in the PUBLIC FORUM or other open environment have the same free speech rights as adults, the question is more complicated with reference to speech within the confines of the public schools. In upholding a student's right to wear a protest armband even in class, the Supreme Court in TINKER V. DES MOINES INDEPENDENT COMMUNITY SCHOOL DISTRICT (1969) observed that "[n]either students [n]or teachers shed their constitutional rights to freedom of speech or expression at the schoolhouse gate" and proceeded to hold content-based restrictions on student speech in the schools invalid unless supported by evidence of actual or potential "disturbance," "disruption," or "disorder."

Both the language in *Tinker* and its "disturbance" standard proved difficult to square, however, with the fact that much of the mission of the schools involves controls on communication, of which the most obvious is the hardly unconstitutional practice of rewarding certain answers and penalizing others. As a result, subsequent cases, themselves frequently criticized as too much of a departure from *Tinker* and too easy an acquiescence to teacher or administrator authority, have tempered the *Tinker* approach. In BETHEL SCHOOL DISTRICT V. FRASER (1986) the Court upheld disciplinary action against a high-school student who had made a sexually suggestive, but plainly not legally obscene, speech in a school assembly, and in HAZELWOOD SCHOOL DISTRICT V. KUHLMEIER (1988), the Court allowed the school to exercise content-based control over a school-sponsored student newspaper produced on school property with school resources, the writing and editing of which was part of a journalism course offered by the school. More significantly, *Hazelwood* explicitly substituted a seemingly more lenient "reasonableness" standard for the *Tinker* "disturbance" standard, although it remains too early to assess the actual import of the new approach. It does seem clear that the recent cases represent a willingness to defer to decisions of school authorities more than has been the case in the past and a consequent willingness to allow school authorities at the primary and secondary level to choose to have an "indoctrination" rather than a "market place of ideas" model as the major purpose of primary and secondary education. Thus, the recent trend will likely result in little judicial review of content-based restrictions on student speech within the primary and secondary schools. But the Court's unwillingness to overrule *Tinker*, combined with decisions like BOARD OF EDUCATION V. PICO (1982), dealing (unclearly) with political censorship of school libraries, indicates that judicial intervention remains appropriate where the content-based restrictions are excessively viewpoint based or where they stem not from the decisions of primary professionals such as teachers and principals, but rather from the selective involvement of more political and less professional elected officials.

FREDERICK SCHAUER
(1992)

Bibliography

GARVEY, JOHN   1979   Children and the First Amendment. *Texas Law Review* 57:321–366.
———   1981   Freedom and Choice in Constitutional Law. *Harvard Law Review* 94:1756–1794.
YUDOF, MARK G.   1984   Library Book Selection and the Public Schools: The Quest for the Archimedean Point. *Indiana Law Journal* 59:527–564.

CHILDREN'S RIGHTS

The law of childhood is complex, but as a general legal proposition, a child is someone who has not yet reached the age of civil majority. Each state has the authority to determine the age of majority for its own residents, and in most states that age is now eighteen. Prior to 1971, the age of majority was typically twenty-one, but after the ratification of the TWENTY-SIXTH AMENDMENT, which gave eighteen-year-olds the right to vote in federal elections, most states lowered the age of majority, as well as the voting age for state elections.

In general, children have less liberty than adults and are less often held accountable for their actions. Parents have legal power to make a wide range of decisions for the child, although they are held responsible by the state for the child's care and support. Children have a special power to avoid contractual obligations but are not normally entitled to their own earnings and cannot manage their own property. Moreover, persons younger than certain statutory limits are not allowed to vote, hold public office, work in various occupations, drive a car, buy liquor, or be sold certain kinds of reading material, quite apart from what either they or their parents may wish.

Although a variety of civic and personal rights accrue at the age of majority, rights to engage in various "adult" activities may occur either before or after the age of eighteen. For example, many states restrict the legal access of nineteen- and twenty-year-olds to alcoholic beverages. On the other hand, most states permit sixteen- and seventeen-year-olds to secure licenses to drive automobiles. State child labor laws typically permit young people who are sixteen or seventeen to work, particularly outside of school hours, although federal law prohibits the employment of children under eighteen in hazardous occupations. A minor who is self-supporting and living away from home may, through emancipation, obtain a broad range of adult rights.

When advocates speak of children's rights, they may have in mind either of two quite contradictory notions. One notion focuses on children's basic needs, and the obligations to satisfy those needs. The other focuses on autonomy and choice.

At times, the word "right" is used to describe the duties of others—typically parents or state officials—to satisfy what are seen as a child's basic needs. Thus, claims are made that a child has or should have a legal right to education, adequate food and shelter, and even love, affection, discipline, and guidance. The federal Constitution has not been interpreted to give a child a substantive right to adequate education or care, although state law sometimes creates such duties. For example, every state provides for free public education, typically through high school, and many state constitutions require as much. Although the Supreme Court decided in SAN ANTONIO INDEPENDENT SCHOOL DISTRICT V. RODRIGUEZ (1973) that education is not a "fundamental" right, at least for purposes of requiring

strict scrutiny under the EQUAL PROTECTION clause, the Court acknowledged in BROWN V. BOARD OF EDUCATION (1954) that education is "perhaps the most important function of state and local governments." There is no constitutional right to parental love, but opinions such as PIERCE V. SOCIETY OF SISTERS (1925) have suggested that children as well as parents have an interest of constitutional dimension in preserving the parent-child relationship. State child-neglect statutes do impose on parents an obligation to provide adequate custodial care. In all events, a child's "right" to such things as an education or minimally adequate care has little to do with the protection of choice on the part of a particular child. A judge usually does not ask a physically abused child whether she wants to remain with her parents when the responsible authorities believe they cannot protect her from further harm if she remains at home. Compulsory education laws and child labor laws do not give an unhappy eleven-year-old child the legal right to pursue an education by dropping out of school and taking a job.

A second, very different, notion of "children's rights" emphasizes autonomy, choice, and liberty. Claims asserting this sort of right have arisen in a variety of contexts: procedural claims in JUVENILE PROCEEDINGS and in schools (see GOSS V. LOPEZ); choices about abortion or BIRTH CONTROL; access to reading material (see GINSBERG V. NEW YORK); and involvement in political protests (see TINKER V. DES MOINES SCHOOL DISTRICT). Usually the challenge is to some form of state paternalism; but sometimes the minor's claim involves the assertion that he should have the "right" to act independently of his parents. Because the liberty of minors is much more restricted than that of adults, reformers have sometimes asserted that adolescents should have the right to adult status, at least in particular settings. A few have even suggested a children's liberation movement to end the double standard of morals and behavior for adults and children.

The definition of "children's rights" necessarily involves the allocation of power and responsibility among the child, the family, and the state. Taking contemporary constitutional doctrine at face value, three basic principles bear on this allocation. The first principle concerns the children themselves, and the notion that as individuals they have constitutional rights. The Supreme Court declared in IN RE GAULT (1967), the seminal children's rights case, "whatever may be their precise impact, neither the FOURTEENTH AMENDMENT nor the BILL OF RIGHTS is for adults alone."

The second principle concerns parents and the notion that parents have primary authority over the child. Children are part of families, and our traditions emphasize the primacy of the parental role in child-rearing. The rights of children cannot be defined without reference to their parents. The Court has suggested that parental authority also has a constitutional dimension: the state may not intrude too deeply into the parent-child relationship. Drawing on this principle, the Court held in WISCONSIN V. YODER (1972) that Wisconsin could not compel children to attend public schools when their old-order Amish parents believed that public schooling interfered with their raising of their children as their religion dictates. Nor may a state require all children to attend public school when there are private schools that meet legitimate regulatory standards.

The third principle concerns the state. It suggests that the state, in the exercise of its *parens patriae* power, has a special responsibility to protect children, even from their parents. The state's interest in protecting children has frequently been characterized as "compelling" and has been drawn on to justify a variety of child protective measures that constrain the liberty of parents and children alike. "Parents may be free," declared the Supreme Court in PRINCE V. MASSACHUSETTS (1944), "to become martyrs themselves. But it does not follow that they are free, under free and identical circumstances, to make martyrs of their children before they reach the age of full and legal discretion when they can make that choice for themselves."

Any one of these three principles, if taken very far, cuts deeply into the others. For example, to the extent that children, as individuals, are given autonomy rights, limits are necessarily imposed on parental rights to control their behavior or socialization. Recognition of child autonomy also limits the state's right to constrain a child's conduct in circumstances where adult conduct could not be similarly constrained. Some rights of child autonomy would disable the state from having special protective legislation for children. Broad interpretation of the state's *parens patriae* power to intervene to protect children necessarily will diminish both the parental role in child-rearing and the child's role in decision making. Similarly, an expansive interpretation of parents' rights to control and govern their children necessarily limits the state's ability to protect children, or to ensure child autonomy.

The Supreme Court's decisions concerning children's rights evidence these tensions. For example, the *Tinker* decision, emphasizing child autonomy, declared that children have First Amendment rights to engage in peaceful political protest within the schools. On the other hand, the *Ginsberg* decision, emphasizing state protection of children, determined that the state could criminally punish the sale to minors of sexually explicit materials that an adult would have a constitutional right to receive. (See OBSCENITY.) In its decisions concerning juvenile delinquency proceedings, the Court has extended a broad range of procedural rights to minors, and yet also determined that a juvenile court need not provide an accused young person with TRIAL BY JURY. In PARHAM V. J. R. (1979) the Court held that due process does not require a hearing before the commitment of a minor by a parent to a state mental hospital. Similarly, although the *Pierce* and *Yoder* opinions emphasized the primacy of the parental role in child-rearing, *Prince*, in enforcing a child labor law, emphasized the state's *parens patriae* obligation to protect children.

The Supreme Court's decisions involving the abortion rights of minors suggest that a state may not give parents an absolute "veto" over a pregnant minor's decision to have an abortion (PLANNED PARENTHOOD OF CENTRAL MISSOURI V. DANFORTH, 1976), but may require parental notification, at least for younger pregnant teenagers still living at home (*H. L. v. Matheson*, 1981). And in *Planned Parenthood v. Ashcroft* (1983) the Court upheld a state law requiring either parental or judicial consent to a minor's abortion; under the law the court must approve the abortion if the minor is sufficiently mature to make the abortion decision, or, alternatively, if the abortion is in the minor's best interests.

In sum, the Constitution has not been interpreted to prohibit the state from treating children differently from adults. Because children often lack adult capacity and maturity and need protection, and because of the special relationship of children to their families, giving children the same rights and obligations as adults would often do them a substantial disservice. To assume adult roles, children need to be socialized. The Constitution does not prohibit the use of state or parental coercion in this task of socialization. But, because ours is a society where adults are socialized for autonomous choice, there are necessarily some limits, even for children. In determining the contour of children's constitutional rights, then, the Supreme Court appears to be seeking to recognize the moral autonomy of children as individuals without abandoning children to their rights.

ROBERT H. MNOOKIN
(1986)

Bibliography

HAFEN, BRUCE C. 1976 Children's Liberation and the New Egalitarianism: Some Reservations about Abandoning Youth to Their "Rights." *Brigham Young University Law Review* 1976:605–658.

MNOOKIN, ROBERT H. 1978 *Child, Family and State*. Boston: Little, Brown.

———, ed. 1985 *In the Interest of Children*. New York: W. H. Freeman & Co.

TEITELBAUM, LEE E. 1980 Foreword: The Meaning of Rights of Children. *New Mexico Law Review* 10:235–253.

WALD, MICHAEL S. 1979 Children's Rights: A Framework for Analysis. *University of California, Davis, Law Review* 12: 255–282.

YOUTH LAW CENTER 1982 Legal Rights of Children in the

United States of America. *Columbia Human Rights Law Review* 13:675–743.

CHILD SUPPORT RECOVERY ACT
106 Stat. 3403 (1992)

The Child Support Recovery Act (CSRA) provides that anyone who willfully fails to pay "past due support" for a child living in another state may be fined or imprisoned. "Past due support" means court-ordered obligations that either have been unpaid for more than a year or exceed $5,000. Congress enacted the CSRA to assist the efforts of states to collect unpaid child support. Congress estimated that the gap between the child support owed and that actually paid was approximately $5 billion annually. It also expressed concern that this deficit contributes to the increase in the cost of federal welfare assistance, much of which goes to single-parent families.

The constitutionality of the act has been questioned since its passage in 1992. Several federal district courts held that the CSRA exceeded the authority of Congress under the COMMERCE CLAUSE, relying heavily on the Supreme Court's decision in UNITED STATES V. LÓPEZ (1995). By mid-1998, however, every federal court of appeals that had reviewed the act had held it constitutional. Although the states have traditionally regulated domestic relationships, the courts have characterized the CSRA either as a regulation of debts owed in INTERSTATE COMMERCE or as regulation of an activity that substantially affects interstate commerce. Moreover, the CSRA only applies to child support obligations owed by a parent for a dependent child residing in a different state. The courts have also rejected arguments based on the TENTH AMENDMENT and NEW YORK V. UNITED STATES (1992) because the act does not direct state officials to do anything. The CSRA does not interfere with state child support determinations; rather, it is an attempt to enforce those state-determined obligations when the obligations take on an interstate character.

JAY S. BYBEE
(2000)

(SEE ALSO: *Federalism.*)

Bibliography

BURDETTE, KATHLEEN A. 1996 Making Parents Pay: Interstate Child Support Enforcement After *United States v. López. University of Pennsylvania Law Review* 144:1469–1528.

CALHOUN, JANELLE T. 1995 Interstate Child Support Enforcement System: Juggernaut of Bureaucracy. *Mercer Law Review* 46:921–976.

SIFF, ANDREW M. 1997 *United States v. López* and the Child Support Recovery Act of 1992: Why a Nice Idea Must Be

Declared A Casualty of the Struggle to Save Federalism. *Cornell Journal of Law and Public Policy* 6:753–813.

CHILD WITNESSES

See: *Coy v. Iowa; Maryland v. Craig*

CHILLING EFFECT

Law is carried forward on a stream of language. Metaphor not only reflects the growth of constitutional law but nourishes it as well. Since the 1960s, when the WARREN COURT widened the domain of the FIRST AMENDMENT, Justices have frequently remarked on laws' "chilling effects" on the FREEDOM OF SPEECH. A statute tainted by VAGUENESS or OVERBREADTH, for example, restricts the freedom of expression not only by directly subjecting people to the laws' sanctions but also by threatening others. Because the very existence of such a law may induce self-censorship when the reach of the law is uncertain, the law may be held INVALID ON ITS FACE. The assumed causal connection between vague legislation and self-censorship was made by the Supreme Court as early as HERNDON V. LOWRY (1937); half a century later, circulating the coinage of Justice FELIX FRANKFURTER, lawyers and judges express similar assumptions in the language of chilling effects.

The assumption plainly makes more sense in some cases than it does in others. For a law's uncertainty actually to chill speech, the would-be speaker must be conscious of the uncertainty. Yet few of us go about our day-to-day business with the statute book in hand. A statute forbidding insulting language may be vague, but its uncertainty is unlikely to have any actual chilling effect on speech in face-to-face street encounters. Yet a court striking that law down—even in application to one whose insults fit the Supreme Court's narrow definition of FIGHTING WORDS— is apt to speak of the law's chilling effects.

For chilling effects that are real rather than assumed, we must look to institutional speakers—publishers, broadcasters, advertisers, political parties, groups promoting causes—who regularly inquire into the letter of the law and its interpretation by the courts. Magazine editors, for example, routinely seek legal counsel about defamation. Here the uncertainty of the law's reach does not lie in any statutory language, for the law of libel and slander is largely the product of COMMON LAW judges. It was a concern for chilling effects, however, that led three concurring Justices in NEW YORK TIMES V. SULLIVAN (1964) to advocate an absolute rule protecting the press against damages for the libel of a public official. The majority's principle in the case, which would allow damages when a newspaper defames an official knowing that its statement is false, or in reckless disregard of its truth or falsity, may, indeed, chill the press. Even slight doubt about information may make an editor hesitate to publish it, for fear that it may turn out to be false—and that a jury years later will decide it was published recklessly. The concern is not to protect false information, but that doubtful editors will play it safe, suppressing information that is true.

Conversely, when the Justices are persuaded that the law's threat will not have the effect of chilling speech, they are disinclined to use the overbreadth doctrine. A prominent modern example is the treatment of COMMERCIAL SPEECH. Because advertising is profitable, and advertisers seem unlikely to be chilled by laws regulating advertising, such laws are not subject to challenge for overbreadth.

The worry, when a court discusses chilling effects, is that a law's uncertainty will cause potential speakers to censor themselves. Thus, an overly broad law is subject to constitutional challenge even by one whose own speech would be punishable under a law focused narrowly on speech lying outside First Amendment protection. The defendant in court stands as a surrogate for others whose speech would be constitutionally protected—but who have been afraid to speak, and thus have not been prosecuted, and cannot themselves challenge the law. Whether or not this technique amounts to a dilution of the jurisdictional requirements of STANDING or RIPENESS, it allows courts to defend against the chilling effects of unconstitutional statutes that would otherwise elude their scrutiny.

KENNETH L. KARST
(1986)

Bibliography

AMSTERDAM, ANTHONY G. 1960 The Void-for-Vagueness Doctrine in the Supreme Court. *University of Pennsylvania Law Review* 109:67–116.
NOTE 1970 The First Amendment Overbreadth Doctrine. *Harvard Law Review* 83:844–927.
SCHAUER, FREDERICK 1978 Fear, Risk and the First Amendment: Unraveling the "Chilling Effect." *Boston University Law Review* 5:685–732.

CHIMEL v. CALIFORNIA
395 U.S. 752 (1969)

In *Chimel* the Supreme Court considerably narrowed the prevailing scope of SEARCH INCIDENT TO ARREST, by limiting the search to the person of the arrestee and his immediate environs. The Court thus ended a divisive, decades-long debate on the subject.

The principle that officers executing a valid arrest may simultaneously search the arrestee for concealed weapons or EVIDENCE has never been challenged; it is rooted in COMMON LAW, and was recognized by the Court in WEEKS V. UNITED STATES (1914) as an emergency exception to the FOURTH AMENDMENT's warrant requirement. That the search may extend beyond the person to the premises in which the arrest is made was recognized in AGNELLO V. UNITED STATES (1925). The extension, too, has never been challenged; it seems sensible to permit officers to eliminate the possibility of a suspect's seizing a gun or destroying evidence within his reach though not on his person. The permissible scope of a warrantless search of the premises has, however, embroiled the Court in controversy.

Some Justices would have allowed a search of the entire place, arguing that after an arrest, even an extensive search is only a minor additional invasion of privacy. The opposing camp, led by Justice FELIX FRANKFURTER, condemned such wholesale rummaging: to allow a search incident to arrest to extend beyond the need that justified it would swallow up the rule requiring a search warrant save in EXIGENT CIRCUMSTANCES. The latter view finally prevailed in *Chimel*, when the Court ruled that the search must be limited to the arrestee's person and "the area from which he might gain possession of a weapon or destructible evidence." It may not extend into any room other than the one in which the arrest is made, and even "desk drawers or other closed or concealed areas in that room itself" are off-limits to the officers if the suspect cannot gain access to them.

JACOB W. LANDYNSKI
(1986)

CHINESE EXCLUSION ACT
22 Stat. 58 (1882)

Although Chinese IMMIGRATION to California probably raised both wages and living standards of white laborers, economic, political, and cultural arguments were adduced against the foreigners. Assimilation was said to be impossible: the Chinese were gamblers, opium smokers, and generally inferior. Anti-Chinese feeling became the hub for many political issues, and agitation for legislation increased. Senator John Miller of California contended that failure to enact exclusion would "empty the teeming, seething slave pens of China upon the soil of California." Although most of the nation was indifferent, opposition to exclusion was weak and disorganized; Congress thus passed its first exclusion law in 1882. The act prohibited Chinese laborers from entering the United States for ten years, although resident ALIENS might return after a temporary absence. Nonlaboring Chinese would be admitted only upon presentation of a certificate from the Chinese government attesting their right to come. Other sections provided for deportation of illegal immigrants and prohibited state or federal courts from admitting Chinese to CIT-IZENSHIP. Further exclusion acts or amendments passed Congress—eleven by 1902. The most important of these were the Scott Act of 1888 prohibiting the return of any departing Chinese and the Geary Act of 1892 which extended the 1882 law. (See CHAE CHAN PING V. UNITED STATES.)

DAVID GORDON
(1986)

CHINESE EXCLUSION CASE

See: *Chae Chan Ping v. United States*

CHIPMAN, NATHANIEL
(1752–1843)

Federalist jurist and statesman Nathaniel Chipman was instrumental in securing Vermont's admission to the Union in 1791 as the first state with no history as a separate British colony. An ally and correspondent of ALEXANDER HAMILTON, Chipman was three times chief justice of Vermont and also the first federal judge in the Vermont district. He was professor of law at Middlebury College (1816–1843) and author of *Principles of Government* (1793; revised edition 1833).

DENNIS J. MAHONEY
(1986)

CHISHOLM v. GEORGIA
2 Dallas 419 (1793)

The first constitutional law case decided by the Supreme Court, *Chisholm* provoked opposition so severe that the ELEVENTH AMENDMENT was adopted to supersede its ruling that a state could be sued without its consent by a citizen of another state. Article III of the Constitution extended the JUDICIAL POWER OF THE UNITED STATES to all controversies "between a State and citizens of another State" and provided that the Supreme Court should have ORIGINAL JURISDICTION in all cases in which a state should be a party. During the ratification controversy, anti-Federalists, jealous of state prerogatives and suspicious about the consolidating effects of the proposed union, had warned that Article III would abolish state sovereignty. Ratificationists, including JOHN MARSHALL, JAMES MADISON, and ALEXANDER HAMILTON (e.g., THE FEDERALIST #81) had argued that the clause intended to cover only suits in which a state had given its sovereign consent to being sued or had instituted the suit. Here, however, with Justice JAMES IREDELL alone

dissenting, the Justices in SERIATIM OPINIONS held that the states by ratifying the Constitution had agreed to be amenable to the judicial power of the United States and in that respect had abandoned their SOVEREIGNTY.

The case arose when Chisholm, a South Carolinian executor of the estate of a Tory whose lands Georgia had confiscated during the Revolution, sued Georgia for restitution. The state remonstrated against the Court's taking jurisdiction of the case and refused to argue on the merits. The Justices, confronted by a question of sovereignty, discoursed on the nature of the Union, giving the case historical importance. Iredell, stressing the sovereignty of the states respecting reserved powers, believed that no sovereign state could be sued without its consent unless Congress so authorized. Chief Justice JOHN JAY and Justice JAMES WILSON, delivering the most elaborate opinions against Georgia, announced for the first time from the bench the ultra-nationalistic doctrine that the people of the United States, rather than the states or people thereof, had formed the Union and were the ultimate sovereigns. From this view, the suability of the states was compatible with their reserved sovereignty, and the clause in Article III neither excluded suits by outside citizens nor required state consent.

The decision, which seemed to open the treasuries of the states to suits by Tories and other creditors, stirred widespread indignation that crossed sectional and party lines. A special session of the Massachusetts legislature recommended an amendment that would prevent the states from being answerable in the federal courts to suits by individuals. Virginia, taking the same action, condemned the Court for a decision dangerous to the sovereignty of the states. The Georgia Assembly would have defied the decision by a bill providing that any United States officer attempting to enforce it should "suffer death, without benefit of clergy, by being hanged." Though the state senate did not pass the bill, Georgia remained defiant. Congress too opposed the decision and finally agreed on a remedy for it that took the form of the Eleventh Amendment.

LEONARD W. LEVY
(1986)

Bibliography

MATHIS, DOYLE 1967 *Chisholm v. Georgia*: Background and Settlement. *Journal of American History* 54:19–29.

CHOATE, JOSEPH H.
(1832–1917)

A highly conservative lawyer and leader of the American bar, Joseph Hodges Choate often appeared before the Supreme Court in defense of property interests and removed from the concerns of a populace he inimitably referred to as the "Great Unwashed." In MUGLER V. KANSAS (1887), Choate sought in vain to convince the Court to embrace laissez-faire, but he succeeded in wresting, in OBITER DICTUM, future judicial examination of the reasonableness of exercises of STATE POLICE POWER. Choate unequivocally endorsed constitutional rights in private property, a position the Court would soon partly accept. Indeed, his most famous victory came in POLLOCK V. FARMERS' LOAN & TRUST COMPANY (1895), which he argued with WILLIAM GUTHRIE. Labeling the income tax "communistic" and heaping reactionary invective upon his opponent, JAMES COOLIDGE CARTER, Choate constructed a framework for the Court's decision; he attacked the tax as a DIRECT TAX on income from real property, history and judicial precedent to the contrary.

DAVID GORDON
(1986)

Bibliography

HICKS, FREDERICK C. 1931 Joseph Hodges Choate. *Dictionary of American Biography*, Vol. 4. New York: Scribner's.

CHOICE OF LAW

In the system of American FEDERALISM, some transactions and phenomena are governed by supreme federal law and others by state law. In the latter situations, multistate transactions frequently raise the question which state's law is to be applied. "Choice of law" refers to the process of making this determination. Choice of law may usefully be viewed as an issue of distribution of legislative or lawmaking powers "horizontally" among the states in those areas not governed by overriding federal law.

A basic principle of choice of law theory under the Constitution is that determination of the allocation of lawmaking power among the states in such circumstances is, itself, an issue of state law. Each state has its own law on choice of law, which may differ from the choice of law doctrines of other states and which is applied in actions brought in that state both in state courts and in DIVERSITY JURISDICTION cases in federal courts. Thus the outcome of litigation involving a multistate transaction may in theory be determined by the choice of the forum in which the suit is brought. The basic principle might have been the contrary—that is, that conflicts of state laws within the federal system should be resolved by a comprehensive supreme federal law of choice of law, binding on the states. Such a body of national conflict of laws doctrine might have been derived from the FULL FAITH AND CREDIT clause,

the COMMERCE CLAUSE, or the DUE PROCESS clause of the FOURTEENTH AMENDMENT. Alternatively, supreme federal choice of law doctrine might have been developed as FEDERAL COMMON LAW pertaining to the mutual relationships among the states in the federal union. Or Congress, under various ENUMERATED POWERS, might have enacted federal choice of law principles. None of these courses has been followed; the law of choice of law in the federal system has not developed, judicially or legislatively, as supreme federal law. The states remain the primary determiners of the legal aspects of their mutual relationships within the federal union.

A state's law of choice of law, like all state law, is subject to constitutional limitations. Two such provisions have occasionally been applied so as to limit state choice of law principles, but in general these are not significant limitations.

In an occasional early case the Supreme Court held that the application of the forum's own law to a multistate transaction violated due process, even though the forum state did have a legitimate interest in having its law prevail. Under more recent doctrine there would be no due process violation in such circumstances. The modern principle, enunciated in *Allstate Insurance Co. v. Hague* (1981), is that "for a State's substantive law to be selected in a constitutionally permissible manner, that State must have a significant contact or significant aggregation of contacts, creating state interests, such that choice of its law is neither arbitrary nor fundamentally unfair." The due process clause can also limit a state's choice of law doctrine where there would be unfair surprise to a litigant in the choice of law otherwise proposed to be made.

The Court also has occasionally held that the full faith and credit clause requires a state to apply the law of another state even though the forum state does have a legitimate interest in applying its own law. (Thus in a case of claims for benefits against a fraternal benefit association, the Court held that a national interest in having a single uniform law determine the mutual rights and obligations of members required all states to apply the law of the place where the association was incorporated.) In general, however, the full faith and credit clause does not require that a forum state apply the law of another state unless it would violate due process for the forum to apply its own law.

Other provisions of the Constitution are potentially applicable as limitations on state choice of law doctrine. The commerce clause might be the basis for channeling state choice of law principles regarding multistate commercial transactions. The EQUAL PROTECTION clause and the PRIVILEGES AND IMMUNITIES clause of Article IV might be held to limit distinctions made in state choice of law doctrine based upon the residence or domicile of parties to a transaction. These constitutional provisions have not been so developed.

HAROLD W. HOROWITZ
(1986)

Bibliography

SYMPOSIUM 1981 Choice-of-Law. *UC Davis Law Review* 14: 837–917.
———— 1981 Choice of Law Theory after *Allstate Insurance Co. v. Hague. Hofstra Law Review* 10:1–211.

CHOICE OF LAW AND CONSTITUTIONAL RIGHTS

CHOICE OF LAW (also called conflict of laws or conflicts law) is a body of legal DOCTRINE that seeks to provide a basis for choosing a substantive rule (for example, in tort or contract law) over the conflicting rule of another place. Rules conflict when their applications would produce opposing results in the same case, and when the relation of each place to the controversy makes it plausible for the rule of either place to govern. Conflicts law is usually state COMMON LAW, applied either by state courts or by federal courts in exercise of the latter's DIVERSITY JURISDICTION.

Courts periodically engage in conflicts localism. That is, they choose local state substantive law when the forum state's relation to the controversy is clearly less important than that of the place providing conflicting law. These decisions unfairly damage nonforum litigants, exhibit disrespect to nonforum governments, and undermine principles of order and uniformity in the law. The FULL FAITH AND CREDIT clause, the DUE PROCESS and EQUAL PROTECTION clauses of the FOURTEENTH AMENDMENT, the COMMERCE CLAUSE, and the PRIVILEGES AND IMMUNITIES clause of Article IV could in various ways be read to protect these interests. But the Supreme Court rarely intervenes under the Constitution.

The Court makes serious use of only the first two of the clauses listed above, merging them into a single test. According to *Allstate Ins. Co. v. Hague* (1981), "[F]or a State's substantive law to be selected in a constitutionally permissible manner, that State must have a significant contact or significant aggregation of contacts creating state interests, such that choice of its law is neither arbitrary nor fundamentally unfair."

Applying the *Hague* test in *Phillips Petroleum Co. v. Shutts* (1985), the Court held unconstitutional the attempt of Kansas courts in a nation-wide CLASS ACTION to apply local law to some claims that had no connection with the state. Despite the result, the Court's analysis in *Shutts* reinforced its minimalist view of the Constitution in choice of law. The Court deemed Kansas to have failed the combined full faith and credit and due process test only after concluding that Kansas had no interest in regulating the claims and that application of Kansas law to the claims would disturb the reasonable expectations of the defendant. Not only do state and lower federal courts remain free to apply local substantive law when demonstrating state interest, however modest, in determining the merits of the controversy; they may be free to apply their law even when the state has no such interest, when there is no showing that such would disturb the reasonable expectations of a party.

Commentators have criticized the Court's reluctance to correct conflicts abuse, and they have offered a variety of constitutional theories for more extensive oversight of choice of law. Yet the Court's restraint may be defensible. Constitutional justifications for greater Supreme Court intervention share so fully the mainstream values of choice of law that, should the Court begin to give serious weight to the former, it might be unable to find a logical stopping point short of constitutionalizing the entire subject—an option the Court has disdained.

GENE R. SHREVE
(2000)

Bibliography

LAYCOCK, DOUGLAS 1992 Equal Citizens of Equal and Territorial States: The Constitutional Foundations of Choice of Law. *Columbia Law Review* 92:249–337.
REESE, WILLIS L. M. 1978 Legislative Jurisdiction. *Columbia Law Review* 78:1587–1608.
SHREVE, GENE R. 1996 Choice of Law and the Forgiving Constitution. *Indiana Law Journal* 71:271–296.
WEINBERG, LOUISE 1982 Choice of Law and Minimal Scrutiny. *University of Chicago Law Review* 49:440–488.

CHRISTIAN RIGHT

See: Religious Fundamentalism

CHURCH OF JESUS CHRIST OF LATTER DAY SAINTS v. UNITED STATES
136 U.S. 1 (1890)

The Mormon Church was granted a charter of incorporation in February 1851 by the so-called State of Deseret; later an act of the territorial legislature of Utah confirmed the charter. In 1887 Congress, having plenary power over the TERRITORIES, repealed the charter and directed the seizure and disposal of church property.

Justice JOSEPH P. BRADLEY wrote for the Court. He held that the power of Congress over the territories was sufficient to repeal an act of incorporation. He also held that once the Mormon Church became a defunct CORPORATION, Congress had power to reassign its property to legitimate religious and charitable uses, as near as practicable to those intended by the original donors. The claim of RELIGIOUS FREEDOM could not immunize the Mormon Church against the congressional conclusion that, because of its sponsorship of polygamy, it was an undesirable legal entity.

Chief Justice MELVILLE WESTON FULLER dissented, joined by Justice STEPHEN J. FIELD and Justice L. Q. C. LAMAR. Fuller objected to according Congress such sweeping power over property.

RICHARD E. MORGAN
(1986)

CHURCH OF THE LUKUMI BABALU AYE, INC. v. CITY OF HIALEAH
508 U.S. 520 (1993)

The Lukumi religion, of West African origin, migrated to Cuba in the nineteenth century with the slave population, and became known as Santería; in our own time Lukumi has migrated to Florida. Several important rituals require the sacrifice of food animals to *orishas*, the Lukumi pantheon of spiritual beings. This practice led the City of Hialeah to enact several ordinances prohibiting animal sacrifice. The Supreme Court unanimously held that these ordinances violated the free exercise clause of the FIRST AMENDMENT because they had "targeted" religious practices. Justice ANTHONY M. KENNEDY wrote for the Court.

The city argued that the ordinances were valid means to protect public health and prevent cruelty to animals. But, the Court said, the "targeting" of religion was demonstrated by the ordinances' references to "sacrifice" and to "certain religions," and more generally by their overinclusiveness (e.g., forbidding ritual slaughtering even in licensed slaughterhouses) and underinclusiveness (e.g., exempting Kosher slaughtering and leaving unregulated both hunting and slaughtering for food purposes). Kennedy also said "targeting" was evident in statements of city council members indicating a motivation to stamp out the Lukumi religion. Justice ANTONIN SCALIA, joined by Chief Justice WILLIAM H. REHNQUIST, dissociated himself from this view, saying that subjective motive was irrelevant; "targeting" was to be found in the words of the ordinances.

Justices DAVID H. SOUTER and HARRY A. BLACKMUN (joined by Justice SANDRA DAY O'CONNOR), concurring, suggested reconsideration of the holding in EMPLOYMENT DIVISION, DEPARTMENT OF HUMAN RESOURCES OF OREGON V. SMITH (1990) that the free exercise clause has no application to incidental effects on RELIGIOUS LIBERTY caused by laws of general application. If, as *Lukumi* suggests, "targeting"

can be proved by showings of overinclusiveness and underinclusiveness, government officials will be well advised to offer legitimate (nontargeted) reasons for the actions that have restricted religious freedom. A judicial inquiry into "targeting" may, as in *Lukumi*, lead to an inquiry into the weight of asserted government interests. Such inquiries have the potential to undermine the "rule" of *Smith*, even if *Smith* escapes overruling.

KENNETH L. KARST
(2000)

Bibliography
KARST, KENNETH L. 1993 Religious Freedom and Equal Citizenship: Reflections on *Lukumi*. *Tulane Law Review* 69:335–372.

CIRCUIT COURTS

The JUDICIARY ACT OF 1789 fashioned a decentralized circuit court system. The boundaries of the three circuits coincided with the boundaries of the states they encompassed, a practice that opened them to state and sectional political influences and legal practices. The act assigned two Supreme Court Justices to each circuit to hold court along with a district judge in the state where the circuit court met. (After 1794, a single Justice and a district judge were a quorum.) The circuit-riding provision brought federal authority and national political views to the new and distant states, but also compelled the Justices to imbibe local political sentiments and legal practices.

For a century questions about the administrative efficiency, constitutional roles, and political responsibilities of these courts provoked heated debate. In the JUDICIARY ACT OF 1801, Federalists sought to replace the Justices with an independent six-person circuit court judiciary, but one year later the new Jeffersonian Republican majority in Congress eliminated the circuit judgeships and restored the Justices to circuit duties, although they left the number of circuits at six. (See JUDICIARY ACTS OF 1802.) Subsequent territorial expansion prompted the addition of new circuits and new Justices until both reached nine in the Judiciary Act of 1837. Slave state interests opposed further expansion because they feared the loss of their five-to-four majority on the high court. Congress in 1855 did create a special circuit court and judgeship for the Northern District of California to expedite land litigation.

Significant structural and jurisdictional changes accompanied the CIVIL WAR and RECONSTRUCTION. The Judiciary Act of 1869 established a separate circuit court judiciary and assigned one judge to each of the nine new circuits that stretched from coast to coast. Justices retained circuit-riding duties although the 1869 act and subsequent legislation required less frequent attendance.

Historically, these courts had exercised ORIGINAL and APPELLATE JURISDICTION in cases involving the criminal law of the United States, in other areas where particular statutes granted jurisdiction, and in cases resting on diversity of citizenship. The Judiciary Act of 1869 strengthened the appellate responsibilities of the circuit courts by denying litigants access to the Supreme Court unless the amount in controversy exceeded $5,000. The Jurisdiction and Removal Act of 1875 established a general FEDERAL QUESTION JURISDICTION and made it possible for, among others, interstate CORPORATIONS to seek the friendly forum of the federal as opposed to the state courts. The 1875 measure also transferred some of the original jurisdiction of the circuit courts to the district courts. However, because the circuit courts were given increased appellate responsibilities, along with only modest adjustments in staffing, their dockets became congested. The resulting delay in appeals, combined with similar congestion in the Supreme Court, persuaded Congress in 1891 to establish the Circuit Courts of Appeals which became the nation's principal intermediate federal appellate courts. (See CIRCUIT COURTS OF APPEALS ACT.) Although the old circuit courts became anachronisms, Congress delayed abolishing them until 1911.

Throughout the nineteenth century Supreme Court Justices held ambivalent attitudes toward circuit duty. The Justices complained about the rigors of circuit travel and the loss of time from responsibilities in the nation's capital, but most of them recognized that circuit judging offered a unique constitutional forum free from the immediate scrutiny of their brethren on the Court. "It is only as a Circuit Judge that the Chief Justice or any other Justice of the Supreme Court has, individually, any considerable power," Chief Justice SALMON P. CHASE observed in 1868.

Circuit court judges contributed to the nationalization of American law and the economy. Justice JOSEPH STORY, in the First Circuit, for example, broadly defined the federal ADMIRALTY AND MARITIME JURISDICTION. In perhaps the most important circuit court decision of the nineteenth century, Story held, in *De Lovio v. Boit* (1815), that this jurisdiction extended to all maritime contracts, including insurance policies, and to all torts and injuries committed on the high seas and in ports and harbors within the ebb and flow of the tide. This decision, coupled with Story's opinion eight years later in *Chamberlain v. Chandler* (1823), expanded federal control over admiralty and maritime-related economic activity and added certainty to contracts involving shipping and commerce.

The circuit courts extended national constitutional protection to property, contract, and corporate rights. Justice WILLIAM PATERSON's 1795 decision on circuit in VAN HORNE'S LESSEE V. DORRANCE was the first significant statement in the federal courts on behalf of VESTED RIGHTS. But in 1830 Justice HENRY BALDWIN anticipated by seven years the PUBLIC USE doctrine later embraced by the Supreme Court. In *Bonaparte v. Camden & A. R. Co.* he held that state legislatures could take private property only for public use, and that creation of a monopoly by a public charter voided its public nature. As new forms of corporate property emerged in the post-Civil War era, the circuit courts offered protection through the CONTRACT CLAUSE. In the early and frequently cited case of *Gray v. Davis* (1871) a circuit court held, and the Supreme Court subsequently affirmed, that a legislative act incorporating a railroad constituted a contract between the state and the company, and a state constitutional provision annulling that charter violated the contract clause.

The circuit courts' most dramatic nationalizing role involved commercial jurispru:dence. Through their DIVERSITY JURISDICTION the circuit courts used SWIFT V. TYSON (1842) to build a FEDERAL COMMON LAW of commerce, thus encouraging business flexibility, facilitating investment security, and reducing costs to corporations. After the Civil War these courts eased limitations on the formation and operation of corporations in foreign states (*In Re Spain*, 1891), supported bondholders' rights, allowed forum shopping (*Osgood v. The Chicago, Danville, and Vincennes R. R. Co.*, 1875), and favored employers in fellow-servant liability cases.

Ambivalence, contradiction, and frustration typified circuit court decisions involving civil and political rights. In 1823 Justice BUSHROD WASHINGTON, in CORFIELD V. COR-YELL, held that the PRIVILEGES AND IMMUNITIES clause guaranteed equal treatment of out-of-state citizens as to those privileges and immunities that belonged of right to citizens of all free governments, and which had at all times been enjoyed by citizens of the several states. After 1866 some circuit judges attempted to expand this narrow interpretation. Justice JOSEPH P. BRADLEY held, in *Live-Stock Dealers' & Butchers' Ass'n v. Crescent City Live-Stock Landing & Slaughter-House Co.* (1870), that the FOURTEENTH AMENDMENT protected the privileges and immunities of whites and blacks as national citizens against STATE ACTION. In 1871 the Circuit Court for the Southern District of Alabama, in *United States v. Hall*, decided that under the Fourteenth Amendment Congress had the power to protect by appropriate legislation all rights in the first eight amendments. And in *Ho Ah Kow v. Nunan* (1879) Justice STEPHEN J. FIELD struck down as CRUEL AND UNUSUAL PUNISHMENT, based on the Eighth Amendment and the EQUAL PROTECTION clause of the Fourteenth Amendment, a San Francisco ordinance that required Chinese prisoners to have their hair cut to a length of one inch from their scalps.

These attempts to nationalize civil rights had little immediate impact. The Supreme Court in 1873 rejected

Bradley's reading of the Fourteenth Amendment, and in 1871 the Circuit Court for the District of South Carolina in *United States v. Crosby* concluded that the right of a person to be secure in his or her home was not a right, privilege, or immunity granted by the Constitution. Neither the Supreme Court nor any other circuit court adopted the theory of congressional power to enforce the Fourteenth Amendment set forth in *Hall*. Justice Field's *Nunan* opinion was most frequently cited in dissenting rather than majority opinions.

Political rights under the FIFTEENTH AMENDMENT fared only slightly better. In *United States v. Given* (1873) the Circuit Court for the District of Delaware held that the Fifteenth Amendment did not limit congressional action to cases where states had denied or abridged the right to vote by legislation. In the same year, however, Justice WARD HUNT, in *United States v. Anthony*, concluded that the right or privilege of voting arose under state constitutions and that the states might restrict it to males.

Despite a regional structure and diverse personnel, these circuit courts placed national over state interests, reinforced the supremacy of federal power, promoted national economic development, and enhanced the position of interstate corporations. However, in matters of civil and political rights they not only disagreed about the scope of federal powers but also confronted a Supreme Court wedded to a traditional state-centered foundation for these rights.

KERMIT L. HALL
(1986)

Bibliography

FRANKFURTER, FELIX and LANDIS, JAMES M. 1927 *The Business of the Supreme Court: A Study in the Federal Judicial System.* Pages 3–86. New York: Macmillan.
HALL, KERMIT L. 1975 The Civil War Era as a Crucible for Nationalizing the Lower Federal Courts. *Prologue: The Journal of the National Archives* 7:177–186.
SWISHER, CARL B. 1974 *The Taney Period, 1836–1864.* Volume IV of *The Oliver Wendell Holmes Devise History of the Supreme Court of the United States.* Pages 248–292. New York: Macmillan.

CIRCUIT COURTS OF APPEALS ACT
26 Stat. 826 (1891)

The first substantial revision of the federal court system since its formation (except for the abortive JUDICIARY ACT OF 1801), this act established a badly needed level of courts just below the Supreme Court: the UNITED STATES COURTS OF APPEALS. Senator WILLIAM EVARTS led the reform

movement to relieve pressure on the Supreme Court docket by providing intermediate appellate review for most district and circuit court decisions. By keeping the CIRCUIT COURTS but abolishing their APPELLATE JURISDICTION, Congress maintained two courts with substantially similar JURISDICTION, causing confusion until the circuit courts were abolished in the JUDICIAL CODE of 1911. The act established direct Supreme Court review, bypassing the courts of appeals, in cases of "infamous" crimes (an ill-considered description that actually increased the Court's business and had to be deleted in 1897), and introduced the principle of discretionary Supreme Court review by WRIT OF CERTIORARI.

The basic structure of today's system of appellate review of federal court decisions remains as it was established in the 1891 Act.

DAVID GORDON
(1986)

Bibliography

FRANKFURTER, FELIX and LANDIS, JAMES M. 1927 *The Business of the Supreme Court.* New York: Macmillan.

CITIES AND THE CONSTITUTION

Cities, unlike STATES, are not mentioned in the Constitution. Many other important collective institutions in our society, such as CORPORATIONS, are not mentioned in the Constitution either. In its effort to determine the constitutional status of cities, the Supreme Court has had to decide whether to treat cities like states or like corporations. In fact, the Court has been required to answer two separate questions concerning the constitutional status of cities. First, do cities, like private corporations, have rights that are protected from governmental power by the Constitution? Second, do cities, like states, exercise governmental power which is limited by the Constitution?

At the time the Constitution was written and adopted, there was no legal distinction between cities and other corporations. Neither WILLIAM BLACKSTONE's *commentaries*, published the decade before the CONSTITUTIONAL CONVENTION OF 1787, nor the first treatise on corporations, published by Stuart Kyd in 1793, categorized corporations in a way that would distinguish the Corporation of the City of New York, for example, from manufacturing and commercial concerns or from universities. Each of these entities was considered a lay corporation, formed by its members and given legal status by a grant of power from the state. The ability of these corporations to pursue the purposes for which their charter was granted was a right that needed protection from governmental power. At the same time, however, all corporations wielded power delegated to them by the state and, therefore, posed a danger of abuse that required subjection to popular control.

The Supreme Court's first important attempt to settle the constitutional status of corporations created a distinction between cities and other corporations. In DARTMOUTH COLLEGE V. WOODWARD (1819) Justice JOSEPH STORY articulated a public/private distinction for American corporations, classifying cities with states and distinguishing them from private corporations. "Public corporations," he said, "are generally esteemed such as exist for public political purposes only, such as towns, cities, parishes, and counties; and in many respects they are so, although they involve some private interests; but strictly speaking, public corporations are such only as founded by the government for public purposes, where the whole interests belong also to the government."

When considering whether cities should have rights that protect them against state control, the Supreme Court has largely accepted Justice Story's proposition that the cities' whole interest belongs to the government; it has treated cities as if they were the state itself. At least insofar as they are considered "public" entities, cities, unlike private corporations, have virtually no constitutional protection against STATE ACTION. The Supreme Court dramatically summarized the nature of state power over cities in *Hunter v. Pittsburg* (1907):

Municipal corporations are political subdivisions of the State created as convenient agencies for exercising such of the governmental powers of the State as may be entrusted to them. . . . The State, therefore, at its pleasure may modify or withdraw all such powers, may take without compensation such property, hold it itself, or vest it in other agencies, expand or contract the territorial area, unite the whole or part with another municipality, repeal the charter and destroy the corporation. . . . In all these respects the State is supreme, and its legislative body, conforming its actions to the state constitution, may do as it will, unrestrained by any provision of the Constitution of the United States.

The Court in *Hunter* indicated, however, that there might be a limit to state power over cities, one it articulated in terms of a public/private distinction within the concept of a city. To some extent, cities act like private corporations, and this private aspect of city government, the Court said, could receive the same constitutional protection as other private interests. Even Justice Story had recognized in *Dartmouth College* that cities are not purely public entities but "involve some private interests" as well. But the proposition that cities are entitled to protection from state power under the Constitution in their "proprietary" (as contrasted to their "governmental") capacities has not yielded them much constitutional protection. The Supreme Court has never struck down a state statute on

the grounds that it invaded such a private sphere. Indeed, in *Trenton v. New Jersey* (1923) Justice PIERCE BUTLER, noting that such a sphere could not readily be defined, expressed doubt whether there was a private sphere that limited the states' power over their own municipalities.

Whatever limited protection the Court has given cities under the Constitution has involved their public and not their private capacities. In GOMILLION V. LIGHTFOOT (1960) the Court held that the FIFTEENTH AMENDMENT restricted the state's ability to define the boundaries of its cities in a way that infringed on its citizens' VOTING RIGHTS; the Court narrowed the extravagant description of state power over cities in *Hunter* by construing the Court's language in that case to be applicable only to the particular constitutional provisions considered there. But the Court has not subsequently expanded on its distinction between the Fifteenth Amendment and other constitutional provisions, such as the FOURTEENTH AMENDMENT and the CONTRACT CLAUSE, as vehicles for limiting state power over cities. No subsequent case has given cities constitutional protection against state power.

From 1976 to 1985, during the short life of NATIONAL LEAGUE OF CITIES V. USERY (1976), the Supreme Court articulated the most expansive constitutional protection ever given cities, again a protection for their public and not their private activities. By treating them as if they were states the Court limited the power of the federal government to regulate cities; it held that cities, like states, were immunized from federal control under the TENTH AMENDMENT insofar as federal interference "directly impaired their ability to structure integral operations in areas of traditional governmental functions." In GARCIA V. SAN ANTONIO METROPOLITAN TRANSIT AUTHORITY (1985), however, *National League of Cities* was overruled. One reason for OVERRULING *National League of Cities*, the Court said, was that there was no practical way to make a public/private distinction between "traditional governmental functions" and other state and city functions. Hence, the Court reasoned, there was no principled basis for choosing some areas of state or city activity over others to be immune from federal control as a constitutional matter.

There is a second question concerning the constitutional status of cities: to what extent are cities like states, and, therefore, subject to those constitutional provisions that affect the power of states? The Supreme Court's answer to this question has been complex.

For some purposes, the Court has treated cities like states. City power is like state power, for example, in that it is equally limited by the DUE PROCESS and EQUAL PROTECTION clauses of the Fourteenth Amendment and by the dormant COMMERCE CLAUSE. On the other hand, the Court has held that cities are not like states for purposes of the ELEVENTH AMENDMENT (dealing with states' immunity from suits in federal court). In a number of nonconstitutional cases the Supreme Court has also sought to distinguish cities from states. "We are a nation not of city-states but of States," the Court said in *Community Communications Co. v. City of Boulder* (1982), holding cities, like private corporations but unlike states, liable to federal antitrust laws.

Indeed, sometimes the Court has treated cities in a way that distinguishes them from both states and corporations. In MONELL V. DEPARTMENT OF SOCIAL SERVICES (1978) the Supreme Court interpreted SECTION 1983, TITLE 42, UNITED STATES CODE to allow damage suits against cities when they commit constitutional violations. City action is like state action in that cities are subject to constitutional limitations applicable to states. But states, unlike cities, have immunities under the Eleventh Amendment against suits in federal court to enforce these constitutional limitations. Thus, under *Monell*, cities are liable under section 1983 for constitutional violations in situations in which neither the states (because of the Eleventh Amendment) nor private corporations (because their power is not subject to constitutional limitations) would be liable.

Finally, at times cities are considered like states and private corporations simultaneously. Both cities and states can act in the marketplace just as private corporations do. Thus in *White v. Massachusetts Council of Construction Employers* (1983) the Supreme Court held that the commerce clause does not restrict a city's ability to require its contractors to hire city residents as long as it is acting as a market participant and not as a market regulator. The Court thus extended to cities the immunity from commerce clause restrictions that it had previously provided states when they act as market participants. The practical effect of the *White* case, however, is limited. In *United Building & Construction Trades Council v. Camden* (1984) the Court held that the privileges and immunities clause, unlike the commerce clause, limited a city's ability to require its contractors to hire city residents whether or not it acts as a market participant. In *Camden* the Court treated cities like states but distinguished them from corporations; the power of states and cities, unlike that of corporations, is restrained by the privileges and immunities clause of the Constitution.

The cities' historic link with corporations and their assimilation in the nineteenth century to the status of states have given them a divided status under the Constitution. Although the predominant linkage has been between cities and states, there remain occasions when the prior linkage with corporations is emphasized. The Court's ability to conceptualize cities as either states or corporations (indeed, to conceptualize them as both simultaneously or as distinguishable from both) opens up a multitude of possibilities for the Court as it defines the relationship between cities and the Constitution in the future.

GERALD E. FRUG
(1986)

Bibliography

CLARK, GORDON 1985 *Judges and the Cities: Interpreting Local Autonomy.* Chicago: University of Chicago Press.
FRUG, GERALD 1980 The City as a Legal Concept. *Harvard Law Review* 93:1059–1154.
HARTOG, HENDRIK 1983 *Public Property and Private Power: The Corporation of the City of New York in American Law, 1730–1870.* Chapel Hill: University of North Carolina Press.
MICHELMAN, FRANK 1977–1978 Political Markets and Community Self-Determination: Competing Judicial Models of Local Government Legitimacy *Indiana Law Journal* 53:145–206.

CITIZENSHIP
(Historical Development)

The concept of citizenship articulated during the AMERICAN REVOLUTION and adjusted to the special circumstances of an ethnically diverse federal republic in the nineteenth century developed from English theories of allegiance and of the subject's status. Enunciated most authoritatively by Sir EDWARD COKE in CALVIN'S CASE (1608), English law held that natural subject status involved a perpetual, immutable relationship of allegiance and protection between subject and king analogous to the bond between parent and child. All persons born within the king's allegiance gained this status by birth. Conquest or NATURALIZATION by Parliament could extend the status to the foreign-born, but subjects adopted in such a manner were by legal fiction considered bound by the same perpetual allegiance as the native-born. The doctrine "once a subject, always a subject" reflected Coke's emphasis on the natural origins of the subject-king relationship and militated against the emergence of concepts of voluntary membership and EXPATRIATION.

The appearance of new SOCIAL COMPACT ideas modified but did not entirely supersede traditional concepts. By the mid-eighteenth century, Lockean theorists derived subject status from the individual's consent to leave the state of nature and join with others to form a society. To such theorists the individual subject was bound by the majority and owed allegiance to the government established by that majority. Barring the dissolution of society itself or the consent of the majority, expressed through Parliament, individual subjects were still held to a perpetual allegiance.

Colonial conditions eroded these ideas. Colonial naturalization policies especially contributed to a subtle transformation of inherited attitudes. Provincial governments welcomed foreign-born settlers in order to promote population growth vital to physical security and economic prosperity. Offering political and economic rights in exchange for the ALIEN's contribution to the general welfare of the community, the colonists underscored the contractual, consent-based aspects of membership that had been subordinated in English law to older notions of perpetual allegiance. Imperial administrators, concerned to protect England's monopoly of colonial trade, declared in 1700 that colonial naturalization could confer subject status only within the confines of the admitting colony; although a parliamentary statute of 1740 established administrative procedures whereby a colonial court could vest an alien with a subject status valid throughout the empire, such actions merely reinforced the conclusion that the origins, extent, and effects of subject status were determined not by nature but by political and legal compacts.

When Americans declared independence in 1776 they initially relied on the traditional linkage of allegiance and protection to define citizenship in the new republican states. Congress's resolution of June 24, 1776, declared that all persons then resident in the colonies and deriving protection from the laws were members of and owed allegiance to those colonies. Lockean theory was also useful, for if each colony were considered a separate society merely changing its form of government, then loyalist minorities could still be considered subject to the will of patriot majorities. Yet forced allegiance clashed with the idea that all legitimate government required the free consent of the governed. Wartime TREASON prosecutions contributed to a gradual reformulation of the theory of citizenship that stressed the volitional character of allegiance. Employing a doctrine stated most clearly in the Pennsylvania case of *Respublica v. Chapman* (1781), American courts came to hold that citizenship must originate in an act of individual consent.

Republican citizenship required the consent of the community as well as of the individual, and legislators concerned with establishing naturalization policies concentrated on defining the proper qualifications for membership. This preoccupation obscured the ill-defined nature of the status itself. The Revolution had created a sense of community that transcended state boundaries; the ARTICLES OF CONFEDERATION implied that state citizenship carried with it rights in other states as well (Article IV). Framers of the United States Constitution perpetuated this ambiguity: section 2 of Article IV provided that "The citizens of each State shall be entitled to all PRIVILEGES AND IMMUNITIES of citizens in the several States." Questions concerning the nature and relationship of state and national citizenship would not be resolved until the CIVIL WAR.

The Revolutionary idea that citizenship began with the individual's consent extended logically to the idea of expatriation. Although some states acknowledged this principle, it raised delicate questions of federal relations after 1789. The problem appeared as early as 1795 in *Talbot v. Janson*, when the United States Supreme Court wrestled with the question whether a Virginia expatriation procedure could release a citizen from national as well as state allegiance. Unwilling to resolve that issue, the Court looked to Congress to provide a general policy of expatriation. Although the propriety of such a measure was discussed a number of times during the antebellum period, congressional action foundered on the same issue of federal relations. As long as the question of the primacy of state or United States citizenship remained open, the idea that citizenship rested on individual choice would be more valid for aliens seeking naturalization than for persons whose citizenship derived from birth.

The problematic character of dual state and national citizenship appeared in its most intractable form in disputes over the status of free blacks. Many northern states acknowledged free blacks as birthright citizens, though often at the cost of conceding that important political rights were not necessarily attached to that status. From the 1820s on, slave states increasingly resisted the contention that such citizenship carried constitutional guarantees of "privileges and immunities" in their own jurisdictions. ROGER B. TANEY's opinion in DRED SCOTT V. SANDFORD (1857) that national citizenship was restricted to white state citizens of 1789, persons naturalized by Congress, and their descendants alone marked the final effort, short of SECESSION, to restrict the scope of citizenship.

The FOURTEENTH AMENDMENT finally defined national citizenship as the product of naturalization or birth within the JURISDICTION of the United States, leaving state citizenship dependent upon residency. On July 27, 1868, Congress declared that the right of expatriation was a fundamental principle of American government, thus allowing persons born to citizenship the same right as aliens to choose their ultimate allegiance.

JAMES H. KETTNER
(1986)

Bibliography

KETTNER, JAMES H. 1978 *The Development of American Citizenship, 1608–1870.* Chapel Hill: University of North Carolina Press.

ROCHE, JOHN P. 1949 *The Early Development of United States Citizenship.* Ithaca, N.Y.: Cornell University Press.

CITIZENSHIP
(Theory)

Article I, section B, of the Constitution authorizes Congress "to establish a uniform Rule of NATURALIZATION." The power afforded Congress in this spare textual authorization has long been interpreted as plenary, effectively insulating from constitutional challenge congressional decisions about whom to admit to the national community. The theory of national community expressed through this constitutional interpretation was summarily sketched by the Supreme Court nearly a century ago in *Nishimura Eiku v. United States* (1891): "It is an accepted maxim of international law, that every sovereign nation has the power, inherent in SOVEREIGNTY, and essential to self-preservation, to forbid the entrance of foreigners within its domain, or to admit them only in such cases and upon such conditions as it may see fit to prescribe."

This still regnant theory of sovereignty has become, for most people, entirely natural and unimposed. Its inchoate justification, articulated in abstract terms, does have a natural and necessary air: one can understand nations asserting an absolute right to decide whom to admit or to exclude as advancing the universal right to form communities and the right to keep them distinctive and stable. While nations have grown significantly more interconnected and while the world's creatures are one for some important purposes, the notion of protecting the right to form and maintain special communities within larger communities resonates with our understanding of how America became a nation. Still, even for one who believes in protecting the national community, a moral question remains: what constitutes membership in the political community to be protected?

In a strictly positive sense, the answer is that citizenship in this country has been conferred by birth (either in the United States or abroad to American parents) or by naturalization. Although only "a natural born Citizen" can be President, naturalized citizens are otherwise the formal equals of citizens by birth. Moreover, the Constitution extends many of its protections to "persons" or "people" so that ALIENS are protected in much the same way as citizens even before they are naturalized.

But the United States has been a national community not readily inclined to ask what constitutes membership in the political community—or perhaps more accurately, not genuinely curious about the answer or willing to give it constitutional significance. Congress has long presumed that those who currently share citizenship (citizens and, during most but not all historical periods, documented residents) constitute the community to be protected and maintained.

The judiciary, in turn, has long deferred to whatever Congress decides. This deference, while varying across the range of immigration law disputes, radically diverges from the political relationship between judiciary and legislature that informs most constitutional jurisprudence. Consider a range of congressional "membership" decisions and the corresponding judicial response: Exclusion decisions and procedures are treated as extraconstitutional; congressional power to classify aliens is effectively unconstrained by EQUAL PROTECTION values; DEPORTATION is treated as a civil and not a criminal proceeding, thereby denying certain constitutional protections expressly limited or interpreted to apply only to criminal proceedings; the power to detain remains unlimited by any coherent set of values, and is available effectively to imprison individuals and groups for long periods and under disreputable conditions; immigration judges remain intertwined with government agencies responsible for administering and enforcing immigration law. In so deferring to Congress, the judiciary either denies the constitutional relevance of the always amending character of the national community or indulges absolutely Congress's habitual response to what constitutes membership in the political community.

If together Congress and the courts "freed" us from being genuinely curious about ourselves, they were not without help in constructing this reality. It has been commonplace for many to deny that citizenship does or should play a central role in our political community. No less a figure in recent constitutional jurisprudence than ALEXANDER M. BICKEL insisted that citizenship "was a simple idea for a simple government"; others entirely ignored the question, as if a view on membership in the process of self-determination were not itself constitutive of the national community's very nature. But, of course, citizenship in the United States never has been a simple idea. Naturalization laws, implementing the FOURTEENTH AMENDMENT, were not extended to persons of African descent until 1870; citizens of Mexican descent were deported in 1930 raids; citizens of Japanese descent were interned during WORLD WAR II because of their ancestry; women citizens were not allowed to vote until 1920; Puerto Ricans and people of other conquered territories were afforded only second-class citizenship status. Yet the relationship of these and other events to our conception of United States citizenship has been far more often ignored than attended to, as if the denial of contradictory acts would somehow save the regnant theory of national community.

These efforts notwithstanding, the experience of community is beginning to challenge the prevailing constitutionalized attitude toward membership in the political community. The presence of millions of undocumented workers—sharing neighborhoods, burdens, and laws—has prompted intense and frequently conflicting responses to the general question of citizenship and its role in the political community. In PLYLER V. DOE (1982) the Supreme Court compelled the state of Texas to provide the children of undocumented workers with a free public education. At the same time, attention to the relationship of citizenship to the political community has led the Court to intensify its scrutiny of laws that deny documented residents access to certain occupations. State laws barring aliens from permanent civil service positions and from the practice of law and civil engineering have been struck down. But where the position is intimately related to the process of democratic self-government (the so-called political function exception), the Court has upheld laws requiring police, public teachers, and probation officers to be citizens.

What this communitarian challenge foreshadows defies facile forecasting; a theory so long dominant as ours toward community membership and sovereignty resists predictable or simple change. Still, in its unwillingness to be silenced, in its refusal to accept uncritically the regnant theory, today's challenge focuses attention on our history, and on the relationship of work to full political life. At least in this sense, there is the hope that we will no longer blithely disregard the values formally expressed in our vision of citizenship. After all, whom we acknowledge as full members of the political community tells us much about who we are and why we remain together as a nation.

GERALD P. LÓPEZ
(1986)

CITIZENSHIP
(Update 1)

American citizenship can be obtained in three ways. The most common way, citizenship by birth in the United States (jus soli), is secured by the FOURTEENTH AMENDMENT citizenship clause. Although customary exceptions to this principle exist (e.g., children born on foreign vessels or of diplomatic personnel), this birthright citizenship has been understood (wrongly, I have argued) to extend even to native-born children of ALIENS in the country illegally or on a temporary visa.

A second route to citizenship is through NATURALIZATION. To naturalize, one must be a resident alien who has resided in the United States continuously for five years (a longer period than in Canada and the Scandinavian countries); be of good moral character; and demonstrate an ability to speak, read, and write English and a basic knowledge of United States government and history. These requirements are relaxed for certain individuals, such as spouses of U.S. citizens.

The third route to citizenship is through parentage (jus sanguinis). Statutory law enumerates a number of parentage categories, sometimes augmented by RESIDENCY REQUIREMENTS, that confer eligibility for citizenship on the child. The Supreme Court held in *Rogers v. Bellei* (1971) that in regulating this form of citizenship, Congress is not limited by the citizenship clause of the Fourteenth Amendment. In recent years Congress has liberalized eligibility.

Dual and triple citizenships, which arise as a result of the combination of the American jus soli rule with the jus sanguinis rules of other nations, are tolerated and legally protected. Still, the government discourages multiple citizenship; aliens who wish to naturalize must renounce any prior allegiance, which may or may not effectively terminate their foreign citizenships.

U.S. citizenship, once acquired, is almost impossible to lose without the citizen's expressed consent. The Supreme Court has severely restricted the government's power to denationalize a citizen for disloyalty, divided allegiance, or other reasons. Birthright citizens cannot be deprived of their citizenship unless the govenment proves that they specifically intended to renounce it. Naturalized citizens who procured their citizenship through fraud or misrepresentation are subject to DENATURALIZATION, but to prevail the government must satisfy demanding standards, most recently defined in *Kungys v. United States* (1988). This tiny risk of denaturalization is the only permissible difference between naturalized and other citizens.

As a result of a steady expansion of the equal protection and due process principles, legal resident aliens today enjoy almost all the significant rights and obligations that citizens enjoy, including access to most public benefits. Only five differences are worth noting. Three of them are political: citizens, but not aliens, may vote, serve on juries, and serve in certain high elective ofices and certain high (and not so high) appointive ones. Modern practice (many states in the nineteenth century permitted aliens to vote) and political inertia, more than sound policy, probably account for the durability of these differences. A fourth difference, which congress has considered eliminating, is that citizens can bring their noncitizen family members to the United States more easily than aliens can. Finally, aliens are subject to DEPORTATION, although the actual risk of deportation for a long-term resident alien who does not engage in serious criminal behavior is very low.

This progressive convergence of the citizen and resident-alien statuses suggests some devaluation of American citizenship. As public philosophy, this devaluation carries with it certain dangers for the polity. But it also represents an immense gain for the liberal values of inclusiveness and equal treatment. By maximizing individual opportunity and preventing the formation of a legally disabled underclass, the equality and due process principles have fostered the social mobility and optimism that seem essential to the success of American democracy. Moreover, the constitutional JURISPRUDENCE through which this has been achieved is probably irreversible, reflecting fundamental dynamics in domestic law and international relations that enjoy widespread support.

The conception of political membership has grown steadily more fluid, functional, and context-dependent. Before the rise of the modern nation-state, political membership was based upon kinship and ethnic ties. Today, membership is a far more complex, variegated, multipurpose idea. For purposes such as voting, citizenship is the crucial status, whereas mere territorial presence suffices for attributing most constitutional rights. For purposes of participation in an economic common market, membership is constituted by supranational groupings, exemplified by the recently established United States-Canada free-trade zone and the still-evolving European Community.

We live in an increasingly integrated world. Transnational economic relationships are ubiquitous, international travel has become inexpensive, migratory pressures are enormous, environmental problems are often global, scientific and cultural exchanges are highly valued, and political cooperation among nations is more essential than ever before. Even within America's borders, citizenship represents an increasingly hollow ideal. It neither confers a distinctively advantageous status nor demands much of the individuals who possess it.

National citizenship, however, is not anachronistic. It provides a focus of political allegiance and emotional energy on a scale capable of satisfying deep human longings for solidarity, symbolic identification, and community. This is especially important in a liberal polity whose cosmopolitan aspirations for universal principles of human rights must somehow be balanced against the more parochial social commitments to family, ethnicity, locality, region, and nation. Although these political and emotional aspects of citizenship remain significant, American society seems resolved that little else of consequence shall be allowed to turn on citizenship. But within that general understanding and social consensus, the precise role of citizenship and the special rights and obligations that should attach to it are open questions. Here, only one proposition seems certain: Today's conceptions of citizenship may not be adequate to meet tomorrow's needs.

PETER H. SCHUCK
(1992)

Bibliography

BRUBAKER, W. R., ed. 1989 *Immigration and the Politics of Citizenship in Europe and North America.* New York: University Press of America.

SCHUCK, PETER and SMITH, ROGERS 1986 *Citizenship Without Consent: Illegal Aliens in the American Polity.* New Haven, Conn.: Yale University Press.

CITIZENSHIP
(Update 2)

The Supreme Court has declared American citizenship "a most precious right," regarded by many as "the highest hope of civilized men." Recognition of the importance of U.S. citizenship led the Court to hold in AFROYIM V. RUSK (1967) that Congress may not deprive a person of U.S. citizenship (other than in the case of wrongful NATURALIZATION) unless the person has a specific intent to relinquish it. American citizens may not be deported, and have the right to enter or return to the United States. Most citizens take these rights for granted, but they mark a significant distinction between the statuses of citizen and ALIEN.

The fundamental norm of U.S. citizenship law is the principle of *jus soli*—that all persons born in the United States are citizens at birth. The language of the FOURTEENTH AMENDMENT—written to overcome Chief Justice ROGER BROOKE TANEY's opinion in DRED SCOTT V. SANDFORD (1857)—affirmed the COMMON LAW rule of *jus soli*. In UNITED STATES V. WONG KIM ARK (1898), decided at the height of constitutionalized American racism, the Court held that the children of Chinese immigrants born in the United States were citizens at birth, despite federal law prohibiting the naturalization of their parents.

Citizenship may also be acquired by descent (*jus sanguinis*) and through naturalization. Since 1790, federal statutes have permitted aliens in the United States to naturalize, and have granted citizenship at birth to persons born to American parents outside the United States. These sources of citizenship are not secured by the Fourteenth Amendment, and traditionally the Court has recognized broad congressional authority to distribute citizenship by statute largely immune from judicial scrutiny. However, in *Miller v. Albright* (1998), the Court was sharply divided over the constitutionality of a federal statute permitting U.S. citizen mothers to pass citizenship to NONMARITAL CHILDREN born outside the United States on easier terms than U.S. citizen fathers. A majority of the Justices indicated that they would invalidate the statute in a properly presented case.

Citizenship is at the same time universalistic and exclusionary. The Constitution forbids Congress from granting TITLES OF NOBILITY; in this republic, the office of citizen defines the class of governors. The concept of citizenship therefore pushes toward universal suffrage. So too, by defining membership in a polity, citizenship suggests a core class of right holders. In a famous formulation, T. H. Marshall noted that "[c]itizenship is a status bestowed on those who are full members of a community. All who possess the status are equal with respect to the rights and duties with which the status is endowed."

But formal equality on paper has rarely guaranteed equal treatment in life. Throughout American history large classes of citizens have been citizens in name only. Most adult Americans were not eligible to vote at the time of the Constitution's adoption, and discrimination based on race, gender, wealth, and other grounds has created huge political and economic inequalities among nominally "equal" citizens.

So too, laws regulating access to citizenship have included racial exclusions for more of our history than not. The naturalization act of 1790 limited eligible classes to "white persons." Following the CIVIL WAR, the statute was amended to include persons of "African descent"—a formulation that continued to prohibit Asian immigrants from naturalizing. The racial bars on naturalization were not fully removed until 1952. For several decades early in this century, federal law provided that citizen women who married foreigners lost U.S. citizenship for so long as the MARRIAGE lasted.

Despite this history, the constitutional claim of equal citizenship is a powerful one, and distinctions that seem natural in one era become unconstitutional denials of equal citizenship in another. But it is here that the exclusionary aspect of citizenship arises. By drawing a circle and designating those within the circle sovereign and equal, the concept of citizenship perforce treats those outside the circle (aliens) as less than full members. Justice BYRON R. WHITE recognized this implication of citizenship in *Cabell v. Chávez-Salido* (1982): "Self-government . . . begins by defining the scope of the community of the governed and thus of the governors as well: Aliens are by definition those outside of this community."

Does the Constitution necessarily link rights and citizenship? The term "citizen" does not appear in the BILL OF RIGHTS; and it has long been bedrock constitutional law that aliens residing in the United States are protected by the Fourteenth Amendment's guarantee of EQUAL PROTECTION OF THE LAWS, under the rule of YICK WO V. HOPKINS (1886), and enjoy most of the rights secured by other provisions of the Constitution. Furthermore, the Court has applied STRICT SCRUTINY to state regulations based on alienage (with an exception for political rights and offices). At the same time the Court has adopted a virtually toothless STANDARD OF REVIEW for federal statutes that draw distinctions on the basis of alienage. The Court's deference to Congress extends both to explicit regulations of IMMIGRATION and to statutes distinguishing aliens from citizens in the granting of federal benefits. As the Court stated expressly in *Mathews v. Díaz* (1976), "Congress regularly makes rules that would be unacceptable if applied to citizens[;] [and the] fact that an Act of Congress treats aliens differently from citizens does not in itself imply that such disparate treatment is 'invidious.'" Perhaps it is not an oxymoron to suggest that constitutional norms supply a "second-class citizenship" for aliens in the United States.

As the nation-state comes under challenge both from below (with claims for autonomy for subnational groups) and from above (with the establishment of supranational legal orders), the concept of citizenship has come under renewed focus. Proposals have been made to make citizenship "mean more"; and landmark changes in U.S. welfare policy in 1996 did just that by disentitling most future immigrants from federally supported welfare programs. Other proposals, of dubious constitutionality, would deny BIRTHRIGHT CITIZENSHIP to children born in the United States to undocumented aliens. Policies that grant significant benefits to citizens denied to aliens apparently have provided a substantial incentive to naturalization. The interesting question for those who seek to pour more content into citizenship is whether naturalizations based on a desire to preserve access to social programs in fact serve that goal.

The increasing frequency of dual nationality poses new questions for the meaning of citizenship. At the beginning of the twentieth century, dual nationality was disfavored. Prevailing INTERNATIONAL LAW norms pursued the goal of ensuring that every person was a member of one and only one nation-state. But migration and state practice have made dual nationality a more common phenomenon, arising usually from birth in one state to parents who are citizens of another state. In a significant shift in state practice, a number of countries are now permitting citizens who naturalize elsewhere to retain their original citizenship. Because the United States continues to admit large numbers of immigrants, it will likely face increasing numbers of dual nationals. The Constitution says nothing explicit about dual nationality. The Fourteenth Amendment's principle of *jus soli* (coupled with the laws of foreign states) is an important cause of dual nationality. Congress's Article I, section 8 power to adopt naturalization laws permits the federal government to either embrace, ignore, or seek to deter dual nationality of persons who attain U.S. citizenship by naturalization.

In the end, we face a constitutional conundrum. As a democracy, the United States needs a *demos* both as a location of SOVEREIGNTY and from which to designate a class of governors. (Although in the nineteenth century a number of states permitted ALIEN SUFFRAGE, those laws had been repealed by the early twentieth century.) But the Constitution does not define rights in terms of citizenship; rights are generally guaranteed as human rights, irrespective of status. Indeed, the Constitution imposes no specific obligations on citizens; and other than JURY SERVICE, there are precious few obligations imposed by law on citizens *qua* citizens. Aliens, then, benefit from a kind of constitutional citizenship, even if the citzenry is deemed the source of the Constitution and the day-to-day governance of the republic is reserved to citizens.

T. ALEXANDER ALEINIKOFF
(2000)

Bibliography

BRUBAKER, ROGERS   1992   Citizenship as Social Closure. Pages 21–34 in *Citizenship and Nationhood in France and Germany*. Cambridge, Mass.: Harvard University Press.

KARST, KENNETH L.   1977   The Supreme Court, 1976 Term—Foreword: Equal Citizenship under the Fourteenth Amendment. *Harvard Law Review* 91:1–68.

MARSHALL, T. H.   1964   Citizenship and Social Class. Pages 65–122 in *Class, Citizenship, and Social Development: Essays by T. H. Marshall*. Garden City, N.Y.: Doubleday & Company, Inc.

SMITH, ROGERS   1997   *Civic Ideals: Conflicting Visions of Citizenship in U.S. History*. New Haven, Conn.: Yale University Press.

WALZER, MICHAEL   1989   Citizenship. Pages 211–219 in Terence Ball, James Farr, and Russell L. Hanson, eds., *Political Innovation and Conceptual Change*. Cambridge, Mass.: Cambridge University Press.

CITY COUNCIL OF LOS ANGELES v. TAXPAYERS FOR VINCENT
466 U.S. 789 (1984)

A Los Angeles ordinance prohibited the posting of signs on public property. Supporters of a candidate for city council sued to enjoin city officials from continuing to remove their signs from utility poles; they were joined as plaintiffs by the company that made and posted the signs for them. Of the 1,207 signs removed during one week of the campaign, 48 supported the candidate; most were commercial signs. The Supreme Court, 6–3, rejected constitutional attacks on the ordinance on its face and as applied.

The case seemed to call for analysis according to the principles governing rights of access to the PUBLIC FORUM—rights particularly valuable to people of limited means. Instead, Justice JOHN PAUL STEVENS, for the Court, applied the set of rules announced in UNITED STATES V. O'BRIEN (1968), suggesting the possibility that those rules might in the future be applied routinely to FIRST AMENDMENT cases involving regulations that are not aimed at message content. Here the government interest in aesthetic values was substantial; the city had no purpose to suppress a particular message; and the law curtailed no more speech than was necessary to its purpose. In a bow to public forum reasoning, Stevens noted that other means of communication remained open to the plaintiffs.

The dissenters, led by Justice WILLIAM J. BRENNAN, ar-gued that the assertion of aesthetic purposes deserved careful scrutiny to assure even-handed regulation, narrowly tailored to aesthetic objectives that were both comprehensively carried out and precisely defined. The City had made no such showing here, they contended.

Critics of the decision have suggested that it is part of a larger inegalitarian trend in BURGER COURT decisions concerning the FREEDOM OF SPEECH and FREEDOM OF THE PRESS, a trend exemplified by BUCKLEY V. VALEO (1976) and HUDGENS V. NLRB (1976).

KENNETH L. KARST
(1986)

CITY OF . . .

See: entry under name of city

CIVIL DISOBEDIENCE

Civil disobedience is a public, nonviolent, political act contrary to law usually done with the aim of bringing about a change in the law or policies of the government. The idea of civil disobedience is deeply rooted in our civilization, with examples evident in the life of Socrates, the early Christian society, the writings of Thomas Aquinas and Henry David Thoreau, and the Indian nationalist movement led by Gandhi.

The many occurrences of civil disobedience throughout American history have had a profound impact on the legal system and society as a whole. The Constitution does not provide immunity for those who practice civil disobedience, but because the United States is a representative democracy with deep respect for constitutional values, the system is uniquely responsive to acts of civil disobedience. Examples of civil disobedience in American history include the Quakers' refusal to pay taxes to support the colonial Massachusetts Church, the labor movement's use of the tactic in the early twentieth century, and citizens' withholding of taxes in protest of military and nuclear expenditures.

The fundamental justification for civil disobedience is that some persons feel bound by philosophy, religion, morality, or some other principle to disobey a law that they feel is unjust. As MARTIN LUTHER KING, JR., wrote in his *Letter from Birmingham Jail*, "I submit that an individual who breaks a law that his conscience tells him is unjust, and willingly accepts the penalty by staying in jail to arouse the conscience of the community over its injustice, is in reality expressing the very highest respect for law." Civil disobedience is most justifiable when prior lawful attempts to rectify the situation have failed; and when the acts of civil disobedience are done to force the society to recognize the problem; when performed openly and publicly; and when the actor will accept the punishment. Many proponents urge that civil disobedience be used only in the most extreme cases, arguing that the Constitution provides many opportunities to voice one's grievances without breaking the law.

Opponents of civil disobedience see it as a threat to democratic society and the forerunner of violence and anarchy. The premise of stable democracy, they contend, is that the minority will accept the will of the majority. Opponents argue that the lack of a coherent theory of civil disobedience can result in the abuse of the tactic.

Civil disobedience may be designed to change the Constitution itself. The responsiveness of the Constitution to the voice of dissent and civil disobedience is particularly evident in two movements in our history: the women's suffrage movement and the antislavery movement. These movements brought about great constitutional changes through a variety of political strategies, including civil disobedience.

The women's suffrage movement began in the first part of the nineteenth century. Increasing numbers of women were becoming active in political parties, humanitarian societies, educational societies, labor agitation groups, antislavery associations, and temperance associations. By 1848, the women had organized the National Women's Rights Convention at SENECA FALLS where ELIZABETH CADY STANTON and Lucretia Mott led the women in writing the Declaration of Sentiments. A main tenet of the declaration was that women should be granted the right to vote in order to preserve the government as one that has the consent of the governed. The women used a variety of tactics in their struggle to obtain the franchise, including conventional political tactics, lobbying at the national, state, and local levels, and petitions. An important tactic in the women's fight was the use of civil disobedience, which helped gain support and publicity for their cause. The methods of civil disobedience included voting in elections (which was illegal), refusing to pay taxes, and PICKETING the White House.

A visible act of civil disobedience used by the women's movement was to register and vote in elections. A prominent example occurred in 1872 when SUSAN B. ANTHONY and fourteen other women registered and voted in Rochester, New York. They were accused and charged with a crime "of voting without the lawful right to vote." The women argued that the FOURTEENTH AMENDMENT and FIFTEENTH AMENDMENT gave them the legal right to vote. This legal argument was dismissed by the Supreme Court in MINOR V. HAPPERSETT (1875), when the Court held that women were CITIZENS but were not entitled to vote. Once the Court refused to recognize the argument based on existing amendments, the suffragist organization concentrated their efforts on the fight for passage of a constitutional amendment that would ensure women the right to vote.

Another, more isolated instance of civil disobedience was performed by activist Abby Smith. Abby Smith refused to pay her property taxes until she was given the right to vote at the town meeting. This simple instance of a woman standing up for her rights served to publicize the women's cause to a certain extent.

A final tactic of the WOMAN SUFFRAGE MOVEMENT that amounted to both civil disobedience and lawful dissent was the practice of picketing the White House in order to gain presidential support for the proposed amendment. Although the women had a legal right to picket, the policemen at the time treated them with contempt, as if they were lawbreakers. The women were jailed for exercising constitutional rights, and it was not until later that they were vindicated by the courts.

During the antislavery movement in the mid-1850s, civil disobedience gained considerable acceptance in some parts of the country. Opposition to slavery reached new peaks after the passage of the Fugitive Slave Law of 1850. The act provided for a simplified procedure to return escaped slaves to their masters, with provisions excluding TRIAL BY JURY and writs of HABEAS CORPUS from fugitive slave cases, and providing a financial incentive for federal commissioners to decide cases in favor of southern claimants. Throughout the North, meetings were held where citizens denounced the new law and vowed their disobedience to the act. Many based their views on philosophical, legal, or religious grounds. Those publicly opposing the act included Lewis Hayden, William C. Nell, Theodore Parker, Daniel Foster, and Henry David Thoreau. Some commentators believe that a clear and direct line runs from the antislavery crusaders to the Fourteenth Amendment. The acts of civil disobedience to the Fugitive Slave Act represented the feelings of a substantial portion of the country at the time. This opinion was eventually transformed into the THIRTEENTH, Fourteenth, and Fifteenth Amendments, which abolished slavery, guaranteed the former slaves' citizenship, and protected their right to vote. Civil disobedience remains a potentially significant tool for effecting constitutional change.

The Constitution has been used to justify civil disobedience. Examples in our recent history include the CIVIL RIGHTS MOVEMENT and military resistance. Some of the best-known uses of civil disobedience occurred during the civil rights movements of the 1950s and 1960s. Martin Luther King, Jr., and his followers felt compelled to disobey laws that continued the practice of SEGREGATION; they opposed the laws on moral, ethical, and constitutional grounds. In fact, some of the laws they allegedly disobeyed were unconstitutional. Although the movement initially attempted to change the system through conventional legal and political channels, it eventually turned to the tactics of civil disobedience in order to bring national attention to its cause. By appealing to the Constitution as justification for their acts of civil disobedience, the civil rights leaders made important contributions to the development of constitutional law in the areas of EQUAL PROTECTION, DUE PROCESS, and FREEDOM OF SPEECH.

The civil rights movement's tactics included SIT-INS, designed to protest the laws and the practice of segregated lunch counters and restaurants. Black students entered restaurants and requested to be served in the white part of the establishment. When they refused to leave upon the owner's request, they were arrested on grounds of criminal TRESPASS.

Quite a few of these cases were heard by the Supreme Court, where the blacks argued that the equal protection clause of the Fourteenth Amendment made these laws unconstitutional. In *Peterson v. City of Greenville* (1963) ten black students had been arrested after they refused to leave a segregated restaurant. The Supreme Court reversed their convictions, holding that the laws requiring segregation violated the equal protection clause of the Fourteenth Amendment. The court reasoned that there was sufficient STATE ACTION because of the existence of the statute, which indicated the state policy in favor of segregation. Many factually similar cases were reversed on the authority of the *Peterson* decision. In addition to using the equal protection clause, the courts sometimes held that the laws as applied to black citizens were VOID FOR VAGUENESS or for lack of NOTICE.

The sit-ins, freedom rides, and continued demonstrations eventually swayed public opinion and contributed to the passage of the CIVIL RIGHTS ACT OF 1964, which prohibited discrimination in many areas of life. Under the act, many acts that had previously amounted to civil disobedience became protected by law.

In addition to the successes achieved in RACIAL DISCRIMINATION law, the civil rights movement and its acts of civil disobedience have contributed to the FIRST AMENDMENT law regarding freedom of speech and FREEDOM OF ASSEMBLY AND ASSOCIATION. For example, in COX V. LOUISIANA (1964) peaceful civil rights demonstrators were convicted of disturbing the peace. The Court struck down the BREACH OF THE PEACE statute for vagueness and OVERBREADTH, thus expanding constitutional rights to free speech and assembly.

Although the civil rights movement involved acts of civil disobedience on a massive scale, resistance to the country's military policy has traditionally involved more solitary acts. Still, the resisters have based many of their arguments on constitutional provisions. These arguments have not always been successful, but the protesters succeeded in calling attention to causes such as opposition to war and military policy.

Those opposed to the country's military policy have used both indirect and direct methods of civil disobedience. Examples of indirect methods include DRAFT CARD BURNING, supplying false information on tax forms, and trespassing on government grounds. Although the protesters gained publicity from these tactics, the disobedient's claims of freedom of speech and RELIGIOUS LIBERTY under the First Amendment usually have not been accepted by the courts. A well-known example of the use of indirect civil disobedience is the Catonsville Nine case in which protesters entered the office of the local Selective Service Board and destroyed government records. Their defense, based on philosophical and moral grounds, was held insufficient by the courts.

Direct forms of civil disobedience to war have included resistance to the draft and refusal to pay taxes. The disobedience surrounding the draft has taken many forms, but many legal challenges have focused on the SELECTIVE SERVICE ACT. In several cases, the men who refused induction argued that the CONSCIENTIOUS OBJECTION provision was unconstitutional as it applied to the individual. They argued that to construe the provision as requiring a belief in a supreme being was a violation of the free exercise clause of the First Amendment. The Court has avoided the constitutional questions in these cases by giving a broad construction to statutory exemptions of the conscientious objectors. Another direct form of civil disobedience used to protest the country's involvement in war has been to withhold the payment of taxes, arguing that to support a war that one does not believe in is in violation of the free exercise clause. The Supreme Court has never decided the constitutional issues in these cases. Although both direct and indirect forms of civil disobedience in resistance to military policy have been equally unsuccessful in presenting legal challenges to laws, they have been successful in publicizing the disobedients' grievances.

The debate concerning the morality or justification for the use of civil disobedience as a method of effecting change in society will never be fully resolved. However, civil disobedience remains a significant and often successful tactic used in many movements in American society. The use of civil disobedience, when incorporated with other conventional political strategies, can lead to profound changes in the Constitution itself or in the interpretation of the document. American society's positive response to certain acts of civil disobedience can be seen in the civil rights movement, the women's suffrage movement, and the antislavery movement. Although not all acts of civil disobedience yield substantial changes, our democratic system provides the opportunity for civil disobedience to contribute to significant changes in society.

ROBERT F. DRINAN, S.J.
(1986)

Bibliography

FORTAS, ABE 1968 *Concerning Dissent and Civil Disobedience.* New York: World Publishing Co.
GREENBERG, JACK 1968 "The Supreme Court, Civil Rights, and Civil Dissonance." *Yale Law Journal* 77:1520–1544.
KALVEN, HARRY, JR. 1965 *The Negro and the First Amendment.* Columbus: Ohio State University Press.
WEBER, DAVID R., ed. 1978 *Civil Disobedience in America.* Ithaca, N.Y.: Cornell University Press.

CIVIL FORFEITURE

Forfeiture refers to the government's uncompensated confiscation of PROPERTY that is implicated in crime. The property may be used to commit crime, be its product, or be obtained with its fruits. A home, for example, that is bought with money from a robbery or illegal drug sales is subject to forfeiture. The government may prosecute the culprit criminally and, on his conviction, confiscate his property as part of his punishment, or it may proceed against the property in a civil suit by means of a procedure that is at war with the Constitution.

Unlike EMINENT DOMAIN, forfeiture excludes any compensation for the confiscated property. In the case of civil forfeiture, unfairness and injustice always prevail. "Civil forfeiture," declared the president of the National Association of Criminal Defense Attorneys, "is essentially government thievery." If the civil forfeiture laws of the states and the federal government are a license to steal, the cops are the robbers. Police shake down suspects, confiscate their cash, and make no arrests. At airports, law enforcement officers routinely take cash from travelers who supposedly fit a drug-smuggler profile or otherwise look suspicious. The promise of forfeiture lures officers and prosecutors to seize what they can, because they are able to keep for law enforcement purposes most of what they seize, or they can use the assets for whatever they need—weapons, helicopters, cellular phones, salary increases, bulletproof vests, or new police cars with which to conduct the war against crime.

About 80 percent of all civil forfeiture cases are uncontested, quite likely because most of the suspects are in fact guilty. But many forfeiture victims are innocent. One Floridian, for example, bought a new sailboat for $24,000. Customs officers, who often suspect boat owners of smuggling drugs, seized his sailboat and conducted a seven-hour search, during which time they ripped out its woodwork, smashed its engine, ruptured its fuel tank, and drilled holes in its hull, many below the water line. The officers, who found no drugs, damaged the boat beyond repair, forcing the innocent owner to sell it for scrap. Law enforcement officers seize money, cars, houses, land, and businesses, yet the victims often cannot afford to contest a forfeiture because of the high cost of lawyers. Legal fees can easily run to considerably more than the value of most forfeitures. As one defense attorney declared, "Sue to get your car back? Forget it. If they take your car, it's gone. Unless I get pissed off and take a case for the sweet pleasure of revenge, I'm not going to handle anything less than $75,000 in assets, from which I'd get one-third." A Connecticut family, whose grandson kept controlled substances in his room, lost their home and denounced the government's greed as "Nazi justice." A man who ran an air charter service innocently carried a passenger whose luggage contained drug money. As a result of the search by drug enforcement agents, who caused damage of at least $50,000 for which the Drug Enforcement Agency (DEA) is not liable, the owner of the charter service had to declare BANKRUPTCY, lost his business, and became a truck driver.

Civil forfeitures have a peculiar character—the government sues the supposedly guilty property, not its owners. Thus, in *United States v. One 6.5 mm. Mannlicher-Carcano Military Rifle* (1966), the government sued the rifle that was used to assassinate President JOHN F. KENNEDY. As the Court observed, the law ascribes "to the property a certain personality, a power of complicity and guilt in the wrong." In another case the Court explained, "Traditionally, forfeiture actions have proceeded upon the fiction that the inanimate objects themselves can be guilty of wrongdoing. Simply put, the theory has been that if the object is 'guilty,' it should be held forfeit." The innocence of its owner is irrelevant as a matter of law. The guilt attaches to the thing by which a wrong has been done, and the government profits from the wrong. Forfeitures are an important source of government revenue, and because no person is found guilty in a civil forfeiture case, the forfeiture is held not to constitute punishment—a blatant misconception. A tiny trace of marijuana suffices to justify the forfeiture of a vessel, vehicle, or home.

Civil forfeiture is attractive to the nation's lawmakers because it is much more likely to be successful than a criminal forfeiture proceeding in which the defendant has the benefits of all the rights of the criminally accused guaranteed by the Constitution, plus the presumption that he is innocent until the government proves otherwise beyond a reasonable doubt. In a civil forfeiture case, the government does not have to establish the person's guilt; he is not a party to the case. The obligation of the government is simply to show that a probable causal connection exists between the property and the commission of a crime. Hearsay, circumstantial evidence, and anything more than a hunch can be used to establish PROBABLE CAUSE. That done, the burden shifts to the owner of the property or to its claimant to establish by a preponderance of evidence that the property is "innocent." Owners or claimants have no way to exercise their constitutional rights. In civil forfeitures, the property that is sued has no rights. Civil forfeiture is swift, cheap, and pretty much a sure thing from the government's standpoint.

The leading American case, decided in 1974, involved the Pearson Yacht Company, which had rented its vessel to someone who left the remains of one marijuana cigarette, which the state discovered on searching the ship. The company had no knowledge that its yacht had been used in violation of state law, yet the Court held against the company and in favor of the forfeiture. The Court, ruling that the innocence of the company mattered not at all, reasoned that the law proceeded not against the owner of the property but against the yacht itself, because the yacht was the guilty party. Intellectual flimflammery characterizes the law of civil forfeiture.

LEONARD W. LEVY
(2000)

(SEE ALSO: *Double Jeopardy.*)

Bibliography
LEVY, LEONARD W. 1996 *A License to Steal: The Forfeiture of Property.* Chapel Hill: University of North Carolina Press.

CIVIL LIBERTIES

WILLIAM BLACKSTONE described civil liberty as "the great end of all human society and government . . . that state in which each individual has the power to pursue his own happiness according to his own views of his interest, and the dictates of his conscience, unrestrained, except by equal, just, and impartial laws." As a matter of law, civil liberties are usually claims of right that a citizen may assert against the state. In the United States the term "civil liberties" is often used in a narrower sense to refer to RELIGIOUS LIBERTY, personal privacy, and the right to DUE PROCESS OF LAW, or to other limitations on the power of the state to restrict individual freedom of action. In this sense, civil liberties may be distinguished from rights to equality (sometimes called "civil rights"), although the latter have increasingly been recognized as important elements of individual freedom because they permit participation in society without regard to race, religion, sex, or other characteristics unrelated to individual capacity.

The concept of civil liberties is a logical corollary to the ideas of LIMITED GOVERNMENT and RULE OF LAW. When government acts arbitrarily, it infringes civil liberty; the rule of law combats and confines these excesses of power. The concept "government of laws, not of men" reflects this idea as does the vision of justice as fairness.

Although civil liberties are usually associated in practice with democratic forms of government, liberty and democracy are distinct concepts. An authoritarian government structure may recognize certain limits on the capacity of the state to interfere with the autonomy of the individual. Correspondingly, calling a state democratic does not tell us about the extent to which it recognizes civil liberty. Thus, "civil liberties" does not refer to a particular form of political structure but to the relationship between the individual and the state, however the state may be organized. But civil liberties do presuppose order. As Chief Justice CHARLES EVANS HUGHES said in COX V. NEW HAMPSHIRE (1941), "Civil liberties imply the existence of an organized society maintaining public order without which liberty itself would be lost in the excesses of unrestrained abuses."

In the final analysis, civil liberties are based on the integrity and dignity of the individual. This idea was expressed by George C. Marshall, who was chief of staff to the American army in WORLD WAR II and later served as secretary of state: "We believe that human beings have . . . rights that may not be given or taken away. They include the right of every individual to develop his mind and his soul in the ways of his own choice, free of fear and coercion—provided only that he does not interfere with the rights of others."

There are two principal justifications for preferring individual liberties to the interests of the general community—justice and self-interest. At the very least, justice requires norms by which persons in authority treat those within their power fairly and evenly. Self-interest suggests that our own rights are secure only if the rights of others are protected.

Because these two justifications for civil liberties are abstractions to most people, they are often subordinated to more immediate concerns of the state or the majority. In America, even administrations relatively friendly to civil liberty have perpetrated some of the worst violations. The administration of FRANKLIN D. ROOSEVELT interned Japanese Americans during World War II. ABRAHAM LINCOLN suspended the right of HABEAS CORPUS. And as Leonard W. Levy has reminded us, THOMAS JEFFERSON was far more of a libertarian as a private citizen than when he was in power. Nevertheless, civil liberties have been more broadly defined and fully respected in the United States than in other nations.

The roots of American civil liberties can be traced to

ancient times. The city-state of Athens made a lasting contribution to civil liberty. In the sixth century B.C., Solon, the magistrate of Athens, produced a constitution that, while flawed, gave the poor a voice in the election of magistrates and the right to call public officials to account. Solon is also credited with first expressing the idea of the rule of law. But Athens knew no limits on the right of the majority to adopt any law it chose, and there was no concept of individual rights against the state. Greek philosophers introduced the idea of "natural law" and the derivative concept of equality; all Athenians (except slaves) were equal citizens, for all possessed reason and owed a common duty to natural law.

The Romans also contributed to civil liberties, first through a rudimentary SEPARATION OF POWERS of government and later by the further development of natural law. Justinian's *Institutes* recites, "Justice is the fixed and constant purpose that gives every man his due." Nevertheless, the Roman emperors were autocratic in practice; there were no enforceable rights against the state, which practiced censorship, restricted travel, and coerced religion.

In the Middle Ages there was little manifestation of civil liberties. But the idea of a pure natural law was carried forward in Augustine's *City of God.* On the secular side, the contract between feudal lords and their vassals established reciprocal rights and responsibilities whose interpretation was, in some places, decided by a body of the vassal's peers.

Among English antecedents of civil liberties, the starting point is MAGNA CARTA (1215), the first written instrument that exacted from a monarch rules he was bound to obey. Although this document reflected the attempt of barons to secure feudal privileges, basic liberties developed from it—among them the security of private property, the security of the person, the right to judgment by one's peers, the right to seek redress of grievances from the sovereign, and the concept of due process of law. Above all, as Winston Churchill said, Magna Carta "justifies the respect in which men have held it" because it tells us "there is a law above the king."

Another great charter of English liberty was the 1628 PETITION OF RIGHT, a statute that asserted the freedom of the people from unconsented taxation and arbitrary imprisonment. The HABEAS CORPUS ACT OF 1679 was another major document of English liberty. The BILL OF RIGHTS of 1698 which also influenced American constitutional law, declared that parliamentary elections ought to be free and that Parliament's debates ought not to be questioned in any other place, and it condemned perversions of criminal justice by the last Stuart kings, including excessive BAIL and CRUEL AND UNUSUAL PUNISHMENTS.

The experience of the American colonies was important to the development of civil liberties in the United States.

The COLONIAL CHARTERS set up local governments that built upon English institutions, and the colonists jealously opposed any infringements upon their rights. The VIRGINIA CHARTER OF 1606 reserved to the inhabitants "all liberties, Franchises and Immunities . . . as if they had been abiding and born, within this our Realm of England."

The MASSACHUSETTS BODY OF LIBERTIES of 1641 expressed in detail a range of fundamental rights later to be adopted in the American BILL OF RIGHTS. Rhode Island was the first colony to recognize religious liberty, largely through the efforts of its founder, ROGER WILLIAMS. The Puritans banished Williams from Massachusetts in 1635 for unorthodoxy, and he settled in Providence. There the plantation agreement of 1640 protected "liberty of Conscience," and this doctrine appeared in the Colony's charter in 1663. The Pennsylvania charter and those of other colonies were also influential in protecting individual rights. ZENGER'S CASE (1735), in which a jury acquitted a New York publisher on a charge of SEDITIOUS LIBEL, was a milestone in securing the freedom of the press.

By the time of the American Revolution, the colonists were familiar with the fundamental concepts of civil liberty that would be included in the Constitution and Bill of Rights. Unlike the contemporary French experience, where the promise of the Declaration of the Rights of Man went largely unfulfilled for want of institutional safeguards, the American Constitution of 1787 embodied a republican government elected by broad suffrage that was reinforced by judicial review and by CHECKS AND BALANCES among the three branches of government.

The original Constitution, a document devoted mainly to structure and the allocation of powers among the branches of the national government, contains some explicit safeguards for civil liberty. It provides that the "privilege" of habeas corpus, which requires a judge to release an imprisoned person unless he is being lawfully detained, may not be "suspended." The EX POST FACTO and BILL OF ATTAINDER clauses require the Congress to act prospectively and by general rule. Article III guarantees a jury trial in all federal criminal cases, defines TREASON narrowly, and imposes evidentiary requirements to assure that this most political of crimes will not be lightly charged.

Apart from the omission of a bill of rights, which was soon rectified, the Constitution's principal deficiency from a civil liberties standpoint was its countenance of slavery. Without mentioning the term, in several clauses it recognized the legality of that pernicious institution. DRED SCOTT V. SANDFORD (1857) cemented the legally inferior status of blacks and contributed to CIVIL WAR by ruling that slaves or the descendants of slaves could not become citizens of the United States. The EMANCIPATION PROCLAMATION (1863) and the THIRTEENTH AMENDMENT (1865) freed the slaves, but the reaction that occurred after the end of RECON-

STRUCTION in 1877 and decisions such as the CIVIL RIGHTS CASES (1883) and PLESSY V. FERGUSON (1896) undercut their purposes. The movement toward civil equality did not gain new momentum until the middle of the twentieth century.

The civil liberties of Americans are embodied primarily in the BILL OF RIGHTS (1791), the first ten amendments to the Constitution. JAMES MADISON proposed the amendments after the debates on RATIFICATION OF THE CONSTITUTION revealed wide public demand for additional protection of individual rights. The FIRST AMENDMENT guarantees the freedoms of speech, press, assembly, petition, and religious exercise, as well as the SEPARATION OF CHURCH AND STATE. The FOURTH AMENDMENT protects the privacy and security of home, person, and belongings and prohibits unreasonable SEARCHES AND SEIZURES. The Fifth, Sixth, and Eighth Amendments extend constitutional protection to the criminal process, including the right to due process of law, TRIAL BY JURY, CONFRONTATION, of hostile witnesses, assistance of legal counsel, the RIGHT AGAINST SELF-INCRIMINATION, and protection against DOUBLE JEOPARDY and cruel and unusual punishment. The TENTH AMENDMENT reserves to the states and to the people powers not delegated to the federal government. Although the Bill of Rights was originally applicable only to the federal government, most of its provisions now have been applied to the states through the due process clause of the FOURTEENTH AMENDMENT. (See INCORPORATION DOCTRINE.) The amendment also provides a generalized guarantee of EQUAL PROTECTION OF THE LAWS as well as a virtually unenforced right to certain PRIVILEGES AND IMMUNITIES. Finally, the FIFTEENTH AMENDMENT and NINETEENTH AMENDMENT guarantee VOTING RIGHTS regardless of race or sex.

A practical understanding of civil liberties in the United States may be aided by illustrations of three main dimensions of the subject: freedom of speech, due process, and equal protection.

The First Amendment provides that "Congress shall make no law . . . abridging the freedom of speech, or of the press." The almost universal primacy given free speech as a "civil liberty" rests on several important values: the importance of freedom of speech for self-government in a democracy, its utility in probing for truth, its role in helping to check arbitrary government power, and its capacity to permit personal fulfillment of those who would express and receive ideas and feelings, especially unpopular ones, without fear of reprisal.

Consistent with the First Amendment, even revolutionary speech that is not "directed to inciting or producing imminent lawless action and is likely to incite or produce such action" is immunized from government control. (See INCITEMENT.) Similarly, highly offensive political speech and defamations of public officials and PUBLIC FIGURES that are not intentionally or recklessly false are protected. (See

LIBEL AND THE FIRST AMENDMENT.) Because effective advocacy is enhanced by group membership, the First Amendment has also been interpreted to protect freedom of association from interference, absent a compelling state justification. The First Amendment provides particularly strong protection against PRIOR RESTRAINT—INJUNCTIONS or other means of preventing speech from ever being uttered or published.

Freedom of speech is not absolute. In addition to the limits just noted, OBSCENITY, child PORNOGRAPHY, and FIGHTING WORDS likely to provoke physical attacks are unprotected. All forms of speech, furthermore, are subject to reasonable time, place, and manner restrictions. The amendment has been interpreted to afford a lesser degree of protection to speech that is sexually explicit (although not obscene), to COMMERCIAL SPEECH, to SYMBOLIC SPEECH such as nonverbal displays intended to convey messages, and to DEMONSTRATIONS (for example, PICKETING) that combine speech and action.

The concept of fair procedure, embodied in the due process clauses of the Fifth and Fourteenth Amendments, has been viewed as an element of civil liberties at least since Magna Carta, when the king was limited by "the LAW OF THE LAND." In principle, the guarantee of due process prevents government from imposing sanctions against individuals without sufficiently fair judicial or administrative procedures. Justice LOUIS D. BRANDEIS said: "In the development of our liberty insistence upon procedural regularity has been a large factor." Violations of this constitutional guarantee cover a wide range of official misconduct in the criminal process, from lynchings, to coerced confessions, to criminal convictions of uncounseled defendants, to interrogation of suspects without cautionary warnings. Beyond criminal cases, due process principles have been applied to protect juveniles accused of delinquency and individuals whose government jobs or benefits have been terminated. Whatever the context, civil liberty requires that individual interests of liberty and property not be sacrificed without a process that determines facts and liability at hearings that are fairly established and conducted. (See PROCEDURAL DUE PROCESS OF LAW, CRIMINAL; PROCEDURAL DUE PROCESS OF LAW, CIVIL).

The guarantee of equal protection is interpreted to forbid government, and in some cases private entities, to discriminate among persons on arbitrary grounds. The central purpose of the equal protection clause was to admit to civil equality the recently freed black slaves, and leading judicial decisions such as SHELLEY V. KRAEMER (1948) and BROWN V. BOARD OF EDUCATION (1954) and legislative enactments such as the CIVIL RIGHTS ACTS of 1866 and 1964 were particularly addressed to the condition of racial minorities. The constitutional guarantee of equality has been extended to women and to DISCRETE AND INSULAR

MINORITIES—ethnic and religious groups, ALIENS, and children of unwed parents—whom the Supreme Court has deemed unable to protect their interests through the political process. In recent years, the Court has rejected attempts to broaden this category of specially protected groups. It has denied special protection to homosexuals, older persons, and the mentally retarded. The Court has also expressed the antidiscrimination ideal in holding that it is unconstitutional for a legislative districting system to accord votes in some districts significantly greater weight than votes in others.

A vexing equality issue is whether benign classifications of racial minorities or women are consistent with civil liberty on the theory that they prefer groups that historically were, and often still are, discriminated against. Against the background of slavery and legally enforced SEGREGATION, the Supreme Court has upheld AFFIRMATIVE ACTION programs for blacks that prefer them for employment and university admissions on the ground that a wholly "color blind" system would "render illusory the promise" of *Brown v. Board of Education*. It has also upheld some forms of preference for other minorities and for women. There is deep division over these programs. It is often charged that they are themselves an obnoxious use of racial or sexual classifications. Justice HARRY A. BLACKMUN responded to these contentions in REGENTS OF UNIVERSITY OF CALIFORNIA V. BAKKE (1978) by stating that "[i]n order to get beyond racism, we must first take account of race.... We cannot—we dare not—let the Equal Protection Clause perpetuate racial supremacy."

Some liberties in the United States are traceable to a natural law tradition that long antedated the Constitution and are only indirectly reflected in its text. In the American experience, for example, the VIRGINIA DECLARATION OF RIGHTS aserted that "all men are by nature equally free and independent, and have certain inherent rights ... namely, the enjoyment of life and liberty, with the means of acquiring and possessing property." This sentiment was reflected in the DECLARATION OF INDEPENDENCE, which spoke of "inalienable rights," and in the Constitution itself, which embodied these principles. In CALDER V. BULL (1798) Justice SAMUEL CHASE expressed his view that NATURAL RIGHTS "form the very nature of our free Republican governments." Over the years the Supreme Court has recognized a number of rights not explicitly grounded in the constitutional text, including, for a season, FREEDOM OF CONTRACT, and, in recent years, the RIGHT TO TRAVEL, and the FREEDOM OF ASSOCIATION. The Court's most celebrated recent decisions of this kind have recognized a series of rights that reflect values of personal privacy and autonomy. These include the rights to marriage and to BIRTH CONTROL, to family relationships and to ABORTION. These liberties are fundamental conditions of the ability of a person to master his or her life. (See FREEDOM OF INTIMATE ASSOCIATION.)

The Supreme Court's decisions enunciating some of these rights have been challenged as unrooted in the original intention of the Framers and therefore subjective and illegitimate. But the Constitution was not frozen in time. Chief Justice JOHN MARSHALL said in MCCULLOCH V. MARYLAND (1819) for a unanimous Court that it is an instrument "intended to endure for ages to come and, consequently, to be adapted to the various crises of human affairs." In the twentieth century, Justice BENJAMIN N. CARDOZO agreed: "The great generalities of the Constitution have a content and a significance that vary from age to age." Further, the NINTH AMENDMENT contemplated that the provisions of the Bill of Rights explicitly safeguarding liberty were not meant to be exhaustive: "The enumeration in the Constitution, of certain rights, shall not be construed to deny or disparage others retained by the people." Finally, the structure of the Constitution, and the premises of a free society, imply certain liberties, such as the freedom of association and the right to travel.

The uncertainty and even illogic of Supreme Court decisions protecting certain groups and rights—why illegitimate children and not homosexuals, why a right to travel and not a right to housing—should not be viewed as merely the product of politics or prejudice. There are inevitably disagreements and inconsistencies over the proper boundaries of civil liberties and the proper judicial role in their recognition. Filling in the "majestic generalities" of the Constitution has always been a long-range and uncertain task.

An example of the difficulty is CAPITAL PUNISHMENT—the question whether there is a constitutional right not to be executed even for a heinous crime. This liberty is widely accepted throughout the world, but the United States Supreme Court has not recognized it as a constitutional right, instead permitting states to impose sentences of death for murder, subject to due process limitations. Many consider capital punishment inherently a violation of civil liberties because of the randomness in its application, its finality in the face of inevitable trial errors, its disproportionate use against racial minorities, and its dehumanizing effect on both government and the people. The struggle over this and other claims of civil liberty continues in public opinion, legislatures, and the courts.

Another source of American civil liberties is the doctrine of separation of governmental powers, illuminated most notably in the eighteenth century by the *philosophe* MONTESQUIEU. Anticipating John Acton's dictum that absolute power corrupts absolutely, the Supreme Court recognized in LOAN ASSOCIATION V. TOPEKA (1875) that the "theory of our governments, State and National, is opposed to the deposit of unlimited power anywhere. The executive, the legislative, and the judicial branches of these governments are all of limited and defined powers." In the same vein, individual rights are enhanced by the existence of a diverse population. THE FEDERALIST #51 states: "In a free government the security for civil rights [consists] in the multiplicity of interests."

The Supreme Court has enforced the principle of separation of powers. In YOUNGSTOWN SHEET TUBE CO. V. SAWYER (1952) it denied that the President had constitutional power, even in time of national emergency, to seize private companies without legislative authorization. Two Justices rested on the separation of powers doctrine in NEW YORK TIMES CO. V. UNITED STATES (1971) by holding that under all but extraordinary circumstances the President lacks inherent power to enjoin news organizations from publishing classified information. And in UNITED STATES V. NIXON (1974), while ruling that Presidents possess an EXECUTIVE PRIVILEGE to maintain the secrecy of certain communications, the Court rebuffed President RICHARD M. NIXON's attempt to withhold White House tapes from the Watergate special prosecutor. In form, these decisions dealt with questions of allocation of governmental powers; in fact they were civil liberties decisions effectuating a structure designed, in Justice Brandeis's words, "to preclude the exercise of arbitrary power."

Neither the original Constitution nor the Bill of Rights guaranteed the right to vote, a cornerstone of democratic government as well as a civil liberty; slaves, women, and those without property were disfranchised. During the early nineteenth century states gradually rescinded property qualifications; the Fifteenth Amendment (1868) barred voting discrimination by race or color, and the Nineteenth Amendment (1920) outlawed voting discrimination on the ground of sex. Nevertheless, various devices were employed to prevent nonwhites from voting. These were curtailed by the VOTING RIGHTS ACT OF 1965, the TWENTY-FOURTH AMENDMENT's invalidation of POLL TAXES as a qualification for voting, and the Supreme Court's decision in HARPER V. VIRGINIA BOARD OF ELECTIONS (1966). The TWENTY-SIXTH AMENDMENT (1971) extended the franchise to all citizens eighteen years of age and older.

A controversial question is presented by the relationship between the right to property and civil liberties. As the Supreme Court stated in GRIFFIN V. ILLINOIS (1956), "Providing equal justice for poor and rich, weak and powerful alike is an age-old problem." Although some would reject any such link between economics and liberty, others disagree. ALEXANDER HAMILTON stated that "a power over a man's subsistence is a power over his will." More recently, Paul Freund, recognizing that economic independence provides a margin of safety in risk or protest, commented that the effective exercise of liberty

may require "a degree of command over material resources."

To a limited extent the Supreme Court has concurred. It has prohibited discrimination against the poor in cases involving voting rights and ACCESS TO THE COURTS. It has also afforded procedural protection against loss of government entitlements, including a government employee's interest in his job and a recipient's interest in welfare benefits. On the other hand, the Court has refused to recognize a generalized constitutional right to economic security. The Court has permitted reduction of welfare benefits below a standard of minimum need, has permitted courtroom filing fees to keep indigents from obtaining judicial discharge of debts, and has refused to recognize a constitutional right to equalized resources for spending on public education. The Court said in DANDRIDGE V. WILLIAMS (1970): "In the area of economics and social welfare, a State does not violate [equal protection] merely because the classifications made by its laws are imperfect." The idea that civil liberties imply a degree of economic security is not yet a principle of constitutional law.

Invasions of liberty are usually committed by government. But individuals may also be victimized by private power. The authority of medieval lords over their vassals was not merely economic. Today large institutions such as corporations, labor unions, and universities may seek to limit the speech or privacy of individuals subject to their authority. For this reason federal and state legislation bars RACIAL DISCRIMINATION and other forms of arbitrary discrimination in the hiring, promotion, and firing of employees, in the sale and rental of private housing, and in admission to academic institutions. The courts likewise have recognized that private power may defeat civil liberties by barring the enforcement of private RESTRICTIVE COVENANTS not to sell real estate to racial minorities and by barring private censorship and interference with freedom of association when those restrictions are supported by STATE ACTION.

Civil liberties can never be entirely secure. Government and large private institutions often seek to achieve their goals without scrupulous concern for constitutional rights. In the eighteenth century Edmund Burke wrote: "Of this I am certain, that in a democracy the majority of citizens is capable of exercising the most cruel oppression upon the minority." More recently, Charles Reich observed that civil liberties are an "unnatural state for man or for society because in a short-range way they are essentially contrary to the self-interest of the majority. They require the majority to restrain itself." The legal rights of minorities and the weak need special protection, particularly under conditions of stress.

The first such condition is economic stringency. Mass unemployment and high inflation exacerbate ethnic rivalries and discrimination, and at times are offered to justify the repression of dissent. Minorities pay the heaviest price. The victims include the dependent poor, whose government benefits are often among the first casualties during economic recession.

War also strains the Bill of Rights, for a nation threatened from without is rarely the best guardian of civil liberties within. As noted, President Abraham Lincoln suspended habeas corpus during the Civil War and President Franklin D. Roosevelt approved the internment of Japanese Americans during World War II. In addition, President WOODROW WILSON presided over massive invasions of free speech during WORLD WAR I; MCCARTHYISM, the virulent repression of dissent, was a product of the Cold War of the late 1940s and early 1950s; and President LYNDON B. JOHNSON authorized prosecution of protestors during the VIETNAM WAR. More recently, the deterioration of deatente in the 1980s has led to interference with peaceful demonstrations, widespread surveillance of Americans, politically motivated travel bans and visa denials, and censorship of former government officials.

A third perennial source of trouble for civil liberties in America has been religious zeal. Anti-Catholic and Anti-Semitic nativism paralleled slavery during the nineteenth and twentieth centuries. The Scopes trial (1925), in which a public school teacher was convicted for teaching evolution, was the result of fundamentalist excesses. On the other hand, religious sentiments have often buttressed civil liberties by, for example, supporting the extension of civil rights to racial and other minorities and endorsing the claims of conscientious objectors to conscription in the armed services, even during wartime. But zealous groups threaten to infringe civil liberties when they seek government support to impose their own religious views on nonadherents. This has taken many forms, including attempts to introduce organized prayer in public schools, to outlaw birth control and abortion, and to use public tax revenues to finance religious schools.

If civil liberties exist simply as abstractions, they have no more value than the barren promises entombed in many totalitarian constitutions. To be real, rights must be exercised and respected. The political branches of government—legislators and executive officials—can be instrumental in protecting fundamental rights, and especially in preventing their sacrifice to the supposed needs of the nation as a whole. Yet majoritarian pressures on elected representatives are great during times of crisis, and the stress on liberty is most acute.

The vulnerability of politically accountable officials teaches that freedom is most secure when protected by life-tenured judges insulated from electoral retribution. The doctrine of JUDICIAL REVIEW, which gives the courts final authority to define constitutional rights and to invalidate offending legislation or executive action, is the most important original contribution of the American political system to civil liberty.

Since Chief Justice John Marshall wrote for a unanimous Supreme Court in MARBURY V. MADISON (1803) that the power of judicial review is grounded in the Constitution, tension has existed between this checking authority and the nation's commitment to majority rule. Challenges to the legitimacy of judicial review have been rejected with arguments based on the SUPREMACY CLAUSE in Article VI of the Constitution, on the pragmatic need for national uniformity, and on history. Thus, ROSCOE POUND, the longtime dean of Harvard Law School, concluded that the claim that judicial review is usurpation is refuted by the "clear understanding of American Lawyers before the Revolution, based on the seventeenth-century books in which they had been taught, the unanimous course of decision after independence and down to the adoption of the Constitution, not to speak of the writings of the two prime movers in the convention which drafted the instrument."

Judicial review reinforces the principle that even in a democracy the majority must be subject to limits that assure individual liberty. This principle is the essential premise of the Bill of Rights—the need to counteract the majoritarian pressures against liberty that existed in the eighteenth century and have persisted throughout American history. In the words of the Spanish writer Josea Ortega y Gassett, "[Freedom] is the right which the majority concedes to minorities and hence it is the noblest cry that has ever resounded in this planet." Further, the democratic political process requires civil liberties in order to function—the rights to vote, to speak, and to hear others. Elected legislatures and executive officials cannot be relied on to protect these rights fully and thus to assure the integrity of the democratic process; an insulated judiciary is essential to interpret the Constitution.

The role of the Supreme Court and other courts in exercising judicial review is valid even though their decisions may not reflect the view of the people at a given time. American democracy contemplates limitations on transient consensus and imposes long-term restrictions on the power of legislative majorities to act, subject to a constitutional amendment, because the democracy established by the Constitution is concerned not merely with effectuating the majority's will but with protecting minority rights. Further, as Burt Neuborne has pointed out, federal judges have a democratic imprimatur: "They are generally drawn from the political world; they are appointed by the President and must be confirmed by the Senate." It is for these reasons that James Madison viewed courts as the "natural guardian for the Bill of Rights."

The central role of independent courts in the enforcement of civil liberties has provoked efforts to weaken judicial review. The abolitionists, dissatisfied with federal judges who protected the rights of slaveholders, clamored for jury trials for alleged fugitive slaves; populists have long urged the popular election of judges; and Franklin D. Roosevelt sought to pack the Supreme Court to bend it to popular will. More recently, bills have been introduced in Congress to limit the JURISDICTION OF THE FEDERAL COURTS and to bar some legal remedies that are indispensable to the effectuation of certain constitutional rights. Whatever the perceived short-term advantages of such schemes to one group or another, the long-term effect would be erosion of judicial review and a consequent undermining of civil liberty.

The centrality of courts to the constitutional plan must not obscure the equally important role of legislatures. They can enhance or weaken civil liberty and, absent a declaration of unconstitutionality, their actions are final. During the period of the WARREN COURT, it was widely assumed that the judiciary alone would defend individual rights because legislatures were subject to immediate pressures from the electorate that prevented them from taking a long and sophisticated view of American liberties and protecting minorities and dissenters. But during the 1960s Congress prohibited discrimination in employment, housing, access to PUBLIC ACCOMMODATIONS, and voting; it passed the FREEDOM OF INFORMATION ACT; and it provided legal services for the poor. A few years later it enacted laws aimed at protecting the privacy of personal information. Congress can authorize expenditures, create and dismantle administrative agencies, and enact comprehensive legislation across broad subject areas—powers beyond the institutional capacity of courts.

Legislatures can also impair civil liberties in ways other than restricting judicial review. In recent years battles have raged in Congress over the Legal Services Corporation, the FREEDOM OF INFORMATION ACT, the VOTING RIGHTS ACT, school prayer, tuition tax credits to support private schools, the powers of the Central Intelligence Agency and the Federal Bureau of Investigation, and many other issues. This congressional agenda reflects an intense national debate over the meaning and scope of civil liberties in the 1980s.

Whatever the forum, the security of civil liberty requires trained professionals to press the rights of people. Throughout American history the services of paid counsel have been supplemented by lawyers who volunteer out of ideological commitment or professional obligation. Publicly supported legal services organizations and legislative provision for awarding attorneys' fees to prevailing plaintiffs in CIVIL RIGHTS cases have encouraged the growth of a sophisticated bar that litigates constitutional issues. Vital support for the defense of civil liberties is also provided by private organizations such as the AMERICAN CIVIL LIBERTIES UNION (ACLU) and more specialized groups such as the National Association for the Advancement of Colored People, the National Organization for Women, and public interest law firms ranging across the political spectrum. These bodies engage in litigation, legislative lobbying, and public education in order to advance the rights of their constituencies or constitutional rights generally.

History shows that civil liberties are never secure, but must be defended again and again, in each generation. Examples of frequently repetitive violations of civil liberties involve police misconduct, school book censorship, and interference with free speech and assembly. For instance, the ACLU found it necessary to assert the right of peaceful demonstration when that right was threatened by Mayor Frank Hague's ban of labor organizers in New Jersey in the 1930s, by Sheriff Bull Connor's violence to civil rights demonstrators in Alabama in the 1960s, by the government's efforts to stop antiwar demonstrators in Washington in the 1970s, and by the 1977–1978 effort of the city of Skokie, Illinois, to prevent a march by American Nazis.

The continuing defense of civil liberties is indispensable if often thankless. Strong and determined opponents of human rights have always used the rhetoric of patriotism and practicality to subvert liberty and to dominate the weak, the unorthodox, and the despised. Government efficiency, international influence, domestic order, and economic needs are all important in a complex world, but none is more important than the principles of civil liberties. As embodied in the Constitution and the Bill of Rights, these principles reflect a glorious tradition extending from the ancient world to modern times.

NORMAN DORSEN
(1986)

Bibliography

BRANT, IRVING 1965 *The Bill of Rights.* Indianapolis: Bobbs-Merrill.

CHAFEE, ZECHARIAH, JR. 1941 *Free Speech in the United States.* Cambridge, Mass.: Harvard University Press.

———— 1956 *The Blessings of Liberty.* Philadelphia: Lippincott.

DEWEY, ROBERT E. and GOULD, JAMES A., eds. 1970 *Freedom: Its History, Nature, and Varieties.* London: Macmillan.

DORSEN, NORMAN 1970 The Rights of Americans: What They Are—What They Should Be. New York: Pantheon.

————, ed. 1984 *Our Endangered Rights.* New York: Pantheon.

EMERSON, THOMAS I. 1970 *The System of Freedom of Expression.* New York: Random House.

HAIMAN, FRANKLYN 1981 *Speech and Law in a Free Society.* Chicago: University of Chicago Press.

HAND, LEARNED 1960 *The Spirit of Liberty.* New York: Knopf.

MARSHALL, BURKE, ed. 1982 *The Supreme Court and Human Rights.* Washington, D.C.: Forum Series, Voice of America.

MULLER, HERBERT J. 1963 *Freedom in the Western World from the Dark Ages to the Rise of Democracy.* New York: Harper & Row.

SCHWARTZ, BERNARD 1971 *The Bill of Rights: A Documentary History.* New York: Chelsea House/McGraw-Hill.

TRIBE, LAURENCE H. 1978 *American Constitutional Law.* Mineola, N.Y.: Foundation Press.

CIVIL LIBERTIES
(Update 1)

The significant increase in the constitutional protection of CIVIL RIGHTS and civil liberties that has occurred since the late 1950s has brought dramatically renewed focus to the question of the appropriate scope of JUDICIAL POWER. Some argue that the federal judiciary, especially the Supreme Court, should play an active role in helping to shape public values—pushing a sometimes reluctant populace to make more meaningful the broad constitutional guarantees of liberty and equality. Others warn of the antidemocratic nature of JUDICIAL REVIEW. Constitutional decision making often invalidates the policy choices of popularly elected officials in favor of the rulings of life-tenured unelected judges. Schools are desegregated, prisons are ordered restructured, ABORTION regulations are voided, and SCHOOL PRAYERS are prohibited—regardless of how the majority of Americans feel about these decisions.

This countermajoritarian "difficulty" has led to consistent demands for a more passive judiciary. Only if violations of the Constitution are unambiguous, involving significant deprivations of clearly understood civil liberties, the argument goes, should the independent federal judiciary intervene. Otherwise, American democracy should be allowed a loose rein. The choices of the majority, even in most areas that implicate liberty and equality interests, should be considered determinative. And most fundamentally, they should be respected by courts.

How one comes out on this perennial debate, of course, has a major impact upon how one regards the performance of the judiciary in the post-WORLD WAR II era. The VINSON COURT (1946–1953) exercised its authority to invalidate governmental practices relatively rarely. As a result, for example, the criminal prosecution of communists under the Smith Act was upheld and the continued implementation of the SEPARATE BUT EQUAL DOCTRINE by the states went largely undisturbed by the Court.

The WARREN COURT (1954–1969), however, took a much different tack. Following BROWN V. BOARD OF EDUCATION (1954, 1955), the Court launched a virtual constitutional revolution. In fairly rapid succession the Court handed down decisions not only combating RACIAL DISCRIMINATION on a number of fronts but also requiring the REAPPORTIONMENT of legislatures, the application of the bulk of the provisions of the BILL OF RIGHTS against the states through the INCORPORATION DOCTRINE, giving more content to the FIRST AMENDMENT's speech and press guarantees, protecting VOTING RIGHTS, prohibiting orchestrated public school prayer, assuring the poor some measure of ACCESS TO THE COURTS, and bolstering the demands of PROCEDURAL DUE PROCESS. Other institutions of government, both state and federal, were forced to comply with the Justices' aggressive, and often inspiring, vision of the equal dignity of black and white, rich and poor, high and low.

The almost breathless pace of change wrought by the Warren Court led to significant calls for a judicial counterrevolution. President RICHARD M. NIXON named jurists to the Court whom he believed would strictly construe the Constitution. In his view, this meant that the Court would interfere far less frequently with the political branches of government. In many ways, however, the BURGER COURT (1970–1986) failed to fit the bill of STRICT CONSTRUCTION. Some Warren-era doctrines—CRIMINAL PROCEDURE guarantees and legal protections for the poor, for example—were pared back. But the Supreme Court, if anything, became even more accustomed to enforcing its vision of constitutional mandate against other government actors. Important women's rights, including a right to choose to have an abortion, were recognized for the first time. Protections for FREEDOM OF SPEECH were expanded. More surprisingly, perhaps, the Burger Court aggressively patrolled what it considered the appropriate division and SEPARATION OF POWERS among the branches of the federal government. By striking down the LEGISLATIVE VETO procedure in IMMIGRATION AND NATURALIZATION SERVICE V. CHADHA (1983), for example, the Court voided, in one stroke, more federal legislative enactments than it had previously in its entire history. The Burger Court may not have been an inspiring Court; it was, however, a powerful one.

The REHNQUIST COURT, of course, has yet to sketch fully its vision of judicial authority. WILLIAM H. REHNQUIST was confirmed as CHIEF JUSTICE in 1986. ANTONIN SCALIA joined the Court in the same year. ANTHONY M. KENNEDY replaced Justice LEWIS F. POWELL in early 1988. Although it is true that a few terms do not a Court make, significant signs are beginning to appear which suggest that the Rehnquist Court may reject much of the activism of its two immediate predecessors. It is possible that the Court will, in the coming decade, intentionally reduce its role in protecting civil liberties through the interpretation of what Justice WILLIAM J. BRENNAN has termed the "majestic generalities" of the Constitution and the Bill of Rights. There is increasing reason to believe that after thirty years of political turmoil over the role of the judiciary in American government, a passive Court may be in the making.

Consider a few prominent examples. In 1986 the Supreme Court dramatically announced a halt to the growth of a favorite Burger Court product, the RIGHT OF PRIVACY. The decision in BOWERS V. HARDWICK (1986) refused to afford constitutional protection to the private, consensual homosexual acts of an adult male. Michael Hardwick had been arrested—though the prosecution was subsequently dropped—for violating Georgia's sodomy statute by having sexual relations with another adult man in his own bedroom. Hardwick claimed that the Georgia law violated the right to privacy. Earlier decisions like GRISWOLD V. CONNECTICUT (1965), which protected the right to use contraceptives, and ROE V. WADE (1973), recognizing the right to terminate a pregnancy, had characterized the right to privacy as "fundamental" and "deeply rooted in this Nation's history and tradition."

The Court in *Bowers* declared that it was not "incline[d] to take a more expansive view of [its] authority to discover new fundamental rights. . . . The Court is most vulnerable and comes nearest to illegitimacy when it deals with judge-made constitutional law having little or no cognizable roots in the language or design of the Constitution." The majority of the Court claimed that if it were to give credence to claims such as that made by Hardwick, it would be "tak[ing] to itself further authority to govern the country without express constitutional authority." The adjective "further" assumes that the Supreme Court has already moved beyond any supportable role in the constitutional structure. It may also suggest that if *Bowers* is the reversal of a significant trend of decision making in the privacy arena, others will not be far behind.

In the same year, the Supreme Court upheld a municipal ZONING ordinance making it illegal to locate an "adult" theater within a thousand feet of a residential area, single-family dwelling, church, park, or school. The opinion in RENTON (CITY OF) V. PLAYTIME THEATRES, INC. (1986) carried many of the suggestions of the diminished JUDICIAL ROLE that appeared in *Bowers*. As a result, the decision allowed the regulation of constitutionally protected (nonobscene) speech in order to "maintain property values . . . and preserve the . . . quality of the city's neighborhoods."

Perhaps even more telling, though, was the crux of the Court's rationale. The fact that the statute "may" have been motivated, at least in part, by the city's desire to restrict "the exercise of First Amendment rights" was ruled beyond the scope of the Court's review; "[T]his Court will not strike down an otherwise constitutional statute on the basis of an alleged illicit legislative motive." Furthermore, the Court declared that it is beyond the judicial function

to "appraise the wisdom of the city's decision. . . . The city must be allowed a reasonable opportunity to experiment with solutions to admittedly serious problems." This language is at least somewhat surprising in a case involving the regulation of speech that is, as even the Court admits, protected by the First Amendment. In an earlier time, one can almost imagine Justice HUGO L. BLACK reminding in dissent that legislatures retain a great deal of leeway for experimentation without violating the Bill of Rights.

In the context of public education, the Supreme Court has taken these declarations of deference to local decision makers considerably farther. In BETHEL SCHOOL DISTRICT V. FRASER (1986) the Court sustained a school's suspension of a student for making a sexually suggestive nominating speech at a voluntary assembly, concluding flatly that the "determination of what manner of speech in . . . school assembly is inappropriate properly rests with the school board." And in HAZELWOOD SCHOOL DISTRICT V. KUHLMEIER (1988), in which the Court upheld the censorship of a high school newspaper, it determined that judicial oversight must be reduced in order to give local school administrators the opportunity to "disassociate" themselves from the messages contained in school-sponsored student publications. Accordingly, principals may constitutionally exercise editorial control over high school newspapers "so long as their actions are reasonably related to legitimate pedagogical concerns."

The Supreme Court's controversial abortion ruling in WEBSTER V. REPRODUCTIVE HEALTH SERVICES (1989) reflects a major change in emphasis as well. Although a majority refused to overrule *Roe v. Wade*, the Court recognized considerably greater authority in state governments to regulate the abortion process. Chief Justice Rehnquist's PLURALITY OPINION characterized the Court's prior abortion decisions as "unsound in principle, and unworkable in practice." *Roe*'s privacy protections are, in his view, "not found in the text of the Constitution or in any place else one would expect to find a constitutional principle." Moreover, they result in the Justices of the Supreme Court acting as the country's "ex officio medical board," accepting or rejecting medical practices and standards throughout the United States. Surely, the Chief Justice wrote, the goal of constitutional adjudication is not "to remove inexorably politically divisive issues from the ambit of the legislative process."

Justice Scalia was even clearer in his declarations that the Supreme Court has no business deciding sensitive policy issues like abortion. He described *Roe* as asserting a "self-awarded sovereignty over a field where [the Court] has little proper business since the cruel questions posed are political . . . not juridical." As a result, he would overrule the 1973 abortion decision outright, returning the difficult human rights issue to the legislatures for determination.

Other examples—such as the Supreme Court's rulings that minors and mentally retarded defendants can be subjected to CAPITAL PUNISHMENT—could be mentioned. No doubt, though, these few instances constitute far less than a major cross-sampling of the Court's work. In the past several terms the Court has occasionally ventured into new arenas of judicial purview. These areas have primarily involved separation of powers claims rather than classic civil liberties issues. But the Justices have also bolstered the protection afforded to some economic rights and, even more surprising, tentatively entered the difficult thicket of the GERRYMANDER.

Still, the likelihood is strong that a significant trend is afoot. The present Supreme Court seems determined to reduce its role as a policymaker in American government. If new and difficult civil liberties claims are pressed, the judiciary may be less inclined to impose its will on the more democratically accountable branches of government. Even the Court's higher-profile constitutional decisions reflect something of this tendency. In the controversial and widely noted FLAG DESECRATION case, *Texas v. Johnson* (1989), a majority of the Court voted to reverse a state conviction based upon the burning of a flag. Justice Kennedy's influential concurring opinion, however, emphasized that the Court "cannot here ask another branch to share responsibility . . . for we are presented with a clear and simple statute to be judged against a pure command of the Constitution." This desire to defer to other government actors—if possible—may be the hallmark of the judiciary in the years to come. As a matter of democratic theory, that choice may be a wise one. For this constitutional democracy, however, the verdict may be significantly more complex.

GENE R. NICHOL
(1992)

(SEE ALSO: *Desegregation; Freedom of the Press; Prisoners' Rights; Religious Liberty; Separation of Church and State; Sexual Orientation; Sexual Preference and the Constitution.*)

Bibliography

DWORKIN, RONALD   1986   *Law's Empire*. Cambridge, Mass.: Harvard University Press.

FISHER, LOUIS   1988   *Constitutional Dialogues*. Princeton, N.J.: Princeton University Press.

GARVEY, J. and ALEINIKOFF, ALEXANDER   1989   *Modern Constitutional Theory: A Reader*. St. Paul, Minn.: West Publishing Company.

GREENWALT, KENT   1988   *Religious Convictions and Political Choice*. New York: Oxford University Press.

LEVINSON, SANFORD   1988   *Constitutional Faith*. Princeton, N.J.: Princeton University Press.

MACKINNON, CATHERINE   1987   *Feminism Unmodified*. Cambridge, Mass.: Harvard University Press.

NAGEL, ROBERT   1989   *Constitutional Cultures*. Berkeley: University of California Press.

PERRY, MICHAEL   1988   *Morality, Politics and Law*. New York: Oxford University Press.

SYMPOSIUM   1987   The Bork Nomination. *Cardozo Law Review* 9:1–530.

TRIBE, LAURENCE   1988   *American Constitutional Law*, 2nd ed. New York: Foundation Press.

CIVIL LIBERTIES
(Update 2)

It is generally thought that one of the principal functions of courts in the American political system is to protect civil liberties. Yet "civil liberties" is an ill-defined concept. The prevalent modern conception of the term focuses on rights like FREEDOM OF SPEECH, VOTING RIGHTS, CRIMINAL PROCEDURE safeguards, and sexual autonomy. Yet the Framers of the FOURTEENTH AMENDMENT thought that ECONOMIC LIBERTIES were the most important civil liberties—the FREEDOM OF CONTRACT, to buy and sell PROPERTY, to pursue a lawful occupation, and to protect those FUNDAMENTAL RIGHTS through the judicial process. For most of the period between the adoption of the Fourteenth Amendment in 1868 and the NEW DEAL revolution of the 1930s, it was these economic rights that won the greatest solicitude in the Supreme Court. During the so-called *Lochner* era—named for LOCHNER V. NEW YORK (1905)—the Court invalidated maximum hour laws, minimum wage laws, union protective laws, and other economic LEGISLATION, on the ground of undue interference with liberty of contract.

The modern conception of civil liberties is generally traced to a famous footnote in UNITED STATES V. CAROLENE PRODUCTS CO. (1938), though earlier hints of the shift appear in a handful of cases from the 1920s and 1930s. In the *Carolene Products* footnote, the Court identified a special role for itself in protecting rights constitutive of the democratic process, such as speech and voting, as well as groups habitually disadvantaged in that process, such as racial and religious minorities. Over the next thirty years, the Court refrained from protecting the old civil liberties of contract and property, while gradually expanding its commitment to the new civil liberties of speech, voting, criminal procedure, sexual autonomy, and racial equality. By the end of the 1960s, a revolution in constitutional DOCTRINE and in the Court's perception of its role in the American political system had taken place.

The CIVIL RIGHTS and civil liberties revolutions of the WARREN COURT raise three important questions for CONSTITUTIONAL THEORY. First, how much responsibility do court decisions bear for the fundamental changes that have taken place in American society and culture since WORLD WAR II—changes like the civil rights and gender revolutions? For example, would it be more accurate to say that BROWN V. BOARD OF EDUCATION (1954) caused or reflected the CIVIL RIGHTS MOVEMENT? Second, is it possible convincingly to distinguish the civil liberties activism of the Warren Court from the now-repudiated economic activism of the *Lochner* era? Third and relatedly, how valid are the claims of modern conservative critics that activist JUDICIAL REVIEW contains an inherently liberal political bias?

As to the causal consequences of legal doctrine, it is noteworthy that the Court often has claimed for itself a vital role in the protection of minority groups from majoritarian oppression. Justice HUGO L. BLACK, in CHAMBERS V. FLORIDA (1940), stated that courts stand "as havens of refuge for those who might otherwise suffer because they are helpless, weak, outnumbered, or because they are nonconforming victims of prejudice and public excitement." Similarly, legal scholars frequently assert that *Brown* played a critical role in inspiring the civil rights movement of the 1960s. Critics have suggested, though, that the Justices possess an obvious incentive to inflate their contributions to social change and that American CONSTITUTIONAL HISTORY refutes the romantic image of the Court as savior of oppressed minorities. On this view, the Court sanctioned rather than attacked SLAVERY in the antebellum period, legitimized SEGREGATION for most of the Jim Crow era, validated the Japanese American internment during World War II, failed to protect free speech during either the First or the Second Red Scares, and approved SEX DISCRIMINATION until after the emergence of the modern women's movement.

Even the most celebrated examples of the Court's supposed role as savior of oppressed minorities are less than compelling, on this view. The landmark decision in *Brown* was rendered possible by a broad array of political, social, economic, and ideological forces inaugurated or accelerated by World War II; by the time the Court interceded against school segregation, half the nation already was on its side. Similarly, ROE V. WADE (1973), extending constitutional protection to ABORTION, was decided at the crest of the women's movement and was supported by half the nation from the day it was handed down. Finally, the Court protected gay rights for the first time in ROMER V. EVANS (1996) only after a social and political gay-rights movement had made substantial inroads against traditional attitudes toward divergent SEXUAL ORIENTATIONS.

Whatever the practical consequences of the revolution in civil rights and civil liberties doctrine, the Court's decisions have been intensely controversial. Critics have assailed the Justices for undermining democracy by writing their own value preferences into the Constitution, ignoring traditional constitutional constraints such as text and ORIGINAL INTENT, and assuming for the Court the role of solving societal problems that were going unaddressed by the political branches. Defenders of the Court's expanded civil liberties role generally have replied in one of two ways. Some have argued that certain rights are too fundamental to be left to the political process, and regardless of whether they are textually enshrined in the Constitution, the legitimacy of the entire political system depends on their being validated in court.

Other defenders have advocated a more constrained role for the Court, which validates its protection of rights fundamental to the democratic process, such as speech or voting, while continuing to repudiate *Lochner*-style interventions in behalf of economic rights. This position, known as political process theory, derives from the famous footnote in *Carolene Products* and has received its fullest elaboration in John Hart Ely's landmark book, *Democracy and Distrust* (1980). According to this view, courts act legitimately when protecting rights and groups unlikely to receive a fair hearing in the political process. For example, the self-interest of legislators seeking reelection often biases the political process against affording due recognition to the right of the political opposition to speak freely and have its political strength fairly measured. According to political process theory, judicial intervention in this context is vital to maintaining the integrity of the democratic process. Critics, however, have questioned the capacity of political process theory to provide a principled distinction between the contested value choices implicated in defining a properly functioning political process and those involved, for example, in resolving substantive constitutional disputes over abortion, SCHOOL PRAYERS, and AFFIRMATIVE ACTION. For these critics, the only difference between the Warren Court's protection of democratic values such as speech and voting and the *Lochner*-era Court's protection of economic liberties lies in the competing political agenda of the Justices.

This criticism leads naturally to a third question that has dominated the popular debate over judicial review since the heyday of the Warren Court—does judicial review contain an inherently liberal political bias? Conservative critics largely have succeeded in winning this rhetorical battle; even liberal newspaper journalists generally seem to accept the view that JUDICIAL ACTIVISM is a practice engaged in only by liberal judges. A broader historical perspective tends to refute this view. For much of the Court's history, it was advocates of PROGRESSIVE CONSTITUTIONAL THOUGHT who challenged judicial review for blocking economic redistribution, whether in the form of a mildly progressive income tax, debtor relief laws, minimum wage and maximum hour legislation, or union protective measures.

Perhaps of greater present relevance, the performances

of the BURGER COURT and the REHNQUIST COURT have corroborated the politically double-edged nature of judicial activism. Conservative activism has invalidated race-based affirmative action, minority voting districts, HATE SPEECH regulation, environmental land-use restrictions, and CAMPAIGN FINANCE reform. Liberal activism, on the other hand, has undermined school prayer, abortion regulation, restrictions on indecent speech, and discrimination against African Americans, women, and gays. Thus, judicial review has no intrinsic political bias.

Still, the conservative critics of the Court's expanded civil liberties role may have a point. To observe that judicial review is a politically double-edged sword is not to deny that the practice has any systematic bias, only to suggest that the bias operates along an axis other than partisan politics. Justices of the U.S. Supreme Court (indeed of any state or federal court) are overwhelmingly upper-middle-class or upper-class and extremely well-educated, usually at the nation's most elite universities. Moreover, unlike legislators who generally share a similar cultural background, federal judges enjoy a relative political insulation that significantly reduces any offsetting obligation to respond to the nonelite political preferences of their constituents. Throughout most of American history, this elite cultural bias yielded a constitutional jurisprudence that was somewhat more protective of PROPERTY RIGHTS than was majoritarian politics. Since the constitutional revolution of the 1930s, though, social and cultural issues largely have displaced economic ones from the forefront of the constitutional agenda. And on these issues, a culturally elite bias has roughly correlated with a politically liberal one. That is, on the culture-war issues of school prayer, abortion, PORNOGRAPHY, gay rights, and FLAG DESECRATION, liberal opinion tends to be strongly correlated with years of education and economic class.

This point about the culturally elite bias of judicial review is not inconsistent with the earlier one about the limited capacity and inclination of the Justices to deviate from majoritarian norms. Dominant social mores set the broad boundaries within which judicial review operates; the Court never strays far from them. Thus it is implausible to expect the Court to have invalidated racial segregation before the dramatic transformation in American racial attitudes spawned by World War II; forbidden sex discrimination before the rise of the women's movement; or banned prayer from the public schools before the gradual undermining of the nation's unofficial Protestant establishment. Yet within the parameters established by dominant public opinion, the Justices enjoy some room for maneuver. Plainly the Court's decisions invalidating school prayer or flag-burning prohibitions and protecting the procedural rights of alleged criminals have not commanded majority support. Within the limited playing field that

dominant opinion establishes for judicial review, then, the culturally elite values of the Justices may bias outcomes on certain issues in a particular direction.

MICHAEL J. KLARMAN
(2000)

Bibliography

BICKEL, ALEXANDER 1962 *The Least Dangerous Branch.* New Haven, Conn.: Yale University Press.

ELY, JOHN HART 1980 *Democracy and Distrust.* Cambridge, Mass.: Harvard University Press.

FRIEDMAN, BARRY 1993 Dialogue and Judicial Review. *Michigan Law Review* 91:577–682.

KLARMAN, MICHAEL J. 1994 *Brown,* Racial Change, and the Civil Rights Movement. *Virginia Law Review* 80:7–150.

——— 1996 Rethinking the Civil Rights and Civil Liberties Revolutions. *Virginia Law Review* 82:1–66.

MCCLOSKEY, ROBERT 1994 *The American Supreme Court,* 2nd ed. Chicago, Ill.: University of Chicago Press.

ROSENBERG, GERALD N. 1991 *The Hollow Hope: Can Courts Bring About Social Change?* Chicago, Ill.: University of Chicago Press.

CIVIL LIBERTIES AND THE ANTISLAVERY CONTROVERSY

Two civil liberties issues linked the freedom of communication enjoyed by whites with the cause of the slave: the mails controversy of 1835–1837 and the gag controversy of 1836–1844.

By 1835, southern political leaders, anxiety-ridden by threats to the security of slavery, were in no mood to tolerate a propaganda initiative of the American Anti-Slavery Society, which began weekly mailings of illustrated antislavery periodicals throughout the South. The first mailing was seized and burned by a Charleston, South Carolina, mob, an action condoned by Postmaster General Amos Kendall. President ANDREW JACKSON recommended legislation that would prohibit mailings of antislavery literature to the slave states. Senator JOHN C. CALHOUN denounced this as a threat to the SOVEREIGNTY of the states, while some northern political leaders objected to it on the grounds that it inhibited the FIRST AMENDMENT rights of FREEDOM OF SPEECH and FREEDOM OF THE PRESS of their constituents. In ensuing debates, the POSTAL POWER under Article I, section 8, and the First Amendment became the center of debates on Jackson's counterproposal, which would have mandated interstate cooperation in suppressing abolitionist mailings. Ironically, in 1836, Congress apparently inadvertently enacted legislation making it a misdemeanor to delay delivery of mail. But by 1837, abolitionists abandoned the campaign for more promising antislavery ventures.

The gag controversy proved to be longer-lived. Opponents of SLAVERY had been petitioning Congress ever since 1790 on various subjects relating to slavery, such as the international and interstate slave trade. Such petitions were routinely either tabled or shunted to the oblivion of committees. Southerners in Congress were extremely inhospitable to such petitions, especially when the Anti-Slavery Society discontinued its mails campaign in favor of a stepped-up petition and memorial drive in 1836 focusing on the abolition of slavery in the DISTRICT OF COLUMBIA. To cope with the resulting flood of unwelcome petitions, Calhoun proposed that each house, acting under the rules of proceedings clause of Article I, section 5, refuse to receive petitions concerning slavery, rather than receiving and then tabling them. More moderate congressmen, however, adopted alternate resolutions providing for automatic tabling of such petitions. This only stimulated the antislavery societies to more successful petition drives. In response, each house annually adopted evermore stringent gag rules, the House of Representatives making its a standing rule in 1840.

Congressman JOHN QUINCY ADAMS, the former President who represented a Massachusetts district in the House, carried on an eight-year struggle to subvert the gags; he slyly introduced abolitionist petitions despite the standing rule. Enraged southern congressmen determined to stop his impertinence by offering a motion to censure him in 1842. The move backfired because it gave Adams a splendid forum to defend the First Amendment FREEDOM OF PETITION and to dramatize the threat to whites' CIVIL LIBERTIES posed by the attempted suppression of the antislavery movement. The Adams censure resolution failed. Proslavery congressmen then succeeded in censuring another antislavery Whig, Joshua Giddings of Ohio, for introducing antislavery resolutions in the House in 1842. He resigned his seat, immediately ran for reelection in what amounted to a referendum on his antislavery position, and was overwhelmingly reelected. Recognizing that the gags were not only tattered and ineffectual but now also counterproductive, stimulating the very debate they were meant to choke, Congress let them lapse in 1844.

WILLIAM M. WIECEK
(1986)

Bibliography

WIECEK, WILLIAM M. 1977 *The Sources of Antislavery Constitutionalism in America, 1760–1848.* Ithaca, N.Y.: Cornell University Press.

CIVIL–MILITARY RELATIONS

The Constitution has a twofold impact on civil-military relations: first, through its specific provisions on this subject: and second, through the overall structure of government and division of powers it prescribes.

Several provisions of the Constitution deal directly with civil-military relations. The second clause of Article I, section 6, prohibits members of Congress from simultaneously holding other federal office. Article I, section 8, gives Congress the power to declare war, to grant LETTERS OF MARQUE AND REPRISAL, to make rules concerning captures, to raise and to support armies, to provide and to maintain a navy, to make rules for the regulation of the armed forces, to provide for calling the militia into federal service, and to provide for organizing, arming, and disciplining the militia. Article I, section 10, limits the military powers of the states. Article II, section 2, makes the President COMMANDER-IN-CHIEF of the armed forces and authorizes the appointment of officers. The SECOND AMENDMENT protects the right of the people to keep and bear arms, in order to constitute a "well-regulated militia." And the THIRD AMENDMENT severely restricts the quartering of troops in private homes.

These provisions constitute only a skeletal framework for the relations between civil government and military forces and between the military and society. Some of them (for example, those dealing with the quartering of troops, the two-year limit on appropriations for the army, the incompatibility of congressional and military office) have become obsolete, meaningless, or unobserved in practice. When written, however, these provisions reflected a broad consensus, expressed in the debates and actions of the CONSTITUTIONAL CONVENTION and the state ratifying conventions. Three key views underlay that consensus. The Framers believed that military power and military usurpation should be feared, that soldiering should be an aspect of CITIZENSHIP, and that control of military power should be divided between state and national governments and between President and Congress.

The "supremacy of the civil over the military," said Justice FRANK MURPHY in DUNCAN V. KAHANAMOKU (1945), "is one of our great heritages." At the time of the framing of the Constitution, everyone agreed on the need to insure civil authority over the military. One of the indictments of George III in the DECLARATION OF INDEPENDENCE was that he had "affected to render the Military independent of and superior to the Civil Power." Several state constitutions, including the Virginia and Massachusetts Bills of Rights, contained declarations that the military should in all cases and at all times be subordinate to and governed by the civil power. CHARLES PINCKNEY vainly proposed inclusion of similar language in the federal Constitution, and the lack of such a provision was the target of much criticism in the state conventions. Objections were also raised because the Constitution had no provision guarding against the dangers of a peacetime standing army.

In practice civil supremacy prevailed for two reasons: the deeply ingrained antimilitary attitudes continuously prevalent in American political culture, and the equally deeply ingrained ideal of the apolitical, nonpartisan, impartial military professional that gained ascendancy in the officer corps after the CIVIL WAR. In the early nineteenth century, the line between professional officer and professional politician was unclear, and individual military officers were often involved in politics. After WORLD WAR II many military officers were appointed to high civil positions in government. Yet at no time, in peace or war, did serious challenges to civilian authority issue from the central military institutions. When, as in the Civil War and the KOREAN WAR, individual military leaders challenged or seemed to challenge the authority of the President, they were removed from command. The Supreme Court, in EX PARTE MILLIGAN (1866), also limited military power by holding that martial law may operate only in situations where actual conflict forces civil courts to close. The Court has also narrowly defined the extent to which American civilians accompanying the armed forces overseas are subject to military justice, as in REID V. COVERT (1957).

In the 1780s there was general agreement that the militia should be the principal source of defense for a free society. Some members of the Constitutional Convention proposed prohibiting a standing army in peacetime or limiting the size of such an army. These proposals were rebutted both in the debates and in THE FEDERALIST by arguments that there was no way to prevent another nation with a standing army from threatening the United States, and that inability to maintain such a force would invite aggression. Everyone agreed, however, that in keeping with the tradition dating from the English BILL OF RIGHTS of 1689, the power to establish military forces rested with Congress. There was widespread belief that appropriations for the army should be limited to one year, and a two-year limit was approved only because it seemed likely that Congress might assemble only once every two years. The Constitution is silent on the means Congress may employ to recruit military manpower. CONSCRIPTION was, however, an accepted eighteenth-century practice, and the Supreme Court has held that the power to "raise and support" armies included, "beyond question," the power "to classify and conscript manpower for military service" in peace or in war.

The early consensus on the central role of the militia did not extend to the question of who should control it. Traditionally, the militias had been state forces, and it was widely accepted that they should remain under state control in time of peace. The national government, however, needed the power to call on the militia to deal with invasions or insurrections. Experience in the Revolution also had demonstrated the need to insure that the militia meet minimum national standards. JAMES MADISON remarked that control over the militia "did not seem in its nature to be divisible between two distinct authorities," but in the end that control was divided: the national government took responsibility for organizing, arming, and disciplining the militia, and the state governments were responsible for the appointment of officers and training. In the debates that led to this shared control, the most repeated and persuasive argument of the nationalists was the need to have a well-organized and disciplined militia under national control so as to reduce reliance on a standing army. Support in the state conventions for what subsequently became the SECOND AMENDMENT was based on similar reasoning.

In the Militia Act of 1792, Congress did not effectively exercise its powers to organize, arm, and discipline the militia. In effect, the states retained sole control over the militia in peacetime. When required, the militia was called into federal service for the limited constitutional purposes of executing the laws, suppressing insurrections, and repelling invasions. Even in wartime, however, the assertion of federal control was controversial because the states guarded their power to appoint officers. In addition, militia units could not be used outside the United States. Thus in the nineteenth century the militia was under state control in peace and under dual control in war. Laws passed between 1903 and 1933 in effect put the militia, now called the National Guard, under dual control in peace and national control in war. Federal support was greatly expanded, federal standards were more effectively imposed, and provision was made to order the National Guard into federal service in war under the army clause of the Constitution, thus precluding any assertion of state power.

In Great Britain the king was the COMMANDER-IN-CHIEF of the army and navy and in some states the governors played similar roles. The Federal Convention gave the President command of the national military forces and of the militia when in federal service. War Presidents, most notably ABRAHAM LINCOLN, FRANKLIN ROOSEVELT, and LYNDON B. JOHNSON, actively directed military operations. The commander-in-chief clause is unique in the Constitution in assigning power in terms of an office rather than a function. It is, consequently, unclear to what extent it gives the President powers extending beyond military command. In *The Federalist*, ALEXANDER HAMILTON wrote that the clause grants "nothing more than the supreme command and direction of the military and naval forces"; yet he also wrote that the clause makes the executive responsible for the "direction of war" and gives him "the power of directing and employing the common strength." The latter definition might justify a President's seizing a steel plant to insure the continuation of war production; the former clearly would not. Beginning with Lincoln, Presidents have, however, used the clause to justify the exercise of a wide range of war powers.

The ineligibility clause of the Constitution expressly prohibits appointment of congressmen to civil positions created while they are in Congress. The Framers specifically exempted military positions, because, in case of a war, citizens capable of conducting it might be members of Congress. The incompatibility clause, on the other hand, applies to both civil and military offices. Enforced in the nineteenth century, this prohibition against simultaneously holding legislative position and military office has been frequently and systematically violated in the twentieth century by congressmen holding reserve commissions in the military services.

The more fundamental provisions in the Constitution regarding the distribution of power have had an equal effect on shaping civil-military relations, complicating, and at times frustrating, the achievement of civilian control over the military. FEDERALISM required that authority over the militia be divided between state and national governments. This division has enhanced the power of the militia by giving them two masters that might be played off against each other. The division of control over the national forces between Congress and President has worked in comparable fashion. Military officers testifying before congressional committees have some freedom to determine how far they should go in defending the policies of their commander-in-chief and how far they should go in expressing their own views. Military officers working in implicit cooperation with influential members of Congress may be able to undermine policies of the President. In addition, the commander-in-chief clause has at times been interpreted to encourage a direct relationship between the President and the uniformed heads of the armed services, bypassing the civilian secretaries of those departments. The Framers clearly intended to establish firm civilian control over the military, and many specific provisions are designed to secure that goal. Yet, by limiting the power of each branch of the government, the constitutional system effectively limits the power those branches can exercise over the military.

SAMUEL P. HUNTINGTON
(1986)

Bibliography
HUNTINGTON, SAMUEL P. 1957 *The Soldier and the State: The Theory and Politics of Civil-Military Relations.* Cambridge, Mass.: Harvard University Press.
RIKER, WILLIAM H. 1957 *Soldiers of the States: The Role of the National Guard in American Democracy.* Washington, D.C.: Public Affairs Press.
SMITH, LOUIS 1951 *American Democracy and Military Power.* Chicago: University of Chicago Press.

CIVIL RIGHTS

The core of the concept "civil rights" is freedom from RACIAL DISCRIMINATION. Although the term, not improperly, often refers to freedom from discrimination based on nationality, alienage, gender, age, sexual preference, or physical or mental handicap—or even RELIGIOUS LIBERTY, immunity from official brutality, FREEDOM OF SPEECH, the RIGHT OF PRIVACY, and additional rights found in the Constitution or elsewhere—other terms can characterize these rights. Sometimes they are referred to as CIVIL LIBERTIES or by particular names (for example, gender or handicap discrimination). Although the racial discrimination cases have influenced doctrinal development in many of these other areas, standards governing them often differ at the levels of both judicial scrutiny and appropriate remedies. Racial discrimination deserves separate treatment.

The constitutional law of civil rights begins in the THIRTEENTH, Fourteenth, and FIFTEENTH AMENDMENTS. These "CIVIL WAR amendments" were adopted during RECONSTRUCTION to effect a radical revision of the status of blacks and a sharp change in relations between national and state governments. Until the end of the Civil War, the situation of black people had been dominated by SLAVERY in the South and a regime under which, in the words of the Supreme Court in DRED SCOTT V. SANDFORD (1857), they had no rights that a white man was bound to respect. Their legal rights or disabilities derived from state law, subject to no meaningful control by the national government. The Civil War amendments changed that. The Thirteenth Amendment abolished slavery; the Fourteenth, among other things, prohibited states from denying to any person DUE PROCESS OF LAW or EQUAL PROTECTION OF THE LAWS. (Other provisions of the Fourteenth Amendment had little practical effect). The Fifteenth Amendment protected VOTING RIGHTS against governmentally imposed racial discrimination.

Each amendment empowered Congress to adopt enforcing legislation. Such laws were enacted—most notably the CIVIL RIGHTS ACT OF 1866—but they were not implemented, were interpreted restrictively, or fell into disuse following the COMPROMISE OF 1877 which assured the Presidential election of RUTHERFORD B. HAYES in exchange for his pledge to withdraw Union troops from the South and end Reconstruction. During the same period southern states, effectively free from national control, implemented BLACK CODES, and later Jim Crow laws, which returned black people to a status that was only nominally free. No significant national civil rights law was adopted again until the mid-1960s.

Between Reconstruction and the mid-twentieth century, the judiciary sporadically found significant content in the Civil War amendments; yet racial SEGREGATION and discrimination remained pervasive in the South and widespread elsewhere. During the same period, the Fourteenth Amendment was interpreted expansively to protect burgeoning business enterprise. Between BROWN V. BOARD OF EDUCATION (1954) and the CIVIL RIGHTS ACT OF 1964, the main period of the modern civil rights revolution, the doctrinal potential of the amendments to advance the cause of black people became largely realized. Implementation became the main task, taking the form of comprehensive civil rights statutes, lawsuits brought by the United States and private parties, and administrative enforcement. As a result of this process, some whites have charged that remedies for blacks violate *their* constitutional rights: for example, that AFFIRMATIVE ACTION constitutes "reverse discrimination," or that SCHOOL BUSING for integration injures them. Justice OLIVER WENDELL HOLMES' aphorism, "the life of the law has not been logic: it has been experience," is as least as true of civil rights law as of any other branch of law.

The concept of "equal protection of the laws" underwent its greatest evolution between 1896, when PLESSY V. FERGUSON upheld a state law requiring SEPARATE BUT EQUAL segregation of whites and blacks in intrastate rail travel, and 1954, when *Brown v. Board of Education* held that segregated public EDUCATION denied equal protection. Although *Plessy* dealt only with intrastate transportation and *Brown* only with education, each was quickly generalized to other aspects of life.

The very factors which the Supreme Court invoked to uphold segregation in 1896 were reassessed in *Brown* and used to justify a contrary result. The *Plessy* majority held that the framers of the Civil War amendments did not intend to eliminate segregation in rail travel which the Court characterized as a social, not a political activity. It thereby distinguished STRAUDER V. WEST VIRGINIA (1880), in which the Supreme Court had held that excluding blacks from juries violated the Fourteenth Amendment because it stigmatized them. *Plessy* dismissed the argument that segregating blacks from whites could justify segregating Protestants from Catholics, because that would be unreasonable; racial segregation was reasonable, for state court decisions and statutes had authorized segregation in schools. Finally, the Court addressed what today is called social psychology, writing that although *Plessy* claimed segregation connoted black inferiority, whites would not consider themselves stigmatized if they were segregated by a legislature controlled by blacks. Any harmful psychological effects of segregation were self-inflicted.

Plessy became so deeply ingrained in jurisprudence that as late as 1927, in GONG LUM V. RICE, a Court in which

Holmes, LOUIS D. BRANDEIS, and HARLAN F. STONE sat unanimously agreed that racial segregation in education "has been many times decided to be within the constitutional power of the state legislature to settle, without the intervention of the federal courts under the Federal Constitution."

Other Supreme Court decisions, however, offered hope that some day the Court might come to a contrary conclusion. In YICK WO V. HOPKINS (1886) the Court invalidated as a denial of equal protection a city ordinance which, under the guise of prohibiting laundries from operating in wooden buildings, where virtually all Chinese laundries were located, excluded Chinese from that business. In BUCHANAN V. WARLEY (1917) it invalidated racial zoning of urban land under the due process clause. Later it struck down state laws prohibiting blacks from participating in primary elections. By 1950, in SWEATT V. PAINTER and MCLAURIN V. OKLAHOMA STATE REGENTS, the Court invalidated segregation in law school and graduate education, without holding segregation unconstitutional per se and without abandoning the separate-but-equal formula. These and other decisions foreshadowed *Brown* and undermined precedents approving segregation.

Brown contradicted or distinguished *Plessy* on every score. It read the legislative history of the Civil War Amendments as inconclusive on the question of school segregation, pointing out that although after the Civil War public education had been undeveloped and almost nonexistent for blacks, it had become perhaps the most important function of state government. In effect the amendment was treated as embodying a general evolutionary principle of equality which developed as education became more important. The Court treated early precedents as not controlling school segregation and drew from the 1950 graduate school cases support for a contrary result.

In contrast to *Plessy*'s dismissal of the psychological effects of segregation, *Brown* held that "to segregate them [black children] from others of similar age and qualifications solely because of their race generates a feeling of inferiority as to their status in the community that may affect their hearts and minds in a way unlikely ever to be undone." The Court cited social science literature in support of this response to *Plessy*. This portion of the opinion provoked much adverse commentary, some condemning the decision as based on social science, not law. But of course, *Plessy* had come to its sociological conclusions without any evidence at all.

In BOLLING V. SHARPE, a companion case to *Brown*, the Court decided that the Fifth Amendment's due process clause prohibited school segregation in the District of Columbia. Any other result, the Court said, would be "unthinkable."

The contending arguments in *Plessy* and *Brown* not only exemplify the possibilities of legal advocacy but also raise the question how "equal protection" could be interpreted so differently at different times. After all, the arguments remained the same, but first one side prevailed, then the other. The reason for the change lies in the development of American history. Indeed, *Brown* suggests as much in describing how much public education had changed between Reconstruction and 1954, how essential education had become for personal development, and how much blacks had achieved. By 1954 black citizens had fought for their country in two major World Wars, the more recent of which was won against Nazi racism; had moved from concentration in the South to a more even distribution throughout the country; and had achieved much socially, politically, economically, and educationally, even though their status remained below that of whites.

The courtroom struggle leading to *Brown* showed that blacks were ready to participate effectively in securing their full liberation. It culminated a planned litigation campaign, building precedent upon precedent, directed by a group of mostly black lawyers headed by THURGOOD MARSHALL, then head of the NAACP LEGAL DEFENSE AND EDUCATIONAL FUND and later a Justice of the United States Supreme Court. This campaign had many ramifications, not the least of which was to become a model for development of public interest law, which grew rapidly in the 1970s.

The nation owed black people a debt which it acknowledged officially in several ways. In the late 1940s and in *Brown* itself the solicitor general of the United States joined counsel for black litigants in calling upon the Supreme Court to declare segregation unconstitutional. That the country was generally prepared to accept this argument was further evidenced in the 1947 Report of President HARRY S. TRUMAN's Committee on Civil Rights. The committee called for the end of racial segregation and discrimination in education, PUBLIC ACCOMMODATIONS, housing, employment, voting, and all other aspects of American life.

Despite the storm of controversy stirred by the 1954 decisions, they are firmly rooted in constitutional law and nowadays there is no longer significant criticism of their results. *Brown* was quickly followed by decisions applying its principles to all other forms of state imposed racial segregation. Courts soon ordered desegregation of parks, beaches, sporting events, hospitals, publically owned or managed accommodations, and other public facilities.

But *Brown* could not affect the rights of blacks against privately imposed discrimination, for the equal protection clause is a directive to the states. The admonition that "no state" shall deny equal protection was not addressed to private employers, property owners, or those who managed privately owned public accommodations. In the CIVIL RIGHTS CASES (1883) the Supreme Court made clear not only that the equal protection clause did not apply to private action but that Congress in enforcing the Fourteenth Amendment might not prohibit private persons from discriminating. As a consequence, national civil rights laws could not apply to private restaurants, hotels, transportation, employment, and housing—places where people spend most of their lives.

In 1960 the SIT-INS, freedom rides, and DEMONSTRATIONS burst upon the national scene, aimed first at racial exclusion from privately owned public accommodations and then at other forms of discrimination. This phase of the civil rights struggle sought to move antidiscrimination precepts beyond the limitation of state power to prohibitions against private discrimination. The cases arising out of these efforts necessarily examined the distinction between what is private and what is STATE ACTION, an issue long debated in political theory and constitutional law. On the one hand, it has been argued that privately asserted rights derive from power conferred and enforced by the state and that at bottom there is no such thing as a "private" right. According to this reasoning, applying the TRESPASS laws to enforce an owner's privately held preference against black patronage of his lunch counter would be prohibited by the Fourteenth Amendment: the owner's property interest is a function of state law; the law of trespass is a state creation; prosecution and its consequences are state conduct. Pursuing such reasoning, lawyers for sit-in demonstrators identified the governmental components of otherwise private action, arguing that the Fourteenth Amendment, therefore, protected blacks who were denied service on racial grounds and later prosecuted for refusing to leave the premises. They had some legal support for this argument. Even before 1954 the Supreme Court had held in MARSH V. ALABAMA (1946) that religious proselytizing on company town property was protected by the FIRST AMENDMENT against prosecution for trespass because the town was a governmental entity, notwithstanding private ownership. Similarly, the equal protection clause had been interpreted to forbid enforcement by state courts or racially RESTRICTIVE COVENANTS against purchase or occupancy of real estate by blacks or other minorities. These cases, and their rationales, followed to the end of their logic, would mean that governmental enforcement of private discrimination violates the equal protection clause.

But the courts were not prepared to follow the reasoning to its logical conclusion. In cases in which blacks were arrested and prosecuted for entering or remaining on privately owned public accommodations where they were not wanted because of race, the Supreme Court first avoided deciding whether there was state action by ruling for the defendants on various other grounds, for example, lack of evidence or VAGUENESS of the law. In other cases the Court found state action in special circumstances: a private owner segregated because required by law; an ordinance required segregated toilets, which tended to encourage exclusion of blacks; a private restaurant leased premises from a state agency; private security guards who enforced segregation were also deputy sheriffs. But the Court balked at finding state action in prosecution for trespass to enforce a proprietor's personal decision to discriminate. The resistance grew out of a fear that to extend the state action doctrine would make most private decisions subject to government control. Moreover, if one could not call upon the state to enforce private preferences, personal force might be employed.

Other legal theorists would have differentiated between conduct prohibited by the amendment and that which is not by factoring into the decision-making process the concept of privacy. They would find, for example, that impermissible state action existed in racial exclusion from a restaurant but not from a private home. The policy against racial discrimination would prevail in the restaurant case, where there was no countervailing interest of privacy, but in the private home case the privacy interest would outweigh strictures against racial discrimination.

In 1964 the Court held that the Civil Rights Act of that year invalidated convictions of sit-in demonstrators, even those convicted before its passage. The fundamental question of precisely what level of state involvement in private conduct constitutes state action was left undecided.

The uncertain scope of the state action doctrine was underscored by the constitutional basis advanced for congressional power to pass the 1964 Civil Rights Act. Congress relied on the COMMERCE CLAUSE in addition to the Fourteenth Amendment because the commerce clause does not require state action to justify congressional regulation. The initial Supreme Court decisions upholding the 1964 Civil Rights Act, HEART OF ATLANTA MOTEL V. UNITED STATES (1964) and KATZENBACH V. MCCLUNG (1964), relied on the commerce clause, and upheld applications of the law in cases of minimal effect upon commerce.

The impulse to define fully the meaning of state action was further damped by developments in Thirteenth Amendment law. The Thirteenth Amendment has no state action limitation and, therefore, covers private as well as state action. But early efforts to apply it to discrimination as a BADGE OF SERVITUDE were rejected by the Court, which held that the amendment forbade only slavery itself. The Civil Rights Act of 1866 had made illegal private racially discriminatory refusals to contract or engage in real estate transactions. But not until 1968 did the Supreme Court interpret these laws to forbid private discrimination. By the mid-1960s, through the civil rights acts of that period and the new judicial interpretation of Reconstruction leg-

islation, it was no longer necessary to discover state action in ostensibly private conduct in order to prevent discrimination. With the passing of this need, concerted efforts to expand the courts' views of the state action concept came to a halt.

The contrast between the promise of the Constitution and its performance was nowhere better highlighted than in *Brown* itself. The Supreme Court treated constitutional right and remedy in two separate opinions, *Brown I* and *Brown II*, decided in 1955. *Brown I* decided only that racial segregation was unconstitutional, postponing decisions on the means and the pace of school desegregation. *Brown II* proclaimed that school segregation need not end immediately; it had to be accomplished with ALL DELIBERATE SPEED. The Court required a "prompt and reasonable" start, and permitted delay only for the time necessary for administrative changes. Opposition to desegregation, the Court said, would not justify delay. Nevertheless, southern schools actually integrated at an extremely slow pace. Not until 1969, when the Court announced that the time for "deliberate speed" had passed, did school integration proceed rapidly.

While the "deliberate speed" decision contributed to a sense that desegregation was not urgent and procrastination was tolerable, it is difficult to believe that a different formula would have materially affected the pace of integration. Armed physical opposition in Little Rock and elsewhere in the South was aimed at integration at any time, with or without deliberate speed. One hundred members of Congress signed the SOUTHERN MANIFESTO denouncing the Supreme Court, and Congress came within a single vote of severely restricting the Court's JURISDICTION. Congressional legislation implementing *Brown* would not be adopted until after the civil rights movement of the 1960s.

The refusal of school districts to desegregate was not susceptible to remedy because there was almost no one who would bring integration suits. No southern white lawyers would bring school suits until the 1970s; in many a southern state, there was only a handful of black lawyers with minimal resources; civil rights organizations were few, small, and overburdened; the United States Justice Department and the Department of Health, Education, and Welfare had no authority to bring suit. As a consequence, where school boards resisted or claimed to be in compliance with *Brown*, there was hardly any way to compel change. These conditions, not "deliberate speed," kept school segregation in place. Real opportunities for the judiciary to speed the pace of integration had to await political change. That change came in the 1960s, with the pro-civil rights policies of Presidents JOHN F. KENNEDY and LYNDON B. JOHNSON, culminating in the Civil Rights Act of 1964.

Supreme Court opinions stating in OBITER DICTUM that integration must be achieved rapidly began to be issued at the end of the 1960s. In the 1970s courts began to hand down detailed orders requiring the end of segregation "root and branch." Because black and white families were segregated residentially, the only way to integrate schools in many communities was to combine in single attendance zones areas separated by some distance, thus employing SCHOOL BUSING. Numerical standards also were employed to measure whether acceptable levels of integration had been reached. These techniques—particularly busing and RACIAL QUOTAS—have stimulated controversy and political opposition.

The integration of the 1970s in most instances was carried out as quickly as possible when courts ordered it. Although the deliberate speed doctrine had by then been overruled, such rapid desegregation met its literal requirements. In a typical case, the revision of boundaries and regulations and the reassignment of students and teachers took a few months. Conditions in the nation, not "deliberate speed," caused the long delay.

Brown, of course, concerned states where segregation had been required or permitted by statute. By the 1970s the Supreme Court faced the issue of northern segregation which was not caused by state statute. It differentiated between "de facto" segregation (resulting from racially segregated housing patterns) and "de jure" segregation (resulting from deliberate official decisions). Some commentators argued that there is no such thing as de facto segregation, for children always are assigned to schools by governmental action. But only where some intent to discriminate was demonstrated did the courts require desegregation. However, where an intent to discriminate has been shown in part of a district, a presumption has been held to arise that single-race schools elsewhere in the district have been the product of such intent. Under this doctrine many northern districts have been desegregated.

Often a city school district is nearly all black and surrounded by white suburban districts. The Court held in MILLIKEN V. BRADLEY (1974) that integration across district lines may not be ordered without proof of an interdistrict violation. A number of lower courts have found such violations and have ordered integration across district lines.

All of these standards were implemented, particularly in the 1970s, by the Departments of Justice and Health, Education, and Welfare (later the Department of Education). The private bar brought a considerable number of cases facilitated by congressional legislation authorizing the award of counsel to prevailing parties in school segregation, to be paid by defendants. But the intimate relation between politics and implementation of constitutional civil rights became apparent once more in the 1980s when a new administration opposed to busing and numerical standards for gauging integration virtually ceased bringing school cases to court, undertook to modify or revoke INJUNCTIONS in already decided cases, and opposed private plaintiffs in others.

Following *Brown* and in response to the demonstrations of the 1960s, the Civil Rights Acts of 1964, 1965, and 1968 were enacted with the goal of implementing the ideals of the Civil War amendments. But results of these laws varied according to their political, social, and legal settings. Public accommodations, for example, integrated easily; housing has been intractable. Affirmative action policies have been devised to assure certain levels of minority participation, but they have stimulated opposition by whites who claim they are being disfavored and illegally so. Controversy has also developed over the question of whether antidiscrimination orders might be entered only upon a showing of official discriminatory intent, or whether such orders are also justified to remedy the racially discriminatory effects of official policies. Affirmative action and discriminatory intent, the twin central legal issues of civil rights in the 1980s, have in common a concern with distributive fairness. Both issues have been contested in political, statutory, and constitutional arenas.

In general, the courts have sustained the constitutionality of affirmative action as a congressional remedy for past discriminations and as an appropriate judicial remedy for past statutory or constitutional violations. In medical school admissions, for example, four Justices of the Supreme Court thought a fixed racial quota favoring minorities violated the Civil Rights Act of 1964, and a fifth Justice found an equal protection violation; a different majority, however, concluded that an admissions policy favoring racial and other diversity, which assured the admission of a substantial but not fixed number of minorities, would be valid as an aspect of a university's First Amendment exercise of academic freedom. The Court, with three dissents, has sustained a congressionally mandated quota assuring ten percent of certain government contracts to minority contractors. And in school integration numerical measures of integration have been commonplace. In employment and voting as well, affirmative action has been incorporated into efforts to undo discrimination and has been upheld by the courts. (See REGENTS OF UNIVERSITY OF CALIFORNIA V. BAKKE; FULLILOVE V. KLUTZNICK.)

The courts usually have required a showing of discriminatory intent in order to establish an equal protection violation, but intent may be inferred from conduct. In any event, the intent requirement may be dispensed with where Congress has legislated to make discriminatory results adequate to trigger corrective action.

The public accommodations portions of the 1964 Act

prohibited discrimination in specific types of establishments (typified by those providing food or amusement) that affect INTERSTATE COMMERCE. An exception for private clubs reflected uncertainty about the lack of power (perhaps arising out of countervailing constitutional rights of association) and the desirability of controlling discrimination in such places. But the meaning of "private" in this context has not been explicated. Clubs where a substantial amount of business is conducted may not be exempt and an amendment has been proposed to make this clear.

Immediately following passage of the law the Department of Justice and private plaintiffs brought successful suits against recalcitrant enterprises. Most public accommodations complied rapidly. Large national enterprises that segregated in the South integrated because they could not afford the obloquy of resistance, threat of boycott, and consequent loss of business in the North. Many small southern businesses opened to all without problems. Even proprietors who wished to continue discriminating soon bowed to the law's commands. Today one rarely hears of public accommodations discrimination.

Before adoption of the civil rights legislation of the 1960s, the only significant federal regulations of employment discrimination were the Fifth Amendment and Fourteenth Amendment, which prohibited federal and state employment discrimination, and executive order prohibition of discrimination by certain government contractors. The Railway Labor Act and the NATIONAL LABOR RELATIONS ACT were construed to forbid discrimination by covered unions. But all such limitations were difficult to enforce. The Civil Rights Act of 1964 and the 1968 Equal Employment Opportunity (EEO) Act were the first effective prohibitions against discrimination in employment. Private suits (with counsel fees payable to prevailing plaintiffs), suits by the Equal Employment Opportunity Commission against private defendants, and suits by the Justice Department against state and local government are the primary mechanisms of enforcement. As elsewhere in modern civil rights law, the two most important issues with constitutional overtones under this law have been whether a plaintiff must prove that discrimination was intentional and whether courts may award affirmative relief, including racial quotas. As to intent, the EEO statute has been interpreted to forbid hiring and promotion criteria that have an adverse impact on a protected group but bear no adequate relationship to ability to perform the job. Thus, an intelligence test for coal handlers, or a height requirement for prison guards, which screen out blacks or women and do not indicate ability to do the job, violate the statute even absent a showing of intent to discriminate. On the other hand, when the statute is not applicable, a plaintiff can secure relief under the Constitution only by showing intentional discrimination.

Affirmative action in the form of hiring and promotion goals and timetables have been prescribed by courts and all branches of the federal government with enforcement responsibility. Moreover, some private employers have adopted these techniques as a matter of social policy or to head off anticipated charges of discrimination. The legality of such programs has been upheld in the vast majority of cases. Affirmative action has substantially increased minority and female participation in jobs it covers but continues to be attacked by nonprotected groups as unconstitutional, illegal, or unwise. In 1984 the Supreme Court held that the EEO Act prohibits enjoining layoffs of black beneficiaries of a consent decree requiring certain levels of black employment where that would result in discharging whites with greater seniority.

Although the Fifteenth Amendment expressly protects the right to vote against racial discrimination and the Fourteenth Amendment's equal protection clause also has been interpreted to do so, voting discrimination was widespread and blatant well into the 1960s, and to some extent it still persists. Apart from physical violence and intimidation, which lasted until the mid-1960s, a long line of discriminatory devices has been held to be in violation of the Constitution and statutes, only to be succeeded by new ones. Very early, southern states adopted GRANDFATHER CLAUSES, requiring voters to pass literacy tests but exempting those who were entitled to vote in 1866, along with their lineal descendants—which meant whites only. When the courts struck down the grandfather clause, it was succeeded by laws permitting registration only during a very brief period of time without passing a literacy test. Thereafter even those who could pass the test were not permitted to register. Very few blacks could take advantage of this narrow window, but the stratagem was not outlawed until 1939. Most southern states through the 1920s had laws prohibiting blacks from voting in party PRIMARY ELECTIONS. In the South, the Democratic party excluded blacks, and the winner of the Democratic primary always was elected. These laws were held unconstitutional in the 1940s and 1950s on the grounds that the party primary was an integral part of the state's electoral system, despite its nominal autonomy. As the white primary fell, laws and practices were widely adopted requiring registrants to read and understand texts like the Alabama State Constitution or to answer registrars' questions such as "how many bubbles are there in a bar of soap." These tests were held unconstitutional. Racial GERRYMANDERING, a not uncommon practice where blacks in fact voted, also was enjoined as unconstitutional. Other impediments to voting were not motivated solely by racial considerations but affected blacks disproportionately, such as the POLL TAX, later prohibited by constitutional amendment. LITERACY TESTS also lent themselves to discriminatory administration.

The VOTING RIGHTS ACT OF 1965 invalidated any and all

racially discriminatory tests and devices. But, more important, states in which there was a history of voting discrimination (identified by low registration or voter turnout) could not adopt new voting standards unless those standards were certified as nondiscriminatory by the Department of Justice. This prohibition ended the tactic of substituting one discriminatory device for another. Where they were needed, federal officials could be sent to monitor registration and voting or, indeed, to register voters.

Although the 1965 law significantly reduced racial discrimination in the electoral process, abuses persisted in the forms of inconvenient registration procedures, gerrymandering, occasional intimidation, and creation of MULTIMEMBER DISTRICTS. This last device has its roots in post-Reconstruction efforts to dilute black voting strength. The use of single-member districts to elect a city council would result in the election of blacks from those districts where blacks constitute a majority. By declaring the entire city a multimember district, entitled to elect a number of at-large candidates, the majority white population can, if votes are racially polarized, elect an all-white council—a result that has occurred frequently. The Supreme Court required a showing of discriminatory intent if such a voting system were to be held unconstitutional. But the interplay between Court and Congress produced an amendment of the Voting Rights Act in 1982, permitting proof of a violation of the act by a showing of discriminatory effect.

Affirmative action has been an issue in voting as in other areas. The Supreme Court has held that, upon a showing of past voting discrimination, the attorney general may condition approval of legislative redistricting upon a race-conscious drawing of district lines to facilitate election of minority candidates.

Until 1968, the most important federal prohibition of housing discrimination was the equal protection clause, which was held in SHELLEY V. KRAEMER (1948) to prohibit judicial enforcement of restrictive covenants among property owners forbidding occupancy of property by members of racial minorities. The Fifth and Fourteenth Amendments prohibit racial segregation in public housing, but the construction of public housing has virtually ceased.

The Fair Housing Act of 1968 marked the completion of the main statutory efforts to satisfy the prescriptions of President HARRY S. TRUMAN's 1947 Committee on Civil Rights. On the eve of the law's passage, the Supreme Court interpreted the Civil Rights Act of 1866 to forbid refusals to engage in real property transactions on racial grounds. Nonetheless, the 1866 and 1968 acts have been the least effective of the civil rights acts. Their failure owes to deep, persistent opposition to housing integration, to a lack of means of enforcement commensurate with the extent of the problem, and to a shortage in the housing market of houses in the price range which most minority buyers can afford. Because the housing market is atomized, a single court order cannot have widespread effect. (Housing is thus unlike education, where an entire district may be desegregated, or employment, where government agencies and other large employers can be required to take steps affecting thousands of employees.)

An effort to address the relationship between race and economics in housing foundered at the constitutional level when the Court held that large-lot zoning—which precluded construction of inexpensive housing, thereby excluding minorities—was not invalid under the Constitution absent a demonstration of racially discriminatory intent. The 1968 Fair Housing Act authorizes judicial relief when such laws produce discriminatory effects, without demonstration of intent. Nevertheless, economic factors and political opposition have prevented the statutory standard from having a significant practical impact. In several states where state law has invalidated such zoning, the actual change in racial housing patterns has been slight.

Some legislative efforts to desegregate housing have run into constitutional obstacles. A municipality's prohibition of "For Sale" signs to discourage panic selling by whites in integrated neighborhoods has been held to violate the First Amendment. A judge's award of damages for violation of the Fair Housing Act has been held to violate the Sixth Amendment right of TRIAL BY JURY (subsequently, contrary to civil rights lawyers' expectations, jury verdicts often have been favorable to plaintiffs). A large governmentally assisted housing development's racial quota, set up with the aim of preventing "tipping" (whites moving out when the percentage of blacks exceeds a certain point), was still being contested in the mid-1980s.

From constitutional adoption, through interpretation, and judicial and statutory implementation, the law of civil rights has interacted with the world that called it into being. No great departures from settled doctrine are to be anticipated in the near future. But similar assertions might have been made confidently at various points in the history of civil rights, only to be proved wrong in years to come.

JACK GREENBERG
(1986)

(SEE ALSO: *Civil Rights Movement.*)

Bibliography

BLACK, CHARLES L., JR. 1967 Foreword: State Action, Equal Protection, and California's Proposition 14. *Harvard Law Review* 81:69–109.

EASTLAND, TERRY and BENNETT, WILLIAM J. 1979 *Counting by Race.* New York: Basic Books.

GREENBERG, JACK 1968 The Supreme Court, Civil Rights and Civil Dissonance. *Yale Law Journal* 77:1520–1544.

JOINT CENTER FOR POLITICAL STUDIES 1984 *Minority Vote Dilution,* Chandler Davidson, ed. Washington, D.C.: Howard University Press.

KIRP, DAVID L. 1983 *Just Schools: The Idea of Racial Equality in American Education.* Berkeley: University of California Press.

KLUGER, RICHARD 1975 *Simple Justice: The History of Brown v. Board of Education and Black America's Struggle for Equality.* New York: Knopf.

KONVITZ, MILTON R. 1961 *Century of Civil Rights.* New York: Columbia University Press.

KUSHNER, JAMES A. 1983 *Fair Housing: Discrimination in Real Estate, Community Development, and Revitalization.* New York: Shepard's/McGraw-Hill.

SCHLEI, BARBARA and GROSSMAN, PAUL 1983 *Employment Discrimination Law,* 2nd ed. Washington, D.C.: Bureau of National Affairs.

U.S. COMMISSION ON CIVIL RIGHTS 1981 *Affirmative Action in the 1980's: Dismantling the Process of Discrimination.* Washington, D.C.: U.S. Commission on Civil Rights.

CIVIL RIGHTS
(Update 1)

In contemporary legal discourse, civil rights refer principally to legislative and judicial proscriptions against racial SEGREGATION and RACIAL DISCRIMINATION—although some branches of civil rights law concern SEX DISCRIMINATION and discrimination based on religion, ethnicity, national origin, physical or mental handicap, and SEXUAL ORIENTATION. The primary sources of civil rights are the CIVIL WAR amendments to the Constitution and congressional legislation enacted pursuant to these amendments. In common usage, however, the term civil rights includes antidiscrimination legislation enacted under Congress's other constitutional powers, federal regulations, executive orders, and state laws, as well as judicial decisions interpreting all of these sources.

There have been two major periods of civil rights activity. The first, commonly referred to as RECONSTRUCTION, began at the end of the CIVIL WAR and lasted little more than a decade. The beginning of the second period, sometimes called the Second Reconstruction, is often placed at 1954, with the Supreme Court's decision in BROWN V. BOARD OF EDUCATION (1954).

Although all three branches of the national government have participated in establishing the scope of civil rights, in recent years the Supreme Court has been the focus of continuing interest and often heated debate. The Court has played a highly visible role in determining the applicability of formal civil rights guarantees to social activity, and since *Brown,* the Court has been widely seen as the institution primarily responsible for articulating the morality of racial equality. This perception is ironic, considering the Court's role in eviscerating civil rights legislation during the first RECONSTRUCTION—a history that seems especially vivid in light of some of the Court's recent decisions narrowing the substantive content of civil rights.

Civil rights jurisprudence generally involves two broad issues: defining the right that has allegedly been violated and determining the scope of the remedy once a violation has been found. In theory, the latter follows the former because the Supreme Court often says that the nature of the violation determines the scope of the remedy. However, in practice, the relation between the two is not so neatly defined. First, civil rights remedies do not ineluctably follow the finding of a violation. For example, although the Court in *Brown v. Board of Education* determined that segregation violated the constitutional rights of black school children, the aggrieved children were forced to await *Brown II v. Board of Education* (1955) before the Court issued a remedy. Even this remedy was partial; school boards were not required to eliminate the violation immediately, but "with all deliberate speed." It is also not clear that determining the scope of civil rights remedies actually follows the determination that a violation has occurred. The reverse may occasionally be true: commentators often speculate that the Court's decision to reject a claim of constitutional injury has been influenced by concerns over its ability to administer a manageable and effective remedy. Whatever the exact sequence may be, the narrowed conception of civil rights that evolved during the midstages of the Second Reconstruction has been accompanied by a correspondingly limited scope for remedial policies.

Recent conflicts over civil rights issues reflect the ongoing effort to derive specific resolutions from general principles set forth in the Constitution—an effort that historically has produced shifting and sometimes contradictory interpretations. The THIRTEENTH AMENDMENT, for example, renders SLAVERY and its badges and incidents unconstitutional, whereas the FOURTEENTH AMENDMENT guarantees equal CITIZENSHIP and equality before the law. The late-nineteenth-century Court determined that neither PRIVATE DISCRIMINATION nor state-mandated segregation implicated these civil guarantees. Yet these principles are currently interpreted to permit statutory regulation of private discrimination and to prohibit state-sponsored racial segregation.

Thus, although it seems clear that equality before the law is a basic civil right guaranteed by the Fourteenth Amendment, this ideal has historically offered no clear basis for determining the scope of civil rights because equality is subject to multiple interpretations. In the modern civil rights era, equality has been interpreted to forbid racial discrimination, but even this formula offers no clear basis for determining the scope of civil rights. For example, it is not clear whether the proscription against racial discrimination applies only to explicit racial categories or whether it applies more broadly to policies, practices, and customs that appear, on their face, neutral, but exact similar exclusionary effects. It is also not clear whether race-conscious efforts to remedy the effects of racial discrimination are consistent with or a violation of the prohibition. It is also not clear which background circumstances and conditions are relevant and which are not in determining whether an act or policy is discriminatory. Anatole France's oft-quoted saw that "Law in its majestic equality forbids the rich and poor alike from sleeping under bridges" illustrates the transparency of purely formal conceptions of equality that do not acknowledge the importance of social and economic inequality.

Post-1986 developments manifest a ripening of conflict over the question of whether civil rights law contemplates only formal equality or whether it contemplates something more. Judges, scholars, legislators, and laymen have debated whether racial equality requires only the cessation of practices that explicitly discriminate on the basis of race or whether it also demands a full dismantling of practices, policies, and structures that continue to produce racial inequality. The opposing approaches to these questions derive from competing conceptualizations of civil rights: the antidiscrimination approach and the antidomination approach.

The antidiscrimination approach focuses on achieving formal equality through the eradication of racial classifications and purposeful discrimination. It emphasizes individual-centered harms and colorblind remedies. In contrast, the antidomination view tends to look beyond formally manifested or intentional discrimination to the circumstances and conditions of inequality. Ultimately, this wider perspective envisions the creation of legal remedies and social practices that will foster greater RACIAL BALANCE throughout society.

Many, if not most, civil rights decisions are consistent with either approach. However, rough distinctions between the two are apparent in current debates over the extent to which pervasive conditions of racial inequality implicate civil rights and bear on the scope of civil rights remedies. The doctrinal arenas in which this conflict is most apparent have involved discriminatory intent and AFFIRMATIVE ACTION.

Although the scope of the intent doctrine was largely determined in the 1970s, its full impact has become increasingly apparent in subsequent years. Discriminatory intent was first articulated as the *sine qua non* of an EQUAL PROTECTION claim in WASHINGTON V. DAVIS (1976). In this case, plaintiffs challenged the use of a reading and writing test to screen applicants for employment in Washington, D.C., as police officers. Not shown to measure skills necessary for effective performance as a police officer, the test served as an effective barrier to black recruitment. The Court nevertheless determined that an equal-protection claim could be sustained only if the test had been adopted with the intent to discriminate against minority applicants. This intent standard, as further clarified in later cases, could not be satisfied even where the employer adopting the challenged policy or practice did so with full knowledge of its disproportionate impact. In recent years, the discriminatory-intent doctrine has, in effect, provided a presumption of constitutionality to most racially unequal conditions because it is the unusual case in which some discriminatory intent is manifest in a governmental decision. Thus, racial inequalities that have historically burdened nonwhite communities and that continue to exist today in employment, education, housing, and criminal justice generally do not implicate civil rights. Although the Supreme Court has acknowledged that such disparities often result from societal discrimination, unless a particular discriminatory decision can be identified and isolated, such inequalities are not seen to raise any civil rights issues and thus require no remedy.

Many commentators and some members of the Court have criticized the Court's use of the discriminatory-intent test to distinguish inequalities that violate the Constitution from those that do not. They assert that the presence of explicit intent should not exhaust the definition of constitutional injury. Some point out that the model of discrimination contemplated by the intent requirement is simply anachronistic. In the aftermath of *Brown's* rejection of formal white supremacy, few decision makers currently adopt policies that explicitly discriminate against blacks.

Even on its own terms, the intent standard is inadequate, for racial animus may play a role in decision making, yet be difficult to prove. Indeed, racial motivation may remain hidden even to the actor. Yet another problem is that the intent standard tends to focus inquiry on a single allegedly discriminatory actor when there are often multiple actors, many of whom have acted without animus, but who, in the aggregate, perpetuate the discriminatory effects of past discrimination.

The principle of purposeful discrimination also fails to address inequality that is reproduced by social practices that have now become ingrained in American society. Critics have argued that the intent standard embodies a superficial conceptualization of formal equality in that its critical scope focuses only on the most external aspects of racial discrimination. This framework virtually excludes consideration of racial categories that are effectively created through apparently neutral practices. Sometimes referred to as "procedural discrimination," practices and policies that do not discriminate on their face, but predictably produce racial disparities throughout society are more common sources of inequity than are formal racial categories. Unvalidated standardized tests, subjective evaluation procedures, nepotism, word-of-mouth hiring practices, and even the high-school diploma requirements can unfairly limit the opportunities of minorities. Whether intentional or unthinking, these practices disadvantage and burden minorities in ways that are closely related to the formal discriminations of the past.

Such criticisms are informed by a view that the moral and political objective of the Fourteenth Amendment is to empower the national government to eliminate the effects of white supremacy. Eliminating intentional discrimination does not fully satisfy this mandate, as purposeful harm is simply one of many means of perpetuating white supremacy.

Despite the effective limits that the intent standard places on the scope of civil rights litigation, defenders marshal several arguments to justify its currency. One is that intentional discrimination prevailed during the period preceding *Brown*, and it is this form of discrimination that is now understood as incompatible with the nation's ideals. Institutionally, the intent standard is justified because intentional racial discrimination is precisely the kind of perversion of democracy that the Court is empowered to correct. Remedying these harms and eliminating these tendencies justify and exhaust the moral and ideological commitment of civil rights. Any other rule, it is argued, would involve judicial overreaching and undue interference with myriad governmental and private practices that sometimes produce racially disproportionate results. Moreover, it would stretch the Court's institutional and symbolic resources to fashion appropriate remedies if a broader standard were used. In sum, there is no ideological, political, or moral justification to move beyond intentional discrimination. Racially disparate results do not themselves speak to civil rights; it is racially unequal treatment that constitutes the crux of the injury. Under this view, the intent standard thus effectively mediates between legitimate and illegitimate conceptions of civil rights.

The intent standard, along with other doctrines in current vogue with the Supreme Court's majority, represents a refusal to extend constitutional protections to preclude institutional and systemic discrimination. Although aggregate views of racial disparities suggest that racial separation and stratification are still common in employment, housing, voting, and the criminal justice system, this view is rendered irrelevant by the Court's current framework that seeks one actor when there are often several and current and demonstrably direct causes when many are historical and cumulative.

Those who support an antidomination view of racial equality note that aggregate views of race paint a picture of society that resembles conditions prevailing during periods in which white supremacy was more openly advocated and racial discrimination more explicitly practiced. They regard these disparities as raising legitimate civil rights issues not only because of their probable connection to the more explicit policies of the not-too-distant past, but also because of the devastating effect on the life chances of minorities and the likelihood that such conditions will reproduce themselves for generations to come.

Earlier decisions suggested that the Court might be receptive to this view. For example, in GRIGGS V. DUKE POWER CO. (1971), the Court ruled that an employment practice that disproportionately harmed minorities constituted EMPLOYMENT DISCRIMINATION under the CIVIL RIGHTS ACT OF 1964, whether or not the practice was adopted with the intent to discriminate. The fact that the practice disparately burdened minorities was enough to require the employer to produce evidence that the practice was a business necessity.

In subsequent years, however, the Court increasingly disfavored such systemic views of discrimination. An ominous indication of the full implications of this trend was suggested by MCCLESKEY V. KEMP (1987) and was reinforced in *Wards Cove Packing Co. v. Antonio* (1989).

In *McCleskey v. Kemp*, Justice LEWIS F. POWELL accepted the validity of a study indicating that African Americans in Georgia who killed whites were significantly more likely to receive the death penalty than were blacks who killed blacks or whites who killed either whites or blacks. Nonetheless, the Court determined that these statistics did not substantiate an equal-protection challenge to the Georgia death penalty. Aggregate statistics could not be used because they could not support an inference that intentional racial discrimination had influenced the disposition of the defendant's particular case. Moreover, other factors, such as the state's interests in imposing the death penalty, in maintaining prosecutorial discretion, and in protecting the integrity of jury deliberations, precluded the defendant from gaining access to information needed to prove that racial discrimination affected the disposition of his case.

Although *McCleskey v. Kemp* might have been reconciled as consistent with the distinction that the Court drew between constitutional claims (in which systemic claims were generally disfavored) and statutory claims (in which the Court had adopted a more flexible approach toward such claims), *Wards Cove* demonstrates that the Court's rejection of systemic claims is not limited to constitutional claims. In *Wards Cove*, the Court significantly narrowed *Griggs* to require, in part, that employees challenging employment practices that create racial disparities must specify and isolate each practice and its effects.

McCleskey and *Wards Cove* are two of several cases

that illustrate how the Court in the 1980s has employed various analytical and normative preferences to reject the appeal for systemic relief. Its techniques include viewing causation as isolated rather than interrelated, demanding showings of contemporary rather than historical explanations for racial disparities, and embracing merely formal rather than substantive equality as the objective of civil rights law.

The predominance of the intent standard has significantly affected the development of affirmative action, another area in which the conflict between competing visions of civil rights has been most apparent over the past decade. Affirmative action, while largely referring to race-conscious remedial measures, also encompasses more general efforts to dismantle segregation and to cease the reproduction of racial inequality. GREEN V. COUNTY SCHOOL BOARD OF NEW KENT (1968) best represents this broader conceptualization of affirmative action. In this case, the Supreme Court determined that a "free choice" policy was insufficient to remedy the dual school system created by the defendant school board's previous de jure segregation. Equality required not only a cessation of discriminatory practices, but in addition, an affirmative effort to dismantle the racial segregation that had been created through express governmental policy and that would likely be maintained by the practices that were institutionally and societally ingrained.

The current controversy over affirmative action centers on the extent to which this task of dismantling a dual society should be undertaken by governmental and private entities in various contexts. Affirmative efforts have been made to integrate public and private industries, higher education, and professional trades. Affirmative-action plans have been developed as remedies following findings of discrimination; some were included in consent decrees and still others were developed voluntarily, sometimes under the threat of suit, but other times out of genuine commitments to increase the numbers of underrepresented groups in various walks of life.

Critics of affirmative action vigorously assailed the use of race-conscious strategies to benefit minority individuals who had not themselves been shown to be victims of discrimination. Their principal argument is that affirmative action is simply "disease as cure," in that it makes use of race classification to distribute opportunities on the basis of race rather than on individual merits. This is precisely the harm that was imposed on racial minorities and that cannot be justified on nondiscrimination grounds. They argue, moreover, that whites harmed by such efforts are in fact victims of racial discrimination and that the use of race-conscious efforts to correct racial imbalances violates the Fourteenth Amendment.

Affirmative action has been most often justified by

supporters as necessary to remedy the effects of past discrimination. Most of the arguments boil down to a view that a full remedy for racial discrimination requires affirmative efforts to restructure racial hierarchy by redistributing educational, economic, and employment opportunities across racial groups. Affirmative action has also been characterized as essential to the nondiscrimination principle. In this view, it is a bottom-line effort to minimize the effects of racial bias that works its way into evaluation systems that have historically favored dominant values and interests. Some argue that affirmative action serves as reparation for past discrimination, whereas others justify affirmative action as essential to creating a future society that is not racially stratified. In the words of one Justice, "to get beyond race, we must first take race into account."

Despite the polarized nature of the ongoing affirmative-action debate, affirmative action is a doctrinal area in which the fluctuating majorities on the Court and its shifting sensibilities since 1986 are best illustrated. Indeed, the Court has only recently reached an apparent consensus on the constitutionality of affirmative action.

The much awaited decision in REGENTS OF UNIVERSITY OF CALIFORNIA V. BAKKE (1978) produced something of a stalemate: state universities were permitted to use race as one factor in admission decisions; but, absent some evidence of past discrimination on their part, they could not set aside seats for which only minorities could compete. After Bakke, the constitutional status of affirmative action remained murky. In subsequent cases, a shifting majority upheld affirmative-action plans adopted by the federal government in construction contracts (in FULLILOVE V. KLUTZNICK, 1980) and in private industry (in UNITED STEELWORKERS OF AMERICA V. WEBER, 1979). However, growing concerns over the rights of whites disadvantaged by these efforts finally came to the fore in FIREFIGHTERS' LOCAL #1784 V. STOTTS (1984), in which the Court precluded federal courts from ordering a city employer subject to an affirmative-action CONSENT DECREE to protect the jobs of less-senior minorities by laying off more-senior whites.

Foes of affirmative action subsequently interpreted Stotts to ban all affirmative-action remedies that benefitted persons other than actual victims of discrimination. The U.S. Justice Department, after urging the Court to make such a ruling, used Stotts as a basis for challenging affirmative-action programs operated by hundreds of cities and states pursuant to consent decrees. Yet Stotts failed to produce a clear consensus regarding the constitutionality of affirmative action. Subsequent Court decisions upholding other affirmative-action plans benefitting "non-victims" indicated that Stotts was not read as encompassing a broad rejection of race-conscious remedies.

Despite these decisions, however, there remained on the Court a vocal opposition to such race-conscious measures. That slim majorities upheld these measures suggested that the constitutionality of affirmative action remained highly contested and subject to limitation. In 1989, a majority finally coalesced in CITY OF RICHMOND V. J. A. CROSON CO. (1989) to hold that race-conscious affirmative-action programs were subject to STRICT SCRUTINY. The city of Richmond adopted a thirty percent set-aside program for minority contractors. Although Richmond was fifty percent black, only one sixty-seventh of one percent of all city contracts had gone to minority contractors. The Court held that the city could not undertake an affirmative-action program to correct such gross disparities without some evidence that black contractors had been discriminated against in the past and that this discrimination had caused the disparities. Particularly striking is the Court's refusal to recognize the relevance of Congress's previous findings of industry-wide discrimination, and its willingness to reduce centuries of white supremacy to the same plane as two decades of affirmative action. Such findings could not be "shared," but had to be proven anew in Richmond.

Croson demonstrates how the combination of the intent requirement and the application of strict scrutiny to affirmative action combine to create the tragic irony that institutional and systemic perpetuation of racial inequality escapes constitutional scrutiny, while efforts to break these patterns and practices are constitutionally prohibited.

Moreover, *Croson* represents a decisive victory of the more formal antidiscrimination approach over the more contextual antisubordination approach, at least where Congress has not adopted the latter approach. (See METRO BROADCASTING V. FCC.)

Critics argue that traditional protections for nonwhites are being eroded while the civil rights laws are being interpreted vigorously to preclude some of the more effective remedies. This claim is not implausible when one compares, for example, the language in *Croson* (explaining how the Court's deep commitment to eliminate all forms of racial discrimination mandates a rejection of even remedial race classifications) with the Court's willingness in PATTERSON V. MCLEAN CREDIT UNION (1989) to interpret the CIVIL RIGHTS ACT OF 1866 to leave a private employer's racial harassment unremedied under this statute. Although the contrasting protections in each of these cases might be reconciled by focusing on the distinctions between the separate doctrinal categories under which these cases arise, it is hard to ignore the apparent trend in which minorities are receiving less protection against traditional forms of race discrimination while the racially privileged are receiving more.

The Court's recent race jurisprudence also suggests that civil rights litigation no longer occupies the status of "high priority litigation." The Court seems to have rejected the view that civil rights plaintiffs play a special role as private attorneys general seeking to effectuate society's highest interest in eradicating discrimination, root and branch. In technical interpretations, the Court has narrowed the availability of remedies and simultaneously shifted advantages to employers and often to white males. Most troubling are rule 11 cases, in which courts have levied severe penalties against civil rights litigants for bringing suits that were judged to be "frivolous." Although rule 11 of the FEDERAL RULES OF CIVIL PROCEDURE lay dormant until it was raised in 1983, nearly half of all rule 11 sanctions have involved civil rights and public-interest cases. Other research also suggests civil rights cases are also disproportionately likely to be dismissed given the heightened pleading threshold placed on such claims. The overall effect of these "techinical" opinions has been to raise the risk and cost of litigating civil rights claims at precisely the same time that shifts in substantive rules make it unlikely that a plaintiff will prevail. The probable consequence of such decisions is the chilling of the civil rights bar. The long-term consequence may be that law may cease to serve as a meaningful deterrent to discriminatory behavior.

These recent developments have led many to conclude that the Second Reconstruction is largely a dead letter and that the period is now more aptly described as a post-civil rights era. Indeed, the parallels with the Second Reconstruction seem to confirm the cyclical nature of civil rights protection and, more troubling, the cyclical nature of its decline.

KIMBERLÉ CRENSHAW
(1992)

Bibliography

FREEMAN, ALAN   1990   Antidiscrimination Law: The View from 1989. *Tulane Law Review* 64:1407–1441.

LAWRENCE, CHARLES   1987   The Id, the Ego, and Equal Protection: Reckoning with Unconscious Racism. *Stanford Law Review* 39:317–387.

ORTIZ, DANIEL   1989   The Myth of Intent in Equal Protection. *Stanford Law Review* 41:1105–1150.

SCHNAPPER, ERIC   1983   Perpetuation of Past Discrimination. *Harvard Law Review* 96:828–864.

STRAUSS, DAVID A.   1986   The Myth of Colorblindness. *Supreme Court Review* 1986:99–134.

TRIBE, LAURENCE H.   1988   *American Constitutional Law*, 2nd ed. New York: Foundation Press.

WILLIAMS, PATRICIA   1989   The Obliging Shell: An Informal Essay on Formal Equal Opportunity. *Michigan Law Review* 87:2128–2151.

CIVIL RIGHTS
(Update 2)

The field of civil rights generally refers to the various areas of American law concerned with a person's right to be free from discrimination based on his or her identity as a member of a particular social group. In the classical liberal political tradition, "civil rights" historically meant the universally held legal rights of all citizens to participate in civil society—for example, to make contracts, pursue occupations, own and convey property—and more recently has included the "political" right to vote in civic elections. The contemporary notion of civil rights as protection for minority groups is linked to the struggle, first by African Americans and then others, to expand the equal enjoyment of (supposedly) universally held rights to disempowered groups in American society. Today, civil rights law, in one form or another, encompasses discrimination based on race, gender, disability, primary language, ethnicity, national origin, family structure, religion, and SEXUAL ORIENTATION.

There are multiple sources of civil rights law. The Constitution contains provisions abolishing SLAVERY (the THIRTEENTH AMENDMENT), prohibiting the denial of VOTING RIGHTS on the basis of race, sex, or failure to pay a POLL TAX (the FIFTEENTH AMENDMENT, the NINETEENTH AMENDMENT, and the TWENTY-FOURTH AMENDMENT), and guaranteeing the EQUAL PROTECTION OF THE LAWS (the FOURTEENTH AMENDMENT and analogous state constitutional provisions). Federal legislative enactments prohibit discrimination on designated bases and in a variety of contexts, including most notably PUBLIC ACCOMMODATIONS, employment, education, lending, and housing. Civil rights law also includes the rules promulgated by federal ADMINISTRATIVE AGENCIES constituted under and charged with enforcement of various federal civil rights statutes. In addition to federal law, an often overlapping complex of state constitutional law and state and local enactments, ordinances, and administrative rules outlaw discrimination on a wide variety of bases and in diverse social contexts.

Federal constitutional law is relevant to civil rights law in several ways. First, and most importantly, the federal Constitution is a substantive source of civil rights protection. The equal protection clause of the Fourteenth Amendment provides that "no State shall . . . deny to any person within its jurisdiction the equal protection of the laws." The courts have used this open-ended language to craft a general body of civil rights law. While federal and state legislatures may provide greater protection, the constitutional standards set a legal minimum.

The courts early on interpreted equal protection narrowly, to prohibit only the most explicit forms of exclusion of blacks by the government. In PLESSY V. FERGUSON (1896), the Supreme Court upheld a state law requiring SEGREGATION of whites and blacks in rail cars. Articulating what became known as the SEPARATE BUT EQUAL DOCTRINE, the Court interpreted the equal protection clause to permit formal and explicit racial segregation. Under the Court's logic, no denial of equal protection of the laws was manifest in racial segregation so long as equal facilities were provided. Of course, the racial segregation to which African Americans were subjected hardly offered equal facilities. Nevertheless, *Plessy* became the constitutional authority for the legality of the systemic racial segregation that characterized the post-RECONSTRUCTION domination of African Americans in many sectors of American society.

The modern era of civil rights begins with the Court's repudiation of the separate-but-equal doctrine in BROWN V. BOARD OF EDUCATION (1954). According to the *Brown* opinion, segregated schools were inherently unequal. Relying on SOCIAL SCIENCE RESEARCH suggesting that segregation inflicted on black children a stigma of inferiority that impeded their education, the Justices ruled that state-mandated school segregation constituted unequal treatment in violation of the equal protection clause.

Brown marked the starting point for a massive increase in litigation challenging various social practices as violating constitutional equal protection guarantees. It also has symbolized, for generations of lawyers, the possibility of employing law for progressive social change. Widely viewed as the American legal system's ratification of the goals of the CIVIL RIGHTS MOVEMENT, *Brown* is associated with the historic dismantling of the formal system of racial segregation that marked not only education, but also public parks, carriers, employment, recreation, and housing in the United States. After decades of expansion and contraction, however, the potential for using constitutional doctrine as a mandate for overcoming continuing inequality has been largely tamed by the narrow interpretations that conservative Court majorities have accorded equal protection doctrine since the mid-1970s.

The potential substantive reach of the equal protection clause is limited at the outset by the Court's continued allegiance to the STATE ACTION doctrine mandating that the equal protection clause applies only to discrimination deemed to be governmental in nature. Therefore, any protection against discrimination by private actors depends on the existence of applicable LEGISLATION. Legislative bodies may, but are not constitutionally compelled to, prohibit various forms of discrimination by private parties. Under the Court's interpretation of the Constitution, however, private discrimination, no matter how pervasive or oppressive, is beyond the purview of the equal protection clause.

The WARREN COURT, which decided *Brown*, often found state action in contexts in which private actors played particularly powerful roles in the lives of individuals. The more conservative BURGER COURT and REHNQUIST COURT have since imposed strict barriers to litigation in the name of the state action doctrine, significantly limiting the potential reach of constitutional antidiscrimination norms. One consequence is that, even in the field of education at issue in *Brown*, continuing racial segregation and new resegregation is beyond constitutional reach because, as the Court ruled in MISSOURI V. JENKINS (1990), racial school segregation that cannot be traced to intentional governmental action must be deemed privately caused.

Another key restriction on the potential reach of the equal protection clause is the judicially imposed requirement that, unless the government has overtly based a decision on race or another constitutionally prescribed ground, the plaintiff must prove that he or she was a victim of "intentional" discrimination to make out a violation of the equal protection clause. Since the fall of the open and official racial apartheid that marked American life, particularly in the South, prior to the late 1960s, decisionmakers have rarely made race an explicit consideration. In WASHINGTON V. DAVIS (1976), the Court held that the disparate racial impact of a standardized written test for choosing police officers did not establish an equal protection violation, for there was no showing that the test had been chosen or its use continued for racially discriminatory purposes. Under this doctrine, a plaintiff must show that a governmental entity intentionally made a decision on the basis of a racial criterion in order to render equal protection norms against RACIAL DISCRIMINATION applicable. The Court chose the "intent" standard to govern constitutional equal protection analysis, even though various civil rights statutes permit "disparate impact" along with intent to make out a violation. Under the disparate impact approach of Title VII of the CIVIL RIGHTS ACT OF 1964, for example, proof of discrimination can be based on the employer's use of a criterion for decisionmaking that results in the disproportionate exclusion of blacks or other protected groups and that cannot be proved necessary to the legitimate needs of the employer. Adoption of the intent standard has meant that constitutional antidiscrimination doctrine is, as a practical matter, virtually useless in litigating against contemporary forms of racial stratification.

The equal protection clause has also been interpreted since *Brown* to apply beyond the context of race and national origin. In CRAIG V. BOREN (1976), the Court held that gender classifications should also be subject to heightened constitutional scrutiny, although a lesser standard known as "intermediate" scrutiny. In a notably vigorous application of this standard, the Court held in UNITED STATES V. VIRGINIA (1996) that the male-only admission policy at the Virginia Military Institute was unconstitutional SEX DISCRIMINATION. In *Clark v. Jeter* (1988), the Court extended the intermediate scrutiny standard to classifications based on the marital status of the subject's parents (or ILLEGITIMACY; see NONMARITAL CHILDREN). The Court has thus far refused to recognize age, wealth, or sexual orientation as SUSPECT CLASSIFICATIONS, meaning that such criteria have no special constitutional significance.

In one of the most controversial civil rights decisions in recent times, the Court in BOWERS V. HARDWICK (1986) exemplified its unwillingness to extend heightened constitutional protections to certain minorities. The Court refused to strike down a state sodomy statute's criminalization of sexual practices between consenting adults on the ground that it violated the constitutional RIGHT OF PRIVACY. The *Bowers* opinion not only refused to extend protection against discrimination to sexual minorities, but seemed to give constitutional legitimacy to the most anachronistic stereotypes and prejudices that underlie the marginalization of sexual minorities in American society. However, in ROMER V. EVANS (1996), the Court struck down a state constitutional amendment prohibiting municipalities from protecting sexual minorities from discrimination, holding that such a REFERENDUM reflected animosity toward a particular group and was unrelated to any legitimate state objective. *Evans* demonstrates that, despite the *Bowers* result, sexual minorities will receive at least some protection from explicit governmental action aimed at them.

In addition to providing substantive civil rights protection, equal protection has also been interpreted to limit legislative action to address historical discrimination. The conservative Court majorities of the last two decades have embraced what might be called a "colorblindness" interpretation of the equal protection clause, so named because it purports to require that the government be blind to race in its decisionmaking processes. According to the colorblindness approach, the equal protection clause protects individuals from personal evaluations based on a proscribed criterion (such as race or gender) rather than vindicates the interests of historically subordinated groups (such as African Americans or women). From this perspective, the equal protection clause protects whites, men, and other historically privileged groups in the same ways that it protects African Americans, women, and other disadvantaged groups.

In the AFFIRMATIVE ACTION cases, the colorblindness approach has meant that governmental attempts to remedy past discrimination through policies giving preference to minorities with respect to various governmental benefits are deemed constitutionally equivalent to race-conscious policies that harm racial minorities. As the Court ruled in RICHMOND (CITY OF) V. J. A. CROSON CO. (1989), STRICT SCRU-

TINY applies to all racial classifications, whether malign or benign. Accordingly, the City of Richmond's affirmative action policy for hiring construction contractors was struck down on the ground that there was insufficient proof that the huge under-representation of racial minorities in the construction contracting business was the result of past racial discrimination— although there had been congressional findings of discrimination nationwide in the construction industry, and Richmond, the capital of the Confederacy, had long enforced racial apartheid in virtually all sectors of public life. ADARAND CONSTRUCTORS, INC. V. PEÑA (1995) extends the same strict scrutiny to analogous affirmative action of the federal government.

In addition to including a significant body of civil rights protections and setting limits on legislative remedial action, the Constitution is relevant to civil rights law because, like any other federal legislative or executive action, civil rights acts of Congress must be authorized by some provision of the Constitution. For example, in the CIVIL RIGHTS CASES (1883), the Court struck down the CIVIL RIGHTS ACT OF 1875, which prohibited racial discrimination in public accommodations. The Court held that the FOURTEENTH AMENDMENT, SECTION 5—granting Congress power to enforce the equal protection clause and other substantive guarantees of the amendment—did not authorize Congress to remedy any discriminatory practice that did not independently constitute a violation of the Fourteenth Amendment. As a substantive matter, the Fourteenth Amendment did not prohibit private discrimination by innkeepers, railroad carriers, and others. Consequently, when Congress came to enact the Civil Rights Act of 1964—prohibiting race and gender discrimination in public accommodations, employment, and education by public and private parties—it relied on the COMMERCE CLAUSE, granting Congress power to regulate INTERSTATE COMMERCE, and the SPENDING POWER, permitting Congress to attach conditions to the receipt of federal funds. The reach of federal civil rights law depends, indirectly, on the future interpretation of these constitutional grants of congressional power and the resolution of FEDERALISM concerns raised by their expansive reach.

Finally, constitutional law is relevant to the field of civil rights in a less formal and a more ideological way. As an abstract matter, the idea of "civil rights" in a democratic society embodies the public meanings of equality and democratic self-determination. The special status of constitutional law in American civic ideology gives special significance to the courts' determination in particular cases the civil rights necessary for justice under democratic principles. The content of "civil rights" is not self-evident, and in fact has been hotly contested throughout American history.

Writers in a new scholarly movement, CRITICAL RACE THEORY, began in the 1990s to challenge many of the core assumptions of the civil rights tradition. According to these writers, judicial interpretations of constitutional requirements for equality constitute and embody a particular way of interpreting the world, a special language for distinguishing the relevant from the irrelevant in the social landscape. The judicial interpretation of the significance and meaning of race, gender, sexual orientation, disability, and other features of a person's identity necessarily is part of the broader struggle over the exercise of social power generally in American society. The structure of antidiscrimination law—with its premise that racial power is manifest in isolated, individual, intentional, and irrational acts—forms a narrative partly of justice and liberation, but partly also of legitimation and apologia. It paints a false picture of a world in which, separate from any race-conscious acts of decisionmakers, things operate according to rational and culturally neutral norms, thereby mistaking the norms of dominant social groups for universal standards of merit.

GARY PELLER
(2000)

Bibliography

BELL, DERRICK A. 1992 *Race, Racism, and American Law*, 3rd ed. Boston: Little, Brown.
BRANCH, TAYLOR 1988 *Parting the Waters: America in the King Years, 1954–63*. New York: Simon & Schuster.
—— 1998 *Pillar of Fire: America in the King Years, 1963–65*. New York: Simon & Schuster.
CRENSHAW, KIMBERLÉ; GOTANDA, NEIL; PELLER, GARY; and THOMAS, KENDALL, eds. 1995 *Critical Race Theory: The Key Writings that Formed the Movement*. New York: The New Press.
DANIELSEN, DAN and ENGLE, KAREN, eds. 1995 *After Identity: A Reader in Law and Culture*. New York: Routledge.
MACKINNON, CATHARINE A. 1989 *Toward a Feminist Theory of the State*. Cambridge, Mass.: Harvard University Press.
MALCOLM X 1990 *Malcolm X Speaks: Selected Speeches and Statements*. New York: Grove Weidenfeld.
SPANN, GIRARDEAU A. 1993 *Race Against the Court: The Supreme Court & Minorities in Contemporary America*. New York: New York University Press.
WILLIAMS, PATRICIA J. 1991 *The Alchemy of Race and Rights: The Diary of a Law Professor*. Cambridge, Mass.: Harvard University Press.

CIVIL RIGHTS ACT OF 1866 (FRAMING)
14 Stat. 27

Responding to the BLACK CODES, Congress in 1866 passed its first CIVIL RIGHTS bill to enforce the THIRTEENTH AMENDMENT. The bill's definition of national CITIZENSHIP superseded the decision in DRED SCOTT V. SANDFORD (1857), which had excluded blacks. A citizen was any person not an Indian or of foreign allegiance born in any state or territory, regardless of color. All citizens were to enjoy full and EQUAL PROTECTION of all laws and procedures for the protection of persons and property, and be subject to like punishments without regard to former slave status. In all jurisdictions citizens were to have equal rights to sue, contract, witness, purchase, lease, sell, inherit, or otherwise convey personal or real property. Anyone who, "under color of any law ... or custom," prevented any person from enjoying those rights, or who subjected any person to discriminatory criminal punishments because of race or previous involuntary servitude, was subject to MISDE-MEANOR prosecutions in federal courts. Congress further authorized the REMOVAL OF CASES from state to federal courts of persons denied civil rights and of federal officer defendants, prosecuted by states, protecting civil rights; that provision connected the civil rights bill to the FREED-MEN'S BUREAU and the HABEAS CORPUS statutes. All federal officials could initiate proceedings under the bill. Federal judges were to appoint special commissioners to enforce judgments under the bill (a use of fugitive slave law processes for opposite purposes). Alternatively, judges could employ the army or state militias, under the President's command, as posses. Last, Congress expanded the Supreme Court's APPELLATE JURISDICTION to include questions of law arising from the statute.

President ANDREW JOHNSON's powerful veto of the Civil Rights Bill, though overridden by Congress, touched both honorable traditions of the states' monopoly of rights and ignoble concepts of race hierarchy. He insisted that the bill would create a centralized military despotism and invoked the recent EX PARTE MILLIGAN (1866) decision. Congress, he argued, was creating black citizens of the same states it was excluding from representation.

Though trenchant, the veto never touched on the question of the remedies available to injured citizens or the nation, when states failed to carry out their duty to treat their own citizens equally. If no statutory remedies existed, then both nation and states were returned to the conditions of 1860. Anxious to make clear the fact of the nation's advance from that pitiable condition, the Congress pushed ahead with a FOURTEENTH AMENDMENT proposal and, in 1867, resorted to military reconstruction as a desperate stop-gap.

But the Fourteenth Amendment, unlike the Thirteenth (which the Civil Rights Act enforced) constrained only STATE ACTION, at least according to Supreme Court judgments commencing with the *Slaughterhouse* case (1873). In May 1870, the Congress "re-enacted" the 1866 Civil Rights law, this time under the Fourteenth and FIFTEENTH AMENDMENTS (though section 16 of the 1870 law still punished discriminatory felonious private acts). In 1874, a re-

vision of the federal statutes appeared, breaking up the text of the 1866 statute into scattered sections.

HAROLD M. HYMAN
(1986)

(SEE ALSO: *Section 1983, Title 42, United States Code.*)

Bibliography

HOWE, M. A. DEWOLFE 1965 Federalism and Civil Rights. [Massachusetts Historical Society] *Proceedings* 77:15–27.
HYMAN, HAROLD M. and WIECEK, WILLIAM M. 1982 *Equal Justice under Law: Constitutional Development 1835–1875.* Chaps. 9–11. New York: Harper & Row.
KACZOROWSKI, ROBERT J. 1971 Nationalization of Civil Rights: Theory and Practice in a Racist Society, 1866–1883. Ph.D. diss., University of Minnesota.

CIVIL RIGHTS ACT OF 1866
(Judicial Interpretation)

Judicial interpretation has transformed the Civil Rights Act of 1866 from a simple effort to dismantle the BLACK CODES into one of the most important existing CIVIL RIGHTS laws. In assessing judicial treatment of the act, it is helpful to consider section one of the act separately from section three. Other sections have not led to noteworthy judicial development. Section one of the act, which granted all persons the same rights as white persons to make and enforce contracts, sue, be parties, give EVIDENCE, inherit, purchase, lease, sell, hold, and convey real and personal property, and to the full and equal benefit of all laws and proceedings for the security of person and property, was reenacted in modified form by the Civil Rights Act of 1870, was divided into two sections by the REVISED STATUTES of 1874, and survives as sections 1981 and 1982 of Title 42, United States Code. Section three of the act, which set forth the procedures for vindicating rights protected by section one, was scattered throughout the United States Code. Portions of it survive as CIVIL RIGHTS REMOVAL statutes and as part of section 1988 of Title 42. Judicial interpretation of the 1866 act is not unrelated to these statutory reshufflings. Cut adrift from their moorings in the entire 1866 act, the act's remnants are amenable to many more interpretations than the original provision.

Cases decided in the years immediately following the 1866 act's passage are particularly important in ascertaining its original meaning. The REVISED STATUTES of 1874 would strip the act's descendants of any close resemblance to the original measure. And once the courts became accustomed to applying the FOURTEENTH AMENDMENT, much of the 1866 act would become superfluous. In addition, ratification of the Fourteenth Amendment eliminated most doubts about the act's constitutionality.

Prior to ratification of the Fourteenth Amendment, most courts were willing to sustain the act under Congress's THIRTEENTH AMENDMENT power to proscribe SLAVERY. But at least Kentucky's highest court in *Bowlin v. Commonwealth* (1867) declared the act unconstitutional. Other courts avoided such a declaration only by interpreting the act not to prohibit some forms of RACIAL DISCRIMINATION that the act's words arguably covered.

In the reported interpretations of the act, for example, courts divided over whether states could continue to outlaw marriages between whites and blacks. State courts in Tennessee (1871), Indiana (1871), and Alabama (1878) found marriage not to be a contract within the meaning of section 1, and therefore rejected attacks on antimiscegenation laws that relied on the 1866 act. State courts in Louisiana (1874) and Alabama (1872) relied at least in part on the 1866 act to find intermarriage legal, but the Alabama case was soon overruled. Not until LOVING V. VIRGINIA (1967) did the Supreme Court hold the Fourteenth Amendment to ban antimiscegenation laws.

State courts also divided over whether the 1866 act abrogated state laws prohibiting blacks from testifying against whites. The Kentucky court found Congress's effort to do so unconstitutional, but an 1869 Arkansas decision found the act to authorize such testimony. In 1869, the California Supreme Court relied on the 1866 act's evidentiary provision to dismiss an INDICTMENT against a mulatto, because Chinese witnesses had testified at his trial and state law prohibited them from testifying against white men. But a year later, despite the 1866 act, the California court sustained the state's evidentiary ban on testimony by Chinese against whites.

After the 1870s, section 1 diminished in importance. The state laws against which it most successfully operated, laws mandating racial discrimination in areas covered by section 1, could also be attacked directly under the Fourteenth Amendment. And with section 1 and the Fourteenth Amendment undermining the most egregious provisions of the Black Codes, there remained only one important area to which section 1 might be applied—private discrimination. When the CIVIL RIGHTS CASES (1883), UNITED STATES V. HARRIS (1883), and UNITED STATES V. CRUIKSHANK (1876) limited Congress's Thirteenth and Fourteenth Amendment power to legislate against private racial discrimination, there was doubt about whether section 1 constitutionally could be applied to private discrimination. One early lower federal court opinion, *United States v. Morris* (1903), suggested the 1866 act's applicability to private discrimination, but Supreme Court statements in *Virginia v. Rives* (1880) and CORRIGAN V. BUCKLEY (1926) suggested that the act did not apply to private conduct. (See STRAUDER V. WEST VIRGINIA, 1880.),

Hurd v. Hodge (1948), a companion case to SHELLEY V. KRAEMER (1948), gave section 1 some new life. The court applied section 1 to prohibit courts in the DISTRICT OF COLUMBIA from enforcing a racially RESTRICTIVE COVENANT. The breakthrough came in JONES V. ALFRED H. MAYER CO. (1968), where the Court held both that Congress meant the 1866 act to proscribe private discrimination and that Congress constitutionally could outlaw private discrimination under the Thirteenth Amendment. As the result of *Jones, Johnson v. Railway Express Co.* (1974), and RUNYON V. MCCRARY (1976), the remnants of the 1866 act were transformed from historical relics into federal laws broadly prohibiting private racial discrimination in the sale or lease of all housing, in schools, in employment and in virtually all other contracts. In many respects the 1866 act's newly discovered coverage exceeds that of comprehensive modern civil rights laws. *General Building Constructors Association, Inc. v. Pennsylvania* (1982) limited the 1866 act's reach by holding that liability may not be imposed under the act without proof of intentional discrimination.

Section 3 of the 1866 act traveled a less visible path through the courts. Its primary significance has been to determine when a violation of former section 1 authorizes an original or removal action in federal court. (See REMOVAL OF CASES.) In BLYEW V. UNITED STATES (1872), over the dissents of Justices JOSEPH P. BRADLEY and NOAH SWAYNE, the Court held that Kentucky's testimonial disqualification of black witnesses did not confer ORIGINAL JURISDICTION on a lower federal court to hear a state murder case at which the black witnesses were to testify. In a series of civil rights removal cases, the Court held that what had been section 3 authorized removal to federal court where state laws expressly mandated a racial distinction that prevented blacks from receiving equal justice, as when blacks were excluded from juries. But the Court found removal not to be authorized where the same result was achieved through other than formal state statutory command.

Under section 3's remnants, actions that arise under state law but are removed to federal court are tried in federal court by applying state law. In *Robertson v. Wegmann* (1978), however, the Court misconstrued the shred of the 1866 act commanding this result to require application of state law to cases arising under *federal* law. The same remnant, section 1988, also has been relied on in *Sullivan v. Little Hunting Park, Inc.* (1969) to authorize damages for violations of section 1 rights and in *Tomanio v. Board of Regents* (1980) to require the use of state statutes of limitations in federal civil rights cases.

THEODORE EISENBERG
(1986)

Bibliography

BARDOLPH, RICHARD 1970 *The Civil Rights Record.* Pages 84–87, 94–96, 200–201, 532–533. New York: Thomas Y. Crowell.
CARR, ROBERT K. 1947 *Federal Protection of Civil Rights.* Ithaca, N.Y.: Cornell University Press.

EISENBERG, THEODORE 1981 *Civil Rights Legislation*. Charlottesville, Va.: Michie Co.

CIVIL RIGHTS ACT OF 1875
18 Stat. 335

On his deathbed Senator CHARLES SUMNER (Republican, Mass.) implored a congressional friend, "You must take care of the civil rights bill,—my bill, the civil rights bill, don't let it fail." Since 1870 Sumner had sought to persuade Congress to enact a law guaranteeing to all people, regardless of race or religion, the same accommodations and facilities in public schools, churches and cemeteries incorporated by public authority, places of public amusement, hotels licensed by law, and common carriers. Sumner had contended that racial SEGREGATION was discriminatory, that SEPARATE BUT EQUAL facilities were inherently unequal, and that compulsory equality would combat prejudice as much as compulsory segregation fostered it. Opponents claimed that the FOURTEENTH AMENDMENT protected the privileges of United States CITIZENSHIP only, not those of state citizenship to which the bulk of CIVIL RIGHTS attached. Opponents also claimed that Congress had no constitutional power to protect civil rights from violation by private persons or businesses.

School DESEGREGATION was unpopular among northern Republicans and hated by southern Democrats. After the election of 1874 resulted in a Democratic victory in the House, supporters of Sumner's bill settled for "half a loaf" by consenting to the deletion of the provisions on education, churches, and cemeteries. A black congressman from South Carolina agreed to the compromise because the school clause jeopardized the Republican party in the South and subordinated the educational needs of blacks to their right to be desegregated. Teaching the "three Rs" to the children of former slaves was more important than risking their educational opportunities by demanding their admission to "white" schools.

In February 1875 the lame-duck 43rd Congress, 2nd session, voting along party lines in both houses, passed the modified bill which President ULYSSES S. GRANT signed into law on March 1. The Civil Rights Act of 1875, the last Reconstruction measure and the last civil rights act until 1957, was the most important congressional enactment in the field of PUBLIC ACCOMMODATIONS until the CIVIL RIGHTS ACT OF 1964. The act of 1875 affirmed the equality of all persons in the enjoyment of transportation facilities, in hotels and inns, and in theaters and places of public amusement. Theoretically such businesses, though privately owned and operated, were like public utilities, exercising public functions for the benefit of the public and subject to public regulation. Anyone violating the statute was civilly liable for $500 damages and, on conviction in federal court, subject to a fine of not more than $1,000 or imprisonment for not more than one year. In 1883 the Supreme Court held the statute unconstitutional in the CIVIL RIGHTS CASES.

LEONARD W. LEVY
(1986)

Bibliography

KONVITZ, MILTON R. 1961 *A Century of Civil Rights*. New York: Columbia University Press.

CIVIL RIGHTS ACT OF 1957
71 Stat. 634

Although this law marked the end of an eighty-two-year period of congressional inactivity in the field of CIVIL RIGHTS, it accomplished little. The act created the CIVIL RIGHTS COMMISSION but granted it only investigative and reporting powers. The act also created a separate CIVIL RIGHTS DIVISION within the Department of Justice to be headed by an additional assistant attorney general. More substantively, the act made it unlawful to harass those exercising their VOTING RIGHTS in federal elections and provided for federal initiation of proceedings against completed or potential violations. Offenders receiving more than slight penalties were entitled to TRIAL BY JURY, a watering-down provision inserted by Senate opponents.

The act is as significant for important deletions from the original bill as for what was ultimately enacted. Southern senators managed to eliminate a provision authorizing the ATTORNEY GENERAL to seek injunctive relief against all civil rights violators, a provision opponents feared would enhance the federal presence in school DESEGREGATION disputes and one they characterized as reimposing Reconstruction on the South. The emasculated act was viewed as a victory for southern segregationists. It was not even worth a filibuster.

THEODORE EISENBERG
(1986)

Bibliography

BRAUER, CARL M. 1977 *John F. Kennedy and the Second Reconstruction*. New York: Columbia University Press.

CIVIL RIGHTS ACT OF 1960
74 Stat. 86

The insignificance and ineffectiveness of the CIVIL RIGHTS ACT OF 1957 generated pressure in the next Congress to enact a more effective CIVIL RIGHTS law. And the CIVIL

RIGHTS COMMISSION established by the 1957 act added to the pressure by issuing a report documenting the abridgment of black VOTING RIGHTS in the South.

As enacted, the 1960 act required state election officers to retain for twenty-two months records relating to voter registration and qualifications in elections of federal officials. Where courts found patterns or practices of abridgment of the right to vote on account of race, they were authorized to declare individuals qualified to vote and to appoint federal voting referees to take EVIDENCE and report to the court on the treatment of black voters.

In a provision originally aimed at interference with school DESEGREGATION decrees, the act imposed criminal penalties for obstruction of all court orders. It also created a federal criminal offense of interstate flight to avoid prosecution for destroying buildings or other property.

Like the 1957 act, the 1960 act is noteworthy for its failure to include a proposed provision authorizing the United States to initiate actions on behalf of persons deprived of civil rights.

THEODORE EISENBERG
(1986)

Bibliography

BRAUER, CARL M. 1977 *John F. Kennedy and the Second Reconstruction.* New York: Columbia University Press.

CIVIL RIGHTS ACT OF 1964
78 Stat. 241

The Civil Rights Act of 1964 signified many changes. For JOHN F. KENNEDY, prompted by southern resistance to DESEGREGATION orders and violent responses to peaceful CIVIL RIGHTS protests, proposing the measure symbolized an aggressive new attitude toward RACIAL DISCRIMINATION. For LYNDON JOHNSON, who supported the act after Kennedy's assassination, it marked a turn away from southern regionalism and toward national leadership on civil rights matters. For Congress, the act ended a century of nonexistent or ineffective civil rights laws and was the first civil rights measure with respect to which the Senate invoked CLOTURE. For blacks, the act was the first major legislative victory since Reconstruction and the most far-reaching civil rights measure in American history.

The act consists of eleven titles. Titles I and VIII reinforce voting rights provisions of the CIVIL RIGHTS ACTS OF 1957 and 1960 and limit the use of LITERACY TESTS to measure voter qualifications. (See also VOTING RIGHTS ACT OF 1970.) Titles III and IV, in provisions deleted from the bills that became the 1957 and 1960 acts, authorize court actions by the ATTORNEY GENERAL to challenge segregated public facilities and schools. Title V amends provisions governing the CIVIL RIGHTS COMMISSION. Title IX authorizes appeal from orders remanding to state courts civil rights cases that have been removed to federal court and authorizes the Attorney General to intervene in EQUAL PROTECTION cases. Title X establishes a Community Relations Service to assist communities in resoving discrimination disputes. Title XI deals with miscellaneous matters. The most important parts of the law are Title II, forbidding discrimination in PUBLIC ACCOMMODATION; Title VI, forbidding discrimination in federally assisted programs; and Title VII, forbidding EMPLOYMENT DISCRIMINATION. In 1972, Congress extended Title VII's coverage to most government employees. It does not cover religious institutions.

Congress shaped the 1964 act with a keen awareness of previously declared constitutional limitations on ANTIDISCRIMINATION LEGISLATION. Title II's ban on discrimination in public accommodations and Title VII's ban on employment discrimination are limited to those entities whose operations affect INTERSTATE COMMERCE. By limiting these provisions to establishments and employers affecting commerce, Congress sought to avoid the CIVIL RIGHTS CASES' (1883) determination that Congress lacks power under the FOURTEENTH AMENDMENT to outlaw discrimination by private citizens, even in such a quasi-public area as that of public accommodations. Unlike its power to enforce the Fourteenth Amendment, Congress's COMMERCE CLAUSE power is not limited to STATE ACTION. In HEART OF ATLANTA MOTEL, INC. V. UNITED STATES, (1964) and KATZENBACH V. MCCLUNG (1964) the Court upheld Title II as a valid exercise of the commerce power and the power to regulate interstate travel. Under the Court's subsequent decision in JONES V. ALFRED H. MAYER CO. (1968), much of Title II and Title VII would be valid as congressional enforcement of the THIRTEENTH AMENDMENT. Title VI's ban on discrimination in federally assisted programs was tied to another constitutional provision, Congress's TAXING AND SPENDING POWER.

Judicial interpretation seems to have avoided another potential constitutional problem attending Title VII. Under a 1972 amendment to Title VII, employers must accommodate an employee's religious practices if the employer is able to do so without undue hardship. In *Trans World Airlines, Inc. v. Hardison* (1977), the Supreme Court held that the statute does not require an employer to bear more than a DE MINIMIS cost to accommodate an employee's religious preferences. If Title VII were interpreted to mandate substantial concessions to religiously based employee work preferences, it might raise serious problems under the FIRST AMENDMENT'S ESTABLISHMENT OF RELIGION clause.

With the 1964 act's constitutional vulnerability minimized shortly after enactment, the way was clear for its development. Title II, banning racial discrimination in public accommodations, was the act's symbolic heart, providing immediate and highly visible evidence that blacks, as equal citizens, were entitled to equal treatment in the public life of the community. But Title II generated little litigation, for compliance was swift throughout the South once the principle of equal access was established. Equalizing employment opportunity was a goal that would take longer to accomplish. Thus in operation, Title VII has dwarfed all other titles combined, frequently generating a huge backlog of cases in the agency charged with Title VII's administration, the Equal Employment Opportunity Commission (EEOC), and leading to thousands of judicial decisions.

The proof necessary to establish a Title VII violation repeatedly occupies the Supreme Court. Two leading cases, *McDonnell Douglas Corp. v. Green* (1973) and GRIGGS V. DUKE POWER CO. (1971), approve alternative methods of proof in Title VII cases. Under *McDonnell Douglas*, a plaintiff alleging discrimination by an employer must, after exhausting the necessary remedies with the EEOC or a state antidiscrimination agency, show that the plaintiff applied and was rejected for a job for which the plaintiff was qualified, and that the employer continued to try to fill the position. An employer must then justify its actions. Under *Griggs*, in an extension of Title VII not necessarily contemplated by the 1964 Congress, proof that an employment selection criterion has a disproportionate adverse impact on minorities requires the employer to show that the selection standard is required by business necessity. After *Griggs*, statistically based Title VII cases, and threats to bring such cases, became a widespread method for pressuring employers to hire more minority and female workers. Few employers are both able to prove the business necessity of employment tests or other hiring criteria and willing to incur the expense of doing so.

The 1964 act, particularly Title VII, is not without its ironies. First, opponents of the act amended it to include sex discrimination in the hope that such an amendment would weaken the bill's chances for passage. But the bill passed with the additional ban that revolutionized at least the formal status of female workers. And in the case of sex discrimination, Title VII reaches beyond traditional refusals to hire or obvious pay disparities. When the Court held in *General Electric Co. v. Gilbert* (1976) that excluding pregnancy from a health plan does not constitute discrimination on the basis of sex, Congress amended Title VII to overturn the result. *Los Angeles Department of Water and Power v. Manhart* (1978) marks some sort of outer limit on Title VII's protection of female workers. The Court held Title VII to proscribe a requirement that females, who live longer than males and therefore can expect to receive greater total retirement benefits from a pension plan, contribute more to a pension than males contribute.

In the case of sex, religion, or national origin discrimination, Title VII provides a defense if these factors constitute a bona fide occupational qualification, a defense sometimes difficult to separate from that of business necessity. The Supreme Court found in *Dothard v. Rawlinson* (1977) that a bona fide occupational qualification justifies requiring male prison guards for at least some classes of male prisoners.

Second, although the BURGER COURT generally has been viewed as conservative in the field of civil rights, Title VII owes much of its practical importance to Chief Justice WARREN E. BURGER's opinion for the Court in *Griggs v. Duke Power Co. Griggs* removed the requirement that discriminatory intent be an element of Title VII cases. This holding, in addition to its significance for Title VII, has been incorporated in other areas, including discrimination in housing under the CIVIL RIGHTS ACT OF 1968. *New York City Transit Authority v. Beazer* (1979), in which the Court refused to invalidate an employment selection standard (exclusion of drug users) with disparate impact on minorities, may signify some retrenchment from the full force of the *Griggs* principle. And in *International Brotherhood of Teamsters v. United States* (1977), the Court refused to extend *Griggs* to invalidate seniority systems that predate Title VII. But the Court never has directly questioned *Griggs*. In UNITED STEELWORKERS OF AMERICA V. WEBER (1979), the Burger Court concluded that Title VII permitted at least some private AFFIRMATIVE ACTION employment programs.

Although Title VII deservedly receives most of the attention paid to the 1964 act, Title VI is also an important antidiscrimination law. In REGENTS OF THE UNIVERSITY OF CALIFORNIA V. BAKKE (1978) it provided the setting for the Court's first important pronouncement on affirmative action programs. Many subsequent antidiscrimination laws, such as Title IX of the EDUCATION AMENDMENT OF 1972, the AGE DISCRIMINATION ACT OF 1975, and the REHABILITATION ACT of 1973 are modeled after Title VI. Title VI is the principal antidiscrimination measure for programs receiving federal funds that are not affected by other antidiscrimination measures. In the case of public institutions, however, there is much overlap between Title VI's prohibitions and those contained in the Fourteenth Amendment. The Supreme Court has been ambiguous in describing the relationship between the two. In *Bakke*, a majority of Justices suggested that Title VI and the Constitution are coterminous, but it did not purport to overturn the Court's earlier holding in LAU V. NICHOLS (1974), widely read as extending Title VI to cases of discrimination not banned by the Constitution.

The contributions of the 1964 act to racial equality defy precise measurement, but surely they have been weighty. Beyond the tangible changes the act brought to the public life of southern communities and to the entire American workplace lie enormous changes in attitudes and everyday personal relations. Those who believe that "you can't legislate morality" would do well to ponder the lessons of the Civil Rights Act of 1964.

THEODORE EISENBERG
(1986)

(SEE ALSO: *Firefighters Local Union No. 1784 v. Stotts.*)

Bibliography

DORSEN, NORMAN; BENDER, PAUL; NEUBORNE, BURT; and LAW, SYLVIA 1979 *Emerson, Haber and Dorsen's Political and Civil Rights in the United States,* 4th ed. Vol. II:581–608, 902–1062, 1172–1220. Boston: Little, Brown.

LARSON, ARTHUR and LARSON, LEX K. 1981 *Employment Discrimination.* New York: Matthew Bender.

SCHLEI, BARBARA L. and GROSSMAN, PAUL 1976 *Employment Discrimination Law.* Washington, D.C.: Bureau of National Affairs.

SULLIVAN, CHARLES A.; ZIMMER, MICHAEL J.; and RICHARDS, RICHARD F. 1980 *Federal Statutory Law of Employment Discrimination.* Indianapolis: Bobbs-Merrill.

CIVIL RIGHTS ACT OF 1968
82 Stat. 696

This act capped the modern legislative program against RACIAL DISCRIMINATION that included the CIVIL RIGHTS ACT OF 1964 and the VOTING RIGHTS ACT OF 1965. Title VIII of the act, which constitutes the nation's first comprehensive OPEN HOUSING LAW, prohibits discrimination in the sale, rental, financing, and advertising of housing, and in membership in real estate brokerage organizations. Ironically, soon after Title VIII's enactment, the Supreme Court, in JONES V. ALFRED H. MAYER CO. (1968), construed a remnant of the CIVIL RIGHTS ACT OF 1866 to outlaw private racial discrimination in housing. In dissent in *Jones,* Justice JOHN M. HARLAN, joined by Justice BYRON R. WHITE, relied in part on Title VIII's passage to challenge the need for the Court's decision. The 1968 act also contained criminal penalties to protect civil rights activity and comprehensive measures to protect rights of AMERICAN INDIANS. Different portions of the act, including antiriot provisions, represented a backlash against antiwar demonstrations, CIVIL RIGHTS protest, and other forms of domestic unrest.

Like the Civil Rights Act of 1964, the 1968 act survived a southern filibuster in the Senate. Efforts by House opponents to delay consideration of the bill backfired. The delay led to the bill's consideration in the aftermath of Dr. MARTIN LUTHER KING, JR.'s assassination. Given that the bill passed the House by a small margin, the delay may have made all the difference.

THEODORE EISENBERG
(1986)

Bibliography

HARVEY, JAMES C. 1973 *Black Civil Rights During the Johnson Administration.* Jackson, Miss.: University and College Press of Mississippi.

CIVIL RIGHTS ACT OF 1991
105 Stat. 1071 (1991)

In 1989, the Supreme Court handed down a half-dozen decisions making it more difficult to prevail on claims arising under several pieces of ANTIDISCRIMINATION LEGISLATION. Congress responded by passing the Civil Rights Act of 1990, only to have President GEORGE H. W. BUSH veto it and an override effort fail. Civil rights legislation reintroduced in the spring of 1991 might have suffered a similar fate, but for the bruising confirmation hearing of Supreme Court Justice CLARENCE THOMAS. In the wake of the hearings, which cast the administration in a negative light with regard to CIVIL RIGHTS while simultaneously revealing fractures within the civil rights coalition, both sides sought compromise. The Civil Rights Act of 1991 was quickly passed and signed into law on November 21, 1991.

Broadly speaking, the act sought to achieve two goals: (1) restore civil rights law to its pre-1989 contours; and (2) end inconsistencies in the remedies available under different antidiscrimination statutes. The latter it achieved by providing that, as under 42 U.S.C. § 1981, parties prevailing upon a claim of intentional discrimination under either Title VII or the AMERICANS WITH DISABILITIES ACT could recover compensatory and PUNITIVE DAMAGES, albeit subject to certain caps. As to the former, the act's success was more limited.

The act responded to a number of Court decisions, and as a result, consists of many bits and pieces. Among these, two stand out. First, the act reworked the Court's restrictive reading of section 1981 announced in PATTERSON V. MCCLEAN CREDIT UNION (1989). In *Patterson,* the Court reaffirmed the holding in RUNYON V. MCCRARY (1976) that section 1981 prohibits RACIAL DISCRIMINATION in the making and enforcement of private contracts, but held that it offered no relief from workplace discrimination that occurred after the formation of a contract. In contrast, the 1991 act insists that section 1981 applies to "the enjoyment of all benefits, privileges, terms, and conditions of the contractual relationship." Second, the 1991 act responded to *Wards Cove Packing Co. v. Atonio* (1989). In

Wards Cove, the Court undermined the disparate impact approach developed in GRIGGS V. DUKE POWER COMPANY (1971) for showing systematic, as opposed to intentional, discrimination. It did so out of concern that a robust disparate impact DOCTRINE would encourage employers to adopt hiring quotas in order to avoid potential liability. The 1991 act went some distance toward undoing the changes wrought by *Wards Cove*, but stopped short of restoring the doctrine to its previous vigor. For example, the act accepted an increased burden imposed by the Court on those bringing claims by adopting the requirement that plaintiffs disaggregate sources of discrimination and establish "causation," while it potentially eased the burden on employers by failing to define what exactly they needed to show in order to establish a "business necessity" justification for otherwise discriminatory practices.

The Civil Rights Act of 1991 slowed the conservative assault on civil rights laws. Nevertheless, by virtue of its various compromises, the act achieved limited success in restoring antidiscrimination law to its pre-1989 state.

IAN F. HANEY LÓPEZ
(2000)

Bibliography

GUERON, NICOLE   1995   Note: An Idea Whose Time Has Come: A Comparative Procedural History of the Civil Rights Acts of 1960, 1964, and 1991, *Yale Law Journal* 104:1201–1234.
LEWIS, HAROLD, JR.   1997   *Civil Rights and Employment Discrimination Law.* St. Paul, Minn.: West.

CIVIL RIGHTS CASES
109 U.S. 3 (1883)

In an opinion by Justice JOSEPH P. BRADLEY, with only Justice JOHN MARSHALL HARLAN dissenting, the Supreme Court ruled that Congress had no constitutional authority under either the THIRTEENTH or the FOURTEENTH AMENDMENT to pass the CIVIL RIGHTS ACT OF 1875. Holding that act unconstitutional proved to be one of the most fateful decisions in American history. It had the effect of reinforcing racist attitudes and practices, while emasculating a heroic effort by Congress and the President to prevent the growth of a Jim Crow society. The Court also emasculated the Fourteenth Amendment's enforcement clause, section five. The tragedy is that the Court made the Constitution legitimize public immorality on the basis of specious reasoning.

The *Civil Rights Cases* comprised five cases decided together, in which the act of 1875 had been enforced against innkeepers, theater owners, and a railroad company. In each of the five, a black citizen was denied the same accommodations, guaranteed by the statute, as white citizens enjoyed. The Court saw only an invasion of local law by the national government, contrary to the powers reserved to the states under the TENTH AMENDMENT. Bradley began his analysis with the Fourteenth Amendment, observing that its first section, after declaring who shall be a citizen, was prohibitory: it restrained only STATE ACTION. "Individual invasion of individual rights is not the subject-matter of the amendment." Its fifth section empowered Congress to enforce the amendment by appropriate legislation. "To enforce what? To enforce the prohibition," Bradley answered. He ignored the fact that the enforcement section applied to the entire amendment, including the CITIZENSHIP clause, which made all persons born or naturalized in the United States and subject to its jurisdiction citizens of the United States and of the states in which they reside. As Harlan pointed out, citizenship necessarily imports "equality of civil rights among citizens of every race in the same state." Congress could guard and enforce rights, including the rights of citizenship, deriving from the Constitution itself. Harlan reminded the Court of its opinion in STRAUDER V. WEST VIRGINIA (1880), where it had said that "a right or immunity created by the constitution or only guarantied by it, even without any express delegation of power, may be protected by congress."

But Bradley took the view that the legislative power conferred upon Congress by the Fourteenth Amendment does not authorize enactments on subjects "which are within the domain of state legislation. . . . It does not authorize congress to create a code of municipal law for regulation of private rights." Congress can merely provide relief against state action that violates the amendment's prohibitions on the states. Thus, only when the states acted adversely to the rights of citizenship could Congress pass remedial legislation. But its legislation could not cover the whole domain of CIVIL RIGHTS or regulate "all private rights between man and man in society." Otherwise, Congress would "supersede" the state legislatures. In effect the Court was saying that the Reconstruction amendments had not revolutionized the federal system. In effect the Court also warned the states not to discriminate racially, lest Congress intervene, as it had in the CIVIL RIGHTS ACT OF 1866, which the Court called "corrective" legislation against state action. In the cases under consideration, however, the discrimination derived from purely private acts unsupported by state authority. "The wrongful act of an individual, unsupported by any such authority, is simply a private wrong" that Congress cannot reach. Congress can, of course, reach and regulate private conduct in the normal course of legislation, penalizing individuals; but, Bradley explained, in every such case Congress possesses under the Constitution a power to act on the subject.

Under the Thirteenth Amendment, however, Congress

can enact any legislation necessary and proper to eradicate SLAVERY and "all badges and incidents of slavery," and its legislation may operate directly on individuals, whether their acts have the sanction of state authority or not. The question, then, was whether the Thirteenth Amendment vested in Congress the authority to require that all persons shall have equal accommodations in inns, public conveyances, and places of public amusement. The Court conceded that the amendment established "universal civil and political freedom throughout the United States" by abolishing slavery, but it denied that distinctions based on race or color abridged that freedom. Where, Bradley asked, does slavery, servitude, or badges of either arise from race discrimination by private parties? "The thirteenth amendment," he declared, "has respect, not to distinctions of race, or class, or color, but to slavery." The act of the owner of an inn, or theater, or transportation facility in refusing accommodation might inflict an ordinary civil injury, recognizable by state law, but not slavery or an incident of it. "It would be running the slavery argument into the ground," Bradley insisted, "to make it apply to every act of discrimination which a person may see fit to make" as to his guests, or those he will take in his coach, or those he will admit to his concert. On the theory that mere discrimination on account of race or color did not impose badges of slavery, the Court held that the Thirteenth Amendment, like the Fourteenth, did not validate the Civil Rights Act of 1875.

The case involved questions of law, history, and public policy. Harlan, dissenting, had the weight of argument as to all three, but Bradley had the weight of numbers. It was an 8–1 decision, and the eight scarcely bothered to answer the dissenter. Ignoring him might have been more discreet than trying to rebut him. He met their contentions head-on, starting with a strenuous objection to their parsimonious interpretation of national powers under the Thirteenth and Fourteenth Amendments, both of which expressly made affirmative grants of power. By contrast, Harlan demonstrated, the Court had generously construed the Constitution to support congressional enactments on behalf of slaveholders. The fugitive slave acts, which operated on private individuals, were based on a clause in the Constitution, Article 4, section 2, paragraph 3, that did not empower Congress to legislate at all. The clause merely provided that a fugitive slave be delivered up upon the claim of his owner, yet the Court sustained the acts of 1793 (PRIGG V. PENNSYLVANIA, 1842) and of 1850 (ABLEMAN V. BOOTH, 1859), implying a national power to enforce a right constitutionally recognized. The Thirteenth Amendment, as the majority admitted, established a constitutional right: civil freedom for citizens throughout the nation. And, as the majority admitted, the abolition of slavery reached the BADGES OF SERVITUDE, so that the

freedmen would have the same rights as white men. Similarly, the act of 1875 reached badges of servitude, because it, like the amendments to the Constitution, aimed at erasing the assumption that blacks were racially inferior. For Harlan, RACIAL DISCRIMINATION was a badge of servitude. Bradley had distinguished the act of 1866 from the act of 1875 on the ground that the earlier statute aimed at protecting rights that only the states might deny. Harlan replied that citizens regardless of race were entitled to the same civil rights.

Harlan also demonstrated that the rights allegedly violated by purely private parties were denied by individuals and CORPORATIONS that exercised public functions and wielded power and authority under the state. Relying on a broad concept of state action, he sought to prove that the parties whom the majority regarded as private were, in contemplation of law, public or quasi-public. A railroad corporation, an innkeeper, and a theater-manager had denied accommodations to black citizens. Railroads and streetcars were common carriers, that is, they were public highways, performing state functions; they were public conveyances which, though privately owned, had been established by state authority for a public use and were subject to control by the state for the public benefit. Free citizens of any race were entitled to use such facilities. Similarly, the COMMON LAW defined innkeepers as exercising a quasi-public employment that obligated them to take in all travelers, regardless of race. Theaters were places of public amusement, licensed by the public, of which the "colored race is a part," and theaters were clothed with a public interest, in accord with MUNN V. ILLINOIS (1877). Congress had not promiscuously sought to regulate the entire body of civil rights nor had it entered the domain of the states by generally controlling public conveyances, inns, or places of public amusement. Congress had simply declared that in a nation of universal freedom, private parties exercising public authority could not discriminate on ground of race; in effect the statute reached state instrumentalities whose action was tantamount to state action.

Under the Thirteenth Amendment, Congress could reach badges of servitude; under the Fourteenth, it could reach racial discrimination by state agencies. Contrary to the Court's assertion, Congress had not outlawed racial discrimination imposed by purely private action. It had aimed at such discrimination only in public places chartered or licensed by the state, in violation of the rights of citizenship which the Fourteenth Amendment affirmed. The amendment's fifth section empowered Congress to pass legislation enforcing its affirmative as well as its prohibitory clauses. Courts, in the normal exercise of JUDICIAL REVIEW, could hold unconstitutional state acts that violated the prohibitory clauses. Accordingly, section five was not restricted to merely corrective or remedial national legislation. Congress, not the Court, said Harlan, citing MCCULLOCH V. MARYLAND (1819), might choose the means best adopted to implementing the ends of the two amendments. Harlan insisted that Congress

> may, without transcending the limits of the constitution, do for human liberty and the fundamentals of American citizenship, what it did, with the sanction of this court, for the protection of slavery and the rights of the masters of fugitive slaves. If fugitive slave laws, providing modes and prescribing penalties whereby the master could seize and recover his fugitive slave, were legitimate exertions of an implied power to protect and enforce a right recognized by the constitution, why shall the hands of congress be tied, so that—under an express power, by appropriate legislation, to enforce a constitutional provision granting citizenship—it may not, by means of direct legislation, bring the whole power of this nation to bear upon states and their officers, and upon such individuals and corporations exercising public functions, assumed to abridge the supreme law of the land.

Some old abolitionists, deploring a ruling that returned the freedmen to a "reign of contempt, injury, and ignominy," denounced the "new DRED SCOTT decision," but most were resigned to defeat. Racial segregation was common throughout the country. Not surprisingly *The Nation* magazine, which approved of the decision, observed that the public's general unconcern about the decision indicated "how completely the extravagant expectations as well as the fierce passions of the war have died out." The Court served "a useful purpose in thus undoing the work of Congress," said the *New York Times,* and *Harper's Weekly* agreed. Public opinion supported the Court, but justice and judicial craftsmanship were on the side of Harlan, dissenting.

LEONARD W. LEVY
(1986)

Bibliography

KONVITZ, MILTON R. 1961 *A Century of Civil Rights.* New York: Columbia University Press.

WESTIN, ALAN F. 1962 The Case of the Prejudiced Doorkeeper. Pages 128–144 in Garraty, John A., *Quarrels That Have Shaped the Constitution.* New York: Harper & Row.

CIVIL RIGHTS COMMISSION

THE CIVIL RIGHTS ACT OF 1957 created the Commission on Civil Rights to investigate alleged deprivations of VOTING RIGHTS, to study and collect information concerning denials of EQUAL PROTECTION, and to appraise federal laws and policies with respect to equal protection of the laws. Subsequent legislation restated and expanded the commission's concerns to include denials of rights on the basis of color, race, religion, national origin, sex, age, or handicap. Initially, the commission was to issue a series of reports and expire upon issuance of its final report, but Congress repeatedly has extended the commission's reporting duties and life. The commission lacks power to enforce any antidiscrimination or other CIVIL RIGHTS laws.

By the standards of later civil rights legislation, creation of the commission seems an innocuous event. But at the time even this mild gesture drew substantial southern opposition. The commission's "snoopers," one southern congressman argued, "would cause inestimable chaos, confusion, and unrest among [the South's] people and would greatly increase the tension and agitation between the races there."

Because of the commission's advisory nature, measuring its accomplishments is difficult. In the 1960s, the commission's early reports helped to inform Congress about the need for voting rights legislation. And it clearly has served the function, added to its mandate in 1964, of a national clearinghouse for information about denials of equal protection. But the commission also has played a somewhat larger political role. In most administrations the commission's views are more egalitarian than the President's. The commission thus serves as a gadfly that both makes official sounding pronouncements and commands media attention. Administrations hear the commission even if they do not always listen to it.

THEODORE EISENBERG
(1986)

Bibliography

UNITED STATES COMMISSION ON CIVIL RIGHTS 1961 *Report.* Pages xv–xviii. Washington, D.C.: U.S. Government Printing Office.

CIVIL RIGHTS DIVISION

Created by Order of the Attorney General No. 3204, February 3, 1939, the Civil Rights Section (originally named the Civil Rights Unit) of the Justice Department became the federal government's principal CIVIL RIGHTS litigation unit. The order creating the Section called for a study of federal law to assess its utility in enforcing civil rights. The study, which stated the legal basis and goals of the Section's early civil rights enforcement efforts, suggested the need for TEST CASES to resolve uncertainties about the scope and constitutionality of the only statutory weapons then available to the Section, the surviving Reconstruction-era civil rights legislation. The Section's test cases include UNITED STATES V. CLASSIC (1941), an important precedent establishing authority to prosecute offenses relating to PRIMARY ELECTIONS, and SCREWS V. UNITED STATES (1945), which allowed the application of the criminal provisions of the CIVIL RIGHTS ACT OF 1866 to misconduct by state police officers.

The Civil Rights Section's growth reflects a general increase in national concern with civil rights matters. As of 1947, the Section is reported never to have had more than eight or ten lawyers and professional workers on its staff. In 1950, the section more than doubled in size. The CIVIL RIGHTS ACT OF 1957 upgraded the Section to the status of Division by providing for an additional assistant attorney general. By 1965, the Division had eighty-six attorneys and ninety-nine clerical workers. By 1978, there were 178 attorneys and 203 support personnel.

The Division's principal activity consists of litigation. It enforces the CIVIL RIGHTS ACT OF 1957, 1960, 1964, and 1968, the VOTING RIGHTS ACT OF 1965, the Equal Credit Opportunity Act, the 1866 act's criminal provisions, laws prohibiting PEONAGE and involuntary servitude, and various other laws. It does so through direct actions or through AMICUS CURIAE appearances in private cases. An administration's civil rights priorities are reflected in the categories of cases emphasized by the Division. In the early 1960s the Division emphasized voting rights cases. From 1965 to 1967, DESEGREGATION of education was its priority issue. By 1967, employment litigation became a priority item. Creation of a Task Force on Sex Discrimination in 1977 reflected a growing concern with sex discrimination.

THEODORE EISENBERG
(1986)

Bibliography

CARR, ROBERT K. 1947 Federal Protection of Civil Rights: Quest for a Sword. Ithaca, N.Y.: Cornell University Press.

CIVIL RIGHTS MOVEMENT

Because the basic rights of CITIZENSHIP were not equally available to all Americans at the nation's inception, civil rights movements involving groups excluded from full political participation have been a continuing feature of U.S. history. Males without property, African Americans, and women are among the groups that have engaged in sustained struggles to establish, protect, or expand their rights as American citizens. These struggles have resulted in fundamental departures from the limited conceptions of citizenship and the role of government that prevailed during the early national era.

The term "civil rights movement" more narrowly refers to the collective efforts of African Americans to advance in American society. These efforts are aspects of a broader, long-term black freedom struggle seeking goals beyond CIVIL RIGHTS, but they have had particularly important impact on dominant conceptions of the rights of American

citizens and the role of government in protecting these rights. Although the Supreme Court in the DRED SCOTT decision of 1857 negated the citizenship status of African Americans, the subsequent extensions of egalitarian principles to African Americans resulted in generalized expansions of the scope of constitutionally protected rights. In particular, both the FOURTEENTH AMENDMENT and the FIFTEENTH AMENDMENT to the Constitution, despite retrogressive Court decisions such as PLESSY V. FERGUSON (1896), ultimately served as foundations for major civil rights reforms benefiting black Americans and other groups. During the twentieth century, African Americans have participated in many racial advancement efforts that have enlarged the opportunities and protections available to individuals in other groups. More recently, as a result of sustained protest movements of the period after WORLD WAR II, the term "civil rights" has come to refer not only to governmental policies relating to the equal treatment of individuals but also to policies equalizing the allocation of resources among groups. In short, the modern civil rights movement in the United States has redefined as well as pursued rights.

The National Association for the Advancement of Colored People (NAACP), an interracial group founded in 1909, has been the most enduring institution directing the course of twentieth-century American civil rights movements. Although many organizations later challenged the NAACP's priorities and its reliance on the tactics of litigation and governmental lobbying, the group's large membership and its increasingly effective affiliate, the NAACP LEGAL DEFENSE & EDUCATIONAL FUND, made civil rights reforms into principal black political objectives. Among the outgrowths of NAACP-sponsored legal suits were the Supreme Court's SMITH V. ALLWRIGHT (1944) decision outlawing white primary elections and the BROWN V. BOARD OF EDUCATION (1954, 1955) decision against segregated public schools. These landmark cases helped to reverse earlier Court decisions—such as Plessy—that limited the scope of civil rights protections.

In the years after the Brown decision, other civil rights organizations departed from the NAACP's reform strategy and placed more emphasis on protest and mass mobilization. Starting with the Montgomery bus boycott of 1955–1956, southern blacks, aided by northern allies, successfully used boycotts, mass meetings, marches, rallies, sit-ins, and other insurgent tactics to speed the pace of civil rights reform. The Southern Christian Leadership Council (SCLC), founded in 1957 and led for many years by MARTIN LUTHER KING, JR., and the Student Nonviolent Coordinating Committee (SNCC), founded in 1960, spearheaded a series of mass struggles against white racial domination in the South. The NAACP also supplied many of the participants and much of the legal support for these struggles, while the predominantly white Congress of Racial Equality (CORE) contributed activists and expertise in the use of Gandhian nonviolent tactics. Although DESEGREGATION was initially the main focus of southern mass movements, economic and political concerns were evident from their inception.

King and the SCLC played especially important roles in mobilizing mass protest campaigns in the Alabama cities of Birmingham and Selma in 1963 and 1965. SCLC leaders orchestrated clashes between nonviolent demonstrators and often brutal law enforcement personnel. Such highly publicized confrontations made northern whites more aware of southern racial inequities, particularly the pervasive and antiquated Jim Crow system of public SEGREGATION. As the southern struggle's best-known spokesperson, King sought to link black civil rights aspirations with widely accepted, long-established political principles. During 1961 he identified the democratic ideals of the Founding Fathers as an unrealized "noble dream." "On the one hand, we have proudly professed the principles of democracy, and on the other hand, we have sadly practiced the very antithesis of those principles," he told an audience at Lincoln University. Speaking at the 1963 March on Washington, he insisted that the DECLARATION OF INDEPENDENCE and the Constitution were "a promissory note" guaranteeing all Americans "the unalienable rights of life, liberty, and the pursuit of happiness." By exposing the contradictions between American ideals and southern racial realities, the SCLC's southern campaigns strengthened northern white support for civil rights reforms.

Although the SNCC was an outgrowth of the student sit-in movement of 1960, its most significant activities were concentrated in the rural areas of Mississippi and Alabama. In these areas, SNCC staff members worked with indigenous black leaders seeking to overcome economic and political oppression. During the first half of the 1960s, SNCC concentrated its efforts on the achievement of voting rights for southern blacks and federal protection for civil rights workers. SNCC organizers also helped to create new institutions, such as the Mississippi Freedom Democratic party and the Lowndes County (Alabama) Freedom Organization, under local black leadership. By 1966, the "black power" slogan, popularized by SNCC's chair Stokely Carmichael, summarized the group's emerging ideas of a struggle seeking political, economic, and cultural objectives beyond narrowly defined civil rights reforms.

By the late 1960s, organizations such as the NAACP, SCLC, and SNCC faced increasingly strong challenges from "black nationalist" leaders and new militant organizations, such as the Black Panther party. Often influenced by Malcolm X and by Pan-African ideologies, proponents of "black liberation" saw civil rights reforms as insufficient because they did not address the problems of poor blacks. Black nationalists also pointed out that African American citizenship had resulted from the involuntary circumstances of enslavement. In addition, racial-liberation proponents often saw the African American freedom struggle in international terms, as a movement for "human rights" and national "self-determination" rather than for civil rights.

The most significant legislation to result from the mass struggles of the 1960s were the CIVIL RIGHTS ACT OF 1964 and the VOTING RIGHTS ACT OF 1965. (Congress also passed notable civil rights bills in 1968, 1972, and 1990.) Taken together, these laws greatly enhanced the civic status of blacks, women, and other minority groups and placed greater responsibility on the federal government to protect such groups from discriminatory treatment. Although the 1964 and 1965 acts were in some respects simply restatements of protections specified in the constitutional amendments enacted during RECONSTRUCTION, the impact of the new legislation was greater because of the expanded scope of federal regulatory powers and the continued militancy by victims of discrimination.

Since the mid-1960s, national civil rights policies have evinced awareness that antidiscrimination legislation was not sufficient to achieve tangible improvements in the living conditions of many blacks or to bring about equalization of the distribution of resources and services among racial groups in the United States. In 1968 the National Advisory Commission on Civil Disorders (the Kerner Commission) concluded that despite civil right reforms, the nation was "moving toward two societies, one black, one white—separate and unequal." By the time of this report, the liberal coalition that had supported passage of the major civil rights legislation was divided over the role, if any, government should play in eliminating these persistent racial inequities. A "white backlash" against black militancy and claims that black gains had resulted in "reverse discrimination" against whites undermined support for major new civil rights initiatives during the 1970s and 1980s.

Although militant protest activity declined after the 1960s, civil rights movements have remained a significant feature of American political life. The increased black participation in the American political system that resulted from previous struggles lessened black reliance on extralegal tactics, but civil rights issues continued to stimulate protest, particularly when previous gains appeared to be threatened. Furthermore, women, homosexuals, disabled people, and other groups suffering discriminatory treatment have mobilized civil rights movements and created organizations of their own, thereby contributing to the continuing national dialogue regarding the scope of civil rights and the role of government.

During the 1970s and 1980s, debate continued over the appropriateness of employment AFFIRMATIVE ACTION programs and court-ordered compensatory remedies for historically rooted patterns of discrimination. Nevertheless, despite contention regarding these issues and notwithstanding the conservative political climate of the period, most national civil rights policies established during the 1960s have survived. Moreover, civil rights advocates have continued to press, with limited success, toward implementation of policies for group advancement rather than individual rights, tangible gains rather than civil status, and equality of social outcomes rather than equality of opportunity. The modern African American freedom and liberation struggles of the 1960s therefore produced a major but still controversial shift in prevailing norms regarding the nature of civil rights in the United States.

CLAYBORNE CARSON
(1992)

(SEE ALSO: *Race Consciousness; Racial Discrimination; Racial Preference.*)

Bibliography

BRANCH, TAYLOR 1988 *Parting the Waters: America in the King Years, 1954–63.* New York: Simon and Schuster.

CARSON, CLAYBORNE 1981 *In Struggle: SNCC and the Black Awakening of the 1960s.* Cambridge, Mass.: Harvard University Press.

GRAHAM, HUGH DAVIS 1990 *The Civil Rights Record.* New York: Oxford University Press.

KLUGER, RICHARD 1975 *Simple Justice: The History of Brown v. Board of Education and Black America's Struggle for Equality.* New York: Knopf.

LAWSON, STEVEN F. 1985 *In Pursuit of Power: Southern Blacks and Electoral Politics.* New York: Columbia University Press.

CIVIL RIGHTS PRACTICE

Civil rights practice, as discussed herein, refers to litigation brought pursuant to federal CIVIL RIGHTS legislation. Many civil rights statutes exist, some of modern origin and some dating from the RECONSTRUCTION era following the CIVIL WAR. The statutes protect individuals from deprivations of constitutional rights by government and from various kinds of discrimination by private individuals. SECTION 1983, TITLE 42, U.S. CODE, passed in 1871, is the primary vehicle for litigating deprivations of constitutional rights. ANTIDISCRIMINATION LEGISLATION, passed in the 1960s and later, creates protection from private discrimination on certain grounds in particular contexts, such a PUBLIC ACCOMMODATIONS, EMPLOYMENT, and housing. Although the structure and scope of these statutes differ, they are all enforced primarily through private litigation for damages or injunctive relief. The different statutes may also authorize other enforcement mechanisms—criminal prosecutions, civil actions, or administrative enforcement by the government—and these can play an important role in effectuating the purposes of the legislation. But given constraints on government resources, private enforcement is essential.

There are many substantive hurdles to recovery under the various civil rights statutes, some imposed by Congress and many by the Supreme Court in its decisions. Limitations on constitutional rights such as the RIGHT OF PRIVACY or DUE PROCESS OF LAW, stringent proof requirements, and defenses such as absolute and qualified immunity, are but a few examples of the challenging issues a litigant may confront. Because of the complexities in civil rights practice, effective private enforcement usually requires that the plaintiff retain an attorney. In a small number of cases, the plaintiff can join with others in a CLASS ACTION lawsuit, but most likely, the plaintiff as an individual will seek REPRESENTATION.

In 1976, Congress realized that the prevailing American rule, in which each party bears its own attorneys' fees, was a significant impediment to private enforcement of civil rights legislation. In that year, Congress enacted the Attorneys' Fees Awards Act, which permitted "prevailing parties" in civil rights actions to recover their attorneys' fees from the losing parties. In practice, this fee-shifting favors plaintiffs much more than defendants, despite the neutrality of the language. The legislative history of the Attorneys' Fees Awards Act reveals that Congress was aware that civil rights cases often present issues with less monetary value than other types of litigation an attorney might undertake. Congress believed that in the absence of fee-shifting, civil rights plaintiffs with low damages or claims in which predominantly equitable remedies are sought would lack the means to vindicate their rights. The difficulty and the economics of their cases would make them unable to compete with litigants presenting other types of legal work.

Since passage of the Attorneys' Fees Awards Act, the Court has decided numerous cases interpreting the statute. Although a number of the Court's decisions have bolstered recovery of fees, some of the Court's decisions have undercut the incentives the Fees Act gives attorneys to represent civil rights plaintiffs. One example of such a decision is *Evans v. Jeff D.* (1986). There, the Court held that a waiver of fees as part of a settlement is consistent with the purposes of the Fees Act. The decision has affected the strategies of both civil rights plaintiffs' attorneys and defense attorneys. Plaintiffs' attorneys practicing in nonprofit settings are vulnerable to requests for fee waivers, because the rules by which they operate often prevent them from entering into agreements that give their clients a disincentive to waive their fees. In the private sector, plaintiffs' attorneys have protected themselves by fee agreements that provide for a contingent recovery or payment of an hourly fee in the event of a settlement that includes a waiver. Defendants commonly make lump sum offers, out of which fees will be paid. Often the result is a partial waiver of fees. Because most cases ultimately are settled, the result of *Jeff D.* is that civil rights lawyers who seek to make a living at the practice must take cases with damages high enough to compensate the attorney in the event of settlement. Cases with lower predictable damages—for example, those based on constitutional violations or adverse employment actions against blue-collar or temporary workers, or cases involving equitable relief—are not so likely to be accepted by attorneys.

City of Burlington v. Dague (1992) is another case that has sapped the vitality of certain types of civil rights practice. By this decision, the Court withdrew the discretion of judges to award fees in addition to the hourly rate. Unfortunately, some types of civil rights litigation are so expensive that compensation for the hours spent does not begin to pay for the litigation. In the VOTING RIGHTS area, for example, even assessing the viability of a case involves significant SOCIAL SCIENCE RESEARCH. Studies can cost in the tens of thousands of dollars. Plaintiffs cannot afford these costs, and so the attorney must forward them. Without the possibility of extra compensation for the financial risks undertaken by the attorney, there is a significant disincentive to litigate those cases. Some voting rights litigation is handled by nonprofit or private organizations, whose own resources defray costs; also, the U.S. Department of Justice plays a significant role in voting rights litigation because of the department's preclearance responsibilities. However, if a plaintiff does not succeed in placing the case with a nonprofit firm or the Department of Justice for litigation, it is extremely difficult to obtain private counsel. The disincentives to private representation narrow the scope of voting rights issues that are addressed by litigation.

Because civil rights legislation encompasses so many different types of claims, the practice areas differ greatly. Just as some types of civil rights practice have been hard hit by the decisions discussed above, other practices have seemingly been unaffected and are thriving. The Court has not focused on the heterogeneity of civil rights cases as it has decided issues affecting fees and damages. Unless the Court takes account of the varying impacts of its decisions on certain types of practice, the incentives promised by the Fees Act will be greatly diluted.

JULIE DAVIES
(2000)

Bibliography

DAVIES, JULIE 1997 Federal Civil Rights Practice in the 1990's: The Dichotomy Between Reality and Theory. *Hastings Law Journal* 48:197–270.

LANDSBERG, BRIAN K. 1997 *Enforcing Civil Rights, Race Discrimination and the Department of Justice.* Lawrence: University Press of Kansas.

SCHWAB, STEWART J. and EISENBERG, THEODORE 1987 The Reality of Constitutional Tort Litigation. *Cornell Law Review* 72:641–695.

——— 1988 Explaining Constitutional Tort Litigation: The Influence of the Attorneys Fees Statute and the Government as Defendant. *Cornell Law Review* 73:719–781.

SELMI, MICHAEL 1996 The Value of the EEOC: Reexamining the Agency's Role in Employment Discrimination Law. *Ohio State Law Journal* 57:1–64.

WASBY, STEPHEN L. 1995 *Race Relations Litigation in an Age of Complexity.* Charlottesville, Virginia: University Press of Virginia.

CIVIL RIGHTS REMOVAL

Since the CIVIL RIGHTS ACT OF 1866, federal CIVIL RIGHTS laws have allowed REMOVAL OF CASES from state to federal courts. The 1866 and 1870 acts provided for removal to federal court of state criminal or civil cases affecting persons who were denied or could not enforce in state court rights guaranteed by the acts. In the REVISED STATUTES of 1874, Congress restated the removal power to encompass violations of "any law providing for . . . equal civil rights." Early removal cases, typified by STRAUDER V. WEST VIRGINIA (1880), allowed removal when state courts denied rights by enforcing state statutes but refused removal when state courts denied rights by following uncodified practices. With the vanishing of the BLACK CODES, removal became an insignificant remedy.

In the 1960s, civil rights protesters often were arrested under state TRESPASS, traffic, and other minor laws and were subjected to unfair state court proceedings. After a pause of eighty years, the Court again considered civil rights removal. In *Georgia v. Rachel* (1966) civil rights SIT-IN demonstrators being prosecuted for trespass in state court sought removal. The Court held removal authorized only for violations of "any law providing for specific civil rights stated in terms of racial equality." But, bending the *Strauder-Rives* line, the Court did not require that a state statute be the basis for the alleged deprivation of federal rights. The Court allowed removal on the grounds that the state prosecution violated the CIVIL RIGHTS ACT OF 1964, which outlaws even attempts to punish persons exercising rights of equal access to PUBLIC ACCOMMODATIONS.

On the same day, however, the Court decided in *City of Greenwood v. Peacock* (1966) that workers engaged in a voter registration drive could not rely on various voting statutes that prohibit RACIAL DISCRIMINATION to remove their state prosecutions for obstructing the public streets. The mere likelihood of prejudice was not enough to justify removal under the statute. The majority evidently shrank from the prospect of wholesale removal of criminal prosecutions of black defendants from southern state courts to federal courts. *Peacock* effectively precludes widespread modern use of civil rights removal.

THEODORE EISENBERG
(1986)

Bibliography

AMSTERDAM, ANTHONY G. 1965 Criminal Prosecutions Affecting Federally Guaranteed Civil Rights: Federal Removal and Habeas Corpus Jurisdiction to Abort State Court Trial. *University of Pennsylvania Law Review* 113:793–912.

CIVIL RIGHTS REPEAL ACT
28 Stat. 36 (1894)

From the middle of the 1860s to 1875, Congress was favorably disposed toward ANTIDISCRIMINATION LEGISLATION and even enacted some such measures over presidential veto. But many of the provisions enacted encountered restrictive interpretations to outright invalidation in the Supreme Court. The Repeal Act of 1894 symbolizes formal reconvergence of congressional and judicial attitudes towards CIVIL RIGHTS statutes.

In 1892 the Democratic party, for the first time after the CIVIL WAR, gained control of both houses of Congress and the presidency. In the Repeal Act of 1894, which repealed portions of the Enforcement Act of 1870 and the FORCE ACT OF 1871, Congress eliminated most civil rights measures that had not already been undermined by the Court. The repealed provisions had provided for federal control of federal elections through the appointment of federal election officials, a control method revived in the CIVIL RIGHTS ACTS of 1960 and 1964 and the VOTING RIGHTS ACT OF 1965.

THEODORE EISENBERG
(1986)

Bibliography

EISENBERG, THEODORE 1981 *Civil Rights Legislation.* p. 741. Charlottesville, Va.: Michie Co.

CIVIL WAR

The Civil War was the greatest constitutional crisis in the nation's history. It tested the nation-state relationship and the powers of Congress, the President, and the courts. By ultimately destroying SLAVERY, the conflict removed the most destructive element in the constitutional system and produced promises of equality under law throughout the United States. The addition of the THIRTEENTH AMENDMENT, FOURTEENTH AMENDMENT, and FIFTEENTH AMENDMENT dramatically changed the structure of the federal system in important respects. In the short run these amendments ended slavery and gave state and national CITIZENSHIP to over four million black men, women, and children. They also opened the door for black participation in politics. By the mid-twentieth century the amendments would place a great many individual rights under federal protection.

The was also finally settled the long-debated question of SOVEREIGNTY. When a state and the national government clashed over ultimate authority, the national government would prevail. This primacy did not mean, however, that the states were stripped of power or influence. Both state and national governments involved themselves energetically and successfully in war-making and hence increased both their influence and their stature before the people. State and federal taxation increased along with state and federal expenditures for public projects. The war thus produced an ironic dual legacy: freedom for black Americans and a vital federal system in which states would retain significant, though no longer unique, influence over the amount of freedom these freedmen would exercise.

Because Congress was in recess when the conflict began, the President had to cope with the crisis alone. ABRAHAM LINCOLN answered secessionist rhetoric with a powerful argument that sustained national authority by noting the danger of anarchy in SECESSION and by emphasizing the sovereignty of people, not states. "A majority, held in restraint by constitutional checks, and limitations, and always changing easily, with deliberate changes of popular opinions and sentiments, is the only true sovereign of a free people," Lincoln said. To preserve the constitutional system that embodied this process, Lincoln was willing to lead the Union into war.

Lincoln marshaled northern resources to fight secession. He called for troops, paid $2 million from the treasury, pledged federal credit for $250 million more, and proclaimed a blockade of southern ports. These initiatives raised the constitutional problem of whether the conflict was legitimate at all, for Lincoln had acted without statutory authority and only Congress had power to declare war. In the March 1863 PRIZE CASES, the Supreme Court gave its answer on the disposition of several ships seized by the Union navy after Lincoln's 1861 blockade. The constitutional question was whether the President could blockade the South without a DECLARATION OF WAR by Congress. Emphasizing the distinction between an international war, which Congress had to declare, and a civil war thrust upon the President and demanding immediate response, the Court defined the war as an insurrection, thus recognizing the President's power to subdue the rebellion without recognizing the Confederacy as an independent nation. The Court also justified Lincoln's action on the basis of the Militia Act of 1795, which allowed the President to call up the federal militia to stop insurrections. Presidents JOHN QUINCY ADAMS, JAMES K. POLK, MILLARD FILLMORE, and FRANKLIN PIERCE had established precedents in exercising this power, and the 1827 case of MARTIN V. MOTT had sustained it.

Executive authority over CIVIL LIBERTIES, the rights of civilian justice, FREEDOM OF SPEECH, and FREEDOM OF THE PRESS provoked the most criticism. Fearing prorebel judges and juries in border states, Lincoln in 1861 suspended the privilege of the writ of HABEAS CORPUS in the area between New York and Washington. This action gave the military control over civil liberty. Union soldiers arrested men near Baltimore for recruiting rebels and burning bridges linking Washington to the North. Chief Justice ROGER BROOKE TANEY went to Baltimore especially to challenge Lincoln's suspension of the writ. Congress, not the President, retained constitutional suspension authority, Taney claimed. But over fifty pamphlets quickly surfaced to debate the issue, and authoritative voices supported Lincoln. Lincoln ignored Taney, and habeas corpus remained suspended. In fact, in 1862 suspension of the writ was expanded to cover the entire North.

The Union army arrested about 15,000 people; however, the vast majority were taken as rebel territory was occupied. The number of northern civilians subject to military law owing to the suspension of habeas corpus was limited, perhaps to a few hundred, and press, platform, and pulpit continued to sound with criticism of the "Lincoln dictatorship." On the other hand some newspapers, including the *National Zeitung*, the Philadelphia *Evening Journal*, the Chicago *Times*, and the New York *World*, were temporarily shut down, and the editors of others were arrested, held for short periods of time, and then released—a practice that often restrained their criticism. Furthermore, Lincoln defended the suspension policy with sweeping rhetoric that may have had its own chilling effect on criticism: "The man who stands by and says nothing when the peril of his government is discussed cannot be misunderstood. If not hindered he is sure to help the enemy."

In the most famous civil liberties case of the time, a leading Ohio Democratic congressman, Clement Vallandigham, was arrested in Ohio in 1863 for protesting General Burnside's prohibition of "declaring sympathy for the enemy." Tried and convicted by a military tribunal, Val-

landigham was banished to the Confederacy after the Supreme Court denied itself jurisdiction of the case in Ex Parte Vallandigham (1864). Vallandigham and his arrest were popular causes, however, and the Democratic party sought votes with some success as the party of civil liberties throughout the conflict. Still, when northern voters had to choose between Lincoln's suspensions and Vallandigham's defiance, they usually sided with Lincoln and his explanation that preserving the constitutional system as a whole in wartime required limiting speech that threatened the war effort. The Confederate government also suspended the writ of habeas corpus, provoking protest from state-sovereignty radicals, but such protest did little to weaken the Confederacy.

The abiding health of the constitutional system in the North during the war was demonstrated by the ongoing electoral process, within which civil liberty restrictions could be discussed and debated and through which the voters might throw out of office the very government that was restricting civil liberties. In Dixie, too, elections continued for the Confederate Congress, although not for the presidency, which had a six-year term, beginning in 1861. One advantage the North had over the South was an established political system that generated alternatives, focused political discussion, used patronage to keep intraparty rivalries in line, and kept opposition to the administration within reasonable bounds. Confederate political quarrels, lacking party apparatus, became personal and hence more intense.

LEGISLATIVE POWER also expanded during the war, as Congress and executive cooperated to preserve and strengthen national authority. Legislators enacted a series of military drafts that brought national authority directly into the life of every American. Congress endorsed Lincoln's habeas corpus suspension in March 1863, although the tardiness of the Indemnity Act suggests the sensitivity of voters to the issue. Congress established the Joint Committee on the Conduct of the War to investigate generals perceived as not vigorous enough or not in accord with REPUBLICAN PARTY policies. Lincoln used committee pressure to prod generals toward advanced measures. The one major division between executive and legislative branches, over RECONSTRUCTION, began with the antiLincoln diatribe of the Wade-Davis Manifesto, but soon found Lincoln and Congress working out their differences, agreeing on the need to protect freedmen and provide them with economic support through the Freedmen's Bureau Act. Wade and Davis both supported Lincoln for reelection in 1864, and just before his death Lincoln was apparently contemplating a change in his Reconstruction policies that would have moved him closer to Congress. The two branches still debated which southern governments should be restored to the Union—those following Lincoln's plan or Congress's alternative—but both agreed that once war ended Congress would effectively control the Reconstruction process.

There was no disagreement about the wartime economic program. The first federal income tax law, the creation of the first national currency in the Greenback Act of 1862, the development of a national banking system, the taxing out of existence of state-based currency, the huge subsidy to build railroads to the Pacific Ocean, the opening up of millions of acres to homesteading with the HOMESTEAD ACT, the establishment of the Department of Agriculture, and the MORRILL ACT, which helped found and sustain major universities throughout the nation, all received Lincoln's unequivocal approval.

None of this national government activity was accompanied by federal regulation. The first national regulative agency, the Interstate Commerce Commission of 1887, lay twenty-two years into the postwar era. But people now accepted Congress's constitutional authority to shape the economy. Despite the Jeffersonian rhetoric of the Democratic party, it was the old Hamiltonian program and Hamiltonian views of national power, now infusing Whig and Republican political economy, that shaped national government policymaking. State governments, too, became more active. Some states set up public health boards and railroad oversight commissions. In the South, Reconstruction state governments established the region's first public schools. Cities also expanded their activities, having seen what government energy might accomplish.

The death of slavery was the largest constitutional change of the war. The conflict helped to resolve a growing contradiction within the constitutional system itself. On the one hand, the Constitution of 1787 recognized and protected slavery in several of its provisions. FEDERALISM left states free to determine whether they would be free or slave. The Supreme Court had declared the territories open to slavery. Democratic presidents had endorsed proslavery demands. On the other hand, by 1860 slavery had become, in many northern eyes, a major threat to constitutional liberties and the operation of the political/constitutional system.

The prewar era saw proslavery attempts to stifle antislavery voices—in Congress through gag rules, in the free states through anti-abolitionist mobs, and in politics generally through the prohibition of antislavery arguments in the slave states and the territories. All these efforts helped generate sectional parties. In addition, the South used threats of secession to protect slavery, thus hardening northern hostility to the peculiar institution and to what it termed "the Slave Power Conspiracy." People did not have to be racial egalitarians to be enemies of slavery. The threat to individual rights and the political process made slavery a target of northern hostility. The Constitution thus was at war with itself—promising open elections, free debate, the right to petition, the whole process of government by consent, on the one hand, and protecting slavery, on the other. The war ended the conflict.

Freed from obstruction by southern congressmen, the wartime northern Congress not only enacted much nationalizing legislation but also attacked slavery whenever the Constitution put it within congressional reach. Congress ended slavery in the DISTRICT OF COLUMBIA and in the territories. Then, acting on the theory that slaves might be contraband of war, Congress turned on the South and passed laws first confiscating property used directly to attack the Union (First Confiscation Act, August 1861) and then taking all slaves of rebels (Second Confiscation Act, July 1862). But these two laws freed no slaves, for the judicial procedures to prove disloyalty were too cumbersome. The laws did, however, demonstrate growing support for executive action against slavery.

Lincoln had two arenas in which he might act. In civilian areas his emancipation goals were restrained by the Constitution, which let states choose freedom or slavery. He asked border slave states to free their slaves. When that effort failed, he turned his attention to places still in rebellion, places where his constitutional war powers could operate. The EMANCIPATION PROCLAMATION of January 1, 1863, freed slaves wherever the Union advanced after that day, and it permitted freedmen to acquire claims on citizenship by serving as soldiers.

Emancipation ended the national government's protection for slavery, which had existed since 1787. With the adoption of the Thirteenth Amendment in 1865, the national government promised to eradicate, not defend, slavery. The death of slavery ended the reason for secession and for obstructing open debate in Congress and in the polity at large. It also meant that the institution that had most conspicuously challenged the ideal of equal justice under law was gone. As the Civil War ended, a robust constitutional system of active states and a proven nation awaited new challenges to that ideal.

PHILLIP S. PALUDAN
(1992)

(SEE ALSO: *Confederate Constitution; Confiscation Acts; Constitutional History, 1861–1865; Executive Power; Executive Prerogative; Jeffersonianism; War Powers; Whig Party.*)

Bibliography

BELZ, HERMAN 1978 *Emancipation and Equal Rights: Politics and Constitutionalism in the Civil War Era.* New York: Norton.

—— 1984 *Lincoln and the Constitution: The Dictatorship Question Reconsidered.* Fort Wayne, Ind.: Louis Warren Lincoln Library.

FEHRENBACHER, DON E.   1979   Lincoln and the Constitution. In Cullom Davis, ed., *The Public and Private Lincoln*. Carbondale: University of Southern Illinois Press.

HYMAN, HAROLD   1973   *A More Perfect Union: The Impact of the Civil War and Reconstruction on the Constitution*. New York: Knopf.

———, and WIECEK, WILLIAM   1982   *Equal Justice Under Law: Constitutional Development, 1835–1875*. New York: Harper & Row.

MCKITRICK, ERIC   1967   Party Politics and the Union and Confederate War Efforts. In Walter Dean Burnham and William Chambers, eds., *The American Party System*. New York: Free Press.

NEELY, MARK E., JR.   1991   *The Fate of Liberty: Abraham Lincoln and Civil Liberties*, New York: Oxford.

PALUDAN, PHILLIP S.   1988   *"A People's Contest": The Union and Civil War, 1861–1865*. New York: Harper & Row.

RANDALL, JAMES G.   (1926) 1951   *Constitutional Problems Under Lincoln*, rev. ed. Urbana: University of Illinois Press.

CIVIL WAR AMENDMENTS

See: Fifteenth Amendment; Fourteenth Amendment; Thirteenth Amendment